D-ROM FOR BUSINESS COMMUNICATION

This interactive CD-ROM includes:

- Unique video scenarios that set up each episode.
- Highly interactive exercises with feedback based on the decisions students make.
- Video conclusions for both good and bad endings.
- Additional guidance and discussion questions.

Video sets the scene.

VIDEO WINDOW

PERILS OF PAULINE

EPISODE II: Writing Bad-News Message

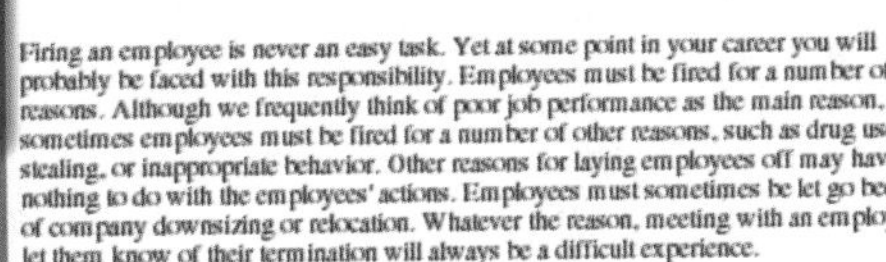

Firing an employee is never an easy task. Yet at some point in your career you will probably be faced with this responsibility. Employees must be fired for a number of reasons. Although we frequently think of poor job performance as the main reason, sometimes employees must be fired for a number of other reasons, such as drug use, stealing, or inappropriate behavior. Other reasons for laying employees off may have nothing to do with the employees' actions. Employees must sometimes be let go bec[...] of company downsizing or relocation. Whatever the reason, meeting with an employ[...] let them know of their termination will always be a difficult experience.

It is also one that must be handled very carefully. Leaving a job will result in a period [...] transition that is usually very stressful. It is true that sometimes employees are actuall[...] relieved to be let go from a job, and it may be best for both parties if the person mov[...] to a job where they are happier and better suited. However, a terminated employee w[...] feels that their termination was uncalled for, unfair, or the result of discrimination or [...] reasons that are not related to job performance could take legal action against the com[...] Firing an employee is never a task to be taken lightly.

Let us see if you can help Pauline navigate through this difficult challenge. In the introductory video, you will see how Pauline's boss, Sylvia, asks her to inform one c[...] workers, Brian, of the termination of his employment. Pauline will have to compose [...] effective letter and then meet with Brian in person to discuss the matter with him. No[...] that soon after Pauline is asked by her boss to fire Brian, she already makes a mistak[...] the process. It may seem very small at first, but news of a potential layoff is somethi[...] everyone in the company wants to know about. Can you catch her first mistake? Tak[...] look at the introductory video now.

Click the ▶ in the Video Window to start the video.

After watching the video, proceed to the Exercise.

EPISODE THEMES

- INTRODUCTION (Pilot episode)
- 1. CONDUCTING A MEETING (Chapters 1 & 19)
- 2. VERBAL AND NONVERBAL COMMUNICATION (Chapter 2)
- 3. INTERCULTURAL COMMUNICATION (Chapter 3)
- 4. USING TECHNOLOGY EFFECTIVELY (Chapter 4)
- 5. BRAINSTORMING SESSION (Chapter 5)
- 6. WRITING DIRECT REQUESTS (Chapters 6, 7, 8 & 9)
- 7. PERSUASIVE MESSAGES (Chapter 11)
- 8. SUCCESSFUL RESUMES (Chapter 12)
- 9. THE JOB INTERVIEW (Chapter 13)
- 10. GIVING A FORMAL SPEECH (Chapter 14 - 18 & 20)
- WRITING BAD-NEWS MESSAGE (Chapter 10)
- 12. RESOLVING CONFLICTS (Chapter 19)

In each episode, Pauline finds herself confronted with real-world communication challenges. Students see what the consequences are when employees fail to communicate effectively.

Interactive skills-based activities follow each episode.

VIDEO WINDOW

Now let us examine the general flow of a good termination letter. Take a look at pages 311 and 313 in your Bovee and Thill textbook. In addition, here are some notes to help further explain how good termination letters are constructed.

1. **Open with a neutral statement related to the subject of the letter.** The goal is to get the reader to read the entire letter because you have taken grea[...] care to maintain goodwill. If the reader gets upset in the opening, the chances ar[...] less that he/she will read on. A neutral statement offers neither positive or negati[...] information and **does not** state the purpose of the letter. A neutral opening related to the topic of the letter **does**, however, identify the letter's topic.
2. **State the reasons for the termination (or negative information).** By giving the reasons before the stated negative information, the reader is coming to the conclusion him/herself. If the negative is stated first, the reader may read th[...] reasons with a defensive stance. All readers want to know the reasons and should know them. Their frame of mind as they read the negative news that follows will depend on what you have just said in this section.
3. **Clearly state the negative information.** You cannot assume that the reader is clear on the purpose of the letter just from the reasons for the negative. You must clearly state the negative.
4. **Offer alternatives or help.** To maintain goodwill, be of assistance to the reader. In the case of denying credit, offer an alternative means of doing business until the credit can be established (cash). In the case of denying employment, offer to keep the application on file for a specific time period or offer a hot line for available jobs. If there is no room in the inn, offer to make calls to surrounding inns to help locate a room. If you do not have the requested product, suggest another of your product lines or another product from a competitor. Include telephone numbers. In the case of a termination, offer assistance on resume development. Offering assistance **after** stating the negative news immediately turns the message from negative to positive and forward looking.
5. **Close with a goodwill statement leading away from negative.** Never end your letter by referring to the negative. You will leave your reader focusing on the negative and associating it with your company.

Click the "View Letter" button below to view the letter in a separate window.

View Letter

You may be interested to see the likely outcome of a well constructed [...] button below to load the "Good Ending" video. You will see that a l[...] guidelines is effective. Meeting with an employee to discuss the situ[...] uncomfortable affair, but at least with an effectively written letter, th[...] [...] of avoiding accusations and focusing instead on the future.

Good Ending

Once the video has loaded, click the ▶ in the Video Window to view th[...]

After watching the video, please proceed to the Discussion Questions.

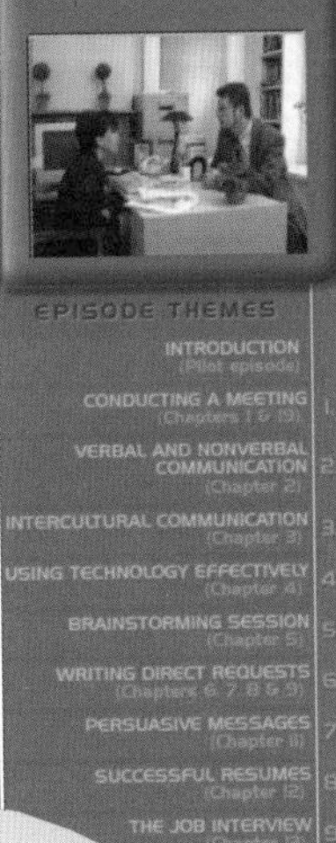

Additional guidance and reinforcement is provided.

Depending on the choices students make, they will see a good ending or a bad ending.

Additional discussion questions are provided.

BUSINESS COMMUNICATION TODAY

SIXTH EDITION

Courtland L. Bovée

Professor of Business Communication
C. Allen Paul Distinguished Chair
Grossmont College

John V. Thill

Chief Executive Officer
Communication Specialists of America

Prentice Hall
Upper Saddle River, New Jersey 07458

With immense gratitude, we dedicate this book to our publishing mentor,
Seibert G. Adams

Editor-in-Chief: Natalie Anderson
Vice-President/Editorial Director: James Boyd
Marketing Manager: Debbie Clare
Senior Editor: Linda Schreiber
Assistant Editor: Kristen Imperatore
Editorial Assistant: Sue Galle
Production Editor: Lynda P. Hansler
Associate Managing Editor: Judy Leale
Manufacturing Buyer: Kenneth J. Clinton
Manufacturing Supervisor: Arnold Vila
Manufacturing Manager: Vincent Scelta
Permissions Coordinator: Monica Stipanov
Design Manager: Patricia Smythe
Interior Design: Lorraine Castellano
Cover Design: Joan O'Connor
Cover Art: Guy Crittenden/Digital Productions, Inc.
Production/Composition: York Production Services

Upper Saddle River, New Jersey 07458

Library of Congress Cataloging-in-Publication Data
Bovée, Courtland L.
Business communication today / Courtland L. Bovée, John V. Thill. —6th ed.
p. cm.
Includes bibliographical references and index.
ISBN 0-13-084513-2
1. Business communication—United States—Case studies. 2. Communication in organizations—United States—Case studies. 3. Business writing—United States—Case studies. I. Thill, John V. II. Title.
HF5718.B66 1999
658.4'5—dc21 99-20812
CIP

Prentice-Hall International (UK) Limited, *London*
Prentice-Hall of Australia Pty. Limited, *Sydney*
Prentice-Hall Canada, Inc., *Toronto*
Prentice-Hall Hispanoamericana, S.A., *Mexico*
Prentice-Hall of India Private Limited, *New Delhi*
Prentice-Hall of Japan, Inc., *Tokyo*
Prentice-Hall (Singapore) Pte. Ltd.
Editora Prentice-Hall do Brasil, Ltda., *Rio de Janeiro*

Printed in the United States of America

10 9 8 7 6 5

CONTENTS IN BRIEF

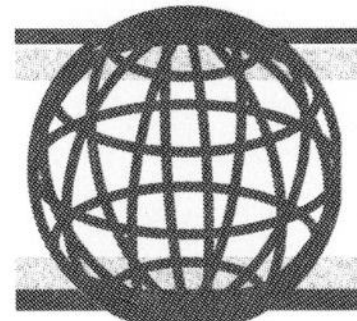

CONTENTS

Chapter 9: Writing Persuasive Messages 286

PART 4: INFORMATION AND TECHNOLOGY 335

CHAPTER 10: Communicating Information through the Internet and Other Technologies 336

PART 5: REPORTS AND ORAL PRESENTATIONS 437

CHAPTER 13: Communicating through Reports 438

CHAPTER 14: Planning, Organizing, and Writing Reports and Proposals 468

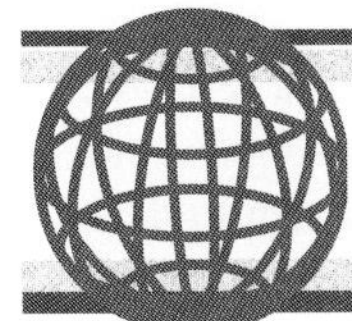

PREFACE

Presenting vivid insights into real-life business situations and employing a lively, conversational writing style, *Business Communication Today,* Sixth Edition, captures the dynamics of business communication like no other textbook. It also captures the interest of students and teachers alike: In the 14 years since the first edition of *Business Communication Today* was published, millions of students have learned about business communication from this text. We believe this edition will continue its tradition of being the number-one-selling text in the field.

Survey after survey places good communication skills at the top of the list of employee qualifications that are in high demand today. Simply put, those with outstanding communication skills will have an advantage in the workplace, and *Business Communication Today* gives them that crucial edge. By using an involving writing style and eye-opening graphics to crystallize chapter concepts, we draw students into the subject matter, help them understand the importance of excellent communication skills, and prepare them to obtain and pursue satisfying business careers.

This sixth edition of *Business Communication Today* is the centerpiece of a comprehensive teaching and learning package. The text covers all the basic principles and goals as recommended by the Association of Collegiate Business Schools and Programs, the American Assembly of Collegiate Schools of Business (AACSB), and the International Association for Management Education. Moreover, it fully integrates issues critical to successful business communication. Among the many important topics discussed in *Business Communication Today*, the following are given extensive coverage: ethics, cultural diversity, technology, teamwork, law, audience-centered messages, and the writing process.

A Thorough Revision

Successful companies know that they must continually reinvent themselves and their products to meet the ever-changing needs of their customers. This means that companies must listen to the people who use their products daily and incorporate their valuable recommendations in future product enhancements and revisions. In this sixth edition, we have accomplished all of this. But, we have also done more.

As the market leader, this text has once again raised the standards by which other business communication texts will be measured. For example, the new Part 4, "Information and Technology," is the result of both our own research findings and our conversations with many of today's business leaders who have strongly recommended that we teach students how to process and communicate information in today's high-tech environment. Furthermore, the new integrated exercises and case studies exemplify the type of comprehensive, critical thinking students will need to use when communicating on their jobs. In fact, these changes and more make *Business Communication Today,* Sixth Edition, our most comprehensive revision to date. Following is a closer look at some of the new features we have added to this edition.

NEW! Streamlined and Reorganized Text

This edition streamlines and reorganizes the text, reducing the number of regular chapters from 20 to 18, and making it easier to cover the entire text in one term. Material previously covered in Chapters 1 and 2 has been combined into Chapter 1. The chapter on writing direct requests has been combined with the chapter on writing routine, good-news, and goodwill letters, shortening the letter-writing chapters from four to three. The discussion of interpersonal communication skills such as listening and working in teams has been expanded and moved to Chapter 2. And the discussion of the writing process now begins one chapter earlier.

NEW! Part 4: Information and Technology

A new three-chapter part on information and technology has been created: Chapter 10, "Communicating Information through the Internet and Other Technologies," discusses how businesses today are using new technologies to communicate, the advantages these new technologies provide in the workplace, and the challenges they create; Chapter 11, "Finding, Evaluating, and Processing Information," is entirely new and presents a detailed, six-step business research process students can use for the remainder of their business studies and on the job; Chapter 12, "Communicating Information through Graphs and Other Visuals," includes a new multimedia presentation in addition to all new colorful graphs and visual aids that have been prepared using popular software. See "Part-by-Part Changes" for a complete overview of the content of each of these chapters.

NEW! Focus on Integrated Learning

This edition adds two new features—integrated exercises and integrated critical thinking cases—to help students understand the interrelationship and trade-offs involved in communicating effectively. Each chapter now includes two to three exercises (identified with a special icon) that integrate current chapter material with material covered earlier in the text. Integrated topics include channel and media selection, message timing, information overload, communication etiquette, audience-centered messages, message filtering, ethics, communication barriers, message organization, prewriting techniques, writing skills, and more.

New end-of-part case studies, "A Case for Critical Thinking," integrate material covered in the part with current communication issues faced by popular companies:

- Pillsbury's Recipe for Candid Talk (employee feedback and communication barriers)
- Caution: E-Mail Can Bite (Microsoft and communication privacy)
- How Boeing Blew It (miscommunication and bad news)
- Yahoo! The Little Search Engine That Could (virtual communication)
- Duplicating Success at Kinko's (professional-looking reports and presentations)
- Games Recruiters Play (unusual interviewing situations)

Each integrated case includes three critical thinking questions plus an Internet exercise that expands student learning.

NEW! Greater Emphasis on the Communication Process

Because communication product and processes are interrelated, we have reorganized the material in many of the text's chapters into a series of easy-to-follow steps while still maintaining a strong product orientation. Students will appreciate this logical approach, which includes a seven-step process for planning, organizing, and revising business messages (Chapters 4–6), a sequential approach to developing persuasive messages (Chapter 9), a six-step research process for finding, evaluating, and processing information (Chapter 11), a three-step process for planning, organizing, and writing reports and proposals (Chapter 14), and a three-step process for giving speeches and oral presentations (Chapter 16).

NEW! Tools for Learning

Three new learning tools have been added to this sixth edition to reinforce and apply chapter material:

- *Exploring the Best of the Web.* New end-of-chapter Internet exercises give students hands-on experience in using the rich business communication resources available on the World Wide Web. The exercises are directly tied to the "Best of the Web" features showcased in the chapter.
- *Did You Know?* Each chapter includes three intriguing business communication facts. These facts are closely related to the chapter material and are boxed and strategically placed in the margin. This feature is designed to stimulate student interest and extend student learning.
- *Numbered Learning Objectives and Summary of Learning Objectives.* Each chapter begins with a list of objectives summarizing what students should learn by studying the chapter. These objectives guide the learning process and help motivate students to master the material. The end-of-chapter "Summary of Learning Objectives" restate these learning objectives and summarize chapter highlights to reinforce learning of basic concepts.

Features Link Concepts to the Real World

Business Communication Today, Sixth Edition, paints a realistic picture of the world of business communication that appeals to instructors and to students, and it offers the most up-to-date look at business communication of any book in its field. Designed to hold students' attention, each chapter presents practical communication advice and tips from women and men working in real companies—people with experience who cope daily with communication problems and opportunities. These role models capture students' imagination because they symbolize success; they aren't newcomers in entry-level positions, but people who have proved their abilities and who hold positions that students find inspiring.

Because it encourages students to view themselves as part of an actual organization when completing assignments, this text is the next best thing to on-the-job training. It shows how standard approaches to routine assignments can help students complete work quickly and efficiently. At the same time, it stresses that every situation is different and advises students to think for themselves.

Communication Close-Ups and Communication Challenges

This text offers students the opportunity to learn from other people's successes and failures.

Each chapter begins with an instructive "Communication Close-Up" featuring a communication expert who, in his or her own words, applies the chapter's concepts to common business situations. That expert reappears from time to time throughout the chapter to dramatize the connection between the chapter's contents and life on the job. This on-the-scene, internal company information was gathered through personal interviews with our business associates, friends, and contacts, and it gives *Business Communication Today* the ring of truth that students are so eager for.

Projects called "Communication Challenges" conclude each chapter and are related to the situations described in the "Communication Close-Ups." Each chapter has one individual challenge (to give students "on-the-job" practice applying principles they have just learned) and one team challenge (to give students experience with the collaborative approach so prevalent in business today). These challenges are exclusive to *Business Communication Today*, providing a dimension of reality unmatched by any other textbook in the field.

New "Communication Close-Ups" and "Communication Challenges" added to this sixth edition include features on companies such as Sheraton Hotels Hawaii, SGI, Black Entertainment Television, Corporate Dynamics, Recreational Equipment Incorporated (REI), and Anderson Business Resources.

Real-Company Cases

Business Communication Today was the first business communication textbook to include letter, memo, and e-mail cases featuring real companies almost exclusively, and we continue this tradition. Over 50 percent of the cases in this sixth edition are new. Examples include

- Measuring suppliers: Inside letter requesting reviews at Microsoft
- Suffering artists: Memo refusing high-tech shoes at American Ballet Theater
- Missed target: "Bad news" poll results at the *Journal of the American Medical Association*
- Outsourcing: Kelley Services offers solutions
- Stroke awareness: Letter to Genentech requesting funds for educational campaign
- Relief requested: BestBank customer plea to Colorado Attorney General

Real-World Communication Issues

The boundaries of business communication are always expanding. In addition to covering all the traditional subjects, *Business Communication Today*, Sixth Edition, examines many current issues and provides material to help students successfully manage the following issues.

Ethics

Adhering to high ethical standards takes on a new importance in this age of wavering business behavior. Ethical questions addressed in this book include

- How much to emphasize the positive in business messages (Chapter 4)
- How to handle negative information in recommendation letters (Chapter 7)
- Where to draw the line between persuasion and manipulation in sales letters (Chapter 9)
- How to construct visual aids in a form that will convey a company's point of view without misleading the audience (Chapter 12)

Taking an ethical position in the face of pressures and temptations requires more than courage—it requires strong communication skills.

Cultural Diversity

The changing nature of the domestic work force requires strong communication skills to relate to older workers, women, members of various socioeconomic groups, immigrants, and others. Moreover, with such developments as European common currency and the North American Free Trade Agreement (NAFTA), and with the growth of worldwide information access via the Internet, the continuing globalization of business necessitates strong skills to communicate effectively with people from other countries (Chapter 3).

Communication Technology

Students will be expected to know how to use the Internet and other communication technologies once they enter the workplace. E-mail, electronic meetings, and videoconferencing are changing the way businesspeople communicate.

In fact, more and more people are interacting through computers today than face to face, and this trend will continue. To survive in today's business world, students need to master high-tech communication skills. They also need to understand that advances in communication technology bring with them additional challenges such as information overload, privacy, data security, clarity, and new rules for communication etiquette (Chapters 1, 5, 6, and 10). Even the job of referencing documents from electronic media must be mastered (Component Chapter B).

Law

The increasing tendency of people to sue makes it important to understand the legal implications of written and oral communication. For example, students need to understand the pitfalls of writing recommendation letters (discussed in Chapter 7). Other issues include the laws that govern sales letters and collection messages (discussed in Chapter 9), and the legality of employment interview questions (discussed in Chapter 18).

Employment Search

More and more people are making radical mid-career job changes, whether by choice or because their companies are downsizing and flattening hierarchies. These people need to master new communication skills to compete in today's job market. New text coverage explains how to prepare electronic and HTML résumés, and the discussion of using the Internet to find job openings and employer information has been updated (Chapter 17). The unit is completed by highlighting what today's employers are looking for in job candidates and by providing students with practical advice so they can prepare for job interviews (Chapter 18).

Real-World Insights

Boxed and strategically placed throughout the text, 35 special features extend the chapter material. Since the first edition of *Business Communication Today* was published, we have been searching through publications and interviewing respected authorities to provide insights into the business world that are not found in other textbooks. These special features center on four well-integrated themes.

Sharpening Your Skills

Practical pointers and confidence-building guidelines help students improve writing and speaking skills in special features such as

- Send Me a Memo on It; or Better Yet, Don't
- Writing Headings That Spark Reader Interest
- Sixteen Tough Interview Questions: What to Say When You're Stopped in Your Tracks
- Use Plain English, Please!

Focusing on Ethics

By examining critical ethical issues that face business communicators in today's workplace, students gain instruction on how to identify areas of ethical vulnerability, how to steer clear of ethical perils, and when to seek ethical advice. Special features cover a wide range of topics, including

- The Tangled Web of Internet Copyrights
- Warning: Deceptive Résumés Can Backfire
- Visual Aids That Lie: The Use and Abuse of Charts and Graphs
- Doublespeak: Why No One Knows What Anyone's Saying Anymore

Communicating across Cultures

Tested techniques help students communicate successfully both in the global arena and across the growing cultural diversity at home. Cultural issues are explored in special features such as

- Actions Speak Louder Than Words All Around the World
- Should Companies Stress English Only on the Job?
- Good Ways to Send Bad News Around the World
- How Direct Is Too Direct?

Keeping Pace with Technology

Specific techniques offer students guidance for using technological applications to improve business communication. Special features present a well-balanced selection of technological topics, including

- E-Mail Etiquette: Minding Your Manners Online
- High-Tech Job Hunting: The Secrets of Finding Employment on the World Wide Web
- From Digits to Dust
- Canning Spam

Each special feature includes two questions, ranging from discussion topics to application exercises.

Real-World Internet Resources

The World Wide Web, a component of the Internet, contains a wealth of valuable resources. To acquaint students with Web sites that relate to the content of *Business Communication Today*, a "Best of the Web" feature describing an especially useful site is included in each chapter. Examples of the "Best of the Web" feature include

- Polish Your Skills in Audience Analysis
- Check Out Materials at this Library 24 Hours a Day
- Avoid Embarrassment by Avoiding Common Errors
- Link Your Way to a Better Job Search

Real-Company Photographs

Yet another distinctive feature of this book is its use of photographs (most of them from real companies). Each photo is accompanied by a caption that describes how it relates to business communication. The photos cover a rich assortment of people, organizations, and events, and all of them give students an intimate glimpse into the real-life application of the topic being studied.

Reliable and Effective Pedagogy Sparks Student Learning and Real-World Competencies

Having an accurate picture of how businesspeople communicate is important, but students need more if they are to develop usable skills. What skills and competencies do students need to be successful in the workplace? According to the SCANS (Secretary's Commission on Achieving Necessary Skills) report from the Department of Labor, students need effective interpersonal skills, information gathering and processing skills, systems design and improvement skills, technological skills, and time and resource management skills. *Business Communication Today*, Sixth Edition, includes an extraordinary number of pedagogical devices that simplify teaching, facilitate learning, stimulate critical thinking, maintain student interest and enjoyment, and emphasize the skills and competencies necessary for students to make the transition from academia to the workplace.

In-Depth Critiques

Throughout *Business Communication Today*, Sixth Edition, you will find up-to-date sample documents, many collected from our consulting work. These documents are superb business examples that provide students with benchmarks for achievement. Many of these documents are fully formatted letters or memos presented on company letterhead; other documents are fully formatted e-mail messages. All "In-Depth Critiques" are accompanied by a caption explaining the particular business situation and by a sentence-by-sentence analysis that helps students see precisely how to apply the principles discussed in the text. Additional documents are displayed in the text, some including poor and improved examples to illustrate common errors and effective techniques for correcting them.

Documents for Analysis

Students can critique and revise 29 documents in 11 chapters. Documents include letters, memos, e-mail messages, a letter of application, a résumé, and visual aids. This hands-on experience in analyzing and improving documents will help students revise their own.

Checklists

To help students organize their thinking when they begin a communication project, make decisions as they write, and check their own work, we have included 29 checklists throughout the book and located them as closely as possible to the related discussions. These checklists are reminders, however—not "recipes." They provide useful guidelines for writing, without limiting creativity. Students will find them handy when they are on the job and need to refresh their memory about effective communication techniques.

Critical Thinking Questions

End-of-chapter Critical Thinking Questions (144 in all) are designed to get students thinking about the concepts introduced in each chapter. They may also prompt students to stretch their learning beyond the chapter content. Not only will students find them useful when studying for examinations, but instructors may also draw on them to promote classroom discussions about issues that have no easy answers.

Exercises and Cases

A wide variety and wealth of exercises (202) and cases (128), many of them e-mail and memo-writing tasks, provide real-world, on-the-job assignments. In addition, each chapter includes an individual and team-based communication challenge that ties the chapter-opening vignette to real-life communication issues and reinforces chapter material. A special exercise or a case (marked with an icon) requires access to the World Wide Web and gives students practice in using the Internet to solve communication problems.

Margin Notes

Short summary statements that highlight key points and reinforce learning appear in the margins of *Business Communication Today*, Sixth Edition. They are no substitute for reading the chapters, but are useful for quickly getting the gist of a section, rapidly reviewing a chapter, and locating areas of greatest concern.

Lively, Conversational Writing Style

Read a few pages of this textbook and then read a few pages of another textbook. We think you will immediately notice the difference. The lucid writing style in *Business Communication Today*, Sixth Edition, makes the material pleasing to read and easy to comprehend. It stimulates interest, promotes learning, and exemplifies the principles presented in this book. We have also carefully monitored the reading level of *Business Communication Today* to make sure it is neither too simple nor too difficult.

Book Design

The state-of-the-art design is based on extensive research and invites students to delve into the content. It makes reading easier, reinforces learning, and increases comprehension. The boxed special features and other elements do not interfere with the flow of textual material, a vital factor in maintaining attention and concentration. The design of this book, like much communication, has the simple objective of gaining interest and making a point.

This text has been attractively printed, and the dramatic use of full color throughout the book gives it exceptional visual appeal. In addition, students will learn from carefully crafted illustrations of important concepts in each chapter: graphs, charts, tables, and photographs.

Part-by-Part Changes

With an eye to emphasizing and integrating important topics, we have critically evaluated virtually every sentence in the text, making literally hundreds of refinements. Members of the academic and business communities have carefully reviewed it, and we have tested it in the classroom. Instructors, businesspeople, and students have all praised its thorough coverage of subject matter, its up-to-date examples, its flexible organization, and its authentic portrayal of business. Here is an overview of the major content changes in the sixth edition:

Part 1: Foundations of Business Communication *(Chapter 1: Understanding Business Communication; Chapter 2: Listening, Working in Teams, and Understanding Nonverbal Communication; Chapter 3: Communicating Interculturally)* combines and reorganizes material previously discussed in Chapters 1 and 2 into Chapter 1, providing a more logical flow of material and reducing discussion of communication concepts and theories; strengthens emphasis of six vital communication themes that recur throughout the book: open communication climate, ethics, intercultural messages, audience-centered thinking, wise and responsible use of technology, and efficient and effective message preparation and flow; moves discussion of interpersonal skills to Chapter 2 so students can practice these skills when completing team challenges and group exercises; increases discussion of collaborative writing, running productive meetings, working in teams, improving listening skills, and giving effective feedback; expands discussion of high- and low-context cultures in Chapter 3, and emphasizes the importance of understanding and respecting cultural differences in today's workplace.

Part 2: The Writing Process *(Chapter 4: Planning Audience-Centered Business Messages; Chapter 5: Organizing and Composing Audience-Centered Business Messages; Chapter 6: Revising Audience-Centered Business Messages)* starts discussion on the writing process one chapter earlier; completely reorganizes chapters, redistributes material, in-text examples, and exercises to increase coverage and achieve a better balance between chapters; increases discussion of audience analysis and channel and medium selection; streamlines and simplifies the writing process into seven steps (three stages) for a more logical approach; now begins writing-skills exercises in Chapter 4, giving students three full chapters of practice; strengthens discussion of improving communication effectiveness by controlling style and tone, carefully selecting words, and creating effective sentences; moves and expands discussion of using bullets and lists to composition chapters; now updates and integrates material previously discussed in the technology chapter into the writing process; and strengthens composition and organization process with increased in-text examples and new supporting figures.

Part 3: Letters, Memos, E-Mail, and Other Brief Messages *(Chapter 7: Writing Routine, Good-News, and Goodwill Messages; Chapter 8: Writing Bad-News Messages; Chapter 9: Writing Persuasive Messages)* now shortens letter-writing chapters from four to three by combining the chapter on writing direct requests with the chapter on writing routine, good-news, and goodwill letters; reorganizes combined chapter material by message type; Chapter 7 now focuses on messages more suitable for the direct organizational plan, whereas Chapter 8 now focuses on messages more suitable for the indirect organizational plan; increases discussion of differences between the direct and indirect organizational plans and includes a supporting figure to highlight these differences; reorganizes Chapter 9 and expands discussion of components required to build a strong persuasive argument; adds new figure on the AIDA organizational plan and a new checklist on developing persuasive messages; strengthens discussion of using persuasive tools and semantics to reinforce arguments; adds new material on dealing with audience resistance and avoiding common mistakes when crafting persuasive arguments; places greater emphasis on the importance of an audience-centered tone; adds new figure to clarify the difference between product features and consumer benefits; moves business summaries to Chapter 13; replaces nearly half of all end-of-chapter letter-writing cases; and adds end-of-chapter exercises in addition to the case assignments in all chapters in the past.

Part 4: Information and Technology *(Chapter 10: Communicating Information Through the Internet and Other Technologies; Chapter 11: Finding, Evaluating, and Processing Information; Chapter 12: Communicating Information Through Graphs and Other Visuals),* an entirely new text part, provides students with information management skills they will need to compete in today's workplace. It includes mostly new material and centralizes research techniques and information management skills previously discussed in many chapters, providing students with tools they can use early in the course. Chapter 10 now focuses on how businesses are using the Internet to communicate; updates and expands coverage of new communication technologies including intranets, extranets, and speech recognition software; now explains how search engines work and clarifies the difference between push and pull technology; adds a new table of popular search engines by category; adds a new checklist on high-tech etiquette; and elaborates on technology-related communication issues in the workplace such as information overload, privacy, data security, and employee productivity.

Chapter 11 is entirely devoted to a new six-step research process for finding, evaluating, and processing business information. The step-by-step process shows students how and where to begin business research—where to look for different types of business information, how to conduct an effective library and online database search using boolean and proximity operators, and how to evaluate and finalize sources; expands coverage of taking notes, conducting interviews, giving appropriate source credit, and outlining; adds new material on how to paraphrase; adds several new figures and tables to diagram the research process; and teaches students how to stay focused and keep research materials organized.

Chapter 12 combines graphics, visual aids, and multimedia presentation material previously discussed in two chapters into one; adds new discussion of how to design and deliver electronic business presentations using popular software; includes detailed steps, basic design principles, and a variety of new model slides and handouts; and adds all-new graphs and visuals in addition to a new checklist for creating effective visual aids.

Part 5: Reports and Oral Presentations *(Chapter 13: Communicating through Reports; Chapter 14: Planning, Organizing, and Writing Reports and Proposals; Chapter 15: Completing Formal Reports and Proposals; Chapter 16: Giving Speeches and Oral Presentations)* now presents a clear definition and differentiation of the types of informational and analytical reports used in business applications. It now focuses entirely on a step-by-step approach for planning, organizing, and writing reports; moves material on research to Part 4 and restructures material to improve information flow; and simplifies discussion of organizing material based on logical arguments. The chapter on public speaking and oral presentations adds new material on overcoming anxiety, choosing words carefully, and handling audience questions effectively; and includes new material on using visual aids effectively in reports and oral presentations.

Part 6: Employment Messages *(Chapter 17: Writing Résumés and Application Letters; Chapter 18: Interviewing for Employment and Following Up)* updates all sample résumés and expands discussion of preparing and adapting résumés to electronic and HTML format; adds greater emphasis on adopting the "you" attitude when drafting résumés and application letters; includes new discussion of posting résumés online; now explains the résumé scanning process; adds a new reference table for online job searches; expands discussion of adopting the AIDA organizational plan for job application messages; adds new material on what employers look for in job candidates; explains how to use the Internet to find competitive salary information; highlights increased use of situational interviews in the workplace; and updates and expands sample interview questions.

Part 7: Special Topics in Business Communication *(Component Chapter A: Format and Layout of Business Documents; Component Chapter B: Documentation of Report Sources)* moves the entire section on using source information to Chapter 11 in order to incorporate discussion of note taking, copyrights, and fair use in the six-step research process. It now provides an entirely new chapter on the *Chicago* style, *APA* style, and *MLA* style.

Web Site for Students

The PHLIP/Companion Web site at http://www.prenhall.com/bovee offers a wealth of materials and technological experience for students:

- The *Interactive Study Guide* provides a variety of chapter-by-chapter multiple-choice, true/false, and essay questions tied to the chapter objectives so that students can quiz themselves on topics covered in the text.

Students can take advantage of the online hints feature, receive immediate feedback on their answers, and then e-mail the results to their professor or teaching assistant.

- *Current Events and Examples* provide an array of current articles with an exercise built around them as well as additional examples in business communication that are presented with helpful learning objectives and discussion points.
- *Internet Exercises* direct students to Web sites to analyze real companies, perform research, and answer thought provoking questions.
- A *Study Hall* offers four major areas: (1) "Ask the Tutor" allows students to post questions or comments to a threaded conference message board maintained for their course, (2) the "Career Center" offers many resources for employment help and includes assistance in preparing a letter of application and a résumé, (3) the "Writing Center" offers tools and techniques for writing more effectively, (4) and the "Study Skills Center" helps students develop their ability to learn more effectively and to achieve greater success in college.
- The *Research Area* provides tutorials for developing skills in using the vast resources of the Internet.

Study Guide

An accompanying study guide provides chapter-by-chapter exercises designed to reinforce comprehension of key concepts presented in this text and to promote good language and writing skills. Features include Master Key Concepts, Quiz Yourself, Build Your Skills, Develop Your Word Power, plus 20 lessons on English essentials.

An Unsurpassed Instructional Resource Package

The instructional package accompanying this text is specially designed to simplify the task of teaching and learning. The supplementary package for the sixth edition of *Business Communication Today* has been thoroughly revised, and several new and exciting features have been added.

Instructor's Resource Manual

This comprehensive paperback book is an instructor's tool kit. Among the many things it provides are sample syllabi, lesson plans, and class activities for each chapter, suggested solutions to exercises, suggested solutions and fully formatted letters for every case in the letter-writing chapters, sections on collaborative writing and cooperative learning groups, and a grammar pretest and posttest. All lectures for *Business Communication Today*, Sixth Edition, have been completely rewritten and are now keyed to PowerPoint slides and color acetate transparencies. This manual is also available electronically to faculty at the book's Web site.

PowerPoint Lecture Presentation Slides

A set of over 320 new slides is available on PowerPoint 97. These colorful slides highlight and reinforce the major concepts of the text. Keyed to the Instructor's Resource Manual, these electronic slides include fade-outs, flying bullets, hypertext links, and many dazzling effects.

Acetate Transparency Program

A set of 100 large-type color transparency acetates, available to instructors on request, helps bring concepts alive in the classroom and provide a starting point for discussing communication techniques. All transparencies are keyed to the Instructor's Resource Manual.

Test Bank

This manual is organized by text chapters and includes a mix of multiple-choice, true/false, and fill-in questions for each chapter—approximately 1,500 objective items in all, carefully written and reviewed to provide a fair, structured program of evaluation.

Prentice Hall Custom Test, Windows Version

Based on a state-of-the-art test generation software program developed by Engineering Software Associates (ESA), *Prentice Hall Custom Test* is suitable for your course and can be customized to your class needs. You can originate tests quickly, easily, and error free. You can create an exam, administer it traditionally or online, evaluate and track students' results, and analyze the success of the examination—all with a simple click of the mouse.

Communication Briefings Video Series and Video Guide

Accompanying the text is a series of videos from Communication Briefings, a firm known for its monthly newsletter and its video series. The video set is available without charge to adopters of *Business Communication Today*. Included in the series are the following videos:

Everyone's Teamwork Role
Communicating for Results: How to Be Clear, Concise, and Credible
Better Business Grammar
Make the Phone Work for You
Listen and Win: How to Keep Customers Coming Back

How to See Opportunity in a Changing Workplace
Resolving Conflicts: Strategies for a Winning Team
Make Presentations Work for You

In addition, a separate video guide is available. Features include synopses of each video and discussion questions. To order the set, please call 1-800-388-8433.

Interactive CD-ROM

Have students learn valuable lessons about communicating effectively in a variety of business situations prior to experiencing them first-hand. The "Perils of Pauline" is an exciting interactive CD-ROM that uses custom video scenarios linked with exercises and activities. Your students help Pauline, a recent college graduate, deal with real-world communication predicaments in her first job. Students must use their knowledge from the text to answer questions, and based on their responses, they are shown likely outcomes of their choices with video clips. This interactive CD-ROM can be packaged with the text for a nominal cost.

New York Times Supplement

This supplement, published twice a year, offers a collection of *New York Times* articles to help keep your class current through additional discussion topics and project ideas.

Career Search Supplement

Beginning Your Career Search, by James O'Rourke, offers straightforward, practical advice on how to write a résumé, where and how to find company information, and how to conduct yourself during an interview. Also included are sample introductory, cover, follow-up, and "thank you" letters.

Internet Supplement

Surfing for Success in Business Communication: An Internet Guide is a brief discipline-specific guide to the Internet, and can be packaged with the text at no additional cost. Students will get answers to frequently asked questions, such as how to get up and running, how to get their message out in style, how to conduct job research and prepare résumés, and how to find their way on the information superhighway, and they will get to participate in distance learning (updated annually).

Business Communication Update Newsletter for Faculty

Delivered exclusively by e-mail every month, the newsletter provides interesting materials that can be used in class, and it offers practical ideas about teaching methods. To receive a complimentary subscription, simply send a blank message by e-mail to majordomo@po.databack.com today. In the message area, insert the following two lines:

subscribe bcu
end

Authors' E-Mail Hotline for Faculty

Integrity, excellence, and responsiveness are our hallmarks. This means providing you with textbooks that are academically sound, creative, timely, and sensitive to instructor and student needs. As an adopter of *Business Communication Today*, you are invited to use our E-Mail Hotline. We want to be sure you're completely satisfied, so if you ever have a question or a concern related to the text or its supplements, please e-mail us at bovee-thill@uia.net. We'll get back to you as quickly as possible.

Web Site for Faculty

Visit the PHLIP/Companion Web site at http://www.prenhall.com/bovee. The site includes downloadable resources, including the Instructor's Resource Manual and Lecture Presentation Slides (PowerPoint 97). Also included is an archive of teaching materials, faculty Internet resources, and a moderated conference and chat group that provides opportunities for asking questions, making suggestions, and sharing new teaching ideas. The faculty Web site is password-protected to prevent student access.

WebCT

In addition to the wealth of resources and information found on the companion Web sites, we now offer WebCT with this text at an additional cost.

WebCT allows you to create your own full-length, online course, or to simply produce online materials to supplement existing courses. For more information, contact your Prentice Hall sales representative.

Personal Acknowledgments

Business Communication Today, Sixth Edition, is the product of the concerted efforts of a number of people. A heartfelt thanks to our many friends, acquaintances, and business associates who agreed to be interviewed so that this textbook could continue to feature real people at actual companies: Clarence Wooten Jr. and Andre Forde, Metamorphosis Studios; Virginia Johnson, Minnesota Mining & Manufacturing; Michiru Tamanai and Kayomi Kaneda, Sheraton Hotels Hawaii; Jeff Hagen, General Mills; Julian Santoyo, Community Health Group; Adrianne Proeller, Turner Broadcasting System; Silva Raker, The Nature

Company; Yia Eason, Olmec Toys; Jeanne Anderson, AT&T Language Line Services; Kim Daus, Silicon Graphics; Charley Shin, Gosh Enterprises; Curtis Symonds, BET Holdings; Wesley Van Linda, Narada Records; Dierdre Ballou, San Diego Wild Animal Park; Mark Landiak, Corporate Dynamics; Leann Anderson, Anderson Business Resources; Doug Halm, Recreational Equipment Incorporation (REI); and Jodi DeLeon, Microsoft.

We are grateful to Barbara Schatzman for her remarkable talents and valuable contributions; to Lianne Downey for her unique insights and perspectives; to Joe Glidden for his dedication and expertise; to Jackie Estrada for her noteworthy talents and wise counsel; and to Terry Anderson for her breadth of knowledge and outstanding communication skills.

We appreciate the useful contributions of Deborah Valentine, Emory University; Anne Bliss, University of Colorado, Boulder; Carolyn A. Embree, University of Akron; Carla L. Sloan, Liberty University; Doris A. Van Horn Christopher, California State University, Los Angeles; and Susan S. Rehwaldt, Southern Illinois University.

Recognition and thanks to Mary Leslie, Don Fitzgerald, Donald Anderson, and Quentin Decker at Grossmont College.

We also feel it is important to acknowledge and thank the Association for Business Communication, an organization whose meetings and publications provide a valuable forum for the exchange of ideas and for professional growth.

Thanks to the many individuals whose valuable suggestions and constructive comments have contributed to the success of this book. The authors are deeply grateful for the efforts of Robert Allen, Northwest Connecticut Community College; Lois J. Bachman, Community College of Philadelphia; Jane Bennett, Dekalb College; Mary Bresnahan, Michigan State University; Julian Caplan, Borough of Manhattan Community College; Donald Crawford, West Georgia College; Susan Currier, California Polytechnic State University; David P. Dauwalder, California State University, Los Angeles; Carol David, Iowa State University; Rod Davis, Ball State University; Earl A. Dvorak, Indiana University, Bloomington; Norma J. Gross, Houston Community College; Florence Grunkemeyer, Ball State University; Maxine Hart, Baylor University; Susan Hilligoss, Clemson University; Louise C. Holcomb, Gainesville Junior College; J. Kenneth Horn, Southwestern Missouri State University; Randolph H. Hudson, Northeastern Illinois University; Edna Jellesed, Lane Community College; Betty Johnson, Stephen F. Austin State University; Paul J. Killorin, Portland Community College; Lorraine Krajewski, Louisiana State University; Patricia Kuriscak, Niagara County Community College; Reva Leeman, Portland Community College; Ethel A. Martin, Glendale Community College; Kenneth R. Mayer, Cleveland State University; Gertrude M. McGuire, University of Montevallo; Willie Minor, Phoenix College; Evelyn P. Morris, Mesa Community College; Linda Munilla, Georgia Southern College; Tom Musial, Saint Mary's University; Alexa North, Georgia State University; Devern Perry, Brigham Young University; Paul Preston, University of Texas, San Antonio; Thomas P. Proietti, Monroe Community College; Nelda Pugh, Jefferson State College; Richard David Ramsey, Southeastern Louisiana University; Lillian E. Rollins, Dekalb College; W. J. Salem, Central Michigan University; Grant T. Savage, Texas Tech University; Dorothy Sibley, Brevard Community College; Roberta M. Supnick, Western Michigan University; Sumner B. Tapper, Northeastern University; Vincent Trofi, Providence College; Linda N. Ulman, University of Miami; Dona Vasa, University of Nebraska; Ruth A. Walsh, University of South Florida; John L. Waltman, Eastern Michigan University; Kathryn Jensen White, University of Oklahoma; Mimi Will, Foothill College; J. Douglas Andrews, University of Southern California; Jane Beamish, North Country Community College; Pauline Ann Buss, William R. Harper College; James L. Godell, North Michigan University; Kenneth Gorman, Winona State University; Francis N. Hamlet, Longwood College; William Hendricks, Temple University; Elizabeth Jenkins, Pennsylvania State University; Barbara Jewell, Pierce College; Elaine Krajewski, Louisiana State University; Reeva Leeman, Portland Community College; Virgil R. Pufahl, University of Wisconsin, Platteville; Jim Rucker, Fort Hays State University; Carla L. Sloan, Liberty University; Jeremiah J. Sullivan, University of Washington; Rose Ann Swartz, Ferris State University; Janet Adams, Mankato State University; Sauny Dills, California Polytechnic State University; and Claudia Rawlins, California State University, Chico; Janet Adams, Mankato State University; Bill Hendricks, California University, Pennsylvania; Carol Lutz, University of Texas, Austin; Glynna Morse, Georgia College, Georgia; and David Victor, East Michigan University.

A special debt is owed to the following individuals who reviewed the fifth edition in preparation for the sixth edition: J. Douglas Andrews, University of Southern California; Lillie Anderton-Lewis, North Carolina A&T State University; Dr. Colleen Vawdrey, Utah Valley State College; Nanette Clinch Gilson, College of Business, San Jose State University; and Susan Eisner, Ramapo College.

We want to extend our warmest appreciation to the devoted professionals at Prentice Hall. They include Sandra

Steiner, President; James Boyd, Vice President/Editorial Director; Natalie Anderson, Editor-in-Chief; Linda Schreiber, Senior Editor; Kristen Imperatore, Assistant Editor; Debbie Clare, Marketing Manager; all of Prentice Hall Business Publishing, and the outstanding Prentice Hall sales representatives. Finally, we thank Judy Leale, Associate Managing Editor, and Lynda P. Hansler, Production Editor, for their dedication. We are grateful to copyeditor Margo Quinto, designer Lorraine Castellano, permissions coordinator Monica Stipanov, and photo researcher Melinda Alexander for their superb work.

Courtland L. Bovée
John V. Thill

Foundations of Business Communication

Chapter 1
Understanding Business Communication

Chapter 2
Listening, Working in Teams, and Understanding Nonverbal Communication

Chapter 3
Communicating Interculturally

UNDERSTANDING BUSINESS COMMUNICATION

AFTER STUDYING THIS CHAPTER, YOU WILL BE ABLE TO

1. Explain the importance of having good communication skills in today's workplace
2. Highlight the difference between the formal and informal communication channels
3. Discuss the process of communication
4. Identify eight major communication barriers between people and within organizations
5. List six factors that contribute to effective business communication
6. Explain the meaning of *media richness*

Andre Forde

Clarence Wooten Jr.

COMMUNICATION CLOSE-UP AT METAMORPHOSIS STUDIOS

Clarence Wooten Jr. and Andre Forde were barely in their twenties when they opened their own multimedia design firm in 1993. At the time, Wooten was producing animated presentations for architects, and Forde was designing educational software. However, they shared a dream of having their own company—a company that could challenge industry giants such as Sega and Microsoft, a company that would be an energizing oasis for creative people. They wanted their company to be open and nurturing, unlike the stifling corporate environments they had both experienced firsthand.

Today, their dream is a reality. Metamorphosis Studios is considered an up-and-coming competitor, thanks to its cutting-edge designs of interactive software, multimedia presentations, corporate Web pages, and edutainment products. Moreover, the company's unique working environment is attracting the industry's most talented professionals. That's because the company is a "virtual corporation"—for all practical purposes, located in cyberspace. The partners created this virtual corporation by default, when they decided to hire freelancers because they couldn't afford the enormous expense required for an in-house staff.

A core group of eight creative specialists work regularly for Metamorphosis, along with dozens of others who come aboard for specific projects. To get a feeling for the creative skills of first timers, and to gauge their level of self-motivation, Wooten uses newcomers on a test project before hiring them as regular contributors. Based all over the country, these freelancers are linked by phone, fax, and the Internet. In fact, many potential workers contact Metamorphosis after seeing its Web page (at http://www.mstudios.com), which showcases products, services, creative talent, and clients. "We design our Web page with great

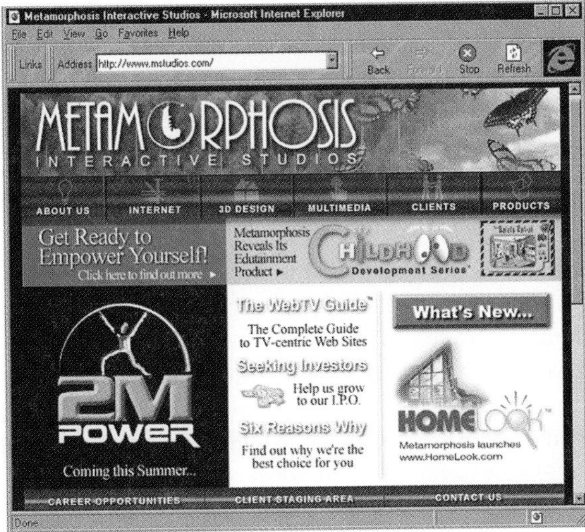

At Metaphorphosis Studios, open communication is the key. Whether it's through the company's Web page, face-to-face meetings, weekly bulletins, or e-mail, the communication flows freely. Wooten and Forde are committed to overcoming communication barriers both inside and outside the company by planning ahead for communication opportunities, keeping the environment responsive and nonthreatening, and encouraging everyone to share their ideas.

care," says Wooten, "because we want to show that we understand the medium and that our creative designs can compete with anyone's."

A typical project takes three to six months or more to complete and requires frequent communication and coordination with each far-flung member of the creative team. Indeed, the company's open communication methods enable Metamorphosis to produce its trademark creative products on time and within budget.

Communication on a project begins when Wooten and Forde assemble the entire team for a kickoff meeting. Such face-to-face interaction enables team members to establish a rapport while exchanging ideas on creative strategies. During these meetings, the partners encourage feedback with informal, give-and-take discussions. "We hang out, crash on the floor, and coordinate our efforts," say Wooten. "Participation in exchanging ideas is more than encouraged—it's expected. It's a democracy, and we listen." Wooten believes that when they have an opportunity to share ideas and give feedback, creative specialists tend to be more productive, more enthusiastic, and best of all, more creative than when they're just told what to do. So he works hard to make sure that this climate of open communication and feedback continues among team members throughout the project.

Some freelancers, particularly the technical specialists, are reluctant communicators who are much less likely than the creative specialists to offer feedback. But Wooten maintains two-way communication by sending out a biweekly bulletin to everyone via electronic mail, updating everyone on all aspects of the project, and asking for comments and reactions.

Many people are stimulated by knowing how an entire project is progressing (even beyond their own individual roles); however, others feel so overloaded by unnecessary information that effective communication is actually blocked. So in addition to his update bulletins, Wooten sends individualized messages to team members. He takes care to make these communications clear and concise. He's specific both when asking for what he needs and when providing information. At the same time, he communicates a feeling of enthusiasm and trust in the freelancer, strengthening the person's commitment and team spirit.

Of course, Wooten's audience of freelancers are likely to be immersed in their work, no matter what time of the day or night he might try to contact them. This kind of competition for attention can be another formidable barrier to communication. But Wooten overcomes this problem by using e-mail, because it's read only when the receiver chooses to access it.

Wooten and Forde understand the importance of effective communication. They encourage two-way communication, build a solid foundation of trust, elicit feedback at every turn, and send messages that are clear and specific. Metamorphosis Studios is proving that cyberspace can be a productive environment when both workers and managers operate with trust and communicate effectively.[1] ■

COMMUNICATION, BUSINESS, AND YOU

Organizations such as Metamorphosis bend over backward to see that communication both inside and outside the company is open, honest, and clear. They understand that their success depends on the ability of their employees and managers to communicate effectively. And they know that communication and effective communication are not the same thing. **Communication** is the process of sending and receiving messages. *Effective communication,* however, occurs when individuals achieve a shared understanding, stimulate others to take actions, and encourage people to think in new ways.

Communication enables organizations to function.

Your ability to communicate effectively increases productivity, both yours and your organization's: You can anticipate problems, make decisions, coordinate work flow, supervise others, develop relationships, and promote products and services. You can shape the impressions you make on your colleagues, employees, supervisors, investors, and customers. And you can perceive and respond to the needs of these **stakeholders** (the various groups you interact with).[2] Whether you work for a virtual corporation such as Metamorphosis, run your own business, invest in a company, buy or sell products, design computer chips, run for public office, or raise money for charities, your communication skills determine your success.[3]

Employers want people who can communicate.

In fact, your chances of being hired by an organization are better if you have strong communication skills. Consider this: Out of 120 job descriptions appearing in one issue of the *National Business Employment Weekly* (published by *The Wall Street Journal*), almost every listing included this requirement: "The persons we seek must have strong oral and written communication skills." From chief financial officer to product manager, from senior economist to personnel analyst, from senior sales representative to petroleum buyer—these positions will be filled by people who can communicate well.[4]

THE BASIC FORMS OF COMMUNICATION

In this course, you will learn how to select the best form of communication for your message.

Communication occurs in many forms. You can pick up the phone and have a conversation with your supervisor or leave her a voice-mail message if she is unavailable. You can choose, instead, to write her a memo and send it by e-mail. In turn, she can respond to your message in the form of her choice. Your supervisor may decide to forward your message to other employees or managers, and they may communicate it to customers and other outsiders. The process is fluid; the form in which a message is communicated changes constantly. Communication can be formal or informal, spoken or written, and internal or external. In fact, it can even be a simple smile.

Nonverbal Communication

Nonverbal communication is the process of communicating without words.

The most basic form of communication is **nonverbal communication:** all the cues, gestures, facial expressions, spatial relationships, and attitudes toward time that enable people to communicate without words. Anthropologists theorize that long before human beings used words to talk things over, our ancestors communicated with one another by using their bodies. They gritted their teeth to show anger; they smiled and touched one another to indicate affection. Although we have come a long way since those primitive times, we still use nonverbal cues to express superiority, dependence, dislike, respect, love, and other feelings.[5]

Nonverbal communication differs from verbal communication in fundamental ways. For one thing, it's less structured, so it's more difficult to study. You can't pick up a book on nonverbal language and master the vocabulary of gestures, expressions, and inflections that are common in our culture. Even experts don't really know how people learn nonverbal behavior. No one teaches a baby to cry or smile, yet these forms of self-expression are almost universal. Other types of nonverbal communication, such as the meaning of colors and certain gestures, vary from culture to culture.

Nonverbal communication also differs from verbal communication in terms of intent and spontaneity. You generally plan your words. When you say, "Please get back to me on that order by Friday," you have a conscious purpose; you think about the message, if only for a moment. However, when you communicate nonverbally, you sometimes do so unconsciously. You don't mean to raise an eyebrow or to blush. Those actions come naturally. Without your consent, your emotions are written all over your face. Of course, as Chapter 2 discusses in greater detail, good communicators recognize the value of nonverbal communication and use it to enhance the communication process.

Actions speak louder than words.

Verbal Communication

Although you can express many things nonverbally, there are limits to what you can communicate without the help of language. If you want to discuss past events, ideas, or abstractions, you need symbols that stand for your thoughts. **Verbal communication** consists of words arranged in meaningful patterns. The ever-growing English language currently contains about 750,000 words, although most people in the United States recognize only about 20,000 of them.[6] To create a thought with these words, you arrange them according to the rules of grammar, putting the various parts of speech in the proper sequence. You then transmit the message in spoken or written form, anticipating that someone will hear or read what you have to say.

Language is composed of words and grammar.

Speaking and Writing

As Figure 1.1 illustrates, businesspeople tend to prefer oral communication channels to written ones. The trade-offs between speaking and writing are discussed in more depth in Chapter 4, but in general, talking to somebody is quicker and more convenient than writing a memo or a letter. Furthermore, when you're speaking or listening, you can pick up added meaning from nonverbal cues and benefit from immediate feedback.

Even though oral communication is the preferred medium, there are times when written communication is more appropriate and effective: when the information you are conveying is very complex, when a permanent record is needed for future reference, when the audience is large and geographically dispersed, and when immediate interaction with the audience is either unimportant or undesirable. The most common types of written communication are letters, memos, reports, and proposals.

Businesspeople rely more heavily on oral than on written communication for sharing information on a day-to-day basis, but they often put important messages in writing.

Over the past few decades, technological advances have led to the development of electronic communication. Voice mail, teleconferencing, e-mail, and computer networks have revolutionized both oral and written communication and have become vital elements in achieving organizational goals. However, as Chapter 10 and numerous examples throughout this book will point out, each form of communication also has its limitations. Protocols must be followed, and individuals must learn when it is appropriate to use each form.[7]

Figure 1.1
The Percentage of Communication Time Businesspeople Spend on Various Communication Channels

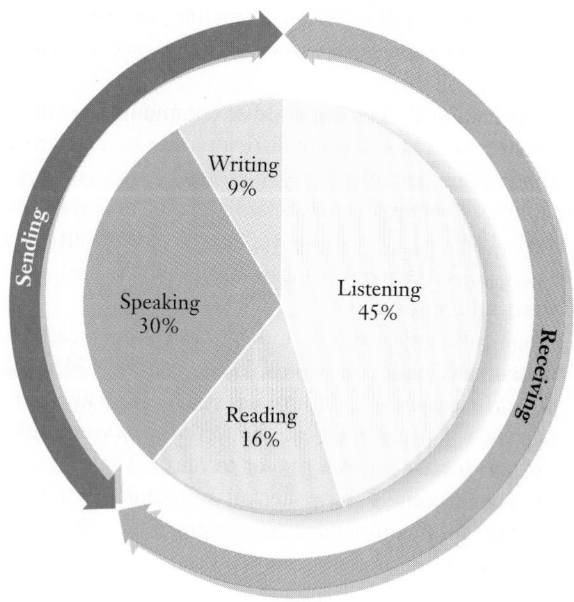

Listening and Reading

Take another look at Figure 1.1. In addition to underscoring the importance of oral communication, it illustrates another interesting fact: People spend more time *receiving* information than transmitting it. Listening and reading are every bit as important as speaking and writing.

As Chapter 2 will point out, most of us aren't very good listeners. Immediately after hearing a ten-minute speech, we typically remember only half of what was said. A few days later, we've forgotten three-quarters of the message. Worse, we often miss the subtle, underlying meaning entirely. To some extent, our listening problems stem from our education, or lack of it. We spend years learning to express our ideas, but few of us ever take a course in listening. Nevertheless, developing better listening abilities is crucial for anyone who wants to foster the understanding and cooperation necessary in today's workplace.[8]

To absorb information, you must concentrate, evaluate, and retain what you read or hear.

Employees who don't listen pose obvious problems for companies. Some of the most sophisticated training in communication occurs in the airline industry, where failure to process information correctly can be fatal. To learn from others' mistakes, new pilots at most major airlines analyze cockpit tapes recorded on flights that have crashed. After hearing the tape from a plane that went down near Portland, Oregon, trainees at one airline identified the following communication problems: (1) The captain ignored the second officer's warning that fuel was running short; (2) the first officer never spoke up; and (3) no one corrected the captain when he made the wrong assumption about the amount of fuel remaining in each tank. By studying these and other communication problems, pilot trainees learn to listen for what should have been said but wasn't.[9]

Employees' reading skills can also leave a good deal to be desired. Look at Baldor Electric, a maker of industrial motors. When the company began having a serious problem on its assembly line, the company's chairman was puzzled. When he went to the plant to investigate, he found that many of Baldor's veteran employees couldn't read. In the days when assembly lines churned out the same product over and over, illiteracy wasn't an issue; a worker could learn by watching someone else. But in the new era of high-tech manufacturing, a single production line can produce a dozen items, each item has its own set of directions, and these directions have to be read—whether from manuals or computer monitors. Baldor's employees who could not read were becoming the company's biggest source of error.[10]

FUNCTIONS AND FORMS OF ORGANIZATIONAL COMMUNICATION

Whether an organization is large, small, or a virtual corporation like Metamorphosis, the sharing of information among the parts of an organization, as well as between the organization and the outside world, is the glue that binds the organization together. As a member of an organization, you are a link in the information chain. Whether you're a top manager or an entry-level employee, you have information that others need to perform their jobs. At the same time, others have information that is crucial to you.

Each organization has its own approach to transmitting information, both within the organization and to the outside world.

In a business that has only five or six employees, much information can be exchanged casually and directly by phone, e-mail, fax, or interoffice memo (see Figure 1.2). In a giant organization such as PepsiCo, with hundreds of thousands of employees scattered around the world, transmitting the right information to the right people at the right time is a real challenge. To meet this challenge, organizations rely on internal and external communication channels.

Internal Communication

Internal communication refers to the exchange of information and ideas within an organization. Communication among the members of an organization is essential for effective functioning. As an employee, you are in a position to observe firsthand things that your supervisors and co-workers cannot see: a customer's immediate reaction to a product display, a supplier's momentary hesitation before agreeing to a delivery date, a funny whirring noise in a piece of equipment, or a slowdown in the flow of customers. Managers and co-workers need these little gems of information in order to do their jobs. If you don't pass that information along, nobody will—because nobody else knows.

You are a contact point in both the external and internal communication networks.

Of course, some companies are better at communicating than others. At top-performing companies, communication is a way of life. For example, AT&T's audio news service delivers information to managers and employees by offering callers a choice of reports on specific subjects. AT&T also distributes a daily newsletter to employees and mails a monthly magazine to employees' homes. IBM encourages all U.S. employees to communicate any concerns electronically, using confidential and secure online systems. Because managers and employees at such companies communicate freely, employees develop a clear sense of the organization's mission, and managers are able to identify and react quickly to potential problems. In these firms, management *is* communication.[11] To maintain a healthy flow of information, effective managers use both formal and informal communication channels.

Formal Communication Channels

The **formal communication network** is aligned with the official structure of an organization, which is typically shown as an organization chart like the one in Figure 1.3. Such charts summarize the lines of authority; each box represents a link in the chain of command, and each line represents a formal channel for the transmission of official messages. Information may travel down, up, and across an organization's formal hierarchy.

The formal flow of information follows the official chain of command.

When managers depend on formal channels for communicating, they risk encountering **distortion**, or misunderstanding. Every link in the communication chain opens up a chance for error. So by the time a message makes its way all the way up or down the chain, it may

Figure 1.2
In-Depth Critique: Internal Communication by Memo

As a supplier to vacation spots such as Disney theme parks, Personalized Products, Inc. (PPI) produces souvenirs and toys printed with a wide variety of common names. In this memo, sales manager Tom Beatty reports first-quarter sales to Jacqueline Rogeine, vice president of finance.

INTERNAL MEMORANDUM

TO: Jacqueline Rogeine
FROM: Tom Beatty
DATE: April 10, 2000
SUBJECT: First-Quarter Sales to Disney

The first paragraph gives the reader specific information related to the subject.

Our first-quarter sales to Disney theme parks show a continuing tend toward growth, although margins remain thin. We supplied 38 retail outlets with 52 licensed or personalized items. Revenues rose 34.6% from the first quarter last year, so the severe winter evidently had less impact than we originally expected.

The second paragraph presents an easy-to-read chart of data selected from the overall report.

Although you can look over the attached raw data, the items below enjoyed continued popularity:

Product & Number	2000 First Quarter	1999 First Quarter	Percent Increase
Minnie's Tea Set (M30)	$ 122,460	$ 102,477	19.5
Mickey's Mighty Ball (B44)	249,425	204,112	22.2
"My-Name" Note Cards (P26)	121,689	98,934	23.0
"Needs-a-Name" Doll (D88)	534,827	407,332	31.3
Character T-shirt (P102)	1,147,638	804,231	42.7
TOTAL	$2,176,039	$1,617,806	34.6

The third and fourth paragraphs provide pertinent information related to other areas in the company.

I'm recommending to Ted in marketing that we supply our field reps with character T-shirts (P102) to present to buyers. We can break $1.5 million with this product if we keep promoting it.

Our Asian suppliers assure us that they can keep the products moving our way; however, we need to carefully monitor the spelling of all names. I recommend that we request a fax to proof before signing off on imprinting any item produced overseas.

The final paragraph summarizes the information, asks for follow-up by a certain time, and ends on a positive note.

In general, the figures suggest continued strong growth with no appreciable change in our investment ratio other than adjusting for inflation. After you look aver the numbers, let me know whether you have any questions or concerns before the board meets next month. If the trend continues, 2000 may prove to be a record-setting year for PPI.

The communication climate suffers when information gets distorted or is ignored or when management limits the flow of information to and from employees.

bear little resemblance to the original idea. As a consequence, people at lower levels may have only a vague idea of what top management expects of them, and executives may get an imperfect picture of what's happening lower down the chain.

The formal communication chain has another potential disadvantage: Information may become **fragmented.** Unless management encourages communication across the organization and diligently communicates down the hierarchy, only the person at the very top can see

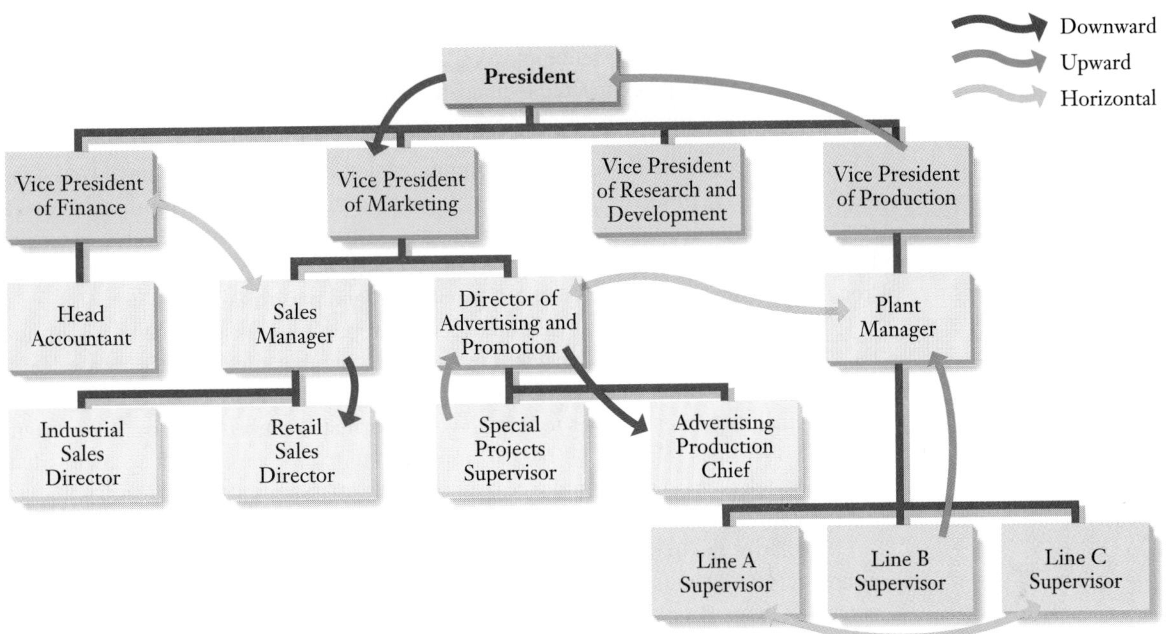

Figure 1.3
Formal Communication Network

the "big picture." People lower down in the organization obtain only enough information to perform their own isolated tasks. They don't learn much about other areas, so their flexibility is limited, and they're unable to suggest ideas that cut across organizational boundaries.

Consider this: In a recent poll of 638 employees conducted by a Chicago-based independent research organization, 90 percent of the employees said they had good ideas on how their companies could run more successfully. Yet, more than 50 percent said a lack of management interest and of effective means for sharing their ideas prevented them from communicating their ideas to management.[12] One way to encourage employee contributions is to make sure communication flows freely down, up, and across the organization chart.

Downward Information Flow In most organizations, decisions are made at the top and then flow down to the people who will carry them out. This downward information flow might occur in a casual conversation or in a formal interview between a supervisor and an individual employee, or it might occur in a meeting, in a workshop, on videotape, or even on voice mail. Downward flow also occurs via messages written for e-mail, memos, training manuals, newsletters, bulletin board announcements, and policy directives. From top to bottom, each person in the organization must be careful to understand each message, apply it, and pass it along. As pointed out by Phil Stein, vice president of H&E Do-It-Yourself Centers (in Victorville, California): "The general manager has to be able to communicate just as well as I do . . . has to be able to communicate our thoughts, our policies, and our regulations to the store managers. A store manager has to be able to communicate with the people on the floor. The 'good morning smile' has to filter all the way down."[13]

Managers direct and control the activities of lower-level employees by sending messages down through formal channels.

Most of what filters downward is geared toward helping employees do their jobs. Even though the trend today is to involve as many people as practical in the decision-making process, once the decisions have been made, it is generally management's responsibility to make sure the word gets out. Typical messages include briefings on the organization's mission and strategies, instructions on how to perform various jobs, explanations of policies and procedures, feedback on employee performance, and motivational pep talks. In hard times, it's especially important to let employees know how the organization is doing, what problems it faces, and what's expected to happen. Likewise, in good times it's important to share the organization's success with those who have made it possible.

Messages directed upward provide managers with the information they need in order to make intelligent decisions.

Upward Information Flow Upward communication is just as vital as downward communication. To solve problems and make intelligent decisions, managers must learn what's going on in the organization. Because they can't be everywhere at once, executives depend on lower-level employees to furnish them with accurate, timely reports on problems, emerging trends, opportunities for improvement, grievances, and performance.

The danger, of course, is that employees will report only the good news. People are often afraid to admit their own mistakes or to report data that suggest their boss was wrong. Companies try to guard against this rose-colored-glasses syndrome by creating reporting systems that require employees to furnish vital information on a routine basis. For example, Southwest Airlines relies on its 14,000 employees to report back to management whatever customers tell them. And, if employees want to bring an issue straight to the top without talking to their manager first, they can.[14]

Similarily, the management at Herman Miller, a Michigan manufacturer of office furniture, gets 2,000 suggestions a year from the company's 5,300 employees and accepts 53 percent of them. People who submit suggestions are publicly honored at departmental meetings; those who submit the most outstanding ideas qualify for the "Idea Club," whose members are invited to a special annual dinner with the CEO. The savings or profits created by the suggestions are set aside and spent for something that benefits all the employees.[15]

Official channels also permit messages to flow from department to department.

Horizontal Information Flow In addition to flowing upward and downward along the chain of command, communication flows from one department to another, either laterally or diagonally. This horizontal flow of information helps employees share information and coordinate tasks, and it is especially useful for solving complex and difficult problems.[16] For example, in the organization depicted in Figure 1.3, the sales manager might write a memo or send e-mail to the vice president of finance, outlining sales forecasts for the coming period; or the plant manager might phone the director of advertising and promotion to discuss changes in the production schedule.

The amount of horizontal communication that occurs through formal channels depends on the degree of interdependence among departments. The most recent trend has been toward more cross-functional interaction. For example, Boeing used hundreds of "design-build" teams that integrated design engineers and production workers to develop its 777 airplane. In the past, the two groups worked independently, and engineers often came up with designs that production workers thought were too costly or unbuildable. By using integrated teams, however, Boeing addressed these types of problems early on, saving the company time and money.[17]

Informal Communication Channels

The informal communication network carries information along the organization's unofficial lines of activity and power.

Formal organization charts illustrate how information is supposed to flow. In actual practice, however, lines and boxes on a piece of paper cannot prevent people from talking with one another. Every organization has an **informal communication network**—a *grapevine*—that supplements official channels. As people go about their work, they have casual conversations with their friends in the office. They joke and kid around and discuss many things: their apartments, their families, restaurants, movies, sports, and other people in the company. Although many of these conversations deal with personal matters, about 80 percent of the information that travels along the grapevine pertains to business.[18]

DID YOU KNOW?

Between 75 and 95 percent of the information traveling the grapevine is accurate.

Some executives are wary of the informal communication network, possibly because it threatens their power to control the flow of information. However, savvy managers tap into the grapevine, using it to spread and receive informal messages.[19] One service, called In

SHARPENING YOUR SKILLS

PSSST! I HEARD IT THROUGH THE GRAPEVINE

Gossip. It's with us whether we like it or not. Why else would the *National Enquirer* be a top-selling tabloid? Why else would talk shows be so popular? Anyone who has ever worked in an organization knows where to go to get the real scoop—the office grapevine. It's the fastest internal communication channel around. and news travels along it in all directions.

"Forget about trying to stop the grapevine," notes Elaine Re, president of a communications firm based in New York and London. "It's a natural part of life, and it's healthy because it gives people a chance to vent their feelings." Experts such as Re agree that it's okay for management to listen in to stay on top of employee concerns and fears, but they disagree over whether managers should use the grapevine as a testing ground.

Planting the Seed It's a simple, cheap way to check an idea. At least, that's how some managers see the grapevine. They casually mention their new idea to the employee who has the fastest tongue, and then they wait for the word to spread. In no time, responses find their way back to the source. If the responses are positive, the managers go ahead with the new plan; if they are negative, then it's back to the drawing board.

Critics of this practice point out that using the grapevine in this way shows a complete lack of understanding of how even an accurate message can become twisted as it travels. Keeping an ear cocked to the vine is one thing, but if you have something to communicate, use the normal channels. Besides, if you regularly supply your employees with real information, you won't need the grapevine.

A Flight Plan for Success Continental Airlines' CEO Gordon Bethune went straight to his employees when he wanted to turn the company around. Continental had been floundering for a decade, and many employees were skeptical of the whole change effort. Bethune knew that communication was a major part of getting employees to accept the new programs. Here are some normal-channel communication devices he used to help keep employees knowledgeable while he turned the airline around from worst to first:

- Daily newsletters to all employees (hard copy or e-mail); four-page monthly newsletter
- Weekly Friday voice-mail update to all employees
- Meetings of all employees three times a year at all eight company locations
- Monthly meetings inviting employees to ask questions of the CEO and company president in a forum structure
- Toll-free number for employees to submit questions
- Fifty-page quarterly journal with comprehensive articles
- Videocassettes with stories about the state of the business and plans for the future (distributed to all employees)

Of course, wise managers like Bethune know that keeping apprised of employee concerns and getting accurate information back to them quickly is one way to put those concerns and fears to rest. They don't rely on the grapevine to do their job. Instead, they count on it for one thing only—gossip. By the way, did you hear the story about the office manager who . . . ?

1. Do you think it is a good idea to use the grapevine to test a new idea? Why or why not?
2. Suppose you are the manager of a sporting goods store and you are thinking about changing the store hours. The change will affect everybody's schedule. How will you go about communicating your idea to the employees? Why might you want feedback?

Touch, helps executives keep up with grapevine news by providing an 800 number that employees can call anonymously with any problems or worries. The recorded messages are either summarized or transcribed verbatim for top management.[20] Because eliminating the grapevine is virtually impossible, sophisticated companies minimize its importance by making certain that the official word gets out.

The grapevine is an important source of information in most organizations.

External Communication

The external communication network links the organization with the outside world of customers, suppliers, competitors, and investors.

Just as internal communication carries information up, down, and across the organization, **external communication** carries it into and out of the organization. Companies constantly exchange messages with customers, vendors, distributors, competitors, investors, journalists, and community representatives. Sometimes this external communication is carefully orchestrated—especially during a crisis. At other times it occurs informally as part of routine business operations.

Informal Contacts with Outsiders

Every employee informally accumulates facts and impressions that contribute to the organization's collective understanding of the outside world.

As a member of an organization, you are automatically an informal conduit for communicating with the outside world. In the course of your daily activities, you unconsciously absorb bits and pieces of information that add to the collective knowledge of your company. What's more, every time you speak for or about your company, you send a message. Many outsiders may form their impression of your organization on the basis of the subtle, unconscious clues you transmit through your tone of voice, facial expression, and general appearance.

Top managers rely heavily on informal contacts with outsiders to exchange information that might be useful to their companies. Although much of the networking involves interaction with fellow executives, plenty of high-level managers recognize the value of keeping in touch with "the real world." For example, when Stanley Gault was chairman of Rubbermaid, he cornered travelers in airports to ask for ideas on new products. Xerox executives spend one day each month handling customer complaints. Senior executives at Hyatt Hotels serve as bellhops, Disney managers all take their turns in 80- to 100-pound character costumes at one of the theme parks, and even the chairman of Intuit (producer of Quicken financial software) spends a few hours each month working the customer-service phone lines. As Wal-Mart founder Sam Walton used to say when someone asked why he visited Kmart stores: "It's all part of the educational process. I'm just learning."[21]

Formal Contacts with Outsiders

Of course, although informal contacts with outsiders are an important vehicle for learning about customers needs, companies must often communicate with outsiders in a more formal manner.

Carefully constructed letters like the one displayed in Figure 1.4 convey an important message to outsiders about the quality of your organization. Whether by phone, fax, videotape, or letter, good communication is the first step in creating a favorable impression. Consider, for instance, the merger announcement made by Daimler-Benz and Chrysler. A great deal of thought and planning went into the press releases and shareholder communication announcing one of the biggest industrial mergers in history.[22] In fact, because messages such as statements to the press, letters to investors, advertisements, price increase announcements, and litigation updates require careful planning, they are often drafted by a team of individuals whose sole job is to create and manage the flow of formal messages to outsiders.

The marketing and public relations departments are responsible for managing much of the organization's formal communication with outsiders.

The Role of Marketing and Public Relations As a consumer, you are often on the receiving end of marketing messages, via face-to-face or telephone conversations with salespeople, direct-mail solicitations, television and radio commercials, newspaper and magazine ads, banner ads on the Internet, product brochures, and mail-order catalogs. Although these messages are highly visible, they represent just the tip of the iceberg when it comes to marketing communication. In addition to advertising and selling products, the typical marketing department is also responsible for product development, physical distribution, market research, and customer service, all of which involve both the transmission and the reception of information.

Marketing focuses on selling goods and services, whereas public relations is more concerned with developing the organization's overall reputation.

Public relations is closely related to marketing and is often confused with it, but the focus of public relations differs. Marketing has three basic responsibilities: to find out who customers are and what they want, to develop products that satisfy those needs, and to get the products into the customers' hands. The public relations (PR) department (also called the

Montana's Save the Wolves Foundation seeks to raise funds for relocating wolves captured from other states into selected wilderness areas of Montana. The foundation communicates externally with representatives of the mass media to try to educate the public and garner support.

Figure 1.4
In-Depth Critique: External Communication by Letter

Save the Wolves Foundation
4542 Audubon Highway • Viper, MT 32400
(406) 266-6223 • Fax (406) 723-3229
<http://www.wolves.org>

March 13, 2000

Mr. Sam Davis, Managing Editor
Montana Times Magazine
468 West Times Drive
Helena, Montana 59601

Dear Mr. Davis:

Thank you for your recent editorial supporting the Montana wolf relocation program. We are as dedicated to preserving domestic livestock herds as are the ranchers who own them. However, killing the wolf predators is both a short-term and a short-sighted solution. We'd like your readers to have some additional information, besides the excellent points you made.

Every one of the 32 wolves we've captured and relocated this year has been examined by a veterinarian. The wolves receive inoculations to prevent rabies, among other diseases. Therefore, the relocated wolves pose little threat of disease to wildlife, their pack, or the occasional domestic animal or human who might encounter them.

In the wilderness areas where they will be relocated, wolves help keep the population of caribou, moose, and deer under control, and they cull injured or sick animals from the herd. However, wolves fear human beings and will avoid people whenever possible. Our North American wolves do not attack humans.

In addition, your readers will be interested to know a little more about wolves in general. Wolves have strong family ties and often mate for life. Female wolves give birth to about four to six pups, and both parents supply food and help train the pups. In fact, the wolf pack is usually a family group. And just as families call to their children, wolves sometimes howl to keep their pack together.

We invite those of your readers who would like to join our efforts to call 1-800-544-8333 to receive more information.

Sincerely,

Carroll Paulding

Carroll Paulding
President

sg

The first paragraph refers to what prompted the communication and ends by clearly stating the purpose of the letter to the editor. The paragraph identifies the two audiences receiving information: the editor of the magazine and magazine readers.

The second and third paragraphs provide specific information on the relocation program and reassure readers of their personal safety.

The fourth paragraph seeks to establish a special connection, or link (sometimes called rapport in oral communication), with the readers.

Finally, the letter ends with a clearly stated invitation placed where readers will notice it.

corporate communication department) manages the organization's reputation with various groups, including employees, customers, investors, government agencies, and the general public. Professional PR people may have a background in journalism, as opposed to marketing. They view their role as disseminating news about the business to the organization's various audiences.

Whereas marketing messages are usually openly sponsored and paid for by the company, public relations messages are carried by the media if they are considered newsworthy. The communication tools used by PR departments include news releases, lobbying programs, special events, booklets and brochures about the organization, letters, annual reports, audiovisual materials, speeches and position papers, tours, and internal publications for employees.

Crisis Communication One of the most visible functions of the PR department is to help management plan for and respond to crises, which can range from environmental accidents or sabotage situations to strikes, massive product failure, major litigation, or even an abrupt change in management. If handled improperly, a crisis can destroy a company's reputation, drain its financial strength, erode morale, and invite protracted investigations, heavy fines, and negative publicity.

The way a company handles a crisis can have a profound impact on the organization's subsequent performance.

Look at the 1997 United Parcel Service (UPS) strike. Experts agree that UPS damaged itself by allowing as many as a dozen human resources executives answer questions from the press. "Details were too complicated," note experts. "UPS had too many people delivering messages. It's too bad, because the company had a great story to tell."[23]

Most experts recommend handling a crisis with candor and honesty.

Recognize the impact of a crisis on employees.

To avoid this confusion, most communication experts suggest selecting (in advance) a communications team and a knowledgeable spokesperson to handle the many requests for information that arise during a crisis. The individuals selected should be able to speak honestly and remain calm when a crisis hits. Furthermore, the experts recommend that the company's top managers be visible in the hours immediately following the initial crisis to demonstrate that the company will do whatever it takes to control the situation, to find the cause, and to prevent a future occurrence. Finally, experts recommend that managers minimize the impact of any crisis on employees by communicating honestly, openly, and often—using caution when sharing personal opinions (see Table 1.1).[24]

When TWA Flight 800 crashed, the company's management was caught off guard. Having a crisis communication plan in place means preparing for even the worst kinds of disasters.

TABLE 1.1

WHAT TO DO IN A CRISIS

When a Crisis Hits:

Do	Don't
Do be prepared for trouble. Identify potential problems. Appoint and train a response team. Prepare and test a crisis management plan. Do get top management involved as soon as the crisis hits. Do set up a news center for company representatives and the media, equipped with phones, computers, and other electronic tools for preparing news releases. ■ Issue at least two news updates a day, and have trained personnel on call to respond to questions around the clock. ■ Provide complete information packets to the media as soon as possible. ■ To prevent conflicting statements and to provide continuity, appoint a single person, trained in advance, to speak for the company. ■ Tell receptionists to direct all calls to the news center. Do tell the whole story—openly, completely, and honestly. If you are at fault, apologize. Do demonstrate the company's concern by your statements and your actions.	Don't blame anyone for anything. Don't speculate in public. Don't refuse to answer questions. Don't release information that will violate anyone's right to privacy. Don't use the crisis to pitch products or services. Don't play favorites with media representatives.

TWA was criticized for not taking many of these actions when Flight 800 crashed off the coast of Long Island in July 1996, killing all 230 people on board. Critics accused TWA of taking too long to release the names of people on board and criticized the company for being unresponsive to the media. Furthermore, many felt that CEO Jeffrey Erickson waited too long before addressing the public about the crash. TWA was simply not prepared for the crisis: Erickson was in London at the time of the crash, two of his top executives who might have been able to handle the situation in his absence had resigned only a month before, the human resources executive who heads TWA's "trauma team" of crisis volunteers was on vacation, and the executives who *were* available communicated poorly with the media about who was in charge. The company was caught off guard, and it suffered a huge public relations blow as a result. Not only did the company lose customers, but its stock price plummeted from $23 to $6 per share.[25]

The Process of Communication

By now you can see that communication is the lifeblood of an organization. It includes the structure through which messages pass and the way information is presented, as well as the actual content of the messages themselves. Whether you are speaking or writing, listening or reading, communication is more than a single act. It's a dynamic, transactional (two-way) process that can be broken into six phases:

The communication process consists of six phases linking sender and receiver.

1. *The sender has an idea.* You conceive an idea and want to share it.
2. *The sender transforms the idea into a message.* When you put your idea into a message that your receiver will understand, you are **encoding,** deciding on the

message's form (word, facial expression, gesture), length, organization, tone, and style, all of which depend on your idea, your audience, and your personal style or mood.

3. *The sender transmits the message.* To physically transmit your message to your receiver, you select a **communication channel** (verbal or nonverbal, spoken or written) and **medium** (telephone, computer, letter, memo, report, face-to-face exchange, and so on). The channel and medium you choose depend on your message, the location of your audience, your need for speed, and the formality of the situation.

4. *The receiver gets the message.* For communication to occur, your receiver must first get the message. If you send a letter, your receiver has to read it before understanding it. If you're giving a speech, the people in your audience have to be able to hear you, and they have to be paying attention.

5. *The receiver interprets the message.* Your receiver must cooperate by **decoding** your message, absorbing and understanding it. Then the decoded message has to be stored in the receiver's mind. If all goes well, the message is interpreted correctly; that is, the receiver assigns the same basic meaning to the words as you intended and responds in the desired way.

Feedback is your audience's response; it enables you to evaluate your message's effectiveness.

6. *The receiver reacts and sends feedback to the sender.* **Feedback** is your receiver's response, the final link in the communication chain. After getting the message, your receiver responds in some way and signals that response to you. Feedback is the key element in the communication process because it enables you to evaluate the effectiveness of your message. If your audience doesn't understand what you mean, you can tell by the response and refine your message.

As Figure 1.5 illustrates, the communication process is repeated until both parties have finished expressing themselves.[26] The process is effective only when each step is successful. In other words, ideas cannot be communicated if any step in this process is skipped or is completed incorrectly.

Figure 1.5
The Communication Process

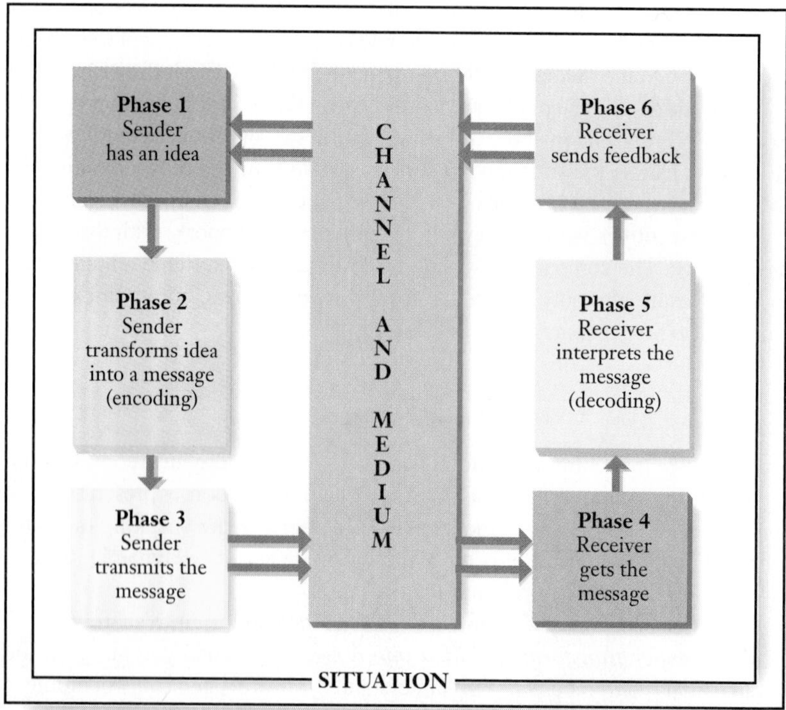

Communication Barriers

Even if you successfully complete these six steps, other hurdles may prevent you from communicating effectively. Communication is successful only when the receiver understands the message as intended by the sender. **Noise** is any interference in the communication process that distorts or obscures the sender's meaning. Noise takes the form of various communication barriers and can exist between individuals as well as within organizations.[27]

Communication barriers exist between individuals and within organizations.

Communication Barriers between People

When you send a message, you intend to communicate meaning, but the message itself doesn't contain meaning. The meaning exists in your mind and in the mind of your receiver. To understand each other, you and your receiver must share similar meanings for words, gestures, tone of voice, and other symbols. Effective communicators do all they can to deal with barriers such as differences in perception and language, poor listening, emotional interference, cultural differences, and physical distractions.

Differences in Perception and Language

The world constantly bombards us with sights, sounds, scents, and so on. Our minds organize this stream of sensation into a mental map that represents our **perception** of reality. Even when two people have experienced the same event, their mental images of that event will not be identical. Because your perceptions are unique, the ideas you want to express differ from other people's. As a sender, you choose the details that seem important to you, a process known as **selective perception**. As a receiver, you try to fit new details into your existing pattern. If a detail doesn't quite fit, you are inclined to distort the information rather than rearrange the pattern.

Perception is people's individual interpretation of the sensory world around them.

Language is an arbitrary code that depends on shared definitions. However, there's a limit to how completely any two people can share the same meaning for a given word. Take the simple word *cookie*, for example. Your idea of a cookie is a composite of all the cookies you have ever tasted or seen: oatmeal cookies, chocolate chip cookies, sugar cookies, and so on. Someone from another culture may have an entirely different range of cookie experiences: meringues, florentines, spritz. You both agree on the general concept of cookie, but the precise images in your minds differ.

Your definitions of words may differ dramatically from those of other people.

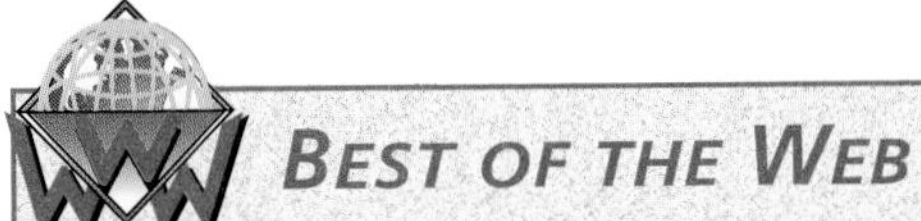

Beef Up Your Internet Language Skills

Your success in Internet communication depends on how well you understand the language. That's where Netlingo can help. Keep the site's "pocket dictionary" floating toolbar on your desktop while you surf, and you'll have instant access to definitions of common Net terms, which aren't always what you'd expect them to be. For instance, you know from this chapter that *cookie* means different things in different cultures, but do you know what *cookie* means to a Netizen? Better look it up.

http://www.netlingo.com

Note: If you receive an error message when you try to get to a site on the Web, go to http://www.inference.com or http://www.cyber411.com. Insert the name of the site in the space provided, and press "search." If the site you're seeking is still operating, the results of your research will usually provide a hot link to it.

At Home Depot, Carolyn Fushima needs to communicate with the employees she supervises, regardless of differences in their age, their gender, or their cultural or ethnic backgrounds.

Poor Listening

Listening ability decreases when information is difficult to understand and when it has little meaning for the listener.

Although most of us think we know how to listen, Chapter 2 will show that in reality many of us are poor listeners. We all let our minds wander now and then, plus we are especially likely to drift off when we are forced to listen to information that is difficult to understand or that has little direct bearing on our own lives. If we are tired or concerned about other matters, we are even more likely to lose interest.

Emotional Interference

It's difficult to shape a message when you are upset, hostile, or fearful. Your ideas and feelings often get in the way of being objective. Likewise, if the other person is emotional, he or she may ignore or distort your message. Although it's practically impossible to avoid all communication when emotions are involved, you should be alert to the greater potential for misunderstanding that accompanies emotional messages.

Cultural Differences

Communicating with someone from another country is probably the most extreme example of how different backgrounds and cultures may impede communication. In fact, it may be one of the hardest communication barriers to overcome—especially when your receiver's age, education, social status, economic position, religion, or life experience also differs substantially from yours (see Chapter 3). Figure 1.6 shows how shared experience contributes to shared meaning and understanding; the portion of each diagram where the circles overlap represents the level of understanding between the sender and the receiver.

Physical Distractions

Your audience is more likely to receive your message accurately if nothing physical interrupts or distorts the message.

Communication barriers are often physical: bad connections, poor acoustics, illegible copy. Although noise of this sort seems trivial, it can block an otherwise effective message. Your receiver might be distracted by an uncomfortable chair, poor lighting, health

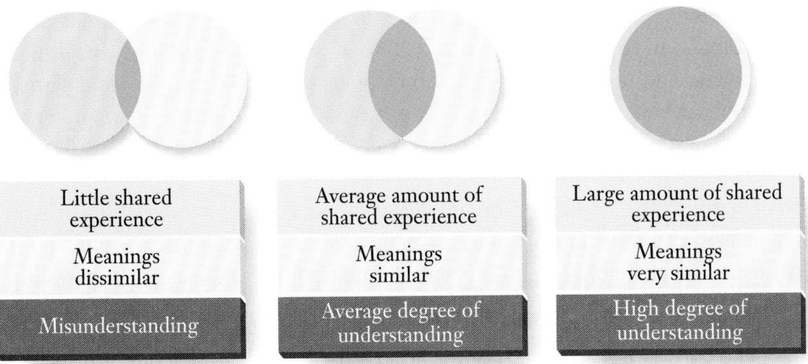

Figure 1.6
How Shared Experience Affects Understanding

problems, or some other irritating condition. These annoyances don't generally block communication, but they may reduce the receiver's concentration.

Communication Barriers within Organizations

Business communication is especially subject to noise because the material is often complex and controversial. Furthermore, the number of business messages delivered each day is staggering, and the opportunities for feedback are often limited, making it difficult to correct misunderstandings when they do occur. By understanding the types of communication barriers that exist in organizations, you can increase your chances of overcoming them.

Information Overload and Message Competition

Ohail Shafi's workday starts long before he arrives at his office. He's the director of corporate information technology at Harsco, an industrial service and product supplier. Before leaving his home, Shafi checks his e-mail (sometimes more than 50 messages a day). As he begins his one-hour commute, he pops a casette tape into his car stereo and listens to

This Planet Advertising employee finds it difficult to cope with the daily glut of faxes, memos, reports, e-mail, and other messages he receives.

technical conferences he didn't have time to attend. He turns on his cellular phone and checks his voice-mail messages (sometimes 20 to 30 a day). At the office, his desk is piled high with papers, and his computer desktop displays today's latest news and statistics because Shafi subscribes to a 24-hour Internet personal news service. Like many executives, Shafi is overwhelmed with the volume of messages from all sources. And it's getting worse.[28]

Today's businesspeople are plagued by message overload.

A recent study by the Gallup organization found that, on a typical day, the average white-collar worker sends and receives as many as 190 messages (see Figure 1.7).[29] The problem is that new technology isn't replacing more traditional forms; it's just adding to the load. As a result, people like Shafi are inundated with messages, and they will ignore the ones they deem unimportant, delay responding to them, or answer them incompletely or inaccurately. Consider this: When one executive returned from vacation and found 2,000 e-mail messages waiting for him, he simply deleted them all.[30]

Incorrect Filtering

Filtering is screening out or abbreviating information before passing the message on to someone else.

Filtering is screening out or abbreviating information before a message is passed on to someone. In business, the filters between you and your receiver are many: secretaries, assistants, answering machines, and voice mail, to name a few. Just getting through by telephone can take a week if you're calling someone who's protected by these gatekeepers, or filters. Worse yet, information theory tells us that "every relay doubles the noise and cuts the message in half."[31] That means your message may be distilled and probably distorted before it's passed on to your intended receiver.

Closed or Inadequate Communication Climate

A management style that is directive and authoritarian blocks the free and open exchange of information that characterizes effective communication. Likewise, having two few channels will block communication, whereas having too many channels will distort messages as they move upward, downward, or horizontally through the organization.

Figure 1.7
Message Mania

Message mania is occurring because many people "bundle" or send the same message in more than one form to make sure it gets through.

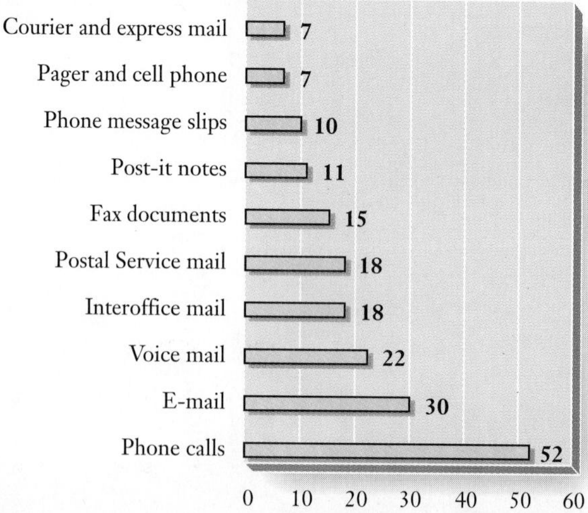

How to Overcome Barriers and Improve Communication

Think about the people you know. Which of them would you call successful communicators? What do these people have in common? Chances are, the individuals on your list share these five traits:

Effective communication requires perception, precision, credibility, control, and congeniality.

- *Perception*. They are able to predict how you will receive their message. They anticipate your reaction and shape the message accordingly. They read your response correctly and constantly adjust to correct any misunderstanding.
- *Precision*. They create a "meeting of the minds." When they finish expressing themselves, you share the same mental picture.
- *Credibility*. They are believable. You have faith in the substance of their message. You trust their information and their intentions.
- *Control*. They shape your response. Depending on their purpose, they can make you laugh or cry, calm down, change your mind, or take action.
- *Congeniality*. They maintain friendly, pleasant relations with you. Regardless of whether you agree with them, good communicators command your respect and goodwill. You are willing to work with them again, despite your differences.

Effective communicators work hard at perfecting the messages they deliver. When they make mistakes, they learn from them. If a poorly written memo does not get the response they hoped for, they change their approach the next time around. If a meeting they are running gets out of control or becomes unproductive, they do things differently at the next one. If they find themselves having to explain themselves over and over ... uate their choice of communication medium ...

Throughout this book, you will lear... coming chapters we'll present real-life e... explain what's good or bad about them. A... tice that six themes keep surfacing as eff... proving your communication skills: (1) fo... mitting to ethical communication; (3) unde... communication; (4) adopting an audience... technology wisely and responsibly to obt... processing your messages effectively and ... guidelines.

Fostering an Open Communic...

...ganization's communication climate affects the quantity and quality of the information that passes through the pipeline.

An organization's communication climate is ... ture of values, traditions, and habits that give ... companies tend to choke off the upward flow o... consuming and unproductive. Other companies ...phosis, work to maintain an open communication climate. They encourage candor and honesty, and their employees feel free to confess their mistakes, to disagree with the boss, and to express their opinions.

Modify the Number of Organizational Levels

One way to foster an open communication climate is to reduce the number of levels in the organization's structure. The fewer the links in the communication chain, the less likely it is that misunderstandings will occur.[32] In other words, a flat structure (having fewer

A modular office layout such as this one at Continental Packaging Products encourages an open communication climate.

levels) and a wide span of control (having more people reporting to each supervisor) are less likely to introduce distortion than a tall structure and a narrow span of control.

To keep in touch with employees and to encourage an open climate, effective managers
- Get out of their offices
- Talk with and listen to management and non-management groups

Molex, a $1.5 billion global manufacturer of electronic-connector products, is a perfect example of how a company uses its organizational structure to foster an open communication environment. Unlike other companies its size, Molex keeps its structure relatively flat to encourage communication at all levels. Officers at Molex work in cubicles, just as regular employees do, and they are accessible to everyone.[33] Although flat is not necessarily better, more and more companies are flattening their structure in an effort to cut costs, boost productivity, and get closer to customers. Flatter structures enable managers to share information with colleagues and employees and to include employees in decision making, goal setting, and problem solving.[34]

On the other hand, designing too few formal channels and having too many people report to a single individual can block effective communication. To overcome structural barriers, offer opportunities for communicating upward, downward, and horizontally (using such techniques as employee surveys, open-door policies, newsletters, memos, e-mail, and task groups).

Facilitate Feedback

Make feedback useful by
- Planning how and when to accept it
- Being receptive to your audience's responses
- Encouraging frankness
- Using it to improve communication

Giving your audience a chance to provide feedback is crucial to maintaining an open communication climate. According to a recent American Express survey, the thing employees wanted the most from their employers was personal feedback (money was rated second). But, eager to avoid conflict or to be cast in the role of critical boss, many managers avoid giving frank feedback to underperforming employees until it's too late.[35] Still, as Clarence Wooten knows from his experience at Metamorphosis Studios, feedback isn't always easy to get, even when you encourage it. In some cases, you may have to draw out the other person by asking questions. If you want to know specific things, ask specific questions, but also encourage your audience to express general reactions; you can often garner useful information that way.

Of course, if you encourage people to be open and to tell you what they really think and feel, then you have to listen to their comments, and you must do so objectively. You can't say "Please tell me what you think" and then get mad at the first critical comment. Your goal is to find out whether the people in your audience have understood and accepted your message. If you find that they haven't, don't lose your temper, and try not to react defensively. After all, the fault is at least partially yours. Instead of saying the same thing over again, only louder this time, try to find the source of the misunderstanding. Then revise your message. Sooner or later, if you keep trying, you'll succeed. You may not win the audience to your point of view, but at least you'll make your meaning clear, and you'll part with a feeling of mutual respect.

No one is more familiar with this process than Jack Welch, CEO of General Electric. A fierce believer in the power of his people, Welch encourages near-brutal candor in his meetings so he can collect unfiltered information and make sure that the organization's triumphs and failures are openly shared. As Welch puts it, "the idea flow from the human spirit is absolutely unlimited. All you have to do is tap into that well."[36]

Committing to Ethical Communication

The second guideline for effective communication is a commitment to **ethics,** the principles of conduct that govern a person or a group. Unethical people are essentially selfish and unscrupulous, saying or doing whatever it takes to achieve an end. Ethical people are generally trustworthy, fair, and impartial, respecting the rights of others and concerned about the impact of their actions on society. Former Supreme Court Justice Potter Stewart defined ethics as "knowing the difference between what you have a right to do and what is the right thing to do."[37]

Ethics are the principles of conduct that govern a person or a group.

Ethics plays a crucial role in communication. Language itself is made up of words that carry values. So merely by saying things a certain way, you influence how others perceive your message, and you shape expectations and behaviors.[38] **Ethical communication** includes all relevant information, is true in every sense, and is not deceptive in any way.

When sending an ethical message, you are accurate and sincere. You avoid language that manipulates, discriminates, or exaggerates. You do not hide negative information behind an optimistic attitude, you don't state opinions as facts, and you portray graphic data fairly. You are honest with employers, co-workers, and clients, never seeking personal gain by making others look better or worse than they are. You don't allow personal preferences to influence your perception or the perception of others, and you act in good faith. On the surface, such ethical practices appear fairly easy to recognize. But deciding what is ethical can be quite complex (see "Focusing on Ethics: Ethical Boundaries: Where Would You Draw the Line?").

Recognize Ethical Choices

Every company has responsibilities to various groups: customers, employees, shareholders, suppliers, neighbors, the community, and the nation. Unfortunately, what's right for one group may be wrong for another.[39] Moreover, as you attempt to satisfy the needs of one group, you may be presented with an option that seems right on the surface but somehow feels wrong. When people must choose between conflicting loyalties and weigh difficult trade-offs, they are facing a dilemma.

An **ethical dilemma** involves choosing among alternatives that aren't clear-cut (perhaps two conflicting alternatives are both ethical and valid, or perhaps the alternatives lie somewhere in the vast gray area between right and wrong). Suppose you are president of a company that's losing money. You have a duty to your shareholders to try to cut your losses and to your employees to be fair and honest. After looking at various options, you conclude that you'll have to lay off 500 people immediately. You suspect you may have to lay off another

Conflicting priorities and the vast gray areas between right and wrong pose ethical problems for an organization's communicators.

FOCUSING ON ETHICS

ETHICAL BOUNDARIES: WHERE WOULD YOU DRAW THE LINE?

At the very least, you owe your employer an honest day's work for an honest day's pay: your best efforts, obedience to the rules, a good attitude, respect for your employer's property, and a professional appearance. Such duties and considerations seem clear-cut, but where does your obligation to your employer end? The ethics involved in some situations seem perfectly umambiguous . . . until you think about them. For instance, where would you draw the line in communication situations such as the following?

- Writing your résumé so that an embarrassing two-year lapse won't be obvious
- Telling your best friend about your company's upcoming merger right after mailing the formal announcement to your shareholders
- Hinting to a co-worker (who's a close friend) that it's time to look around for something new, when you've already been told confidentially that she's scheduled to be fired at the end of the month
- Saying nothing when you witness one employee taking credit for another's successful idea
- Preserving your position by presenting yourself to supervisors as the only person capable of achieving an objective
- Buying one software package for use by three computer operators
- Making up an excuse when (for the fourth time this month) you have to pick up your child from school early and miss an important business meeting
- Calling in sick because you're taking a few days off and you want to use up some of the sick leave you've accumulated.

At times, your ethical obligation to act in the best interests of your employer may involve more than a simple honest day's work. For example, where would you draw the line in the following situation? You're returning from a bidder's conference, and you spot a competitor's product design in an airport wastebasket. Is it unethical to take advantage of your luck? Once on the plane, you're seated behind two of your competitor's engineers, who are loudly discussing their product's new design. Is it unethical if you can't help overhearing? Then you discover you're seated next to another competitor's chief engineer. He's openly studying detailed drawings of an exciting new product; he carelessly leaves the drawings in his seat when he gets up to use the restroom. How unethical could it be to take a quick glance? When the plane finally lands, the same engineer accidentally leaves his drawings behind as he makes a mad dash for a connecting flight. Again, would it be unethical to take a look?

Is it really unethical to take advantage of a competitor's carelessness in order to benefit your employer? Is it really unethical to betray an employer's confidence or to tell your employer a lie? Wherever you are, whatever the circumstances, you owe your employer your best efforts. Nonetheless, time and again, it will be up to you to decide whether those efforts are ethical.

---

1. As an employer, what ethical behavior would you expect from your employees that isn't mentioned here?
2. As the supervisor of the office typing pool, you must deal with several typists who have a tendency to gossip about their co-workers. List five things you might do to resolve the situation.

---

100 people later on, but right now you need those 100 workers to finish a project. What do you tell them? If you confess that their jobs are shaky, many of them may quit just when you need them most. However, if you tell them that the future is rosy, you'll be stretching the truth.

Unlike a dilemma, an **ethical lapse** is making a clearly unethical or illegal choice. Suppose you have decided to change jobs and have discreetly landed an interview with your boss's largest competitor. You get along great with the interviewer, who is impressed enough with you to offer you a position on the spot. Not only is the new position a step up from your current job, but the pay is double what you're getting now. You accept the job and agree to start next month. Then as you're shaking hands with the interviewer, she asks you to bring along profiles of your current company's ten largest customers when you report for work. Do you comply with her request? How do you decide between what's ethical and what is not?

Make Ethical Choices

One place to look for guidance is the law. If saying or writing something is clearly illegal, you have no dilemma: You obey the law. However, even though legal considerations will resolve some ethical questions, you'll often have to rely on your own judgment and principles. If your intent is honest, the statement is ethical, even though it may be factually incorrect; if your intent is to mislead or manipulate the audience, the message is unethical, regardless of whether it is true. You might look at the consequences of your decision and opt for the solution that provides the greatest good to the greatest number of people, and one that you can live with.[40]

Laws provide ethical guidelines for certain types of messages. Ask yourself how you would feel if you were on the receiving end of the message.

Motivate Ethical Choices

Some companies lay out an explicit ethical policy by using a written **code of ethics** to help employees determine what is acceptable. In addition, many managers will use *ethics audits* to monitor ethical progress and to point up any weaknesses that need to be addressed. They know that being ethical is simply the right thing to do. Plus, it's contagious. Others will follow your example when they observe you being ethical and see the success you experience both in your interpersonal relationships and in your career.[41]

Organizations can foster ethical behavior

- By helping top managers become more sensitive communicators
- By using ethics audits
- By rewarding ethical actions

Understanding the Difficulties Involved in Intercultural Communication

The third guideline contributing to a positive communication climate is understanding intercultural communication. Not only are more and more businesses crossing national boundaries to compete on a global scale, but the makeup of the global and domestic work force is changing rapidly. European, Asian, and U.S. firms are establishing offices around the world and creating international ties through global partnerships, cooperatives, and affiliations.[42]

Global companies must understand the laws, customs, and business practices of many countries, and they must deal with business associates and employees who perhaps speak many languages. Domestically, firms are also working with more and more employees of diverse cultural backgrounds. In the United States, women and ethnic minorities are entering the work force in record numbers. By 2005, 47.7 percent of the U.S. work force will be women, 11.6 percent will be African American, 11 percent will be Hispanic, and 5.5 percent will be Asian American and other minorities (see Figure 1.8).[43] So whether you work abroad or at home, to compete successfully in today's multicultural environment, you will need to overcome the communication barriers not only of language but of culture as well.

The increases in international business dealing and in the diversity of the work force create communication challenges.

Chapter 3 discusses intercultural communication in detail. You'll see how the need for intercultural understanding has grown, whether your company operates within national boundaries or does business around the world. You'll learn about specific cultural differences and see how they affect communication. And you'll discover how understanding others' backgrounds, spheres of knowledge, personalities, and perceptions helps overcome barriers created by cultural differences.

Adopting an Audience-Centered Approach to Communication

The fourth guideline contributing to effective communication is adopting an **audience-centered approach**, or keeping your audience in mind at all times during the process of communication. Because you care about your audience, you take every step possible to

Using an audience-centered approach means keeping your audience in mind at all times when communicating.

Figure 1.8
Ethnic Composition of the U.S. Work Force

Hispanic and Asian American employees are making up a greater proportion of the U.S. work force.

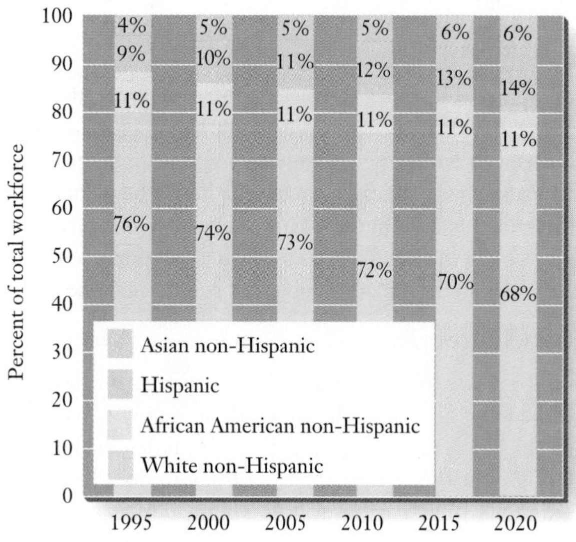

get your message across in a way that is meaningful to your audience. In fact, empathizing with and being sensitive to your audience's feelings is the best way to overcome such communication barriers as differences in perception and emotional interference. If you are aware of others' feelings, you'll be able to choose neutral words, understand their views, and perhaps empathize with their position by trying to view the situation through their eyes.

Your audience-centered approach will help you incorporate into your messages the other four factors of effective communication: an open climate, an ethical commitment, an intercultural understanding, and an effective and efficient message.

In reality, the audience-centered approach is more than an approach to business communication; it's actually the modern approach to business in general (behind such concepts as total quality management and total customer satisfaction). By focusing your attention on your audience, you accomplish the other factors that contribute to effective communication. Because you want to know what your audience's needs are and what they think of your message, you work for an open communication climate inside and outside your organization. Because you sincerely wish to satisfy the needs of your audience, you approach communication situations with good intentions and high ethical standards. Because you need to understand your audience, you do whatever it takes to understand intercultural differences and barriers. Finally, because you value your audience's time and make a practice of anticipating your audience's expectations, you create and process your oral and written messages effectively and efficiently and use technology wisely and responsibly to obtain and share information—the fifth guideline to effective communication.

Using Technology Wisely and Responsibly to Obtain and Share Information

Technology has such an impact on business communication that you have no choice but to master it.

In today's world information moves through an array of media at the speed of a neural impulse. As lightning-fast signals streak to, from, and past your organization, you not only have to think about what you are going to say and how you are going to say it, but you also have to decide which technological tools you'll use to do so. Throughout this book we'll present numerous examples of the types of technological tools you'll encounter on the job and how to use those tools effectively and wisely.

In Chapters 4 through 6, for example, we'll discuss how to use technology to compose, revise, and distribute your message. In Chapter 10 we'll explain how technology is changing the way people work and communicate, both internally and externally. In Chapter 11 we'll explore some of the best ways to obtain and analyze data. And in Chapter 12 we'll show you how to organize and present your data in visuals that communicate your message unequivocally and instantly. In short, you'll find that when used wisely and responsibly, technology can be an invisible ally, helping you improve the effectiveness of your business communication.[44]

Creating and Processing Your Messages Effectively and Efficiently

Earlier in this chapter we discussed the six-phase process of communication. Three of the six steps we presented involve transforming your idea into a message and transmitting it. In Chapters 4 through 6, we'll explain the writing process. We'll show you how to plan messages, generate ideas, organize your thoughts, and turn your words into effective business messages—the sixth guideline for effective communication.

Learn about Your Audience

Ask why you are preparing the message and for whom you are preparing it.

Creating an effective message is difficult if you are unfamiliar with your audience or if you don't know how your message will be used. For example, if you're writing a report on the consumer market for sports equipment and you don't know the purpose of the report, it's hard to know what to say. What sort of sports equipment should you cover? Should you include team sports as well as individual sports? Should you subdivide the market geographically or according to price ranges? How long should the report be? Should it provide conclusions and recommendations or simply facts and figures? Unless you know why the report is needed, you can't really answer those questions intelligently, so you are forced to create a very general document, one that covers a little bit of everything.

Likewise, you need to know something about the biases, education, age, status, and style of your receiver in order to create an effective message. If you're addressing strangers, try to find out more about them; if that's impossible, try to project yourself into their position by using your common sense and imagination. Whatever the tactic, the point is to write and speak from your audience's point of view.

Communicate from your audience's point of view.

Adapt Your Message to Your Audience

As Chapter 4 will show, the best way to create messages carefully is to adapt your message to your audience so that you can help them understand and accept it. If you're writing for a specialist in your field, for example, you can use technical terms that might be unfamiliar to a layperson. On the other hand, if you're communicating to someone who might not share your understanding of a topic or someone who might not have your wealth of experience, you can minimize language barriers by using specific and accurate words—ones your audience will understand. Decisions about the content, organization, style, and tone of your message all depend, at least to some extent, on the relationship between you and your audience. If you don't know your audience, you will be forced to make these decisions in the dark, and at least part of your message may miss the mark.

Include only the information that is useful to your audience, and organize it in a way that encourages its acceptance.

Develop and Connect Your Ideas

Deciding what to say is the first hurdle in the communication process. Many people make the mistake of trying to convey everything they know about a subject. Unfortunately, when a message contains too much information, it's difficult to absorb. As you decide what to include and what to leave out, keep in mind that if you try to explain something without first giving the receiver adequate background, you'll create confusion. Likewise, if you recommend actions without first explaining why they are justified, your message may provoke an emotional response that inhibits understanding.

To make your message memorable

- Use telling statistics
- Use words that evoke a physical, sensory impression
- Tie the message to your audience's frame of reference

It's also important to make written messages visually appealing and easy to understand by balancing general concepts with specific illustrations. When you come to an important point, say so. Use specific details such as numbers, tables, and figures, and try using memorable words such as colors, objects, scents, sounds, and tastes to create a picture in your audience's mind. You can also call attention to an idea visually by using headlines, bold type, and indented lists and by using charts, graphs, maps, diagrams, and illustrations, as Chapter 12 will point out.

Furthermore, be sure to show how new ideas are related to concepts that already exist in the minds of your audience, as Carroll Paulding did when he said in his letter (see Figure 1.4), "and just as families call to their children, wolves sometimes howl to keep their pack together." Such connections help make the new concepts acceptable.

Finally, as Chapters 5 and 6 will discuss in detail, keep your messages as brief and as clean as possible. With few exceptions, one page is easier to absorb than two, especially in a business environment where so many messages compete for attention. However, because it's important to develop each main idea adequately, you're better off covering three points thoroughly rather than skimming through eight points superficially. Remember, by highlighting and summarizing your key points, you help your audience understand and remember the message.

The key to brevity is to limit the number of ideas, not to shortchange their development.

Reduce the Number of Messages

Organizations save time and money by sending only necessary messages.

Limiting the number of messages you send is another way to make the messages you do send more effective. One useful way to reduce the number of messages is to think twice before sending one. It takes time and resources to produce letters and memos, so organizations have to be concerned with how many messages they create. If a written message merely adds to the information overload, it's probably better left unsent or handled some other way—say, by a quick telephone call or a face-to-face chat. By holding down the number of messages, organizations will maximize the benefits of their communication activities.

DID YOU KNOW?

Experts estimate that more than 94 million e-mail users send over 5.5 trillion e-mail messages annually.

Choose the Correct Channel and Medium

Even the most carefully constructed message will fail to produce results if it does not reach your audience. As far as possible, try to eliminate potential sources of interference. Begin by eliminating the number of channels a message must pass through before it reaches its intended target. Then make sure your choice of communication channel and medium doesn't interfere with your message.

The careful choice of channel and medium helps focus your audience's attention on your message.

When you plan a message, think about the amount of feedback you want to encourage, and choose a form of communication that suits your needs. Some channels and media are more compatible with feedback than others. **Media richness** is the value of a medium in a given communication situation. Richness is determined by a medium's ability to (1) convey a message by means of more than one informational cue (visual, verbal, vocal), (2) facilitate feedback, and (3) establish personal focus (see Figure 1.9). Face-to-face communication is the richest medium because it is personal, it provides both immediate verbal and nonver-

To ensure effective communication, use richer media for messages that are complex, ambiguous, and nonroutine.

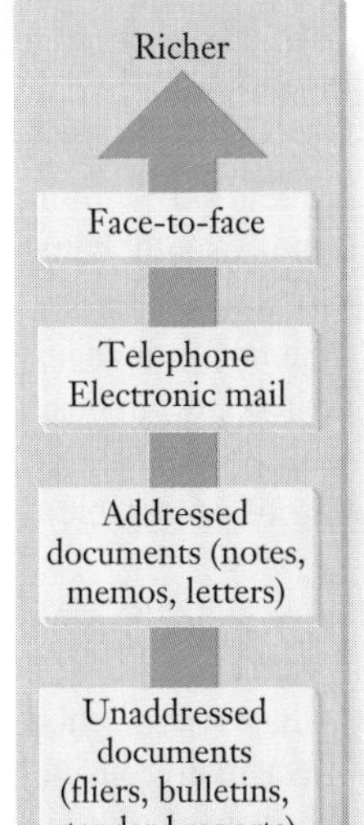

Figure 1.9
A Continuum of Media Richness

bal feedback, and it conveys the emotion behind the message. But it's also one of the most restrictive because you and your audience must be in the same place at the same time.[45]

In Chapter 4, we'll discuss how your choice among a face-to-face conversation, a telephone call, or a written document depends on the location of the audience, the importance of the message, and how much you need the nonverbal feedback that only body language can reveal. Choose the richest media for nonroutine, complex messages. Use rich media to extend and humanize your presence throughout the organization, to communicate caring to employees, and to gain employee commitment to organizational goals. Use leaner media to communicate simple, routine messages. You can send information such as statistics, facts, figures, and conclusions through a note, memo, or written report, as Tom Beatty did in his internal memo (see Figure 1.2).

Your choice of a communication channel and medium depends on the
- Message
- Audience
- Need for speed
- Situation

DID YOU KNOW?

Americans use about 8 million tons of paper each year, and this amount is expected to increase.

Strengthen Your Communication Skills

Recognizing the importance of efficient communication, many companies today train employees in communication skills. Some companies offer seminars and workshops on handling common oral communication situations (such as dealing with customers, managing subordinates, and getting along with co-workers), as well as training in computers and other electronic means of communication.

Focus on building skills in the areas where you've been weak.

Even though you may ultimately receive training on the job, you can start mastering business communication skills right now, in this course. Perhaps the best place to begin is with an honest assessment of where you stand. In the next few days, watch how you handle the communication situations that arise. Try to figure out what you're doing right and what you're doing wrong. Then in the months ahead, try to focus on building your competence in areas where you need the most work.

Practice using all communication skills so that you can learn from your mistakes.

One way to improve your skills is to practice. Lack of experience in writing or speaking can prevent you from developing effective messages. Perhaps you have a limited vocabulary or are uncertain about questions of grammar, punctuation, and style. Perhaps you're simply frightened by the idea of writing something or of appearing before a group. People aren't "born" writers or speakers. Their skills improve the more they speak and write. Someone who has written ten reports is usually better at it than someone who has written only two reports. You learn from experience, and some of the most important lessons are learned through failure. Learning what *not* to do is just as important as learning what *to* do. One of the great advantages of taking a course in business communication is that you get to practice in an environment that provides honest and constructive criticism. A course of this kind also gives you an understanding of acceptable techniques, so you can avoid making costly mistakes on the job.

This book has been designed to provide the kind of communication practice that will prepare you for getting the job you want, boosting your chances for a promotion, starting your own business, or succeeding at whatever you choose to do in the future. As you progress through this book, you will also meet many business communicators such as Clarence Wooten of Metamorphosis. Their experiences will give you an insight into what it takes to communicate effectively on the job.

COMMUNICATION CHALLENGES AT METAMORPHOSIS STUDIOS

Although you've been with Metamorphosis Studios from the beginning as a graphics animator, you've never felt as disconnected as you do now. Every day you find 30 new e-mail messages waiting, a stack of mail several days old sits unopened on your desk, and several unread company bulletins fill your in-basket. All you can think about is the end-of-the-month deadline for the MSNBC launch. "Microsoft used to be a competitor and now they're ordering graphics from us," you think, but it brings you no pleasure. It seems that all the fun is gone.

You go back a long way with your good friend, CEO Clarence Wooten. He took a chance on hiring you, and you've always given him 150 percent. In fact, he stuck his head in the door last week to ask how the graphics were shaping up. Although you said everything was "great," you later kicked yourself for not mentioning something about the information overload. The stress of not keeping up with the flow of communication is beginning to take its toll on you in lost productivity. You vow that next time Clarence gives you the opportunity, you'll speak up.

INDIVIDUAL CHALLENGE: "How's it going, Tom?" Startled, you raise your head to see that Clarence has dropped in. He drapes himself across a chair. You take a deep breath. What will you tell him?

TEAM CHALLENGE: Clarence Wooten takes your information about communication overload as a serious threat to both the harmony and the future profitability of Metamorphosis. He tells his partner, Andre Forde, about the problem, and together they decide to hold a series of meetings to brainstorm ideas on ways to pare down the enormous amounts of information and yet make sure that key people have everything they need to work well together. They contact a professor of management communication at a nearby university. Dr. Sharon Bienvenu has a reputation for excellent work as a corporate consultant. She has suggested that Clarence and Andre not attend the first meeting so that employees will feel free to speak openly.

The brainstorming group includes elements from every facet of Metamorphosis. The team will consist of two freelancers, Barbara McCall and Louis Corrigan, flown in from Dallas and Chicago; two technical support people, Raji Raasad and Alice Smollen from the main office; and two animation specialists, Tom Webster and Sandra Wooten. Assume one of these key roles and discuss the problem and possible solutions with Dr. Bienvenu. Prepare a list of key issues and suggestions, considering that your first audience will be the owners of Metamorphosis.[46] ■

SUMMARY OF LEARNING OBJECTIVES

1. **Explain the importance of having good communication skills in today's workplace.** Good communication skills shape the impressions you make on others. They enable you to perceive and respond to your audience's needs and to influence your audience to think in a particular way. Because successful communicators are understood by others, they are often exceptionally effective and productive employees, and they tend to advance rapidly in their careers.
2. **Highlight the difference between the formal and informal communication channels.** The formal communication channel is patterned after a company's official organizational structure. Information that passes through formal channels flows up and down the hierarchy, as well as across the lines of authority. In actual practice, however, each organization has a powerful informal communication network that encompasses all the casual conversations and messages occurring between employees regardless of their position in the hierarchy. Because the informal network winds through the hierarchical structure in no set pattern, it is often called the grapevine.
3. **Discuss the process of communication.** Communication is a six-phase process: The sender has an idea, transforms the idea into a message, and transmits the message; the receiver gets the message, interprets the message, and reacts to the message by sending feedback.
4. **Identify eight major communication barriers between people and within organizations.** The eight major barriers to communication are differences in perception and language; poor listening; emotional interference; cultural differences; physical distractions; information overload and message competition; incorrect filtering; and closed or inadequate communication climate.
5. **List six factors that contribute to effective business communication.** Effective communicators overcome communication barriers by fostering an open communication climate, committing to ethical communication, increasing their intercultural awareness, adopting an audience-centered approach, using technology wisely and responsibly to obtain and share information, and creating and processing their messages effectively.
6. **Explain the meaning of *media richness*.** Media richness is a medium's ability to convey a message by means of more than one informational cue, to facilitate feedback, and to establish personal focus. Face-to-face communication is the richest medium because it is personal, provides both immediate verbal and nonverbal feedback, and conveys the emotion behind the message.

CRITICAL THINKING QUESTIONS

1. Why do you think good communication in an organization improves employees' attitudes and performance? Explain briefly.
2. Whenever you report negative information to your boss, she never passes it along to her colleagues or supervisors. You think the information is important, but who do you talk to? Your boss? Your boss's supervisor? A co-worker who also reports to your boss? A co-worker who reports to a different boss? Briefly explain your answer.
3. You've just been promoted to manager and you've developed a good rapport with most of your employees, but Richardson and Blake are always going to your supervisor with matters that should go through you. Both employees have been at the company for at least ten years longer than you have, and both know your supervisor very well. Should you speak with them about this situation? Should you speak with your supervisor? Explain briefly.
4. Because of your excellent communication skills, your boss always asks you to write his reports for him. When you overhear the CEO complimenting him on his logical organization and clear writing style, he responds as if he'd written all those reports himself. You're angry, but he's your boss. What can you do? Briefly explain your answer.
5. As long as you make sure that everyone involved receives some benefit and that no one gets hurt, is it okay to make a decision that's just a little unethical? Briefly explain your answer.
6. Which communication channels are more susceptible to noise, written or spoken? Why?
7. How can you impress on your employees the importance of including negative information in messages?
8. Under what circumstances might you want to limit the feedback you receive from an audience of readers or listeners? Explain briefly.

DOCUMENT FOR ANALYSIS

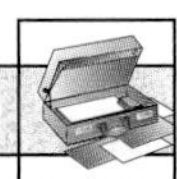

Read the following document; then (1) analyze the strengths and weaknesses of each sentence and (2) revise the document so that it follows this chapter's guidelines.

It has come to my attention that many of you are lying on your time cards. If you come in late, you should not put 8:00 on your card. If you take a long lunch, you should not put 1:00 on your time card. I will not stand for this type of cheating. I simply have no choice but to institute a time-clock system. Beginning next Monday, all employees will have to punch in and punch out whenever they come and go from the work area.

The time clock will be right by the entrance to each work area, so you have no excuse for not punching in. Anyone who is late for work or late coming back from lunch more than three times will have to answer to me. I don't care if you had to take a nap or if you girls had to shop. This is a place of business, and we do not want to be taken advantage of by slackers who are cheaters to boot.

It is too bad that a few bad apples always have to spoil things for everyone.

EXERCISES

1. For the following tasks, identify the necessary direction of communication (downward, upward, horizontal), suggest an appropriate type of communication (casual conversation, formal interview, meeting, workshop, videotape, newsletter, memo, bulletin board notice, and so on), and briefly explain your suggestion.
   a. As personnel manager, you want to announce details about this year's company picnic.
   b. As director of internal communication, you want to convince top management of the need for a company newsletter.
   c. As production manager, you want to make sure that both the sales manager and the finance manager receive your scheduling estimates.
   d. As marketing manager, you want to help employees understand the company's goals and its attitudes toward workers.
2. An old college chum phoned you out of the blue to say: "Truth is, I had to call you. You'd better keep this under your hat, Chris, but when I heard my company was buying you guys out, I was dumbfounded. I had no idea that a company as large as yours could sink so fast. Your group must be in pretty bad shape over there!" Your stomach turned suddenly queasy, and you felt a chill go up your spine. You'd heard nothing about any buyout, and before you could even get your college friend off the phone, you were wondering what you should do. Of the following, choose one course of action and briefly explain it.
   a. Contact your CEO directly and relate what you've heard.
   b. Ask co-workers whether they've heard anything about a buyout.
   c. Discuss the phone call confidentially with your immediate supervisor.
   d. Keep quiet about the whole thing (there's nothing you can do about the situation anyway).
3. Your boss often uses you as a sounding board for her ideas. Now she seems to want you to act as an unofficial messenger, passing her ideas along to the staff and informing her of their responses. Are you comfortable with this arrangement? Write a short paragraph explaining your feelings.[47]
4. In less than a page, explain why you think each of the following is or is not ethical.
   a. Deemphasizing negative test results in a report on your product idea
   b. Taking a computer home to finish a work-related assignment
   c. Telling an associate and close friend that she'd better pay more attention to her work responsibilities or management will fire her
   d. Recommending the purchase of excess equipment to use up your allocated funds before the end of the fiscal year so that your budget won't be cut next year
5. For weeks, you've noticed one of your colleagues taking office supplies home at night. She's been taking pens, markers, file folders, and paper clips, and last night she took an inexpensive calculator. This morning, you asked her whether she thought taking all these supplies was okay with the company. She said, "Oh, it's nothing. Everybody does it; the management expects it. I put in a lot of overtime I don't charge for, and I work hard for this company. It just keeps everything a little more balanced." What do you do next? Explain briefly.
6. Technological devices such as faxes, cellular phones, electronic mail, and voice mail are making businesspeople easily accessible at any time of day or night, at work and at home. What kind of impact might frequent intrusions have on their professional and personal life? Please explain your answer in less than a page.
7. As a manufacturer of aerospace, energy, and environmental equipment, Lockheed Martin has developed a code of ethics that it expects employees to abide by. Visit Lockheed Martin's Web site at http://www.Lmco.com/exeth/ethset.html and review the six important virtues and the company's code of ethics (scroll down). In a brief paragraph, describe three specific examples ofthings you could do that would violate these provisions. Now scroll down and study the list of "Warning Signs" of ethics violations and take the "Quick Quiz." In another brief paragraph, describe how you could use this advice to avoid ethical problems as you write business letters, memos, and reports. Submit both paragraphs to your instructor.
8. Top management has asked you to speak at an upcoming executive meeting to present your arguments for a more open communication climate. Which of the following would be most important for you to know about your audience before giving your presentation? (Briefly explain your choice.)
   a. How many top managers will be attending
   b. What management style members of your audience prefer
   c. How firmly these managers are set in their ways
9. What would be the most efficient way (phone call, interview, memo, or newsletter) of handling the following communication situations? (Briefly explain your answers.)
   a. Informing everyone in the company of your department's new procedure for purchasing equipment
   b. Leaving final instructions for your secretary to follow while you're out of town
   c. Disciplining an employee for chronic tardiness
   d. Announcing the installation of ramps for employees using wheelchairs
10. Write a memo introducing yourself to your instructor. Include such things as your background, interests, achievements, and goals. Keep it under one page, and use Figure 1.2 as a model for the format.
11. Your boss has asked you to research and report on corporate child-care facilities. Of course, you'll want to know who (besides your boss) will be reading your report. List four or five other things you'll want to know about the situation and about your audience before starting your research. Briefly explain why the items on your list are important.

12. Briefly describe a miscommunication you've had with a coworker, fellow college student, friend, or family member. Can you identify what barriers prevented your successful communication? Please explain.
13. Basing your decisions on the varying richness of communication media, such as face-to-face interviews, telephone conversations, written messages (such as memos, letters, and reports), and bulletins or newsletters, advise your employees on how best to send the following messages, and explain your rationale for each.
    a. A technical report on the durability of your production equipment
    b. A reminder to employees about safety rules
    c. A performance evaluation of an employee who has been consistently missing deadlines
    d. A confirmation of tomorrow's luncheon meeting with an important client
    e. The quarterly statistics on inventory control
    f. Your resignation before joining another company
14. Selecting the site for your company's new plant was presented to you as an opportunity to prove yourself; there was even the hint of promotion. You've been in charge of everything, from soil specifications to reviewing architectural proposals. Finally, after all your research, all your negotiations with local landowners, all the cost calculations, and all the money you've already spent on ecological, social, and community impact studies, you are about to recommend the Lansing River site as the best location for the new plant. Now, right before your big presentation, you discover a mistake in your cost calculations; the site acquisition costs appear to be $50,000 more than you calculated, nearly 10 percent over budget.

    You see yourself during the presentation, revealing this last-minute screw-up: You feel like a fool, and you see your career sliding downhill fast. Perhaps you should deemphasize the mistake for now, just until after the presentation and things get rolling. You're not sure there really is a mistake, and with the presentation scheduled in less than 15 minutes, you don't have time to recheck all your figures. By letting it go for now, you'll be acting for the good of the company.

    You fervently believe that the Lansing River site is the best location for your company's new plant, even with the possible extra expense. However, if you can't present a clean, unqualified solution, management will never go for it. You've been around long enough to know that once a project starts, its budget often runs over original estimates anyway, so you could work the extra cost into the budget later. On your way to the meeting room, you make your final decision. In a few paragraphs, explain the decision you made.
15. Whenever your boss asks for feedback on an idea, she blasts anyone offering criticism, no matter how gently the news is broken to her. This defensive reaction has caused people to start agreeing with everything she says. You believe the situation is unhealthy for the company and for your boss. So, despite the likelihood of her reacting defensively, you want to talk to her about it. List some of the things you'll say when you meet with her tomorrow.

Exploring the Best of the Web

Beef Up Your Internet Language Skills, page 17

1. In addition to *cookie,* try looking up any Internet terms that have you baffled. If you can't think of any, scan the lists until you learn something new. Then test your knowledge by trying to use the new terminology correctly among friends or classmates (the best way to remember new terms). Now try keeping the pocket dictionary on the desktop while you surf other sites.
2. Do you think the Internet is creating a new language recognized and understood worldwide? How might this new language benefit the business world? Can you think of any terms coined by Net users that have spilled over into everyday usage? Does this kind of lingo exclude certain groups, or does it broaden everyone's knowledge?

Listening, Working in Teams, and Understanding Nonverbal Communication

After studying this chapter, you will be able to

1 List the six general categories of nonverbal communication
2 Summarize the skills involved in being an effective listener
3 Highlight seven characteristics of effective feedback
4 Describe the four phases of group decision making
5 List six ways leaders can make meetings more productive
6 Explain the win-win strategy to resolving conflict

Communication Close-up at 3M

Excellent speaking and listening skills probably had a lot to do with the once-in-a-career promotion that advanced 3M's Virginia Johnson from marketing administration manager in Austin, Texas, to director of human relations at company headquarters in St. Paul, Minnesota. Johnson had plenty of opportunities to hone her communication skills. In addition to her marketing job, she served for several years as head of 3M's Meeting Management Institute, traveling the nation to show executives how to make their meetings more effective. She found that effectiveness always comes down to those two basic skills: speaking and listening. But, whereas most businesspeople are fairly good speakers, they're often poor listeners.

Listening is important at all levels of business, but it is especially vital for meeting leaders and participants, says Johnson. In fact, most of what a leader does to prepare for and conduct a successful meeting (determining the purpose, creating an agenda, keeping the ball rolling, summarizing the results) is to help participants "listen" more effectively.

Virginia Johnson

"If a leader speaks more than 15 or 20 percent of the time, he or she is not being effective," explains Johnson, and the participants have probably stopped listening out of sheer boredom. Instead, a meeting leader should spend most of the time listening to others, because "the role of the facilitator is to help other people get their opinions or questions out and responded to. Speeches are not meetings." Through 3M-funded research, Johnson also learned that a good meeting leader can help people listen by using visual aids

To be successful at 3M, employees are skilled in oral communication. Their skills are constantly put to the test, whether they're dealing with clients or customers, or participating in meetings.

that enable participants to visualize and retain information. Sticking to the agenda also helps, and summarizing the results reinforces or clarifies what everyone has heard.

Of course, half the responsibility for a successful meeting belongs to the participants. When Johnson attends meetings, she keeps herself actively involved. "If it's a formal meeting, I'll take notes to help me listen and for later recall," says Johnson. "At creative sessions, I may have to listen intently or shout out my responses." Either way, she uses her knowledge of group dynamics to get more out of the time she spends in meetings (top executives spend about 38 percent of a 61-hour workweek in meetings).

Before calling a meeting, Johnson determines whether her goals can best be accomplished through a meeting or a memo. "You can't accomplish some things without getting your people together—when you want to provide them with direct access to an expert, for example, or show that avenues of communication in the company are open," she explains. "Meetings here at 3M serve other needs too. They allow us to share information, build teams, brainstorm solutions, reach decisions, and train people." Johnson's favorite test of the need for a meeting is to write one 25-word sentence stating what she expects people to know, do, and believe after attending. "If I can't create that sentence, the need for a meeting isn't apparent." However, if a meeting is needed, she goes on to develop her agenda and then gathers the visual aids she'll use to help present the main points.

"For me," says Johnson, "the toughest meeting to run is the creative session—trying to bring out the child in adults. Achieving fantasy and free thinking by breaking down management roles is very demanding." At a meeting to generate new ideas for sales training, Johnson used something she calls a "brainwriting sheet." She asked the eight sales managers in the meeting to write down three things about sales training they'd like to see added or changed. Then the managers exchanged sheets and added three more ideas. "After a few rounds of this, they'd forgotten their jobs and titles and were busy scribbling. Each round triggered new ideas."

Johnson understands how important it is to know your audience. In meetings she tries to identify nonverbal signals, to stay in control of the situation, and to be sensitive to listeners' needs (which must be met before they'll actually hear and absorb what's being said). She also tries to slow down nonstop talkers, stimulate quiet participants, and draw out information using various types of questions. "My personal style is to be natural and extemporaneous," says Johnson. "My agenda, visuals, and notes help me achieve that tone."

Johnson's new position puts her at the head of a department charged with smoothing human relations. Keeping everyone happy at a company with thousands of employees is no easy task. So more than ever, Johnson will be relying on her listening and speaking skills to meet that challenge.[1] ■

UNDERSTANDING THE IMPORTANCE OF NONVERBAL COMMUNICATION

DID YOU KNOW?

Nonverbal cues provide 93 percent of the meaning exchanged in any interaction: 35 percent from tone, and 58 percent from gestures, expressions, and other physical cues.

Virginia Johnson tries to identify nonverbal signs during her meetings because she knows that the old maxim is true: People's actions often do speak louder than their words. In fact, most people can deceive others much more easily with words than they can with their bodies. Words are relatively easy to control; body language, facial expressions, and vocal characteristics are not. By paying attention to these nonverbal cues, you can detect deception or affirm a speaker's honesty.

Nonverbal communication is more reliable and more efficient than verbal communication.

Because nonverbal communication is so reliable, people generally have more faith in nonverbal cues than they do in verbal messages. If a person says one thing but transmits a conflicting message nonverbally, listeners almost invariably believe the nonverbal signal.[2] Remember, the meaning of nonverbal communication lies with the observer, who both reads specific signals and interprets them in context of a particular situation and a particular culture. Chances are, if you can read other people's nonverbal messages correctly, you can interpret their underlying attitudes and intentions and respond appropriately.

Nonverbal communication is important for another reason: It can be efficient from both the sender's and the receiver's standpoint. You can transmit a nonverbal message without even thinking about it, and your audience can register the meaning unconsciously. At the same time, when you have a conscious purpose, you can often achieve it more economically with a gesture than you can with words. A wave of the hand, a pat on the back, a wink—all are streamlined expressions of thought. Although nonverbal communication can stand alone, it usually blends with speech, carrying part of the message. Together, the two modes of expression are a powerful combination, augmenting, reinforcing, and clarifying each other.

People use nonverbal signals to support and clarify verbal communication.

The Types of Nonverbal Communication

According to one estimate, there are more than 700,000 forms of nonverbal communication.[3] For discussion purposes, however, these forms can be grouped into the following general categories:

The face and eyes command particular attention as a source of nonverbal messages.

- *Facial expressions and eye behavior.* Your face is the primary site for expressing your emotions; it reveals both the type and the intensity of your feelings.[4] Your eyes are especially effective for indicating attention and interest, influencing others, regulating interaction, and establishing dominance. In fact, eye contact is so important in the United States that even when your words send a positive message, averting your gaze can lead your audience to perceive a negative one.[5] Although the eyes and the face are usually a reliable source of meaning, people sometimes manipulate their expressions to simulate an emotion they do not feel or to mask their true feelings. As Chapter 3 will explain, maintaining eye contact is not important in some cultures. In fact, it can be considered impolite.

- *Gestures and postures.* By moving your body, you can express both specific and general messages, some voluntary and some involuntary. Many gestures—a wave of the hand, for example—have a specific and intentional meaning, such as "hello" or "good-bye." Other types of body movement are unintentional and express a more general message. Slouching, leaning forward, fidgeting, and walking briskly are all unconscious signals that reveal whether you feel confident or nervous, friendly or hostile, assertive or passive, powerful or powerless.

Body language and tone of voice reveal a lot about a person's emotions and attitudes.

- *Vocal characteristics.* Like body language, your voice carries both intentional and unintentional messages. On a conscious level, we can use our voices to create various impressions. Consider the sentence "What have you been up to?" If you repeat that question four or five times, changing your tone of voice and stressing various words, you can convey quite different messages. However, your vocal characteristics also reveal many things that you are unaware of. The tone and volume of your voice, your accent and speaking pace, and all the little *um*'s and *ah*'s that creep into your speech say a lot about who you are, your relationship with the audience, and the emotions underlying your words.

DID YOU KNOW?

In Turkey, it's considered rude to cross your arms while facing someone.

- *Personal appearance.* Your appearance helps establish your social identity. People respond to others on the basis of their physical appearance. Because you see yourself as others see you, these expectations are often a self-fulfilling prophecy. When people think you're capable and attractive, you feel good about yourself, and that feeling affects your behavior, which in turn affects other people's perceptions of you. Although an individual's body type and facial features impose limitations, most people are able to control their attractiveness to some degree. Grooming, clothing, accessories, "style"—all modify a person's appearance. If your goal is to make a good impression, adopt the style of the people you want to impress.

Physical appearance and personal style contribute to one's identity.

- *Touching behavior.* Touch is an important vehicle for conveying warmth, comfort, and reassurance. Even the most casual contact can create positive feelings. This fact was revealed by an experiment in which librarians alternately touched and avoided the hands of students while returning their library cards. Although the contact lasted only half a second, the students who had been touched reported far more positive feelings about themselves and the library, even though many of them didn't even remember being touched.[6] Perhaps because it implies intimacy, touching behavior is governed in various circumstances by relatively strict customs that establish who can touch whom and how. The accepted norms vary, depending on the gender, age, relative status, and cultural background of the persons involved. In business situations, touching suggests dominance, so a higher-status person is more likely to touch a lower-status person than the other way around. Touching has become controversial, however, because it can sometimes be interpreted as sexual harassment.

Your use of touch, your attitude toward time, and your use of space (all of which are affected by culture) help establish your social relationships.

COMMUNICATING ACROSS CULTURES

ACTIONS SPEAK LOUDER THAN WORDS ALL AROUND THE WORLD

"He wouldn't look me in the eye. I found it disconcerting that he kept looking all over the room but rarely at me," said Barbara Walters after her interview with Libya's Colonel Muamar el-Qaddafi. Like many people in the United States, Walters was associating eye contact with trustworthiness, so when Qaddafi withheld eye contact, she felt uncomfortable. In fact, Qaddafi was paying Walters a compliment. In Libya, *not* looking conveys respect, and looking straight at a woman is considered nearly as serious as physical assault.

Nonverbal communication varies widely between cultures, even between subcultures, and the differences strongly affect communication in the workplace. Whether you're trying to communicate with your new Asian American assistant, the Swedish managers who recently bought out your company, the young African American college student who won a summer internship with your firm, or representatives from the French company you hope will buy your firm's new designs, your efforts will depend as much on physical cues as on verbal ones. Most Americans aren't usually aware of their own nonverbal behavior, so they have trouble understanding the body language of people from other cultures. The list of differences is endless:

- In Thailand it's rude to place your arm over the back of a chair in which another person is sitting.
- Finnish female students are horrified by Arab girls who want to walk hand in hand with them.
- Canadian listeners nod to signal agreement.
- Japanese listeners nod to indicate only that they have understood.
- British listeners stare at the speaker, blinking their eyes to indicate understanding.
- People in the United States are taught that it's impolite to stare.
- Saudis accept foreigners in Western business attire but are offended by tight-fitting clothing and by short sleeves.
- Spaniards indicate a receptive friendly handshake by clasping the other person's forearm to form a double handshake.
- Canadians consider touching any part of the arm above the hand intrusive, except in intimate relationships.

It may take years to adjust your nonverbal communication to other cultures, but many options can help you prepare. Books and seminars on cultural differences are readily available, as are motion pictures showing a wide range of cultures. You can always rent videos of films and TV shows from other countries. Examining the illustrations in news and business magazines can give you an idea of expected business dress and personal space. Finally, remaining flexible and interacting with people from other cultures who are visiting or living in your country will go a long way toward lowering the barriers presented by nonverbal communication.

---

1. Explain how watching a movie from another country might help you prepare to correctly interpret nonverbal behavior from that culture.
2. One of your co-workers is originally from Saudi Arabia. You like him, and the two of you work well together. However, he stands so close when you speak with him that it makes you very uncomfortable. Do you tell him of your discomfort, or do you try to cover it up?

- *Use of time and space*. Like touch, time and space can be used to assert authority. Some people demonstrate their importance by making other people wait; others show respect by being on time. People can also assert their status by occupying the best space. In U.S. companies, the chief executive usually has the corner office and the prettiest view. Apart from serving as a symbol of status, space can determine how comfortable people feel talking with each other. When others stand too close or too far away, you are likely to feel ill at ease. However, as Chapter 3 will point out, attitudes toward punctuality and comfort zones vary from culture to culture.

How to Improve Your Nonverbal Communication Skills

To improve your nonverbal communication skills, pay more attention to the kinds of signals just discussed. It is particularly important to avoid giving others conflicting signals. For instance, if you tell an employee that you are free to talk to about her raise but your nonverbal signals suggest that this is not the best time to discuss the subject, she will be confused. So try to be as honest as possible in communicating your emotions. Here are some additional tips for honing your nonverbal skills:[7]

You can improve nonverbal skills by paying more attention to cues, both yours and those of others.

- Smile genuinely. A fake smile is obvious because the timing isn't right and the wrinkles don't follow.
- Be aware that people may give false nonverbal cues.
- Keep appropriate distance and use touch only when appropriate.
- Respect status with your eye contact.
- Adopt a handshake that matches your personality and intention.

Remember, few gestures convey meaning in and of themselves; they have to be interpreted in clusters, and they should reinforce your words.

Improving Your Oral Communication Skills

Virginia Johnson's job at 3M may involve more oral communication than many jobs do, but her experience is by no means unusual. Speaking and listening are the communication skills people use most. Given a choice, people would rather talk to each other than write to each other. Talking takes less time and needs no composing, keyboarding, rewriting, duplicating, or distributing.

More important, oral communication provides the opportunity for feedback. When people communicate orally, they can ask questions and test their understanding of the message; they can share ideas and work together to solve problems. Talking things over helps

Oral communication saves time and provides opportunities for feedback and social interaction.

This speaker uses gestures and facial expressions to emphasize important points and reveal her attitude toward topics.

people in organizations build morale and establish a group identity. Plus, oral communication satisfies our common need to be part of the human community, and it makes us feel good.

Whether you're using the telephone, engaging in a quick face-to-face conversation with a colleague, or attending a meeting, oral communication is the vehicle you use to get your message across. When communicating orally, make it your goal to work on improving two key skills: speaking and listening.

Speaking

The spontaneous quality of oral communication limits your ability to edit your thoughts.

Because speaking is such an ingrained activity, we tend to do it without much thought, but that casual approach can be a problem in business. You have far less opportunity to revise your spoken words than to revise your written words. You can't cross out what you just said and start all over. Your dumbest comments will be etched into the other person's memory, regardless of how much you try to explain that you really meant something else entirely. Moreover, you can't go back and reread what was just said. If you let your attention wander while someone else is speaking, you miss the point. You either have to muddle along without knowing what the other person said or admit that you were daydreaming and ask the person to repeat the comment.

People often judge the substance of a remark by the speaker's appearance and style.

Another problem is that people tend to confuse your spoken message with you as an individual. They're likely to judge the content of what you say by your appearance and delivery style. Nobody will reject your sales letter because you're wearing white socks with a blue suit or because you say "um" a lot. However, people might very well reject your oral presentation on those grounds.

Learn to think before you speak.

Apply the "you" attitude to oral communication.

To improve your speaking skills, be more aware of using speech as a tool for accomplishing your objectives in a business context. To do this, break the habit of talking spontaneously, without planning *what* you're going to say or *how* you're going to say it. Before you speak, think about your purpose, your main idea, and your audience. Organize your thoughts, decide on a style that suits the occasion (for example, formal or informal, lecture or conversation) and your audience (supervisor or assistant, client or colleague), and edit your remarks mentally. Perhaps the most important thing you can do is to remember the "you" attitude, earning other people's attention and goodwill by focusing on them. Try to predict how the other person will react and organize the message accordingly. Your audience may not react the way you expect, so have alternative approaches ready. As you speak, watch the other person, judging from verbal and nonverbal feedback whether your message is making the desired impression. If it isn't, revise it and try again.

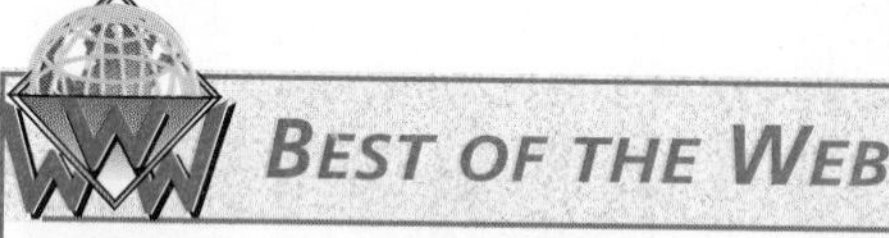

Check Out Books at This Library—It's a Snap!

Here's one Web site that will help you improve your everyday speaking and writing skills. Visit LibrarySpot, a virtual library resource center for just about anyone needing reference books and business resources. And it's all in one convenient location. Be sure to click on the virtual reference desk. Remember, this library never closes!

http://www.libraryspot.com

Listening

Speaking is, of course, only one side of the oral communication story. If you're typical, you spend over half your communication time listening.[8] Nevertheless, listening is one of the most underrated skills in the business world. In fact, businesses lose millions of dollars each year because of miscommunications stemming from a failure to listen to and understand customers' needs.[9]

The ability to listen is a vital skill in business.

Because listening is such a routine, everyday activity, few people think of developing their listening skills. Yet, unlike hearing, listening demands total concentration; it's an active search for meaning.[10] "Many people confuse hearing with active listening," notes one communication consultant. "Hearing is an automatic, physical function. Because you heard the words doesn't necessarily mean you were listening to the message."[11] It's not that we don't mean to listen with our full minds in gear. It's just that most of us have so many things pulling at our brain cells at once that we often don't give our full attention.

Effective listening means listening as though you were a doctor gathering new symptoms from a patient or a pilot in touch with the control tower during a storm. Good listeners welcome new information and new ideas, and the payoff is that they stay informed, up to date, and out of trouble. Good listening also increases the impact when you do speak, and it gives you a negotiating edge. Effective listening supports effective relationships within an organization, enhances the organization's delivery of products, alerts the organization to the innovation growing from both internal and external forces, and allows the organization to manage the growing diversity both in the work force and in the customers it serves.[12]

Someone who believes in the importance of good listening is Jennifer Lawson, executive vice president of programming for PBS. Called on to unite 341 stations across the country, Lawson has learned that "if you want to change a bureaucracy from within, the most important thing you can do is listen. You have to give people a chance to vent their frustrations with a new system, and then build on the basis of that." Lawson advises people "to ask the right questions and be genuinely interested in the answers."[13]

Nevertheless, most people listen poorly. In fact it's well documented that people listen at a 25 percent efficiency rate, or less, and the average person remembers only about half of what's said during a ten-minute conversation and forgets half of that within 48 hours.[14] Furthermore, when questioned about material they've just heard, people are likely to get the facts mixed up. That's because effective listening requires a conscious effort and a willing mind. When it comes down to it, most people prefer to talk rather than listen. Some executives even admit that they take notes in meetings to make it look as if they are listening. They fail to recognize that listening effectively, although a difficult skill to master, is one of the best ways to improve one's communication skills and get ahead. It enhances performance, and better performance leads to raises, promotions, status, and power.[15]

Most people need to improve their listening skills.

The Three Types of Listening

Different situations call for different listening skills. When you attend a briefing on the company's new medical insurance, you listen mainly for content. You want to know what the policy is. As the speaker describes the prescription drug plan, you begin to listen more critically, assessing the benefits of the new plan relative to your own needs. Later, as a friend talks to you about his medical problems, you listen empathically, trying to understand his feelings.

To be a good listener, vary the way you listen to suit various situations.

These three types of listening differ not only in purpose but also in the amount of feedback or interaction that occurs. The goal of **content listening** is to understand and retain the speaker's message. You may ask questions, but basically information flows from the speaker to you. Your job is to identify the key points of the message. It doesn't matter whether you

When you're preoccupied with note taking, such as this group at Career Pathways, it's impossible to actively listen to the speaker.

The three forms of listening:
- Content listening enables you to understand and retain the message.
- Critical listening enables you to evaluate the information.
- Active listening is used to draw out the other person.

agree or disagree, approve or disapprove—only that you understand.[16] When you listen to a regional sales manager's monthly report on how many of your products sold that month, you are listening for content.

The goal of **critical listening** is to both understand and evaluate the meaning of the speaker's message at several levels: logic of the argument, strength of the evidence, and validity of the conclusions; the implications of the message for you or your organization; the speaker's intentions and motives; the omission of any important or relevant points. Critical listening generally involves interaction as you try to uncover the speaker's point of view. You are bound to evaluate the speaker's credibility as well.[17] When the regional sales manager presents sales projections for the next few months, you listen critically, evaluating whether the estimates are valid and what the implications are for your manufacturing department.

The goal of **active, or empathic, listening** is to understand the speaker's feelings, needs, and wants so that you can appreciate his or her point of view, regardless of whether you share that perspective. By listening in an active or empathic way, you help the individual vent the emotions that prevent a dispassionate approach to the subject. Avoid the temptation to give advice. Try not to judge the individual's feelings. Just let the other person talk.[18] You listen empathically when your regional sales manager tells you about the problems he had with his recreational vehicle while vacationing with his family.

Regardless of whether the situation calls for content, critical, or active listening, all three types of listening can be useful in work-related situations, so it pays to learn how to apply them.

What Happens When You Listen

By understanding the process of listening, you will begin to understand why oral messages get lost so often. Listening involves five related activities, which most often occur in sequence:[19]

- *Attending:* physically hearing the message and taking note of it. This reception can be blocked by interfering noises, impaired hearing, or inattention.
- *Interpreting:* assigning meaning to sounds according to your own values, beliefs, ideas, expectations, roles, needs, and personal history. The speaker's frame of reference may be quite different from yours, so you may need to determine what the speaker really means.
- *Remembering:* storing a message for future reference. As you listen, you retain what you hear by taking notes or by making a mental outline of the speaker's key points.
- *Evaluating:* applying critical thinking skills to weigh the speaker's remarks. You separate fact from opinion and evaluate the quality of the evidence.
- *Responding:* reacting once you've evaluated the speaker's message. If you're communicating one-on-one or in a small group, the initial response generally takes the form of verbal feedback. If you're one of many in an audience, your initial response may take the form of applause, laughter, or silence. Later on, you may act on what you have heard.

Listening involves five steps: attending, interpreting, remembering, evaluating, and responding.

Because listening requires a mix of physical and mental activities, it is subject to a variety of physical and mental barriers. A large part of becoming a good listener is the ability to recognize and correct these barriers. (See Chapter 3 for a discussion of intercultural barriers.)

Barriers to Listening

Prejudgment is one of the most common and difficult barriers to listening because it is an automatic process. People could not operate in life without holding some assumptions. However, in new situations, these assumptions are often incorrect. In addition, some people listen defensively, viewing every comment as a personal attack. If someone says, "Golly, it's warm in here," defensive listeners might assume that the person is blaming them for mismanaging the thermostat. Their immediate reaction is to prove that the speaker is wrong and they're right. To protect their self-esteem, they may distort a message by tuning out anything that doesn't confirm their view of themselves.

When you jump to conclusions, you close your mind to additional information.

Many listeners are also guilty of self-centeredness. For example, the minute a speaker mentions *his* or *her* problem, self-centered listeners take control of the conversation and talk about *their* problem. They trivialize the speaker's concerns by pointing out that their own difficulties are twice as great. They can top the positive experiences as well. No matter what subject is being discussed, they know more than the speaker does—and they're determined to prove it.

Self-centered listeners shift their attention from the speaker to themselves.

Another common barrier to effective listening is to listen selectively, also known as *out-listening.* You have experienced out-listening if you've ever sat in a meeting and let your mind wander to such things as whether you brought your dry-cleaning ticket to work. You stay tuned out until you hear a word or phrase that gets your attention once more. The problem with out-listening is that it leaves you not with a memory of what the speaker *actually* said but with a memory of what you *think* the speaker probably said.[20]

One of the reasons people's minds tend to wander is that they think faster than they speak. Most people talk at about 120 to 150 words per minute in most situations. However, studies indicate that depending on the subject and the individual, people can process information at 500 to 800 words per minute.[21] This disparity between rate of speech and rate of thought allows the listener's mind to wander. Some people use this time to pull their arguments together; others just tune out completely. The important thing is to recognize these

Your mind can process information more than four times faster than the rate of speech.

counterproductive tendencies in yourself and to work at ways to improve your listening skills. Try using this extra brainpower to stay focused by evaluating what has been said and summarizing the main ideas in your own mind.

Strategies for Effective Listening

You can improve your listening ability by becoming more aware of the practices that distinguish good listeners from bad (see Figure 2.1). To improve your listening skills, follow these steps:[22]

- Look beyond the speaker's style by asking yourself what the speaker knows that you don't.
- Depersonalize your listening so that you decrease the emotional impact of what's being said and are better able to hold your rebuttal until you've heard the total message.
- Fight distractions by closing doors, turning off radios or televisions, and moving closer to the speaker.
- Listen for concepts and key ideas as well as for facts, and know the difference between fact and principle, idea and example, and evidence and argument.
- Stay ahead of the speaker by anticipating what will be said next and by thinking about what's already been said.
- Look for unspoken messages. Often the speaker's tone of voice or expressions will reveal more than the words themselves.
- Review the key points. Do they make sense? Are the concepts supported by facts?

Figure 2.1
Distinguishing Good Listeners from Bad Listeners

THE BAD LISTENER	THE GOOD LISTENER	TO LISTEN EFFECTIVELY
Tunes out dry subjects	Opportunizes; asks "What's in it for me?"	Find areas of interest
Tunes out if delivery is poor	Judges content; skips over delivery errors	Judge content, not delivery
Tends to enter into argument	Doesn't judge until comprehension is complete; interrupts only to clarify	Hold your fire
Listens for facts	Listens for central themes	Listen for ideas
Takes extensive notes	Takes fewer notes	Take selective notes
Fakes attention	Works hard; exhibits active body state	Work at listening
Is distracted easily	Fights or avoids distractions; knows how to concentrate	Block out competing thoughts
Resists difficult expository material	Uses heavier material as exercise for the mind	Paraphrase the speaker's ideas
Reacts to emotional words	Interprets emotional words; does not get hung up on them	Stay open-minded
Tends to daydream with slow speakers	Listens between the lines; weighs the evidence; mentally summarizes	Capitalize on the fact that thought is faster than speech

- Keep an open mind by asking questions that clarify understanding; reserve judgment until the speaker has finished.
- Don't interrupt. Interruptions can be deadly when you're trying to get to the bottom of a problem. A person who already has difficulties communicating can be thrown off course by constant interruptions.
- Evaluate and criticize the content, not the speaker.
- Provide feedback. Let the speaker know you're with him or her. Maintain eye contact. Provide appropriate facial expressions. Paraphrase or summarize when the speaker reaches a stopping point.
- Take meaningful notes that are brief and to the point.

One way to assess your listening skills is to pay attention to how you listen. When someone else is talking, are you really hearing what is said, or are you mentally rehearsing how you will respond? Above all, try to be open to the information that will lead to higher-quality decisions, and try to accept the feelings that will build understanding and mutual respect. Becoming a good listener will help you in many business situations—especially those that are emotion laden and difficult.

Effective listening involves being receptive to both information and feelings.

Giving Feedback

In Chapter 1, we discussed how facilitating feedback is one way to foster an open communication environment. Knowing how to give constructive criticism or feedback is an important communication skill that will help you improve the way you work with others. Here are some guidelines for developing effective feedback skills:[23]

Learn how to give both positive and negative feedback.

- *Focus on specific behaviors.* Feedback should be specific rather than general.
- *Keep feedback impersonal.* No matter how upset you are, keep feedback job related, and never criticize someone personally.
- *Use "I" statements.* Instead of saying, "You are absent from work too often," say, "I feel annoyed when you miss work so frequently."
- *Keep feedback goal oriented.* If you have to say something negative, make sure it's directed toward the recipient's goals. Ask yourself whom the feedback is supposed to help. If the answer is essentially you, bite your tongue.
- *Make feedback well timed.* Feedback is most meaningful when there is a short interval between the recipient's behavior and the receipt of feedback about that behavior.
- *Ensure understanding.* If feedback is to be effective, you need to make sure the recipient understands it.
- *Direct negative feedback toward behavior that is controllable by the recipient.* There's little value in reminding a person of some shortcoming over which he or she has no control.

Working in Teams and Small Groups

Your speaking and listening skills are also put to the test when you work in teams and small groups. A **team** is a unit of two or more people who work together to achieve a goal. Team members have a shared mission and are collectively responsible for their work.[24]

Team members have a shared mission and are collectively responsible for their work.

In a recent survey of Fortune 1000 executives, 83 percent said their firms are working in teams or moving in that direction.[25] One reason for this rising trend is that teams have the potential to unleash vast amounts of creativity and energy in workers by embracing the con-

Earth and Environmental Services in San Francisco encourages its employees to work collaboratively so they can benefit from the knowledge of other team members.

cept of **participative management,** or involving employees in the company's decision making. Companies are looking for people who can interact successfully in small groups and make useful contributions while working in teams. When Hewlett-Packard studied its most successful managers to identify the personality traits that contribute to their effectiveness, the company found that all the managers were good at team building. This finding prompted the company to emphasize team-building skills in its management development program.[26]

The combined knowledge and skills of team members can lead to high performance and good decisions.

At their best, teams can be an extremely useful forum for making key decisions. Theoretically, the interaction of the participants should lead to good decisions based on the combined intelligence of the group. That is, teams generally achieve performance levels that exceed what would have been accomplished had the members worked independently. Whether a team is organized to solve a problem or to work on a specific activity, the participants gain a sense of involvement and importance. Because they share in the final product, they are committed to seeing it succeed.

At their worst, teams are unproductive and frustrating, and they waste everyone's time. Some may actually be counterproductive, because they may arrive at bad decisions. As we shall see, when people are pressured to conform, they may abandon their sense of personal responsibility and agree to ill-founded plans.

Understanding Group Dynamics

The interactions and processes that take place when a team meets, the **group dynamics,** also affect the outcome. Although teams are assembled to achieve a work-related task, some members may have a **hidden agenda**—private motives that affect the group's interaction. Sam might want to prove that he's more powerful than Sherry; Sherry might be trying to share the risk of making a decision; Don might be looking for a chance to postpone doing "real" work; and Rachel might be looking for approval from her peers. Each person's hidden agenda either contributes to or detracts from the group's ability to perform its task. It is of course unethical for any group member to make decisions solely on the basis of his or her hidden agenda.

Role Playing

The roles people play in small groups fall into three categories (see Figure 2.2). Members who assume **self-oriented roles** are motivated mainly to fulfill personal needs; they tend to be less productive than the other two types. Far more likely to contribute to group goals are those who assume **group-maintenance roles** to help members work well together and those who assume **task-facilitating roles** to help members solve the problem or make the decision.

Each member of a group plays a role that affects the outcome of the group's activities.

To a great extent, the roles individuals assume in a group depend on their status in that group. The people with more status play dominant roles; those with less status play more passive parts. Status depends on many variables, including personal attractiveness, competence in a particular field, past successes, education, age, social background, and organizational position. It also varies from group to group: You may have a good deal of status in one group (say, a college fraternity) and less status in another (say, a Fortune 500 company).

In most groups, a certain amount of "politics" occurs as people try to establish their relative status. One or two people typically emerge as the leaders, but often an undercurrent of tension remains as members of the group vie for better positions in the pecking order. These power struggles often get in the way of the real work. One person might refuse to go along with a decision simply because it was suggested by a rival. Until roles and status have stabilized, the group may have trouble accomplishing its goals.

Group members' personal motives may interfere with the group's efforts to accomplish its mission.

Group Norms

A group that meets regularly develops unwritten rules governing the behavior of its members. To one degree or another, people are expected to conform to these norms. For example, there may be an unspoken agreement that it's okay to be 10 minutes late for meetings but not 15 minutes late. In the context of work, the most productive groups tend to develop norms that are conducive to business.

Figure 2.2
Roles People Play in Groups

SELF-ORIENTED ROLES	GROUP-MAINTENANCE ROLES	TASK-FACILITATING ROLES
Controlling: dominating others by exhibiting superiority or authority **Withdrawing:** retiring from the group either by becoming silent or by refusing to deal with a particular aspect of the group's work **Attention seeking:** calling attention to oneself and demanding recognition from others **Diverting:** focusing group discussion on topics of interest to the individual rather than on those relevant to the task	**Encouraging:** drawing out other members by showing verbal and nonverbal support, praise, or agreement **Harmonizing:** reconciling differences among group members through mediation or by using humor to relieve tension **Compromising:** offering to yield on a point in the interest of reaching a mutually acceptable decision	**Initiating:** getting the group started on a line of inquiry **Information giving or seeking:** offering (or seeking) information relevant to questions facing the group **Coordinating:** showing relationships among ideas, clarifying issues, summarizing what the group has done **Procedure setting:** suggesting decision-making procedures that will move the group toward a goal

Some groups are more cohesive than others. When the group has a strong identity, the members all observe the norms religiously. They're upset by any deviation, and individuals feel a great deal of pressure to conform. This sense of group loyalty can be positive: Members generally have a strong commitment to one another, and they're highly motivated to see that the group succeeds. However, such group loyalty can also lead members into **groupthink**, the willingness of individual members to set aside their personal opinions and to go along with everyone else, even if everyone else is wrong, simply because belonging to the group is more important to them than making the right decision. Because decisions based on groupthink tend to result from group loyalty and conformity rather than from carefully considered opinion and fact finding, groupthink can lead to poor-quality decisions and ill-advised actions. Groupthink can even induce people to act against their own sense of ethics.

Because they feel pressured to conform, members of a group may agree to unwise decisions.

Group Decision Making

Group decision making passes through four phases: orientation, conflict, emergence, and reinforcement.

Groups usually reach their decisions in a predictable pattern. The process can be viewed as passing through four phases. In the *orientation phase,* group members socialize, establish their roles, and begin to define their task or purpose. In the *conflict phase,* members begin to discuss their positions on the problem. If group members have been carefully selected to represent a variety of viewpoints and expertise, disagreements are a natural part of this phase. The point is to *brainstorm,* or air all the options and discuss the pros and cons fully. At the end of this phase, group members begin to settle on a single solution to the problem.

In the *emergence phase,* members reach a decision. Consensus is reached when members find a solution that is acceptable enough for all members to support it (even if they have reservations). In other words, no member actively opposes it. Those who advocated different solutions put aside their objections, either because they're convinced that the majority solution is better or because they recognize that arguing is futile. This consensus usually happens only after all members have had an opportunity to communicate their positions and feel that they have been listened to. Finally, in the *reinforcement phase,* group feeling is rebuilt and the solution is summarized. Members receive their assignments for carrying out the group's decision and make arrangements for following up on those assignments.[27]

These four phases almost always occur, regardless of what type of decision is being considered. Group members naturally use this decision-making process, even when they lack experience or training in group communication.

Using Technology to Enhance Group Decision Making

The use of videoconferencing—which allows people in several different locations to "meet" via video and audio links—has skyrocketed in the corporate world as companies try to cut travel costs and speed products to market. In fact, its growing popularity means that a job candidate may now be asked at the spur of the moment to sit down for an interview via videoconference hookup with a prospective employer in another city. Similarly, a salesperson may be required to make a presentation to a roomful of customers via a videoconference hookup, or a newly formed work team with members in offices around the world may be asked to brainstorm on camera.[28]

Group decision-making software (also called *electronic meeting systems*) is one form of videoconferencing technology designed to save time and streamline the decision-making process. Such systems can make the process more democratic by putting everyone on equal footing. The concept is simple: Issues are presented to participants, who then keyboard their comments, all of which are anonymously displayed on a large projection screen in the room.

The major advantages of group decision software are anonymity, honesty, and speed. Participants can anonymously type any message they want and it flashes on the screen for all to see. Anonymity allows people to be brutally honest, without penalty. In addition, experts claim that this approach is as much as 55 percent faster than traditional face-to-face meetings because chitchat is eliminated. Still, there are drawbacks. First, you have to be a good typist. Also, those with the best ideas don't get credit for them. Finally, the process lacks the information richness of face-to-face oral communication. For a closer look at electronic decision making, see "Keeping Pace with Technology: Electronic Meetings: Work Together—Wherever You Are—to Get the Results You Want."

KEEPING PACE WITH TECHNOLOGY

ELECTRONIC MEETINGS: WORK TOGETHER—WHEREVER YOU ARE—TO GET THE RESULTS YOU WANT

Imagine a meeting at which everyone shares ideas, but no one knows who contributed them: a meeting in which people aren't talking, but typing. It's called a computer-supported, or electronic, meeting, and it's been popular with big corporations since IBM introduced the technology in the 1980s. Thanks to computer conferencing, the Internet, groupware, and a variety of new, affordable software packages, some day soon you may attend a virtual meeting in the morning and then in the afternoon enter the electronic decision room, where you and your colleagues will brainstorm ideas.

Here's How It Works Attending a *virtual meeting* means joining (by computer) an ongoing dialogue between two or more individuals communicating over telephone lines via computer modems. The exchange is similar to e-mail, but it's interactive (like chat rooms); that is, everyone sees everyone else's message as soon as it's sent. Participants, who may be separated by miles, can exchange ideas as if they were in the same room.

Electronic meeting rooms take virtual meetings one step further. A dedicated meeting room is filled with special equipment called electronic meeting systems (EMS), group decision support systems, and electronic voting systems. The simplest of these setups includes a large viewing screen, personal computers, and individual keypads (one for each participant). In general, the participants are all together, and the meeting is led by a trained facilitator who asks questions while participants type their responses.

With a simple keypad system, participants can view all responses, they can vote on an idea, and the results will be immediately displayed on the large screen—as a graph, as a simple number tally, or as a complex breakdown of categories and voting trends. Discussion follows, along with subsequent votes on every aspect of the issues at hand. At the end of the meeting, the system provides a printed summary for everyone.

Are Electronic Meetings More Productive? Studies shows that electronic meetings are up to 55 percent faster than traditional meetings. Here's why. Participants stay focused on issues that need to be addressed, and detailed statistical data can help guide decision making. Plus, everyone is given a chance to speak at the same time (responses are typed simultaneously). "It's the great equalizer," notes one communication expert. "Employees can share opinions anonymously—and honestly—without fear of displeasing superiors." Such meetings also tend to flatten the corporate hierarchy, because participants are judged on what they say not on who they are.

In addition, many managers have found that employees open up more in computer conferences than they do at in-person meetings or in memos. Furthermore, electronic meetings help build consensus among members, and participants are more satisfied with the result because the process engenders a sense of true shared decision making.

Still, electronic meetings are not designed to replace the synergy and spontaneity of face-to-face meetings. In fact, even during electronic meetings the keyboards are sometimes set aside for vigorous group discussion. After all, the purpose of the electronic meeting format isn't to dwell on the technology; it's to use the technology to enhance the group process, to gather information, to elicit peoples' honest thoughts and ideas, and to engage them in dialogue.

1. What advantages do in-person, face-to-face meetings have over electronic meetings?
2. What potential risks face employees and companies that don't keep up with trends in electronic meeting technology?

Videoconferencing systems, like this one from Picturetel, are growing in popularity as the technology improves and the costs come down.

Whereas traditional groupware and similar networked collaboration tools have been around for some time, more and more companies are now developing large-scale work spaces on the Internet. As Chapter 10 will discuss in detail, they use these areas for online discussions, videoconferencing, and data sharing. The primary benefits of Web-based collaboration are that it's easy, it's cost effective, and it allows you to do multiple activities in a seamless fashion. "There is a greater sense that you're cooperating with others because it's easy to follow a thread of discussion and see interactions," notes Mellanie Hills, author of "Intranet as Groupware."[29]

For example, at KPMG Consulting, Web-based collaboration has already progressed beyond simple information sharing. Recently, eight KPMG employees scattered around the globe wrote, edited, and commented on a report using WebFlow Corp's SamePage. This software tool allows users, in real time, to draft different sections of a document while editing other sections and participating in a Web-based discussion about the document—all at the same time.[30]

Writing in Teams

Collaborative writing is common in many organizations.

In many organizations besides KPMG, the process of preparing a message is a team effort. **Collaborative writing,** or team writing, means working with other writers to produce a single document. Team writing is used in any number of business situations. For instance, you sit down with your boss to plan a memo, work independently during the writing phase, and then ask your boss to review the message and suggest revisions. You might even participate in an all-out team effort to write a company's business plan or a major report.

Guidelines for Effective Team Writing

Because team writing can involve many people—a project manager, researchers, writers, typists, graphic artists, and editors—one of the first things you must do when starting a collaborative writing project is to get organized. Your team will select a leader, clarify goals, and resolve conflict.[31] Before anyone begins to write, your team will agree on the purpose of the project and the audience. You'll also plan the organization, format, and style of the document. Keep in mind that even though several individuals are involved, the final project must look and sound as if it had been prepared by one writer. The following guidelines will help you produce a document that is both clear and punctual:[32]

Make sure the final document "speaks with one voice."

- Select members who have strong interpersonal skills, who understand group dynamics, and who care about the project.
- Clarify goals and individual expectations.
- Identify a group leader who will keep members informed and intervene when necessary.
- Create a sense of ownership and shared responsibility for the document.
- Use the same word-processing program to facilitate combining files if separate team members are writing segments.
- Assign specific roles and establish clear lines of reporting.
- Establish a timeline and deadlines for every part of the project.
- Establish communication standards that are accurate and open and that create an atmosphere of trust.
- Use electronic tools such as groupware, e-mail, and computer conferencing to communicate quickly and effectively with other team members.

Collaborative Writing Challenges

Because collaborative writing brings multiple perspectives and various skills to a project, the result is often a better product than an individual working alone could have produced. Still, collaborative writing isn't without challenges. To begin with, team members often come from different backgrounds and have different work habits or concerns: A technical expert may focus on accuracy and meeting scientific standards; an editor may focus on organization and coherence; a manager may focus on schedules, cost, and corporate goals. So in addition to being able to write, you must be able to attend meetings regularly, plan and organize efficiently, accept responsibility, volunteer willingly, contribute ideas freely, elicit and listen to ideas, cooperate, and resolve conflicts.

You must also be able and willing to overcome differences in writing styles, working styles, and personality traits. In addition, you must be flexible and open to the opinions of others—focusing on your team's objectives instead of your own.[33] This means you must recognize that people express themselves differently and that not everything will be phrased exactly as you would have said it. In short, you can enhance your collaborative writing efforts by improving your interpersonal skills. In the next sections we discuss how to make meetings—both collaborative writing and other kinds—more productive and how to handle difficult interpersonal situations.

When you write collaboratively, pay attention to group dynamics.

Making Your Meetings More Productive

Meetings are a prime tool for problem solving, developing ideas through giving and getting feedback, identifying opportunities, and deciding how to maximize the company's resources. Whether you're meeting virtually or in person, much of the oral communication you'll do in the workplace will take place in small-group meetings. Your ability to contribute to the group and the organization as a whole will depend on how well you have mastered oral communication skills. As more and more companies increase their use of teams to solve problems and work collaboratively on projects, chances are that the num-

DID YOU KNOW?

The typical British manager spends almost 20 years in meetings during his or her career, and more than 25 percent of that time is spent traveling to and from the meeting site.

ber of meetings you'll attend will also increase. Already, more than 25 million meetings take place every day in the world of business.[34]

Unfortunately, however, many meetings are unproductive for everyone involved. In a recent research study, senior and middle managers reported that only 56 percent of their meetings were actually productive and that 25 percent of the meetings they attended could have been handled by a phone call or a memo.[35] Given these demoralizing statistics, no wonder companies today are focusing on making their meetings more productive. The three most frequently reported problems with meetings are getting off the subject, not having an agenda, and meeting for too long.[36]

Arranging the Meeting

Before calling a meeting, ask yourself whether it is really needed.

The key to productive meetings is careful planning of purpose, participants, agenda, and location. You want to bring the right people together in the right place for just enough time to accomplish your goals. Virginia Johnson of 3M warns that the biggest mistake in holding meetings is not having a specific goal. So before you call a meeting, satisfy yourself that one is truly needed. Perhaps your purpose doesn't require the interaction of a group, or maybe you could communicate more effectively in a memo or through individual conversations.

Meetings are called to solve problems or to share information.

In general, the purpose of a meeting is either informational or decision making, although many meetings combine both purposes. An informational meeting is called so that the participants can share information and, possibly, coordinate actions. This type of meeting may involve individual briefings by each participant or a speech by the leader followed by questions from the attendees. Decision-making meetings are mainly concerned with persuasion, analysis, and problem solving. They often include a brainstorming session that is followed by a debate on the alternatives. These meetings tend to be somewhat less predictable than informational meetings. When planning a decision-making meeting, remember that your purpose is to develop a course of action that the group can support. Therefore, each participant must be aware of the nature of the problem and the criteria for its solution.

Selecting the Participants and the Location

In many organizations, being invited to this or that meeting is a mark of status. As the one calling the meeting, you may be reluctant to leave someone out. Despite the pressure to include everyone even remotely concerned, try to invite only those whose presence is essential. The number of participants should reflect the purpose of the meeting. If the session is purely informational and one person will be doing most of the talking, you can include a relatively large group. However, if you're trying to solve a problem, develop a plan, or reach a decision, try to limit participation to between 6 and 12 people.[37] The more people who attend, the more comments and confusion you're likely to get, and the longer the whole thing will take.

Limit the number of participants, but include all key people.

Although you don't want to invite too many people, be sure to include those who can make an important contribution and those who are key decision makers. Holding a meeting to decide an important matter is pointless if the people with the necessary information aren't there. If your purpose is to develop the schedule for launching a new product, you'd better be sure you've invited someone from production as well as all the marketing people. Otherwise, you may end up with a great promotional campaign but nothing to sell.

Decide where you'll hold the meeting, and reserve the location. For work sessions, morning meetings are usually more productive than afternoon sessions. Consider the seating arrangements. Are rows of chairs suitable, or do you need a conference table? Give some attention to such details as room temperature, lighting, ventilation, acoustics, and refreshments. These things may seem trivial, but they can make or break a meeting.

Give attention to the small details that help participants focus on the task at hand.

Setting and Following the Agenda

Although the nature of a meeting may sometimes prevent you from developing a fixed agenda, at least prepare a list of matters to be discussed. Distribute the agenda to the participants several days before the meeting so they will know what to expect and can come prepared to respond to the issues at hand.

Prepare and distribute a detailed agenda well in advance of the meeting.

Agendas include the names of the participants and the time, place, and order of business (see Component Chapter A). Some executives argue that the most important items should be scheduled first, but others favor an arrangement that provides warm-up time to accommodate latecomers. Regardless of the order of business, make sure the agenda is specific. For example, the phrase "development budget" doesn't tell very much, whereas the longer explanation "to discuss the proposed reduction of the 1999–2000 development budget in light of our new product postponement" helps all committee members prepare in advance with facts and figures.

Agendas also help you start and end your meetings on time. Starting and ending on time sends a signal of good organization and allows attendees to meet other commitments. In fact, one of Virginia Johnson's favorite solutions for improving meetings is simply telling people what time the meeting will end. Another important use of the agenda is to move the meeting forward. This means you have to stick to it. People often get off track, either by design or because of distractions. When they do, a good agenda and an effective leader will bring them back in line.

In short, a productive agenda should answer these key questions: (1) What do we need to do in this meeting to accomplish our goals? (2) What conversations will be of greatest importance to all the participants? (3) What information must be available in order to have these conversations?[38]

Getting Everyone Involved

Whether the meeting is conducted electronically or conventionally, its success depends largely on how effective the leader is. If the leader is prepared and has selected the participants carefully, the meeting will generally be productive. Moreover, according to 3M's Virginia Johnson, listening skills are especially important for meeting leaders. The leader's ability to listen well facilitates good meetings.

As meeting leader, you're responsible for keeping the ball rolling and staying on track. A good meeting is not a series of dialogues between individual members and the leader. Instead, it is a cross-flow of discussion and debate, with the leader occasionally guiding, mediating, probing, stimulating, and summarizing, but mostly letting the others thrash out their ideas. That's why, as leader, it's important for you to avoid being so domineering that you close off suggestions. On the other hand, don't be so passive that you lose control of the group. If the discussion lags, call on those who haven't been heard from. Pace the presentation and discussion so that you'll have time to complete the agenda. As time begins to run out, interrupt the discussion and summarize what has been accomplished.

The meeting leader's duties:

- Pacing the meeting
- Following the agenda
- Stimulating participation and discussion
- Summarizing the debate
- Reviewing recommendations
- Circulating the minutes

Even though you are responsible for following a set agenda, don't be too rigid. Allow enough time for discussion, and give people a chance to raise related issues. If you cut off discussion too quickly or limit the subject too narrowly, no real consensus can emerge.

One way you can improve the productivity of a meeting is by using **parliamentary procedure**, a time-tested method for planning and running effective meetings. Anyone belonging to an organization should understand the basic principles of parliamentary procedure. Used correctly, it can help groups in several important ways:[39]

- Transact business efficiently
- Protect individual rights
- Maintain order
- Preserve a spirit of harmony
- Help the organization accomplish its goals

The most common guide to parliamentary procedure is *Robert's Rules of Order,* available in various editions and revisions. Also available are less technical guides based on "Robert's Rules." You can determine how strictly you want to adhere to parliamentary procedure. For small groups you may be quite flexible, but for larger groups you'll want to use a more formal approach.

As the meeting gets under way, you'll discover that some participants are too quiet and others are too talkative. To draw out the shy types, ask for their input on issues that particularly pertain to them. You might say something like, "Roberto, you've done a lot of work in this area. What do you think?" For the overly talkative, simply say that time is limited and others need to be heard from. The best meetings are those in which everyone participates, so don't let one or two people dominate your meeting while others doodle on their notepads. As you move through your agenda, stop at the end of each item, summarize what you understand to be the feelings of the group, and state the important points made during the discussion.

At the conclusion of the meeting, tie up the loose ends. Either summarize the general conclusion of the group or list the suggestions. Wrapping things up ensures that all participants agree on the outcome and gives people a chance to clear up any misunderstandings. Before the meeting breaks up, briefly review who has agreed to do what by what date. Then be sure to follow up. As soon as possible after the meeting, make sure all participants receive a copy of the minutes or notes, showing recommended actions, schedules, and responsibilities. (Component Chapter A includes an example of the format for minutes of meetings.) The minutes will remind everyone of what took place and will provide a reference for future actions.

Participants also have responsibilities during meetings. If you've been included in the group, try to contribute to both the subject of the meeting and the smooth interaction of the participants. Use your listening skills and powers of observation to size up the interpersonal dynamics of the people, then adapt your behavior to help the group achieve its goals. Speak up if you have something useful to say, but don't monopolize the discussion. (To review the tasks that contribute to productive meetings, see this chapter's Checklist for Meetings.)

HANDLING DIFFICULT INTERPERSONAL SITUATIONS

Regardless of how well you learn to communicate, you're bound to face difficult interpersonal situations on the job from time to time. Improving your listening habits will help you cope with some of the difficult situations that inevitably arise in business. But in gen-

CHECKLIST FOR MEETINGS

A. Preparation
1. Determine the meeting's objectives.
2. Work out an agenda that will achieve your objectives.
3. Select participants.
4. Determine the location, and reserve a room.
5. Arrange for light refreshments, if appropriate.
6. Determine whether the lighting, ventilation, acoustics, and temperature of the room are adequate.
7. Determine seating needs: chairs only or table and chairs.

B. Conduct
1. Begin and end the meeting on time.
2. Control the meeting by following the announced agenda.
3. Encourage full participation, and either confront or ignore those who seem to be working at cross-purposes with the group.
4. Sum up decisions, actions, and recommendations as you move through the agenda, and restate main points at the end.

C. Follow-Up
1. Distribute the meeting's notes or minutes on a timely basis.
2. Take the follow-up action agreed to.

eral, you'll need a great deal of communication skill to maintain your composure and achieve your goals when the stakes are high and emotions are aroused—especially if you're trying to resolve conflict or overcome resistance.

Resolving Conflict

Conflict is not necessarily bad, as long as it is handled in a constructive fashion.

Many business dealings involve conflict. People in organizations often compete for scarce resources or clash over differences in goals and values. Misunderstandings based on cultural differences may arise. These conflicts can be valuable, forcing important issues into the open and bringing out creative ideas about solving problems.

Although conflict itself can be positive, some approaches to resolving conflict are destructive. If you believe that the only solution is for one party to win and the other party to lose (win-lose strategy), the outcome of the conflict will surely make someone unhappy. Unfortunately, some conflicts degenerate to the point that both parties would rather lose than see the other party win (lose-lose strategy). On the other hand, if you approach the conflict with the idea that both parties can satisfy their goals at least to some extent (win-win strategy), then no one loses. The principle behind the win-win strategy is that the parties in conflict can better solve their problems by working together than by waging war. However, for the win-win strategy to work, everybody must believe that it's possible to find a solution both parties can accept, that cooperation is better for the organization than competition, that the other party can be trusted, and that higher status doesn't entitle one party to impose a solution.

Look for win-win solutions to conflict.

One of the first steps to finding a win-win solution is to preserve the "you" attitude by considering the other person's needs. Before you meet, try to find out what might be acceptable to the other party. For example, if you're buying a new car, get the wholesale list price so that you know the dealer's break-even cost. You can extend the "you" attitude by searching for mutually satisfactory solutions. Keep your eyes and ears open; ask questions that will help you understand the other person's wants. Look for compromises that result in joint gain.[40]

The important thing to remember about resolving conflict is that both parties can usually get what they want if both are willing to work together. In many cases, the resolution process is chiefly an exchange of opinions and information that gradually leads to a mutually acceptable solution. Here are seven measures a manager can take to successfully resolve conflict:

- Deal with minor conflict before it becomes major conflict.
- Get the persons most directly involved in the conflict to participate in solving it, and make sure they know that you expect them to communicate with each other.
- Get feelings out in the open before dealing with the main issues; try to understand each party's motivations, biases, and vested interests.
- Seek reasons for the problem before seeking solutions, but don't blame either party; make sure that reasons are based on fact, not on differing perceptions.
- Don't let anyone become locked into a position before considering other solutions.
- Don't let anyone avoid a fair solution by hiding behind the rules.
- Try to get the parties to fight together against an "outside force" instead of against each other.

By applying these techniques, a manager can turn potentially disastrous conflict into an opportunity for creative change.

Overcoming Resistance

Part of dealing with conflict is learning how to persuade other people to accept your point of view. In a business situation, reason usually prevails. Sometimes, however, you encounter people who react emotionally. When you face irrational resistance, you may well become frustrated, but the best strategy is to remain calm and detached so that you can avoid destructive confrontations and present your position in a convincing manner.

When you encounter resistance or hostility, try to maintain your composure and address the other person's emotional needs.

Start by expressing understanding. Most people are ashamed when they react emotionally, especially in business situations. They're insulted when you say, "You're being emotional," and they respond by rejecting you and your viewpoint. Show that you sympathize; you don't necessarily have to agree with someone who is reacting emotionally, but respond with understanding and acceptance. You might say, "I can understand that this change might be difficult, and if I were in your position, I might be reluctant to do it myself." The point is to make the other person relax and talk about his or her anxiety so that you have a chance to offer reassurance.[41]

Be aware that the person's resistance and behavior might be the result of cultural differences. What seems like irrational behavior to you might seem perfectly rational to the other person. For example, people in mainstream American culture try not to react emotionally in a business setting, but in other cultures emotional reactions at work may be quite acceptable. (See Chapter 3 for more on cultural barriers.)

Make the person aware of her or his resistance. When you encounter a noncommittal, silent reaction, you know that you aren't getting through to the other person. Although not actively resisting you, the person is tuning you out, possibly without even being aware of why. In such situations, continuing to present your own point of view is futile. Deal directly with the resistance, but not in an accusing way. You might say, "You seem cool to this idea. Have I made some faulty assumptions somewhere?" This sort of question will force the person to face up to her or his resistance and define it.[42]

Seek to understand so that you can be understood.

Evaluate others' objections fairly. Don't just continue repeating yourself. Focus instead on what the other person is saying. Listen carefully to both the words and the feelings being expressed. Get the person to open up so that you can understand the basis for his or her resistance. The person may raise some legitimate points. If your suggestions are going to create problems for people, you'll have to discuss ways of minimizing those problems.[43]

When you're trying to convince someone of your viewpoint, hold your arguments until the other person is ready for them. Your success in getting your points across depends as much on the other person's frame of mind as it does on your arguments. You can't assume that a strong argument will speak for itself. By becoming more audience-centered, you will learn to address the other person's emotional needs first.

COMMUNICATION CHALLENGES AT 3M

As director of 3M's human relations department, Virginia Johnson constantly faces demands for effective communication—with her own staff, with executives throughout the company, in one-on-one interviews, and in meetings. Her department (an offshoot of human resources) is charged with making sure the company meets all its legal responsibilities to employees (through equal-hiring, affirmative action, and family-leave policies, for instance). Johnson's department is also the place employees can bring problems they would feel uncomfortable discussing with supervisors. So Johnson is sometimes supporting employees and sometimes explaining management's perspective, but she's always striving to achieve a balanced and fair conclusion that meets everyone's needs. Work like this requires every person in her eight-member department to be a good listener and a good speaker.

INDIVIDUAL CHALLENGE Several members of your department have been confused by Johnson's way of doing things, which is slightly different from her predecessor's. A fellow staffer explains to you that when Johnson's predecessor retired, he was "a well-loved man throughout the company. They all miss him." Johnson wants to clear the air and establish her own way of doing things. As Johnson's assistant, you have been asked to advise her whether to (1) write a memo clarifying procedures, (2) call each of the eight department members into her office for one-to-one discussions, or (3) hold a meeting of the entire department. Decide on the best approach and explain your reasoning in a brief memo to Johnson.

TEAM CHALLENGE Using Johnson's "brainwriting sheet" technique for generating new ideas, write down three things you'd like to change about your school. Then exchange sheets with your classmates, and add three more items. After a few rounds, list all the recommendations on the board (combining similar items and eliminating duplicates). Then group the ideas into categories. Conduct a classroom meeting to discuss the ideas and to decide on the ten most important ones. Using the memo format in Figure 1.2 on page 8 as a model, draft a memo to your college president highlighting your top ten recommendations. Be sure to include some of the supporting rationale you discussed during your classroom meeting.[44] ■

SUMMARY OF LEARNING OBJECTIVES

1. **List the six general categories of nonverbal communication.** The six categories of nonverbal communication include facial expressions and eye behavior, gestures and postures, vocal characteristics, personal appearance, touching behavior, and use of time and space.
2. **Summarize the skills involved in being an effective listener.** You can improve your listening skills by finding areas of interest with the speaker; judging content, not delivery; reserving judgment until the speaker has finished; taking selective notes; paying attention; keeping an open mind; fighting distractions; paying attention to the speaker's body language; paraphrasing what the speaker says; and practicing.
3. **Highlight seven characteristics of effective feedback.** Effective feedback focuses on specific behavior, is impersonal, uses "I" statements, is goal oriented, is well timed, ensures understanding, and addresses behavior that is controllable by the recipient.
4. **Describe the four phases of group decision making.** In the orientation phase, group members socialize and define their task. In the conflict phase, members begin to discuss their positions

on the problem. In the emergence phase, they reach a decision, and in the reinforcement phase they summarize their decision while rebuilding group feeling.

5. **List six ways leaders can make meetings more productive.** You can make your meetings more productive by planning carefully, selecting the right participants, choosing a good location, setting and following an agenda, getting everyone involved, and keeping things under control.
6. **Explain the win-win strategy to resolving conflict.** The principle behind the win-win strategy is to find a solution that is beneficial to all parties involved. This is done by considering the other person's needs as well as your own and by creatively seeking new alternatives through a process of mutual brainstorming and open communication.

CRITICAL THINKING QUESTIONS

1. How can nonverbal communication help you run a meeting? How can it help you call a meeting to order, emphasize important topics, show approval, express reservations, regulate the flow of conversation, and invite a colleague to continue with a comment?
2. Have you ever made a comment you later regretted? Describe the circumstances of your verbal blunder, and explain the consequences.
3. When communicating across cultures, U.S. businesspeople tend to be impatient. What are the drawbacks of such impatience? How would you suggest dealing with this trait? Explain.
4. Should meeting leaders always use a participatory style, or are there some circumstances when this might not be advisable? Explain your answer.
5. During your meeting with members of your project team, one member keeps raising objections to points of style in a rough draft of your group's report. At this rate, you'll be here for hours debating whether to use the word *criteria* or the word *parameters* on page 27. What should you do? Explain your answer.
6. Is conflict in a team good or bad? Explain your answer.
7. At your last department meeting, three people monopolized the entire discussion. What might you do at your next meeting to encourage the other department members to voluntarily participate?
8. Why is it a good idea to paraphrase what a speaker says? Do you need to do this out loud?

EXERCISES

With a partner, attend a local community or campus meeting to observe group decision making. You will use your observations and notes to answer exercises 1–8, so read these questions carefully before attending the meeting. Check the agenda in advance to make sure the meeting will involve discussion items that will require group action (such as a vote).

1. Evaluate the meeting with regard to (a) the leader's ability to clearly articulate the meeting's goals, (b) the leader's ability to engage members in a meaningful discussion, (c) the group's dynamics, and (d) the group's listening skills. Prepare a memo summarizing your evaluations.
2. How did the group make decisions? Did they vote? Did they reach decisions by consensus? Did the naysayers get an opportunity to voice their objections?
3. How well did the individual participants listen? How could you tell?
4. Did any of the participants change their mind during the meeting? Why might that have happened?
5. Identify some of the communication barriers discussed in Chapter 1 that you observed during the meeting.
6. Analyze a copy of the meeting agenda. Did it have a meeting start time or end time? Was the agenda specific enough so that, as an outsider, you knew what items they were going to discuss? If not, how would you improve the agenda?
7. Did it appear that any of the meeting members had a personal hidden agenda? How could you tell?
8. Compare the notes you took during the meeting with those of your partner. What differences do you notice? How do you account for these differences?
9. Identify some of your bad listening habits and make a list of ways you could correct them. For the next 30 days, review your list and jot down any improvements you've noticed as a result of your effort.
10. Your company is opening a new office in Japan, and you are unfamiliar with Japanese culture and business practices. Suggest some ways you and your co-workers could learn more about the cultural differences that might affect work relationships. Briefly explain your suggestions.
11. Every month, each employee in your department is expected to give a brief oral presentation on the status of his or her project. However, your department has recently hired an employee with a severe speech impediment that prevents people from understanding most of what he has to say. As department manager, how will you resolve this dilemma? Please explain your answer.
12. Select a business letter and envelope that you have received at work or home. Analyze their appearance. What nonverbal messages do they send?
13. Visit the 3M home page on the Internet at http://www.3m.com. Click on "Advanced Meeting Solutions," and click on the "3M Ideaboard." What advantages does a digital whiteboard offer? Draft a short internal memo to your boss outlining the product's advantages using the memo format in Figure 1.2 on page 8.

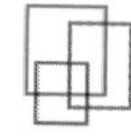

14. Describe a recent conflict you had with a peer at work or at school, and explain how you resolved it. Did you find a solution that both of you could accept?
15. Review the guidelines for developing effective feedback skills on page 45, and explain why it's important to adopt an audience-centered approach when giving feedback to others.

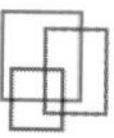

Exploring the Best of the Web

Check Out Books at This Library—It's a Snap!, page 40

Visit LibrarySpot at http://www.libraryspot.com, and explore this resource center. Click on "My Virtual Ref. Desk" and then click on "Quick Ref/Research." Discover some interesting facts. Go back to the home page, click on "Dictionaries," and click on the "Phrase Finder" to learn a thing or two. There's so much information at this site, you're bound to get lost in the stacks.

1. How can you use the links at this Web site to enhance your everyday communication skills?
2. Sometimes the best way to get people involved in a meeting is to throw out an interesting fact or two. Find five business facts or statistics that you think others might be interested in and try them out at your next meeting.

COMMUNICATING INTERCULTURALLY

AFTER STUDYING THIS CHAPTER, YOU WILL BE ABLE TO

1. Discuss three trends that have made intercultural business communication so important
2. Name three main barriers to intercultural communication
3. Identify nine ways people can differ culturally
4. Explain the principal difference between high-context and low-context cultures
5. List things you can do to learn about a particular culture
6. Describe six ways you can overcome cultural barriers to written communication

COMMUNICATION CLOSE-UP AT SHERATON HOTELS HAWAII

Michiru Tamanai

Kayomi Kaneda

Michiru Tamanai and Kayomi Kaneda love bringing together people from different cultures. Tamanai is the director of training and Kaneda is the training administrator for Sheraton Hotels Hawaii. Together, they've taught thousands of Sheraton employees how to improve customer satisfaction by being sensitive to cultural differences. As Tamanai sees it, having a broad cultural perspective is a necessary skill for businesspeople today. "The business world is becoming more global," she says. "Distance and time wise, we are closer than ever. . . . But we are still learning to understand each other's mindset. We need to develop cultural awareness in order to be successful."

That's especially true in the hospitality industry, where success depends on satisfying customers from a variety of cultural backgrounds. In Hawaii, the number of Japanese tourists alone doubled in the past decade, and today they account for over 60 percent of Sheraton's guests. But as business has soared, language and cultural barriers have made it increasingly difficult for employees to meet guests' needs, creating frustration and job dissatisfaction among employees. In response, Sheraton started a program providing all guest-contact employees with six hours of Japanese language training and two hours of cultural sensitivity training. In the past few years, over 3,500 employees have been trained, and both employee and customer satisfaction have increased as a result.

According to Kaneda, a common mistake employees make is assuming that international guests have the same behavior and communication patterns as themselves. For instance, guests from the United States usually complain right away when they are unhappy about the hotel service, because the United States is a low-context culture; that is, its members rely mostly on verbal communication to convey their messages. On the other hand, guests from high-context cultures, such as Japan, rely less on verbal communication and more on circumstances and nonverbal actions to communicate their messages. So rather than complain directly to the employees, Japanese guests expect employees to anticipate their

Because over 60 percent of the guests of Sheraton Hotels Hawaii come from Japan, all hotel employees receive extensive training in the Japanese culture as part of the hotel's intercultural training program.

needs. Other behavioral differences are more overt. For example, when a hotel receptionist pulls out a chair for a Japanese woman, the woman's husband will typically sit down first, thinking the receptionist has pulled it out for him.

Gestures are another big difference. In fact, Japanese guests find some Western forms of nonverbal communication offensive, including leaning on a wall, using an index finger to summon someone, or moving things with one's feet. So Tamanai and Kaneda instruct employees to avoid these offensive behaviors and to communicate in ways that guests are accustomed to. After all, making guests feel comfortable is an important part of Sheraton Hotels Hawaii's cultural sensitivity training program.

But the program has other goals too. For instance, Tamanai and Kaneda strive to improve communications among Sheraton's diverse employees, whose cultural backgrounds include Chinese, Korean, Japanese, Native Hawaiian, Philippine, and American. Their goal is for all employees to treat each other as *ohana,* or extended family. And this is not an easy task, because there are so many differences.

Take meetings, for example. Employees from the United States and Europe tend to be more enthusiastic about meetings than employees from the Philippines or Japan, because open heated discussions are more common in Western countries than in the East. Unfortunately, Westerners may wrongfully perceive this difference as a lack of interest on the part of their Eastern associates. To avoid such ethnocentrism, Tamanai and Kaneda encourage managers and employees to focus on each other's core competencies. Fortunately, their efforts have paid off; employee satisfaction is up, and employee turnover is down.

Of course, employees aren't the only ones satisfied at Sheraton. The company's cultural training programs are turning out to be a real competitive advantage in Hawaii. Several Japanese guidebooks, which Japanese tourists rely on heavily when they travel, list Sheraton as "Japanese friendly," an accolade that Tamanai says is very good for business. In addition, the number of repeat guests is increasing. In fact, management is so pleased with the success of the programs that plans are now under way to offer employee training in additional languages and cultures.

Such a positive effect on business comes as no surprise to Tamanai and Kaneda. As far as they are concerned, effective intercultural communication is a necessity no matter what business you're in. "Businesses need to promote a multicultural work environment for global competitiveness," Tamanai advises. "This means respecting different cultures, values, work styles, and backgrounds." To be successful, Kaneda adds, you must also possess a "sincere desire for understanding others and patience."[1] ■

THE IMPORTANCE OF INTERCULTURAL BUSINESS COMMUNICATION

The globalization of business is accelerating as more companies cross national borders to find customers, materials, and money.

Sheraton Hotels Hawaii is by no means alone in its multinational focus. Thanks to technological advances in communication and transportation, companies today can quickly and easily span the globe in search of new customers, new sources of materials, and new sources of money. Even firms that once thought they were too tiny to expand into a neighboring city have discovered that they can tap the sales potential of overseas markets with the help of fax machines, the Internet, overnight delivery services, and e-mail (see Figure 3.1).

Just how important is intercultural business communication in the global marketplace? Consider these facts and trends:

- Ninety-five percent of the world's consumers live outside the United States.[2]
- The level of U.S. exports has grown steadily in recent years to well over $800 billion.[3]
- Relaxed trade barriers are accelerating the pace of international trade. The North American Free Trade Agreement (NAFTA) has created a single market of 400 million people, and discussions are under way to extend this agreement throughout the Americas.[4]
- Capital, products, and employees have been flowing freely across the borders of the European Community for years, creating a unified market of 367 million people. Now that 11 of its members have joined forces under a unified currency, the euro, this group will become an even greater force in the world economy.[5]
- In a single year, U.S. companies invested approximately $30 billion in non-U.S. facilities and equipment, employing more than 20 million people outside the United States.[6] Likewise, companies from all over the world are setting up shop in the United States.[7]
- Technology and the Internet allow people of different cultures to work together seamlessly. Today, multicultural teams collaborate and share information on projects without leaving their desks. Already, a few companies have established work teams that "follow the sun": Projects move around the globe, from the United States to Asia and Europe and back again, so that work is being done 24 hours a day. Computer programs that can translate language as it is input will expedite this new way of working.[8]

In short, the relaxation of trade barriers, the resulting rise in international business, and the increased use of new technologies means that the global marketplace will continue to become a dizzying combination of countries and cultures.

UNDERSTANDING CULTURE AND CULTURAL DIFFERENCES

Culture is a shared system of symbols, beliefs, attitudes, values, expectations, and norms for behavior.

You belong to several cultures. The most obvious is the culture you share with all the people who live in your own country. You also belong to other cultural groups, including an ethnic group, probably a religious group, and perhaps a profession that has its own special language and customs. **Culture** is a shared system of symbols, beliefs, attitudes, values, expectations, and norms for behavior. All members of a culture have similar assumptions about how people should think, behave, and communicate, and they all tend to act on those assumptions in much the same way.

Subcultures are distinct groups that exist within a major culture.

Some cultures are made up of many diverse and disparate groups; others tend to be more homogeneous. Distinct groups that exist within a major culture are more properly referred to as **subcultures.** Indonesia, for example, is home to a wide variety of ethnic and religious subcultures; by comparison, Japan is much more homogeneous because it has only a few sub-

Wickman Hospital Products, Inc., a large U.S. company, is interested in developing a client base in Mexico. Wickman's marketing department suggested a direct-mail campaign supplemented with personalized e-mail communications. Each Mexican hospital was initially sent a letter of introduction, detailed product information, and a carton of sample products. A week later, the following e-mail message was sent.

Figure 3.1
In-Depth Critique: E-Mail Is One of the Technologies Shrinking the World

E-Mail

Comments: authenticated sender is <jackson@wickman.com>
From: "Timothy A. Jackson" <jacksont@wickman.com>
To: jHerrera@stlukeshosp.org
Date: Thurs, 19 June 1999, 10:30:23, CDT
Subject: Wickman Hospital Products, Inc.
Return-Receipt-To: jacksont@wickman.com

The header containing routing information, subject, and so forth is a common feature of most e-mail programs.

Dear Sr. Herrera:

Wickman Hospital Products is eager to serve you. Did you have time to look over the materials we sent you recently? You may be especially interested in our fine line of disposable pads and bedding.

The message begins politely and with a reminder of previous communication.

For your convenience, Charles Garrison can give you detailed information about any of our products. You can contact him by e-mail, phone, or post:

This paragraph gives helpful information, suggests actions, and provides an address for each action.

E-mail	garrison@wickman.com
Phone	(800) 773-4558
Post	Charles Garrison Customer Representative Wickman Hospital Products P.O. Box 511 Columbus, Ohio, 43216-0508 USA

You can also place an order right away, browse through our entire line of products, and review product specifications. Just visit our Internet home page: <http://www.wickman.com>. You can count on delivery within 48 hours of the time we receive your e-mail, Internet order form, or phone call.

Please let us help you supply St. Luke's Hospital with the finest products available.

Timothy A. Jackson, International Sales
Wickman Hospital Products

The letter closes by urging use of the Internet. When this message is sent, the angle brackets placed around the Uniform Resource Locator, or URL, convert the Web address to a live link (also called a hot link). The URL appears in a distinctive color, and the angle brackets are no longer visible. To visit the linked Web page, the recipient merely clicks on the URL.

cultures.[9] Groups that might be considered subcultures in the United States are Mexican Americans, Mormons, wrestling fans, Russian immigrants, and Harvard graduates.

Recognizing Cultural Differences

As discussed in Chapter 1, cultural differences can be a difficult communication barrier to overcome. When you write to or speak with someone from another culture, you encode your message using the assumptions of your own culture. However, the receiver decodes the message according to the assumptions of the other culture, so your meaning may be misunderstood. The greater the difference between the sender's culture and the receiver's culture, the greater the chance for misunderstanding.[10]

People differ in cultural background, language, gender, age, physical ability, family status, and educational background.

Whether you're in another country or in your own country, you're likely to come into contact with people from a variety of backgrounds and whose culture and language differ from yours. Of course, people also differ in terms of their gender, age, physical abilities, family status, and educational background. Together with culture and language, these elements shape how people view the world. They also affect how business messages are conceived, planned, sent, received, and interpreted.

Cultural diversity is the degree to which the population is made up of people from varied national, ethnic, racial, and religious backgrounds.

The U.S. work force has grown more and more diverse, partly because of immigration.

Few countries have an entirely homogeneous population. A country's work force reflects its **cultural diversity,** the degree to which the population is made up of people from various national, ethnic, racial, and religious backgrounds. In the United States, for example, the high degree of cultural diversity in the domestic work force has been partially shaped by immigration, with new arrivals from Europe, Canada, Latin America, and Asia.[11] As you communicate with members of an increasingly diverse domestic work force, you'll face language and cultural barriers that can interfere with your message exchange.

Consider the communication challenge that Mazda's managers faced when the Japanese auto manufacturer opened a plant in the United States. Mazda officials passed out

Solectron is a U.S. company that's making it big as an electronics contract manufacturer. It assembles printed circuit boards and complete computers for companies like IBM, Hewlett-Packard, and Compaq. Because the U.S. work force is increasing in cultural diversity, companies such as Solectron benefit from learning about intercultural communication.

company baseball caps and told their U.S. employees that they could wear the caps at work, along with their mandatory company uniform (blue pants and khaki shirts). The employees assumed that the caps were a *voluntary* accessory, and many decided not to wear them. Their decision upset the Japanese managers, who regarded it as a sign of disrespect. Managers acknowledged that the caps were voluntary but believed that employees who really cared about the company would want to wear the caps. However, the U.S. employees had a different view: They resented being told what they should want to do, and they began cynically referring to all Mazda's directives as "mandatory-voluntary."[12]

Similarly, when a U.S. computer sales representative wanted to make a good impression while calling on a client in China, he brought an expensive grandfather clock as a gift. Unfortunately, the differences between the sender's culture and the receiver's culture interfered with the communication process. Instead of being pleased, the Chinese client was deeply offended, because in China receiving a clock as a gift is considered bad luck.[13] Problems like these arise when we assume, wrongly, that other people's attitudes and lives are like ours.

Like the Mazda managers and the salesperson, you may find yourself trying to bridge differences in both language and culture as you exchange business messages with customers, suppliers, investors, competitors, and business associates from other lands. By bridging these differences, you can successfully achieve **intercultural communication,** the process of sending and receiving messages between people of different cultures. As a graduate of one intercultural training program said, "I used to think it was enough to treat people the way I wanted to be treated. But [after taking the course] . . . I realized you have to treat people the way *they* want to be treated."[14] Acknowledging and accommodating cultural differences without expecting persons from either culture to give up their identity is an important step toward communicating effectively (see "Communicating across Cultures: Test Your Intercultural Knowledge").[15]

Intercultural communication is the process of sending and receiving messages between people of different cultures.

Effective intercultural communication depends on recognizing ways in which people differ.

In the following sections you'll see how cultural differences show up in social values, ideas of status, decision-making habits, attitudes toward time, use of space, cultural context, body language, manners, and legal and ethical behavior. Without an understanding of these differences, U.S. businesspeople can unknowingly act improperly and unacceptably when abroad, hurting their own reputations and that of their organization.[16]

Social Values

Although the United States is home to millions of people having different religions and values, the major influence is the Puritan work ethic. The predominant U.S. view is that money solves many problems, that material comfort (earned by individual effort) is a sign of superiority, and that people who work hard are better than those who don't. By and large, people in the United States assume that people from other cultures also dislike poverty and value hard work. The fact is, however, that many societies condemn materialism, and some prize a more carefree lifestyle.

People from the United States emphasize hard work, material success, and efficiency more than many people in other countries do.

As a culture, people in the United States are goal oriented. They want to get their work done efficiently, and they assume that everyone else does too. They think they're improving things if they can figure out a way for two people using modern methods to do the same work as four people using the "old way." In countries such as India and Pakistan, where unemployment is high, creating jobs is more important than working efficiently. Executives in these countries would rather employ four workers than two, and their values influence their actions as well as the way they encode and decode messages.

Roles and Status

Culture dictates the roles people play, including who communicates with whom, what they communicate, and in what way. For example, in many countries women still don't play a prominent role in business, so female executives who visit these countries may find that

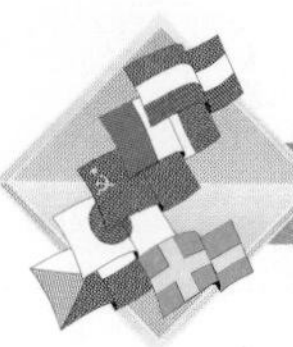

COMMUNICATING ACROSS CULTURES

TEST YOUR INTERCULTURAL KNOWLEDGE

Never take anything for granted when you're doing business in a foreign country. All sorts of assumptions that are valid in one place can trip you up elsewhere if you fail to consider that customs may vary. Here are several true stories about businesspeople who blundered by overlooking some simple but important cultural differences. Can you spot the erroneous assumptions that led these people astray?

1. You're tired of the discussion and you want to move on to a new topic. You ask your Australian business associate, "Can we table this for a while?" To your dismay, your colleague keeps right on discussing just what you want to put aside. Are Australians that inconsiderate?
2. When your fragrance company decides to sell its line of men's cologne in North Africa, it uses its tried-and-true North American ad, which pictures a man and his dog in a rural setting. The fragrance bombs in North Africa. What did your company not realize?
3. You finally made the long trip overseas to meet the new German director of your division. Despite slow traffic, you arrive only four minutes late. His door is shut, so you knock on it and walk in. The chair is too far away from the desk, so you pick it up and move it closer. Then you lean over the desk, stick out your hand and say, "Good morning, Hans, it's nice to meet you." Of course, you're baffled by his chilly reaction. Why?
4. Your meeting went better than you'd ever expected. In fact, you found the Japanese representative for your new advertising agency to be very agreeable; she said yes to just about everything. When you share your enthusiasm with your boss, he doesn't appear very excited. Why?
5. You've finally closed the deal, after exhausting both your patience and your company's travel budget. Now, two weeks later, your Chinese customers are asking for special considerations that change the terms of the agreement. How could they do this? Why are they doing it? And, most important, what should you do?

In each case the problems have resulted from inaccurate assumptions. Here are the explanations of what went wrong:

1. To "table" something in Australia means to bring it forward for discussion. This is the opposite of what Americans usually mean. The English that's spoken in Australia is closer to British than to American English. If you must do business in Australia, become familiar with the local vocabulary. Note the tendency to shorten just about any word whenever possible and to add "ie" to it is a form of familiar slang: for example, *brolly* (umbrella) and *lollie* (candy). And yes, it's true: "G'day" is the standard greeting. Use it always.
2. Muslim people consider a dog to be either a sign of bad luck or a symbol of uncleanliness—not exactly appealing for a men's cologne ad.
3. You've just broken four rules of German polite behavior: punctuality, privacy, personal space, and proper greetings. In time-conscious Germany, you should never arrive even a few minutes late. Also, Germans like their privacy and space, and they adhere to formal greetings of "Frau" and "Herr," even if the business association has lasted for years.
4. With the Japanese, "yes" may not always mean yes in the Western sense. The Japanese (and Asian people in general) will use the word *yes* to confirm they have heard or understood something but not necessarily to indicate that they agree with it. You'll seldom get a direct no. Some of the ways the Japanese say no indirectly include "It will be difficult," "I will ask my supervisor," " I'm not sure," "We will think about it," and "I see."
5. For most Americans, the contract represents the end of the negotiation. For the Chinese, however, it's just the beginning. Once a deal is made, the Chinese view their counterparts as trustworthy partners who can be relied on for special favors—such as new terms in the contract.

they're not taken seriously as businesspeople. When they're in modern western Europe, women can usually behave as they would in the United States, but they should be more cautious in Latin American and eastern European countries, and they should be extremely cautious in the Middle East and the Far East.[17]

Culture also dictates the way people refer to each other. In the United States, people show respect for superiors and top managers by addressing them as "Mr. Roberts" or "Mrs. Gutierrez." However, in China, it's customary to show respect for organizational rank by addressing businesspeople according to their official titles, such as "President" or "Manager."[18]

People from other cultures demonstrate their status differently than people in the United States do.

Concepts of status also differ. Most U.S. executives send status signals that reflect materialistic values. The big boss has a large corner office, deep carpets, an expensive desk, and handsome accessories. In other cultures, status is communicated in other ways. The highest-ranking executives in France sit in the middle of an open area, surrounded by lower-level employees. When Japanese businessmen check into a hotel, senior executives must be placed on higher floors than junior executives.[19] And, in the Middle East, fine possessions are reserved for the home, and business is conducted in cramped and modest quarters. An executive from another culture who assumed that such office arrangements indicate a lack of status would be making a big mistake.

Did You Know?

In Japan, the seat directly behind the driver (in an automobile) is the seat of honor.

Decision-Making Customs

In the United States and Canada, businesspeople try to reach decisions as quickly and efficiently as possible. The top people are concerned with reaching an agreement on the main points, and they leave the details to be worked out later by others. In Greece, this approach would backfire. A Greek executive assumes that anyone who ignores the details is being evasive and untrustworthy. Spending time on each little point is considered a mark of good faith. Similarly, Latin Americans prefer to make their deals slowly, after much discussion. And the Japanese look for a group consensus before making a decision. So Tamanai and Kaneda train their employees to be patient when waiting on tables, because Japanese customers often take longer to decide what to order than American customers do.

Many cultural groups take longer than U.S. and Canadian businesspeople to reach decisions, and many rely more heavily on group consensus.

Cultures also differ in terms of who makes the decisions. In the United States, many organizations are dominated by a single figure who says yes or no to the major deals. It is the same in Pakistan, where you can get a decision quickly if you reach the highest-ranking executive.[20] In other cultures, decision making is shared. In China and Japan, the negotiating team arrives at a consensus through an elaborate, time-consuming process. Agreement must be complete; there is no majority rule. And, as do businesses everywhere, Chinese and Japanese firms expect their managers to follow the same decision-making process regardless of whether they're in Beijing, Tokyo, or Toledo.

Concepts of Time

Differing perceptions of time are another factor that can lead to misunderstandings. German and U.S. executives see time as a way to plan the business day efficiently, focusing on only one task during each scheduled period. Because time is so limited, German and U.S. executives try to get to the point quickly when communicating.

However, executives from Latin America and Asia see time as more flexible. In their cultures, building a foundation for the business relationship is more important than meeting a deadline for completing a task. Seen in this light, it's not surprising that people in such cultures do not observe strict schedules. Instead, they take whatever time is needed to get to know each other and explore the background issues.[21]

Although businesspeople in the United States, Germany, and some other nations see time as a way to organize the business day efficiently, other cultures see time as more flexible.

If a salesperson from Chicago called on a client in Mexico City and was kept waiting 30 minutes in the outer office, that salesperson would assume that the client attached a low priority to the visit and would feel angry and insulted. In fact, the Mexican client wouldn't have meant to imply anything at all by the delay. In Mexico, a wait of 30 minutes is a matter of course; the workday isn't expected to follow a rigid, preset schedule.[22]

Concepts of Personal Space

Like time, space means different things in different cultures. The classic story of a conversation between a U.S. executive and a Latin American executive is that the interaction may begin at one end of a hallway and end up at the other, with neither party aware of having moved. During the conversation the Latin American executive instinctively moves closer to the U.S. executive, who unconsciously steps back, resulting in an intercultural dance across the floor.

People from various cultures have different "comfort zones."

People in Canada and the United States usually stand about five feet apart during a business conversation. This distance is uncomfortably close for people from Germany or Japan. But to Arabs or Latin Americans, this distance is uncomfortably far. Because of these differing concepts of personal space, a Canadian manager may react negatively (without knowing exactly why) when an Arab colleague moves closer during their conversation. And the Arab colleague may react negatively (again, without knowing why) when the Canadian manager backs away.

As pictured here outside Amtex Enterprises, U.S. executives commonly maintain a five-foot comfort zone during business discussions. However, senior businessmen in Jerusalem are more comfortable conducting business up close.

Cultural Context

One of the ways people assign meaning to a message is according to its **cultural context,** the pattern of physical cues and implicit understanding that convey meaning between two members of the same culture. However, people convey contextual meaning differently from culture to culture. In a **high-context culture** such as South Korea or Taiwan, people rely less on verbal communication and more on the context of nonverbal actions and environmental setting to convey meaning. For example, a Chinese speaker often begins by creating a context with generalizations that form a web (or frame) to receive and support a given topic. The Chinese speaker is likely to expect the receiver to discover the meaning in a message that uses indirectness and metaphor.[23] Thus, a series of exchanges appearing to say one thing on the surface might say quite another thing just beneath it. In addition, the rules of everyday life are rarely explicit in high-context cultures; as they grow up, individuals learn how to recognize situational cues (such as gestures and tone of voice) and how to respond as expected.[24]

Although U.S. businesspeople rely mostly on words to convey meaning, people in other cultures rely on situational cues and implicit understanding.

In a **low-context culture** such as the United States or Germany, people rely more on verbal communication and less on circumstances and cues to convey meaning. An English speaker feels responsible for transmitting the meaning of the message and often places sentences in chronological sequence to establish a cause-and-effect pattern.[25] Furthermore, expectations are usually spelled out in a low-context culture through explicit statements such as "Please wait until I'm finished" or "You're welcome to browse." In this way, a businessperson in a low-context culture not only explains his or her own actions but also cues the other person about what to do or what to expect next.[26]

Because the written word is highly valued in low-context cultures, agreements are considered binding. High-context cultures, by contrast, put less emphasis on the written word and consider personal pledges more important than contracts. They also have a tendency to view law with flexibility, whereas low-context cultures would adhere to the law strictly.[27]

Another differentiating factor between the two is the way in which business is conducted. In a high-context culture, business is conducted in what appears to be a social atmosphere. That's because developing trust is critical to the business relationship; without trust, a deal cannot be consummated.[28] Imagine the confusion and frustration of someone from a low-context culture trying to sell products to a client from a high-context culture. The salesperson could get the unintended message that the potential customer who likes to socialize is not really interested in the product, when the customer's intention is exactly the opposite. By misinterpreting this cue, the salesperson would lose potential sales.

Body Language

Gestures help members of a culture clarify confusing messages, but as Kaneda teaches her employees, differences in body language are a major source of misunderstanding during intercultural communication. Furthermore, it's a mistake to assume that someone from another country who speaks your language has mastered the body language of your culture. You need to be aware of some of the basic differences in the way people supplement their words with body movement. Take the signal for *no*. People in the United States and Canada shake their heads back and forth; people in Bulgaria nod up and down; people in Japan move their right hand; people in Sicily raise their chin. Or take eye contact. Businesspeople in the United States assume that a person who won't meet their gaze is evasive and dishonest. However, in many parts of Latin America and Asia, keeping your eyes lowered is a sign of respect, and among many Native American groups, a child's maintaining eye contact with adults is a sign of disrespect.[29]

Variations in the meaning of body language can cause problems because people are unaware of the messages they are transmitting.

Sometimes people from different cultures misread an intentional signal sent by body language; at other times they overlook the signal entirely or assume that a meaningless gesture is significant. An Arab man indicates a romantic interest in a woman by running a hand backward across his hair; most Westerners would not understand the significance of the gesture.[30] On the other hand, an Egyptian might mistakenly assume that a Westerner who exposes the sole of his or her shoe is offering a grave insult. The more open you are to nonverbal messages, the better you will be able to communicate in your own and other cultures.[31]

Social Behavior and Manners

The rules of polite behavior vary from country to country.

What is polite in one culture may be considered rude in another. In Arab countries it's impolite to take gifts to a man's wife but acceptable to take gifts to his children. In Germany giving a woman a red rose is considered a romantic invitation—inappropriate if you are trying to establish a business relationship with her. In India you might be invited to visit someone's home "any time." If you're not familiar with the culture, you may be reluctant to make an unexpected visit, and you might therefore wait for a definite invitation. But your failure to take the invitation literally is an insult, a sign that you do not care to develop the friendship.

In any culture, rules of etiquette may be formal or informal. Formal rules are the specifically taught "rights" and "wrongs" of how to behave in common social situations, such as table manners at meals. When formal rules are violated, members of a culture can explain why they feel upset. In contrast, informal social rules are more difficult to identify and are usually learned by watching how people behave and then imitating that behavior. Informal rules govern how males and females are supposed to behave, when it is appropriate to use a person's first name, and so on. When informal rules are violated, members of a culture are likely to feel uncomfortable, although they may not be able to say exactly why.[32]

Legal and Ethical Behavior

People often encounter differing standards of legal and ethical behavior in the course of doing business in other countries.

From culture to culture, what is considered legal and ethical behavior varies widely. In some countries companies are expected to pay government officials extra fees for approving government contracts. These payments aren't illegal or unethical; they are routine. However, the same payments are seen as bribes in the United States, Sweden, and many other countries, where they are both illegal and unethical. In fact, U.S.-based companies are generally not allowed to bribe officials anywhere in the world. (The U.S. Foreign Corrupt Practices Act, which governs company payments to foreign officials, allows a few exceptions, such as small payments that speed but don't actually influence government actions.)[33]

When you conduct business around the world, you may also find that other legal systems differ from what you're accustomed to. In the United Kingdom and the United States, someone is presumed innocent until proven guilty, a principle that is rooted in English common law. In Mexico and Turkey, someone is presumed guilty until proven innocent, a principle that is rooted in the Napoleonic code.[34] These distinctions can be particularly important if your firm must communicate about a legal dispute in another country.

Corporate Cultural Differences

Organizational culture is the way companies do things. In other words, it influences the way people treat and react to each other. It shapes the way people feel about the company and the work they do; the way they interpret and perceive the actions taken by others; the expectations they have regarding changes in their work or in business; and how they view those changes.

When organizations with entirely different ways of doing things join forces, their cultures sometimes clash.

Today, more U.S. companies than ever are trying to form alliances with foreign companies, and more than half of these partnerships fail.[35] One of the reasons behind these failures is culture clash, which is what happens when two groups holding different beliefs about what is really important, how to make decisions, how to organize resources, and how to communicate join forces.[36]

Look at Daimler-Benz and Chrysler. When these two companies announced their engagement in 1998, employees and investors alike were stunned. Except for the fact that both companies make cars, they couldn't be more different in culture and product. Pegged as a middle-class company that is willing to take chances, Chrysler sells over 2.3 million Jeeps, vans, rugged pickup trucks, and cars annually—mostly to U.S. customers. Daimler-Benz, by contrast, is slow moving and intensely conservative, with annual sales of about 726,000 cars that ooze quality and luxury and appeal to an elite group of mostly European buyers.[37] Usually, this type of operational difference is just the tip of the culture-clash iceberg. With the employees of each company speaking two different languages and coming from two different backgrounds, miscommunication is bound to occur.

DID YOU KNOW?

The single most common reason for failed mergers and acquisitions is culture clash.

Dealing with Language Barriers

As U.S. companies—both big and small—look for new global markets, they're beginning to realize that they can't get by with speaking only English anymore. Even though English is widely spoken in the global business marketplace, the language of business, as the adage goes, is the language of the customer. Increasingly, that language may not be English—even in the United States.[38]

English is the most prevalent language in international business, but it's a mistake to assume that everyone understands it.

One out of every seven people in the United States speaks a language other than English when at home. After English, Spanish is by far the most commonly spoken language, followed by French, German, Italian, and Chinese. Also, because of immigration patterns, some areas of the United States have a higher concentration of non-English speakers than others. New Mexico has more Spanish-speaking residents than any other state; Maine has more French-speaking residents; and Michigan has more Arabic-speaking residents.[39]

When U.S. businesspeople deal with individuals who use English as a second language (and some 650 million people fall into this category), misunderstandings involving vocabulary, pronunciation, or usage are likely. Although some of these millions are extremely fluent, others have only an elementary command of English. Although you may miss a few subtleties when dealing with those less fluent in your own language, you are still able to communicate. However, don't assume that the other person understands everything you say. Your message can be mangled by slang, idioms, and local accents.

Watch for clues to be sure that your message is getting through to people who don't speak your language.

Slang and Idioms

Languages never translate from one to another on a word-for-word basis. Languages are idiomatic; that is, they are constructed with phrases and word groupings that can run counter to the usual patterns of the language's framework and can have meanings far different from their individual components when translated literally. When words are translated literally, communication can break down. So it's crucial for you to consider the meaning of the message and the way it will appear to the receiver when translating from one language into another.

For example, if a U.S. executive tells an Egyptian executive that a certain product "doesn't cut the mustard," chances are communication will fail. Likewise, when companies translate their product names and advertising slogans into a foreign language, things don't always go exactly as planned. For instance, the advertising slogan "Come alive with Pepsi" was once mistranslated for German audiences as "Come out of the grave" and for Thai audiences as "Bring your ancestors back from the dead."[40]

When speaking to people less fluent in your language, try to choose words carefully to convey only their most specific denotative meaning. For example, the phrase "big bucks" to some may mean a great deal of money, but to others it could mean a herd of large deer or physically large currency.[41] Even when the words make sense, their meanings may differ according to the situation. For example, suppose you are dining with a German woman who speaks English quite well. You inquire, "More bread?" She says, "Thank you," so you pass the bread. She looks confused; then she takes the breadbasket and sets it down without taking any. In German, *thank you* (*danke*) can also be used as a polite refusal. If the woman had wanted more bread, she would have used the word please (*bitte* in German).

Local Accents and Pronunciation

Differences in pronunciation, vocal inflections, and vocabulary can pose problems when you're speaking to people from other cultures.

Even if the other person speaks your language, you may have a hard time understanding the pronunciation if the person isn't proficient. One group of English-speaking Japanese employees who transferred to Toyota's U.S. office had to enroll in a special course to learn that "Jeat yet?" means "Did you eat yet?" and that "Cannahepya?" means "Can I help you?"

Furthermore, many nonnative English speakers can't distinguish between the English sounds *v* and *w,* so they say "wery" for "very." At the same time, many people from the United States cannot pronounce the French *r* or the German *ch*. Also, the different ways in which people use their voices can lead listeners to misunderstand their intentions. Russian speakers, for instance, speak in flat, level tones in their native tongue. When they speak English, they maintain this pattern, and non-Russian listeners may assume that the speakers are bored or rude. Middle Easterners tend to speak more loudly than Westerners and may therefore mistakenly be considered more emotional. On the other hand, the Japanese are soft-spoken, a characteristic that implies politeness or humility to Western listeners.

Possible Remedies

When you deal with people who don't speak your language at all, you have three options: You can learn their language, use an intermediary or a translator, or teach them your language. Of course, Michiru Tamanai knows that becoming fluent in a new language requires a major commitment. So she advises her employees: "Don't worry about whether you get the formal language right; sincerity of the heart is the most important thing. They will understand."

If you have a long-term business relationship with people of another culture, it is helpful to learn their language.

Nevertheless, at the U.S. State Department, foreign service officers take six months of language training and then continue their studies at their foreign posts. Even the Berlitz method, famous for the speed of its results, requires a month of intensive effort. Language courses can be quite expensive as well. So unless you're planning to spend several years abroad or to make frequent trips over an extended period, learning another language may take more time and more money than you can afford.

DID YOU KNOW?

There are more than 8,000 natural languages in the world, but only some 200 nations.

A more practical approach to dealing with people who don't speak your language is to use an intermediary or a translator. An experienced translator can analyze a message, understand its meaning in the cultural context, consider how to convey the meaning in another language, and then use verbal and nonverbal signals to encode or decode the message for someone from another culture. World trade centers, colleges, and universities are good sources for translators. If your company has an overseas subsidiary, you may want to seek help from local employees who are bilingual.

You can also hire bilingual professionals such as advertising consultants and lawyers. Whenever possible, arrange to meet the translator ahead of time to give him or her a sense of what you are presenting as well as to discuss specific words or concepts that could be confusing. Try to be aware of double meanings in what you say and of jargon that, if taken literally in translation, won't make sense.[42]

Some companies protect themselves against poor translations by using a technique called *back-translation.* Once a translator encodes a message into another language, a different translator retranslates (back-translates) the same message into the original language. This back-translation is then compared with the original message to discover any errors or discrepancies.

The third approach is to offer English language training programs for employees. Tenneco is one U.S.-based company that instituted an English language training program—in this case, for its Spanish-speaking employees in a New Jersey plant. The training concentrated on practical English for use on the job, and thanks to the classes, accidents and grievances declined and productivity improved.[43]

Some multinational companies, on the other hand, ask all their employees to use English when writing to employees in other countries, regardless of where they're located. For example, Nissan employees use English for internal memos to colleagues around the world, even though the corporation is based in Japan. Similarly, English is the official business language of Philips, the global electronics giant based in the Netherlands.[44] Of course, requiring employees to use a specific language when they're on the job can create tension and a host of other problems, an issue discussed in "Communicating across Cultures: Should Companies Stress English Only on the Job?"

Dealing with Ethnocentric Reactions

Although language and cultural differences are significant barriers to communication, these problems can be overcome by maintaining an open mind. Unfortunately, many people lapse into **ethnocentrism,** the tendency to judge all other groups according to their own group's standards, behaviors, and customs. When making such comparisons, people too often decide that their group is superior.[45]

Ethnocentrism is the tendency to judge all other groups according to one's own group's standards, behaviors, and customs and to see other groups as inferior by comparison.

By reacting ethnocentrically, you ignore the distinctions between your own culture and another person's culture. You assume that others will act the same way you do, that they will operate from the same assumptions, and that they will use language and symbols the same way you do. If they do not, you may mistakenly believe that they are in error, that their way is invalid, or that it's inferior to your own. An ethnocentric reaction makes you lose sight of the possibility that your words and actions will be misunderstood. It also makes you likely to misinterpret or belittle the behavior of others.

Ethnocentric people are often prone to **stereotyping**—attempting to predict individuals' behavior or character on the basis of their membership in a particular group or class. When someone first starts to investigate the culture of another group, he or she may stereotype characteristics as a way of understanding the common tendencies of that group's members, but the next step is to move beyond the stereotypes to relationships with real people. Unfortunately, when ethnocentric people stereotype an entire group of people, they do so on the basis of limited, general, or inaccurate evidence, and they frequently develop biased attitudes toward the group.[46] They fail to communicate with individuals as they really are. Instead of talking with Abdul Karhum, unique human being, ethnocentric people think only about talking to an Arab. Although they've never met an Arab, they may already believe that all Arabs are, say, hagglers. Abdul Karhum's personal qualities become insignificant in the face of such preconceptions. Everything he says and does will be forced to fit the preconceived image, even if it's wrong.

Stereotyping is the attempt to categorize individuals by trying to predict their behavior or character on the basis of their membership in a particular group.

Often, both parties in an intercultural exchange are guilty of ethnocentrism, stereotyping, and prejudice. Little wonder, then, that misunderstandings arise. Fortunately, a healthy dose of open-mindedness can prevent a lot of problems.

Tips for Communicating with People from Other Cultures

You may never completely overcome linguistic and cultural barriers or ethnocentric tendencies, but you can communicate effectively with people from other cultures if you work at it. Once you've acknowledged that cultural differences exist, the next step is to learn as much

COMMUNICATING ACROSS CULTURES

SHOULD COMPANIES STRESS ENGLISH ONLY ON THE JOB?

When Frances Arreola read the memo announcing that employees should speak only English on the job, she was outraged. Arreola, a lens inspector for Signet Amoralite, a lens-manufacturing firm in southern California, remembers having been punished and humiliated by elementary school teachers for speaking in her native Spanish. She is now fluent in both English and Spanish but feels that the English-only rules stressed in some corporate cultures constitute discrimination.

More than half of Signet Amoralite's 900 employees are Asian, Filipino, or Hispanic. The company defends its English-only rule on the grounds that "speaking in another language that friends and associates cannot fully understand can lead to misunderstandings, is impolite, and can even be unsafe." The company claims that the English-only requirement is not written policy, just a guideline, and that violating it carries no punishment.

Nevertheless, this policy—and ones like it at hundreds of companies throughout the United States—is incorporated into the company's culture, and it is considered by critics to violate federal laws against discrimination on the basis of national origin. According to Equal Employment Opportunity Commission rules, employers can establish language restrictions only when such restrictions are required by valid business necessities.

A similar situation occurred at the Allied Insurance Agency in Amarillo, Texas. Two clerks at the agency, Rosa Gonzales and Ester Hernandez, were hired partially because both are fluent in Spanish and were therefore able to communicate with Spanish-speaking customers. However, the agency's owners became irritated when the two women chatted with each other in Spanish during the workday. Both women were subsequently let go after they refused to sign a pledge that would make Allied "an English-speaking office except when we have customers who can't speak our language." Since then, the agency has been boycotted by two Hispanic groups and has been threatened with lawsuits.

Managers are caught in the middle. On the one side are employees who are disturbed by co-workers' speaking to each other in a language they don't understand, an act they consider to be rude. According to Allied Insurance's owners, the women's chatting in Spanish was "almost like they were whispering behind our backs." On the other side are employees who feel they have a right to speak in a more familiar language as long as it doesn't affect their work. "I'm not doing it to offend anybody. It just feels comfortable," says Gonzales. What is a manager to do?

The best solution, according to experts, is to offer culture sensitivity training that will eliminate misconceptions on both sides and create a more open corporate culture. Native English speakers often assume that nonnative speakers don't want to make the effort to learn and use English. More commonly, however, nonnative speakers are highly motivated to learn English because they believe it will improve their chances for advancing in the work world. "They tend to speak English as often as they can," says Michael Adams, who helps run culture sensitivity programs for employees at the University of California at San Francisco. "When they speak another language, it's done in order to help a fellow employee understand something."

Colleagues may empathize if they step into the nonnative speaker's shoes. They can be asked to imagine traveling overseas and encountering someone from their home country. What language would they converse in? Would that be rude, or would it simply be more comfortable?

1. If a company hires an employee knowing that she is not fluent in English, should the company have a right to establish a policy like Amoralite's? Why or why not?
2. If you took a job in another country where you weren't fluent in the native language, would you feel compelled to learn the language even if your employer did not require you to? If your employer did suddenly decide to implement a one-language policy at work, how do you think you would react?

as possible about those cultures with which you plan to do business. You can also develop general skills for dealing with cultural diversity in your own and in other countries. If you'll be negotiating across cultures, it's important to learn how to conduct yourself and what to expect. Finally, you'll want to consider how to handle both written and oral communication with people from other cultures.

When speaking to people from another culture, take time to research their preferences for the direct or indirect approach to communication.

Learning about a Culture

Learning as much as possible about another culture will enhance your ability to communicate with its members.

When you're preparing to do business with people from a particular culture, you'll find that you can communicate more effectively if you study that culture in advance. If you're planning to live in another country or to do business there repeatedly, you might want to learn the language. The same holds true if you'll be working closely with a subculture that has its own language, such as Vietnamese Americans. Even if you're doing business in your own language, you show respect by making the effort to learn the subculture's language. In addition, you'll learn something about the culture and the customs of its people. If you don't have the time or the opportunity to learn a new language, at least learn a few words. Although foreign language software won't make you fluent overnight, it's an excellent means of learning the basics.

In addition to learning the language, read books and articles about the culture and talk to people who have done business with that culture's members. Concentrate on learning something about the culture's history, religion, politics, values, and customs. Find out about a coun-

BEST OF THE WEB

Learn a Country's Way of Life

Learning the customs of behavior in a country is a good first step to understanding cultural differences. Excite's City Net is your link to intercultural knowledge. Click on several of the countries listed, click on the "Fact Sheet," and read the listed customs. Then follow the links to learn more about the country and culture. Did you know it's sometimes easier to communicate by fax in Japan than by telephone? (Most Japanese can read at least some English.) And, while you're in Japan, never blow your nose in public; just delicately dab it with a tissue, if you must.

http://www.city.net/countries

CHECKLIST FOR DOING BUSINESS ABROAD

A. Social Customs
   1. How do people react to strangers? Are they friendly? Hostile? Reserved?
   2. What words and gestures do people use to greet each other?
   3. What are the appropriate manners when you enter and leave a room? Should you bow? Nod? Shake hands?
   4. How are names used for introductions? How are introductions handled (by age, gender, authority)?
   5. What are the attitudes toward touching people?
   6. How do you express appreciation for an invitation to lunch or dinner or to someone's home? Should you bring a gift? Send flowers? Write a thank-you note?
   7. Does custom dictate how, when, or where people are expected to sit in social or business situations?
   8. Are any phrases, facial expressions, or hand gestures considered rude?
   9. How close do people stand when talking?
   10. How do you attract the attention of a waiter in a restaurant? Do you tip the waiter?
   11. When is it rude to refuse an invitation? How do you politely refuse?
   12. What are the acceptable eye contact patterns?
   13. What gestures indicate agreement? Disagreement? Respect?
   14. What topics may be discussed in a social setting? In a business setting? What topics are unacceptable?

B. Concepts of Time
   1. How is time expressed?
   2. What are the generally accepted working hours?
   3. How do businesspeople view scheduled appointments?
   4. How do people react to time in social situations?

C. Clothing and Food
   1. What occasions require special clothing? What colors are associated with mourning? With love? With joy?
   2. Are some types of clothing considered taboo for one sex or the other?
      a. What is appropriate business attire for men?
      b. What is appropriate business attire for women?
   3. What are the attitudes toward human body odors? Are deodorants or perfumes used?
   4. How many times a day do people eat? How are hands or utensils used when eating?
   5. What types of places, food, and drink are appropriate for business entertainment?
   6. Where is the seat of honor at a table?

D. Political Patterns
   1. How stable is the political situation? How does it affect business inside and outside the country?
   2. How is political power manifested? Military power? Economic strength?
   3. What are the traditional institutions of government?
   4. What channels are used for expressing political opinion?
      a. What channels are used to express official governmental positions?
      b. What channels are used to express unofficial governmental positions?
   5. What media of information are important? Who controls them?
   6. In social or business situations, is it appropriate to talk politics?

E. Work Force Diversity
   1. Is the society homogeneous?
   2. What minority groups are represented?
   3. What languages are spoken?
   4. How diverse is the work force?
   5. What are the current and projected immigration patterns? How do these trends influence the composition of the work force?

F. Religion and Folk Beliefs
   1. To which religious groups do people belong? Is one predominant?
   2. How do religious beliefs influence daily activities?
   3. Which places have sacred value? Which objects? Which events?
   4. Is there a tolerance for minority religions?
   5. How do religious holidays affect business and government activities?
   6. Does religion affect attitudes toward smoking? Drinking? Gambling?
   7. Does religion require or prohibit eating specific foods? At specific times?
   8. Which objects or actions portend good luck? Bad luck?

G. Economic and Business Institutions
   1. What are the primary resources and principal products?

2. What kinds of vocational and technological training are offered?
3. What are the attitudes toward education?
   a. Do most businesspeople have a college degree?
   b. Are women educated as well as men?
4. Are businesses generally of one type?
   a. Are they large public corporations?
   b. Are they government owned or controlled?
   c. Are they family businesses?
5. Is it appropriate to do business by telephone? By fax? By e-mail?
6. Do managers make business decisions unilaterally, or do they involve employees?
7. Are there any customs related to exchanging business cards?
8. How are status and seniority shown in an organization? In a business meeting?
9. Are businesspeople expected to socialize before conducting business?

H. Ethics, Values, and Laws
1. Is money or a gift expected in exchange for arranging business transactions? What are the legal, ethical, and business consequences of giving what's expected? Of not giving?
2. What ethical issues might affect business transactions?
3. What legal issues might affect business transactions?
4. Is competitiveness or cooperation of greater importance?
5. What are the attitudes toward work? Toward money?
6. Is politeness more important than factual honesty?
7. How is a *friend* defined? What are the responsibilities of a friend?
8. What qualities are admired in a business associate? In a friend?

---

try's subcultures, especially its business subculture, and any special rules or protocol. Here is a brief sampling of intercultural communication tips from seasoned business travelers:

- In Spain let a handshake last five to seven strokes; pulling away too soon may be interpreted as rejection. In France, however, the preferred handshake is a single stroke.
- Don't give a gift of liquor in Arab countries.
- In Pakistan don't be surprised when businesspeople excuse themselves in the middle of a meeting to conduct prayers. Muslims pray five times a day.
- Allow plenty of time to get to know the people you're dealing with in Africa; they're suspicious of people in a hurry.
- You'll insult your hosts if you turn down food, drink, or hospitality of any kind in Arab countries. But don't accept too quickly, either. A polite refusal (such as "I don't want to put you to any trouble") is expected before you finally accept.
- Stress the longevity of your company when dealing with German, Dutch, and Swiss firms.

These are just a few examples of the variations in customs that make intercultural business so interesting. This chapter's Checklist for Doing Business Abroad can help you start your investigation of another culture by examining its social customs, concepts of time, clothing and food, political patterns, work force diversity, religion and folk beliefs, economic and business institutions, ethics, values, and laws.

Developing Intercultural Communication Skills

As Y. A. Cho, chief operating officer of Korean Airlines, notes, "In dealing with American businesspeople, I'm amazed at how naive most are about other cultures and the way that others do business."[47] Learning all you can about a particular culture is a good way to figure out how to send and receive intercultural messages effectively. However, remember two important points: First, don't expect ever to understand another culture completely. No matter how much you study German culture, for example, you'll never be a German or share the experiences of having grown up in Germany. Second, don't fall into the overgeneralization trap; don't look at people as stereotypical "Italians" or "African Americans" and then never move beyond that view. The trick is to learn useful general information and, at the same time, to be aware of and open to variations and individual differences.

Learning general intercultural communication skills will help you adapt in any culture, an ability that is especially important if you interact with people from a variety of cultures or subcultures.

These guidelines are especially important if you interact with people from a variety of cultures or subcultures. You may not have the time or the interest to learn a lot about every culture, but you can communicate more effectively if you develop general skills that help you adapt in any culture:[48]

- *Assume differences until similarity is proven.* Don't assume that others are more similar to you than they actually are.
- *Take responsibility for communication.* Don't assume it's the other person's job to communicate with you.
- *Withhold judgment.* Learn to listen to the whole story and accept differences in others without judging them.
- *Show respect.* Learn how respect is communicated—through gestures, eye contact, and so on—in various cultures.
- *Empathize.* Before sending a message, put yourself in the recipient's shoes. Imagine the other person's feelings and point of view; consider what he or she is trying to communicate and why.
- *Tolerate ambiguity.* Learn to control your frustration when placed in an unfamiliar or confusing situation.
- *Look beyond the superficial.* Don't be distracted by such things as dress, appearance, or environmental discomforts.
- *Be patient and persistent.* If you want to communicate with someone from another culture, don't give up easily.
- *Recognize your own cultural biases.* Learn to identify when your assumptions are different from the other person's.
- *Be flexible.* Be prepared to change your habits and attitudes when communicating with someone from another culture.
- *Emphasize common ground.* Look for similarities to work from.
- *Send clear messages.* Make both your verbal and nonverbal signals clear and consistent.
- *Increase your cultural sensitivity.* Learn about variations in customs and practices so that you'll be aware of potential areas for miscommunication.
- *Deal with the individual.* Communicate with each person as an individual, not as a stereotypical representative of another group.
- *Learn when to be direct.* Investigate each culture so that you'll know when to send your message in a straightforward manner and when to be indirect.
- *Treat your interpretation as a working hypothesis.* Once you think you understand a foreign culture, carefully assess the feedback provided by recipients of your communication to see if it confirms your hypothesis.

These skills will help you communicate with anybody, regardless of culture. For more ideas on how to improve communication in the workplace, see this chapter's Checklist for Communicating with a Culturally Diverse Work Force.

Negotiating across Cultures

Whether you're trying to make a sale, buy a business, or rent an office, negotiating with people from other cultures can test your communication skills. Moran, Stahl & Boyer International, a company specializing in cross-cultural training, proposes that culture con-

CHECKLIST FOR COMMUNICATING WITH A CULTURALLY DIVERSE WORK FORCE

A. Accepting Cultural Differences

1. Adjust the level of communication to the education level of your employees.
2. Encourage employees to openly discuss their culture's customs so that differences won't seem strange or inexplicable.
3. Create a formal forum for all employees to become familiar with the specific beliefs and practices of the cultures represented in the company work force.
4. Provide training to help employees recognize and overcome ethnocentric reactions and stereotyping.
5. Make available books, articles, and videotapes about various cultures so that interested employees can learn more.
6. Help stamp out negative or stereotyped labels by paying attention to how people identify their own groups.

B. Handling Oral and Written Communications

1. Define and explain key terms that people will need to know on the job.
2. Repeat and recap information frequently to emphasize important points.
3. Use familiar words whenever possible.
4. Don't cover too much information at one time.
5. Be specific and explicit, using descriptive words, exact measurements, and examples when possible.
6. Give the reason for asking employees to follow a certain procedure and explain what will happen if the procedure is not followed.
7. Use written summaries and visual aids (when appropriate) to clarify your points.
   - **a.** Give employees written information they can take away to go over later.
   - **b.** Use pictures that show actions (especially when explaining safety procedures).
   - **c.** Use international symbols (such as ⊘), which are understood cross-culturally.
   - **d.** Augment written material with video presentations to make the material more memorable.
8. Demonstrate and encourage the right way to complete a task, use a tool, and so on.
9. Reduce barriers caused by language differences.
   - **a.** Offer managers training in the language of the employees they supervise.
   - **b.** Offer employees training in the language that most people in the company (and customers) use.
   - **c.** Ask bilingual employees and managers to serve as translators when needed, but rotate this assignment to avoid resentment.
   - **d.** Recruit bilingual employees and managers or have trained translators available to give the organization more flexibility in dealing with linguistic differences.
   - **e.** Print important health and safety instructions in as many languages as needed to enable all employees to understand.

C. Assessing How Well You've Been Understood

1. Be alert to facial expressions and other nonverbal signs that indicate confusion or embarrassment.
2. Encourage employees to ask questions in private and in writing.
3. Observe how employees use the information you've provided to do their jobs, and review any points that may have been misunderstood.
4. Research the nonverbal reactions of other cultures so that you're prepared to spot the subtle signs of misunderstanding.

D. Offering Feedback to Improve Communication

1. Focus on the positive by explaining what *should* be done rather than on the negative by discussing what *shouldn't* be done.
2. Offer feedback in terms of the person's behaviors and the situation, rather than a judgment about the person.
3. Be supportive as you offer feedback, and reassure individuals that their skills and contributions are important.

---

sists of two levels: S*urface culture,* the obvious level, includes things such as food, holidays, and styles; *deep culture* consists of the attitudes and values on which culture is based.[49] The differences resulting from deep culture can be hidden pitfalls for the uninformed negotiator.

People from other cultures often have different approaches to negotiation and may vary in their tolerance for open disagreement.

For one thing, you may find that your approach to negotiation differs from the approach of the people you're negotiating with. For example, negotiators from the United States tend to take a relatively impersonal view of negotiations. They see their goals in economic terms and usually presume trust of the other party, at least at the outset. By contrast, Chinese and Japanese negotiators prefer a more sociable negotiating atmosphere. If you want to sell successfully in China, you'd better be patient and master *guanxi,* the Chinese term for "personal relationship."[50] In both countries you must forge personal ties as the basis for building trust throughout the negotiating process. To both Chinese and Japanese negotiators, any immediate economic gains are less important than establishing and maintaining a long-term relationship. Conversely, French negotiators are likely to be somewhat less personal. They may favor an atmosphere of formal hospitality and start by distrusting the other party.[51]

Cultures also differ in their tolerance for open disagreement. Although U.S. negotiators typically enjoy confrontational, debate-oriented negotiation, Japanese negotiators shun such tactics. To avoid the unpleasant feelings that might result from open conflict, Japanese companies use a go-between or a third party to assist in the negotiation. Chinese negotiators also try to prevent public conflict. They make concessions slowly and stay away from proposal-counterproposal methods. If you try to get members of a Chinese negotiating team to back down from their position, you will cause them to lose face—and you will very likely lose the deal.

In addition, negotiators from other cultures may use different problem-solving techniques, protocol, schedules, and decision-making methods. If you learn about your counterparts' culture before you start to negotiate, you'll be better equipped to understand their viewpoints. Moreover, showing flexibility, courtesy, patience, and a friendly attitude will go a long way toward finding a solution that works for both sides.

Handling Written Communication

Because so many international business letters are written in English, U.S. firms don't always worry about translating their correspondence. However, many other forms of written communication must be translated. Advertisements are almost always translated into the language of the culture in which the products are being sold. Warranties, repair and maintenance manuals, and product labels require translation, as well. For example, the warranty for a Hewlett-Packard laser jet printer cartridge is written in five languages: English, French, Spanish, Italian, and Japanese. In addition, many multinational companies translate policy and procedure manuals for use in overseas offices. Reports from foreign branches to the home office may be written in one language and then translated into another. One multinational company, E. I. Du Pont de Nemours & Company, translates roughly 70,000 pages of documents each year.[52]

Most routine business correspondence is written in English, but marketing messages are generally translated into the language of the country where the product is to be sold.

Unless you are personally fluent in the language of your intended audience, you will ordinarily write in your own language and, if needed, have your letters or other written materials translated by a professional translator. Remember, to overcome barriers to written communication, follow these recommendations:[53]

- Use short, precise words that say exactly what you mean.
- Rely on specific terms and concrete examples to explain your points.
- Avoid using slang, idioms, jargon, and buzzwords. Abbreviations, acronyms (such as CAD/CAM), and unfamiliar product names may also lead to confusion.
- Construct sentences that are shorter and simpler than those you might use when writing to someone fluent in your own language.
- Use short paragraphs. Each paragraph should stick to one topic and be no more than eight to ten lines long.
- Help readers follow your train of thought by using transitional phrases. Precede related points with expressions such as *in addition* and *first, second, third.*

Your word choice should reflect the relationship between you and your audience. In general, U.S. businesspeople will want to be somewhat more formal in their international correspondence than they would be when writing to people in their own country. In many cultures, writers use a more elaborate style, so your audience will expect more formal language in your letter. Consider the letter in Figure 3.2. This letter might sound stilted to a U.S. reader, but it is typical of business letters in many other countries. In Germany, business letters usually open with a reference to the business relationship and close with a compliment to the recipient. Of course, be careful not to carry formality to extremes, or you'll sound unnatural.

International business letters generally have a formal tone and a relatively elaborate style.

This letter was written by a supplier in Germany to a nearby retailer. The tone is more formal than would be used in the United States, but the writer clearly focuses on his audience.

Figure 3.2
In-Depth Critique: Translated German Business Letter

Mister
Karl Wieland
Business Leader
Black Forest Gifts
Friedrichstrasse 98

70174 Stuttgart
GERMANY

May 15, 2000

Very honorable Mister Wieland,

Because the tourist season will begin soon, we would like to seize the opportunity to introduce our new line of hand-carved cuckoo clocks to you. Last year you were so friendly as to buy two dozen of our clocks. In recognition of our good business relationship, we now offer you the opportunity to select the new models before we offer this line to other businesses for purchase.

As you know, our artisans use only the best wood. According to time-honored patterns that are passed on from generation to generation, they carefully carve every detail by hand. Our clockworks are of superior quality, and we test every clock before it is painted and shipped. We give you a guarantee of five years on all Furtwangen Handcrafts clocks.

Enclosed you will find a copy of our newest brochure and an order form. To express our appreciation, we take over the shipping costs if you order before June 15.

We continue to wish you a lot of success in your new Stuttgart location. We are convinced that you will satisfy your regular clientele with your larger exhibition area and expanded stock and will gain many new visitors.

With friendly greetings

Frederick Semper

Frederick Semper

The addressee's title, *Geschäfts-führer*, literally means "business leader": A common English translation would be "managing director."

By offering the retailer an early selection of products, a five-year guarantee, and free shipping costs for an early order, Herr Semper shows his concern for his audience.

The closing compliment is typical of German business letters.

Also note that, in German business letters, the sender's title is not included under the typed name on the closing block.

Letter writers in other countries also use various techniques to organize their thoughts. If you are aware of some of these practices, you'll be able to concentrate on the message without passing judgment on the writers. Letters from Japanese businesspeople, for example, are slow to come to the point. They typically begin with a remark about the season or weather. This is followed by an inquiry about your health or congratulations on your success. A note of thanks for your patronage might come next. After these preliminaries, the main idea is introduced (see Figure 3.3).

Figure 3.3
In-Depth Critique: Translated Japanese Business Letter

This letter was written by a Japanese banker to a large business customer. Notice how the banker emphasizes developing a long-term business relationship.

Sakura International Trade Bank Company, Ltd.
Marunouchi 1-5-32
Chiyoda-ku, Tokyo, Japan

Tel: (0565) 28-2121
Telex: 4537854 Sakura I
Cable: Sakura Tokyo

東京都千代田区丸の内1 - 5 - 32
さくら国際商業銀行

電話 (03) 5628-2121 大代表
テレックス 4537854 Sakura I
外電略号 Sakura Tokyo

The addressee's name and address do not appear above the salutation. This information appears on the envelope only.

Dear Sir:

Before getting to the point of the letter, the first paragraph mentions the season, congratulates the reader, and thanks the reader for his patronage.

With the season of fall upon us, let us congratulate your company on its growing prosperity. We are very grateful for your continued patronage.

It is a great pleasure to notify you that we decided to set your line of credit at five hundred million yen. We wish that this new line of credit will contribute to the further development of your business. If you find that you require additional credit, we would be willing to consider the details at a later date.

The tone is not only more formal than U.S. businesspeople are accustomed to, but it is also exceedingly polite.

With this brief letter, I have quickly notified you of the arrangement of the new line of credit. We most humbly assure you of our every effort to satisfy all your banking needs, so we solicit your further patronage.

Sincerely,

The date is part of the closing block, instead of coming at the top of the letter, and the writer's title precedes his name.

February 10, 2000

Vice President
Tomoaki Kagota

Handling Oral Communication

If you've ever studied another language, you know it's easier to write in that language than to conduct a conversation. Some transactions, however, simply cannot be handled without face-to-face contact. In many countries, business relationships are based on personal relationships, and, until you establish rapport, nothing happens. When speaking in English to people who speak English as a second language, you may find these guidelines helpful:

Face-to-face communication lets you establish a personal relationship with people from other cultures and gives you the benefit of immediate feedback.

- *Try to eliminate noise.* Pronounce words clearly, stop at distinct punctuation points, and make one point at a time.
- *Look for feedback.* Be alert to signs of confusion in your listener. Realize that nods and smiles don't necessarily mean understanding. Recognize that gestures and expressions mean different things in different cultures. If the other person's body language seems at odds with the message, take time to clarify the meaning.
- *Rephrase your sentence when necessary.* If someone doesn't seem to understand you, choose simpler words; don't just repeat the sentence in a louder voice.
- *Clarify your true intent with repetition and examples.* Try to be aware of unintentional meanings that may be read into your message.
- *Don't talk down to the other person.* Try not to overenunciate, and don't "blame" the listener for not understanding. Use phrases such as "Am I going too fast?" rather than "Is this too difficult for you?"
- *Use objective, accurate language.* Avoid throwing around adjectives such as *fantastic* and *fabulous,* which people from other cultures might consider unreal and overly dramatic.
- *Listen carefully and patiently.* Let other people finish what they have to say. If you interrupt, you may miss something important. You'll also show a lack of respect. If you do not understand a comment, ask the person to repeat it.
- *Adapt your conversation style to the other person's.* For instance, if the other person appears to be direct and straightforward, follow suit.
- *Clarify what will happen next.* At the end of the conversation, be sure that you and the other person agree on what has been said and decided. If appropriate, follow up by writing a letter or a memo summarizing the conversation and thanking the person for meeting with you.

In short, take advantage of the other person's presence to make sure that your message is getting across and that you understand his or her message too. As Kayomi Kaneda instructs the Sheraton employees, "Try to observe their nonverbal cues in order to anticipate their needs."

COMMUNICATION CHALLENGES AT SHERATON HOTELS HAWAII

Employee diversity at Sheraton Hotels Hawaii helps to create a rich and dynamic working environment. However, it can also lead to communication difficulties between employees on an interpersonal level as well as between management and employees on a companywide level. Different employees, depending on the cultural context they are most familiar with, may interpret a single message several different ways.

Individual Challenge: As a member of Michiru Tamanai's training staff, you have been asked to deliver a brief oral presentation to a group of 20 new employees on the importance of respecting cultural differences. These employees come from many cultural backgrounds, including Korean, Japanese, Filipino, Iranian, Kenyan, and American. Drawing on what you have learned in the chapter, develop an outline for your presentation. List the topics that you feel are most important to address, and jot down some ideas about how to deliver your message to such a diverse group. Keep in mind that you'll want to ensure smooth communication and a productive work environment.

TEAM CHALLENGE: Michiru Tamanai has just received a fax from the hotel manager confirming that the entire hotel has been reserved for IBM's annual international sales meeting to take place in three months. During the meeting, individuals of practically every nationality, culture, and language will be staying at the hotel. As members of Tamanai's training staff, you are responsible for developing a plan to make sure the hotel is ready for this big event. Your first job is to brainstorm every conceivable thing that will help this diverse cultural group feel welcome at Sheraton Hotels Hawaii. Don't worry about costs for now. Rather, think about the things you might want if you were staying at a hotel in a country whose customs and language were unfamiliar to you.[54] ■

SUMMARY OF LEARNING OBJECTIVES

1. **Discuss three trends that have made intercultural business communication so important.** The relaxation of trade barriers, the resulting rise in international business, and the increased use of new technologies have increased opportunities to communicate with someone who speaks a different language or belongs to a different culture. Developing good intercultural business communication skills will become increasingly important if you are to succeed in the multicultural, global marketplace.
2. **Name three main barriers to intercultural communication.** The biggest barriers to effective intercultural communication are cultural differences, language problems, and ethnocentric reactions.
3. **Identify nine ways people can differ culturally.** Cultural differences can show up in social values, ideas of status, decision-making habits, attitudes toward time, use of space, cultural context, body language, manners, and legal and ethical behavior.
4. **Explain the principal difference between high-context and low-context cultures.** In a high-context culture, information is conveyed implicitly. People rely less on verbal communication and more on nonverbal actions and environmental settings to convey meanings. In a low-context culture, the written word is highly valued. People rely more on verbal communication and less on circumstances and cues to convey meaning.
5. **List things you can do to learn about a particular culture.** You can learn about a culture by reading books and articles, talking to people who are part of that culture or who have done business with the culture's members, visiting the country, learning the language, and studying the country's history, religion, politics, values, and customs.
6. **Describe six ways you can overcome cultural barriers to written communication.** To overcome cultural barriers to written communication use short, precise words; rely on specific terms and concrete examples; avoid using slang, idioms, jargon, and buzzwords; use short, simple sentences; use short paragraphs that stick to one topic; and use transitional phrases.

CRITICAL THINKING QUESTIONS

1. Your office in Turkey desperately needs the supplies that have been sitting in Turkish customs for a month. Should you bribe a customs official to speed up delivery? Explain.
2. What actions might you take to minimize the potential problems of differing concepts of time between your office in New York and your office in Venezuela?
3. A Canadian retail chain is opening a new store in Tijuana, Mexico (a border city south of San Diego, California). What cultural differences might this retailer's managers encounter when they start to hire and train local employees?
4. Your company has relocated to a U.S. city where a Vietnamese subculture is strongly established. Many of your employees will be from this subculture. What can you do to improve communication between your management and the Vietnamese Americans you are currently hiring?
5. What are some of the intercultural communication issues to consider when deciding whether to accept an overseas job with a firm that's based in your own country? A job in your own country with a local branch of a foreign-owned firm? Explain.
6. How do you think company managers from a country that has a relatively homogeneous culture might react when they have to do business with the culturally diverse staff of a company in a less homogeneous country? Explain your answer.
7. You're anxious to begin negotiating a deal with a Chinese-owned company to sell its line of athletic wear in the United States. Even though the owners speak English fairly well, what are some of the intercultural differences you might encounter during your negotiations with the Chinese?
8. You prepared for months for your business trip to Barcelona, Spain. You even enrolled in an evening Spanish language course at your local community college. You also read as much as you could about the Spanish culture. So you can't understand why your first evening at a Barcelona cafe with your new Spanish client didn't go as well as you'd hoped it would. You couldn't understand 95 percent of the menu items, and

your client used words you never learned. How can you explain this outcome after all the time you spent studying the language and culture?

EXERCISES

1. You represent a Canadian toy company that's negotiating to buy miniature truck wheels from a manufacturer in Osaka, Japan. In your first meeting, you explain that your company expects to control the design of the wheels as well as the materials that are used to make them. The manufacturer's representative looks down and says softly, "Perhaps that will be difficult." You press for agreement, and to emphasize your willingness to buy, you show the prepared contract you've brought with you. However, the manufacturer seems increasingly vague and uninterested. What cultural differences may be interfering with effective communication in this situation? Explain.
2. A U.S. manager wants to export T-shirts to a West African country, but a West African official expects a special payment before allowing the shipment into his country. How can the two sides resolve their different approaches without violating U.S. rules against bribing foreign officials? On the basis of the information presented in Chapter 1, would you consider this situation an ethical dilemma or an ethical lapse? Please explain.
3. Some executives believe the Foreign Corrupt Practices Act puts U.S. firms at a disadvantage. They point out that non-U.S. firms are allowed to make payments that are often part of the normal process of winning lucrative government contracts in other countries. Does this law hurt U.S. competitiveness overseas? Write a paragraph arguing for or against imposing this standard on U.S. firms, regardless of where in the world they do business.
4. You've been assigned to host a group of Swedish college students who are visiting your college for the next two weeks. They've all studied English and speak the language well. What can you tell them that will help them fit into the culture on your campus? Make a brief list of the important formal and informal behavioral rules they should understand to communicate effectively with students on your campus. Next to each item, note one problem that might occur if the Swedish visitors don't consider that rule when communicating.
5. Choose a specific country, such as India, Portugal, Bolivia, Thailand, or Nigeria; the less familiar you are with it, the better. Research the culture and write a brief summary of what a U.S. manager would need to know about concepts of personal space and rules of social behavior in order to conduct business successfully in that country.
6. As the director of marketing for a telecommunications firm based in Germany, you're negotiating with an official in Guangzhou, China, who's in charge of selecting a new telephone system for the city. You insist that the specifications be spelled out in detail in the contract. However, your Chinese counterpart argues that in developing a long-term business relationship, such minor details are unimportant. What can you do or say to break this intercultural deadlock and obtain the contract without causing the official to lose face?
7. Although English is the international language of business, the English spoken in the United States differs from that spoken in Great Britain. By going to the library or interviewing someone who's lived in Great Britain, research five specific phrases that have different meanings in these two cultures. What problems would you have if you were unaware of the different meanings and misinterpreted these phrases during a business conversation?
8. Germany is a low-context culture; by comparison, France and England are more high-context. These three translations of the same message were posted on a lawn in Switzerland: The German sign read, "Walking on the grass is forbidden"; the English sign read, "Please do not walk on the grass"; and the French sign read, "Those who respect their environment will avoid walking on the grass."[55] How does the language of each sign reflect the way information is conveyed in the cultural context of each nation? Write a brief (two- to three-paragraph) explanation.
9. When a company knows that a scheduled delivery time given by an overseas firm is likely to be flexible, managers may buy in larger quantities or may order more often to avoid running out of product before the next delivery. Identify three other management decisions that may be influenced by differing cultural concepts of time, and make notes for a short (two-minute) presentation to your class.
10. Team up with two other students and list ten examples of slang (in your own language) that would probably be misinterpreted or misunderstood during a business conversation with someone from another culture. Next to each example, suggest other words you might use to convey the same message. Do the alternatives mean *exactly* the same as the original slang or idiom?
11. Differences in gender, age, and physical abilities contribute to the diversity of today's work force. Working with a classmate, role-play a conversation in which
    a. A woman is being interviewed for a job by a male personnel manager
    b. An older person is being interviewed for a job by a younger personnel manager
    c. A person using a wheelchair is being interviewed for a job by a person who can walk

    How did differences between the applicant and the interviewer shape the communication? What can you do to improve communication in such situations?
12. Imagine that you're the lead negotiator for a company that's trying to buy a factory in Prague, the Czech Republic. Your parents grew up near Prague, so you understand and speak the language fairly well. However, you wonder about the advantages and disadvantages of using a translator anyway. For example,

you may have more time to think if you wait for an intermediary to translate the other side's position. Decide whether to hire a translator, and then write a brief (two- or three-paragraph) explanation of your decision. Be sure to address the issue of message filtering in your decision (see Chapter 1).

13. Your boss wants to send a message welcoming employees recently transferred to your department from your Hong Kong branch. They all speak English, but your boss asks you to review his message for clarity. What would you suggest your boss change in the following paragraph? (Briefly explain your decisions.) Would you consider this message to be audience centered? Why or why not?

    I wanted to welcome you ASAP to our little family here in the states. It's high time we shook hands in person and not just across the sea. I'm pleased as punch about getting to know you all, and I for one will do my level best to sell you on America.

14. Suppose you transferred to a college in another country. How would you learn appropriate classroom behavior? List what you would need to know. For example, you might want to find out how to approach your instructors when you have questions. To get the answers to these questions, draft a letter to a college student in another nation.

15. One of your new co-workers is from Italy. Each morning, he greets you with a pleasant "buon giorno." You'd love to be able strike up a little conversation in Italian; it would surely make Antonio feel more welcome at his new job. Go to the Travlang Web site at http://www.travlang.com and click on "Foreign Languages for Travelers," then click on the Italian flag. Learn how to say some basic words, time and dates, and dining terms in Italian.

EXPLORING THE BEST OF THE WEB

Learn a Country's Way of Life, page 75

1. Select five countries and learn about their cultural customs by clicking on the "Fact Sheet" of each one. (Note: Not all countries have a fact sheet.) List at least two new things that you learned about each country's traditions or lifestyle. Share your lists with your classmates.
2. Select one of the countries you visited and search the Internet for more information about the customs and culture of that country. Use any of the search engines listed in Chapter 10. What additional information were you able to find out about the culture of that country?

Part 1 A Case for Critical Thinking

PILLSBURY'S RECIPE FOR CANDID TALK

No matter how many speeches and assurances managers give about how much they appreciate employee input, that sliver of fear remains—the fear that today's candid conversation will influence tomorrow's performance review. If you're like most employees, giving frank feedback means figuring out how to offer constructive criticism without offending your boss. It's something few employees are willing to do—unless they're working for Pillsbury.

Staying in Touch

Frustrated with existing communication channels (a whistleblower hotline for reporting fraud and the usual suggestion-box programs), Lou de Ocejo, Pillsbury's senior vice president of human resources, wanted to motivate employees to expose inefficiencies, douse brush fires, and, most important, stay in touch. So he installed InTouch, a toll-free, third-party voice-mail system that allows employees to talk about anything with the comfort of anonymity, and without the fear of reprisal. In addition, employees are assured that senior management will address the issues they raise. Here's how it works.

At the Tone, Please Tell Us What You Really Think!

When employees call, a recorded voice asks whether they want to remain anonymous, whether they'd like to receive a personal phone call, or whether they want to address their message to a

Pillsbury invites customers to share their comments with the company via its Web site.

specific person. If they choose anonymity, an outside service transcribes their recorded message (no worries that the boss will recognize a voice or handwriting) and sends the transcript to Pillsbury executives, who review each and every one. If an employee leaves a name and requests contact (27 percent of callers do), someone will follow up.

In response to the hotline, de Ocejo sends out management letters answering questions and reporting any changes made on the basis of the employee's message. Managers also post responses to employee comments on company bulletin boards. Furthermore, all recorded comments are paraphrased to ensure that employees can't be identified through a particular word choice. All in all, keeping in touch has paid off for both management and employees, although initially getting them to use it was a bit of a challenge.

Cooking Up a Way to Make Pillsbury Listen

As with any new system, employees were cynical at first. Even managers were worried, because they didn't know what they were going to hear from employees. Once the word got out that the system was safe, however, the calls came pouring in—more than 2,300 in the first five years. Employees began leaving messages about faulty work systems, ineffective supervisors, and new product ideas. Even de Ocejo was stunned to see how much genuinely useful knowledge had been bottled up for fear of ridicule or recrimination.

In fact, the calls have prodded some 200 product and cost-savings ideas. These big changes aren't the crux of InTouch, however; some 99 percent of the calls are about more mundane matters that just need to be addressed (such as a report that a new delivery route isn't working, or a request for an ATM machine on the 31st floor).

De Ocejo admits that the hotline will never be preferable to one-on-one frank conversation. But he hopes employees will now feel free to talk candidly during in-person conversations and that managers will become better listeners and problem solvers for their workers.

1. Why don't more companies install anonymous employee-feedback systems like InTouch?
2. What is the best way to encourage employee feedback?
3. Prejudgment is one of the most common barriers to listening. How does Pillsbury's InTouch system eliminate that barrier?
4. Visit Pillsbury's Web site at http://www. pillsbury.com. Click on "The Pillsbury Story," and find out why Pillsbury is "A Great Place to Work." Read about "Working at Pillsbury," and learn how the company en courages diversity. Find out what it takes to be on the team. Review the list of desired skills. Which ones have you already read about in this textbook?

The Writing Process

PLANNING AUDIENCE-CENTERED BUSINESS MESSAGES

AFTER STUDYING THIS CHAPTER, YOU WILL BE ABLE TO

1. Describe the three stages of the composition process
2. Name four criteria that will help you test the purpose of your message
3. Explain why it is important to analyze your audience when composing business messages and list four ways you can develop your audience's profile
4. Name six ways to satisfy your audience's informational needs
5. Discuss five ways to establish a good relationship with your audience
6. List eight things to consider when selecting communication channels and media

COMMUNICATION CLOSE-UP AT GENERAL MILLS

Betty Crocker never had to deal with Boo*Berry monster cereal. Most of the lengthy letters Betty received in the 1920s, when General Mills first invented her, were from women who wanted to know why their bread wasn't rising or why their meringues were weeping. To respond, General Mills established a special department to write formal, polite replies to customers. But a lot more than Betty's hairstyle has changed since then.

As director of consumer services for General Mills, Jeff Hagen deals not only with Boo*Berry but also with Count Chocula, Frankenberry, and 2,500 other products. Hagen must also deal with 800 numbers, computerized correspondence software, voice-mail information lines, e-mail, and the company's Web site, http://www.genmills.com. He manages a staff of 65 full-time employees who respond to between 700,000 and 1,000,000 contacts from consumers every year. And that's okay, because he's got every base covered—almost. "We're not out there waving signal flags," he admits, but his staff will respond in whatever medium consumers choose.

Jeff Hagen

Today's consumers are as likely to be men as women, and most of them call rather than write. Of course, Betty still gets letters, but now so do the Trix Rabbit and Sonny the Cuckoo Bird (the Rabbit and Sonny usually get e-mail from the kids' Web site that General Mills sponsors at www.youruleschool.com). If a message is from a kid, Hagen's staff makes sure the reply is in "kid language." Yes, Hagen even trains people to think about how the Trix Rabbit might respond to questions. As Hagen explains, "He wouldn't sound like a lawyer. He'd be funny; he'd be weird."

This ability to respond to consumers in their own language is the key to Hagen's success. For instance, e-mail is typically brief and sometimes irreverent, so Hagen encourages

Over the years, in recognition of its customers' changing interests and needs, General Mills has changed the appearance of Betty Crocker, its fictitious spokesperson. The latest Betty Crocker has been digitally "morphed" from the seven previous pictures and from the pictures of 75 real women selected across the United States. Now possessing features that appear more ethnically diverse, she has become the fuzzy reflection of us all.

his Internet team to write responses that are "professional but not stuffy." It's a tough line to walk, he admits, but "if they're writing to you in short grunts, you don't want to write back sounding like a novel."

Hagen's staff inputs the information from every contact into a sophisticated computer tracking program. "Let's say somebody calls who can't find Boo*Berry cereal in their area," explains Hagen. The call is coded as "Boo*Berry, question or request, availability." The program automatically suggests a form reply, with alternative choices varying slightly in tone or content. The system then prints the selected letter and attachments, personalizes it with the consumer's name, and signs it with a digitized replica of the staff member's actual signature.

In the case of missing Boo*Berry, the staffer checks availability on a database, and if it's not in the consumer's area, the staffer offers to ship the cereal to the consumer in four-packs or case lots. "Even if we're talking to people on the phone, we follow up with a confirmation letter saying this is what we discussed," says Hagen. The follow-up not only puts an order form in the customer's hands but also gives General Mills an opportunity to explain why not every product can be on every store shelf.

"Our goal is to respond to every contact we have," says Hagen, whether it's a person in Iowa who's in love with Boo*Berry or the woman in New York who wants to know if she needs to follow the directions for high-altitude cooking because she lives on the twentieth floor. The response from General Mills must demonstrate understanding, knowledge, professionalism, and efficiency—and that takes careful planning.[1] ■

UNDERSTANDING THE COMPOSITION PROCESS

Like Jeff Hagen and his staff, you'll face a variety of communication assignments in your career, both oral and written. Some of your tasks will be routine, needing little more than jotting down a few sentences on paper or keyboarding a brief e-mail message; others will be more complex, requiring reflection, research, and careful document preparation. Regardless

To compete for attention, business messages must be lively, concise, and readable.

of their size or complexity, the number of business messages increases daily, all of which are competing for your audience's attention. Therefore, your business messages will have to be livelier, easier to read, more concise, and more interesting than ever before.

Of course, making your business messages interesting does not mean using the same techniques you would use in a creative writing class. Your purpose is not to dazzle your readers with your extensive knowledge or powerful vocabulary. Instead, your messages need to be audience-centered, concise, and purposeful. In fact, the goal in effective business writing is to express your ideas rather than to impress your audience. One of the best ways to do so is to follow a systematic writing process.

The composition process is flexible; it is not a fixed prescription of sequenced steps.

Although some communicators reject any structured composition process as artificial, the fact is that your final message (the product) and the way you achieve it (the process) are irrevocably linked; so to be successful, you must concentrate on both.[2] Keep in mind that there is no "single" best writing process. The steps you take will vary with the situation, the communication, and the organization. Nevertheless, effective business communicators perform a series of general steps when composing a written communication. As Figure 4.1 shows, this **composition process** may be viewed as seven separate steps that fall into three simple categories, or stages: (1) planning, (2) organizing and composing, and (3) revising.

- *Planning*. Good planning is the first step to successful business writing. Abraham Lincoln once said, "If I had eight hours to chop down a tree, I'd spend six sharpening my axe."[3] The more time you spend sharpening your writing axe, the more effective your message will be. During the planning phase, you think about the fundamentals of your message: your reason for communicating and your audience. You analyze your audience so that you can tailor your message to their needs and expectations. Then you select the communication channel and the medium that both suit your needs and meet your audience's expectations. Therefore, the three steps of the planning stage are (1) defining your purpose, (2) analyzing your audience and adapting your message, and (3) selecting the appropriate communication channel and medium. These three steps will be the focus of our discussion for the remainder of this chapter.
- *Organizing and composing*. After the planning stage, the next step is to organize your ideas and begin composing your first draft, committing your thoughts to words, creating sentences and paragraphs, and selecting illustrations and details to support your main idea. The two steps of this stage are (4) organizing your message and (5) composing your message; they are discussed in Chapter 5.
- *Revising*. Having formulated your thoughts and composed your first draft, you step back to see whether you have expressed your ideas adequately. You review the content and organization of your message and its overall style, structure, and readability. You revise and rewrite until your message comes across as clearly and as effec-

Figure 4.1
The Composition Process

Good communicators realize that steps in the composition process often occur out of order, as they jump back and forth from one stage to another.

PLANNING	ORGANIZING AND COMPOSING	REVISING
1. Define purpose 2. Analyze audience 3. Select channel and medium	4. Organize message 5. Compose message	6. Edit and rewrite message 7. Produce and proofread message

tively as possible. Then you proofread the message for details such as grammar, punctuation, and format. So the two steps of the revision stage are (6) editing and rewriting your message and (7) producing and proofreading your message. These final steps are discussed in Chapter 6.

Because many business messages today are composed under pressure and on a schedule that is anything but realistic, allocating your time among these three stages can be a challenge. In some cases, your audience may expect you to get your message out in record time—sometimes only minutes after speaking with a client or attending a meeting. Whether you have 30 minutes or two days, try to give yourself enough time to plan, compose, and revise your message. Then stick to your schedule. As a general rule, try using roughly half of your time for planning, gathering material, organizing, and immersing yourself in the subject matter. Use less than a quarter of your time for composing and more than a quarter of the time for revising (so that you don't shortchange important final steps such as polishing and proofing).[4]

As you work through the three-stage process presented in Chapters 4, 5, and 6, it's best to view the process not as a list of how-to directives or a fixed sequence of steps but as a way to understand the various tasks involved in effective composition.[5] Even though the process can seem intimidating at times, try not to rush in and start writing. Many businesspeople are not effective writers simply because they fail to complete the entire seven steps; some don't even go beyond the old write-once-and-I'm-finished routine. Effective communicators, on the other hand, do complete all seven steps, although they don't necessarily complete them in 1-2-3 order. Some jump back and forth from one step to another; some compose quickly and then revise; others revise as they go along. But for the sake of organization, we'll start at the beginning, with step 1.

DID YOU KNOW?

Other than job-related skills, writing abilities are among the most difficult to find in job candidates. A survey of 150 executives with the largest 1,000 U.S. companies showed that effective writing skills are as difficult to find as effective leadership and management skills.

STEP 1: DEFINING YOUR PURPOSE

When planning a business message, think about your purpose. Obviously you want to maintain the goodwill of the audience and create a favorable impression for your organization, but you also have a particular goal you want to achieve. That purpose may be clear and straightforward (such as placing an order), or it may be more difficult to define. When the purpose is unclear, it pays to spend a few minutes thinking about what you hope to accomplish.

Suppose your boss asks you to write a memo describing the company's policy on vacation time. This is a fairly broad topic. What should you say? Knowing the purpose of your message helps you make important decisions about it. For instance, when you know your purpose, you include only the information necessary to accomplish your objective. Everything else is irrelevant and should be eliminated. Even though the extraneous information may be interesting, including it in your message will reduce the impact of your message by overloading your audience and diverting their attention from the important point.

The purpose of the message helps you decide whether to proceed, how to respond to your audience, which information to focus on, and which channel and medium to use.

Another reason you need a clear purpose is to decide whether to proceed. Frankly, many business messages serve no practical purpose and shouldn't be composed at all. Even if your message is witty, you can rapidly use up your credibility by writing memos that merely fill up filing cabinets. So when you're tempted to fire off a message, ask yourself: "Is this really necessary? Will it make a difference?" If you suspect that your ideas will have very little impact, hold off. Wait until you have a more practical purpose.

Common Purposes of Business Messages

All business messages have a **general purpose:** to inform, to persuade, or to collaborate with your audience. The purpose determines both the amount of audience participation you need and the amount of control you have over your message (see Figure 4.2). If your

Your general purpose may be to inform, to persuade, or to collaborate.

SHARPENING YOUR SKILLS

SEND ME A MEMO ON IT; OR BETTER YET, DON'T

Most managers dislike memos. They dislike writing them. They dislike reading them. They complain loudly about how many they receive and how unorganized, wordy, and pointless these communications typically are. Yet, at company after company, memorandums continue to drift into in-boxes, pile up in drawers, and weigh down briefcases for the journey home. After all, with today's technology, it's so easy to sit down at the keyboard, type out your great managerial thought, and send it in an electronic blink to, say, 15 or 20 people.

If everyone's complaining about getting too many memos, why do employees continue to send them? One reason is that the memo remains the single best device for communicating substantial chunks of detailed information—especially if your communication consists largely of numbers or if you are going to need a written record. But some employees have an ulterior motive behind their memos.

For instance, some employees feel uncomfortable communicating face to face or over the phone. They are afraid that what they have to say will be confrontational. For them, sending a memo can be a way to begin a difficult conversation. Others send memos for political reasons, good and bad. They want credit for their ideas, or they want to cover their you-know-what. Be on guard. If someone you usually communicate with in person or over the phone starts sending you memos instead, something has happened, and probably for the worse.

Regardless of the motive, before you write a memo make sure you have a well-defined purpose in mind. Who is your audience? What do you want them to do? If possible, try to find out in advance from the intended recipients what information they want. Then try to write clearly and keep your sentences short. When it comes to choosing your words, aim for simplicity and get right to the point. Remember, you are trying to put an idea across, not to impress the audience with your knowledge.

Keep in mind that before you e-mail your memo, fax it, or drop it into an interoffice mailbox, you should "sleep" on your idea for a night or two. You may find that you'll awaken with a better plan or decide to correct something that you may later regret having said—especially if you wrote the memo when you were angry or tired. One final word of caution. Committing a matter to paper may be dangerous. If your company is investigated or sued, some lawyer for the other side could some day end up waving that document in your face.

1. Most employees express themselves best when given time to think and edit. The downside is that including too much thought in your memos can make them go on and on. How can memos provide a complete thought yet still be concise?
2. Do you think it's a good idea to give your immediate supervisor a copy of all your interoffice memos? Please explain.

message is intended strictly to inform, you require little interaction with your audience. Your readers or listeners absorb the information and accept it or reject it, but they don't contribute to message content; you control the message. If your message is persuasive, you require a moderate amount of audience participation, so you need to retain a moderate amount of message control. Finally, if you seek collaboration from your audience, you require maximum audience participation, so your control of the message is minimal. Rather than adhere to a rigid plan, you need to adjust to new input and unexpected reactions.

To determine the specific purpose, think of how the audience's ideas or behavior should be affected by the message.

In addition to having a general purpose, your messages also have a **specific purpose.** Ask yourself, "What should my audience do or think after reviewing this message?" Then state your purpose as precisely as possible, identifying the members of the audience who should respond.

How to Test Your Purpose

Once you've established your purpose, pause for a moment to consider whether it's worth pursuing at this time. There's no point in creating a message that is unlikely to accomplish its goals. Before you decide to pursue the message, ask yourself these questions:

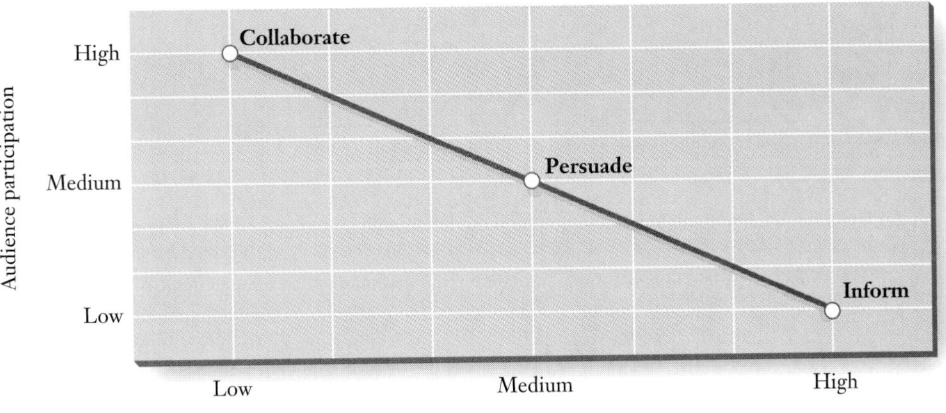

Figure 4.2
The Relation between the General Purpose of a Business Message and Communicator Control

- *Is the purpose realistic?* Most people resist change. So if your purpose involves a radical shift in action or attitude, you'll do better to go slowly. Instead of suggesting your whole program at once, consider proposing the first step and viewing your message as the beginning of a learning process.
- *Is this the right time?* An idea that is unacceptable when profits are down, for example, may easily win approval when business improves. If an organization is undergoing changes of some sort, you may want to defer your message until things stabilize and people can concentrate on your ideas.
- *Is the right person delivering the message?* Even though you may have done all the work yourself, your boss may have a better chance of accomplishing results because of her or his higher status. Achieving your objective is more important than taking the credit. In the long run, people will recognize the quality of your work. Also bear in mind that some people are simply better writers or speakers than others. If the stakes are high and you lack experience or confidence, you might want to play a supporting role rather than take the lead.
- *Is the purpose acceptable to the organization?* As the representative of your company, you are obligated to work toward the organization's goals. Say you're a customer service representative who answers letters from customers (much as Jeff Hagen's staff does at General Mills). If you receive an abusive letter that unfairly attacks your company, your initial reaction might be to fire back an angry reply. Would top managers want you to counterattack, or would they want you to regain the customer's goodwill? Your response should reflect the organization's priorities.

Defer a message, or do not send it at all if
- The purpose is not realistic
- The timing is not right
- You are not the right person to deliver the message
- The purpose is not acceptable to the organization

Step 2: Analyzing Your Audience and Adapting Your Message

Once you are satisfied that you have a legitimate purpose in communicating, take a good look at your intended audience. Who are the members? What are their attitudes? What do they need to know? And why should they care? The answers to such questions will indicate something about the material you'll cover and the way you'll cover it.

Ask yourself some key questions about your audience:
- Who are they?
- What is their probable reaction to your message?
- How much do they already know about the subject?
- What is their relationship to you?

Develop Your Audience's Profile

If you're communicating with someone you know well, perhaps your boss or a co-worker, audience analysis is relatively easy. You can predict the person's reactions pretty well without a lot of research. On the other hand, if your audience is made up of strangers, you'll have

Polish Your Skills in Analyzing an Audience

Businesses and organizations often find it useful to join formally into an association in order to share information, keep abreast of new developments, and advance their common interests. Thanks to electronic media, such associations can communicate quickly with memberships of all sizes, and they are able to disseminate information to people all over the world. Even without formally affiliating with an organization, a company may find contact information on the World Wide Web that leads to potential audiences or markets that might otherwise have gone unexplored. Many associations post descriptions of their membership on their Web sites. These summaries can help a business develop an audience profile that will allow it to target its message more effectively, thus saving time and money. You'll find an extensive list of associations and organizations with live links at Internet Public Library's Associations on the Net.

http://www.ipl.org/ref/AON

to do some investigating to learn about them before you can give them the information they need, meet their expectations, or anticipate their reactions (see Figure 4.3).

Identify the Primary Audience

When several people will be receiving your message, try to identify those who are most important to your purpose. If you can reach these decision makers or opinion molders, the other members of the audience will fall into place. Ordinarily, those with the most organizational status are the key people, but occasionally someone will surprise you. A person in a relatively low position may have influence in one or two particular areas.

Determine Audience Size and Composition

The size of your audience also influences your message. If you are writing a report for wide distribution, you'll probably choose a more formal style, organization, and format than you would if you were directing the report to only three or four people in your department. At the same time, however, you'll want to respond to the particular concerns of individuals. The head of marketing needs different facts about a subject than the head of production or finance needs, and so on.

Figure 4.3
Audience Analysis

Here's a quick way to help you remember some of the things you'll need to know about your audience if you want to deliver a truly customized message—which is what today's audiences demand.

Analyze	Who is your audience?
Understand	What is the audience's knowledge of the subject?
Demographics	What are the ages, genders, and educational background of your audience?
Interests	What interests does your audience have?
Environment	Is your audience friendly or hostile?
Needs	What information does your audience need?
Customize	How can you customize your message to connect with your audience?
Expectations	What does your audience expect?

U.S. companies must often translate messages for audiences in other countries. At this 7-Eleven in Japan, a clerk is scanning boxed meals with a hand-held computer. Whether the company needs to translate an advertising slogan, food labels, or a company name, the adaptation is done with great care.

If your audience is composed of people with different cultural backgrounds, education, status, and attitudes, they will likely react differently to the same message. So as you compose your message, look for the common denominators that tie audience members together, and try to include a variety of evidence that touches on everyone's area of interest. Keep in mind that communicating successfully with an intercultural audience goes beyond avoiding idioms, jargon, long words, complicated sentences, and gestures. To be clearly understood across cultures, consider how your audience thinks and learns as well as what they expect in terms of style.[6]

Focus on the common interests of the audience, but be alert to their individual concerns.

Gauge the Audience's Level of Understanding

If you and your audience share the same general background, you can assume they will understand your material without any difficulty. If not, you'll have to decide how much you need to educate them. The trick is to provide the information they need without being stodgy or obvious. In general, you're better off explaining too much rather than too little, particularly if you're subtle about it. The audience may get a bit impatient, but at least they'll understand your message. It may be that most of your audience has roughly the same general level of understanding. If not, gear your coverage to the key decision makers.

Estimate the Audience's Probable Reaction

In Chapter 5 we'll discuss how your approach to organizing your message depends on your audience's probable reaction. For instance, if you expect a favorable response with little criticism or debate, you can be straightforward about stating your conclusions and recommendations. You can also use a bit less evidence to support your points. On the other hand, when you face a skeptical audience, you may have to introduce your conclusions and recommendations more gradually and provide more proof.

A gradual approach and plenty of evidence are required to win over a skeptical audience.

In addition to considering the audience's general reaction, try to anticipate how key decision makers will respond to specific points. From experience, you may know that the boss is especially concerned about certain issues: profits, market share, sales growth, or whatever. By anticipating this bias, you can incorporate evidence in your presentation that will address those issues.

Satisfy Your Audience's Informational Needs

Five questions to ask yourself that will help you satisfy the audience's information needs:

- What does the audience want to know?
- What does the audience need to know?
- Have I provided all desired and necessary information?
- Is the information accurate?
- Have I emphasized the information of greatest interest to the audience?

As Jeff Hagen points out, the key to effective communication is determining your reader's informational needs and then responding to them. A good message answers all the audience's questions. But if you don't know what your audience wants to know, you're likely to serve them fruit punch and peanut butter when they're expecting champagne and caviar.

Find Out What the Audience Wants to Know

By restating a vague request in more specific terms, you can get the requester to define his or her needs more precisely.

In many cases the audience's information needs are readily apparent. When Jeff Hagen and his staff at General Mills answer messages requesting information about products or recipes, all they normally have to do is respond to the consumers' questions. In other cases, an audience may not be particularly good at telling you what is needed. Your boss might say, "Find out everything you can about the Polaroid Corporation, and write a memo on it." That's a pretty big assignment. Ten days later, you submit your 25-page report, and, instead of heaping you with praise, your boss says, "I don't need all this. All I want is Polaroid's five-year financial record."

One good way to pin down a vague request is to restate the request in more specific terms. If your boss says, "Find out everything you can about Polaroid," you might respond, "You want me to track down their market position by product line and get sales and profit figures by division for the past five years, right?" Another way to handle a vague request is to get a fix on its priority. You might ask, "Should I drop everything else and devote myself to this for the next week?" Asking a question or two forces the person to think through the request and define more precisely what is required.

Anticipate Unstated Questions

Include any additional information that might be helpful, even though the requester didn't specifically ask for it.

Try to think of information needs that your audience may not even be aware of. Suppose your company has just hired a new employee from out of town, and you've been assigned to coordinate this person's relocation. At a minimum, you would write a welcoming letter describing your company's procedures for relocating employees. With a little extra thought, however, you might decide to include some information about the city: perhaps a guide to residential areas, a map or two, brochures about cultural activities, or information on schools and transportation facilities.

Providing the little extras can be a big help to your audience. In some cases, you may even be a better judge of their information needs than they are. You may even tell them something they consider important but wouldn't have thought to ask. Although adding information of this sort lengthens your message, it creates goodwill.

Provide All the Required Information

Test the completeness of your document by making sure it answers all the important questions: who, what, when, where, why, and how.

Once you've defined your audience's needs, be certain to satisfy those needs completely. One good way to test the thoroughness of your message is to use the journalistic approach: Check to see whether your messages answer *who, what, when, where, why,* and *how*. Here's an example of a letter that fails to pass the test. It's a request for information from a large hotel:

> Dear Ms. Hill:
>
> I just got back from a great vacation in Hawaii. However, this morning I discovered that my favorite black leather shoes are missing. Since I wore them in Hawaii, I assume I left them at the Hawaii Sands Hotel. Please check the items in your "lost and found" and let me know whether you have the missing shoes.

Although the style of the letter is fine and the letter is grammatically correct, it won't get the desired results because the author fails to tell Hill everything she needs to know. The *what* could be improved by a detailed description of the missing shoes (size, brand, any distinguishable marks or trim). Hill doesn't know *when* the writer stayed at the Hawaii Sands, what room the writer stayed in (*where*), or *how* to return the shoes. Hill will have to write or call the sender to get the missing details, and the inconvenience may be just enough to prevent her from complying with the request.

Whenever you request any action, take particular care to explain exactly what you are expecting. Until readers get a clear picture of what they're supposed to do, they can't possibly do it. If you want them to send you a check for $5, tell them; if you want them to turn in their time cards on Friday by 3:00 p.m., say so. If you want somebody to do something, be specific when stating your request, and cover all the essential points.

When you want to induce action
- Be specific
- Cover all the essential points

Be Sure the Information Is Accurate

There's no point in answering all your audience's questions if the answers are wrong. In business, you have a special duty to check the accuracy of information before making a written commitment, especially if you're writing to someone who is outside the company. Your organization is legally bound by any promises you make, so make sure your company is able to follow through. Whether you're promising delivery by a given date or agreeing to purchase an item, if you have any doubt about the organization's ability or willingness to back up your promises, check with the appropriate people *before* you make the commitment. If you send the letter first and check for approval later, you may get some nasty surprises. Unreliability is embarrassing, and it damages your company's reputation.

Be certain that the information you provide is accurate and that the commitments you make can be kept.

Of course, honest mistakes are possible. You may sincerely believe that you have answered someone's questions correctly and then later realize that your information was incorrect. If that happens, the most ethical thing for you to do is to contact the person immediately and correct the error. Most people will respect you for your honesty.

You can minimize mistakes, however, by trying to be accurate and by double-checking everything you write or say. Check first to be certain that the organization can meet any commitments you make involving other people. Then check again to be certain you haven't made any errors of fact or logic. If you are using outside sources of information, ask yourself whether they are current and reliable. If your sources are international, be aware that cultures can view accuracy differently. A German bank may insist on balancing the books to the last penny, whereas an Italian bank may be more lenient. Such attitudes toward accuracy clearly influence the reliability of any information presented.[7] Be sure to review any mathematical or financial calculations. Check all dates and schedules, and examine your own assumptions and conclusions to be certain they are valid.

This executive (standing far left) at Alfresco Company tries to stay in touch with his audience by anticipating their unstated questions and explaining exactly what he expects of them.

Communicate Ethically

Unethical communication does not always involve exaggerating or telling lies to the audience. Oftentimes, messages can be unethical simply because information is omitted. Of course, for legal and other sound business reasons, messages may not be able to contain every detail about every matter. Still, it's important to include accurate details in proper context to satisfy your audience's informational needs.

Good ethics will help you determine how much detail to include in your message.

Just how much detail should you include? Keep in mind that *complete* is a relative term. Even though most people don't want to be buried in an avalanche of paperwork, include enough detail so that your audience is not misled. For example, is it ethical to note that a production quota was met for the first time without telling your audience that the quota has been substantially reduced? Likewise, is it ethical to overstate this year's sales by using confusing graphs with inappropriate scales? Deciding how much detail to include is one of the toughest challenges you will face when communicating in the business world. If there's any doubt about how much information your audience needs, offer the information that you believe best fits your definition of complete, and then offer to provide more upon request.

Emphasize Ideas of Greatest Interest to the Audience

Try to figure out what points will especially interest your audience; then give those points the most attention.

When deciding how to respond to your audience's information needs, remember that some points will be of greater interest and importance than others. Say that you're summarizing a recent conversation you had with one of your company's oldest and best customers. The emphasis you give each point of the conversation depends on the audience's concerns. The head of engineering might be interested in the customer's reaction to the design features of your product. Someone in the shipping department might be concerned about comments on delivery schedules. In other words, pick out the points that will have the most impact on your audience and emphasize them.

If you don't know the audience, or if you're communicating with a large group of people, you'll have to use your common sense to identify points of particular interest. Such factors as age, job, location, income, or education can give you a clue. Suppose you're trying to sell memberships in the Book of the Month Club. How would you adjust your sales message for college students? For suburban homemakers? For retired residents of Sun City, Arizona? For traveling sales representatives? For auto mechanics? All these people would need to know the same facts about membership, but each group would be more interested in some facts than in others. Economy might be important to college students or retired people, and convenience might attract sales representatives or homemakers. Remember that your main goal as a business communicator is to tell your audience what they need to know (see Figure 4.4).

Satisfy Your Audience's Motivational and Practical Needs

Be aware of audience resistance to your motivational message.

Some types of messages, particularly persuasive messages, are intended to motivate audience members to change their beliefs or behavior. The problem is that people resist ideas that conflict with their existing beliefs and practices. If you try to sell financial planning services to someone who has always managed her own finances, she has to rethink her way of doing things. She is being asked to give up a system she's familiar with for one that's entirely new. Faced with such a choice, people sometimes reject the new information without even listening.[8] They may screen out threatening ideas or distort your message to fit their preconceived map of reality. In Chapters 5 and 9 we'll discuss how to arrange the information in your message to overcome this resistance.

Presenting the required information in a convenient format will help your audience understand and accept your message.

Keep in mind that many business messages are directed toward people who are themselves in business—your customers, suppliers, and co-workers—and that their days are

Scott DeGraeve knows that his primary customers are busy people who prefer to spend their time doing something other than pushing a grocery cart down supermarket aisles. So in this letter to potential customers, he emphasizes the things that are likely to be of greatest interest to them; quality, convenience, and saving time and money.

Figure 4.4
In-Depth Critique: An Audience-Centered Letter

July 15, 1999

Dear Friend,

Have you shopped at Scotty's lately? If you haven't, you may not know that we've added over 500 new products from which you can choose. Our total offering now exceeds 7,000 products. And you can always count on our consistently high level of quality on produce, meat, and baked goods—at prices competitive with the major grocery stores.

Now we've made it even easier for you to give us a try. Our **Top 200** sample list includes the highest-volume items that we offer and the ones found in most people's homes. Try using this list. All the item numbers are marked so that you can order right off this simplified format. Selecting from this great mix of products may **eliminate a trip to the store for you this week.** Plus, you will get to experience what it is like having Scotty's come to your door!

In addition to our expanded product line, Scotty's now offers FREE delivery for computer orders over $100 placed any time. Compare our prices. We do all the time, and we know they are competitive. To give you an incentive to try us, we are providing a fantastic offer of **$20 off your first order** of $75 or more. We know that once you try Scotty's, you'll want to keep using us for all your grocery needs.

So look over our product list and give us a call. We look forward to hearing from you soon.

Sincerely,

Scott DeGraeve

Scott DeGraeve
President

P.S. It's prime produce season, and Scotty's has the best. **Please make us prove it!**

Even though the generic salutation indicates that this is a form letter, the tone of the letter indicates that DeGraeve is in touch with his customers' needs.

DeGraeve adopts the "you" attitude throughout this letter by focusing on the benefits the customer will enjoy by using Scotty's service.

He uses boldfaced words to draw the reader to the most significant benefits without overdoing it.

Sometimes, P.S. remarks are the first thing a reader will look at. Here again, DeGraeve focuses on the customer by stating "make us prove it [to you]."

filled with distractions. So make your message as convenient as possible for your audience. Try to be brief. In general, a one-page letter is more manageable than a two-page one, and a three-page memo is more likely to be read than a ten-page report. If your written or oral message has to be long, Part 5 of this textbook will give you plenty of tips on how to make it easy for your audience to follow longer messages.

Establish a Good Relationship with Your Audience

The first step toward establishing a good relationship with the audience is to think about who you are and who they are. Are you friends of long standing with common interests, or are you total strangers? Are you equal in status, experience, and education, or are you clearly unequal? Your answers to these questions will help you define your relationship with the audience so that you can give the right impression in your message. Perhaps the most important thing you can do to establish a good relationship with your audience is to avoid trying to be someone you're not. People can spot falseness very quickly, and they generally don't like it. If you just try to be yourself, you'll sound sincere.

Use the "You" Attitude

Once you've thought about the kind of relationship you want to establish, remember to center your efforts on your audience. Try to project yourself into your audience's shoes. What do they want from you? What are their expectations? How will they feel about what you have to say?

The "you" attitude is best implemented by expressing your message in terms of the audience's interests and needs.

By using an audience-centered approach, you try to see the subject through your audience's eyes. Then you can project this approach in your messages by adopting a **"you" attitude**—that is, by speaking and writing in terms of your audience's wishes, interests, hopes, and preferences. Talk about the other person, and you're talking about the thing that most interests him or her. Too many business messages have an "I" or "we" attitude, which causes the sender to sound selfish and uninterested in the receiver. The message tells what the sender wants; the recipient is expected to go along with it.

On the simplest level, you can adopt the "you" attitude by replacing terms that refer to yourself and your company with terms that refer to your audience. In other words, use *you* and *yours* instead *of I, me*, and *mine* or *we, us*, and *ours:*

INSTEAD OF THIS	USE THIS
To help us process this order, we must ask for another copy of the requisition.	So that your order can be filled promptly, please send another copy of the requisition.
We are pleased to announce our new flight schedule from Atlanta to New York, which is any hour on the hour.	Now you can take a plane from Atlanta to New York any hour on the hour.
We offer the printer cartridges in three colors: black, blue, and green.	Select your printer cartridge from three colors: black, blue, and green

Avoid using *you* and *yours*
- To excess
- When assigning blame
- If your organization prefers a more formal style

Using *you* and *yours* requires finesse. If you overdo it, you're likely to create some rather awkward sentences. You also run the risk of sounding like a high-pressure carnival barker at the county fair.[9] The "you" attitude is not intended to be manipulative or insincere. It is an extension of the audience-centered approach. In fact, the best way to implement the "you" attitude is to be sincere in thinking about your audience. It isn't just a matter of using one pronoun as opposed to another; it's a matter of genuine empathy. You can use *you* 25 times in a single page and still ignore your audience's true concerns. Look back at the letter in Figure 4.4. The first paragraph uses the pronoun *you* correctly and effectively. The second paragraph also displays effective use of the "you" attitude by explaining how the potential customer will benefit from Scotty's service.

The word *you* does not always indicate a "you" attitude, and the "you" attitude can be displayed without using the word *you.*

In the final analysis, it's the thought and sincerity that count, not the pronoun. If you're talking to a retailer, try to think like a retailer; if you're dealing with a production supervisor, put yourself in his or her position; if you're writing to a dissatisfied customer, imagine how you would feel at the other end of the transaction. The important thing is your attitude toward the members of your audience and your appreciation of their position.

On some occasions, you'll do better to avoid using *you*. For instance, when someone makes a mistake and you want to point it out impersonally to minimize the possibility of ill will, you might say, "We have a problem," instead of "You caused a problem." Using *you* in a way that might sound dictatorial is also impolite:

INSTEAD OF THIS	USE THIS
You should never use that kind of paper in the copy machine.	That type of paper doesn't work very well in the copy machine.
You must correct all five copies before noon.	All five copies must be corrected by noon.
You need to make sure the staff follows instructions.	The staff may need guidance in following instructions.

Keep in mind the attitudes and policies of your organization as well. Some companies have a tradition of avoiding references to *you* and *I* in their memos and formal reports. If you work for a company that expects a formal, impersonal style, confine your use of personal pronouns to informal letters and memos.

DID YOU KNOW?

In Japan, people are uncomfortable with the personal touch and the "you" attitude. In fact, Japanese writers refer to their audience's company rather than to their receiver: "*Your company* [not *you*] will be pleased with the survey results."

Emphasize the Positive

Another way of establishing a good relationship with your audience is to emphasize the positive side of your message.[10] Focus on the silver lining, not on the cloud. Stress what is or will be instead of what isn't or won't be. Most information, even bad news, has at least some redeeming feature. If you can make your audience aware of that feature, you will make your message more acceptable.

Explain what you have done, what you can do, and what you will do—not what you haven't done, can't do, or won't do.

INSTEAD OF THIS	USE THIS
It is impossible to repair this vacuum cleaner today.	Your vacuum cleaner will be ready by Tuesday.
We apologize for inconveniencing you during our remodeling.	The renovations now under way will help us serve you better.
We never exchange damaged goods.	We are happy to exchange merchandise that is returned to us in good condition.

In addition, when you're criticizing or correcting, don't hammer on the other person's mistakes. Avoid referring to failures, problems, or shortcomings. Focus instead on what the person can do to improve:

When you are offering criticism or advice, focus on what the person can do to improve.

INSTEAD OF THIS	USE THIS
The problem with this department is a failure to control costs.	The performance of this department can be improved by tightening up cost controls.
You filled out the order form wrong. We can't send you the paint until you tell us what color you want.	So that your order can be processed properly, please check your color preferences on the enclosed card.
You broke the dish by running cold water on it right after you took it from the oven.	These dishes are sensitive to temperature shock and should be allowed to cool gradually after they are removed from the oven.

Show your audience how they will benefit from complying with your message.

If you're trying to persuade the audience to buy a product, pay a bill, or perform a service for you, emphasize what's in it for them. Don't focus on why *you* want them to do something. Instead of saying, "Please buy this book so that I can make my sales quota," say, "The plot of this novel will keep you in suspense to the last page." Instead of saying, "We need your contribution to the Boys and Girls Club," say, "You can help a child make friends and build self-confidence through your donation to the Boys and Girls Club." An individual who sees the possibility for personal benefit is more likely to respond positively to your appeal.

Avoid words with negative connotations; use meaningful euphemisms instead.

In general, try to state your message without using words that might hurt or offend your audience. Substitute mild terms (euphemisms) for those that have unpleasant connotations. Instead of advertising "cheap" merchandise, announce your bargain prices. Don't talk about "pimples and zits"; refer more delicately to complexion problems. You can be honest without being harsh. Gentle terms won't change the facts, but they will make those facts more acceptable:

INSTEAD OF THIS	USE THIS
toilet paper	bathroom tissue
used cars	resale cars
high-calorie food	high-energy food
elderly	senior citizen

On the other hand, don't carry euphemisms to extremes. If you're too subtle, people won't know what you're talking about. "Derecruiting" workers to the "mobility pool" instead of telling them that they have six weeks to find another job isn't really very helpful. When using euphemisms, you walk a fine line between softening the blow and hiding the facts. It would not be ethical to speak to your community about relocating refuse when you're really talking about your plans for disposing of toxic waste. Such an attempt to hide the facts would very likely backfire, damaging your business image and reputation. In the final analysis, people respond better to an honest message delivered with integrity than they do to sugar-coated double-talk.

Establish Credibility

People are more likely to react positively to your message when they have confidence in you.

If you're unknown to your audience, you'll have to earn their confidence before you can win them to your point of view. Because the success of your message may depend on the audience's perception of you, their belief in your competence and integrity is important. You want people to believe that you know what you're doing and that your word is dependable.

An audience's faith in you has a profound impact on their acceptance of your message. In one experiment, separate groups of U.S. college students heard the same prerecorded talk recommending leniency toward juvenile delinquents. One group was told that the speaker was a judge, another that he was a former juvenile offender out on bail on a drug charge. As you might guess, most of the "judge's" audience (73 percent) said that they agreed with the speaker, but only 29 percent of the "offender's" audience agreed with the speaker.[11]

If you're communicating with a familiar group, your credibility has already been established, so you can get down to business immediately. However, even in this situation you may have to overcome people's preconceptions about you. Some members of the audience may have trouble separating your arguments from your personality or your field. If they

FOCUSING ON ETHICS

DOUBLESPEAK: WHY NO ONE KNOWS WHAT ANYONE'S SAYING ANYMORE

If there's one product U.S. businesses can produce in large amounts, it's doublespeak. Doublespeak is language that only pretends to say something but that in reality hides, evades, or misleads. Like most products, doublespeak comes in many forms, from the popular buzzwords that everyone uses but no one really understands—such as "competitive dynamics" and "empowerment"—to words that try to hide meaning, such as "reengineering," "synergy," and "restructure."

With doublespeak, bribes and kickbacks are called "rebates" or "fees for product testing," junk and used-car-parts dealers have become "auto dismantlers and recyclers," and travel agents are called "vacation specialists," "destination counselors," or "reservation specialists." Plus, just about everyone's job title has the word "chief" in it. Try these titles on for size: Chief Nuclear Officer, Chief Learning Officer, Chief Cultural Officer, Chief Ethics Officer, Chief Turnaround Officer, and Chief Creative Officer. After all the "operations improvement" that corporations have undergone, you have to wonder who all those "chiefs" are leading. Never before have so few been led by so many.

With doublespeak, banks don't have "bad loans" or "bad debts"; they have "nonperforming credits" that are "rolled over" or "rescheduled." And corporations never lose money; they just experience "negative cash flow," "deficit enhancement," or "negative contributions to profits."

Of course, no one gets fired these days. If you're high enough in the corporate pecking order, you "resign for personal reasons." But for those below the lofty heights of corporate power, you're "involuntarily terminated" as the result of "downsizing," "work force adjustments," and "headcount reductions." Some companies even "assign candidates to a mobility pool," "implement a skills mix adjustment," or "eliminate redundancies in the human resources area." Others, like one automobile company that closed an entire assembly plant and eliminated over 8,000 jobs, call it " a volume-related production schedule adjustment."

But don't worry, if you're "dehired," "deselected," "surplused," or "uninstalled," corporations will offer you a "career change opportunity," or "vocational relocation." In fact, hardly anyone is laid off these days. "We don't characterize it as a layoff," said one corporate doublespeaker (sometimes called a spin doctor). "We're managing our staff resources. Sometimes you manage them up, and sometimes you manage them down."

1. The president of one company just learned that some of his employees have been playing a popular game called "buzzword bingo," in which participants ridicule doublespeak by tracking the jargon their bosses use during staff meetings on bingo-like cards. Some managers are complaining that it's getting out of control. In fact, as one meeting dragged on, employees tried to steer the conversation to use all the buzzwords on their cards. What can managers do to avoid these silly games?
2. Visit one of the following buzzword bingo Web sites and print out a card or two. Read the current business section of your favorite newspaper. How many buzzwords did you find?

http://www.ksquared.net/~key/ietf-bingo.cgi
http://buzzword-bingo.com/play/index.html

---

think of you as, say, a "numbers person," they may question your competence in other areas. As you develop your message, you can overcome these prejudices by providing ample evidence for any material outside your usual area of expertise.

But what if your audience consists of complete strangers? Even worse, what if they start off with doubts about you? In these cases, you will need to devote the initial portion of your message to gaining credibility. First and foremost, show an understanding of the audience's situation by calling attention to the things you have in common. If you're communicating with someone who shares your professional background, you might say, "As a fellow engineer (lawyer, doctor, teacher, or whatever), I'm sure you can appreciate this situation." Another approach is to use technical or professional terms that identify you as a peer.

To enhance your credibility
- Show that you understand the other person's situation
- Establish your own credentials or ally yourself with a credible source
- Back up your claims with evidence, not exaggerations
- Use words that express confidence
- Believe in yourself and your message

You can also gain the audience's confidence by explaining your credentials, but you need to be careful that you don't sound pompous. In general, one or two aspects of your background are all you need to mention. Possibly your title or the name of your organization will be enough to impress the audience with your abilities. If not, perhaps you can mention the name of someone who carries some weight with your audience. You might begin a letter with "Professor Goldberg suggested that I contact you," or you could quote a recognized authority on a subject, even if you don't know the authority personally. The fact that your ideas are shared by a credible source adds prestige to your message.

Your credibility is also enhanced by the quality of the information you provide. If you support your points with evidence that can be confirmed through observation, research, experimentation, or measurement, your audience will recognize that you have the facts, and they will respect you. Exaggerated claims, on the other hand, are unethical and do more harm than good. Here's an example from a mail-order catalog advertising rose bushes: "You'll be absolutely amazed at the remarkable blooms on this healthy plant. Gorgeous flowers with brilliant color and an intoxicating aroma will delight you week after week." Terms such as *amazing, incredible, extraordinary, sensational,* and *revolutionary* exceed the limits of believability, unless they're backed up with some sort of proof.

You also risk losing credibility if you seem to be currying favor with insincere compliments. So support compliments with specific points:

INSTEAD OF THIS	USE THIS
My deepest heartfelt thanks for the excellent job you did. It's hard these days to find workers like you. You are just fantastic! I can't stress enough how happy you have made us with your outstanding performance.	Thanks for the fantastic job you did filling in for Gladys at the convention with just an hour's notice. Despite the difficult circumstances, you managed to attract several new orders with your demonstration of the new line of coffeemakers. Your ded ication and sales ability are truly appreciated.

The other side of the credibility coin is too much modesty and not enough confidence. Many writing authorities suggest that you avoid such words as *if, hope,* and *trust*, which express a lack of confidence on your part:

INSTEAD OF THIS	USE THIS
We hope this recommendation will be helpful.	We're glad to make this recommendation.
If you'd like to order, mail us the reply card.	To order, mail the reply card.
We trust that you'll extend your service contract.	By extending your service contract, you can continue to enjoy top-notch performance from your equipment.

The ultimate key to being believable is to believe in yourself. If you are convinced that your message is sound, you can state your case with authority so that the audience has no doubts. When you have confidence in your own success, you automatically suggest that your audience will respond in the desired way. If you lack faith in yourself, however, you're likely to communicate an unsteady attitude that undermines your credibility.

Be Polite

Being polite is another good way to earn your audience's respect. By being courteous to your audience, you show consideration for their needs and feelings. You express yourself with kindness and tact.

Undoubtedly, you'll be frustrated and exasperated by other people many times in your career. When that happens, you'll be tempted to say what you think in blunt terms. Nevertheless, venting your emotions will rarely improve the situation and may jeopardize the goodwill of your audience. Instead, be gentle when expressing yourself:

Although you may be tempted now and then to be brutally frank, try to express the facts in a kind and thoughtful manner.

INSTEAD OF THIS	USE THIS
I've seen a lot of dumb ideas in my time, but this takes the cake.	This is an interesting suggestion, but I'm not sure it's practical. Have you considered the following possible problems?
You really fouled things up with that last computer run.	Let me tell you what went wrong with the last computer run so that we can make sure things run smoothly next time.
You've been sitting on my order for two weeks now. When can I expect delivery?	As I mentioned in my letter of October 12, we are eager to receive our order as soon as possible. Please let us know when to expect delivery.
I told you before you hired the guy that he wouldn't work out. You made your bed; now lie in it.	We all make mistakes about people from time to time, and maybe this was one of them. Why don't you give the new person a few more weeks to get adjusted?

Of course, some situations require more diplomacy than others. If you know your audience well, you can get away with being less formal. However, when you are corresponding with people who outrank you or with those outside your organization, an added measure of courtesy is usually needed. In general, written communication requires more tact than oral communication. When you're speaking, your words are softened by your tone of voice and facial expression. You can adjust your approach depending on the feedback you get. Written communication, on the other hand, is stark and self-contained. If you hurt a person's feelings in writing, you can't soothe them right away. In fact, you may not even know that you have hurt the other person, because the lack of feedback prevents you from seeing his or her reaction.

Use extra tact when writing and when communicating with higher-ups and outsiders.

In addition to avoiding things that give offense, try to find things that might bring pleasure. Remember a co-worker's birthday, send a special note of thanks to a supplier who has done a good job, acknowledge someone's help, or send a clipping to a customer who has expressed interest in a subject. People remember the extra little things that indicate you care about them as individuals. In this impersonal age, the human touch is particularly effective.

Being courteous means taking the time to do a little extra for someone.

Another simple but effective courtesy is to be prompt in your correspondence. If possible, answer your mail within two or three days. If you need more time to prepare a reply, write a brief note or call to say that you're working on an answer. Most people are willing to wait if they know how long the wait will be. What annoys them is the suspense.

Promptness is a form of courtesy.

Use Bias-Free Language

Most of us think of ourselves as being sensitive, unbiased, ethical, and fair. But being fair and objective isn't enough; to establish a good relationship with your audience, you must also *appear* to be fair.[12] **Bias-free language** avoids unethical, embarrassing blunders in language related to gender, race, ethnicity, age, and disability.

Avoid biased language that might offend your audience.

Gender Bias Women's roles in business have changed over the years, and good communicators make every effort to change sexist language.[13] For example, the word *man* used to denote humanity, describing a human being of either gender and any age. Today, however, *man* is associated more with an adult male human being. Some of the most commonly used words contain the word *man*, but some simple solutions exist:

UNACCEPTABLE	PREFERABLE
mankind	humanity, human beings, human race, people
if a man drove 50 miles at 60 miles per hour	if a person (or someone or a driver) drove 50 miles at 60 miles per hour
man-made	artificial, synthetic, manufactured, constructed, of human origin
manpower	human power, human energy, workers, work force

Here are some simple ways to replace occupational terms that contain the word *man* with words that can represent people of either gender:

UNACCEPTABLE	PREFERABLE
businessman	business executive, business manager, businessperson
salesman	sales representative, salesperson, sales clerk
insurance man	insurance agent
foreman	supervisor

Replace words that inaccurately exclude women or men.

Avoid using female-gender words such as *authoress* and *actress*; *author* and *actor* denote both women and men. Similarly, avoid special designations, such as *woman doctor* or *male nurse*. Use the same label for everyone in a particular group. Don't refer to a woman as a *chairperson* and then call the man a *chairman*.

The pronoun *he* has also traditionally been used to refer to both males and females. Here are some simple ways to avoid this outdated usage:

UNACCEPTABLE	PREFERABLE
The average worker . . . he	The average worker . . . he or she
The typical business executive spends four hours of his day in meetings.	Most business executives spend four hours a day in meetings.

Avoid identifying certain roles with a specific gender:

UNACCEPTABLE	PREFERABLE
the consumer . . . she	Consumers . . . they
the nurse/teacher . . . she	nurses/teachers . . . they

If you're discussing categories of people, such as bosses and office workers, avoid referring to the boss as *he* and the office worker as *she*. Instead, reword sentences so that you can use *they*, or reword them so that you don't have to use any pronoun. In today's business world, it's also appropriate sometimes to use *she* when referring to a boss and *he* when referring to an office worker.

Another way to avoid bias is to make sure you don't always mention men first. Vary the traditional pattern with *women and men, she and he, her and his*.

Finally, identify women by their own names, not by their role or marital status—unless it is appropriate to the context:

UNACCEPTABLE	PREFERABLE
Phil Donahue and Marlo	Phil Donahue and Marlo Thomas
Phil Donahue and Ms. Thomas	Mr. Donahue and Ms. Thomas

The preferred title for women in business is Ms., unless the individual asks to be addressed as Miss or Mrs. or has some other title, such as Dr.

Racial and Ethnic Bias The guidelines for avoiding racial and ethnic bias are much the same as those for avoiding gender bias. The central principle is to avoid language suggesting that members of a racial or an ethnic group have stereotypical characteristics:

Eliminate references that reinforce racial or ethnic stereotypes.

UNACCEPTABLE	PREFERABLE
disadvantaged black children	children from lower-income families
Jim Wong is an unusually tall Asian.	Jim Wong is tall.

The best solution is to avoid identifying people by race or ethnic origin unless such a label is relevant:

UNACCEPTABLE	PREFERABLE
Mario M. Cuomo, Italian American politician and ex-governor of New York	Mario M. Cuomo, politician and ex-governor of New York

Age Bias As with gender, race, and ethnic background, mention the age of a person only when it is relevant:

Avoid references to an individual's age or physical limitations.

UNACCEPTABLE	PREFERABLE
Mary Kirazy, 58, has just joined our trust department.	Mary Kirazy has just joined our trust department.

When referring to older people, avoid such stereotyped adjectives as *spry* and *frail.*

Disability Bias There is really no painless label for people with a physical, mental, sensory, or emotional impairment. However, if you must refer to such individuals in terms

If you make an assumption about people's gender based on their job, you're likely to be wrong in today's work environment. Avoid gender bias by using newer occupational terms that apply to both women and men alike.

Always refer to people first and their disabilities second.

of their limitations, avoid using terms such as *handicapped, crippled*, or *retarded,* and be sure to put the person first and the disability second:[14]

UNACCEPTABLE	PREFERABLE
Crippled workers face many barriers on the job.	Workers with physical disabilities face many barriers on the job.

Most of all, avoid mentioning a disability unless it is pertinent. When it is pertinent, present the whole person, not just the disability, by showing the limitation in an unobtrusive manner:

UNACCEPTABLE	PREFERABLE
An epileptic, Tracy has no trouble doing her job.	Tracy's epilepsy has no effect on her job performance.

The 1990 Americans with Disabilities Act guarantees equal opportunities for people who have or have had a condition that might handicap them. The goal of bias-free communication is to abandon stereotyped assumptions about what a person can do or will do and to focus on an individual's unique characteristics. So describe people without disabilities as *typical* rather than *normal*. People having disabilities are certainly *atypical* but not necessarily *abnormal*.[15]

Project the Company's Image

Subordinate your own style to that of the company.

Even though establishing a good relationship with the audience is your main goal, give some thought to projecting the right image for your company. When you communicate with outsiders, on even the most routine matter, you serve as the spokesperson for your organization. The impression that you make can enhance or damage the reputation of the entire company. Thus, your own views and personality must be subordinated, at least to some extent, to the interests and style of the company.

Say you've just taken a job with a hip, young retail organization called Rappers. One of your first assignments is to write a letter canceling additional orders for clothing items that have been identified as slow sellers. Your goal is to cancel the order while maintaining the goodwill of the vendor (the business selling you the clothes).

Dear Ms. Bataglia:

I am writing to cancel our purchase order 092397AA for the amount of $12,349. Our contract with your organization specifies that we have a 30-day cancellation clause which we wish to invoke. If any shipments went out before you received this notification, they will be returned; however, we will remunerate freight charges as specified in the contract.

I am told we have ordered from you since our inception in 1993. Your previous service to us has been quite satisfactory; however, recent sales of the "Colored Denim" line have been less than previously forecast. We realize that our cancellation may have a negative impact, and we pledge to more accurately predict our needs in the future.

We maintain positive alliances with all our vendors and look forward to doing further business with you. Please keep us informed of new products as they appear.

After reading your draft, you realize that the letter may be misinterpreted. Its formal tone may leave a feeling of ill will with the vendor, and it certainly doesn't reflect the corporate culture of your new employer. You try again.

Dear Ms. Bataglia:

We appreciate the relationship we've had with you since 1993. Your shipments have always arrived on time and in good order.

However, our recent store reports show a decline in sales for your "Colored Denim" line. Therefore, we're canceling our purchase order 092397AA for $12,349. If you'll let us know the amounts, we'll pay the shipping charges on anything that has already gone out.

We're making lots of changes at Rappers, but one thing remains the same—the positive relationship we have with vendors such as you. Please keep us informed of your new lines as they appear so that we can look forward to doing business with you in the future.

This version reflects the more relaxed image of your new company. You can save yourself a great deal of time and frustration if you master the company style early in your career.

Step 3: Selecting the Appropriate Channel and Medium

An equally important part of planning audience-centered business messages is selecting the appropriate communication channel and medium to deliver your message. Your channel and medium selection can make the difference between effective and ineffective communication.[16] In fact, your choice will govern the style, tone, and overall composition of your message.

Different types of messages require different communication channels.

For instance, you wouldn't write an e-mail message with the same level of formality that you would use in a memo (see Figure 4.5). Similarily, drafting a few notes for a conversation

Figure 4.5
In-Depth Critique: A Typical E-Mail Message

In her e-mail message, Glenda Anderson responds to a consumer who has written General Mills to ask about a product. Anderson is careful to maintain a tone of courtesy and friendliness.

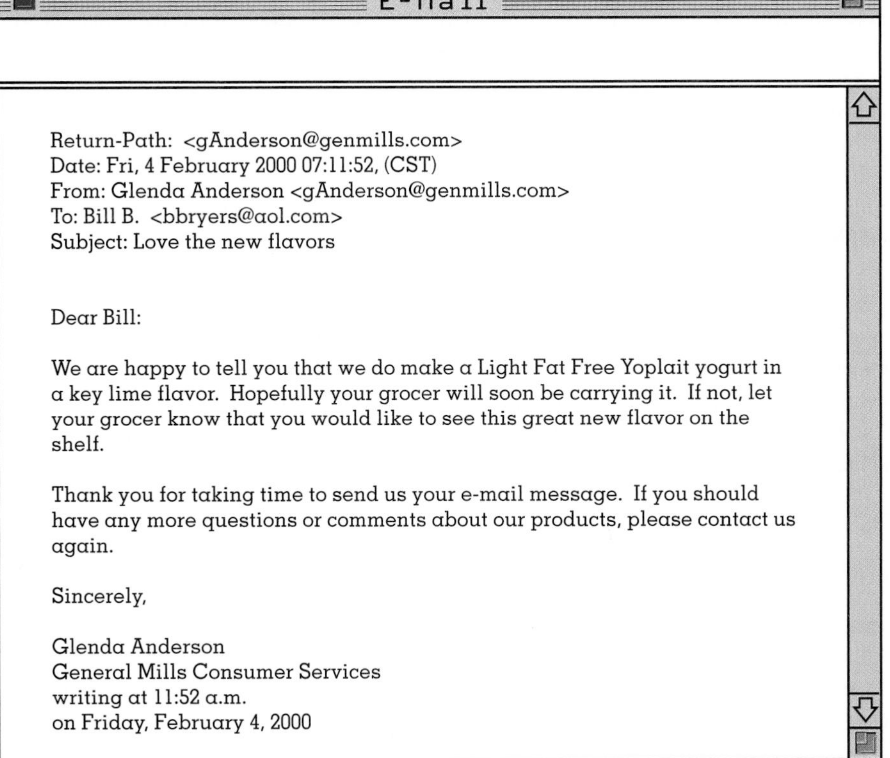

E-Mail

Return-Path: <gAnderson@genmills.com>
Date: Fri, 4 February 2000 07:11:52, (CST)
From: Glenda Anderson <gAnderson@genmills.com>
To: Bill B. <bbryers@aol.com>
Subject: Love the new flavors

Dear Bill:

We are happy to tell you that we do make a Light Fat Free Yoplait yogurt in a key lime flavor. Hopefully your grocer will soon be carrying it. If not, let your grocer know that you would like to see this great new flavor on the shelf.

Thank you for taking time to send us your e-mail message. If you should have any more questions or comments about our products, please contact us again.

Sincerely,

Glenda Anderson
General Mills Consumer Services
writing at 11:52 a.m.
on Friday, February 4, 2000

E-mail messages contain four pieces of information: date, from, to, and subject.

Glenda Anderson states her business right away.

E-mail messages are often brief and to the point.

A courteous attitude and friendly style keep the lines of communication open.

with an employee would be less formal than drafting a letter of reprimand for inappropriately using the company telephone. Thus, before you begin drafting your message, select your channel and medium so that you can tailor your message to match their specific characteristics.

When choosing a channel for your message (oral or written), and a medium within that channel (face-to-face conversation, telephone conversation, e-mail, voice mail, fax, videotape, written report), do your best to match your selections to your message and to your intentions.[17] Begin by examining the unique benefits and characteristics of each. Then choose a channel and medium that will help you reach your goal and that will be most appropriate for your audience. For example, if your purpose is to put together a company softball team, you may decide to use e-mail so that you can send your message simultaneously to everyone in the office.

When selecting a medium, keep in mind that every medium has limitations that filter out parts of the message. For example, flyers and bulletin boards are nondynamic and ineffective for communicating extremely complex messages, but they're perfect for simple ones. Moreover, every medium influences your audience's perception of your intentions. If you want to emphasize the formality of your message, use a more formal medium, such as a memo or a letter. If you want to emphasize the confidentiality of your message, use voice mail rather than a fax, send a letter rather than a memo, or address the matter in a private conversation rather than during a meeting. If you want to instill an emotional commitment to corporate values, consider a visual medium such as a videotape or videoconference. If you require immediate feedback, face-to-face conversation is your best choice.[18] However, if you'll need a written record, you'll probably want to write a memo or a letter.

Time is another factor you will need to consider in selecting a medium. How urgent is your message? If it's very urgent, you'll probably choose to use the phone, fax, or next-day mail. Plus you'll need to consider cost. There is usually a trade-off between time and cost. For instance, you wouldn't think twice about telephoning an important customer overseas if you just discovered your company erroneously sent the customer the wrong shipment. But you'd probably choose to fax or e-mail a routine order acknowledgment to your customer in Australia. You'll also want to consider tone and confidentiality. Although e-mail messages and faxes offer both speed and low cost, they aren't very formal or confidential.

In addition to formality, confidentiality, feedback, complexity, time, and cost, you'll need to consider which communication channel your audience expects or prefers and whether you'll need a permanent record of the communication.[19] For instance, what would you think if your college tried to deliver your diploma by fax? It would seem a bit strange, wouldn't it? You'd expect the college to hand it to you at graduation or mail it to you (if you weren't present). In addition, some cultures tend to favor one channel over another. For example, the United States, Canada, and Germany emphasize written media, whereas Japan emphasizes oral media—perhaps because its high-context culture carries so much of the message in nonverbal cues and "between the lines" interpretation.[20] Table 4.1 outlines some of the basic considerations that will help you choose between an oral and a written channel and the types of media available to each.

Oral Communication Media

Primary oral communication media include face-to-face conversation (the richest medium), telephone calls, speeches, presentations, and meetings. Your choice between a face-to-face conversation and a telephone or videoconference call would depend on audience location, message importance, and your need for the sort of nonverbal feedback that only body language can reveal.

TABLE 4.1

When choosing among the following channels and media, consider the urgency, formality, complexity, confidentiality, emotional content, and cost of sending your message as well as your audience's expectations and your need for a permanent record.

An Oral Channel Is Best When	A Written Channel Is Best When
You want immediate feedback from the audience	You don't need immediate feedback
Your message is relatively simple and easy to accept	Your message is detailed, is complex, and requires careful planning
You don't need a permanent record	You do need a permanent, verifiable record
You can assemble the audience conveniently and economically	You are trying to reach an audience that is large and geographically dispersed
You want to encourage interaction to solve a problem or reach a decision	You want to minimize the chances for distortion that occur when a message is passed orally from person to person
Oral Media Include	**Written Media Include**
■ Face-to-face conversation, speeches, meetings	■ Letters, memos, reports, proposals
■ Telephone and voice mail	■ Electronic mail
■ Audiotape and videotape	■ Regular and special mail
■ Teleconference and videoconference	■ Faxes

The chief advantage of oral communication is the opportunity it provides for immediate feedback. This is the channel to use when you want the audience to ask questions and make comments or when you're trying to reach a group decision. It's also the best channel if there's an emotional component to your message and you want to read the audience's body language or hear the tone of their response.[21]

In general, use oral communication if your purpose is to collaborate with the audience.

In general, the smaller the audience, the more interaction among the members. If your purpose involves reaching a decision or solving a problem, select an oral medium geared toward a small audience. Be sure the program is relatively informal and unstructured so that ideas can flow freely. Gatherings of this sort can be arranged quickly and economically.

When selecting a medium for your message, you have many choices today. Speed and cost are two important criteria.

At the opposite extreme are formal presentations to large audiences, which are common at events such as sales conventions, shareholder meetings, and ceremonial functions. Often, these major presentations take place in a big facility, where the audience can be seated auditorium style. Their formality makes them unsuitable for collaborative purposes requiring audience interaction.

Written Communication Media

Written communication increases the sender's control but eliminates the possibility of immediate feedback.

Written messages also take many forms. At one end are the scribbled notes people use to jog their own memories; at the other are elaborate, formal reports that rival magazines in graphic quality. Regardless of the form, written messages have one big advantage: They let you plan and control the message. A written format is appropriate when the information is complex, when a permanent record is needed for future reference, when the audience is large and geographically dispersed, and when immediate interaction with the audience is either unimportant or undesirable.

Although many types of written communication are specialized, the most common are letters, memos, and reports (see Figure 4.6). For extensive coverage of letters and memos, see Chapters 7 through 9. Reports are thoroughly discussed in Chapters 13 through 15. In addition, Component Chapter A presents a detailed discussion of the accepted formats for business documents.

Letters and Memos

Most letters and memos are relatively brief documents, generally one or two pages. Memos are the workhorses of business communication, used for the routine, day-to-day exchange of information within an organization. You often use memos to designate responsibility, communicate the same material to many people, communicate policy and procedure, confirm oral agreements or decisions, and place specific information on record.

Letters and memos are organized according to their purpose; the relationship between writer and reader dictates their style and tone.

In general, memos lack a salutation and use a TO, FROM, DATE, and SUBJECT format to emphasize the needs of readers who most likely have time only to skim messages. Good memos discuss only one topic, and their tone is conversational. Because of their open construction and informal method of delivery (e-mail or interoffice mail), memos are less private than letters.

In contrast, letters frequently go to outsiders, and they perform an important public relations function in addition to conveying a particular message. Many organizations rely on form letters (and sometimes form memos) to save time and money on routine communication. Form letters are particularly handy for such one-time mass mailings as sales messages about products, explanations of policies and procedures, information about organizational activities, goodwill messages such as seasonal greetings, and acknowledgments of job applications. A variation of the form letter is the **boilerplate,** a standard paragraph that can be selected to suit an occasion or audience. Letters containing boilerplates are used for slightly more individualized messages, such as General Mills's replies to inquiries about its products and activities.

DID YOU KNOW?

In a typical corporation, 85 percent of the letters, memos, and reports are written by someone other than the higher-level managers who sign them. Most of the time, managers reject first drafts of such documents for stylistic reasons. In fact, the average draft goes through five revisions before it is finally approved.

Both letters and memos can be classified by function into three categories: routine, good-news, and goodwill messages; bad-news messages; and persuasive messages. In Chapters 7 through 9 we'll elaborate on how the function and nature of each of these message types determine their organization.

Reports and Proposals

Reports are generally longer and more formal than letters and memos, and they have more components.

Reports and proposals are factual, objective documents that may be distributed to either insiders or outsiders, depending on their purpose and subject. They come in many formats, including preprinted forms, letters, memos, and manuscripts. In length, they range from a few

When Jeff Hagen responds to a consumer, he is careful to show respect, make the message as personal as possible, and match the customer's tone, in this case by keeping the approach light and cheerful.

Figure 4.6
In-Depth Critique: A Typical Letter

General Mills Consumer Services
P.O. Box 1113, Minneapolis, MN 55440

March 13, 2000

Mr. Julius Croghan
231 Ruffin Avenue
Cedar Spring, South Carolina 29302

Dear Mr. Croghan:

Thank you very much for your delightful comments. It was kind of you to share your thoughts, and you've brightened our day here at General Mills.

Many of our products have long attracted loyal fans. I'm happy to see that you are among that group.

At General Mills, customer feedback is critical to our success. It's through communications like yours that we become aware of consumer concerns and preferences.

I have enclosed gift coupons and hope you will continue to use and enjoy our products.

Sincerely,

Jeffrey N Hagen

Jeffrey N. Hagen
Director, Consumer Services

Web site http://www.genmills.com

Jeff Hagen uses letterhead stationery but doesn't let that make his message too formal or unfriendly.

The formal salutation indicates Hagen's respect for a customer he doesn't know.

The body of the letter is brief but still includes friendly remarks designed to maintain goodwill.

The close is an optimistic look at the future.

to several hundred pages, and they are generally more formal in tone than a typical business letter or memo. (Reports and proposals are discussed in detail in Chapters 13–15.)

Electronic Communication Media

The availability of electronic mail, regular mail, overnight mail, fax, audiotape, teleconferencing, videoconferencing, and dozens of other options complicate the choices you have to make as a communicator.

When it comes to one particular message or document, you may have two or three technological options. The trick is to pick the tool that does the best overall job in each situation. Although oral messages can be in person and face to face, they can also be transmitted electronically using voice mail, teleconferencing, audiotape, videotape, closed-circuit television, and so on. Similarly, although written messages can be handwritten, typed, or printed, they can also be transmitted electronically using faxes, e-mail (see figure 4.7), computer conferencing, and so on. Electronic media are useful when you need speed, when you're physically separated from your audience, when you need to overcome time-zone barriers, when you need to reach a dispersed audience personally, and when you are not concerned about confidentiality. Although no hard rules dictate which tool to use in each case (partly because technology keeps changing), here are a few pointers that will help you determine when to select electronic media over traditional oral or written media:[22]

In general, use electronic communication for speed, to overcome time-zone barriers, and to reach a widely dispersed audience personally.

- *Voice mail* can be used to replace short memos and phone calls that need no response. It is most effective for short, unambiguous messages.
- *Teleconferencing* is best for informational meetings, but it's ineffective for negotiation. It's an efficient alternative to a face-to-face meeting, but it can't simulate completely. For example, it discourages the "secondary" conversations that usually occur during a meeting of more than four or five people—which can help participants focus on a topic, but which can prevent participants from sharing valuable information.
- *Videotape* is often effective for getting a motivational message out to a large number of people. By communicating nonverbal cues, it can strengthen the sender's image of

Figure 4.7
In-Depth Critique: A Brief E-Mail Message Conveying Time-Sensitive Material

The president of a chain of Texas-based pet stores, Pet Paradise, has asked his administrative assistant, Maria Hernandez, to notify all 47 store managers that their February 4 meeting in San Antonio has been rescheduled for February 25. Hernandez could phone or fax the message, but either of those methods would take considerable time. By choosing e-mail, Hernandez minimizes her own efforts and gets the important news to each manager almost immediately.

E-Mail

Date: Tues, February 1, 2000, 01:21:34
To: storemanagers@petparadise.com
From: Maria Hernandez<mhernandez@petparadise.com>
Subject: Postponement and rescheduling of Friday meeting

Because Hernandez has all managers' e-mail addresses in one file, she needs to key in only the name of that file to reach each manager.

All Pet Paradise store managers:

The managers' meeting scheduled for this Friday, February 4, has been postponed. Vice President Andrew Melendez had an emergency appendectomy this morning at St. Francis Hospital in San Antonio and is doing well.

Hernandez first states the critical message and then gives the reason for postponement.

The managers' meeting has been rescheduled for February 25, from 8:00 a.m. until noon, with the same agenda as previously distributed. Mr. Melendez expects to attend the February 25 meeting.

She then gives information on the rescheduled meeting and tries to anticipate the managers' questions.

You can contact me with any questions.

Maria Hernandez

sincerity and trustworthiness; however, it offers no opportunity for immediate feedback.

- *Fax* messages can be used to overcome time-zone barriers when a hard copy is required. A fax has all the characteristics of a written message, except that it may lack the privacy of a letter, and depending on the quality of the audience's machine (thermal versus plain paper, for example), the message may appear less crisp, perhaps even less professional, than other written messages.
- *E-mail* has the advantages of speed, low cost, and increased access to other employees. This medium is best at communicating brief, noncomplex information that's time sensitive, but its effectiveness depends on the skills of the people using it.
- *Computer conferencing* offers democracy; that is, more attention is focused on an idea than on who communicates it. However, too much emphasis on the message (to the neglect of the person communicating it) can threaten corporate culture, which needs a more dynamic medium of communication.

Message planning is the first stage of the composition process. The three steps presented in this chapter encompass valuable tasks that help you establish a solid foundation before you begin to organize and compose your message. Use this chapter's Checklist for Planning Audience-Centered Business Messages not as a recipe for well-planned messages but as a reminder of what tasks and choices to address as you develop your business messages. Also remember that the steps discussed in this chapter may be useful at any time during the composition process. You will need to review them and modify them if the original purpose of your message or the nature of your audience changes.

CHECKLIST FOR PLANNING AUDIENCE-CENTERED BUSINESS MESSAGES

A. Define Your Purpose
  1. Determine whether the purpose of your message is to inform, persuade, or collaborate.
  2. Identify the specific behavior you hope to induce in the audience.
  3. Make sure that your purpose is worthwhile and realistic.

B. Analyze Your Audience
  1. Identify the primary audience.
  2. Determine the size and composition of the group.
  3. Determine the audience's level of understanding.
  4. Analyze the audience's probable reaction to your message.
  5. Analyze the audience's informational, motivational, and practical needs.
     - **a.** Find out what the audience wants to know.
     - **b.** Anticipate unstated questions.
     - **c.** Provide all required information and make sure it's accurate, ethical, and convenient.
  6. Establish a good relationship with your audience.
     - **a.** Adopt an audience-centered approach by using the "you" attitude.
     - **b.** Emphasize the positive aspects of your message.
     - **c.** Establish your credibility to gain the audience's confidence.
     - **d.** Use a polite tone.
     - **e.** Use bias-free language.
     - **f.** Project your company's image.

C. Consider the Following Message Factors When Selecting Your Channel and Medium
  1. Formality
  2. Length
  3. Urgency
  4. Confidentiality
  5. Complexity
  6. Cost
  7. Need for feedback
  8. Need for permanent record
  9. Audience size
  10. Audience expectations

COMMUNICATION CHALLENGES AT GENERAL MILLS

Although Jeff Hagen writes many of the form letters his department uses, he can't write them all. So a few senior staff members work on keeping the company's communications current and relevant as new products and new issues arise. That team is always facing bigger challenges.

INDIVIDUAL CHALLENGE: The Trix Rabbit has been getting a lot of e-mail lately. When the Web site was still new, Internet team members would log into the tracking software, look up the suggested reply, and then cut and paste paragraphs into the e-mail program, shuffling them around to make them personal and appropriate to the medium. Now Hagen has asked you to develop a form reply to people who simply want to say, "I just love this product." But this form reply must come via e-mail from the Trix Rabbit.

TEAM CHALLENGE: Hagen would like to increase the number of visitors to the company's Web site at http:/www.genmills.com. He's decided to sponsor a contest to entice company employees to generate ideas for promoting the Web site to outsiders. Of course, Hagen has drafted a proposal discussing the contest, requirements, rules, prizes—you name it. But now he's asked you and several employees to recommend the best channel and media to deliver his message to the employees. Furthermore, he's open to all suggestions—oral, written, traditional memos, e-mail, and so on. What will you recommend and why?[23]

SUMMARY OF LEARNING OBJECTIVES

1. **Describe the three stages of the composition process.** The three stages of the composition process are planning your message, organizing and composing your message, and revising your message.
2. **Name four criteria that will help you test the purpose of your message.** A message is more likely to accomplish its purpose if it is realistic, is acceptable to the organization, is delivered by the right person, and is delivered at the right time.
3. **Explain why it is important to analyze your audience when composing business messages, and list four ways you can develop your audience's profile.** Analyzing your audience places you in a better position to satisfy their informational needs and establish a good relationship with them. You can develop your audience's profile by identifying the primary audience, determining their size and composition, gauging their level of understanding, and estimating their probable reaction.
4. **Name six ways to satisfy your audience's informational needs.** To satisfy your audience's informational needs: find out what they want to know; anticipate unstated questions; provide all required information; make sure all information is accurate; communicate ethically; and emphasize ideas of greatest interest to them.
5. **Discuss five ways to establish a good relationship with your audience.** You can establish a good relationship with your audience by using the "you" attitude, emphasizing the positive, establishing your credibility, being polite, and using bias-free language.
6. **List eight things to consider when selecting communication channels and media.** In addition to formality, confidentiality, feedback, complexity, time, and cost, you'll need to consider which communication channel your audience prefers and whether you'll need a permanent record of the communication.

CRITICAL THINKING QUESTIONS

1. Some writers argue that planning messages wastes time because they inevitably change their plans as they go along. How would you respond to this argument? Briefly explain.
2. Your supervisor has asked you to prepare a message that, in your opinion, serves no worthwhile purpose. What do you do? Explain.
3. As editor of your company's newsletter, how would you go about discovering the needs of your fellow employees? Write a one-page explanation.
4. When composing business messages, how can you be yourself and project your company's image at the same time?
5. As personnel manager, what medium would you use for presenting employee benefits to new employees? Explain your answer.
6. As a member of the public relations department, what medium would you recommend using to inform the local community that your toxic-waste cleanup program has been successful? Why?
7. Considering how fast and easy it is, should e-mail replace meetings and other face-to-face communication in your company? Why or why not?
8. The company president has asked you to draft a memo to the board of directors informing them that sales in the newly acquired line of gourmet fruit jams have far exceeded anyone's expectations. As purchasing director, you happen to know that sales of moderately priced jams have declined substantially (many customers have switched to the more expensive jams). You were not directed to add that tidbit of information. What should you do?

DOCUMENT FOR ANALYSIS

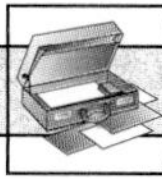

Establishing a Good Relationship with Your Audience

Read the following document; then (1) analyze the strengths and weaknesses of each sentence and (2) revise the document so that it follows this chapter's guidelines.

I am a new publisher with some really great books to sell. I saw your announcement in *Publishers Weekly* about the bookseller's show you're having this summer, and I think it's a great idea. Count me in, folks! I would like to get some space to show my books. I thought it would be a neat thing if I could do some airbrushing on T-shirts live to help promote my hot new title, *T-Shirt Art*. Before I got into publishing, I was an airbrush artist, and I could demonstrate my techniques. I've done hundreds of advertising illustrations and have been a sign painter all my life, so I'll also be promoting my other book, hot off the presses, *How to Make Money in the Sign Painting Business.*

I will be starting my PR campaign about May 2000 with ads in PW and some art trade papers, so my books should be well known by the time the show comes around in August. In case you would like to use my appearance there as part of your publicity, I have enclosed a biography and photo of myself.

P.S. Please let me know what it costs for booth space as soon as possible so that I can figure out whether I can afford to attend. Being a new publisher is mighty expensive!

EXERCISES

1. For each of the following communication tasks, state a specific purpose (if you have trouble, try beginning with "I want to . . .").
   a. A report to your boss, the store manager, about the outdated items in the warehouse
   b. A memo to clients about your booth at the upcoming trade show
   c. A letter to a customer who hasn't made a payment for three months
   d. A memo to employees about the office's high water bills
   e. A phone call to a supplier checking on an overdue parts shipment
   f. A report to future users of the computer program you have chosen to handle the company's mailing list
2. Make a list of communication tasks you'll need to accomplish in the next week or so (for example, a job application, a letter of complaint, a speech to a class, an order for some merchandise). For each, determine a general and a specific purpose.
3. List five messages you have received lately, such as direct-mail promotions, letters, e-mail messages, phone solicitations, and lectures. For each, determine the general and the specific purpose; then answer the following questions: (a) Was the message well timed? (b) Did the sender choose an appropriate channel and medium for the message? (c) Did the appropriate person deliver the message? (d) Was the sender's purpose realistic?
4. Barbara Marquardt is in charge of public relations for a cruise line that operates out of Miami. She is shocked to read a letter in a local newspaper from a disgruntled passenger, complaining about the service and entertainment on a recent cruise. Marquardt will have to respond to these publicized criticisms in some way. What audiences will she need to consider in her response? What channels and media should she choose? If the letter had been published in a travel publication widely read by travel agents and cruise travelers, how might her course of action differ?
5. For each communication task below, write brief answers to three questions: Who is my audience? What is my audience's general attitude toward my subject? What does my audience need to know?
   a. A final-notice collection letter from an appliance manufacturer to an appliance dealer, sent ten days before initiating legal collection procedures
   b. An unsolicited sales letter asking readers to purchase computer disks at near-wholesale prices
   c. An advertisement for peanut butter
   d. Fliers to be attached to doorknobs in the neighborhood, announcing reduced rates for chimney lining or repairs
   e. A cover letter sent along with your résumé to a potential employer
   f. A request (to the seller) for a price adjustment on a piano that incurred $150 in damage during delivery to a banquet room in the hotel you manage
6. Rewrite the following message so that it includes all the information that the reader needs. (Make up any necessary details.)

   I am pleased to offer you the position of assistant buyer at Fontaine and Sons at an annual salary of $15,500. I hope to receive notice of your acceptance soon.
7. Frank Kroll has been studying a new method for testing the durability of the electric hand tools his company manufactures. Now he needs to prepare three separate reports on his findings: first, a report for the administrator who will decide whether to purchase the new equipment needed for using this method; second, a report for the company's engineers who design and develop the hand tools; and third, a report for the trainers who will be showing workers how to use the new equipment. To determine the audience's needs for each of these reports, Frank has listed the following questions: (1) Who are the readers? (2) Why will they read my report? (3) Do they need introductory or background material? (4) Do they need definitions of terms? (5) What level or type of language is needed? (6) What level of detail is needed? (7) What result does my report aim for? Put yourself in Frank's shoes, and answer those questions for each of the three audiences:
   a. The administrator

b. The engineers
c. The trainers

8. Choose an electronic device (videocassette recorder, personal computer, telephone answering machine) that you know how to operate well. Write two sets of instructions for operating the device: one set for a reader who has never used that type of machine and one set for someone who is generally familiar with that type of machine but has never operated the specific model.

9. Visit the Web site http://www.ceoexpress.com. Browse this site and make a list of the many ways the links provided at this site can help you analyze your audience. Be creative. For instance, you might have to plan a trip to understand your audience's culture really well. Compare your list with those of your classmates.

10. Substitute a better phrase for each of the following:
   a. You claim that
   b. It is not our policy to
   c. You neglected to
   d. In which you assert
   e. We are sorry you are dissatisfied
   f. You failed to enclose
   g. We request that you send us
   h. Apparently you overlooked our terms
   i. We have been very patient
   j. We are at a loss to understand

11. Rewrite these sentences to reflect your audience's viewpoint.
   a. We request that you use the order form supplied in the back of our catalog.
   b. We insist that you always bring your credit card to the store.
   c. We want to get rid of all our 15-inch monitors to make room in our warehouse for the 19-inch screens. Thus we are offering a 25 percent discount on all sales this week.
   d. I am applying for the position of bookkeeper in your office. I feel that my grades prove that I am bright and capable, and I think I can do a good job for you.
   e. As requested, we are sending the refund for $25.

12. Revise these sentences to be positive rather than negative.
   a. To avoid the loss of your credit rating, please remit payment within ten days.
   b. We don't make refunds on returned merchandise that is soiled.
   c. Because we are temporarily out of Baby Cry dolls, we won't be able to ship your order for ten days.
   d. You failed to specify the color of the blouse that you ordered.
   e. You should have realized that waterbeds will freeze in unheated houses during winter. Therefore, our guarantee does not cover the valve damage and you must pay the $9.50 valve-replacement fee (plus postage).

13. Provide euphemisms for the following words and phrases:
   a. stubborn
   b. wrong
   c. stupid
   d. incompetent
   e. loudmouth

14. Rewrite each of the following to eliminate bias:
   a. For an Indian, Maggie certainly is outgoing.
   b. He needs a wheelchair, but he doesn't let his handicap affect his job performance.
   c. A pilot must have the ability to stay calm under pressure, and then he must be trained to cope with any problem that arises.
   d. Candidate Renata Parsons, married and the mother of a teenager, will attend the debate.
   e. Senior citizen Sam Nugent is still an active salesman.

15. Your supervisor, whom you respect, has asked you to withhold important information that you think should be included in a report you are preparing. Disobeying him could be disastrous for your relationship and your career. Obeying him could violate your personal code of ethics. What should you do? On the basis of the discussion in Chapter 1, would you consider this situation to be an ethical dilemma or an ethical lapse? Please explain.

16. How can the material discussed in this chapter also apply to meetings as discussed in Chapter 2? (Hint: Review the section headings in Chapter 4 and think about making your meetings more productive.)

17. Last week you thought of a perfect solution to the inventory back-order problems that have been plaguing your company for months. You spent the entire week drafting a memo even your business communication instructor would call "excellent." But now you're stuck. You can't decide to whom you should address the memo. Your boss? The department vice president? The company president? You grab a company organizational chart to help guide you, but you notice that things don't really work around the office they way this chart indicates. Briefly explain why a company's formal and informal communication channels (discussed in Chapter 1) should both be considered when addressing office memos.

EXPLORING THE BEST OF THE WEB

Polish Your Skills in Analyzing an Audience, page 96

Think of a letter you'd like to write to a group (such as the Sierra Club, International Association of Business Communicators, or Mothers Against Drunk Driving). Write down your general purpose and your specific purposes. Then, on the basis of the information you glean from the organization's Web site, write your audience's profile: (a) Describe the audience's size and composition, (b) identify the primary audience, (c) estimate the audience's probable reaction to your letter, and (d) gauge the audience's level of understanding of your message.

If you don't already have an organization in mind, use the subject areas in Associations on the Net (http://www.ipl.org/ref/AON) to select one. Clicking on the name of a group that interests you will take you directly to that organization's Web site. You can also use AON's search function to find the URL for a specific organization.

ORGANIZING AND COMPOSING AUDIENCE-CENTERED BUSINESS MESSAGES

AFTER STUDYING THIS CHAPTER, YOU WILL BE ABLE TO

1 Explain why good organization is important to both the communicator and the audience
2 Differentiate between the topic and the main idea of a message
3 Discuss five prewriting techniques to help you identify the main idea of your message
4 Compare the direct and indirect patterns for organizing ideas and explain under what circumstances each is generally used
5 Cite seven techniques for maintaining a conversational tone in business messages
6 Discuss how to develop effective sentences and coherent paragraphs

COMMUNICATION CLOSE-UP AT COMMUNITY HEALTH GROUP

Although most people think accountants spend their days crunching numbers, Julian Santoyo says it just isn't true anymore. "Machines have taken care of a lot of that," explains the chief financial officer for Community Health Group (CHG), a nonprofit health maintenance organization (HMO) in Chula Vista, California. "Now, the more successful financial people are people who communicate and offer recommendations that support business decisions," he says. To do that, Santoyo writes memos, reports, letters, e-mail, and even news releases.

Julian Santoyo

As a nonprofit organization, CHG is one of the few HMOs in the country to serve low-income recipients of government-funded medical care (known as "Medi-Cal" in California). As do commercial HMOs, CHG charges a monthly fee for each member and then contracts with doctors, hospitals, and other health-care professionals to provide the actual medical services members require. The difference is that CHG's member fees are paid by the government.

Most of CHG's 55,000 members are Hispanic or Asian, and many are non-English-speaking. Santoyo says that his co-workers reflect this diversity: 60 percent are Hispanic, 30 percent are Anglo, and 10 percent are from a variety of cultural backgrounds. Some prefer Spanish as a primary language; others prefer English. In addition to crossing language bar-

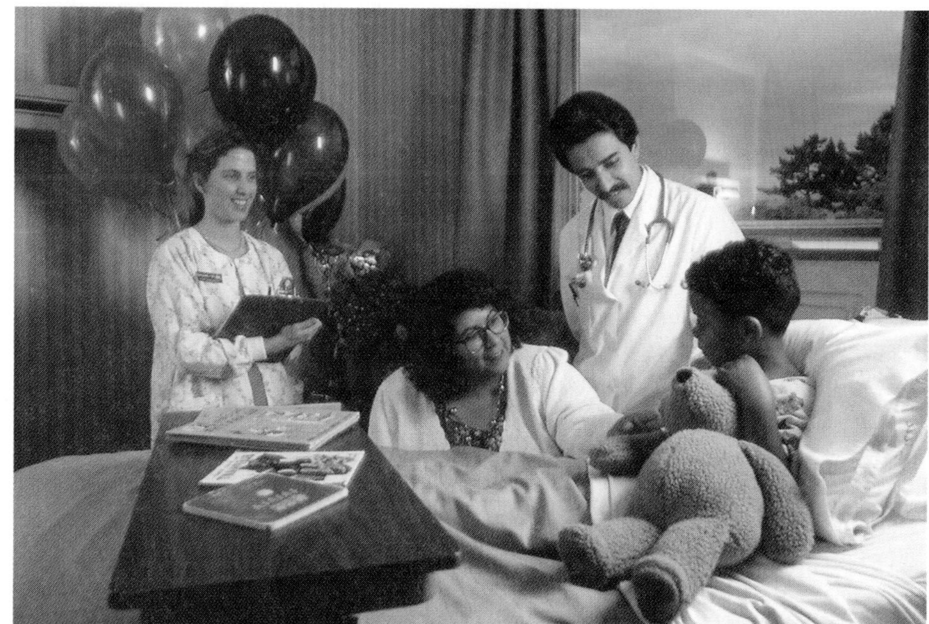

Because the majority of CHG's patients and staff members are Hispanic and Asian, employees work hard to overcome language and cultural barriers. Even when dealing with other businesses, CHG workers strive for clarity by carefully avoiding jargon and acronyms. To be as clear as possible, they strive for sound organization and a straightforward style.

riers, CHG's business spans the medical, insurance, government, and sales industries—all fields riddled with insider jargon and confusing acronyms and abbreviations. To be clearly understood, says Santoyo, he has to be particularly aware of the audience for each message.

"I need to take the numbers, the specific actuarial data or accounting data, and convert that information into something that's user friendly and understandable," he says. "That means that I have to be flexible in how I structure my communication."

He starts with an outline. If he thinks his audience will agree with him, he puts the main idea up front. If what he's writing is controversial or likely to be viewed with skepticism, he builds up to his main point. He makes these decisions before starting his first draft. The goal is to structure the message so that his readers can easily understand it, believe it, and use the information contained in it.

As Santoyo explains, it often takes two or three drafts to organize his message correctly. "You write it out, put it down, you come back later, and you look at it," explains Santoyo, "because when you're writing, there's a lot of information that you're familiar with and that you assume everyone knows. A short time later or a day later, you look at your document again and that 'familiar' feeling is gone and you think, 'Well, maybe I need to add this exhibit, or I need to elaborate on this point a little bit more, because I don't really think I'm getting the point across, or I could write it a little bit better, rewording it a certain way.' If it's an important memo, I always recommend waiting at least half a day to distribute it."

Santoyo generally writes in a less formal style, in keeping with CHG's small size and casual atmosphere. He tries to avoid using technical terms. "If I'm going to use an acronym, I'll only use one that I know the audience is familiar with, or I'll define it somewhere in the text." As part of his audience-centered approach, Santoyo often uses the word *we* to reflect CHG's team approach, as in, "We have to keep costs down because . . . "

To maintain his credibility, Santoyo never stretches his facts. "Never cry wolf," he advises. "Never exaggerate a point because you want to make sure something gets done. After a few times, your audience will get wise to you and you'll end up like the kid in the story: You'll be someone's lunch." He believes in building credibility over time. "You have to have a good reputation; you see, that's all you have. You can't just say, 'Hey, I'm an honest guy,' and then go around with hidden agendas, because no matter how smart you think you are, a bright executive or co-worker is going to see through your smoke and mirrors . . . and they'll lose confidence in you." Then you'll have to work twice as hard for the same results.[1] ■

STEP 4: ORGANIZING YOUR MESSAGE

Like Julian Santoyo, all business communicators face the problem of conveying a complicated web of ideas in an understandable fashion. People don't remember dissociated facts and figures, so successful communicators rely on organization to make their messages meaningful.[2] Before thinking about *how* to achieve good organization, however, think about *what* it means and *why* it's important.

What Good Organization Means

The definition of good organization varies from country to country. But in the United States and Canada, it generally means creating a linear message that proceeds point by point. If you've ever received a disorganized message, you're familiar with the frustration of trying to sort through a muddle of ideas. Consider this letter from Jill Saunders, the office manager at Boswell & Sons, mapmakers:

> Our president, Mr. Boswell, was in an accident last year, and he hasn't been able to work full-time. His absence has affected our business, so we don't have the budget we used to. His two sons are working hard, so we aren't bankrupt by any means, and soon Mr. Boswell will be coming back full-time.
>
> Boswell & Sons has been doing business with ComputerTime since I was hired six years ago. Your building was smaller then, and it was located on the corner of Federal Avenue and 2nd N.W. Mr. Boswell bought our first laser printer there. I still remember the day. It was the biggest check I'd ever written. Of course, over the years, I've gotten used to larger purchases.
>
> We have seven employees. Although all of them aren't directly involved in producing the maps we sell, they all need to have their computers working so that they can do their jobs. The CD-ROM drive we bought for my assistant, Suzanne, has been a problem. We've taken it in for repairs three times in three months to the authorized service center, and Suzanne is very careful with the machine and hasn't abused it. She likes playing interactive adventure games on lunch breaks. It still doesn't work right, and she's tired of hauling it back and forth. We're all putting in longer hours to make up for Mr. Boswell's not being here, and none of us has a lot of spare time.
>
> This is the first time we've returned anything to your store, and I hope you'll agree that we deserve a better deal.

This letter displays a lack of organization that U.S. and Canadian readers find frustrating. By taking a closer look at what's wrong, you can identify the four most common faults responsible for such organization problems:

Most disorganized communication suffers from problems with content, grouping, or sequence.

- *Taking too long to get to the point.* Saunders didn't introduce the topic, the faulty CD-ROM drive, until the third paragraph. Then she waited until the final paragraph to state her purpose: requesting an adjustment. Solution: Make the subject and purpose clear.
- *Including irrelevant material.* Saunders introduced information that has no bearing on her purpose or her topic. Does it matter that the computer store used to be smaller or that it was in a different location? What difference does it make whether Saunders's boss is working only part-time or whether her assistant likes playing com-

puter games during lunch? Solution: Include only information that is related to the subject and purpose.

- *Getting ideas mixed up*. Saunders seems to be making
has money to spend, (2) it's an old customer, (3) it pays b
numerous items at the store, (5) the CD-ROM drive do
wants an adjustment. However, the ideas are in the wro
logical to begin with the fact that the machine doesn't w
should be combined under the general idea that the com
Solution: Group the ideas and present them in a logical
- *Leaving out necessary information*. The customer servic
know the make, model, and price of the CD-ROM dri
purchased; the specific problems the machine has had;
covered by the warranty. Saunders also failed to specify
do. Does she want a new CD-ROM drive of the same
simply her money back? Solution: Include all the neces

Achieving good organization can be a challenge. Nevert
these common faults, you can communicate clearly, logically,
you state all information as truthfully, honestly, and fairly as p
lutions changes Saunders's letter so that the message can be e
municated (as shown in Figure 5.1).

Why Good Organization Is Important

You might be asking yourself whether it matters that a message is well organized, as long as its point is eventually made. Why not just let the ideas flow naturally and trust that the audience will grasp the meaning? However, if you consider the cost of misinterpreted messages (such as wasted time reading and rereading unclear messages, poor decision making, and shattered business relationships), you begin to realize the value of clear writing and good organization.[3]

Being well organized helps you compose your messages more quickly and efficiently. In business, the objective is to get work done, not to produce messages. In fact, when the chief executives in one survey were asked what they would most like to improve about their own business writing, they mentioned speed of composition more often than any other factor.[4]

If you think about what you're going to say and how you're going to say it before you begin to write, your draft will go more quickly, because you won't waste time putting ideas in the wrong places or composing material you don't need. You can use your organizational plan to get some advance input from your audience so that you can be sure you're on the right track *before* you spend hours working on a draft. If you're working on a large, complex project, you can use the plan to divide the writing job among co-workers to finish the assignment as quickly as possible. In addition to saving your time, good organization saves your audience time because they receive only the information they need, presented as accessibly and as succinctly as possible.

Good Organization Helps Your Audience Understand Your Message

As CHG's Julian Santoyo points out, you want your information to be "user friendly and understandable." Read the following excerpt from a letter requesting detailed information from a hotel in order to finalize plans for a future conference. How well can the hotel manager understand the needs of the writer?

The main reason for being well organized is to improve the chances that people will understand exactly what you mean.

> I am chair of the planning committee for our annual conference and was considering your hotel as a possible site. I know that summer is a busy time, but we

Figure 5.1
In-Depth Critique: Letter with Improved Organization

This letter from Boswell & Sons asking about ComputerTime's exchange policy is organized to give all needed information in a sequence that helps the reader understand the message.

Route 7, Hancock Highway, Clear Lake, Iowa 50428
Voice: (515) 788-4343 E-mail: boswell@aol.com Fax: (515) 788-4344

September 13, 2000

Customer Service
ComputerTime
556 Seventh Avenue
Mason City, Iowa 50401

Dear Customer Service Representative:

The first paragraph clearly states the purpose of this letter.

Boswell & Sons bought an Olympic Systems, Model PRS-2, CD-ROM drive from your store on November 15, 1999, during your pre-Christmas sale, when it was marked down to $199.95. We didn't use the unit until January, because it was bought for my assistant, who unexpectedly took six weeks' leave from mid-November through December. You can imagine her frustration when she first tried using it and it didn't work.

The second paragraph explains the situation so that the reader will understand the problem. The writer includes no irrelevant information, and the ideas are presented logically.

In January, we took the drive to the authorized service center and were assured that the problem was merely a loose connection. The service representative fixed the drive, but in April we had to have it fixed again—another loose connection. For the next three months, the drive worked reasonably well, although the response time was occasionally slow. Two months ago, the drive stopped working again. Once more, the service representative blamed a loose connection and made the repair. Although the drive is working now, it isn't working very well. The response time is still slow, and the motor seems to drag sometimes.

The third paragraph states precisely what adjustment is being requested.

What is your policy on exchanging unsatisfactory merchandise? Although all the repairs have been relatively minor and have been covered by the one-year warranty, we are not satisfied with the drive. We would like to exchange it for a similar model from another manufacturer. If the new drive costs more than the old one, we will pay the difference, even though we generally look for equipment with heavy business discounts.

The letter includes all the necessary information.

Boswell & Sons has done business with your store for six years and until now has always been satisfied with your merchandise. We are counting on you to live up to your reputation for standing behind your products. Please let us hear from you soon.

Sincerely,

Jill Saunders

Jill Saunders

lv

are committed to a summer conference because of scheduling problems. Can your hotel handle 350 guests for four nights? Do you have three large meeting rooms so we can have concurrent training sessions? What about dining facilities? Also, there is some concern about shuttle service to and from the airport.

From what you've read, is it possible for the hotel to send accurate, helpful information to the letter writer? What are the exact dates of the conference? Is the conference this year or next? Will each guest want a single room? What does the writer want to know about the dining facilities? What is the concern about shuttle service? Now look at the revised version:

> The National Association of Accountants (NAA) is considering your hotel as a site for our annual summer conference to be held August 21–24, 2001, but we need some detailed information before coming to a final decision. Please respond to the following questions:
>
> 1. Can your hotel accommodate 350 persons for the nights of August 21, 22, 23, and 24 (with approximately three-quarters of the attendees preferring single rooms)? What convention room rates can you offer?
> 2. Are three meeting rooms available on those dates (each accommodating at least 125 persons)?
> 3. Our preference for dining is to be able to eat together. Does your hotel have banquet facilities that can handle 350 persons at breakfast, lunch, and dinner? Also, please send menu suggestions and prices.
> 4. Does your hotel have a complimentary shuttle to and from the airport? How often does it run? If no complimentary shuttle is available, what other forms of transportation are available, and what is the cost to and from the airport?

This version contains the same topics as the initial letter, but it's organized so that the main point (the conference dates) is clear at the outset. The letter follows with the precise needs of this particular group indented and numbered. As this revised version shows, a well-organized message satisfies the audience's need for information.

Good Organization Helps Your Audience Accept Your Message

Good organization also helps you get your ideas across without upsetting the audience.

Good organization helps motivate your audience to accept your message. Say that you're Jill Saunders (the customer with the unsatisfactory CD-ROM drive) and you get the following reply from Linda Davis, a customer service representative at the computer store:

> Your letter has been referred to me for a reply. I'm sorry, but we are unable to grant your request for a CD-ROM drive. Our store does not accept returns on sale equipment or on equipment that was purchased over six months ago. Because you bought the drive on sale ten months ago, we cannot help you. I suggest that you have it repaired before the warranty runs out. We do hope that you will understand our position and that you will continue to shop at our store. As you said yourself, this is the first problem you've ever had with our equipment.

How do you feel about the computer store now? Although Davis's letter appears at first glance to be logical enough, she's made no effort to select and organize her points in a diplomatic way. With greater care in choosing and presenting her ideas, Davis could have come up with something more acceptable, like the letter in Figure 5.2. This letter is still unlikely to satisfy the customer totally, but isn't the bad news a little easier to take?

As the letter in Figure 5.2 shows, you can soften refusals, leave a better impression, and be more convincing by organizing messages diplomatically. You can also use good organization to enhance your credibility and add authority to your messages. In a recent survey of chief executives, 89 percent said that they interpret clear, well-organized writing as an indication of clear thinking.[5]

Good Organization Saves Your Audience Time

Well-organized messages are efficient because they contain only relevant information.

Well-organized messages are efficient. They contain only relevant ideas, so your audience doesn't waste time on superfluous information. Effective organization is the foundation of brevity.

Moreover, all the information in a well-organized message is in a logical place. The audience can follow the thought pattern without a struggle. Because the organization is clear and logical, they can save even more time, if they want to, by looking for just the information they need instead of reading everything.

Figure 5.2
In-Depth Critique: Letter Demonstrating a Diplomatic Organization Plan

This letter from ComputerTime responds to the inquiry from Boswell & Sons about the unsatisfactory CD-ROM drive. Although the information is effectively negative, the letter diplomatically achieves a positive feeling.

COMPUTERTIME
556 Seventh Avenue, Mason City, IA 50428
(515) 979-8870 / Comptime@netins.net

September 17, 2000

Ms. Jill Saunders
Boswell & Sons
Route 7, Hancock Highway
Clear Lake, IA 50401

Dear Ms. Saunders:

The letter begins with a neutral statement that the reader should not find objectionable.

Thank you for letting us know about your experience with the Olympic CD-ROM drive that you bought last November. It's important that we learn of unusual problems with the equipment we stock.

The refusal is stated indirectly and is linked with a solution to the reader's problem.

As you know, regularly priced equipment returned to ComputerTime within 30 days is covered by the unconditional refund that has been our tradition for 22 years. Your drive, however, is still covered by the manufacturer's warranty. Your needs will receive immediate attention if you write to

Mr. George Bender
Olympic Systems
P.O. Box 7761, Terminal Annex
Los Angeles, CA 90010

From experience, I know that the people at Olympic truly care about having satisfied customers.

The letter closes on an appreciative note and confidently assumes normal dealings in the future.

We, too, value your business, Ms. Saunders. Please don't miss our holiday sale in early November, which will feature more of the low prices and high-quality equipment that you've come to rely on.

Sincerely,

Linda Davis

Linda Davis
Customer Service

hg

How Good Organization Is Achieved

To organize a message
- Define your ideas
- Group the ideas
- Put the ideas in sequence

Understanding the *need* for good organization is half the battle. Knowing *how* to organize your messages well is the other half. Julian Santoyo of Community Health Group achieves good organization by following the three-step process: (1) define your ideas, (2) group the ideas, (3) establish their sequence by selecting either a direct or an indirect approach.

When Terry and Donna Plunkett investigated franchise opportunities with Critter Care of America, they began the process by sending an inquiry letter to the franchisor. Now, as successful owners of this Colorado pet-sitting franchise, they know that well-organized communications can expedite the entire franchising process.

Define the Main Idea

In Chapter 4 we explained that all business messages have a general purpose and a specific purpose. In addition to these purposes, every business message can be boiled down to one main idea. Regardless of the issue's complexity, one central point sums up everything. This is your theme, your main idea. Everything else in the message either supports this point or demonstrates its implications. A topic and a main idea are different (see Table 5.1). The **topic** is the broad subject of the message, whereas the **main idea** makes a statement about the topic. For example, you might give a presentation on the topic of company health clubs, with the aim of persuading management to build an on-site facility. Your main idea might be that

The topic is the broad subject; the main idea makes a statement about the topic.

TABLE 5.1

PURPOSE, TOPIC, AND MAIN IDEA

Purpose General	Specific	Topic	Main Idea
To inform	To teach customer service representatives how to file an insurance claim	Filing insurance claims	Proper filing by employees saves the company time and money
To persuade	To get top management's approval for increased spending on research and development	Funding for research and development	Competitors spend more than we do on research and development.
To collaborate	To get the human resources and accounting departments to jointly devise an incentive system that ties wages directly to profits	Incentive pay	Tying wages to profits will automatically reduce compensation costs in tough years while motivating employees to be more productive.

the costs of providing a company health club would be more than offset by gains in productivity and reductions in insurance costs.

When you're preparing a brief letter, memo, or meeting agenda, the main idea may be pretty obvious, especially if you're dealing with simple facts that have little or no emotional content for the audience. In such cases, the main idea may be nothing more than "Here is what you wanted." If you're responding to a request for information about the price and availability of your company's products, your main idea would be something like "We have these items at competitive prices."

The main idea is the "hook" that sums up why a particular audience should do or think as you suggest.

However, finding the angle, or "hook," is more complicated when you're trying to persuade someone or when you have disappointing information to convey. In these situations, look for a main idea that will establish a good relationship between you and your audience. One way to do this is by focusing on some point of agreement or common interest.

In longer documents and presentations, in which a mass of material needs to be unified, the problem of establishing a main idea becomes still more challenging. You need to identify a generalization that encompasses all the individual points you want to make. For tough assignments such as these, you may need to take special measures to come up with a main idea.

For longer messages, determining the main idea often requires creative thinking.

Use Prewriting Techniques The process of identifying the main idea and establishing supporting details often requires a good deal of creative thinking. One of the best ways to generate ideas is to **brainstorm**, letting your mind wander over the possibilities and testing various alternatives against your purpose, your audience, and the facts at your disposal. The important thing to remember about prewriting techniques such as brainstorming is to be completely creative and uncensored (see "Sharpening Your Skills: Overcoming Your

SHARPENING YOUR SKILLS

OVERCOMING YOUR FEAR OF THE BLANK PAGE

For some people, writing is a breeze. For many others, however, putting words on a page or on a screen is a real struggle. They may even get stuck so often that they develop a mental block. Are you one of those people? If so, here are some ways to overcome writer's block:

- *Use positive self-talk.* Writer's block comes from worrying about being unable to write well or easily and from believing that writing is too difficult, too time consuming, or too complicated. Replace such negative ideas about writing by telling yourself that you're a resourceful, capable person who knows how to do the job. As proof that you really can write when you want to, recall past examples of your writing that were successful.
- *Know your purpose.* What do you want to accomplish with this particular piece of writing? Without a clear purpose, writing can indeed be impossible.
- *Visualize your audience.* Picture their backgrounds, interests, knowledge of the subject, and vocabulary, including the technical jargon they're familiar with. Visualization can help you choose an appropriate slant for your writing.
- *Create a productive environment.* When you're blocked, you're easily distracted by sights, sounds, and other elements in your environment. Make sure you write in a place that is for writing only, and make that environment pleasant. Then set "appointments" with yourself, during which you do nothing but write. A writing appointment for, say, 9:30 to 12:00 seems less imposing than an indefinite writing session. Also, be sure to build in break times to keep your mind fresh.
- *Make an outline or a list.* Even if making a formal outline makes you restless, jot down at least a few notes about how your ideas fit together. As you go along, you'll probably revise these notes, which is fine, as long as you end up with a plan that gives direction and coherence to your writing.
- *Just start.* Put aside all worries, fears, and distractions—everything that gives you an excuse to postpone writing.

Fear of the Blank Page"). You'll have plenty of opportunities to edit and polish your thoughts later on.

Here are a few approaches that successful communicators use to facilitate the free flow of ideas. Experiment until you find a prewriting method that fits your creative style.

Some techniques for establishing the main idea:
- Storyteller's tour
- Random list
- FCR worksheet
- Journalistic approach
- Question-and-answer chain

- *Storyteller's tour.* Turn on your tape recorder and pretend that you've just run into an old friend on the street. She says, "So, what are you working on these days?" Give her an overview of your message, focusing on your reasons for communicating, your major points, your rationale, and the implications for your intended audience. Listen critically to the tape; then repeat the exercise until you are able to give a smooth, two-minute summary that conveys the gist of your message. The summary should reveal your main idea.
- *Random list.* On a computer screen or a clean sheet of paper, list everything that pops into your head that pertains to your message. Once you begin your list, your thoughts will start to flow. When you've exhausted the possibilities, study the list for relationships. Sort the items into groups, as you would sort a deck of cards into suits. Look for common denominators; the connection might be geographic, sequential, spatial, chronological, or topical. Part of the list might break down into problems, causes, and solutions; another part, into pros and cons. Regardless of what categories finally emerge, the sorting process will help you sift through your thoughts and decide what's important and what isn't. To help you decide what's important, try to select points that will most benefit your audience.
- *FCR worksheet.* If your subject involves the solution to a problem, you might try using an FCR worksheet to help you visualize the relationships among your findings (F), your conclusions (C), and your recommendations (R). For example, you might find

---

Then start putting down any thoughts you have about the topic. Don't worry about whether these ideas can actually be used; just let your mind range freely.

- *Write the middle first.* You don't have to start at the beginning. Start wherever your enthusiasm is greatest and your ideas are most developed. If your thoughts take you in a different direction, feel free to follow them, making notes about any ideas you want to come back to later. When you've finished with this first section, pick out another; but don't worry about sequence. The idea is to get all your thoughts in writing.
- *Push obstacles aside.* You may well get stuck at some point, but you can easily get unstuck. First, don't worry about it. These things happen. Second, get rid of any distractions. Third, if you're stuck on one thought or sentence or paragraph, go on to one that's easier for you. You can always come back later. Fourth, prime the pump; that is, simply write about why you're stuck: "I'm stuck because . . ." Before you know it, you'll be writing about your topic. Also try talking aloud about your problem. Finally, try brainstorming. Make notes about things you haven't yet covered. Soon enough, you'll feel the urge to write.
- *Read a newspaper or a magazine.* Perhaps the most overlooked and underestimated way to oil your writing joints is through reading. Try reading an article that uses a style similar to yours and one that you'll enjoy—that way you'll read it more closely.

When deadlines loom, you may become paralyzed with panic. But if you keep things in perspective, you'll survive. Concentrate on the major ideas first, and save the details for later, after you have something on the page.

1. Procrastination is a skill that many writers have developed into a fine art. List the ways you procrastinate, and discuss what you can do to break these habits.
2. One reason for writer's block is negative self-talk. Analyze your own writing experiences. What negative self-talk do you use? What might you do to overcome this tendency?

that you're losing sales to a competitor who offers lower prices than you do (F). From this information, you might conclude that your loss of sales is due to your pricing policy (C). This conclusion would lead you to recommend a price cut (R). To make an FCR worksheet, divide a computer screen or a sheet of paper into three columns. List the major findings in the first column, then extrapolate conclusions and write them in the second column. These conclusions form the basis for the recommendations, which are listed in the third column. An analysis of the three columns should help you focus on the main idea.

- *Journalistic approach*. For informational messages, the journalistic approach may provide a good point of departure. The answers to six questions—who, what, when, where, why, and how—should clarify the main idea.
- *Question-and-answer chain*. Perhaps the best approach is to look at the subject from your audience's perspective. Ask yourself: "What is the audience's main question? What do they need to know?" Examine your answers to those questions. What additional questions emerge? Follow the chain of questions and answers until you have replied to every conceivable question that might occur to the audience. By thinking about your material from their point of view, you are likely to pinpoint the main idea.

Gear your main idea to the length of the message.

Limit the Scope Whether the audience expects a one-page memo or a one-hour speech, select a main idea that can be developed within that framework. Once you have a tentative statement of your main idea, test it against the length limitations that have been imposed for your message.

There's a limit to how much you can communicate in a given number of words. What can be accomplished depends on the nature of the subject, audience members' familiarity with the topic, their receptivity to your conclusions, and your existing credibility. In general, presenting routine information to a knowledgeable audience that already knows and respects you takes fewer words. Building consensus about a complex and controversial subject takes longer, especially if the audience is composed of skeptical or hostile strangers.

Although you adjust your message to fit the time or space available, don't change the number of major points. Regardless of how long the message will be, stick with three or four major points—five at the very most. According to communication researchers, that's all your audience will remember.[6]

If you're delivering a long message—say, a 60-minute presentation or a 20-page report—you can develop the major points in considerable detail. You can spend about ten minutes or ten paragraphs (or over three pages of double-spaced, typewritten text) on each of your key points and still have room for the introduction and conclusion. Instead of introducing additional points, you can deal more fully with complex issues, offer a variety of evidence, and overcome resistance. If your message is brief—four minutes or one page—you'll have only a minute or a paragraph each for the introduction, conclusion, and major points. The amount of evidence you can present is limited, too, so your main idea will have to be both easy to understand and easy to accept.

The scope of your message (its length and detail) also determines the amount and depth of information gathering you can do. The information you'll need for various business messages will cover a broad range. You may need only to glance at your calendar to confirm a meeting, or you may need to spend weeks conducting formal research for a complicated report. Gathering information for reports and proposals is thoroughly discussed in Chapter 11.

Group Your Ideas

Although prewriting techniques will help generate your main idea, they won't necessarily tell you how to develop it or how to group the supporting details in the most logical and effective way. To decide on the final structure of your message, you need to visualize how all

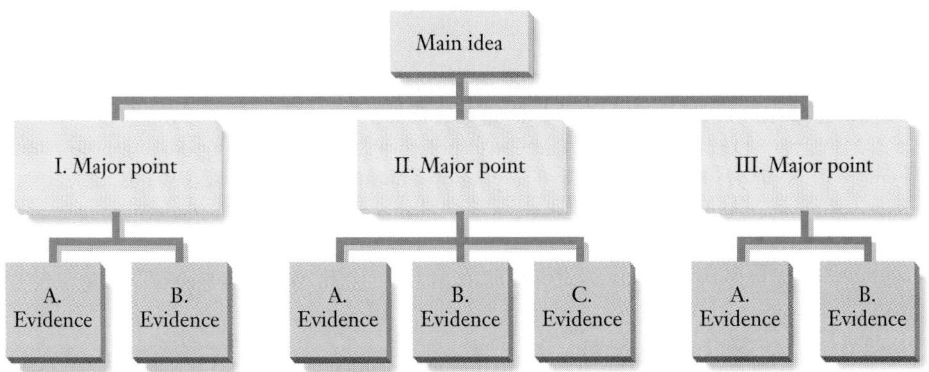

Figure 5.3
"Organization Chart" for Organizing a Message

the points fit together. One way to do so is to construct an outline. Whether you use the outlining features provided with word-processing software or simply jot down three or four points on the back of an envelope, making a plan and sticking to it will help you cover the important details.

An outline or a schematic diagram will help you visualize the relationship among parts of a message.

When you're preparing a long, complex message, an outline is indispensable because it helps you visualize the relationships among the various parts. Without an outline, you may be inclined to ramble. As you're describing one point, another point may occur to you, so you describe it. One detour leads to another, and before you know it, you've forgotten the original point. With an outline to guide you, however, you can communicate in a more systematic way, covering all the necessary ideas in an effective order and with proper emphasis. Following an outline also helps you insert the transitions between points so that your message is coherent and the audience will understand the relationships among your ideas.

You're no doubt familiar with the basic alphanumeric outline, which uses numbers and letters to identify each point and indents them to show which ideas are of equal status. (Chapter 14 tells more about the various formats that can be used in this type of outlining.) A more schematic approach illustrates the structure of your message in an "organization chart" similar to one that depicts a company's management structure (see Figure 5.3). The main idea is shown in the highest-level box, and like a top executive, it establishes the big picture. The lower-level ideas, like lower-level employees, provide the details. All the ideas are logically organized into divisions of thought, just as a company is organized into divisions and departments.[7]

The main idea is the starting point for constructing an outline.

Start with the Main Idea The main idea, placed at the top of an organization chart, helps you establish the goals and general strategy of the message. This main idea summarizes two things: (1) what you want your audience to do or think and (2) why they should do so. Everything in the message should either support the main idea or explain its implications.

The main idea should be supported by three to five major points, regardless of the message's length.

State the Major Points In an organization chart, the boxes directly below the top box represent the major supporting points, corresponding to the main headings in a conventional outline. These are the "vice presidential" ideas that clarify the message by expressing it in more concrete terms. To fill in these boxes, break the main idea into smaller units. In general, try to identify three to five major points. If you come up with more than seven main divisions of thought, go back and look for opportunities to combine some of the ideas. The next task is deciding what to put in each box. Sometimes the choices are fairly obvious. At other times you may have hundreds of ideas to sort through and group together. In either case, be sure to keep in mind both your purpose and the nature of the material.

If your purpose is to inform and the material is factual, the groupings are generally suggested by the subject itself. They are usually based on something physical that you can visualize or measure: activities to be performed, functional units, spatial or chronological relationships, or parts of a whole. When you're describing a process, the major supporting points are almost inevitably steps in the process. When you're describing a physical object, the vice presidential boxes correspond to the components of the object. When you're giving a historical account, each box represents an event in the chronological chain.

When your purpose is to persuade or to collaborate, the major supporting points may be more difficult to identify. Instead of relying on a natural order imposed by the subject, develop a line of reasoning that proves your central message and motivates your audience to act. The boxes on the organization chart then correspond to the major elements in a logical argument. Basically, the supporting points are the main reasons your audience should accept your message.

Illustrate with Evidence The third level on the organization chart shows the specific evidence you'll use to illustrate your major points. This evidence is the flesh and blood that helps your audience understand and remember the more abstract concepts you're presenting. Say you're advocating that the company increase its advertising budget. To support this point, you could provide statistical evidence that your most successful competitors spend more on advertising than you do. You could also describe a specific case in which a particular competitor increased its ad budget and achieved an impressive sales gain. As a final bit of evidence, you could show that over the past five years, your firm's sales have gone up and down in unison with the amount spent on advertising.

If you're developing a long, complex message, you may need to carry the organization chart (or outline) down several levels. Remember that every level is a step along the chain from the abstract to the concrete, from the general to the specific. The lowest level contains the individual facts and figures that tie the generalizations to the observable, measurable world. The higher levels are the concepts that reveal why those facts are significant.

Each major point should be supported with enough specific evidence to be convincing, but not so much that it's boring.

The more evidence you provide, the more conclusive your case will be. If your subject is complex and unfamiliar or if your audience is skeptical, you'll need a lot of facts and figures to demonstrate your points. On the other hand, if your subject is routine and the audience is positively inclined, you can be more sparing with the evidence. You want to provide enough support to be convincing but not so much that your message becomes boring or inefficient.

A brain trust of outside business advisers helps Grace McGartland generate ideas for her consulting firm. Once the brainstorming sessions are over, however, McGartland must organize the ideas logically so that she can communicate them effectively to others.

TABLE 5.2

SIX TYPES OF DETAIL

Type of Detail	Example	Comment
Facts and figures	Sales are strong this month. We have received two new contracts worth $5 million and have a good chance of winning another with an annual value of $2.5 million.	Most common form of detail in business messages. Adds more credibility than any other form of development. May become boring if used in excess.
Example or illustration	We've spent the past four months trying to hire recent accounting graduates for our internal audit staff, and, so far, only one person has agreed to join our firm. One woman told me that she would love to work for us, but she can get $5,000 more a year elsewhere.	Adds life to a message, but one example does not prove a point. Idea must be supported by other evidence as well.
Description	Upscale hamburger restaurants are designed for McDonald's graduates who still love the taste of a Big Mac but who want more than convenience and low prices. The adult hamburger establishments feature attractive waitresses, wine and beer, half-pound burgers, and substantial side dishes, such as nachos and potato skins. "Atmosphere" is a key ingredient in the formula for success.	Useful when you need to explain how something looks or functions. Helps audience visualize the subject by creating a sensory impression. Does not prove a point, but clarifies points and makes them memorable. Begins with overview of object's function; defines its purpose, lists major parts, and explains how it operates; relies on words that appeal to senses.
Narration	Under former management, the company operated in a casual style. Executives came to work in blue jeans, meetings rarely started on time, and lunch rarely ended on time. When Mr. Wilson took over as CEO, however, the company got religion—financial religion. A Harvard MBA who favors Brooks Brothers suits, Mr. Wilson has embarked on a complete overhaul of the operation. He has cut the product line from 6,000 items to 1,200 and has chopped $12 million off expenses.	Good for attracting attention and explaining ideas, but lacks statistical validity.
Reference to authority	I talked with Jackie Lohman in the Cleveland plant about this idea, and she was very supportive. As you know, Jackie has been in charge of that plant for the past six years. She is confident that we can speed up the number 2 line by 150 units per hour if we add another worker.	Bolsters a case and adds variety and credibility. Works only if "authority" is recognized and respected by audience.
Visual aids	Graphs, charts, tables	Essential when presenting specific information. Used more often in memos and reports than in letters.

Another way to keep the audience interested is to vary the type of detail. As you plan your message, try to incorporate the methods described in Table 5.2. Switch from facts and figures to narration; add a dash of description; throw in some examples or a reference to authority. Reinforce it all with visual aids. Think of your message as a stew: a mixture of ingredients seasoned with a blend of spices. Each separate flavor adds to the richness of the whole.

Choose between the Direct and Indirect Approaches

Once you've defined and grouped your ideas, you're ready to decide on their sequence. When you're addressing a U.S. or Canadian audience with minimal cultural differences, you have two basic options:

Use direct order if the audience's reaction is likely to be positive and indirect order if it is likely to be negative.

- Direct approach *(deductive).* Put the main idea first, followed by the evidence. Use this approach when your audience will feel neutral about your message or will be pleased to hear from you.
- Indirect approach *(inductive).* Put the evidence first and the main idea later. Use this approach when your audience is likely to be displeased about what you have to say.

These two basic approaches may be applied either to short messages (memos and letters) or to long ones (reports, proposals, presentations; discussed in Part 5).

To choose between the two alternatives, you must first analyze your audience's likely reaction to your purpose and message. Your audience's reaction will fall somewhere on the continuum shown in Figure 5.4. As CHG's Julian Santoyo knows, the direct approach is generally fine when your audience will be receptive—eager, interested, pleased, or even neutral. But if they're likely to be resistant to your message—displeased, uninterested, or unwilling—you'll usually have better results with the indirect approach.

Bear in mind, however, that each message is unique. You can't solve all your communication problems with a simple formula. If you're sending bad news to outsiders, for example, an indirect approach is probably best. On the other hand, you might want to get directly to the point in a memo to an associate, even if your message is unpleasant. The direct approach might also be the best choice for long messages, regardless of the audience's attitude, because delaying the main point could cause confusion and frustration.

Table 5.3 summarizes how your approach may differ depending on the message type and likely audience reaction. Note that in each message type, the opening, the body, and the close all play an important part in getting your message across. When used with good judgment, these basic types of business messages can be powerful tools of communication.[8] Just remember that the first priority is to make the message clear.

The direct approach is effective for messages that will please the reader or will cause no particular reaction.

Routine, Good-News, and Goodwill Messages The most straightforward business messages are routine, good-news, and goodwill messages. If you're inquiring about products or placing an order, your audience will usually want to comply. If you're announcing a price cut, granting an adjustment, accepting an invitation, or congratulating a colleague, your audience will most likely be pleased to hear from you. If you're providing routine information as part of your regular business, your audience will probably be neutral, neither pleased nor displeased.

Aside from being easy to understand, these kinds of messages are easy to formulate. In most cases you get right down to business. The direct approach is the most natural approach, perhaps the most useful and businesslike. You can state your point or request directly, without searching for some creative introduction. By starting off with the positive point, you put your audience in a good frame of mind and encourage them to be receptive to whatever else

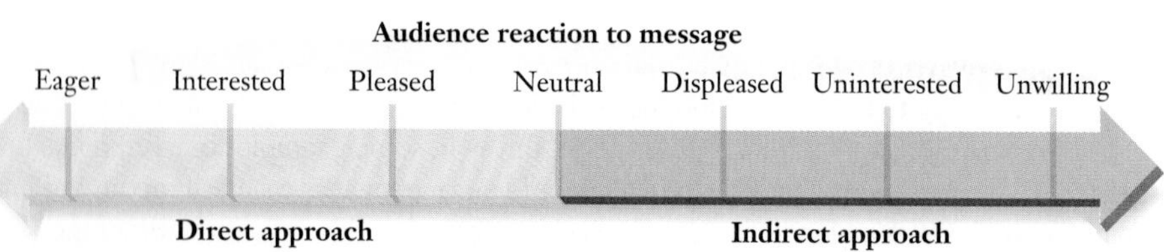

Figure 5.4
Audience Reaction and Organizational Approach

TABLE 5.3

CHOOSING BETWEEN THE DIRECT AND INDIRECT APPROACHES

Message Type	Likely Audience Reaction	Approach	Opening	Body	Close
Routine, good-news, and goodwill messages	Pleased or neutral	Direct	Begin with the main idea, the request, or the good news.	Provide necessary details.	Close with a cordial comment, a reference to the good news, or a statement about the specific action desired.
Bad-news messages	Displeased	Indirect	Begin with a neutral statement that acts as a transition to the reasons for the bad news.	Give reasons to justify a negative answer. State or imply the bad news, and make a positive suggestion.	Close cordially.
Persuasive messages	Uninterested or unwilling	Indirect	Begin with a statement or question that captures attention.	Arouse the audience's interest in the subject. Build the audience's desire to comply.	Request action.

you have to say. This approach also emphasizes the pleasing aspect of your message by putting it right up front, where it's the first thing recipients see. Routine, good-news, and goodwill messages are discussed in greater detail in Chapter 7.

Bad-News Messages If you're turning down a job applicant, refusing credit, or denying a request for an adjustment, your audience will be disappointed; in these cases it's best to use the indirect approach—putting the evidence first and the main idea later. You may be tempted to blurt out an unpleasant message in the most direct and unvarnished manner, believing that you're just being businesslike or that the audience is too far away or unimportant to matter. In many cases, however, bluntness is more expedient than practical. Astute businesspeople know that every person encountered has the potential to be a customer, a supplier, or a contributor or to influence someone who is a customer, a supplier, or a contributor. Such communicators take a little extra care with their bad-news messages.

If you have bad news, try to put it somewhere in the middle, cushioned by other, more positive ideas.

The challenge lies in being honest but kind. You don't want to sacrifice ethics and mislead the audience; at the same time, you don't want to be overly blunt. To achieve a good mix of candor and kindness, imagine you're talking face to face with someone you want to remain on good terms with, and then focus on some aspect of the situation that makes the bad news a little easier to take (see Figure 5.5).

The first and last sections of a message make the biggest impression. If Levasseur had refused in the first sentence of the letter in Figure 5.5, the reader might never have bothered to go on to the reasons or might have been in the wrong frame of mind to consider them. By putting

Figure 5.5
In-Depth Critique: Letter Delivering Bad News

The following letter shows how Jamie Levasseur, advertising manager at Paradigm Enterprises, responded when asked to act as industry chairperson for a dinner sponsored by the National Conference of Christians and Jews. Note how she cushions the bad news.

676 Fifth Avenue, Ninth Floor
New York, New York 10103
VOICE: 212/397-8888
FAX: 212/397-8877

March 6, 2000

Ms. Joyce Leland
Public Relations Officer
National Conference of Christians and Jews
2237 Welch Avenue
Houston, Texas 77219

Dear Ms. Leland:

Your invitation to act as industry chairperson for NCCJ's upcoming Anniversary Citation Dinner is a great honor. I thoroughly enjoyed serving in the role last year. Your members are a fine group with high ideals, and working with them was a privilege.

This year I'm involved with a remodeling project here at Paradigm that is consuming all my time—and then some. Therefore, although I would enjoy repeating the experience of working with NCCJ, I believe that someone else would be better able to give the assignment the attention it deserves.

Perhaps one of my colleagues would have the time to do the job the way it ought to be done. Enclosed is a brief list of colleagues (with address and phone information) who have voiced some interest in working with NCCJ. We want the advertising industry to be well represented.

I wish you and the rest of your committee the greatest success in achieving the goals set this year by NCCJ.

Sincerely,

Jamie Levasseur

Jamie Levasseur
Advertising Manager

sw

Enclosure

The letter begins with a neutral statement that provides a transition to the refusal.

The midsection explains the reason for the refusal and then states the bad news.

The writer takes care to introduce a positive thought.

The letter closes on a cordial note.

the explanation before the refusal, Levasseur focused attention on the reasons. Of course, you have to be sincere about your reasons. A reader can spot a phony excuse in a minute.

The indirect approach is neither manipulative nor unethical. As long as you can be honest and reasonably brief, you're better off opening a bad-news message with a neutral point and putting the negative information after the explanation. Then if you can close with something fairly positive, you're likely to leave the audience feeling okay—not great, but not hostile either. When you're the bearer of bad tidings, that's often about all you can hope for. This type of message is discussed further in Chapter 8.

Persuasive Messages The indirect approach is also useful when you know that your audience will resist your message (will be uninterested in your request or unwilling to comply without extra coaxing). Such resistance might be the likely reaction to a sales or collection letter, an unsolicited job application, or a request for a favor of some kind. In such cases, you have a better chance of getting through to the person if you lead off with something catchy. This doesn't mean that you should go in for gimmicks, but do try to think of something that will make your audience receptive to what you have to say. Mention a possible benefit, or refer to a problem that the recipient might have. Pose a question, or mention an interesting statistic.

Using the indirect approach gives you an opportunity to get your message across to an uninterested or skeptical audience.

Although you might argue that people are likely to feel manipulated by the indirect approach, the fact remains that you have to capture people's attention before you can persuade them to do something. If you don't, you really have no way to get the message across. You also have to get your audience to consider with an open mind what you have to say; to do this, you have to make an interesting point and provide supporting facts that encourage the audience to continue paying attention. Once you have them thinking, you can introduce your real purpose. Persuasive messages are discussed at greater length in Chapter 9.

Step 5: Composing Your Message

Once you've completed the planning process and have organized your message, you're ready to begin composing your first draft. If your schedule permits, put your outline or organization chart aside for a day or two; then review it with a fresh eye, looking for opportunities to improve the flow of ideas. When you feel confident that your structure will achieve your purpose with the intended audience, you can begin to write.

Composition is easiest if you've already figured out what to say and in what order, although you may need to pause now and then to find the right word. You may also discover as you go along that you can improve on your outline. Feel free to rearrange, delete, and add ideas, as long as you don't lose sight of your purpose. As you compose your first draft, pay some attention to your style and tone. Select words that match the tone you're trying to achieve. Try to create effective sentences and to develop coherent paragraphs. But don't worry about getting everything perfect. Just put down your ideas as quickly as you can. You'll have time to revise and refine the material later. Remember, good business writing is learned by imitation and practice. So as you read business journals, newspapers, even novels, make a note of words, phrases, style, or paragraphs you think are effective and keep them in a file. Then look through the file before you draft your next letter or report. Try using some of these ideas in your document. You may be surprised how helpful they are.

Composition is the process of drafting your message; polishing it is a later step.

Controlling Your Style and Tone

Style is the way you use words to achieve a certain **tone,** or overall impression. You can vary your style—your sentence structure and vocabulary—to sound forceful or passive, personal or impersonal, colorful or colorless. The right choice depends on the nature of your message and your relationship with the reader. Although style can be refined during the revision phase (see Chapter 6), you'll save time and a lot of rewriting if you use a style that allows you to achieve the desired tone right from the first.

When composing the message, vary the style to create a tone that suits the occasion.

Your use of language is one of your credentials, a badge that identifies you as being a member of a particular group. Try to make your style clear, concise, and grammatically correct, and try to make it conform to the norms of your group. Every organization has its own stylistic conventions, and many occupational groups share a particular vocabulary.

The tone of your business messages may span a continuum from informal to conversational to formal. CHG's Julian Santoyo writes in a somewhat informal style, appropriate for his company's size and atmosphere. Most business messages fall around the conversational level of formality, using plain language that is neither stiff nor full of slang.

Avoid Obsolete and Pompous Language

Obsolete formal phrases can obscure meaning.

The language of business used to be much more formal than it is today, and a few out-of-date phrases remain from the old days. Perhaps the best way to determine whether you're using them is to ask yourself, "Would I say this if I were talking with someone face to face?"

OBSOLETE	UP-TO-DATE
in due course	today, tomorrow (or a specific time)
permit me to say that	(permission is not necessary, just say what you wish)
we are in receipt of	we have received
pursuant to	(omit)
in closing, I'd like to say	(omit)
the undersigned	I; me
kindly advise	please let us know
we wish to inform you	(just say it)
attached please find	enclosed is
it has come to my attention	I have just learned; Ms. Garza has just told me
our Mr. Lydell	Mr. Lydell, our credit manager
please be advised that	(omit)

The use of pompous language suggests that you are a pompous person.

Pompous language is similar to out-of-date phrases. People use big words, trite expressions, and overly complicated sentences when they are trying to impress somebody. But as Table 5.4 and the following examples show, pompous words sound stiff, puffed up, and roundabout.

POOR	IMPROVED
Upon procurement of additional supplies, I will initiate fulfillment of your order.	I will fill your order when I receive more supplies.
Perusal of the records indicates a substantial deficit for the preceding accounting period due to the utilization of antiquated mechanisms.	The records show a company loss last year due to the use of old equipment.

Use a Conversational Tone

Although various situations require various tones, most business communicators today use a conversational tone that sounds businesslike without being stuffy. Rather than trying to impress the reader with an extensive vocabulary, good communicators focus on being sensible,

TABLE 5.4

POMPOUS VERSUS CONVERSATIONAL LANGUAGE

Pompous	Conversational	Pompous	Conversational
accompany	go with	in order to	to
accordingly	so	in the event that	if
aforementioned	these, the	numerous	many
appeared to be	seemed	possessed	had
attributable	due	prior to	before
compensate	pay	provided that	if
considerable	large	purchase	buy
facilitate	help	a number of	a few, several, many
foregoing	this, these	stated	said
furthermore	also, in addition	terminate	end
inasmuch as	because	utilize	use
indicate	show	visualize	see

logical, and objective as they provide supporting facts and a rationale. In addition, they avoid intimacy, humor, and preaching or bragging:

To achieve a warm but businesslike tone

- Don't be too familiar
- Use humor only with great care
- Don't preach
- Don't brag

- *Intimacy.* Don't mention things about anyone's personal life unless you know the individual very well. Avoid phrases that imply intimacy, such as "just between you and me" and "as you and I are well aware." Be careful about sounding too folksy or chatty; such a familiar tone may be interpreted as an attempt to seem like an old friend when, in fact, you're not.
- *Humor.* Using humor can backfire, especially if you don't know your readers very well. What seems humorous to you may be deadly serious to others. Chances are slim that when you're communicating across cultures, your audience will appreciate your humor or even realize that you're trying to be funny.[9] Keep in mind that in written communication, there is often a lag time between when you compose your message and when it's read. Today's humor may not be very funny one week or one month from now.
- *Preaching and bragging.* Few things are more irritating than people who assume that they know it all and we know nothing. If, for some reason, you have to tell your audience something obvious, try to make the information unobtrusive. Place it in the middle of a paragraph, where it will sound like a casual comment as opposed to a major revelation. Likewise, bragging about your accomplishments or the size or profitability of your organization may be especially annoying (unless, of course, your audience belongs to your organization). You're likely to evoke a negative reaction with comments like "We at McMann's, which is the oldest and most respected firm in the city, have a reputation for integrity that's beyond question."

Your conversational tone may become less or more formal, depending on the situation. For instance, if you're addressing an old friend, your conversational tone may tend more toward an informal level. Of course, in business messages, your tone would never be as informal as it would with family members or school friends. On the other hand, if you're in a large organization and you're communicating with your superiors or if you're communicating to customers, your conversational tone would tend to be more formal and respectful. Consider the formality and pompous tone of this letter:[10]

Dear Ms. Navarro:

Enclosed please find the information that was requested in our telephone communication on May 14. As was mentioned at that time, Midville Hospital has significantly more doctors of exceptional quality than any other health facility in the state.

As you were also informed, our organization has offices located throughout the state. In the event that you need a specialist, our professionals will refer you to the most appropriate party. You are also entitled to utilize one of our numerous programs that will assist you and your family in achieving the highest level of health possible.

Please contact me in the event that you have questions or would like additional information.

Most sincerely yours,
Samuel G. Berenz

Now review Figure 5.6 to see how the letter can be rewritten in both a professional and an informal tone.

Use Plain English

Plain English is close to spoken English and can be easily understood.

Plain English is a way of writing and arranging technical materials so that your audience can understand your meaning. Because it's close to the way people normally speak, plain English is easily understood by anyone with an eighth- or ninth-grade education. If you've ever tried to make sense of an obtusely worded legal document or credit agreement, you can understand why governments and corporations today are endorsing plain-English initiatives.[11] In fact, these initiatives have already led to plain-English loan and credit-card application forms, insurance policies, investment documents, and real estate contracts (see "Sharpening Your Skills: Use Plain English, Please!" on pages 144–145).

These two business letters to Gabriella Navarro deliver the same information included in the letter above, but they omit the formal tone.

PROFESSIONAL TONE (RECOMMENDED FOR MOST BUSINESS COMMUNICATION)	INFORMAL TONE (USE ONLY WITH FRIENDS AND CLOSE BUSINESS ASSOCIATES)
Dear Ms. Navarro: I am sending along the information you requested on Friday. As I mentioned, Midville Hospital has more doctors than any hospital in the state. In addition, we have a vast network of doctors and other health professionals with offices throughout Massachusetts and in parts of New Hampshire and Rhode Island. If you need a specialist, they can refer you to the right one. You and your family can also participate in numerous programs, such as smoking-cessation classes, a 24-hour hotline with a registered nurse to answer your questions seven days a week, health fairs, and more. Feel free to call anytime between 9:00 and 5:00 Monday through Friday if you would like more information. Sincerely, Samuel G. Berenz	Dear Gabriella: Just sending along the information we talked about on Friday. As I said, Midville Hospital has more doctors than any hospital in the state. We also have an impressive network of doctors and other professionals with offices near your work or home. Need a specialist? They'll refer you to the right one. You and your family can also get health-wise, thanks to our numerous programs, such as classes to help you quit smoking or improve your overall fitness. We even have a health hotline designed to answer your health questions all day, every day. Want to know more? Just call. I'm at the office between 9:00 and 5:00, Monday through Friday. Take care, Sam

Figure 5.6
Professional versus Informal Tone

As an example, plain English has benefited mutual fund company Fidelity Investments, whose documents have been rewritten, reorganized, and redesigned to emphasize important sections and to include more graphics in an attempt to make them easier to comprehend.[12] Even software programmers are trying to simplify their language to communicate with product users. Indeed, people are sometimes amazed at what their audience can't grasp—like the programmer who exclaimed, "You mean he doesn't understand what pop out to DOS means?"[13]

Of course, plain English has some limitations. It lacks the precision necessary for scientific research, intense feeling, and personal insight. Moreover, it fails to embrace all cultures and dialects equally. Needless to say, it's intended for areas where English is the primary language; however, the lessons of plain English can also help you simplify messages intended for audiences who may speak English only as a second or even third language. For example, you will communicate more clearly and precisely with your intercultural audience by choosing words that have only one interpretation.[14]

Selecting the Best Words[15]

As a business communicator, you have to pay attention to correctness and effectiveness when choosing your words. Editors and grammarians occasionally have questions—and even disputes—about correct usage. The "rules" of grammar and usage are constantly changing to reflect changes in the way people speak. For example, many experts now prefer to treat the word *data* as a singular noun when it refers to a body of information, even though, technically, it is the plural form of *datum*. You be the judge: Which of the following sentences sounds better?

The two key aspects of word choice are
- Correctness
- Effectiveness

The data on our market share is consistent from region to region.

The data on our market share are consistent from region to region.

Although debating the finer points of usage may seem like nitpicking, using words correctly is important. If you make grammatical or usage errors, you lose credibility with your audience. Poor grammar is a mark of ignorance, and—rightly or wrongly—nobody puts much faith in an ignorant source. Even if an audience is broad minded enough to withhold judgment of the writer or speaker, grammatical errors are distracting.

If you have doubts about what is correct, don't be lazy. Look up the answer, and use the proper form of expression. Check the grammar and usage guide in this book (see Appendix I), or consult any number of special reference books and resources available in libraries, in bookstores, and on the Internet. Most authorities agree on the basic conventions.

If in doubt, check it out.

Just as important as using the correct words is choosing the *best* words for the job at hand. Word effectiveness is generally more difficult to achieve than correctness, particularly in written communication. Writers like CHG's Julian Santoyo have to work at their craft, using proven writing techniques to polish their style. The rest of this section discusses some of these techniques.

Use Functional and Content Words Correctly

Words can be divided into two main categories. *Functional words* express relationships and have only one unchanging meaning in any given context. They include conjunctions, prepositions, articles, and pronouns. Your main concern with functional words is to use them correctly. *Content words* are multidimensional and therefore subject to various interpretations. They include nouns, verbs, adjectives, and adverbs. These words carry the meaning of a sentence. Content words are the building blocks; functional words are the mortar. In the following sentence, all the content words are in italics:

Functional words (conjunctions, prepositions, articles, and pronouns) express relationships among content words (nouns, verbs, adjectives, and adverbs).

Some objective observers of the *cookie market give Nabisco* the *edge* in *quality,* but *Frito-Lay is lauded* for *superior distribution.*

SHARPENING YOUR SKILLS

USE PLAIN ENGLISH, PLEASE!

The goal of good writing should be to communicate, not to confuse; to make yourself understood, not to hide behind words. Take this example:

> The applicability of the general information and administrative procedures set forth below accordingly will vary depending on the investor and the record-keeping system established for a shareholder's investment in the Fund. Participants in 401(k) and other plans should first consult with the appropriate persons at their employer or refer to the plan materials before following any of the procedures below.

With prose like that, no wonder investors simply roll such documents into fly swatters or throw them away, turning to brokers, accountants, and lawyers for answers and direction. But that's all changing. Today's consumers have had enough. They want to be able to comprehend the leases, mortgages, and sales contracts they sign and the investments they purchase.

Even Security and Exchange Commission chairman Arthur Levitt Jr. has looked at a prospectus (initial document offering a security for sale) and found he couldn't understand it. "I realized the SEC did a good job requiring disclosure, but not enough to make sure documents were in a form most investors could understand." So in January 1998, the SEC mandated companies to write all investment documents in plain English. And two months later it authorized investment funds to use a three- to six-page document called a profile rather than a lengthy prospectus.

All new prospectus language must follow six basic writing principles:

- Use active voice.
- Use short sentences.
- Use everyday words.
- Use lists to present complex material.
- Avoid legal jargon.
- Do not use multiple negatives.

Both functional words and content words are necessary, but your effectiveness as a communicator depends largely on your ability to choose the right content words for your message. So let's take a closer look at two important dimensions for classifying content words.

Content words have both a denotative (explicit, specific) meaning and a connotative (implicit, associative) meaning.

Connotation and Denotation Content words have both a denotative and a connotative meaning. The **denotative meaning** is the literal, or dictionary, meaning; the **connotative meaning** includes all the associations and feelings evoked by the word. Consider *dirt,* a

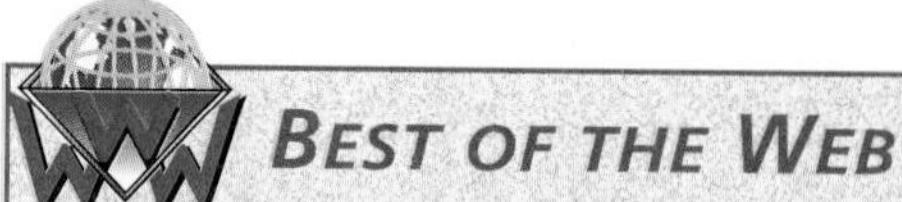

BEST OF THE WEB

Connect Now with a Virtual Library

You can have more than 200 essential sources of information right at your fingertips with the Virtual Reference Desk. The site includes an almanac, an encyclopedia, a dictionary, a thesaurus, an atlas, a Zip Code directory, a virtual newspaper, a weather site, an e-mail address locator, 260 search engines in 19 categories, and more.

http://www.refdesk.com/outline.html

Take our example paragraph. In plain English, this 60-word mess becomes one simple thought: "If you are investing through a large retirement plan or other special program, follow the instructions in your program material."

Although some companies are concerned that writing documents in plain English will compromise disclosure and increase a company's liability, many companies are finding that it doesn't. "In many ways, we reduced our liability because we have created a document that is much clearer and less ambiguous," notes one employee of Bell Atlantic. Others agree. Even Citibank discovered that after it introduced a plain-English promissory note, the number of company collection lawsuits fell dramatically. The clearer writing simply made it easier for borrowers to understand their obligations.

If clear writing makes such good sense, who's against the plain-English movement? Some lawyers purposely choose to be obscure so that they can control and limit access to vital information. After all, it helps if the other side doesn't know what they're signing. And some lawyers don't want sales managers to be able to look at a statute and decide for themselves whether a rebate program is legal. They prefer to have such people call a lawyer to interpret the legal gobbledegook.

Other legal professionals disagree. They want to see lawyers speak plain English—not the King's English. So some state bar associations are strongly endorsing the plain-language movement. Take the State Bar of Texas. It offers sarcastic "legaldegook" awards for especially atrocious writing. And the Michigan Bar has embraced a goal to abolish legalese by 2000. Even law schools are jumping on the bandwagon by investing heavily in programs designed to teach students to write more like E. B. White and George Orwell.

In fact, the plain-English initiative has generated such momentum that in 1998, President Clinton signed an executive order requiring federal agencies to communicate in writing that is "clearer and easier to understand." Agencies are now required to use plain language in any new document explaining how to get a benefit or to comply with a requirement. In addition, all new regulations must use simple wording, and by 2002 all existing letters and notices must be revised. Imagine—an Internal Revenue Code in plain English.

1. How does writing in plain English affect a company's image?
2. If plain English involves simple, concise language, why don't more companies draft their documents using it?

---

word that has many connotations. A disapproving parent remarks, "Just look at you; you're covered in dirt." An investigative reporter tells the editor, "I've uncovered some interesting dirt on that politician." An Iowa farmer says, "My land is good; you've never seen darker dirt." The word is the same, but the connotations are different.

Some words have more connotations than others. If you say that a student has failed to pass the test, you're making a strong statement; you suggest that the person is inferior, incompetent, and second-rate. On the other hand, if you say that the student has achieved a score of 65 percent, you suggest something else. By replacing the word *failed,* you avoid a heavy load of negative connotations.

In business communication, avoid using terms that are high in connotative meaning. Words that have relatively few possible interpretations are less likely to be misunderstood. Furthermore, because you are usually trying to deal with things in an objective, rational manner, avoid emotion-laden comments.

Abstraction and Concreteness In addition to varying in connotative impact, content words also vary in their level of abstraction. An *abstract word* expresses a concept, quality, or characteristic instead of standing for a thing you can touch or see. Abstractions are usually broad, encompassing a category of ideas. They are often intellectual, academic, or philosophical. *Love, honor, progress, tradition,* and *beauty* are abstractions. *Concrete terms* are anchored in the tangible, material world. They stand for something particular: *chair, table, horse, rose, kick, kiss, red, green, two.* These words are direct, clear, and exact.

The more abstract a word, the more it is removed from the tangible, objective world of things that can be perceived with the senses.

You might suppose that concrete words are better than abstract words, because they are more precise. However, try to rewrite this sentence without using the italicized abstract words:

> We hold these *truths* to be *self-evident*, that all men are *created equal*, that they are *endowed* by their Creator with certain *unalienable Rights*, that among these are *Life, Liberty,* and the *Pursuit of Happiness.*

As you can see, the Declaration of Independence needs abstractions, and so do business messages. Abstractions permit us to rise above the common and tangible. They allow us to refer to such concepts as *morale, productivity, profits, quality, motivation,* and *guarantees*.

In business communication, use concrete, specific terms whenever possible; use abstractions only when necessary.

Even though they're indispensable, abstractions can be troublesome. They tend to be fuzzy and subject to many interpretations. They also tend to be boring. It isn't always easy to get excited about ideas, especially if they're unrelated to concrete experience. The best way to minimize such problems is to blend abstract terms with concrete ones, the general with the specific. State the concept, then pin it down with details expressed in more concrete terms. Save the abstractions for ideas that cannot be expressed any other way.

Take a sample of your writing and circle all the nouns. How many of them point to a specific person, place, or object? The ones that do are concrete and specific. Look at the vague nouns; can you replace them with terms that are more vivid? Now underline all the adjectives. How many of them describe the exact color, size, texture, quantity, or quality of something? Bear in mind that words such as *small, numerous, sizable, near, soon, good,* and *fine* are imprecise. Try to replace them with terms that are more accurate. Instead of referring to a *sizable loss,* talk about a *loss of $32 million*.

Find Words That Communicate

Wordsmiths are journalists, public relations specialists, editors, letter and report writers—anyone who earns a living by crafting words. Unlike poets, novelists, or dramatists, wordsmiths don't try for dramatic effects. They are mainly concerned with being clear, concise, and accurate in their use of language. To reach this goal, they emphasize words that are strong and familiar, and they avoid hiding their message under unnecessary syllables. When you compose your message, do your best to think like a wordsmith.

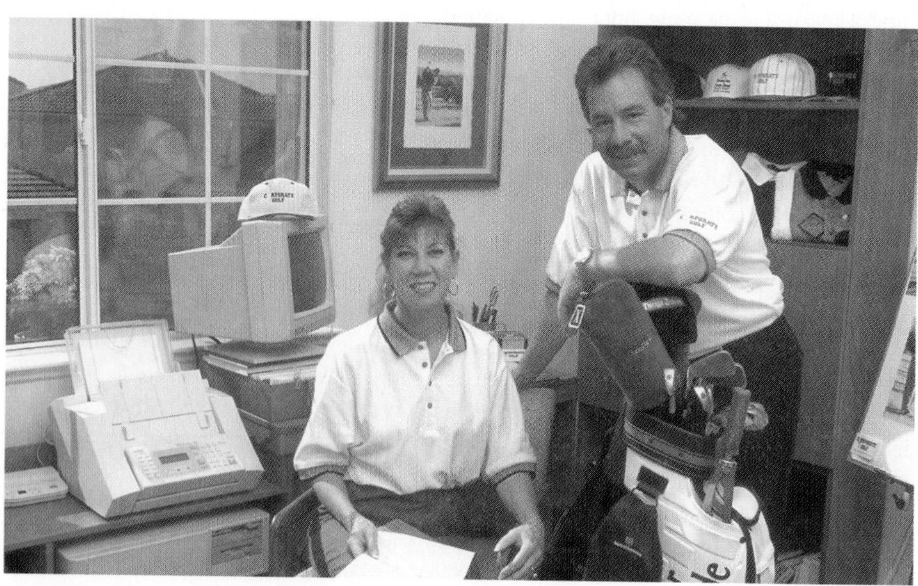

Nena Renaud and Bill Bryan use printers, scanners, and a multifunction desktop system to streamline the preparation and delivery of their business messages.

Strong Words Nouns and verbs are the most concrete words in any message, so use them as much as you can. Although adjectives and adverbs obviously have parts to play, use them sparingly. They often call for subjective judgments, and business communication strives to be objective. Verbs are especially powerful because they carry the action; they tell what's happening in the sentence. The more dynamic and specific the verb, the better. Instead of settling for *rise* or *fall,* look for something more meaningful and descriptive, such as *soar* or *plummet.*

Nouns and verbs are more concrete than adverbs and adjectives.

Given a choice of words, choose the one that most clearly and specifically expresses your thought:

AVOID WEAK PHRASES	USE STRONG TERMS
wealthy businessperson	tycoon
business prosperity	boom
hard times	slump

Familiar Words You'll communicate best with words that are familiar to your readers. At the same time, bear in mind that words familiar to one reader might be unfamiliar to another:

Familiar words are preferable to unfamiliar ones, but try to avoid overworked terms (clichés).

AVOID UNFAMILIAR WORDS	USE FAMILIAR WORDS
ascertain	find out, learn
consummate	close, bring about
peruse	read, study
circumvent	avoid
increment	growth, increase
unequivocal	certain

Avoid Worn-Out Phrases and Clichés

Although familiar words are generally the best choice, beware of terms and phrases so common that they have become virtually meaningless. Most people use these phrases not because they think it makes their speech and writing more vivid and inviting but because they don't know how to express themselves otherwise.[16] Because clichés are used so often, readers tend to slide right by them to whatever is coming next:

bottom of the barrel	an uphill battle	writing on the wall
call the shots	taken by storm	an arm and a leg
a new ballgame	worst nightmare	fall through the cracks

Also handle technical or professional terms with care. Used in moderation, they add precision and authority to a message. However, many people simply don't understand them, and even a technically sophisticated audience will be lulled to sleep by too many. Let your audience's vocabulary be your guide. If they share a particular jargon, you may enhance your credibility by speaking their language. When addressing a group of engineers, you might refer to *meteorological effects on microwave propagation.* When addressing an ordinary audience, you'd probably do better referring to the *effects of weather on radio waves.*

DID YOU KNOW?

The phrase *Achilles' heel*—used to describe the weak spot that every person has regardless of how tough she or he may be—got its start when one mother decided to give her son a kind of immortality. As the story goes, hours after Achilles was born, his mother dipped him into the mysterious waters of the river Styx to coat him with supernatural protection. Yet, Achilles was killed during the Trojan War. He died from a wound to his heel—the part his mother held when she dipped him.

Creating Effective Sentences

In English, words don't make much sense until they're combined in a sentence to express a complete thought. Thus, *Jill, receptionist, the, smiles,* and *at* can be organized into "Jill smiles at the receptionist." Now you can begin exploring the possibilities for improvement, looking at how well each word performs its particular function. Nouns and noun equivalents are the

Every sentence contains a subject (noun or noun equivalent) and a predicate (verb and related words).

topics (or subjects) you're communicating about, and verbs and related words (or predicates) make statements about those subjects. In a complicated sentence, adjectives and adverbs modify the subject and the statement, and various connectors hold the words together.

The Three Types of Sentence

To give your writing variety, use the three types of sentences:

- Simple
- Compound
- Complex

Sentences come in three basic varieties: simple, compound, and complex. A **simple sentence** has a single subject and a single predicate, although it may be expanded by nouns and pronouns serving as objects of the action and by modifying phrases. Here's a typical example (with the subject underlined once and the predicate verb underlined twice):

> Profits have increased in the past year.

A **compound sentence** expresses two or more independent but related thoughts of equal importance joined by *and, but,* or *or*. In effect, a compound sentence is a merger of two or more simple sentences (independent clauses) that deal with the same basic idea. For example:

> Wage rates have declined by 5 percent, and employee turnover has been high.

The independent clauses in a compound sentence are always separated by a comma or by a semicolon (in which case the conjunction—*and, but, or*—is dropped).

A **complex sentence** expresses one main thought (the independent clause) and one or more subordinate thoughts (dependent clauses) related to it, often separated by a comma. The subordinate thought, which comes first in the following sentence, could not stand alone:

> Although you may question Gerald's conclusions, you must admit that his research is thorough.

When constructing a sentence, use the form that best fits the thought you want to express. The structure of the sentence should match the relationship of the ideas. If you have two ideas of equal importance, express them as two simple sentences or as one compound sentence. However, if one of the ideas is less important than the other, place it in a dependent clause and form a complex sentence. This compound sentence uses a conjunction to join two ideas that aren't truly equal:

> The chemical products division is the strongest in the company, and its management techniques should be adopted by the other divisions.

In the complex sentence that follows, the first thought has been made subordinate to the second. Note how much more effective the second idea is when the cause-and-effect relationship has been established:

> Because the chemical products division is the strongest in the company, its management techniques should be adopted by the other divisions.

In complex sentences, the placement of the dependent clause should be geared to the relationship between the ideas expressed. If you want to emphasize the idea, put the dependent clause at the end of the sentence (the most emphatic position) or at the beginning (the second most emphatic position). If you want to downplay the idea, bury the dependent clause within the sentence.

> **Most Emphatic:** The handbags are manufactured in Mexico, *which has lower wage rates than the United States.*
>
> **Emphatic:** *Because wage rates are lower there,* the handbags are manufactured in Mexico.
>
> **Least Emphatic:** Mexico, *which has lower wage rates,* was selected as the production point for the handbags.

To make your writing as effective as possible, balance all three sentence types. If you use too many simple sentences, you can't properly express the relationships among ideas.

If you use too many long, compound sentences, your writing will sound monotonous. On the other hand, an uninterrupted series of complex sentences is hard to follow.

Sentence Style

Of course, sentence style varies from culture to culture. German sentences are extremely complex, with lots of modifiers and appositives; Japanese and Chinese languages don't even have sentences in the same sense that Western languages do.[17] Basically, whether a sentence in English is simple, compound, or complex, it should be grammatically correct, efficient, readable, interesting, and appropriate for your audience. In general, strive for straightforward simplicity. For most business audiences, clarity and efficiency take precedence over literary style. The following guidelines will help you achieve these qualities in your own writing.

Rely on the Active Voice Active voice makes your writing more vigorous and concise and generally easier to understand.[18] You're using **active voice** when the subject (the "actor") comes before the verb and the object of the sentence (the "acted upon") follows the verb: "John rented the office." You're using **passive voice** when the subject follows the verb and the object precedes it: "The office was rented by John." As you can see, the passive verb combines the helping verb *to be* with a form of the verb that is usually similar to the past tense. Using passive verbs makes sentences longer and deemphasizes the subject. Active verbs produce shorter, stronger sentences:

Active sentences are stronger than passive ones.

Avoid Passive Sentences	Use Active Sentences
Sales were increased by 32 percent last month.	Sales increased by 32 percent last month.
The new procedure is thought by the president to be superior.	The president thinks the new procedure is superior.
There are problems with this contract.	This contract has problems.
It is necessary that the report be finished by next week	The report must be finished by next week.

Of course, in some situations, using the passive voice makes sense. You may want to be diplomatic when pointing out a problem or error of some kind, so you might say, "The shipment was lost" rather than "You lost the shipment." The passive version seems less like an accusation because the emphasis is on the lost shipment rather than on the person responsible. Similarly, you may want to point out what's being done without taking or attributing either the credit or the blame, so you might say something like "The production line is being analyzed to determine the source of problems." In other cases, you may want to avoid personal pronouns in order to create an objective tone. So in a formal report you might say, "Criteria have been established for evaluating capital expenditures."

Use passive sentences to soften bad news, to put yourself in the background, or to create an impersonal tone.

Emphasize Key Thoughts In every message, some ideas are more important than others. You can emphasize these key ideas through your sentence style. One obvious technique is to give important points the most space. When you want to call attention to a thought, use extra words to describe it. Consider this sentence:

Emphasize parts of a sentence by
- Giving them more space
- Putting them at the beginning or at the end of the sentence
- Making them the subject of the sentence

> The chairperson of the board called for a vote of the shareholders.

To emphasize the importance of the chairperson, you might describe her more fully:

> The chairperson of the board, who has considerable experience in corporate takeover battles, called for a vote of the shareholders.

You can increase the emphasis even more by adding a separate, short sentence to augment the first:

> The chairperson of the board called for a vote of the shareholders. She has considerable experience in corporate takeover battles.

Another way to emphasize an idea is to place it at either the beginning or the end of a sentence:

LESS EMPHATIC	MORE EMPHATIC
We are cutting the *price* to stimulate demand.	To stimulate demand, we are cutting the *price.*

You can also call attention to a thought by making it the subject of the sentence. In the following example, the emphasis is on the person:

> *I* can write letters much more quickly using a computer.

In this version, the computer takes center stage:

> The *computer* enables me to write letters much more quickly.

Techniques like this one give you a great deal of control over the way your audience interprets what you have to say.

DID YOU KNOW?

Triplets tend to be pleasing to the ear. When describing or listing items, try groups of three. But be sure there's a logical order to the three items such as *morning, noon, and night* or *concise, informative, and well-written,* and place the most powerful word last in the phrase.

Vary the Sentence Length Variety is the key to making your message interesting. When you write, you create a rhythm with your words and sentence structure that emphasizes important points, enlivens the writing style, and makes the information appealing for the reader. Although good business writers use short sentences most of the time, too many short sentences in a row can make your writing choppy. Conversely, if all your sentences move at the same plodding gait, you're likely to lull your reader to sleep. So, to be interesting, use a variety of both short and long sentences.

Break long sentences into shorter ones to improve readability.

Long sentences are usually harder to understand than short sentences because they are packed with information that must all be absorbed at once. On the other hand, long sentences are especially well suited for grouping or combining ideas, listing points, and summarizing or previewing information. Medium-length sentences (those with about 20 words) are useful for showing the relationships among ideas. Short sentences are tailor-made for emphasizing important information. Most good business writing has an average sentence length of 20 words or fewer. This figure is the average, not a ceiling. (Of course, for audiences abroad, varying sentence length can create translation problems for the reader, so stick to short sentences in international messages.)[19]

Questions are another way to punch up your writing, because they stop the motion: The answer starts it up again. Consider the following:

> Frank Deitch is an excellent employee who fully deserves the Employee of the Year Award. Why? The answer is simple. He understands every aspect of his position and is results driven.

Lists are effective tools for highlighting and simplifying material.

Use Bullets and Lists An effective alternative to using straight sentences is to set off important ideas in a **list,** a series of words, names, or items. Lists can show the sequence of ideas or visually heighten their impact. In addition, they facilitate the skimming process for busy readers, simplify complex subjects, highlight the main point, break up the page visually, and give the reader a breather.

When creating a list, you can separate items with numbers, letters, or bullets (a general term for any kind of graphical element that precedes each item). Bullets are generally preferred over numbers unless the sequence of events is critical (in other words, the steps in a process must be completed in a specific order). For example, these three steps need to be performed in the order indicated, and the numbers make that clear:

1. Find out how many employees would like on-site day-care facilities.
2. Determine how much space the day-care center would require.
3. Estimate the cost of converting a conference room for the on-site facility.

When using lists, make sure to introduce them clearly so that people know what they're about to read. Consider the following example:

> The board of directors met to discuss the revised annual budget. To keep expenses in line with declining sales, the directors voted to:
>
> - Cut everyone's salary by 10 percent
> - Close the employee cafeteria
> - Reduce travel expenses

Note that the items in the sample lists are phrased in parallel form. In other words, if one item begins with a verb, all subsequent items begin with a verb. If one is a noun phrase, all should be noun phrases.

Developing Coherent Paragraphs

A paragraph is a cluster of sentences all related to the same general topic. It is a unit of thought. A series of paragraphs makes up an entire composition. Each paragraph is an important part of the whole, a key link in the train of thought. As you compose your message, think about the paragraphs and their relationship to one another.

Paragraphs are functional units that revolve around a single thought.

When you're talking to someone face to face, you develop your paragraphs informally, using tone of voice and gestures to signal the relationships among ideas. You pause to indicate that you have completed one topic and are ready to begin another, a new "paragraph." In a written document, on the other hand, paragraphs are developed more formally. Each paragraph is separated from other units of thought by the typographical device of skipping a line or indenting the first line.

Elements of the Paragraph

Paragraphs vary widely in length and form. You can communicate effectively in one short paragraph or in pages of lengthy paragraphs, depending on your purpose, your audience, and your message. The typical paragraph contains three basic elements: a topic sentence, related sentences that develop the topic, and transitional words and phrases.

Most paragraphs consist of a topic sentence, related sentences, and transitional elements.

Topic Sentence Every properly constructed paragraph is **unified;** it deals with a single topic. The sentence that introduces that topic is called the **topic sentence.** In informal and creative writing, the topic sentence may be implied rather than stated. In business writing, the topic sentence is generally explicit and is often the first sentence in the paragraph. The topic sentence gives readers a summary of the general idea that will be covered in the rest of the paragraph. The following examples show how a topic sentence can introduce the subject and suggest the way that subject will be developed:

The topic sentence
- Reveals the subject of the paragraph
- Indicates how the subject will be developed

> The medical products division has been troubled for many years by public relations problems. [In the rest of the paragraph, readers will learn the details of the problems.]
>
> Relocating the plant in New York has two main disadvantages. [The disadvantages will be explained in subsequent sentences.]
>
> To get a refund, you must supply us with some additional information. [The details will be described.]

Related Sentences The sentences that explain the topic sentence round out the paragraph. These related sentences must all have a bearing on the general subject, and they must provide enough specific details to make the topic clear:

> The medical products division has been troubled for many years by public relations problems. Since 1997 the local newspaper has published 15 articles that portray the division in a negative light. We have been accused of everything from mistreating laboratory animals to polluting the local groundwater. Our facility has been described as a health hazard. Our scientists are referred to as "Frankensteins," and our profits are considered "obscene."

Paragraphs are developed through a series of related sentences that provide details about the topic sentence.

The developmental sentences are all more specific than the topic sentence. Each one provides another piece of evidence to demonstrate the general truth of the main thought. Also, each sentence is clearly related to the general idea being developed; the relation between the sentences and the idea is what gives the paragraph its unity. A paragraph is well developed when it contains enough information to make the topic sentence convincing and interesting.

Each paragraph should cover a single idea. Use transitional words and phrases to show readers how paragraphs and the ideas within them are related.

Transitional Elements In addition to being unified and well developed, effective paragraphs are **coherent;** that is, they are arranged in a logical order so that the audience can understand the train of thought. When you complete a paragraph, your readers automatically assume that you've finished with a particular idea. Coherence is achieved through the use of transitions that show the relationship between paragraphs and among sentences within paragraphs. Transitions show how one thought is related to another and help readers understand the connections you are trying to make. You can establish transitions in various ways:

Some transitional devices:
- Connecting words (conjunctions)
- Repeated words or phrases
- Pronouns
- Words that are frequently paired

- Use connecting words: *and, but, or, nevertheless, however, in addition,* and so on.
- Echo a word or phrase from a previous paragraph or sentence: "A system should be established for monitoring inventory levels. *This system* will provide . . ."
- Use a pronoun that refers to a noun used previously: "Ms. Arthur is the leading candidate for the president's position. *She* has excellent qualifications."
- Use words that are frequently paired: "The machine has a *minimum* output of . . . Its *maximum* output is . . ."

Some transitional elements serve as mood changers; that is, they alert the reader to a change in mood from the previous paragraph. Some announce a total contrast with what's gone on before; some announce a causal relationship; and some signal a change in time. They all prime the reader for the change. At least a dozen words will do this job for you: *but, yet, however, nevertheless, still, instead, thus, therefore, meanwhile, now, later, today, subsequently,* and several more. Use them.[20]

Five Ways to Develop a Paragraph

Five ways to develop paragraphs:
- Illustration
- Comparison or contrast
- Cause and effect
- Classification
- Problem and solution

Paragraphs can be developed in many ways. Five of the most common techniques are illustration, comparison or contrast, cause and effect, classification, and problem and solution. Your choice of technique depends on your subject, your intended audience, and your purpose. In actual practice, you'll often combine two or more methods of development in a single paragraph. To add interest, you might begin by using illustration, shift to comparison or contrast, and then shift to problem and solution.

Before settling for the first approach that comes to mind, consider the alternatives. Think through various methods before committing yourself. If you fall into the easy habit of repeating the same old paragraph pattern time after time, your writing will be boring.

Illustration When you develop a paragraph by illustration, you give examples that demonstrate the general idea:

> Some of our most popular products are available through local distributors. For example, Everett & Lemmings carries our frozen soups and entrees. The J. B. Green Company carries our complete line of seasonings, as well as the frozen soups. Wilmont Foods, also a major distributor, now carries our new line of frozen desserts.

Comparison or Contrast Similarities or differences among thoughts often provide a strong basis for paragraph development. Here's an example developed by contrast:

> In previous years, when the company was small, the recruiting function could be handled informally. The need for new employees was limited, and each manager could comfortably screen and hire her or his own staff. Today, however, Gambit Products must undertake a major recruiting effort. Our successful bid on the Owens contract means that we will be doubling our labor force over the next six months. To hire that many people without disrupting our ongoing activities, we will create a separate recruiting group within the human resources department.

Cause and Effect When you develop a paragraph using the cause-and-effect technique, you focus on the reasons for something:

> The heavy-duty fabric of your Wanderer tent probably broke down for one of two reasons: (1) A sharp object punctured the fabric, and without reinforcement, the hole was enlarged by the stress of erecting the tent daily for a week; or (2) the fibers gradually rotted because the tent was folded and stored while still wet.

Classification Paragraphs developed by classification show how a general idea is broken into specific categories:

> Successful candidates for our supervisor trainee program generally come from one of several groups. The largest group, by far, consists of recent graduates of accredited data-processing programs. The next largest group comes from within our own company, as we try to promote promising clerical workers to positions of greater responsibility. Finally, we do occasionally accept candidates with outstanding supervisory experience in related industries.

Problem and Solution Another way to develop a paragraph is to present a problem and then discuss the solution:

> Selling handmade toys by mail is a challenge because consumers are accustomed to buying heavily advertised toys from major chains. However, if we develop an appealing catalog, we can compete on the basis of product novelty and quality. In addition, we can provide craftsmanship at a competitive price: a rocking horse made from birchwood, with a hand-knit tail and mane; a music box with the child's name painted on the top; a real Indian teepee, made by Native American artisans.

Paragraph Length and Headings

Some ideas are simply too big to be handled conveniently in one paragraph. Unless you break up the thoughts somehow, you'll end up with a three-page paragraph that's guaranteed to intimidate even the most dedicated reader. It's a fact that short paragraphs (of 100 words or fewer) are easier to read than long ones, and they make your writing look inviting. Direct-mail letters almost always use very short paragraphs because the writers know that their letters will be read more carefully that way. Even in memos, letters, and reports, you may want to emphasize an idea from time to time by isolating it in a short, forceful paragraph.

Short paragraphs are easier to read than long ones.

DID YOU KNOW?

Closing paragraphs should be as strong as opening ones. Even though closing paragraphs are the last ones your readers will see, they're the first they'll remember. Some people read the first paragraph, skim the body, and read the closing. Others read only the beginning and closing paragraphs. So don't risk weakening your message. Make your closing paragraph strong.

What do you do when you want to package a big idea in a short paragraph? Break the idea into subtopics and treat each subtopic in a separate paragraph, being careful to provide plenty of transitional elements. Take a look at Figure 5.7. By breaking the single paragraph into three shorter ones, the writer has done a good job of revising this draft—but many other approaches might be as effective. There is no such thing as the "right" way to develop a paragraph. As you write your message, try to use a variety of paragraph lengths. You might even use a one-sentence paragraph occasionally for emphasis.

Headings are another effective tool for organizing your material into short sections. They act as labels to group related paragraphs together. They not only help the reader understand you but can also serve as shortcuts, highlighting the material the reader may want to read or skip. Effective headings grab the reader's attention and make the copy easier to read. They should be informative, inviting, and in some cases intriguing.

Headings are similar to the subject line in memos and e-mail correspondence. Whereas subject lines merely identify the purpose of the memo or e-mail, headings also advise the reader about the material included in the paragraph. Both should be brief and put the reader

The openings to these two e-mail messages are identical except for their paragraph length. Which one is easier to read?

Date: Thursday, 26 September 2000, 11:14:09, EST
To: "Lee Gifford" ⟨lgifford@research.marketpix.com⟩
From: "Jeffrey Coombs" ⟨jeffc@hmr.com⟩
Subject: Donner Profile
Cc: "Donna Holland" ⟨Holland@hmr.com⟩
Bcc:
Attachments:

Mr. Gifford, here is the information you requested on the Donner Corporation:

Donner Corporation faced a major transformation, growing from a small, single-product company to a large, broadly based corporation in just three years. This changeover involved much more than simply adding on to the plant and hiring more people, because the quality of the existing staff and products was not good enough for a first-rate operation. The task therefore required both physical expansion and quality improvement. The physical expansion alone represented a major undertaking. The investment in facilities required $18 million. Over a three-year period, the organization spent more on the new plant and equipment than it had spent in the past seventeen years of its operation. To raise its competitive capability, the company had to develop new programs and organizational units and, at the same time, expand and upgrade its existing operations. It also needed to double the size of its staff by recruiting high-caliber people from many fields. This staffing had to be accomplished in an increasingly competitive labor market and without benefit of an experienced human resources department.

Date: Thursday, 26 September 2000, 11:14:09, EST
To: "Lee Gifford" ⟨lgifford@research.marketpix.com⟩
From: "Jeffrey Coombs" ⟨jeffc@hmr.com⟩
Subject: Donner Profile
Cc: "Donna Holland" ⟨Holland@hmr.com⟩
Bcc:
Attachments:

Mr. Gifford, here is the information you requested on the Donner Corporation:

Donner Corporation faced a major transformation, growing from a small, single-product company to a large, broadly based corporation in just three years. This changeover involved much more than simply adding on to the plant and hiring more people, because the quality of the existing staff and products was not good enough for a first-rate operation. The task therefore required both physical expansion and quality improvement.

The physical expansion alone represented a major undertaking. The investment in facilities required $18 million. Over a three-year period, the organization spent more on the new plant and equipment than it had spent in the past seventeen years of its operation.

To raise its competitive capability, the company had to develop new programs and organizational units and, at the same time, expand and upgrade its existing operations. It also needed to double the size of its staff by recruiting high-caliber people from many fields. This staffing had to be accomplished in an increasingly competitive labor market and without benefit of an experienced human resources department.

Figure 5.7
Effect of Paragraph Length on Readability

CHECKLIST FOR ORGANIZING AND COMPOSING BUSINESS MESSAGES

A. Organize Your Message
  1. Recognize good organization.
    a. Subject and purpose are clear.
    b. Information is directly related to subject and purpose.
    c. Ideas are grouped and presented logically.
    d. All necessary information is included.
  2. Achieve good organization.
    a. Define the main idea.
      i. Stimulate your creativity with brainstorming techniques.
      ii. Identify a "hook" that will motivate the audience to respond to your message in the way you intend.
      iii. Evaluate whether the main idea is realistic given the length limitations imposed on the message.
      iv. Collect any necessary information.
    b. Decide what to say.
      i. Start with the main idea.
      ii. State the major points.
      iii. Illustrate with evidence.
    c. Organize the message to respond to the audience's probable reaction.
      i. Use the direct approach when your audience will be neutral, pleased, interested, or eager.
      ii. Use the indirect approach when your audience will be displeased, uninterested, or unwilling.

B. Compose Your Message
  1. Generate ideas.
    a. Get ideas down as quickly as you can.
    b. Rearrange, delete, and add ideas without losing sight of your purpose.
  2. Vary the style to create a tone that suits the occasion.
    a. Use the appropriate level of formality.
    b. Avoid being overly familiar, using inappropriate humor, including obvious flattery, sounding preachy, bragging, or trying to be something you're not.
    c. Avoid obsolete and pompous language.
  3. Select the best words.
    a. Use plain English.
    b. Use concrete words that avoid negative connotations.
    c. Rely on nouns, verbs, and specific adjectives and adverbs.
    d. Choose words that are strong and familiar while avoiding clichés.
  4. Create effective sentences.
    a. Use simple, compound, and complex sentences, choosing the form that best fits the thought you want to express.
    b. Write mainly in the active voice, but use the passive voice to achieve specific effects.
    c. Emphasize key points through sentence style; give important points the most space.
    d. Vary the sentence length, but aim for an average of 20 words.
    e. Use lists.
  5. Create effective paragraphs.
    a. Be sure each paragraph contains a topic sentence, related sentences, and transitional elements.
    b. Choose a method of development that suits the subject: illustration, comparison or contrast, cause and effect, classification, problem and solution.
    c. Vary the length and structure of sentences within paragraphs.
    d. Mix paragraphs of different lengths, but aim for an average of 100 words.

right into the context of the message. For a reminder of the tasks involved in organizing and composing your message, see this chapter's Checklist for Organizing and Composing Business Messages.

Use headings to grab the reader's attention and divide material into short sections.

Shaping Your E-Mail Messages

Even though e-mail may have a reputation for speed and informality, you'll want to take time to compose your e-mail messages carefully. Organization and style are just as important for e-mail messages as for any other type of message. Although e-mail may at times seem transitory, it can emulate "snail mail" by having conventional business language, a respectful style, and a more formal format (including a traditional greeting, formalized headings, and a formal closing and signature), or it can be as informal and casual as a conversation between old friends.[21] Just be sure that the style you select is appropriate for the situation.

The formality of your e-mail depends on your audience and their culture.

How formal you make your message depends on both your audience and your purpose. Consider your reader's interests, needs, and feelings. For instance, when communicating with someone in another culture, take into account cultural differences. Be sure to give metric measurements (followed by English-system equivalents); spell out what format or system you're using for dates, times, numbers, and money; and generally use greetings that are more formal.[22] (For an in-depth discussion of e-mail etiquette, see Chapter 10).

Make responding easy.

As with any business communication, do your best to use correct spelling and proper grammar. Some e-mail old-timers insist that spelling and grammar take a backseat to your readiness to communicate.[23] But in business communication, e-mail needs to be as clear and as easy to understand as possible. In addition, make responding to your message easy by clearly stating the type of response you need. Word your message so that your audience can respond as briefly as possible, perhaps with a yes or a no. Also, ask for your audience's response early in your message, perhaps even in your subject line.[24]

Make Your Subject Line Informative

When your readers are deciding which messages to spend time on, they look at who each message is from, they check the subject line, and they may scan the first screen. If your message can't attract your reader's attention by that time, your e-mail will probably go unread and will perhaps be deleted.[25]

E-mail's subject line offers you an opportunity to gain your reader's interest.

An interesting subject line does more than just describe or classify the content of your message. By applying key words, humor, quotations, or questions, you can grab your reader's attention.[26] You have 25 to 30 characters to build interest for your message (longer lines are often truncated). Try wording your subject line so that it tells your reader what to do. For example: *Send figures for July sales* is much more informative than *July sales figures*. Of course, you don't want to use wild statements just to attract your reader's attention. Using *urgent* in your subject lines too often will soon have an effect quite different from the one intended.

Personalize Your E-Mail Message[27]

Use a greeting to make your e-mail more personal.

Even though your header displays whom your message is to and from, adding a greeting makes your e-mail message more personal. Naturally, whether you use a formal greeting (*Dear Professor Ingersoll*) or a more casual one (*Hi Marty!*) depends on your audience and your purpose. Your closing and signature also personalize your e-mail message. In most cases, use simple closings, such as *Thanks* or *Regards,* rather than more traditional business closings such as *Sincerely yours*. Of course, you may want to use a more formal closing for international e-mail.

After a simple closing, you can include a signature in several ways.

For your signature, you can simply type your name or initials on a separate line. You might put one or two hyphens before your name to set it off from the body of your e-mail. Or you may want to use a *signature file,* a short identifier that may include your name, company, postal address, fax number, other e-mail addresses, and sometimes even a short quotation or thought. Some users believe you should include only the information needed to contact you. Once you create a signature file, you can save it in your mail program and add it to e-mail messages without retyping it. You can also use a digital copy of your handwritten signature, which is becoming acceptable as legal proof of business transactions, especially when accompanied by a date stamp that is automatically inserted by your mail program.

The following message is typical of those sent using the Eudora Pro software package.

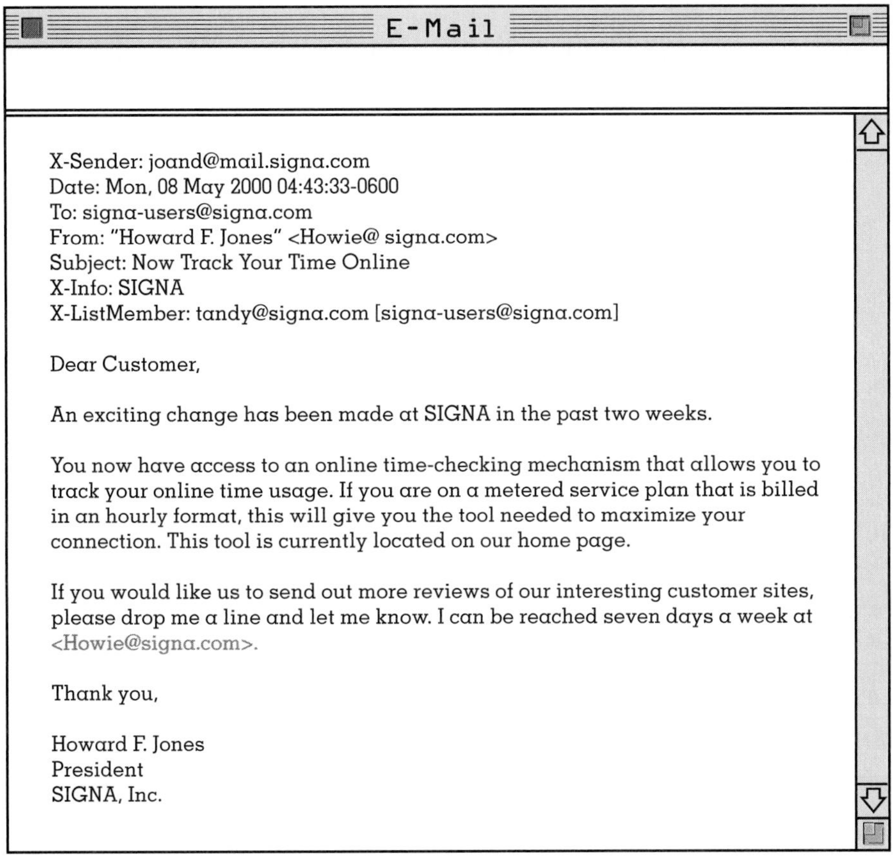

Figure 5.8
In-Depth Critique: On-Screen E-Mail Message

E-Mail

X-Sender: joand@mail.signa.com
Date: Mon, 08 May 2000 04:43:33-0600
To: signa-users@signa.com
From: "Howard F. Jones" <Howie@ signa.com>
Subject: Now Track Your Time Online
X-Info: SIGNA
X-ListMember: tandy@signa.com [signa-users@signa.com]

Dear Customer,

An exciting change has been made at SIGNA in the past two weeks.

You now have access to an online time-checking mechanism that allows you to track your online time usage. If you are on a metered service plan that is billed in an hourly format, this will give you the tool needed to maximize your connection. This tool is currently located on our home page.

If you would like us to send out more reviews of our interesting customer sites, please drop me a line and let me know. I can be reached seven days a week at <Howie@signa.com>.

Thank you,

Howard F. Jones
President
SIGNA, Inc.

The subject line captures customer interest.

Line length is well under 80 characters.

Jones has a friendly tone in this message to his customers.

The "you" attitude is apparent in the focus of the message as well as in the request for feedback.

Make Your E-Mail Easy to Follow

Some readers receive more e-mail than they can read, so in addition to making your subject line informative, make your e-mail easy to follow. Because e-mail is read on-screen, keep your audience's terminal in mind (see Figure 5.8). Computers and e-mail systems vary, so you want to ensure that your readers won't be confused by message lines that run off the screen or that wrap incorrectly. Press the *Enter* key at the end of each line, making sure your line has fewer than 80 characters (or fewer than 60 characters if your message is likely to be forwarded, because forwarding often indents messages a tab length). And, don't use font features such as boldface and italics—unless you're certain your reader's computer and e-mail software can reproduce such features.[28]

Consider how your message will appear on your audience's screen.

Your e-mail will be easier to follow if you keep your message short and concise by using short, focused paragraphs that are organized in a logical fashion. Whenever possible, try to limit your message to one screen or window. Of course, some e-mail messages will be longer than one screen; a few may even be longer than several screens. When it's necessary to send a long e-mail message, consider writing like a newspaper reporter, from the top down. Start with the "headline" statement and fill in the details in descending order of importance. That way you'll be sure to get your point across as early as possible, in case your reader doesn't have the time or interest to finish reading your message.[29]

Consider writing e-mail from the top down.

COMMUNICATION CHALLENGES AT COMMUNITY HEALTH GROUP

A recent newspaper article played on fears that HMOs might deny some people medical care to save costs, and Julian Santoyo is concerned because CHG was mentioned along with numerous other HMOs. Because CHG's member fees are paid by taxpayers (through the state government), management must correct any damage to CHG's public reputation.

Santoyo has facts at his fingertips that set CHG apart from other HMOs: CHG has been serving the indigent Hispanic and Asian communities for nearly 15 years; CHG's staff reflects this diversity (so staff members are able to understand members and speak their language); and CHG sinks its profits back into improving services (for example, adding a telephone advice nurse for members and supplying transportation to and from appointments—important because many of CHG's members can't afford cars). Also, CHG encourages members and physicians to practice preventive medicine to stave off illnesses and to keep medical visits down. Yes, CHG saves costs—but by encouraging good health, not by denying services.

TEAM CHALLENGE: Santoyo will be working with management to present this information, and he's asked you and some other employees to help him develop the best approach. Should a letter be sent to the local news media, to state government officials, or to both? If both, should they receive the same letter? Why or why not? Once you've decided these factors, make an outline of the message. Will you use the direct approach or the indirect approach? Why? What is the main idea? How will you gain and hold the audience's interest? How will you conclude the message?

INDIVIDUAL CHALLENGE: Following the outline you've developed, draft a one-page version of the message in the form you've chosen, for the audience you've identified. Using the facts supplied, choose the proper style and level of formality to create a message that will counteract the article's negative publicity.[30] ■

SUMMARY OF LEARNING OBJECTIVES

1. **Explain why good organization is important to both the communicator and the audience.** Good organization helps communicators compose messages more quickly and efficiently. Not only does it help the audience understand and accept the message, it also saves the audience time.
2. **Differentiate between the topic and the main idea of a message.** The topic is the broad subject of a message. The main idea makes a statement about the topic, either supporting it or explaining it.
3. **Discuss five prewriting techniques to help you identify the main idea of your message.** To identify the main idea, you can summarize it in a storyteller's tour, produce and then sort a random list of ideas, use an FCR worksheet, clarify it by using the journalistic approach, or use a question-and-answer chain to look at the subject from your audience's perspective.
4. **Compare the direct and indirect patterns for organizing ideas and explain under what circumstances each is generally used.** The direct approach puts the main idea first, followed by the evidence, and is generally used when the audience will want to comply or will be pleased to hear from you. The indirect approach puts the evidence first and the main idea later. It is generally used when the audience will be displeased about what you have to say.
5. **Cite seven techniques for maintaining a conversational tone in business messages.** To maintain a conversational tone, you should avoid being too familiar, using humor, or preaching. You should use plain English, strong words, familiar words, and functional and content words correctly.
6. **Discuss how to develop effective sentences and coherent paragraphs.** To create effective sentences, you should choose the sentence form that fits the thought you want to express, rely on the active voice, emphasize key thoughts, vary sentence length, and use lists. To develop coherent paragraphs, you should include enough information to make the topic sentence convincing and interesting, monitor your paragraph length, arrange paragraphs in a logical order, use transitions to show the relationships between paragraphs, and (where applicable) use headings.

CRITICAL THINKING QUESTIONS

1. When organizing the ideas for your business message, how can you be sure that what seems logical to you will also seem logical to your audience?
2. Do you think that cushioning bad news is manipulative?
3. Would you use a direct or an indirect approach to ask employees to work overtime to meet an important deadline? Please explain.
4. Which approach would you use to let your boss know that you'll be out half a day this week to attend your father's funeral—direct or indirect? Why?
5. Is it ever okay to use an indirect approach when writing e-mail? How can you put off the bad news when you have to state your purpose in the subject line? Explain.
6. What specific techniques of style could you use to create a formal, objective tone? An informal, personal tone?

7. In what business situations might you want to use words of high connotative value?
8. Evaluate this comment: "I already have more work than I can handle. I don't have any extra time to spend listing or outlining my messages. I generally get right to the point—without wasting words."

DOCUMENT FOR ANALYSIS

Define and Group Ideas

A writer is working on an insurance information brochure and is having trouble grouping the ideas logically into an outline. Prepare the outline, paying attention to appropriate subordination of ideas. Rewrite if necessary to give phrases a more consistent sound.

Accident Protection Insurance Plan

- Coverage is only pennies a day
- Benefit is $100,000 for accidental death on common carrier
- Benefit is $100 a day for hospitalization as result of motor vehicle or common carrier accident
- Benefit is $20,000 for accidental death in motor vehicle accident
- Individual coverage is only $17.85 per quarter; family coverage is just $26.85 per quarter
- No physical exam or health questions
- Convenient payment—billed quarterly
- Guaranteed acceptance for all applicants
- No individual rate increases
- Free, no-obligation examination period
- Cash paid in addition to any other insurance carried
- Covers accidental death when riding as fare-paying passenger on public transportation, including buses, trains, jets, ships, trolleys, subways, or any other common carrier
- Covers accidental death in motor vehicle accidents occurring while driving or riding in or on automobile, truck, camper, motor home, or nonmotorized bicycle

EXERCISES

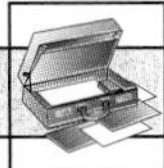

1. Suppose you are preparing to recommend that top management install a new heating system (using the cogeneration process). The following information is in your files. Eliminate topics that aren't essential; then arrange the other topics so that your report will give management a clear understanding of the heating system and a balanced, concise justification for installing it.

   History of the development of the cogeneration heating process
   Scientific credentials of the developers of the process
   Risks assumed in using this process
   Your plan for installing the equipment in your building
   Stories about its successful use in comparable facilities
   Specifications of the equipment that would be installed
   Plans for disposing of the old heating equipment
   Costs of installing and running the new equipment
   Advantages and disadvantages of using the new process
   Detailed ten-year cost projections
   Estimates of the time needed to phase in the new system
   Alternative systems that management might wish to consider

2. Indicate whether the direct or the indirect approach would be best in each of the following situations; then briefly explain why. Would any of these messages be inappropriate for e-mail? Explain.
   a. A letter asking when next year's automobiles will be put on sale locally
   b. A letter from a recent college graduate requesting a letter of recommendation from a former instructor
   c. A letter turning down a job applicant
   d. An announcement that because of high air-conditioning costs, the plant temperature will be held at 78 degrees during the summer
   e. A final request to settle a delinquent debt
3. If you were trying to persuade people to take the following actions, how would you organize your argument?
   a. You want your boss to approve your plan for hiring two new people.
   b. You want to be hired for a job.
   c. You want to be granted a business loan.
   d. You want to collect a small amount from a regular customer whose account is slightly past due.
   e. You want to collect a large amount from a customer whose account is seriously past due.
4. Suppose that end-of-term frustrations have produced this e-mail message to Professor Anne Brewer from a student who feels he should have received a B in his accounting class. If this message were recast into three or four clear sentences, the teacher might be more receptive to the student's argument. Rewrite the message to show how you would improve it:

   I think that I was unfairly awarded a C in your accounting class this term, and I am asking you to change the grade to a B. It was a difficult term. I don't get any money from home, and I have to work mornings at the Pancake House (as a cook), so I had to rush to make your class, and those two times that I missed class were because they wouldn't let me off work because of special events at the Pancake House (unlike some other students who just take off when they choose). On the midterm examination, I originally got a 75 percent, but you said in class that there were two different ways to answer the third question and that you would change the grades of students who used the "optimal cost" method and had been counted off 6 points for doing this. I don't think that you took this into account, because I got 80 percent on the final, which is clearly a B. Anyway, whatever you decide, I just want to tell you that I really enjoyed this class, and I thank you for making accounting so interesting.

5. Rewrite the following letter to Mrs. Bruce Crandall (1597 Church Street, Grants Pass, Oregon 97526) so that it conveys a helpful, personal, and interested tone:

   We have your letter of recent date to our Ms. Dobson. Owing to the fact that you neglected to include the size of the dress you ordered, please be advised that no shipment of your order was made, but the aforementioned shipment will occur at such time as we are in receipt of the aforementioned information.

6. Write a concrete phrase for each of these vague phrases:
   a. sometime this spring
   b. a substantial saving
   c. a large number attended
   d. increased efficiency
   e. expanded the work area
7. List terms that are stronger than the following
   a. ran after
   b. seasonal ups and downs
   c. bright
   d. suddenly rises
   e. moves forward
8. As you rewrite these sentences, replace the clichés with fresh, personal expressions:
   a. Being a jack-of-all-trades, Dave worked well in his new selling job.
   b. Moving Leslie into the accounting department, where she was literally a fish out of water, was like putting a square peg into a round hole, if you get my drift.
   c. I knew she was at death's door, but I thought the doctor would pull her through.
   d. Movies aren't really my cup of tea; as far as I am concerned, they can't hold a candle to a good book.
   e. It's a dog-eat-dog world out there in the rat race of the asphalt jungle.
9. Suggest short, simple words to replace each of the following.
   a. inaugurate
   b. terminate
   c. utilize
   d. anticipate
   e. assistance
   f. endeavor
   g. ascertain
   h. procure
   i. consummate
   j. advise
   k. alteration
   l. forwarded
   m. fabricate
   n. nevertheless
   o. substantial
10. Rewrite each sentence so that it is active rather than passive:
   a. The raw data are submitted to the data-processing division by the sales representative each Friday.
   b. High profits are publicized by management.
   c. The policies announced in the directive were implemented by the staff.
   d. Our computers are serviced by the Santee Company.
   e. The employees were represented by Janet Hogan.
11. Write up-to-date versions of these phrases; write none if you think there is no appropriate substitute:
   a. as per your instructions
   b. attached herewith
   c. in lieu of
   d. in reply I wish to state
   e. please be advised that
12. In the following paragraph, identify the topic sentence and the related sentences (those that support the idea of the topic sentence):

   Each year McDonald's sponsors the All-American Band, made up of two high school students from each state. The band marches in Macy's Thanksgiving Day parade in New York City and the Rose Bowl Parade in Pasadena. Franchisees are urged to join their local Chamber of Commerce, United Way, American Legion, and other bastions of All-Americana. McDonald's tries hard to project an image of almost a charitable organization. Local outlets sponsor campaigns on fire prevention, bicycle safety, and litter cleanup, with advice from Hamburger Central on how to extract the most publicity from their efforts.[31]

   Now add a topic sentence to this paragraph:

   Your company's image includes what a person sees, hears, and experiences in relation to your firm. Every business letter you write is therefore important. The quality of the letterhead and typing, the position of the copy on the page, the format, the kind of typeface used, and the color of the typewriter ribbon—all these factors play a part in creating an impression of you and your company in the mind of the person you are writing to.[32]

13. Write a paragraph on each of the following topics: one by illustration, one by comparison or contrast, one by discussion of cause and effect, one by classification, and one by discussion of problem and solution:
   a. Types of cameras (or dogs or automobiles) available for sale
   b. Advantages and disadvantages of eating at fast-food restaurants
   c. Finding that first job
   d. Good qualities of my car (or house, or apartment, or neighborhood)
   e. How to make a dessert recipe (or barbecue a steak or make coffee)
14. Visit the Security Exchange Commission's (SEC) plain-English Web site at http://www.sec.gov/news/handbook.htm and review the online handbook. In a brief sentence or two, summarize what the SEC means

by the phrase "plain English." Find a piece of company literature (an instruction manual, annual report, warranty, or contract) that you think should be rewritten in plain English. Circle the paragraphs or sentences that are the most difficult to understand. Share these examples with your classmates.

15. Rewrite the following paragraph using a bulleted list:

With our alarm system, you'll have a 24-hour security guard who signals the police at the suggestion of an intruder. You'll also appreciate the computerized scanning device that determines exactly where and when the intrusion occurred. No need to worry about electrical failure, either, thanks to our backup response unit.[33]

16. Reorder the following customer service list according to which points you think would interest your readers (potential customers) the most.

1. Friendly manner on the telephone
2. Thorough knowledge of service
3. Calm disposition even during a crisis
4. Willingness to work overtime for the customer[34]

17. Using the Bosewell & Sons letter on page 126 (Figure 5.1), draw an organizational chart similar to the one shown in Figure 5.3 (see page 133), filling in the main idea, the major points, and the evidence provided in this letter. (Note: Your diagram may be smaller.)

18. Think of some popular clichés and explain why using them can become a language barrier, especially when you are communicating with an intercultural audience.

19. Which barriers to communication discussed in Chapter 1 can you overcome by using the principles presented in this chapter?

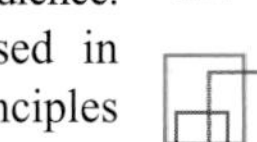

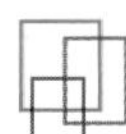

EXPLORING THE BEST OF THE WEB

Connect Now with a Virtual Library, page 144

Your boss heard about a new educational software program called "ADI 4," developed by a French branch of Sierra On-line. She wants to write a letter of inquiry about this product. She also wonders what other software the company offers. She asks you to find out the French company's name and address and to gather as much information as you can about its product line. She also requests that you get her an up-to-date currency exchange rate. Use the Virtual Reference Desk to gather the data your boss needs. *Hint:* You might want to begin your search with the "Quick Reference" index pages.

REVISING AUDIENCE-CENTERED BUSINESS MESSAGES

AFTER STUDYING THIS CHAPTER, YOU WILL BE ABLE TO

1 Briefly discuss the steps involved in editing a message
2 List five ways to make messages more concise
3 Name nine ways to improve your writing style
4 Identify seven issues to keep in mind when critiquing someone else's writing style
5 Discuss how technology can be used to compose, revise, and design messages
6 Identify five design elements and briefly explain how they can change the appearance and overall effectiveness of a message

COMMUNICATION CLOSE-UP AT TURNER BROADCASTING SYSTEM

"Make sure that it's *Turner Broadcasting System* and not '*Systems,*' " coaches corporate communications manager Adrianne Proeller when asked to talk about her work at the Atlanta-based media giant (now owned by Time Warner). According to the company's corporate style manual, *TBS* or *Turner* is okay for subsequent references. "That's one of the first things you do when editing," says Proeller. "You make sure you get the name of the company right."

Not only does Proeller write speeches and statements for TBS president R. E. (Ted) Turner, she has enough other public relations duties to keep her busy during frequent ten-hour days. She enjoys her job, even when she's revising a document for the second or third time, weeding out weak verbs, simplifying complicated sentences, and eliminating unnecessary facts. She revises everything she writes, a task that she says "just comes with the territory."

Adrianne Proeller

The "territory" Proeller covers on a daily basis includes writing letters, memos, speeches, press releases, executive biographies, corporate fact sheets, and company histories. She also writes sample questions and answers for corporate executives before media interviews. "The Q & A prepares the executive for just about every possible question that might be asked," explains Proeller. Company founder Ted Turner is a favorite media topic, and so are the conglomerate's highly visible international divisions, which include Cable News Network (CNN), CNN Headline News, TBS Superstation, Turner Network Television (TNT), Turner Classic Movies (TCM), Hanna-Barbera Productions, TNT Latin America, TNT & Cartoon Asia, New Line Cinema, and Castlerock Entertainment. TBS also owns the Atlanta Braves baseball team, the Atlanta Hawks basketball team, and other sports and en-

Communication is the profession of many employees of Turner Broadcasting System and its international division (such as CNN). Whether working with Adrianne Proeller in corporate communications at TBS, writing press releases for the Atlanta Braves, or delivering news stories on CNN, these professionals understand the importance of careful revision. The most successful communicators make sure their messages are the best they can be.

tertainment ventures. Reporters are always asking questions, and the answers executives give could turn up on tomorrow's front page or today's broadcast news. So Proeller has to be certain her memos and press releases are clear and accurate.

That doesn't mean she always has time to let her writing "cool off" before she takes a second look—which is the ideal way to approach revision. "If I have the luxury to print it out instead of just looking at it on my computer screen, then I'm doing well," laughs Proeller. Whether the document is on screen or in hard copy, however, she rereads it through completely, asking herself: "What am I trying to say? Is it getting across? Is there anything that could make this better? Could anything make it stronger? Is there anything missing?"

For clarity, Proeller often narrows her communication to one primary message; then, to gain her reader's attention, she makes sure that this key idea is mentioned in the first paragraph. Because TBS is an international company, she also checks her copy for any cultural references that could be considered narrow minded or biased. For instance, did she mistakenly assume a U.S. perspective? *Domestic sales* would confuse European readers, so Proeller replaces it with *U.S.-based sales* when sending memos overseas.

"Mr. Turner is very much an internationalist," Proeller explains. "A few years ago he sent around a memo to all of CNN saying that because we're an international network, he didn't want any use of the word *foreign*. In fact, I could be fined for saying that—literally fined money (about $50). Most newsrooms have a national desk and a foreign desk; Turner has a national desk and an international desk." Of course, employees have poked a little fun at the rule, joking, "Excuse me, I have an international substance in my eye." However, they don't laugh at Turner's international success.

During her revision, Proeller checks the corporate style book for the proper formats and for company updates (for example, *TBS Superstation* used to be *TBS SuperStation*, and before that it was *Superstation TBS*). She also reconsiders her word choices. "I'm always trying to cut out unnecessary words, and I'm a big believer in strong verbs." She simplifies sentences that are too cumbersome and eliminates secondary messages if a document is too long. Overall, she makes sure the writing is positive, even when referring to TBS's competitors. That is company policy, Proeller says, because competitors of one division are often customers of another.

"Every document that passes your desk is a reflection on you," Proeller believes. "Your reputation, both internally and externally, is built one little bit at a time. I think typos are unforgivable, but beyond that, you want every document to be the best it can be. If you're not putting 100 percent of your thought into looking at it once it has been drafted—for all of the different aspects of style and content and accuracy—you're risking your professional image."[1] ■

STEP 6: EDITING AND REWRITING YOUR MESSAGE

Once you've completed the first draft of your message, you may be tempted to breathe a sigh of relief and get on with the next project. Resist the temptation. As professional communicators like Adrianne Proeller are aware, the first draft is rarely good enough. Most writers don't initially say what they want to say or say it as well as they could. You owe it to yourself and to your audience to review and refine your messages before sending them. In fact, many writing authorities suggest that you plan to go over a document at least three times: once for content and organization, once for style and readability, and once for mechanics and format.

You might wonder whether all this effort to fine-tune a message is worthwhile. The fact is, people in business care very much about saying precisely the right thing in precisely the right way. Their willingness to go over the same document at least three times shows just how important it is to communicate effectively.

Although the tendency is to separate revision from composition, editing is an ongoing activity that occurs throughout the composition process. You edit and revise as you go along; then you edit and revise again after you've completed the first draft. While editing, you constantly search for the best way to say something, probing for the right words, testing alternative sentences, reshaping, tightening, and juggling elements that already exist. The letter in Figure 6.1 has been edited using the proofreading marks shown in Appendix II. The letter in Figure 6.2 shows how the letter looks with all the revisions incorporated.

Keep in mind that the basic editing principles discussed here apply to both written and oral communication. However, the steps involved in revising a speech or an oral presentation are slightly different, as Chapter 16 explains.

Evaluating Your Content and Organization

After a day or two, review your message for content and organization.

Ideally, let your draft age a day or two before you begin the editing process so that you can approach the material with a fresh eye. Then read through the document quickly to evaluate its overall effectiveness. You're mainly concerned with content, organization, and flow. Compare the draft with your original plan. Have you covered all points in the most logical order? Is there a good balance between the general and the specific? Do the most important ideas receive the most space, and are they placed in the most prominent positions? Have you provided enough support and double-checked the facts? Would the message be more convincing if it were arranged in another sequence? Do you need to add anything? Be sure to consider the effect your words will actually have on readers (not just the effect you *plan* for them to have).

In the first phase of editing, spend a few extra moments on the beginning and ending of the message. These are the sections that have the greatest impact on the audience. Be sure that the opening of a letter or memo is relevant, interesting, and geared to the reader's probable reaction. In longer messages, check to see that the first few paragraphs establish the subject, purpose, and organization of the material. Review the conclusion to be sure that it summarizes the main idea and leaves the audience with a positive impression.

This letter responds to Louise Wilson's request for information about the Commerce Hotel's frequent-guest program.

Figure 6.1
In-Depth Critique: Sample Edited Letter

November 12, 2000

Miss Louise Wilson
Corporate Travel Department
Brother's Electric Corporation
2300 Wacker Drive
Chicago, IL 60670

Dear Miss Wilson:

Thank you for your interest in ~~I enjoyed our recent conversation regarding~~ the *frequent-guest* ~~FG~~ program ~~and am~~ *at the Commerce Hotel.* *We are* delighted to hear that the people at Brother's Electric are thinking about joining. ~~Incidentally, we are planning a special Thanksgiving weekend rate, so keep that in mind in case you happen to be in San Francisco for the Holiday.~~

The enclosed brochure explains the details of the *frequent-guest* ~~FG~~ program. *As a Corporate member, Brother's Electric will be entitled to a 20 percent discount on all rooms and services.* ~~Your FG ID card is enclosed. Use it~~ whenever you make reservations with us *use the enclosed ID card* to obtain *your* ~~a~~ corporate discount. ~~We will see to it that~~ your executives ~~are treated~~ *will receive* ~~with~~ special courtesy, ~~and that they get to~~ *including free* use *of* the health club ~~free~~. *Organizations enrolled in the frequent-guest program also qualify for discounts on* ~~We also have excellent~~ convention facilities and banquet rooms. ~~should you want to book a convention or meeting here. We hope you and your company will~~ Take advantage of these ~~outstanding world class amenities~~ *facilities the next time you book a convention.* Please call me if you have any questions. I will be happy to answer them.

Sincerely,

Mary Cortez
Account Representative

Content and organization: In the first paragraph, stick to the point (the main idea). In the middle, highlight the key advantage of the frequent-guest program, and, in subsequent paragraphs, discuss details. Eliminate redundancies.

Style and readability: Reword to stress the "you" viewpoint. Clarify the relationships among ideas through placement and combination of phrases. Moderate the excessive enthusiasm, and eliminate words (such as *amenities*) that may be unfamiliar to your reader.

Mechanics and format: To prevent confusion, spell out the abbreviated phrase *FG*.

Reviewing Your Style and Readability

Once you're satisfied with the content and structure of the message, look at its style and readability. Ask yourself whether you have achieved the right tone for your audience. Look for opportunities to make the material more interesting through the use of strong, lively words and phrases as discussed in Chapter 5.

Figure 6.2
In-Depth Critique: Final Revised Letter

The revised letter gives the requested information in a more organized fashion, has a friendlier style, and has clearer mechanics.

COMMERCE HOTEL

333 Sansome Street ➢ San Francisco, CA 94104
(800) 323-7347 ➢ (415) 854-2447 ➢ Fax (415) 854-7669
www.CommerceHotel.com

November 12, 2000

Miss Louise Wilson
Corporate Travel Department
Brother's Electric Corporation
2300 Wacker Drive
Chicago, IL 60670

Dear Miss Wilson:

Thank you for your interest in the frequent-guest program at the Commerce Hotel. We are delighted to hear that the people at Brother's Electric are thinking about joining.

The enclosed brochure explains the details of the frequent-guest program. As a corporate member, Brother's Electric will be entitled to a 20 percent discount on all rooms and services. To obtain your corporate discount, use the enclosed ID card whenever you make reservations with us. Your executives will receive special courtesy, including free use of the health club.

Organizations enrolled in the frequent-guest program also qualify for discounts on convention facilities and banquet rooms. Take advantage of these facilities the next time you book a convention. Please call me if you have any questions. I will be happy to answer them.

Sincerely,

Mary Cortez

Mary Cortez
Account Representative

The first paragraph now provides a "you" attitude, spells out what was previously abbreviated, and contains no irrelevant material.

The second paragraph now clarifies the benefits of the frequent-guest program and personalizes those benefits by using the "you" attitude.

The last paragraph now combines a final benefit with more information about services available. It also concludes with a friendly tone.

At the same time, be particularly conscious of whether your message is clear and readable. You want the audience to understand you with a minimum of effort. Check your vocabulary and sentence structure to be sure you're relying mainly on familiar terms and simple, direct statements. You might even apply a readability formula to gauge the difficulty of your writing.

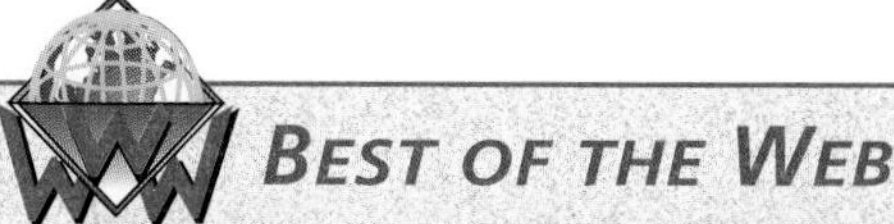

Improve Your Writing Style with Proven Techniques

You can improve your writing quickly and easily with *The Elements of Style* by William Strunk Jr. This classic book is now available in online format. The book includes rules of usage, principles of composition, commonly misused words and expressions, commonly misspelled words, and dozens of before-and-after examples.

http://www.columbia.edu/acis/bartleby/strunk

The most common readability formulas measure the length of words and sentences to give you a rough idea of how well educated your audience must be to understand your message. Figure 6.3 shows how one readability formula, the Fog Index, has been applied to an excerpt from a memo. (The "long words" in the passage have been underlined.) As the calculation shows, anyone who reads at a ninth-grade level should be able to read this passage

Figure 6.3
The Fog Index

1. **Select writing sample.**
   Keep the sample between 100 and 125 words long.

   I called Global Corporation to ask when we will receive copies of its <u>insurance policies</u> and <u>engineering</u> reports. Cindy Turner of Global said that they are putting the <u>documents together</u> and will send them by Express Mail next week. She told me that they are late because most of the <u>information</u> is in the hands of Global's <u>attorneys</u> in Boston. I asked why it was in Boston; we had <u>understood</u> that the account is serviced by the carrier's Dallas branch. Turner explained that the account <u>originally</u> was sold to Global's Boston <u>division</u>, so all paperwork stays there. She promised to <u>telephone</u> us when the package is ready to ship.

2. **Determine average sentence length.**
   Count the number of words in each sentence. Treat independent clauses (stand-alone word groups containing subject and predicate) as separate sentences. For example, "In school we studied; we learned; we improved" counts as three sentences. Then add all word counts for each sentence to get the total word count, and divide that by the number of sentences. This excerpt has an average sentence length of 14:

   $$18 + 21 + 21 + 7 + 13 + 12 + 5 + 2 = 99 \text{ words} \div 8 \text{ sentences} = 12$$

3. **Determine percentage of long words.**
   Count the number of long words—that is, all words that have three or more syllables (underlined in excerpt). Omit proper nouns, combinations of short words (such as *butterfly* and *anyway*), and verbs that gain a third syllable by adding *-es* or *-ed* (as in *trespasses* and *created*). Divide the number of long words by the total number of words in the sample. The percentage of long words in this excerpt is 10 percent:

   $$11 \text{ long words} \div 109 \text{ total words} = 10 \text{ percent}$$

4. **Determine the grade level required to read the passage.**
   Add the numbers for average sentence length and percentage of long words. Multiply this sum by 0.4, and drop the number following the decimal point. The number of years of schooling required to easily read this excerpt is 9:

   $$14 \text{ words per sentence} + 10 \text{ percent long words} = 24 \times 0.4 = 9.6 - 0.6 = 9 \text{ (Fog Index)}$$

with ease. For technical documents, you can aim for an audience that reads at a twelfth- to fourteenth-grade level; for general business messages, your writing should be geared to readers at the eighth- to eleventh-grade level. The Fog Index of such popular business publications as the *Wall Street Journal* and *Forbes* magazine is somewhere between 10 and 11.

Of course, readability indexes can't be applied to languages other than English. Counting syllables makes no sense in other languages. For example, compare the English *forklift driver* with the German *Gabelstaplerfahrer*. Also, Chinese and Japanese characters don't lend themselves to syllable counting at all.[2]

Readability depends on word choice, sentence length, sentence structure, organization, and the message's physical appearance.

Readability formulas are easy to apply; many are commonly done on a computer. However, they ignore some important variables that contribute to reading ease, such as sentence structure, the organization of ideas, and the appearance of the message on the page.[3] To fully evaluate the readability of your message, ask yourself whether you have effectively emphasized the important information. Are your sentences easy to decipher? Do your paragraphs have clear topic sentences? Are the transitions between ideas obvious?

Rewriting Your Message

Ernest Hemingway once said, "There's no such thing as writing—only rewriting." Yet, once most businesspeople finish the writing stage, they make one of two mistakes: They shuffle words around on the page rather than actually make improvements, or they think rewriting is too time consuming and send the document out the moment that last period hits the page.[4]

With a minimal amount of solid rewriting, you'll end up with a stronger document. As you edit your business message, you'll find yourself rewriting sentences, passages, and even whole sections to improve their effectiveness. Of course, you're probably also facing a deadline, so try to stick to the schedule you set during the planning stage of the project. Do your best to revise and rewrite thoroughly but also economically.

As you rewrite, concentrate on how each word contributes to an effective sentence and how that sentence develops a coherent paragraph. Sometimes you'll find that the most difficult problem in a sentence can be solved by simply removing the problem itself. When you find yourself with a troublesome element, ask, "Do I need it at all?" Probably not. In fact,

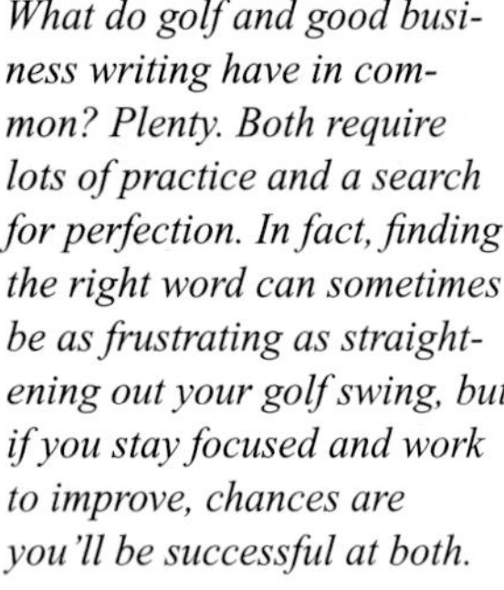

What do golf and good business writing have in common? Plenty. Both require lots of practice and a search for perfection. In fact, finding the right word can sometimes be as frustrating as straightening out your golf swing, but if you stay focused and work to improve, chances are you'll be successful at both.

you may find that it was giving you so much grief because it was trying to do an unnecessary job.[5] Once you remove the troublesome element, the afflicted sentence will spring to life and breathe normally. Of course, before you delete anything, you'll probably want to keep copies of your previous versions. As TBS's Adrianne Proeller points out, someone can come back to you and say, " 'Hey, I didn't approve that.' So it's very important to keep a paper trail."

DID YOU KNOW?

A person's written communication is probably more self-revealing than any other single item in the workplace. The words you use repeatedly give a clue about how you see yourself and think about others.

Write Concisely

Clutter is the disease of writing. Three-fourths of the executives who participated in one survey complained that most written messages are too long.[6] Many business documents are swollen with words and phrases that do no new work. In fact, most first drafts can be cut by 50 percent.[7]

Because executives are more likely to read documents that efficiently say what needs to be said, it's especially important to weed out unnecessary material. You do so by examining every word you put on paper and stripping every sentence to its cleanest components: You eliminate every word that serves no function, replace every long word that could be a short word, and remove every adverb that adds nothing to the meaning already carried in the verb. For instance, *very* can be a useful word to achieve emphasis, but more often it's clutter. There's no need to call someone very methodical. Either someone is methodical or not. As you begin your editing task, keep the following three goals in mind: simplify, prune, and strive for order.

Eliminate Unnecessary Words and Phrases Some words and combinations of words have more efficient, one-word equivalents. Here are some combinations to avoid:

Be on the lookout for
- Inefficient phrases
- Redundancies
- Unneeded relative pronouns and articles

COMBINATIONS TO AVOID	EFFICIENT EQUIVALENTS
for the sum of	for
in the event that	if
on the occasion of	on
prior to the start of	before
in the near future	soon
have the capability of	can
at this point in time	now
due to the fact that	because
in view of the fact that	because
until such time as	when
with reference to	about

Relative pronouns such as *who, that,* and *which* frequently cause clutter, and sometimes even articles are excessive (mostly too many *the*'s). Consider the following:

TIGHTEN FROM	TIGHTEN TO
Cars that are sold after January will not have a six-month warranty.	Cars sold after January will not have a six-month warranty.
Employees who are driving to work should park in the underground garage.	Employees driving to work should park in the underground garage.

However, well-placed relative pronouns and articles serve an important function by preventing confusion. For example, without *that,* the following sentence is ambiguous:

Confusing: The project manager told the engineers last week the specifications were changed.
Clearer: The project manager told the engineers last week *that* the specifications were changed.
Clearer: The project manager told the engineers that last week the specifications were changed.

Short words are generally more vivid than long ones and improve the readability of a document.

Use Short Words and Infinitives Another way to prune your prose is by using short words. Short words are generally more vivid and easier to read than long ones are. The idea is to use short, simple words, *not* simple concepts.[8]

AVOID LONG WORDS	USE SHORT WORDS
During the preceding year, the company accelerated productive operations.	Last year the company sped up operations.
The action was predicated on the assumption that the company was operating at a financial deficit.	The action was based on the belief that the company was losing money.

Use infinitives to replace some phrases.

By using infinitives in place of some phrases, you not only shorten your sentences but make them clearer as well:

POOR	IMPROVED
If you want success as a writer, you must work hard.	To be a successful writer, you must work hard.
He went to the library for the purpose of studying.	He went to the library to study.
The employer increased salaries so that she could improve morale.	The employer increased salaries to improve morale.

Avoid needless repetition.

Eliminate Redundancies Some word combinations are redundant. That is, the words tend to say the same thing. For instance, "visible to the eye" is redundant because *visible* is enough; nothing can be visible to the ear. Likewise, "surrounded on all sides" is redundant because *surrounded* implies on all sides. Also, look closely for double modifiers. Do you really need to say "modern, up-to-date equipment," or would "modern equipment" do the job?

When editing your message, be on the lookout for these common redundancies:

absolutely complete	basic fundamentals	follows after	reduce down
free and clear	refer back	repeat again	collect together
future plans	return back	important essentials	midway between
end result	actual truth	final outcome	uniquely unusual

Avoid starting sentences with *it* and *there.*

Watch for Indefinite Pronoun Starters If you start a sentence with an indefinite pronoun (an expletive) such as *it* or *there,* odds are that the sentence could be shorter:

Poor	**Improved**
It would be appreciated if you would sign the lease today.	Please sign the lease today.
There are five employees in this division who were late to work today.	Five employees in this division were late to work today.

Eliminate Awkward Pointers To save words, business writers sometimes direct their readers' attention elsewhere with such expressions as *the above-mentioned, as mentioned above, the aforementioned, the former, the latter,* and *respectively*. These words cause the reader to jump from one point in the message to another, a process that hinders effective communication. A better approach is to be specific in your references, even if you must add a few more words:

Be specific in your reference.

Poor	**Improved**
Computer supplies for legal secretaries and beginning accountants are distributed by the Law Office and Accounting Office, respectively.	Computer supplies for legal secretaries are distributed by the Law Office; those for beginning accountants are distributed by the Accounting Office.

Improve Your Writing Style

Good writing doesn't come naturally, though most people think it does. Writers must constantly ask, "What am I trying to say?" Surprisingly they often don't know. Then they must look at what they have written and ask, "Have I said what I wanted to say? Will the message be clear to someone encountering the subject for the first time?" If either answer is no, it's usually because the writer hasn't been careful enough.[9]

Carelessness can take any number of forms. Perhaps the sentence is so cluttered that the reader can't unravel it; perhaps it is so shoddily constructed that the reader can interpret it in several ways; perhaps the writer switches pronouns or tense in midsentence so that the reader loses track of who is talking or when the event took place; perhaps sentence B is not a logical sequel to sentence A; or perhaps the writer uses an important word incorrectly by not taking the trouble to look it up.[10]

Writing is hard work. A clear sentence is no accident. Very few sentences come out right the first time, or even the third time. The following advice will help you improve your writing style. Of course, nothing will substitute for actual practice. The more you write (whether on the job or for pleasure), the better writer you'll become.

Break Up Strung-Out Sentences A strung-out sentence is a series of two or more sentences unwisely connected by *and*—in other words, a compound sentence taken too far. If you find yourself stuck in a long sentence, you're probably trying to make the sentence do more than it can reasonably do, such as express two dissimilar thoughts. You can often improve your writing style by separating the string into individual sentences:

In many cases, the parts of a compound sentence should be separated into two sentences.

Poor	**Improved**
The magazine will be published January 1, and I'd better meet the deadline if I want my article included.	The magazine will be published January 1. I'd better meet the deadline if I want my article included.

Avoid Hedging Sentences Sometimes you have to write *may* or *seems* to avoid stating a judgment as a fact. Nevertheless, when you have too many such hedges, you aren't really saying anything:

Don't be afraid to present your opinions without qualification.

These soft sculptures created and pieced together by Monita Somers and Ann Carlson can show up in the most unexpected places. So can errors in your written messages. Before you send your messages, take time to revise them. Pay attention to the details—as the makers of these dolls do—until you are satisfied that your message is clear and readable.

POOR	IMPROVED
I believe that Mr. Johnson's employment record seems to show that he may be capable of handling the position.	Mr. Johnson's employment record shows that he is capable of handling the position.

When you use the same grammatical pattern to express two or more ideas, you show that they are comparable thoughts.

Express Parallel Ideas in Parallel Form When you have two or more similar (parallel) ideas to express, try to use a **parallel construction**; that is, use the same grammatical pattern. The repetition of the pattern tells readers that the ideas are comparable and adds a nice rhythm to your message. In the following examples, parallel construction makes the sentences more readable:

POOR	IMPROVED
Miss Simms had been drenched with rain, bombarded with telephone calls, and her boss shouted at her.	Miss Sims had been drenched with rain, bombarded with telephone calls, and shouted at by her boss.
Ms. Reynolds dictated the letter, and next she signed it and left the office.	Ms. Reynolds dictated the letter, signed it, and left the office.
To waste time and missing deadlines are bad habits.	Wasting time and missing deadlines are bad habits.
Interviews are a matter of acting confident and to stay relaxed.	Interviews are a matter of acting confident and staying relaxed.

Parallelism can be achieved through a repetition of words, phrases, clauses, or entire sentences:

Parallel Words: The letter was approved by Clausen, Whittaker, Merlin, and Carlucci.

Parallel Phrases: We have beaten the competition in supermarkets, in department stores, and in specialty stores.

Parallel Clauses: I'd like to discuss the issue after Vicki gives her presentation but before Marvin shows his slides.

Parallel Sentences: In 1998 we exported 30 percent of our production. In 1999 we exported 50 percent.

Correct Dangling Modifiers Sometimes a modifier is not just an adjective or an adverb but an entire phrase modifying a noun or a verb. Be careful to construct your sentences so that this type of modifier refers to something in the main part of the sentence in a way that makes sense. Consider this sentence:

Make sure that modifier phrases are really related to the subject of the sentence.

> Walking to the office, a red sports car passed her.

The construction implies that the red sports car has both an office and the legs to walk there. The modifier is said to be dangling because it has no real connection to the subject of the sentence—in this case, the sports car. This is what the writer is trying to say:

> A red sports car passed her while she was walking to the office.

Flipping the clauses produces another correct sentence:

> While she was walking to the office, a red sports car passed her.

Dangling modifiers make sentences confusing and sometimes ridiculous:

Poor	Improved
Working as fast as possible, the budget was soon ready.	Working as fast as possible, the committee soon had the budget ready.
After a three-week slump, we increased sales.	After a three-week slump, sales increased.

The first example shows one frequent cause of dangling modifiers: passive construction in the independent clause. When the clause is made active instead of passive, the connection with the dangling modifier becomes more obvious.

Passive construction is often the cause of dangling modifiers.

Avoid Long Sequences of Nouns When nouns are strung together as modifiers, the resulting sentence is hard to read. You can clarify the sentence by putting some of the nouns in a modifying phrase. Although you add a few more words, your audience won't have to work as hard to understand the sentence.

Stringing together a series of nouns may save a little space, but it causes confusion.

Poor	Improved
The window sash installation company will give us an estimate on Friday.	The company that installs window sashes will give us an estimate on Friday.

Avoid Camouflaged Verbs Watch for word endings such as *-ion, -tion, -ing, -ment, -ant, -ent, -ence, -ance,* and *-ency*. Most of them change verbs into nouns and adjectives. In effect, the words that result are camouflaged verbs—the heart of weak construction. Getting rid of these camouflaged verbs will strengthen your writing:

Turning verbs into nouns or adjectives weakens your writing style.

AVOID CAMOUFLAGED VERBS	USE VERBS
The manager undertook implementation of the rules.	The manager implemented the rules.
Verification of the shipments occurs weekly.	Shipments are verified weekly.

Another bad habit is to transform verbs into nouns (*we performed an analysis of* instead of *we analyzed*). When possible, use verbs instead of noun phrases. Using verbs livens up your writing and prunes your prose.

AVOID WORDY NOUN PHRASES	USE VERBS INSTEAD
reach a conclusion about	conclude
make a discovery of	discover
give consideration to	consider

Subject and predicate should be placed as close together as possible, as should modifiers and the words they modify.

Keep Words Together That Work Together To avoid confusing readers, keep the subject and predicate of a sentence as close together as possible. When subject and predicate are far apart, readers have to read the sentence twice to figure out who did what.

POOR	IMPROVED
A 10 percent decline in market share, which resulted from quality problems and an aggressive sales campaign by Armitage, the market leader in the Northeast, was the major problem in 1994.	The major problem in 1994 was a 10 percent loss of market share, which resulted from both quality problems and an aggressive sales campaign by Armitage, the market leader in the Northeast.

The same rule applies to other parts of speech. Adjectives, adverbs, and prepositional phrases usually make the most sense when they're placed as close as possible to the words they modify:

POOR	IMPROVED
We will deliver the pipe soon that you ordered last Tuesday.	We will soon deliver the pipe that you ordered last Tuesday.

Business writing shouldn't be gushy.

Moderate Your Enthusiasm An occasional adjective or adverb intensifies and emphasizes your meaning, but too many can ruin your writing.

POOR	IMPROVED
We are extremely pleased to offer you a position on our staff of exceptionally skilled and highly educated employees. The work offers extraordinary challenges and a very large salary.	We are pleased to offer you a position on our staff of skilled and well-educated employees. The work offers challenges and an attractive salary.

Writing in Groups and Critiquing the Writing of Another

In Chapter 2 we discussed guidelines and challenges for effective team writing. We explained that before you begin writing collaboratively, your team must agree on the purpose of the project and on the audience, as well as on the organization, format, and style of the document.

Enthusiasm for his products helped propel Junki Yoshida's enterprises to $50 million in annual revenue. To propel your messages, use an occasional sprinkle of enthusiasm; just make sure you don't overdo it.

Whether you're writing in teams or reviewing a document prepared by someone else for your signature, at times you will need to critique the writing of another. When you do that, you will want to provide specific, constructive comments so that you can help the person communicate effectively. To help the writer make meaningful changes, you need to say more than simply "This doesn't work" or "This isn't what I wanted" or "I don't see what you're trying to say."[11] When critiquing a document, concentrate on three elements:[12]

When critiquing the writing of another
- Keep your comments constructive
- Question any facts that appear incorrect or illogical
- Make sure the message is clear and the language is unambiguous

- *Does the document accomplish the intended purpose?* Is the purpose clearly stated? Does the body support the stated purpose? You might outline the key points to see whether they support the main idea. Is the conclusion supported by the data? Are the arguments presented logically? If the document fails to accomplish its purpose, it must be rewritten. Be sure to determine whether the directions given with the initial assignment were clear and complete. Making sure that directions are specific and understandable saves time both for the writer and for the person giving the critique.
- *Is the factual material correct?* A proposal to provide nationwide computer-training services for $15 million would be disastrous if your intention was to provide those services for $150 million. Be sure you pay strict attention to detail. All factual errors must be corrected.
- *Does the document use unambiguous language?* Readers must not be allowed to interpret the meaning in any way other than intended. If you interpret a message differently from what a writer intended, the writer is at fault, and the document must be revised to clarify problem areas.

If any of these elements needs attention, the document must be rewritten or revised. However, once these elements are deemed satisfactory, the question is whether to request other changes. Of course, minor changes can be made at any time in the critiquing process.

But if these three criteria are in fact met, consider these additional points before requesting a major revision:[13]

- *Can the document truly be improved?* The answer to this question is usually yes—given enough time.
- *Can you justify the time needed for a rewrite or a revision?* Will deadlines be missed? Will other priorities suffer from a delay? For example, if a production line is down and the document in question is a description of what's wrong or how to fix it, any polishing beyond accuracy and clarity is secondary to getting the production line running again.
- *Will your request have a negative impact on morale?* Are the changes to be made a purely personal preference? If unexplained or inconsistent changes are regularly made to a person's writing efforts, that writer can become demoralized. (Of course, consistent style preferences can always be suggested for future use.)

Writing in teams often means that two or more people will develop and revise a single document. Software known as *groupware* offers a range of features that make team writing efficient. For example, groupware (which is installed in a computer network environment) allows many people to compose and edit a single document at the same time from different locations. In addition, groupware will keep track of each person's revisions so that if you later have a question or recommendation, you can easily identify the author of that revision (see Figure 6.4).

Groupware also lets people attach electronic notes to each other's sections, enforces a common format for all sections, and takes care of other issues that come up in any collaborative writing project. Most word-processing software today includes similar revision features. In fact, it's impractical to produce or revise your written messages today without using technology.

STEP 7: PRODUCING AND PROOFREADING YOUR MESSAGE

Even after you have rewritten your message from start to finish, you're not done yet. Once you're satisfied with your message's content and organization, style and readability, word choice, sentence style, and paragraph development, you'll want to produce your message in some form that allows you to check it for accuracy, appearance, and detail. (You might want to refresh your memory about the details of grammar and usage by reviewing Appendix I.) Then you'll want to proofread your document to ensure that it's letter perfect (see "Sharpening Your Skills: How to Proofread Like a Pro: Tips for Creating the Perfect Document").

Your credibility is affected by your attention to the details of mechanics and format.

Although grammar, spelling, punctuation, and typographical errors may seem trivial to some people, most readers will view your attention to detail as a sign of your professionalism. Whether you're writing a one-paragraph memo or a 500-page report, if you let mechanical errors slip through, the reader automatically wonders whether you're unreliable in more important ways. Adrianne Proeller of TBS says, "When I get a college résumé and I see a typo on it, I instantly disregard that résumé." Companies such as the *New Yorker* magazine take great pride in their editorial standards. When the *New Yorker* misspelled *Tucson* as "Tuscon," it ended up giving Arizona $66,000 worth of free advertising to set things right.[14]

Also, give some attention to the fine points of format. Have you followed accepted conventions and company guidelines for laying out the document on the page? Have you included all the traditional elements that belong in the documents of the type you are creating?

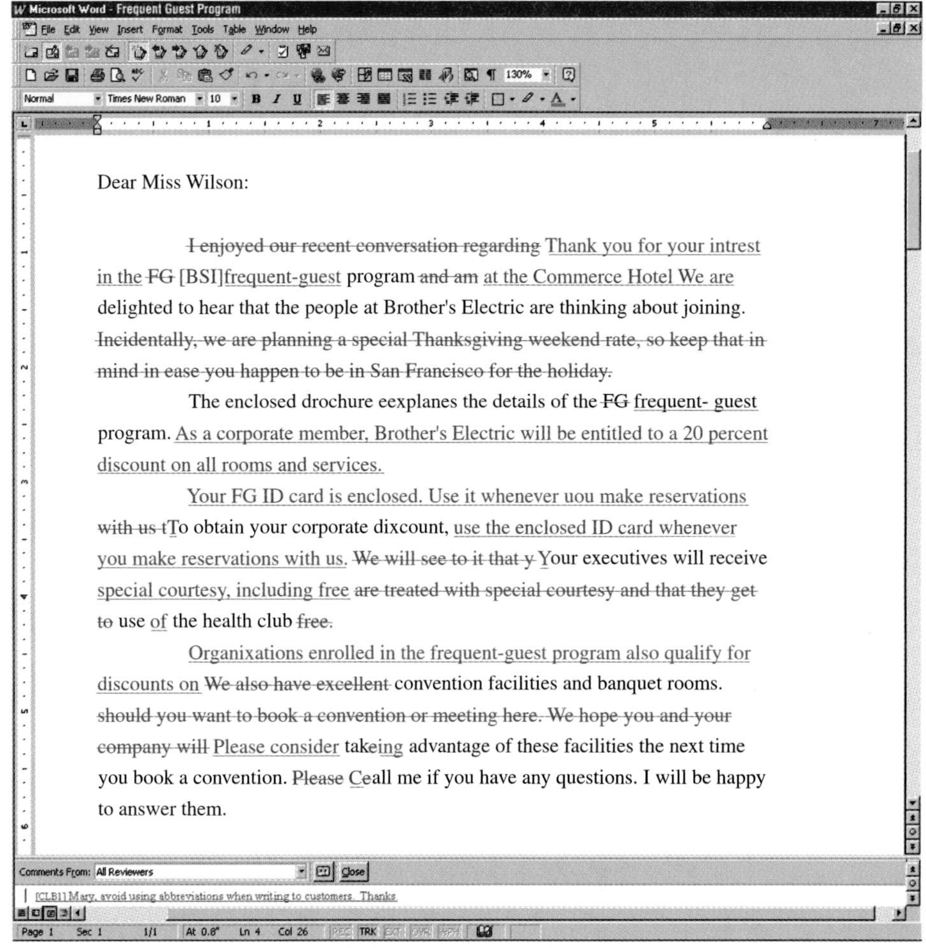

Dear Miss Wilson:

~~I enjoyed our recent conversation regarding~~ Thank you for your intrest in the ~~FG~~ [BSI]frequent-guest program ~~and am~~ at the Commerce Hotel We are delighted to hear that the people at Brother's Electric are thinking about joining. ~~Incidentally, we are planning a special Thanksgiving weekend rate, so keep that in mind in case you happen to be in San Francisco for the holiday.~~

The enclosed drochure eexplanes the details of the ~~FG~~ frequent- guest program. As a corporate member, Brother's Electric will be entitled to a 20 percent discount on all rooms and services.

Your FG ID card is enclosed. Use it whenever uou make reservations ~~with us t~~To obtain your corporate dixcount, use the enclosed ID card whenever you make reservations with us. ~~We will see to it that y~~ Your executives will receive special courtesy, including free ~~are treated with special courtesy and that they get to~~ use of the health club ~~free.~~

Organixations enrolled in the frequent-guest program also qualify for discounts on ~~We also have excellent~~ convention facilities and banquet rooms. ~~should you want to book a convention or meeting here. We hope you and your company will~~ Please consider takeing advantage of these facilities the next time you book a convention. ~~Please~~ Ceall me if you have any questions. I will be happy to answer them.

Figure 6.4
Software tools such as revision marks keep track of proposed editing changes and provide a history of a document's revisions.

Have you been consistent in handling margins, page numbers, headings, exhibits, source notes, and other details? To resolve questions about format and layout, see Component Chapter A. In the remaining sections of this chapter, we'll show you how technology can help you compose, revise, produce, and distribute written documents.

Using Technology to Compose and Revise Your Message

The most common means for creating printed documents is word-processing software.

Word-processing software is the dominant tool for creating printed documents. Composing a document on your computer involves keyboarding, of course, but that's just the beginning. Technology offers many ways to get text into your document, and you're no longer limited to just text, either. The right software makes it relatively easy to add a wide variety of graphic elements to your document—and even audio notes if you have the right equipment.

Entering Text

Word processors help make entering text as painless as possible, giving you the ability to delete and move text easily. For example, if you compose numbered lists or outlines on a computer, the software will automatically renumber the remaining segments if an entry is

SHARPENING YOUR SKILLS

HOW TO PROOFREAD LIKE A PRO: TIPS FOR CREATING THE PERFECT DOCUMENT

You've carefully revised and polished your document, and it's been sent off to the word-processing department to be put into final form. You can breathe a sigh of relief, but only for the moment: You'll still be proofreading what comes out of the printer. To ensure that any document is error free, always proofread the final version. Following are some hints to help make your proofreading more effective.

- *Multiple passes.* Go through the document several times, focusing on a different aspect each time. The first pass might be to look for omissions and errors in content; the second pass could be for layout, spacing, and other aesthetic features; a final pass might be to check for typographical, grammatical, and spelling errors.
- *Tricks for recognizing errors.* In normal reading, your perceptual processes have been trained to ignore transposed letters, improper capitalization, misplaced punctuation, and the like. To short-circuit these normally helpful processes, try some tricky techniques. Professional proofreaders recommend (1) reading each page from the bottom to the top, starting at the last word in each line, (2) placing your finger under each word and reading it silently, (3) making a slit in a sheet of paper that will reveal only one line of type at a time, and (4) reading the document aloud and pronouncing each word carefully.
- *Impartial reviews.* Have a friend or colleague proofread the document for you. Others are likely to catch mistakes that you continually fail to notice. (All of us have blind spots when it comes to reviewing our own work.)
- *Typos.* Look for the most common typographical errors (typos): transposition (such as *teh*), substitution (such as *ecomonic*), and omission (such as *productvity*).
- *Mechanics.* Look for errors in spelling, grammar, punctuation, and capitalization. If you're unsure about something, look it up in a dictionary, a usage book, or another reference work.
- *Accuracy.* Double-check the spelling of names and the accuracy of dates, addresses, and all numbers (quantities ordered, prices, and so on). It would not do to order 500 staplers when you want only 50.
- *Distance.* If you have time, set the document aside and proofread it the next day.
- *Vigilance.* Avoid reading large amounts of material in one sitting, and try not to proofread when you're tired.
- *Focus.* Concentrate on what you're doing. Try to block out distractions, and focus as completely as possible on your proofreading task.
- *Caution.* Take your time. Quick proofreading is not careful proofreading.

Proofreading may require patience, but it adds credibility to your document.

---

1. What qualities does a person need to be a good proofreader? Are such qualities inborn, or can they be learned?
2. Proofread the following sentence:

   aplication of thse methods in stores in San Deigo nd Cinncinati have resultted in a 30 drop in roberies an a 50 precent decling in violnce there, acording ot thedevelpers if the securty sytem, Hanover brothrs, Inc.

---

removed. (Outlines will be discussed in detail in Chapter 14.) Other helpful features include automatic page numbering and dating. When you insert a date code into a document, the software automatically fills in today's date each time you open or print that document. This feature is especially handy if you use form letters. Be careful though; sometimes you'll want to keep the original date intact, especially if you're keeping a history of your correspondence.

In addition to the benefits of word-processing software, computers offer other interesting possibilities for text entry. If you don't know how to keyboard or don't like to, your worries may be over sooner than you think. Alternative interfaces such as handwriting and speech entry are making rapid progress. *Pen-based computers* let you write with an electronic stylus on a special pad that converts your handwriting to text the computer can recognize. The CrossPad from A.T. Cross is a sort of electronic clipboard; slip in a pad, pick up the special pen, and store as many as 50 handwritten pages in the clipboard's memory. Connect the pad to your computer and a facsimile of the handwritten pages is zapped into the PC. Similarly, palm computers let you input data by scribbling directly on their screens. Using handwriting-recognition software, the palm computer exchanges data with your desktop or notebook computer.[15]

Technology provides several options for entering text into a document:

- Keyboarding (typing)
- Pen-based computers
- Voice-recognition systems
- Scanning and OCR

Some of the text that business communicators use in their documents is "prewritten," already appearing in other documents. Say that you want to announce to the media that you've developed a new product or hired an executive. Such announcements—called press releases—usually end with a standard paragraph about the company and its line of business. Any standard block of text used in various documents without being changed is called a *boilerplate*. With a good word processor, you don't have to retype the boilerplate each time you write a press release; you simply store the paragraph the first time you write it and then pop it into a document whenever you need it. Using boilerplates saves time and reduces mistakes because you're not retyping the paragraph every time you use it. A related concept applies to manipulating existing text. If you're a national sales manager compiling a report that includes summaries from your four regional managers, you can use your word processor's *file merge* capability to combine the four documents into one, saving yourself the trouble of retyping all four.

A boilerplate is any standard block of text used in various documents without being changed.

Using a boilerplate or file merge capability assumes that the text you want to include is in electronic format; that is, it's saved on a computer disk. But sometimes you have only printed versions of the document. In such cases you can use a *scanner*, a device that essentially takes a picture of a printed document and converts it to an electronic format that your computer can handle. Scanners produce just a visual image of the document, though, and the process requires an additional step if you want to use the words from the document as normal input to your word processor. A technology called *optical character recognition (OCR)* lets your computer "read" the scanned image, picking out the letters and words that make up the text.

With pen-based computers you can permanently record your ideas anywhere. When you return to your office, simply download your notes into your PC, convert them to text, and then, cut and paste them directly into your documents.

KEEPING PACE WITH TECHNOLOGY

FROM DIGITS TO DUST

Froma Joselow was getting ready to bang out a newspaper story when the invisible intruder struck. Joselow, a financial reporter at the Providence *Journal-Bulletin,* had just inserted a disk into her computer when the machine's familiar whir was pierced by a high-pitched beep. Each time she tried to call a file to the screen, the warning DISK ERROR flashed instead. "I got that sinking feeling," remarked Joselow. "Every writing project of mine was on that disk."

Joselow's disk had been stricken by a deadly virus—the kind that lurks in the computer, waiting for an opportunity to attach to software. When the virus copied itself onto Joselow's disk, it scrambled the contents and turned her words and sentences into electronic confetti.

Because computer viruses can travel from one place to another as fast as a phone call, a single strain can quickly turn up in thousands of computers, oceans apart. The infection that struck Joselow hit more than 100 disks at the *Journal-Bulletin* as well as an estimated 100,000 other disks across the United States. Once a computer has been infected, the invader can sometimes be eradicated with a special antivirus program that searches out and erases every bit of foreign material. But to remain effective, the software must be updated regularly; yesterday's antivirus tools don't cut it in today's virus-infested world.

Fortunately, an epidemic has been avoided so far. No killer virus has penetrated the U.S. electronic funds transfer system (which is essential to the operation of U.S. banks). No stock exchange or commodity exchange computer centers have crashed. No insurance company rolls have been wiped out. No pension funds have had their records scrambled. And no air-traffic control systems have ground to a halt. But some experts warn that the worst is yet to come. In fact, the ranks of those who would dismiss the virus threat as a Chicken Little scare are getting smaller with every outbreak.

Viruses aren't the only thing threatening today's data. For years, computer scientists told us that digital 1s and 0s could last forever. Computers, we were told, would help us manage the information explosion by storing oceans of data that, at some later date, could be recalled at the click of a mouse. Now they're discovering that the media we're using to carry our precious information on into the future are turning out to be far from eternal. Consider this: Up to 20 percent of the information carefully collected on Jet Propulsion Laboratory computers during NASA's 1976 Viking mission to Mars has been lost. And some POW and MIA records and casualty counts from the Vietnam War, stored on Defense Department computers, can no longer be read.

"Forget forever," notes one computer expert. "Under less-than-optimal storage conditions, digital tapes and disks—including CD-ROMs and optical drives—might deteriorate about as fast as newsprint, in 5 to 10 years." And the biggest worry is CD-ROMs. Unlike paper records, CD-ROMs don't usually show decay until it's too late. Experts are just beginning to realize that stray magnetic fields, oxidation, humidity, and material decay can quickly erase the information stored on these disks.

Scanning and OCR technologies raise the legal and ethical issues of plagiarism and image manipulation. Of course, people have had the ability to copy words and images for quite some time, but the new computer tools make copying and altering material even easier. Now you can scan a photo from your files, retouch it as you see fit, and then include it in your own document. Photo-retouching software enables you to make products and people appear better than they really are. You can even depict situations or events that never actually happened. As technology continues to expand these options, business communicators will continue to face new and challenging ethical issues.

Revising Text

When it's time to revise and polish your message, your word processor can help, starting with the basics of adding, deleting, and moving text. *Cut and paste* is a term used to indicate cutting a block of text out of one section of a document and pasting it in somewhere else.

And thanks to the unrelenting pace of technology, chances are good that software needed to get at much of today's data might not be readily available in 10 years. Anyone who has tried wrestling information from a $5^1/_4$ inch floppy disk knows that.

In fact, if you use a PC, sooner or later you are likely to lose data. Whether it's one file or the contents of your entire hard drive, you can prevent your digits from turning to dust by taking these precautions:

- *Keep your PC clean.* Protect your investment by keeping food and drink away from your equipment.
- *Maintain your hard drive.* Scan your drive for errors often and correct them. Defragment your hard drive once a year, but only after performing a complete system backup.
- *Install surge protectors.* Make sure your protectors have a UL1449 rating of 330 volts or less. Install a backup power supply.
- *Exit your system correctly.* Shut down all applications before you turn off your computer; then shut down your computer in proper sequence.
- *Register your hardware and software.* Send in your registration cards so that you are eligible for customer support and are notified about major problems or upgrades.
- *Prevent loss from viruses.* Install and use a good virus scanning program and update it at least quarterly. Run a virus scan on everything that comes into your computer, including new software, floppy disks, and every download from the Internet. Don't open e-mail attachments from strangers.
- *Back up your system regularly.* Make sure you flag all important files and keep a regular backup schedule. Back up your entire system before installing any new software.
- *Store your backups properly.* Store your backup media offsite in a cool, dry cabinet away from heat, humidity, light, dust, and smoke. Keep them away from electric motors, speakers, phone handsets, monitors, TV screens, and transformers, as these devices can potentially cause electromagnetic radiation and erasure. Serious PC users may want to consider online backup services, a safe and inexpensive option.
- *Keep your copies clean and organized.* Label your backup media clearly. Twice a year buy and use new backup media, and clean the magnetic heads on your backup hardware. Do a test restore monthly to make sure your backups are usable.

By taking these steps, you can substantially reduce your risk should a data disaster strike.

---

1. Your office has just decided to go paperless. All written communications, reports, policies, and so on are to be written and stored electronically. You're concerned about this policy, especially after reading this article. Write a short memo to the president of the company expressing your concern.
2. Trade memos with a classmate; review and edit each other's writing. Then answer the bulleted questions in the section "Writing in Groups and Critiquing the Writing of Another."

The *search and replace function* helps you track down words or phrases and change them if you need to. This function can be a great time saver in long documents if you need to change a word or phrase that appears in several places. Be careful, though; choosing the "replace all" option can result in some unintended errors. For example, finding *power* and replacing all occurrences with *strength* will also change the word *powerful* to *strengthful*.

AutoCorrect is another handy feature. It allows you to store words you commonly misspell or mistype, along with their correct spelling. So if you frequently type "teh" instead of "the," AutoCorrect will automatically correct your typo for you.

Beyond the many revision tools, three advanced software functions can help bring out the best in your documents. A *spell checker* compares your document with an electronic dictionary stored on your disk drive, highlights words that it doesn't recognize, and suggests correct spelling. Spell checkers are a wonderful way to weed major typos out of your documents, but it's best not to use them as replacements for good spelling skills. If you use *their*

Spell checkers, grammar checkers, and computerized thesauruses can all help with the revision process, but they can't take the place of good writing and editing skills.

when you mean to use *there,* your spell checker will fly right past the error, because *their* is spelled correctly. If you're in a hurry and accidentally omit the *p* at the end of *top,* your spell checker will read *to* as correct. Or if you mistakenly type the semicolon instead of the *p,* your spell checker will read *to;* as a correctly spelled word. Plus, some of the "errors" detected may actually be proper names, technical words, words that you misspelled on purpose, or simply words that weren't included in the spell checker's dictionary. It's up to you to decide whether each flagged word should be corrected or left alone.

A computer *thesaurus* gives you alternative words, just as your printed thesaurus does. Not only can a computer thesaurus give you answers faster and more easily than a printed thesaurus, but it may be able to do things that your printed thesaurus could never do. The electronic version of the *American Heritage Dictionary* provides a thesaurus and a special WordHunter function that gives you a term when all you know is part of the definition. If you're racking your brain to remember the word that means a certain quantity of paper, you simply type *quantity AND paper* and then WordHunter searches for every definition in the dictionary that includes those two terms. In a few seconds, the word *ream* pops into view, and you say, "Aha! That's the word I was looking for."

DID YOU KNOW?

The punctuation world is entering a new period. European-style punctuation, which favors the period over the hyphen, is rapidly crossing more borders. Many U.S. companies are abandoning traditional telephone punctuation for the likes of 800.555.1212. They claim that their mad dash to dots is not just a fashionable whim, but rather an attempt to be consistent all over the world.

The third major revision tool is the *grammar checker,* which tries to do for your grammar what a spell checker does for your spelling. The catch here is that checking your spelling is much easier than checking your grammar. A spell checker simply compares each word in your document with a list of correctly spelled words. A grammar checker has to determine whether you're using words correctly and constructing sentences according to the complex rules of composition. Because the program doesn't have a clue about what you're trying to say, it can't tell whether you've said it correctly. Moreover, even if you've used all the rules correctly, a grammar checker still can't tell whether your document communicates clearly. However, grammar checkers can perform some helpful review tasks and point out things you should consider changing, such as passive voice, long sentences, and words that tend to be misused or overused. Some programs even run readability formulas for you (see Figure 6.5).

Figure 6.5
Readability Indexes Using a Grammar Checker

Here are the readability statistics that the program Grammatik computed for a paragraph in one document.

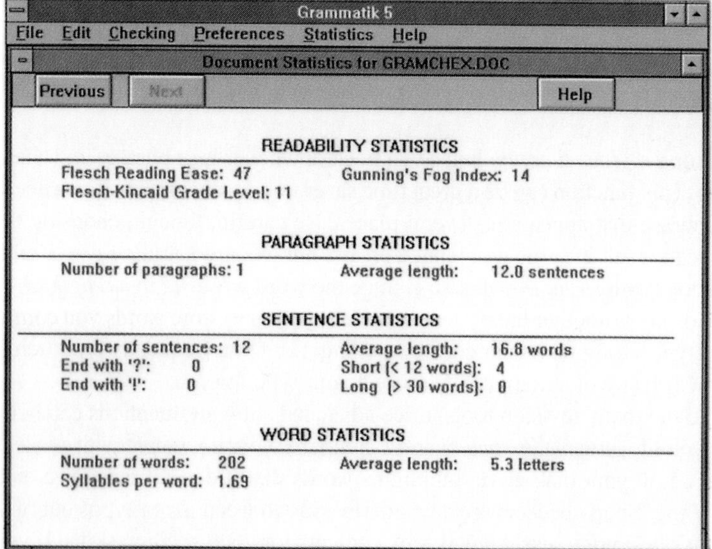

By all means, use any software that you find helpful when revising your documents. Just remember that it's unwise to rely on grammar or spell checkers to do all your revision work. What these programs can do is identify "mistakes" you may overlook on your own. It's up to you to decide what, if anything, needs to be done, and it's up to you to catch the mistakes that these computer programs can't.[16] For a reminder of the tasks involved in revision, see this Chapter's checklist for Revising Business Messages.

Adding Graphics, Sound, and Hypertext to Documents

You can use graphics software to add visual elements to your message.

Computers can do some amazing things with text entry, but that's only part of the story. With the right equipment, you can add full-color pictures and even sound recordings to your documents. The software for creating business visuals falls into two basic groups: presentation software and graphics software. *Presentation software* helps you create overhead transparencies and computerized slide shows for meetings. (Presentations will be discussed in detail in Chapters 12 and 16.) *Graphics software* ranges from products that can create simple diagrams and flowcharts to comprehensive tools geared to artists and graphic designers. You can create your pictures from scratch, use *clip art* (collections of uncopyrighted images), or scan in drawings or photographs. Much of the graphic design and artwork that you see in business publications was created with software packages such as CorelDRAW!

Inserting your visuals into a document used to be a chore, but increasing standardization of computer file formats has made the task somewhat easier. Say you want to distribute some ideas you have for a new corporate logo, and you want to include your sketches in a memo. You've already created several logos in CorelDRAW!, but your memo is in Microsoft Word. No problem—you simply save the CorelDRAW! file in a special transfer format, then switch to your memo in Microsoft Word and activate a command to insert the picture. The logos pop into your memo, and you can shrink or enlarge them to fit.

Adding sound bites to your documents is an exciting new way to get your message across. Several systems now allow you to record a brief message or other sound and attach it to particular places in a document. For instance, you can add sound annotations, instead of written ones. Then, when you click on the special speaker icon, a recorded comment, such as "Please convert this paragraph to a bulleted list" will play. Of course, to actually hear the sound, the person receiving the memo has to load the memo into his or her computer and have a sound card installed.

Your document can have live links to other documents and to the Internet.

You can also insert HyperText Markup Language (HTML) into your document. HyperText Markup Language is an Internet publishing format that hyperlinks documents together, making it easy for users to jump from one document to another. By clicking on a link in the document, you can go directly to a Web site (provided you have an active Internet hookup) or you can jump to another section in the document (or even to a different document).

Think of the possibilities this tool adds to your messages. Say, for example, you're preparing a report on this year's budget. Rather than include pages and pages of prior years' budget detail for all readers, you can submit the report on a computer disk and include a hyperlink in the file. Then, when the user clicks on the hyperlink, a document containing the prior years' budget detail will open. By using hyperlinks, you can customize your documents to meet the individual information needs of your readers—just as you can on a Web page. Of course, you'll have to make sure that the file, or the software program used to open that file, is either included with your electronic document or installed on the recipient's computer. (Electronic reports will be discussed in detail in Chapter 10.)

DID YOU KNOW?

When computer data are lost, 47 percent of the time the cause is mechanical failure or power problems; 32 percent of the time it's human error; and 14 percent of the time it's software problems. Viruses account for only 7 percent of the loss, but they are the fastest-growing cause of data destruction.

CHECKLIST FOR REVISING BUSINESS MESSAGES

A. Editing and Rewriting Your Message
  1. Content and organization
    a. Review your draft against the message plan.
    b. Cover all necessary points in logical order.
    c. Organize the message to respond to the audience's probable reaction.
    d. Provide enough support to make the main idea convincing and interesting.
    e. Eliminate unnecessary material; add useful material.
    f. Be sure the beginning and ending are effective.
  2. Style and readability
    a. Make sure you've achieved the right tone.
    b. Increase interest with lively words and phrases.
    c. Make sure your message is readable.
      i. Check vocabulary.
      ii. Check sentence structure.
      iii. Consider using a readability index.
  3. Conciseness
    a. Eliminate unnecessary words and phrases.
    b. Watch for indefinite pronoun starters.
    c. Eliminate awkward pointers.
  4. Clarity
    a. Break up strung-out sentences.
    b. Avoid hedging sentences.
    c. Express parallel ideas in parallel form.
    d. Correct dangling modifiers.
    e. Avoid long sequences of nouns.
    f. Avoid camouflaged verbs.
    g. Keep subject and verb close together; keep adverbs, adjectives, and prepositional phrases close to the words they modify.
    h. Moderate your enthusiasm.

B. Producing and Proofreading Your Message
  1. Design elements
    a. Use appropriate white space around headings, in margins, between columns, at line endings, in paragraph indents or between unindented paragraphs, and between lines of type.
    b. Choose margins and line justification that won't darken your document.
    c. Use headings to break up long passages of text and to guide your readers through your message.
    d. Select typefaces that complement the tone of your message.
    e. Use only as many type styles as you actually need, avoiding any style that slows the reader's progress.
  2. Design decisions
    a. Be consistent, balanced, restrained, and detail oriented.
    b. Avoid last-minute compromises.
  3. Technology
    a. Become familiar with the many features of word-processing software to help you enter, edit, and revise your text.
    b. Be conservative when adding graphics, sound, or hypertext; make sure your reader has similar technology.
  4. Mechanics and format
    a. Review sentences to be sure they are grammatically correct.
    b. Correct punctuation and capitalization errors.
    c. Correct spelling and typographical errors.
    d. Review the format to be sure it follows accepted conventions.
    e. Use the format consistently throughout the message.
  5. Electronic grammar and spell checkers
    a. Use electronic grammar and spell checkers to point out errors you might overlook.
    b. Be aware of program limitations so that you don't rely too heavily on electronic checkers.

Using Technology to Design Your Message

Once you've planned, composed, edited, and rewritten your message, give some thought to its design. Most word-processing programs include several elements to help you assemble your finished pages, combining text and graphics so that the appearance is both professional and inviting. But if you want a first-class report with photos and drawings, you should consider **desktop publishing (DTP)** software. Desktop publishing software includes additional specialized tools for formatting, drawing, design, and layout.

In general, the software most appropriate for assembling finished pages with graphics elements is desktop publishing (DTP), although word-processing software can handle graphics to a limited extent.

Whether you use word-processing or DTP software to design your message, it's important that you balance graphics and text. Consider the memo shown in Figure 6.6. The bar chart in this memo is centered to give a formal impression, and the color used in the graphic is balanced by the letterhead logo.

Figure 6.6
In-Depth Critique: The Importance of Appearance

An attractive, contemporary appearance can help you get your message across effectively.

9408 Sepulveda Way • Los Angeles, California 97402 • (805) 555-4103

A colorful letterhead can add to a professional appearance.

MEMO

DATE: April 14, 2000
TO: Alden Maxwell, Vice President, Marketing
FROM: Louise Ellison, Manager, Promotions
SUBJECT: Using sports as a selling tool for promoting our new calcium-plus soft drink

After doing a little research, I'm more convinced than ever that sponsoring a sporting event would be an excellent way to build awareness of our new calcium-plus soft drink.

The experiences of other companies show that sports sponsorship is an extremely cost-effective approach to promotion. For example, Volvo found that it can reach as many people by spending $3 million on tennis tournaments as it can by spending $25 million on media advertising.

A contemporary typeface can help your document appear lively.

If we decide to go forward with a sponsorship, our first priority should be to identify a sport that is popular with our target customers. As the chart below indicates, auto racing is currently the number-one sport among corporate sponsors, possibly because it appeals to both men and women:

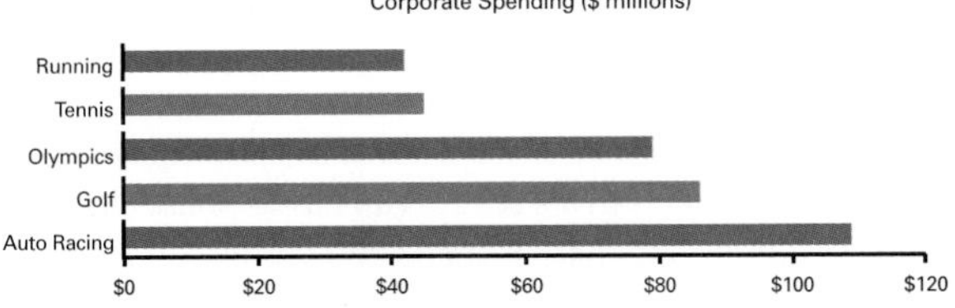

Colorful graphics are great for drawing attention to important points.

Although the "mainstream" sports currently receive the lion's share of corporate dollars, we might achieve more impact with a lesser-known event. Timberline Company has really scored with its sponsorship of the Iditarod dog-sled race across Alaska, a contest that appeals to customers for rugged footwear.

Balancing graphics, text, and color creates a polished appearance that lends credibility to your message

Over the next few days, I plan to do some more research to identify sporting events that would give us the most exposure among health-conscious women, who represent our primary market. I hope to pinpoint three or four possibilities and prepare some preliminary cost estimates for discussion at the Tuesday staff meeting.

Computer software can help you add a first-class look to your most important business documents.

The manner in which you package your ideas has a lot to do with how successful your communication will be. A document that looks tired and out of date will give that impression to your readers—even if your ideas are innovative. Today's computer software makes it easy for anyone to produce great-looking documents in a hurry. Both word processors and desktop publishing software can help you in three ways:

- *Adding a first-class finish*. From selecting attractive typefaces to adding color graphics, you can use your computer tools to turn a plain piece of text into a dazzling and persuasive document. Used improperly, however, these same tools can turn your document into garish, high-tech rubbish. Knowing how to use the tools of technology is a key issue for today's business communicators.
- *Managing document style*. The many design and formatting choices at your fingertips might make it difficult to maintain consistency throughout your document. Most word processors today use *styles,* which are formatting commands that you can save and apply as needed. Some high-end word processors and DTP packages use *style sheets,* collections of formatting rules that can save a lot of formatting effort. For instance, using your style sheet can ensure that each section you add to your report is formatted consistently with the other sections (with the same typeface, margins, word spacing, and so on). You can also use style sheets to ensure a consistent look for all the documents created by everyone in a department or even in an entire company.
- *Generating supporting elements*. If you've ever written a report with footnotes or endnotes, an index, and a table of contents, you know how much work creating such supporting elements can be. Fortunately, computers can help keep track of your footnotes, renumbering them every time you add or delete references. For indexes and tables of contents, you simply flag the items you want to include, and the software assembles the lists for you.

Design Elements

Most readers have trouble comprehending long, uninterrupted pages of text. Design elements such as white space, headings, and boldface type help the reader by providing visual clues to the importance of various ideas and their relationships.[17] Keep in mind that if you're composing a half-page memo, a boatload of design elements will only confuse your audience.

White space is free of text and artwork.

White Space Space free of text or artwork is known as **white space**. It provides contrast, and perhaps even more important, it gives readers a resting point. White space includes the open area surrounding headings, the margin space, the vertical space between columns, the space created by ragged line endings, the paragraph indents or extra space between unindented paragraphs, and the horizontal space between lines of type. You need to decide how much white space to allow for each of these areas.

Margins and Line Justification Margins define the space around your text and between text columns. They're influenced by the way you place lines of type, which can be set (1) justified (flush on the left and flush on the right), (2) flush left with a ragged-right margin, (3) flush right with a ragged-left margin, or (4) centered.

Justified type "darkens" your message's appearance, because the uniform line lengths lack the white space created by ragged margins. It also tends to make your message look more like a form letter and less like a customized message. Justified type is often considered more difficult to read, because large gaps can appear between words and because more words are hyphenated. Excessive hyphenation is distracting and hard to follow. Even so, many magazines and newspapers use justified type because word density is higher.

Flush-left–ragged-right type "lightens" your message's appearance. It gives a document an informal, contemporary feeling of openness. The space between words is the same, and only long words that fall at the ends of lines are hyphenated.

Flush-left–ragged-right type gives your message an open feeling.

Centered type lends a formal tone to your message. However, centering long blocks of type slows reading because your audience has to search for the beginning of each line. The same problem is true of flush-right–ragged-left type. These two approaches are usually avoided for passages of text.

Headings and Captions Headings and subheadings are usually set larger than the type used for text and are often set in a different typeface. They invite readers to become involved in your message, so avoid centering heads that contain more than two lines. Like centered text, centered headings slow your readers as they search for the beginning of each line; flush-left heads are better. Because headings and subheadings clue readers into the organization of your message's content, you want to link them as closely as possible to the text they introduce. You can do so by putting more space above the heading than below it.

Headings help your readers quickly identify the content and organization of your message.

Next to headings, captions are the most widely read part of a document. They tie photographs and illustrations into the rest of your message. Although usually placed below the exhibits they describe, captions can also be placed beside or above their exhibits. Make sure that the width of your captions is pleasing in proportion to the width of the exhibit, the surrounding white space, and the text.

Typefaces **Typeface** refers to the physical design of letters, numbers, and other characters. Most computers offer innumerable choices of typefaces. Each typeface influences the tone of your message, making it look authoritative, friendly, expensive, classy, casual, and so on. So choose typefaces that are appropriate for your message.

Serif typefaces have small crosslines (called serifs) at the ends of each letter stroke.[18] (See Figure 6.7.) Serif faces such as Times Roman (which is built into most laser printers) are commonly used for text; they tend to look busy and cluttered when set in large sizes for headings or other display treatments. Typefaces with rounded serifs can look friendly; those with squared serifs can look official.

Serif typefaces are commonly used for text.

Sans serif typefaces have no serifs. Faces such as Helvetica (which comes with most laser printers) are ideal for display treatments that use larger type. Sans serif faces can be difficult to read in long blocks of text. They look best when surrounded by plenty of white space—as in headings or in widely spaced lines of text.

Sans serif typefaces are commonly used for headings.

Figure 6.7
Common Typefaces

Although serif typefaces are considered easier to read than sans serif, both have their place in document design.

Serif Typeface	Sans Serif Typeface
Times Roman is often used for text.	Helvetica is often used for headings.
TIMES ROMAN IS HARDER TO READ IN ALL CAPS.	HELVETICA IS A CLEANER FACE EVEN IN ALL CAPS.

Limit the number of typefaces used in a single document.[19] In general, avoid using more than two typefaces on a page. Many great-looking documents are based on a single sans serif typeface for heads and subheads, with a second serif typeface for text and captions. Using too many typefaces clutters the document and reduces your audience's comprehension.

Type Styles *Type style* refers to any modification that lends contrast or emphasis to type. Most computers offer not only underlining but also boldface, italic, and other highlighting and decorative styles. Using boldfaced type for subheads breaks up long expanses of text. Just remember that too much boldfacing will darken the appearance of your message and make it look heavy. You can set isolated words in boldface type in the middle of a text block to draw more attention to them. If you draw more attention than a word warrants, however, you might create a "checkerboard" appearance.

Avoid using type styles that slow your readers down.

Use italic type for emphasis. Although italics are sometimes used when irony or humor is intended, quotation marks are usually best for that purpose. Italics can also be used to indicate a quote and are often used in captions.

Be careful to avoid any style that slows your audience's progress through your message. Underlining can interfere with your reader's ability to recognize the shapes of words, and using all capitals slows reading.[20] Shadowed or outlined type can seriously hinder legibility, so use these styles judiciously.

Make sure the size of your type is proportionate to the importance of your message and the space allotted. Small type in a sea of white space appears lost. Large type squeezed into a small area is hard to read and visually claustrophobic.

Effective Design

For effective design, pay attention to
- Consistency
- Balance
- Restraint
- Detail

Effective design guides your readers through your message, so be sure to be consistent, balanced, restrained, and detail-oriented:

- *Consistency*. Throughout a message (and sometimes even from message to message), be consistent in your use of margins, typeface, type size, and spacing (for example, in paragraph indents, between columns, and around photographs). Also be consistent when using recurring design elements, such as vertical lines, columns, and borders.
- *Balance*. To create a pleasing design, balance the space devoted to text, artwork, and white space.
- *Restraint*. Strive for simplicity in design. Don't clutter your message with too many design elements, too much highlighting, or too many decorative touches.
- *Detail*. Track all details that affect your design and thus your message. Headings and subheadings that appear at the bottom of a column or a page can offend readers when the promised information doesn't appear until the next column or page. A layout that appears off balance can be distracting, and any typographical errors can sabotage an otherwise good-looking design.

Avoid last-minute compromises. Don't reduce type size or white space to squeeze in text. On the other hand, avoid increasing type size or white space to fill space. If you've planned your message so that your purpose, your audience, and your message are clear, you can design your document to be effective.[21] Start by thinking about your medium: press release, magazine or newsletter article, brochure, direct-mail package, slide presentation, formal report, business letter, or internal memo. Once you've decided on a medium, try to make it look as interesting as you can while making it as easy as possible to read and understand.

Using Technology to Distribute Your Message

Technology does some of its most amazing feats when it's time to distribute your documents. For multiple copies of your document, you can print as many as you like on your office printer or print a single copy and reproduce it with a *photocopier*. For high-volume and complex reproduction (involving colors or photographs, for instance), you'll want to take your document to a *print shop,* a company that has the special equipment needed for such jobs.

When you need to send the same document (sales letter, invoice, or other customer communication) to a large number of people, *mail merge* automatically combines a standard version of the document with a list of names and addresses. It will produce one copy for each person on your mailing list, saving you the trouble of inserting the name and address each time. The names and addresses can come from your own customer databases or from mailing lists you can rent from firms that specialize in collecting names and addresses.

Fax machines (and computers equipped with fax modems) are an integral part of the business communication process, providing fast transmission of printed documents all over the world.

Fax machines have had a major impact on the distribution of printed documents. Using regular telephone lines, you can transmit (fax) an exact reproduction (a facsimile) of a document from one machine to another. Broadcast faxing saves considerable time; it allows you to enter mailing lists into your fax machine and transmit your document to the fax machines of all members on the list. Fax machines are indispensable for international business, particularly because they overcome the delay problems of regular mail and the time-zone problems of trying to contact someone by telephone.[22] Personal computers can be equipped with *fax modems,* which combine data transmission with fax capabilities.

Many companies now distribute information on CD-ROM or computer disk rather than on paper. For instance, several of Hewlett-Packard's product catalogs are available either on CD-ROM or in printed form. CD-ROMs hold a large amount of information, and their small size saves money in postage and shipping.

Of course, one of the most popular methods for distributing documents is over the Internet. Most Internet browser software allows you to attach documents of all sizes and types to e-mail messages. If you are sending multiple documents or long documents over the Internet, you can use special software to encode or compress your message, reducing the file size so that it can be transmitted faster. Before doing that, however, make sure your recipients have similar software so that they can decode or uncompress the message and convert it back into its original file format.

Technology gives today's business communicators more options for composing, revising, designing, and distributing messages, but it also requires more decisions and more skills. In Chapter 10 we'll discuss communicating through technology in depth, including such aspects as the Internet, e-mail, company intranets, videoconferencing, electronic reporting, hi-tech etiquette, and information overload. Then, in Chapter 11 we'll elaborate on using technology and the Internet to conduct research, and in Chapter 12 we'll explain how technology can be used to develop visual aids.

COMMUNICATION CHALLENGES AT TURNER BROADCASTING SYSTEM

One of Adrianne Proeller's tasks is to send out internal memos announcing new employees hired by TBS. You're one of the newest—hired right out of college—and Proeller has asked you to provide the information she needs to write the official announcement.

INDIVIDUAL CHALLENGE: Decide which job you've been hired for (communications assistant, sales trainee, technical engineer, marketing associate, or any other you choose) and determine what qualifications you'll bring to the position (you may need to invent some). For help, consult library references such as the *Dictionary of Occupational Titles,* which describes positions and qualifications. Then draft a routine memo to Proeller that supplies her with everything she needs to write her announcement. This is one of your first on-the-job tasks, so you want your memo to look good. Scrutinize your first draft for content, organization, style, and readability. Then produce a second draft.

TEAM CHALLENGE: In a small group, exchange copies of your memos so that everyone can mark suggestions for revision on each group member's memo. Then compare your efforts. Did everyone spot the same errors? Where did you disagree? Is it a good idea to let others review your work?[23] ■

SUMMARY OF LEARNING OBJECTIVES

1. **Briefly discuss the steps involved in editing a message.** Editing is an ongoing activity that occurs throughout the composition process. It involves evaluating the message's content and organization, reviewing its style and readability, and rewriting the message to make it clear and concise.
2. **List five ways to make messages more concise.** To make messages more concise, you should eliminate unnecessary words and phrases, use short words and infinitives, eliminate redundancies, replace indefinite pronoun starters, and eliminate awkward pointers.
3. **Name nine ways to improve your writing style.** To improve your writing style you should break up strung-out sentences, avoid hedging sentences, use parallel construction, correct dangling modifiers, avoid long sequences of nouns, avoid camouflaged verbs, keep words together that work together, moderate your enthusiasm, and practice.
4. **Identify seven issues to keep in mind when critiquing someone else's writing style.** When critiquing someone else's writing style, you should first make sure that the document accomplishes its intended purpose, verify that the factual material is correct, and point out all ambiguous language so that it can be eliminated. Then ask yourself whether the document can truly be improved, whether the time needed to rewrite it can be justified, and whether asking for a rewrite could have a negative impact on morale. Finally, make sure your comments are constructive and professional.
5. **Discuss how technology can be used to compose, revise, and design messages.** Technology can assist you with entering and revising text, storing documents and text for future use, and finding errors. In addition, you can use technology to jazz up your documents by adding graphics, sound, and hypertext as well as to design and format your documents' style. Finally, you can use technology to distribute your messages to any number of people all over the globe and in a variety of formats.
6. **Identify five design elements and briefly explain how they can change the appearance and overall effectiveness of a message.** White space provides contrast and gives readers a resting point. Margins define the space around the text and contribute to the amount of white space. Headings and captions invite readers to become involved in the message. Typefaces influence the tone of the message, and type styles provide contrast or emphasis.

CRITICAL THINKING QUESTIONS

1. You have so little time to complete your current project that you have to skip a few of the tasks in the composition process. You've already cut as many corners as you can in the planning and composing stages. Which tasks in the revision phase would be the best to bypass: editing, rewriting, producing, or proofreading? Explain.
2. Why is it important to let your draft "age" a day before you begin the editing process?
3. What are some challenges you might encounter when writing in teams?
4. Why are companies interested in collaborative technologies such as teleconferencing and groupware?
5. Is it important for everyone in the company to know how to use the latest technological tools for document preparation? Why or why not?
6. When you are designing a formal business letter, which design elements do you have to consider and which are optional?
7. Evaluate this comment: "Before I began using a word processor, I used to crank out memos one, two, three. I'd draft them on paper and my secretary would have them ready for my signature by the next morning. Now I'm supposed to use the computer for everything—including keyboarding and editing my own memos. I thought all this technology stuff would save me time. It's hasn't."
8. Given the choice of only one, would you prefer to use a grammar checker or a spell checker? Why?

DOCUMENTS FOR ANALYSIS

Read the following documents; then (1) analyze the strengths and weaknesses of each sentence and (2) revise each document so that it follows the guidelines in Chapters 4 through 6.

Document 6.A

The move to our new offices will take place over this coming weekend. For everything to run smooth, everyone will have to clean out their own desk and pack up the contents in boxes that will be provided. You will need to take everything off the walls too, and please pack it along with the boxes.

If you have alot of personal belongings, you should bring them home with you. Likewise with anything valuable. I do not mean to infer that items will be stolen, irregardless it is better to be safe than sorry.

On Monday, we will be unpacking, putting things away, and then get back to work. The least amount of disruption is anticipated by us, if everyone does their part. Hopefully, there will be no negative affects on production schedules, and current deadlines will be met.

Document 6.B

Dear Ms. Giraud:

Enclosed herewith please find the manuscript for your book, *Careers in Woolgathering*. After perusing the first two chapters of your 1,500-page manuscript, I was forced to conclude that the subject matter, handicrafts and artwork using wool fibers, is not coincident with the publishing program of Framingham Press, which to this date has issued only works on business endeavors, avoiding all other topics completely.

Although our firm is unable to consider your impressive work at the present time, I have taken the liberty of recording some comments on some of the pages. I am of the opinion that any feedback that a writer can obtain from those well versed in the publishing realm can only serve to improve the writer's authorial skills.

In view of the fact that your residence is in the Boston area, might I suggest that you secure an appointment with someone of high editorial stature at the Cambridge Heritage Press, which I believe might have something of an interest in works of the nature you have produced.

Wishing you the best of luck in your literary endeavors, I remain

Arthur J. Cogswell
Editor

Document 6.C

For delicious, air-popped popcorn, please read the following instructions: The popper is designed to pop 1/2 cup of popcorn kernels at one time. Never add more than 1/2 cup. A half cup of corn will produce three to four quarts of popcorn. More batches may be made separately after completion of the first batch. Popcorn is popped by hot air. Oil or shortening is not needed for popping corn. Add only popcorn kernels to the popping chamber. Standard grades of popcorn are recommended for use. Premium or gourmet type popping corns may be used. Ingredients such as oil, shortening, butter, margarine, or salt should never be added to the popping chamber. The popper, with popping chute in position, may be preheated for two minutes before adding the corn. Turn the popper off before adding the corn. Use electricity safely and wisely. Observe safety precautions when using the popper. Do not touch the popper when it is hot. The popper should not be left unattended when it is plugged into an outlet. Do not use the popper if it or its cord has been damaged. Do not use the popper if it is not working properly. Before using the first time, wash the chute and butter/measuring cup in hot soapy water. Use a dishcloth or sponge. Wipe the outside of the popper base. Use a damp cloth. Dry the base. Do not immerse the popper base in water or other liquid. Replace the chute and butter/measuring cup. The popper is ready to use.

EXERCISES

1. Revise the following sentences, using shorter, simpler words:
   a. The antiquated calculator is ineffectual for solving sophisticated problems.
   b. It is imperative that the pay increments be terminated before an inordinate deficit is accumulated.
   c. There was unanimity among the executives that Ms. Jackson's idiosyncrasies were cause for a mandatory meeting with the company's personnel director.
   d. The impending liquidation of the company's assets was cause for jubilation among the company's competitors.
   e. The expectations of the president for a stock dividend were accentuated by the preponderance of evidence that the company was in good financial condition.
2. Rewrite each sentence so that the verbs are no longer camouflaged:
   a. Adaptation to the new rules was performed easily by the employees.
   b. The assessor will make a determination of the tax due.
   c. Verification of the identity of the employees must be made daily.
   d. The board of directors made a recommendation that Mr. Ronson be assigned to a new division.
   e. The auditing procedure on the books was performed by the vice president.
3. Shorten these sentences by adding more periods:
   a. The next time you write something, check your average sentence length in a 100-word passage, and if your sentences average more than 16 to 20 words, see whether you can break up some sentences.
   b. Don't do what the village blacksmith did when he instructed his apprentice as follows: "When I take the shoe out of the fire, I'll lay it on the anvil, and when I nod my head, you hit it with the hammer." The apprentice did just as he was told, and now he's the village blacksmith.

c. Unfortunately, no gadget will produce excellent writing, but using a yardstick like the Fog Index gives us some guideposts to follow for making writing easier to read because its two factors remind us to use short sentences and simple words.
d. Know the flexibility of the written word and its power to convey an idea, and know how to make your words behave so that your readers will understand.
e. Words mean different things to different people, and a word like *block* may mean city block, butcher block, engine block, auction block, or several other things.

4. Cross out unnecessary words in the following phrases:
a. consensus of opinion
b. new innovations
c. long period of time
d. at a price of $50
e. still remains

5. Use infinitives as substitutes for the overly long phrases in these sentences:
a. For living, I require money.
b. They did not find sufficient evidence for believing in the future.
c. Bringing about the destruction of a dream is tragic.

6. Rephrase the following in fewer words:
a. in the near future
b. in the event that
c. in order that
d. for the purpose of
e. with regard to
f. it may be that
g. in very few cases
h. with reference to
i. at the present time
j. there is no doubt that

7. Condense these sentences to as few words as possible:
a. We are of the conviction that writing is important.
b. In all probability, we're likely to have a price increase.
c. Our goals include making a determination about that in the near future.
d. When all is said and done at the conclusion of this experiment, I'd like to summarize the final windup.
e. After a trial period of three weeks, during which time she worked for a total of 15 full working days, we found her work was sufficiently satisfactory so that we offered her full-time work.

8. Remove all the unnecessary modifiers from these sentences:
a. Tremendously high pay increases were given to the extraordinarily skilled and extremely conscientious employees.
b. The union's proposals were highly inflationary, extremely demanding, and exceptionally bold.

9. Rewrite these sentences so that they no longer contain any hedging:
a. It would appear that someone apparently entered illegally.
b. It may be possible that sometime in the near future the situation is likely to improve.
c. Your report seems to suggest that we might be losing money.
d. I believe Nancy apparently has somewhat greater influence over employees in the word processing department.
e. It seems as if this letter of resignation means you might be leaving us.

10. Rewrite these sentences to eliminate the indefinite starters:
a. There are several examples here to show that Elaine can't hold a position very long.
b. It would be greatly appreciated if every employee would make a generous contribution to Mildred Cook's retirement party.
c. It has been learned in Washington today from generally reliable sources that an important announcement will be made shortly by the White House.
d. There is a rule that states that we cannot work overtime without permission.
e. It would be great if you could work late for the next three Saturdays.

11. Present the ideas in these sentences in parallel form:
a. Mr. Hill is expected to lecture three days a week, to counsel two days a week, and must write for publication in his spare time.
b. She knows not only accounting, but she also reads Latin.
c. Both applicants had families, college degrees, and were in their thirties, with considerable accounting experience but few social connections.
d. This book was exciting, well written, and held my interest.
e. Don is both a hard worker and he knows bookkeeping.

12. Revise the following sentences to delete the awkward pointers:
a. The vice president in charge of sales and the production manager are responsible for the keys to 34A and 35A, respectively.
b. The keys to 34A and 35A are in executive hands, with the former belonging to the vice president in charge of sales and the latter belonging to the production manager.
c. The keys to 34A and 35A have been given to the production manager, with the aforementioned keys being gold embossed.
d. A laser printer and a dot-matrix printer were delivered to John and Megan, respectively.
e. The walnut desk is more expensive than the oak desk, the former costing $300 more than the latter.

13. Rewrite these sentences to clarify the dangling modifiers:
a. Running down the railroad tracks in a cloud of smoke, we watched the countryside glide by.
b. Lying on the shelf, Ruby saw the seashell.
c. Based on the information, I think we should buy the property.
d. Being cluttered and filthy, Sandy took the whole afternoon to clean up her desk.
e. After proofreading every word, the memo was ready to be signed.

14. Rewrite the following sentences to eliminate the long strings of nouns:

a. The focus of the meeting was a discussion of the bank interest rate deregulation issue.
b. Following the government task force report recommendations, we are revising our job applicant evaluation procedures.
c. The production department quality assurance program components include employee training, supplier cooperation, and computerized detection equipment.
d. The supermarket warehouse inventory reduction plan will be implemented next month.
e. The State University business school graduate placement program is one of the best in the country.

15. Rearrange the following sentences to bring the subjects closer to their verbs:
a. Trudy, when she first saw the bull pawing the ground, ran.
b. It was Terri who, according to Ted, who is probably the worst gossip in the office (Tom excepted), mailed the wrong order.
c. William Oberstreet, in his book *Investment Capital Reconsidered,* writes of the mistakes that bankers through the decades have made.
d. Judy Schimmel, after passing up several sensible investment opportunities, despite the warnings of her friends and family, invested her inheritance in a jojoba plantation.
e. The president of U-Stor-It, which was on the brink of bankruptcy after the warehouse fire, the worst tragedy in the history of the company, prepared an announcement for the press.

16. Explore the Web site, Anatomy of English Language at http://www.dsoe.com./explore/english, and jot down two rules pertaining to parts of speech or style that will help you edit your work. Be sure to review these rules each time you compose or edit a message.

17. Your accounting firm has composed a five-page form letter that describes the firm's services, its policies, and a bit of its history. Each time you send this form letter to a new client, you customize it to adapt the message to your audience. Review the seven steps in the writing process discussed in Chapters 4 through 6. What are some of the things you should consider when customizing this letter for a new client?

18. An employee has come to work more than an hour late three times this week. You just put the finishing touches on an e-mail message notifying her that her behavior is inexcusable. Before you send the message, however, you change your mind and decide to send the message in a letter addressed to her home. What changes might you have to make now that you've selected a different medium (letter instead of e-mail)?

EXPLORING THE BEST OF THE WEB

Improve Your Writing Style with Proven Techniques, page 167

The following paragraph is an excerpt from a letter sent by a local water utility to its customers. Using Strunk's *Elements of Style* as a guide, what changes would you make in the company's message?

> To assure the continued efficient functioning of our water delivery system (which is so important to the people and businesses of this area) we are asking your cooperation in conserving water. Private residences and commercial establishments should restrict water usage on weekdays between the hours of 10 a.m. and 2 p.m. and 12 p.m. and 4 p.m., respectively. We are sure that you won't mind saving water. It is a very worth while goal for each and every one of us, we thank you in advance for your efforts.

Part 2 A Case for Critical Thinking

CAUTION! E-MAIL CAN BITE

Bill Gates, chairman of Microsoft, has discovered what other CEOs around the globe are just starting to grasp about e-mail: It can—and will—bite.

In May 1998, the U.S. Justice Department filed a landmark antitrust case against Microsoft, claiming that the software giant had tried ruthlessly and illegally to crush competitors and to monopolize access to the Internet. What's the evidence for the allegations? Millions of pages of internal memos and e-mail messages—dashed off years ago by Gates and his top lieutenants. Now, some Microsoft executives wish they could take them back.

Like Gates, others have discovered that in today's litigious environment, electronic mail and internal memos can contain the most damaging information. Look at Staples. When the Federal Trade Commission (FTC) challenged Staples's $4 billion

The U.S. Justice Department used Chairman Bill Gates' own memos and e-mail to strengthen its case against Microsoft.

acquisition of Office Depot, the two companies argued in federal court that the deal wouldn't hurt competition. But internal company documents proved the competition would suffer, so the FTC blocked the merger. Similarly, a subsidiary of Chevron recently spent $2.2 million to settle a sex discrimination lawsuit based, in part, on an e-mail message that made jokes about women and that was circulated to about 30 employees.

What Makes E-Mail So Good . . . And So Dangerous? One of the greatest features—and dangers—of e-mail is that it's treated far more informally than other forms of business communication. Because of its perceived impermanence, people often use it to express opinions they would never put in a letter. As one attorney puts it, "Increasingly, I see entire cases built on e-mail correspondence, in large part because people don't take it as seriously as written correspondence; rather, they treat e-mail in a more conversational way." Yet, despite years of telling workers that their e-mail isn't private, companies still see e-mail containing conversations that used to take place by the water cooler, in the elevator, or over lunch.

Most large companies maintain strict document-retention policies, but only a few extend these policies to cover e-mail. In fact, a recent survey of 800 corporate human resource managers found that barely half of the companies had written policies governing e-mail use, and of those, only one quarter were actually enforcing the policies. Some top managers worry that monitoring e-mail will trigger employee complaints of Big Brother in the workplace. Furthermore, the cost of managing e-mail is high, and determining a policy is difficult. For instance, what e-mail should be considered appropriate? What is inappropriate? And how long should you keep it?

Digital Immortality Some people describe the management of their e-mail in one word: chaos. Here's why. For one thing, purging old e-mail isn't as easy as it seems; e-mail is actually more permanent than traditional memos, letters, or reports because—short of reformatting the hard drive—computers don't actually erase anything. Instead, deletion programs hide the files and label them "deletable." If the computer needs the space, the deletable file will be overwritten by a new one. But most computers these days have so much capacity that a file might never be erased. And even if it is, countless copies of the message can be floating around anywhere.

Companies using networks often store many backup copies of each computer's hard drive in several places; these backup copies often contain information that was sent to the electronic trash bin long ago. Furthermore, when an e-mail message is sent, it bounces from one routing computer to another as it makes its way across the Internet to the recipient. Each of those steps is another place where prying eyes can peek at a message or where a backup can be made. Of course, all these backups are great if you lose a file when your system crashes. They're not great, however, if you are trying to get rid of e-mail messages that sneer or call the boss a dope.

Catch-22 While experts advise companies to keep important messages and purge the rest, some judges disagree. They are increasingly ready to penalize companies they think haven't done enough to save or uncover e-mail. For instance, in one lawsuit Sprint Corp. was penalized for "spoilation of evidence"—or in layman terms, not keeping e-mail and other documents that were relevant to its business practices.

What do you do if you receive more than 100 e-mails a day as Bill Gates does? Should you be expected to keep and remember every message? Furthermore, just because something is mentioned in an e-mail between managers, does that make it company policy?

No way, says one Microsoft attorney. "An e-mail message in a company like Microsoft is a conversation; it's where ideas are explored, and sometimes shot down," and "because it's both informal and not conclusive, you can't really look at any single e-mail or excerpt out of context." Of course, that's what Microsoft's attorneys must now prove. In fact, the government's case against Microsoft is really about much more than an alleged monopoly. It's also about the way we communicate.

Developing an E-Mail Policy As more and more businesses use e-mail to revolutionize their links to clients, suppliers, and customers, companies will have to figure out how to deal with this internal communication challenge. That is, they must find a way to take advantage of new communication media such as e-mail without getting tripped up by the informal, candid, and sometimes inflammatory remarks such media can foster. One good way to start tackling this challenge is to develop company e-mail policy. Consider this advice from experts:

- Immediately establish an e-mail retention policy: Only essential e-mail should be saved.
- Keep each user's e-mail in a designated directory or area on the computer network.

- Don't forward e-mail without the sender's express permission.
- Use extreme care when forwarding e-mail that is protected by attorney-client privilege. Sending privileged material to an unauthorized party, even if done accidentally, may result in a waiver of the privilege.
- Avoid using obscenities and making derogatory remarks.
- Delete any copyrighted material that you don't have permission to use. Make sure that employees understand that copyrighted material includes not only text but also pictures, video, and sound.
- Establish procedures for handling complaints about inappropriate or offensive e-mail.
- Clearly establish that the computer and e-mail system belong to the company and may be used only for business purposes.

1. You are a member of a special task force of employees and administrators that has finally reached consensus on a companywide e-mail policy. The policy will become effective in three months, and it's rather extensive. Now your group must decide how to communicate this policy to all company employees. Break into smaller groups (say four to five), and, using everything you've learned in Chapters 4 through 6, develop a list of criteria the task force should consider to help them select the best channel, medium, and approach (direct or indirect) for delivering this complex message.
2. Why do most people treat e-mail so casually?
3. Using the effective writing principles discussed in Chapters 4 through 6, write a short memo to your instructor highlighting several things that can be done to prevent lawsuits when composing e-mail messages.
4. Learn about the Electronic Communications Privacy Act (ECPA) by visiting the Web site http://www.people.virginia.edu/~klb6q/infopaper/ECPA.html. Write a brief e-mail message to your instructor summarizing what the act covers and prohibits and describing the protection it affords online system users.

Letters, Memos, E-Mail, and Other Brief Messages

CHAPTER 7

WRITING ROUTINE, GOOD-NEWS, AND GOODWILL MESSAGES

AFTER STUDYING THIS CHAPTER, YOU WILL BE ABLE TO

1 Discuss why it's generally appropriate to use the direct organizational plan for routine, good-news, and goodwill messages
2 Describe the basic format for writing routine requests
3 Describe the basic format for writing routine positive replies
4 Highlight the main elements to include in direct requests for claims and adjustments
5 Discuss the main differences in the explanatory section of a favorable response to a routine claim for adjustment when the company, the customer, or a third party is at fault
6 Explain why goodwill messages are important and how to make them effective

COMMUNICATION CLOSE-UP AT THE NATURE COMPANY

When Silva Raker was studying zoology, she never dreamed that the lizards, birds, and leopards she would spend her life with would be made of sterling silver, paper, and glass. Nevertheless, after graduation Raker landed a job in The Nature Company's warehouse. Soon she was traveling the world as a buyer for the international retail chain, and now she's been promoted to vice president of merchandise. Raker's strong communication skills help her coordinate the work of buyers and retail sales staff with that of the designers and architects who keep the atmosphere lively and interesting inside The Nature Company's stores (whether they're in the United States, Canada, France, the United Kingdom, or Japan). "I do a lot of communicating just to keep everyone informed," says Raker. And, like most busy executives, she makes plenty of direct requests.

Silva Raker

First of all, "you need to be polite and genuine," advises Raker. Her formal training as a zoologist and her travels for The Nature Company have convinced her that "the world's a pretty connected place . . . a web of people working together." She believes that treating people well is as important in business as it is in any other setting—and part of that treatment means considering people's needs and problems when you are making a direct request.

One year Raker ordered a thousand sterling silver lizard earrings from an artist who hand-cast them in his basement, one pair at a time. Because The Nature Company's mission is "to provide fine-quality products devoted to the observation, understanding, and appreciation of the natural world," its customers have come to expect true-to-life merchandise that reflects nature's fascinating diversity. They loved the realistic lizards, which dangled by their tails from the wearer's ears. Raker knew from early sales projections that she could sell ten times her original order. She decided to ask the artist to produce not 1,000, but 10,000, pairs

At The Nature Company, direct requests are common, both inside and outside the organization. Whether employees are dealing with customers face to face, composing memos to co-workers, or writing letters to suppliers, they make an effort to consider and understand their audience's needs and problems when making a request.

of earrings, and she wanted to ask him to do so in time to capture the Christmas market. It was already August, but if he could make the deadline, both the artist and The Nature Company would earn a nice sum from the popular lizards.

Raker understood that she would be asking the artist to expand his business substantially, to a level he probably hadn't planned to reach for many years—if ever. For such a serious request, Raker says, "You really have to establish a rapport with people, and trust." They need to know that if they expand their staff or buy new equipment, you'll still be doing business with them in the future. You want to explain how a positive response will benefit them. But at the same time, cautions Raker, "You want to make sure you don't promise more than you can deliver."

In her letter, Raker got right to the request, explaining the reasons behind it and pointing out the benefits of complying with it. She also made sure to compliment the artist on his product: "You've really got something great here. Here's the response we're getting."

Raker says she tries to imagine all the ways a request might be misunderstood (something she learned from buying merchandise in other countries); then she writes her request to avoid those misunderstandings. With the lizard artist, she also wanted to establish a personal rapport and a feeling of partnership. So she included questions she might ask a partner, such as, "How many earrings can you produce in a week? Tell me about your setup and your staff. What are the limiting factors? Is there a component that you can't get enough of?" She let the artist know that she cared about his business and that she would be available to offer support and advice as he increased his production. "I tried to present my request as more of a challenge rather than an impossible task," Raker recalls.

As a result of her skillful presentation, the artist accepted the challenge. He developed a method for gang-casting the earrings and met Raker's request for the Christmas season by delivering 10,000 pairs of lizard earrings—which sold even better than expected. The artist still supplies The Nature Company with some of its best-selling items.

Whether writing memos requesting cooperation from co-workers or writing letters requesting information or services from people outside the company, Raker phrases her direct requests clearly, simply, and with knowledge of her audience's point of view. She also projects a certain enthusiasm into her writing, which lets her readers know that the request involves "something that's going to matter." She's found that people sense and appreciate her concern for their needs. As a result, they're eager to cooperate, and Raker reaps positive replies to her direct requests.[1] ■

STRATEGIES FOR ROUTINE REQUESTS AND POSITIVE MESSAGES

Whether you're ordering lizard earrings for The Nature Company or congratulating an employee on a job well done, chances are that in the course of everyday business you'll compose a lot of **routine, good-news,** and **goodwill messages.** In fact, most of a typical employee's communication is about routine matters: orders, information, claims and adjustments, credit, employees, products, operations, and so on. Sometimes you'll communicate these messages orally; other times you'll put these messages in writing. Regardless of your channel choice, understanding how to organize and write routine messages is an important part of communicating effectively.

Most routine, good-news, and goodwill messages are of interest to the reader because they contain information necessary to conduct day-to-day business. If your message requires no special tact or persuasion, if you're addressing an audience with minimal cultural differences, and if you can assume that your audience will be interested in what you have to say or will be neutral (neither pleased nor displeased), then use the direct, or deductive, plan to organize your message. Begin with a clear statement of the main idea, follow with neces-

COMMUNICATING ACROSS CULTURES

HOW DIRECT IS TOO DIRECT?

Is it possible to be too direct, even if you're simply requesting information? At an event in Mexico, the president of the United States spoke bluntly of political realities, whereas the president of France spoke more abstractly—his style more grand, his words more beautiful. One man addressed the issues directly; the other was less direct. Which one had greater impact?

Neither speech changed global relationships, but the U.S. president was seen as a product of his outspoken culture, whereas the French president was seen as at least making his listeners feel better for a while. Countries such as France, Mexico, Japan, Saudi Arabia, Italy, and the Philippines all tend toward high-context cultures (see discussion in Chapter 3). That is, people in those countries depend on shared knowledge and inferred messages to communicate; they gather meaning more from context and less from direct statement.

Although people in the United States believe that being direct is civil, considerate, and honest, people in high-context cultures view that same directness as abrupt, rude, and intrusive—even dishonest and offensive. You might think you're doing a good thing by offering a little honest and constructive criticism to your Mexican assistant, but doing so may actually hurt his or her dignity and might even be devastating. In fact, in high-context cultures, be careful to avoid saying outright, "You are wrong." People in such cultures know when they've made a mistake, but by putting it into words, you cause them to lose face.

When making requests outside the United States, consider whether your message might be too direct. To determine whether your international audience will appreciate a direct or an implied message, consider factors such as your audience's attitudes toward destiny, time, authority, and logic.

- *Destiny.* Do people in this culture believe they can control events themselves? Or are events seen as predetermined and uncontrollable? If you're supervising employees who believe that a construction deadline is controlled by fate,

sary details, and close with a cordial statement or a request for the action you want. If your audience will be displeased, uninterested, or unwilling, then use an indirect organizational plan for your message by putting the evidence first and the main idea later.

For routine requests and positive messages
- State the request or main idea
- Give necessary details
- Close with a cordial request for specific action

Look back at Table 5.3 on page 137. Spend a few moments reviewing the criteria and circumstances for selecting the best organizational plan for your message. In this chapter we'll elaborate on the types of messages that are appropriate for the direct approach. Then in Chapter 8 we'll explain how and when to use the indirect approach for bad-news messages, and in Chapter 9 we'll focus on organizational plans for persuasive messages. Keep in mind that regardless of the message type, communicating across cultural boundaries can be frustrating, especially if you're not familiar with the cultural differences involved. So before selecting an organizational plan for your message, learn about the customs of your audience and follow them to the degree possible. (See "Communicating across Cultures: How Direct Is Too Direct?")

Routine Requests

A request is routine if it's part of the normal course of business and you anticipate that your audience will comply. By using the direct organizational approach for routine requests, you place the request first, where it stands out and gets the most attention. Getting right to the point, however, should not be interpreted as a license to be abrupt or tactless. Even though you expect a favorable response, the tone of your initial request is important. Instead of demanding immediate action ("Send me your catalog no. 33A"), soften your request with words such as *please* and *I would appreciate*. An impatient demand for rapid service isn't necessary because you can generally assume that your audience will comply with your request once the reason for it is understood.

Assume that your reader will comply once he or she understands your purpose.

---

your crisp e-mail message requesting them to stay on schedule may be hard for them to understand; it may even be insulting.

- *Time.* Do people in this culture believe that time is exact, precise, and not to be wasted? Or do they view time as relative, relaxed, and necessary for developing interpersonal relationships? If you believe that time is money and you try to get straight to business in your memo to your Mexican manager, your message may be overlooked in the confusion over your lack of relationship skills and your disregard for social propriety.
- *Authority.* Do the people in this culture conduct business more autocratically or more democratically? In Mexico, rank and status are highly valued, so when communicating downward, you may need to be even more direct than you're used to being in the United States. And when communicating upward, you may need to be much less direct in Mexico than you're used to being in the U.S.
- *Logic.* Do the people in this culture pursue logic in a straight line from point A to point B? Or do they communicate in circular or spiral patterns of logic? If you organize a speech or a letter in a straightforward and direct manner, your message may be considered illogical, unclear, and disorganized.

The issue may be a question not only of how direct to be in written messages but also of whether to write at all; perhaps a phone call or a visit would be more appropriate. By finding out how much or how little a culture tends toward high-context communication, you will be able to decide whether to be direct or to rely on nuance when communicating with people in that culture.

1. Research a high-context culture such as Japan, Korea, or China, and write a one- or two-paragraph summary of how someone in that culture would go about requesting information.
2. When you are writing in American English to someone in a high-context culture, would it be better to (a) make the request directly in the interest of clarity or (b) try to match your audience's unfamiliar logic and make your request indirectly? Explain your answer.

Begin with the Request

Although you may be tempted to begin your request with a personal introduction such as "I am the vice president of merchandise at a large international company, and I am looking for quality products that . . . ," Silva Raker knows that this type of beginning is usually a mistake. It buries the essence of the message—the specific request—and it may get lost.

Word the request itself carefully so that it states exactly what you want.

If you're requesting something, state what you want in the first sentence or two and let the explanation follow. Be specific. For example, if you request " the latest census figures" from a government agency, be sure to state whether you want a page or two of summary figures or a detailed report running several thousand pages.

Provide Necessary Details and Justification

In the middle section of the request
- Call attention to how the reader will benefit from granting your request
- Give details of your request

Use the middle section of your message to explain the original request as well as how your audience might benefit from complying. For example, when Silva Raker writes letters to potential suppliers, she might make the first sentence of her message's middle section audience-centered by stating a benefit to the reader. True, she's looking for product information, but she's also telling her unknown readers why she needs the information and explaining how long-term business and personal relationships might evolve. For instance, Raker might write, "By keeping The Nature Company informed about your products, you can help create a new distribution channel for your business."

Another possible approach for the middle section of a routine request is to ask a series of questions, particularly if your inquiry concerns machinery or complex equipment. For instance, you might ask about technical specifications, exact dimensions, and the precise use of a complex tool. If your request is relatively simple, however, such as inquiring about the shipping options when ordering a book or compact disk from Amazon.com, use the middle section of your message to state your questions or provide information. Keep in mind that you should ask the most important questions first. If cost is your main concern, you might begin with a question such as "What is the cost for shipping the CDs by Priority Mail?" Then you may want to ask more-specific but related questions about, say, the cost of shipping partial orders.

Ask the most important question first; then ask related, more specific questions.

When you prepare questions
- Ask only questions that are related to your main request
- Don't ask for information you can find yourself
- Make your questions open-ended and objective
- Deal with only one topic in each question

So that your request can be handled quickly, ask only the questions that are central to your main request. Avoid asking for information that you can find on your own, even if it takes considerable time. If your questions are simple yes-or-no questions, you may even want to provide respondents with a form or with boxes they can check to indicate their answers. If you need a more elaborate answer, pose an open-ended question. For example, "How fast can you ship the CDs?" is more likely to elicit the information you want than "Can you ship the CDs?"

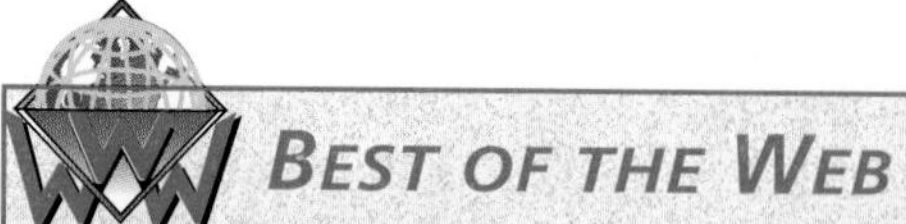

Compose Your Messages with Confidence

Garbl's Writing Resources Online covers virtually every problem faced by a writer. The site includes grammar guides, reference sources, style and usage help, and links to online writing experts who will answer your questions.

http://pw1.netcom.com/~garbl1/writing.html

Now that these two homerun sluggers have broken Babe Ruth's record, they are sure to receive all kinds of direct requests for personal appearances and product endorsements.

If you're requesting several items or answers, number the items and list them in logical order or in descending order of importance. Deal with only one topic in each question. When you have an unusual or complex request, state the request and then provide supporting details. If the question needs amplification, keep each topic in a separate, short paragraph. You may even want to use paragraph headings. You make the reader's job easier when you break down your needs this way.

Use numbered lists when you're requesting several items or answers.

End with a Courteous Close and a Request for Specific Action

Close your letter with two important elements: (1) a request for some specific response (complete with any time limits that apply) and (2) an expression of appreciation or goodwill. Help your reader respond easily by including your phone number, office hours, and other contact information. However, don't thank the reader "in advance" for cooperating. If the reader's reply warrants a word of thanks, send it after you've received the reply. See this chapter's Checklist for Writing Routine Requests to review the direct organizational pattern for routine requests.

Close with
- A request for some specific response
- An expression of appreciation
- Information about how you can be reached

Positive Messages

When you're responding positively to a request or sending a good-news or goodwill message, you'll most likely use the direct organizational approach. That's because the reader will generally be interested in what you have to say. Your goal in these situations is to communicate the good news, answer all questions, provide all required details, and leave your reader with a good impression of you and your firm. Keep in mind that even though you may be doing someone a favor by responding to a request, be courteous, be upbeat, and maintain a you-oriented tone.

Use the direct organizational plan for positive messages.

Begin with the Main Idea

By beginning your positive message with the main idea or good news, you're preparing your audience for the detail that follows. Try to make your opening clear and concise. Although the following introductory statements make the same point, one is cluttered with unnecessary information that buries the purpose, whereas the other is brief and to the point:

CHECKLIST FOR WRITING ROUTINE REQUESTS

A. Direct Statement of the Request
1. Phrase the opening to reflect the assumption that the reader will respond favorably to your request.
2. Phrase the opening clearly and simply so that the main idea cannot be misunderstood.
3. Write in a polite, undemanding, personal tone.
4. Preface complex requests with a sentence or two of explanation.

B. Justification, Explanation, and Details
1. Justify the request, or explain its importance.
2. Explain the benefit of responding.
3. State desired actions in a positive and supportive, not negative or dictatorial, manner.
4. Itemize parts of a complex request in a logical or numbered series.
5. List specific questions that you can't answer through your own efforts.
   a. Limit each question to one topic.
   b. Word questions to get the type of answers you need.

C. Courteous Close with Request for Specific Action
1. Courteously request a specific action.
2. Make it easy to comply by including your contact information: name, address, phone and fax numbers (with area code), and e-mail address.
3. Indicate gratitude.
4. Clearly state any important deadline or time frame for the request.

INSTEAD OF THIS	WRITE THIS
I am pleased to inform you that after deliberating the matter carefully, our human resources committee has recommended you for appointment as a staff accountant.	You've been selected to join our firm as a staff accountant, beginning March 20.

Before you begin, have a clear idea of what you want to say.

The best way to write a clear opening is to have a clear idea of what you want to say. Before you put one word on paper, ask yourself this: What is the single most important message I have for the audience?

Provide Necessary Details and Explanation

The middle part of a positive message is typically the longest section. Even though your response or reason for communicating can usually be expressed in a sentence or two, you'll need more space and time to explain your point completely so that the audience will experience no confusion or lingering doubt. In addition to providing details in the middle section, maintain the supportive tone established at the beginning. This tone is easy to continue when your message is purely good news, as in this example:

> Your educational background and internship have impressed us, and we believe you would be a valuable addition to Green Valley Properties. As discussed during your interview, your salary will be $3,300 per month, plus benefits. In that regard, you will meet with our benefits manager, Paula Sanchez, at 8:00 a.m. on Monday, March 20. She will assist you with all the paperwork necessary to tailor our benefit package to your family situation. She will also arrange for various orientation activities to help you acclimate to our company.

Embed negative information in a positive context.

If your routine message must convey mildly disappointing information, put the negative portion of your message into as favorable a context as possible. Look at the following example:

INSTEAD OF THIS	WRITE THIS
No, we no longer carry the Sportsgirl line of sweaters.	The new Olympic line has replaced the Sportsgirl sweaters that you asked about. Olympic features a wider range of colors and sizes and more contemporary styling.

Notice how the bluntly negative explanation has been replaced with a more complete description that emphasizes how the audience can benefit from the change. Be careful, though: You can use negative information in this type of message only if you're reasonably sure the audience will respond positively. Otherwise, as Chapter 8 will point out, you'll use the indirect approach.

End with a Courteous Close

Your message is most likely to succeed if your audience is left with the feeling that you have their personal welfare in mind. You accomplish this by either highlighting a benefit to the audience or expressing appreciation or goodwill. If follow-up action is required, clearly state who will do what next. See the Checklist for Writing Positive Messages to review the primary tasks involved in this type of business message.

Make sure the audience understands what to do next and how that action will benefit them.

ORDERS

Messages placing orders and acknowledging receipt of orders are considered some of the simplest types of routine messages.

CHECKLIST FOR WRITING POSITIVE MESSAGES

A. Initial Statement of the Good News or Main Idea
  1. If message is mixed, present the good news first.
  2. Respond promptly.
  3. Avoid such trite and obvious statements as "I am pleased to," "We have received," "This is in response to," or Enclosed please find."
  4. Convey an upbeat, courteous, you-oriented tone.

B. Middle, Informational Section
  1. Imply or express interest in the request or provide details of the good news.
  2. List all information in an orderly manner. If possible, answer all questions and requests in the order posed.
     a. Adapt replies to the reader's needs.
     b. Indicate what you have done and will do.
     c. Include any necessary details or interpretations that the reader may need in order to understand your answers.
  3. If you cannot comply with part of the request, perhaps because the information is unavailable or confidential, tell the reader why and offer other assistance.
  4. Embed negative statements in positive contexts or balance them with positive alternatives.
  5. Inform or remind the reader of the general benefits of doing business with your firm. Avoid exaggerations or flamboyant language.

C. Warm, Courteous Close
  1. If further action is required, tell the reader how to proceed and encourage the reader to act promptly.
  2. Avoid clichés ("Please feel free to").
  3. Offer additional service, but avoid implying that your answer is inadequate, by using doubtful statements such as "I trust that" or "I hope."
  4. Express goodwill or take an optimistic look into the future, if appropriate.

Placing Orders

Most companies today use computer-generated order forms.

When placing an order, you need not excite your reader's interest; just state your needs clearly and directly. Most orders refer to a product that the reader knows about, so they're usually processed without objection.

Most companies today use computer-generated order forms that provide a list of goods offered with a description of each item and information such as the catalog number, name or trade name, color, size, and unit price. Your job is simple: Fill in the quantity, compute the total amount due, and provide the shipping address.

Electronic ordering via computer networks and over the Internet is moving companies in the direction of paperless order processing. Still, if you need to draft an order letter, try to follow the same format as you would on an order blank, presenting specific information about the items you want in column form, double-spacing between the items, and totaling the price at the end. In your letter be sure to specify the delivery address, especially if it is not the address from which you send your letter. (Sometimes the billing and delivery addresses are different.) Also indicate how the merchandise is to be shipped: by truck, air freight, parcel post, air express, or delivery service. Unless you specify the mode of transportation, the seller chooses.

In any letter sent with payment, mention the amount enclosed, explain how the amount was calculated, and if necessary, explain to what account the amount should be charged. Again, the order form provides an excellent model. Here's an example:

The general request is stated first.

Please send the following items to the above address by air freight. I am ordering from your current spring–summer catalog:

All necessary details are provided (in a format similar to an order form).

COUNT	STOCK I.D.	DESCRIPTION	PRICE PER ITEM	PRICE TOTAL
10	342	Navajo bracelets (turquoise and silver tubular beads)	$ 8.95	$ 89.50
10	343	Navajo necklaces (turquoise and silver tubular beads)	11.95	119.50
10	344	Navajo loop earnings (turquoise and silver)	9.95	99.50
10	574	Navajo hand-woven rugs (Windsong pattern, 20″ × 38″)	16.99	169.90
5	575	Navajo hand-woven rugs (Windsong pattern, 42″ × 65″)	49.95	249.75
3	595	Navajo hand-woven rugs (Sundance pattern, 5′5″ × 8′2″)	99.99	299.97
		TOTAL SALES		$1,028.12
		SHIPPING		46.00
		AMOUNT DUE		**$1,074.12**

Information about shipping was provided in the catalog, so the writer calculated the amount due.

When placing international orders, use the transposed format: day/month/year.

If you are placing an order with an international company, remember that in most countries the day is placed before the month, as follows:

OTHER COUNTRIES	UNITED STATES
15.3.2000 or 15.3.00	3/15/2000 or 3/15/00
15 March 2000	March 15, 2000

A final suggestion about placing orders: Be thorough and clear. If you supply unclear or insufficient information, your reader must make an extra effort to get the missing details. The resulting delays and cross-communications will hold up delivery of your order and may lead to mistakes in filling it.

When placing orders, be thorough and clear.

Acknowledging Orders

Many order acknowledgments today are in the form of brief statements similar to the e-mail notice this customer received after purchasing a book from Amazon.com:

Subj: Your Amazon.com order (#001-8975234-141987)
Date: 9-17-99 18:54:55 EDT
From: orders@amazon.com
To: McFall@AOL.com

We thought you'd like to know that the following item has been shipped to:

Gail McFall
1554 Oakwood Drive
Wheeling, Illinois 60090

using U.S. Priority (comp. upgrade)

Your order #001-8975234-141987 (received September 16, 1999 11:28 PDT)

Ordered	Title	Price	Shipped	Amount
1	High Tech, High Hope	$19.57	1	$19.57
		Subtotal		19.57
		Shipping & Handling		3.95
		Total		$23.52

This completes your order. If you have any questions, please contact us via e-mail (orders@amazon.com), FAX (1-206-694-2950) or phone (1-800-201-7575 for U.S. customers or 1-206-694-2992 for international customers).

Thank you for shopping at Amazon.com.

If you need to draft a more elaborate acknowledgment, begin by expressing appreciation for the order and briefly describing the merchandise ordered. Provide details about the order in

Placing a direct order at Amazon.com is as easy as point and click.

CHECKLIST FOR ORDERS*

A. Information for Order Requests

1. Provide a general description of the order in the opening.
2. Include all order specifications in the body: quantity, price (including discounts), size, catalog or product number, product description, delivery instructions, arrangements for payment (method, time, deposits), and cost totals.
   - **a.** Indicate how and where to send the shipment (sometimes billing and delivery addresses are different).
   - **b.** Use a format that presents information clearly and makes it easy to total amounts.
   - **c.** Double-check the completeness of your order and the cost totals.
3. State when you expect delivery and specify any time limits in the closing.

B. Information for Order Acknowledgments

1. In the opening, express appreciation for the order and welcome the new customer.
   - **a.** Describe the merchandise ordered in general terms.
   - **b.** Indicate in your first sentence that you are fulfilling the reader's request.
2. In the body, provide all important details about the order.
   - **a.** Necessary educational information about the product.
   - **b.** Details of shipment, including approximate arrival time.
   - **c.** Charges (shipping, insurance, credit charges, or discounts for quick payment).
   - **d.** Information about related products, and credit application, if appropriate.
3. In the closing, remind the reader of the benefits to be derived from the order.

*These items are in addition to the basic tasks associated with writing routine requests and positive responses.

the body of the letter, and when closing, be sure to remind the reader of the benefits he or she will enjoy from the merchandise. (To remind yourself of the tasks involved in placing and acknowledging orders, see this chapter's Checklist for Orders.)

ROUTINE REQUESTS FOR INFORMATION AND ACTION

When making a routine request, say
- What you want to know
- Why you want to know
- Why it is in the reader's interest to help you

When you need to know about something, to elicit an opinion from someone, or to suggest a simple action, you usually need only ask. In essence, simple requests say, "This is what I want to know or what I want you to do, why I'm making the request, and why it may be in your interest to help me." If your reader can do what you want, such a straightforward request gets the job done with a minimum of fuss.

A routine request follows the standard direct plan. Start with a clear statement of your reason for writing; then provide whatever explanation is needed to justify the request. Close with a specific account of what you expect, and include a deadline if appropriate. Despite their simple organization, routine requests deserve a tactful touch. Many organizations send hundreds or even thousands of routine requests in e-mail, memos, and letters to employees, customers, clients, and shareholders. So the potential for creating a positive impression is second only to the risk of causing ill will through ambiguous wording or a discourteous tone. As with any business message, keep your purpose in mind. That is, ask yourself what you want recipients to understand or to do as a result of reading the message. As you prepare the request, remember that it is possible even in the briefest note to create confusion and hard feelings.

Exactly what do you want the reader to understand or to do as a result of reading your request for action?

Requests to Company Insiders

Although requests to fellow employees are often oral and rather casual, some messages are better put in writing. A clear, thoughtfully written memo or e-mail message can save time and questions by helping readers understand precisely what is required. The memo in

Interior Design Decisions (IDD) provides interior office designs for businesses. The company recently decided to upgrade its wellness and benefits program, but it will have to charge employees a nominal fee for use of a sports complex. This memo seeks employee input about the new program and the fee.

Figure 7.1
In-Depth Critique: Memo Requesting Action from Company Insiders

INTERIOR DESIGN DECISIONS

INTERNAL MEMORANDUM

To: All Employees
From: Tony Ramirez, Human Resources
Date: October 15, 1999
Subj: New Wellness Program Opportunity

The benefits package committee has asked me to contact everyone about an opportunity to save money and stay healthier in the bargain. As you know, we've been meeting to decide on changes in our benefits package. Last week, we sent you a memo detailing the Synergy Wellness Program.

In addition to the package as described in the memo (life, major medical, dental, hospitalization), Synergy has sweetened the pot by offering IDD a 10 percent discount. To meet the requirements for the discount, we have to show proof that at least 25 percent of our employees participate in aerobic exercise at least three times a week for at least 20 minutes. (Their actuarial tables show a resulting 10 percent reduction in claims.)

After looking around, we discovered a gymnasium just a few blocks south on Haley Boulevard. Sports Midwest will give our employees unlimited daytime access to their indoor track, gym, and pool for a group fee that comes to approximately $4.50 per month per employee if at least half of us sign up.

In addition to using the track and pool, we can play volleyball, jazzercise, form our own intramural basketball teams, and much more. Our spouses and children can also participate at a deeply discounted monthly fee. If you have questions, please e-mail or call me or any member of the committee. Let us know your wishes on the following form.

Sign and return the following no later than **Friday, October 29.**

= =

______ Yes, I will participate in the Synergy Wellness program and pay $4.50 a month.
______ Yes, I am interested in a discounted family membership.
______ No, I prefer not to participate.

Signature ______________________________

Employee ID Number ______________________________

The readers are busy, so the purpose of the communication is stated in the first paragraph.

The second and third paragraphs present the situation that makes the inquiry necessary.

The final paragraph lists reader benefits, requests action, and provides an easy-to-use response form.

Figure 7.1 was sent to all employees of a relatively small interior design firm. This matter-of-fact memo assumes some shared background. Such a style is appropriate when you're communicating about a routine matter to someone in the same company.

A request in memo form
- Provides a permanent record
- Saves time and questions
- Tells precisely what is needed

When used well, memos and e-mail messages can communicate efficiently, concisely, and powerfully. When misused, these messages can waste time and effort, can swell the ocean of information that offices must deal with, and can even tarnish your business reputation. So avoid writing frequent, long, and unneeded messages.

Requests to Other Businesses, Customers, and Other Outsiders

Requests to outsiders often spell out in detail
- What exactly is needed
- How filling the request will benefit them

Businesses often ask other businesses, customers, or other individuals outside the organization to provide information or to take some simple action: attend a meeting, return an information card, endorse a document, confirm an address, or supplement information on an order. These messages are often short and simple, like this request for information:

> Would you please supply me with information about the lawn services you provide. Pralle Realty owns approximately 27 pieces of rental property in College Station, and we're looking for a lawn service to handle all of them. We are making a commitment to provide quality housing in this college town, and we are looking for an outstanding firm to work with us.
>
> **1. Lawn care:** What is your annual charge for each location for lawn maintenance, including mowing, fertilizing, and weed control?
>
> **2. Shrubbery:** What is your annual charge for each location for the care of deciduous and evergreen bushes, including pruning, fertilizing, and replacing as necessary?
>
> **3. Contract:** How does Agri-Lawn Service structure such large contracts? What additional information do you need from us?
>
> We hope to hear from you by February 15. We want to have a lawn-care firm in place by March 15.

The overall request is stated at the beginning. Phrased politely in question form, it requires no question mark.

The explanation for the request keeps the reader's attention by hinting at the possibility of future business.

To avoid burdening the reader with an impossibly broad request, the writer asks a series of specific questions, itemized in a logical sequence.

To avoid receiving useless yes-or-no answers, the writer asks some open-ended questions.

The courteous close specifies a time limit.

In more complex situations, readers might be unwilling to respond unless they understand how the request benefits them. So be sure to include this information in your explanation.

The purpose of some routine requests to customers is to reestablish communication.

Sometimes businesses need to reestablish a relationship with former customers or suppliers. Frequently, customers don't complain when they are unhappy about some purchase or about the way they were treated: They simply stay away from the offending business. A letter of inquiry encouraging them to use idle credit accounts offers them an opportunity to register their displeasure and then move on to a good relationship. In addition, a customer's response to an inquiry may provide the company with insights into ways to improve its products and customer service. Even if they have no complaint, customers still welcome the personal attention. Such an inquiry to the customer might begin this way:

> When a good charge customer like you has not bought anything from us in six months, we wonder why. Is there something we can do to serve you better?

Similar inquiry letters are sent from one business to another. For example, a sales representative of a housewares distributor might send the same type of letter to a retailer.

Replies to Requests for Information and Action

If your answer to a request is yes or is straightforward information, the direct plan is appropriate. However, if the answer is no or if the message will be displeasing to the audience, you'll want to use the indirect approach for communicating the bad news (see Chapter 8). Regardless of the organizational plan you use, your prompt, gracious, and thorough handling of a request will positively influence how people think about your company and its products, your department, and yourself. Readers' perceptions are the reason Silva Raker of The Nature Company is so sensitive to the tone of her memos, letters, and other messages. Raker makes it a point to adopt the "you" attitude in all her business correspondence.

Admittedly, complying with a request isn't always easy. The information may not be immediately at hand, and decisions to take some action must often be made at a higher level. Fortunately, however, many requests are similar. For example, a human resources department gets a lot of routine inquiries about job openings. Companies usually develop form responses to handle repetitive queries like these. Although form responses are often criticized as being cold and impersonal, you can put a great deal of thought into wording them, and you can use computers to personalize and mix paragraphs. Thus, a computerized form letter prepared with care, like the one in Figure 7.2, may actually be more personal and sincere than a quickly dictated, hastily typed "personal" reply.

When you're answering requests and a potential sale is involved, you have three main goals: (1) to respond to the inquiry and answer all questions, (2) to leave your reader with a good impression of you and your firm, and (3) to encourage the future sale. The following letter succeeds in meeting all three objectives:

Three main goals when a potential sale is involved:

- Respond to the immediate request
- Convey a good impression of you and your firm
- Encourage a sale

You requested a copy of our brochure "Entertainment Unlimited," and Blue Ocean Com-munications is pleased to send it to you. This booklet describes the vast array of entertainment options available to you with an Ocean Satellite Device (OSD).

A clear, conversational statement of the main point is all that's required to start.

On page 12 of "Entertainment Unlimited," you'll find a list of the 138 channels that the OSD brings into your home. You'll have access to movie, sport, and music channels; 24-hour news channels; local channels; and all the major television networks. OSD gives you a clearer picture and more precise sound than those old-fashioned dishes that took up most of your yard—and OSD uses only a small dish that mounts easily on your roof.

Key information is presented immediately, along with resale and sales promotion.

More music, more cartoons, more experts, more news, and more sports are available to you with OSD than with any other cable or satellite connection in this region. Yes, it's all there, right at your fingertips.

Highlighting this product's benefits encourages readers to take one more step toward a purchase.

Just call us at 1-800-786-4331, and an OSD representative will come to your home to answer your questions. You'll love the programming and the low monthly cost. Call us today!

The personal close confidently points toward the sale.

Routine Messages Involving Claims and Adjustments

Satisfied customers bring additional business to the firm; angry or dissatisfied customers do not. In addition, angry customers complain to anyone who'll listen, creating poor public relations. So even though **claims** (or formal complaints) and **adjustments** (or claim settlements) may seem unpleasant, progressive organizations such as The Nature Company treat requests for claims and adjustments as golden opportunities to build customer loyalty.[2]

Figure 7.2
In-Depth Critique: Memo Replying to Requests

Julian Zamakis wrote to McBride Department Stores for information on employment opportunities and received the following encouraging reply.

—McBride—
Department Stores

781 Westchester Boulevard, Hartford, Connecticut 06108
(203) 758-7733 • Fax (203) 758-7703

February 21, 2000

Mr. Julian Zamakis
40106 Glastonbury Lane
Granby, CT 06035

Dear Mr. Zamakis:

Thanks for your letter requesting information on the professional career tracks at McBride Department Stores. As a retail chain with 47 stores in the New England states, we value those recent college graduates who accept entry-level professional positions each year. Your interest is important to us, so we are pleased to provide information on two professional career paths we offer here.

The sales management track places college graduates on the sales floor, dealing with customers and supervising all salesclerks in a given department. The first assignment is usually in a small department, but after two or three years' experience and satisfactory performance, the sales manager has an opportunity to be assigned to a substantially larger department. Part of a sales manager's responsibilities are meeting sales quotas, setting up displays, and handling customer complaints.

The merchandising track places college graduates as assistant buyers, where they work closely with an experienced buyer, reviewing sales figures, formulating the buying plan and budget, and following up on the sales of the merchandise selected. After three to five years' experience and satisfactory performance, the assistant buyer has an opportunity to be promoted to a buyer position.

In a year or so, when you're closer to receiving your degree, come in and talk with us about opportunities with McBride Stores. By asking questions while you're still preparing for your professional career, you'll improve your chances of pursuing the career you want.

Sincerely,

Haley Middleton

Haley Middleton
Human Resources Manager

ss

A brief statement indicates that the requested information will be provided and comments positively on the value of new college graduates to the company.

Specific information is given in answer to the questions posed by the writer.

A warm, personalized closing generates goodwill for McBride and encourages the letter writer to keep in touch—with the possibility that McBride may hire this person in the future.

Direct Requests for Claims and Adjustments

You are entitled to request an adjustment whenever you receive a product or experience service that doesn't live up to the supplier's standards.

Suppose you've waited four months for your new custom office furniture to arrive. It's finally delivered, but you notice that the order is wrong. The fabric on the side chairs was supposed to be beige stripes, not solid brown. And the desk you ordered had two pencil drawers, not one. Your best course of action is to communicate at once with someone at the office furniture company who can make the correction. A phone call or visit may solve the problem, but a written claim letter is better because it documents your dissatisfaction.

Your first reaction to a clumsy mistake or a defective product is likely to be anger or frustration, but the person reading your letter probably had nothing to do with the problem. A courteous, clear, concise explanation will impress the reader much more favorably than an abusive, angry letter. Asking for a fair and reasonable solution will increase your chances of receiving a satisfactory adjustment.

Tone is of primary importance; keep your claim businesslike and unemotional.

In most cases, and especially in your first letter, assume that a fair adjustment will be made, and follow the plan for direct requests. Begin with a straightforward statement of the problem, and give a complete, specific explanation of the details. In the middle section of your claim letter, provide any information the adjuster will need to verify your complaint about faulty merchandise or unsatisfactory service. In your closing, politely request specific action or a sincere desire to find a solution, and suggest that the business relationship will continue if the problem is solved satisfactorily.

In your claim letter
- Explain the problem and give details
- Provide backup information
- Request specific action

Companies usually accept the customer's explanation of what's wrong, so ethically it's important to be entirely honest when filing claims for adjustment or refund. Also, be prepared to back up your claim with invoices, sales receipts, canceled checks, dated correspondence, catalog descriptions, and any other relevant documents. Send copies and keep the originals for your files.

Be prepared to document your claim. Send copies and keep the original documents.

If the remedy is obvious, tell your reader exactly what will return the company to your good graces—for example, an exchange of merchandise for the right item or a refund if the item is out of stock. If you're uncertain about the precise nature of the trouble, you could ask the company to make an assessment. Be sure to supply your contact information and the best time to call so that the company can discuss the situation with you if necessary.

DID YOU KNOW?

Dissatisfied customers tell an average of ten other people about their negative experience, but satisfied customers tell an average of only five other people about their positive experience.

The following letter was written to a gas and electric company. As you read it, compare the tone with that in Figure 7.3. If you were the person receiving the complaint, which version would you respond to more favorably?

> We have been at our present location only three months, and we don't understand why our December utility bill is $115.00 and our January bill is $117.50. Businesses on both sides of us, in offices just like ours, are paying only $43.50 and $45.67 for the same months. We all have similar computer and office equipment, so something must be wrong.
>
> Small businesses are helpless against big utility companies. How can we prove that you read the meter wrong or that the November bill from before we even moved in here got added to our December bill? We want someone to check this meter right away. We can't afford to pay these big bills.

It's generally a good idea to suggest specific and fair compensation when asking for an adjustment. However, in some cases you wouldn't request a specific adjustment but would ask the reader to resolve the problem. In other situations you may need to make a strong case for your claim or request for adjustment. Perhaps your printer stopped working one week after the warranty expired. These types of nonroutine claims will be discussed in detail in Chapter 9.

Favorable Responses to Claims and Adjustment Requests

Few people go to the trouble of requesting an adjustment unless they actually have a problem. So the most sensible reaction to a routine claim is to assume that the customer's account of the transaction is an honest statement of what happened—unless the same customer repeatedly submits dubious claims or the dollar amount in the dispute is very large. Once the complaint is made, respond promptly. Of course, you'll want to investigate the problem first,

In general, it pays to give customers the benefit of the doubt.

Figure 7.3
In-Depth Critique: The Importance of Tone

Most people would react much more favorably to this version of the complaint letter about high utility bills. As this rational and clear approach demonstrates, a courteous approach is best for any routine request. If you must write a letter that gives vent to your anger, go ahead; then tear that one up and write a letter that will actually help solve the problem.

The European Connection
Specialist Purveyors of European Antiques
for over 30 years
P.O. Box 804 • Cayucos, California 93430
Telephone: (805) 979-7727 Fax: (805) 979-2828
EuroConnect@nemesis.net

February 23, 2000

Customer Service Representative
City of San Luis Obispo Utilities
955 Morro Street
San Luis Obispo, CA 93401

Dear Customer Service Representative:

The utility meter in our store may not be accurate. Please send someone to check it.

We have been at our current location since December 1, almost three months. Our monthly bill is nearly triple those of neighboring businesses in this building, yet we all have similar storefronts and equipment. In December we paid $115.00, and our January bill was $117.50; the highest bills that neighboring businesses have paid were $43.50 and $45.67.

If your representative could visit our store, he or she could do an analysis of how much energy we are using. We understand that you regularly provide this helpful service to customers.

We would appreciate hearing from you this week. You can reach me by calling 979-7727 during business hours.

Sincerely,

Laura Covington

Laura Covington
Proprietor

The problem is stated clearly and calmly in the first paragraph.

The second paragraph explains the particulars of the situation so that the person reading the letter will understand why the writer thinks a problem exists.

The last paragraph requests specific action and makes responding easy by providing a phone number.

to determine what went wrong and why. Likewise, you'll want to determine whether the company, the customer, or a third party is at fault. Here's some practical advice to follow when your response is favorable, depending on whether the company, the customer, or a third party is at fault.

When the Company Is at Fault

Put yourself in the shoes of the furniture store that shipped the custom furniture to you. The usual human response to a bad situation is to say, "It wasn't my fault!" However, businesspeople who receive requests for claims or adjustments can't take that stance. Even when the company's terms of adjustment are generous, a grudging tone can actually increase the customer's dissatisfaction.

An ungracious adjustment may increase customer dissatisfaction.

If you're responding favorably, protect your company's image and try to regain the customer's goodwill by referring to your company's errors carefully. Don't blame an individual or a specific department, such as shipping for placing the wrong furniture order on the truck. And avoid such lame excuses as "Nobody's perfect" or "Mistakes will happen." Don't promise that problems will never happen again; such guarantees are unrealistic and often beyond your control. Instead, explain your company's efforts to do a good job; in so doing, you imply that the error was an unusual incident.

Imagine that a large mail-order clothing company has decided to create a form letter to respond to the hundreds of claims it receives each year. The most common customer complaint is not receiving exactly what was ordered. The form letter can be customized through word processing and individually signed:

> Your letter concerning your recent Klondike order has arrived and has been forwarded to our director of order fulfillment. Your complete satisfaction is our goal; when you are satisfied, we are satisfied. Our customer service representative will contact you soon to assist with the issues raised in your letter.
>
> Whether you're skiing or driving a snowmobile, Klondike Gear offers you the best protection from wind, snow, and cold—and Klondike has been taking care of your outdoor needs for over 27 years! Because you're a loyal customer, enclosed is a $5 gift certificate. You may wish to consider our new line of quality snow goggles.
>
> Thank you for taking the time to write to us. Your input helps us better serve you and all our customers.

This letter exemplifies the following points:

You may send form letters in response to claims, but word them carefully so that they are appropriate in a variety of circumstances.

- Because a form letter like this is sent to people with various types of requests or complaints, it cannot start with a clear good-news statement.
- The letter starts instead with what might be called a "good attitude" statement; it is you-oriented to put the customer at ease.
- At no time does this letter suggest that the customer was mistaken in writing to Klondike about the order in question.
- The letter includes some resale and sales promotion, made more personal by the use of *you.*
- The letter closes with a statement of the company's concern for all its customers.

By contrast, a claim letter written as a personal answer to a unique situation would start with a clear statement of the good news: the settling of the claim according to the customer's request. Here is a more personal response from Klondike Gear:

> Here is your heather-blue wool-and-mohair sweater (size large) to replace the one returned to us with a defect in the knitting on the left sleeve. Thanks for giving us the opportunity to correct this situation. Customers' needs have come first at Klondike Gear for 27 years. Our sweaters are handmade by the finest knitters in this area.
>
> Our newest catalog is enclosed. Browse through it, and see what wonderful new colors and patterns we have for you. Whether you are skiing or driving a snowmobile, Klondike Gear offers you the best protection available from wind, snow, and cold. Let us know how we may continue to serve you and your sporting needs.

When the Customer Is at Fault

When complying with an unjustified claim, let the customer know that the merchandise was mistreated, but maintain a respectful and positive tone.

Say that a customer is technically wrong (he washed a dry-clean-only sweater in hot water) but feels he's right ("The washing instructions were impossible to find!"). You can refuse the claim and attempt to justify your refusal, or you can simply do what the customer asks. As you try to decide which course to take, remember that if you refuse to make an adjustment you may lose that customer as well as many of the customer's friends, who will hear only one side of the dispute. It makes sense, therefore, to weigh the cost of making the adjustment against the cost of losing future business from one or more customers.

DID YOU KNOW?

A federal study found that encouraging customer complaints increased the likelihood of those customers' continuing to do business with the organization. If the company responded immediately, apologized, and guaranteed to fix the problem, the probability of the customer's remaining a customer was 95 percent.

If you choose not to contest the claim, start off with a statement of the good news: You're replacing the merchandise or refunding the purchase price. The explanatory section needs more attention, however. Your job is to make the customer realize that the merchandise was mistreated without falling into a tone that is condescending ("Perhaps you failed to read the instructions carefully") or preachy ("You should know that wool shrinks in hot water"). The dilemma is this: If the customer fails to realize what went wrong, you may commit your firm to an endless procession of returned merchandise; but if you insult the customer, your cash refund will have been wasted because the customer will make his or her next purchase elsewhere. Keep in mind that a courteous tone is especially important to the success of your message, regardless of the solution you propose (see Figure 7.4).

When a Third Party Is at Fault

At times, a customer will submit a legitimate claim regarding a defect or damage that was not caused by either of you. If the merchandise was damaged while in transit, the carrier is responsible. If the defect was caused by the manufacturer, you have a claim for replacement from that firm.

Three options when a third party is at fault:

- Honor the claim
- Honor the claim but explain what went wrong
- Refer the customer to the third party for satisfaction of the claim

When a third party is at fault, you have three options: (1) Honor the customer's claim with the standard good-news letter and no additional explanation; (2) honor the claim but explain that you were not at fault; or (3) take no action on the claim and suggest that your customer file against the firm that caused the defect or damage. Common business sense tells you that the third option is almost always a bad choice. (The exception is when you're trying to dissociate yourself from any legal responsibility for the damaged merchandise, especially if it has caused a personal injury, in which case you would send a bad-news message.)

Of the other two options, the first is more attractive. By honoring the claim without explanation, you are maintaining your reputation for fair dealing at no cost to yourself; the carrier or manufacturer that caused the damage in the first place will reimburse you. Nevertheless, you may want to provide an explanation to the customer, possibly to correct any impression that the damage was caused by your negligence. In that case, you can still write the standard good-news letter, but stress the explanation. (This chapter's Checklist for Claims and Adjustments will remind you of the tasks involved in such messages.)

ROUTINE CREDIT REQUESTS AND APPROVALS

These days much of our economy runs on credit. Hardly anyone carries cash around anymore; instead, everyone carries a wallet full of plastic credit and debit cards. Likewise, businesses of all sizes operate on credit—30 days, 60 days, even long-term payment schedules. Because credit is so common in today's business environment, most credit requests and approvals are routine and follow the direct organizational approach.

Making Routine Credit Requests

The first step in requesting credit is to get an application form.

If your credit rating is sound, your application for business credit may be as direct as any other type of simple request. Whether the application is directed to a local bank, a supply

Without being offensive, this letter educates a customer about how to treat his in-line skates.

Figure 7.4
In-Depth Critique: Letter Responding to a Claim When the Buyer Is at Fault

20901 El Dorado Hills
Laguna Niguel, CA 92677
(714) 332-7474 • Fax: (714) 336-5297
skates@speed.net

February 7, 2000

Mr. Steven Cox
1172 Amber Court
Jacksonville, FL 32073

Dear Mr. Cox:

Thank you for letting us know about the problem with your in-line skates. Although your six-month warranty has expired, we are mailing you a complete wheel assembly replacement free of charge. The enclosed instructions make removing the damaged wheel line and installing the new one relatively easy.

The "Fastrax" (model NL 562) you purchased is our best selling and most reliable skate. However, wheel jams may occur when fine particles of sand block the smooth rotating action of the wheels. These skates perform best when used on roadways and tracks that are relatively free of sand. We suggest that you remove and clean the wheel assemblies (see enclosed directions) once a month and have them checked by your dealer about every six months.

Because of your Florida location, you may want to consider our more advanced "Glisto" (model NL 988) when you decide to purchase new skates. Although more expensive than the Fastrax, the Glisto design helps shed sand and dirt quite efficiently and should provide years of trouble-free skating.

Enjoy the enclosed copy of "Rock & Roll," with our compliments. Inside, you'll read about new products, hear from other skaters, and have an opportunity to respond to our customer questionnaire.

We love hearing from our skaters, so keep in touch. All of us at Skates Alive! wish you good times and miles of healthy skating.

Sincerely,

Candace Parker

Candace Parker
Customer Service Representative

Enclosure

A brief statement acknowledges the problem and conveys the good news.

Here, the writer explains the problem without blaming the customer and suggests ways to avoid future problems.

The writer uses the opportunity to encourage the customer to "trade up," showing how to turn negative feelings about a product into future sales.

Finally, the writer adds value by enclosing a newsletter that invites future response from the customer.

The letter ends on a positive, "feel good" note that conveys an attitude of excellent customer service.

company, a wholesaler, a manufacturer, or a national credit-card company, the information needed is the same. You might phone the company to ask for a credit application or write a letter as simple as this:

> We would like to open a credit account with your company. Please send an application blank, and let us know what references you will need.

CHECKLIST FOR CLAIMS AND ADJUSTMENTS*

A. Claims and Adjustment Requests

1. In the opening, include a straightforward statement of the problem.
   - **a.** Write a claim letter as soon as possible after the problem has been identified.
   - **b.** Maintain a confident, factual, fair, unemotional tone.
2. In the body, tell specifics of the problem. Include any necessary details.
   - **a.** Present facts honestly, clearly, and politely.
   - **b.** Eliminate threats, sarcasm, exaggeration, and hostility, and use a nonargumentative tone to show confidence in the reader's fairness.
   - **c.** Make no accusation against any person or company, unless you can back it up with facts.
   - **d.** To gain the reader's understanding, praise some aspect of the good or service, or at least explain why the product was originally purchased.
   - **e.** If appropriate, clearly state what you expect as a fair settlement, or ask the reader to propose a fair adjustment.
   - **f.** Provide copies of necessary documents (invoices, canceled checks, confirmation letters, and the like); keep the originals.
3. In the closing, briefly summarize desired action.

B. Favorable Responses to Claims and Adjustment Requests

1. In the opening, immediately state your willingness to honor the reader's claim, without negative comment.
   - **a.** Accept your reader's account as entirely accurate unless good business reasons demand a different interpretation of some points.
   - **b.** Thank the reader for taking the time to write.
2. In the body, explain how you will remedy the problem.
   - **a.** Minimize or, if possible, omit any disagreements with your reader's interpretation of events.
   - **b.** If appropriate, provide an objective, nonvindictive, impersonal explanation.
   - **c.** Apologize only under extreme circumstances; then do so crisply and without an overly apologetic tone.
   - **d.** Maintain a supportive tone through such phrases as "Thank you for," "May we ask," "Please let us know," and "We are glad to work with you."
   - **e.** Admit your firm's faults carefully. Avoid shifting the blame to others, implying general company inefficiency, and making unrealistic promises about the future.
   - **f.** Be careful when handling the customer's role in producing the problem.
3. In the closing, remind the reader how you have honored the claim and clarify any actions that your reader must take.
   - **a.** Encourage the customer to look favorably on your company or the product in question.
   - **b.** Encourage the customer to continue buying other goods from you but avoid seeming greedy.
   - **c.** Clarify any actions that your reader must take.

*These items are in addition to the basic tasks associated with writing routine requests and positive responses.

The second step is to supply the necessary information.

Before you get a credit account, you'll have to supply such information as the name of your company, the length of time you've been in business, the name of your bank, and the addresses of businesses where you have existing accounts. Businesses trying to establish credit are also expected to furnish a financial statement and possibly a balance sheet. In general, the lender wants proof that your income is stable and that you can repay the loan. You might put this information in your original letter, but it will probably be requested again on the standard credit application form.

Approving Routine Credit Requests

Letters approving credit are good-news messages and the first step in what may be a decades-long business relationship. So, as in the credit request, use the direct approach. Begin your letter by informing the reader that his or her application for credit with your firm has been approved. In the middle section, include a reasonably full statement of the credit arrangements: the upper limit of the account, dates that bills are sent, possible arrangements for partial monthly payments, discounts for prompt payments, interest charges for unpaid balances, and due dates. Stress the advantages of prompt payment. Include or attach any legally required disclosure statements as well as a full explanation of your firm's credit policies and expectations of payment. State the terms positively and objectively, not negatively or in an authoritarian manner:

State credit arrangements factually and in terms of the benefits to the reader.

INSTEAD OF THIS	WRITE THIS
Your credit balance cannot exceed $5,000.	With our standard credit account, you can order up to $5,000 worth of fine merchandise.
We expect your payment within 30 days of receipt of our statement.	Payment is due within 30 days after you receive our statement.

In the final section of the letter, highlight the benefits of buying from you and motivate the customer to use the new account. Because the letter approving credit is considered a legal document, check the wording for accuracy, completeness, and clarity. The following letter was written both to approve credit and to bring in customers:

Include resale and sales promotion information in a credit-approval letter.

Congratulations! Your credit application to Jake's Building Center has been approved, with $3,000 in credit available to you. Just use the enclosed card when you shop at any of our three Jake's Building Centers. With this card, you can purchase tools, appliances, paint, plumbing and electrical supplies, lawn products, and much more.

The good-news opening gets right to the point.

Statements are sent out on the 20th of each month and list each credit purchase, the total amount due, and the monthly payment due. If you pay the total amount by the 15th of the following month, no interest is charged. If you elect to pay the smaller monthly amount, interest will be calculated at the monthly rate of 1 1/2 percent on the amount still owed and will be added to your next statement.

An objective statement of the terms constitutes a legal contract. Positive, you-oriented wording avoids an authoritarian tone.

Jake's Building Centers are located in Murphysboro, Pinkneyville, and Carbondale, with free delivery within 50 miles of each store. Come to us for everything you need to build, repair, or remodel your home or business. Count on our high quality and low prices whenever you purchase one of our top-of-the-line products. Come see us for your next building project!

The courteous close notes a range of customer benefits, promoting the store's products and services.

INQUIRIES ABOUT PEOPLE AND POSITIVE RESPONSES

The need to inquire about people arises often in business. For example, some companies ask applicants to supply references before awarding credit, contracts, jobs, promotions, scholarships, and so on. If you're applying for a job and your potential employer asks for references, you may want to ask a close personal or professional associate to write a letter of recommendation. Or, if you're an employer considering whether to hire an applicant, you may want to write directly to the person the applicant named as a reference.

Because such inquiries are routine and you can confidently assume that the reader will honor your request, organize your inquiry using the direct approach. Use the same approach if you're responding to an inquiry about someone and your comments are mostly positive.

Recommendation and Reference Requests

Always ask for permission before you use someone's name as a reference.

Companies ask applicants to supply references who can vouch for their ability, skills, integrity, character, and fitness for the job. Before you volunteer someone's name as a reference, it's a good idea to ask that person's permission. Some people won't let you use their names, perhaps because they don't know enough about you to feel comfortable writing a letter or because they have a policy of not providing recommendations. In any event, you are likely to receive the best recommendation from persons who agree to write about you, so check first.

Refresh the memory of any potential reference you haven't been in touch with for a while.

When asking a close personal or professional associate to serve as a reference, begin your message by clearly stating that you're applying for a position and that you would like the person to write a letter of recommendation. If you haven't had contact with the person for some time, use the opening to refresh the person's memory. Recall the nature of the relationship you had, the dates of association, and any special events that might bring a clear, favorable picture of you to mind.

If you're applying for a job, a scholarship, or the like, include a copy of your résumé to give the reader an idea of the direction your life has taken. After reading the résumé, your reader will know what favorable qualities to emphasize and will be able to write the recommendation that best supports your application. If you don't have a résumé, include in your letter any information about yourself that the reader might use to support a recommendation, such as a description of related jobs you've held.

Close your letter with an expression of appreciation and the full name and address of the person to whom the letter should be sent. When asking for an immediate recommendation, you should also mention the deadline. You'll make a response more likely if you enclose a stamped, preaddressed envelope. The letter in Figure 7.5 covers all these points.

Letters Responding to a Recommendation Request

If you're asked to write a letter of recommendation, you'll want to convince the readers that the person being recommended has the characteristics for the job or other benefit. It is important, therefore, that your letter contains all the relevant details:

- The full name of the candidate
- The job or benefit that the candidate is seeking
- Whether the writer is answering a request or taking the initiative
- The nature of the relationship between the writer and the candidate
- Facts relevant to the position or benefit sought
- The writer's overall evaluation of the candidate's suitability for the job or benefit sought

Recommendation letters are usually confidential; that is, they're sent directly to the person or committee who requested them and are not shown to the candidate. However, recent

In Joanne Tucker's letter requesting a recommendation, she adds important information about some qualifications that might be of special interest to Strategic Investments.

Figure 7.5
In-Depth Critique: Letter Requesting a Recommendation

Joanne Tucker
1181 Ashport, Tate Springs, Tennessee 38101
(901) 369-2093

March 14, 2000

Professor Lyndon Kenton
School of Business
University of Tennessee, Knoxville
Knoxville, Tennessee 37916

Dear Professor Kenton:

May I have a letter of recommendation from you? I recently interviewed with Strategic Investments and have been called for a second interview for their Analyst Training Program (ATP). They have requested at least one recommendation from a professor, and I immediately thought of you.

As you may recall, I took BUS 485, Financial Analysis, from you in the fall of 1998. I enjoyed the class and finished the term with an "A." Professor Kenton, your comments on assertiveness and cold-calling impressed me beyond the scope of the actual course material. In fact, taking your course helped me decide on a future as a financial analyst.

My enclosed résumé includes all my relevant work experience and volunteer activities. But I'd also like to add that I've handled the financial planning for our family since my father passed away several years ago. Although initially, I learned by trial and error, I have increasingly applied my business training in deciding what stocks or bonds to trade. This, I believe, has given me a practical edge over others who may be applying for the same job.

If possible, Ms. Blackmon in Human Resources needs to receive your letter by March 30. For your convenience, I've enclosed a preaddressed, stamped envelope.

I appreciate your time and effort in writing this letter of recommendation for me. It will be great to put my education to work, and I'll keep you informed of my progress.

Sincerely,

Joanne Tucker

Joanne Tucker

Enclosure

This letter opens with the direct approach; Joanne Tucker assumes that Professor Ken-ton will honor the request and names the potential employer involved (Strategic Investments).

The next section gives enough information for Professor Kenton to recall his former student.

Tucker not only includes her résumé but also mentions experience that may set her apart from other candidates.

The close includes information on the person expecting the recommendation.

litigation has made it advisable in some situations to prepare a carefully worded letter that satisfies both parties.

Oddly enough, the most difficult recommendation letters to write are those for truly outstanding candidates. Your audience will have trouble believing uninterrupted praise for someone's talents and accomplishments. So illustrate your general points with a specific

Two devices for convincing the reader when the candidate is outstanding:

- Use examples
- Use comparisons with the "competition"

Many of these graduating Boston University students will ask their college professors to write letters of recommendation on their behalf.

example or two that point out the candidate's abilities, and discuss the candidate's abilities in relation to the "competition."

A serious shortcoming cannot be ignored, but beware of being libelous:

- Include only relevant, factual information
- Avoid value judgments
- Balance criticisms with favorable points

Most candidates aren't perfect, however. Omitting reference to a candidate's shortcomings may be tempting, especially if the shortcomings are irrelevant to the demands of the job in question. Even so, you have an obligation to your audience, to your own conscience, and even to the better-qualified candidate who's relying on honest references to refer to any shortcoming that is serious and related to job performance.

Of course, the danger in writing a critical letter is that you might engage in libel—that is, make a false and malicious written statement that injures the candidate's reputation. On the other hand, if that negative information is truthful and relevant, it may be unethical and illegal to omit it from a recommendation. So if you must refer to a shortcoming, you can best protect yourself by sticking to the facts and placing your criticism in the context of a generally favorable recommendation, as in Figure 7.6.

A recommendation letter presenting negatives can be carefully worded to satisfy both the candidate and the person or company requesting information.

DID YOU KNOW?

In a recent survey, 75 percent of respondents said their companies had refused to provide reference information out of fear of lawsuits.

To explore the topic further, see "Focusing on Ethics: Recommendation Letters: What's Right to Write?" on pages 224–225. You can also avoid trouble by asking yourself the following questions before mailing a recommendation letter:

- Does the person receiving this frank, personal information have a legitimate right to the information?
- Is all the information I have presented related directly to the job or other benefit being sought?
- Have I put the candidate's case as strongly as I honestly can?
- Have I avoided overstating the candidate's abilities or otherwise misleading the reader?
- Have I based all my statements on firsthand knowledge and provable facts?

GOOD NEWS AND GOODWILL MESSAGES

Most businesses spend a good deal of effort developing and maintaining good relationships with customers, clients, employees, and the general public. Savvy companies recognize that it's good business to spread the word about such positive developments as the opening

In this letter, the writer supports her statements with facts and steers clear of vague, critical judgments.

Figure 7.6
In-Depth Critique: Recommendation Letter

S I N G H
Marketing Systems
789 E. Eisenhower Parkway, Ann Arbor, Michigan 48108-3275
Voice: (313) 930-3905 ■ Fax: (313) 930-3906
www.singh.com

November 15, 1999

Mr. Henry Paltrow
Marketing Director
Massy Young, Inc.
767 Canal Street, Suite B
Houston, TX 77061

Dear Mr. Paltrow:

I am pleased to recommend Zhe-Sheng Cheng for the marketing position at Massy Young, Inc. Zhe-Sheng has worked summers with us for the past two years, while working toward his degree in marketing and advertising.

As his supervisor, in addition to knowing his work here at SMS, I also know that Zhe-Sheng has served as secretary for the International Business Association at the University of Michigan. In addition, he tutored other international students in the university's writing center. His fluency in three languages and thorough knowledge of other cultures will make him an immediate contributor to your international operation. Although a quiet, introspective young man, Zhe-Sheng will not hesitate to contribute ideas when invited to do so. In addition, because Zhe-Sheng learns quickly, he will have no problem learning your company's routine.

I believe Zhe-Sheng will make an excellent addition to the staff of Massy Young. If you would like to further discuss Zhe-Sheng's qualifications, please call or fax me at the numbers above. I can be hard to catch at my desk, so you might want to contact me at Jenai.Singh@aol.com so that I can call you.

Sincerely,

Jenai L. Singh

Jenai L. Singh
Senior Partner

The candidate's full name and the main point are clearly stated.

The duration and nature of the relationship are specified to give weight to the evaluation.

A summary of the writer's supportive evaluation provides a good close. The phone number and invitation to discuss the candidacy constitute another helpful touch.

of new facilities, the appointment of a new executive, the introduction of new products or new customer services, or the sponsorship of community events. In addition, they send goodwill messages to employees, customers, clients and the general public. Because good news is welcome by all, it's appropriate to use the direct approach when organizing these messages.

FOCUSING ON ETHICS

RECOMMENDATION LETTERS: WHAT'S RIGHT TO WRITE?

You were Frank Walker's supervisor for four years. When he left the company recently, he asked you to write a letter of recommendation for him. However, your company's legal experts said, "Don't do it."

Why Not Give Recommendations? Why? Because thousands of lawsuits have been filed (and won) by employees, charging former employers with making slanderous (oral) and libelous (written) statements in job recommendations. In one seven-year period in California, employees won 72 percent of libel and related suits they brought against employers, and the average award was $582,000. One employer lost its case for saying an employee had "suddenly resigned," which implied (according to the court) that the employee had resigned under "a veil of suspicion." Another employer lost its case for saying an employee was fired "for causes." Furthermore, when employees prove that actual malice is involved, damage awards skyrocket.

To make things more complicated, a recent court ruling has held an employer liable for *omitting* information about a former employee. So companies may well be confused about what sort of information should or should not be included in a recommendation. Even though some states have passed laws protecting companies against lawsuits when the employer acted in good faith, legal and human resources experts often advise companies to centralize all recommendations to maintain better control over what's being said. The cautious approach is to supply only dates of employment and titles of positions held—and to give that information only to people who have a legitimate right to know (or who have written authorization from former employees).

What If You Want to Give a Recommendation? You have an ethical dilemma: Frank Walker was a terrific employee, a good friend, and someone you'd really like to help succeed. How can you refuse his request for a recommendation when you believe he really deserves it? The experts suggest two alternatives. The first option is to write the letter of recommendation with Walker so that the contents satisfy both

Good News about Employment

Finding suitable job applicants and then selecting the right person is a task fraught with hard choices and considerable anxiety. In contrast, writing a letter to the successful applicant is a pleasure. Most of the time, such a letter is eagerly awaited, so the direct approach is appropriate:

> Welcome to Lake Valley Rehabilitation Center. A number of excellent candidates were interviewed, but your educational background and recent experience at Memorial Hospital make you the best person for the position of medical records coordinator.
>
> As we discussed, your salary is $26,200 a year. We would like you to begin on Monday, February 1. Please come to my office at 8:00 a.m. I will give you an in-depth orientation to Lake Valley and discuss the various company benefits available to you. You can also sign all the necessary employment documents.
>
> After lunch, Vanessa Jackson will take you to the medical records department and help you settle into your new responsibilities at Lake Valley Rehabilitation Center. I look forward to seeing you first thing on February 1.

This letter takes a friendly, welcoming tone, and it explains the necessary details: job title, starting date, salary, and benefits. The explanation of the first day's routine helps allay the bewilderment and uncertainty that might afflict the new employee.

A letter telling someone that she or he got the job is a legal document, so make sure all statements are accurate.

Although letters like these are pleasant to write, they constitute a legal job offer. You and your company may be held to any promises you make. So attorneys sometimes recommend stating salary as a monthly amount and keeping the timing of performance evaluations and raises vague; you want to avoid implying that the newly hired employee will be kept on, no matter what, for a whole year or until the next scheduled evaluation.[3]

of you. Then, to be certain you're not violating company policy, discuss the letter with your human resources department before releasing it. (Walker's agreement with the contents should reassure the legal department.)

If your employer is still uncomfortable, the second option is to ask Walker to list you as a *personal* reference. This removes your company from any responsibility for statements you make, and gives you the freedom to say what you like. Even so, whether you're acting as a company or as a personal reference, you can be held personally responsible for your comments. In fact, a common legal defense among corporations is to prove that the person who made the recommendation was acting outside company policy and should therefore be accountable for the entire amount of the lawsuit.

What If You'd Rather Not Give a Recommendation? Of course, if it had been Sharon Brown who had asked for a recommendation, you'd be facing a different ethical dilemma. Brown wasn't the greatest employee, so do you owe her potential employer the whole story? Negative information could get you sued by Brown, and leaving out negative information could make you liable for "failure to disclose" or "negligent referral" in a lawsuit filed by the hiring company. Of course, what was negative in one job situation could be irrelevant in another, so you may have no reason to convey the negative information at all. Again, consult your human resources or legal department to be sure you're supplying sufficient information, and to be certain your wording is impersonal.

Regardless of the circumstances, be sure to (1) comment only on your own direct experience working with any former employee, (2) make all comments in writing, and (3) limit your remarks to provable facts (that is, don't exaggerate). Remember that honesty, integrity, and prudence are the foundations of legality and good business ethics.

1. One of your former employees was often late for work but was an excellent and fast worker and got along well with everyone. Do you think it's important to mention the tardiness to potential employers? If so, how will you handle it?
2. Step outside yourself for a moment and write a letter of recommendation about yourself from a former employer's perspective. Practice honesty, integrity, and prudence.

Good News about Products and Operations

Imagine that So-Good Foods has successfully introduced a new line of vegetable chips (carrot, turnip, and yam chips—not the same old potato chips). To maintain its position on supermarket shelves, So-Good decides to offer a new discount program to stores that buy large quantities of its vegetable chips. It supplements the personal visits of its sales force with a good-news message describing the new program to existing customers. The letter begins by trumpeting the news, fills in the details of the discount program in the middle, and closes with a bit of resale information and a confident prediction of a profitable business relationship.

When the audience for a good-news message is large and scattered, however, it's usually easier to communicate through the mass media. When McDonald's opened its first restaurant in Moscow, it sent announcements to newspapers, magazines, radio stations, and television networks. The specialized documents used to convey such information to the media are called **news releases**. Written to match the style of the medium they are intended for, news releases are typed on plain $8\frac{1}{2}$-by-11-inch paper or on special letterhead, not on regular letterhead, and they're double spaced for print media or triple spaced for electronic media. Figure 7.7 illustrates the correct format. The content of this news release follows the customary pattern for a good-news message: good news, followed by details and a positive close. However, it avoids explicit references to any reader, displaying the "you" attitude by presenting information presumed to be of interest to all readers. To write a successful news release, keep the following points in mind:[4]

Specially formatted news releases convey good news to the media, which in turn disseminate it to the public.

- Include no marketing or sales material in your news release.

Figure 7.7
In-Depth Critique: News Release Format

This news release demonstrates the proper format for the targeted medium (in this case, print).

Provide your own suggestion for a title or leave two inches so that the editor can insert a headline.

This release for a newspaper starts with a dateline and a summary.

Put a release on one page if you can, but indicate carry-over if there's a second page.

NEWS RELEASE

Media Please Call
Public Relations
(214) 792-4847

Customers Please Call
(800) I FLY SWA or
en Español (800) 221-0016

SOUTHWEST AIRLINES HEATS UP WINTER WITH $99 FARE SALE

Travel on Southwest Airlines for $99 or Less

DALLAS--Dec. 1, 1998--From today through Dec. 16, 1998, Customers may purchase travel on Southwest Airlines for $99 or less, each way, based on roundtrip purchase*. Oakland to Baltimore is $99 each way, based on roundtrip purchase; Los Angeles to Tampa is $99 each way; and Chicago to Phoenix is $99 each way.

Shorter flights also are available at a great savings. Albuquerque to Phoenix is just $39 each way, based on roundtrip purchase. It's just $49 each way between Austin and Dallas, $39 each way between Baltimore/Washington and Manchester, $39 each way between Ft. Lauderdale and Orlando, and $49 between Los Angeles and Oakland. (*Flights to and from the Florida cities of Ft. Lauderdale, Tampa, Jacksonville, and Orlando will not be available from March 12 through April 2, 1999.)

"A ticket on Southwest Airlines makes a great gift for the holidays," said Joyce Rogge, Southwest's vice president of marketing. "You can send a friend or loved one clear across the country at a price you can afford. We love to see our Customers saving money, particularly during the 'season of giving.'"

Tickets must be purchased by Dec. 16, 1998 and are good for travel through April 2, 1999. Fares are listed each way with roundtrip purchase and do not include airport taxes of up to $12 roundtrip or a Federal fee of $2 per segment. Tickets must be purchased at least seven days before departure and require at least a one-night stay. Seats are limited and will not be available on some flights that operate during very busy travel times or the Christmas and New Year holiday periods. Tickets are nonrefundable, but if unused, may be applied toward future travel on Southwest Airlines. Fares are subject to change until ticketed.

Southwest Airlines was ranked the best overall airline among the ten largest domestic carriers in the November 1997 issue of *Money* magazine. *Money* rated Southwest number one in safety, Customer Service, ontime arrival, and baggage handling.

SOUTHWEST AIRLINES CO. P.O. BOX 36611 LOVE FIELD DALLAS, TEXAS 75235-1611 214/792-4000

- Put your most important idea first (Don't say "Calco's president, James Grall announced today that the company will move its headquarters to the Main Street office." Instead, start with the news: "Calco will move its headquarters to the Main Street office, President James Grall announced today.")
- Be brief (break up long sentences and keep paragraphs short).
- Eliminate clutter such as redundancy and extraneous facts.
- Be as specific as possible.
- Avoid adjectives and adverbs (understatement goes a long way with the media).

In addition to issuing written news releases, many large companies hold news conferences or create their own videotapes, which are sent to television stations and networks.

Goodwill Messages

Goodwill is the positive feeling that encourages people to maintain a business relationship.

You can enhance your relationships with customers and other businesspeople by sending friendly, unexpected notes with no direct business purpose. Jack Welch, CEO of General

As busy as he is, CEO Jack Welch takes the time to write personal goodwill messages to General Electric employees.

Electric, is known for his handwritten notes to all employees, from managers to hourly workers. Welch writes employees personal notes to inspire and motivate as often as to stir and demand action. Consider this message Welch wrote to a manager who had turned down a promotion because he didn't want to move his teenager to a different school: "Bill," wrote Welch, "we like you for a lot of reasons—one of them is that you are a very special person. You proved it again this morning. Good for you and your lucky family . . ."[5]

Goodwill messages have a positive effect on business, because people prefer to deal with organizations that are warm and human and interested in more than just money. Of course, to be effective, goodwill messages must be sincere and honest. Otherwise, they appear as if the writer is interested only in personal gain and not in benefiting customers or fellow workers. One way to come across as sincere is to avoid exaggeration and back up any compliments with specific points:

Make sure your compliments are grounded in reality.

INSTEAD OF THIS	WRITE THIS
Words cannot express my appreciation for the great job you did. Thanks. No one could have done it better. You're terrific! You've made the whole firm sit up and take notice, and we are ecstatic to have you working here.	Thanks again for taking charge of the meeting in my absence. You did an excellent job. With just an hour's notice, you managed to pull the legal and public relations departments together so that we could present a united front in the negotiations. Your dedication and communication abilities have been noted and are truly appreciated.

Note also the difference in the words used in these two examples. Your reader would probably regard the more restrained praise as being be more sincere.

Congratulations

Taking note of significant events in someone's personal life helps cement the business relationship.

One prime opportunity for sending goodwill messages is to congratulate someone for a significant business achievement: for example, being promoted or attaining an important civic position (see Figure 7.8).

Figure 7.8
In-Depth Critique: Letter Congratulating a Business Acquaintance

This sample congratulatory note moves swiftly to the subject: the good news. It gives reasons for expecting success and avoids such extravagances as "Only you can do the job!"

Office DEPOT, Inc.
2200 Old Germantown Road, Delray Beach, FL 33445 407/278-4800

March 3, 2000

Mr. Ralph Lambert, President
Lambert, Cutchen & Browt, Inc.
14355 Pasadena Parkway
Pasadena, TX 74229

Dear Mr. Lambert:

Congratulations on your firm's recent selection to design and print media advertisements for the National Association of Business Suppliers (ABS). We learned of your success at our convention in Atlanta last month.

We have long believed that the success of individual franchises is directly linked to the healthy growth of the industry at large. We can think of no better firm to help our industry achieve wide recognition than Lambert, Cutchen & Browt.

We have admired your success in promoting associations of other industries such as soft drinks, snack foods, and recycling. Your "Dream Vision 2000" ads for the bottling industry were both inspirational and effective in raising consumer awareness, and we look for similar positive responses to your ABS campaign.

Again, accept our warm congratulations. We look forward to seeing the results of the survey you conducted during our convention. And we will follow your media campaign with great interest.

Sincerely,

Janice McCarthy

Janice McCarthy
Director, Media Relations

tw

The reason for congratulating the reader is expressed early and concisely.

The compliment becomes more effective when coupled with statements that show your knowledge of the recipient's work.

The letter ends with a personal note of congratulations. It expresses interest in following the future success of the individual or business.

Highlights in people's personal lives—weddings and births, graduations, success in nonbusiness competitions—are another reason for sending congratulations. You may congratulate business acquaintances on their achievements or on their spouse's or children's achievements. You may also take note of personal events, even if you don't know the reader well. Of course, if you're already friendly with the reader, you can get away with a personal tone.

Some alert companies develop a mailing list of potential customers by assigning an employee to clip newspaper announcements of births, engagements, weddings, and graduations or by obtaining information on real estate transactions in the local community. Then they introduce themselves by sending out a form letter that might read like this:

> Congratulations on your new home! Our wish is that it brings you much happiness.
>
> To help you commemorate the occasion, we have enclosed a key chain with your new address engraved on the leather tab. Please accept this with our best wishes.

In this case, the company's letterhead and address are enough of a sales pitch. This simple message has a natural, friendly tone, even though the sender has never met the recipient.

Messages of Appreciation

An important managerial quality is the ability to see employees (and other business associates) as individuals and to recognize their contributions. People often value praise more highly than monetary rewards. A message of appreciation may also become an important part of an employee's personnel file:

A message of appreciation documents a person's contributions.

> Thanks for creating computerized spreadsheets to track our marketing efforts and sales by both region and product. Your personal understanding of the scope of this division's responsibilities is evident in the detail and thoroughness of the spreadsheets. I particularly appreciate the historical data you included and the fine documentation and training you provided so that the data included in the spreadsheets can be consistent over time—regardless of who is working on them.
>
> Your talents in conceptualizing the scope of the project, executing it on time, and following through with the final details are a great asset to our division.
>
> cc: Employee file, Human Resources

With its references to specific qualities and deeds, this note may provide support for future pay increases and promotions.

Suppliers also like to know that you value some exceptional product or the service you received. Long-term support deserves recognition, too. Your praise doesn't just make the supplier feel good; it also encourages further excellence. The brief message that follows expresses gratitude and reveals the happy result:

Anyone who does you or your organization a special favor should receive written thanks.

> Thank you for sending the air-conditioning components via overnight delivery. You allowed us to satisfy the needs of two customers who were getting very impatient with the heat.
>
> Special thanks to Susan Brown who took our initial call and never said, "It can't be done." Her initiative on our behalf is greatly appreciated.

When you write a message of appreciation to a supplier, try to mention specifically the person or people you want to praise. Your expression of goodwill might net the employee some future benefit. In any case, your message honors the company that the individual represents.

Condolences

In times of serious trouble and deep sadness, written condolences and expressions of sympathy leave their mark. Granted, this type of message is difficult to write, but don't let the difficulty of the task keep you from responding promptly. Those who have experienced a health problem, the death of a loved one, or a business misfortune like to know that they're not alone.

Begin condolences with a brief statement of sympathy, such as "I was deeply sorry to hear of your loss." In the middle, mention the good qualities or the positive contributions made by the deceased. State what the person or business meant to you. In closing, you can offer your condolences and your best wishes. One considerate way to end this type of message is to say something that will give the reader a little lift, such as a reference to a brighter future.

You're not obligated to offer help to the reader; a good condolence message is often help enough. However, if you want to and can offer assistance, do so. Remember, the bereaved and grieving often suffer financially as well as emotionally, and reestablishing a business or a life often takes a great deal of time and effort. A simple gesture on your part may mean much to the reader.

Here are a few general suggestions for writing condolence messages:

- *Keep reminiscences brief.* Recount a memory or an anecdote (even a humorous one), but don't dwell on the details of the loss, lest you add to the reader's anguish.
- *Write in your own words.* Write as if you were speaking privately to the person. Don't quote "poetic" passages or use stilted or formal phrases. If the loss is a death, refer to it as such rather than as "passing away" or "departing."
- *Be tactful.* Mention your shock and dismay, but keep in mind that the bereaved and distressed loved ones take little comfort in such lines as, "Richard was too young to die" or "Starting all over again will be so difficult." Try to strike a balance between superficial expressions of sympathy and heartrending references to a happier past and a possibly bleak future.
- *Take special care.* Be sure to spell names correctly and to be accurate in your review of facts. Try to be prompt.
- *Write about special qualities of the deceased.* You may have to rely on reputation to do this, but let the grieving person know the value of his or her loved one.
- *Write about special qualities of the bereaved person.* A pat on the back helps a bereaved family member feel more confident about handling things during such a traumatic time.[6]

In condolence messages, try to find a middle path between being superficial and causing additional distress.

Above all, don't let the fear of saying something wrong keep you from saying anything at all. A supervisor, George Bigalow, sent the following condolence letter to his administrative assistant, Janice Case, after learning of the death of Janice's husband:

> My sympathy to you and your children. All your friends at Carter Electric were so very sorry to learn of John's death. Although I never had the opportunity to meet him, I do know how very special he was to you. Your tales of your family's camping trips and his rafting expeditions were always memorable.

As a reminder of the tasks involved with this type of message, see the Checklist for Writing Goodwill Messages.

DIRECTIVES AND INSTRUCTIONS

Directives tell employees what to do; instructions tell readers how to do something.

Directives are memos that tell employees *what* to do. Instructions tell people inside and outside the company *how* to do something and may take the form of e-mail messages, memos, letters, or even booklets. Directives and instructions are both considered routine messages because readers are assumed to be willing to comply.

The goal in writing directives and instructions is to make the point so obvious and the steps so self-explanatory that readers won't have to ask for additional help. Directives and instructions are especially important within companies: Faulty internal directives and bungled instructions are expensive and inefficient. The following directive does a good job of explaining what employees are expected to do:

> New security badges will be issued to all employees between January 20 and January 24. Each employee must report in person to the human resources office (Building B, Room 106) to exchange the old (red) security badges for the new (yellow) security badges. The electronic security system will not recognize the old badges on February 1 and thereafter.

CHECKLIST FOR WRITING GOODWILL MESSAGES

A. Planning

1. Choose the appropriate type of goodwill message for your purpose.
   a. Offer congratulations to make the reader feel noticed.
   b. Express praise or thanks to show your appreciation for good performance.
   c. Offer condolences to show appreciation for the deceased or for the person suffering a loss.
2. Be prompt when sending out goodwill messages so that they lose none of their impact.
3. Send a written goodwill message rather than a telephone message, because a written message can be savored more than once; but keep in mind that a telephone message is better than none at all.

B. Format

1. Use the format most appropriate to the occasion.
   a. Use letter format for condolences and for any other goodwill message sent to outsiders or mailed to an employee's home.
   b. Use memo format for any goodwill messages sent through interoffice mail, except for condolences.
   c. Use a preprinted greeting card for condolences (with a brief handwritten message added).
2. Handwrite condolences (and replies to handwritten invitations); otherwise, type the goodwill message.
3. Use special stationery, if available.
4. For added impact, present congratulations in a folder with a clipping or photo commemorating the special event.

C. Opening

1. State the most important idea first to focus the reader's attention.
2. Incorporate a friendly statement that builds goodwill, right at the beginning.
3. Focus on the good qualities of the person or situation.

D. Middle

1. Provide sufficient details, even in a short message, to justify the opening statement.
2. Express personalized details in sincere, not gushy, language.
3. Be warm but concise.
4. Make the reader, not the writer, the focus of all comments.

E. Close

1. Use a positive or forward-looking statement.
2. Restate the important idea, when appropriate.

If you are unable to make this exchange between January 20 and January 24, contact Theresa Gomez before January 15 either by phone at 4-6721 or by e-mail at tgomez@biotech.com.

This directive is brief and to the point. Drawn-out explanations are unnecessary because readers are expected simply to follow through on a well-established procedure. Yet it also covers all the bases, answering these questions: Who? What? When? Where? Why? How?

Instructions answer the same questions, but they differ from directives in the amount of explanation they provide. Silva Raker of The Nature Company might write a simple three-sentence directive to suppliers to tell them of a change in the company's credit policies; however, a detailed set of instructions would be more appropriate for explaining the procedure necessary to apply for credit and to submit credit applications.

When writing instructions, you have one goal: to provide a clear, self-sufficient explanation so that readers can perform the task independently. Make your instructions clear by:

- Including a list of equipment and materials.
- Dividing the process into short, simple steps presented in order of occurrence.
- Presenting the steps in a numbered list, or in paragraph format, using words indicating time or sequence, such as *first* and *then*. If the process involves more than ten steps, divide them into groups or stages identified with headings.
- Phrasing each step as a command ("Do this" instead of "You should do this").
- Indicating how readers may tell whether a step has been performed correctly or is complete.

- Including diagrams of complicated devices and referring to the diagrams in appropriate steps.
- Summarizing the importance of the process and the expected results in a conclusion.
- Testing your instructions. Ask someone else to read them to see if they make sense and are easy to follow.

Keep in mind that when writing instructions, take nothing for granted. Assuming that readers know nothing about the process you're describing is better than risking confusion and possible damage or harm by overlooking some basic information.

COMMUNICATION CHALLENGES AT THE NATURE COMPANY

The Nature Company's two Canadian stores are doing so well that the company has decided to open three more: one in Vancouver, one in Toronto, and one in Ottawa. Silva Raker is busy working with the designers and architects to create an in-store atmosphere uniquely suited to each location—The Nature Company's trademark design with a few extra touches to reflect the local region's flora and fauna.

INDIVIDUAL CHALLENGE: Getting ready for three new store openings outside the United States has created lots of extra work for Raker's staff. Nearly everyone has worked overtime, including weekends, and Raker wants to hire Jim Moody as a new staff member. She's impressed with his résumé and interview. Now she'd like to know whether Moody responds well under pressure. As public relations coordinator for Brentwell Logging in Snohomish, Washington, Moody may have dealt with pressured situations. Write a letter inquiring about Moody (making up any necessary details), to his Brentwell supervisor, Henry Watrous (at 1552 10th Avenue, Snohomish, WA 98290).[7]

TEAM CHALLENGE: Buyers in the merchandise department have already increased orders to stock the new stores, but in recent conversations with the retail staff at the established Canadian stores, Raker was clued in to a few products that are very popular among the company's northern clientele. Raker has handed your team a list of four of these extra-popular items, supplied by four separate vendors: glow-in-the-dark firefly T-shirts (which retail for $16.95 in adult sizes and $12.95 in child sizes), three-dimensional polar bear puzzles ($19.95), a digital display international-time clock ($39.95), and Greek wind chimes ($65.00). Your team is to develop a form letter explaining the circumstances and requesting a 20 percent increase in your original order from each of these vendors. Choose one of these items to use in a sample letter, making up company and individual names, wholesale prices, and quantities.

SUMMARY OF LEARNING OBJECTIVES

1. **Discuss why it's generally appropriate to use the direct organizational plan for routine, good-news, and goodwill messages.** Because most routine, good-news, and goodwill messages generally are of interest to the reader, it's appropriate to use the direct organizational approach as long as your message requires no special tact or persuasion and you are addressing an audience with minimal cultural differences.
2. **Describe the basic format for writing routine requests.** Open by stating your specific request. In the middle, justify your request, explain its importance, ask relevant questions, highlight benefits to the reader for responding, state desired actions in a positive manner, and include contact information. Close by requesting some specific response and an expression of goodwill.
3. **Describe the basic format for writing routine positive replies.** Begin with the good news or main idea. Use the middle to answer the request and provide details. End with a courteous close and an expression of goodwill.
4. **Highlight the main elements to include direct requests for claims and adjustments.** Include a straightforward statement of the problem in the opening. Tell the specifics, include any necessary details, and state the remedy you are seeking in the body. Close courteously with a brief summary of the desired action.
5. **Discuss the main differences in the explanatory section of a favorable response to a routine claim for adjustment when the company, a customer, or a third party is at fault.** When the company is at fault, explain your company's efforts to do a good job and refer to your errors carefully. If the customer is at fault, inform the customer that the merchandise was mistreated, but don't be condescending. If a third party is at fault, briefly explain that you have chosen to honor the claim even though the problem was not caused by your negligence.
6. **Explain why goodwill messages are important and how to make them effective.** Goodwill messages help develop and maintain good relationships with employees, customers, clients, and the general public. They have a positive effect on business and are most effective when they are honest and sincere.

CRITICAL THINKING QUESTIONS

1. When organizing your requests, why is it important to know whether any cultural differences exist between you and your audience? Explain.
2. For U.S. and Canadian requests, why is it inappropriate to begin with a brief personal introduction? Please explain your answer.
3. Every time you send a direct-request memo to Ted Jackson, he delays or refuses to comply. You're beginning to get impatient. Should you send Jackson a memo to ask what's wrong? Complain to your supervisor about Jackson's uncooperative attitude? Arrange a face-to-face meeting with Jackson? Bring up the problem at the next staff meeting? Explain.
4. As a local retailer, would you take the time to reply to requests for information and action when no potential sale is involved? Why or why not?
5. You have a complaint against one of your suppliers, but you have no documentation to back it up. Should you request an adjustment anyway? Why or why not?
6. Your company's error cost an important business customer a new client; you know it and your customer knows it. Do you apologize, or do you refer to the incident in a positive light without admitting any responsibility? Briefly explain.
7. When checking on a reference, why should you need the applicant's permission to contact a source? Explain your answer.
8. You've been asked to write a letter of recommendation for an employee who is disabled and uses a wheelchair. The disability has no effect on the employee's ability to do the job, and you feel confident about writing the best recommendation possible. Nevertheless, you know the prospective company and its facilities aren't well suited to wheelchair access. Do you mention the employee's disability in your letter? Explain.

DOCUMENTS FOR ANALYSIS

Read the following documents; then (1) analyze the strengths and weaknesses of each sentence and (2) revise each document so that it follows this chapter's guidelines.

Document 7.A: Requesting Routine Information from a Business

Our college is closing its dining hall for financial reasons, so we want to do something to help the students prepare their own food in their dorm rooms if they so choose. Your colorful ad in *Collegiate Magazine* caught our eye. We need the following information before we make our decision.

1. Would you be able to ship the microwaves by August 15th? I realize this is short notice, but our board of trustees just made the decision to close the dining hall last week and we're scrambling around trying to figure out what to do.
2. Do they have any kind of a warranty? College students can be pretty hard on things, as you know, so we will need a good warranty.
3. How much does it cost? Do you give a discount for a big order?
4. Do we have to provide a special outlet?
5. Will students know how to use them, or will we need to provide instructions?

As I said before, we're on a tight time frame and need good information from you as soon as possible to help us make our decision about ordering. You never know what the board might come up with next. I'm looking at several other companies, also, so please let us know ASAP.

Document 7.B: Writing Direct Requests for Claims and Adjustments

At a local business-supply store, I recently purchased your "Negotiator Pro" for my computer. I bought the CD because I saw your ad for it in *MacWorld* magazine, and it looked as if it might be an effective tool for use in my corporate seminar on negotiation.

Unfortunately, when I inserted it in my office computer, it wouldn't work. I returned it to the store, but since I had already opened it, they refused to exchange it for a CD that would work or give me a refund. They told me to contact you and that you might be able to send me a version that would work with my computer.

You can send the information to me at the letterhead address. If you cannot send me the correct disk, please refund my $79.95. Thanks in advance for any help you can give me in this matter.

Document 7.C: Responding to Claims and Adjustment Requests When the Customer Is at Fault

We read your letter requesting your deposit refund. We couldn't figure out why you hadn't received it, so we talked to our maintenance engineer as you suggested. He said you had left one of the doors off the hinges in your apartment in order to get a large sofa through the door. He also confirmed that you had paid him $5.00 to replace the door since you had to turn in the U-Haul trailer and were in a big hurry.

This entire situation really was caused by a lack of communication between our housekeeping inspector and the maintenance engineer. All we knew was that the door was off the hinges when it was inspected by Sally Tarnley. You know that our policy states that if anything is wrong with the apartment, we keep the deposit. We had no way of knowing that George just hadn't gotten around to replacing the door.

But we have good news. We approved the deposit refund, which will be mailed to you from our home office in Teaneck, New Jersey. I'm not sure how long that will take, however. If you don't receive the check by the end of next month, give me a call.

Next time, it's really a good idea to stay with your apartment until it's inspected as stipulated in your lease agreement. That way, you'll be sure to receive your refund when you expect it. Hope you have a good summer.

Document 7.D: Letter of Recommendation

Your letter to Tanaka Asata, President of SONY, was forwarded to me because I am the human resources director. In my job as head of HR, I have access to performance reviews for all of the SONY employees in the United States. This means, of course, that I would be the person best qualified to answer your request for information on Nick Oshinski.

In your letter of the 15th, you asked about Nick Oshinski's employment record with us because he has applied to work for your company. Mr. Oshinski was employed with us from January 5, 1992 until March 1, 1997. During that time, Mr. Oshinski received ratings ranging from 2.5 up to 9.6 with 10 being the top score. As you can see, he must have done better reporting to some managers than to others. In addition, he took all vacation days, which is a bit unusual. Although I did not know Mr. Oshinski personally, I know that our best workers seldom use all the vacation time they earn. I do not know if that applies in this case.

In summary, Nick Oshinski performed his tasks well depending on who managed him.

EXERCISES

1. Revise the following short e-mail messages so that they are more direct and concise; develop a subject line for each revised message.
   a. I'm contacting you about your recent order for a High Country backpack. You didn't tell us which backpack you wanted, and you know we make a lot of different ones. We have the canvas models with the plastic frames and vinyl trim and we have the canvas models with leather trim, and we have the ones that have more pockets than the other ones. Plus they come in lots of different colors. Also they make the ones that are large for a big-boned person and the smaller versions for little women or kids.
   b. Thank you for contacting us about the difficulty you had collecting your luggage at the Denver airport. We are very sorry for the inconvenience this has caused you. As you know, traveling can create problems of this sort regardless of how careful the airline personnel might be. To receive compensation, please send us a detailed list of the items that you lost and complete the following questionnaire. You can e-mail it back to us.
   c. Sorry it took us so long to get back to you. We were flooded with résumés. Anyway, your résumé made the final ten, and after meeting three hours yesterday, we've decided we'd like to meet with you. What is your schedule like for next week? Can you come in for an interview on June 15 at 3:00 p.m.? Please get back to us by the end of this work week and let us know if you will be able to attend. As you can imagine, this is our busy season.
   d. We're letting you know that because we use over a ton of paper a year and because so much of that paper goes into the wastebasket to become so much more environmental waste, starting Monday, we're placing white plastic bins outside the elevators on every floor to recycle that paper and in the process, minimize pollution.
2. Rewrite the following sentences so they are direct and concise.
   a. We wanted to invite you to our special 40 percent off by-invitation-only sale. The sale is taking place on November 9.
   b. We wanted to let you know that we are giving a tote bag and a free Phish CD with every $50 donation you make to our radio station.
   c. The director planned to go to the meeting that will be held on Monday at a little before 11:00 a.m.
   d. In today's meeting, we were happy to have the opportunity to welcome Paul Eccelson. He reviewed some of the newest types of order forms. If you have any questions about these new forms, feel free to call him at his office.
3. Select the most effective medium for communicating these written messages.
   a. A notice to all employees about the placement of recycling bins by the elevator doors
   b. The first late-payment notice to a good customer who usually pays his bills on time
4. Send a free electronic greeting card from the My Sentiments Fine Art Greeting Cards collection at http://www.artcards.com. You can choose from a variety of backgrounds and can even add music. Many languages are available. Recipients will receive an e-mail notice that a greeting is waiting for them.

EXPLORING THE BEST OF THE WEB

Compose Your Messages with Confidence, page 202

Consider the following scenario. Recently, you wrote a direct request for a software catalog. Your boss brings you a draft of the letter. Visibly annoyed, he points to this sentence: "None of these great programs are available anywhere else!" He insists that *none* always means "no one" and therefore is always used with a singular verb. He wants you to replace *are* with *is*. You are reluctant to cause trouble, but you are pretty sure that *none* can take either a singular or a plural verb, depending on the sentence. Use Garbl's Writing Resources Online http://pw1.netcom.com/,garbl1/writing.html to resolve the problem. What do the experts say? Should you change your verb? What should you tell your boss?

PLACING ORDERS

1. Wakeboard mania: Letter from Performance Ski & Surf ordering more equipment Your boss is amazed. Bill Porter, owner of Performance Ski & Surf, hasn't seen sporting equipment sell this rapidly in Orlando, Florida, since in-line skating became popular. But since May, you haven't been able to keep wakeboards in stock. It doesn't seem to matter much which brand—Wake Tech, Neptune, or Full Tilt—your customers, locals and tourists alike, are snapping them up and heading out to the water. These boards are outselling traditional trick water skis by 20 to 1.

"Maybe it's because they don't require big, fast boats," you suggest. "I heard they're using fishing trawlers out in Seattle, and they're still catching wind because the slower boats make bigger wakes to launch from."

Porter nods thoughtfully as he gazes at a photograph of professional wakeboarder Dean Lavelle at nearby Lake Butler. He's holding the same kind of rope any water skier holds, but he's 15 feet in the air. His short, stubby, fiberglass wakeboard (which is strapped to his feet) is higher than his head and from the grimace on his face, it looks as if he's in mid-flip.

"I just hope none of these kids get hurt trying to imitate the pros," Butler says.

"Nah," you say. "Extreme sports—it's the way of the '90s. Look at what happened to snowboarding. You'll see wakeboarders at the Olympics soon."

Your task: Butler has asked you to order another 12 Wake Techs, 8 Neptunes, and 10 Full Tilts. "Don't worry about colors or models; we'll be lucky to get this order filled at all from what I hear." He suggests you draft a form letter for the three orders and he'll supply the addresses and account numbers when you're finished.[8]

REQUESTING ROUTINE INFORMATION AND ACTION

2. Shrinking vacation: E-mail to a *Los Angeles Times* advice column "Hey," you exclaim (to no one in particular) after ripping open your paycheck and glancing at the stub. "They cheated me!"

LaDonna sticks her head up from the next cubicle. "What are you screaming about?"

"They ripped me off for vacation time!" you fume, waving the slip under LaDonna's nose. "Look right there, in the little square. It says I've only got 45.36 accrued hours for vacation and sick time. What happened to the 71 hours I had two weeks ago?"

Your colleague just smiles sweetly at you. "You didn't read the memo they sent around, did you?"

"What memo?" You're really not interested in memos right now. You're just wondering how soon you can get in to see the boss—or maybe you should go straight to personnel.

"The memo that explained the new company policy. Every time we're late"—she looks at you pointedly—"and that includes late coming back from lunch, they're going to deduct the time from our sick leave and vacation time. Looks like you've been busted."

"They can't do this to me! It's not fair!" you sputter. "I'll take it to the labor commissioner!"

"Hey, if you really think it's not fair, why don't you write to that column in the *L.A. Times*," your colleague suggests. LaDonna always did enjoy office controversies.

"What column?" you mumble morosely, resigning yourself to your fate. You've been counting in your head and they're probably accurate with their figures. You never could get anywhere on time, and you estimate you've been late about 10 times in the last 14 working days—that is, if you count the extra 15 minutes you took for lunch a few times. And you thought no one had noticed!

"It's called 'Shop Talk.' Here, I have a copy. Check it out."

You look over the column, and it's all about work-related problems, in a question-and-answer format. But the answers are supplied by real attorneys, working for a variety of law firms in and around southern California and specializing in employment law, employee benefits, employee rights, and so on. What harm could it do? You just might have a point of contention: No one discussed the tardies with you before deducting the vacation time, and you received no detailed listing of the dates and exact amounts of time you were late. Is this a legal action for an employer to take?

Your task: Write an e-mail message to *The Los Angeles Times* and send it to shoptalk@latimes.com, including your initials and home town as requested. Keep in mind the column's published request that questions raise issues of general interest, and don't forget the disclaimer that answers provided do not constitute legal advice. But if the attorney answering your query says that your employer's action was illegal, you might have a pretty good argument for talking your way back into your vacation time.[10]

3. Blockbuster shake-up: Memo from top brass requesting info from retail managers Everyone knew there was trouble at Blockbuster's new headquarters in Dallas when CEO Bill Fields, a former Wal-Mart whiz, suddenly resigned. Then Sumner Redstone and Tom Dooley (chairman and deputy chairman of Blockbuster's parent company, Viacom) flew in to assess the damage wrought by Fields's departure. They started by giving orders—particularly to you, Fields's former executive assistant.

Before Fields resigned to take a position with Hudson's Bay Company, in Canada, his strategy had been to boost Blockbuster's sagging video rentals by establishing a new niche as a "neighborhood entertainment center." Using tricks he'd learned at Wal-Mart, he ordered the reconfiguration of more than 1,000 Blockbuster outlets, surrounding the cash registers with flashy displays of candy, potato chips, new and used videotapes for sale, magazines, and tie-in toys. His stated goal was to add $1 in retail purchases to every rental transaction. Meanwhile, he also relocated Blockbuster's headquarters from Florida to Dallas, losing 75 percent of the company's top staff when they declined to make the move. Then, Fields initiated the construction of an 818,000-square-foot warehouse 25 miles outside Dallas to centralize a new, highly sophisticated distribution operation (Fields's special expertise) for Blockbuster's 3,600 North American outlets. But revenues were still falling.

Redstone and Dooley's new plan is to get Blockbuster back into its core business—video rentals—ignoring gloomy analysts who say satellite dishes and cheap tape sales are slowly sinking the rental industry. "This is still a healthy, growing business," Dooley insists. He believes that consumers coming in to rent videos were confused by the array of retail products that greeted them. "We want people to think of Blockbuster as the place to go to rent tapes," he says.

Dooley and Redstone have been hiring new headquarters staff at the rate of about 50 persons per week; they've been to the warehouse construction site; they've ordered outlets to rearrange merchandise to emphasize tape rentals; and now they've turned to you. "We've got a job you'll love," Dooley smiles. "We know you can handle it."

Your task: Briefly state the purpose of your message. Then draft a memo that will pick the brains of retail managers in the stores that Fields reconfigured. Dooley wants to know whether customers walk out when current hits aren't available, whether the emphasis on retail products affected cash flow, and whether sales and rental figures have changed now that the clutter has been removed. Ask them: Where's the cash coming from—tape rentals, tape sales, or candy bars? Dooley says, "I want a full report from every manager by the end of next week!" To get that kind of cooperation, you'd better organize your questions effectively.[11]

4. Training is murder: Letter to Norwest Banks requesting information on Red Herring mystery troupe As a sales training manager for Jarvis Office Products in Denver, you've tried just about everything to get your sales reps' attention during training seminars. Usually their eyes glaze over within the first hour. After a seminar, sales figures rise slightly for a while; then they slump back to the normal average. This year you're determined to try something new.

Recently, a friend of yours mentioned an idea that's so outlandish, it might work. She'd heard of a theatrical troupe in Colorado Springs, Red Herring Productions, that performs murder mysteries for company seminars, helping management put points across with a certain unforgettable "zing." They call this "pointimation," your friend said. She thought their Web address was something like "Red Herring Productions-dot-com."

Turns out she was right. The approach looks promising. Cast members show up in character to schmooze with your participants for a while. Then they hook them with a staged murder and a subsequent team organization to decipher clues and solve the "whodunnit" mystery.

The company writes its own scripts, everything from the Wild West "Murder at the Buffalo Chip," with gunslingers, church ladies, and gamblers, to the Rockin' '50s "Murder on Location" of a movie set. "The CEO Murder" sounds a little too close to home, but surely something like "Invaded by Murder," with an alien landing in the middle of your meeting, would wake up your staff!

You click to the "Red Herring Educational Services Products" page and discover a special-purpose mystery on "Selling to Your Client's View of the World." It promises to cover nine common client personality types. Another click and you find a list of Red Herring's customers and some testimonials: "You made me look great as a meeting planner . . ."; "It was a roaring success . . . "; "I haven't laughed so hard in a long time. The performers stayed in character all day! I didn't want to stop; not even for breaks!"

That one, from a meeting planner at Norwest Banks, is the one that gets you. You try to imagine your cynical sales pros being that captivated by *anything*. . .

Your task: Write a letter to the meeting planning department (no name is given) at Norwest Banks (887 Dove Creek Drive, Colorado Springs, CO 80901), asking for comments on Red Herring's services. You don't want to look like a fool; after all, once Lizzie the gun moll comes swaggering into your meeting room, there'll be no turning back![12]

5. Please tell me: Request for information about a product You're a consumer, and you've probably seen hundreds of products that you'd like to buy (if you haven't, look at the advertisements in your favorite magazine for ideas). Choose a big-ticket item that is rather complicated, such as a stereo system or a vacation in the Caribbean.

Your task: You surely have some questions about the features of your chosen product or about its price, guarantees, local availability, and so on. Write to the company or organization that's offering it, and ask four questions that are important to you. Be sure to include enough background information so that the reader can answer your questions satisfactorily.

If requested to do so by your instructor, mail a copy of your letter (after your instructor has had an opportunity to review it) to the company or organization. After a few weeks, you and your classmates may wish to compare responses and to answer this question: How well do companies or organizations respond to unsolicited inquiries?

REPLYING TO REQUESTS FOR INFORMATION AND ACTION

6. Mercedes merchandise: Form letter announcing a new upscale catalog Mercedes-Benz owners take their accessories seriously, which is why so many of them are upset when they purchase "rip-off" Mercedes baseball caps that fall apart. Such merchandise is produced by "sweatshop entrepreneurs," your boss's term for merchandisers who pirate the Mercedes logo, paste it onto cheap caps, and then sell their wares at swap meets and in flea markets. When the logo falls off, you get the irate letters.

You're working for Steve Beaty, vice president of accessories marketing for Mercedes-Benz. This is big business; today nearly every brand of automobile offers accompanying goods for proud owners: ties, T-shirts, watches, shoes, hats, jackets, sweaters. Most are sold right in the showrooms, and they're extremely popular, whether they be Saturn sneakers or Land Rover tweeds. Some of the upscale auto manufacturers have been striving to provide logo-bearing clothing and gadgets that meet their customers' high-class budgets and tastes. But simply raising prices has backfired. The second most common customer complaint you've been receiving is, "Why should I pay twice the price for an ordinary shirt just because it carries the Mercedes triangle?"

Beaty agrees with these customers, so he went to work with other company executives to produce a brand-new, 55-page, glossy, full-color *Mercedes-Benz Personal & Automotive Accessories* catalog loaded with expensive loot. Mercedes-Benz has recruited world-class, top-of-the-line manufacturers and designers to produce merchandise worthy of the company's highly refined clientele. The new catalog presents Wittnauer watches, Caran D'Ache ballpoints, Bally bomber jackets, and silk boxers designed by artist Nicole Miller—all emblazoned with the triangle logo or images of Mercedes-Benz models, past and present. The catalog even features a $3,300 collapsible aluminum mountain bike for slipping into the trunk of your 500SL.

Your task: Beaty wants you to develop a form letter—a very classy one, of course—to send with a copy of the new catalog to all the customers who have sent complaints about shoddy or overpriced merchandise during the last year or so. He thinks they'll be quite happy with this reply.[13]

7. Red dirt to go: E-mail to a mainland customer from Paradise Sportswear Robert Hedin would agree with whoever said that it's possible to turn a failure into a success. But he'd probably add with a chuckle that it could take several failures before you finally hit "pay dirt." As the owner of Paradise Sportswear in Hawaii, Hedin was nearly done in by Hurricane Iniki in 1992, which wiped out his first silk-screened and airbrushed T-shirt business. He tried again, but then Hawaii's red dirt started seeping into his warehouse and ruining his inventory. Finally, a friend suggested that he stop trying to fight Mother Nature. Hedin took the hint: He mortgaged his condo and began producing Red Dirt Shirts, all made with dye created from the troublesome local dirt.

Bingo: So popular are Hedin's Red Dirt Sportswear designs, they're being snapped up by locals and tourists in Hedin's eight Paradise Sportswear retail outlets and in every Kmart on the islands. Last year Hedin added a new line: Lava Blues, made with real Hawaiian lava rock.

"You can make 500 shirts with a bucket of dirt," grins Hedin as he shows you around the operation on your first day. He's just a few years away from the usual retirement age, but he looks like a kid who's finally found the right playground.

Recently Hedin decided to capitulate to all the requests he's received from retail outlets on the mainland. Buyers kept coming to the islands on vacation, discovering Hedin's "natural" sportswear, and plaguing him in person, by mail, and by e-mail, trying to set up a deal. For a long time, his answer was no; he simply couldn't handle the extra work. But now he's hired you.

As special sales representative, you'll help Hedin expand slowly into this new territory, starting with one store. Wholesaling to the local Kmarts is easy enough, but handling all the arrangements for shipping to the mainland would be too much for the current staff. So you'll start with the company Hedin has chosen to become the first mainland retailer to sell Red Dirt and Lava Blues sportswear: Surf's Up in Chicago, Illinois—of all places. The boss figures that with less competition than he'd find on either coast, his island-influenced sportswear will be a big hit in Chicago, especially in the dead of winter.

Your task: Write a positive response to the e-mail received from Surf's Up buyer Ronald Draeger, who says he fell in love with the Paradise clothing concept while on a surfing trip to Maui. Let him know he'll have a temporary exclusive and that you'll be sending a credit application and other materials by snail mail. His e-mail address is surfsup@insnet.com.[14]

8. Window shopping at Wal-Mart: Writing a positive reply via e-mail The Wal-Mart chain of discount stores is one of the most successful in the world: designing, importing, and marketing across national borders. In particular, Wal-Mart rarely fails to capitalize on a marketing scheme, and its online shopping page is no exception. To make sure the Web site remains effective and relevant, the

Webmaster asks various people to check out the site and give their feedback. As administrative assistant to Wal-Mart's director of marketing, you have just received a request from the Webmaster to visit Wal-Mart's Web site and give feedback on the shopping page.

Your task: Visit Wal-Mart at http://www.wal-mart.com and do some online "window shopping." As you browse through the shopping page, consider the language, layout, graphics, ease of use, and background noise. Then compose a positive reply to the Webmaster, and send your feedback to cserve@wal-mart.com. Print a copy of your e-mail message for submission to your instructor.

WRITING DIRECT REQUESTS FOR CLAIMS AND ADJUSTMENTS

9. Spoiled in Argentina: Claim from California peach growers When President Carlos Menem of Argentina took office, he and his economy minister, Domingo Cavallo, decided that competition from foreign producers would stimulate Argentine business to provide better products at competitive prices. To the delight of Argentine shoppers, import tariffs were lowered and goods began pouring in from all over the world: calculators and copy machines, scissors and automobiles, bicycles, toothpicks—and peaches.

When Menem's new policies took effect, California peach growers responded eagerly to the opening of the new market. Individual growers banded into the California Peach Growers Association to ship their fruit to Edcadassa, the Argentine firm that oversees all imported goods while they await customs clearance at Ezeiza international airport.

As supervisor of the Argentine project for the growers association, you were extremely pleased with the success of the first few shipments; everything had gone smoothly. Then word came back from angry Argentine buyers that instead of the fresh, firm California peaches they had expected, the peaches that arrived at their stores were ready for the garbage bin. They refused to pay for the rotten fruit, and your growers lost $50,000.

You made inquiries and discovered that Edcadassa was overwhelmed by the level of imported goods flowing into Argentina (an average of 150 tons a day, compared with 60 tons two years before). Your peach shipment was lost in the confusion, and by the time it was cleared through customs, three weeks late, the peaches were already rotten. You'd shipped the fruit when it was at the perfect stage to make the journey, await the normal customs delay, and ripen gently in the supermarkets of Buenos Aires, so you believe that the responsibility for the shipment's destruction rests with Edcadassa.

Your task: Write a letter to Edcadassa (Columbia 4300, 1425 Buenos Aires, Argentina) requesting full compensation for the ruined peaches.[15]

10. Bolga boo-boo: E-mail to Getrade (Ghana) Ltd. from Pier 1 Imports The way you heard it, your employer, Pier 1 Imports, sent a buyer to Accra, Ghana, to find local handicrafts to slake your customers' insatiable thirst for African art. Free-market reforms in Ghana during the 1980s helped ease export procedures, but so far the local entrepreneurs who sprang forward to take advantage of the change are having trouble meeting demand from large-quantity buyers like Pier 1 (and your rival, Cost Plus). The shipment that just arrived from Getrade (Ghana) Ltd., one of your best Ghanaian suppliers, is a good example of what's been going wrong.

Your customers love bowl-shaped Bolga baskets, traditionally woven by the Fra-fra people of northern Ghana. You can't keep the baskets in stock. So this was to be a huge shipment—3,000 Bolga baskets. You sympathize with Ladi Nylander, chairman and managing director of Getrade, who is trying hard to adapt to the specific tastes of his U.S. buyers. He's hiring local artisans to carve, shape, and weave all sorts of artifacts—often from designs provided by Pier 1. In this case, your order spelled out that Getrade was to ship 1,000 green, 1,000 yellow, and 1,000 magenta baskets in the traditional shape.

Your overseas buyer heard that the Body Shop ordered similar baskets but with mixed-color patterns and a flatter shape. Pier 1 may have received the Body Shop's order, because what you received was 3,000 mixed-color, flat Bolga baskets.

Your task: As assistant buyer, it's your job to compose the e-mail message alerting Getrade to the mix-up. You decide that if you want the mistake corrected, you'd better direct your message to Nylander at Nylander@Getrade.co.za. If you're lucky, it may be simply that the Body Shop got your order and you got theirs.[16]

RESPONDING FAVORABLY TO CLAIMS AND ADJUSTMENT REQUESTS

11. Good news from "Freddy Pumpkin": Letter from Teleline, granting an adjustment on a phone bill The March phone bill was a bit of a shock to Allen White (of 723 Amber Court, Cambridge, MA 02140), and April's bill was no better. The statements for both months listed $40 worth of calls that White was sure he had not made. Finally, in May, when the mystery calls totaled $100, White figured out that his four-year-old son was placing calls to "Freddy Pumpkin," a 900 telephone line advertised on children's television shows. The irate Mr. White paid the telephone bill but fired off a letter of protest to Mr. Robert H. Lorsch, president of Teleline, a company that operates children's phone-line services.

White's letter distressed Mr. Lorsch, who feels that Teleline offers a legitimate service. Children who call the firm's 900 numbers hear a taped message featuring cartoon or fantasy characters. At $2.45 for the first minute and 45 cents for each additional minute, the calls aren't cheap; but they aren't a big problem unless a child develops a serious habit. Teleline receives fewer than 12 complaints a month. The company is careful to state its prices in its television ads for the phone lines, and it warns children to ask their parents for permission before calling.

Your task: Draft a letter for Mr. Lorsch's signature offering to refund $90 of Mr. White's money—half of what he paid for the calls during March, April, and May.[17]

12. Satisfaction guaranteed: Letter from L. L. Bean granting a claim As a member of L. L. Bean's customer service department in Freeport, Maine, you've handled plenty of claims in your day. The famous mail-order sporting goods and clothing company processes thousands of orders every month, and inevitably, some items are returned. Your job is to respond to the customer either by exchanging the merchandise or by refunding the person's money, regardless of why the item was returned. L. L. Bean guarantees satisfaction, no questions asked.

Today you have received a package from Arvin Bummel (212 North Star, Traverse City, MI 49684). When you open it, you find (1) one Maine guide shirt, stiff as a board and two sizes smaller than it ought to be; (2) one pair of whipcord trousers, also stiff and shrunken; and (3) a nasty letter from Mr. Bummel saying that he expects better from L. L. Bean. According to him, the clothes were ruined the first time he washed them. He wants L. L. Bean to replace the shirt and pants. You are not surprised that the clothes are ruined, because the label plainly says, "Dry-clean only." Regardless, $108.50 worth of clothes are now unwearable.

Your task: In the spirit of good customer relations, write to Mr. Bummel and grant his claim. You may want to suggest gently that he look for clothing that is washable.

MAKING ROUTINE CREDIT REQUESTS

13. Beanie Babies: Letter requesting credit from Ty, Inc. Bubbles (the fish), Inch (the worm), Ziggy (the zebra)—if you hear another parent ask for them, you're going to walk out the door of Sandy's Gifts and never return. No, not really. You love the brightly colored, fuzzy little bean-bag toys just as much as anyone, but you hate seeing adults look as disappointed as their kids when you tell them you don't carry them.

"You mean you don't even have Bongo the monkey? Or Pinky the flamingo?"

"Sorry, not yet," you apologize. "But we've had so many requests, we're hoping to have them in stock soon. If you leave your name and phone number . . ."

Sandy Applegate, the store's owner, is sympathetic when you tell her what's been happening, but she doesn't know what to do. Her cash flow situation just doesn't allow for any new stock purchases until after Christmas. Who would have thought the $5 bean-bag animals (called "Beanie Babies" by manufacturer Ty, Inc.) would be so popular?

"But think of the sales we're missing," you interject. "Won't they give you credit?"

"Well, we've never done business with them before," Sandy says thoughtfully, "but you might have a point. After all, Sandy's Gifts has been in business for almost 10 years, at the same location. How many retail shops can say that today? And our credit with other vendors is excellent. Why don't you give it a try? You've been wanting to learn more about managing the store, haven't you?"

She's right. This is a great opportunity!

Your task: Write a letter for Sandy's signature to New Account Sales, Ty, Inc., P.O. Box 5377, Oakbrook, IL 60522, requesting credit to purchase two dozen Beanie Babies. Introduce the store and then discuss its reputation and the reasons Ty might like to comply.[18]

14. Please, Mr. Spear: Fax requesting credit for movie-scene banquet ingredients A few months ago you landed the most exciting job you could imagine, as a production assistant for Meg McComb, one of the best-known movie food stylists in Hollywood. But some days it's just a little too exciting. Like today. Your boss has been hired at the eleventh hour to concoct a twelfth-century feast for a period costume drama directed by Kenneth Branagh. The food, for 150 actors, must look authentic and must be ready by shooting time tomorrow, 1 P.M.

McComb is a pro, and you have full confidence in her as she races about the office, handing out assignments to a cluster of nervous assistants. You know that she knows what to do with a banquet for 150 if the shooting is canceled at the last moment (feed it to friends), and how to handle temperamental ingredients (avoid them) and star-quality special requests (indulge them if the budget's right). For director Branagh, she previously created a circa-1948 wedding banquet for *Dead Again.* But after four days of shooting, her fancy tower of cheeses melted into what McComb called a *quesadilla muerte.* Then Branagh cut the scene from the movie anyway. For *Apollo 13,* McComb spent a full week recreating a 1969 picnic complete with hams and gelation-molds, and for *Star Trek: The Next Generation,* she found puffy green cakes at an Oriental market that earned her fame as the inventor of "algae puff hors d'oeuvres."

Zipping by your desk, McComb tosses you a catalog of food retailers, blurting only one word, "Asparagus." Thank goodness the set is in Hollywood, not London. She means asparagus for 150, and luckily most of your produce suppliers are in California.

Flipping through the pages, you come across Mr. Spear, a combination grower and shipper in the San Joaquin Valley that specializes in overnight retail shipments of jumbo spears, picked in the morning, shipped in the afternoon, and on your table the next day—three pounds for $16.95, plus shipping. Quick work with your calculator indicates you need about 75 pounds, or $424 worth, if you have to pay retail. It's already noon.

You've never worked with Mr. Spear before, but you need the grower to ship the asparagus without prepayment in order to get it to McComb's kitchens by 10 A.M. tomorrow. Standard office practice is to ask for a wholesale price and free shipping when ordering such large amounts. But if these terms aren't available, you'll pay full retail price as long as Mr. Spear can meet the deadline. You'll have to pass on the extra cost to Branagh's ever-growing production budget.

Your task: The folks at Mr. Spear will want to review Meg McComb's credentials before they'll ship on credit, so you'd better fax your request immediately and include a copy of McComb's highly impressive client list. Call the number they list in the catalog, 800-677-7327, to get the fax number.[19]

APPROVING ROUTINE CREDIT REQUESTS

15. Virtual audio imager: Good news from Brown Innovations On Saturday afternoons in a store selling music CDs, multimedia computers, stereo speakers, and other consumer electronics—all with display models ready to demonstrate their sound capabilities—there can be such a cacophony that no one can hear anything, including the sales pitch. Brown Innovations' virtual audio imager eliminates this problem by creating an "isolated" listening region directly beneath the speakers. In a game arcade, for instance, players can hear their own radical sound effects, but not everyone else's. In the stereo store, the rap music demo on the boombox doesn't interfere with the salesperson across the store trying to explain the benefits of a laser printer.

Ever since a small item about the virtual audio imager appeared in *Newsweek*, both the Boston and Chicago offices of Brown Innovations have been swamped with orders. From where you sit, it looks as if every music store, arcade, and electronic equipment store in the nation wants to install the new equipment to cut down on noise pollution.

The applications for credit are streaming in by the hundreds. As an accounts receivable supervisor, you've already reviewed 25 today, and you have just one more on your desk, a credit purchase for two virtual audio imagers from Stevens Stereo in Albuquerque, New Mexico. The financial statements have already been reviewed and approved, and the store's history is good.

Your task: Write a letter to Paul Ramirez, manager (Stevens Stereo, 87714 Malaga Road, Albuquerque, NM 87103), telling him his application has been approved and his order is being processed.[20]

INQUIRING ABOUT PEOPLE

16. Measuring suppliers: Inside letter requesting reviews at Microsoft "Why do you do reviews with employees?" Roxanna Frost, group program manager for Microsoft's Executive Management and Development Group is asking those of you from the Employee Services Group who are gathered in her presence. You think it's a dumb question, but Kevin Ostic, manager of business and technology in your group, pipes up, "It's all about improving clarity in terms of goals and expectations."

Right, Kev, and two more brownie points for you, you think gloomily. You've never been good at coming up with the right answers at the right moment, even if your title is "communications manager"—but you know you're darn good at everything else. And just give you a little time to think things through . . .

But you don't have any more time. Frost is pushing on, "Right—so everyone can talk about accomplishments and improvements. The same should go for suppliers. There's a gap between what we want our suppliers to do and the feedback they're getting." She's eyeing you pointedly. But hey, it's not your fault that 60 percent of the employee services your group monitors (travel assistance, 401(k) programs, the library onsite at Microsoft's Redmond, Washington, campus) are provided by outsourcers—that is, independent contractors. Lots of departments at Microsoft outsource for services and products. Why is she looking at you like that?

Within seconds, you know: She wants you to write a *formal letter* to all departments at Microsoft that use outside suppliers. You must ask them to evaluate each supplier for the same five qualities used to evaluate employees (financial value, delivery, quality, customer satisfaction, and innovation). Each quality should be rated on a scale of 1 (poor) to 5 (great). She wants the evaluations repeated every six months, and she wants them to be written up in a formal letter format for mailing to each supplier. The departments are to forward their letters to Frost's office (for Microsoft record keeping), where her staff will handle the mailing. She also suggests that your letter give managers some ideas for gently introducing the new policy to suppliers.

Your task: First you'll have to suppress your concern that Microsoft's ratings may be more feedback than suppliers want, and more work for department managers. But you've got time to think . . . and your mind is already busy concocting a direct request letter that's less commanding than Frost's orders to you. (That's what you get for working at a company that likes to keep employees challenged.)[21]

17. Faxes and farmers: Staples' memo inquiring about a manager's qualifications for boondocks duty For years, Staples and its superstore competitors have clustered in large cities, selling cut-price supplies to small businesses that need to compete with corporations that buy supplies in bulk. The superstores have helped level the playing field for city-based business owners. But now the market is heading for the boondocks, following the entrepreneurs who've moved out of the metropolis and into the bucolic countryside. These business owners still view the world as their marketplace, but they want country air and wide-open spaces. Now they just need someone to sell them fax paper, computer components, and lamination services.

You need someone, too—someone to staff the Lebanon, New Hampshire, Staples expansion, a new 24,000-square-foot store to replace the first Staples in the community, population 12,600. That's nearly 2 square feet per citizen, you calculate idly, sitting in your office at Staples' headquarters in Westborough, Massachusetts. As director of human resources, you have been charged by Staples' chairman, Thomas Stemberg, with finding people who understand the rural market, where stores grow fast and where profits shoot up like corn in July.

Right now, you're looking for a special manager, one who knows office supplies but can also relate to customers like Walter Boyd, owner of a six-room inn who travels an hour to Lebanon to purchase essentials such as file cabinets, and Mimi Murray-Eastman, who brings in her hand-painted bookmarks for lamination before sending them to customers. The résumé of Karen Osterweil looks promising. It was sent to you by a Staples manager in Grand Rapids, Michigan, where Osterweil works as assistant manager. She wants to transfer to the East. And two years ago, she spent her summer breaks from MSU working at a farmers' co-op in her hometown. "I want to do anything I can to help this fine employee receive the recognition she deserves," writes the manager, Hallie Riggola.

Your task: The résumé offers no contact information for the farmers' cooperative, so you have to write a confidential memo to Riggola asking her to question Osterweil about her previous co-op experience, but discreetly. You don't want this employee to know yet that she's being considered for a promotion and transfer to the new store.[22] Which organizational pattern will you use (direct or indirect) when writing your message? Briefly explain.

CONVEYING POSITIVE INFORMATION ABOUT PEOPLE

18. On a course for Harvard: Reply to a request for a recommendation letter After working for several years for Zoe Coulson in Campbell Soup Company's department of consumer affairs, one of your co-workers, Angela Cavanaugh, has decided to apply for admission to the Harvard Business School's M.B.A. program. She has asked Coulson, a Harvard graduate, to write a letter of recommendation for her. Here are the facts about Angela Cavanaugh:

1. She has an undergraduate degree in journalism from the University of Iowa, where she was an honors student.
2. She joined Campbell directly after graduating and has worked for the firm for the past five years.
3. Her primary responsibility has been to answer letters from consumers; she has done an outstanding job.
4. Her most noteworthy achievement has been to analyze a year's worth of incoming mail, categorize the letters by type and frequency, and create a series of standardized replies. The department now uses Cavanaugh's form letters to handle approximately 75 percent of its mail.
5. Although Cavanaugh has outstanding work habits and is an excellent writer, she lacks confidence as a speaker. Her reluctance to present her ideas orally has prevented her from advancing more rapidly at Campbell. This could be a problem for her at Harvard Business School, where skill in classroom discussion influences a student's chances of success.

Your task: Because you have worked closely with Cavanaugh, Zoe Coulson has asked you to draft the letter, which Coulson will sign.[23]

CONVEYING GOOD NEWS ABOUT EMPLOYMENT

19. Cold comfort: E-mail offering a regional sales position with Golight Winter in Nebraska ranch country is something to sneeze at—and to shiver over. That's why rancher Jerry Gohl invented the Golight, a portable spotlight that can be mounted on a car or truck roof and rotated 360 degrees horizontally and 70 degrees vertically *by remote control.* No more getting out of the truck in freezing, predawn temperatures to adjust a manual spotlight in order to check on his livestock in the dark. In fact, for Gohl, there's hardly any time left to check the livestock at all these days: His invention has become so popular that three-year-old Golight, Inc., expects to sell more than $2 million worth of the remote-controlled lights next year.

The company expanded fast, with Golights becoming popular all over the world among hunters, boaters, commuters who fear dark-of-night roadside tire changes, and early-morning fishing enthusiasts who can scope out the best shoreline sites by controlling the spotlight from inside their warm and cozy vehicles. Sales reps have been hired for every part of the country and overseas, but Gohl has been holding out for just the right person to replace him in the Nebraska territory. After all, the company president knows better than anyone what the local ranchers need and how they think—that's why his invention was such a success there. He doesn't want to jinx his good fortune by choosing the wrong replacement.

Finally, last week he met a young man named Robert Victor who seems to fit the bill. Robert grew up on a Nebraska ranch, helping his dad with those 4 A.M. chores. He's young, but he's felt the bite of Nebraska's cold, he knows the rancher mind, and best of all, he's been bringing in top dollar selling agricultural equipment in Montana for the past few years. Now he wants to return to his home state. Gohl liked him from the first moment they shook hands. "He's got the job if he wants it," the boss tells you. "Better send him some e-mail before someone else grabs him. He can start as soon as he's settled."

Your task: Compose the message communicating Gohl's offer to Robert Victor: salary plus commission as discussed, full benefits (paid vacation, health and dental insurance) if he's still around in six months. His e-mail address is rvictor@ism.net. Sign with your name, as Gohl's personnel manager.[24]

CONVEYING GOOD NEWS ABOUT PRODUCTS AND OPERATIONS

20. Learn while you earn: Memo announcing Burger King's educational benefits Your boss, Herb Schervish, owner of a Burger King store in Detroit's downtown Renaissance Center, is worried about employee turnover. He needs to keep 50 people on his payroll to operate the outlet, but recruiting and retaining those people is tough. The average employee leaves after about seven months, so Schervish has to hire and train 90 people a year just to maintain a 50-person crew. At a cost of $1,500 per hire, the price tag for all that turnover is approximately $62,000 a year.

Schervish knows that a lot of his best employees quit because they think that flipping burgers is a dead-end job. But what if it weren't a dead end? What if a person could really get someplace flipping burgers? What if Schervish offered to pay his employees' way through college if they remained with the store? Would that keep them behind the counter?

He's decided to give educational incentives a try. Employees who choose to participate will continue to earn their usual salary, but they will also get free books and college tuition, keyed to the number of hours they work each week. Those who work from 10 to 15 hours a week can take one free course at nearby Wayne County Community College; those who work 16 to 25 hours can take two courses; and those who work 26 to 40 hours can take three courses. The program is open to all employees, regardless of how long they have worked for Burger King, but no one is obligated to participate.

Your task: Draft a memo for Mr. Schervish to send out announcing the new educational incentives.[25]

21. Daily blast: Disney & Microsoft target the Internet kids They're known as the "Internet Generation"—kids between the ages of 3 and 15 who are growing up in an era when the Information Superhighway leads right into the family den. And two of the most ubiquitous companies in the world, Microsoft and Disney, have their corporate eyes on this lucrative market-in-the-making.

The two companies first teamed up with Disney's Daily Blast, a multimedia, interactive Web site designed to attract and hold the interest of the gradeschool set (kids 3 to 12 years old). After a month-long free trial, Disney offered its "smorgasbord" of games, stories, news items and quizzes, comic books, and other colorful and noisy activities to subscribers for $4.95 per month. Your boss, Disney Online President Jake Winebaum, told the news media at the time that, although nearly everything on the Web is free and that's what consumers expect, he was confident that families would be willing to subscribe to bring "quality family programming" into their homes via the tool kids are most eager to explore: the Internet.

But just in case subscriptions were slow, Disney signed an agreement with Microsoft to provide the Daily Blast for Channel 6 on the Microsoft Network (MSN). That guaranteed Disney at least 2 million customers, for which Microsoft is paying the equivalent subscription fees. Moreover, Microsoft agreed to share the marketing costs to promote the Daily Blast. The arrangement was to be exclusive for ten months, after which other networks could sign similar agreements with Disney.

Those ten months are nearly up, and now Disney and the Microsoft Network are cooking up a new scheme. They've unveiled plans this week to produce a kind of Daily Blast for kids 12 to 15 years old. Holding their interest won't be easy, but the two companies are confident they can use what they've learned from the Daily Blast experience to avoid pitfalls. After all, some of their early subscribers are growing up, and the companies would love to keep their attention—as would advertisers on the site. As yet unnamed, the new site will again be offered on a subscription basis and as a ten-month exclusive on MSN. It will feature more-sophisticated games and comics, news items and other information features that will help kids with their homework, and plenty of graphics, sounds, and interactive quizzes—all geared to appeal to their audience's "aging" tastes and trend consciousness. The executives believe that parents, who pay for the subscriptions, will love and support the site as a "safe" and educational Internet experience for their offspring.

"These kids have grown up with PCs, and for them computers are completely second nature," Winebaum tells you confidently. He should know; he has two kids in this age group. "They will own this medium, and you can quote me on that," he adds.

Your task: Winebaum has asked you to help him draft the news release announcing the new Disney-Microsoft venture. It will have to pass through both companies for approval, of course, and before it's released they will need to agree on a name for the new site. But he wants to be ready. Where the Internet, Disney, and Microsoft are concerned, timing is crucial, and sooner is always better than later. Leave space for the site name to be added later if you must. And remember: At this stage, the plans are top secret; this draft is CONFIDENTIAL: FOR YOUR EYES ONLY.[26] Bring your completed draft to class and exchange it with those of your classmates. Edit each other's work. (Be sure to review the guidelines in Chapter 6 for critiquing the work of another.)

WRITING GOODWILL MESSAGES

22. Good work: E-mail congratulating Netscape's unofficial recruiting team Despite the meager 1.6 percent growth in the overall job market, so-called computer techies have become a hot commodity, garnering starting salaries in the high five figures. For computer "nerds" with at least three years' experience, signing bonuses of $6,000–$10,000 are not uncommon. When you add offers of 1,500 to 2,000 company shares, you get a pretty good idea of the employment outlook for those with the necessary computer skills. "We hire the good people first, and figure out what they're going to do later," says Eric Schmidt, chief technology officer at Sun Microsystems. Competition for workers is so intense that "you have to treat your current employees as though you were recruiting them to stave off raids by rivals," he says, citing bonuses offered to employees who help recruit others.

You are Sandra Harmon, director of human resources for Netscape Communications Corp. You used to be among the 150 recruiters interviewing engineering students at the University of Illinois. This spring there were 330 recruiters. You were particularly interested in 23-year-old Juan Jose Mata, a graduate student in electrical and computer engineering. You've been in a heated battle with Hewlett-Packard, Oracle, and several others for the talents of this young man. After several trips to your plant, he agrees to a contract. You're not only elated but also grateful to Netscape's computer engineers who courted Mata during his plant trips.

Your task: Now that Mata has signed with Netscape, you want to say "Congratulations, good work!" to the people who made it possible. Draft an e-mail to the following people: Ross Johnson, Tasha Blaken, Fritz Hammel, Andre Gonzalez, and Kia Vallas. Let them know that the company is awarding them $2,000 each for their time and assistance in landing this valuable recruit.[27]

23. Pizza promises: Message from an unknown parent, VF Corporation "We'll fix 'em!" The director of human relations at VF Corporation is grinning at you. "If they think we're going to let them go on in ignorance, then they're wrong. And I know just what will get their attention."

As human relations assistant for the large Greensboro, North Carolina, apparel maker, you've learned to sway with the currents of enthusiasm that flow from this particular superior. He likes to solve problems in a big, splashy way; that's one of the reasons why everyone likes him. He has a knack for turning corporate problems into opportunities for some new, wonderful development no one else had thought of.

For instance, today's problem: Top VF executives are moaning about a spot survey among 40,000 workers at your subsidiaries—the ones producing Lee, Wrangler, and other brands. Apparently, few employees had heard of VF Corporation. They didn't even know they had a corporate parent.

"You watch," your boss enthuses. "By tomorrow, they'll not only know who we are, they'll be singing our praises. And to think you get to break the good news to them!" He gives you another winning smile. You love this job.

Your task: Write an e-mail message for companywide distribution explaining that tomorrow, 15,000 lunchtime pizzas (all shifts) will be delivered to the company's 40,000 employees, compliments of their no-longer-mysterious corporate parent. Try to reflect some of your boss's good nature when putting the point across, But remember: You're representing your company to every single employee.[28]

WRITING DIRECTIVES AND INSTRUCTIONS

24. Mind your own e-mail: An e-mail message about electronic privacy at the *Los Angeles Times* When you stepped into your office at the *Los Angeles Times* this morning, the place was buzzing with the news that a reporter in the paper's Moscow bureau was being disciplined for reading his co-workers' electronic mail. As the story went, the newly hired correspondent was suspected of routinely snooping into his fellow reporters' e-mail. So his supervisors set up a "sting" operation, enlisting the Jerusalem bureau to send messages containing false information about shrinking travel allowances to another Moscow reporter.

The suspect took the bait, apparently using a co-worker's password to intercept the e-mail. When he later mentioned the new travel rules, he was slapped with a reassignment back to Los Angeles, to an as-yet-undesignated job (probably writing obituaries). Word of this action spread rapidly through all the paper's domestic and international bureaus.

The *Los Angeles Times* has always observed strict discipline with regard to journalistic ethics. But because journalists have always held confidentiality in such high regard, everyone assumed that e-mail privacy needed no enforcement. Now that's changing.

As an employee of the newspaper's legal department, you're developing instructions for handling violations of e-mail privacy. Management has decided on the following penalties: reassignment, suspension without pay, or termination of employment.

Your task: Review the case for critical thinking "Caution! E-Mail Can Bite" on pages 191–193. Then write an e-mail message to bureau managers (who oversee editorial offices spread around the globe)with step-by-step instructions on how to handle employees who violate e-mail privacy rules (use your common sense). The managers will have to use their own judgment in each case, but to avoid legal problems, they'll need some uniform guidelines. Hint: First-time offenders may be warned, but repeated problems should be dealt with more strongly.[9] When composing your message, use bullets or numbers or both to list your guidelines and the consequences of violations.

CHAPTER

WRITING BAD-NEWS MESSAGES

AFTER STUDYING THIS CHAPTER, YOU WILL BE ABLE TO

1 Differentiate between the direct and indirect organizational approaches to bad-news messages
2 Discuss how the tone of your message can contribute to its effectiveness
3 Explain the purpose of a buffer and list several types commonly used
4 List five techniques for saying no as gently as possible
5 Explain when it's appropriate to use the direct approach for delivering bad news
6 Discuss the additional challenges involved when conveying bad news to customers

COMMUNICATION CLOSE-UP AT OLMEC TOYS

When her son was three years old, Yia Eason was worried about his self-image. Little Menelik, who loved all the superheroes, sadly told his mother that he couldn't be one himself because all superheroes were white. "I thought that if he couldn't see himself as a black superhero, then maybe he couldn't see himself being a black scientist or doctor," says Eason. After a fruitless search for a black superhero doll, she talked with other mothers and found that she wasn't alone in feeling left out. So she decided to start her own company, Olmec Toys, and she created SunMan, the first black superhero action figure (who gets his powers from the melanin in his skin).

Today, Olmec Toys is the largest minority-owned toy company in the United States, with annual sales in the $10 million range. The company still specializes in producing dolls created specifically for African American, Hispanic, and Asian American children, but now it also markets educational games, music videos, and even a white doll.

Eason believes that black consumers are predisposed to buy from Olmec once they know that the company is owned and operated by a black mother. "Our studies show that the black consumer doesn't believe that Mattel can make a black doll better than we can," says Eason. So Olmec puts the company's story on the back of every package and in its catalog. But Eason says that, even though this recognition earns sales and loyalty from consumers, people in the toy industry tend to push even harder once they know that Olmec is a small company and is operated by a woman. Because Olmec's sales are only a fraction of the $1.5 billion ethnic toy market and a tiny fraction of the total $17.5 billion U.S. toy industry, Olmec must fight hard to retain shelf space and maintain market share.

Yia Eason

Surviving in the toy business hasn't been easy for Eason, who earned her M.B.A. at Harvard and used to be a financial editor. It's a fast-paced industry, and the competition is fierce. When Eason communicates with her suppliers, customers, banks, investors, and em-

As a small company specializing in ethnic toys, Olmec must maintain strong relationships with customers, employees, and investors. One way it builds and retains these relationships is by focusing on audience feelings. By explaining the reasons for any bad news and by focusing on the positive aspects of a negative situation, people at Olmec communicate their understanding and demonstrate their goodwill.

ployees, she strives to show strength and determination as well as to foster goodwill and build lasting relationships. And she's especially careful when her messages must contain bad news.

Having a single item out of stock can cost a toy company not only an immediate sale but also a long-term relationship with a retailer, especially one who's a potential first-time customer who simply turns to another toy company and is never heard from again. When Olmec receives an order or a request for a product that's no longer being produced, Eason's reply states up front that the item is not available. Then she immediately describes in-stock items that are similar. As a way of pleasing the customer and nurturing a long-term relationship, she concludes her letter by offering a discount or more attractive payment terms for any substitute items that are ordered.

Fierce competition in the consumer marketplace often leads to financial problems, especially for small retail stores. When a retailer places an order on credit but has numerous unpaid invoices, Eason is both firm and compassionate in the face of pleading, begging, and sometimes even threats. First she expresses her appreciation for previous business with the retailer. Then she states her reasons for adhering to Olmec's accounting department guidelines. Finally, she expresses confidence that the retailer will be able to regain solid financial footing and that their relationship will be able to continue in the future.

Key relationships for Eason are those with her investors and the members of Olmec's board of directors. She believes it's important to stay ahead of any problems, so she delivers any bad news as early as possible. She prefers to meet with the investor or board member face to face, because "we need to look at and address the situation eye to eye." Afterward, she puts in writing exactly what was discussed, emphasizing any positive aspects that were covered in the meeting.

She communicates with unsatisfactory employees as positively as possible. These employees require the highest level of diplomacy, says Eason. So she makes a point of focusing on what the company needs to achieve rather than on what the employee might lack.

Saying no gracefully requires tactful communication. "You always want to be able to go back someday," say Eason. When she must convey bad news, she's appreciative and cordial, but she's also careful to keep her correspondence short. Her brevity emphasizes the finality of her decision, and her warmth shows an interest in future possibilities.[1] ■

STRATEGIES FOR ORGANIZING BAD-NEWS MESSAGES

As Yia Eason can attest, nobody likes bad news. People don't like to get it, and they don't like to give it. In fact, saying no to an idea, a proposition, or a request from a customer, an employee, a shareholder, a salesperson—or even your boss—can put knots in your stomach and cost you hours of sleep.

No is so terse and abrupt, so rude in its unambiguous negativity, that a lot of people have trouble saying it. And for most, it's the toughest word to hear or understand. Furthermore, the delivery can be far more damaging than the answer itself. That's why in business, you must be careful whenever you deliver bad news. It's helpful to remember that the most dangerous "no" is usually the one you don't explain.[2]

Whether you're responding to a complaint, communicating about problems with an order or personnel, or notifying employees about a change in company policies that may affect them negatively, you have three main goals when delivering bad news: (1) Convey the bad news; (2) gain acceptance for it; and (3) maintain as much goodwill as possible with the audience. In addition to these goals, you will want to maintain a good image for your organization and reduce or eliminate the need for future correspondence on the matter. Furthermore you'll want to make the audience feel that they have been taken seriously and that the decision is fair and reasonable.

Accomplishing so many goals in a single message is not easy. But, by carefully choosing your words, adopting an audience-centered tone, and organizing your message to meet your audience's needs and expectations, you can deliver effective bad-news messages.

When Boston Chicken filed for bankruptcy protection in October 1998, security analyst Roger Lipton announced the bad news by holding up a lifeless rubberized chicken. But, Boston Chicken's management had to do more than just communicate the bad news. They had to maintain as much goodwill as possible while convincing shareholders, investors, and employees that this was the company's only alternative.

Creating an Audience-Centered Tone

You've heard it before: It's not *what* you say but *how* you say it that counts. That adage couldn't be truer with bad-news messages. Your tone contributes to your message's effectiveness by supporting three specific goals:

- Helping your audience understand that your bad news represents a firm decision
- Helping your audience understand that, under the circumstances, your decision was fair and reasonable
- Helping your audience remain well disposed toward your business and preserving your audience's ego

When establishing tone, strive for
- Firmness
- Fairness
- Goodwill

If you're communicating bad news to a U.S. or Canadian audience with minimal cultural differences, make liberal use of the "you" attitude. For example, point out how your decision might actually further your audience's goals. Convey concern by looking for the best in your audience. And assume that your audience is interested in being fair, even when they are at fault.

In a bad-news message, the "you" attitude translates into
- Emphasizing the audience's goals instead of your own
- Looking for the best in your audience
- Using positive rather than negative phrasing

You can ease disappointment by using positive words rather than negative, counterproductive words. Just be sure that your positive tone doesn't hide the bad news behind difficult language.[3] Remember, you want to convey the bad news, not cover it up.

INSTEAD OF THIS	SAY THIS
We have received your *broken* clock.	We have received the clock you sent us.
I *cannot understand* what you mean.	Please clarify your request.
The *damage* won't be fixed for a week.	The item will be repaired next week.
There will be a *delay* in your order.	We will ship your order as soon as possible.
You are clearly *dissatisfied*.	We are doing what we can to make things right.
Your account is in *error*.	Corrections have been made to your account.
The breakage was not our *fault*.	The merchandise was broken during shipping.
Sorry for your inconvenience.	The enclosed coupon will save you $5 next time.
We *regret* the misunderstanding.	I'll try my best to be more clear from now on.
I was *shocked* to hear the news.	The news reached me yesterday.
Unfortunately, we haven't received it.	It hasn't arrived yet.
The enclosed statement is *wrong*.	Please recheck the enclosed statement.

When you use language that conveys respect and avoids an accusing tone, you protect the audience's pride. For instance, when refusing an adjustment or a claim, try using third-person, impersonal, passive language to explain your audience's mistakes in an inoffensive way. This approach downplays the doer of the action because the doer is not specified. Say, "The appliance won't work after being immersed in water" instead of "You shouldn't have immersed the appliance in water." When the customer is at fault, the "you" attitude is better observed by avoiding the word *you*.

Sometimes the "you" attitude is best observed by avoiding the word *you*.

Of course, if you are communicating across cultures, you'll want to use the tone, organization, and other cultural conventions that your audience expects. Only then can you avoid the inappropriate or even offensive approaches that could jeopardize your business relationship.[4]

Choosing an Organizational Approach

How you arrange the main idea and the supporting data can also ease your audience's disappointment. The two basic strategies described in Chapters 5 and 7 are the indirect plan, which presents supporting data before the main idea, and the direct plan, which presents the main idea before supporting data (see Figure 8.1).

With the indirect organizational plan, the reasons are given before the bad news; with the direct organizational plan the bad news is given first.

Indirect Organizational Approach

Use this approach when the audience is emotionally involved or will be displeased by the bad news.

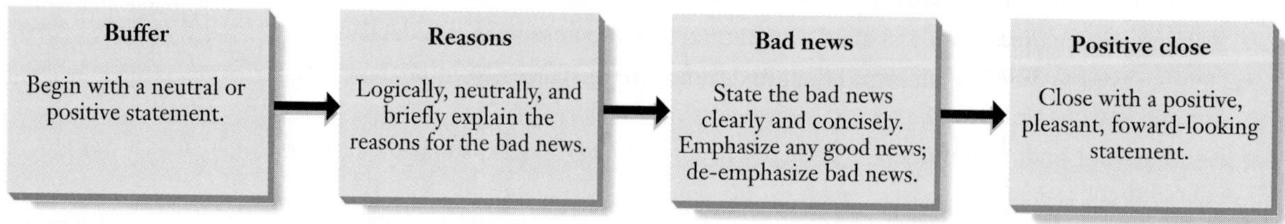

Direct Organizational Approach

Use this approach if you know that the audience prefers the bad news first, if the situation is routine or minor, if the reader is not likely to be disappointed by the news, or if you know that firmness is needed.

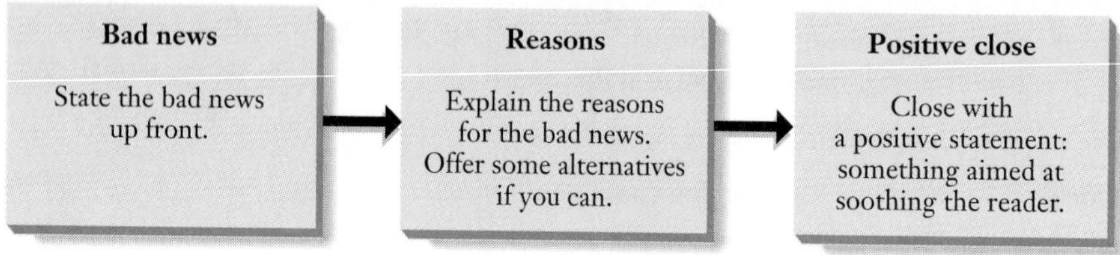

Figure 8.1

Differences between the Indirect and Direct Organizational Plans for Bad-News Messages

As with most business messages, the key to choosing the best approach for bad-news messages is to analyze your audience first. Try to put yourself in their shoes. What is their likely reaction to the news? How important is the message? How well do you know them? Some people like to know the bad news right away; others prefer that the news be softened a bit before they get hit with it. Similarly, some situations are more appropriate for directness than others.

Use the direct plan when your negative answer or information will have little personal impact; use the indirect plan in more sensitive situations.

If you know that the receiver is likely to prefer the bad news first, or if the situation is minor and the news would cause the person little pain or disappointment, use the direct plan. Start with a clear statement of the bad news, proceed to the reasons for the decision, and end with a courteous close. In most cases, however, you'll find that using an indirect approach for delivering bad news is preferable.

Using the Indirect Plan

Beginning a bad news message with a blunt no could keep your audience from reading or listening to your reasons. Instead, ease your audience into the message and give your reasons before delivering the bad news. Presenting the reasons first increases your chances of gaining audience acceptance and gradually prepares the audience for the disappointment to come. The indirect plan follows a four-part sequence: (1) Open with a buffer; (2) continue with reasons supporting the negative decision; (3) follow with a clear, diplomatic statement of the negative decision (the bad news); and (4) end with a helpful, friendly, and positive close—perhaps a statement of interest, encouragement, or goodwill.

Buffer

A buffer is a neutral lead-in to bad news.

The first step in using the indirect plan is to put the audience in an accepting mood by making a neutral, noncontroversial statement closely related to the point of the message; this statement is called a **buffer.** It expresses your appreciation for being thought of, assures the reader of your attention to the request, compliments the reader, or indicates your understanding of the reader's needs. Opening with a buffer sets the stage for the bad news to follow. In a memo telling another supervisor that you can't spare anyone from your customer service staff for a temporary assignment to the order fulfillment department, you might begin with a sentence like this: "Customer service is one of our major concerns at National Investments. In addition, our department shares your goal of processing orders quickly and efficiently."

Use a buffer that is
- Neutral
- Relevant
- Not misleading
- Assertive
- Succinct

If possible, base the buffer on statements made by the person you're responding to. This type of buffer shows the person that you have listened well. If you use an unrelated buffer, you will seem to be "beating around the bush"; that is, you'll appear unethical and will lose your audience's respect. Another goal when composing your buffer is to avoid giving the impression that good news will follow. Building up the audience at the beginning only makes the subsequent letdown even more painful. Imagine your reaction to the following openings:

> Your résumé indicates that you would be well suited for a management trainee position with our company.
>
> Your résumé shows very clearly why you are interested in becoming a management trainee with our company.

The second opening emphasizes the applicant's interpretation of her qualifications rather than the company's evaluation, so it's less misleading but still positive. Here are some other things to avoid when writing a buffer:

- *Avoid saying no.* An audience encountering the blunt refusal right at the beginning usually reacts negatively to the rest of the message, no matter how reasonable and well phrased it is.
- *Avoid using a know-it-all tone.* When you use phrases such as "you should be aware that," the audience expects your lecture to lead to a negative response and therefore resists the rest of your message.
- *Avoid wordy and irrelevant phrases and sentences.* Sentences such as "We have received your letter," "This letter is in reply to your request," and "We are writing in response to your request" are irrelevant. You make better use of the space by referring directly to the subject of the letter.
- *Avoid apologizing.* An apology weakens your explanation of the unfavorable decision.
- *Avoid writing a buffer that is too long.* The point is to briefly identify something that both you and your audience are interested in and agree on before proceeding in a businesslike way.

Table 8.1 shows several types of buffers you could use to open a bad-news message tactfully.

Some critics believe that using a buffer is manipulative, dishonest, and thus unethical. In fact, buffers are unethical only if they're insincere. Breaking bad news with kindness and courtesy is the human way. Consideration for the feelings of others is never dishonest, and that consideration helps your audience accept your message.

After you've composed a buffer, evaluate it by asking yourself four questions: Is it pleasant? Is it relevant? Is it neutral, saying neither yes nor no? Does it provide for a smooth transition to the reasons that follow? If you can answer yes to every question, you can proceed confidently to the next section of your message.

Reasons

If you've done a good job of composing the buffer, the reasons will follow naturally. Cover the more positive points first; then move to the less positive ones. Provide enough detail for the audience to understand your reasons, but be concise; a long, roundabout explanation may make the audience impatient.

TABLE 8.1

TYPES OF BUFFERS

Buffer	Strategy	Example
Agreement	Find a point on which you and the reader share similar views.	We both know how hard it is to make a profit in this industry.
Appreciation	Express sincere thanks for receiving something.	Your check for $127.17 arrived yesterday. Thank you.
Cooperation	Convey your willingness to help in any way you realistically can.	Employee Services is here to smooth the way for all of you who work to achieve company goals.
Fairness	Assure the reader that you've closely examined and carefully considered the problem, or mention an appropriate action that has already been taken.	For the past week, we have carefully monitored those using the photocopying machine to see whether we can detect any pattern of use that might explain its frequent breakdowns.
Good news	Start with the part of your message that is favorable.	A replacement knob for your range is on its way, shipped February 10 via UPS.
Praise	Find an attribute or an achievement to compliment.	Your résumé shows an admirable breadth of experience, which should serve you well as you progress in your career.
Resale	Favorably discuss the product or company related to the subject of the letter.	With their heavy-duty, full-suspension hardware and fine veneers, the desks and file cabinets in our Montclair line have become a hit with value-conscious professionals.
Understanding	Demonstrate that you understand the reader's goals and needs.	So that you can more easily find the printer with the features you need, we are enclosing a brochure that describes all the Panasonic printers currently available.

Present reasons to show that your decision is reasonable and fair.

The goal is to explain *why* you have reached your decision before you explain *what* that decision is. If you present your reasons effectively, they should convince your audience that your decision is justified, fair, and logical. By delivering your reasons before the rejection, you soften the tone of your "no" and enable the other person to understand, retain composure, and save face.

Focus on how the audience might benefit from your negative message.

When giving your reasons, be tactful by highlighting how the decision benefits your audience (instead of focusing on why the decision is good for you or your company). For example, when denying a credit request, show how your decision will keep the person from becoming overextended financially. Facts and figures are often helpful in convincing members of your audience that you're acting in their best interests.

As you explain your reasons, avoid hiding behind company policy to cushion the bad news. If you say, "Company policy forbids our hiring anyone who does not have two years' management experience," you seem to imply that you haven't considered the person on her or his own merits. Although skilled and sympathetic communicators may sometimes quote company policy, they also briefly explain it so that the audience can try to meet the requirements at a later time. Similarly, avoid apologizing when giving your reasons. Apologies are appropriate only when someone in your company has made a severe mistake or has done something terribly wrong. If no one in the company is at fault, an apology gives the wrong impression.

Say, for example, you're refusing the application of a management trainee. A tactfully worded letter might give these reasons for the decision not to hire:

> Because these management trainee positions are quite challenging, our human relations department has researched the qualifications needed to succeed in them. The findings show that the two most important qualifications are a bachelor's degree in business administration and two years' supervisory experience.

The paragraph does a good job of stating the reasons for the refusal:

Well-written reasons are
- Detailed
- Tactful
- Individualized
- Unapologetic
- Positive

- It provides enough detail to make the reason for the refusal logically acceptable.
- It implies that the applicant is better off avoiding a program in which he or she would probably fail, given the background of potential co-workers.
- It doesn't rest solely on company policy. A relevant policy exists but is presented as logical rather than rigid.
- It offers no apology for the decision.
- It avoids negative personal expressions ("You do not meet our requirements").

Sometimes detailed reasons should not be provided.

Although specific reasons help the audience accept bad news, reasons cannot always be given. Don't include reasons when they involve confidential, excessively complicated, or purely negative information or when they benefit only you or your firm (by enhancing the company's profits, for example). Instead, move directly to the next section.

The Bad News

To make bad news less painful to hear
- De-emphasize the bad news visually and grammatically
- Use a conditional statement
- Tell what you did do, not what you didn't do

When the bad news is a logical outcome of the reasons that come before it, the audience is psychologically prepared to receive it. However, the audience may still react emotionally if the bad news is handled carelessly. Three techniques are especially useful for saying no as clearly and as kindly as possible. First, de-emphasize the bad news:

- Minimize the space or time devoted to it.
- Subordinate it in a complex or compound sentence ("My department is already shorthanded, so I'll need all my staff for at least the next two months"). This construction pushes the bad news into the middle of the sentence, the point of least emphasis.
- Embed it in the middle of a paragraph or use parenthetical expressions ("Our profits, which are down, are only part of the picture").

Second, use a conditional (*if* or *when*) statement to imply that the audience could have received, or might someday receive, a favorable answer: "When you have more managerial experience, you are welcome to reapply." Such a statement could motivate applicants to improve their qualifications.

Third, tell the audience what you did do, can do, or will do rather than what you did not do, cannot do, or will not do. Say "We sell exclusively through retailers, and the one nearest you that carries our merchandise is . . ." rather than "We are unable to serve you, so please call your nearest dealer." Here's the same principle applied to the letter rejecting the job applicant: "The five positions currently open have been staffed with people whose qualifications match those uncovered in our research." That type of statement need not be followed by the explicit news that you won't be hiring the reader. By couching the bad news in terms that show how the reader's problem can be solved, you focus on the positive and soften the blow.

When writing a bad-news message, avoid negative wording and personal language.

Of course, when implying bad news, be sure your audience understands the entire message—including the bad news. It would not be ethical to overemphasize the positive. If an implied message might leave doubt, state your decision in direct terms. Just be sure to avoid blunt statements that are likely to cause pain and anger. The following phrases are particularly likely to offend:

INSTEAD OF THIS	USE THIS
I must refuse your request.	I won't be in town on the day you need me.
We must deny your application.	The position has been filled.
I am unable to grant your request.	Contact us again when you have established . . .
We cannot afford to continue the program.	The program will conclude on May 1.
Much as I would like to attend . . .	Our budget meeting ends too late for me to attend.
We *must reject* your proposal.	We've accepted the proposal from AAA Builders.
We must turn down your extension request.	Please send in your payment by June 14.

Positive Close

An upbeat, positive close
- Builds goodwill
- Offers a suggestion for action
- Provides a look toward the future

After giving your audience the bad news, your job is to end your message on an upbeat note. You might propose an attainable solution to the audience's problem: "The human resources department has offered to bring in temporary workers when I need them, and they would probably consider doing the same for you." In a message to a customer or potential customer, an off-the-subject ending that includes resale information or sales promotion is also appropriate. If you've asked someone to decide between alternatives or to take some action, make sure that she or he knows what to do, when to do it, and how to do it with ease. Whatever type of close you choose, follow these guidelines:

- Keep your close as positive as possible. Don't refer to, repeat, or apologize for the bad news, and refrain from expressing any doubt that your reasons will be accepted (avoid statements such as "I trust our decision is satisfactory").
- Encourage additional communication *only* if you're willing to discuss your decision further (avoid phrases such as "If you have further questions, please write").
- Keep a positive outlook on the future. Do not anticipate problems (avoid statements such as "Should you have further problems, please let us know").
- Be sincere. Steer clear of clichés that are insincere in view of the bad news (avoid saying, "If we can be of any help, please contact us").
- Be confident about keeping the person as a customer (avoid phrases such as "We hope you will continue to do business with us").

DID YOU KNOW?

Although 95 percent of CEOs say they have an open-door policy and will reward those who communicate potentially bad news, 50 percent of employees believe that the bad-news messenger runs a real risk where they work.

If you are the one who has to reject the applicant for the management trainee position, you can observe these guidelines by writing a close like this:

> Many companies seek other qualifications in management trainees, so I urge you to continue your job search. You'll certainly find an opening in which your skills and aspirations match the job requirements exactly.

Keep in mind that the close is the last thing the audience has to remember you by. Try to make the memory a positive one. For a reminder of the strategies for delivering bad-news messages, see this chapter's Checklist for Delivering Bad-News Messages.

Using the Direct Plan

Although the indirect approach is preferable for most bad-news messages, you may sometimes want to move right to the point. A bad-news message organized on the direct plan starts with a clear statement of the bad news, proceeds to the reasons for the decision, and ends

CHECKLIST FOR DELIVERING BAD-NEWS MESSAGES

A. Overall Strategy
  1. Use the indirect plan in most cases.
  2. Use the direct plan when the situation is routine (between employees of the same company), when the reader is not emotionally involved in the message, when you know that the reader would prefer the bad news first, or when you know that firmness is necessary.
  3. Adopt an audience-centered tone.
    a. Use positive words.
    b. Use language that conveys respect and avoids an accusing tone.
    c. Be sincere.
    d. Be aware of cultural differences.

B. Buffer
  1. Express appreciation, cooperation, fairness, good news, praise, resale, or understanding.
  2. Introduce a topic that is relevant to the subject and that both you and the reader can agree on.
  3. Eliminate apologies and negative-sounding words *(won't, can't, unable to).*
  4. Keep the buffer brief and to the point.
  5. Maintain a confident, positive, supportive tone.

C. Reasons
  1. Show how the decision benefits your audience.
  2. Avoid apologies and expressions of sorrow or regret.
  3. Offer enough detail to show the logic of your position.
  4. Include only factual information.
  5. Include only business reasons, not personal ones.
  6. Don't hide behind company policy.
  7. Carefully word the reasons so that the reader can anticipate the bad news.
  8. Check the lead-in from the buffer for smoothness.
  9. Make a transition from the favorable to the unfavorable message.
  10. Make a transition from the general to the specific.

D. Bad News
  1. State the bad news as positively as possible, using tactful wording.
  2. De-emphasize the bad news.
    a. Minimize the space devoted to it.
    b. Subordinate it.
    c. Embed it.
  3. Emphasize what the firm did do or is doing rather than what it can't or won't do.

E. Positive, Friendly, Helpful Close
  1. Remind the reader of how his or her needs are being met.
  2. Keep the close as positive as possible.
    a. Eliminate any reference to the bad news.
    b. Avoid apologies and words of regret.
    c. Eliminate words suggesting uncertainty.
  3. Suggest actions the reader might take.
  4. Keep a positive outlook on the future.
  5. Be confident about keeping the person as a customer.

---

with a courteous close. Stating the bad news at the beginning can have two advantages: (1) It makes a shorter message possible, and (2) the audience needs less time to reach the main idea of the message, the bad news itself.

Memos are often organized so that the bad news comes before the reasons. In fact, some managers expect all internal correspondence to be brief and direct, regardless of whether the message is positive or negative. Routine bad-news messages to other companies often follow the direct plan, especially if they relay decisions that have little or no personal impact. Buffers can actually cause ill will in people who see them frequently (such as people searching for employment).[5] In addition, you'll sometimes know from experience that your audience simply prefers reading the bad news first in any message. Of course, the direct plan is also appropriate when you want to present an image of firmness and strength; for example, the last message in a collection series, just before the matter is turned over to an attorney, usually gets right to the point.

Use the direct plan when
- Your boss prefers that internal messages come right to the point
- The message has little personal impact
- You want to make your point emphatically

Thus, in a variety of circumstances you may want to use the direct plan and save your positive comments for the close. Even so, remember that a tactful tone and a focus on reasons will help make any bad-news message easier to accept. (For an idea of how some other

COMMUNICATING ACROSS CULTURES

GOOD WAYS TO SEND BAD NEWS AROUND THE WORLD

Bad news is unwelcome in any language, but the conventions for passing it on to business associates can vary considerably from country to country. To save yourself grief when sending and receiving bad news internationally, be familiar with the customary approach.

For instance, French business letters are very formal and writer oriented (without reference to audience needs or benefits). That's because French businesses traditionally write for one purpose: to establish evidence for any future litigation. The preferred style is prudent, precise, and respectful, even if the writer and reader know each other very well. Letters begin with courteous titles ("Monsieur," "Madame," but not "Dear ___") and close with flowery salutations ("With our anticipated thanks, we beg you to accept, Sir, our sincere greetings," or "Awaiting your reply, we offer you, Sirs, our assiduous greetings"). French business letters never become personal or friendly, and their formal tone is sometimes misinterpreted by Americans as coolness, nonchalance, or indifference.

When the news is bad, French writers take a direct approach. They open with a reference to the problem or previous correspondence and then state the bad news clearly. They don't try to avoid negative words, nor do they refer to the audience's needs, but they often do apologize and express regret for the problem. A bad-news letter in France won't necessarily end on a positive note, but the close remains gracious: "Accept, Sirs, our distinguished greetings."

In Japan all letter writing is regarded as a troublesome task, even when the news is good. To preserve or establish the appropriate level of respect and humility for the relationship between writer and reader, Japanese letter writers select different forms of nouns, pronouns, and verbs, depending on whose actions they're referring to. Also, their letters traditionally open with remarks about the season, taken from books that provide standard phrases for each month: For example, "The season for cherry blossoms is here with us and everybody is beginning to feel refreshed." This opening remark is followed by a reference to the reader's business prosperity or health.

When the message is bad news, these opening formalities serve as a buffer. Explanations and apologies follow; then comes the bad news or refusal. Also, Japanese writers protect the reader's feelings by wording the bad news ambiguously; the vague language can be misinterpreted by Western readers as a condition of acceptance rather than as the refusal it truly is.

British bad-news letters may surprise readers who know that British culture values politeness, tact, and diplomacy. Centuries of business tradition dictate a direct approach for all business letters, even when the message is unsettling. A typical bad-news letter opens with a reference to the subject and continues with a few paragraphs explaining the bad news in an abrupt and blunt, but logical, sequence. The writer then expresses apology and regret, which further emphasizes the bad news. Some British letters end there; others close with a few words wishing the reader success or hoping for continued goodwill. Recently, however, some leading British companies have begun to see the value of considering their audiences' feelings and are using the indirect approach common in the United States.

1. Select a bad-news message and see whether you can redesign it for Japan, France, and Great Britain. How would you change the format for each country? What would you add or delete?
2. Which is more important: (a) learning the language of the customers you do business with or (b) learning their customs? Please explain.

---

cultures handle bad news, see "Communicating across Cultures: Good Ways to Send Bad News around the World").

COMMUNICATING NEGATIVE ANSWERS AND INFORMATION

The businessperson who tries to say yes to everyone probably won't win many promotions or stay in business for long. Occasionally, your response to inquiries must simply be no. It's a mark of your skill as a communicator to be able to say no clearly yet not cut yourself off from future dealings with other people.

Providing Bad News about Products

When you must provide bad news about a product, the situation and the reader will dictate whether to use the direct or the indirect plan. If you were writing to tell your company's bookkeeping department about increasing product prices, you'd use the direct plan. The reader would have to make some arithmetical adjustments when the increases were put into effect but presumably would not be emotionally involved in the matter. However, you would probably use the indirect plan to convey the same information to customers or even to your own sales department, because a change that weakens your products' competitive edge threatens sales representatives' incomes and possibly their jobs.

Use either the direct or the indirect plan for telling the reader bad news about a product.

The e-mail message in Figure 8.2 was written to tell one company's sales managers that its request for a licensing agreement was rejected. The middle section of the memo presents

When Sybervantage pursued licensing agreements with Warner, the company expected to be entering into a lucrative arrangement in which both companies would profit. But Warner rejected the request, and now Sybervantage must adjust its strategic planning and must keep its sales force both motivated and involved.

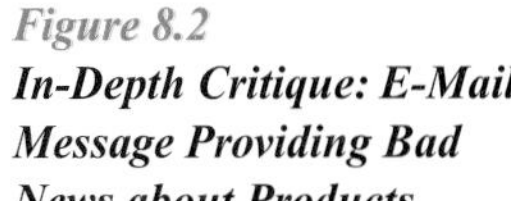

Figure 8.2
In-Depth Critique: E-Mail Message Providing Bad News about Products

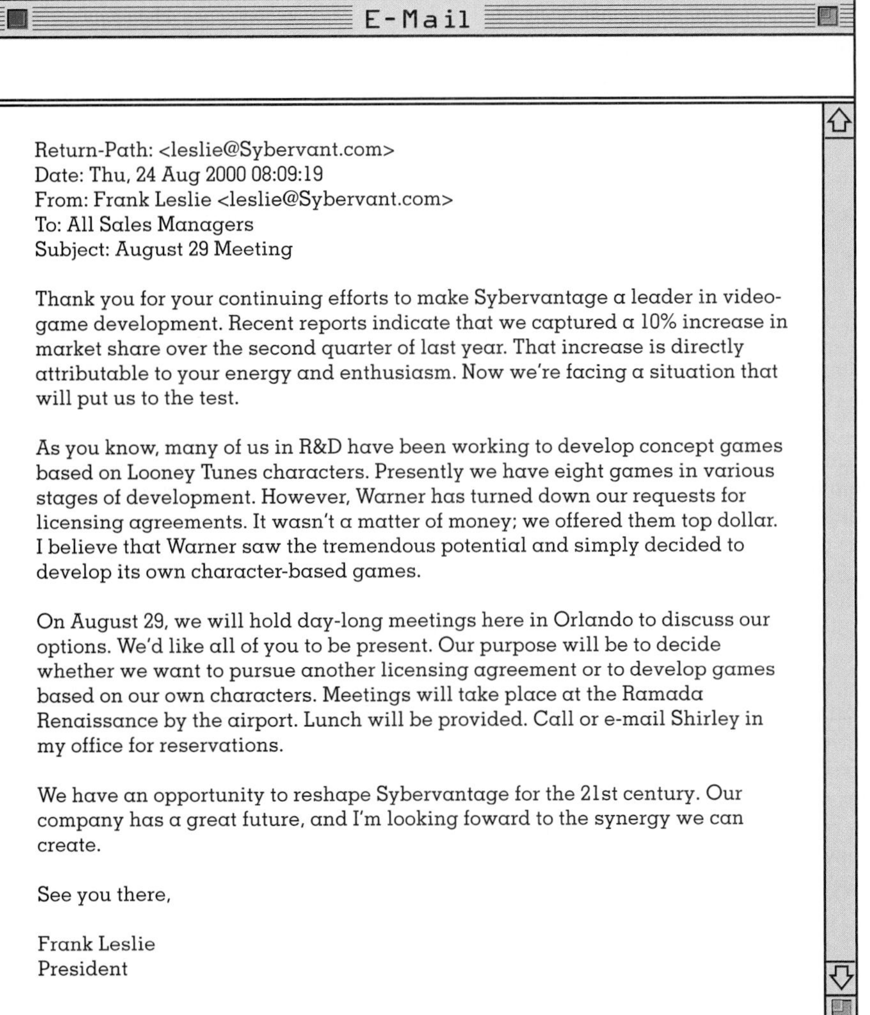

E-Mail

Return-Path: <leslie@Sybervant.com>
Date: Thu, 24 Aug 2000 08:09:19
From: Frank Leslie <leslie@Sybervant.com>
To: All Sales Managers
Subject: August 29 Meeting

Thank you for your continuing efforts to make Sybervantage a leader in video-game development. Recent reports indicate that we captured a 10% increase in market share over the second quarter of last year. That increase is directly attributable to your energy and enthusiasm. Now we're facing a situation that will put us to the test.

As you know, many of us in R&D have been working to develop concept games based on Looney Tunes characters. Presently we have eight games in various stages of development. However, Warner has turned down our requests for licensing agreements. It wasn't a matter of money; we offered them top dollar. I believe that Warner saw the tremendous potential and simply decided to develop its own character-based games.

On August 29, we will hold day-long meetings here in Orlando to discuss our options. We'd like all of you to be present. Our purpose will be to decide whether we want to pursue another licensing agreement or to develop games based on our own characters. Meetings will take place at the Ramada Renaissance by the airport. Lunch will be provided. Call or e-mail Shirley in my office for reservations.

We have an opportunity to reshape Sybervantage for the 21st century. Our company has a great future, and I'm looking foward to the synergy we can create.

See you there,

Frank Leslie
President

The memo begins on a complimentary note to buffer the bad news.

The bad news is presented along with possible explanations.

The third paragraph indicates the action that will be taken to lessen the impact of the bad news and actively involves the readers in the possibility of a solution.

an honest statement of the bad news. The effect of the bad news is diminished by the problem-solving tone, by avoidance of any overt statement that such a setback may affect commissions, and by the upbeat close.

Use either the direct or the indirect plan to tell someone you cannot do what has been requested.

Denying Cooperation with Routine Requests

When people ask you for information or want you to do something and you can't honor the request, you may answer with either the direct plan or the indirect plan. Say that you've asked a company to participate in your research project concerning sales promotion. However, that company has a policy against disseminating any information about projected sales figures. How would you react to the following letter?

> Our company policy prohibits us from participating in research projects where disclosure of discretionary information might be necessary. Therefore, we decline your invitation to our sales staff to fill out questionnaires for your study.
>
> Thank you for trying to include Qualcomm Corporation in your research. If we can be of further assistance, please let us know.

That letter would offend most readers, for several reasons:

- The direct plan is used, even though the reader is outside the company and may be emotionally involved in the response.
- The tone of the first paragraph is unnecessarily negative and abrupt.
- The writer hides behind company policy, a policy that the reader may find questionable.
- The offer to help is an unpleasant irony, given the writer's unwillingness to help in this instance.

Wording, tone, and format conspire to make a letter either offensive or acceptable. The letter that follows conveys the same negative message as the previous letter without sounding offensive:

> We at Qualcomm Corporation appreciate and benefit from the research of companies such as yours. Your study sounds interesting, and we certainly wish we could participate.
>
> Unfortunately, our board requires strict confidentiality of all sales information until quarterly reports are mailed to stockholders. We release press reports at the same time the quarterly reports go out, and we'll be sure to include you in all our future mailings.
>
> Although we cannot release projected figures, we are more than willing to share information that is part of the public record. I've enclosed several of our past earnings reports for your inspection. We look forward to seeing the results of your study. Please let us know if there is any additional way we can help.

The buffer is supportive and appreciative.

Without falling back on references to company policy, the writer fully explains the reason for the policy. The bad news is implied, not stated explicitly.

The close is friendly, positive, and helpful.

As you think about the different impact those two letters might have on you, you can see why effective business writers like Yia Eason take the time and the trouble to give negative messages the attention they deserve.

Declining Invitations and Requests for Favors

When you must say no to an invitation or a requested favor, your use of the direct or the indirect plan depends on your relationship with the reader. For example, suppose the president of the local community college asks your company to host graduation on your corporate grounds but your sales meetings will be taking place at the same time. If you don't know the president well, you'll probably use the indirect plan, as demonstrated in Figure 8.3. However, if you are friends with the president and work frequently on projects for the college, you might use the direct approach:

When turning down an invitation or a request for a favor, consider your relationship to the reader.

> Sandra, thanks for asking us to host your graduation. You know we've always supported the college and would love to do this for you. Unfortunately, our company sales meetings will be going on during the same time. We'll have so many folks tied up with logistics, we won't have the personnel to adequately take care of the graduation.
>
> Have you called Jerry Kane over at the Botanical Gardens? I can't think of a prettier site for graduation. Roberta in my office volunteers over there and knows Jerry. She can fill you in on the details, if you'd like to talk to her first.
>
> Thanks again for considering us. Let's have lunch in mid-June to plan our involvement with the college for the next school year. You can think of all kinds of ways to make me sorry I had to say no! I'll look forward to seeing you and catching up on family news.

This letter gets right to the point but still uses some blow-softening techniques: It compliments the person and organization making the request, suggests an alternative, and looks toward future opportunities for cooperation.

DID YOU KNOW?

It's estimated that nearly 40 percent of business and personal correspondence bypasses the U.S. Postal Service by traveling over the Internet.

DELIVERING BAD NEWS TO CUSTOMERS

When delivering bad news to existing or would-be customers, you have an additional challenge—resale. To make the reader feel good about continuing to do business with your firm, you want to:

- Work toward an eventual sale along the lines of the original order
- Keep instructions or additional information as clear as possible
- Maintain an optimistic, confident tone so that your reader won't lose interest

Reinforcing the customer's confidence in your service or product is an effective way to meet the resale challenge. Just don't overdo it.

The basic goal of a bad-news letter about orders is to protect or make a sale.

Conveying Bad News about Orders

For several reasons, businesses must sometimes convey bad news concerning orders. When Yia Eason must relate bad news to retailers about their orders, she is careful to focus her audience's attention on what she can do rather than on what she cannot do.

When you must back order for a customer, you have one of two types of bad news to convey: (1) You're able to send only part of the order, or (2) you're able to send none of the order. When sending only part of the order, you actually have both good news and bad news. In such situations, the indirect plan works very well. The buffer contains the good news (that part of the order is en route) along with a resale reminder of the product's attractiveness. After the buffer come the reasons for the delay of the remainder of the shipment. A strong close encourages a favorable attitude toward the entire transaction (see Figure 8.4).

Use the indirect plan when telling a customer that you cannot immediately ship the entire order.

Figure 8.3
In-Depth Critique: Letter Declining a Favor

Sandra Wofford asked Infotech to host graduation ceremonies for Whiddier Community College, but Infotech's facilities will be in use on the day of graduation. In the following letter, May Yee Kwan delivers the bad news in a helpful and supportive way.

927 Dawson Valley Road, Tulsa, Oklahoma 74151
Voice: (918) 669-4428 Fax: (918) 669-4429
www.infotech.com

March 5, 2000

Dr. Sandra Wofford, President
Whiddier College
333 Whiddier Avenue
Tulsa, Oklahoma 74150

Dear Dr. Wofford:

Because we appreciate Whiddier College and the many opportunities you have provided to deserving students over the years, we at Infotech have supported the college in many ways. Thank you for considering our grounds for your graduation ceremony.

Our company-wide sales meetings will be held during the weeks of May 29th and June 5th. We will host over 200 sales representatives and their families, and activities will take place at both our corporate campus and the Ramada Renaissance. Therefore we will be unable to devote an adequate support staff for your graduation.

My assistant, Roberta Seagers, suggests you contact the Municipal Botanical Gardens as a possible graduation site. She recommends calling Jerry Kane, director of public relations. If we can help in any other way with graduation, please let us know.

Even though our annual meeting will most likely prohibit us from ever hosting graduation, we remain firm in our commitment to you, President Wofford, and to the fine students you represent. We will continue to be a corporate partner to Whiddier College and will support your efforts as you move into the twenty-first century.

Sincerely,

May Yee Kwan

May Yee Kwan
Public Relations Director

lc

The buffer recaps the request and demonstrates respect.

The reason for the bad news is stated explicitly and in detail.

By suggesting an alternative, Kwan shows that she does care about the college and has given the matter some thought.

The close renews the corporation's support in the future.

Even when you're unable to send the customer any portion of an order, you still use the indirect approach. However, because you have no good news to give, your buffer only confirms the sale and the explanation section states your reasons for not filling the order promptly. For a brief outline of back-order tasks, see this chapter's Checklist for Bad News about Orders.

For a customer whose order for a recliner and ottoman will be partly filled, your letter might read like this one.

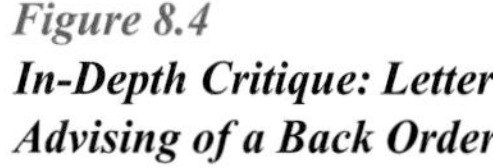

Figure 8.4
In-Depth Critique: Letter Advising of a Back Order

1284 North Telegraph Road
Monroe, MI 48161-5138

September 9, 1999

Dr. Elizabeth Fawnworth
2524 St. Georgen Common
Boston, MA 22290-2827

Dear Dr. Fawnworth:

Thank you for your order of the special edition recliner and matching ottoman. The recliner with custom features will be shipped today. The leather trim you designated turned out beautifully, and we're sure the recliner will make a handsome addition to your study.

The roll-around ottoman has proved to be one of our most popular items. Our plant manager reports that, even though he has almost doubled production this year, we are still experiencing some delays. We estimate that your ottoman will be shipped no later than November 15 to arrive by Thanksgiving.

Remember that all La-Z-Boy products carry a lifetime guarantee. We know you will enjoy your recliner and ottoman for many years. I've enclosed a catalog that includes our latest designs. Please call me at (616) 358-2899 if you'd like to talk about any of our special fabrics or custom designs. We look forward to serving you again in the future.

Cordially,

Suzanne Godfrey

Suzanne Godfrey
Manager, Custom Designs

Enclosure

ek

In the indirect plan, the buffer conveys the good news and confirms the wisdom of the customer's choice.

The reasons for the shipping delay are stated in a way that indicates that the ottoman is a popular choice. The bad news is cushioned by the pledge to take care of the problem by a definite time.

The bad news itself is implied by telling the reader what is being done, not what cannot be done.

The positive close also opens the door to future business.

Refusing Adjustment for Claims and Complaints

Almost every customer who requests an adjustment is emotionally involved; therefore, the indirect plan is usually the best approach for a refusal. Your job as a writer is to avoid accepting responsibility for the unfortunate situation and yet avoid blaming or accusing the customer. To steer clear of these pitfalls, pay special attention to the tone of your letter. Keep in mind that a tactful and courteous letter can build goodwill while denying the claim (see Figure 8.5).

Use the indirect plan in most cases of refusing to make an adjustment.

Figure 8.5
In-Depth Critique: Letter Refusing a Claim

Village Electronics recently received a letter from Daniel Lindmeier, who purchased a portable CD player a year ago. He wrote to say that the unit doesn't work correctly and to inquire about the warranty. Lindmeier believes that the warranty covers one year, when it actually covers only three months.

NUMBER ONE IN ENTERTAINMENT

Village Electronics

68 Lake Itasca Boulevard • Hannover, MN 55341
Voice: (612) 878-1312 • Fax: (612) 878-1316

May 3, 2000

Mr. Daniel Lindmeier
849 Cedar Street
Lake Elmo, MN 55042

Dear Mr. Lindmeier:

Thank you for your letter describing the problem with your portable Sony CD Walkman. We believe, as you do, that electronic equipment should be built to last. That's why we stand behind our products with a 90-day warranty.

Even though your Walkman is a year old and therefore out of warranty, we can still help. Please package your CD player carefully and ship it to our store in Hannover. Include your complete name, address, phone number, and a brief description of the problem along with a check for $35. After examining the unit, we will give you a written estimate of the needed parts and labor. Then just let us know—either by phone or by filling out the prepaid card we will provide—whether you want us to make the repairs.

If you choose to repair the unit, the $35 will be applied toward your bill, payable by check or major credit card. If you decide not to repair the unit, the $35 will pay for the technician's time in examining the unit. Sony also has service centers available in your area. If you would prefer to take the unit to one of them, please see the enclosed list.

Thanks again for inquiring about our service. I've also enclosed a catalog of our latest high-tech electronic gear. For the month of June, Sony is offering a "Trade-Up Special," at which time you can receive trade-in credit for your Walkman when you purchase a newer model. Please visit Village Electronics very soon.

Sincerely,

Walter Brodie

Walter Brodie
President

mk

Enclosure

The buffer covers a point that reader and writer agree on.

The reason puts the company's policy in a favorable light.

The bad news, stated indirectly, tactfully leaves the repair decision to the customer.

A positive alternative action should help soothe the customer.

The close blends sales promotion with acknowledgment of the customer's interests.

When refusing to make an adjustment

- Demonstrate understanding of the complaint
- Explain your refusal
- Suggest alternative action

When refusing to adjust a claim, avoid language that might have a negative impact on the reader. Instead, demonstrate that you understand and have considered the complaint. Then, even if the claim is unreasonable, rationally explain why you are refusing the request (but don't apologize or rely on company policy). End the letter on a respectful and action-oriented note.

CHECKLIST FOR BAD NEWS ABOUT ORDERS*

A. Buffer
   1. Include any details identifying the order.
   2. Extend a welcome to a new customer.
   3. Use resale information on the ordered merchandise to build the customer's confidence in the original choice (except for unfillable orders).
   4. For partial shipments, include the good news about the fulfilled part.

B. Reasons
   1. State the facts without laying blame.
   2. Handle back orders carefully.
      a. Specify shipping dates.
      b. Explain why the item is out of stock, such as high popularity or exceptional demand, which may stimulate the customer's desire for the item.
      c. Reinforce the customer's confidence (for consumers, emphasize resale information such as personal attention, credit, repair services, free delivery, special discounts, telephone shopping, and other services; for dealers, emphasize free counter and window displays, advertising materials, sales manuals, factory guarantees, and nearby warehousing).
      d. Refer to sales promotion material, if desirable.

C. The Bad News
   1. Stress the reader benefit of the decision to buy.
   2. Offer a substitute product, if available.

D. Positive, Friendly, Helpful Close
   1. Adopt a tone that shows you remain in control of the situation and will continue to give customers' orders personal attention.
   2. Use resale information to clinch the sale, especially for back orders.

*These items are in addition to the material included in the Checklist for Delivering Bad-News Messages.

You may be tempted to respond to something particularly outrageous by calling the person responsible a crook, a swindler, or an incompetent. Resist! If you don't, you could be sued for **defamation,** a false statement that tends to damage someone's character or reputation. (Written defamation is called *libel;* spoken defamation is called *slander.*) By this definition, someone suing for defamation would have to prove (1) that the statement is false, (2) that the language is injurious to the person's reputation, and (3) that the statement has been "published."

If you can prove that your accusations are true, you haven't defamed the person. The courts are likely to give you the benefit of the doubt because our society believes that ordinary business communication should not be hampered by fear of lawsuits. However, beware the irate letter intended to let off steam: If the message has no necessary business purpose and is expressed in abusive language that hints of malice, you'll lose the case. To avoid being accused of defamation, follow these guidelines:

Avoid deformation by not responding emotionally.

- Avoid using any kind of abusive language or terms that could be considered defamatory.
- If you wish to express your own personal opinions about a sensitive matter, use your own stationery (not company letterhead), and don't include your job title or position. Take responsibility for your own actions without involving your company.
- Provide accurate information and stick to the facts.
- Never let anger or malice motivate your messages.
- Consult your company's legal department or an attorney whenever you think a message might have legal consequences.
- Communicate honestly, and make sure that what you're saying is what you believe to be true.

For a brief review of the tasks involved when refusing adjustments of claims or complaints, see this chapter's Checklist for Refusals to Make Adjustments.

CHECKLIST FOR REFUSALS TO MAKE ADJUSTMENTS*

A. Buffer
   1. Indicate your full understanding of the nature of the complaint.
   2. Avoid all areas of disagreement.
   3. Avoid any hint of your final decision.

B. Reasons
   1. Provide an accurate, factual account of the transaction.
   2. Emphasize ways that the product should have been handled or the contract followed, rather than the reader's negligence.
      a. Avoid using a know-it-all tone.
      b. Use impersonal, passive language.
      c. Avoid accusing or preaching (*you should have*).
   3. Do not blame or scold the reader.
   4. Do not make the reader appear or feel stupid.

C. The Bad News
   1. Make the refusal clear, using tactful wording.
   2. Avoid any hint that your decision is less than final.
   3. Avoid words such as *reject* and *claim.*
   4. Make a counterproposal for a compromise settlement or partial adjustment (if desirable) in a willing, not begrudging tone, in a spirit of honest cooperation, and without making it sound like a penalty.
   5. Include a resale note for the company or product.
   6. Emphasize a desire for a good relationship in the future.
   7. Extend an offer to replace the product or to provide a replacement part at the regular price.

D. Positive, Friendly, Helpful Close
   1. Eliminate any reference to your refusal.
   2. Refer to enclosed sales material.
   3. Make any suggested action easy for readers to comply with.

*These items are in addition to the material included in the Checklist for Delivering Bad-News Messages.

Refusing to Extend Credit

Use the indirect plan when turning down a credit applicant.

Credit is refused for a variety of reasons, all involving sensitive personal or legal considerations. When denying credit to the applicant with a proven record of delinquent payments and to the applicant with an unstable background, you would probably be justified in offering little hope for future credit approval. You could be more encouraging to other types of applicants. You most certainly would like their current cash business, and you may want their future credit business (see Figure 8.6).

In a letter denying credit to a business
- Be more factual and less personal than in a letter to an individual
- Suggest ways to continue doing business

Denials of business credit, as opposed to denials of individual credit, are less personally sensitive but more financially significant. Businesses have failed because major suppliers have suspended credit at inconvenient times. When refusing to extend credit to a business, explain your reasons as factually and as impersonally as possible (perhaps the firm's latest financial statements don't meet your criteria or its credit rating has fallen below an acceptable minimum). Also, explain the steps that must be taken to restore credit. Emphasize the benefits of continued dealings on a cash basis until the firm's credit worthiness has been established or restored. You might offer discounts for cash purchases or assistance in cooperative merchandising to reduce the firm's inventory and increase its cash flow. Third-party loans are another possibility you might suggest.

Be aware that credit is a legally sensitive subject.

Whether denying credit to business customers or consumers, you need to exercise good judgment to avoid legal action. A faulty decision that unfairly damages a person's reputation may provoke a lawsuit and other bad publicity for your company. Handling credit denials over the phone instead of in writing is no guarantee of avoiding trouble; companies that orally refuse credit must still proceed with caution. For a reminder of the tasks involved in this type of message, see this chapter's Checklist for Credit Refusals.

The following letter refuses credit for the present but points to the possibility of extending credit later. Krueger has taken pains to make the reader feel welcome and to help her realize that her business is appreciated.

Figure 8.6
In-Depth Critique: Letter Refusing Credit

Best Buy
1717 Eastwood Boulevard, Atlanta, Georgia 30317
Voice: (404) 598-4747 • Fax: (404) 598-4748
www.bestbuy.com

September 9, 1999

Ms. Joelle Richards
818 Sandy Springs Road
Atlanta, GA 30328

Dear Ms. Richards:

Your request for a Best Buy card tells us something important: You enjoy the rewards of purchasing top-quality music and electronic equipment at bargain prices. Each year, Best Buy has grown because of a commitment to bringing you the best products at the best price.

Your excellent credit rating puts you in the top 25 percent of credit card customers. Although our Best Buy card requires continuous residence of credit card customers for 12 months, your application will remain in our database so that it will be easier for you to reapply after you've lived a year at your current location.

In the meantime, we want you to know that we value you as a customer at Best Buy. During the month of July, our Atlanta area stores are celebrating the opening of our new location in Duluth just off Interstate 85. Every store in the Metro area will be offering sales, special purchases, and additional discounts on our most popular electronic items. We'll be sending you a flyer soon. Your local paper will have all the details. We appreciate our customers and strive to give them the best at Best Buy.

Sincerely,

Evian Krueger

Evian Krueger
Customer Service Representative

The buffer expresses understanding and offers some subtle resale on the company. It establishes common ground while promoting the store.

The reason for refusal is tempered with the idea that Richards will likely be approved in the future.

The close reminds the reader that she is still a valued customer and promotes the upcoming celebration.

Conveying Unfavorable News about People

From time to time, most managers must convey bad news about people. Letters to prospective employers may be written in direct order. On the other hand, letters to job applicants and employees are often written in indirect order, because the reader will most certainly be emotionally involved.

Use the indirect plan when giving someone bad news about his or her own job; use the direct plan when giving bad news about someone else's job.

CHECKLIST FOR CREDIT REFUSALS*

A. Buffer
  1. Express appreciation for the credit request.
  2. Introduce resale information.

B. Reasons
  1. Explain your general credit criteria.
  2. Carefully present reasons for the refusal.
    a. Clearly state the reasons if the reader will accept them.
    b. Refer to a credit-reporting agency you have used.
    c. Avoid a condescending lecture about how credit is earned.
    d. Phrase reasons in terms of experience with others.
    e. Use "insufficient information" as a reason only if it is true.
    f. To avoid the risk of legal action, omit reasons entirely when dealing with extraordinarily sensitive or combative persons or when the evidence is unusually negative or involves behavioral flaws.
  3. Avoid relying on unexplained company policy.
  4. Stress the benefits of not being overextended.
  5. Encourage a later credit application, if future approval is realistic.
  6. Remind the reader of the benefits of purchasing by cash.

C. The Bad News
  1. Make the refusal clear to the reader.
  2. Offer only honest encouragement about considering the credit application at a later date.
  3. Avoid negative words, such as *must decline.*
  4. Suggest positive alternatives, such as cash and layaway purchases.
  5. Handle refusals of business credit differently.
    a. Recommend cash purchases for small, frequent orders.
    b. Describe cash discounts (include figures).
    c. Suggest reducing inventory so that the business can strengthen its credit rating.
    d. Offer promotional and marketing aid.
    e. Suggest a later review of the credit application, if future approval is realistic.

D. Positive, Friendly, Helpful Close
  1. Encourage the reader to look to the future, when the application may be approved.
  2. Suggest alternative financing sources.
  3. Include sales promotion material only if the customer would not be offended.

*These items are in addition to the material included in the Checklist for Delivering Bad-News Messages.

Refusing to Write Recommendation Letters

In letters informing prospective employers that you will not provide a recommendation, be direct, brief, and factual (to avoid legal pitfalls).

Even though many states have passed laws to protect employers who provide open and honest job references for former employees, legal hazards persist.[6] That's why many former employers still refuse to write recommendation letters—especially for people whose job performance has been, on balance, unsatisfactory. Prospective employers don't usually have a personal stake in the response, so letters refusing to provide a recommendation may be brief and direct:

> We received your request for a recommendation for Yolanda Johnson. According to guidelines from our human resources department, we are authorized to confirm only that Ms. Johnson worked for Tandy, Inc., for three years from June 1996 to July 1999. Best of luck as you interview the administrative applicants.

In letters telling job applicants that you will not write a recommendation, use the utmost tact.

Letters to the applicants themselves are another matter. Any refusal to cooperate may seem a personal slight and a threat to the applicant's future. The only way to avoid ill feelings is to handle the applicant gently:

> Thank you for letting me know about your job opportunity with Coca-Cola. Your internship there and the MBA you've worked so hard to earn should place you in an excellent position to land the marketing job.

> Although we can't write formal recommendations here at PepsiCo, I can certainly send Coke a confirmation of your employment dates. For more in-depth recommendations, be sure to ask the people you worked with during your internship to write evaluations of your work performance, and don't forget to ask several of your professors to write evaluations of your marketing skills.
> Best of luck to you in your career.

This letter deftly and tactfully avoids hurting the reader's feelings because it makes positive comments about the reader's recent activities, implies the refusal, suggests an alternative, and uses a polite close.

Rejecting Job Applications

In a letter turning down a job applicant, treat the reader with respect; by applying for a job, he or she has complimented your company.

It's also difficult to tactfully tell job applicants that you aren't going to offer them employment. But don't let the difficulty stop you from communicating the bad news. Rejecting an applicant with silence is unacceptable. At the same time, poorly written rejection letters do have negative consequences, ranging from the loss of qualified candidates for future openings to the loss of customers (not only the rejected applicants but also their friends and family).[7] When delivering bad news to job applicants, remember three principles:[8]

- *Open with the direct plan.* Job applicants know that good news will most likely come by phone and that bad news will most likely come by letter. If you try to buffer the bad news that your reader is expecting, you will seem manipulative and insincere.
- *Clearly state why the applicant was not selected.* Make your rejection less personal by stating that you hired someone with more experience or whose qualifications match the position requirements more closely.
- *Close by suggesting alternatives.* If you believe the applicant is qualified, mention other openings within your company. You might suggest professional organizations that could help the applicant find employment. Or you might simply mention that the applicant's résumé will be considered for future openings. Any of these positive suggestions may help the applicant be less disappointed and view your company more positively.

A rejection letter need not be long. Remember, sending a well-written form letter that contains these three principles is better than not sending one at all. After all, the applicant wants to know only one thing: Did I land the job? Your brief message conveys the information clearly and with some consideration for the applicant's feelings (see Figure 8.7).

BEST OF THE WEB

Protect Yourself When You Write a Recommendation Letter

A visit to the SOHO Guide can help reduce your legal liability when you write a letter of recommendation. Learn about state job reference requirements (several states have laws that may require you to write a reference). Learn about the types of statements that may form the basis of a lawsuit against you. Find out how to avoid lawsuits for invasion of privacy and violation of state blacklisting laws. Discover what employee information you can usually provide safely. Learn about when you have an absolute legal obligation to provide information about a former employee.

http://www.toolkit.cch.com/text/p05_8610.htm

Figure 8.7
In-Depth Critique: Letter Rejecting a Job Application

After Kate DeCicco interviewed with Bradley & Jackson, she was hopeful about receiving a job offer. Everything went well, and her résumé was in good shape. The following letter was intended to help DeCicco understand that she would have been hired if she'd had more tax experience and that she shouldn't be discouraged.

Bradley & Jackson
CERTIFIED PUBLIC ACCOUNTANTS

223 Brandon Street • Biloxi, Mississippi 39530 • (601) 446-9810 • (601) 466-6235

May 7, 1999

Ms. Kate DeCicco
472 Bellville Way
Biloxi, MS 39530

Dear Ms. DeCicco:

We appreciate your application for the position of tax accountant. Your academic record and previous accounting experience indicate your willingness to work hard. Those of us who had the opportunity to talk with you on your visit believe you have much to offer the right firm.

Because there were over thirty applicants for this position, the selection process was quite difficult. However, after much consideration, we have decided to hire an applicant with over ten years' experience in tax accounting.

Thank you for thinking of us. Your résumé and credentials show you to be a deserving candidate. And your ability to communicate will certainly help you achieve an excellent position in a recognized accounting firm.

Sincerely,

Marvin R. Fichter

Marvin R. Fichter
Human Resources Director

bl

The complimentary opening should help the candidate accept the bad news better.

The explanation of choosing a candidate with ten years' experience implies the bad news that the candidate didn't get the job. It also helps her understand that the deciding factor was experience, not unsatisfactory qualifications.

The positive close offers specific praise, helping the candidate finish the message with her self-confidence intact.

Giving Negative Performance Reviews

A performance review is a manager's formal or informal evaluation of an employee. Few other communication tasks require such a broad range of skills and strategy as that needed for performance reviews, whether positive or negative. The main purpose of these reviews is to improve employee performance by (1) emphasizing and clarifying job requirements, (2) giving employees feedback on their efforts toward fulfilling those requirements, and (3) guiding continued efforts by developing a plan of action, along with its rewards and opportunities. In addition to improving employee performance, performance reviews help companies set organizational standards and communicate organizational values.[9]

In performance reviews, say what's right as well as what's wrong, and explain how the employee can improve performance.

Positive and negative performance reviews share several characteristics: The tone is objective and unbiased, the language is nonjudgmental, and the focus is problem resolution.[10] Also, to increase objectivity, more organizations are giving their employees feedback from multiple sources. In these "360-degree reviews," employees get feedback from all directions in the organization: above, below, and horizontally.[11]

Be aware that employee performance reviews can play an important role in lawsuits. It's difficult to criticize employees face to face, and it's just as hard to include criticism in written performance evaluations. Nevertheless, if you fire an employee for incompetence and the performance evaluations are all positive, the employee can sue your company, maintaining you had no cause to terminate employment.[12] Also, your company could be sued for negligence if an injury is caused by an employee who received a negative evaluation but received no corrective action (such as retraining).[13] So, as difficult as it may be, make sure your performance evaluations are well balanced and honest.

Did You Know?

Supervisors who protect their subordinates from bad news—by praising success and glossing over failure—lose opportunities to improve performance.

When you need to give a negative performance review, remember the following guidelines:[14]

- *Confront the problem right away.* Avoiding performance problems only makes them worse. The one acceptable reason to wait is if you need time to calm down and regain your objectivity.
- *Plan your message.* Be clear about your concerns, and include examples of the employee's specific actions. Think about any possible biases you may have, and get feedback from others. Collect all relevant facts (both strengths and weaknesses).

Performance reviews at New Concept Design and Development Company incorporate feedback from multiple sources. When delivering a negative review, discuss the problems privately and be sure to outline a plan of action that will help the employee improve his or her performance.

- *Deliver the message in private.* Whether in writing or in person, make sure you address the performance problem privately. Don't send performance reviews by e-mail or fax. If you're reviewing an employee's performance face-to-face, conduct that review in a meeting arranged expressly for that purpose, and consider holding that meeting in a conference room, the employee's office, or some other neutral area.
- *Focus on the problem.* Discuss the problems caused by the employee's behavior (without attacking the employee). Compare the employee's performance with what's expected, with company goals, or with job requirements (not with the performance of other employees). Identify the consequences of continuing poor performance, and show you're committed to helping solve the problem.
- *Ask for a commitment from the employee.* Help the employee understand that planning for and making improvements are the employee's responsibility. However, finalize decisions jointly so that you can be sure any action to be taken is achievable. In fact, set a schedule for improvement and for following up with evaluations of that improvement.

Yia Eason would recommend that even if your employee's performance has been disappointing, you would do well to mention some good points in your performance review. Then you must clearly and tactfully state how the employee can better meet the responsibilities of the job (see "Sharpening Your Skills: How to Take the Sting out of Criticism and Foster Goodwill"). If the performance review is to be effective, be sure to suggest ways that the employee can improve.[15] For example, instead of telling an employee only that he damaged some expensive machinery, suggest that he take a refresher course in the correct operation of that machinery. The goal is to help the employee succeed.

SHARPENING YOUR SKILLS

HOW TO TAKE THE STING OUT OF CRITICISM AND FOSTER GOODWILL

People can't improve if they aren't evaluated, but criticism from others is often hard to take. The way you tell someone "You did it wrong" can destroy goodwill and cooperation, or it can build the relationship and improve the person's performance. The following suggestions will help you criticize people constructively.

- *Get all the facts first.* Don't accept hearsay or rumors. Be specific. Find out who did or said what, when, where, why, and how.
- *Don't act in haste.* Never act while you're angry, no matter how upset you or the other person may be. Take time to cool off and think things out before you start to write or speak. Remember that you're in control. Then explain your criticism calmly, rationally, and objectively.
- *Phrase your remarks impersonally.* Criticize the mistake, not the person. Focus your remarks on the action only. Analyze it thoughtfully. You'll help the person retain self-esteem and learn from the mistake.
- *Never criticize in an offhand manner.* Treat the situation seriously. Take the time to state what the problem is in detail. Explain what was wrong and why.
- *Don't ridicule, talk down, or use sarcasm.* An abusive tone will prevent the person from accepting what you have to say. To make the criticism more acceptable, respect your readers or listeners and give them the benefit of the doubt.
- *Make the offense clear.* Don't talk in generalities. Be specific. Let the person know exactly what she or he did wrong.
- *Share responsibility.* Take the sting out of your criticism by sharing some of the blame for the person's mistake. One way to do this is by saying *we,* as in "What do you think we did wrong?"
- *Preface the criticism with a kind word or a compliment.* It will make the other person more receptive and put her or him at ease. Start with a few words of praise or admira-

CHECKLIST FOR UNFAVORABLE NEWS ABOUT PEOPLE

A. Buffer

1. Identify the applicant or employee clearly when writing to a third party.
2. Express the reasons for writing—clearly, completely, and objectively.
3. Avoid insincere expressions of regret.
4. Avoid impersonal business clichés.

B. Reasons

1. Word negative job-related messages carefully to avoid legal difficulties.
   - **a.** Avoid terms with legal definitions (*slanderous, criminal*).
   - **b.** Avoid negative terms with imprecise definitions (*lazy, sloppy*).
   - **c.** Whenever possible, embed negative comments in favorable or semifavorable passages.
   - **d.** Avoid generalities, and explain the limits of your observations about the applicant's or employee's shortcomings.
   - **e.** Eliminate secondhand information.
   - **f.** Stress the confidentiality of your letter.
2. Avoid negative personal judgments.
3. For letters refusing to supply a recommendation to job seekers, suggest another avenue for getting a recommendation.
4. For rejection letters, emphasize the positive qualities of the person hired rather than the shortcomings of the rejected applicant.
5. For performance reviews, describe the employee's limitations and suggest methods for improving performance.

C. The Bad News

1. Understate negative decisions by implying them whenever possible.
2. Avoid statements that might involve the company in legal action.

D. Positive, Friendly, Helpful Close

1. For refusals to supply recommendations and for rejection letters, extend good wishes.
2. For performance reviews, express a willingness to help further.
3. For termination letters, make suggestions for finding another job, if applicable.

---

tion. Say how much you value the person. Put good news first; then introduce bad news.

- *Supply the answer.* When telling a person what she or he did wrong, also explain how to do it right. Don't emphasize the mistake; emphasize how to correct it and how to avoid repeating it.
- *Ask for cooperation; don't demand it.* Asking makes the person feel like a member of your team and provides an incentive to improve.
- *Limit yourself to one criticism for each offense.* Don't drag up past mistakes or rehash any that are done with. Focus on the current one.
- *End on a friendly note.* Until an issue has been resolved on a positive note, it hasn't been resolved. Don't leave things up in the air, to be discussed again later. Settle them now. A friendly close works wonders. Give the other person a pat on the back. Let the last memory of the matter be a good one. The person is much more likely to accept your criticism and to feel friendly toward you.
- *Forgive and forget.* Once the criticism has been made, let the person start with a clean slate. Don't look for more mistakes. Give the person a chance to improve.
- *Take steps to prevent a recurrence.* After telling the person what to do to improve, follow up to make sure she or he is acting on your suggestions and doing things right.

If you follow these guidelines, constructive criticism can benefit you, your company, and—most important—the person you're criticizing.

---

1. Think back over the lessons you've learned in life. In what ways have you benefited when someone has told you the truth about something you were doing wrong?
2. With a partner, role-play a situation in which one of you is the boss and the other an employee. The boss is angry because the employee is repeatedly late for work, takes long lunches, and always leaves five to ten minutes early. However, the employee's work is always excellent. After the role-play, analyze what the boss did right and what areas could use improvement.

Terminating Employment

Carefully word a termination letter to avoid creating undue ill will and grounds for legal action.

When writing a termination letter, you have three goals: (1) to present the reasons for this difficult action, (2) to avoid statements that might involve the company in legal action, and (3) to leave the relationship between the terminated employee and the firm as favorable as possible. For both legal and personal reasons, present specific justification for asking the employee to leave.[16] Make sure that all your reasons are accurate and verifiable. Avoid words that are open to interpretation, such as *untidy* and *difficult.* Make sure the employee leaves with feelings that are as positive as the circumstances allow. You can do this by telling the truth about the termination and by helping as much as you can to make the employee's transition as smooth as possible.[17] To review the tasks involved in this type of message, see this chapter's Checklist for Unfavorable News about People.

HANDLING BAD NEWS ABOUT COMPANY OPERATIONS OR PERFORMANCE

At least three types of situations require bad-news letters about company operations or performance: (1) a change in company policy that will have a negative effect on the reader, (2) problems with company performance, and (3) controversial or unpopular company operations. In trying situations, apologies may be in order. If an apology is appropriate, good writers usually make it brief and bury it somewhere in the middle of the letter. Moreover, they try to leave readers with a favorable impression by closing on a positive note.

Communicating bad news during an airline pilot strike can be emotionally trying—especially if your customers are stranded and have no other way to get home.

When a change in company policy will have a negative effect on the reader, the key is to clearly and carefully state the reasons for the change. The explanation section of the letter convinces readers that the change was necessary and, if possible, explains how the change will benefit them. For example, dropping orthodontic coverage from an employee dental plan could be couched in terms such as "by eliminating this infrequently used benefit we will not have to increase the monthly amount withheld from your paycheck for insurance coverage."

When conveying bad news about the company, focus on the reasons and on possible benefits.

If your company is having serious performance problems, your customers and shareholders want to learn of the difficulty from you, not from newspaper accounts or from rumors. Even if the news leaks out, counter it with your own explanation as soon as possible. Much business is based on mutual trust; if your customers and shareholders can't trust you to inform them of your problems, they may choose to work with someone they can trust. Of course, when you do inform stakeholders, use your common business sense and minimize the bad news by presenting it in as favorable a light as possible. For instance, the loss of a major business customer could be presented as an opportunity to focus on smaller, growing businesses or on new products.

Companies that produce unpopular products or have controversial operations can also find themselves caught in a political crossfire. In such cases, your general strategy might be to present the reasons the company is manufacturing the controversial item or providing the unpopular service. The goal is to show that reason and need (not villainy, carelessness, or greed) are behind the controversial decision.

COMMUNICATION CHALLENGES AT OLMEC TOYS

When Yia Eason formed Olmec Toys to produce ethnic action figures, she could not have foreseen the company's tremendous growth and the many challenges she would face. As each challenge has arisen, she has relied on well-trained and loyal employees and an active board of directors to provide solutions. Talented people who share your vision can be invaluable when you are faced with the task of delivering bad news.

INDIVIDUAL CHALLENGE: Olmec has recently received letters from 23 consumers requesting a "family line" of dolls. The letters specifically request that dolls represent a mother, father, and children to emphasize African American family unity. As director of development and marketing, you think the motivation for the letters is commendable. However, a line of family dolls would not fit with Olmec's line of ethnic action figures.

Draft a bad-news form letter to the consumers who suggested the family line. In your letter, be careful to leave the possibility open for a future family line, and explain that the company is currently concentrating on its successful action figures. Plan carefully how you will open your communication. Will you end on a strong, positive note? Perhaps you will want to emphasize that SunMan and the other action figures already represent family values and that Olmec as a company is committed to promoting positive role models for young people. List your objectives and major points before you begin to draft your bad-news letter.[18]

TEAM CHALLENGE: As a member of Olmec's board of directors, you have just learned that the company will not meet earnings projections for the quarter. Knowing that this news will negatively affect the price of Olmec's stock, you are meeting informally with three other board members. Your task is to suggest language to be included in a news release that will deliver the bad news and yet keep investor confidence high.

Brainstorm ideas with your group. What is the best approach, direct or indirect? What reassurances will you give investors? How will you explain the steps Olmec is taking to correct the earnings slump? You can invent numbers to help you make a convincing argument to both the media and your investors. Then write a memo to Yia Eason in which you suggest the best approach to take in the company's news releases. ■

SUMMARY OF LEARNING OBJECTIVES

1. **Differentiate between the direct and indirect organizational approaches to bad-news messages.** The direct pattern states the bad news before the reasons and does not use a buffer. The indirect pattern begins with a buffer and places the reasons before the bad news, gradually preparing the audience for the disappointment. Both approaches end with a positive close.
2. **Discuss how the tone of your message can contribute to its effectiveness.** By adopting an audience-centered tone, you can help the audience understand that your decision is firm, fair, and reasonable while preserving the audience's ego. Your tone will also help the audience remain well disposed toward your business.
3. **Explain the purpose of a buffer and list several types commonly used.** A buffer sets the stage for the bad news by putting the audience in an acceptance mood. It should be pleasant, relevant, and neutral and should provide a smooth transition to the reasons that follow. Buffers can express agreement, appreciation, cooperation, fairness, good news, praise, resale information, and understanding.
4. **List five techniques for saying no as gently as possible.** You can minimize the space or time devoted to the bad news; subordinate it; embed it; enclose it in a conditional statement to imply a favorable answer later on; and explain what you did, can do, or will do.
5. **Explain when it's appropriate to use the direct approach for delivering bad news.** Use the direct approach if you know that the receiver prefers the bad news first, if the situation is minor and will cause little pain or disappointment, if the receiver is not emotionally involved, or if you know that firmness is necessary.
6. **Discuss the additional challenges involved when conveying bad news to customers.** When delivering bad news to existing or would-be customers, you want to make them feel good about doing business with your firm. You use resale information or promotional material to reinforce the customer's confidence in your service or product.

CRITICAL THINKING QUESTIONS

1. Why is it important to end your bad-news message on a positive note? Explain.
2. If company policy changes, should you explain those changes to employees and customers at about the same time, or should you explain them to employees first? Why?
3. Why is the indirect plan generally more appropriate than the direct plan for delivering bad news?
4. Why should you avoid apologizing when giving reasons for the bad news?
5. Is intentionally de-emphasizing bad news the same as distorting graphs and charts to de-emphasize unfavorable or bad-news data? Why or why not?
6. If the purpose of your letter is to convey bad news, should you take the time to suggest alternatives to your reader? Why or why not?
7. When a company suffers a misfortune, should the impact be softened by letting out the bad news a little at a time? Why or why not?
8. Why is it a good idea to send rejection letters?

DOCUMENTS FOR ANALYSIS

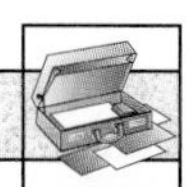

Read the following documents; then (1) analyze the strengths and weaknesses of each sentence and (2) revise each document so that it follows this chapter's guidelines.

Document 8.A: Conveying Bad News about Orders

We want to take this opportunity to thank you for your past orders. We have included our new catalog of books, videos, films, and slides to let you know about our great new products. We included our price list also. Please use this list rather than the old one as we've had a slight increase in price.

Per your request, we are sorry we can't send you the free examination copies of the textbooks you requested. The books, *Communication for Business* and *Winning the Presentation Game*, are two of our new titles that are enjoying brisk sales. It seems everyone is interested in communication skills these days.

We do apologize for not sending the exam copies for free. Our prices continue to rise along with everyone else's, and it's just not feasible to send everyone free copies. If you'd still like to have a look, please notice the prices in the list I've included and don't forget shipping and handling. You can also fax your order to the number shown on the sheet or e-mail your order over the Internet.

I'm sure these books would make a great addition to your collection. Again, we are sorry we couldn't grant your request, but we hope you order anyway.

Document 8.B: Communicating Negative Answers and Information

Your spring fraternity party sounds like fun. We're glad you've again chosen us as your caterer. Unfortunately, we have changed a few of our policies, and I wanted you to know about these changes in advance so that we won't have any misunderstandings on the day of the party.

We will arrange the delivery of tables and chairs as usual the evening before the party. However, if you want us to set up, there is now a $100.00 charge for that service. Of course, you might want to get some of the brothers and pledges to do it, which would save you money. We've also added a small charge for cleanup. This is only $3.00 per person (you can estimate because I know a lot of people come and go later in the evening).

Other than that, all the arrangements will be the same. We'll provide the skirt for the band stage, tablecloths, bar setup, and of course, the barbecue. Will you have the tubs of ice with soft drinks again? We can do that for you as well, but there will be a fee.

Please let me know if you have any problems with these changes and we'll try to work them out. I know it's going to be a great party.

Document 8.C: Refusing Adjustment of Claims and Complaints

I am responding to your letter of about six weeks ago asking for an adjustment on your fax/modem, model FM39Z. We test all our products before they leave the factory; therefore, it could not have been our fault that your fax/modem didn't work.

If you or someone in your office dropped the unit, it might have caused the damage. Or the damage could have been caused by the shipper if he dropped it. If so, you should file a claim with the shipper. At any rate, it wasn't our fault. The parts are already covered by warranty. However, we will provide labor for the repairs for $50.00, which is less than our cost since you are a valued customer.

We will have a booth at the upcoming trade fair there and hope to see you or someone from your office. We have many new models of office machines that we're sure you'll want to see. I've enclosed our latest catalog. Hope to see you there.

Document 8.D: Rejecting Job Applications

I regret to inform you that you were not selected for our summer intern program at Equifax. We had over a thousand résumés and cover letters to go through and simply could not get to them all. We have been asked to notify everyone that we have already selected students for the twenty-five positions based on those who applied early and were qualified.

We're sure you will be able to find a suitable position for summer work in your field and wish you the best of luck. We deeply regret any inconvenience associated with our reply.

EXERCISES

1. Select which approach you would use (direct or indirect) for the following bad-news messages:
   a. A memo to your boss informing her that one of your key clients is taking its business to a different accounting firm
   b. An e-mail message to a customer informing her that one of the books she ordered over the Internet is temporarily out of stock
   c. A letter to a customer explaining that the tape backup unit he ordered for his new custom computer is on back order and that, as a consequence, the shipping of the entire order will be delayed
   d. A letter from the telephone company rejecting a customer's claim that the phone company should reimburse the customer for the costs of a new high-speed modem (Apparently, the phone lines will carry data at only half the modem's speed.)
   e. A memo to all employees notifying them that the company parking lot will be repaved during the first week of June and that the company will provide a shuttle service from a remote parking lot during that period
   f. A letter from a travel agent to a customer stating that the airline will not refund her money for the flight she missed but that her tickets are valid for one year
   g. A form letter from a U.S. airline to a customer explaining that they cannot extend the expiration date of the customer's frequent flyer miles even though the customer was living overseas for the past three years
   h. A letter from an insurance company to a policyholder denying a claim for reimbursement for a special medical procedure that is not covered under the terms of the customer's policy
   i. A letter from an electronics store stating that the customer will not be reimbursed for a malfunctioning cell phone still under warranty (The terms of the warranty do not cover damages to phones that were accidentally placed in the freezer overnight.)
   j. An announcement to the repairs department listing parts that are on back order and will be three weeks late
2. Revise the following statements to de-emphasize the bad news. (*Hint:* Minimize the space devoted to the bad news, subordinate it, embed it, or use the passive voice.)
   a. The airline can't refund your money. The "Conditions" segment on the back of your ticket states that there are no refunds for missed flights. Sometimes the airline makes exceptions, but only when life and death are involved. Of course, your ticket is still valid and can be used on a flight to the same destination.
   b. I'm sorry to tell you, we can't supply the custom decorations you requested. We called every supplier and none of them can do what you want on such short notice. You can, however, get a standard decorative package on the same theme in time. I found a supplier that stocks these. Of course, it won't have quite the flair you originally requested.
   c. We can't refund your money for the malfunctioning lamp. You shouldn't have placed a 250-watt bulb in the fixture socket; it's guaranteed for a maximum of 75 watts.
3. Answer the following questions pertaining to buffers:
   a. You have to tell a local restaurant owner that your plans have changed and you have to cancel the 90-person banquet

scheduled for next month. Do you need to use a buffer? Why or why not?

b. Write an appreciation buffer for a letter declining an invitation to speak at the association's annual fund-raising event.

c. Write a praise buffer for a letter rejecting a job applicant who speaks three foreign languages fluently.

4. When is avoiding the word *you* a better use of the "you" attitude?

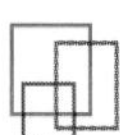

EXPLORING THE BEST OF THE WEB

Protect Yourself When You Write a Recommendation Letter, page 265

1. As the SOHO Guide makes clear, providing references for former employees can leave employers vulnerable to lawsuits. Increasingly, employers are choosing to eliminate this risk by simply refusing to provide any references. Do you think this is a good approach? Why or why not?

2. Follow the links in the SOHO Guide (click on the highlighted text to jump to PO5_8640, PO5_8650, and PO5_8660) to learn more about the ins and outs of requesting and providing references.

   a. What other options does the SOHO Guide describe for employers who want to avoid legal battles?

   b. Are there any conditions under which an employer *must* provide a reference for a former employee?

   c. Do employers who refuse to provide references run any legal risks by adopting such a policy?

   d. If an employer in good faith gives information about a former employee and limits the scope of the information provided to the specific inquiry made, is there any real chance that the law would *not* protect the employer?

   e. Why does the SOHO Guide caution employers to avoid saying that an employee was terminated "for cause" or for "unsatisfactory performance"?

CASES CASES CASES CASES

PROVIDING BAD NEWS ABOUT PRODUCTS

1. Suffering artists: Memo declining high-tech shoes at American Ballet Theater Michael Jordan would never take the court in shoes designed two decades ago, let alone *two centuries ago.* But that's sports and this is ballet, you sigh. Here at the American Ballet Theater (ABT), where you're serving as assistant to Artistic Director Kevin McKenzie, the notion of suffering for the art form has been ingrained since the early 1800s, when the first ballerina rose up *en pointe,* to the tips of her soon-to-be-deformed toes, in order to create the graceful illusion of floating on air. And what an exquisite sight it is!

Many entrepreneurs view this painful situation with hopeful enthusiasm, especially when they discover that dancers worldwide spend about $150 million annually on their "little tiny torture chambers" of cardboard and satin (with glued linen or burlap to stiffen the toes). The pink monstrosities (about $50 a pair) rarely last beyond a single hard performance.

A company the size of ABT spends about $500,000 a year on ballet slippers. Then there's the cost of the on-staff physical therapist, and the trips to chiropractors, podiatrists, and surgeons to relieve bad necks, backs, knees, and feet. Surely there's room for improvement, given the current advantages of orthopedics, space-age materials, and high-tech solutions for contemporary athletes. And now that the old dancers' joke, "If I wanted an easier workout, I'd play football," has been scientifically proven, there's no denying that ballerinas are among the hardest-working athletes in the world.

No one at ABT blames the latest entrepreneur, Eliza Minden of Gaynor Minden Inc., for wanting to provide a solution to the shoe problem. She buttonholed Michael Kaiser, executive director and a member of ABT's Board of Governing Trustees, with a proposal for providing new, high-performance pointe shoes in exchange for an endorsement. It truly is a good idea. It's just a hard sell among the tradition-oriented dancers.

Minden's alternative pointe shoe offers high-impact support and toe cushions. They're only $70 a pair, and supposedly they can be blow dried (like Birkenstocks) back into shape after a performance. When the cost-conscious board member urged the company to give them a try, you were assigned to collect feedback from dancers.

So far, not good. For example, principal ballerina Christine Dunham: She'd rather numb her feet in icy water, dance through "zingers" of toe pain, and make frequent visits to the physical therapist than wear Minden's shoes, she insisted after a brief trial. The others agree. Apparently, they *like* breaking in the traditional satin models with hammers and door slams and throwing them away after a single *Coppelia.* Too stiff, they say of the new shoes. Adds Dunham, "I'm totally settled into what I'm doing."

You've seen those sinewy, wedge-shaped feet bleeding backstage. You feel sorry for Minden; it *was* a good idea. Maybe she should try younger dancers.

Your task: McKenzie has asked you to write an internal memo in his name to Michael Kaiser, executive director of the American Ballet Theater, explaining the dancers' refusal to use the new high-tech Gaynor Minden pointe shoes. In your memo be sure to include the dancers' reasons as well as your own opinion regarding the matter. You'll need to decide whether to use the direct or the indirect approach; include a separate short note to your instructor justifying your selection.[19]

2. The check's in the mail—almost: Letter from Sun Microsystems explaining late payments You'd think that a computer company could install a new management information system without a hitch, wouldn't you? The people at Sun Microsystems thought so too, but they were wrong. When they installed their own new computerized system for getting information to management, a few things—such as payments to vendors—fell through the cracks.

It was embarrassing, to say the least, when Sun's suppliers started clamoring for payment, Terence Lenaghan, the corporate controller, found himself in the unfortunate position of having to tell 6,000 vendors why Sun Microsystems had failed to pay its bills on time—and why it might be late with payments again. "Until we get these bugs ironed out," Lenaghan confessed, "we're going to have to finish some of the accounting work by hand. That means that some of our payments to vendors will probably be late next month too. We'd better write to our suppliers and let them know that there's nothing wrong with the company's financial performance. The last thing we want is for our vendors to think our business is going down the tubes."

Your task: Write a form letter to Sun Microsystem's 6,000 vendors explaining that bugs in their new management information system are responsible for the delays in payment.[20]

3. Feeling at home in Denmark: Letter to Web House critiquing its home page Web House is an award-winning Danish company that designs home pages and other Internet materials for international clients. Christian Broberg has hired you as an independent consultant to critique the company's home page from a U.S. point of view. You'll need to visit the Web House home page at http://www.webhouse.dk and study it from the perspective of a U.S. business manager. Be sure to consider all aspects of clear intercultural communication as discussed in Chapter 3.

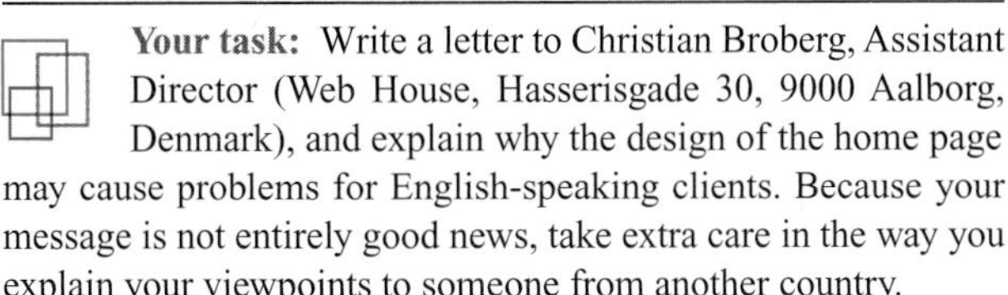

Your task: Write a letter to Christian Broberg, Assistant Director (Web House, Hasserisgade 30, 9000 Aalborg, Denmark), and explain why the design of the home page may cause problems for English-speaking clients. Because your message is not entirely good news, take extra care in the way you explain your viewpoints to someone from another country.

4. Everything old is new again: E-mail message reporting polyester findings Polyester got a bad rap in the 1980s. Now it's making a comeback in both fashion and food. What? Eat and drink from polyester containers? It's an idea whose time has come, according to chemical companies ranging from Dow to Amoco. An ice-cold Coke sipped from a polyester container may be tough for some Americans to swallow, but experts predict that a new generation of plastic may solve many of the problems, such as carbonation loss and heat sensitivity, caused by the containers now being used.

Today's drink bottles use a plastic called PET (polyethylene terephthalate). When stressed by heat, PET is too porous to contain the "fizz." But PET can now be mixed with a recently developed polyester called PEN (polyethylene naphthalate) to create a new generation of tougher plastic. Shell Chemical's director of polyester research and development, David Richardson, believes in the product. "In a few years, I'll be able to fix you a nice meal, and everything in it will come out of a polyester container."

Why make the switch from aluminum or glass to plastic? "Plastic is less deadly than glass when you throw it at a soccer match," says Richard Marion, an executive at Amoco Corporation's Amoco Chemical Company. Airlines like it because it's lightweight. Their little jelly containers used in First Class will weigh less. Consumers like it because it's clear, resealable, lightweight, and easily recycled. Polyester is definitely making a comeback. But one segment of the population is proving resistant to the trend: young adults. In a market research study, students preferred aluminum cans: Of all the container materials, aluminum ranked highest, achieving an 84 percent acceptance rate.

According to the study, students like the feel of the aluminum cans (plastic feels slippery and is harder to hold) and believe that aluminum keeps drinks colder. They also believe that aluminum keeps the carbonation longer, creating a "mouth buzz," whereas plastic lets the fizz out. And finally, they think that aluminum cans look "cool" and that plastic containers look "dorky."

Your market research team has come up with a couple of ways to deal with these perceptions. One approach would be an ad campaign showing "cool" young adults drinking from plastic bottles. Another would be ads showing that new technology is helping the plastic containers to hold in the "fizz."

Your task: As assistant director of marketing for Coca-Cola, write an e-mail message to your boss, Tom Ruffenbach, TomRuf@marketing.coca-cola.com, in which you report your findings and suggest ways to overcome this consumer bias.[21]

DENYING COOPERATION WITH ROUTINE REQUESTS

5. All in the family: E-mail message resigning a position Your brother, Ruben N. Rodriguez Jr., started the family-owned Los Amigos Tortilla Manufacturing, Inc., in 1969 with only $12,000. While Los Amigos developed, you were able to help support the family with your income as marketing director for the Latin American Division of IBM. Today, the Atlanta-based Los Amigos enjoys annual sales of about $4.5 million and its prospects look bright.

Ruben asked you to resign from your position at IBM and work full-time for Los Amigos. You decided to do some research before answering. You found that Hispanic-owned businesses have outperformed U.S. business growth in general. You also learned that many Hispanic corporate executives are leaving big companies to start their own business. You want to be a part of this amazing trend, not only because of the profit potential but also because you love your family and want to help your brother develop the company. You hope your son will become a part of the organization some day. After considering all aspects, you made your decision: You submitted your letter of resignation to IBM. Today, you received e-mail from the division vice president urging you to stay and offering a lucrative incentive package, including an additional week's vacation, an upgrade on your company car, and an increase of $10,000 a year.

Your task: Write an e-mail message to George Packard, your division vice president, at GPackard@lad.ibm.com, thanking him for his offer. Explain the reasons behind your decision to resign and suggest that Consuela Vargas, who has worked with you for five years, would make an excellent marketing director. Vargas not only speaks Spanish and Portuguese but has played a key role in closing deals for IBM in several Latin American countries. Plus, she's a terrific strategic thinker.[22]

6. Navajo Joe's: Letter rejecting interior design proposal Atmosphere is everything at Navajo Joe's coffeehouse in Window Rock, Arizona, in the middle of a Navajo reservation the size of West Virginia. "We've got Starbucks and Hank Williams," brags owner Manny Wheeler, a 26-year-old art history graduate of Arizona State University who grew up on the "big rez." While a student, Wheeler hung out in coffeehouses all over Phoenix. When he came home, he took odd jobs but kept fine-tuning his business plan all the while. He knew Navajos loved their coffee as much as their fry bread, but as far as he knew, nothing resembling an urban-style coffeehouse existed on any reservation. Finally, with a loan from his aunt, furniture from second-hand stores, and decor consisting of Wheeler's original art and cast-offs from his grandmother's yard (an old saddle, rotting wagon harness, and so on), Navajo Joe's was born.

Wheeler has just hired you for your summer break from business school, and he's showing you around the place.

"I like the colors," says the 29-year-old musician whose band, Burn in Effigy, plays weekends here. You look up at the black ceiling and yellow walls, then at the arrow holes in the back wall (no, not a sign of Navajo history, but left over from the archery store that once filled the space). One of Wheeler's paintings catches your eye: a black and gray abstract of a bronc rider painted on a slab of cardboard. "That's my Cubist phase," Wheeler explains. "Dude from Chicago offered me $500 for it. I said it's not for sale." Another wall features Johnny Cash album covers and weird tabloid headlines: "Nude Sunbathers Attacked by Crazed Sea Gulls!" You marvel at the lack of a telephone and the fact that Wheeler drives 250 miles round-trip to Albuquerque three times a month to buy coffee beans. And you can't help noticing the music; sometimes it's country and western, sometimes surf music, sometimes tribal music.

"I look at this coffeehouse as an art piece," Wheeler explains proudly. "You keep adding to it until you have a sense of what works."

Well, you can't argue with success. Somehow Wheeler is appealing to Navajos of all generations. For the younger crowd, it's double lattes with a splash of hazelnut and late-night chess games. For the old timers, Wheeler had to work a little harder. They couldn't figure out that wall menu, with its mochas and Konas and no regular coffee. They walked out scratching their heads. Wheeler considered brewing up some sheepherder's coffee for them, but he finally settled for keeping a warm pot of Farmer Bros. on hand. It worked like a charm.

At the end of your first week, the coffeehouse played host to a pair of business partners from Albuquerque who had heard of Wheeler's success. Luther and Marilyn Busby own Native Design, a big-city interior decorating firm that specializes in Southwestern decor for businesses. They loved Wheeler's operation and insisted on presenting him with a "cost-effective" proposal for sprucing up Navajo Joe's decor. "You'll triple your business," they assured him enthusiastically. You held your breath, but Wheeler was polite. He drawled, "Sure . . . send me a proposal."

Your task: The written proposal finally arrived and Wheeler's reaction was exactly as you expected. But what you didn't plan for was his insistence that you write the rejection letter. "You're a business student, aren't you?" he winks. "Tell 'em they don't know a thing about business on the rez . . . or whatever you think is an appropriate way to say, 'Not in my lifetime!' "[23]

CONVEYING BAD NEWS ABOUT ORDERS

7. Seattle Blend: Letter explaining delays for Cedar Grove compost Ever since word got out about your company's "gourmet compost" (with a little help from your marketing department), Pacific Northwest gardeners can't seem to get enough of Cedar Grove Composting's $20 per cubic yard blend of rotting plant materials, vegetables, and of course, coffee grounds. The fact that your company picks up its composting materials as part of a mandatory recycling program in Seattle and surrounding King County is probably part of the appeal. But some pundits think it has something to do with a nationwide mania for anything rich, aromatic, brown, and expensive coming from Seattle.

"It has a good, rich smell," Mary Heide, manager of Sky Nursery in Shoreline, Washington, told the press, while one of her employees raved about its "rich, brown coffee color—kind of a mocha color from a Seattle point of view." That was it. The orders from gardening retailers started pouring in as their customers heard of the stuff and demanded it for their gardens, despite the fact that your prices are 30 percent higher than everyone else's. It didn't hurt sales, either, when your general manager, Jan Allen, publicized your $3 million, high-speed fans, cooling chambers, and other devices that "air out" the compost as it cures. She told the media that competing brands just "sit around in static piles. Ours has a higher degree of intelligence."

Your task: You are the manager of Cedar Grove's wholesale division, and you have a backlog of requests from retailers who are eager to fulfill their customers' demands. You have to let them know that it's going to take about four weeks to fill their orders. You'd better write this bad-news form letter with as much care and concern as Cedar Grove puts into its compost. First identify the main idea of your message. Then be sure to list some of the evidence you will include in your form letter to support your main idea.[24]

8. Tethered SwimCords: Letter to Italian sports retailer returning order Kelly Greene loved to swim; more than that, she loved the all-over exercise that swimming provides, without the joint hammering of jogging or aerobics. Trouble was, it took only six strokes to swim across the small pool at her apartment complex. She spent most of her time turning and pushing off, so she was actually gliding most of the time and she wasn't getting much exercise. What could she do? She invented SwimCords.

Taking her cue from surfers who use ankle tethers to keep their boards from getting lost in the waves, Greene developed an elastic, Bungee-like leash she could attach to her ankle and the pool's edge. She could swim and swim—and go nowhere. After a few design improvements and an enthusiastic endorsement from the UCLA swim team, Greene opened her new manufacturing business.

Of course, as she explained when she hired you to help process orders, it wasn't an overnight success. She first spent two years as a member of an inventors' guild, learning her way through the patenting process. But now orders for the $29.95 SwimCords are pouring in from all over the United States.

Today you opened a letter from Isabella Caparelli, owner of Sports Italia in Milan, eagerly requesting a sizable shipment of SwimCords. Caparelli spotted them in a U.S. sporting goods store and "has to have them," she writes. You took the letter straight to Greene's office.

"Oh, dear," the inventor fretted. "We're not ready to ship overseas. I knew it would happen soon, but right now—you'll just have to tell her no." She hesitated for a moment, glanced at the letter again, then added, "But mention that we're growing fast and we might be ready to ship them internationally in, say," she glanced at the calendar on her wall, "six months. I just hate to lose an order that big. Do what you can to keep her interest, but don't mislead her, either. I'm learning that honesty pays off faster than any big-ticket sales in this business," she smiled. "Oh, and be sure to send her a free sample."

Your task: Back at your desk, write a polite and encouraging refusal to Isabella Caparelli, the owner of Sports Italia, Via Arimondi 29-20121, Milan, Italy. Enclose a sample SwimCord.[25]

9. Popular product: Letter about delayed shipping from Comfy Interamerican Sheepskins If you're paying big dollars for your automobile, you want to be sure that the interior stays in the best possible condition—which is why Tom Plotkin's business is thriving. The New Zealander identified a virtually untapped U.S. market for sheepskin seat covers in 1987, so he bought Comfy Interamerican Sheepskins in Los Angeles. It was a good move; Comfy has reached $3 million in annual sales to automobile manufacturers, upscale retailers, individual car owners, and even airline pilots who like the feel, the coolness, the protection, and, of course, the status of the expensive seat covers.

Your problem, however, is handling the huge volume of special orders Comfy receives. They're complicated and they require longer production time then routine orders. For instance, last week you took an order from a Corvette owner who wanted his $450, top-of-the-line, customized seat covers in pure white with sewn-on burgundy stripes to match his car's interior. Today you're looking at a letter from a Porsche owner in Baltimore, Maryland. She wants "ivory and midnight black checkerboard patterns" and she's expecting you to ship her seat covers within 24 hours (as your company promises for certain standard, in-stock merchandise). Even when you aren't backlogged, your normal shipping time for custom orders is 14 days. But right now you're running about six days behind.

Your task: Write a letter to Anamarie Haverton (4766 Elkridge Place, Baltimore, MD 21227), explaining the situation.[26]

10. More to come: Letter explaining delay of Tesla videotapes Membership is expanding so rapidly at the nonprofit International Tesla Society that volunteers at the organization's headquarters and museum in Colorado Springs can hardly keep up with the daily mail. Many of the letters are orders for the rare books, diaries, patents, videotapes, audiotapes, and T-shirts advertised in the society's Museum Bookstore catalog.

Inventor Nikola Tesla, who emigrated from Yugoslavia to the United States in 1884, was responsible for the alternating current electrical system now used worldwide (which replaced Edison's direct current system). Called a "genius," a "mental giant," and "a man ahead of his time," Tesla also holds the patent for radio technology (although Guglielmo Marconi got the credit), and he invented a host of other devices that dazzled turn-of-the-century society: remote-controlled submarines, magnetic resonators, and lightning-generating "Tesla coils." For a time, Tesla was so well known he even appeared on the cover of *Time* magazine. Then, for reasons biographers still debate, the world forgot about Nikola Tesla.

Now people are catching up with many of Tesla's ideas—and the thousands of unexploited patents he left behind. Industrial and amateur inventors are developing working models from his drawings and notes for new concepts that may, as A/C power did years ago, revolutionize technology. The International Tesla Society hosts an annual symposium at which inventors can demonstrate their models and attend lectures on the most esoteric aspects of Tesla research. People from many countries attend; others order videotapes of the lectures and workshops.

Last year's symposium was so popular that you've depleted your supply of videotape copies for 17 of the 29 master tapes (this is an all-volunteer operation; no one rushed out to duplicate the missing tapes). Now you've received a letter from a German engineer ordering the complete set. He included $495 in U.S. funds, plus $12.50 for overseas shipping, and, as a Tesla Society member, he's expecting the usual "same-day shipping." It's going to take about two weeks to get copies of the 17 missing tapes.

Your task: Write to Josef Mandelheim, Sonnenstrasse 4, 86669 Erlingshofen, Germany, explaining the back-order situation. With your letter, send the 12 lecture videotapes you have on hand.[27]

REFUSING ADJUSTMENTS OF CLAIMS AND COMPLAINTS

11. Your monkey, your choice: Letter from Duncan's Exotic Pets refusing a damage claim As a well-known exotic animal dealer in the Cincinnati area, your boss, Roger Duncan, has dealt with his share of customers experiencing buyer's regret. Despite his warnings, many of them still buy their exotic pets for the wrong reasons. When Melissa Carpenter bought Binky, the red-tailed guenon monkey, she begged Mr. Duncan to reduce his price to $10,000 because she had "fallen in love with Binky's soulful eyes and adorable button nose." Now she wants to return poor Binky, and you have never seen your boss so angry.

"Listen to this!" fumes Mr. Duncan as he reads you part of Carpenter's letter:

> While I was at work, I locked your monkey in his own room—which I equipped with his own color TV (with cable) and which I spent days wallpapering with animal pictures. Then last night your monkey somehow unlocked the door, ripped out my telephone, opened the refrigerator, smashed eggs all over my kitchen and my new Persian carpet, broke 14 of the china dishes my mother gave me when I got married, and squeezed toothpaste all over my Louis XIV settee I inherited from my grandmother!

"Not only does she demand that I take poor Binky back after she's abused him through her ignorance and neglect," snapped Mr. Duncan, "but she wants me to pay $150,000 in damages for her apartment and her state of mind."

Your boss is so upset that you decide to write to Ms. Carpenter yourself.

Your task: Write to Melissa Carpenter (876 Newton Ave., Cincinnati, OH 45202) and include a copy of her contract. It clearly states Roger Duncan's policy: Refunds only if animals are returned in good health, and absolutely no warranty against damages. Each pet comes with specific care instructions, including warnings about certain idiosyncrasies that could cause problems in the wrong environment.

Despite the fact that Binky is probably traumatized by his experiences, Mr. Duncan has generously agreed to accept his return, refunding Ms. Carpenter's $10,000. However, he will not accept liability for any loss of property or for any claims of mental duress on the part of Ms. Carpenter.[28]

12. Ketchup complaint: Sorry, Mom. Heinz says the labels stay As a mother, a children's media consultant, and the founder of Action for Children's Television, Peggy Charen has written a letter to H.J. Heinz, complaining about a recent move by the company to involve kids in its new ketchup label designs. "I don't think children are the proper target for marketing efforts," the letter complains.

Working in Heinz consumer relations, you've been hearing some ripples of concern among parents ever since Heinz began its campaign by sending art posters and label-design contest rules to classrooms around the nation. Heinz also promoted the design contest with magazine ads asking, "Hey kids, wanna be famous?" At the same time, the company donated $450,000 to the National Endowment for the Arts (NEA) to be used for children's art programs.

In the company's 120 years, this is only the second time the famous ketchup labels have been changed, and Heinz wanted to be sure they would appeal to "families" (meaning the kids, who are now influencing family buying decisions more than ever, according to marketing experts). Among single-parent and working-parent families, screaming, demanding, tantrum-throwing, or simply TV-influenced kids are determining which brands Mom and Dad choose in the supermarket aisles. (Mom and Dad are too tired to fight or care.) Some experts estimate that kids' influence directly affects over $172 billion in annual consumer spending. So the kid's label-design contest was a great way to remind families that ketchup is still as important as salsa, according to Al Banisch, senior product manager for Heinz.

"Heinz took great care to minimize the commerciality, so to speak, of this program," Banisch told a recent meeting of staff from your department. "The materials sent to schools were packed with art facts and art history and art learning. This was really very much an educational exercise."

More than 2,000 classrooms took part, with over 60,000 entries pouring in to be judged by a Heinz panel that included children's horror writer R. L. Stine. The three winners each received $5,000 and the satisfaction of seeing their designs on new bottles: the 17-year-old's oil painting of a tomato, the 12-year-old's American flag with dribbled ketchup stripes, and the 6-year-old's grinning face constructed of two tomatoes, a pickle, and smiling hot-dog mouth.

But Peggy Charen isn't impressed. She praises Heinz's NEA grant but adds that she's worried about kids in the classroom "thinking much too long about ketchup. I don't want my grandchildren thinking ketchup is an important part of their lives." She wants Heinz to stop the commercial use of the children's artwork.

Your task: As consumer relations representatives for H.J. Heinz, your team (break up into groups of about four) has decided to jointly write a letter explaining to Ms. Charen that the three new labels are here to stay. Be sure to highlight the benefits of the contest (as you see them) along with the fact that your company is a strong supporter of art education.[29]

13. Of course they're ugly: Letter from Na-Na boutique refusing a claim over "unsightly" Doc Martens As manager of the trendy Na-Na boutique in Santa Monica, you've sold so many pairs of "Doc Martens"—the clunky, street-combat boots made by Dr. Marten—that your buyer can barely keep them in stock. Even your employees wear them because they're easy on the feet. They cater to comfort first and fashion not at all.

Ugly as Doc Martens are, you can't remember receiving a single customer complaint about the comfy boots until you received this unusual letter from Susan Stone of Ventura:

> Several months ago I purchased a pair of burgundy Doc Martens with black laces, after one of your salespeople convinced me that they're the most comfortable boots around. They look cool with both short and long skirts and with jeans. Then a week ago I got a job as a waitress at the Eggshell Café. After two days of eight-hour shifts, I figured I'd wear my Doc Martens and save what was left of my feet. I got fired. I argued with the manager, pointing out that she lets the girls wear whatever they want—miniskirts or leather or tank tops—but she said, "You're out of here." Why? Customer complaints about my "unsightly footwear."
>
> I was misled by your salesperson, who told me that Doc Martens can be worn anywhere in Los Angeles. I think I'm entitled to a full refund of the $116 that I paid for the boots, plus $1,200 compensation (a month's wages and tips) for losing my job over them.

Ms. Stone says she bought the boots "several months ago," so a full refund is out of the question. Besides, waitress dress codes in Los Angeles are liberal; since Stone had been on the job for only two days, you suspect that her manager used the boots as an excuse to fire an employee who simply wasn't capable. (It's unfortunate, but you know that some managers have difficulty telling fired employees the whole truth.) The fact that Ms. Stone makes no mention of a second chance to improve her wardrobe choice convinces you that she was actually fired for other reasons. In any case, the claim for job-loss compensation seems extreme for a shoe retailer, and you're not about to pay it. The boutique's owner agrees.

Your task: Write a letter to Susan Stone (235 W. Alameda, #42, Ventura, CA 93001) refusing her refund request and her claim for job-loss compensation. As a goodwill gesture, invite her to visit the store for a 20 percent discount on any of the other popular footwear the boutique sells.[30]

14. It's legal: Memo to Salem State College employee defending video surveillance Maybe it was bad employee relations, but it was legal. That's what your school's lawyers told you, as human resources director for Salem State College, after you passed along an angry memo from an employee in the college's Small Business Development Center (SBDC).

In her memo, Nancy Kim expressed her horror and outrage at discovering, too late, that when she slipped behind a divider after hours to change from her office attire into her jogging outfit for the trek home, she had been recorded on videotape by cameras installed in the department for security reasons. The SBDC houses a lot of expensive computer equipment, and your security department believed that the video surveillance was warranted; they had suspicions about a night intruder. However, no one informed the employees who work in the department that the cameras had been installed and were operating 24 hours a day. Your security department may have thought that was a good strategy for catching any dishonest employees red-handed, so to speak. But in light of what happened to Kim, it just seems like a rude and embarrassing misjudgment.

Kim has demanded an apology and $5,000 in damages for the indignity she suffered. Although she hasn't yet contacted her union representatives or a lawyer, she does hint that those will be her next steps. Your legal department insists she has no claim; employees relinquish their privacy rights the minute they step into the workplace. The only federal law limiting employer surveillance is the 1986 Electronic Communications Privacy Act, which prohibits employers from listening in on spoken personal conversations. Otherwise, they can tally phone numbers and call duration, videotape employees, and review e-mail, Internet access, and computer files. Only the state of Connecticut has passed a law also limiting employer surveillance in bathrooms and other areas designated for "health and personal comfort."

The college's attorneys have provided you with a copy of an article quoting Robert Ellis Smith, publisher of *Privacy Journal.* He says, "Employees are at the mercy of employers. . . . There is no protection in the workplace." According to the article, 63 percent of employers in an American Management Association survey of 900 midsize and large companies use some kind of employee surveillance, and 23 percent of them don't tell workers. Moreover, 16 percent use video cameras for their employee monitoring.

Legally, it sounds as if the college is in the right. But personally, you can't help but agree that Kim was wronged. Nevertheless, the legal department wants to discourage Kim from any form of litigation or pursuit of the case with her union representatives or the Massachusetts Labor Relations Committee. In hopes of downplaying the college's concern about the incident, the legal department wants you to handle the response. Go ahead and apologize, say the lawyers, but don't invite further action. This is not going to be easy, you think with a sigh.

Your task: Write an answering memo to Nancy Kim, denying her request for monetary compensation.[31]

15. A taxing matter: Letter from O&Y Tax Service refusing to pay for another's mistake During the mid-April rush at tax time last year, Hilda Black phoned to ask whether she could roll over funds from one retirement account into another without paying taxes on any gain. You answered that such a rollover was not considered a tax event, as long as the transaction was completed in 60 days. You also informed her that when she eventually draws out the funds to supplement her retirement income, she will pay taxes on the portion that represents interest earned on the account.

Today Ms. Black has phoned to say that she is being billed by the Internal Revenue Service for $1,309.72 in penalties and back interest because she failed to declare interest income earned when she cashed in "those bonds that I told you about last April." You explain that bonds are not the same thing as a retirement account. One difference, unfortunately, is that people are required to pay taxes the following April on any interest income or capital gains earned by cashing in bonds.

Your client is not satisfied. She demands "something in writing" to show to her lawyer. Her position is that you misled her, so you should pay the penalties and interest charges, which, of course, are getting larger every day. She is willing to pay the actual tax on the transaction.

Your task: Write to Hilda Black (622 N. Bank Lane, Park Forest, IL 60045), explaining why you are unwilling to pay the penalties and interest charges requested by the IRS. Your position should be that you have done nothing to make yourself vulnerable in this transaction.

16. Many happy returns: Letter from Cliffs Notes refusing a claim in a complicated transaction Like most other publishers, Cliffs Notes of Lincoln, Nebraska, gives full credit to any bookstore that returns unsold copies of its publications, provided that the books are received in salable condition within six months of their original shipment to the bookstore. The bookstore pays postage. Even though most large publishers have return rates of 30 to 50 percent, only about 6 percent of Cliffs Notes' 222 titles are returned.

Still, today's mail includes a large return from the University of Wyoming Bookstore, Laramie, WY 82071, containing the following:

21 copies, *Macbeth*
6 copies, *The Scarlet Letter*
12 copies, *Crime and Punishment*
5 copies, *Hamlet*

All the Cliffs Notes sell for a retail (or list) price of $9.95. Cliffs gives the bookstores a 40 percent discount off the list price.

The cover note from the University of Wyoming Bookstore indicates that 23 copies of *Macbeth* have been sent, but you count only 21. The carton has sustained some damage, but nothing appears to have spilled out. Five of the *Macbeth* booklets are worn to the extent that they cannot be resold. One copy of *Crime and Punishment* is water-stained and cannot be resold. One copy of *The Scarlet Letter* was damaged in shipping, from a combination of careless packing and rough handling in transit.

The shipment also includes four copies of *A Tale of Two Cities,* published by Monarch Notes, one of Cliffs Notes' competitors. Obviously, the company does not owe the bookstore anything for these booklets.

As a customer service representative for Cliffs Notes, you have decided to return the four copies of *A Tale of Two Cities* to the university bookstore (and charge them $2.20 for postage); to return the unsalable copies to them with an explanation; and to tell them that they shipped you only 21 copies, not 23 copies, of *Macbeth.*

Your task: Write a letter to the university explaining your decision.[32]

REFUSING TO EXTEND CREDIT

17. Grand finale: No credit for burials in space by Celestis "I know you'll understand my request," the letter began, "and I'm sure your company has enough money from its wealthy customers to cover my needs temporarily." For many businesses, such a letter might well mean a new customer, but for Celestis, Inc., of Houston, Texas, those words won't start a profitable relationship.

In the first place, this company's business is space burials, or rather, "space memorials." Celestis offers "grand finale" space voyages for a symbolic portion of a person's cremated remains: about a quarter of an ounce, or approximately 1 percent of the total.

By special arrangement with Orbital Sciences Corporation in Virginia, you are able to promise your customers a blast-off aboard a high-flying L-1011 jet, which releases a Pegasus rocket into the atmosphere. The rocket then lifts and releases a small satellite into orbit, containing 30 lipstick-sized ash capsules secured in a honeycomb arrangement. No, you won't scatter customers' ashes in space, nor do you release the $1\frac{1}{2}$-inch capsules

(cluttering space with debris). They remain on the satellite until it reenters and burns up in the earth's atmosphere, some 18 months to 10 years later.

The cost for this service is less than $5,000 per person—a bargain, when you think of the technology involved. So far, your most famous customers have been Gene Roddenberry (creator of the *Star Trek* television series), Timothy Leary (1960s LSD philosopher), and Gerald O'Neill (space colony advocate).

As a member of the Celestis marketing team, you think the concept is terrific and should be accessible to many people. But there's no way the company is going to offer credit for something like this. In fact, all arrangements for the Celestis space memorial must be paid for in advance.

Your task: Write a letter responding to Gerald C. Hertsbacher's request for credit, tactfully explaining why you cannot grant it. He resides at 9760 Sepulveda Blvd., Apt. R, Sherman Oaks, CA 91403).[33]

18. Cash for celebrities: Credit refusal from Stylefile "Of all the nerve," exclaims Elizabeth Harrison, co-owner of Stylefile, a New York public relations agency. "We can put celebrities into the front row of any fashion show in the world—but not on credit!" She tosses the credit request from a relatively obscure designer on your desk, shaking her head in disgust. "Tell him to find an L.A. agency—or maybe one from Peoria. We don't need his business."

We might not need his business now, you think, but today's unknown fashion designer can rise to great heights in no time. After all, even Donna Karan, Todd Oldham, and Jean-Paul Gaultier were nobodies once upon a time. And their current fame could as easily evaporate if they don't play the game right. In the fashion world, playing the game means having famous faces at every show, and seeing that famous faces appear at shows is how the 32-year-old Harrison and her 25-year-old partner, Lara Shriftman, earn their huge fees. Stylefile specializes in "celebrity hunting," luring stars to fashion shows to lend glitz, glamour, and media buzz.

The tactic never fails. For instance, when Harrison snagged rock star/actress Courtney Love to fly to New York for a big-name designer's show the same year Love was nominated for an Oscar, the lead story in *Women's Wear Daily* the following Monday made more fuss over Love's appearance than over the clothes in question.

Armed with their database of 10,000 publicists, managers, agents, and celebrities, Harrison and Shriftman have seen plenty of action. The fee for landing an A-list celebrity like Love, Nicole Kidman, or Leonardo DiCaprio, could easily be as high as $3,000 per star—payable in advance, of course (about $750 for B-list names). Some fashion designers simply keep Stylefile on retainer, which helps Harrison and Shriftman cover expenses for their coast-to-coast flights, late-night dinners at expensive restaurants, designer clothing, parties in Southhampton, stretch limos, and gifts that keep celebrities and their publicists happy and willing to cooperate when Stylefile calls with a request. In return for attending a show, celebrities usually receive free transportation, accommodations, clothing, and, infrequently, some spending money or a trip to the designer's private boutique.

You gaze at the letterhead. Franklin Desuaro. Could be famous someday. Too bad Stylefile can't give him a break; it's his first show and he's only asking for B-list names. He'll be competing against all the other fall shows and probably won't attract much attention unless Hollywood looks interested. But you know Harrison's rules. Once the lights go down and the reviews come out, it's too easy to forget about paying Stylefile for those glamorous faces in the crowd. So no celebrities on credit.

Your task: As Harrison's executive assistant, write a letter for her signature to Mr. Desuaro (836 W. 37th Street, New York, NY 10018) explaining Stylefile's no-credit policy.[34]

19. No more advances: Memo outlining Banc One policy against IRS refund loans A few years ago, Banc One in Columbus, Ohio, joined several banking institutions in offering its customers "IRS refund loans." These loans allowed customers to borrow against their income tax refunds before actually receiving them. As part of the loan agreement, the Internal Revenue Service would send refunds directly to the bank to pay off the loans.

To get such a loan, customers had to file electronic tax returns, making use of newly implemented IRS technology. Once the computerized return was filed, the IRS responded with immediate confirmation of any refund due the taxpayer, and the bank made its loan on the basis of the IRS-verified amount, which would later be repaid directly to the bank. It seemed a foolproof system—until an IRS programming error started creating problems with tax returns from all over the country.

The first year the problem emerged, the IRS was forced to apologize for errors that added up to $3 million in mistakenly confirmed refunds. Banc One lost some money on uncollected loans, but not much. The second year, IRS errors during one 17-day period totaled nearly $40 million, so Banc One cashed out of the IRS refund loan business. Too risky, bank executives decided. If the IRS confirmed a refund that wasn't forthcoming, the bank could be left with an unsecured balance due that the customer might not be able to pay. Collection costs alone could cause the once-secure loans to become highly unprofitable for the bank.

Although news reports have quoted IRS officials as stating that the computer glitch has been corrected, Banc One executives remain firm in their decision to suspend the refund loan program. The only exceptions will be made under special circumstances involving long-term customers with exemplary credit records and with whom the bank has had prior lending experience, so even if the IRS should err in confirming the refund amount, the bank could feel confident that the customer would be able to repay the loan. The bank's advertisements no longer promote the refund loans, but bank officers are expecting to receive numerous requests from customers wanting to borrow against their tax refunds during the first few months of next year.

Your task: As communications director, you have been asked to issue a memo to all branch managers and credit officers, informing them of the bank's new policy. Rather than write a detailed memo of explanation, you decide to include in your memo a model form letter that branch managers can send to customers explaining the policy change.[35]

REFUSING TO WRITE RECOMMENDATION LETTERS

20. Geek Squad fake: He never worked for us Ever since *Newsweek, People,* and the *Wall Street Journal* made a big fuss over the Geek Squad—Minneapolis's 24-hour, "on-site, rapid response computer task force" support consultants—the squad has received some strange correspondence. But the letter on your desk right now makes you think you might be dealing with downright fraud. It's a request for a job reference regarding an individual claiming he was once a member of the Geek Squad. But no one on the team has ever heard of him; this "Sammy Stanton" has obviously lied to his potential employer, Computer Savvy.

Well, you can almost understand why. You've been working on the Squad yourself for only a few months, and it was quite a coup to land the job as "special agent" for the colorful company. Although the computer support firm is only four years old and your boss ("Chief Inspector" Robert Stephens) is only 28, the flair with which he does business has not escaped notice, to say the least. Now pulling in over half a million a year, the company has more than 2,500 clients, including 3M, General Mills, IBM, Cargill, Twentieth Century Fox, and Warner Brothers. You suspect they fell in love with the whole concept: a team of ten computer geeks in signature black suits, white socks, and fedoras, carrying official "Geek Squad" badges and pulling up for a corporate house call, "Ghostbusters" style, in one of the company's black retrofitted ice cream trucks or the 1958 Simca that Stephens is so proud of. Even the company's Web site (http://www.geeksquad.com) is a cool configuration of dossiers for every "special agent," stamped "Top Secret" and complete with front and side view mug shots.

Naturally, Hollywood and the New York publishing houses have come calling. Movie deals, book deals, and even a radio program are in the works. Not bad for a guy who (according to Stephens's dossier) dropped a scholarship from the Art Institute of Chicago to study computer science. He wound up researching virtual reality flight simulators for the Navy and the FAA before starting his consulting company with $200 and lots of imagination.

Now that you think about it, this whole *Dragnet* meets *Ghostbusters* thing may have been a form of artistic expression for Stephens, and the fact that team members are incredibly computer savvy may have been a mere bonus . . . Computer Savvy—Got to finish that letter about Sammy Stanton right away, because out there in the mean city is a computer about to break down, and you know who they're gonna call . . .

Your task: Dash off a quick response to Rosalie Sherman, personnel manager at Computer Savvy (6501 Cathy Avenue N.E., Albuquerque, New Mexico, 87109-3643), explaining that "Sammy Stanton" is no friend to the Geek Squad. Then flip your two-way back on and let 'em know you're ready for the next assignment.[36]

REJECTING JOB APPLICATIONS

21. Try ladybugs: Letter rejecting an application at Fluker Farms cricket ranch It seemed almost like a joke to Richard Fluker back in 1953 when a co-worker invited him to buy into a cricket ranch in Port Allen, Louisiana. Back then, $300 was nothing to sneeze at. But Fluker thought it over and finally agreed to give it a go; after all, crickets were good fishing bait, and fishing was a long-entrenched Louisiana pastime.

Surely the elder Fluker didn't know then that the company he passed on to his son, David Fluker, would one day be looking at a balance sheet showing upwards of $6 million in annual sales. That's not only from crickets, mind you. Fluker Farms has grown along with a general interest in pets (particularly reptiles). The company now ships live crickets, mealworms, and iguanas to pet stores, zoos, and universities around the world, and it has also moved into "dry goods" (as in freeze-dried crickets), as well as reptile leashes and other accessories. Fluker Farms even markets chocolate-covered crickets for brave humans—a big hit at trade shows, especially when the samplers get an 'I Ate A Bug' club button.

But Fluker Farms is no joke, and the number of applicants who want to work for you has increased as the business has grown. As human resources manager for the company, it's your job to screen them.

Last week you interviewed about a dozen candidates for a job in research and development. The company is looking for other bugs it can profit from, testing them as pet food and evaluating their "shelf-life" potential in both live and freeze-dried forms. With pet stores expanding into superstores, the demand for new food varieties is also growing. So the researcher you hire has to understand the feeding habits of reptiles and birds, must be acquainted with insect life cycles, and must possess the kind of imagination that can come up with a new idea and figure out how to make it profitable. That's not an easy spot to fill.

Your task: The candidates you saw all carried excellent credentials, every one of them with multiple degrees and a research background. But only one, Maria Richter, had the right personality for Fluker Farms: the combination of imagination, knowledge, and resourcefulness you're looking for. In addition, she has five years of reptile research, a doctorate in zoology, and a bachelor's degree in marketing. Now you have the onerous task of writing rejection letters to the other candidates. Start with a letter to Werner Speker, whom you liked personally but whose postgraduate work has been mostly with felines, not reptiles. He's at 4265 Broadview Road, Baton Rouge, LA 70815.[37]

HANDLING BAD NEWS ABOUT COMPANY OPERATIONS OR PERFORMANCE

22. Piercing policy: Memo announcing a new dress code at Yo' Bagel You and your spouse loved the first Yo' Bagel shop—those cute logos you dreamed up, the clever recipes, the friendly conversations with regulars who swung in for a slug of coffee and a bagel on the way to work. It was fun, even if the hours were long. Then you added a second shop.

Now you're stuck behind a desk, swamped with food-ordering puzzles (how many tubs of mayo can two bagel shops use in a week? No, make that *this* week—early autumn, no summer crowds . . .), and the phone's ringing again. You know it's the manager of your second store, and you know what she wants. But your attorney says put it in writing first. You sigh as the voice mail picks up the call.

Last week the manager, Mary Bledgewick, cornered you with an urgent plea for help. One of her 16-year-old, after-school employees came in with a pierced tongue, and her customers are "grossed out and complaining."

"I don't know what to tell her," Mary explained. "There must be discrimination laws we shouldn't violate, but customers tell me they can't look at that pierced tongue and think about eating. And frankly, I can't either. Just yesterday, a man stomped out in disgust and called me later to say he'd never eat here again. Should I fire her? Is that legal? She's a sweet girl, though, and a good worker, and at least when she's behind the counter, customers can't see the pierced—"

"That's fine, Mary," you interrupted, shuddering. "I'll look into it."

Your attorney, who refers to piercing as "facial jewelry" and tattoos as "body art," says this type of "exotic adornment and accessorizing" is becoming common. You can't tell your employees not to pierce, but you can prescribe what they wear on the job, as long as the dress code is "not discriminatory." What does that mean? you ask her. She replies that you can legally base your piercing policy on image requirements or safety concerns, but if safety isn't the issue, you'd better allow employees as much self-expression as you—and your customers—can stand. "Keep in mind," she smiles at you, "the girl with the pierced tongue can probably remove the jewelry, even if the thought makes us cringe. And don't forget to prescribe a policy for tattoos, too."

Your task: Write a memo outlining a new dress code policy for Yo' Bagel employees. Of course they can wear clean, neatly pressed shorts or slacks and collar-type shirts in any color. But you'll allow only five earrings at once, and one small nose ring. If they have tattoos, politely suggest they cover them up with clothing. Treat the memo as "bad news" for existing employees; they may not be happy with your new "guidelines."[38]

---

23. Kids are like that: Bad news from Crayola research For six months, you've been working in Binney & Smith's product development department, and in that time, you've probably smelled more Crayolas than you did throughout your entire childhood. Who can forget that distinctive waxy smell? But if all goes well, the next generation will be remembering something far different. Your Magic Scent Crayolas will make sure of that.

The idea for scented crayons isn't new; before you joined the company, Binney & Smith released the first Magic Scent crayons with much hoopla. They quickly flopped. Even though company tests proved otherwise, parents were convinced their kids would try to eat the lusciously fragrant coconut-scented white, bubblegum pink, and chocolate brown. They refused to buy the new food-scented crayons.

But Binney & Smith didn't give up on what you all agreed was a great idea. As a researcher, you've been helping develop new "magic scents": familiar fragrances parents won't fear and kids will still recognize and enjoy, such as Leather Jacket brown and Shampoo pink.

This morning, you have a focus group of a dozen 4- to 11-year-olds set up in the laboratory, each with a selection of unlabeled crayons laid out before them in rainbow order. Parents are hovering in the background, and the videotape is rolling. Just to be sure you get everything down, you've stationed assistants with notebooks all around the table.

"Okay, kids," you announce to quiet the commotion. "Let's all sniff the first crayon, the brown one. What does it smell like to you?"

"Baloney samwich," a little redhead blurts out. "Nah—dead worms!" shouts a boy with an earring. "Smells like paint to me," a girl in plaid says softly. The two four-year-olds nod in agreement.

Well, okay, so Leather Jacket is a little off the mark. Bravely you proceed. By the end of the morning, you know that Cedar Chest smells like "dog doo," "fire," and "DNA"; Shampoo reminded them of "dead flowers"; and New Car struck their little noses as "pollution," "California," and "a vacuum cleaner." Your personal favorite, Lilac, reminded them of "mothballs," while Eucalyptus brought shouts of "cigarettes!" The kids had great fun; your stomach is churning. Not a single child correctly identified any of the fragrances the research team has been working on for months.

Your boss has been busy out of town with another project, but he's expecting you to fax him a memo ASAP describing the results of this morning's test. Maybe after your stomach settles you can find some positive perspective to temper the dismal news.

Your task: Write the memo to Kevin Lee, manager of product research, for faxing to San Francisco. Briefly explain the test results and request hosting an additional focus group to provide some more "useful" information—you hope![39]

---

24. Missed target: "Bad news" poll results at the *Journal of the American Medical Association* The distinguished *Journal of the American Medical Association* isn't looking so distinguished this week. As a staff editor, you've been "privileged" with an early peek at a reader survey that's sure to rock some egos.

Your subscribers, mostly practicing physicians, were asked to choose topics they'd prefer to read about from a list of 73. They gave high ranks to subjects such as alternative medicine, health tips for travel, heart disease, obesity, children's health, advances in critical care, and malpractice liability—the kinds of things their patients ask about.

At an ordinary magazine, such detailed audience feedback would be greeted with enthusiasm by editors, who'd use them as valuable insights to steer the magazine. But publishing at a professional journal is worlds away from the way it is at popular magazines.

Subjects have always been proposed by the *Journal*'s panel of experts. The articles are written by scientists who are conducting research, and then the articles are subjected to peer review before they're accepted for publication. It's the traditional method for publishing scientific papers to let the world know what's happening on the cutting edge. But now it appears that the *Journal*'s experts have been too far out of touch. Have they been suggesting topics based on their knowledge of current research projects rather than on knowledge of audience interest?

Ranking the same list of topics, your "experts" put alternative medicine at number 68, whereas your readers ranked it at number 7. The health aspects of travel were considered even less important by the experts, who ranked it 69th, while readers ranked it 27th. The two groups agreed on only three topics: both ranked managed care, death and dying, and genetics in the top ten.

"What are you going to do?" you ask managing editor George Lundberg.

"I'm going to publish these results, and I'm also going to put out a call for some new articles. I think this item will look good right next to the article by Krimsky and Rothenberg of Tufts and UCLA—the one suggesting that our researcher/authors should disclose their financial interests in their field of research."

Medical research is often funded by drug companies looking for products to market. Whether this funding biases researchers toward their underwriters' viewpoint or allows them to benefit humanity is a hotly debated issue. So publishing the poll results in the same issue of the *Journal*—well, Lundberg has guts, you think admiringly.

"We'll devote the whole issue to ethics," he muses aloud. Then he turns to you with a wicked gleam in his eye, "Meanwhile, you're going to write a memo to our panel of experts, informing them about the survey results. Promise them we'll be meeting with them very soon to discuss some changes."

Your task: Write a memo to the advisory panel members, to be signed by you. Be sure to include the following facts as well as the survey results: (1) You were surprised by the results, (2) you think the reader's opinions are logical and have merit, (3) you're ready for a change, (4) you want to keep faithful subscribers happy, and (5) you'd like to meet with the panel members to discuss this further.[40]

---

25. From junk to robots: E-mail message explaining delay and requesting more money For decades, scientists have worked to make the perfect robot: intelligent, sophisticated, and capable of multiple functions. You believe that creating such robots would be too expensive and too complex. Working at Los Alamos National Laboratory in Los Alamos, New Mexico, you use parts from discarded tape players, worn-out toasters, and Casio watches to fabricate small one-task robots. Your goal is to make robots that are cheap and reliable.

Borrowing movement designs from nature, you built the Solar Spinner to resemble a light-seeking tarantula. Dangled by wires before a window, it wanders over the entire surface as it tries to gobble up more sunshine. Because four tiny brushes are attached to its legs, it cleans windows on its way.

Funded by a grant from the U.S. Army Research Lab at White Sands Missile Range, you are attempting to build a prototype for a robot that can unearth land mines, bombs, and other explosives. Such robots could clear the minefields that continue to maim civilians in previously war-torn countries such as Vietnam, Afghanistan, and Bosnia.

Although you've been working tirelessly for six months on the Mine Sweeper prototype, the desert heat and sandy terrain have slowed the project by six months. Indoors, the Mine Sweeper works just great, but when you get it outside, the sand gets into the mechanisms, locking up the hardware. And the other day 130-degree heat melted the microtape backup system.

The good news is that your team has figured out some solutions to these problems. You think that encasing the robots' joints with elastic plastic will prevent any ground contamination, and putting in a fan should keep the backup system from melting. You'd also like to reprogram the self-check system to detect heat or sand contamination. The bad news is, these solutions will take about six months and cost roughly $225,000.

Your task: You are robot designer Mark Tilden. Write an e-mail message to Chuck Wullenjohn at White Sands Missile Range WullenjohnC@WSMR.army.mil to let him know that the project will need additional funding of $225,000 and an extension of at least six months. Remember to use a positive approach, and inform Wullenjohn that your grant amendment will be ready for his review next week.[41]

9

CHAPTER

WRITING PERSUASIVE MESSAGES

AFTER STUDYING THIS CHAPTER, YOU WILL BE ABLE TO

1 List the components of a well-developed persuasive message
2 Discuss several ways to establish credibility in persuasive messages
3 Describe the AIDA organizational plan for persuasive messages
4 List several tools that help reinforce your position in a persuasive message
5 Discuss four common mistakes people make when putting together persuasive arguments
6 Identify some of the key ingredients of a good persuasive claim or request for adjustment

COMMUNICATION CLOSE-UP AT AT&T'S LANGUAGE LINE SERVICES

His wife was giving birth, and he didn't know what to do, so the anxious father-to-be dialed 911. Trouble was, he spoke no English, and the operator couldn't understand what the emergency was. Neither party panicked, however; the 911 operator simply dialed an 800 number that connected her to AT&T's Language Line Services. In minutes, the AT&T operator set up a three-way call with a Spanish interpreter who helped talk the worried husband through the delivery of his first child.

As sales director for Language Line Services, Jeanne Anderson has collected dozens of true-life stories like this, and they all illustrate the same thing: the benefits of dialing a toll-free number from any telephone and being connected at a moment's notice with an interpreter in any of 140 languages—24 hours a day. Whereas the average day rate for an on-site interpreter is $500 to $700, AT&T's service costs from $1.00 to $3.50 per minute. Over-the-phone interpreters have closed a $12 million business deal in Taiwan, handled a marriage proposal in Russia, located a missing parent in Germany, translated an argument between a husband and wife, and helped hundreds of nurses, doctors, police officers, and business executives communicate with the diverse populations in their own local communities.

Jeanne Anderson

After years of experience writing persuasive messages to help sell Language Line Services, Anderson has developed a few principles she always follows. She had to; as the anecdotes convey, the list of Language Line benefits is long. Just enumerating all the languages and dialects offered—from Asian Fukienese to African Lingala—would fill up a page. Anderson could easily mention so many applications and benefits that a potential customer would be overwhelmed—and unmoved. So she has learned to be selective and to target a persuasive message directly to an audience's needs. Her goal is not to manipulate readers but to help them make an intelligent, informed decision about her message. Of course, she also makes sure she highlights specific benefits that she knows her audience will find attractive.

To persuade potential customers to try Language Line Services, Jeanne Anderson finds out who her audience is and what they're interested in. Then she crafts her letters to get attention, create interest, encourage desire, and motivate action. Whether working as an executive crafting letters to potential clients or as an operator serving current customers, employees of Language Line Services have strong communication skills and use them constantly.

Anderson follows the same principles when writing persuasive memos to her staff or composing persuasive e-mail messages. She says the only difference is in the language and tone. "When I write an internal memo, I try to make sure that my personality comes out. I think all the same principles apply, though, because you really are competing for time with each employee. You want to make your message interesting, and you don't want to make it too long, so that people will have time to read it."

For every persuasive message, Anderson starts by answering two questions that any persuasive writer must ask: "Who is my audience, and what are they going to be interested in?" Once she knows the answers, she starts her message with what she calls a "grabber," or attention-getter, designed specifically for this particular audience. Her next paragraphs build her credibility, create interest, and encourage desire by emphasizing benefits she knows her readers care about. Depending on the nature of the message, Anderson's final paragraph will be some form of "call to action," which may be as simple as "Please respond to this request before Thursday." If she can tie that request to a final "grabber," or benefit, and make it easy for the reader to respond (by including her phone number, extension, or e-mail address), she knows she's written a winning message.

"You really do want to keep it simple," Anderson says, whether your audience is an outside client or a fellow employee. "Even if the first paragraph is interesting, your reader may think, 'Gee, there's just too much detail here. I'll just read this later when I have more time,' and unfortunately, it gets put on that pile—that 'To Do' pile that never gets done!" To keep it simple, Anderson avoids showy language, unfamiliar words, and AT&T lingo. She chooses active words and phrases that are "crisp and succinct," using the terminology of her audience's own industry when appropriate. Moreover, she always stresses the positive—for example, saying to a potential customer, "This service will save you time," instead of "We know you don't have a lot of time."

Anderson's using her own skills with language to help others discover a new way to conquer language barriers—if not to save a life, then to make life simpler for everyone.[1] ■

PLANNING PERSUASIVE MESSAGES

Persuasion is the process of changing people's attitudes or influencing their actions.

Savvy businesspeople like Jeanne Anderson know that work today gets done in an environment where people don't just ask "What should I do?" but "Why should I do it?" That's why Anderson often employs **persuasion**—the attempt to change an audience's attitudes, beliefs, or actions—to accomplish her goals.[2] Simply put, effective persuasion is the ability to present a message in a way that makes readers or listeners feel they have a choice and makes them choose to agree.[3]

Within an organization you may write persuasive messages to
- Sell an idea
- Request a favor
- Gather support
- Request funding for a project

Although most business messages are routine, some circumstances require messages designed to motivate or persuade others. Within an organization, for example, individuals may write persuasive messages to sell a supervisor on an idea for cutting costs, to suggest more efficient operating procedures, to elicit cooperation from competing departments, to win employee support for a new benefits package, to request money for new equipment or funding for a special project, or to request a favor.

Similarly, a variety of messages directed to people outside the organization require persuasive techniques. For example, many persuasive messages are written to request favors, adjustments, or information or to solicit funds and cooperation. In fact, an external persuasive message is one of the most difficult tasks you could undertake. For one thing, people are busy, so they're reluctant to do something new, especially if it takes time and offers no guarantee of any reward in return. For another, competing requests are plentiful. In fact, the public relations departments of many large corporations receive so many persuasive requests for donations to worthy causes that they must sometimes resort to lotteries to decide which to support.

Persuasive requests encounter two problems:
- They frequently offer nothing tangible in return.
- There are many competing requests.

Nevertheless, the most effective leaders have a knack for putting together a persuasive argument. They know how to take the pulse of a group and communicate with people in terms they can understand and embrace.[4] So whether you're selling real estate or just trying to sell your idea to your boss, writing effective persuasive messages is an important skill that will help you get ahead in today's competitive marketplace.

Unlike routine requests (discussed in Chapter 7), persuasive messages aim to influence audiences who are inclined to resist. As a result, persuasive messages are generally longer, are more detailed, and depend heavily on strategic planning—like that carried out by Jeanne Anderson of AT&T's Language Line Services. As with routine messages, you begin a persuasive message by analyzing your audience, considering cultural differences, and choosing between the direct and indirect approaches. With persuasive messages, however, in addition to communicating your main idea and reasons, you need to motivate your audience to do something. To do so, you must establish your credibility, carefully frame your arguments, choose your appeal, and reinforce your position when developing your message.

Analyzing Your Audience

Appeal to the specific needs of your audience.

Chapter 4 introduced you to the basics of audience analysis. Getting ready to persuade can take weeks—even months—as you learn about your audience and the position you intend to argue. That's because everyone's needs differ, and people will respond differently to any given message. Not everyone is interested in economy, for instance, or fair play; as a matter of fact, some people's innermost needs make appeals to status and greed much more effective.

The best persuasive messages are closely connected to your audience's existing desires and interests.[5] To accommodate these individual differences, analyze your audience and then construct a message that appeals to their needs. Begin by considering these important questions: Who is my audience? What do I want them to do? How might they resist? What are

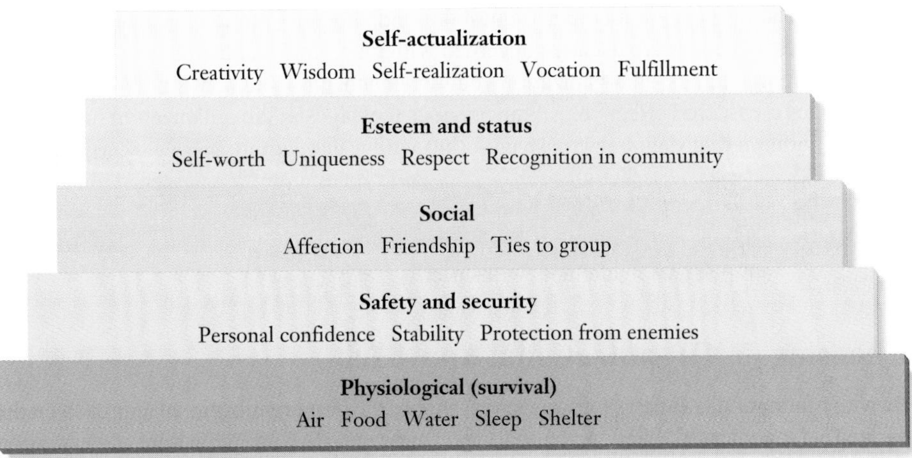

Figure 9.1
Maslow's Hierarchy of Needs

their needs? Are there alternative positions I need to examine? How will my credibility affect the message? What does the decision maker consider the most important issue? How might the organization's culture influence my strategy?

Questions to ask before you begin to write a persuasive message:

- Who is my audience?
- What do I want them to do?
- How might they resist?
- What alternative positions should I examine?
- How will my credibility affect my message?

Some theorists believe that certain needs have priority. Figure 9.1 represents psychologist Abraham Maslow's hierarchy of needs, with the most basic needs appearing at the bottom of the figure. Maslow suggested that only after lower-level needs have been met will a person seek to fulfill needs on higher levels.[6] For example, suppose you supervise someone who consistently arrives late for work. You must either persuade him to change or fire him. First, find out why he's coming in late. Is he oversleeping because he has a second job to support his family (a safety and security need)? Is he coming in late because of a misguided desire to have people notice his arrival (an esteem and status need)? Once you've analyzed the need motivating him to arrive late, you can craft an appeal, a "hook" that will interest him in your message about changing his behavior. If the need for safety and security is behind his tardiness, you might begin by saying, "Your job is very important to you, I know." If he craves esteem and status, you could say, "You've always seemed interested in being given more responsibility, perhaps even a promotion."

To assess various individual needs, you can refer to specific information such as **demographics** (the age, gender, occupation, income, education, and other quantifiable characteristics of the people you're trying to persuade) and **psychographics** (the psychological characteristics of an individual, such as personality, attitudes, and lifestyle). In addition, both types of information are strongly influenced by culture. When analyzing your audience, take into account their cultural expectations and practices so that you don't undermine your persuasive message by using an inappropriate appeal or by organizing your message in a way that seems unfamiliar or uncomfortable to the audience.

Demographics include characteristics such as age, gender, occupation, income, and education.

Psychographics include characteristics such as personality, attitudes, and lifestyle.

Considering Cultural Differences

Cultural differences influence your persuasion attempts.

Your understanding and respect for cultural differences will not only help you satisfy the needs of audience members but will also help them respect you. That's because persuasion is different in different cultures. For example, in France, using an aggressive, hard-sell technique is no way to win respect from your audience. In fact, such an approach would probably antagonize your audience. In Germany, where people tend to focus on technical matters, plan on verifying any figures you use for support, and make sure they are exact. In Sweden, audiences tend to focus on theoretical questions and strategic implications, whereas in the United States audiences are usually concerned with more practical matters.[7]

Every message written for a corporation adds to the corporate tradition.

As with individuals, an organization's culture or subculture heavily influences the types of messages considered effective. All the previous messages in the organization have established a tradition that define persuasive writing within that culture. If you accept and use these traditions, you are essentially establishing one type of common ground with your audience, and you will be rewarded by being accepted into the corporate culture. If you never learn these traditions or if you reject them, you'll have difficulty achieving that common ground, and your persuasion attempts will suffer.

Choosing an Organizational Approach

Use the indirect approach when your audience will react unfavorably to your message. Use the direct approach when your message is long or complex, or when your reader prefers directness.

As with routine and bad-news messages, you choose the best organizational approach on the basis of your audience's likely reaction to your message. Because the nature of persuasion is to convince your audience or to change their attitudes, beliefs, or actions, you'll use the indirect organizational pattern for most persuasive messages. That is, you'll want to explain your reasons and build interest before revealing your purpose.

However, if your audience is objective or if you know that they prefer to hear the "bottom line" first (perhaps because it will save them time), the direct approach might be the better choice. In addition, you'll want to use the direct approach when the corporate culture encourages directness or if your message is long or complex (your reader may become impatient if the main idea is buried seven pages later).

If you're using the direct approach, as Bette McGiboney does in Figure 9.2, keep in mind that even though your audience may be easy to convince, you'll still want to include at least a brief justification or explanation. In other words, don't expect your reader to accept your idea on blind faith. Consider this:

POOR	IMPROVED
I recommend building our new retail outlet on the West Main Street site.	After comparing the four possible sites for our new retail outlet, I recommend West Main Street as the only site that fulfills our criteria for visibility, proximity to mass transportation, and square footage.

Your position relative to your audience's within an organization influences which approach you should use in your persuasive message.

Your amount of authority, expertise, or power in an organization also influences how you organize persuasive messages. Say you are a first-line manager. When writing a persuasive message to top management, you may try to be diplomatic and use an indirect approach—which could backfire if some managers perceive your indirectness as manipulative and time wasting. On the other hand, you may consciously try to save your supervisors time by using a direct approach—with the danger being that some might perceive your directness as brash and presumptuous. Similarly, when writing a persuasive message to employees, you may try to ease into a major change by persuading with an indirect approach, but they might perceive your indirect approach as weak or even wishy-washy. In short, you need to think carefully about your corporate culture and what your audience expects before selecting your approach.

DEVELOPING YOUR PERSUASIVE MESSAGES

Whether you use the direct or the indirect approach, you must convince the reader that your request or idea is reasonable. Effective persuasion involves four distinct and essential components: establishing credibility, framing your arguments in a way that identifies common

Bette McGiboney is administrative assistant to the athletic director of Auburn University. Each year, after season tickets have been mailed, the cost of the athletic department's toll-free number skyrockets as fans call to complain about their seats or about receiving the wrong number of tickets or to order last-minute tickets. The August phone bill is usually over $3,000, in part because each customer is put on hold while operators serve others. McGiboney has an idea that may solve the problem.

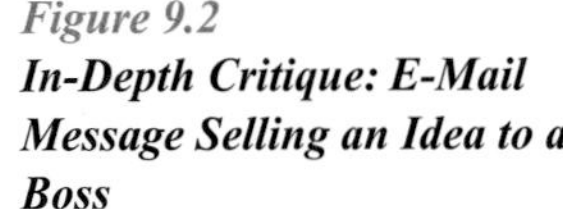

Figure 9.2
In-Depth Critique: E-Mail Message Selling an Idea to a Boss

E-Mail

Date: Wednesday, 22 July 2000, 3:44:05
X-Sender: mcgibon@ath.auburn.edu
To: housel@ath.auburn.edu
From: "Bette McGiboney" mcgibon@ath.auburn.edu
Subject: Savings on toll-free number

Dear David:

As you know, our billing for the toll-free number coming into the ticket office usually runs at least $3,000 for the month of August, compared with an average of $493 for the other eleven months. Tiger fans who call in August usually have at least a five-minute wait on hold. Here's an idea that will not only save us money but also help us manage our time and better serve our fans.

Under this plan, callers will hear the same messages and be offered the same options as before. However, if an operator isn't available when a caller presses "0" for ticket information, a new message will request a name and phone number so that we can return the call within the next two business days.

I estimate that reducing the on-hold time could eliminate at least $2,000 from our August bill (based on a conversation with Tandy Robertson, our AT&T representative). The good news is that the idea costs nothing and can be implemented immediately. We can use quiet times of the day to return phone calls, thus spreading our work more evenly.

I've discussed the idea informally with our operators, and they would like to try it. After football season, we can use our fall interns to call a random selection of customers to see how they liked the new message system. The plan will help us in the following ways:

- Provide better customer service
- Help us manage our time and stress levels
- Save us money on our toll-free line

I've attached a sheet with possible wording for the new message. Please let me know by the end of the month whether you'd like to give this a try.

Thanks,

Bette

This message follows the direct organizational plan. The attention-getter is the main idea (a new plan for handling phone calls from fans). The writer uses the subject line to announce that the proposal will save money.

The next paragraph explains how the new plan will work, creating more interest in the idea.

The third and fourth paragraphs create desire by presenting supporting evidence such as cost savings, and the bulleted benefits draw the reader to the meat of the message.

The last paragraph is a simple and direct request for action within a specific time frame. It also takes care of a chore that might have caused the reader to delay.

ground with your audience, connecting with the audience by using appeals to logic or emotions, and reinforcing your position with vivid language and compelling evidence. The amount of detail you include in each of these components varies proportionately with the complexity of your idea or request.

Establishing Your Credibility

Your credibility is defined by how reliable, believable, and trustworthy you are.

The first hurdle you must overcome is to persuade a skeptical or hostile audience that you know what you're talking about and that you're not trying to mislead them. Your **credibility** is your capability of being believed because you're reliable and worthy of confidence. Without such credibility, your efforts to persuade will seem manipulative. Research strongly suggests that most managers overestimate their own credibility—considerably.[8]

Gain credibility by supporting your argument with facts such as testimonials, documents, guarantees, statistics, and research results.

One of the best ways to gain credibility is to support your message with facts. Testimonials, documents, guarantees, statistics, research results, and the like all provide seemingly objective evidence for what you have to say, so they add to your credibility. The more specific and relevant your proof, the better. Another good way to improve your credibility is to name your sources, especially if they're respected by your audience. Still other ways of gaining credibility include:

Your credibility is improved if you are an expert, enthusiastic, objective, sincere, and trustworthy and if your intentions are good and you establish common ground.

- *Being an expert.* Your knowledge of your message's subject area (or even of some other area) helps you give your audience the quality information necessary to make a decision.
- *Being enthusiastic.* Your excitement about the subject of your message can infect your audience.
- *Being objective.* Your understanding of and willingness to acknowledge all sides of an issue help you present fair and logical arguments in your persuasive message.
- *Being sincere.* Your honesty, genuineness, good faith, and truthfulness help you focus on your audience's needs.
- *Being trustworthy.* Your honesty and dependability help you earn your audience's respect.
- *Having good intentions.* Your willingness to keep your audience's best interests at heart helps you create persuasive messages that are ethical.
- *Establishing common ground.* Those beliefs, attitudes, and background experiences that you have in common with members of your audience will help them identify with you.

Remember, credibility is a process. It takes time to earn it.

Part of Carol Browner's job as head of the Environmental Protection Agency (EPA) is to persuade interest groups that the policies established by the agency are a result of thorough investigation, research, and public input. To accomplish this, Browner supports her persuasive messages with facts and sources. This demonstrates her knowledge and establishes her credibility.

Framing Your Arguments

Once you have gathered enough facts, evidence, and sources to establish your credibility, you're ready to frame your arguments. Most persuasive messages follow the **AIDA** organizational plan, which has four phases: (1) attention, (2) interest, (3) desire, and (4) action (see Table 9.1).

Organize persuasive messages using the AIDA plan:
- Attention
- Interest
- Desire
- Action

- *Attention.* In the attention phase, you convince your audience right at the beginning that you have something useful or interesting to say. Make your opening sentence brief and engaging, without making extravagant claims or threats and without bringing up irrelevant points (see Figure 9.3). Introduce the audience to the problem or idea that makes them want to hear what you have to say. Your audience will want to know "What's in this message for me?" so find some common ground or points of agreement on which to build your case.

Begin every persuasive message with an attention-getting statement that is
- Personalized
- "You" oriented
- Straightforward
- Relevant

- *Interest.* In the interest phase, you explain the relevance of your message to the audience. Continuing the theme that you started with, you paint a more detailed picture with words. Your goal is to get the audience thinking, "This is an interesting idea; could it possibly solve my problems?" In Figure 9.3, the interest section ties together a factual description and the benefits of instituting the new recycling plan. Also, the benefits are related specifically to the attention phase that precedes this section.

In the interest section
- Continue the opening theme in greater detail
- Relate benefits specifically to the attention-getter

- *Desire.* In the desire phase of a persuasive message, you make the audience want to change by explaining how the change will benefit them. You reduce resistance by thinking of questions your audience might have and answering them in advance. If your idea is complex, explain how you would implement it. Also, by backing up claims, you increase your audience's willingness to take the action that you'll suggest in the next section. Remember, whatever evidence you use to prove your claim, make sure it's directly relevant to your point.

In the desire section
- Provide evidence to prove your claim
- Draw attention to any enclosures

- *Action.* In the action phase, you suggest the action you want your audience to take. All persuasive messages end with a section that urges specific action, but the ending is more than a statement such as "Institute this program as soon as possible" or "Send me a refund." In fact, this section offers a good opportunity for one last reminder of the main benefit the audience will realize from taking the action you want. The secret of the action phase is to make the action easy. In sales letters, AT&T's Jeanne Anderson might ask readers to call a toll-free number for more information. You might ask your audience to fill out an enclosed order form or to use a preaddressed, prepaid envelope for donations. Be sure to include a response due date if applicable.

End by
- Suggesting a specific step the audience can take
- Restating how the audience will benefit by acting as you wish
- Making action easy

The AIDA plan is tailor-made for using the indirect approach, allowing you to save your main idea for the action phase. However, it can also be used for the direct approach. In this

TABLE 9.1

THE AIDA ORGANIZATIONAL PLAN

Attention	Get the reader's attention with a benefit that is of real interest or value.
Interest	Build the reader's interest by further explaining benefits and appealing to his or her logic or emotions.
Desire	Build desire by showing how your offer can really help the reader.
Action	Give a strong and simple call to action and provide a convenient means for the reader to take the next step.

Figure 9.3
In-Depth Critique: Persuasive Letter Using the AIDA Plan

Randy Thumwolt uses the AIDA plan in this persuasive memo about a program that could solve two problems at once: (1) the high annual cost of plastics and (2) the rising number of consumer complaints about the company's failure to recycle plastics.

INTERNAL MEMORANDUM

To: Eleanor Tran, Comptroller
From: Randy Thumwolt, Purchasing Director
Date: August 22, 1999
Subject: Cost Cutting in Plastics

As you know, we purchase five tons of plastic product containers each year. The price of the polyethylene terephthalate (PET) tends to rise and fall as petroleum costs fluctuate. You asked me earlier to find some ways to cut our annual costs for plastics. In my memo of January 5, I suggested that we bulk-purchase plastics during winter months, when petroleum prices tend to be lower. Thanks for approving that suggestion. So far, I estimate that we will realize a 10 percent savings this year.

Even so, our costs for plastic containers are exorbitant ($2 million annually). In addition, we have received an increasing number of consumer letters complaining about our lack of a recycling program for the PET plastic containers both on the airplanes and in the airport restaurants. I've done some preliminary research and have come up with the following ideas:

1. Provide recycling containers at all Host Marriott airport restaurants.
2. Offer financial incentives for the airlines to collect and separate PET containers.
3. Set up a specially designated dumpster at each airport for recycling plastics.
4. Contract with A-Batt Waste Management for collection.

I've attached a detailed report of the costs involved. As you can see, our net savings the first year should run about $500,000. I've spoken to Ted Macy in marketing. If we adopt the recycling plan, he wants to build a PR campaign around it.

The PET recycling plan will help build our public image while improving our bottom line. If you agree, let's meet with Ted next week to get things started.

In the attention phase, background information and specific numbers grab the reader's attention.

In the interest phase, the writer clearly describes the problems the company is still facing.

The desire phase makes suggestions in an easy-to-read list and provides detailed support in an attachment.

In the action phase, the writer provides another reader benefit and urges action within a specific time frame.

Using AIDA with the indirect approach allows you to save your idea for the action phase; using it with the direct approach allows you to use your main idea as your attention-getter.

case, you use your main idea as an attention-getter. You build interest with your argument, create desire with your evidence, and emphasize your main idea in the action phase with the specific action you want your audience to take.

If you're composing your message in a memo format or delivering it by e-mail, keep in mind that your subject line is often the first thing that will catch your readers' eye. Your challenge is to make it interesting and relevant enough to capture their attention and make them want to continue reading without revealing your proposal. If you put your request in the subject line, you're likely to get a quick no before you've had a chance to present your arguments.

INSTEAD OF THIS	TRY THIS
Proposal to Install New Phone Message System	Savings on Toll-Free Number

Another thing to keep in mind when presenting your argument or ideas is to limit your objectives. Focus on your primary goal when presenting your case, and concentrate your efforts on accomplishing that one goal. For example, if your main idea is to convince your company to install a new phone messaging system, leave discussions about switching long-distance carriers until another day—unless, of course, it's relevant to your argument.

Choosing Your Appeal

How do you actually convince an audience that your position is the right one, that your plan will work the best, that your company will do the most with a reader's donations? One way is to appeal to the audience's minds or hearts. Most persuasive messages include both emotional and logical appeals. Used together, these two elements have a good chance of persuading your audience into action.

Both emotional and logical appeals are needed to write successful persuasive messages.

Finding the right balance between the two types of appeals depends on four factors: (1) the actions you wish to achieve, (2) your reader's expectations, (3) the degree of resistance you must overcome, and (4) how far you feel empowered to go in selling your point of view.[9] In general, you'll lean toward logic and make your emotional appeal subtle when you are persuading someone to accept a complex idea or recommendation, take a serious step, make a large and important decision, or make a major purchase. By contrast, if you're writing a sales letter or persuading someone to join a cause or make a small donation, you'll rely more heavily on emotions to persuade your audience.

Emotional Appeals

To persuade your audience, you can call on human emotion by basing your argument on the needs or sympathies of audience members, as long as your **emotional appeal** is subtle.[10] You can make use of the emotion surrounding certain words. *Freedom,* for instance, brings forth strong feelings, as do words such as *success, prestige, credit record, savings, free, value,* and *comfort.* Using words like these puts the audience in a certain frame of mind and helps them accept your message. Also, emotion works with logic in a unique way: People need to find rational support for an attitude they've already embraced emotionally.

Emotional appeals are best if subtle.

Logical Appeals

A **logical appeal** calls on human reason. In any argument you might use to persuade an audience, you make a claim and then support your claim with reasons or evidence. When appealing to your audience's logic, you might use three types of reasoning:

Logical appeals can use
- Analogy
- Induction
- Deduction

- *Analogy* is reasoning from specific evidence to specific evidence. To persuade employees to attend a planning session, you might use a town meeting analogy, comparing your company to a small community and your employees to valued members of that community.

- *Induction* is reasoning from specific evidence to a general conclusion. To convince potential customers that your product is best, you might report the results of test marketing in which individuals preferred your product over others. Therefore, if some individuals preferred it, so will others.
- *Deduction* is reasoning from a generalization to a specific conclusion. To persuade your boss to hire additional employees, you might point to industrywide projections and explain that industry activity (and thus your company's business) will be increasing rapidly over the next three months. Therefore, you will need more employees to handle the increase in business.

Of course, regardless of the reasoning method used, an argument or a statement can easily appear to be true when it's actually false. Whenever you appeal to your audience's reason, do everything you can to ensure that your arguments are logically sound.

The Toulmin model of logic helps you uncover hidden assumptions that your audience may not accept.

Using Toulmin Logic As you shape your argument, you'll make it stronger (1) by finding common ground (basing your major argument on points that your audience already accepts) and (2) by stating the points in your case clearly. The four-step Toulmin model of logic can help you test your argument to see whether it is valid and whether you've provided enough strong evidence. By going through the series of steps, you'll discover whether you've made hidden assumptions that your audience may not accept:[11]

1. State your claim clearly.
2. Support your claim with a clear reason.
3. If your audience already accepts your reason (already holds that same belief, value, or principle presented in your reason), you may proceed to your conclusion.
4. If your audience does not already accept your reason, you must support this reason with another clearly stated claim, and support that claim with another clear reason, and so forth until you achieve common ground (find a reason based on beliefs, values, or principles that your audience already agrees with). Only then may you return to step 3.

As you can see, you are basically supporting your claim with evidence that is itself backed by a chain of reasons (all of which your audience must accept before you can move forward). This approach may remind you of the question-and-answer chain discussed briefly in Chapter 5 and at more length in Chapter 14.

Avoid faulty logic such as hasty generalizations, begging the question, attacking your opponent, oversimplifying, assuming a false cause, using faulty analogies, and using illogical support.

Avoiding Faulty Logic In any rational appeal, ethical standards dictate that you provide useful information, facts, and knowledge that can be used in decision making. For this information to be persuasive, your arguments must be relevant, well grounded, and systematic. To make your points lucid and your arguments sound, steer clear of faulty logic:[12]

- *Avoid hasty generalizations.* Make sure you have plenty of evidence before drawing conclusions.
- *Avoid begging the question.* Make sure you can support your claim without simply restating it in different words.
- *Avoid attacking your opponent.* Be careful to address the real question. Attack the argument your opponent is making, not your opponent's character.
- *Avoid oversimplifying a complex issue.* Make sure you present all the facts rather than relying on an "either/or" statement that makes it appear as though only two choices are possible.
- *Avoid assuming a false cause.* Use cause-and-effect reasoning correctly; do not assume that one event caused another just because it happened first.
- *Avoid faulty analogies.* Be careful that the two objects or situations being compared are similar enough for the analogy to hold. Even if A resembles B in one respect, it may not in all respects.

- *Avoid illogical support.* Make sure the connection between your claim and your support is truly logical and not based on a leap of faith, a missing premise, or irrelevant evidence.

Ethical Considerations

The word *persuasion* is used negatively when associated with dishonest and unethical practices, such as coaxing, urging, and sometimes even tricking people into accepting an idea, buying a product, or taking an action they neither want nor need. However, the positive meaning of *persuasion* is influencing your audience members by informing them and by aiding their understanding, which allows them the freedom to choose.[13] Ethical businesspeople inform customers of the benefits of an idea, an organization, a product, a donation, or an action so that customers can recognize how well that idea, organization, product, donation, or action will fill a need they truly have.

Positive persuasion leaves your audience free to choose.

For anyone trying to influence people's actions, knowledge of the law is crucial. However, merely avoiding what is illegal may not always be enough. To maintain the highest standards of business ethics, make every attempt to persuade without manipulating. Choose words that won't be misinterpreted when de-emphasizing negatives, and be sure you don't distort the truth. Show consideration for your audience by adopting the "you" attitude with honest concern for their needs and interests. Your consideration of audience needs is more than ethical; it's the proper use of persuasion. Moreover, it's likely to achieve the response you intended and to satisfy your audience's needs. (See "Focusing on Ethics: Does Some Direct Mail Contain Deliberately Deceptive Copy?")

To maintain the highest ethics, try to persuade without manipulating.

Reinforcing Your Position

Once you have established your credibility, framed your arguments, and chosen your appeal, you can concentrate on strengthening your message with some important persuasive tools. Most effective persuaders supplement numerical data with examples, stories, metaphors, and analogies to make their position come alive. In other words, they use language to paint a vivid picture of the persuader's point of view.[14]

Semantics

Say, for example, you're trying to build your credibility. How do you let your audience know that you're enthusiastic and trustworthy? Simply making an outright claim that you have these traits is sure to raise suspicion. However, you can use *semantics* (the meaning of words and other symbols) to do much of the job for you. The words you choose to state your message say much more than their dictionary definition.[15]

Semantics is the meaning of words and other symbols.

Instead of This	Use This
I think we should attempt to get approval on this before it's too late.	Let's get immediate approval on this.
It seems to me that . . .	I believe . . .
I've been thinking lately that maybe someone could . . .	After careful thought over the past two months, I've decided that . . .
This plan could work if we really push it.	With our support, this plan will work.

Another way semantics can affect persuasive messages is in the variety of meanings that people attribute to certain words. Abstract words are subject to interpretation because they refer to things that people cannot experience with their senses. So use abstractions to enhance the emotional content of a persuasive message. For example, you may be able to sell more flags by appealing to your audience's patriotism (which may be interpreted in many ways) than by describing the color and size of the flags. You may have better luck collecting

Two ways of using semantics are choosing your words carefully and using abstractions to enhance emotional content.

FOCUSING ON ETHICS

DOES SOME DIRECT MAIL CONTAIN DELIBERATELY DECEPTIVE COPY?

What's ethical and what's just smart selling? Some direct-mail campaigns use tokens and stickers to deter consumers from logical analysis and to steer them toward a more childlike state of mind. Others set prices at $29.95 to make audiences think the product costs around $20 instead of $30. One questionable practice involves the "assumptive claim": A letter states, "Here's the information you requested," when no such request was made. Some companies rationalize these methods as "affirmative puffery" and "mild misrepresentation" that do no real harm to the consumer. What do you think?

Ever since Montgomery Ward sold his first oilcloth table covers through the mail in 1872, marketers have proven that direct mail is one of the most profitable and cost-effective forms of advertising. They've also encountered some of the toughest ethical decisions in business. A few laws have been enacted to protect consumers: The federal Deceptive Mailings Preventions Act of 1990 prohibits mailings that resemble government documents, and state privacy legislation governs the nature of consumer information gathered, retained, sold, and traded as mailing lists. For the most part, however, the direct-mail seller must weigh the alternatives: How enthusiastically can I extol the benefits of my product and still maintain good ethical and legal business standards?

Skilled direct-mail copywriters try to catch their audience's attention in the first four seconds, so certain words are highly valued in the trade: *free, urgent, special, immediate, exclusive, limited supply,* and so on. "Irresistible" envelopes, personalized letters, brochures, response cards, and gimmicks such as tokens and stickers tread the narrow line between truth and exaggeration. Going overboard is easy, and professional organizations debate about how far is too far. Some researchers have even begun questioning the potential long-term negative effects of emotion-laden messages that leave a particular segment of the audience feeling depressed, anxious, hostile, or inferior.

One direct-mail expert advised businesses: "If there's a limited supply, say so." If not, you might say, "while current supply lasts" or "until inventory is sold out." This same expert suggested that even if there's no impending price increase (after the current offer expires), it might be profitable to suggest that "prices may never be this low again." Are these approaches legal? Yes. Are they ethical? You'll have to decide for yourself.

1. Plenty of honest, hard-working people use direct-mail campaigns successfully and ethically. From your own mailbox, collect some positive examples of direct-mail selling, and highlight several examples of effective attention-getters.
2. Where would you draw the ethical line for your own direct-mail campaign?

---

an overdue bill by mentioning honesty and fair play than by repeating the sum owed and the date it was due. However, be sure to include the details along with the abstractions; the very fact that you're using abstract words leaves room for misinterpretation.

Other Tools

Other persuasive tools include focusing on your goals, using simple language, anticipating opposition, being specific, being moderate, providing sufficient support, creating a win-win situation, timing your message, and using metaphors and anecdotes.

Using semantics skillfully isn't your only persuasive tool. Here are some additional techniques you can use to strengthen your persuasive messages:[16]

- *Focus on your goal.* Your message will be clearest if you shift your focus away from changing minds and emphasize the action you want your audience to take.
- *Use simple language.* In most persuasive situations, your audience will be cautious, watching for fantastic claims, insupportable descriptions, and emotional manipulation. So speak plainly and simply.
- *Anticipate opposition.* Think of every possible objection in advance. In your message, you might raise and answer some of these counterarguments.
- *Be specific.* Back up your claims with evidence, and when necessary cite actual facts and figures. Let your audience know that you've done your homework.

- *Be moderate.* Asking your audience to make major changes in attitudes or beliefs will most likely evoke a negative response. However, asking audience members to take one step toward that change may be a more reasonable goal.
- *Provide sufficient support.* It is up to you to prove that the change you seek is necessary.
- *Create a win-win situation.* Make it possible for both you and your audience to gain something. Audience members will find it easier to deal with change if they stand to benefit.
- *Time your messages appropriately.* The time to sell roofs is right after the tornado. Timing is crucial in persuasive messages.
- *Speak metaphorically.* Metaphors create powerful pictures. One metaphor can convey a lifetime of experience or a head full of logic.
- *Use anecdotes and stories to make your points.* People can only digest so much factual information. Anecdotes tie it all together—logic and emotions. Don't tell them what kinds of problems users can have if the system crashes. Tell them what happened to Jeff Porte when his hard drive crashed in the middle of his annual sales presentation.

All of these tools will help your persuasive message be accepted, but none of them will actually convince your audience to take the action you want. Whether based on emotion or logic, your argument will need to be strong to persuade people to act.

Dealing with Resistance

The best way to deal with audience resistance is to eliminate it. If you expect a hostile audience, one biased against your plan from the beginning, present all sides—all options and the pros and cons of each. You'll create extra credibility if you present these options before the decision is presented.[17]

To uncover audience objections, try some "What if?" scenarios. Poke holes in your own theories and ideas before your audience does. Then find solutions to the problems you've uncovered. Recognize that people support what they help create. So set about asking your audience for their thinking on the subject before you put your argument together. Let them recommend some solutions. With enough thought and effort, you may even be able to turn problems into opportunities or show how in the long run your proposal will be more economical. Regardless, be sure to be thorough, open, and objective about all the facts and alternatives. Try to avoid these common mistakes people make when putting together persuasive arguments:[18]

- They attempt to make their case with an up-front hard sell. Setting out a strong position at the start of a persuasion effort gives potential opponents something to grab onto—and fight against.
- They resist compromise. Persuasion is a process of give and take. As one expert points out, a persuader rarely changes another person's behavior or viewpoint without altering his or her own in the process.
- They think the secret of persuasion lies in presenting great arguments. In persuading people to change their minds, great arguments matter, but they are only one part of the equation. Creating a mutually beneficial framework for a position, connecting on the right emotional level with the audience, and communicating through vivid language are just as important. Furthermore, they make your argument come alive.
- They assume persuasion is a one-shot effort. Persuasion is a process, not an event. Rarely, if ever, is it possible to arrive at a shared situation on the first try. More often than not, persuasion involves listening to people, testing a position, developing a new position that reflects input from the group, more testing, more compromise, and so on.

Remember, persuasive messages take careful planning and organization. Your success depends on your commitment to being ethical, analyzing your audience's needs, maintaining your own credibility, using semantics carefully, balancing emotion and logic, and choosing the most appropriate organizational plan. Following these guidelines will help you craft strong persuasive messages, no matter what the situation. To review the steps involved in developing persuasive messages, see this chapter's Checklist for Developing Persuasive Messages.

WRITING PERSUASIVE REQUESTS

Make only reasonable requests.

Highlight the direct and indirect benefits of complying with your request.

The most important thing to remember when preparing a persuasive request for action or an adjustment is to keep your request within bounds. Nothing is as distressing as a request so general, all encompassing, or inconsiderate that it seems impossible to grant, no matter how worthy the cause. When making a persuasive request, therefore, take special care to highlight both the direct and the indirect benefits of fulfilling the request. Direct benefits might include a reduced work load for the supervisor who institutes requested flextime or a premium for someone who responds to a survey. Indirect benefits might include better employee morale, enhanced prestige, or the chance to make a meaningful contribution.

Persuasive Requests for Action

Whether you're requesting a favor or a budget increase, use the AIDA organizational plan to frame your message. Begin with an attention-getting device such as showing readers that you know something about their concerns and that you have some reason for making such

CHECKLIST FOR DEVELOPING PERSUASIVE MESSAGES

A. Establish Your Credibility
  1. Support your message with facts and sources.
  2. Demonstrate your knowledge, enthusiasm, objectivity, and sincerity.

B. Frame Your Arguments
  1. Attention
    a. Open with a reader benefit, a stimulating question, a problem, or an unexpected statement.
    b. Find a common ground by discussing something your audience can agree with.
    c. Demonstrate that you understand the audience's concerns.
    d. Introduce a direct or an indirect benefit that can be developed as a central selling point.
  2. Interest and Desire
    a. Elaborate on the main benefit.
    b. Back up your claims with relevant evidence.
    c. Anticipate and answer possible objections. Turn them into opportunities when possible. Otherwise, give assurance that you will handle them as best you can.
  3. Action
    a. Confidently ask for the audience's cooperation.
    b. Make the desired action clear and easy.
    c. Stress the positive results of the action.
    d. Include the due date (if any) for a response, and whenever possible tie it in with audience benefits.
    e. Include one last reminder of the audience benefit.

C. Choose Your Appeal
  1. Use emotional appeals to help the audience accept your message.
  2. Use logical appeals when presenting facts and evidence for complex ideas or recommendations.
    a. Test your logic for validity.
    b. Make sure your audience can accept your chain of reasons.
    c. Avoid faulty logic.
  3. Practice good business ethics.

D. Reinforce Your Position
  1. Use semantics to build credibility and enhance the emotional content of your message.
  2. Use a variety of critical thinking and effective writing tools to strengthen your case.

E. Deal with Resistance
  1. Try "What if?" scenarios and poke holes in your theories.
  2. Let others help you find solutions to problems that you uncover.
  3. Present the pros and cons of all options.

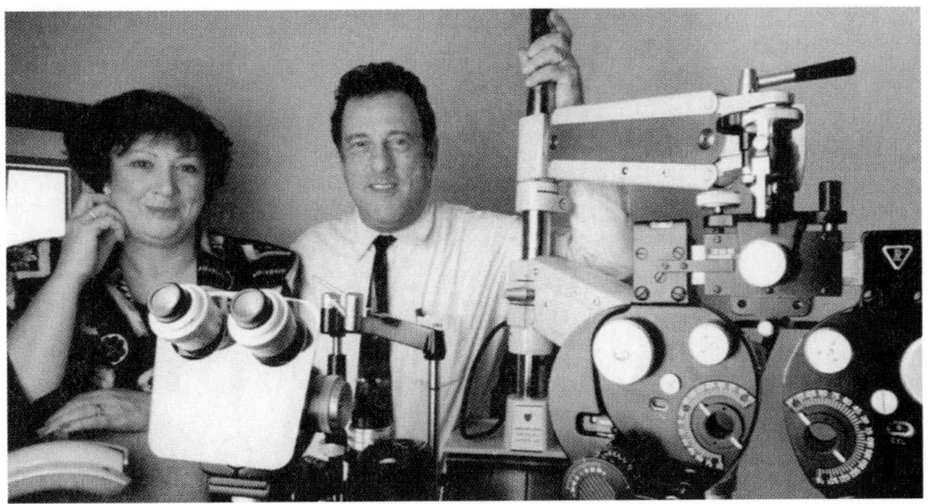

A mix-up with employer identification numbers left optometrist F. Barry Jacobs and his wife Nancy in a drawn-out battle with the IRS. To help resolve the situation, the couple provided the IRS with enough history, facts, and figures to persuade the government that an honest error had been made.

requests. In this type of persuasive message, more than in most others, a flattering comment about your reader is acceptable, especially if it's sincere.

Use the interest and desire sections of your letter or memo to cover what you know about the situation you're requesting action on: the facts and figures, the benefits of helping, and any history or experience that will enhance your appeal. The goals are to give you and your request credibility and to make the reader believe that helping you will indeed help solve a significant problem.

Be careful not to doom your request to failure by asking your reader to do all your work for you: to provide information that you were too lazy to seek, to take an action that will save you from embarrassment or inconvenience, or to provide total financial support for a cause that nobody else is supporting. Once you've demonstrated that your message is relevant to your reader, you can close with a request for some specific action. Take a look at the request in Figure 9.4. Be aware, however, that a persuasive memo is somewhat more subdued than a letter to an outsider might be.

If you're requesting a favor, keep in mind that if the favor is routine—such as asking someone to attend a meeting in your absence—you'll normally use the direct approach and the format for routine messages (see Chapter 7). However, if you're asking someone to chair an event or to serve as the team leader because you can no longer fill that role, you'll probably use persuasive techniques to convince him or her of the value of the project. That means you need to include all necessary information about the project and any facts and figures that will convince the person that his or her contribution will be enjoyable, easy, important, and of personal benefit.

Persuasive Claims and Requests for Adjustments

The goal of a persuasive claim or request for adjustment is to satisfy your expectations for a transaction.

Although persuasive claims and adjustment requests are sometimes referred to as complaint letters, your goal is to persuade someone to make an adjustment in your favor; you're not merely getting a complaint off your chest. You reach your goal by demonstrating the difference between what you expected and what you actually got. Most claim letters begin as routine messages (see Chapter 7). Suppose, however, that your routine claim is denied and you still feel that you have a strong case. You might choose to write a persuasive claim, adding additional evidence and using more attention-getting techniques.

For example, suppose you purchase something, and after the warranty expires, you discover that it was defective. You write the company a routine request asking for a replacement,

Figure 9.4
In-Depth Critique: Persuasive Memo Requesting Action

Ed Alvarez is excited about a new method of packaging bananas to decrease shipping damage and reduce costs. He needs his boss's approval to proceed and her cooperation in coordinating with another department. Here is his memo.

MEMORANDUM

To: Kia Miamoto
From: Ed Alvarez
Date: September 3, 1999
Subject: Money-saving packaging

Earlier this year you expressed concern about our damage problems in transporting our bananas from Chile using wooden crates. Recently, I came across information on plastic-lined reusable boxes that may solve our problem and save us money.

TexCrate, Inc., manufactures the corrugated boxes to any specifications. A heat process is used to affix the 6 ml polyethylene lining to the walls of the boxes. A metal U-bar inside the box provides a hanger for the bananas. The boxes feature slip-on lids that make stacking them in our containers quite easy. They can be fork-lifted using wooden pallets that we already own. We would place a desiccant pouch in each box to prevent "sweating." In addition, small vents can be cut into the lids and sides.

Because of the recent increase in lumber costs, the boxes cost less than the wooden crates. The boxes are also fully recyclable, so they fit in with our "Earth-Friendly" campaign. Randy Farney of TexCrate says we should be able to ship repeatedly in the same boxes for several years. He would like to provide us with six sample boxes to test before our peak season, and he wants our specifications as soon as possible. He'll work up a dollar amount depending on the size we'll need. If we decide to use TexCrate's boxes, we can donate our wooden crates to Habitat for Humanity.

If you agree, I'd like to proceed with the test. Can you authorize someone from R&D to work with me on developing the specs for TexCrate? Please let me hear from you by Wednesday. If we can get the information to TexCrate within the week, we'll be able to conduct the tests and have results by early November. At that time I'll also be able to give you an estimate of our dollar savings so that we'll be ready to make a decision before mid-November—in plenty of time to make any needed changes before our peak season begins in late December.

A solution to an ongoing problem and an additional benefit help get the reader's attention.

By detailing the advantages and adaptability of the boxes, the writer gives the request credibility while increasing interest.

Additional cost and environmental benefits make the new method seem workable and build the reader's desire to try it.

The final paragraph tells the reader exactly what must be done and emphasizes the need to act now.

DID YOU KNOW?

The White House Office of Consumer Affairs estimates that for every complaint a company receives, there are 26 other unsatisfied customers who do not complain.

but your request is denied. You're not satisfied, and you still feel you have a strong case. Perhaps you just didn't communicate it well enough the first time. In cases like these, persuasion is a necessity. You can't threaten to withhold payment, so try to convey the essentially negative information in a way that will get positive results. Fortunately, most people in business are open to fair settlement of your claim. It's to their advantage to maintain your goodwill and to resolve your problem quickly.

The key ingredients of a good persuasive claim are a complete and specific review of the facts and a confident and positive tone. Assume that the other person is not trying to cheat you but also that you have the right to be satisfied with the transaction. Talk only about the complaint at hand, not about other issues involving similar products or other complaints about the company. Your goal is to solve a particular problem; your audience is most likely to help when you focus on the benefits of solving the problem rather than on the horrors of neglecting your complaint.

Make your persuasive claims
- Complete and specific when reviewing the facts
- Confident and positive in tone

As you read the following letter, note the improvements that could be made:

I bought an Audio-Tech sound system a few months ago to provide background music at my gift shop. Now one of the components, the compact disc (CD) player, does not work right. When we play a CD, it repeats and repeats. This is very irritating to me and my customers, and Audio-Tech needs to fix this problem.

This opening fails to clarify for the reader the details of the purchase, the exact product involved, and the problem.

My clerks and I noticed this major mess about a month or so after I bought this fancy unit at the McNally Sound and Light Store in St. Louis, where I buy most of my video and CD stuff—although sometimes I buy through catalogs. When one of the clerks first heard the CD repeat, she tried another CD, and sure enough, it did the same thing, so it is a player problem, not a CD problem. Then we set the CD player on digital so that we could see visually what was going on, and sure enough, the sound was repeating and even skipping.

This paragraph doesn't include any acceptable reasons for Audio-Tech to consider making an adjustment.

When I finally brought the unit back to the store, Henry McNally said that the 60-day warranty had expired, and it was my gift shop's problem, but definitely not his problem. He said I probably had a "lemon."

This paragraph captures the frustration of the store owner, but it cannot persuade the reader, who is still trying to grasp the dimensions of the problem.

This CD unit probably never did work right. I would think that, since I paid hundreds of dollars for this component, it would work for many years. Other stores here on Main Street cannot believe what a bummer it is to hear irritating background music on this Audio-Tech player. They say they will not buy the Audio-Tech brand if you don't replace my unit.

The concluding paragraph touches on what the writer expected of the product, but doesn't state what she wants done; it contains only additional complaining and a vague threat.

BEST OF THE WEB

Lobby Movers and Shakers in the U.S. Government

Sponsored by the Library of Congress, the Thomas site is named in honor of Thomas Jefferson. It offers a smorgasbord of information about Congress, its members and committees, and issues under consideration, and it has links to just about any governmental matter you can conceive. For anyone who wants to lobby government leaders, a visit here could prove most useful. You'll discover information and access information that could take days to find without a computer (if at all). For instance, see whether you can find a link here that will lead you to a current tally of the public debt, all x trillions of it, tracked up to the moment and down to the penny. (Hint: We found this link by clicking on "House Members" and visiting a representative's home page, but there are other ways.)

http://thomas.loc.gov

Figure 9.5
In-Depth Critique: Letter Making a Persuasive Claim

This letter was sent to Audio-Tech Electronics to persuade the company to replace a faulty CD player.

ellie's special place

2201 main street, suite D • chesterfield, missouri 63071 • (314) 778-3345 • fax: (314) 778-3346

January 18, 1999

Mr. Allen Fenwick, Customer Relations
Audio-Tech Electronics
5054 Wicker Place
Chicago, IL 60622

Dear Mr. Fenwick:

As the owner of a small gift shop, I try to provide a pleasant ambiance for customers. For background music, I play "easy listening" and classical music on my Audio-Tech Pro III sound system. I play both CDs and tapes, but the CD player is not working properly. Please replace this CD unit at no charge.

The brief opening clearly describes the problem, the product involved, how the product is used, and what adjustment is requested.

I purchased the Audio-Tech Pro III system on November 15, 1998, from McNally Sound and Light at 16325 Lincoln Drive, St. Louis, Missouri 63158. All parts of the unit worked well for a month or so. I first noticed the problem on December 22: the CD would repeat a phrase two or three times in succession before moving on to the rest of the selection. At first I assumed it was a defective CD. On December 23, two customers asked me to turn off the CD player because it was repeating one musical phrase sporadically throughout a classical selection. The next day I checked the unit by setting it on "digital," and sure enough, every CD I played repeated phrases intermittently.

The next paragraph explains the details of purchase as well as how and when the problem was discovered.

I called Mr. McNally at McNally Sound and Light, but I couldn't bring the unit back until after the Christmas holidays. On January 5, I took the CD unit back to McNally. When I returned on January 17 to pick it up, Mr. McNally told me that he could hear the problem but was unable to fix it. He said it was a manufacturing problem, but since my warranty had expired, he could not replace the unit free of charge.

The involvement of a third party (the dealer) is explained thoroughly.

Enclosed with this letter and the CD component are copies of my original sales form and McNally's January repair order. Please replace, at no charge to me, the defective CD unit. Although the 60-day warranty technically expired on January 1, I discovered the problem well within the warranty period. My original decision to purchase Audio-Tech products was motivated by your reputation for both quality products and exceptional service. So I know you will stand behind your product and replace the faulty machine.

The close refers to attached receipts, restates the adjustment being requested, and provides the reader with a reason to grant the adjustment (the company's reputation for quality and customer service).

Sincerely,

Ellie Chambers

Ellie Chambers

Enclosure

Figure 9.5 is a revised version of this letter, one that should yield much more favorable results. As the figure illustrates, resolving problems is more a matter of reasonable exchange than a struggle between adversaries. For a review of the tasks involved here, see this chapter's Checklist for Persuasive Claims and Requests for Adjustment.

CHECKLIST FOR PERSUASIVE CLAIMS AND REQUESTS FOR ADJUSTMENT

A. Attention

1. For your opening, use one of the following: sincere compliment, rhetorical question, agreeable comment or assertion, statement of the basic problem, or brief review of what has been done about the problem.
2. At the beginning, state something that you and the audience can agree on or that you wish to convince the audience about.

B. Interest and Desire

1. State all necessary facts and details, and interweave them with audience benefits.
2. Provide a description that shows the members of your audience that their firm is responsible for the problem and that your request is factual, logical, and reasonable.
3. Appeal to the audience's sense of fair play, desire for customer goodwill, need for a good reputation, or sense of legal or moral responsibility.
4. Emphasize your goal of having the adjustment granted.
5. Present your case in a calm, logical manner.
6. Tell the audience how you feel; your disappointment with the products, policies, or services provided may well be the most important part of your argument.

C. Action

1. Make sure the action request is a logical conclusion based on the problem and the stated facts.
2. State the request specifically and confidently.
3. Specify a due date for action (when desirable).
4. State the main audience benefit as a reminder of benefits in earlier statements.

WRITING SALES AND FUNDRAISING MESSAGES

Two distinctive types of persuasive messages are sales letters and fundraising letters. These messages often come in special direct-mail packages that can include brochures, reply forms, or other special inserts. Both types of messages are often written by specialized and highly skilled professionals like Jeanne Anderson of AT&T Language Line.

Sales and fundraising letters are distinctive types of persuasive messages that often come in special direct-mail packages.

How do sales messages differ from fundraising messages? Sales messages are usually sent by for-profit organizations persuading readers to spend money on products for themselves. On the other hand, fundraising messages are usually sent by nonprofit organizations persuading readers to donate their money or time to others. Otherwise, sales and fundraising messages are similar: Both compete for business and public attention, time, and dollars.[19] Both attempt to persuade readers to spend their time or money on the value being offered—whether that value is the convenience of a more efficient vacuum cleaner or the satisfaction of helping save children's lives. Both require a few more steps than other types of persuasive messages. And both generally use the AIDA sequence to deliver their message.

Sales and fundraising messages compete for readers' attention, time, and dollars.

Planning Your Sales Message

One of the first things you'll want to do when planning your sales message is to gain a thorough understanding of your product. What does it look like? How does it work? How is it priced? Are there any discounts? How is it delivered and packaged?

When planning a sales message

- Know your product
- Know your audience
- Know your selling points
- Decide on the type of sales campaign

Using the data you collect about your product, try to form a mental image of the typical buyer for the product you wish to sell. Ask yourself: Who is your audience? What's important to them? What might they want to know about the product? Are they driven by bottom-line pricing, or is quality a bigger issue? In other words, as with any persuasive message, you begin by analyzing your audience and focusing on their needs, interests, and emotional concerns.

With a $10,000 loan and a cargo of beachware ordered from a trade show in California, Joni Boldt Ridgway and Kyrle Boldt created "Splash"—five Splash stores actually—in St. Louis. The owners know that producing effective sales messages is just as important to the stores' success as the creative merchandise they stock—some 70 kinds of snowboards, fluorescent bikinis, and lime-green nail polish. Both must get the customer's attention, build interest, increase desire, and motivate action.

Next select the product's selling points or benefits that are most appealing to your particular audience. You'll highlight these points when you compose your persuasive message. At AT&T's Language Line, for instance, Jeanne Anderson emphasizes the ease and cost effectiveness of dialing up one of the 140 languages 24 hours a day.

You'll also need to think about the type of sales campaign you'll conduct. Will you send just a letter, or will you include brochures, samples, response cards, and the like? If you'll send a brochure, how many pages will it run? Will you conduct a multistage campaign, with several mailings and some sort of telephone or in-person follow-up, or will you rely on a single hard-hitting mailing? Generally speaking, expensive items and hard-to-accept propositions call for a more elaborate campaign than low-cost products and simple actions.

Of course, all these decisions depend on the audience you're trying to reach—their characteristics, their likely acceptance of or resistance to your message—and what you're trying to get them to do. In short, knowing your audience will help you get started in many ways: It will lead you to the most effective campaign, help you choose the proper tone and choice of vocabulary, and help you select the prime benefits to highlight in your message.

Determining Selling Points and Benefits

Selling points focus on the product; benefits focus on the user.

Selling points + "you" attitude = benefits.

As Table 9.2 shows, selling points are the most attractive features of an idea or product; benefits are the particular advantages that readers will realize from those features. Selling points focus on the product. Benefits focus on the user. For example, if you say that your shovel has "an ergonomically designed handle," you've described a good feature. But to persuade someone to buy that shovel, say "the ergonomically designed handle will help reduce your risk of back injury." That's a benefit. For your letter and your overall sales efforts to be successful, your product's distinguishing benefit must correspond to your prospects' primary needs or emotional concerns.

Take a look at Figure 9.6 on page 308. The features of the SecureAbel Alarms system are that it can be installed with a screwdriver, has an activator that hooks to your key chain

TABLE 9.2

FEATURES VERSUS BENEFITS

Feature	Consumer Benefit
No money down, no interest payments for 24 months.	You can buy what you want right now at no additional costs.
This printer prints 17 pages a minute.	This printer can turn out one of your 100-page proposals in six minutes.
Our shelter provides 100 adult beds and 50 children's beds for the needy.	Your donation will provide temporary housing for 100 women who don't want to return to abusive husbands.
Your corporate sponsorship of the seminar will pay for the keynote speaker's travel and lodging.	Your corporate sponsorship of the seminar will allow your site manager a five-minute introduction at the beginning of the program to summarize your services.

or belt loop, and has a blinking red light to warn intruders to stay away. The benefits are ease of installation, ease of activation, and a feeling of safety and security—all obtainable without investing in a full-blown permanently installed alarm system. When composing sales messages, be sure to focus on relatively few product benefits. Ultimately, you'll single out one benefit, which will become the hallmark of your campaign. Safety seems to be the key benefit emphasized by SecureAbel Alarms.

Staying within the Law

Whether you're selling a good, a service, or your company's image, remember that the focus of your message is your audience. As with any message, knowing the law can help you avoid serious legal problems. The laws governing sales letters are quite specific:

Know the laws governing sales letters, and avoid both legal and ethical pitfalls by being genuinely concerned about your audience's needs.

- Sales letters are considered binding contracts in many states. So avoid even implying offers or promises that you can't deliver.
- Making a false statement in a sales letter is fraud if the recipient can prove that (1) you intended to deceive, (2) you made the statement regarding a fact rather than an opinion or a speculation, (3) the recipient was justified in relying on the statement, and (4) the recipient was damaged by it (in a legal sense). Misrepresenting the price, quality, or performance of a product in a sales letter is fraud. So is a testimonial by a person misrepresented to be an expert.
- Using a person's name, photograph, or other identity in a sales letter without permission constitutes invasion of privacy—with some exceptions. Using a photo of the members of a local softball team in a chamber of commerce mailer may be perfectly legal if team members are public figures in the community and if using the photo doesn't falsely imply their endorsement. On the other hand, using a photo of your governor, without consent, on a letter about the profits to be made in worm farming could be deemed an invasion of privacy.
- Publicizing a person's private life in a sales letter can also result in legal problems. Stating that the president of a local bank (mentioned by name) served six months in prison for income tax evasion is a potentially damaging fact that may be considered

Figure 9.6
In-Depth Critique: Letter Selling a Product

The following sales letter for SecureAble Alarms uses the AIDA plan to persuade students to buy its dorm-room alarm systems.

SecureAbel Alarms, Inc.
5654 Lakemont Drive • Altoona, PA 16602 • Voice: (814) 983-4424 • Fax: (814) 983-4422 • http://www.secure.com

October 14, 1999

Mr. Samuel Zolezzi
Penn State University, North Halls
104 Warnock Commons
State College, PA 16802

Dear Mr. Zolezzi:

Did you know that one out of four college students becomes a victim of theft? How would you feel if you returned to your dorm and discovered that your hard-earned stereo, computer, or microwave had been stolen? Remember, locked doors won't stop a determined thief.

It happened to me when I was in college. That's why I've developed a portable security system for your dormitory room. It works like an auto alarm and can be installed with an ordinary screwdriver. The small activator hooks to your key chain or belt loop. Just press the "lock" key. A "beep" tells you your room is secure, and a blinking red light warns intruders to stay away.

If a thief tries to break in, a loud alarm sounds. Your possessions will be safe. And, even more important, you can activate the system from your bedside, so you're safe while you sleep.

You'd expect this peace of mind to cost a fortune—something most college students don't have. But we're offering the SecureAbel Dorm Alarm System for only $75. Here's what you'll receive by return mail:

- The patented alarm unit
- Two battery-operated programmable remote units
- A one-year warranty on all parts
- Complete and easy-to-follow installation instructions

Order additional alarm boxes to install on your window or bathroom door for only $50. Act now. Fill out the response card, and mail it along with your choice of payment method in the enclosed envelope. Don't give thieves and criminals a chance. Protect yourself and your belongings. Send in your card today.

Sincerely,

Dan Abel

Dan Abel, President

Enclosures

Beginning with a provocative question draws the reader into the letter and raises the awareness of a need. Benefits have both a logical appeal (protecting possessions) and an emotional appeal (personal safety).

In the second paragraph, the writer seeks to establish a common bond with the reader and explains how the product works by comparing it to something the reader is familiar with, a car alarm.

The third paragraph mentions an additional threat to safety and hence another benefit of the security system.

The bulleted list creates the sense of added value to the offer.

The final paragraph urges quick action.

an invasion of privacy. You would also risk a lawsuit by publicizing another person's past-due debts or by publishing without consent another person's medical records, x-rays, or photograph.

As with other persuasive messages, following the letter of the law isn't always enough. To write sales letters of the highest ethical character, focus on solving your readers' problem rather than on selling your product. If you're genuinely concerned about your audience's needs and interests, you'll find it easier to avoid legal or ethical pitfalls.

Organizing and Composing Your Sales Messages

Most sales letters are prepared according to the AIDA plan used for any persuasive message. You begin with an attention-getting device, generate interest by describing some of the product's unique features, increase the desire for your product by highlighting the benefits that are most appealing to your audience, and close by suggesting the action you want the audience to take.

Getting Attention

Sales letters start with an attention-getting device. Professionals use some common techniques to attract audience attention. One popular technique is opening with a question. Look closely at the following three examples. Which seems most interesting to you?

Certain tried-and-true attention-getting devices are used in sales letters for a wide variety of products.

> How would you like straight A's this semester?
>
> Get straight A's this semester!
>
> Now you can get straight A's this semester, with . . .

If you're like most people, you'll find the first option the most enticing. The question invites your response—a positive response designed to encourage you to read on. The second option is fairly interesting too, but its commanding tone may make you wary of the claim. The third option is acceptable, but it certainly conveys no sense of excitement, and its quick introduction of the product may lead you to a snap decision against reading further.

Another way to open with excitement when you're preparing a sales letter is by emphasizing

- *A piece of genuine news.* "In the past 60 days, mortgage rates have fallen to a 30-year low."
- *A personal appeal to the reader's emotions and values.* "The only thing worse than paying taxes is paying taxes when you don't have to."
- *The most attractive feature plus the associated benefit.* "New control device ends problems with employee pilferage!"
- *An intriguing number.* "Here are three great secrets of the world's most loved entertainers."
- *A sample of the product.* "Here's your free sample of the new Romalite packing sheet."
- *A concrete illustration with story appeal.* "In 1985 Earl Colbert set out to find a better way to process credit applications. After ten years of trial and error, he finally developed a procedure so simple but thorough that he was cited for service to the industry by the American Creditors Association."
- *A specific trait shared by the audience.* "Busy executives need another complicated 'time-saving' device like they need a hole in the head!"
- *A provocative question.* "Are you tired of watching inflation eat away at your hard-earned profits?"
- *A challenge.* "Don't waste another day wondering how you're going to become the success you've always wanted to be!"
- *A solution to a problem.* "Tired of arctic air rushing through the cracks around your windows? Stay warm and save energy with StormSeal Weather-stripping."

A look at your own mail will show you how many products these few techniques can be applied to. Using such attention-getting devices will give your sales letters added impact. (See Figure 9.6 for a typical example.) In addition, sales letters prepared by professionals use a

DID YOU KNOW?

You have approximately seven seconds to get the reader to open mail and read through a letter.

Choose an attention-getter that encourages the reader to read more.

variety of formatting devices to get your attention, including personalized salutations, special sizes or styles of type, underlining, bullets, color, indentions, and so on. Even so, not all attention-getting devices are equally effective. The best is the one that makes your audience read the rest of the letter.

Building Interest

To determine your product's central selling point, ask
- What does the competition offer?
- What is special about my product?
- What are potential buyers really looking for?

In the interest section of your message, you'll highlight your product's key selling point. Say that your company's alarm device is relatively inexpensive, durable, and tamperproof. Although these are all attractive features, you want to focus on only one. Ask what the competition has to offer, what most distinguishes your product, and what most concerns potential buyers. The answers to these questions will help you select the **central selling point**, the single point around which to build your sales message. Build your audience's interest by highlighting this point in your first paragraph, and make it stand out through typography, design, or high-impact writing.[20]

Determining the central selling point will help you define the benefits to potential buyers. Perhaps your company's alarm device has been built mainly to overcome the inability of the competition's product to resist tampering by would-be burglars. Being tamperproof is the feature you choose as your central selling point; the benefit of this feature is that burglars won't be able to break in so easily.

Increasing Desire

You'll want to mention your main benefit repeatedly, in words and pictures (if possible), in the desire section as well as at the end of your letter. It's what you will use to entice prospects to read on and take further action. As you explain the benefits of your product or service, keep in mind that you don't need to provide every detail. The best letters are short (preferably one but no more than two pages). They include enough detail to spur the reader's interest, but they don't try to be the sole source of information. Use bullet points to highlight details whenever possible. You have to assume that your readers are pressed for time and are interested only in what matters most to them.[21]

You might get attention by using a news item to stress this benefit: "Burglaries of businesses in our county have increased 7.7 percent over the past year; police department officials cite burglars' increasing sophistication and familiarity with conventional alarm devices." You might pose a provocative question: "Worried about the reliability of your current alarm system in repelling today's sophisticated burglars?"

In the rest of the letter, continue to stress this theme but also weave in references to other benefits: "You can get this worry-free protection for much less than you might think." Also, "The same technology that makes it difficult for burglars to crack your alarm system makes the device durable, even when it must be exposed to the elements." Remember, sales letters reflect the "you" attitude through references to benefits, so always phrase the selling points in terms of what such features will do for potential customers.

DID YOU KNOW?

Some 70 billion sales messages are sent to U.S. mailboxes every year, and America Online claims that some days it delivers more than 4 million sales messages by e-mail to its customers.

To give force to a message
- Use action terms
- Use colorful verbs and adjectives

Using Action Terms Active words give force to any business message, but they are especially important in sales letters. Compare the following:

INSTEAD OF THIS	WRITE THIS
The NuForm desk chair is designed to support your lower back and relieve pressure on your legs.	The NuForm desk chair supports your lower back and relieves pressure on your legs.

The second version says the same thing in fewer words and puts more emphasis on what the chair does for the user ("supports") than on the intentions of the design team ("is designed to support").

In general, use colorful verbs and adjectives that convey a dynamic image. Be careful, however, not to overdo it: "Your factory floors will sparkle like diamonds" is hard to believe and may prevent your audience from believing the rest of your message.

Talking About Price The price people will pay for a product depends on the prices of similar products, the general state of the economy, and the psychology of the buyer. Price is therefore a complicated issue and often a sensitive one.

Whether the price of your product is highlighted or downplayed, prepare your readers for it. Such words as *luxurious* and *economical* provide unmistakable clues about how your price compares with that of competitors, and they help your readers accept the price when you finally state it.

You can prepare readers for your product's price by subtle choice and arrangement of words.

Here's an example from a sales letter offering a product at a bargain price:

> **All the Features of Name-Brand Pantyhose at Half the Price!**
> Why pay for fancy packaging or that little tag with a famous name on it when you can enjoy cotton lining, reinforced toes, and matchless durability for only $1.99?

In this excerpt the price falls right at the end of the paragraph, where it stands out. In addition, the price issue is featured in a bold headline. This technique may even be used as the opening of a letter if the price is the most important feature and the audience for the letter is value conscious.

If the price is an attractive feature, emphasize it by displaying it prominently.

If price is not a major selling point, you can handle it in several ways. You could leave out the price altogether or mention it only in an accompanying brochure. You could de-emphasize the price by putting the actual figures in the middle of a paragraph close to the end of your sales letter, well after you've presented the benefits and selling points.

To de-emphasize price
- Bury actual figures in the middle of a paragraph near the end
- Mention benefits and favorable money matters before the actual price
- Break a quantity price into units
- Compare the price with the cost of some other product or activity

> Only 100 prints of this exclusive, limited-edition lithograph will be created. On June 1, they will be made available to the general public, but you can reserve one now for only $350, the special advance reservation price. Simply rush the enclosed reservation card back today so that your order is in before the June 1 publication date.

Emphasis on the rarity of the edition signals value and thus prepares the reader for the big-ticket price that follows. The actual price, buried in the middle of a sentence, is tied in with another reminder of the exclusivity of the offer.

The pros use two other techniques for minimizing price. One is to break a quantity price into units. Instead of saying that a case of wine costs $144, you might say that each bottle costs $12. The other is to compare your product's price with the cost of some other product or activity: "The cost of owning your own spa is less than you'd pay for a health-club membership." Your aim is to make the cost seem as small and affordable as possible, thereby eliminating price as a possible objection.

Supporting Your Claims You can't assume that people will believe what you say about your product just because you've said it in writing. You'll have to prove your claims, especially if your product is complicated, expensive, or representative of some unusual approach.

Support for your claims may take several forms. Samples and brochures, often with photographs, are enclosures in the sales package and are referred to in the letter. The letter also describes or typographically highlights examples of how the product has benefited others, includes testimonials (quotations from satisfied customers), or cites statistics from scientific studies of the product's performance. Guarantees of exchange or return privileges, which may also be woven into the letter or set off in a special way, indicate that you have faith in the product and are willing to back it up.

Types of support for product claims:
- Samples
- Brochures
- Examples
- Testimonials
- Statistics
- Guarantees

It's almost impossible to provide too much support. Try to anticipate every question your audience may want to ask. Put yourself in your audience's place so that you can ask, and answer, all the "what ifs."[22]

Motivating Action

After you have raised enough interest and built the audience's desire for your product, you'll want to clearly explain how to take the next step. After all, the overriding purpose of a sales letter is to get your reader to do something. Many consumer products sold through the mail simply ask for a check—in other words, an immediate decision to buy. On the other hand, companies like AT&T's Language Line and companies selling big-ticket and more complex items frequently ask for just a small step toward the final buying decision, such as sending for more information or authorizing a call by a sales representative.

Aim to get the reader to act as soon as possible.

Try to persuade readers to take action, whatever it is, right away. Convince them that they must act now, perhaps to guarantee a specific delivery date. If there's no particular reason to act quickly, many sales letters offer discounts for orders placed by a certain date or prizes or special offers to, say, the first 500 people to respond. Others suggest that purchases be charged to a credit card or be paid off over time. Still others offer a free trial, an unconditional guarantee, or a no-strings request card for information, all in an effort to overcome readers' natural inertia.

Of course, adding a P.S. is one of the most effective ways to boost sales letter response. This is the place to make your final impression, so be sure the information is noteworthy. Use the P.S. to reiterate your primary benefit, make an additional offer, or compel the reader to act quickly by emphasizing a deadline.[23] Finally, use good judgment when distributing your messages to would-be customers (see "Keeping Pace with Technology: Canning Spam"). And keep in mind that motivating action can be a challenge in sales letters and even more of a challenge when you're trying to raise funds.

Planning Fundraising Messages

Fund-raising letters use many of the same techniques that are used in sales letters.

Most of the techniques used to write sales letters can also be used to write fundraising letters, as long as your techniques match your audience, your goals, and the cause or organization you're representing. Be careful to establish value in the minds of your donors. Above

Persuading mass merchants such as Wal-Mart and Kmart to carry your product can be quite a challenge. So when Brass Eagle's CEO, E. Lynn Scott, set out to convince these giants to sell the company's paintballs and accessories, he framed his persuasive argument using the AIDA plan and motivated action by convincing these stores that his products appealed to both kids and adults.

all, don't forget to include the "what's in it for me?" information: for example, telling your readers how good they'll feel by making a donation.[24]

To make sure that your fundraising letters outshine the competition's letters, take some time to get ready before you actually begin writing.[25] You can begin by reading the mail you receive from donors. Learn as much as you can about your audience by noting the tone of these letters, the language used, and the concerns raised. This exercise will help you write letters that donors will both understand and relate to.

You might also keep a file of competing fundraising letters. Study these samples to find out what other fundraisers are doing and what new approaches they're taking. Most important, find out what works and what doesn't. Then you can continue with your other research efforts, such as conducting interviews, holding focus groups, and reading trade journals to find out what people are concerned about, what they're interested in, and what gets their attention.

Finally, before you start writing, know whose benefits to emphasize. Make a two-column list; on one side, list what your organization does, and on the other side, list what your donors want. You'll discover that the two columns are quite different. Make sure that the benefits you emphasize are related to what your donors want, not to what your organization does. Then you can work on stating those donor benefits in specific detail. For example: "Your donation of $100 will provide 15 people with a Christmas dinner."

Be sure to focus on the concerns of your readers, not on the concerns of your organization.

Personalizing Fundraising Messages

Because fundraising letters depend so heavily on emotional appeals, keep your message personal. A natural, real-life lead-in is usually the best. People seem to respond best to slice-of-life stories. In fact, storytelling is perfect when your narrative is unforced and goes straight to the heart of the matter.[26] Professional fundraiser Conrad Squires advises you to "find and use relevant human-interest stories," to "show donors the faces of the people they are helping," and to "make the act of sending a contribution as real and memorable and personal" as you can.[27] Such techniques make people feel the warmth of other lives.[28]

Human-interest stories are the best way to interest your readers in fundraising letters.

So that your letters remain personal, immediate, and effective, steer clear of three common mistakes:[29]

- Avoid letting your letter sound like a business communication of any kind.
- Avoid wasting space on warm-up (the things you write while you're working up to your real argument).
- Avoid assuming that the goals of your organization are more important than your readers' concerns (a deadly mistake).

The last item is crucial when writing fundraising letters. Squires suggests that "the more space you spend writing about the reader, the better response you're likely to get."[30] Here are some examples:

> "You've proven you are somebody who really cares about what happens to children, Mr. Jones."

> "Ms. Smith, your company's kindness can change the world for Meta Singh and his family."

Personalize fundraising letters by
- Writing about your readers
- Helping your readers identify with recipients

It's also up to you to help your donors identify with recipients. A busy company executive may not be able to identify with the homeless man she passes on the street every day. But every human being understands pain; we've all felt it. So do your best to portray that homeless man's pain in words the busy executive can understand.[31]

Strengthening Fundraising Messages

The best fundraising letters do four things: (1) thoroughly explain a specific need, (2) show how important it is for readers to help, (3) spell out exactly what amount of help is being

Strong fundraising letters
- Explain a specific need thoroughly
- Show how important it is for readers to help
- Spell out exactly what amount of help is being requested
- Describe in detail the benefits of helping

requested, and (4) describe in detail the benefits of helping (see Figure 9.7 on page 316).[32] To help you accomplish these four major tasks, here are some fundraising guidelines:[33]

- Do whatever you can to interest your readers at the absolute beginning of your letter. If you can't catch your readers' interest then, you never will.
- Tell your story with simple, warm, and personal language.
- Be sure to give readers an opportunity to accomplish something important.
- Make the need so urgent and strong that your readers will find it hard to say no. "Won't you send a gift now, knowing children's lives are on the line?" Donors want to feel needed. They want the excitement of coming to your rescue.
- Make it extremely easy to respond by asking for a small gift.
- Make the amount of money you want absolutely clear and appropriate to your audience.
- Explain why the money is needed as soon as possible.
- Write no longer than you have to. For example, people expect telegram-type messages to be short. However, for fundraising letters, longer messages are usually the most effective, as long as you keep your sentences and paragraphs short, maximize content, and minimize wordiness.
- Include all the basics in your reply form: your name, address, and telephone number; a restatement of your request and the gift amount; your donor's name and address (or space enough for a label); information on how to make out the check; and information on tax deductibility.

KEEPING PACE WITH TECHNOLOGY

CANNING SPAM

From exasperated consumers to state attorneys general to giant online services, everyone is trying to stamp out those irritating online sales pitches called spam (electronic junk mail). Even the U.S. Senate has jumped into the act by passing a bill that would regulate this scourge of cyberspace. But rather than waiting for the government to step in, you can wage your own counterassault if spam is jamming your e-mail box. Here's how.

Keep a Low Profile The best way to avoid junk e-mail is to stay off the spammers' lists. Unfortunately, that can be difficult. Many junk mailers are fly-by-night operations that use clever tricks to cloak their identity and location. In addition, sneaky marketers use automated "robot" programs that infiltrate online chat rooms and electronic bulletin boards to harvest e-mail addresses for their sales pitches. Still, savvy surfers can use tricks of their own to fool the robots:

- When possible, use a different online identity than your e-mail address. Many Internet service providers allow users to create different screen names. Create one screen name to use only in chat rooms and forums. That way you can keep your original e-mail address hidden from spammers and help keep junk mail out of your primary e-mail account.
- Don't list yourself in your service provider's member directory. Some spammers use this as a convenient, precompiled spam directory.
- To fool the robots trolling through the bulletin boards, alter your e-mail address in an obvious manner, so that a human knows what the real address is but stupid robot programs don't. For example, an e-mail address like Jason@msn.com can become JasonNOSPAM@-NOSPAM.msn.com.

Whatever You Do, Don't Reply Inevitably, no matter how careful you are, you will end up on some spammers' lists. Some of the junk e-mail even comes across with a civil enough tone: "If you don't wish to receive any more e-mail, click on the reply button and ask to be removed."

- Use interesting enclosures. You will decrease returns by using enclosures that simply give more information about a project or the purpose of your organization. To increase returns, use enclosures that are fun or that give the donor something to do, sign, return, or keep.

These guidelines should help you reach the humanity and compassion of your readers by focusing on specific reader benefits, detailing the unique need, emphasizing the urgency of the situation, and spelling out the exact help needed.

Like sales letters, fundraising letters are simply particular types of persuasive messages. Both categories have their unique requirements, some of which only professional writers can master. (See this chapter's Checklist for Composing Sales and Fundraising Letters as a reminder of the tasks involved in writing these messages.)

Writing Collection Messages

The purpose of the collection process is to maintain goodwill while collecting what is owed. Collection is a sensitive issue; it's also closely governed by federal and state laws. The Fair Debt Collection Practices Act of 1978 outlines a number of restrictions on collection procedures. The following practices are prohibited:

- Falsely implying that a lawsuit has been filed
- Contacting the debtor's employer or relatives about the debt
- Communicating to other persons that the person is in debt
- Harassing the debtor (although definitions of harassment may vary)

Although recent legislation obligates senders of junk e-mail to honor recipients' requests to be removed from mailing lists when asked and imposes fines for violators, experts warn that replying directly to the spammer is the worst possible reaction; it can actually land your e-mail address on a "premium" spam list. That's because the spammer knows they've got a live one; someone is actually reading the e-mail at that account.

Drown Out the Noise Consider this: A mass marketer who sends out 14 million pieces of mail has to pay for the paper, printing, and postage, which can cost up to a dollar for each piece. But in cyberspace, spammers send out millions of messages with just a few mouse clicks, at a cost of about a penny to beam out 1,000 messages.

When the barrage of junk e-mail gets to be too much, you can use technology to trash some of the junk. Most e-mail packages and online services offer filtering programs that scan through your mail and try to get rid of stuff you don't want. There are two ways to set up a filter: You can instruct it either to accept e-mail from a list of users or services you've specified or to specifically weed out people or services that you've targeted as offenders. Of course, no filter is perfect; some desirable e-mail may get tossed out in the process.

Fight Back Aside from trying to avoid, ignore, or delete spam, there are some more extreme steps you can take to retaliate against the most obnoxious spammers. You can file a complaint with the Federal Trade Commission, which is running a vigorous campaign to try to quash the worst spammers.

You can also send a complaint to the Internet service provider of the spammer that sent you the annoying pitch. When service providers get lots of complaints about a mass marketer on their system, they can be pressured to shut down the spammer's account and put her or him out of business—at least temporarily. Why temporarily? Because U.S. laws can't be forced on a global medium; spammers can simply relocate offshore and out of reach of U.S. law enforcement.

1. Do you think a law curbing unsolicited e-mail is a violation of free speech? Why or why not?
2. Some people think that recent legislation requiring senders of unsolicited commercial e-mail to include their name, phone, and address actually legitimizes spamming. In other words, it's okay to spam if you include your contact information. Why might they think this way?

Figure 9.7
In-Depth Critique: Letter to Raise Funds

As president of the nonprofit Decatur High School Band Parents Association, Monty Nichols is faced with the daunting task of raising half a million dollars to help send the band to Osaka, Japan, for an international band festival. Nichols and his board have decided to contact local businesses for help. The following letter makes a compelling case for donations.

Decatur High School Band
27 Linwood Lane • Decatur, Illinois 62525
(217) 864-7768

Dear Corporate Friend:

The "you"-oriented opening focuses on the reader's generosity and grabs attention.

You have been a loyal supporter of our award-winning Decatur High School Band, and we appreciate what you've helped us accomplish. Because of you, we were able to participate in three festival competitions this year, and we brought home three "Grand Champion" trophies. Now we have the unprecedented opportunity to represent Decatur in the Osaka International Band Festival in 2001. Only 25 top bands from the United States have been invited, and, thanks to your sponsorship, Decatur High School Band is one of them.

The next three paragraphs create interest by emphasizing benefits to the reader and by providing details of the trip and costs.

Your continued support will help the Decatur High School Band accept Osaka's exciting invitation. The Decatur City Council, the Decatur School Board, and our own Parents Association Board believe that the trip will be an opportunity for our 130 band members to learn about another culture. Even more important, our Decatur ambassadors will bring their experiences back to our community and their classmates in speeches, photographs, and interviews with the local media.

Let us paint your logo on our band trailer as one of our Golden Sponsors. We'll also include your name in all our programs and mailings between now and the time of the trip. You'll be helping band members

The easy-to-read list of benefits creates desire to participate in a worthwhile project.

1. Learn about other cultures
2. Share information abroad about our way of life in the United States
3. Teach others in Decatur what they learn
4. Help Decatur become recognized as a good home for international businesses

We estimate total costs at $500,000. The city of Osaka has pledged $25,000 toward financing the trip, and we have already received pledges from Akworth Nissan and the city for $25,000 each. Our band members will be holding fundraising events such as car washes, bake sales, a spring fair, and many others over the next two years. But your support will make our dream a reality.

The last paragraph urges action by naming additional reader benefits and enclosing a response card.

Please help our young ambassadors make this trip. Mark your pledge card and return it today. You'll receive personal letters from the kids expressing their appreciation. And you'll be proof of our city's motto, "Dreams come true in Decatur."

Cordially,

Monty Nichols

Monty Nichols
President
Decatur High School Band Parents Association

Enclosure

- Using abusive or obscene language
- Using defamatory language (such as calling the person a *deadbeat* or a *crook*)
- Intentionally causing mental distress
- Threatening violence

CHECKLIST FOR COMPOSING SALES AND FUNDRAISING LETTERS

A. Attention

1. Design a positive opening that awakens in the reader a favorable association with the product, need, or cause.
2. Write the opening so that it's appropriate, fresh, honest, interesting, specific, and relevant.
3. Promise a benefit to the reader.
4. Keep the first paragraph short, preferably two to five lines, sometimes only one.
5. Design an attention-getter that uses a human-interest story for fundraising letters or any of the following techniques for sales letters: significant fact about the product, solution to a problem, special offer or gift, testimonial, stimulation of the senses or emotions, reference to current events, concrete illustration, startling fact, agreeable assertion, comparison, event or fact in the reader's life, problem the reader may face, or quotation.

B. Interest

1. State information clearly, vividly, and persuasively, and relate it to the reader's concerns.
2. Develop the central selling point, or explain the urgency of the need for funds.
3. Feature the product or need in two ways: physical description and reader benefits.
   a. Interweave benefits with a physical description, or place benefits first.
   b. Describe the objective details of the need or of the product (size, shape, color, scent, sound, texture, and so on).
   c. Through psychological appeals, present the sensation, satisfaction, or pleasure your reader will gain, translating the product, service, or donation into the fulfillment of needs and desires.
   d. Blend cold facts with warm feelings.

C. Desire

1. Enlist one or more appeals to support the central idea (selling point or fundraising goal).
   a. Provide one paragraph of desire-creating material in a one-page letter with descriptive brochure; provide several paragraphs if the letter itself is two or more pages long, with or without an enclosed brochure.
   b. Emphasize reader benefits.
   c. If the product is valued mainly because of its appearance, describe its physical details.
   d. If the product is machinery or technical equipment, describe its sturdiness of construction, fine crafting, and other technical details in terms that help readers visualize themselves using it.
   e. Include technical sketches and meaningful pictures, charts, and graphs, if necessary.
   f. If the main point is to elicit a donation, use strong visual details, good narrative, active verbs, and limited adjectives to strengthen the desire to help.
2. Anticipate and answer the reader's questions.
3. Use an appropriate form of proof.
   a. Include facts about users' experience with the charitable organization or product, including verifiable reports and statistics from donation recipients or product users.
   b. Provide names (with permission only) of satisfied buyers, users, or donors.
   c. Present unexaggerated testimonials from persons or firms who have used the product or donated funds and whose judgment the reader respects.
   d. For sales letters, provide the results of performance tests by recognized experts, testing laboratories, or authoritative agencies.
   e. For fundraising letters, provide the details of how donations are spent, using recognized accounting or auditing firms.
   f. In sales letters, offer a free trial or a guarantee, and refer to samples if they are included.
4. Note any enclosures in conjunction with a selling point or a reader benefit.

D. Action

1. Clearly state the action you desire.
2. Provide specific details on how to order the product, donate money, or reach your organization.
3. Make action easy through the use of a mail-back reply card, preaddressed envelope, phone number, or promise of a follow-up call or visit.
4. Offer a special inducement to act: time limit or situation urgency, special price for a limited time, premium for acting before a certain date, gift for buying or donating, free trial, no obligation to buy but more information or a suggested demonstration, easy payments with no money down, credit-card payments.
5. Supply a final reader benefit.
6. Include a postscript conveying important donation information or an important sales point (if desired for emphasis).

- Communicating by postcard (not confidential enough)
- Sending anonymous C.O.D. communications
- Misrepresenting the legal status of the debt
- Communicating in such a way as to make the receiver physically ill
- Giving false impressions, such as labeling the envelope "Tax Information"
- Misrepresenting the message as a government or court document

To protect people from unreasonable persecution and harassment by debt collectors, the law also delineates when you may contact a debtor, how many times you may call, and what information you must provide to the debtor (timely responses, accurate records, and understandable documents). However, that doesn't mean you can't be tough in collection letters. As long as what you state is true and lawful, it can't be construed as harassment or misrepresentation.

A debtor's response is likely to be emotional, especially when the debtor is conscientious, so use tact.

Conscientious customers are embarrassed about past-due accounts. In such an emotional state, they may consciously or unconsciously blame you for the problem, procrastinate, avoid the situation altogether, or react aggressively. Your job is to neutralize those feelings by using **positive appeals**, by accentuating the benefits of complying with your request for payment. If positive appeals fail, you may have to consider a **negative appeal**, which stresses the unpleasant consequences of not acting rather than the benefits of acting. Of course, using abusive or threatening language and harassing your customer is ineffective and illegal. Persuasion is the opposite of force, so continue to use a polite and businesslike tone as you point out some of the actions legally available to you.

Steps in the collection series:

- Notification
- Reminder
- Inquiry
- Urgent notice
- Ultimatum

Don't forget that your real aim is to persuade the customer to make the payment. So your best approach is to try to maintain the customer's goodwill. One key to success in collecting is remembering that collection is a process, not just a single demand.[34] As the past-due period lengthens, a series of collection letters reflecting the increasing seriousness of the problem is sent to the customer at predetermined intervals: notification, reminder, inquiry, urgent notice, and ultimatum. At the later stages, the customer's credit and buying history, the amount of money owed, and the customer's overall credit rating determine the content and style of collection messages.

Notification and Reminder

The standardized notification is a sign of trust.

Most creditors send bills to customers on a regular schedule, depending on the terms of the credit agreement. Typically, this standard notification is a form letter or statement, often computerized, stating clearly the amount due, the date due, the penalties for late payment, and the total amount remaining to be paid. The standardized form, far from being an insult to the recipient, indicates the creditor's trust that all will go according to plan.

The reminder notice, which still assumes only a minor problem, may be a standardized form or an informal message.

If the payment has not been received within a few days after the due date, most creditors send out a gentle reminder. Again, the tone of the standardized letter is reassuring, conveying the company's assumption that some minor problem has delayed payment. In other words, the firm still believes that the customer has every intention of paying what is due and need only be reminded. Thus the tone is not too serious:

> Our records show that your September payment is more than a week overdue. If you have recently mailed your check for $154.87, we thank you. If not, please send it in quickly.

Using a different strategy, some companies send out a copy of the unpaid bill at this stage, with a handwritten note or preprinted stamp or sticker indicating that payment has not yet been received.

Inquiry

As frustrating as it may be to send out a reminder and still get no response, don't assume that your customer plans to ignore the debt, especially if the customer has paid bills promptly in the past. So avoid accusations in your inquiry message. However, the time has passed for assuming that the delay is merely an oversight, so you may assume that some unusual circumstance is preventing payment:

The inquiry
- Assumes that something unusual is preventing payment
- Is personalized
- Avoids any suggestion of customer dissatisfaction

> According to our records, we have not received your September payment of $154.87. Because this payment is four weeks overdue, we are quite concerned. You have a history of paying your bills on time, so we must conclude that there is a problem. Please contact us at (800) 536-4995 to discuss this payment, or send us your check for $154.87 right away. We want to help you correct this situation as quickly as possible.

Personalization at this stage is appropriate because you're asking your customer to work out an individualized solution. The letter also avoids any suggestion that the customer might be dissatisfied with the purchase. Instead, it emphasizes the reader's obligation to communicate about the problem and the creditor's willingness to discuss it. Including the writer's name and a phone number helps motivate a response at this stage.

Urgent Notice

The urgent notice stage represents a significant escalation. Convey your desire to collect the overdue payment immediately and your willingness to get serious, but avoid any overt threats. To communicate a sense of urgency, you might resort to a letter signed by a top official in the company or to a negative appeal. However, an urgent notice still leaves an opening for the debtor to make a payment without losing face:

An urgent notice
- Might be signed by a top company official
- Might indicate the negative consequences of noncompliance
- Should leave an opening for payment without loss of face

I was very surprised this morning when your file reached my desk with a big tag marked OVERDUE. Usually, I receive customer files only when a serious problem has cropped up.

An attention-getter focuses on the unusual circumstances leading to this letter.

Opening your file, I found the following facts: Your order for five cases of Panza serving trays was shipped six months ago. Yet we still haven't received the $232.70 due. You're in business too, Mr. Rosen, so you must realize that this debt needs to be paid at once. If you had a customer this far behind, you'd be equally concerned.

The recipient is reminded of the order. Personalization and an attempt to emphasize common ground may motivate the reader to respond.

Please see that a check for $232.70 is mailed to us at once. If you need to work out an alternate plan for payment, call me now at (712) 693-7300.

The preferred action is spelled out; an option is also suggested in case of serious trouble.

Sincerely,

Artis Knight
Vice President

The name of a ranking official lends weight to the message.

Ultimatum

Some people's finances are in such disorder that you won't get their attention until the ultimatum stage. However, don't send an ultimatum unless you intend to back it up and are well supported by company policy. Even then, maintain a polite, businesslike manner and avoid defaming or harassing the debtor.

An ultimatum
- Should state the exact consequences of nonpayment
- Must avoid any hint of defamation or harassment
- Need not take a personal, helpful tone

By itemizing the precise consequences of not paying the bill, you can encourage debtors to reevaluate their priorities. You're no longer interested in hearing why it has taken them so long to respond; you're interested in putting your claim at the top of their list. The tone of the ultimatum need not be so personal or individualized as the inquiry or urgent notice. At this stage, you're in a position of justified authority and should no longer be willing to return to an earlier stage of communication and negotiation:

> On December 12, 1998, you placed a catalog order with Karting Klothes for our extra-large wheeled duffel bag, and you applied for a credit account with us. We approved your application, and on December 17 we mailed the duffel bag to you with an invoice for $92.87. According to our credit application, which you signed, payment is due within 20 days. As of February 1, your payment is significantly overdue.
>
> Karting Klothes sent you reminders on January 2 and again on February 2. In both these letters, we asked you to contact us to discuss your payment. We also asked you to make a partial payment as a show of your good faith. You did neither.
>
> Karting Klothes has already canceled your credit privileges and will turn your account over to a collection agency if we do not receive your payment for $92.87 by March 10. To reinstate your account and to avoid the problems associated with a bad credit rating, mail your check immediately.

This letter outlines the steps that have already been taken, implying that the drastic action to come is the logical follow-up. Although earlier collection messages were based on persuasion, this one is essentially a bad-news letter.

If a letter like this doesn't yield results, the only remaining remedy is to actually begin legal collection procedures. As a final courtesy, you may wish to send the debtor a notice of the action you're about to take. By maintaining until the bitter end your respect for the customer, you may still salvage some goodwill.

COMMUNICATION CHALLENGES AT AT&T'S LANGUAGE LINE SERVICES

The word about AT&T's Language Line Services has spread quickly among hospitals, police departments, city agencies, and businesses looking to expand into overseas markets. Jeanne Anderson's sales and marketing department is busy prospecting for new subscribers, and her staff keeps growing and growing. Anderson has her hands full, and she recently began delegating some of her responsibilities to keep up with the work load.

INDIVIDUAL CHALLENGE: Every December, the sales and marketing department hosts a Holiday Open House Toy and Food Drive for all Language Line employees. Anderson sees the event as a way of bringing old and new members of her department closer together and of helping local charity organizations. But she realizes it's going to take a little persuasion to get her staff to participate; the holidays are a busy time for everyone, and this affair is strictly voluntary. Moreover, she's asking them, as they do every year, to bring finger food and desserts for a potluck buffet, plus a new toy or canned food to donate to the needy. The party will last from 2:00 to 4:00, with music, talk, and maybe even a little dancing.

Anderson has asked you to write a memo to the staff, serving more as a persuasive request for action than as an invitation to a party. She hopes staff members will decide to attend, will bring a toy or food gift, and will contact Laura and Judy (party organizers) to let them know what potluck dish to expect. (Make up any other names or details you need in order to write a convincing memo.)

TEAM CHALLENGE: Language Line Services became so popular so quickly among certain industries that Anderson has had little time to brainstorm ideas about applications for new markets. She has asked your group to help out. Sooner or later, AT&T's current markets will be saturated; before that happens, Anderson wants her staff ready to target new industries. That will require special sales training and new sales literature targeted to each industry—and that means she'll need a budget increase.

First, she has asked you to brainstorm ways Language Line Services might be used by government agencies, service organizations, or any untapped industry you can identify. List the applications and benefits for each industry, then decide which three sound most promising. Anderson wants you to write a persuasive memo to convince upper management that these three markets are so promising that the added expenditures for staff training and industry-specific sales literature will bring profitable returns. She's going to ask for a $50,000 total budget increase to start the three-industry campaign. "Don't worry about financial justification; I'll supply a detailed budget breakdown as an attachment to the memo," she tells you. "You just need to convince them this is an idea they can't refuse."[35] ■

SUMMARY OF LEARNING OBJECTIVES

1. **List the components of a well-developed persuasive message.** The components of an effective persuasive message include establishing your credibility, framing your argument, using logic and emotional appeals to connect with your audience, and reinforcing your position with vivid language and compelling evidence.
2. **Discuss several ways to establish credibility in persuasive messages.** You can establish credibility by supporting your claims with facts, sources, and testimonials, by demonstrating expertise and enthusiasm, and by being objective, sincere, and trustworthy.
3. **Describe the AIDA organizational plan for persuasive messages.** You open by getting *attention* with a reader benefit, a problem, a stimulating question, a piece of news, or an unexpected statement. You build *interest* with facts, details, and additional reader benefits. You increase *desire* by providing more evidence and reader benefits and by anticipating and answering possible objections. You conclude by motivating a specific *action,* emphasizing the positive results of that action, and making it easy for the reader to respond.
4. **List several tools that can help reinforce your position in a persuasive message.** Use semantics, metaphors, anecdotes, timing, moderation, simple language, and facts to reinforce your position. In addition, try to create a win-win situation and stay focused on your goal.
5. **Discuss four common mistakes people make when putting together persuasive arguments.** They resist compromise, focus too much on crafting a great argument instead of creating a win-win situation, go for the hard sell, and assume that persuasion is a one-shot effort.
6. **Identify some of the key ingredients of a good persuasive claim or request for adjustment.** You should include all the necessary facts and details, be logical, appeal to the audience's sense of fair play, calmly express your feelings, stick to the issues at hand, focus on the benefits of solving the problem, and state a specific and reasonable request for action.

CRITICAL THINKING QUESTIONS

1. If you must persuade your audience to take some action, aren't you being manipulative and unethical? Explain.
2. As a manager, how many of your daily tasks require persuasion? List as many as you can think of.
3. Are emotional appeals ethical? Why or why not?
4. Is it honest to use a hook before presenting your request? Explain.
5. Why is it important to maintain goodwill in your collection letter? Briefly explain.
6. Why is it important to present both sides of an argument when writing a persuasive message to a potentially hostile audience?
7. How are persuasive messages different from routine messages?
8. When is it appropriate to use the direct organizational approach in persuasive messages?

DOCUMENTS FOR ANALYSIS

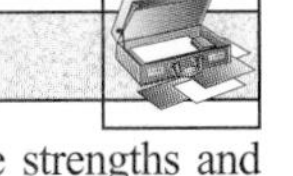

Read the following documents, then (1) analyze the strengths and weaknesses of each sentence and (2) revise each document so that it follows this chapter's guidelines.

Document 9.A: Writing Persuasive Requests for Action

At Tolson Auto Repair, we have been in business for over 25 years. We stay in business by always taking into account what the customer wants. That's why we are writing. We want to know your opinions to be able to better conduct our business.

Take a moment right now and fill out the enclosed questionnaire. We know everyone is busy, but this is just one way we have of making sure our people do their job correctly. Use the enclosed envelope to return the questionnaire.

And again, we're happy you chose Tolson Auto Repair. We want to take care of all your auto needs.

Document 9.B: Writing Persuasive Claims and Requests for Adjustment

Dear Gateway:

I'm writing to you because of my disappointment with my new TelePath x2 Faxmodem. The modem works all right, but the volume is set wide open and the volume knob doesn't turn it down. It's driving us crazy. The volume knob doesn't seem to be connected to anything but simply spins around. I can't believe you would put out a product like this without testing it first.

I depend on the modem to run my small business and want to know what you are going to do about it. This reminds me of every time I buy electronic equipment from what seems like any company. Something is always wrong. I thought quality was supposed to be important, but I guess not.

Anyway, I need this fixed right away. Please tell me what you want me to do.

Document 9.C: Writing Sales and Fund-Raising Letters

We know how awful dining hall food can be, and that's why we've developed the "Mealaweek Club." Once a week, we'll deliver food to your dormitory or apartment. Our meals taste great. We have pizza, buffalo wings, hamburgers and curly fries, veggie roll-ups, and more!

When you sign up for just six months, we will ask what day you want your delivery. We'll ask you to fill out your selection of meals. And the rest is up to us. At "Mealaweek," we deliver! And payment is easy. We accept MasterCard and VISA or a personal check. It will save money especially when compared to eating out.

Just fill out the enclosed card and indicate your method of payment. As soon as we approve your credit or check, we'll begin delivery. Tell all your friends about Mealaweek. We're the best idea since sliced bread!

Document 9.D: Writing Collection Messages

It may not seem like it to you, but your outstanding balance of $429.52 is very important to us. When we grant credit, we do it with the understanding that bills will be paid on time. Our entire operation works smoothly only when we have all our customers paying their bills in a timely fashion.

Perhaps there is some problem which you haven't called us about? We want to please our customers, but even a company with the best of intentions sometimes falls short. Take a minute from your busy day and fill out the enclosed card. We want to know if there is a problem.

Also, take a minute right now to please pay your bill. Thanks for your cooperation. We would hate to turn a valuable customer over to a collection agency.

EXERCISES

1. For over a year, you've tried repeatedly, without success, to collect $6,000 from a client who is able to pay but simply refuses. You're writing one last letter before turning the matter over to your attorney. What sort of things can you say in your letter? What things should you avoid saying? Explain your answers
2. What type of reasoning is at work in the following statement: "We've lost money on 48 of the 52 power plants we've constructed in South America in the last ten years. It's obvious that it's impossible to turn a profit in that market."
3. Analyze the persuasive memo in Figure 9.3 on page 294 by answering the following questions:
   a. What techniques are used to capture the reader's attention?
   b. Does the writer use the direct or the indirect organizational approach?
   c. Is the subject line effective? Why or why not?
   d. Does the writer use an emotional or a logical appeal?
   e. What reader benefits are included?
   f. How does the writer establish credibility?
   g. What tools does the writer use to reinforce his position?
4. Compose effective subject lines for the following persuasive memos:
   a. A request to your supervisor to purchase a new high-speed laser printer for your office. You've been outsourcing quite a bit of your printing to AlphaGraphics and you're certain this printer will pay for itself in six months.
   b. A direct mailing to area residents soliciting customers for your new business "Meals à la Car," a carryout dining service that delivers from most local-area restaurants. All local restaurant menus are on the Internet. Mom and Dad can dine on egg rolls and chow mein while the kids munch on pepperoni pizza.
   c. A special request to the company president to allow managers to carry over their unused vacation days to the following year. Apparently, many managers canceled their fourth-quarter vacation plans to work on the installation of a new company computer system. Under their current contract, vacation days not used by December 31 aren't accruable.
5. It's been over 14 months since your last salary increase. You've been a stellar performer during this period, and you feel it's time to approach the boss for a raise. You have two options for delivering your persuasive message: put it in writing (an internal memo) or arrange a meeting (oral delivery) to make your case. Which will you choose? Why?
6. Visit the Federal Trade Commission Web site http://www.ftc.gov. Click on "Fair Debt Collection Practices Act" and review some of the sections. Explore the site. What does the FTC do, and how does it serve the consumer?

EXPLORING THE BEST OF THE WEB

Lobby Movers and Shakers in the U.S. Government, page 303

1. Follow links to the home page of one of your congressional representatives, or any representative you choose. Draft and send a persuasive but short e-mail message about an issue that concerns you. If you can't think of one, go back to the Thomas home page and review some of the items now under consideration by Congress. You can go as far as your time and interest permit.
2. Now put yourself in the congressional representative's shoes and reread your message. Would it affect your vote? If you could change any aspect of your message, your personal circumstances, your communication medium, or your approach, could you think of a way to be more persuasive? Would more information about the topic help? Where would you go for this information?

WRITING PERSUASIVE REQUESTS FOR ACTION

1. Nap time: Memo requesting space for "day sleepers" at Phidias & Associates It's been one of those days . . . you were dragging by 10 a.m., ready to slump over onto your drafting table at Phidias & Associates architectural firm in San Francisco. Even that incredibly bright bay view outside the office windows hasn't helped perk you up, and the coffee is just giving you stomach pains. How are you supposed to be creatively inspired when you can barely get your eyes to focus and your head feels as if it's full of cotton? No, you weren't out partying last night; you've just been working long, late hours on a rush job for one of the firm's biggest clients. San Francisco is the workaholic city, but this is too much. If only you could stretch out for a little catnap, you'd be good as new in fifteen minutes.

Groggily, your mind brings up the memory of an item you tore out of the *Wall Street Journal* a year ago. You saved it with the vague notion of presenting it during one of those officewide, corporate spirit "pep rallies" your employers are fond of. You rummage around in your desk drawer—ah, there it is. A paragraph or two in the "Work Week" column, all about a minitrend toward "nap rooms" in the workplace. At first, your work ethic was shocked at the concept, but then your creative self started to glow at the thought. After all, didn't they teach you in school that Thomas Edison kept a cot in his office and got his best ideas when he was napping? And the article quotes an expert, William A. Anthony, author of *The Art of Napping* and professor of rehabilitation counseling at Boston University. He says most people aren't sleep deprived, they're "nap ready."

There are plenty of other precedents and pioneers out there in the business world. At *Macworld Magazine,* the human resources director, Shelly Ginenthal, says their two-person nap room was installed in 1986 and usually has a waiting line. It must not be interfering with productivity if they're still using it ten years later, you muse. And here's another firm, Yarde Metals in Bristol, Connecticut, whose president, Bruce Yarde, says, "A quick little nap can rejuvenate you." So he's fighting employee stress with a 25-person nap room. Wow. That's almost like your old kindergarten. And yet another—you like this one best—an architectural firm in Kansas City, Missouri, Gould Evans Goodman Associates, has plans on its drawing boards to add a nap space to its offices. If they can do it in Kansas City, why not here?

Your task: After you've had a good night's sleep, write a memo to Jonas T. Phidias, persuading the senior partner that the distinguished offices of Phidias & Associates could benefit from the addition of a corporate "nap room." Be sure you use your best persuasive skills, though, or you may send the wrong message to your employer. On a separate page, include a short note to your instructor justifying your organizational approach (direct or indirect) and your selection of delivery medium (e-mail or interoffice mail).[36]

2. Selling sales letters: E-mail message promoting a new idea at Sears, Roebuck As marketing manager for Sears, Roebuck, you know that sales messages can make or break a business. One of your company's most difficult tasks is getting customers to read a sales letter. During a recent seminar, you were told about a Web site by *Sales & Marketing Management* magazine. Explore the site at http://www.cmarket.net/features/m19970102.htm and read its material, "Write Sales Letters with Stopping Power." What pointers does this site offer to help grab prospects' attention? Click on "More Direct-Mail Tips." What other important tips can you identify for making your sales letters more effective? You would like everyone in your department to seriously consider browsing this site for its useful advice.

Your task: Write an e-mail message to everyone in your department, selling the idea of the PSALM method to your colleagues.

3. From horses to humans: Memo requesting trip to Flag Is Up Farms As vice president of human resources for Kingston Manufacturing in Atlanta, you try to keep up with new ideas. That's why you bought *The Man Who Listens to Horses,* the autobiography of horse trainer Monty Roberts.

Roberts grew up with horses in the 1930s—champ at age 4, stunt double for Elizabeth Taylor at age 8. But wild mustangs in Nevada taught him what he calls the silent language of "Equus." As a kid, he was fascinated by the patterns of motions, poses, and eye contact a herd's lead mare would use to communicate with the others—even to discipline rowdy youngsters. So he studied and copied her moves and tried them on unbroken horses at home—and it worked beautifully. He spoke their language and they responded.

Roberts, now in his sixties, can achieve "join up" with an untamed horse—saddling and riding it for the first time—in less than half an hour. That's a miracle compared with the brutal meth-

ods normally used to "break" a horse's spirit over the course of weeks so that it obeys—but also fears—humans. Using Equus, Roberts establishes complete rapport, within minutes, so that human and horse work with mutual respect and willing cooperation forever after. This approach is not only faster, it's more humane, safer for handlers, and smarter.

Roberts's horse-trainer father violently opposed this "radical" idea, so Roberts kept his method quiet for decades. Then in 1989, Queen Elizabeth II of England invited him to give a demonstration at the royal stables. She was stunned and impressed. Now all her horses are trained by his method, and he's gone on to demonstrate join-up to thousands of amazed witnesses.

Lives have been changed by the powerful sight of a wild horse—or, more poignantly, a "mad" one—ready to be euthanized who walks over and voluntarily nuzzles Roberts's shoulder after only a few minutes of nonverbal communication. Physically abused women and children (and their abusers) have wept or fainted as Roberts explained what a horse was "telling him" about how it had been beaten or mistreated. And many a tough horse handler and business administrator has come away from these demonstrations with new ideas. Disney, Texaco, Merrill Lynch, and Jaguar have all sent executives to Roberts's 110-acre Flag Is Up Farms in the Santa Ynez Valley (about 30 miles from Santa Barbara).

This is the radical treatment your company needs, you decide. For months, you've been fielding too many complaints from your increasingly multicultural work force about old-school managers. Neither side is "wrong," but they aren't communicating. What managers need is a dramatic demonstration that nonverbal behaviors can be more important than all the words in the world.

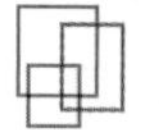

Your task: Write a memo to Kingston president Marvin Montgomery, urging him to send you to visit Flag Is Up Farms as a preview before sending managers to California. Of course, just in case Montgomery calls you into his office after he reads your memo, you'd better be prepared to discuss why nonverbal behaviors can be more important than words. What will you tell Montgomery if he asks?[37]

4. The downsizing dilemma: Persuasive letter at Intermed You've heard the old saying that when your next-door neighbor loses her job, it's a recession; when you lose yours, it's a depression. After 15 years as a loyal employee of Intermed, a surgical equipment manufacturer, you're facing the prospect of downsizing. In a companywide meeting this morning, your CEO informed the work force that Intermed has just been bought out by Urohealth Systems and that a substantial number of layoffs are anticipated in the near future.

As the manager of Intermed's technical support department, you're concerned both for your employees and for yourself. However, you've already learned that Urohealth is basically a holding company that has grown by acquiring smaller, regional companies like Intermed. Urohealth has few hourly or nonexempt employees, so you feel that most of your staff will be kept on. You do know, however, that after Urohealth's last acquisition, dozens of middle managers like yourself disappeared.

You're determined to take a positive approach, so you begin preparing for the inevitable. You know that Intermed has certain policies and procedures for terminations. However, you believe that by taking the initiative, you can negotiate a better deal for yourself. First, you look at your current compensation. You decide to ask for four weeks' severance pay for each year of service. You want to start a bit high and be prepared to settle at somewhere between two and three weeks' pay.

You have been able to purchase company stock over the years. However, you may lose some of your more recent purchases when you are terminated. You consider asking to trade some of your severance pay to be able to keep all your stock. Chances are, the value of the stock will increase after Urohealth takes over. Your 401(k) (personal retirement savings) plan may also be in jeopardy. The company matches your savings each year, provided you are employed for the entire year. You would like the company to add its matching contribution for the entire year, even though you won't be on the payroll through December 31.

Conventional wisdom says it may take up to a year for someone with your skills and experience to find another position. You intend to ask Intermed for outplacement counseling, use of an office, telephone, and office equipment, and payment of your job-hunting expenses for at least 90 days.

Your task: You know you'll get a much better deal by initiating voluntary termination and negotiating your severance package with Intermed before Urohealth takes over. Write a persuasive letter to Shirley Barnett, Intermed's director of human resources, outlining your requests. Address the letter to her at 500 Livingston Street, Northvale, NJ 07647.[38]

5. Ouch, that hurts! Persuasive memo at Technology One requesting equipment retrofit Mike Andrews leaves your office, shutting the door behind him. The pain in his arm is reflected on his face. He's about to file a worker's compensation claim—your third this month. As human resources director for Technology One, a major software development firm, you're worried not only about costs but also about the well-being of your employees.

Mike's complaints are much the same as those already reported by two other computer technicians: sharp pains in the wrist, numbness, and decreased range of motion. You know that the average technician spends at least six hours a day working on the computer, yet you've never had this many complaints in a short time, and the severity of the symptoms seems to be increasing.

You decide to seek the advice of experts. A local sports and orthopedic medicine clinic gives you a detailed description of RSIs, repetitive strain injuries. The symptoms they describe are virtually identical to those exhibited by your technicians. You're distressed to learn that, if the cause of these injuries is not found and corrected, your technicians could require surgery or could even become permanently disabled.

The physical therapist at the clinic feels that exercises and wrist splints may help relieve symptoms and could even prevent new injuries. However, she also recommends that you consult an ergonomic analyst who can evaluate the furniture and equipment your technicians are using.

On her advice, you bring in an analyst who spends an entire day at your facility. After measuring desk and chair height, watching technicians at work, and conducting a detailed analysis of all your equipment, he makes two recommendations: (1) Throw out all your computer keyboards and replace them with ergonomic keyboards, and (2) replace every mouse with a trackball. Suddenly you realize that the RSI complaints began shortly after your controller and purchasing manager bought a truckload of new computer equipment at a local merchant's going-out-of-business sale. You begin to wonder about the quality and design of that equipment, and you ask the analyst what benefits the changes will provide.

The ergonomic keyboard actually splits the traditional rows of keys in half and places the rows of keys at different angles, allowing the wrists to stay straight and relieving pressure on the forearm. The repetitive motions involved in using a mouse further aggravate the symptoms created by use of the traditional keyboard. Using a trackball does not require the repetitive clicking motion of the forefinger.

Your task: You know that replacing peripheral equipment on more than 50 computers will be costly, especially when the existing equipment is nearly new. However, increasing RSIs and disability claims could be even more costly. Write a persuasive memo to Katherine Wilson, your controller, and convince her of the immediate need to retrofit the technicians' computer equipment.[39]

6. Travel turnaround: E-mail message at Travelfest convincing your boss to expand client services As a successful travel agent with Travelfest, Inc., you have been both amazed and troubled by the recent changes in the travel industry. The upset started more than a year ago, when airlines stopped paying the customary 10 percent commission on airline tickets. Instead, airlines paid a flat $25 on one-way domestic flights and $50 on round-trip domestic flights. International flights were not affected.

Travelfest is located in Austin, Texas. It has four offices and more than 80 employees. Headquarters are in the center of downtown, in the lobby of a 35-story office tower. The other three offices are located in major shopping centers in upscale suburbs. The company's business is made up of about 70 percent corporate and business travel and 30 percent leisure travel. However, much of the leisure business comes from corporate customers.

Your boss, Gary Hoover, has been working night and day to make up for declining revenues brought about by the loss of airline commissions. He has tried everything, from direct-mail campaigns to discount coupons to drawings for cruises and weekend getaways. Still, revenues remain flat, and there seems to be no solution in sight.

You've been doing some research and analysis of your office's existing customer profiles. You find that many of your customers are middle- to high-income sophisticated travelers and that, with the expansion of the global economy, foreign travel has increased dramatically in the past 12 months. Your research has triggered some ideas that you believe could substantially increase your revenue from existing customers.

You envision turning your suburban mall office into a travel supermarket. First, since there's such a growth in foreign travel, you'd like to sell videos and audiotape courses in Spanish, Japanese, French, and other languages. You'd like to introduce a line of travel products, including luggage, maps, travel guides, and electronics. You visualize a room with computer terminals where customers would have direct access to the Internet so that they could obtain up-to-date weather reports, currency-exchange rates, and other important information about travel destinations. You're even thinking about a special area for kids, with videos and other educational materials.

You realize your ideas won't generate a lot of direct profit. However, you believe they will get customers in the door, where you and other agents can sell them travel, particularly leisure travel to foreign destinations. If Hoover is willing to try it in your office and it works, he may want to do the same in his other two locations.

Your task: E-mail Gary Hoover at Travelfest's downtown office. Outline your ideas and suggest a meeting to discuss them further and determine what market research he'd like you to perform. Hoover's e-mail address is GHoover@travelnet.com.[40]

7. Teachers' plea: Letter to parents from TCTA urging reduced TV time First you had to convince your own organization, the Texas Classroom Teachers Association (TCTA), that this issue should be addressed by parents, not by legislators. They finally agreed. Now, as director of communications, you've been assigned the task you'd hoped for.

Normally, TCTA is busy lobbying Texas legislators for better education laws or offering legal services to embattled teachers. But when you got your hands on results of a recent study conducted among children in Spain, you knew it called for a letter-writing campaign—but not one aimed at legislators. This time teachers would write to parents, begging them to treat their own children better.

The eight-month study involved parents of 221 children admitted to the pediatric ward of Santa Ana Hospital in Motril, Spain. The parents were asked to fill out a survey about family television viewing. By comparing injuries with hours of television watched, the researchers concluded that for every hour of television a child watched, the risk of injury rose by 34 percent. That seems a sizable increase to you, one that could easily be remedied.

Of course, scientific method demands confirming studies before the results are fully accepted. But on the other hand, every teacher you know would instantly chime in to say that television contributes to all sorts of social and behavioral problems and even impairs intellectual achievement by shortening attention spans, demeaning values, and presenting false images of life that children confuse with reality. Just opinions, mind you, but widely and firmly held—soon to be confirmed by science, you hope.

Meanwhile, the Spanish study is something the TCTA can sink its persuasive teeth into. If you can get parents to reduce their children's television viewing by only an hour or two a day, it could make a difference. Current estimates are that an average child today will have spent between 7 and 10 years watching television by the time he or she reaches the age of 70.

Jose Uberos Fernandez, author of the Spanish research program, stated in the *Archives of Pediatrics and Adolescent Medicine* professional journal, "Paradoxically, a child who spends more time watching television and devotes fewer hours to potentially more dangerous physical activities and games is at greater risk of experiencing events that cause physical injuries. . . . We believe that the depiction of a distorted reality on the television screen, which the child perceives as being real, may be of some help in explaining our findings." Later on in his paper, he adds, "Without any doubt, the effect of television on its viewers is directly related to the number of hours spent in watching per day and the content of the programs watched."

Your task: Mold these study results into a persuasive letter to be sent on TCTA letterhead to all parents of school-age children in the state of Texas. Include TCTA's number (1-888-879-TCTA) for more information.[41]

8. Customer crunch: Letter from Ed's food servers requesting relief Working as a food server at Ed's, a health-conscious eatery on famous Old Highway 101 in Cardiff, California, is a great way to supplement your sparse financial resources as a business student at San Diego State University. From upstairs, you can see the ocean, and during big storms you can even see the waves breaking across the sea-level highway. Last winter, when El Niño lashed the coastline relentlessly, the view was amazing. For weeks, nearly every high tide closed the flooded highway. Before it could open again, bulldozers had to clear the wave-deposited cobbles from the road, pushing back along the shore big mounds that were supposed to help stave off the salty onslaught.

Actually, El Niño was good for Ed's winter business. Lots of San Diegans came out to watch the excitement while your competitors across the highway, who are directly on the shore, lost huge picture windows to the crashing waves. Ed's offered a safe vantage point.

But now it's summer. The waves are still breaking, but now they're much smaller. And the state beach parking lots that were washed away during the storms have been restored. However, there's hardly any beach left—just a narrow strip of mostly rocks with very little sand. Ed's owners are worried.

Normally, beach crowds would cross the highway in the late afternoons for Ed's $4 smoothies and gourmet organic dinners. But there aren't any huge beach crowds this year. As far as you can tell, the locals and some tourists still turn up in healthy numbers for the sunset dinner specials, gazing out to watch dolphins playing in the surf. Nevertheless, your manager has started using what you call a "US West" tactic (in honor of a short-staffing, forced-overtime policy at the telecommunications giant that led to a major strike). As so many companies are doing now, Ed's is saving on overhead by cutting back on the number of servers and kitchen staff. Because of the cutback, customers are waiting longer for their food and for their tables (especially during rush periods), so many are leaving in anger while orders are backing up in the kitchen. You're running twice as hard and getting smaller tips—especially from diners who have to wait up to half an hour for their dinner. No matter how nice you are, it's hard to smoothe their ruffled feathers. You've even lost some faithful regulars who'd been coming to the restaurant for years, bringing all their out-of-town visitors and leaving you healthy tips.

This can't possibly be good for Ed's in the long term. And it's certainly not good for you and your co-workers in the short term!

Your task: Since you're the business major, your fellow servers have nominated you to write a persuasive letter to Ed's owner, Mary Fenwick, explaining why the low-overhead policy should be abandoned. If you write it, they'll sign it, they've promised. Make up any circumstantial details you need. Before you begin, however, jot down the main idea of your message. Then list the major points and supporting evidence you'll include to persuade Fenwick.[42]

9. Korean recognition: E-mail to Garden Grove city council The request seemed reasonable enough: Members of the Korean Chamber of Commerce of Orange County asked the city council of Garden Grove, California, to erect a sign designating a portion of Garden Grove Boulevard as the Korean Business District. Essentially, that's what the neighborhood is, and it has been home to your Korea House restaurant for many years.

But some members of the community complained when the issue was brought up during a city council session. "We should be focusing on the unification of the community as a whole and its general diversity," they proclaimed, "not dividing the city up into little ethnic districts." Some council members were nevertheless intrigued by the prospect of officially creating a new tourist destination by marking the Korean Business District. However, the issue was tabled for later consideration.

As owner of Korea House, you agree with those council members who think the designation would attract visitors. Moreover, the Korean Chamber of Commerce has returned to the city council with an offer to pay for two cement structures, spending up to $30,000 for the design and installation of the signs—one west of Brookhurst Street and another east of Beach Boulevard—to mark the highly concentrated Korean business area.

Your task: As a member of the Korean Chamber of Commerce, you've been asked to support the request with an e-mail message to Cathy Standiford, Garden Grove's deputy city manager, at cstandiford@ch.ci.garden-grove.ca.us.[43]

10. Feng Shui? A tough-sell memo pitching an offbeat approach If you weren't the newest sales agent at McCoy Realty in Niles, Michigan, this wouldn't feel so risky. But you believe in trying new ideas. Considering how much all of you spend on advertising, business cards, promotional flyers, and so on, the $200 to $500 price tag on this idea could pay big dividends.

You've been reading about Feng Shui (pronounced "fung shway"), the ancient Chinese "art of placement." Popular books such as Terah Collins's *The Western Guide to Feng Shui* and Sarah

Rossbach's *Interior Design with Feng Shui* are making it accessible in the United States. They encourage readers to try Feng Shui practices in their homes and offices to improve their health, wealth, family life, career, creativity, personal achievements—even their love life, marriage, parenting, and travel! All these aspects of life are represented by a specific portion of a building or a work space, say the Feng Shui advisers; moreover, people are affected by colors, shapes, materials, and placement of objects in each of those areas.

Well, it sounds complicated, but you love the success stories. One retail shop owner discovered that her display counters were pointing their corners, like arrows, at every customer who started to enter the store. No wonder they all backed right out again! She rearranged the interior and business started booming.

You even saw a television interview with the executive producers of the sitcom *Dharma & Greg,* Chuck Lorre and Dottie Dartland. They'd been assigned a "bad luck" sound stage by Fox Studios; every show produced there had failed. They were worried, so they hired a $275 Feng Shui consultant who advised such "cures" as hanging mirrors in ceilings and painting walls. Did it do the trick? Well, the new show was an instant hit, breaking the curse. And cast and crew get along great.

Your favorite story is about the real estate broker with six houses she couldn't sell for months. After a Feng Shui consultant advised changes, they all sold within 30 days.

You can't help thinking about how difficult it's been to get new listings. You almost never get walk-ins, which newcomers like you would normally be assigned. Could it be those pointy counters? And what about those "loser" houses no one will buy and the sellers can't wait to dump? Could a Feng Shui adviser offer tips on making them more desirable?

Your task: At the risk of being laughed out of town, write a memo persuading your broker, Barbara Tallneck, to bring in a Feng Shui consultant—at least to give a talk to agents in the office.[44]

11. Life's little hassles: Request for satisfaction It's hard to go through life without becoming annoyed at the way some things work. You have undoubtedly been dissatisfied with a product you've bought, a service you've received, or an action of some elected official or government agency.

Your task: Write a three- to five-paragraph persuasive request expressing your dissatisfaction in a particular case. Specify the action you want the reader to take.

WRITING PERSUASIVE CLAIMS AND REQUESTS FOR ADJUSTMENT

12. Relief requested: BestBank customer plea to Colorado Attorney General You are an intern with the Denver Free Legal Clinic, and your job is to screen indigent walk-in clients, directing them to an attorney or paralegal or sometimes writing simple letters on their behalf when the issues don't require legal aid.

As a law student, you value this experience, but 60-year-old Angelina Bigelow's story about BestBank has you riled. In your view, three multimillionaires have fleeced thousands of struggling, poverty-level innocents, raking in huge profits and vanishing in the night like thieves. Disgusting.

Edward P. Mattar, owner of BestBank, Thomas Alan Boyd, president, and Douglas Baetz, owner of an affiliated travel promotion company in Florida, have not been accused of any crimes. But their "virtual bank," which advertised on the Internet and claimed profits five times higher than other banks, was seized by state regulators after they discovered $134 million in soured loans and only $23 million in BestBank reserves to cover them. That's only the most recent in a series of incidents that put the operation under investigation by the Colorado Attorney General's office.

One of BestBank's scams was to sell credit cards to "subprime" borrowers with bad or insufficient credit histories. "You No Longer Need to Worry About Being Without a Credit Card," promises the direct-mail ad Ms. Bigelow shows you. What she and many others didn't read was the fine print: Signing up for her Visa card meant she also agreed to join Mr. Baetz's travel club, at a fee of $498 charged to the new card. An additional $45 fee used up all but $57 of Angelina's new $600 credit limit—putting her in serious debt for her income level. When she couldn't make the unexpected payments, interest charges and $20 late fees started adding up, until she was over her credit limit. Then the bank started adding an additional $20 per month "overlimit fee."

The state's seizure stopped the billings. However, you've made a few calls and learned that Baetz bought these debts; the bills might show up again any day. Your calls also reveal that before they disappeared, Mattar and Boyd paid themselves a combined $9 million in salaries for a six-month period, despite the bank's huge tally of delinquent credit accounts (a disputed figure between $50 million and $215 million).

Angelina Bigelow is distraught and doesn't know how to turn off this debt meter she never intended to start. All she'd wanted was a credit card for identification and emergencies—and to begin building a positive credit history. You promise to help.

Your task: Others among the half-million people who signed up with the bank are sending complaints to the attorney general's office, seeking debt relief as part of the state's resolution of the BestBank matter. Write such a letter on Ms. Bigelow's behalf. She lives at 473 E. Laurel, Englewood, Colorado 80111; her account number is 9978 3888 8893 2274; her current balance is $873.[45]

13. Recall this @#$%& software! E-mail demanding more than refund from Panasonic Interactive Media You've just gotten home from work when you hear a computer-generated voice coming from your eight-year-old daughter's room, uttering profanity you wouldn't want to hear coming from anywhere, let alone from your child's bedroom! Horrified, you rush to her door, opening your mouth to spew out a few well-chosen (but clean) words of your own.

But you stop when you see Tasha's own stricken face, as pink as the walls around her. On her computer screen is the new program you've just bought her, Secret Writer's Society, which is supposed to help seven- to ten-year-olds improve their writing skills—not their vocabularies! "What did you do?" you ask her, trying to control your voice.

"I didn't do anything!" she protests. "That's not what I wrote! See—" she points to five lines of text on the screen, something positively innocent. One of the ways the program is supposed to teach is by reciting back the written lines in the computer-generated voice. "I just double-clicked this," she points again, indicating the option she'd chosen, "and it said all those things!" Her face turns a deeper shade of rose.

You pat her hand comfortingly. "Okay, Honey. But give me that box, will you?" She hands you the box with the 800 number on it. "Why don't you just turn it off for now and we'll talk about this in a little while." You feel a little guilty for having blamed her: where would she have learned those words, some of which you've never even heard? You also dread having to answer her questions about what they might mean. Hurrying off to call the customer service number is a good excuse for avoiding her questions.

Finally, after a long wait on hold, you get a real person at Matsushita's Panasonic Interactive Media, which makes the product. The person tells you that the company is aware of the bug and that your daughter should have single-clicked instead of double-clicked. The bug apparently unleashes words from a filter in the text-to-speech engine that's supposed to prevent the program from uttering any foul words that, say, a mischievous older brother might type in. If you like, they'll send you a new, debugged version.

You're indignant. What about all the other little kids who also own this software and might accidentally double-click the icon? You wouldn't even want a teenager to hear this gutter language! Why aren't they recalling the software? You politely and coldly inform the customer service operator that, no thank you, you'd prefer a refund. And they haven't heard the last from you.

Your task: Write an effective e-mail message to pmi@pana.com demanding a full refund and demanding, furthermore, that Panasonic Interactive Media take the product off the shelves and publicize the problem to warn other parents of what may be lurking on their children's computers.[46]

14. Phone frustration: Persuasive letter to Pacific Bell requesting resolution of telephone service overcharges As a freelance business researcher, your time is valuable, especially when you're using online research sources. These valuable resources are becoming more and more important in your work, so you can't afford to sit around waiting for files to download at 14,400 bits per second (14.4 kbps) or even at 28.8 kbps. You often deal with massive files that can take forever to transfer at these rates. You've determined that an ISDN (Integrated Services Digital Network) connection would be a faster alternative for your online work. You contacted Pacific Bell Telephone in November and requested residential ISDN service (because you work from home).

When the confirming work order arrived, you discovered that PacBell had set up your account as a business service, so you called the service representative to change it to the lower residential rate. As a result, your business service was disconnected, and it took PacBell two weeks to reconnect you. On top of that, when the initial bill arrived, there was a $125 charge for disconnecting the business service and another $75 charge for reinstallation, and no credit for the two weeks of downtime. You have made at least 13 calls to the customer service department about this problem, both locally and at the company's headquarters in Sacramento. You even left a message on the customer feedback section of PacBell's Internet home page. But none of these actions have resolved the situation.

Your task: Compose a persuasive letter to Ms. Claire Abell (PacBell's director of consumer affairs) at 6640 Rosecrans Road, Sacramento, CA 99054, explaining your frustration with this billing problem and asking for an immediate adjustment.[47]

WRITING SALES MESSAGES

15. The bride wore hiking boots: Persuasive letter to We Do bridal superstore When Shari and Randy Almsburg of Dublin, Ohio, decided to tie the knot, they knew just what they wanted.

"We always enjoyed hiking. In fact, we met each other on a hike. That's why we wanted to wrap our wedding plans around our favorite hobby." Enter Tie the Knot, a one-owner company specializing in bizarre wedding plans.

"Actually, the bride wearing a white dress and a pair of hiking boots was NOT our most unusual wedding," explains owner and wedding consultant Todd Dansing (whose own wedding took place a mile high just before the happy couple plunged to earth by parachute). "We recently helped plan an underwater wedding in a shark tank at the aquarium in Chicago for two marine biologists whose work involved feeding the fish. Our main problem there was this huge turtle that kept bumping into the preacher." Dansing tells you of other unusual weddings that took place in airplanes, on boats, under water, and in exotic locations such as Arizona's Painted Desert. Whatever a couple's wedding plans, Todd believes he can find the necessary resources and save them time and money in the process.

Todd's marketing efforts to date have involved mostly word of mouth and free press coverage of his unusual weddings (although reporters kept their distance when two snake handlers from the zoo exchanged vows). But his brother-in-law has invested capital in the business, so Todd hires you to help him tell the world about his services. You suggest that he consider affiliating with an established wedding service or store.

You and Todd visit We Do, a bridal superstore in Dublin, Ohio, and you help Todd see the potential for marketing his offbeat wedding service to this large company. We Do is a 26,000-square-foot matrimonial mecca that sells 600 styles of bridal gowns and everything else couples need for a traditional wedding. The franchise hopes to open 40 stores eventually, so if Todd can strike a deal with We Do, his future profit potential will be high.

Your task: Write a letter for Todd's signature to Carol Feinberg, CEO of We Do. Suggest that Tie the Knot would make a great consultant for couples with offbeat wedding tastes. Emphasize Todd's experience, and point out the ways this venture will provide additional market share for We Do. Think of possible objections, such as Todd's lack of capital and small company size, and try to assure Feinberg that Tie the Knot is the right business to help capitalize on a unique opportunity.[48]

16. Genetic counseling: Letter from International Society of Nurses in Genetics extolling a new service The International Society of Nurses in Genetics (ISNG) keeps members informed about the latest developments in genetic research and their impact on human beings. The National Human Genome Research Institute of the National Institutes of Health expects to "locate" all genes by the year 2005 by mapping them on the human chromosome set. It's a challenging new field spawning an entirely new profession, genetic counseling, and you're the editor of ISNG's newsletter.

Every time a gene is linked to a disease, a new predictive test becomes available. But should healthy people have these tests? That's the first question an informed genetic counselor helps clients answer. The second is: Will results be used for us, or against us? Are employee genetic databanks on the horizon?

Today a "father" can carry a swab of saliva from his child into a lab and find out whether he's the genetic father, with "indisputable accuracy" as far as our scientific and legal institutions are concerned. Long-time family relationships have dissolved as a result. Meanwhile, some women who've discovered they possess genes supposedly related to breast cancer have had healthy breasts removed as a "precaution." And insurance companies have started causing trouble for people with genes suspected to indicate a predisposition to diabetes, hypertension, bipolar disorder, and a host of serious, life-threatening ailments.

But some of the tests are unreliable, experts admit, and only one can definitely save a life: the test for a rare disease causing tumors of the brain, kidney, and eyes. Persons with the gene can watch for tumors and have them treated immediately.

Genetic counseling was born of the need to help patients make informed decisions involving previously undreamed-of medical advances. Genetic counselors are also serving as patient advocates with insurance companies, employers, and family members. And they're trying to help patients ensure that results are kept confidential.

A genetic counselor would have informed the women with "breast cancer genes" that other factors must be considered: environment, heredity, even ethnic background and diet. No one yet knows exactly what *causes* cancer, and genes may be discovered to be merely evidence of some larger, still undiscovered cause.

Nevertheless, people are embracing this new biotechnology. A couple with cystic fibrosis (CF) recently used genetic testing and *in vitro* fertilization to develop five embryos without CF genes. They hope that implanting these embryos in the woman's uterus will produce at least one healthy baby. (An embryo in a petri dish needs to develop only eight cells before two can be removed for testing; embryos that test positive are rejected.) Does genetic testing trigger moral, religious, or scientific challenges? You bet, and it's a different set of challenges for each patient.

Your task: You've decided to print a sample sales letter for use by nurses who have genetic counseling practices. But before you do, briefly describe the audience this letter will be sent to. Who are they? What do you want them to do as a result of the letter? Then, as you draft your letter, be sure to include some of the questions this audience might ask regarding genetic testing to let them know that you understand their needs. Also, be sure to explain how counseling can help them decide whether to undergo genetic testing.[49]

17. Outsourcing: Kelly Services offers solutions Gone are the days of the "Kelly Girl" secretary. Kelly Services now provides technical writers, computer programmers, mechanical engineers, assemblers, data management experts, and, in place of those old clerical jobs, experts in word processing and related software. Companies that downsized in the turbulent '90s are proving a goldmine for Kelly and other temporary employment agencies. Many of these companies outsource their work during busy times to compensate for lean staffing the rest of the year.

Some companies with hiring freezes (often the result of a pending merger or internal reorganization) keep Kelly or other temporary workers busy over the long term, saving themselves the costs of hiring and firing, benefits, taxes, and wages. But is using "temps" for long-term work fair to the workers? Many choose "temp work" not just between jobs, but for long periods in their career. Some like the flexibility and change; others appreciate the opportunity to try out a new employer before agreeing to take a permanent job.

The company's management certainly benefits; they get to sample and test workers before making hiring decisions. Kelly Services earns a fee when its temps are hired permanently, but employers find that's a small price to pay for this valuable preview time, which saves everyone the cost, pain, and suffering caused by a bad hiring decision. For instance, Kelly, a Fortune 500 services company, supplies contract labor for Chrysler, providing temps with office and clerical, information technology, and engineering skills. And Chrysler has awarded Kelly a Chrysler Gold Pentastar Award, rating it "a best-in-class supplier" that provides excellence in "quality, customer satisfaction, technology and delivery."

At Kelly Services, fifth largest staffing service in the world (with 1,600 offices worldwide), your own job as a marketing manager seems secure. The outsourcing industry in which Kelly is a leader is growing explosively (more than 20 percent a year and expected to reach $280 billion worldwide by the year 2000).

As companies face new competitive pressures to provide better service and quality at lower prices, they're turning to outsourcing suppliers with new demands. One company trend, designed to keep down the number of vendors, is to choose a single supplier such as the new Kelly Management Services (KMS) division, to provide "full-service" outsourcing. KMS offers several categories of service, including office services, administrative services, transaction-processing operations, distribution services, and customer service operations. That means an entire department could be staffed completely by temps who appear and disappear as the company's needs change. KMS clients who've tried one service often add others when they see that KMS workers are faster, better, cheaper, and more efficient than permanent employees and departments they've had in the past.

Your task: Write a sales letter to companies similar to Chrysler, explaining what Kelly has to offer.[50]

18. Why cellular users are hanging it up: Sales letter from Sprint Spectrum Never go anywhere without your cell phone? You may change your mind when you discover digital PCS (personal communication services). PCS has been tested in two major U.S. markets and will be available nationwide within the next few years.

Sprint Spectrum is emerging as an early leader in this dynamic market. Its marketing strategy focuses on local storefront sales outlets staffed with knowledgeable, enthusiastic people who relish the idea of head-to-head competition with cellular competitors such as Nynex and Airtouch.

Here's how Sprint Spectrum's lowest-cost service plan compares with similar services offered by Nynex:

Service	Sprint Spectrum	Nynex
Cost of phone	$149 to $199	Free or deeply discounted
Monthly fee	$15	$24.95
First 15 minutes of air	Free	$5.85 peak, $2.85 nonpeak time
Each additional minute	31¢	39¢ peak, 19¢ nonpeak
Activation fee	None	$30 to $50
Answering service	Included	$5.95 per month

Although Sprint Spectrum's lower prices are attractive, the real excitement is in the technology. Any cell phone user who has been cut off in midcall or who has damaged vocal cords from shouting over static interference will appreciate the sound fidelity of PCS. Why the difference? Digital versus analog technology. More than 90 percent of cellular phones use analog technology, which transmits your voice over electromagnetic waves. If the wave is broken, so is your phone call. Not so with PCS.

Before putting its product on the market, Sprint Spectrum conducted its own research into PCS technology. It sent salespeople and technicians out to field-test the equipment under a variety of circumstances. They went into high-rise buildings, parking garages, and subways. They tested the phones on commuter trains, in parked cars, and in moving cars. They made calls from grocery stores, from restaurants, and even on the new "screamer ride" at a local amusement park. Static and cutoffs were virtually nonexistent.

For the past two years, you have been working as a corporate account salesperson for a major cellular provider. You are consistently a top producer and pride yourself on keeping up with the newest technologies. When Sprint Spectrum advertised for experienced salespeople, you jumped at the chance to join tomorrow's technology leader.

After only a month on the job at Sprint Spectrum, you've been able to provide better service at lower cost to many new PCS users and to some of your old customers as well. In addition to basic services, your customers can choose numeric paging, call waiting, call forwarding, and caller ID. Sprint Spectrum does not require a contract and imposes no cancellation fee.

Your task: You believe you have barely scratched the surface of what's possible in selling PCS. You plan to triple your customer base in the next 90 days. At the monthly sales meeting, your boss announces that Sprint Spectrum has just obtained a great mailing list: 100,000 names of individuals who currently use cellular phone service in your sales territory. He is giving each salesperson a share of this list and the opportunity to sell Sprint Spectrum's PCS to these prospects. Compose a direct-mail sales letter designed to convince individual cellular phone users to switch to Sprint Spectrum.[51]

WRITING FUNDRAISING MESSAGES

19. Stroke awareness: Letter to Genentech requesting funds for educational campaign Stroke (a sudden disruption in the brain's blood flow) is the third leading cause of death in the United States and the leading cause of nursing home admissions, because stroke victims who survive are often paralyzed. Until now, stroke was classified as "a catastrophic health event."

Now a new drug developed by Genentech, Inc. offers hope: If t-PA (tissue plasminogen activator) is administered within three hours of the first symptoms, it may prevent paralysis. Use of t-PA is not advisable or effective in all cases, but 80 percent or more of victims could be saved from permanent harm. Trouble is, too few people recognize stroke symptoms or know about the drug. Victims don't get help in time, or they're misdiagnosed by physicians.

You learned all this from your friend Genevieve Marmolejo, whose 49-year-old brother suffered a stroke a few weeks ago while traveling on business. Lee, a musician/inventor, leaned over to gather demonstration equipment and was suddenly struck with terrible pain in his head, accompanied by overall dizziness—two of the five warning signs of stroke. (The other symptoms are sudden weakness or numbness in the face, arm, or leg; dimming or loss of vision; and slurring of speech. Only 57 percent of 1,880 people in a recent study in Cincinnati, where a public awareness campaign is under way, could name even one of these symptoms. Only 8 percent knew three.)

Lee froze, and his business partner, sitting nearby, was immediately concerned. She had him in the care of paramedics and on his way to a hospital within moments. But the hospital diagnosed him with a pinched nerve and sent him away. Twenty-four hours and a three-state commute later, Lee's left side was completely paralyzed. This time a second hospital gave a serious diagnosis: soaring blood pressure, a burst blood vessel at the back of his neck, and a near-miss with the Grim Reaper. Since then, Lee has recovered partial movement, but he's still mostly numb and his career as a guitar player is in jeopardy.

Some patients recover as long as six months later, so Lee's time isn't up. But Genevieve believes a person should "think globally, act locally." She's already drafted materials and a detailed budget for a public information campaign in your hometown, Janesville, Wisconsin. "If there's a drug out there that can save people from stroke paralysis, they need to know," she insists. "This is so new, our family medical book still says your only choice is to keep your blood pressure down and hope it doesn't happen to you." She's come to you, the business major, for help drafting a "beg letter" to Genentech, which helped fund the Cincinnati campaign. She's calculated that she needs $20,000 to start, and she's appointed you "information officer" for the new Janesville Stroke Awareness Campaign.

Your task: Write the letter to Genentech, Inc., DNA Way South, San Francisco, CA 94088, requesting support. But first, take out a sheet of paper and (1) identify you audience, (2) jot down the main idea of your message, and (3) list the major points and supporting evidence you'll use when drafting your letter.[52]

20. Buses for seniors: Fundraising letter from Morris County Senior Center The Morris County Senior Center is one of New Jersey's oldest nonprofit institutions for the elderly. Over the past 50 years, it has relied on financial support from government, businesses, and individuals.

Unfortunately, recent state and federal cutbacks have dug into the organization's budget. In addition, in the last five years two of the county's largest companies, Hardwick Industries and McCarthy Electrical Motors, have moved offshore and shut down local operations. Both businesses were supporters of the center, as were many of the workers who lost jobs.

However, the needs of the center keep growing. For many of the county's roughly 1,000 seniors who live alone, it's the only place where they can meet their peers, use a special library, avoid extreme weather, or get a well-balanced meal. The center is not a nursing home and has no overnight facilities. Most individuals get to the facility on one of the three shuttle-type buses belonging to the center. The buses are also used for various day trips to museums, plays, and similar functions. Occasionally, they are used to help the temporarily disabled get to doctors' offices or pharmacists.

Each bus is more than eight years old. Although not quite unsafe, the buses are showing their age. The constant repairs are stopgap measures at best, and most weeks at least one of the vehicles is inoperable. Monthly repairs are averaging a total of $300 for the three vehicles. In addition, when the vans aren't working, the clients, staff, and budget all suffer. Seniors can't get to the center, trips are canceled, and drivers are sometimes paid for coming to work even though they weren't able to drive.

Conservatively, it would cost about $28,000 to replace each van with a new one: $84,000 total. This includes estimates on how much the center could gain from selling the old vans. It's a fair amount of money, but in the opinion of your board of directors, buying new vans would be better than continuously repairing the old ones or risking the purchase of used ones.

Your task: As director of the center, draft a fundraising letter to send to all of the businesses in the county. Stress the good work the center does and the fact that this is a special fundraising effort. Mention that all the money collected will go directly toward the purchase of the vans.

21. Ears to hear: E-mail soliciting volunteer readers for the blind at Audio International You've been filled with inspiration working as a sighted volunteer at Audio International, Inc., a small Web-design company creating a new site for the blind and visually impaired. CEO George Buys is blind, and all company officers are either visually or otherwise physically challenged. They've put their savings and their ingenuity on the line to provide a free service for others, and you're glad to help where you can.

One of your tasks is preparing print materials for distribution over the Internet. Right now, Audio International needs volunteers with good reading voices to record audio clips of stories appearing in major newspapers and magazines. The company has developed a new software program, 1-Step Audio Publisher 2.0 for Windows 95 and 3.0 for Windows 98, which combines cutting-edge voice-mail technology with Internet audio streaming to create its audio clips. But visually impaired users of the site won't need to purchase the software to benefit; Audio International offers them a demo version that works as a plug-in with major Web browsers and allows them to hear the audio files volunteers will create. If listeners like the service, they can consider purchasing the software.

The company has no grant funding. So far, everything has been financed out of the owners' pockets because, as Buys told you recently, "As a blind person, I know how much this service will mean to people who are print disabled."

In return for their help, volunteers will receive a free copy of 1-Step Audio Publisher for their own use with e-mail or their own Web sites, full instruction and technical support, networking to promote their personal Web sites, and promotional exposure of their vocal skills (great for actors, teachers, ministers, motivational speakers, trainers, writers, publishers, or anyone who loves to read aloud). Every story they record will feature their name, e-mail address, and Web site, if they choose.

Volunteers will need only a few basics: 1-Step Audio Publisher software (provided by Audio International), a sound card, a microphone, a Windows operating system (95 or 98), a Pentium processor, and an ftp account through their ISP (Internet service provider). Once they sign on, they'll receive full details and instructional guidance.

Your task: Write a letter to be distributed by e-mail, targeted to mailing lists of people most likely to benefit as volunteers. Ask interested recipients to call George Buys at(602) 503-2659 or to respond via e-mail to buys@audio-tips.com. Audio International's Web site is http://www.audio-tips.com.[53]

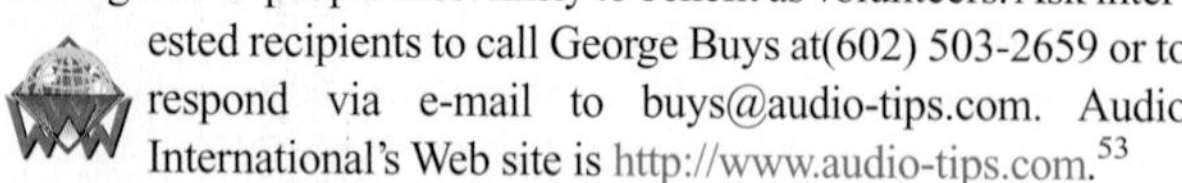

WRITING COLLECTION MESSAGES

22. A firm but gentle nudge: Urgent collection letter at Coast Federal Bank You are the director of marketing at Coast Federal Bank (CFB), a consumer-oriented bank with branches mainly in southern California. Surrounded as it is by some of the top educational institutions in the country, CFB has long considered student loans to be one of its most important products.

You've just finished reviewing this month's collection reports and you realize that, for the sixth straight month, your bad debt ratio has increased; that is, you have more and more loans that are over 90 days past due. In addition, your average collection time has increased by more than 20 days in the same period. This trend disturbs you, and you know that your loan committee (which meets in three days) will be even more disturbed.

When CFB began an aggressive marketing campaign for student loans a little over ten years ago, tuition costs at local public and private universities were less than half what they are today. As the cost of education has skyrocketed (creating a growing demand for financing), your interest rates on these loans have remained virtually unchanged. And with your collection ratio going downhill, you can see profits eroding rapidly.

You're also concerned because many of your student loans were made to parents of college students as part of the PLUS (Parent Loans to Undergraduate Students) program. These parents are some of the bank's best customers: local executives and community leaders with whom you have other important business dealings. You are anxious to maintain your good image and relationship with these customers, so you're hesitant to implement a get-tough collection policy.

You have begun developing a strategy to improve collection of student loans. You plan to stress your loyalty to your customers, your commitment to supporting local educational institutions, and your desire to work with people who will demonstrate good-faith efforts. You believe refinancing and extended payment options may encourage some people to improve their payment records.

You're aware that some more conservative members of the loan committee may want to recommend selling the entire delinquent student loan business to a collection firm. You feel this action would be extremely detrimental to your bank's reputation and long-term growth.

Your task: Develop a customer-relations collection letter designed to encourage your student loan borrowers to improve their payment records. Assume that your bank's computer program will personalize each letter with the customer's name and address. Use a personal tone, and direct your message to the individual customer.[54]

23. One last try: Final-stage collection letter from Arciero Brothers Phil Arciero was ecstatic when his concrete company, Arciero Brothers, was selected as one of the construction subcontractors for a huge entertainment complex being built by Moorfield Construction. Located near one of the country's leading vacation destinations, the complex was designed to include restaurants, theaters, a video arcade, and a kiddyland play park.

With a venture of this magnitude, it wasn't surprising that more than 200 subcontractors were needed to handle the variety of building and infrastructure work. Arciero Brothers specializes in building foundations, sidewalks, and parking lots. Although Arciero has been in business for more than 20 years, the entertainment complex is the largest contract he's ever been awarded.

The project took nearly 24 months to complete. Arciero Brothers was on site throughout the first 21 months of the job. Phil Arciero hired a dozen new employees, including laborers and skilled tradespeople. In addition, he had to buy some extra equipment so that he could handle the new work and still meet the needs of his existing customers.

Moorfield Construction paid Arciero 10 percent of his estimate at the beginning of the job. Interim payments were made monthly, until the total payments reached 85 percent of the contract bid. It was agreed that Moorfield would withhold the final 15 percent until the entire project was approved by the city building inspectors, a common practice in the construction industry.

It's been nearly five months since the entertainment complex passed final inspection and opened for business. You've already paid your workers, drawing against your credit line at the bank to do it. You've either called or written Moorfield Construction once a week requesting payment of the more than $100,000 that is still outstanding on your contract. Moorfield officials say "paperwork foul-ups" are the reason for the slow payment. You're aware that none of the other subcontractors have received their final payments and that some of them are hiring attorneys to file mechanic's liens (legal collection proceedings) directly against the owner of the complex.

Your task: As the controller at Arciero Brothers, you've talked to Phil Arciero about the dilemma. Neither of you wants to jeopardize potential business from Moorfield Construction or from the entertainment complex owners. But to preserve your rights, and to increase your chances of being paid (liens are paid in the order filed), you and Arciero instructed your attorney to file a mechanic's lien. You recommend to Arciero that you write a polite but firm letter to Moorfield, with a copy sent to the owners of the entertainment center, demanding immediate payment of the full amount owed you and informing Moorfield of the lien. Address your letter to Moorfield Construction (9 Corporate Park #600, Irvine, CA 92714), and address the copy to James Penny, Vice President of Finance, Edwards Theaters Inc. (12100 Wilshire Boulevard, Los Angeles, CA 90025).[55]

Part 3 A Case for Critical Thinking

HOW BOEING BLEW IT—ALMOST

The bad news came hard: Production of the 747 jumbo jet at Boeing's factory in Everett, Washington, kept falling further and further behind schedule, and the only way to get the work back on track was to shut down the production line—perhaps for as long as a month.

First the grim-faced managers brought the distressing news about the manufacturing delays to Ron Woodard, president of Boeing's Commercial Airplane Group. Then they told the workers. But nothing was more painful and embarrassing than notifying customers and shareholders of the bad news: that the company would not be able to deliver on sales as promised. Boeing claimed that it had "stubbed its toe," but others felt that it had broken a leg.

Within days after the announcement, the company's stock plummeted 20 percent. And, for the Seattle-based company, it was the start of a sales job like no other: repairing relationships with long-standing customers who would not be receiving their planes on time. Boeing would not only have to instill confidence in the minds of its customers but would also have to persuade them not to run to competition.

The problem, it seems, was born of overambition, miscommunication, a shortage of parts, and a production system that couldn't keep up. Demand for the 747, Boeing's most profitable plane, was lifting off. The competition between Boeing and Europe's Airbus Industrie (Boeing's sole competitor) was savage. Furthermore, for Boeing to turn its back on aircraft sales would be like giving away a large chunk of market share. When your industry has only 200 or fewer potential customers and the life span of your product is about 20 years, if you lose one order to a competitor, you've lost a sale for at least 20 years, and possibly a customer forever.

So Boeing adopted a close-as-many-deals-as-possible mentality to get a head start on Airbus. Signing a record 712 new orders in 1996 alone, executives naively believed that production could be ramped up to meet demand. Salespeople promised customers that orders could be filled in record times. Unfortunately, they never communicated the unrealistic delivery dates to manufacturing—or to Boeing's suppliers, for that matter.

First Boeing cranked up production of its jumbo jets from two planes a month to three and a half. Then to four. Then it shifted several hundred workers from its 767 line to help out on the 747. But having bodies was not enough. The company's capacity was limited; that is, based on current facilities and equipment, Boeing's potential output was too low to meet demand. In addition, the factories were inefficient—something Boeing executives had known for decades. Furthermore, a lack of raw materials and critical parts was making it impossible to meet ramped-up production schedules, forcing too many "jobs" to be done out of sequence and causing bottlenecks in the line. In fact, the 747 line was running more than 14,000 jobs behind schedule (anything less than 3,000 is considered to be manageable). The result? Delays in every part of the system. Boeing finally realized that no number of parts or people was going to get the 747 line back into position. So on September 29, 1997, the manufacturing process at

Boeing's 747-400 plant in Everett, Washington turns out four jets

Boeing, the world's largest aerospace company, shut down—for one full month.

Amazingly, the companies hurt most by Boeing's problems—its customers and suppliers—see a positive side to what happened. Today, Boeing is closer to them then ever before, getting their input on production and working together to negotiate realistic delivery schedules. For example, suppliers meet quarterly with Boeing executives to talk about their respective problems. "It's a wonderful thing," notes one major supplier. "We sit and problem solve and go over these issues. You never could have done that before. . . . Now we're more like a team." In fact, there is a complete mind expansion going on at Boeing. People are learning what they're capable of and what they're not.

1. If you had been a Boeing executive, how would you have broken the bad news to the employees? To the customers? To the shareholders?
2. Would you consider Boeing's promising more orders than it could fill to be an ethical lapse or an ethical dilemma? Please explain.
3. What valuable lesson did Boeing learn from this crisis?
4. Visit Boeing's Web site at http://www.boeing.com. Click on "Doing Business, General Information for Suppliers Doing Business with Boeing, Proper Relationships with Suppliers." Read the Web page. What is your reaction to these supplier policies in light of what you've just read about Boeing's own mishap?

PART

Information and Technology

CHAPTER 10
Communicating Information through the Internet and Other Technologies

CHAPTER 11
Finding, Evaluating, and Processing Information

CHAPTER 12
Communicating Information through Graphs and Other Visuals

COMMUNICATING INFORMATION THROUGH THE INTERNET AND OTHER TECHNOLOGIES

AFTER STUDYING THIS CHAPTER, YOU WILL BE ABLE TO

1. Discuss what individuals can do on the Internet
2. Differentiate between discussion mailing lists and newsgroups
3. Explain how a search engine works
4. Differentiate between an intranet and an extranet
5. Discuss how businesses are using intranets
6. Highlight four communication issues challenging companies in the Information Age

COMMUNICATION CLOSE-UP AT SGI

In the old days, launching a new high-performance computer system at SGI (whose name was recently changed from Silicon Graphics) meant sending engineers on a worldwide road show to train the sales force. This process cost the company valuable product development time, in addition to $3 million for each new product launch. Today, SGI uses a company-wide computer network, or intranet, to deliver new product training to its employees all over the globe. Whether they're in New York or New Delhi, sales representatives can view a live video training presentation on their computers. The video is then archived so that it can be viewed again and again on demand. New product launches now cost about $300,000, and the engineers never have to leave corporate headquarters.

Kim Daus

Video training is just one of the many ways technology helps employees communicate more effectively at SGI. In fact, technology is such a integral part of the company's operation that Kim Daus, senior communications strategist and person responsible for the daily operations of the company intranet, finds it difficult to draw a line between technology and communication. Perhaps that's because the company's intranet allows employees to share information and work together seamlessly from such far-flung locations as Japan, Europe, the Middle East, and South Africa. According to Daus, collaborating over the intranet is *the* way of being a knowledge worker at SGI.

For example, the intranet makes it possible for employees to view live quarterly meetings discussing performance and strategy right from their computers. They can even join in the process by typing in questions. In addition, many messages that used to be delivered on paper or over the telephone are now published online or sent by electronic mail.

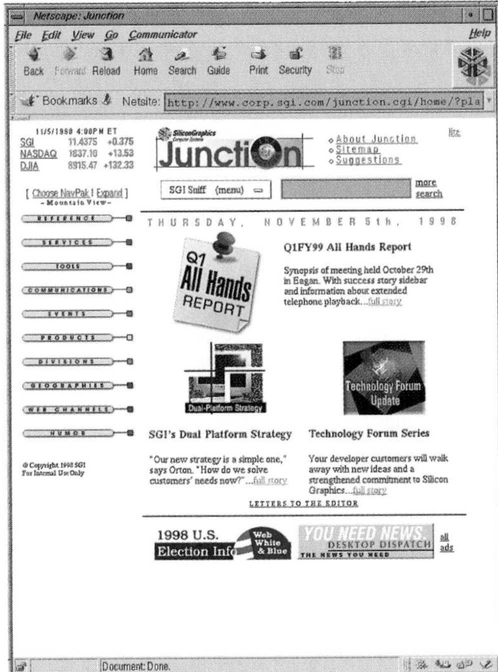

SGI's Web site is an important information source for both employees and customers.

"E-mail has brought huge productivity increases," notes Daus. "I can't imagine being without it." Whether coaching her team of journalists and editors, consulting with managers about how to create effective messages, or drafting stories for the company's newsletters, Daus finds that electronic communication is effective and efficient. Still, she cautions that e-mail isn't the best choice for all business communications. "You need to ask, 'What is the purpose of this message and how should it be delivered?' Sometimes with e-mail you miss the dynamic energy that comes from a meeting of minds."

Technology is also improving external communications at SGI. Through its external computer network, or extranet, the company provides its suppliers with the information and data they need to offer SGI the best possible service. For instance, by making product design information available to suppliers on a continuous basis, production managers can be more certain of getting the specific parts they need at the right times. In addition, Daus says that communicating electronically with suppliers cuts down on printing costs and requires less time than it did in the old days of telephone orders and paper invoices. However, electronic communication doesn't work in every situation, especially when the richness of face-to-face communication is needed.

Despite of all the advantages technology offers, making huge amounts of information available online can create security risks. To protect itself, SGI uses a "Websafe" password system. Daus says the system addresses two issues: "how to keep information safe inside the company, and how to keep it safe from outside the company." By assigning separate passwords to each employee and each supplier, the company can control which data a person or organization may access. For example, one password might allow suppliers access to inventory data while prohibiting access to sensitive product development information. Nevertheless, data security is only one of the challenges the company must deal with.

Because technology is the company's lifeblood, SGI has installed extensive backup systems that bring critical information back online in minutes should the company network crash. Having uninterrupted access to company databases is especially important, because Daus sees technology playing an even bigger role in the company's future. "There's a migration toward more collaborative systems," she says. "We'll see greater interoperability and common standards for data to be created and shared in ways we haven't even thought of."[1] ■

COMMUNICATING IN THE INFORMATION AGE

Advances in communication technology have made it possible to collaborate with others anywhere in the world today.

SGI is just one of the many companies using the Internet, e-mail, voice mail, and faxes to communicate with colleagues, suppliers, and customers. These technologies allow people from opposite ends of the world to work together seamlessly while they send bits and bytes rocketing around the globe 24 hours a day. This global collaboration also enables companies to build their products, run their operations, and deliver their services better, faster, and cheaper. As you can imagine, not only are these technologies changing the way we communicate; they are changing the way we work.

DID YOU KNOW?

The first patent on a working fax machine was granted to Scottish clockmaker Alexander Bain back in 1843—before Alexander Graham Bell was even born. Bain's method for sending a facsimile image cleverly exploited the transmission of electrical signals over telegraph wires.

In many firms, for example, co-workers and even entire departments are no longer in a single location. Today, sophisticated telephone systems, inexpensive fax machines and copiers, and powerful but economical computers make it practical for people to **telecommute,** or work away from a conventional office, whether at home, on the road, or across the country.[2] For some, a tiny computer and a cell phone tucked inside a purse or a shirt pocket have become a portable work space. In fact, it's not uncommon for people today to run their entire business from their car or even from an airplane. Of course, some experts predict that technology will produce even greater changes in the workplace in the near future. Technology, they claim, will permeate every business practice and create advances in communications capabilities that will be far more sophisticated than we can imagine today.[3]

Nevertheless, there are some disadvantages to advances in communication technology. For one thing, the new technology has blurred the line between work life and home life.

Where are you? Your employees? Your clients? Doesn't matter. Thanks to the latest virtual-office technology, staying connected has never been easier.

"Plugged in" and always accessible, more and more employees feel compelled to respond instantly to every message they receive, whether they're at home, on a business trip, or on vacation. For another thing, technology is invading people's privacy. Internet companies are doing whatever they can to learn more about you, your system, and where you go on the Web. Some companies leave cookies (user I.D. files) on your computer when you visit their Web site. Others demand personal information before allowing you access to their Web site or software. Furthermore, technology is producing information overload. The Internet is no longer a rising tide; it's a tidal wave. By pressing a few keys or a single button, anyone can send e-mail and documents to hundreds—even thousands—of people, whether the information is actually needed or not. As a result, today's employees are flooded with far more information than they can effectively process.

Using communication technology away from the office makes it difficult to separate work life from home life.

Of course, as a future businessperson, you'll be expected to know how to use the Internet and other technologies to communicate effectively in the workplace. In addition, you'll need to understand some of the communication challenges companies are facing as a result of these new technologies. In this chapter, we'll explain what you can do on the Internet, and we will provide examples of how businesses are using the Internet to communicate. In addition, we'll explore some of the innovations in other communication technologies. Finally we'll look at information overload, data security, and other workplace challenges.

Technology gives business communicators more options, but it also requires more decisions and more skills.

Understanding the Internet[4]

The Internet is talked about everywhere these days, and this book is no exception. What is this thing that is transforming the way we communicate and do business? Simply put, the **Internet** is a *network:* a group of computers that are connected so they can share information. Sometimes networks are confined to a single building or local area (called *local area networks,* or *LANs*); other times they connect computers in distant locations (called *wide area networks,* or *WANs*). The Internet just happens to be the world's largest network of many electronically connected computers (also known as servers).

The Internet is actually a network of networks.

Started in 1969 by the U.S. Department of Defense, the Internet is a voluntary, cooperative undertaking; no one individual, network, organization, or government owns it. The Internet is accessible to individuals, companies, colleges, government agencies, and other institutions in countries all over the world. To connect to the Internet all you need is a computer with a modem, a standard telephone line, and an *Internet service provider (ISP),* a company that provides access to the Internet. For a flat monthly fee or a per-use fee, you can dial into one of the ISP's host computers, which will link you to any number of the computers that make up the Internet network.

Of course, the most widely used part of the Internet is the **World Wide Web (WWW,** or the **Web**). Developed in 1990, the Web uses a graphical user interface (GUI) system, making it easy for users to search for, display, and save information residing on the Internet. This information is typically stored in a **Web site** located on one of the Internet's many networked computers. An individual Web site can consist of multiple Web pages, and in order to read a Web page you need a Web **browser,** software such as Netscape Navigator or Microsoft's Internet Explorer.

The World Wide Web is the part of the Internet that can accommodate graphics.

The **home page** of a Web site is the primary screen that users first access when visiting a site. Furthermore, each page in a Web site is identified by a unique address known as a **uniform resource locator (URL).** Take http://www.amazon.com, for example. The address begins with *http,* which is an abbreviation for **hypertext transfer protocol,** the communications protocol that allows you to navigate the Web. The second part of the address is the site's registered name (in this case amazon). No other site may use this name. The third part of the address indicates whether the site is hosted by a business (com), educational institution (edu), government (gov), international (int), military (mil), network resources (net), or non-profit organization (org).

When you click on hypertext links, you jump to the location coded behind the colored words or graphics.

Bookmark your favorite Web sites so that you can return to them without having to look up their URL.

Fortunately, you won't have to remember all those URLs, because just about every bit of information on the Web is *hyperlinked* or *hot linked,* which means you can click on words in **hypertext** language (colored, underlined, or highlighted words) with your mouse and automatically jump to another Web page or a different Internet site. Once you get to your new destination you can **bookmark** the site by using a browser feature that places the site's URL in a file on your computer for future use. Then, whenever you click on a bookmark while online, you automatically go to that site's address. Another handy browser feature is the ability to navigate your trail backward or forward at any time by using the *back* and *forward* buttons on your browser software. (See Table 10.2 at the end of this chapter for a glossary of Internet terms.)

What You Can Do on the Internet

You can't really get a picture of what the Internet is until you have a better idea of how you can use it. This section will explain how businesses today are using the Internet to communicate. You can also learn more about the Internet by taking the Internet tour at the Global Village Web site: http://www.globalvillage.com/gcweb/tour.html.

Communicating with Others

The Internet includes these features:

- Telnet
- Internet telephony
- E-mail
- Videoconferencing
- File transfer
- Discussion groups
- Search engines and directories

The original network that evolved into the Internet was designed to improve communication between scientists in the United States. Today, communication remains one of the primary uses for the Internet. Types of communication include Telnet, Internet telephony, e-mail, and videoconferencing.

Telnet **Telnet** is a class of Internet application programs that allow you to connect with a remote host even though your computer is not a permanent part of the network that the host supports. Telnet enables you to run a normal interactive session with other computers on the network as if you were sitting at an on-site terminal. For instance, you would use Telnet to access your local library's card catalog or perhaps your school's network from your home computer.

Internet Telephony It is now possible for Internet users to converse vocally over the Internet. Although the telephone has handled this job for decades, converting traditional voice calls to digital signals and sending them over the Internet is much less expensive than

Create Your Own Web Site

Learn how to create your own Web site using valuable Web development links, utilities, and online tutorials. Through the massive, user-friendly resources provided by the Web Developers' Virtual Library, you'll learn about document and Web page design, navigation, structure, and more. You'll even learn how to have your Web site translated into a foreign language.

http://www.stars.com

calling over standard analog phone lines. It can also be more efficient, because it allows an organization to accommodate more users on a single line at once. The quality of voice conversations over the Internet is still a big problem, but developers of this technology are working out the bugs. Nevertheless, experts say that Internet telephony could capture 4 percent of U.S. telephone company revenues by 2004.[5]

E-Mail Electronic mail, generally called e-mail, is one of the most useful Internet features for business. **E-mail** refers to documents created, transmitted, and read entirely on computer. The document might be a simple text message, or it might include long and complex files or programs. In fact, if you can save a file on your computer, you can probably save it via e-mail. E-mail has changed the style of business communication in dramatic ways. As Kim Daus put it, "I can't imagine being without it."

Electronic mail (e-mail) helps businesses communicate quickly and informally.

In Chapter 5, we discussed how to create effective e-mail messages. Here are some of the advantages of using e-mail:[6]

- *Speed.* E-mail is nearly instantaneous. An e-mail message often arrives at its destination anywhere in the world in a matter of seconds. With e-mail, you can correspond back and forth repeatedly in the time it used to take for one message to be delivered.
- *Cost.* The cost of sending an e-mail message is usually less than the cost of a first-class stamp and considerably less than the cost of overnight delivery services.
- *Portability.* You can receive and send e-mail anywhere you can connect your computer to a phone line.
- *Convenience.* E-mail solves the problem of coordinating phone calls across time zones, and it solves "phone tag" problems (when two people call back and forth leaving messages without ever connecting). Instead of leaving a brief phone message and waiting for a response, you can send and receive detailed, accurate messages. Furthermore, the people you are contacting need not be sitting at the computer or even have the computer turned on when you send a message. As soon as they log on to the Internet, most e-mail software programs will alert them that new mail has arrived. Recent technological advances such as PocketMail (allowing users to send and receive e-mail by holding a small keyboard-equipped device to any telephone), two-way e-mail pagers, and gadgets such as 3Com's wireless Palm Pilot are making this form of communication even more convenient.[7]

E-mail sent to you resides on one of the servers of your Internet service provider. Once you log onto the Internet, your e-mail software program will advise you that have new mail.

- *Record keeping.* You can save and organize e-mail messages you send and receive, so you'll have a good record of the communication on a specific project.
- *Egalitarianism.* With most e-mail systems, anybody can send messages to just about anybody else. Lower-level employees (who may otherwise have no contact with upper management) can send e-mail messages to top managers as easily as to their colleagues—the electronic equivalent of an "open-door" policy.
- *Collaboration.* E-mail encourages greater collaboration among employees, and it may increase productivity by streamlining communication. In addition, e-mail makes it relatively easy for companies to distribute work to temporary workers, independent contractors, or telecommuting employees.[8]
- *Distribution lists.* Within an e-mail program, you can create distribution lists: groups of people to whom you routinely send information. Then, when you want to send a message you specify the name of the list rather than typing all the individual names and addresses again.

KEEPING PACE WITH TECHNOLOGY

E-MAIL ETIQUETTE: MINDING YOUR MANNERS ONLINE

E-mail can be as fast as a phone call and as formal as a document. Because it's too often written hastily, it's often the most abused form of communication. As you write e-mail messages, keep in mind a few rules of etiquette: Be courteous, be brief, and be careful.

Be Courteous

- *Save your company money.* Read, write, and edit your messages offline (before you connect to the Internet). If you have to connect to access your mail program, try writing your message in a word-processing program and using copy-and-paste techniques to transfer it. Clean out your e-mailbox regularly to avoid taking up valuable computer space.
- *Check your e-mail regularly.* Try to check your mail three times a day.
- *Don't spam, or contribute to e-mail overload.* Respect other people's electronic space by sending messages only when necessary and only to those who need to see them. Avoid sending junk mail and trivial e-mail responses.
- *Don't simply reply to a message that was originally sent to multiple recipients.* Be careful about using the "reply" option. When you reply to a message sent to more than one person, your reply will go to all original recipients.
- *Respond quickly.* Explicitly quote the sender's message to provide a context when responding to a previous e-mail.
- *Don't use all capital letters.* This is the online equivalent of shouting. All "caps" are difficult to read.

Be Brief

- *Don't send too much information in one message.* Brevity shows respect for your reader's time. Be concise but not terse. Use short paragraphs to make the message easier to read.
- *Don't send big files without prior notice.* Big files can tie up connections, costing companies time and money. Before sending large files, send the end user a short note requesting permission or offering to send the file by some other means.
- *Avoid adding too many attachments to your e-mail.* Messages burdened with many attachments are difficult to read.

E-mail is not without disadvantages, however. In fact, some of the main benefits of e-mail also create its worst problems. People sometimes include things in e-mail messages that they wouldn't dream of saying in person or typing in a document. This new openness can help companies communicate better and circulate opinions from a wider variety of people, but it can also create tension and interpersonal conflict. Furthermore, because e-mail is so cheap and easy to send, people tend to overuse it, distributing messages more widely than necessary. As a result, some company executives receive hundreds of messages a day, many of which are the electronic equivalent of junk mail (See "Keeping Pace with Technology: E-Mail Etiquette: Minding Your Manners Online"). Besides wasting time, e-mail overuse can overload company networks, resulting in lost messages or even system crashes.

Videoconferencing allows groups to meet via computer in real time.

Videoconferencing In Chapter 2 we discussed how companies are using videoconferencing and groupware to meet and collaborate in real time. By using the Internet and software such as Microsoft's NetMeeting or MCI World Com's Net Conferencing, users can speak in real time and view and share documents electronically. With prices steadily declining and the quality of products continually improving, more and more companies will use videoconferencing in the future.[9]

- *Change the subject line when replying.* In an ongoing communication, it isn't long before recipients can't tell whether they're getting a new message or a recycled one.

Be Careful

- *Edit every message.* Remember, criticism and sarcasm don't come across well in e-mail.
- *Proofread every message.* Make sure that sloppy mechanics are never the cause of misunderstanding.
- *Remember that e-mail isn't always private.* E-mail can go everywhere—and in the blink of an eye. Don't send anything you don't want absolutely everyone to read.
- *Be aware that companies have the right to search company mail boxes.* The 1986 Electronic Communications Privacy Act ensures that internal e-mail is the property of the company that pays for the e-mail system. So watch what you write.
- *Avoid flaming.* Sending angry or unsuitable messages is called flaming. Before sending an e-mail message, read it twice, asking yourself if you would say this to the person's face. If you're upset, wait a few hours or days and think the message over. Once e-mail has been sent there is no way to retrieve it. Never use abusive or obscene language. Remember that in an e-mail message, you may indeed need to criticize the subject matter, but you never need to criticize another person.

The primary rule of e-mail etiquette is the golden rule: Treat others as you would like to be treated. Moreover, if a message is important, controversial, confidential, or easily misunderstood, consider delivering it face to face or by phone instead.

---

1. Experts advise you to ask for permission before forwarding or inserting someone else's e-mail message. Explain briefly why such courteous behavior is a good idea.
2. The people in your department share a printer, which you and your colleagues sometimes use to print out e-mail messages. Since the company owns the e-mail system and the printer, and since you are part of the company, is it okay for you to read any printed e-mail messages waiting to be picked up? Or are they confidential material? Explain your answer in less than half a page.

For a glimpse at how videoconferencing can change the way a company communicates with its customers, consider OnLine Capital, one of the many financial institutions offering home mortgages today. This company uses the Internet to provide prospective home buyers with instant online credit approvals. As soon as a buyer expresses an interest in a home, the realtor can access one of OnLine Capital's Internet loan officers, who immediately joins the group in a virtual meeting (via a videoconferencing system). Over the Internet, the loan officer interviews the buyer, prepares a real-time online loan application, and then either approves or disapproves the loan request—all within 45 minutes.[10]

Transferring Files between Computers

File transfer protocol allows you to download and upload files over the Internet.

File transfer protocol (FTP) is another important feature of the Internet. FTP enables you to **download files** (transfer data from the Internet into your computer) and **upload files** (transfer data from your computer to the Internet). Millions of useful files, including art, music, educational materials, games, maps, photos, software, documents, and books are available for downloading on the Internet. In addition, FTP allows you to attach formatted documents to your e-mail messages. This feature is especially useful in the business world, where employees zap résumés, memos, reports, letters, manuscripts, and so on from their computer to others. When you download a file or an attachment, the FTP software breaks it down, transmits it, and reassembles it on your computer in a usable form.[11] Sometimes users compress, or *zip,* large files into smaller packets to make them easier and faster to transfer. If you receive a zipped file, you must use special software (usually provided with your Web browser) to unzip it before you can read it.

Participating in Discussion Groups

Internet discussion groups allow you to participate in ongoing topical discussions with people all over the world. Two forms of discussion groups, are common on the Internet: *mailing lists* and *Usenet newsgroups.* A **discussion mailing list**, also known as a listserv, is a discussion group to which you subscribe by sending a message to the list's e-mail address. From then on, copies of all messages posted by any other subscriber are sent to you via e-mail. It's like subscribing to an electronic newsletter to which everyone can contribute.[12] For instance, your instructor can create a discussion mailing list for your course. All messages posted by your instructor and other students will be sent to your e-mail address. Once you finish the course, you can unsubscribe or ask to be removed from the mailing list.

The main difference between discussion mailing lists and newsgroups is the way you receive postings or messages.

Usenet newsgroups differ from discussion mailing lists in two key ways. First, messages (called articles) are posted at the newsgroup site. Unlike mailing lists, which are sent to your e-mail address, newsgroup articles must be accessed at the newsgroup's site by using a reader program in your Web browser. In other words, a newsgroup is a *place* you visit to read posted messages, whereas a discussion mailing list *delivers* posted messages to you. Second, messages posted to a newsgroup can be viewed by anyone. In most cases, however, you will have to fill out some preliminary information (such as your name) to post a message. Currently there are over 50,000 newsgroups on just about any topic imaginable, and that number grows daily.[13]

In addition to participating in discussion mailing lists and Usenet newsgroups, many Internet users engage in online **chat,** an online conversation in which any number of computer users can type in messages to each other and receive responses in real time.[14] They can also post messages on "message boards" offered at a wide variety of Web sites.

Searching for Information

One of the most common uses of the Internet is to find and access information. On the Web, you can locate current news, articles, and statistics; company information; tips for running a business, buying a home, or managing your finances; descriptions of products and services for sale; and so on. The amount of information available is almost endless, and the number of Internet Web sites is growing daily. In Chapter 11 we will discuss in detail how to find information on the Internet (as part of the research process), how to improve your search results, and how to evaluate your sources. In this chapter, we will explain how search engines work. By understanding what search engines can and can't do, you will be able to better understand their limitations and maximize your search results. Keep in mind that the term *search engine* is often used interchangeably to describe both search engines and *directories.* They are not the same. Their main difference is in how they compile their listings.

When you search for Web pages using a search engine, you actually search the engine's index, not the entire Web.

Search Engines **Search engines,** also called spiders or crawlers, travel the Web automatically, find new Web sites, and place a copy of these Web pages in their database (commonly called an index or a catalog). Sometimes it can take a while for the spider to find and add new pages to its index. Until a page is indexed, however, it is not available to those searching the Web with this particular search engine. In addition to finding new sites, every month or two the spider returns to previously indexed Web sites to look for changes and to update its index. When a Web surfer enters key search words, the search engine scans its index and

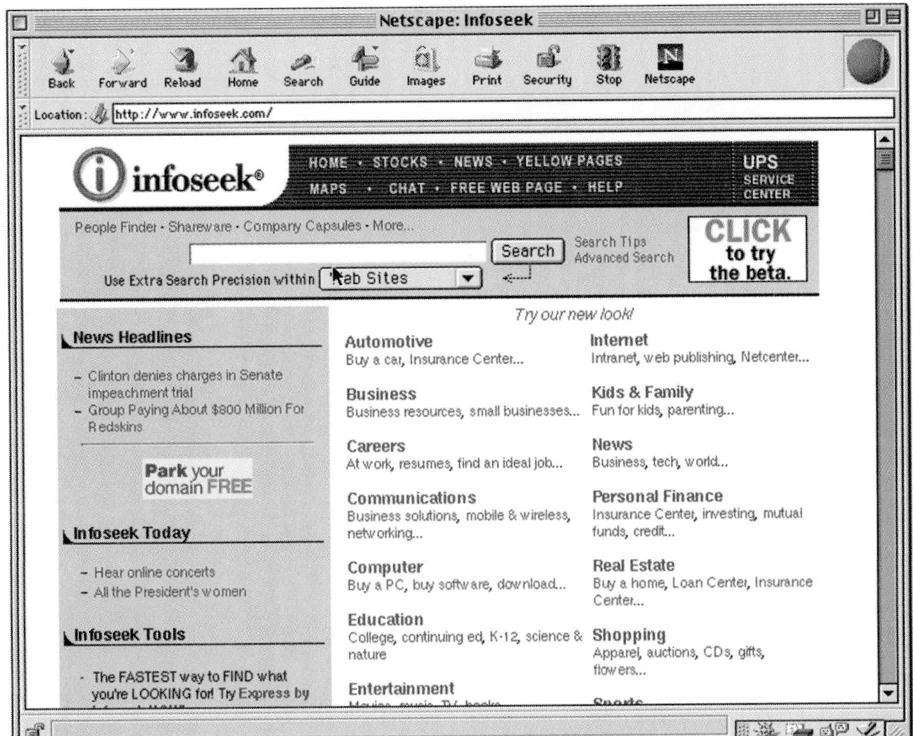

Infoseek, once just a search engine, now offers channels with links to some of the best sites on the Web in addition to other useful Internet resources.

returns the Web page addresses of all documents that match those words. Keep in mind that the engine does not actually go out to the Web each time a search is requested; rather, it only searches the engine's current index.[15]

Another thing to remember is that each search engine has qualities that distinguish it from the others. For instance, some engines index all the pages they find; others index only the most popular pages. Many engines also search Usenet newsgroups if you specify a newsgroup search in your search query. Furthermore, each search engine has its own schedule for updating its index. These differences create significant variations in search results. It is always best, therefore, to try your search on several engines. One effective way to search on multiple engines is to use metacrawlers, special engines that search several search engines at once.

Regardless of which search engine you use, you will get the best results if you spend a few minutes reading the engine's "tips" or "help" page before initiating your search. Getting to know each engine's strengths and weaknesses at the start of your search can save you a lot of time and frustration down the road. Table 10.1 lists some of the more popular search engines available.

Directories The main difference between a search engine and a **directory** is in how Web pages are added to the database or index. A search engine uses an automated robot (software) to find and index Web sites, whereas a directory uses humans to do this job. In other words, someone must actually submit a Web site to the directory, after which humans review the Web site and assign the site to an appropriate category in the directory's index. Because of this key difference, when you use a search engine, you often find more Web sites than when you use a directory. But, directories often yield more-precise results than search engines do.[16]

Directory indexes are prepared by humans, whereas search engine indexes are compiled by automated software.

TABLE 10.1

BEST OF INTERNET SEARCHING

Searchers can get the most dependable results from well-known, commercially backed search engines. These major search engines (and directories) are likely to be well-maintained and upgraded when necessary, to keep pace with the growing Web. Most have simple or advanced search features, plus extras such as interactive maps and weather, travel information, phone and e-mail directories, and company profiles.

Site	Description
	Major Search Engines
Alta Vista	http://altavista.digital.com Indexes data from millions of Web pages and articles from thousands of Usenet newsgroups.
Excite	http://www.excite.com All-purpose site loaded with options.
Fedstats	http://www.fedstats.gov/search.html Simultaneously queries 14 federal agencies for specified statistics and numerical data.
GoTo	http://www.goto.com Companies can pay to be placed higher in this engine's search results.
HotBot	http://www.hotbot.com *Wired* magazine packs all kinds of searching possibilities into this site.
Infoseek	http://www.infoseek.com Sites with red check marks are recommended by Infoseek.
LookSmart	http://www.looksmart.com Closest rival to Yahoo! in terms of being a human-compiled directory. Choose the "Your Town" for local directories.
Lycos	http://www.lycos.com One of the oldest of the major search engines, provides short abstracts for each match.
Northern Light	http://www.northernlight.com Categorizes returns by subject. Has "special collection" of over 2 million documents not readily accessible to search engine spiders.
Snap	http://www.snap.com CNET's Snap does a great job of sifting through and organizing some of the best material on the Web and presenting it in a logical fashion.
WebCrawler	http://www.webcrawler.com Either search the entire site or browse any of the preselected categories.
Yahoo!	http://www.yahoo.com The oldest major Web site directory listing over 500,000 sites.
	Multiple Search Engine Sites—Metacrawlers
Cyber411	http://www.cyber411.com Search up to 16 popular search engines at the same time. The query is reformulated to fit the syntax of each search engine.
Dogpile	http://www.dogpile.com Despite the silly name, just enter one query and this hound sniffs through dozens of FTP, Usenet, and Web sites.
Mamma	http://www.mamma.com Claiming to be the "Mother of All Search Engines," this multilegged spider queries the major search engines for fast results.
MetaCrawler	http://www.go2net.com/search.html One of the oldest, this spider searches six search engines simultaneously.
Metafind	http://www.metafind.com Same as Dogpile, except that searches go only to search engines.
ProFusion	http://www.profusion.com This University of Kansas spider retrieves only the "best" results from selected search engines.

TABLE 10.1, CONTINUED

	Specialty Search Engines
Amnesi	http://www.amnesi.com Can't remember the exact URL of a Web site? Tell Amnesi what you remember, and it will provide a list of sites it thinks match.
DejaNews	http://www.dejanews.com Search thousands of discussion groups found on Usenet from among the several categories.
Education World	http://www.education-world.com Over 50,000 sites of interest to educators, with the ability to narrow searches by appropriate grade level.
Forum One	http://www.forumone.com Allows you to search over 180,000 Web-based discussion forums.
HumanSearch	http://www.humansearch.com Send in a question, and a team of volunteer researchers will try to find an answer—one located on or off the Web.
News Search Engines	If you are still looking for news using "normal" search engines, you'll find using the services listed below to be a much better way to search for the latest news stories from hundreds of sources on the Web: *News Tracker* http://nt.excite.com; *NewsBot* http://newsbot.com; *News Index* http://newsindex.com; *NewsHub* http://newshub.com; *Paperboy* http://www.paperboy.net; *TotalNews* http://totalnews.com.

Portals Both search engines and directories can also become **portals** by adding features to their Web sites. Portals are Internet gateways—your everyday first stop on the Web—that offer some means to navigate the chaos of information on the Internet. Web sites such America Online, Yahoo!, Lycos, Infoseek, Microsoft Service Network, and Netscape are portals. (See "A Case for Critical Thinking: Yahoo! The Little Search Engine That Could," on page 433.)

Users were initially attracted to portals because of their unique search engines. Now, rather than pass surfers along, portals try to keep users at their Web site in order to build a big audience for advertisers—similar to television networks. To hold users' attention, they load their site with free e-mail, weather forecasts, stock reports, news, sports scores, horoscopes, links to other Web sites, and much more.[17]

Push versus Pull Technology In the past, most people obtained information from the Internet by using a search engine, by entering a specific Web site address, or by clicking on hypertext links. These actions are generally referred to as *pulling* information from the Internet.

Push technology automatically delivers information from the Internet to your desktop.

Push technology is just the opposite. You don't have to pull information from the Internet; push technology delivers it to you. When "push" first hit the Internet scene a few years ago, it was expected to become the new norm. It promised Internet users that they would no longer have to think about what Web sites to visit each day or spend time scouring sites for interesting news and desired information. Instead, users could subscribe to theme-related information channels (such as sports, news, and hobbies), and vendors would push this category of information right to their desktops—all day long. In other words, instead of driving to destinations on the information highway, subscribers would get home delivery.[18]

The concept of push technology soon withered, however, simply because recipients still ended up having to dig though the mounds of information that channels were pushing to their desktops. A chief complaint was that the information being pushed was not selective or relevant enough. Many users also discovered that they preferred to gather information proactively, rather than receive a daily dose. Furthermore, the vast amounts of information being pushed to employee's desktops were eating up precious company computer space, glutting their computer networks, and slowing down the network's speed.[19] As a result, push technology fell out of favor.

A personal agent is similar to a private search engine that combs the Internet for your specific interests and delivers the results to your desktop.

Personal Agents Today, personal agents are the next generation of push technology. These software agents mold your desktop information to your personal interests and exclude the types of generic information previously delivered by push channels. Such personalization is not automatic, however. First, users must register with a personal agent Web site (most are free). Next, users must create a detailed profile by entering their individual preferences from a long list of subject categories (these include news, weather forecasts, sports scores and schedules, stock quotations, horoscopes, movie show times, travel alerts, calendar reminders, and even state lottery results). Once a user has completed this process, a personal agent scans a wide range of Web sites, finds information that matches the user's preferences, and delivers it to her or his desktop (or tells the user where to go get it).[20] Eventually the information delivered gets more and more targeted as the user instructs the personal agent to "find more of this" or to "eliminate that."

Take Jessica Nierenbery, for example. Nierenbery subscribes to My Yahoo!, a personal agent service offered by Yahoo!. Each morning when she logs on to the Internet, a tailor-made collection of news and information is waiting for her. This includes the number of new e-mail messages she has waiting for her, a sample of news headlines from local papers she has selected, weather forecasts for her local area, her daily horoscope, and the closing prices of her favorite stocks.[21]

Of course, some personal agents specialize in gathering specific types of information. Company Sleuth at http://www.companysleuth.com, for example, scours the Internet while you sleep and gathers press releases, trademark applications, stock trading information, and newsgroup postings for companies you specify. Each morning, this detective delivers its findings to your desktop in time for your morning coffee.

How Businesses Are Using the Internet to Communicate

Now that you know what individuals can do on the Internet, we'll explore some of the ways businesses are using the Internet to communicate with employees, customers, and suppliers. Company Web sites, for instance, provide all kinds of information. Many companies today use Web sites to advertise their products, take product orders, solicit customer feedback, and recruit employees. They are also using intranets for communicating with selected groups. (See "Keeping Pace with Technology: Create a Winning Web Site.")

Intranets

An intranet is an Internet-type network whose information and access are restricted to a single organization.

Not all Web sites are available to anyone cruising the Internet. Some are reserved for the private use of a single company's employees and stakeholders. In fact, the development of private communication structures based on Internet technology is revolutionizing the way many companies do business. An **intranet** is a private corporate network that connects company computers in various locations. Intranets use the same technologies as the Internet and the World Wide Web, but the information provided and the access allowed are restricted to the boundaries of a companywide computer network. Sensitive corporate data that reside on intranets are protected from unauthorized access through the Internet by a security software called a **firewall,** a special type of gateway that controls access to the company's local net-

An intranet set up by his law firm enables attorney David Beckman to view documents and other legal resources whether he's in his office or in the courtroom.

work. When anyone tries to get into the internal web, the firewall requests a password and other forms of identification. People on an intranet can get out to the Internet, but unauthorized people on the Internet can't get in.

What Are the Advantages of Intranets? As Kim Daus knows, intranets do not require large capital outlays, are incredibly efficient, and are simple to use. In fact, 60 percent of SGI employees believe that their company intranet is essential to their job.[22] Using a Web browser, employees simply point and click their way through large company databases to find the information they are looking for.

Exactly how many companies are using intranets? According to one recent survey by a leading management consulting firm, almost half of the respondents (48 percent) said their companies maintain an active intranet site, and another 37 percent said their companies plan to install one within a few years.[23] Three factors are fueling this intranet boom: (1) the desire to share global knowledge, (2) the need for greater access to company information, and (3) the Web's ease of use and flexibility.[24]

Intranets make it easy for employees to share their knowledge and experience.

Aside from facilitating access to company information, an intranet enables employees to communicate and collaborate. At Arthur Andersen, for instance, global human resources managers use the company's intranet, *AA Online,* to access the company's wealth of expert knowledge and to search the company's online databases.[25] Ford Motor Company uses its intranet to enable engineers and designers worldwide to collaborate in real time on the design of new car models. This collaboration ensures that Ford North America's expertise in aerodynamics is being augmented by Ford Europe's expertise in vehicle ride and road handling without costly and time-consuming travel.[26]

Intranets can link computers that run on different operating systems.

Another big advantage of an intranet is that all company computers can link to it even if they have different internal operating systems. On an intranet, all information is available in a format compatible with Macintosh, PC, or UNIX-based computers. This compatibility virtually eliminates the need to publish internal documents on paper because everyone can

KEEPING PACE WITH TECHNOLOGY

CREATE A WINNING WEB SITE

Which is a more effective way of enticing consumers to buy your custom-designed area rugs: a mailer describing your product and showing a photo of your latest creations or a virtual store that allows consumers to browse your creations and click on the ones they want to see in detail? Many small businesses today are creating Web sites on the Internet to display their products. Some are quite informative. Others are very creative. So if you're considering creating a Web site for your company—whether you build it yourself or hire a consultant to design it for you—here are a few tips for you to consider.

Present a Professional Corporate Image One of the best ways to decide on what to include in your company Web site is by visiting competitors' sites. See what they are up to. How do they present their company image? What types of information do they include? What's missing? How easy is it to navigate the site?

Be sure to provide a company profile that tells people a little bit about your company. Include contact information and news releases or articles about your business so that customers can see how well known or dynamic you are in the industry. Make sure your material is accurate. Remember, successful sites provide information that is both interesting and related to your products. So be sure to identify the key benefits of your product and include product details on a second page.

Make Your Web Site Easy to Use Sites that take forever to load are a major source of user irritation. Keep large graphics to a minimum. Long-winded sites will be quickly passed over as users sit, fidget, and finally give up while waiting for long file transfers. If you're planning to include any large, embedded graphics or photos, provide an option for users to select a text-only interface, or provide small images of photos (called thumbnails) for users to select if they want to view a larger, more detailed photo. Always provide navigational buttons at the bottom of each page so that users can move backward and forward through a multipage site.

Anticipate Your Customers' Questions Plan ahead. Provide enough useful information by asking your sales or service personnel to generate a list of frequently asked questions. Then include this list of questions and answers on your Web

---

access the same information electronically. In addition, employees can find information much more quickly and easily by performing an electronic search on a well-designed intranet than by digging through multiple filing cabinets stuffed with papers.

In fact, thanks to intranets, some companies have even set goals of becoming "paperless." Owens-Corning Fiberglas, for instance, planned no space for filing cabinets in its new headquarters (whereas filing cabinets took up 20 percent of the floor space in their old building). The leader of Owens-Corning's technology transition team says, "This is not a campaign to save trees. This is about operating and running the business much more efficiently."[27]

In short, besides saving paper and floor space, an intranet can save a company time and money by increasing employee communication and collaboration, reducing employee travel, eliminating unnecessary meetings, and making information more accessible.

Many companies are using intranets to
- Publish company documents
- Post job openings
- Provide presentation materials
- Store company records and information
- Offer programs or software

What Types of Information Can You Place on an Intranet? Increasingly sophisticated intranet features are being developed daily, but many companies are currently using intranets to maintain company phone directories, publish company newsletters, and place a variety of company information online. Here are a few examples of the types of business information companies are placing on their intranets:

- *Policy manuals.* The most current version is always available to all employees without having to print hundreds of new copies when policies change.

site. Chances are you'll cover about 90 percent of your customers' concerns. Be sure to provide an active customer feedback mechanism. Incorporating e-mail into your site is one way to get customer input. Another way is to provide open feedback forms, structured survey forms, or even just a telephone or fax number. Remember, users tend to provide both frank and useful input, but only if you ask them for it.

Present Your Message Effectively Keep your text succinct and clear. Break your information into *chewable bites*. Long blocks of text can be overwhelming as well as boring. With every headline, every sentence, ask yourself: If I were reading this instead of writing it, would my interest level stay high? Use bulleted text to list information and highlight material. Remember, surfers want information fast and they want specifics. Bullets satisfy both needs by highlighting contents and by providing detail underneath or on a separate page. Most users want to interact with the message. So be sure to exploit the interactivity of the Internet by establishing key points or links that, when clicked on, will take readers to other pages or Web sites related to your topic.

Promote Your Web Site Be sure to list with one of the Web's search engines, giant indexes where Web users go to find information by entering key words. Most of these listings are free. Maximize the number of times your site will be listed by jamming in as many words as you can that best describe your site. If your site is listed with a few search engines but doesn't get a good ranking during searches, try First Place Software's Web Position Analyzer at http://www.webposition.com. This software queries and analyzes the quality of your site's search returns on most major search engines and offers suggestions to improve your rankings.

In addition to listing with search engines, don't forget about the more traditional approach. Take out an ad in the newspaper or submit a press release announcing your site and listing the site's address, or URL (uniform resource locator). Join newsgroups, and list your company in the Internet Yellow Pages. And remember, don't just sit back and expect your Web site to perform magic. Use it to find out as much as possible about your customers. Keep asking yourself how your company can benefit from all this information.

1. When building a Web site, what information should you include about your company?
2. List some of the ways companies can benefit from having a Web site.

- *Job openings.* New positions are posted, and current employees can submit job applications over the intranet.
- *Presentation materials used by marketing and sales departments.* Sales representatives can download sales and marketing materials at customer sites all over the world. In addition, changes made by marketing representatives at company headquarters are immediately available to field salespeople. Look at SGI. It used to take two to three weeks to get sales material to company field sales representatives. Now this process is almost instantaneous.[28]
- *Company records and information.* Company records and information stored on an intranet are accessible from anywhere in the world; all you need is an Internet connection and the right password. Furthermore, it's easier and faster to find information stored on an intranet. Before SGI installed its intranet, finding desired information manually could take several days.[29]
- *Programs or bits of software that might be useful to other programmers.* Hewlett-Packard maintains a "software vending machine" of code on its intranet. Before creating new code, programmers first check to see whether a program exists that they can use or modify.[30]

Keep in mind that just about any business information that needs to be shared among employees is a good candidate for an intranet; however, no intranet will magically organize

DID YOU KNOW?

Tests show that top-quality VHS tapes stored at room temperature preserve data dependably for only about ten years; the average-quality CD-ROM can become unreliable in only five years.

the information for a company. That's something the company itself must do. In fact, you don't really buy an intranet; rather, you buy the tools and then you create the intranet by weaving together an information infrastructure.

When designing a company intranet, keep these dos and don'ts in mind:[31]

- Do move your information systems onto the intranet gradually.
- Do keep your information current.
- Do borrow ideas from other successful company intranets.
- Don't reinvent the wheel. Why post a list of IRS forms when you can more conveniently link to an IRS Web site containing these resources?
- Don't assume that once you build an intranet people will flock to it. Employees will want to keep using their old familiar systems; it's the company's job to give employees some basic training so they can understand the efficiencies of this new tool.

Remember, an intranet does not automatically solve company problems; if organized properly, however, it will enable employees to access information in ways never before possible.

Extranets

An extranet is similar to an intranet, but it extends the network to people outside the organization.

Once a company has an intranet in place, the cost of adding *extranet* capabilities is minimal, but the benefits can be substantial. An **extranet** is simply an organized network that allows people to communicate and exchange data within a secured network.[32] Unlike intranets, which limit network access to a single organization, extranets allow prequalified people from the outside—such as suppliers and customers—to use the network.

Take Arthur Andersen's KnowledgeSpace. This company extranet is rich in the latest business practices and business news. Company clients can access this information in addition to a special version of Andersen's own internal database by entering the proper security codes given to clients.[33] Some executive search firms and employment agencies are also allowing clients to tap into their private Web sites to search for job prospects. Similarly, doctors and hospitals are using extranets to share best practices among their individual organizations. In the past, they faxed this information to each other, but there was no guarantee that the right person would see a fax or even know it existed before the information became obsolete.[34] In addition to increasing communication with clients, suppliers, and colleagues, extranets can save companies money. Consider this: One management consultant has seen an organization save as much as $70,000 simply by offering online information to its health-care providers and eliminating the need to print special booklets.[35]

While the Internet, intranets, and extranets are advancing the way companies communicate, other technological improvements in more traditional communication devices are also playing an important role in the Information Age.

EXPLORING INNOVATIONS IN OTHER COMMUNICATION TECHNOLOGIES

Technologies for one-to-one oral communication include the basic telephone and options such as faxes, pagers, and voice mail.

Although there is little doubt that new technologies have produced efficiencies in the workplace, some observers wonder whether they've done so at the cost of individuals' relationships with co-workers and clients. Today, phone calls, e-mail, faxes, pagers, and voice mail often take the place of face-to-face business meetings. Furthermore, as high technology permeates everyday life, many users are abandoning politeness and manners in their electronic communications. Not only does improper etiquette negatively affect one's career; it can also strangle a company's success—especially when conducting business overseas.[36] For these reasons, experts caution that before companies throw powerful new communication tools at employees and expect them to use these tools wisely, they must train employees to be responsible communicators (See this chapter's Checklist for High-Tech Etiquette).[37]

Telephone Systems

Business phone systems have become less and less like the phones you use at home; in fact, many act like computers with phones attached. *Call-management* systems give companies better control over both the calls that come in and the calls that go out. For inbound calls, a *PBX* (*private branch exchange*) system can screen and route calls. Some are run by a human operator; others are nearly or completely computerized. For outbound calls, computers can track who called whom, automatically dial numbers from a list of potential customers, and perform other time- and money-saving tasks. To reach employees who are out of the office, a company can equip them with cellular phones or *pagers,* small radio receivers that signal employees to call the office—or home.

DID YOU KNOW?

Statistics show that the average salesperson makes 1,860 phone calls each year, but only 25 percent of all calls are completed on the first try.

Until recently, a number of factors have held back the market for wireless phones in the United States. These factors include incompatible technologies, high infrastructure costs, high user prices, and failure to adopt the "caller pays" system common in most other parts of the world. (Most U.S. wireless phone users have to pay for both incoming and outgoing

CHECKLIST FOR HIGH-TECH ETIQUETTE

A. Leaving Messages on Answering Machines and Voice Mail

1. State whom you are calling, your first and last name, your company and title, the reason for your call, and your phone number (with area code and extension).
2. Be brief when stating your message, and indicate specific callback times.
3. Speak slowly.
4. Deliver bad news personally.
5. Follow up on important messages to make sure they were received.

B. Recording Messages on Answering Machines and Voice Mail

1. Limit menus and options.
2. Give callers an easy way to reach a live person.
3. Test your message.
4. Update greetings frequently, and change your message when going on vacation.

C. Faxing Messages

1. Fax nonpersonal messages only.
2. Use a cover sheet stating the date, number of pages, recipient's name, sender's name, and a phone number to call if there is a transmission error.
3. Sign your fax for a more personal message.
4. Call before faxing urgent messages or before faxing long documents.
5. Check your fax machine regularly to make sure it has adequate paper and cartridges.

D. Sending E-Mail

1. Respect other people's electronic space by sending messages only when necessary.
2. Make your subject line informative.
3. Avoid overusing the label "urgent."
4. Use short paragraphs.
5. Refrain from using all capital letters (shouting).
6. Quote a previous e-mail when responding to questions or requests.
7. Proofread every message.
8. Be careful about using the "reply all" button.
9. Check your e-mail often.
10. Clean out your e-mailbox regularly.

Advances in affordable telecommunications equipment has opened the way for small-business owners to become more active and more competitive away from their home bases.

The use of wireless communication devices is increasing rapidly in the United States.

Communication companies are developing new technology that uses existing phone lines for multiple tasks.

calls.) With advances in wireless communication equipment rolling out almost monthly, however, some experts believe that eventually wireless will get so cheap that it will displace old-fashioned wireline phones. In many cases, this process is already under way. If you walk around any airport, you'll see people standing three feet from a pay phone talking on their portable cell phones. That's displacement.[38]

Of course, existing phone lines will still be used for communication. MCI-WorldCom, for example, will soon provide subscribers with a nationwide, ultrafast Internet access service known as Digital Subscriber Line, or DSL. Aside from communication speed, the biggest advantage of DSL is its ability to use existing copper telephone lines.[39] Similarly, Sprint's new Integrated On-Demand Network (ION) will provide customers with unlimited high-speed access to communications and information. This technology breaks voice and data transmissions into bits and then crams them through the switches, wires, and optical fibers making up today's phone systems. This innovation allows a half dozen people to talk on the phone, send faxes, exchange e-mail, and surf the Web—all at the same time over one phone line—at a fraction of today's costs. Wavelength division multiplexing (WDM) is another recent communication innovation. Telecommunication experts predict that WDM will increase fiber-optic speeds and wireline capacity levels so much that some day every home may have its own direct line to the Internet.[40]

Exactly how much will all this new communication technology cost users? Some experts predict that phone utilities will function much as electric utilities as far as billing goes. With the system always "on" and billable by usage (in this case the amount of information shipped through the line), a three-minute call from New Jersey to California will cost no more than one to the business next door.[41]

Voice Mail and Speech-Recognition Software

The combination of phones and computers has also created an increased use of *voice mail* in the workplace. Much more than a glorified answering machine, voice mail lets you send, store, and retrieve verbal messages to any number of "mailboxes" on the system. Messages can be several minutes long, and you can review your recordings before sending them. To listen to your voice-mail messages, you enter a confidential code; then you can play or delete your messages or forward them to other people on the system. Voice mail solves the time-zone difficulties of across-country and international communication. It can also reduce a substantial amount of interoffice paperwork. (See Figure 10.1 for eight ways to improve your voice-mail communications.)[42]

Even though voice mail can make employees more productive, it's not universally loved. The biggest complaint comes from customers who try to reach a person by phone but first must listen to lengthy recordings and menus only to be transferred to yet more recordings and menus.

Companies are using speech-recognition software to minimize customers' interaction with voice-mail menus.

Many companies are finding that by using speech-recognition software, they can provide callers with better customer service. After decades of painstaking research, software companies have a variety of programs that recognize large vocabularies and perform natural language understanding. Businesses are using these state-of-the-art features to liberate call-in customers from the tedious "press one, press two" phone menus of voice mail. They are replacing Touch-Tone-activated menu systems with the voice of an operator that talks them through the choices or asks, "How can I help you?" But there's a catch—the operator isn't human.[43]

Figure 10.1
Eight Ways to Improve Your Voice-Mail Communications

Much telephone communication today happens through voice mail. Before setting up a voice-mail message, organize your thoughts so that the message will be concise and accurate, and keep in mind that voice-mail messages aren't necessarily private.

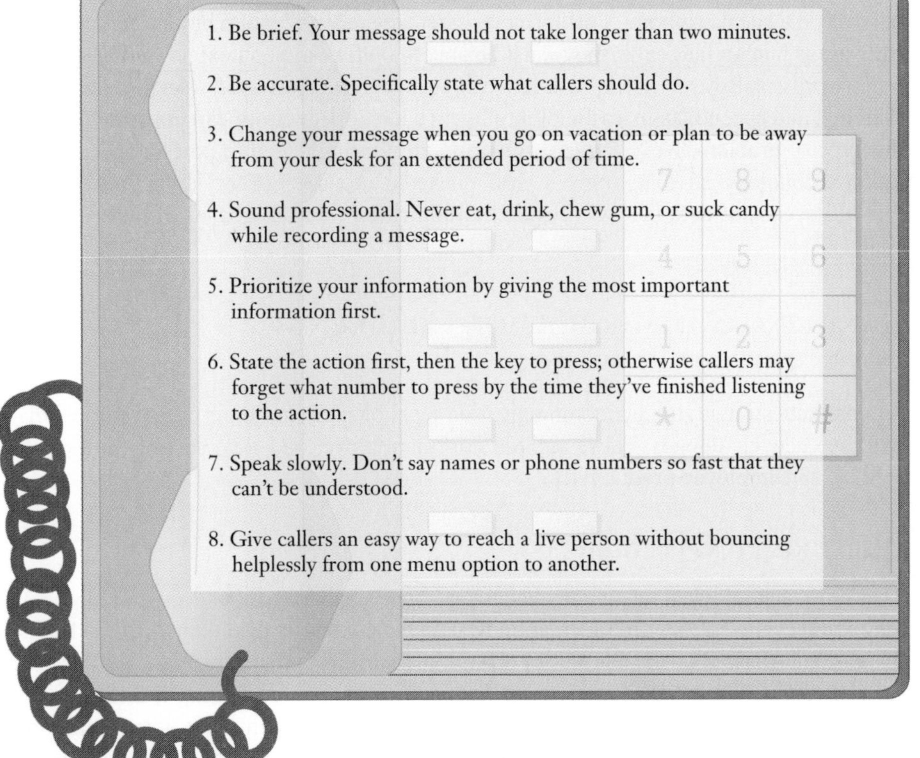

As you speak your request, these programs "listen" to your voice and break it into its phoneme blocks (tiny units of speech). Then they compare your voice blocks against a preloaded template and look for matches. If the system is not sure of the exact match, it responds with a message similar to "Did you say Susan Smith?" These systems disregard superfluous words and phrases such as "uhh," and many have a "bargethrough" feature that allows callers to begin speaking without waiting for the voice prompt to finish talking.[44]

Speech-recognition software can be 97 percent accurate under ideal conditions.

Although newer systems recognize tens of thousands of words and phrases in many languages—some with an accuracy of 97 percent—most speech-recognition systems perform their best under ideal conditions. Put a bunch of people in a room, spark a lively debate, turn on the system, and all of a sudden error rates shoot from a respectable level all the way up to 50 percent—which means that every other word is wrong.[45]

Regardless, companies such as UPS, Bell Canada, Coca-Cola New Zealand, American Express, United Airlines, and dozens of others are currently using these systems to reduce customer wait times without adding more operators or phone lines to handle increased call volume. For instance, UPS uses speech-recognition software to respond to customers' inquiries on the whereabouts of their parcels. Bell Canada uses a system that can service 4 million directory-assistance calls a minute. And Coca-Cola New Zealand uses a speech-recognition system to solve a call volume problem that used to leave both inbound and internal callers in perpetual telephone limbo. Today, Coca-Cola's callers are greeted with the message "Please say the full name of the party you wish to talk to or the name of the department you are looking for."[46]

Scientists are scrambling to perfect the next generation of speech technology. But to do so, they must build recognition systems to work accurately whether speakers have a Japanese or a Spanish accent or whether they are on a cell phone, on a land line, in the airport, or on a speaker phone. Furthermore, scientists recognize that before computers can truly grasp human language, they must be able to understand context as well as words. In other words, software "needs to know a lot about how the world works," says one researcher, and specialists in artificial intelligence have spent entire careers struggling with this type of problem. Nevertheless, scientists are forging ahead to perfect speech-recognition technology so that humans won't have to mouse-click or keypunch their way through oceans of data that will reside in multitrillion-byte databases of the twenty-first century.[47]

HANDLING COMMUNICATION CHALLENGES IN THE INFORMATION AGE

The development of technology is changing business communication, and its effects are both positive and negative.

As companies integrate new communication technologies into their organizations, many will face new challenges. These include information overload, data security, information privacy, and employee productivity.

Information Overload

Thanks to technological advancements, today's workers have instant access to all the data they could ever want; it's an Information Age dream come true. But there are drawbacks to this ease of information exchange. For one thing, a surplus of data is pelting employees and customers like a relentless Seattle rain. For another, people are finding it difficult to discriminate between useful and useless information and between what is truly important and what is routine. In fact, experts worry about the human capacity to absorb this ever-increasing amount of information, especially when the channels are already full and the information is flowing at top speed. Information overload has already hit just about everybody, and experts predict that it's only going to get worse.[48]

What Is Causing Information Overload

A recent study by KPMG management consultants pegged e-mail as the greatest contributor to information overload, but consider this:[49] In addition to e-mail messages, people receive messages by overnight express couriers, fax machines, voice mail, Web sites, snail mail, pagers, and cell phones. Besides these, the average consumer wades through a daily flood of telephone solicitations in addition to being exposed to an endless barrage of television, radio, print, billboard, and even blimp advertisements. Furthermore, the increased use of self-directed teams in the workplace generates hundreds of messages daily, each requesting information or announcing a new process or a new strategy. No wonder people are becoming frustrated.

People are overwhelmed by e-mail, overnight mail, faxes, voice mail, Web sites, snail mail, pagers, and phone calls.

In fact, because today's organizations operate at warp speed, this apparent urgency makes everything—including trivial issues—seem important. Of course, some people handle information overload simply by shifting the time and place they deal with messages. "I'd be lost on Monday," notes one manager, "if I didn't spend an hour or so on Sunday evening cleaning up my e-mail." (See Figure 10.2 for a typical e-mail message.) Others, however, are trying some unique approaches.

How Companies Are Managing Information Overload

While some companies are dealing with information overload by encouraging employees to send fewer e-mail messages and by discouraging the use of the word *urgent,* others are taking more extreme measures. The CEO of Computer Associates, for example, has ordered the company's e-mail system to be shut down for two hours a day. "When it first happened, it was like quitting cigarettes," notes one company manager, "we had 9,000 very edgy employees. But as we got used to it, people found that they had time to think." At SmithKline, business units are charged fees based on the number and length of each unit's e-mail messages. This measure has produced a dramatic decline in the total number of daily messages.

Companies are experimenting with various ways to manage information overload.

Other companies are revising their information distribution systems to more of a pull strategy. Rather than push information, such as news about the company, retirement plan performance reports, recruiting efforts, training programs, and board meeting minutes, they're changing the model so that employees can conveniently find or pull this information from company databases whenever they want it.[50]

Still others are hiring *information architects,* communication specialists who use the principles of instructional design, educational psychology, graphic design, and marketing to reorganize company information into more effective communication. Look at Supercuts, a chain of over 1,100 hair salons. The company worked with information architects to reorganize its operations and procedural manual, which is distributed to store managers nationwide. This manual is filled with crucial information for managing each site's day-to-day operations. Yet at 4,000 pages, it was hardly user friendly. In fact, it was binder overload. By using an information manager, the company remapped the information into graphical boxes, strong headlines, shaded thumbtabs, and callouts at two-thirds the original space, making the information easier to read and access.[51] Information architects also make company Web sites and intranets easier to navigate by applying these same principles.

An information architect effectively organizes a company's information to make it more "user friendly."

Figure 10.2
In-Depth Critique: Electronic Mail

Gretchen Plaxton, a budget analyst at Robson Brothers Manufacturing, encountered some unexpected problems in setting up her computer for an important budget briefing. Her e-mail message was waiting for Li Chau when she returned to her office, and the two women were able to solve Plaxton's problem by closing time.

E-Mail

Date: Thurs, 17 June 1999, 11:45:23, CDT
To: lichau@robson.com
From: gplaxton@robson.com (Gretchen R. Plaxton)
Subject: Help!

Li,

You're not answering your phone, so I guess you're not back from your software demonstration. I really need your expertise! I've spent the better part of this morning trying to get my computer set up for tomorrow's budget briefing, but nothing seems to help. Everything was working fine in my office, but now that I've moved my machine to the conference room, I keep getting application errors in the graphics software!

I have to meet Roland from production for lunch at noon, but I'll be back in the office by 1:00. Can you come look at my machine after that? The budget meeting is set for tomorrow at 9 a.m. sharp! So I can't really wait for the consultant we started on retainer last month (she's tied up until after 4:00). If I can't get things running by end of business today, I'm in deep trouble. I'll be up all night hand drawing flip charts--and with my artistic talent, they won't be pretty!(:<)

If you get back before I do, leave a message on my voice mail, or e-mail me. I'm desperate, Li. Please say you'll come rescue me.

Hope to hear from you soon.

Gretchen

This computer screen shows how a timely message can be sent to anyone connected to the system—whether across the globe or in the same building.

Plaxton has the space to explain the situation so that Chau can respond without needing any more information.

At the end of the second paragraph, Plaxton has included a type of e-mail symbol known as an emoticon—in this case a sideways "sad face" that clues the reader in to how the writer is feeling.

Chau can let Plaxton know whether she will be available and what time would be convenient—again by e-mail—simply by clicking on the reply button and typing in her response.

Data Security

Before computers, a typical company conducted the vast majority of its business on paper. Important files and documents were kept under lock and key, and when something was sent to someone across the office or in another part of the country, security precautions were almost always used. Furthermore, only a limited number of people had access to vital company data. But today's move from paper-based systems to electronic data management poses a real threat to corporate security.[52]

Electronic information poses a real security threat to organizations because it's easy to copy and transmit.

Global networks increase the possibility that crucial information sent over an intranet or the Internet will fall into the wrong hands. Of course, cyberterrorism—orchestrated attacks on a company's information systems for political or economic purposes—is a very real threat. But an even greater security threat is a network without proper safeguards. Vulnerable networks can become a high-tech sieve that lets crooks steal or destroy sensitive data, because digital data are far easier to duplicate and disseminate than are paper documents. Furthermore, a PC without the proper password protections can easily become a fountain of insider information.

Consider this: According to one recent study, 75 percent of companies have suffered financial losses from fraud, theft of proprietary information, and sabotage as a result of breaches in computer security. The study also found that the biggest threat typically comes from inside the organization. Violators include laid-off workers, contractors, consultants, and even good employees who inadvertently destroy, alter, or expose critical data.[53]

Experts advise that, even if companies install the proper security systems, they also take the following security measures: (1) Provide ongoing security education; (2) conduct background checks on all new employees; and (3) maintain clearly defined security policies that at a minimum encourage employees to use passwords, turn computer systems off when not in use, and rely on encryption when sending sensitive e-mail.

At a minimum, companies should take these security measures:

- Install proper security systems
- Educate employees about security
- Perform background checks on new employees
- Encourage employees to use passwords and encryption

Information Privacy and Employee Productivity

Information privacy and employee productivity are two other issues that have surfaced as a result of innovations in communication technologies.

As discussed earlier, many employees erroneously believe that their e-mail and voice-mail messages are private, and they're surprised when e-mail ends up in places they did not intend it to go. Keep in mind that people do not always carefully screen their electronic distribution lists, and they may send information to people who should not have it or do not need it. Even if your message originally goes only where you intended it to go, a recipient can easily forward it to someone else.

Remember, e-mail and voice mail are not very private, and they can be used as evidence in court.

Furthermore, employers have the legal right to monitor everything from an employee's Web access to the content of the employee's e-mail or voice-mail messages. According to a survey by the American Management Association, about 35 percent of major U.S. companies keep tabs on workers by recording phone calls or voice mail and by checking employees' computer files and e-mail.[54]

Both e-mail and voice mail can be used as evidence in court cases, and voice mail doesn't evaporate; it's vulnerable to predators who break into voice mailboxes.[55] Therefore, a good rule of thumb is not to say anything in e-mail or voice mail that you would not want to see published in the *New York Times.*

Maintaining a high level of employee productivity is another challenge companies are facing, because e-mail, voice mail, conference calls, and faxes interrupt employees while they work. Chat or real-time conversation windows can pop up on computer screens and demand immediate conversation. Adding to the productivity problem is the fact that some employees misuse Internet privileges by surfing the Web and visiting non-business-related Web sites during working hours. In fact, in one report, 31 percent of the businesses surveyed cited financial losses from reduced employee productivity as a result of Internet misuse alone.[56] Still, it's hard to be productive if you can't use the Internet when you need it, so restricting employees' access may be counterproductive.

Restrict your use of the Internet to job-related activities during working hours.

Another productivity problem that is related to accessibility is traffic jams. Currently, the Internet is like a single-lane highway with unlimited access points and no traffic control. These features make the Internet's strength, accessibility, a weakness for users who need to move large amounts of data quickly. When traffic gets heavy, things slow down. Furthermore, there is no way to separate high-end Internet users from the millions who use it primarily to send e-mail. Consequently, researchers at more than 100 universities are trying to gather support and funding to add "high-speed" toll lanes to the Internet. Dubbed Internet 2, these new lanes would be used (for a fee) by companies and individuals who need to move huge amounts of data (such as graphics and videoconferencing) quickly and reliably. Of course, there will still be the far-right lanes for the slower traffic (who will still get on for free).[57]

Advocates of Internet 2 want high-speed toll lanes so users can move large amounts of data quickly.

In this chat screen, a record of the conversation is displayed in the top window. Users type their messages in the bottom window.

PREPARING COMPANIES FOR THE NEXT INFORMATION REVOLUTION

Frustrated with the amount of raw data they now have, today's managers aren't really looking for more. Instead, they want information and knowledge, and they want to put this knowledge to work. That's because, in a global economy, managers need to know about their noncustomers, competitors, and potential markets as well as their customers,. Today's companies can no longer afford to only look inward. To be competitive they must shift their focus from inward efficiencies to outward opportunities.

In the information age, organizations need to effectively use the collective knowledge of their employees.

As professor Fernando Bartolome puts it in the book *The Articulate Executive,* "This is the age of information. Organizations will live or die, depending on their ability to process raw data, transform the data into information, distribute the information appropriately, and use it speedily to make decisions today and change them tomorrow as new information reaches the organization."[58] The practice of maximizing a company's collective information is often called *knowledge management.*

Pretty soon we'll use smaller communication devices to plug into the Internet—just about everywhere.

Other experts, such as management guru Peter Drucker, confirm that collecting outside information will become the next communication frontier—the biggest information revolution after the printing press.[59] And information will be even more accessible; some experts predict that someday people will carry around several devices (perhaps a watch, a cellular phone, and a personal digital assistant) that will be enormously more powerful than similar devices today and that will all be able to plug into the Internet. "People will use them to communicate in ways we've never seen before." The Internet, they say, "will become a utility, just like water or electricity." You'll simply plug into it anywhere.[60]

As new communication technologies are developed, companies will have to find ways to make it easier for employees to seek out, sort through, organize, refine, disperse, and share information.[61] *Data-mining*, or focusing on ways to get truly useful information out of huge databases and use it to make decisions, will be one way to accomplish this goal.[62] But technology can't do the thinking. Humans must do that. To be successful, employees will have to know how to find, evaluate, and process information effectively and efficiently—the topic of Chapter 11.

TABLE 10.2

INTERNET GLOSSARY

attachment A file transmitted with an e-mail note.

bookmark A browser feature that places selected URLs in a file for quick access, allowing you to to automatically return to the Web site by clicking on the site's name.

Boolean operators The term *Boolean* refers to a system of logical thought developed by the English mathematician George Boole. It uses the operators AND, OR, and NOT. For the Web, Boolean operators are helpful in conducting searches.

browser Software, such as Netscape Navigator or Microsoft's Internet Explorer, that enables a computer to search for, display, and download the multimedia information that appears on the World Wide Web.

chat A form of interactive communication that enables computer users in separate locations to have real-time conversations; usually takes place at Web sites called chat rooms.

cookie A string of numbers a Web site uses to identify visitors. The cookie can contain information about subscriptions and memberships to online services and other information.

directory Differs from a search engine by using humans (rather than software) to add and categorize Web pages.

discussion mailing lists E-mail lists that allow people to discuss a common interest by posting messages, which are received by everyone in the group. Unlike users of newsgroups, mailing list users must subscribe to a mailing list to post and receive messages. Also called a listserv.

domain name The portion of an Internet address that identifies the host and indicates the type of organization it is. For example, http://www.sun.com is the address for Sun Microsystems. The last portion (sun.com) is the domain name. The "com" part of the domain name reflects the purpose of the organization or entity (in this example, "commercial") and is called the *top-level* domain name. The "sun" part of the domain name is called the *second-level* domain name; it must be registered and is unique on the Internet.

download To transmit a file from one computer system to another. On the Internet, downloading a file means bringing data from the Internet into your computer.

file transfer protocol (FTP) A software protocol that lets you copy or move files from a remote computer—called an FTP site—to your computer over the Internet. File transfer protocol is the Internet facility for downloading and uploading files.

firewall Computer hardware and software that protects part or all of a private computer network attached to the Internet by preventing public Internet users from accessing it.

flaming Giving someone a verbal lashing on the Internet; considered poor etiquette.

frequently asked questions (FAQs) A list of common questions about a particular subject, such as a newsgroup or a Web site.

gopher A text-based Internet navigation program that uses a menu tree to search for subjects. Developed at the University of Minnesota and named after the school's mascot.

home page The primary Web site for an organization or individual; the first hypertext document displayed on a Web site.

hyperlink A hypertext code that automatically allows people to move from one document to another by clicking on the link with a mouse. Also called a hotlink.

TABLE 10.2, CONTINUED

hypertext markup language (HTML) The software language used to create, present, and link pages on the World Wide Web.

hypertext transfer protocol (http) A communications protocol that allows people to navigate among documents or pages linked by hypertext and to download pages from the World Wide Web.

integrated services digital network (ISDN) A communications system that allows people to connect to the Internet and send and receive data in digital form over telephone lines at much higher speeds than on standard lines. Unlike modems, ISDN does not require computer data to be converted into analog voice signals.

Internet A worldwide collection of interconnected networks that enables users to share information electronically and provides digital access to a wide variety of services.

Internet service provider (ISP) A company that provides access to the Internet, usually via public telephone lines.

intranet A private network, set up within a corporation or organization, that operates over the Internet and may be used to link geographically remote sites.

multimedia Typically used to mean the combination of two or more presentation media, such as text, sound, graphics, and motion video.

newsgroups One or more discussion groups on the Internet where people with similar interests can post articles and reply to messages. Also called *Usenet* newsgroups. Unlike mailing lists, which are accessed by e-mail, newsgroups are accessed by a newsgroup reader in your browser. Once you subscribe you can read messages posted by other subscribers and leave messages for other subscribers to read. Newsgroup discussions do not take place in real time.

search engine A server-based application used to search large databases for selected words or phrases. Common search engines use key words to search for information on the World Wide Web.

spam Unsolicited e-mail. From the sender's point of view, it's a form of bulk mail. To the receiver, it seems like junk e-mail.

Telnet A way to access someone else's computer (the host computer), assuming the host has given you permission, and use that computer as if it were right on your desk. A Telnet command request looks like this: telnet the.libraryat.harvard.edu. The result of this fictitious request would be an invitation to log on with a user ID and a prompt for a password. If accepted, you would be logged in like any user who uses this computer every day.

uniform resource locator (URL) Web address that gives the exact location of an Internet resource. It contains information about the server to be contacted and the method and path of access. Example: http://www.patriots.com.

upload On the Internet, uploading a file means sending a file from your computer to the Internet.

Usenet An electronic bulletin board system through which newsgroups are transmitted.

Web site A related collection of Web files that includes a beginning file called a home page. Companies or individuals tell you how to get to their Web site by giving you the *URL* address of their home page. From the home page, you can get to all other pages on their site.

World Wide Web (WWW) A hypertext-based system for finding and accessing Internet resources such as text, graphics, sound, and other multimedia resources.

SUMMARY OF LEARNING OBJECTIVES

1. **Discuss what individuals can do on the Internet.** You can connect to another network using Telnet, hold a telephone conversation, send and receive e-mail, use videoconferencing software, transfer files, participate in discussion mailing lists or newsgroups, search for information, and communicate via intranets and extranets.
2. **Differentiate between discussion mailing lists and newsgroups.** The main difference between discussion mailing lists and newsgroups is in the way you receive and post messages. Subscribers to mailing lists receive copies of all posted messages via e-mail, whereas newsgroup users post and read messages by visiting the newsgroup site.
3. **Explain how a search engine works.** A search engine travels the Web automatically, finds new Web sites, and indexes them.

COMMUNICATION CHALLENGES AT SGI

As senior communications strategist for SGI, Kim Daus helps key communicators make their messages more effective. By examining the purpose and context of a message, Daus helps them structure their messages properly and choose the correct communication channel and medium.

INDIVIDUAL CHALLENGE: You are a member of Daus's staff. Because so many people within the company look to Daus for help with their communications, she relies on you to carefully screen requests and make preliminary recommendations. The following items were sent to you this morning. Evaluate each message, considering the creator and intended receivers, the context of the message, how urgent it is, and whether the creator expects feedback from the receivers. Summarize your assessment, and then recommend a proper communication channel and medium for transmitting the message. (Note: Some may not involve technology.)

Request 1: The vice president of sales and marketing wants to communicate specifications for the next generation of desktop workstations to international sales representatives before the product is launched next quarter.

Request 2: A line supervisor wants to inform his manager of production delays resulting from employee absenteeism. The supervisor would like to discuss ways to boost employee morale and productivity.

Request 3: The CEO wants to congratulate all employees for their hard work, which has resulted in better than expected earnings for the fiscal year.

Request 4: A programmer has discovered several new development tools that have greatly increased her productivity, and she wants to share his findings with the company's other programmers.

Request 5: The production manager wants to notify all of SGI's development partners (third-party suppliers) about the company's new guidelines.

TEAM CHALLENGE: You and three other employees from your department have been assigned to develop a Web page for the company's intranet that will enable employees to get the help and information they need more quickly. You have already identified the following areas that should be addressed: departmental mission statement, contact information, request guidelines, general communication tips, frequently asked questions, appropriate use of communication technology, high-tech etiquette, and links to other communication resources. Your next task is to develop a preliminary plan for the Web site design. Keep in mind that your goal is to make it as easy as possible for employees to communicate effectively. What information will appear on the first page, and why? How will you structure the remaining pages, and how will you link them together? What additional information will you include, and how will you decide what is most relevant? How will you encourage employees to use the site?[63] ■

Once a page has been indexed, it is available to anyone using that search engine. When a surfer enters search words, the search engine scans the current index (not the entire Web) for matches. Different search engines update their indexes differently.

4. **Differentiate between an intranet and an extranet.** Both an intranet and an extranet are based on Internet technology. An intranet, however, restricts access to the boundaries of a companywide computer network, whereas an extranet allows certain people outside the company network to communicate and exchange information.
5. **Discuss how businesses are using intranets.** Businesses are using intranets to publish company newsletters, maintain and distribute company phone directories, publish policy manuals, post job openings, store company records and information such as marketing and sales materials, collaborate and work in teams, and deliver software updates.
6. **Highlight four communication issues challenging companies in the Information Age.** As companies integrate new communication technologies into their operations, they must find ways to handle information overload, data security, information privacy, and employee productivity.

CRITICAL THINKING QUESTIONS

1. Considering how fast and easy it is, should e-mail replace meetings and other face-to-face communication in a company? Why or why not?
2. How could a global corporation such as Coca-Cola take advantage of Internet technology to keep its people around the world in touch with each other?
3. What are the ramifications for companies that are slow to adopt new communication technologies and for employment candidates who have limited experience with such technologies?
4. How is the Internet transforming the way we communicate and do business?

5. E-mail has many advantages, but no communication medium is perfect. What are some of the disadvantages of e-mail?
6. What would be the advantages of using a personal agent on a company intranet?
7. How can communication technology improve your productivity?
8. What do you think is meant by the term *knowledge management*?

EXERCISES

1. For a while you have been thinking about the possibility of working from your home three days a week and going into the office on the remaining two days. You could easily do your work at home. Of course, you'll need your boss's permission. Make a list of the questions you think she might ask you about this arrangement.
2. List the technological skills you already have and could discuss in a job interview. Can you keyboard? Have you used e-mail or online services? Have you surfed the Web? Have you transferred files over the Internet? Can you download a document from the Web? Have you used photocopiers, calculators, answering machines, voice-mail systems? Do you have any experience with videoconferencing equipment? Which software do you have experience using?
3. Interview several local businesspeople or college administrators to find out the following, and write a one-page summary of your findings.
   a. What communication technology they use
   b. What tasks they use the technology for
   c. The advantages of using the technology
   d. The disadvantages of using the technology
   e. How technology has affected their ability to communicate on the job
4. You will be out of town for the next week, attending an important meeting that was called at the last minute. While you're away, you want your clients to be able to get the personal attention they deserve, so you've made arrangements with an associate to cover for you. Of course, not every client will need help before your return on May 16; most of them should be able to leave a message on your voice mail so that you can get back to them next week. Compose a message to record on your voice-mail system letting your clients know that you haven't abandoned them and that they can either leave a message or contact your associate (Bill Comden at 578-3737). Make sure the message is brief but contains all the necessary information.
5. Do you think companies should monitor employees' use of electronic communication such as e-mail, voice mail, and the Internet? Explain your answer.
6. Should there be an Internet 2 for people willing to pay for this service? Why or why not?
7. Many colleges and universities are using the Internet to provide online course work and discussion groups. You can even earn a degree online. What are the advantages and disadvantages of taking a course over the Internet?
8. You just received this e-mail from one of your co-workers. Evaluate this e-mail in terms of the material presented in this chapter and in Chapter 5, "Shaping Your E-Mail Messages."

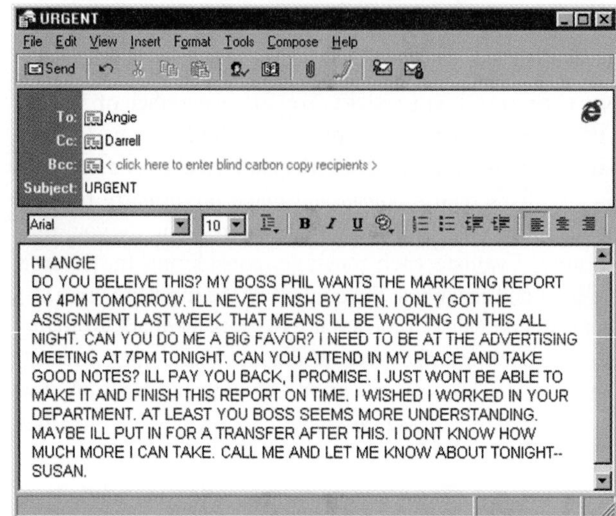
URGENT

File Edit View Insert Format Tools Compose Help

Send

To: Angie
Cc: Darrell
Bcc: < click here to enter blind carbon copy recipients >
Subject: URGENT

HI ANGIE
DO YOU BELEIVE THIS? MY BOSS PHIL WANTS THE MARKETING REPORT BY 4PM TOMORROW. ILL NEVER FINSH BY THEN. I ONLY GOT THE ASSIGNMENT LAST WEEK. THAT MEANS ILL BE WORKING ON THIS ALL NIGHT. CAN YOU DO ME A BIG FAVOR? I NEED TO BE AT THE ADVERTISING MEETING AT 7PM TONIGHT. CAN YOU ATTEND IN MY PLACE AND TAKE GOOD NOTES? ILL PAY YOU BACK, I PROMISE. I JUST WONT BE ABLE TO MAKE IT AND FINISH THIS REPORT ON TIME. I WISHED I WORKED IN YOUR DEPARTMENT. AT LEAST YOU BOSS SEEMS MORE UNDERSTANDING. MAYBE ILL PUT IN FOR A TRANSFER AFTER THIS. I DONT KNOW HOW MUCH MORE I CAN TAKE. CALL ME AND LET ME KNOW ABOUT TONIGHT--SUSAN.

9. Log on to DejaNews at http://www.dejanews.com and search for a newsgroup on your favorite business topic or hobby. Read several of the postings. Try limiting your search by using the Power Search feature.
10. In Chapter 4, we discussed selecting the appropriate electronic communication medium for your message. Review that material. Then, for each of the following tasks, decide which electronic communication medium, if any, you should use to deliver the message. Be prepared to explain your choices in class.
    a. The CEO of a major corporation wants to explain the company's performance to 27,000 employees, who are located in 14 sites across North America and Europe.
    b. A small-business owner wants to convince her bank that the normal loan qualification shouldn't apply in her case and that the bank should approve her request for a $2 million business-expansion loan.
    c. A manager needs to warn three employees that their job performance is below company standards.
    d. A customer wants to inquire about the status of her order.
    e. Five company managers at locations across the United States need to discuss a pending takeover of their company.
    f. Three accountants (at different company locations) need to jointly develop a seminar to be presented at this year's annual accounting convention.
11. Write a persuasive memo to the president of your company convincing her that the company should install an intranet.

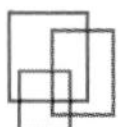

12. Using the information in "Keeping Pace with Technology: Create a Winning Web Site" log on to the Federal Express Web Site–U.S. at http://www.fedex.com/us/ and evaluate the site.

13. Take a look at a demonstration intranet at http://www.intrack.com/intranet/demo.shtml. Study the examples: daily cash receipts and checks, customer information, personnel manual, lists, projects, employee communication, and more. How might a site like this improve your organization?

EXPLORING THE BEST OF THE WEB

Create Your Own Web Site, page 340

1. Think of a Web site you might like to create, either now or in some imaginary future. Picture the kinds of graphics and text you'd use and the overall style and tone (irreverent? funny? serious? all business?) that would be appropriate to your purpose (which you will need to define). How do you think the tools in the Web Developers' Virtual Library (WDVL), at http://www.stars.com, might help you create your imaginary Web site?

2. You may wind up working for a business that hires Web design specialists, but the more you know, the better able you'll be to work with those designers. (You'll also be more employable.) So pursue a link under the "Authoring" list and read about something new to you. For instance, if you still think Java is what you drink in the morning to get you going, look over some of the Java tutorials here. You may never be a programmer, but you'll learn something important. To reward yourself (just for fun), go back to the stars.com home page and follow "The Universe of Stars.com" link to the shimmering Java nebula. Be sure to activate the "2001" audio!

FINDING, EVALUATING, AND PROCESSING INFORMATION

AFTER STUDYING THIS CHAPTER, YOU WILL BE ABLE TO

1. Summarize the six steps of the research process
2. Explain the role of reference librarians
3. List several ways to search databases effectively
4. Briefly discuss the different types of resources you might use to find business information
5. Highlight several things you must do during the interviewing process
6. Discuss the difference between quoting and paraphrasing, and explain the appropriate uses of each

COMMUNICATION CLOSE-UP AT GOSH ENTERPRISES

Charley Shin opened his first Philly cheesesteak restaurant—Charley's Steakery—when he was a junior at Ohio State. Today he is the millionaire owner of Gosh Enterprises, franchisor of over 50 Charley's Steakery restaurants. How did he reach this pinnacle of achievement so early in life? Through hard work and vision—backed up by lots of research and planning.

Shin says that running his first Charley's Steakery (near the Ohio State campus) was "a fun time—a lot of hard work. Going to school and running a restaurant was a bit overwhelming, but I juggled my way through it okay."

Shin and his older sister had come to the United States from South Korea when he was 13. They joined their mother in Columbus, Ohio, where she'd settled two years before. "I don't know if all the immigrants are poor, but we were poor," he recalls. To make ends meet, his mother worked days as a hospital housekeeper and three nights a week at a Japanese steakhouse. In 1980 she bought a small Japanese restaurant, and Shin started washing dishes there when he was 14 or 15 (reading *Forbes* in his spare time). By age 17 he was thinking big. He convinced his mother that the little restaurant wasn't going anywhere and that she should sell it, bank the profits, and wait until he graduated from college so that he could support her. "She, having all the faith in her son, did just that," says Shin. Trouble was, by the time he was a junior, the banked profits were running out. It was time to make his move—and that's how the first Charley's Steakery began.

Charley Shin

A year after it opened, Shin graduated, and a year after that he opened the second Charley's Steakery, followed by a third, and then a fourth and fifth with partners. "At that point, I had to decide on the venue for growth: whether to continue with company-owned restaurants, pursue equity-interested partnerships, or start franchising," explains Shin. Before drafting a new plan for the future, he knew he needed to do some research.

Competing directly with burgers and fries, the Philly cheesesteak sandwich sold at Charley's Steakery outlets is fresh food (not frozen or microwaved). This distinction is just one of the concepts described in the original business plan written at Gosh Enterprises. To guide the company's focus and progress, Shin did considerable amounts of research to develop the company's marketing strategy, franchising policy, location preference, and financial projections.

"Franchising was very interesting to me because it does not require a lot of capital but it has a venue for quick expansion. So, I read a lot of articles," says Shin. "I went to the library almost every day for over a month, and I read everything I could about franchising and the Philly cheesesteak concept." He studied newspaper articles on microfiche, read magazines and books, looked at statistics and trends, and learned what everyone else was doing in the field.

Shin also interviewed a fellow restaurant owner who had long years of experience. The man advised Shin to stick with the "fresh food" concept (instead of precooked or prepackaged sandwiches) and to concentrate on the "captive audience" in shopping-center food courts. Shin now credits this advice as some of the best he ever followed.

After weeks of this research, Shin started writing a formal plan. "I wish there had been a place that could really have given me sound advice about how to write a business plan," he says now. Using what he did know, he wrote an overview, a description of the concept, and a summary of his plans for the future. He hired professionals to help him develop a marketing strategy to include in the plan, but he prepared all the financial statements and projections himself.

Because of Shin's careful research and planning, Gosh Enterprises has done so well that Shin recently directed his senior staff in the preparation of a new three-year plan for future growth. This time, he went all out. Meeting on Saturdays to avoid distractions, Shin and his top people first developed a "work plan" for the writing project. They assigned themselves two months to complete the new business plan, and they divided the research and writing tasks according to their individual expertise.

Shin says he's fortunate that his vice president of franchise operations is an "expert" at preparing business plans; she brought up all the issues to be addressed and made sure all staff members did their part. In fact, Shin thinks business plans are so important that today all his franchise owners must prepare a written business plan during their training. They aren't certified until they complete at least a rough draft.

"The plan is just a road map to where I want to go," explains Shin. "It really disciplines one's thought process. I think it's a lot easier for me to justify in my own mind how I'm going to do certain things; I may have a happy and fuzzy idea in my head, but if I start to write it down on paper, I really have to think things through."[1] ■

ORGANIZING THE RESEARCH PROCESS

Like Charley Shin, you may someday need to gather information on specific companies, industries, trends, issues, or people. This may seem like an overwhelming task considering the amount of information available today. But if you take time to get organized, define the purpose of your research, identify the right questions, and locate the best resources, you'll find that looking for business information can be a rewarding experience.

Over the years, your instructors have assigned carefully designed research projects to help you develop and practice good information literacy and library skills. In this chapter, we'll build on those skills by explaining a research process you can use for the remainder of your college business studies (including this course), on the job, or whenever you are looking for information. In addition, we'll introduce you to some popular resources that you will need to use as a businessperson, and we'll explain where to find them, how to use them, and how to evaluate them.

Develop a plan before you begin to look for information.

When it comes to finding information, many people make the mistake of rushing into the research process without developing a plan. They go to the library, log on to a database or the Internet, type in some key words, produce a bazillion resources, and immediately begin taking notes—on whatever comes up under their topic, such as franchising. Resist the temptation. Bear in mind that good organization and careful planning lay the foundation for all of the research and work you are about to perform. If your foundation is weak, the business decisions you make as a result of your research will be standing on shaky ground indeed.

Use the six-step approach as a guide for finding, evaluating, and processing information effectively and efficiently.

You can adopt an organized approach to research by following these six steps: (1) Identify the right questions; (2) find and access information; (3) evaluate and finalize your sources; (4) process information; (5) analyze and interpret data; and (6) present your findings. In most cases you'll perform these steps sequentially; however, the amount of time you spend on a single step will depend on the nature and volume of information you need, as well as on the purpose of your research. Keep in mind that the research process is cyclical. That is, your discoveries may lead you to additional questions requiring further research and so on. So use the process diagrammed in Figure 11.1 as a guide. And remember, it's fine if you jump around a bit—just make sure you complete all six steps.

STEP 1: IDENTIFYING THE RIGHT QUESTIONS

Why are you looking for information? Do you need to solve a problem? Are you thinking about hiring some salespeople and you'd like to gather some information on managing a sales force? Are you researching a company prior to a job interview? Are you writing your company's annual marketing report?

Businesspeople conduct research for any number of reasons. Sometimes they're only looking for an answer to a simple question or just trying to learn something new. Other times they need to solve a problem or prepare a formal report on a process, product, company, or industry. In the classroom you have generally been able to select your favorite topic for a research project; in the business world you will not be given that option. If your boss says, "I need you to investigate how we can grow this business," you won't be able to raise your hand and request a different topic—at least not if you want to keep your job. As a result, in most cases you will be unfamiliar with the subject matter you are investigating, so first you'll need to gather some preliminary information.

In most cases you will be unfamiliar with your research topic.

Gathering Preliminary Information

Become familiar with your topic by browsing and gathering preliminary information.

The best way to learn about something new is to browse through materials on your topic. Leaf through some books and periodicals, conduct some loosely structured interviews, or log on to one of the databases at the library—or on the Internet—and see what comes up.

Although presented in a stepwise fashion, the research process often requires jumping around, branching off, or looping back through the steps. What's important is to become competent in each of the steps and to complete them all.

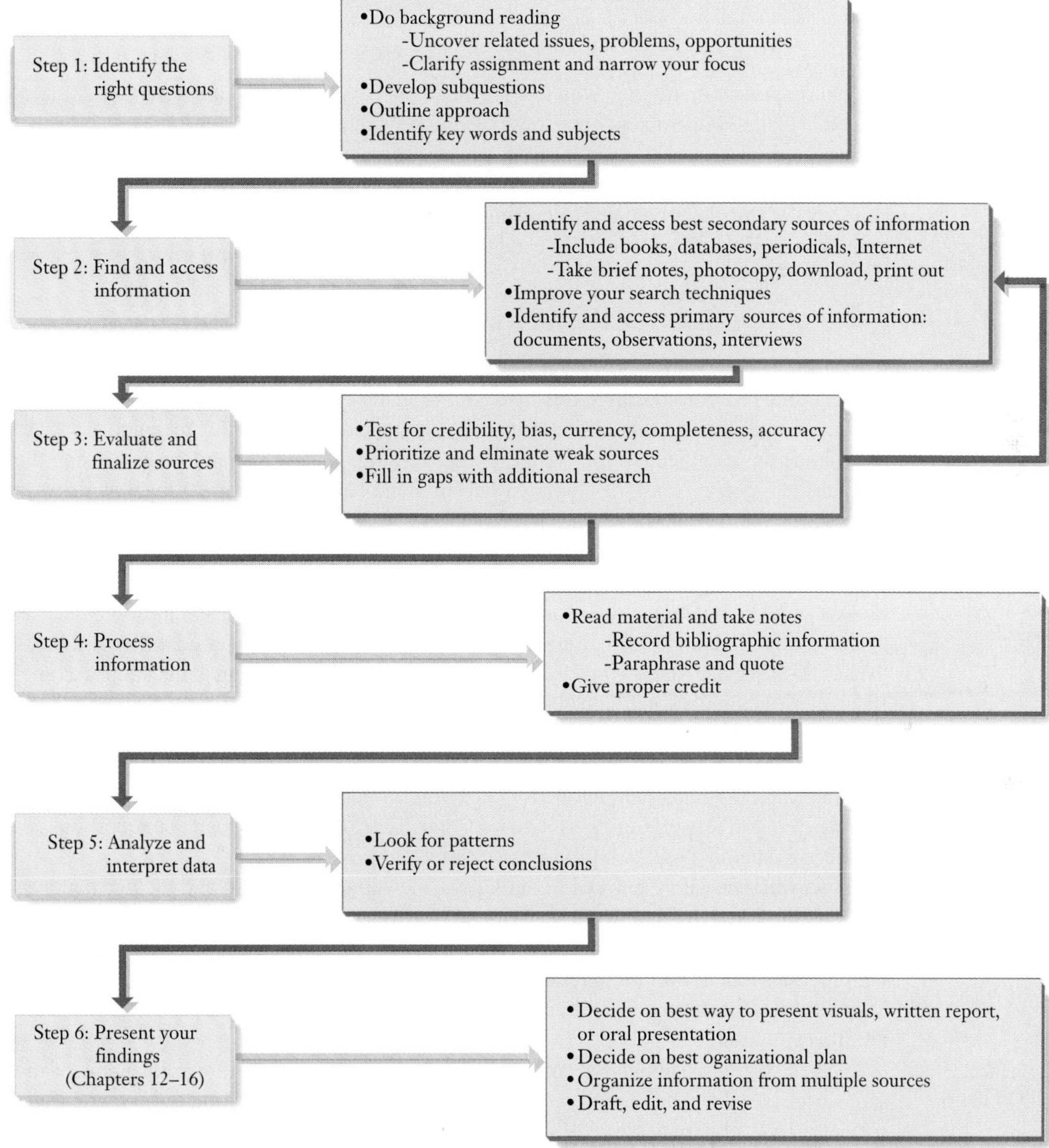

Figure 11.1
Research Process

You may even want to visit your favorite bookstore (both physical and online, such as Amazon.com). Grab a tall iced latte, sit at one of the tables in the back of the bookstore, gather some business books on your topic, and scan their table of contents.

Say, for example, you're Charley Shin and you want to explore ways to expand Charley's Steakery. By browsing some business materials, you might discover that franchising is one way to expand your business. You might even begin to uncover related issues, problems, opportunities, or trends in the franchising industry. As you browse, be sure to keep a written bibliographical list of the helpful resources you find on your topic. In addition, start a list of phrases, terms, and key words that keep surfacing. You'll use them later to locate and access information.

Once you have gathered some preliminary information, use what you have learned to clarify your assignment (if you're performing research at the request of another), and make sure you are on the same page with that person. Then develop a **problem statement**, a statement that defines the problem or purpose of your research—even if it's a simple one. Finally, restate the problem in the form of a main question. For example, Charley Shin could rephrase his original problem statement "Find a way to expand Charley's Steakery" as "How can Charley's Steakery expand?" Phrasing your purpose in the form of a question will help you focus on what information you need to complete your research.

Narrow the focus of your investigation by defining your problem and restating it as a question.

Developing Subquestions and Outlining Your Approach

If the problem you must solve is complex, such as researching the franchise industry as Charley Shin did, you'll want to organize your research efforts by dividing your main question into subquestions. Look back at Chapter 5 and review the prewriting techniques used to help define the main idea of a message. Brainstorming, generating random lists, using the journalistic approach, and developing a question-and-answer chain are all techniques you can use to rephrase your main question into a series of subquestions you must answer.

For example, Charley Shin might take his main question "How can Charley's Steakery expand?" and develop the subquestion "Is franchising a good way to expand Charely's Steakery?" Then he might break down this subquestion into additional subquestions such as "What are the advantages and disadvantages of franchising?" "Is my product franchisable?" "What are the costs?" and so on. Doing so focuses on answering one small question at a time. If you don't subdivide your main question into subquestions, your research efforts will likely end in frustration and perhaps failure.

You can shape your investigation by breaking down your problem into subquestions.

If you are researching a complex problem, in addition to developing subquestions you'll probably want to prepare an outline to guide your research efforts. Outlines can be useful, especially if you're working in a team, your investigation involves many subquestions, or you need to submit a research proposal to your boss.

Two widely used systems of outlining, the alphanumeric system and the decimal system, are illustrated in Figure 11.2. Both are perfectly acceptable, but some companies favor one method over another. Most word-processing programs have exceptionally good outlining programs that allow you to renumber and make changes easily, switch between an outline and report format as you write, and collapse and expand your outline—showing as many levels as you want.

Outline the issues you plan to study using either the alphanumeric or the decimal system.

When writing headings for outlines, use the same grammatical form for items of the same level. Parallel construction shows that the ideas are related, of similar importance, and on the same level of generality. When wording outlines, you must also choose between descriptive (topical) and informative (talking) headings. As Table 11.1 indicates, descriptive headings label the subject that will be discussed, whereas informative headings (in either question or summary form) suggest more about the meaning of the issues. Although outlines with informative headings take a little longer to write, they're generally more useful in guiding your work, especially if written in terms of the questions you plan to answer during your investigation. In addition they're easier for others to review. If other people are going to comment on your outline, they may not have a very clear idea of what you mean by the descriptive heading "Advertising." However, they will get the main idea if you use the informative heading "Did Cuts in Ad Budget Cause Sales Decline?"

Use the same grammatical form for each group of items in your outline.

Informative headings are generally more helpful than descriptive ones.

A good outline should divide a topic into at least two parts; divide the parts into subparts; use a significant, useful basis for subdividing; restrict each subdivision to one category; and make sure that each group is separate and distinct.

Figure 11.2
Two Common Outline Formats

ALPHANUMERIC	DECIMAL
I. First Major Part	1.0 First Major Part
A. First subpoint	1.1 First subpoint
B. Second subpoint	1.2 Second subpoint
1. Evidence	1.2.1 Evidence
2. Evidence	1.2.2 Evidence
a. Detail	1.2.2.1 Detail
b. Detail	1.2.2.2 Detail
3. Evidence	1.2.3 Evidence
C. Third subpoint	1.3 Third subpoint
II. Second Major Part	2.0 Second Major Part
A. First subpoint	2.1 First subpoint
1. Evidence	2.1.1 Evidence
2. Evidence	2.1.2 Evidence
B. Second subpoint	2.2 Second subpoint

Remember, the purpose of your outline is to guide your investigation. Later on, when you've completed your research, you'll use the same format to construct a formal writing outline to help you summarize your findings and prepare a written or oral report.

The outline of issues for analysis is often different from the outline of the final report.

After you've clarified your assignment, developed a problem statement in the form of a question and related subquestions, and completed a research outline (if necessary), you're ready to move on to step 2 of the research process.

STEP 2: FINDING AND ACCESSING INFORMATION

In step 2 you identify the *best* sources of information to use for your research and gather all the information you will need to answer your questions. In most cases you'll begin step 2 by finding *secondary sources* of information that already exist and has been previously collected by others. If secondary information doesn't exist or isn't helpful, you'll need to collect firsthand, or *primary, sources* of information for your specific needs.

Consult secondary and primary sources of information.

TABLE 11.1
TYPES OF OUTLINE HEADINGS

Descriptive (Topical) Outline	Informative (Talking) Outline: Question Form	Informative (Talking) Outline: Summary Form
I. Industry Characteristics	I. What is the nature of the industry?	I. Flour milling is a mature industry.
A. Annual sales	A. What are the annual sales?	A. Market is large.
B. Profitability	B. Is the industry profitable?	B. Profit margins are narrow.
C. Growth rate	C. What is the pattern of growth?	C. Growth is modest.
1. Sales	1. Sales growth?	1. Sales growth averages less than 3 percent a year.
2. Profit	2. Profit growth?	2. Growth in profits is flat.

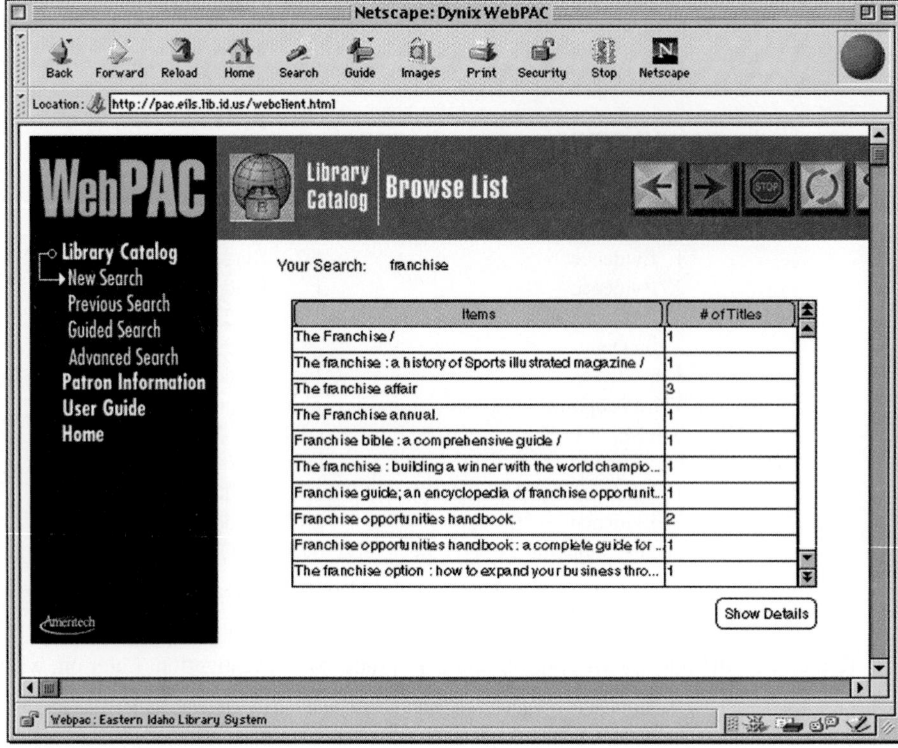

You can search this library's card catalog by accessing its home page on the Internet. Of course you'll have to visit the library to actually check out the book, but checking the Internet first guarantees you won't go home empty-handed.

Secondary Information[2]

Conduct secondary research by locating information that has already been collected, usually in the form of books, periodicals, and reports.

Finding secondary information used to be a simple process. You went to the library and flipped through the card catalog or periodical index to identify books and articles on your subject. It's not that simple anymore, but today you can find a lot more information in a lot less time. Now the two biggest problems you'll have as a business researcher are identifying the best of the many secondary sources of information and prioritizing them.

Reference librarians are there to assist you with your research efforts.

One of the best places to begin your search is the nearest public or university library. There you'll find business books, databases, periodicals, and other helpful materials. In addition, you'll find your most important resource: librarians. Librarians are trained in research techniques, and they spend their days managing information and helping people find materials. They can show you how to use the library's many databases and help you find obscure information. In fact, reference librarians are trained to know where to find just about everything.

Finding Business Information in the Library

At the library, you can find most of the information you need either in print format, on databases or other electronic media, or on microfilm.

The library is full of business resources such as dictionaries, encyclopedias, almanacs, atlases, biographical reference books, handbooks, manuals, journals, and directories of companies and associations. Besides these print materials, the library has databases with journal and newspaper articles in full-text or abstract format and information on microfilm and electronic media. Each of these resources serves a specific function:

- *Business books.* Although not as timely as journal articles, books provide in-depth coverage of a variety of business topics. Because of limited shelf space and budgetary constraints, libraries must be selective when choosing books to put on their shelves. If you need specialized information, you may have better luck finding those types of books at a college library (assuming the college offers courses in those subjects) or at company libraries.

- *Electronic databases.* An **electronic database** is a computer-searchable collection of information, often categorized by subject areas such as business, law, science, technology, and education. Electronic databases can by stored on CD-ROMs or online (which means they are stored on a computer accessible to other computers—generally via a modem). The main advantages of electronic databases over print-based sources are (1) instant access to billions of records of the world's published literature, (2) reduced time to perform a key word and subject search in comparison with a manual search, (3) currency of material, (4) fast turnaround from request to results, and (5) the ability to print out documents (many in full text) for later use in the research process. When using an electronic database, try to get a list of the periodicals or publications it includes in addition to the time period it covers. Then fill in the gaps for any important resources excluded from the database.
- *Newspapers.* Libraries subscribe to only a select number of newspapers and store a limited number of back issues in print, but they frequently subscribe to databases containing newspaper articles in full text (available online, on CD-ROM, or on microfilm). In addition, most newspapers today offer full-text or limited editions of their papers on the Internet.
- *Periodicals.* Most periodicals fall into one of four categories: popular magazines, trade journals, business magazines, and academic journals. Popular magazines are publications that aren't intended for business, professional, or academic use. Trade journals cover particular professions, industries, and occupations, providing news and other information about specific jobs and industries. Business magazines, on the other hand, cover all major industries and professions. They include broader subjects such as management, marketing, consumer trends, international competition, government taxation and regulation, business and the environment, and other business issues. Academic journals are the communication channels for professional researchers and educators. Keep in mind that if your library does not subscribe to a certain periodical, chances are you can find it on one of the many library databases.
- *Directories.* More than 14,000 directories of various kinds, covering everything from accountants to zoos, are published in the United States. Many include membership information for all kinds of special-interest groups. Business directories, for instance, provide entries for companies, products, and individuals and include the name of key contact persons. Directories are considered invaluable for marketers and others such as job seekers who need to establish a prospect list.
- *Almanacs and statistical sources.* Almanacs are handy guides to factual and statistical information. They contain information about countries, politics, the labor force, and so on. Whenever you're looking for specific data about almost any subject, consider starting with an almanac. Even if it doesn't give you the answer, you'll spend no more than a few minutes looking. In addition to almanacs, sources such as the *Statistical Abstract of the United States,* published annually by the U.S. Department of Commerce, contains statistics about life, work, government, population patterns, health issues, business, crime, and the environment. In fact, you'll find more than 1,400 tables of statistics in this resource.
- *Government publications.* By one estimate, 700,000 government employees in the United States specialize in collecting and distributing information.[3] When you want to know the exact provisions of a law, the background of a court decision, or current

DID YOU KNOW?

An average of 1,500 new business books are published annually in the United States.

population patterns and business trends, consult the government documents section of the library. This sort of research can be rather complicated, but a librarian will direct you to the information you need. All you have to know is the name of the government agency you're interested in (U.S. Congress, Ninth Circuit Court of Appeals, Department of Labor, and so on) and some sort of identification for the specific information you need (such as the Safe Drinking Water Act of 1974, *Price v. Shell Oil,* or the latest census). If you know the date and name of a publication containing the document, so much the better.

To research a company, first find out whether it's public or private. You can also look up the company's SIC (or NAICS) code to find information related to the industry.

Keep in mind that if you're looking for information about a specific company, one of the first things you'll need to know is whether the company is public (sells shares of stock to the general public) or private. Public companies generally have more information available than private companies. You can find a list of public companies in the *Directory of Companies Required to File Annual Reports with the Securities and Exchange Commission.*

If you're looking for industry information, you'll need to know the Standard Industrial Classification (SIC) code of that particular industry. The U.S. government requires all companies, from sole proprietorships to corporations, to assign themselves a four-digit industry number when establishing their business. These numbers are the backbone of most business directories. The North American Industry Classification System (NAICS) will eventually replace the SIC system. Both SIC and NAICS codes are available on the Internet in addition to being listed in business reference books.

Some of the more popular resources for company and industry information include the *Statistical Abstract of the United States, Manufacturing USA, U.S. Industrial Outlook, Standard & Poor's Industry Survey, Corporate and Industry Research Reports (CIRR), Moody's Manuals, Hoover's Handbook of American Business,* and *Thomas's Register of American Manufacturers*. These sources and others listed in Figure 11.8, at the end of this chapter, provide information on company and industry statistics, economic forecasts, business concerns, legal issues, competition, and industry performance ratios and averages. Of course, besides these books, the most popular source of company and industry information today is the Internet.

Finding Business Information on the Internet

The Internet is rich in business information ranging from current news, issues, and industry trends to company-related data such as financial performance, products, goals, and employment. In fact, the Web is so vast and changes so constantly that it's easy to get sidetracked. If you've ever been lost in cyberspace, take heart—it happens to everybody.

When doing research on the Internet you need to be selective, because anyone can publish anything and no one checks the information for accuracy.

An important thing to keep in mind when looking for information on the Internet is that anyone (including you) can post anything on a Web site. No one filters it. No one checks it for accuracy. And no one can be really sure of who is producing the information or why they are placing it on the Internet. For that reason, it's best to refrain from seriously surfing the Web for business information until you've had a chance to learn a bit about your topic from journals, books, and commercial databases. That way you'll be able to detect skewed or erroneous information, and you can be more selective in the Web sites and documents you choose to use as a resource.

One good place to start on the Web is the Internet Public Library at http://www.ipl.org. Modeled after a real library, this site will provide you with a carefully selected collection of links to many high-quality business resources that include company profiles, trade data, business news, corporate tax and legal advice, small-business information, prepared forms and documents, biographies of executives, financial reports, job postings, online publications, and so on. (For a closer look at the permission needed for citing information from electronic sources, see "Focusing on Ethics: The Tangled Web of Internet Copyrights.")

DID YOU KNOW?

Approximately every 30 seconds a new Web page is placed on the World Wide Web.

BEST OF THE WEB

Check Out Materials at This Library 24 Hours a Day

Start your business research by visiting the Internet Public Library. Visit the reference center and explore the many online references available. These cover topics such as business, economics, law, government, science, technology, computers, education, and more. Got a question? There's even a librarian on staff to help you. After all, librarians are one of your most important resources when conducting research.

http://www.ipl.org

If you are looking for specific company information, your best source may be the company's Web site (if it maintains one). Web sites generally include detailed information about the company's products, services, history, mission, strategy, financial performance, and employment needs. Furthermore, many sites provide links to related company information, such as SEC filings, press releases, and more.

You can find all kinds of information about a company on its Web site.

FOCUSING ON ETHICS

THE TANGLED WEB OF INTERNET COPYRIGHTS

Copyright laws, which restrict the copying of some kinds of materials, have existed since soon after Gutenberg invented the printing press. U.S. copyright law currently states that "original works of authorship fixed in a tangible medium of expression" created after January 1, 1978, are automatically copyrighted. It is illegal to copy such works without the author's permission. The law obviously applies to books, music, paintings, and other works that can be seen or heard, but how it applies to works in electronic form on computers and networks is much less clear.

Is it a copyright infringement if you download a file from the Internet to your computer? Does making a file available on the Internet automatically place it in the public domain, giving anyone the right to copy and distribute it without restriction? Interest in revisions and interpretations of copyright laws concerning the Internet ranges from publishers and creators (who want strict controls on dissemination of their products) to Internet users (who do not want copyright controls to hamper the free flow of information). Many cases involving alleged copyright violations are currently being heard in courts around the world.

While the legal and ethical issues get sorted out, IBM and other companies are introducing products that make it difficult to copy Internet files. Two of the techniques available are encryption and watermarking. Encryption involves garbling the information so that a user must have a password or decoder to make the information usable. With watermarking, the information includes a visible image that identifies the owner of the information. Microsoft, which holds electronic rights to a large number of artworks, uses watermarking to identify images.

Because we have no clear definition of how copyright laws apply to electronic information, the safest approach is to assume that any information from the Internet is copyrighted and to contact the author or owner for permission to use it. Keep in mind that ignorance is no excuse; you can be prosecuted even if you unknowingly violate a copyright. "Copyright law has no exemption for innocent infringement," according to Michael Grow, a Washington, D.C., attorney. And if you are putting information on the Internet, be aware that it is very easy for anyone to copy and reuse the information with or without your permission.

1. What should you do if you can't find the author or owner of some online information that you'd like to use in a report?
2. How might ethical and legal concerns slow the development of online libraries and other information resources?

Press releases and general news about companies are also available at news release sites.

Subscribers to online database research systems can conveniently access the information these services provide through the Internet.

Small companies and privately held companies generally don't have much public information written about them.

You can obtain press releases and general company news from news release sites such as PR Newswire (http://www.prnewswire.com) and Business Wire (http://www.businesswire.com). These sites offer free databases of news releases from companies subscribing to their services. News release sites are also good places to look for announcements of new products, management changes, earnings, dividends, mergers, acquisitions, and other company information. If you subscribe to a commercial online database system (such as those listed in Figure 11.8), you can also use the Internet to access company and business information from the provider's database.

Keep in mind that a lot of information you may want simply isn't on the Web. For instance, there may be nothing about small organizations except an address and a phone number. Furthermore, even if the information exists on the Web, you may not be able to find it. Current scientific research shows that there are over 320 million Web pages, and even the best search engines are acquainted with only 100 million of those pages.[4] This means that the one page you need might not be among the 33 percent found, and there may be no way to find it. In fact, as millions of pages are added to the Web each year, finding a specific piece of information will only get tougher unless current search tools are improved. Can search engines do better? Researchers say it's probably impossible to index the entire Web.[5]

DID YOU KNOW?

The FBI estimates that U.S. companies lose more than $250 billion worth of information every year, and few companies are prepared to prevent such losses.

Besides, even if search engines turn up what you're looking for, they will also turn up a mountain of stuff you won't need. Say you're looking for information about a job as a writer. The search engine may turn up information on being an accountant at an insurance company. Why? Because the insurance company described itself on the Web as one of the largest *writers* of insurance policies. You can produce better-targeted search results by learning how to conduct an effective database search.

Conducting an Effective Database Search

Whether you are using a library database or an Internet search engine, follow these search strategies and tips to conduct an effective database search:[6]

Improve your database search results by
- Selecting the right database
- Choosing effective search terms
- Using Boolean and proximity operators and wildcards

1. *Select an appropriate database or databases.* In most cases you'll want a good business database. However, the journals covering your topic may be located in the database that includes journals on psychology, computers, or medicine.
2. *Use multiple search engines.* As discussed in Chapter 10, not all search engines are the same. Don't limit yourself to a single search engine, especially if you are looking for less popular topics. To improve your results, read the help file and learn how the search engine works.
3. *Choose search terms by translating concepts into key words and phrases.* For instance, if you want to determine the "effect of TQM on company profits," you should select the key words TQM, total quality management, profits, sales, companies, and corporations. Remember, use synonyms or word equivalents whenever possible, and use quotation marks around phrases to look for the entire phrase instead of separate words.
4. *Do not use a long phrase when a short phrase or a single term will do.* The computer searches for the words exactly as you have keyed them in. If the words occur, but not in the same order, you may miss relevant hits.
5. *Do not use stopwords.* These are words the computer disregards and will not search for. Database documentation will identify any stopwords in addition to the common ones: *a, an, the, of, by, with, for,* and *to.*
6. *Do not use words contained in the name of the database.* Words such as *business* or *finance* in the ABI Inform database (see Figure 11.8) will work, but they will slow down the processing time and will not add precision to your results.

7. *Do enter variations of your terms.* Use abbreviations (CEO, CPA), synonyms (man, male), related terms (child, adolescent, youth), different spellings (dialog, dialogue), singular and plural forms (man, men), nouns and adjectives (manager, management, managerial), and open and compound forms (online, on line, on-line).
8. *Specify a logical relationship between the key words.* In other words, does the document need to have both "companies" and "corporations" or is either fine? Do you need to have both "profits" and "companies" in the same document, or is it more important to have "TQM" or "total quality management" and "profits" or "sales"?
9. *Evaluate the precision and quality of your search results and refine or redo your search if necessary.* The general rule of thumb is that if you end up with more than 60 to 100 references to sort through, you probably need to refine your search strategy. Experts recommend that if your first page of results doesn't have something of interest, you've probably entered the wrong words or too few words. In addition, pay attention to whether you are searching in the title, subject, or document field of the database. Each will return different results.

Of course, having too much information can be as bad as having no information. Another way to enhance your search results is by using Boolean operators, proximity operators, and wildcards.

Boolean Operators Boolean operators include the words AND, OR, and NOT. As Table 11.2 shows, the AND operator narrows a search because it indicates that all the key words (joined by the word AND) must be found in the same document or Web page. By contrast, the OR operator broadens the search because it indicates that either key word must be present. Finally, the NOT operator (sometimes expressed as AND NOT) narrows a search because it indicates that a certain key word must not appear in the document or Web page.

Boolean operators can help you create complex, precise search strategies. For example you could create a search strategy such as "(marketing or advertising) AND (organizations or associations) AND NOT consultants." In plain English, this means that qualifying documents or Web sites must have either the word *marketing* or *advertising* and must have either the word *organizations* or *associations,* but they can't have the word *consultants*. Say, for example, you are trying to search for the *gross national product of Jordan* and you keep getting sports sites about Michael Jordan. By using the operator NOT to exclude the word *Michael*, you'll trim a few hundred thousand irrelevant results right away.

Many search engines automatically include Boolean operators in their search strategies even though you can't see them on the screen. For instance, some search engines insert the OR operator between key words. Others may insert the word AND. For this reason, either insert these operators yourself (in most cases they will override the automatic operators inserted by the engine) or review the instructions to learn the inner workings of the specific search engine you are using.

Proximity Operators and Wildcards Proximity operators let you specify how close one of your key words should be to another. The most common proximity operator is NEAR, which tells the database engine to find documents where one key word is within a certain number of key words of another. For example, the search phrase "marketing NEAR/2 organizations" means that *marketing* must be within two words of *organizations.*

Wildcard characters help you find plurals and alternate spellings of your key words. For example, by using a question mark in the word *organi?ations,* you'll find documents with both *organisations* (British spelling) and *organizations*. Similarly, by using an asterisk at the end of the stem *chair**, you'll find *chairman, chairperson, chairs,* and *chairlift.*

TABLE 11.2

IMPROVING YOUR SEARCH RESULTS

Search Operator	Effect	Strategy	Results
AND	Narrows the results. Searches for records containing both of the words it separates. Words separated by AND may be anywhere in the document—and far away from each other.	Rock AND roll	Music
OR	Broadens the results. This is a scattergun search that will turn up lots of matches and is not particularly precise. Searches for records containing either of the words it separates.	Rock OR roll	Igneous rocks; gemstones; crescent rolls; music
NOT	Limits the results. Searches for records containing the first word(s) but not the second one.	Snow skiing NOT water skiing	Snow skiing; cross-country skiing
NEAR	Proximity operator. Searches for words that all appear in a specified word range.	Snow NEAR/2 skiing	Terms in which *skiing* is within 2 words of *snow*
ADJ	Adjacency operator. Searches for records in which second word immediately follows first word (two words are next to each other).	Ski ADJ patrol	Ski patrol
?	Wildcard operator for single character; matches any one character.	Ski?	Skit; skid; skin; skip
*	Wildcard operator for string of characters.	Ski*	Ski; skiing; skies; skill; skirt; skit; skinny; skimpy
" "	Exact match. Searches for string of words placed within quotation marks.	"1999 budget deficit"	1999 budget deficit

Keeping Track of Your Progress

As you find and review your secondary source materials, you'll want to take some brief notes to keep track of your progress. For instance, you'll want to write down enough information to distinguish one source from the next. In addition, you'll want to identify the main idea or theme of each source and perhaps write a comment or two on which subquestion the article addresses and whether or not it was helpful. You might write, for example: "Article discusses current franchise trends and includes statistics on number of new franchises started each year," or "Chapter 3 gives itemized steps to follow when investigating franchise opportunities."

If you use the Internet to find secondary material, bookmark relevant Web sites or download or print out the actual Web pages. If the library database you are using includes material in full text, print out helpful articles; otherwise print out a copy of your search results and ask the librarian for assistance in finding the articles listed.

The goal of your initial note taking is to keep track of your sources so that you can select the best ones to use.

To record your comments, use note cards or Post-It Notes, or write on the actual material itself—but only if it is a printout or a photocopy. Develop a system that works for you. You'll use these brief notes in step 3 of the research process to evaluate and finalize your sources. Then in step 4, you'll take detailed notes—ones that you will use to write your final report or presentation.

In addition to taking brief notes, prepare a detailed bibliography of each source you intend to use later by using one of the systems explained in Component Chapter B, "Documentation of Report Sources." If you photocopy an article, be sure to record on the photocopy all the bibliographic material you'll need to properly cite that source later on.

Primary Information

Conduct primary research by collecting basic information yourself.

When the information you need is not available from secondary sources, you collect and interpret the data yourself by doing primary research; that is, you go out into the real world to gather information yourself. Often the most useful references are *internal sources,* such as company reports, memos, brochures, newsletters, annual reports, and information stored in company databases ranging from sales performance figures and customer profiles to financial results.

The five main ways of collecting primary data are examining documents, making observations, conducting experiments, surveying people, and conducting interviews.

Documents, Observations, and Experiments

Documentary evidence and historical records are sources of primary data.

In business a great deal of information is filed away for future reference. By scouring a company's files, you can often piece together an accurate, factual, historical record from the tidbits of evidence revealed in various letters, memos, and reports. Business documents that qualify as primary data include sales reports prepared by field representatives, balance sheets and income statements, policy statements, correspondence with customers and suppliers, and contracts.

A single document may be both a secondary source and a primary source. When citing summaries of financial and operations data from an annual report, for example, you're using it as a secondary source because somebody has already summarized the information for you. The same report, however, would be considered a primary source if you were analyzing its design features or comparing it with annual reports from other years or from other companies.

Observation applies your five senses and your judgment to the investigation.

Informal observations are another common way to gather primary data in business. For instance, you can observe people performing their jobs or observe other business operations. In general, observation is a useful technique when you're studying objects, physical activities, processes, the environment, or human behavior. However, it can be expensive and time consuming, and the value of the observation depends on the reliability of the observer.

Experiments, another source of primary data, are far more common in technical fields than in general business. That's because an experiment requires extensive manipulation of the factors involved, which is often very expensive. Keep in mind that when conducting an experiment, it's important to carefully control the factors (called variables) that you're *not* testing.

Surveys

Often the best way to get information is to ask people with relevant experience and opinions. Surveys, which include everything from a single interview to the distribution of thousands of questionnaires, are a good way to find out what a cross section of people think about a given topic. For instance, Charley Shin may want to survey fast-food customers to keep up with their dining preferences.

Two important criteria to keep in mind when conducting a survey are *reliability* and *validity*. A survey is reliable if it would produce identical results if the same study were repeated. A survey is valid if it measures what it intended to measure. For these reasons one

Marketing surveys are a common way of gathering data directly from consumers.

Developing an effective questionnaire requires care and skill.

of the most crucial elements of a survey is the questionnaire. To develop one, begin by making a list of the points you're trying to determine. Then break these points into specific questions, choosing an appropriate type of question for each point (Figure 11.3 shows some variations). The following guidelines will help you produce valid results:[7]

- *Provide clear instructions.* Respondents need to know exactly how to fill out the questionnaire.
- *Keep the questionnaire short and easy to answer.* Ask only questions that are relevant to your research and keep in mind that people are most likely to respond if they can complete the questionnaire within 10 to 15 minutes.
- *Formulate questions that provide easily tabulated or analyzed answers.* Remember, numbers and facts are easier to summarize than opinions.
- *Avoid leading questions.* Questions that lead to a particular answer bias your survey. If you ask, "Do you prefer that we stay open in the evenings for customer convenience?" you'll get a yes answer. Instead, ask, "What time of day do you normally do your shopping?"
- *Ask only one thing at a time.* A compound question such as "Do you read books and magazines regularly?" doesn't allow for the respondent who reads one but not the other.
- *Pretest the questionnaire.* Have a sample group identify questions that are subject to misinterpretation.

If you're mailing your questionnaire rather than administering it in person, include a persuasive cover letter that explains why you're conducting the research. Try to convince the person that her or his response is important to you. Remember, however, that even under the best of circumstances you may not get more than a 10 to 20 percent response.

Interviews

An interview is any planned conversation that has a specific purpose and involves two or more people.

Getting answers straight from an expert on a subject can be a great way to collect information. **Interviews**—planned conversations with a predetermined purpose that involve asking and answering questions—are frequently overlooked as useful sources of information.

Figure 11.3
Types of Survey Questions

QUESTION TYPE	EXAMPLE
Open-ended	How would you describe the flavor of this ice cream?
Either-or	Do you think this ice cream is too rich? _____ Yes _____ No
Multiple choice	Which description best fits the taste of this ice cream? (Choose only one.) a. Delicious b. Too fruity c. Too sweet d. Too intensely flavored e. Bland f. Stale
Scale	Please make an X on the scale to indicate how you perceive the texture of this ice cream. ←——————————————→ Too light Light Creamy Too creamy
Checklist	Which flavors of ice cream have you had in the past 12 months? (Check all that apply.) _____ Vanilla _____ Chocolate _____ Strawberry _____ Chocolate chip _____ Coffee
Ranking	Rank these flavors in order of your preference, from 1 (most preferred) to 5 (least preferred): _____ Vanilla _____ Cherry _____ Maple nut _____ Chocolate ripple _____ Coconut
Short-answer questions	In the past month how many times did you buy ice cream in the supermarket? _________ In the past month how many times did you buy ice cream in ice cream shops? _________

Before you decide to do one, however, ask yourself whether an interview is really the best way to get the information you need. Although doing an interview may seem like an easy way to get information, as Figure 11.4 shows, a successful interview requires careful planning and a lot of time.

In a typical information interview, the interviewer seeks facts that bear on a decision or contribute to basic understanding. The action is controlled by the interviewer, who asks a list of questions designed to elicit information from the interviewee. When you are conducting an interview, it's important to decide in advance what kind of information you want and how you will use it. This planning will save you time and build goodwill with the people you interview.

To accomplish their objectives, interviewers develop a communication plan.

Planning the Interview Planning an interview is similar to planning any other form of communication. You begin by stating your purpose, analyzing the other person, and formulating your main idea. Then you decide on the length, style, and organization of the interview. Having

A successful interview requires careful planning and organization to ensure you get the information you really need.

1. Contact people to interview.
   - Introduce yourself and your purpose.
   - Arrange a time and place.
   - Decide whether to use a tape recorder, and get the subject's permission.
2. Plan the interview.
   - Think about the sequence of your questions.
   - Choose the most important questions.
   - Plan smart questions that are easy to understand.
3. Conduct the interview.
   - Dress appropriately.
   - Arrive a few minutes early.
   - Be respectful and polite.
   - Be ready to ask new questions in response to the answers you get.
   - Thank the subject.
4. Use the information wisely.
   - Review notes as soon as possible after the interview.
   - Organize the results, looking for important themes or information.

Figure 11.4
The Interviewing Process

a plan will enable you to conduct the interview efficiently, even if you find it advantageous to deviate from the plan during the interview. Being *efficient* means you get as much information as you can in as little time as possible. Being *effective* means you get the right kind of information. In other words, you want to develop an efficient set of effective questions.

Preparing the Interview Questions The kinds of answers you get will be influenced, to some extent, by the questions you ask, how you ask them, and the subject's cultural and language background. Race, gender, age, educational level, and social status are all potential factors of influence. Know your subject before you start writing questions.[8] In addition, be aware of ethical implications. For example, asking someone to divulge personal information about a co-worker may be asking that person to make an unethical choice. Always be careful about confidentiality, politics, and other sensitive issues.

If your questions might require research or extensive thinking, or if you'd like to quote the interviewee in writing, consider providing a list of questions a day or two before the interview. Having the questions before the interview will give the person time to prepare more complete (and therefore more helpful) answers. You might want to tape record the interview if the topic is complex or if you plan to quote or paraphrase the interviewee in a written document.

Organize an interview much as you would organize a written message.

As do other types of business communication, good interviews have an opening, a body, and a close. The opening establishes rapport and orients the interviewee to the remainder of the session. You might begin by introducing yourself, asking a few polite questions, and then explaining the purpose and ground rules of the interview. The body of the interview is used for asking questions. In the close of the interview you summarize the outcome, preview what will come next, and underscore the rapport that has been established.

Use the close to sum up the interview and leave the interviewee with a cordial feeling

Follow these guidelines and you'll come up with a great set of interview questions:[9]

- *Think about the sequence.* Arrange your questions in a way that helps uncover layers of information or that helps the subject tell you a complete story.

- *Rate your questions and highlight the ones you really need answers to.* If you start to run out of time during the interview, you may have to skip less important questions.
- *Ask smart questions.* If you ask a question that your subject perceives to be less than intelligent, the interview could go downhill in a hurry.
- *Use a mix of question types.* As Figure 11.5 suggests, most questions fall along a continuum of openness. **Open-ended questions** invite the interviewee to offer an opinion, not just a yes, no, or one-word answer: "What do you think your company wants most from suppliers?" This kind of question is useful when you want to learn the reasons behind a decision rather than just the facts. You can learn some interesting and unexpected things from open-ended questions, but they diminish your control of the interview. **Direct open-ended questions** such as "What have you done about . . ." suggest a response and give you more control while still giving the interviewee some freedom in framing a response. **Closed-ended questions** require yes or no answers or call for short responses. Question such as "Did you meet your sales quota?" produce specific information, save time, require less effort from the interviewee, and eliminate bias and prejudice in answers. On the other hand, they also limit the respondent's initiative and may prevent important information from being revealed. **Restatement questions** mirror a respondent's previous answer and invite the respondent to expand on that answer; "You said you dislike sales quotas. Is that correct?" They also signal to the interviewee that you're paying attention.

Four basic types of interview questions:
- Open-ended questions
- Direct open-ended questions
- Closed-ended questions
- Restatement questions

- *Limit the number of questions.* Don't try to cover more questions than you have time for. People can speak at a rate of about 125 to 150 words (about one paragraph) per minute. If you're using a mix of question types, you can probably handle about 20 questions in a half-hour. Bear in mind that open-ended questions take longer to answer than other types do.

Don't try to cover more questions than you have time for.

Edit your questions as needed to make them neutral and easy to understand. Then practice them several times to make sure you're ready for the interview.

Using the Interview Information When you've concluded the interview, take a few moments to write down your thoughts, go over your notes, and organize your material. Your notes will probably be a disorganized pile of quotes, statistics, phrases, key words, and other bits of information. That's because taking notes during an interview isn't like taking notes from a book; you can't think through each point carefully before you write it down. Look for important themes, helpful facts or statistics, and direct quotes. Fill in any blanks while the interview is fresh in your mind.

Carefully review your interview notes immediately after the interview and fill in the gaps before you forget.

If you made a tape recording, *transcribe* it (take down word for word what the person said) or take notes from the tape in the same basic way you take notes while listening to someone in person.

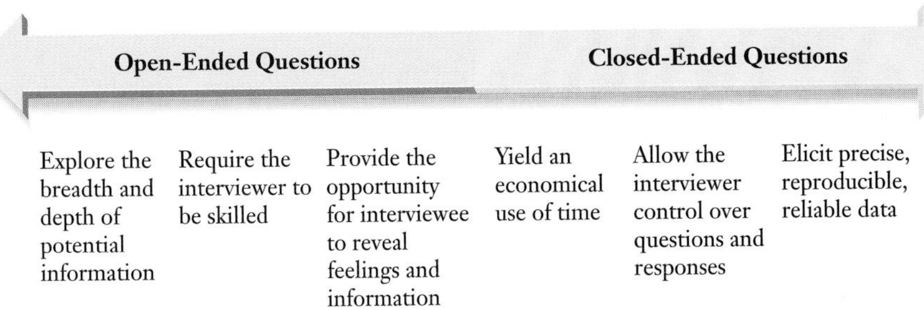

Figure 11.5
Choosing Questions with the Appropriate Degree of Openness

CHECKLIST FOR CONDUCTING EFFECTIVE INTERVIEWS

A. Preparation

1. Decide on the purpose and goals of the interview.
2. Outline your interview on the basis of your goals and the interview category.
   - **a.** Set the level of formality.
   - **b.** Choose a structured or an unstructured approach.
3. Determine the needs of your interviewee, and gather background information.
4. Formulate questions as clearly and concisely as possible.
   - **a.** Ask questions in an order that helps your subject tell you a complete story.
   - **b.** Ask intelligent questions that show you've done your homework.
   - **c.** Use a mix of question types.
5. Select a time and a site.
6. Inform the interviewee of the nature of the interview and the agenda to be covered.
7. Provide a list of questions in advance if the interviewee will need time to research and formulate quality answers.

B. Conduct

1. Be on time for the interview appointment.
2. Remind the interviewee of the purpose and format.
3. Clear the taking of notes or the use of a tape recorder with the interviewee.
4. Use your ears and eyes to pick up verbal and nonverbal cues.
5. Follow the stated agenda, but be willing to explore relevant subtopics.
6. Close the interview by restating the interviewee's key ideas and by reviewing the actions, goals, and tasks each of you has agreed to.

C. Follow-up

1. Write a thank-you memo or letter that provides the interviewee with a record of the meeting.
2. Review notes and revise them while the interview is fresh in your mind.
3. Transcribe tape recordings.
4. Monitor progress by keeping in touch with your interviewee.

Conducting interviews by e-mail is becoming increasingly popular.

Interviews don't necessarily have to take place in person. As more and more people get connected online, e-mail interviews are becoming more common. Perhaps one of the biggest advantages is that e-mail gives subjects a chance to think through their responses thoroughly, rather than rushing to fit the time constraints of an in-person interview.[10] (As a reminder of the tasks involved in interviews, see this chapter's Checklist for Conducting Effective Interviews.)

STEP 3: EVALUATING AND FINALIZING YOUR SOURCES

When it comes to choosing your actual sources from the piles of material you've gathered in step 2, be selective. Avoid dated or biased material. If possible, check on who collected the data, the methods they used, their qualifications, and their professional reputations.[11] Common sense will help you judge the credibility of the sources you plan to use.

Ask questions about the reference works you use:
- Are they up to date?
- Are they objective?
- Who collected the data? How?
- What are the authors' qualifications and reputations?

The goal of step 3 of the research process is to evaluate the usefulness of the information you found and to select the sources that are credible. To do so, ask yourself the following questions about each piece of material:

- *Does the source have a reputation for honesty and reliability?* Naturally, you'll feel more comfortable with information from a source that has established a reputation for accuracy. But the fact that the source has a good reputation doesn't mean you should let your guard down completely; even the finest reporters and editors make mistakes. Find out how articles are accepted for publication and whether the publication has an editorial board.

- *Is the source potentially biased?* Some of the information you'll find in your research will have been produced and distributed by people or organizations with a particular point of view. Bias isn't necessarily bad; in fact, getting people to believe one thing and not another is the purpose of much of the world's communication efforts. If you gather information from the Tobacco Institute or the American Association of Retired Persons, you have a fairly clear idea of what these organizations stand for and what biases their messages may have. However, organizations with neutral names, such as the Heritage Foundation, People for the American Way, or the U.S. Committee for Energy Awareness, aren't as easy to categorize. Without knowing what these organizations stand for, you're at their mercy when it comes to interpreting the information they produce. Also, an organization's source of funding may influence its information output. Again, there is nothing inherently unethical about an organization's having a point of view; you just need to be aware of it when you interpret the information.
- *Where did the source get its information?* Many secondary sources are themselves derived from other sources, making you even further removed from the original data. If a newspaper article says that pollutants in a local river dropped by 50 percent in the last year, chances are the reporter who wrote the article didn't make those measurements directly. He or she got the number from someone else.
- *Can you verify the material independently?* A good way to uncover mistakes or biases is to search for the same information from another source. Verification can be particularly important when the information goes beyond simple facts to include projections, interpretations, and estimates.
- *Is the material current?* Check the publication date of a source and make sure you are using the most current information available. Timeliness is especially important if you are using statistics or citing law from a source.
- *Is the author credible?* Is the author known in her or his field, or is the author an amateur or merely someone with an opinion to air? Look for information about the author or publisher to help you make that determination.
- *What was the purpose of the material?* Was it designed to inform others of new research, summarize existing research, advocate for a position, or stimulate discussion? Or was it designed to promote or sell a product? Be sure to distinguish between advertising and informing.
- *Is the material complete?* Determine whether the information you are viewing is the entire text or whether it's a selection from a fuller document. If it's a selection, which parts were excluded? Do you need more detail?
- *Will the source's claims stand up to thoughtful scrutiny?* Finally, step back and ask yourself whether the things you read or hear make sense and whether the material is relevant to your needs. If a researcher claims that the market for a particular product will triple in the next five years, ask yourself what will have to happen for that prediction to come true. Will three times as many customers buy the product? Will existing customers buy three times as much as they currently buy? Why? Is this information important to your research?

Of course, you probably won't have time to conduct a thorough background check on all your sources, so focus your efforts on the most important or most suspicious pieces of information.

At the end of step 3, you should have two piles of information: those sources you want to use and those you have eliminated. At this point in the process, it's a good idea to review

The Bureau of Labor Statistics is an excellent resource for current economic and job-related data.

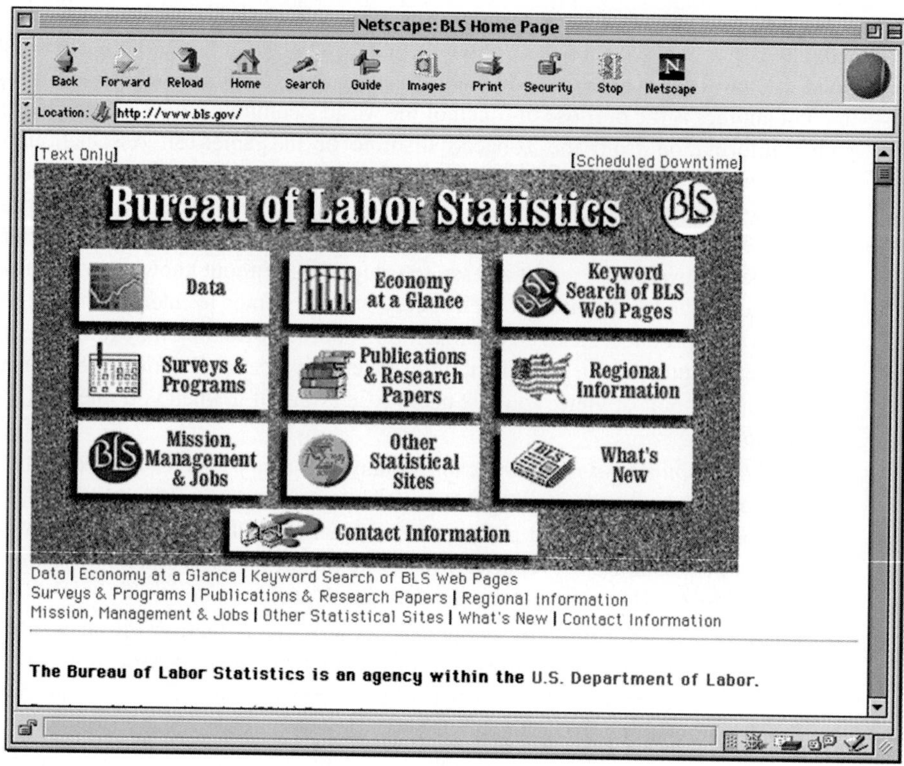

the pile of information you intend to use and ask yourself, Do I have enough of the right kinds of information to answer all my questions? Do I need more? If so, what types of information am I missing?

Stop when you reach the point at which additional effort provides little new information.

How will you know when you have enough? In theory, research can be never ending. But you'll know you have enough when you have answered all the questions that began the research project and you begin noticing that sources are becoming redundant.[12] Keep in mind that too much information can be a deterrent when it comes to taking notes and processing the information. If you find that you do need more information, go back to step 2 and fill in the gaps. Otherwise, if you're satisfied with your findings, proceed to step 4.

STEP 4: PROCESSING INFORMATION

Finding all this information is just the first part of the research process. Now it's time to start using what you've found. Of course, in some cases you may only need to read the material carefully and meet with your boss to discuss your findings. This simple processing is usually all that's needed when you've been asked to find the answer to a simple question—even though finding the answer required a lot of information gathering and work on your part. In most cases, however, you'll be asked to submit a written report or to give an oral presentation on your findings. That means you'll need to go through your research and do some extensive note taking. In step 4 you'll read your material, paraphrase the information, and quote when necessary. (Reports and oral presentations will be discussed in detail in Chapters 13–16.)

Reading the Material and Taking Notes

Before reading your material for purposes of taking notes, organize it into a logical order. For instance, you might want to divide the material by subquestions and then chronologically within each grouping. This way, when you read your material you can focus on a specific topic and read the most current information first. Afterward you can read earlier documents to fill in the history, gather background material, or find older statistics to analyze trends. Keep in mind that when you read a document for the purposes of taking notes, you need not read each and every word. Instead, read the topic sentences first (generally the first sentence of a business article) to decide whether the paragraph may contain useful information. If it does, then read the entire paragraph.

Decide whether a document contains useful information before reading it carefully to take notes.

Because a good amount of your information will be in the form of either computer printouts generated from electronic databases or photocopies, feel free to mark up these documents. Highlight key phrases, facts, or segments or write comments in the margins. Then record your notes on cards or enter your notes directly into a computer. The recording system that most students use (and many instructors recommend) is taking notes on 3-by-5-inch index cards, noting only one thought, quote, or other piece of information per card. The advantages of note cards is that they are easy to use, to carry around, and to sort and arrange.

Until recently, people generally agreed that taking notes on the computer was slower and more cumbersome than using index cards. Computers simply didn't have the tools to make this task easy, and they tended to get in the way more than they helped. However, the portability of laptops and advances in software make it easier today to take notes by computer. Figure 11.6 shows a sample word-processing table used to record the same information traditionally recorded on a note card. By recording notes in electronic format instead of on handwritten cards, the researcher can easily search for words (using the "find" function), sort the cards by column headings, and copy information directly into the document draft.

When deciding whether to use note cards or computer software for taking notes, select whichever system works best for you.

Of course, you may find that using a combination of index cards (to capture information while you're reading it) and computer software (to manage the information once you've captured it or to take notes directly from the source) is the best solution. Whichever method you choose, be sure to take complete notes so that you can avoid backtracking to look up something you forgot.

On each note card write only one fact. Indicate whether the information is a direct quote (use quotation marks, ellipses, and brackets as necessary), a paraphrase of someone else's idea, or your own idea. At the top of the card, write the general subject of the material (either a simple phrase or identifying numbers from your outline) for your own reference and for sorting purposes. Finally, carefully record bibliographic information so that you can cite the source later. If you are collecting several pieces of information from each source, you might prepare a bibliography card for each source, number the source, and then use the numbers to cross-reference your note cards. Thus, notes taken from source 75 will be written on notecards numbered 75.1, 75.2, and so on.

Each note card or computer entry should contain

- Only one fact
- A subject heading
- Complete source information or a cross-reference to bibliography cards

Quoting and Paraphrasing

You can take two kinds of notes: direct quotations or paraphrases. Use direct quotations when the original language will enhance your argument or when rewording the passage would lessen its impact. However, try not to quote sources at great length. Too much quoting creates a choppy patchwork of varying styles, and it appears as if you have lost control over the material.

One way to avoid the choppiness from a series of quotations is to **paraphrase** material, or express it in your own words. When you paraphrase, you present information to the reader in a fresh and condensed manner and demonstrate your complete understanding of the

Express material in your own words unless quoting the original language will have a greater impact.

Whether you use a computer or note cards, taking clear, complete notes is an important step in the research process.

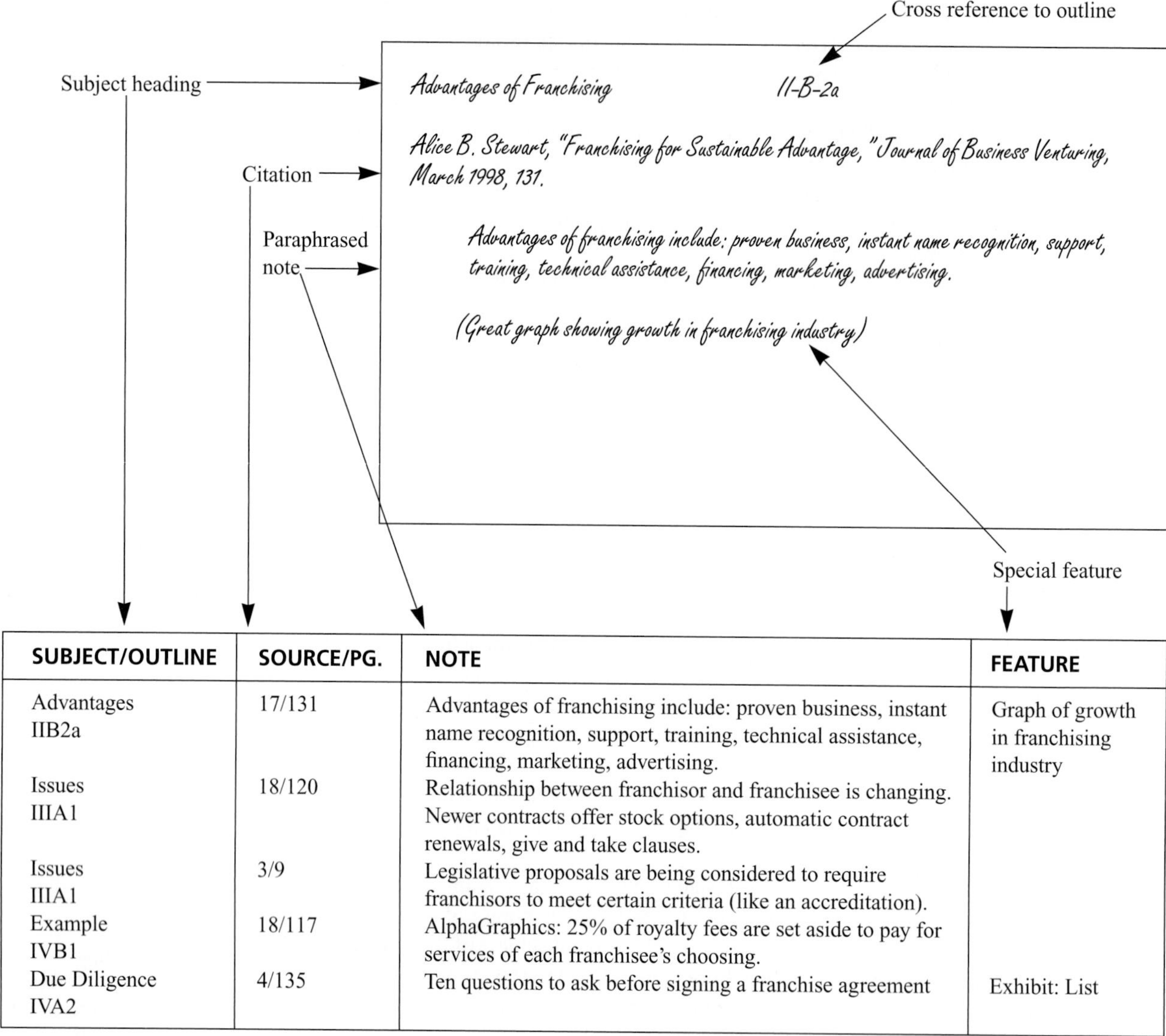

SUBJECT/OUTLINE	SOURCE/PG.	NOTE	FEATURE
Advantages IIB2a	17/131	Advantages of franchising include: proven business, instant name recognition, support, training, technical assistance, financing, marketing, advertising.	Graph of growth in franchising industry
Issues IIIA1	18/120	Relationship between franchisor and franchisee is changing. Newer contracts offer stock options, automatic contract renewals, give and take clauses.	
Issues IIIA1	3/9	Legislative proposals are being considered to require franchisors to meet certain criteria (like an accreditation).	
Example IVB1	18/117	AlphaGraphics: 25% of royalty fees are set aside to pay for services of each franchisee's choosing.	
Due Diligence IVA2	4/135	Ten questions to ask before signing a franchise agreement	Exhibit: List

Sources:
3: Alby Gallun, "Franchise Owners Must Play by the Rules," *Business Journal-Milwaukee,* 23 January 1998, 9.
4: Timothy Bates, "Survival Patterns Among Newcomers," *Journal of Business Venturing,* March 1998, 133–135.
17: Alice B. Stewart, "Franchising for Sustainable Advantage," *Journal of Business Venturing,* March 1998, 131.
18: Andrew E. Serwer, "Trouble in Franchise Nation," *Fortune,* 6 March 1995, 115–128.

Figure 11.6
Sample Note Taking

material you are presenting. In fact, paraphrasing may actually increase your comprehension of the source material, because in recasting a passage you will have to think carefully about its meaning—more carefully than if you merely copied it word for word.[13]

To paraphrase effectively:[14]

- Reread the original passage until you fully understand its meaning.
- Record your paraphrase on a note card or in an electronic format.

- Use business language and jargon that your audience is familiar with.
- Check your version with the original source to verify that you have not altered the meaning.
- Use quotation marks to identify any unique terms or phrases you have borrowed exactly from the source.
- Record the source (including the page number) on your note card so that you can give proper credit if you use this material in a report.

In short, a good paraphrase should accomplish three goals: (1) It should be shorter than the original text; (2) it should be presented in your own words; and (3) it should not alter or distort the meaning of the original text.[15]

A good paraphrase should
- Condense the material
- State the material in your own words
- Not change the meaning of the material

Whether you use direct quotes or paraphrase, to maintain your credibility and ethics you'll need to give proper credit to the original source.

Documenting Sources and Giving Credit

Whenever you quote or paraphrase, you can avoid **plagiarism**—the use of someone else's words or ideas without proper credit—by documenting the original source using one of the systems explained in Component Chapter B, "Documentation of Report Sources." Documenting your sources through footnotes, endnotes, or some similar system applies to books, articles, tables, charts, diagrams, song lyrics, scripted dialogue, letters, speeches—anything that you take from someone else (See "Focusing on Ethics: How to Avoid Plagiarizing"). Even if you paraphrase the material, it's best to give credit to the person you obtained the original information from. However, you do not have to cite a source for general knowledge or for specialized knowledge that's generally known among your readers. For example, everyone knows that Franklin Roosevelt was elected to the presidency of the United States four times. You can say so on your own authority, even if you've read an article in which the author says the same thing.

Always give proper credit when you use someone else's material or ideas.

It's not necessary to give source credit for material that is general knowledge.

Although ideas belong to no one person, the way they're expressed provides the livelihood for many scholars, consultants, and writers. To protect the interests of these people, most countries have established copyright laws. If you transgress those laws, you or your company could be sued, not to mention embarrassed. In addition to covering printed materials, copyright law covers audiovisual material, many forms of artistic expression, computer programs, maps, mailing lists, even answering machine messages. However, copyright law does not protect

- Titles, names, short phrases, and slogans
- Familiar symbols or designs
- Lists of ingredients or contents
- Ideas, procedures, methods, systems, processes, concepts, principles, discoveries, or devices (although it does cover their description, explanation, or illustration)

A work is considered copyrighted as soon as it's put into fixed form, even if it hasn't been registered.[16]

Merely crediting the source is not always enough. According to the *fair use doctrine* you can use other people's work only as long as you don't unfairly prevent them from benefiting as a result. For example, if you reproduce someone else's copyrighted questionnaire in a report you're writing, even if you identify the source thoroughly you're preventing the author from selling a copy of that questionnaire to your readers.

The fair use doctrine offers guidelines for determining how copyrighted material may be used.

In general, avoid relying to such a great extent on someone else's work. However, when you can't avoid it, contact the copyright holder (usually the author or publisher) for permission to reprint. You'll usually be asked to pay a fee.

Fair use is decided in the courts on a case-by-case basis, so you won't find any hard-and-fast rules about when to get permission. You do not need permission to use materials published before 1907, news articles more than three months old, or materials originally published by the government. Nor do you need permission to use copies as the basis for "criticism, comment, news reporting, teaching, scholarship, or research."[17]

When deciding whether you may use someone else's work without permission, remember that the courts (if they get involved) will consider the length of your quotation in relation to the total length of the work from which it was taken, the type of work you took it from, your purpose, and the effect of your action on the original author's efforts to distribute the work. If you think you may be infringing on the author's rights, write for permission and provide a credit line. In any case, be sure to acknowledge the original author's work with a source note.

Analyze your results by calculating statistics, drawing reasonable and logical conclusions, and, if appropriate, developing a set of recommendations.

STEP 5: ANALYZING AND INTERPRETING DATA

After you've completed your research and note taking, you're ready to analyze any data you've accumulated and interpret the findings. By themselves, the data you've collected won't offer much meaning or insight. You'll need to search for relationships among the facts and bits of evidence you've compiled. It's the *analysis* of these facts and the *interpretation*

FOCUSING ON ETHICS

HOW TO AVOID PLAGIARIZING

Is it right to kidnap someone else's ideas, words, or original research? *Plagiarism* (a word derived from the Latin for "kidnapping") occurs when one person misappropriates, without permission or acknowledgment, any ideas, facts, words, or structures that were reported or originated by others. In general, you're flirting with plagiarism when your business documents fail to alert your audience that you have

- Repeated someone else's information word for word
- Paraphrased another's material too closely
- Lifted a series of phrases and put them together with your own words
- Borrowed a unique term that originated elsewhere

Of course, plagiarism is completely unacceptable in the academic world, where term papers, research projects, and other materials must include the proper documentation to indicate when information is taken from other sources. Plagiarism is similarly unacceptable in the business world, although authorship is cited differently.

For example, many organizations downplay the role of individual writers. Whereas creators of academic documents take great pains to give the name of every individual who contributed ideas, criticism, or words, some companies prefer to list an entire department, division, or company as the author of a business document. When your company follows this convention, it's usually not necessary to give credit to any individuals if you cite internal documents in your own report.

Another example is the memo, letter, or other document that you write but that is issued under someone else's name, such as that of your supervisor. In contrast to the college environment, where putting your name on a term paper written by another student would be considered plagiarism, putting a supervisor's name on a business report written by an employee would rarely be seen as plagiarism. After all, drafting documents on behalf of a supervisor is a legitimate part of the employee's job in most organizations.

As a business communicator, you'll often face decisions about how and when to use information from other sources as you draft reports, letters, memos, speeches, articles, manuals, brochures, and other materials. In general, using quotation marks when quoting from a source—and then citing the original source—enables you to properly credit the person whose words you're using. It also tells your audience where to look if they want more information. Similarly, even if you paraphrase from a source, it's important to indicate who originated the information you are using. Although your company may have more specific guidelines, here are a few general tips on how to handle situations that commonly arise when you

of the findings that give you the information you need in order to answer your questions or solve a problem.

Much of the information you compile during the research phrase will be in numerical form. However, statistical information in its raw state is of little practical value. It must be manipulated so that you and your readers can interpret its significance. Look at the data from various angles and try to detect patterns by fitting pieces together to form tentative conclusions. This process will enable you to answer the questions you generated in step 1. As you proceed with your analysis, either verify or reject your conclusions.

The same set of data can be used to produce three kinds of averages: mean, median, and mode.

One useful way of looking at numerical data is to find the **average**, which is a number that represents a group of numbers. Three useful averages are the *mean,* the *median,* and the *mode* (as shown in Figure 11.7). The **mean** is the sum of all the items in the group divided by the number of items in that group. The **median** is the "middle of the road" average, or the midpoint of a series (with an equal number of items above and below). The **mode** is the number that occurs more often than any other in your sample. It's the best average for answering a question such as "What is the usual amount?"

Trend analysis involves examining data over time in order to detect patterns and relationships.

Besides looking at these averages, it's also helpful to look for a **trend,** a steady upward or downward movement in a pattern of events taking place over time. Trend analysis is common in business. By looking at data over a period of time, you can detect patterns and relationships that will help you answer important questions.

plan business documents that include information from other sources:

- *Repeating information from another company document.* If you reuse information that appeared in other company documents, your audience may believe that you've independently verified the repeated material and eliminated any errors that were in the original report. To avoid such misunderstandings, it's best to mention where the material appeared earlier. That way, your readers can check the source for further details.
- *Using the same sources as a noncompany document.* Consulting someone else's sources for further information is perfectly acceptable. Plagiarism deals with the way information is reported or analyzed, not with whether you can access the sources used by someone else. When you approach cited sources to get the same information yourself, you're being absolutely ethical.
- *Repeating information protected by copyright.* When you want to repeat information from books, published articles, songs, and other copyrighted materials, be sure to avoid infringing on the originators' legal rights. Even when you document your sources, you may find that your use of outside information has inadvertently violated copyright laws. Although ideas can't be copyrighted, words, illustrations, graphs, maps, cartoons, poetry, and other creative expressions of ideas can be legally protected against unauthorized use by others. To be safe, talk to your company's attorney before you repeat information or reprint artwork that is protected by copyright.

At the very least, people often lose respect for someone who has been caught stealing the words of another. At worst, plagiarism in business documents can lead to more serious consequences. For example, a scientific researcher lost government funding when the National Institutes of Health found that he had published as his own the conclusions and experimental protocol from another researcher's manuscript. In another case, a *Denver Post* art critic was fired after editors found that she had falsely claimed authorship of two short stories that had been written by others.

Consider how you would feel if you saw your words used without proper credit. On the other hand, you would probably feel flattered if a business report mentioned your work and cited you as the source. So to avoid even unintentional plagiarism, the best approach in most cases is to acknowledge the contributions of others by citing sources carefully and completely.

1. How might you indicate to listeners that a specific passage in your speech was taken word for word from a document written by someone else?
2. If you were the general manager of a marketing research firm, what rules might you establish to help your staff avoid unintentional plagiarism when writing analytical reports for clients?

Figure 11.7
Three Types of Average: Mean, Median, and Mode

SALES-PERSON	SALES	
Wilson	$ 3,000	
Green	5,000	
Carrick	6,000	
Wimper	7,000	Mean
Keeble	7,500	Median
Kemble	8,500	Mode
O'Toole	8,500	Mode
Mannix	8,500	Mode
Caruso	9,000	
Total	$63,000	

A correlation is a statistical relationship between two or more variables.

Once you have identified a trend, you'll want to look for a cause. To do this, you could look for a **correlation,** a statistical relationship between two or more variables. For example, if the salespeople with the largest accounts consistently produced higher sales, you might assume that those two factors were correlated, or related in a predictable way. However, your conclusion might be wrong. Correlations are useful evidence, but they do not necessarily prove a cause-and-effect relationship. To be certain that factors are correlated, you might have to collect more evidence.

STEP 6: PRESENTING YOUR FINDINGS

If the purpose of your research is not self-enlightenment and you must present your findings to others, you'll need to select the best format to convey your information. For instance, in some cases a simple letter or e-mail message will do. At other times you'll need to write a memo or a report or give a formal oral presentation. If you have statistical data that you have gathered from resources such as those listed in Figure 11.8, you may want to construct tables and graphs to include in your report or to use during an oral presentation. In the next five chapters, we'll show you how to do all this.

In Chapter 12 we'll discuss how to plan, design, and produce graphics and other visual aids. Then in Part 5, we'll devote four chapters to presenting information in reports. You'll learn how businesses use reports to communicate information (Chapter 13); how to plan, organize, and write reports and proposals (Chapter 14); how to assemble and format a formal report (Chapter 15); and how to present information orally (Chapter 16).

Figure 11.8
Major Business Resources

Use the following list as a guide for finding basic information and statistics about companies, industries, and people. Many of these resources are available in both print and electronic database format.

COMPANY, INDUSTRY, AND PRODUCT RESOURCES (PRINT)

- *Brands and Their Companies/Companies and Their Brands.* Data on over 281,000 consumer products and 51,000 manufacturers, importers, marketers, and distributors.
- *Corporate and Industry Research Reports (CIRR).* Collection of industry reports produced by industry analysts for investment purposes. Unique coverage includes industry profitability, comparative company sales, market share, profits, and forecasts.
- *Directory of Companies Required to File Annual Reports with the Securities and Exchange Commission.* List of U.S. publicly held companies.
- *Dun's Directory of Service Companies.* Information on 205,000 U.S. service companies.
- *Forbes.* Annual Report on American Industry published in first January issue of each year.

Figure 11.8, continued

- *Hoover's Handbook of American Business.* Profiles of over 500 public and private corporations.
- *Manufacturing USA.* Data series has listings for nearly 25,000 companies, including detailed information on over 450 manufacturing industries.
- *Market Share Reporter.* Data covering products and service categories originating from trade journals, newsletters, and magazines.
- *Moody's Industry Review.* Data on 4,000 companies in about 150 industries. Ranks companies within industry by five financial statistics (revenue, net income, total assets, cash and marketable securities, and long-term debt) and includes key performance ratios.
- *Moody's Manuals.* Weekly manual of financial data in each of six business areas: industrials, transportation, public utilities, banks, finance, and over-the-counter (OTC) industrials.
- *Service Industries USA.* Comprehensive data on 2,100 services grouped into over 150 industries.
- *Standard & Poor's Industry Surveys.* Concise investment profiles for broad range of industries. Coverage is extensive, with a focus on current situation and outlook. Includes some summary data on major companies in each industry.
- *Standard & Poor's Register of Corporations, Directors and Executives.* Index of major U.S. and international corporations. Lists officers, products, sales volume, and number of employees.
- *Thomas's Register of American Manufacturers.* Information on thousands of U.S. manufacturers indexed by company name and product.
- *U.S. Industrial Outlook.* Annual profiles of several hundred key U.S. industries. Each industry report covers several pages and includes tables, graphs, and charts that visually demonstrate how an industry compares with similar industries, including important component growth factors and other economic measures.

COMPANY, INDUSTRY, AND PRODUCT RESOURCES (ONLINE)

- Hoover's Online http://www.hoovers.com. Profiles of publicly listed U.S. companies traded on major stock exchanges and more than 1,200 large private companies. Search by ticker symbol, company name, location, industry, or sales.
- NAICS Codes http://www.census.gov/epcd/www/naics.html. North American Industry Classification System.
- SEC filings http://www.freegar.com. SEC filings including 10Ks, 10Qs, annual reports, and prospectuses for 3,500 U.S. public companies.
- SIC codes http://www.procurement_library/tools/sic_browse.html. List of business and industry classification codes.
- Yahoo! http://dir.yahoo.com/Business_and_Economy/companies/directories/.

DIRECTORIES AND INDEXES (PRINT)

- *Books in Print.* Index of 425,000 books in 62,000 subject categories currently available from U.S. publishers. Indexed by author and by title.
- *Directories in Print.* Information on over 16,000 business and industrial directories.
- *Encyclopedia of Associations.* Index of thousands of associations listed by broad subject category, by specific subject, by association, and by geographic location.
- *Reader's Guide to Periodical Literature.* Periodical index categorized by subject and author.
- *Ulrich's International Periodicals Directory.* Lists title, publisher, editor, phone, and address of over 140,000 publications such as popular magazines, trade journals, government documents, and newspapers. Great for locating hard-to-find trade publications.

PEOPLE (PRINT)

- *Dun & Bradstreet's Reference Book of Corporate Management.* Professional histories of people serving as the principal officers and directors of more than 12,000 U.S. companies.
- *Who's Who in America.* Index of living U.S. citizens who have gained prominence in their fields. Related text, *Who's Who in the World,* covers global achievers.

TRADEMARKS (PRINT/ONLINE)

- *Official Gazette of the United States Patent and Trademark Office.* Weekly publication (one for trademarks and one for patents) provides official record of newly assigned trademarks and patents, product descriptions, and product names.
- United States Patent and Trademark Office http://www.uspto.gov. Trademark and patent information records.

STATISTICS AND FACTS (PRINT)

- *Industry Norms and Key Business Ratios (Dun and Bradstreet).* Industry, financial, and performance ratios.
- *Information Please Almanac.* Compilation of broad-range statistical data with strong focus on labor force.

Figure 11.8, continued

- *Robert Morris Associates' Annual Statement Studies.* Industry, financial, and performance ratios.
- *Statistical Abstract of the United States.* U.S. economic, social, political, and industrial statistics.
- *The World Almanac and Book of Facts.* Compilation of facts on economic, social, educational, and political events for major countries of the world.

STATISTICS AND FACTS (ONLINE)

- Bureau of Economic Analysis http://www.bea.doc.gov. Large collection of economic and government data.
- FedStats http://www.fedstats.gov. Access to full range of statistics and information from over 70 U.S. government agencies.
- STAT-USA http://www.stat-usa.gov. Large collection of economic and government data.
- U.S. Census Bureau http://www.census.gov. Demographic data on both consumers and businesses based on 1990 census.
- U.S. Bureau of Labor Statistics http://bls.gov. Extensive national and regional information on labor and business, including employment, industry growth, productivity, Consumer Price Index (CPI), and overall U.S. economy.

COMMERCIAL DATABASES (REQUIRE SUBSCRIPTIONS)

- ABI Inform. Database with over 1,500 scholarly and trade journals in business, management, industry, and economics (full text and abstracts).
- Dialog. Over 900 main databases that include areas such as business and finance, news and media, medicine, pharmaceuticals, reference, social sciences, government and regulation, science and technology, and more.
- Electric Library. Hundreds of full-text newspapers, magazines, newswires, maps, and photographs.
- LEXIS-NEXIS. More than1.4 billion documents in more than 8,000 databases.
- UMI ProQuest Direct. More than 5,000 journals, periodicals, magazines, newspapers, and other information sources.

COMMUNICATION CHALLENGES AT GOSH ENTERPRISES

Charley Shin always keeps one eye on the consumer marketplace and one eye on his plans for expansion. He learned the importance of paying attention to the customer's perspective shortly after opening the first Charley's Steakery. The restaurant was named simply "Charley's"—until Shin realized that the name didn't communicate what kind of food customers could expect from "Charley." When he spelled it out with a sign that said "Charley's Steakery," business increased by 50 percent.

That's why, in addition to the three-year growth plan, Shin wants to take another look at fast-food trends. Charley's Steakery made its reputation by serving fresh sandwiches with everything prepared to order—no frozen, microwaved entrees. This "fresh-food" concept has been popular with customers since 1986. Is it still important to them? Some of his burger-selling competitors have returned to greasier, less healthy cuisine (boosting business tremendously, they claim), but Shin isn't so sure their numbers are giving an accurate picture; a double-digit increase in sales doesn't mean much if it's preceded by a huge plummet, as in the case of one competitor.

INDIVIDUAL CHALLENGE: As part of Shin's marketing staff, you've been asked to begin setting up the study. First task: Develop a problem statement and state it as a question. Write your statement on paper and present it to the rest of your team.

TEAM CHALLENGE: After the team members have presented their ideas and the problem statements have been agreed on, your team needs to write a preliminary outline for the investigation you will be developing. You can structure the outline either in statement form or in question form.[18] ■

SUMMARY OF LEARNING OBJECTIVES

1. **Summarize the six steps of the research process.** In step 1 you identify questions and develop subquestions so that you can narrow your focus. In step 2 you find and access secondary and primary sources of information. You evaluate and finalize your sources in step 3 by testing for credibility, bias, currency, and completeness, and you fill in any gaps. Then you process the information in step 4 by reading the material and taking notes, which you analyze and interpret in step 5. Finally, in step 6 you present your findings.
2. **Explain the role of reference librarians.** The primary role of reference librarians is to help people find materials and information and to teach people how to use the library resources. They can also help researchers improve their search strategies and improve their search results.
3. **List several ways to search databases effectively.** To search databases effectively you should select the appropriate databases for your needs, use multiple search engines (if searching the Internet), use variations of your terms, avoid stopwords and words contained in the name of the database, and avoid long phrases if short ones will do. In addition you should use Boolean operators, proximity operators, and wildcards.
4. **Briefly discuss the different types of resources you might use to find business information.** Popular secondary business resources include business books, periodicals, newspapers, directories, almanacs, government publications, and electronic databases. Primary business resources include internal documents, observations, experiments, surveys, and interviews.
5. **Highlight several things you must do during the interviewing process.** First you gather background information, contact your subjects, and make all necessary scheduling arrangements. Then you plan the interview by formulating a mix of intelligent questions and arranging them in a logical, sequential order. During the interview you should dress appropriately, arrive early, take good notes, be aware of verbal and nonverbal cues, and follow the agenda but be ready to stray a bit to explore relevant subtopics. After the interview, you should thank the interviewee, review and revise your notes, and process and use the information wisely.
6. **Discuss the difference between quoting and paraphrasing, and explain the appropriate uses of each.** Quoting is copying material word for word and is used when the original language would enhance the impact of the passage or when rewording it would alter its meaning. Paraphrasing is presenting material in your own words without altering or distorting its meaning; it is used in all occasions unless quoting is necessary. Whether you're quoting or paraphrasing, always give proper credit to the source.

CRITICAL THINKING QUESTIONS

1. What are the advantages and disadvantages of knowing a lot about the problem you are researching? Explain.
2. After an exhaustive study of an important problem, you have reached a conclusion that you know your company's management will reject. What will you do? Explain your answer.
3. Why is browsing an important part of the research process?
4. Why might you not want to use the Internet in the beginning stage of your research?
5. Why do you need to evaluate your sources?
6. How will you know when you are finished with the research process?
7. Analyze any recent school or work assignment that required you to conduct research. How did you approach your investigation? Did you rely mostly on primary sources or on secondary sources? Now that you've studied this chapter, can you identify two ways to improve the research techniques you used during that assignment? Briefly explain.
8. You're conducting an information interview with a high-level executive in another division of your company. Partway through the interview, this person shows clear signs of impatience. How should you respond? Explain your answer.

EXERCISES

1. Assume that your college president has received many student complaints about campus parking problems. You are appointed to chair a student committee organized to investigate the problems and recommend solutions. The president gives you the file labeled "Parking: Complaints from Students," and you jot down the essence of the complaints as you inspect the contents. Your notes look like this:

   —Inadequate student spaces at critical hours
   —Poor night lighting near the computer center
   —Inadequate attempts to keep resident neighbors from occupying spaces
   —Dim marking lines
   —Motorcycles taking up full spaces
   —Discourteous security officers
   —Spaces (usually empty) reserved for college officials
   —Relatively high parking fees
   —Full fees charged to night students even though they use the lots only during low-demand periods
   —Vandalism to cars and a sense of personal danger
   —Inadequate total space
   —Resident harassment of students parking on the street in front of neighboring houses

   Your first job is to organize for committee discussion four or five areas that include all (or most) of these specific complaints. Choose the main headings for your outline, and group these specific complaints under them.
2. Your instructor has given you the assignment to write a research paper on a topic of your choice. You decide to search for information using both the library databases and the Internet. Develop a search strategy.

a. What are some key words and phrases you might use?
b. Which Boolean operators would you use to narrow your search?
c. Which wildcard operators might you use?

3. Deciding how to collect primary data is an important part of the research process. Which one or more of the five methods of data collection (examining documents, making observations, surveying people, conducting experiments, and performing interviews) would you use if you were researching these questions?
   a. Has the litter problem on campus been reduced since the cafeteria began offering fewer take-out choices this year than in past years?
   b. Has the school attracted more transfer students since it waived the formal application process and allowed students at other colleges simply to send their transcripts and a one-page letter of application?
   c. Has the number of traffic accidents at the school's main entrance been reduced since a traffic light was installed?
   d. Has student satisfaction with the campus bookstore improved now that students can order their books over the Internet and pick them up at several campus locations?
4. After years of work, you've almost completed your first motion picture, the story of a group of unknown musicians finding work and making a reputation in a difficult world. Unfortunately, some of your friends leave the first complete screening saying that the 132-minute movie is simply too long. Others can't imagine any more editing cuts. You decide to test the movie on a regular audience, members of which will be asked to complete a questionnaire that may or may not lead to additional editing. You obtain permission from a local theater manager to show your film at two special times. Design a questionnaire that you can use to solicit valid answers.
5. Your boss has asked you to analyze sales for the first nine months of this year. Using the following data from company invoices, calculate the mean for each quarter and all averages for the year to date. Then identify and discuss the quarterly sales trends.

January	$24,600	June	$26,800
February	25,900	July	29,900
March	23,000	August	30,500
April	21,200	September	26,600
May	24,600		

6. Find the following information and properly cite your source using the formats discussed in Component Chapter B. (*Hint:* Start with Figure 11.8, Major Business Resources, at the end of this chapter.)
   a. Contact information for the American Management Association
   b. Median weekly earnings of men and women by occupation
   c. Current market share for Perrier water
   d. Performance ratios for office supply retailers
   e. Annual stock performance for Hewlett-Packard
   f. Number of franchise outlets in the United States
   g. Composition of the U.S. work force by profession
7. Prepare a list of the most important magazines and professional journals in the following fields of study:
   a. Marketing/advertising
   b. Insurance
   c. Communications
   d. Accounting
8. Locate the SIC and NAICS codes for the following industries:
   a. Hotels and motels
   b. Breakfast cereals
   c. Bottled water
   d. Automatic vending machines
9. Select any public company and find the following information:
   a. Names of the company's current officers
   b. List of the company's products or services
   c. Current issues in the company's industry
   d. Outlook for the company's industry as a whole
10. Use at least three Internet search engines to find information on a topic of your choice. Which search engine appears to be the most useful for this topic?
11. Plan to conduct an informational interview with a professional working in your chosen career area. Plan the structure of the interview and create a set of interview questions. Conduct the interview. Using the information you gather, write a memo to another student describing the tasks, pitfalls, and advantages this career entails. (Your reader is a person who plans to enter this career.)
12. Your boss has asked you to do some research on franchising. Actually, he's thinking about purchasing a few Subway franchises and he needs some information. Visit Amazon.com at http://www.amazon.com and review the site. On the home page, perform a key word search on "franchise." Explore some of the books by clicking on "read more about this title."
    a. Use the information to develop a list of subquestions to help you narrow your focus.
    b. Write down the names of three books you might purchase for your boss.
    c. How can this Web site assist you with your research efforts?
13. Review the material on how to write instructions in Chapter 7. Now that you are an expert on finding company information, write a brief set of instructions (in a logical, step-by-step format) to help others who might need to research a company. Include in your instructions any resources you think might help others find the following company information: SIC/NAICS code, public or private status, contact information, brands or products, and news about that company.
14. Write an e-mail direct request to a public company of your choice asking for a copy of its latest annual report.

15. Because of the success of your pizza delivery service, you're considering whether to expand. You'll need at least one additional delivery van, but you know that buying one will lead to other expenses such as maintenance, insurance, and so on. Before you can make your decision, you will need to investigate the main question: "What investments will I need make to expand my pizza delivery service?" Use some of the prewriting techniques discussed in Chapter 5 to develop a list of subquestions you must consider to answer this main question.

Exploring the Best of the Web

Check Out Materials at This Library 24 Hours a Day, page 375

Visit the reference center of the Internet Public Library and explore the Business and Economics Reference section. Click on *Business Directories.*

1. Select five companies and use the links provided to find contact information (address, phone, Web site, officers' names, and so on) for each of your companies.
2. Go back to the main reference center and click on *Reference.* Follow some of the reference links. How might these links help you when performing business research?

Communicating Information through Graphs and Other Visuals

AFTER STUDYING THIS CHAPTER, YOU WILL BE ABLE TO

1. Cite the advantages of preparing visual aids before preparing text
2. Explain why business professionals use graphs and other visual aids
3. List several popular types of graphics and discuss when to use them
4. Discuss five principles of graphic design to keep in mind when preparing visual aids
5. Name four qualities to look for before including a visual aid in a report or presentation
6. List several popular types of presentation visuals

Communication Close-up at Black Entertainment Television

As the old saying goes, a picture is worth a thousand words. Curtis Symonds, knows that this adage is especially true in the business world. He is executive vice president of affiliate sales and marketing for BET Holdings (parent company of Black Entertainment Television). Whether Symonds is developing materials to market the BET on Jazz network to cable television companies or speaking before a convention of minority business owners, he uses visual aids to help his audience grasp his most important ideas.

Symonds first went to work for the cable television industry in 1980. By 1984 he was the director of marketing for the ESPN sports network. Then in 1988 he joined BET Holdings, where he has remained ever since. During that time Symonds has helped BET expand from its original television network to a media group consisting of four cable television networks, three magazines, several jazz-theme restaurants, and a national line of sportswear.

Curtis Symonds

In a highly competitive marketplace, that kind of success depends on establishing a quick and lasting connection with your audience. Symonds uses visual aids strategically to engage his customers and hold their attention. "You want to draw the person into the setting so that you can convey the information that most meets their needs," he says. For Symonds, doing so often means using tables and graphs to present detailed data to cable company executives. BET's networks compete with many other networks for space on local cable channels, so Symonds must provide solid evidence that BET offers viewers more of what they want in cable programming. "Research drives our business," he says. "We need to show that we understand the viewer in each specific local market."

BET videotapes the popular Planet Groove *show at its Washington studio.*

To convince cable executives of the quality and appeal of BET's programs, Symonds turns research data into graphs that depict the viewing habits of local customers. Then he tailors his sales presentation to demonstrate how the BET networks fit with those viewing habits. Symonds also uses graphs to show how the popularity of BET programming has increased over time among various demographic groups. By presenting this type of information visually, Symonds enables cable companies to see how they might be able to profit from investments in the BET Network, BET on Jazz, BET Pay-Per-View, or BET Movies.

Still, Symonds is careful not to use too many visual aids in his presentations. "A lot of people overdo their use of visuals," he says. "They either try to give too much information or try to illustrate every point. But when you do this, you run the risk of losing your audience." So Symonds's own formula for success is to be "short, sweet, and direct."

In fact, he's learned that understanding your audience is the key to developing effective visual aids. "It's important to make your visuals relevant to your specific audience," he advises. For example, when speaking to small groups, Symonds may use nothing but his own facial expressions, gestures, and enthusiasm to make his point. When speaking to a large audience such as a trade convention, however, he often uses overhead transparencies or electronic presentations for their efficiency and visual appeal. And when he's addressing a technology-savvy audience, Symonds finds that multimedia presentations involving computer graphics, sound, and full-motion video are most effective.

In every situation, Symonds takes the time to consider the audience's needs and expectations before choosing how to present his message. This preparation allows him to convey his most important points as quickly as possible. "I use visual aids like a storybook," he says. "I want to make it as easy as possible for my audience. If I develop my visuals in a proper manner, I can bring my audience to me, like a fisherman reeling in a fish."[1] ■

PLANNING VISUAL AIDS

Conveying an important idea is the main reason businesspeople like Curtis Symonds include graphs and other visuals in their reports and proposals. But which do you prepare first: visuals or text? Suppose you've just completed the research for an important report or oral presentation, and you're about to begin the composition phase. Your first impulse might be to start with the introduction and proceed page by page until you've completed the text or script. Almost as an afterthought you might throw in a few visual aids—tables, charts, graphs, schematic drawings, illustrations, photographs—to illustrate the words.

A visual aid is an illustration in tabular, graphic, schematic, or pictorial form.

Although fitting visual aids to completed text makes some sense, many experienced businesspeople prefer to begin with the visual aids. This approach has three advantages.

First, much of the fact finding and analytical work is already in tabular or graphic form, so you already have a visual point of departure. Sorting through and refining your visuals will help you decide exactly what you're going to say. Second, by starting with the visual aids, you develop a graphic story line that can be used for both a written report and an oral presentation. Finally, because the text or script explains and refers to the tables, charts, and graphs, you save time by having them ready before you start to compose, particularly if you plan to use quite a few visuals.

Why Business Professionals Use Visual Aids

Visual aids help communicators get through to an audience.

You may be wondering why business professionals use visual aids at all. Of course, carefully prepared visuals can make your report or presentation more interesting. More important, however, pictures are an effective way to communicate with diverse audiences common in today's business environment. In fact, you may even find yourself trying to communicate with people who have little or no interest in your ideas. Furthermore, in the numbers-oriented world of work, people rely heavily on images. They think in terms of trend lines, distribution curves, and percentages. An upward curve means good news in any language, be it English or Japanese. Finally, visual aids attract and hold people's attention in addition to helping them understand and remember the message. Consider this: In one study, 36 audiences were exposed to oral presentations with and without graphic aids, with the following results:

- In presentations that included visual aids, the speaker was able to persuade the audience to accept the message two-thirds of the time. Speakers who did not use visuals won the audience to their point of view only half the time.
- The audience reached a consensus 79 percent of the time when graphics were used, but they agreed on a decision only 58 percent of the time when graphics weren't used.
- Meetings involving graphic presentations were 28 percent shorter than meetings involving no graphics.[2]

Although the study focused on oral presentations, to a considerable degree its results pertain to written reports as well.

Despite their value, Curtis Symonds recommends that you use visual aids selectively and include only those elements that support your primary message. In other words, use illustrative material in a report or presentation to supplement the written or spoken word, not to replace it. You do so by restricting your use of visual aids to situations in which they do the most good. Table 12.1 helps you identify those situations.

The Process of "Visualizing" Information

When you begin to compose a report or a presentation, you usually have a lot of raw data that can be molded into any number of messages. As you sort through the information you've compiled during the research phase, you begin to see relationships and draw conclusions. This process helps you decide on your message.

Decide on the Message

When planning visual aids
- Decide what you want to say
- Pick out the points that can best be made visually
- Judge whether you have too many or too few graphics

Suppose you've been asked to compare your company's recent sales with those of a competitor. You have the following data on market share for the past month:

Sales Region	Your Company's Share	Competitor's Share
North	10%	25%
South	40	8
East	32	32
West	20	23

TABLE 12.1

WHEN TO USE VISUAL AIDS

Purpose	Application
To clarify	Support text descriptions of "graphic" topics: quantitative or numerical information; explanations of trends; descriptions of procedures, relationships, locations; or composition of an item
To simplify	Break complicated descriptions into components that can be depicted with conceptual models, flowcharts, organization charts, or diagrams
To emphasize	Call attention to particularly important points by illustrating them with line, bar, and pie charts
To summarize	Review major points in the narrative by providing a chart or table that sums up the data
To reinforce	Present information in visual and written form to increase reader's retention
To attract	Make material seem more interesting by decorating the cover or title page and by breaking up the text with visual aids
To impress	Build credibility by putting ideas into visual form to convey the impression of authenticity and precision
To unify	Depict the relationship among points—for example, with a flowchart

What message can you derive from this set of data? Some of the possibilities:

- The two companies perform differently in different regions. Your company is strongest in the South, where your competitor is weakest.
- The two companies' performances are similar in the East and West.
- Both companies are uneven in their market share from region to region.

All these messages are true, and all of them might be useful. Your job is to decide which interpretation of the data is most useful for your purposes. As you sort through your facts, looking at various interpretations, you will find that an outline of a message begins to emerge. Some of these facts lend themselves to a prose presentation; others may be expressed more easily in graphic form.

Identify Points That Require Visual Support

Once you have an outline in mind, you can begin to identify which points to illustrate graphically. Ask yourself how to visually dramatize the key elements of your message. Think of each main point as a separate scene, and then try to visualize a chart or graph that would communicate the point to your audience.

Analyze raw data to identify the points that support your main idea.

Take your analysis a step further by considering other visual aids. Undoubtedly, some of the supporting items on your outline involve detailed facts and figures. This sort of information may be confusing and tedious when presented in paragraph form, but tables and graphs can conveniently organize and display such detail. If some points in your outline require a detailed description of physical relationships or procedures, you might even use flowcharts, drawings, or photographs to clarify the discussion. As you think about how to convey your message, you begin to envision the balance between verbal and graphic elements.

Use visual aids to simplify, clarify, and emphasize important information.

Maintain a Balance between Illustrations and Words

When planning the illustrations for your report or presentation, aim to achieve a reasonable balance between the verbal and the visual. The ideal blend depends on the nature of the subject. Some topics are more graphic than others and require more visual aids.

In general, use visual aids only to supplement the story you are telling in words.

Keep in mind that illustrating every point dilutes the effectiveness of all your visual aids. For example, telling your audience every paragraph or two to consult a table or chart is more likely to obscure than to illuminate the thread of your argument. Furthermore, readers tend to assume that the amount of space allocated to a topic indicates its relative importance. So by using visual aids to illustrate a minor point, you may be sending a misleading message about its significance.

When deciding on the mix of words and visuals, give some thought to your readers' needs and thought patterns. Some people ignore the visuals and focus on the words; others do the opposite. If you know that your audience prefers one form of communication over the other—or has special communication needs—you can adjust the balance accordingly. When General Mills redesigned its Hamburger Helper package, management decided to include both drawings and step-by-step photographs of the cooking directions. These visual aids were particularly useful for audiences who speak English as their second language. The illustrations also provided additional help for people with limited cooking experience. "It's critically important that customers can read the directions, because if they don't have a successful experience with the food, they won't buy the product again," says Craig Shulstad, a General Mills spokesperson.[3]

DID YOU KNOW?

The mind favors information shown as pictures and quickly forgets information shown as words or numbers. In fact, research shows that we dream in pictures, not in words.

Another factor to consider when deciding on the number of visuals to include is your production schedule. If you're producing the report or presentation without the help of an art department or appropriate computer-graphics tools, you may want to restrict the number of illustrations. Making charts and tables takes time, particularly if you're inexperienced. Furthermore, constructing visual aids requires a good deal of both imagination and attention to detail.

Of course, deciding on the appropriate type of graph can be a challenge. For instance, using the market share data from our earlier example, what kind of graph would you use to visually communicate the differences between your company and your competitor's? Pie charts? Bar charts? Both could work in this case. Keep in mind that most types of graphs are not interchangeable. As we will see in the next section, different types of graphs best depict different types of data.

SELECTING THE RIGHT GRAPHIC FOR THE JOB

Choose a type of graphic that best presents your message.

Once you've selected which points to illustrate graphically, your next step is to select the type of graph that will present your data most clearly and effectively to your audience:

- To present detailed, exact values, use tables.
- To illustrate trends over time, use a line chart or a bar chart.
- To show frequency or distribution, use a pie chart, segmented bar chart, or area chart.
- To compare one item with another, use a bar chart.
- To compare one part with the whole, use a pie chart.
- To show correlations, use a line chart, a bar chart, or a scatter (dot) chart.
- To show geographic relationships, use a map.
- To illustrate a process or a procedure, use a flowchart or a diagram.

Here's a closer look at each of these graphic types.

Tables

When you have to present detailed, specific information, choose a **table,** a systematic arrangement of data in columns and rows. Tables are ideal when the audience needs the information that would be either difficult or tedious to handle in the main text.

Use tables to help your audience understand detailed information.

Most tables contain the standard parts illustrated in Figure 12.1. Every table includes vertical columns and horizontal rows, with useful headings along the top and side. Tables projected onto a screen during an oral presentation should be limited to three column heads and six row heads; tables presented on paper may include from one or two heads to a dozen or more. If the table has too many columns to fit comfortably between the margins of the page, turn the paper horizontally and insert it in the report with the top toward the binding.

Although formal tables set apart from the text are necessary for complex information, you can present some data more simply within the text. You make the table, in essence, a part of the paragraph, typed in tabular format. Such text tables are usually introduced with a sentence that leads directly into the tabulated information. Here's an example:

This table shows how Amazon.com stacks up against rival Barnes & Noble:

Feature	Amazon.com	Barnes & Noble
Number of stores	1 Web site	1,011
Titles per superstore	3.1 million	175,000
Book returns	2%	30%
Sales per employee (annual)	$375,000	$100,000
Inventory turnovers per year	24	3
Long-term capital requirements	Low	High
Cash flow	High	Low

Source: "Amazon.com the Wild World of E-Commerce," Business Week, 14 December 1998, 110.

Use word tables
- To summarize survey results
- To compare items with some standard

Although many tables are strictly numerical, tables that also use words can be just as useful. Some tables contain no numbers at all. They are particularly appropriate for presenting survey findings or for comparing various items against a specific standard.

When preparing a numerical table, be sure to

- Use common, understandable units, and clearly identify the units you're using: dollars, percentages, price per ton, or whatever.

TABLE 1 Title

	*Multicolumn Head**		*Single-Column Head*	*Single-Column Head*
Stub head	***Subhead***	***Subhead***		
Row head	XXX	XXX	XX	XX
Row head				
Subhead	XX	XXX	XX	XX
Subhead	XX	XXX	XX	XX
Total	XXX	XXX	XX	XX

Source: (In the same format as a text footnote; see Component Chapter B).

*Footnote (for explanation of elements in the table; a superscript number or small letter may be used instead of an asterisk or other symbol).

Figure 12.1
Parts of a Table

- Express all items in a column in the same unit, and round off for simplicity.
- Label column headings clearly and use a subhead if necessary.
- Separate columns or rows with lines or extra space to make the table easy to follow.
- Provide column-to-row totals or averages when relevant.
- Document the source of the data below the table using the same format as a text footnote (see Component Chapter B).

Line and Surface Charts

Use line charts
- To indicate changes over time
- To plot the relationship of two variables

A **line chart** illustrates trends over time or plots the relationship of two variables. In line charts showing trends, the vertical, or *y,* axis shows the amount, and the horizontal, or *x,* axis shows the time or the quantity being measured. Ordinarily, both scales begin at zero and proceed in equal increments; however, in Figure 12.2 the vertical axis is broken to show that some of the increments have been left out. A broken axis is appropriate when the data are plotted far above zero, but be sure to clearly indicate the omission of data points.

A simple line chart may be arranged in many ways. One of the most common is to plot several lines on the same chart for comparative purposes, as shown in Figure 12.3. Try to use no more than three lines on any given chart, particularly if the lines cross. Another variation of the simple line chart has a vertical axis with both positive and negative numbers (see Figure 12.4). This arrangement is handy when you have to illustrate losses.

Figure 12.2
Line Chart with Broken Axis

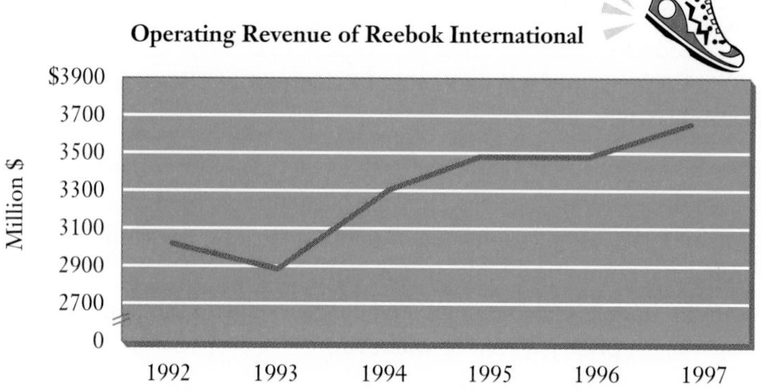

Figure 12.3
Line Chart with Multiple Lines

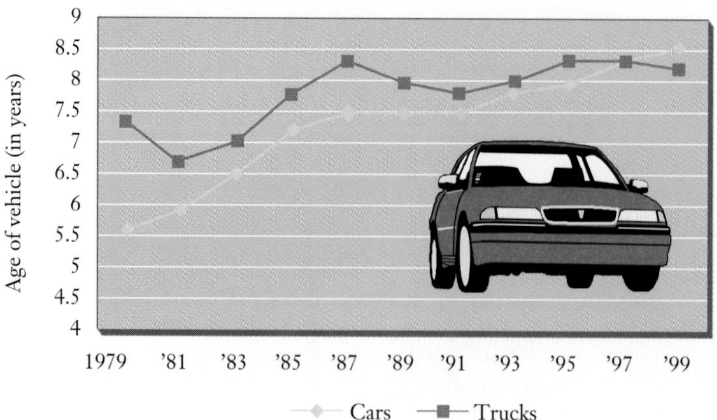

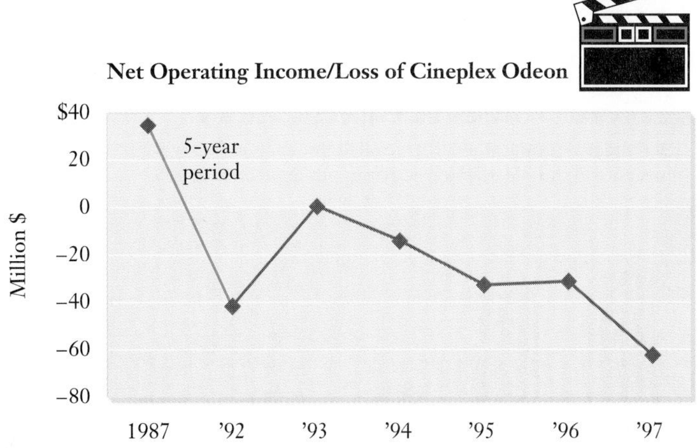

Figure 12.4
Line Chart with Positive and Negative Values on Vertical Axis

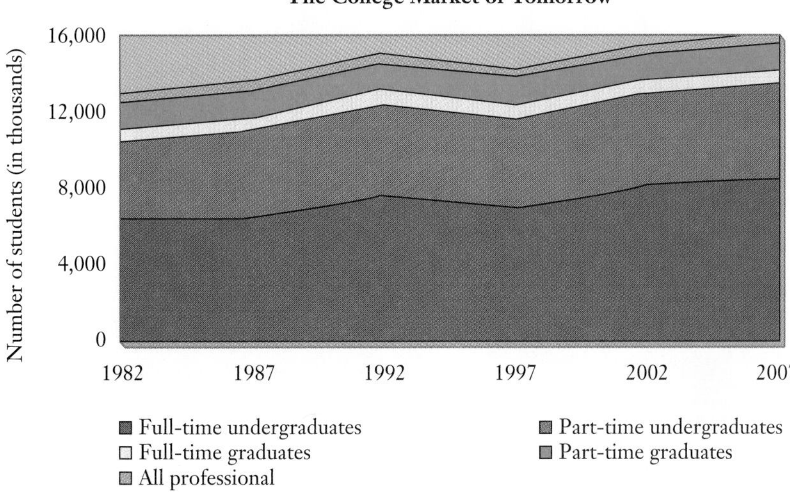

Figure 12.5
Surface Chart

A **surface chart,** also called an **area chart,** is a form of line chart with a cumulative effect; all the lines add up to the top line, which represents the total (see Figure 12.5). This form of chart helps you illustrate changes in the composition of something over time. When preparing a surface chart, put the most important segment against the baseline, and restrict the number of strata to four or five.

A surface chart is a kind of line chart showing a cumulative effect.

Bar Charts, Pictograms, and Gantt Charts

A **bar chart** portrays numbers by the height or length of its rectangular bars, making a series of numbers easy to read or understand. Bar charts are particularly valuable when you want to

- Compare the size of several items at one time
- Show changes in one item over time
- Indicate the composition of several items over time
- Show the relative size of components of a whole

Bar charts, in which numbers are visually portrayed by rectangular bars, can take a variety of forms.

As Figure 12.6 shows, bar charts can be singular, grouped, segmented, or a combination of chart types. Grouped bar charts compare more than one set of data (using a different

Figure 12.6
The Versatile Bar Chart

Four variations on the bar chart are the single bar chart (Where the College Students Are), the grouped bar chart (Eating Occasions), the segmented bar chart (Targeted Talk), and the combined bar chart (line and bar) (Commercial Superhighway).

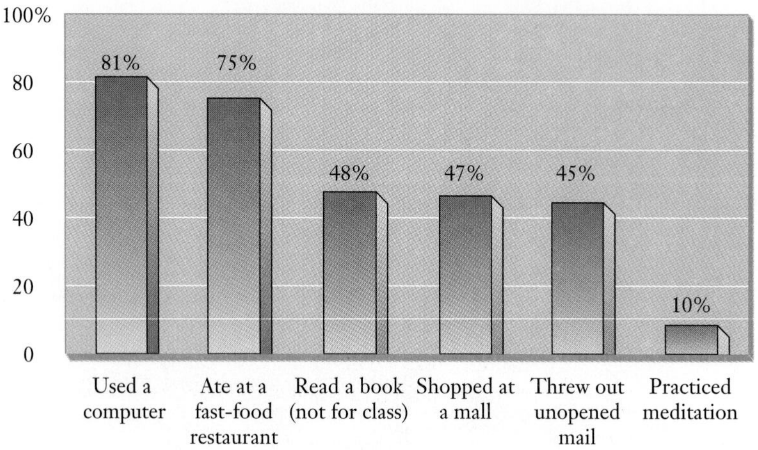

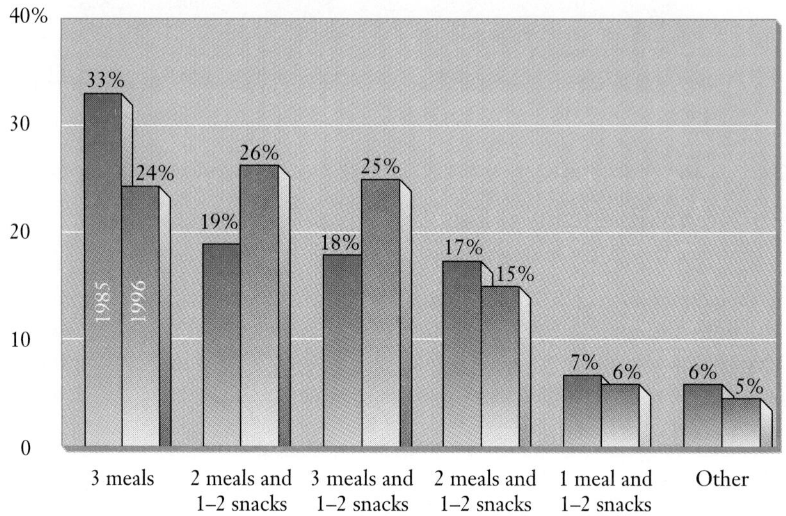

color or pattern for each set). Segmented bar charts, also known as stacked bar charts, show how individual components contribute to a total number (using a different color or pattern for each component). Combination bar and line charts compare quantities that require different intervals.

You can be creative with bar charts in many ways. You might align the bars either vertically or horizontally or you might even use bar charts to show both positive and negative quantities. Be careful, however, to keep all the bars in the chart the same width; different widths

Figure 12.6, continued

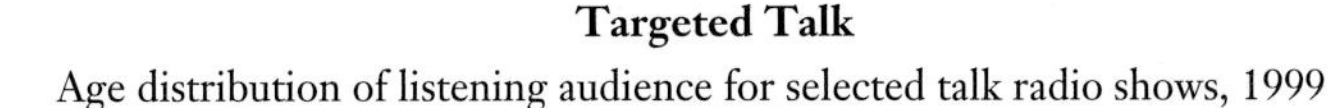

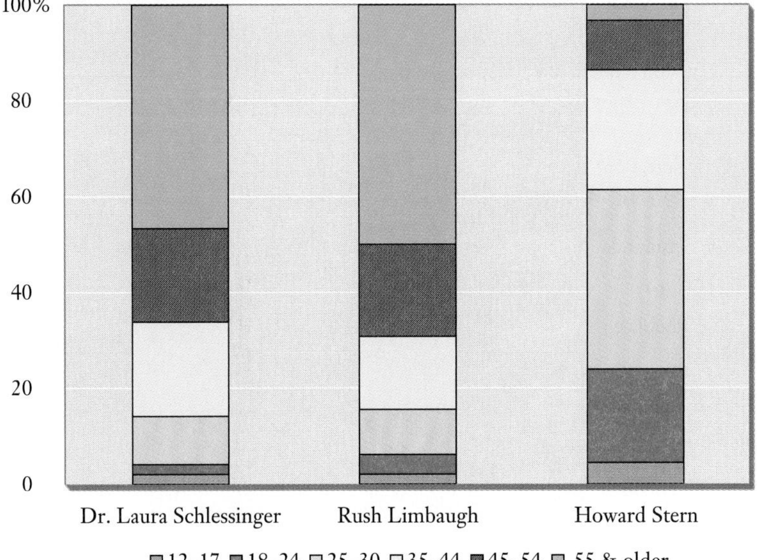

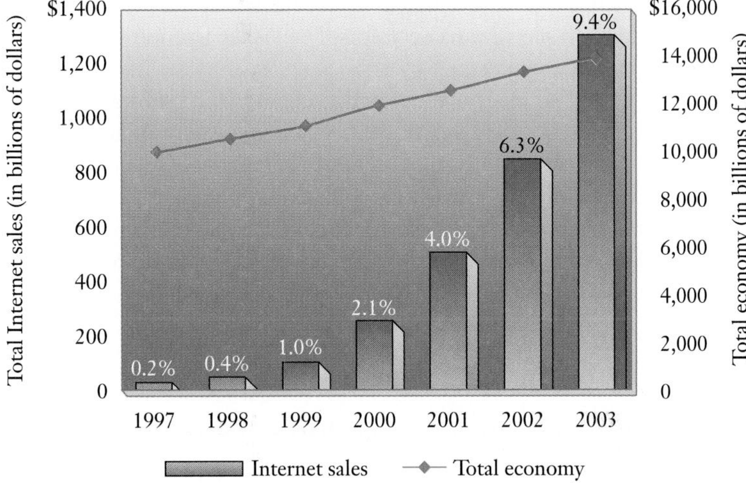

could suggest a relative importance to the viewer. In addition, space the bars evenly and place them in a logical order such as chronological or alphabetical. Keep in mind that most computer software (such as Microsoft Excel, which was used to produce the graphs in this chapter) will generate charts from data tables. The software will place the data in a graph based on the order that is used in the table. So plan ahead, and if you don't like the way the computer interprets your data graphically, go back to the data table and adjust the order there first.

You can also convert the bars into a line of symbols, with the number or length of symbols indicating the relative value of each item (see Figure 12.7). A chart that uses symbols instead of words or numbers to portray data is known as a **pictogram**. The chief value of pictograms is their novelty and ability to convey a more literal, visual message. You can easily

Figure 12.7
Pictogram

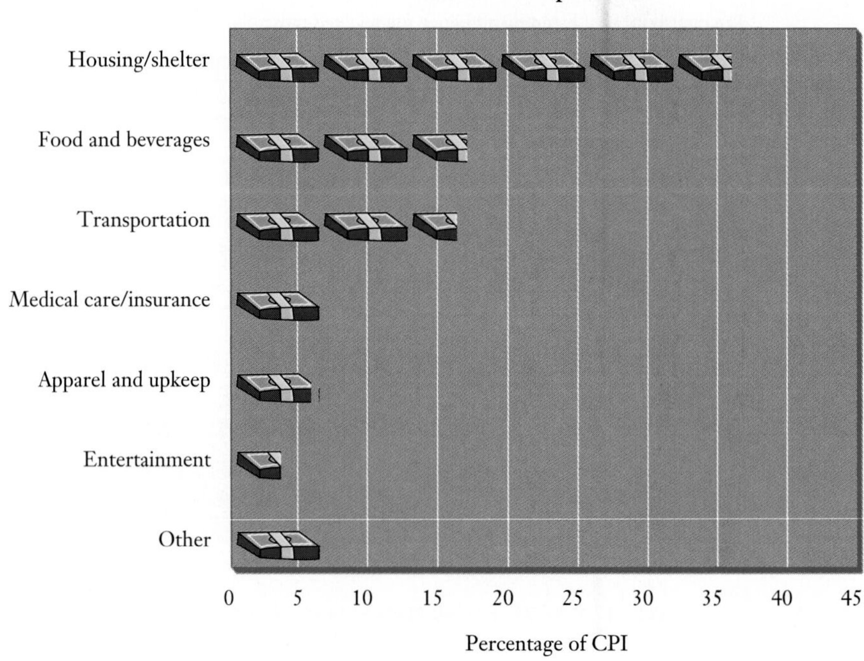

prepare pictograms by using software such as Excel and substituting a piece of clip art for the graphical bar. Although pictograms occasionally enhance a report, they tend to be less useful than other types of bar charts.

Closely related to the bar chart is the **timeline chart**, which shows how much time is needed to complete each task in a given project. When you want to track progress toward completing a project, you can use a type of timeline chart known as a **Gantt chart** (named for management theorist Henry L. Gantt). The Gantt chart in Figure 12.8 shows the activities involved in designing the prototype and conducting the marketing research for product number 1575, which is running on schedule. The maroon bars indicate completed tasks; the blue bars indicate activities not yet completed; the black diamond is a milestone—in this case the prototype's due date.

Pie Charts

Use pie charts to show the relative sizes of the parts of a whole.

Like segmented bar charts and area charts, a **pie chart** shows how parts of a whole are distributed. Each segment represents a slice of a complete circle, or *pie.* As you can see in Figure 12.9, pie charts are an effective way to show percentages or to compare one segment with another. You can combine pie charts with tables to expand the usefulness of such visuals.

When composing pie charts, try to restrict the number of slices in the pie. Otherwise, the chart looks cluttered and is difficult to label. If necessary, lump the smallest pieces together in a "miscellaneous" category. Ideally, the largest or most important slice of the pie, the segment you want to emphasize, is placed at the twelve o'clock position; the rest are arranged clockwise either in order of size or in some other logical progression.

Use different colors or patterns to distinguish the various pieces. If you want to draw attention to the segment that is of the greatest interest to your readers, use a brighter color for that segment, draw an arrow to the segment, or explode it; that is, pull the segment away from the rest of the pie. In any case, label all the segments and indicate their value in either percentages or units of measure so that your readers will be able to judge the value of the

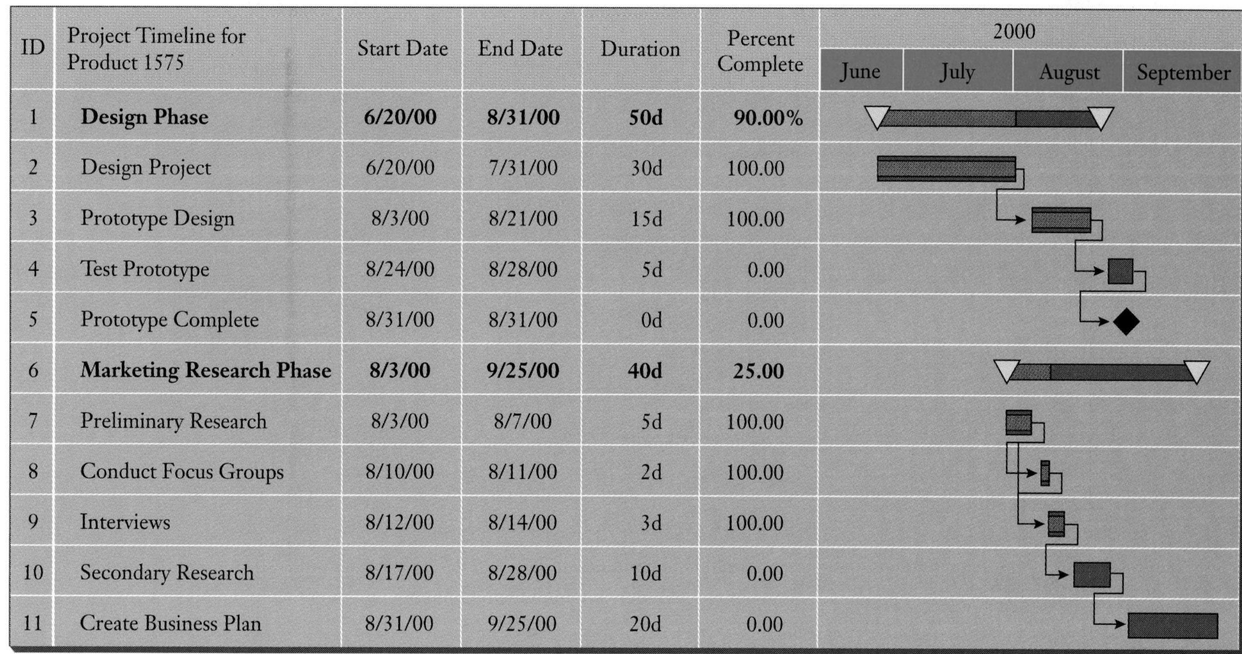

ID	Project Timeline for Product 1575	Start Date	End Date	Duration	Percent Complete
1	**Design Phase**	**6/20/00**	**8/31/00**	**50d**	**90.00%**
2	Design Project	6/20/00	7/31/00	30d	100.00
3	Prototype Design	8/3/00	8/21/00	15d	100.00
4	Test Prototype	8/24/00	8/28/00	5d	0.00
5	Prototype Complete	8/31/00	8/31/00	0d	0.00
6	**Marketing Research Phase**	**8/3/00**	**9/25/00**	**40d**	**25.00**
7	Preliminary Research	8/3/00	8/7/00	5d	100.00
8	Conduct Focus Groups	8/10/00	8/11/00	2d	100.00
9	Interviews	8/12/00	8/14/00	3d	100.00
10	Secondary Research	8/17/00	8/28/00	10d	0.00
11	Create Business Plan	8/31/00	9/25/00	20d	0.00

Figure 12.8
Gantt Chart

wedges. Remember, the segments must add up to 100 percent if percentages are used or to the total number if numbers are used.

Flowcharts and Organization Charts

If you need to show physical or conceptual relationships rather than numerical ones, you might want to use a flowchart or an organization chart. A **flowchart** illustrates a sequence of events from start to finish; it is indispensable when illustrating processes, procedures, and sequential relationships. The various elements in the process you want to portray may be represented by pictorial symbols or geometric shapes, as shown in Figure 12.10.

Use flowcharts

- To show a series of steps from beginning to end
- To show sequential relationships

An **organization chart**, as the name implies, illustrates the positions, units, or functions of an organization and the way they interrelate. An organization's normal communication channels are almost impossible to describe without the benefit of a chart like the one in Figure 12.11.

Use organization charts to depict the interrelationships among the parts of an organization.

Maps

For certain applications, maps are ideal. One of the most common uses is to show concentrations of something by geographic area. In your own reports, you might use maps to show regional differences in such variables as your company's sales of a product, or you might indicate proposed plant sites and their relationship to key markets.

Use maps

- To represent statistics by geographic area
- To show location relationships

Most U.S. office supply stores carry blank maps of various regions of the world, including all or part of the United States. You can illustrate these maps to suit your needs, using dots, shading, color, labels, numbers, and symbols. In addition, popular software such as Excel and CorelDraw! come with regional, country, and world map templates. You just insert the columns of data and assign the data to a state or a country; the software will do the rest. Figure 12.12 on page 412 was prepared using Excel's built-in map feature, the map template for the United States, and the projected state populations for 2025.

Figure 12.9
Pie Chart Combined with Table

Ten Factors Drive Overall Airline Satisfaction

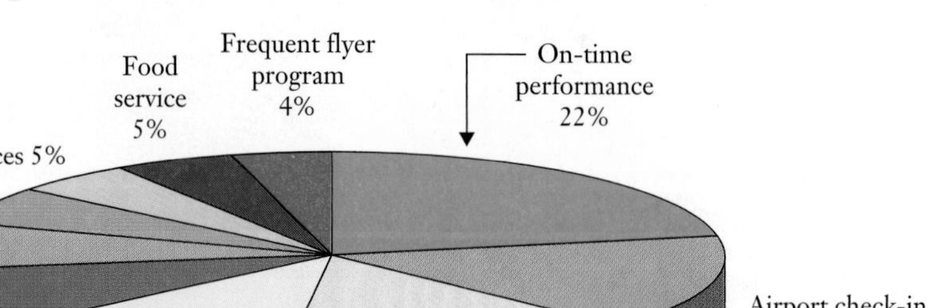

% of Contribution to Overall Satisfaction with the Flight

Which Airline Has the Best On-Time Record

On-Time Arrivals Nov 1997–Oct 1998	
Carrier	*% On Time*
Southwest	80.8
American	79.8
US Airways	79.5
Delta	78.4
TWA	76.9
Continental	76.5
United	73.7
Alaska	73.2
America West	69.3
Northwest	69.3

Drawings, Diagrams, and Photographs

Use drawings and diagrams to show

- How something looks or works
- How something is made or used

Although less commonly used than other visual aids, drawings, diagrams, and photographs can also be valuable elements in business reports and presentations. Drawings and diagrams are most often used to show how something looks or operates. Figure 12.13 was prepared using Visio software and explains the benefits of converged communication networks over traditional networks. Diagrams can be much clearer than words alone when it comes to giving your audience an idea of how an item looks or can be used. In industries such as engineering and architecture, computer-aided design (CAD) systems produce detailed diagrams and drawings. A variety of widely available software programs for microcomputers provide a file of symbols and pictures of various types that can be used (sparingly) to add a decorative touch to reports and presentations.

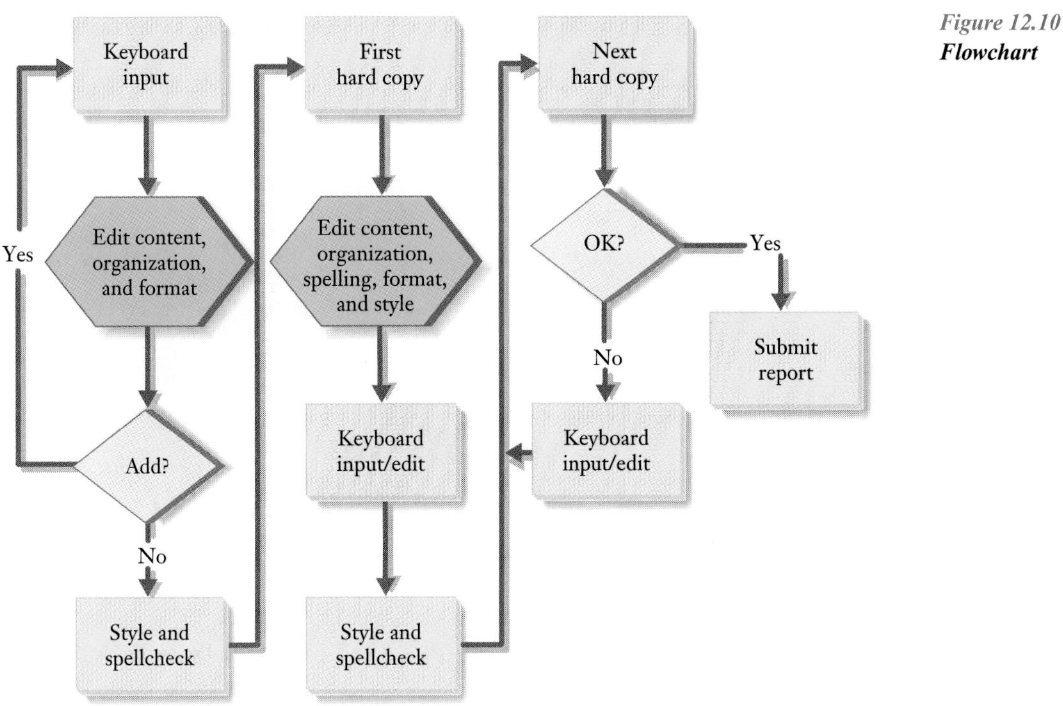

Figure 12.10
Flowchart

Administration and Faculty of Atlantic College

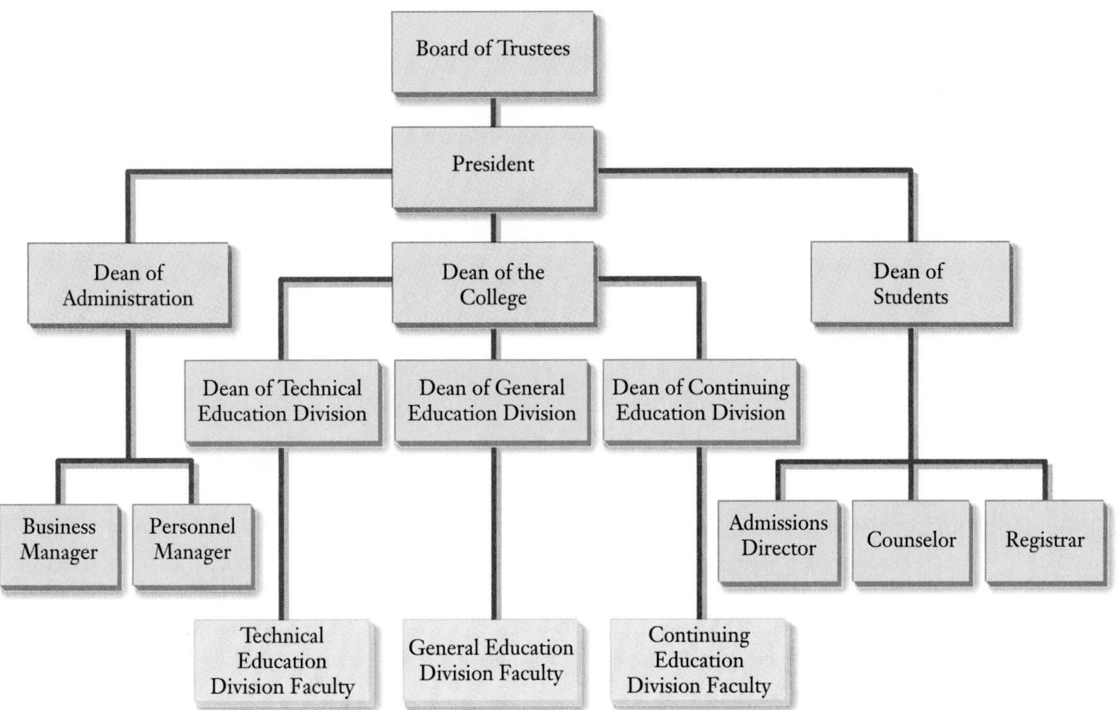

Figure 12.11
Organization Chart

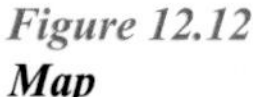

Figure 12.12
Map

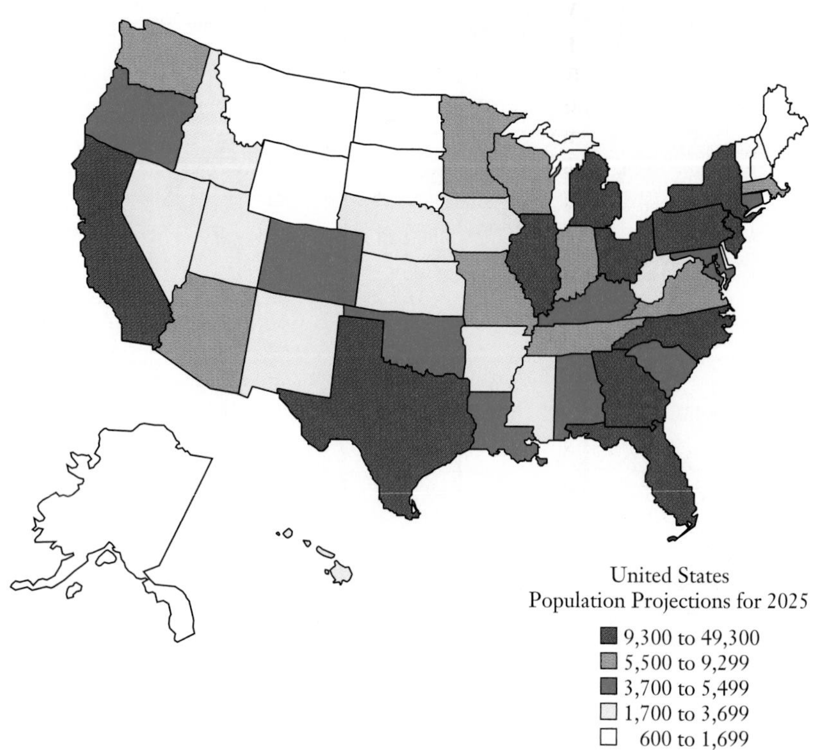

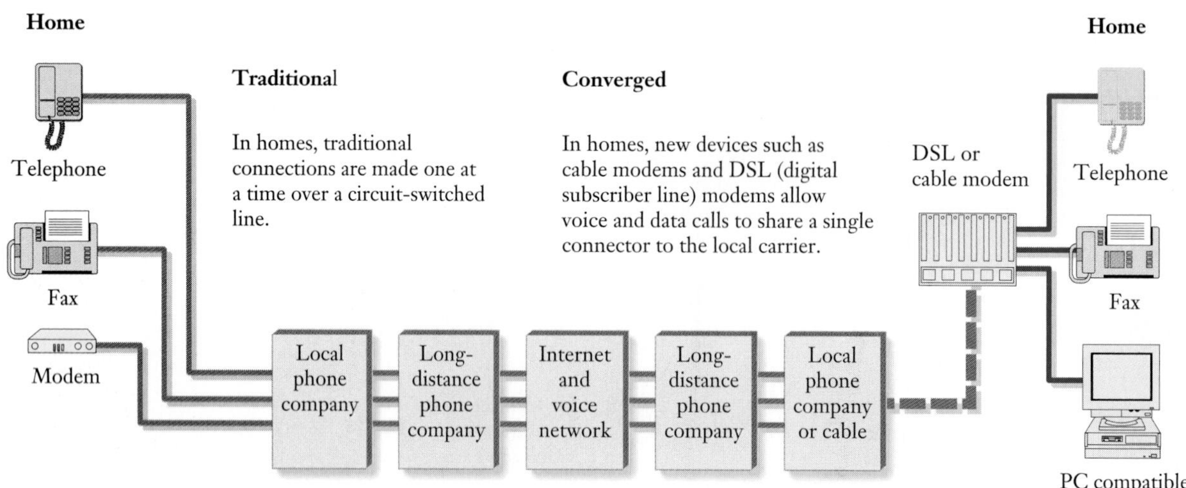

Figure 12.13
Diagram

Photographs have always been popular in certain types of business documents, such as annual reports, where their visual appeal is used to capture the interest of readers. As the technology for reproducing photographs improves and becomes less expensive, even analytical business reports for internal use are beginning to include more photographs. Digital cameras now make it easy to drop photographic images directly into a report or presentation. Furthermore, the collection of available photographs that you can import, crop, and clip grows daily. CD-ROMs provide an abundance of image libraries, and, of course, the Internet is another terrific resource for images. In most cases you can download pictures off the Internet for free; just be sure to give proper credit as you would for any material that you use from another source. To find specific photographs, images, or designs on the Internet, try the Web site AltaVista Photo Finder, http://image.altavista.com/cgi-bin/avncgi.

Use photographs
- For visual appeal
- To show exact appearance

Nothing can demonstrate the exact appearance of a new facility, a piece of property or equipment, or a new product the way a photograph can. However, in some situations a photograph may show too much detail. This is one of the reasons repair manuals, for instance, frequently use drawings instead of photos. With a drawing, you can select how much detail to show and focus the reader's attention on particular parts or places.

While technology has made it easier to use photographs in reports and presentations, it also presents an important ethical concern. Software tools such as Photoshop and CorelDraw! make it easy for computer users to make dramatic changes to photos—without leaving a clue that they've been altered. Making small changes to photos has been possible for a long time, of course (more than a few people have blemishes airbrushed out of their yearbook photos), but computers make drastic changes easy and undetectable. You can remove people from photographs, put Person A's head on Person B's body, and make products look more attractive than they really are. As you do when using other technological tools, stop and ask yourself where the truth lies before you start making changes.[4]

Designing and Producing Graphics for Reports

Professional-looking graphics used to be extremely expensive and time consuming to produce, but personal computer technology has changed all that. Graphics that used to cost hundreds of dollars and take several days to complete can now be done in minutes for little cost. Instead of relying on graphic designers, businesspeople are turning out their own professional-looking visual aids by turning to **computer graphics:** charts and graphs created and produced using a computer program.

Computer-graphics systems cut the time and cost involved in producing visual aids.

Creating Graphics with Computers

With today's powerful computers, it's faster and easier than ever to produce good-looking graphics. Software programs such as CorelDraw!, PowerPoint, Painter, Excel, Lotus 1-2-3, and Visio—to name a few—allow you to create freehand drawings, manipulate existing images, and display numbers in graphic form.

Presentation-graphics programs, drawing programs, painting programs, and spreadsheet programs can all be used to develop visual aids.

Aside from speed, accuracy, and ease of use, another big advantage of using software to prepare graphics is the ability to save the results and use the graphics over and over again in multiple reports. If you spend a lot of time working with numbers, you'll find that a spreadsheet program is particularly handy because it can serve as both an analytical tool and a communication tool. As you enter numerical data into the spreadsheet, you can use the graphics program to automatically calculate trend lines and growth curves. Later on, if you change the data or enter additional data, the program will automatically redraw the charts to reflect any changes. For example, if you track sales or profits by month, you can easily add the latest month's figures to your spreadsheet and create a new graph showing the cumulative pattern. (You'll want to save the new graph under a different file name so that you can preserve earlier graphs.)

A computer-graphics system does more than draw charts; it also enhances your analytical capabilities.

BEST OF THE WEB

Design Effective Computer Graphics

Mambo is a jump station to more than 65 Web sites containing the latest information about the imaginative world of computer graphics. The site provides links to company, university, and government labs displaying colorful portfolios; Usenet groups; and software companies. It also includes frequently asked questions (FAQs), bibliographies, conferences, and utilities.

http://mambo.ucsc.edu/psl/cg.html

For all the power and possibilities they offer, computer-graphics tools are not without some potential drawbacks. Using this equipment efficiently and effectively requires skills that many businesspeople may not possess, including the ability to use hardware and software and to make good design decisions. Many software products have become easier to use,

KEEPING PACE WITH TECHNOLOGY

CREATING COLORFUL VISUAL AIDS WITH COMPUTERS FOR MAXIMUM CLARITY AND IMPACT

More and more people are learning to use graphics software to create striking, attractive visual aids. No matter which type of software you use, your results are likely to look more professional than anything you draw by hand. Once you've designed your visual, you can also use your computer and software to plan the colors.

You know from your own experience that color can make a point more effectively than black and white. However, there's more to using color than simply picking hues that appeal to you. To choose an effective color scheme, ask yourself these questions:

- *What colors will best convey the effect I want?* As a general rule, bright, solid colors are more pleasing to the eye and easier to distinguish than pastel or patterned colors. Yellow, blue, and green are usually good choices. Just keep in mind that too many colors may overwhelm the message. Use color as an accent: bright colors for emphasis and darker or lighter colors for background information. Color can also visually connect related points or set apart points that represent significant change or differences.
- *Are these colors appropriate for my message, purpose, and audience?* Liking red is not a good reason for using it in all your graphic designs. It's too "hot" for some people and conveys the wrong message in some instances; for example, using red to show profits in an annual report might confuse readers because they're likely to associate your graphic with "red ink," or losses. Also, remember that people in other cultures will make color associations that differ from yours.
- *Is my audience familiar with these colors?* Unless your aim is to shake up your audience, avoid uncommon colors or unusual combinations. In general, conventional colors are best for conventional audiences. However, young or trendy audiences probably won't be jarred by unfamiliar colors or color combinations.
- *Can I improve the effect by changing any of the colors?* When you have the opportunity to use more than one color, choose ones that contrast. Colors without contrast blend together and obscure the message. At the same time, be sparing in your use of vivid or highly saturated colors.

Of course, your color choices may be limited or dictated in certain situations. Some organizations specify the exact color or combination to be used on company logos and other official symbols or illustrations. At other times you'll be free to decide but most continue to offer more and more options—type of graph, color and design of the background, typefaces, line weights, and so on. Most businesspeople lack the visual arts training to make informed design decisions; moreover, making all those choices takes time.

Fortunately, many graphics software programs can simplify the situation by making many of these decisions for you. Some products provide *templates* (prepared designs), clip art, and wizards (automated design generators). You simply fill in the blanks with the information you want, and the software makes all the design choices for you. (Be careful with templates, however. Even though they are designed by professional graphic artists, some are "overdesigned" and inappropriate for serious business uses, and some clutter the image with overly fancy borders and backgrounds that can distract the audience from the real message.)

Before you take advantage of any computer-graphics tools, think about the kind of image you want to project. The style of your visual aids communicates a subtle message about your relationship with the audience. A simple, hand-drawn diagram is fine for a working meeting but inappropriate for a formal presentation or report. On the other hand, elaborate, full-color visuals may be viewed as extravagant for an informal memo but may be entirely appropriate for a message to top management or influential outsiders. In other words, the image you want to project should determine your production technique (see "Keeping Pace with Technology: Creating Colorful Visual Aids with Computers for Maximum Clarity and Impact").

A visual aid's level of sophistication should match the communication situation.

on any combination of colors that works best for the visual aid you're preparing. That's when you'll find graphics software especially useful.

Depending on the capabilities of your software and your computer monitor, you can try out various colors and combinations and see the results immediately. Even the most basic program offers three colors. More sophisticated programs can give you thousands or even millions of color and shading choices.

To start, choose a template and select a background color from the program's "palette" of available colors. Then choose a dominant color to set the tone for the overall color scheme. Continue adding colors as necessary, until you find the combination that works best. Because you can test many colors and combinations with a quick click of the mouse, you can come to a final decision more quickly (and with less effort) than if you had to do it without the software.

A final factor to consider in choosing colors is how the graphics will be output. Will the graphics be printed or projected? You can print out a hard copy or an acetate transparency using a color printer or color plotter. You can also create full-color slides using a film recorder, or you can project the image from your computer screen through an overhead projector to a large viewing screen. Always prepare samples ahead of time to make sure you are getting your desired results. Colors can come out quite differently on paper than on the computer screen, for example, and what looks good on the monitor may not be effective when projected.

1. Would you use green or red to shade a visual aid showing the geographic areas where your firm does business? Would you use green or red to shade the areas where your firm does not do business? Why?
2. How can you use color in a line chart to help your audience differentiate between current and projected sales? Between expected and actual sales? Explain your answers.

Understanding the Art of Graphic Design

Although you may not think of yourself as being the "artistic type," chances are you have a better sense of design than you realize. Most people seem to subconsciously recognize good design when they see it, even if they don't know how to achieve the same effects on their own.[5]

Few of us have studied the "language" of line, mass, space, size, color, pattern, and texture. When arranged in certain ways, these elements of visual design are pleasing to the eye. More important for the business communicator, however, they have a meaning of their own. A thick line implies more power than a thin one; a bold color suggests strength; a solid mass seems substantial. To create effective visual aids, become conscious of both the aesthetic and the symbolic aspects of graphic art so that you won't send the wrong message. Here are a few principles to be aware of:

The elements of design convey meaning in subtle ways.

When designing visual aids, observe the principles of continuity, contrast, emphasis, simplicity, and experience.

DID YOU KNOW?

The use of color in visuals accelerates learning, retention, and recall by 55 percent to 78 percent, and it increases motivation and audience participation up to 80 percent.

- *Continuity.* An audience views a series of visual aids as a whole and assumes that you'll use the elements of design in a consistent way from one page to the next. You'll confuse people if you make arbitrary changes in color, shape, size, texture, position, scale, or typeface. If, for instance, your first chart shows results for division A in blue, the audience will expect division A to be shown in blue throughout the report or presentation.
- *Contrast.* The audience also expects that visual distinctions will match verbal distinctions. If you're contrasting A and B, depict them in a visually contrasting manner: red versus blue, black versus white. On the other hand, if you want to indicate similarities between two items, make the visual distinction between them more subtle. You might have a pie chart in which two similar items are shown in two shades of blue and a dissimilar item is shown in yellow. When using similar colors, consider using shaded colors (also called *graduated* or *variant*) to allow one color to dissolve into the next, giving it an airbrush effect in addition to dimension or depth. Keep in mind that accent colors are an effective way to draw attention to key elements. Just don't overdo them or they lose their effect.
- *Emphasis.* An audience assumes that the most important point will receive the most visual emphasis. Therefore, present the key item on the chart in the most prominent way—through color, position, size, or whatever. Visually downplay less important items. Avoid using strong colors for unimportant data, and de-emphasize background features such as the grid lines on a chart.
- *Simplicity.* Limit the number of colors and designs, and take care to avoid *chartjunk,* a term coined by information expert Edward Tufte to describe decorative elements that clutter documents (and confuse readers) without adding any relevant information.[6] Computers make it far too easy to add chartjunk, from clip art illustrations to three-dimensional bar charts that display only two dimensions of data (see Figure 12.14).
- *Experience.* Culture, education, and other experiences condition people to expect things to look certain ways, and these expectations can affect the way people respond to your visuals. Green is easily associated with money in the United States but not in countries that print currency in red, blue, yellow, and other colors. A red cross on a white background, the logo of the International Red Cross, symbolizes emergency medical care in many countries. However, because the cross is also a Christian symbol, the International Red Cross uses a red crescent in Islamic countries.[7]

Of course, the best time to think about the principles of good design is before preparing your visual aids; making changes after the fact increases the amount of time required to produce them.

These two charts show the same information, but the second one is cluttered with useless decoration. The three-dimensional bars don't show anything more than the simple two-dimensional bars in the first chart.

Figure 12.14
Simplify Graphics to Avoid Clutter and Confusion

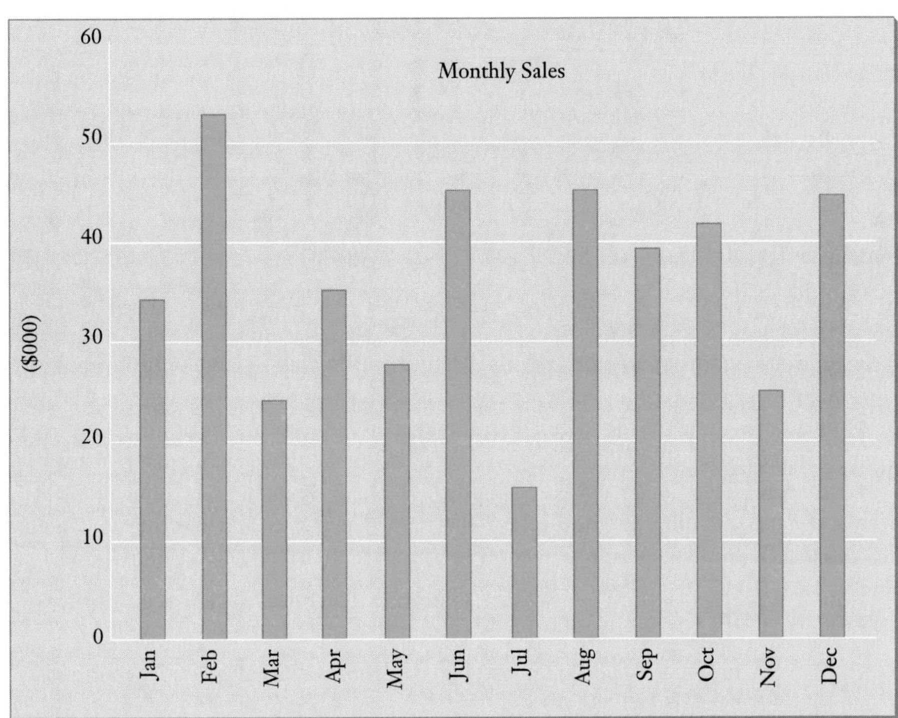

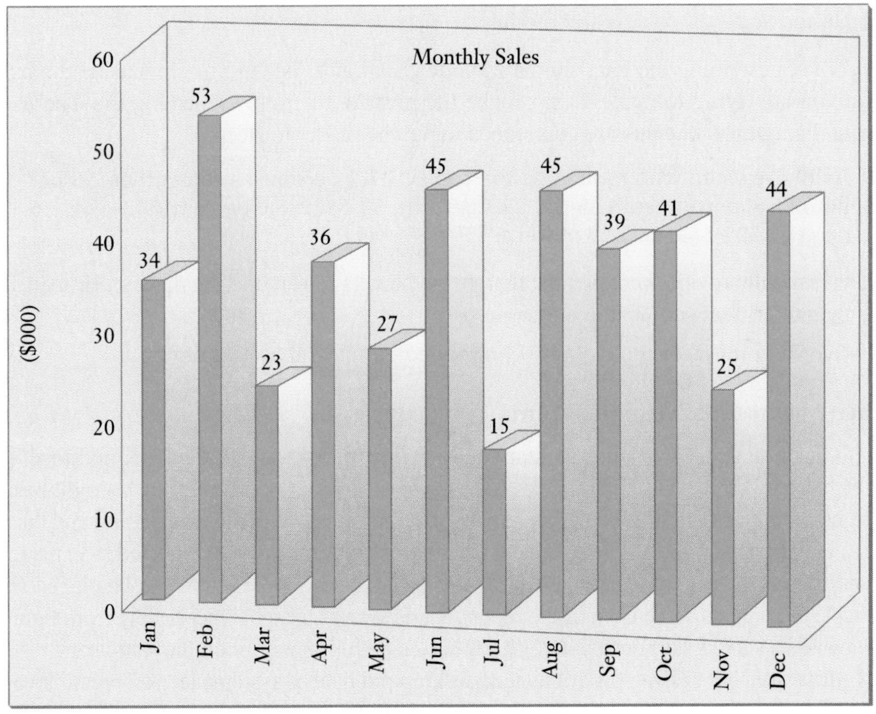

Fitting Graphics into the Text

Once you've produced your visual aids, you face the problem of displaying them in an appropriate way. Fit your visuals into your text in a manner that is convenient for your audience and practical from a production standpoint.

To some extent, your approach to integrating text and visuals depends on the type of report you're preparing. If you're working on a glossy public relations document, you'll handle the visual aids as though they were illustrations in a magazine, positioning them to attract interest and tell a story of their own. However, in most business documents, where the visual aids clarify the text, you'll tie them closely to the discussion.

Introduce Illustrations in the Text

To tie visual aids to the text
- Introduce them in the text
- Place them near the points they illustrate
- Choose a meaningful title and legend for each one

Every illustration you use should be clearly referred to by number in the text of your report. Some report writers refer to all visual aids as exhibits and number them consecutively throughout the report; many others number tables and figures separately (everything that isn't a table is regarded as a figure). In a very long report with numbered chapters (as in this book), illustrations may have a double number (separated by a period or a hyphen) representing the chapter number and the individual illustration number within that chapter.

In-text references tell readers why the illustration is important.

Help your readers understand the significance of any visual aids by referring to them before they appear in the text. The reference helps readers understand why the table or chart is important. The following examples show how you can make this connection in the text:

> Figure 1 summarizes the financial history of the motorcycle division over the past five years, with sales broken into four categories.
>
> Total sales were steady over this period, but the mix of sales by category changed dramatically (see Figure 2).
>
> The underlying reason for the remarkable growth in our sales of low-end motorcycles is suggested by Table 4, which provides data on motorcycle sales in the United States by region and model.

When describing the data shown in your visual aids, be sure to emphasize the main point you are trying to make. Don't make the mistake of simply repeating the data to be shown. Paragraphs like this are guaranteed to put the reader to sleep:

> Among women who replied to the survey, 17.4 percent earn less than $5 per hour; 26.4 percent earn $5–$7; 25.7 percent, $8–$12; 18.0 percent, $13–$24; 9.6 percent, $25–$49; and 2.9 percent, $50 and over.

The visual will provide these details; there is no need to repeat them in the text. Instead, use round numbers that sum up the message:

> Over two-thirds of the women who replied earn less than $12 per hour.

Place Visual Aids Near the Points They Illustrate

Put a visual aid as close as possible to its in-text reference to help readers understand the illustration's relevance.

Try to position your visual aids so that your audience won't have to flip back and forth too much between the visuals and the text. Ideally, it is best to place each visual aid right beside or right after the paragraph it illustrates so that readers can consult the explanation and the visual aid at the same time. Make sure each visual is clearly and correctly referred to in the text. If you have four or more visual aids, prepare a separate list of them that can be placed with the table of contents at the front of the report. Some writers list tables separately from figures. The two lists should start on separate pages unless both lists will fit on the same page.

Most word-processing programs and desktop publishing systems let you create layouts with artwork and text on the same page. If you don't have these programs, or choose not to integrate your visuals with text, then put the visual aids on separate pages and include them with the text after the report has been prepared. Of course, having visual aids on separate pages raises the question of where to put them. Some writers prefer to cluster them at the end of the report, either as a separate section or as an appendix. Others group them at the end of each chapter. Still others prefer to place them as close as possible to the paragraphs they illustrate. Although a case can be made for each approach, the best one is generally to place the page with a visual aid right after the page referring to it. This arrangement encourages readers to look at the visual aids when you want them to, in the context you have prepared.

Choose Titles and Legends with a Message

Titles and legends should
- Reinforce the point you want to make
- Be specific

One of the best ways to tie your visual aids to the text is to choose titles (or captions) and descriptions (or legends) that reinforce the point you want to make. This precaution is especially necessary when the visual aids are widely separated from the text.

The title of a visual aid, when combined with labels and legends on the piece itself, should be complete enough to tell the reader what the content is. The title "Petroleum Tanks in the United States" is sufficient if it's the title of a line chart labeled "Year" along the horizontal axis and "Number (in thousands)" along the vertical axis. However, if the visual aid is a map overlaid with dots of different sizes, the title needs to explain a bit more: "Concentrations of Petroleum Tanks in the United States in 1999." A legend might then explain how many petroleum tanks each size of dot represents.

When you place a visual aid next to the text discussion that pertains to it, clear labeling and a good title are usually enough; the text can explain the visual aid's significance and details. However, when you place a visual aid elsewhere or when the illustration requires considerable explanation that would disrupt the flow of the text, you may need to add a description (or legend). Legends are generally written as one or more complete sentences, and they do more than merely repeat what's already clear from the title and figure labels. It's better to be too specific than too general when you're identifying the content of an illustration. As a check, ask yourself whether you've covered the who, what, when, where, why, and how of the illustration.

If you're using informative headings in your report, carry this style over into the titles and legends. In other words, instead of using a **descriptive title**, which identifies the topic of the illustration, call attention to the conclusion that ought to be drawn from the data by using an **informative title**. Here's the difference:

DESCRIPTIVE TITLE	INFORMATIVE TITLE
Relationship between Petroleum Demand and Refinery Capacity in the United States	Shrinking Refinery Capacity Results from Stagnant Petroleum Demand

Regardless of whether your titles and legends are informative or descriptive, phrase them consistently throughout the report. At the same time, be consistent in your format. If the title of the first visual aid is typed entirely in capital letters, type all the remaining titles that way as well. Although an employer may specify the placement of titles, as a general rule place all table titles at the top. Figure titles may be placed at the top or the bottom. When using legends, make them all roughly the same length. (For a review of the important points to remember when creating visual aids, see this chapter's Checklist for Creating Effective Visual Aids.)

Checking Over the Visual Aids

Before you give your visual aids a final stamp of approval, take a few extra minutes to review them. Ask yourself: Is it necessary? Is it accurate? Is proper credit given? Is it honest?

CHECKLIST FOR CREATING EFFECTIVE VISUAL AIDS

A. Preparation
  1. Proper types of graphics are selected for the data and for the objective of the message.
  2. Visual aids contribute to overall understanding of the subject.
  3. Visuals depict data accurately.
  4. Visuals portray information honestly.
  5. Proper credit is given, if required, and citations follow proper bibliographic form.
  6. Material is appropriate for intended audience.

B. Design
  1. Design elements are consistent and meet audience expectations.
  2. Color is used effectively.
  3. Important points are emphasized.
  4. Visuals are simple and easy to understand.
  5. Headings, labels, titles, and legends are clear and descriptive or informative.
  6. Space is used appropriately.
  7. Data units are clearly identified and understandable.
  8. Typeface and font are clear and readable.
  9. Clip art is used sparingly.

C. Layout
  1. Reasonable balance exists between words and visuals.
  2. Illustrations are clearly referenced in text and are assigned a number or letter.
  3. Visuals are placed close to the points they illustrate.
  4. Visuals appear balanced on the page.
  5. Captions are short, precise, and informative.

Is It Necessary?

Avoid cluttering a report with too many visual aids.

A few well-placed visual aids can clarify and dramatize your message, but an avalanche of illustrations may bury it. So avoid the temptation to overload your reports with unnecessary tables, graphs, and charts. Remember that your audience is busy. Don't give people information they don't need simply because you want to impress them or because you've fallen in love with the computer-graphics system.

Is It Accurate?

Proofread visual aids for errors in data and for consistency with the text.

Before you release the final product, make sure that every number is correct, that every line is plotted accurately, that every scale is drawn to reflect reality, and that every bit of information is consistent with the text.

If you rely on others to prepare the visual aids, you may be tempted to let them catch all the errors. Resist the temptation. Even the most conscientious staff members will miss a few mistakes, particularly because they may lack the information necessary to spot a data point that doesn't make sense. When you're proofreading, also be sure to check the source notes and the content notes for accuracy.

Is Proper Credit Given?

Cite the source of any data you use to create the visual aid.

You may be the creator of the actual graphic design, but if you use someone else's data, you need to give credit by citing the source of any data you use in creating a visual. Identify the actual source of data, such as the name of the journal the information came from, or refer simply to the nature of the information (for example, "interviews with 50 soybean farmers"). If the data are "primary" (meaning you gathered the data for your own purposes), say so. Source notes for illustrations should appear right below the visual material (as shown in Figure 12.1). To avoid cluttering your graphic, you could use a shortened citation on the graphic itself and include a complete citation elsewhere in the report.

Is It Honest?

Accuracy and honesty are two distinct qualities. You can have all the numbers right and still give your audience a false impression by presenting those numbers in a distorted way. Graphs and charts, in particular, tend to oversimplify some numerical relationships, and deliberately leaving out important data points that don't fit your needs is highly unethical.

To prevent your graphs and charts from creating a false impression, be sure to
- Include all key data points
- Mention any important outside influence on the data
- Maintain a consistent scale of measurement

Another possible source of distortion is omitting an outside influence on the data being portrayed. Suppose you develop a bar or line chart that shows big improvements in your company's profits. Your audience might attribute this gain to lasting changes in the way the company does business, even though the source of the improvement might actually be a one-time change in accounting methods. If events not shown on the graph or chart are actually responsible for creating the results, let your audience know. A footnote is helpful, but the best solution is to revise the visual aid to create a more realistic picture of events.

The choice of scale on a graph or chart also introduces the possibility of distortion. As Figure 12.15 illustrates, you can transform modest results into dramatic ones by compressing the horizontal scale or by expanding the vertical scale, but you abandon good business ethics and mislead your audience in the process. So be sure that the visual impression you create is an honest representation of the facts. Choose a scale that conveys a realistic picture of what's happening. Likewise, maintain the same scale in successive charts comparing the same factors (see "Focusing on Ethics: Visual Aids That Lie: The Use and Abuse of Charts and Graphs").

When you are the audience interpreting the data presented in a visual format, remember to consider the possibilities for distortion. Ask yourself whether any important data might have been omitted. Look closely at the scale. Don't let a pretty curve fool you. Bear in mind that visual images tend to oversimplify reality.

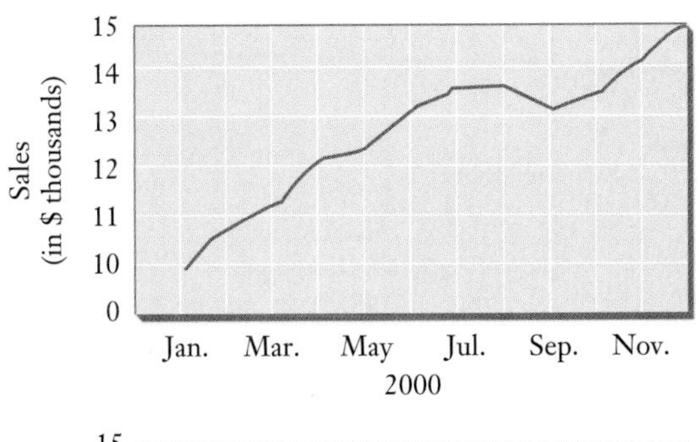

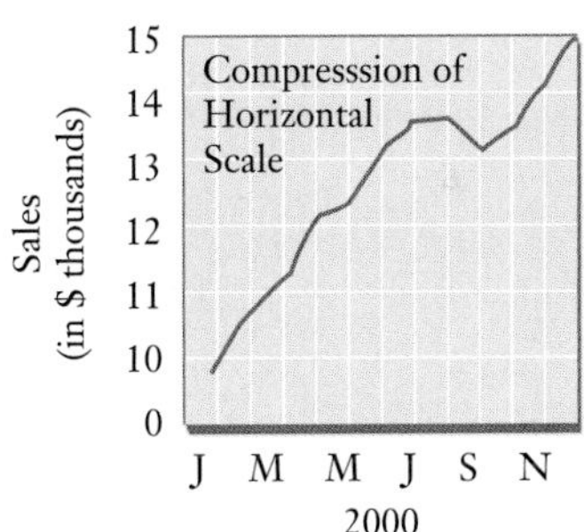

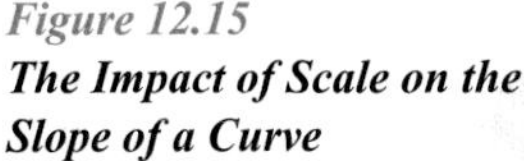
Figure 12.15
The Impact of Scale on the Slope of a Curve

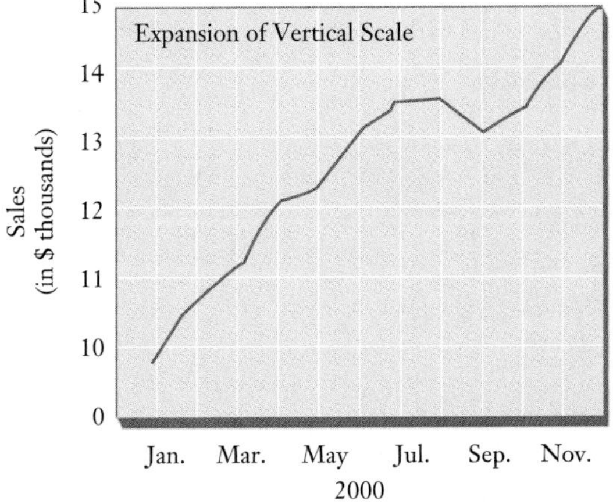

FOCUSING ON ETHICS

VISUAL AIDS THAT LIE: THE USE AND ABUSE OF CHARTS AND GRAPHS

The ease with which computers help people create visual displays of numerical information raises some important ethical issues. Here's a quick example of how easy it is to obscure information or otherwise mislead an audience (the data are all fictional in this example). The line graph in Chart A shows the number of insecticide poisionings by age from 0 to 20. Chart B shows the same data, with one crucial difference: The vertical axis is scaled to fit the data. By expanding the axis way beyond the data, Chart A can create the impression that accident levels are far below the "maximum."

Chart C demonstrates another way graphs can "lie." By showing incidence levels for just four ages, the chart hides the facts that 4- and 5-year-olds suffered the most poisonings and that more 3-, 4-, and 5-year-olds died from poisioning than victims in any other age group. Six-year-olds appear to be the age hardest hit, but they aren't.

When it comes to presenting information, a good way to make ethical decisions is to ask what the audience needs to know in order to make an informed choice. If the audience needs the information, you need to show it.

1. How might your choice of a base unit affect your reader's perception of progress when viewing a Gantt chart?
2. Can you construct a pie chart from data that have been rounded up to equal more than 100 percent? Explain.

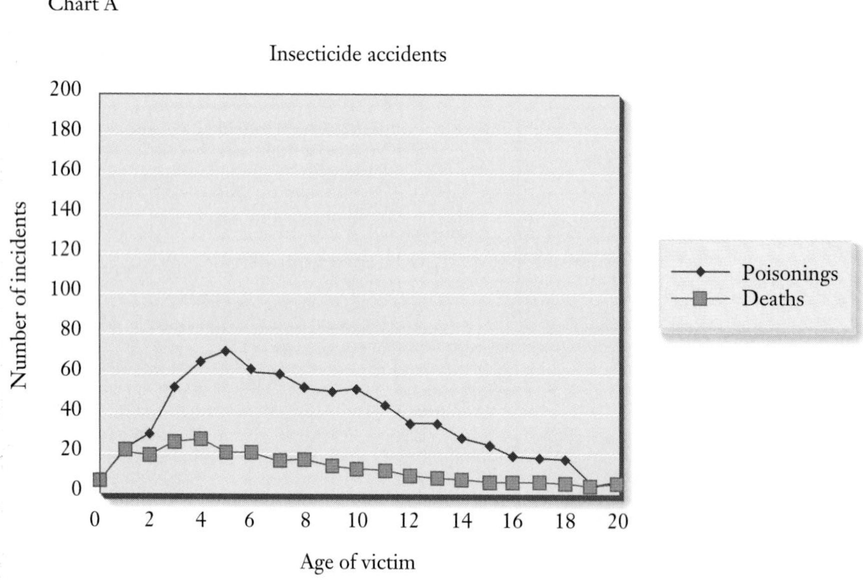

DESIGNING AND PRODUCING VISUALS FOR ORAL PRESENTATIONS

Just as with reports, you can help your audience get the picture by using visuals in oral presentations. When used effectively, visuals create interest and clarify important points. More important, however, visual aids dramatically increase the audience's ability to absorb and remember information. Keep in mind that audiences remember only 10 percent of a

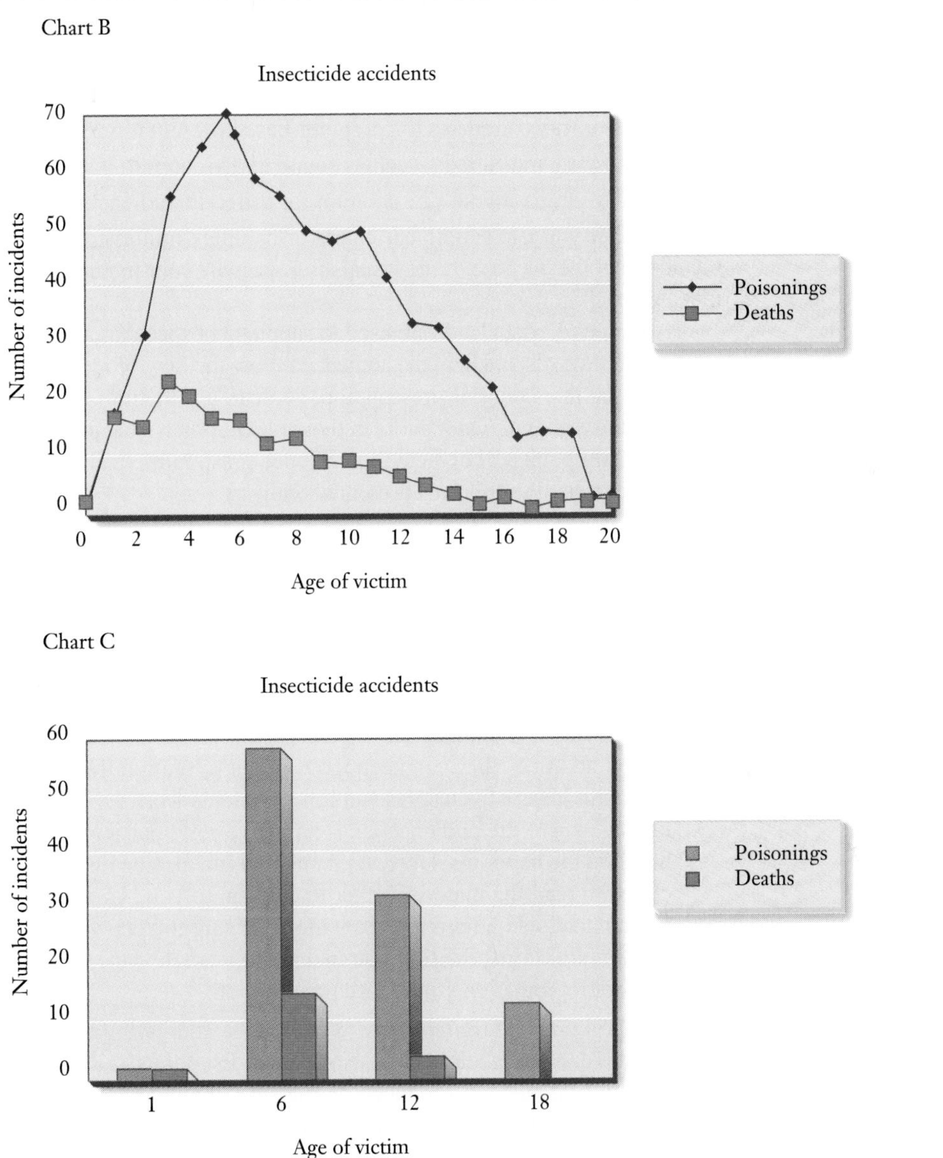

speaker's message when it's presented solely through words, but they remember 50 percent when the information is supported with visual aids such as slides and overhead transparencies.[8]

From a purely practical standpoint, visuals are a convenience for the speaker. They are an effective tool for remembering the details of the message (no small feat in a lengthy presentation). In addition, speakers who use presentation visuals often appear better prepared and more professional than speakers who do not use visuals.

Visual aids help both the speaker and the audience remember the important points.

Of course, creating lively visual materials for oral presentations is not as hard as it used to be, thanks to popular computer software such as Microsoft's PowerPoint, Lotus's Freelance Graphics, Harvard Graphics, and CorelDraw! These products make it easy for you to

- Organize visuals in a logical manner and provide continuity throughout
- Repeat graphical elements on every visual, such as a border, a company logo, or a background
- Select appropriate formats for your presentation, ranging from paper handouts to slides or transparencies to computer-based presentations
- Incorporate multimedia such as sound and video into your presentation
- Modify or adapt your presentation for different audiences

Whether you use simple bar charts or complex multimedia in oral presentations, remember that the purpose of the visuals is to *support* your message—they should not be the message itself.

Two kinds of visual aids:
- Text visuals help listeners follow the flow of ideas.
- Graphic visuals present and emphasize important facts.

Two types of visual aids are used to supplement speeches and presentations. Text visuals consist of words and help the audience follow the flow of ideas. Because text visuals are simplified outlines of your presentation, you can use them to summarize and preview the message and to signal major shifts in thought. Graphic visual aids, on the other hand, illustrate the main points. They help the audience grasp numerical data and other information that would be hard to follow if presented orally.

Types of Presentation Visuals

In preparing visual aids for oral presentations, you have a variety of media to choose from.

Visual aids for documents are usually limited to paper. For speeches and presentations, however, you have a variety of media to choose from:

- *Handouts.* Printed handouts are used to distribute an agenda, an outline of the program, an abstract, a written report, or supplementary materials such as tables, charts, and graphs to your audience. Listeners can refer to the handout while you are speaking. In addition, they can keep the handout to remind them afterward of the subject and main ideas of your presentation. Handouts work especially well in informal situations where the audience takes an active role; participants often make their own notes on the handouts. However, handouts can also be distracting; people may be inclined to read the material rather than listen to you. As a result, many speakers distribute handouts after the presentation. Be sure to keep your handouts simple. Limit the amount of information you include to a single page, and summarize key points without reproducing your entire presentation.
- *Chalkboards and whiteboards.* When you're addressing a small group of people and want to draw out their ideas, use a board to list points as they are mentioned. Because these visual aids are produced on the spot, the boards provide flexibility. However, they're too informal for some situations.
- *Flip charts.* Large sheets of paper attached at the top like a tablet can be propped on an easel so that you can flip the pages as you speak, with each chart illustrating or clarifying a point. You might have a few lines from your outline on one, a graph or diagram on another, and so on. By using felt-tip markers of various colors, you can also record ideas generated during a discussion. Remember, keep it simple: Try to limit each flip-chart page to three or four graphed lines or to five or six points in list format.
- *Overheads.* One of the most common visual aids in business is the overhead transparency, which can be projected on a screen in full daylight. Because you don't have to dim the lights, you don't lose eye contact with your audience. Transparencies are easy to make using a typed original on regular paper, a copying machine, and a page-

size sheet of plastic. Special markers can be used to write on transparencies. In that respect, they're similar to whiteboards and flip charts, but they have the added advantage of enabling you to face the audience. Opaque projections are similar to transparencies but do not require as much preparation. You could use an opaque projector to show the audience a photograph or an excerpt from a report or manual.

- *Slides.* The content of 35-millimeter slides may be text, graphics, or pictures. If you're trying to create a polished, professional atmosphere, you might find this approach worthwhile, particularly if you'll be addressing a crowd and don't mind speaking in a darkened room. Remember, however, that you may need someone to operate the projector and that you'll need to coordinate the slides with your speech. Take a few minutes before your speech to verify that the equipment works correctly and that your slides are positioned correctly in the tray.
- *Electronic presentations.* With special projection equipment, a personal computer can be turned into a large-screen "intelligent chalkboard" that allows you to create and modify your visual aids as the presentation unfolds. For live presentations, an increasing number of businesses now use LCD (liquid crystal display) projectors or display panels. These products grab the images from your computer screen and display them on the same projection screens used for viewing slides. This approach has the advantage of including real-time manipulation of numbers, animation, video clips, and even sound. By using presentation software you can prepare a multimedia show that captures and involves your audience, replacing flip charts, cumbersome overheads, and chalkboards. Most presentation software packages today allow you to incorporate photos, sound, video, and animation into your multimedia presentations.[9]
- *Other visual aids.* In technical or scientific presentations, a sample of a product or material allows the audience to experience your subject directly. Models built to scale are convenient representations of an object. Audiotapes are often used to supplement a slide show or to present a precisely worded and timed message. Filmstrips and movies can capture the audience's attention with color and movement. Television and videotapes are good for showing demonstrations, interviews, and other events. In addition, filmstrips, movies, television, and videotapes can be used as stand-alone vehicles (independent of a speaker) to communicate with dispersed audiences at various times.

As with all visual aids, the crucial factor is how you use them. Properly integrated into an oral presentation, they can save time, create interest, add variety, make an impression, and illustrate points that are difficult to explain in words alone.

Use visual aids to highlight your spoken words, not as a substitute for them.

How to Build an Electronic Presentation

Whether you use Microsoft PowerPoint, Lotus Freelance Graphics, CorelDraw!, or another popular presentation program, creating an **electronic presentation**—a series of computerized slides—can be an effective way to deliver your message orally. Think of an electronic slide as a single page of information. When you build an electronic presentation, you design each slide to cover one point or one graph, much as you would when designing overhead transparencies. In Chapter 16 we'll discuss how to write and deliver oral presentations. For now, we'll focus on the actual mechanics of preparing the visuals or slides for the presentation.

You begin designing your slides by selecting a template or by preparing a custom design for your master slide. You'll use this master slide as the background for your entire presentation. Each time you call up a new slide to add text or graphs, a copy of this master slide will appear. The big advantage is that you can easily program the master slide for the font and color you'll use throughout your presentation as well as for items you want to appear on

The master slide stores design elements that will appear on all presentation slides, ensuring uniformity and consistency.

Figure 12.16
Electronic Slide Presentation for Piece of Cake Bakery Café

all the slides, such as a title or a company logo. Thus, having a master slide ensures that your slides are uniform and easy to follow.

Most presentation software packages allow you to select from a variety of slide layouts, such as graphic slides, bullet slides, title slides, combination slides, and so on. By selecting a preformatted slide, you simply add the words or graphics and the software conveniently places them on the slide using the predetermined layout—another effective way to control the uniformity of your presentation.

Once you've constructed all the slides to be included in your presentation you organize them in a proper sequence so that your material flows in a logical order. Here again, the software makes it easy by allowing you to move slides around; you simply view all the slides in what is commonly known as *slide sorter view* and drag any slide to a different position in the presentation. (Figure 12.16 is a Microsoft PowerPoint presentation in slide sorter view.) Next, you're ready to add some automation. In a simple show, you'll use transitions—special effects such as fading in or fading out—between slides (other transitions include checkerboard motion, dissolving, wiping, or uncovering from different directions). These special effects make your presentation flow smoothly from slide to slide and keep the audience's attention.

Use transitions between slides to give your electronic presentation a more professional look.

Use the "build" feature to help your audience focus on one bullet point at a time.

In addition to transitions between slides, you can select special features called "builds" for your bullet points. Rather than have all your bullet points appear on a slide at once (making it difficult to focus on a single point), you can use builds to make your bullet points appear one at a time, as if they were marching across the screen. You can even use special effects to have one bullet point disappear as another appears, or you can produce a similar effect by altering the intensity of the text's color for one bullet as you discuss it while fading the text of the others into the background.

Finally, you can get fancy by adding sound effects, morphed graphics, video, and so on. You can even automate your program to move from one slide to the next without speaker intervention. Automation is especially useful for running the presentation on television monitors in large places such as conventions and trade shows, where the slide show, in effect, is the only information presented.

Another useful feature of presentation software is the ability to link your slide presentation to other files on your computer. Hypertext markup language and integrated software packages such as Microsoft Office allow you to jump between files and software programs—even Web pages—to illustrate fine details without having to incorporate each detail into a slide. So if you're discussing a Web site, for example, you can click on a link you placed on the slide (while designing it) and go directly to that Web site, making that site, in effect, a part of your presentation. This feature is especially useful if a member of the audience poses a question that could best be answered by displaying a spreadsheet, diagram, or graph stored on your computer. Of course, you'll have to anticipate your audience's questions so that you can prepare these additional slides in advance.

DID YOU KNOW?

The average person can hold only about seven ideas (or "chunks" of meaningful information) in his or her working memory.

Once you've built your slide show, you can use additional presentation software features to create handouts, speaker's notes, outlines, and so on. As shown in Figure 12.17, audience handouts can be actual copies of the slides with plenty of white space for note taking, or they can be scaled-down copies of the slides, fitting several slides on a page. Speaker's notes are a helpful tool to use when delivering your presentation. You can input notes such as "Don't forget to explain the impact of last year's bad weather on sales" and coordinate these notes with a thumbnail sketch of the slide you'll show while delivering that message.

Other useful features of electronic presentation software:

- Handouts
- Speaker's notes
- Outlines

Figure 12.17
Presentation Handouts

By now you can see that the possibilities are plentiful when it comes to using presentation software. Still, having too many visuals that are too complicated or too flashy can detract from your message. Furthermore, if your message is too complex or poorly written, you'll lose the audience's interest no matter how glitzy your presentation looks. Keep in mind that technology has made snazzy special effects so accessible that many speakers rely on them too much, and audiences are increasingly underwhelmed by them.

Tips for Designing Effective Presentation Visuals

Visual aids are most effective when they are simple.

Whether you're using electronic slides, overheads, a flip chart, or a chalkboard, simplicity is the key to effectiveness when designing visual aids. Because people can't read and listen at the same time, your presentation visuals should be simple enough for the audience to understand them within a moment or two. In other words, don't let the visuals steal the show. A simple flip chart, a series of slides, a videotaped demonstration, or even some words scrawled on paper and projected on a screen can help you make your points.

As a rule, text visuals are most effective when they consist of no more than six lines, with a maximum of six words on each line. Produce them in large, clear type, using uppercase and lowercase letters, with extra white space between lines of text. Make sure the type is large enough to be seen from any place in the room. Avoid using script or decorative fonts that are hard to read from a distance, and limit the number of fonts you use. Phrase list items in parallel grammatical form. Use telegraphic wording ("Profits Soar," for example) without being cryptic ("Profits"); you are often better off including both a noun and a verb in each line item.

Many speeches and presentations begin with several text visuals. The first is usually the equivalent of a title page: It announces the subject and signals the audience that the presentation is under way. The second typically lists the three or four major points you'll cover, providing a road map of what's to come. The remaining text visuals are used to cover the key points of your presentation.

You can use any of the graphic visuals you might include in a formal report, such as charts, diagrams, maps, drawings, and tables. However, graphic visuals used in oral presentations should be simplified versions of those that appear in written documents. Eliminate anything that is not absolutely essential to the message. Too much graphic detail is difficult to read on a screen. To help the audience focus immediately on the point of each graphic visual, use headings that state the message in one clear phrase or sentence: "Earnings have increased by 15 percent."

Visual aids are counterproductive if the audience can't clearly see or understand them within a few moments.

When you present visual aids, you want people to read what's there while they are listening to your explanation. To accomplish that goal:

- Be sure that all members of the audience can see the visual aids.
- Check the equipment in advance to make sure it's in good working order.
- Have a backup plan in case the technology fails.
- Allow the audience time to read a visual aid before you begin your explanation.
- Limit each visual aid to one idea.
- Illustrate the main points, not the entire presentation.
- Use borders, pointers, and boxes to highlight important information.
- Use clip art sparingly to add color and excitement to your presentation.
- Avoid visual aids that conflict with your verbal message.
- Don't put the visual up until you're ready to talk about it. When you've finished discussing the point illustrated by the visual aid, remove it from the audience's view.[10]

Remember, you want the audience to listen to you, not study the visual aids. The visual aids are there to supplement your words—not the other way around. Visual aids are an excellent way to remind your audience of main points and to keep your presentation on track. But unless you keep control, visuals have a potential to distract your listeners from you as the primary source of information and authority. Furthermore, the more sophisticated the visuals, the stronger you must be, to keep them from upstaging you.[11]

COMMUNICATION CHALLENGES AT BLACK ENTERTAINMENT TELEVISION

Jazz music is known around the world as a truly original American art form. Noticing a programming opportunity, BET Holdings developed a unique cable network called BET on Jazz. The network offers a wide range of jazz-related programming, including videos, documentaries, and talk shows. Recently, a major cable television service provider in the western United States approached BET about including BET on Jazz in its network offerings. Curtis Symonds has asked you to take the lead in developing an informative sales presentation to be delivered to cable company executives. The financial details will be worked out later. For now, Symonds wants you to focus on presenting the following information:

- The types of programs offered on BET on Jazz
- The most popular shows and peak viewing times for BET on Jazz in various cable markets throughout the United States
- The types of sponsors who advertise on BET on Jazz in local markets
- The annual growth of jazz music sales on the West Coast over the past 20 years
- The total estimated number of West Coast viewers for BET on Jazz
- The growth in popularity of music programming on cable television in the United States over the past 20 years

INDIVIDUAL CHALLENGE: Develop a plan for your presentation. What is your goal? What type of presentation do you think the cable company executives will expect? Will you use simple media—such as transparencies—or will you use a high-tech multimedia format? What types of visual aids will be most effective for each of the different types of information you want to present, and why? How will you check your visuals for content, accuracy, and relevancy?

TEAM CHALLENGE: Discuss your presentation ideas with several of your classmates. Working together as a team, develop a plan for a presentation that incorporates the best ideas from each of the group members. Think about where all the pieces of information should be placed so that the presentation has maximum impact on the audience. Develop a storyboard to outline the presentation, depicting the various types of visual aids you plan to use.[12] ■

SUMMARY OF LEARNING OBJECTIVES

1. **Cite the advantages of preparing visual aids before preparing text.** First, by using data already existing in tabular or graphic form, you can plan what you are going to say. Second, by starting with visual aids, you can develop a story line for both written and oral presentations. Finally, it's easier to refer to your visuals and to explain them effectively in your text if you've already prepared them.
2. **Explain why business professionals use graphs and other visual aids.** Visual aids make reports and presentations more interesting. In addition, they facilitate the communication and interpretation of numbers, trends, distributions, and percentages. Furthermore, they help people understand and remember a message. And finally, they help you draw attention to important points.
3. **List several popular types of graphics and discuss when to use them.** Tables communicate facts and detail in an easy-to-read format. Line charts illustrate trends over time or plot the relationships of two or more variables. Surface charts illustrate the cumulative effect of trends. Bar charts and pictograms portray numbers by the height or length of their rectangular bars and facilitate comparisons of size in addition to showing changes over time. Gantt charts track progress toward completing a project. Pie charts show percentages or how the parts of a whole are distributed. Flowcharts illustrate a sequence of events. Organization charts illustrate positions and functions in an organization. Maps show concentrations by geographic area. Drawings or diagrams show how something looks or operates.
4. **Discuss five principles of graphic design to keep in mind when preparing visual aids.** When preparing visual aids you

should (1) use elements of design consistently so you don't confuse your audience; (2) use color effectively to show contrasting or similar information; (3) use design elements to draw attention to key elements and to visually downplay less important items; (4) avoid clutter; and (5) try to match design selections with audience expectations, such as green for U.S. currency.

5. **Name four qualities to look for before including a visual aid in a report or presentation.** Before finalizing a visual aid, ask yourself these four questions: (1) Is it necessary? In other words, does it help explain the material? (2) Is it accurate? (3) Does it give proper credit by citing the source of any data used to create the visual? (4) Is it honest? In other words, does it portray the data without distorting it or giving false impressions?
6. **List several popular types of presentation visuals.** Popular presentation visuals include handouts, chalkboards, whiteboards, flip charts, overheads or transparencies, 35-mm slides, electronic presentations, models, audiotapes, and movies or videotapes.

CRITICAL THINKING QUESTIONS

1. What similarities do you see between visual aids and nonverbal communication? Explain your answer.
2. You're writing a report to the director of human resources on implementing participative management throughout your company. You want to emphasize that since the new approaches were implemented six months ago, absenteeism and turnovers have been sharply reduced in all but two departments. How do you visually present your data in the most favorable light? Explain.
3. Besides telling readers why an illustration is important, why refer to it in the text of your document?
4. When you can't use color in a printed document, what can you do to visually accentuate your major point in a line chart? In a bar chart? In a pie chart? In a table? Explain your answers.
5. When you read a graph, how can you be sure that the visual impression you are receiving is an accurate reflection of reality? Please explain.
6. How might companies use a Web site to supplement or even replace some live presentations?
7. How can you tell whether you've selected the right graphic for the job?
8. What are some of the advantages and disadvantages of distributing handouts before a presentation, and what can you do to minimize the disadvantages?

DOCUMENTS FOR ANALYSIS

Document 12.A

Examine the pie charts in Figure 12.18 and point out any problems or errors you notice.

Figure 12.18
Pie Charts for Analysis (Document 12.A)

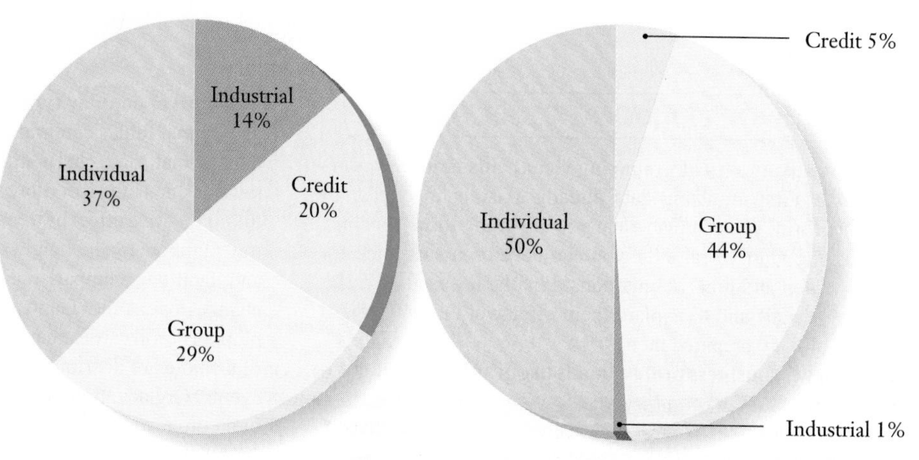

Document 12.B

Examine the line chart in Figure 12.19 and point out any problems or errors you notice.

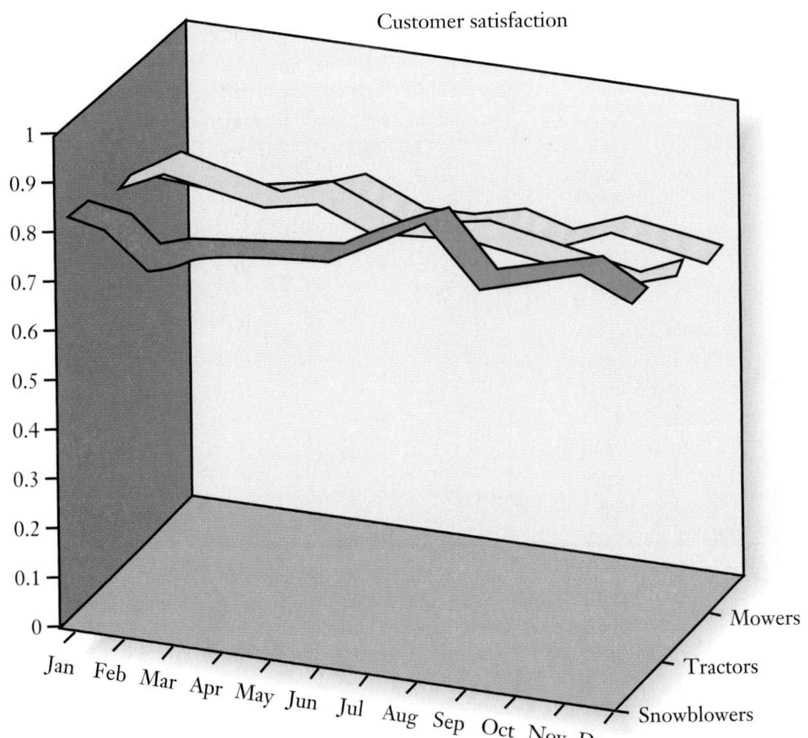

Figure 12.19
Line Chart for Analysis (Document 12.B)

EXERCISES

1. As a market researcher for a statewide chain of car dealerships, you're examining car and truck ownership and lease patterns among single drivers in various age groups. By discovering which age groups have the highest percentages of owners, you will be better able to target advertising that promotes the leasing option. Using the following information, prepare a bar graph comparing the number of owners with the number of leasers in each age category. Be sure to label your graph, and include combined totals for owners and leasers ("total drivers"). Then prepare a pie chart showing the proportion of owners and leasers in the one age group that you think holds the most promise for leasing a new vehicle. Write a sentence that prepares your company's management for the information shown in the pie chart.

Age group	Number of owners (in 000s)	Number of leasers (in 000s)
18–24	1,830	795
25–29	1,812	1,483
30–34	1,683	1,413
35–44	1,303	1,932
45–54	1,211	1,894
55–64	1,784	1,435
65–74	3,200	1,142
75+	3,431	854

2. As director of new business development for a growing advertising agency, you're interested in how companies spend their advertising dollars. Create a pie chart based on the following information, which shows U.S. national advertising

spending by media category. Summarize these findings (in two or three sentences) for publication in a report to top management.

Media type	Expenditure (in $ billions)
Television	$ 42.5
Newspaper	38.4
Direct mail	38.4
Miscellaneous	22.6
Radio	12.3
Yellow Pages	10.8
Magazines	9.0
Business papers	3.8
Outdoor	1.3
Total[13]	$179.1

3. The pet food manufacturer you work for is interested in the results of a recent poll of U.S. pet-owning households. Look at the statistics that follow and decide on the most appropriate scale for a chart; then create a line chart of the trends in cat ownership. What conclusions do you draw from the trend you've charted? Draft a paragraph or two discussing the results of this poll and the potential consequences for the pet food business. Support your conclusions by referring readers to your chart.

   In 1980, 22 million U.S. households owned a cat. In 1985, 24 million households owned a cat. In 1990, 28 million households owned a cat. In 1995, 32 million households owned a cat.

4. You're preparing the annual report for FretCo Guitar Corporation. For each of the following types of information, what form of visual aid would you choose to illustrate the text? Explain your choices.
   a. Data on annual sales for the past 20 years
   b. Comparison of FretCo sales, product by product (electric guitars, bass guitars, amplifiers, acoustic guitars), for this year and last year
   c. Explanation of how a FretCo acoustic guitar is manufactured
   d. Explanation of how the FretCo Guitar Corporation markets its guitars
   e. Data on sales of FretCo products in each of 12 countries
   f. Comparison of FretCo sales figures with sales figures for three competing guitar makers over the past 10 years
5. Team up with a classmate to design graphics based on a comparison of the total tax burden of the U.S. taxpayer with that of people in other nations. One teammate should sketch a horizontal or vertical bar chart and the other should sketch a pictogram from the estimates that follow. Then exchange visual aids and analyze how well each conveys the situation of the U.S. taxpayer. Would the bar chart look best with vertical or horizontal bars? Why? What scale is best? How does the symbol used in the pictogram enhance or obscure the meaning or impact of the data? What suggestions can each student make for improving the other's visual aid?

   Estimates show that Swedish taxpayers spend 51 percent of their incomes on taxes, British taxpayers spend 48 percent, French taxpayers spend 37 percent, Japanese taxpayers spend 28 percent, and U.S. taxpayers spend 27 percent.

6. Here are last year's sales figures for the appliance and electronics megastore where you work. Construct visual aids based on these figures that will help you explain to the store's general manager seasonal variations in each department.

Store Sales in 1999 (in $ thousands)			
Month	Home Electronics	Computers	Appliances
January	$68	$39	$36
February	72	34	34
March	75	41	30
April	54	41	28
May	56	42	44
June	49	33	48
July	54	31	43
August	66	58	39
September	62	58	36
October	66	44	33
November	83	48	29
December	91	62	24

7. Look back at Figure 12.9, part of which compares the on-time arrival records of major U.S. airlines. What type of visual aid would most effectively communicate the performance data shown in the table? Make a sketch and discuss your choice of visual aid as well as your choice of scale. How could you emphasize the airline with the best on-time performance record?
8. You work for C & S Holdings, a company that operates coin-activated, self-service car washes. Research shows that the farther customers live from a car wash, the less likely they are to visit. You know that 50 percent of customers at each of your car washes live within a 4-mile radius of the location, 65 percent live within 6 miles, 80 percent live within 8 miles, and 90 percent live within 10 miles. B & T's owner wants to open two new car washes in your city and has asked you to prepare a report recommending locations. Using a map of your city, choose two possible locations for car washes and create a visual depicting the customer base surrounding each location.
9. Create an organization chart for your school. You will probably need to consult your school library or administration office for documents listing the various offices and departments. Figure 12.11 can serve as a model for how to structure your chart.
10. Re-create the line chart in Figure 12.2 as a bar chart and as a pie chart. Which of these three formats does the best job of conveying the information? Are any of the formats definitely inappropriate for this information? Explain your answers.
11. With a team of three or four other students, brainstorm and then sketch at least three types of visual aids you can use to compare the populations of all 50 states in the United States.

You can use any of the graphic ideas presented in this chapter, as well as any ideas or examples you find from other sources.

12. One of the best places to see how data can be presented visually is in government statistical publications, and today one of the best ways to access government publications is on the Internet. The International Trade Administration (ITA), a branch of the U.S. Department of Commerce, publishes annual reports about emerging economies on its Web site. Current economic data for such countries as India, Poland, South Korea, and Turkey are available at http://www.ita.doc.gov. Click on "Regions and Countries," and then "Web sites and offices around the globe." Then click on a country of your choice. Click on "Trade Statistics," and then click on various statistical links that will show data presented in a number of ways. Using what you learned in this chapter, evaluate a line chart, a bar chart, and a pie chart. Do the charts present the data clearly? Are they missing any elements? What would you do to improve the charts? Print out a copy of the report to turn in with your answers, and indicate which visuals you are evaluating.

13. How can visual aids help people overcome some of the barriers to communication discussed in Chapter 1? Please explain.

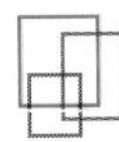

14. How can using visual aids in reports and oral presentations help you deliver bad-news messages more effectively?

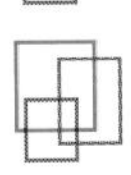

Exploring the Best of the Web

Design Effective Computer Graphics, page 414

Visit the Mambo Web site at http://mambo.ucsc.edu/psl/cg.html.

1. Find some information there that might help you visually enhance a business report. Write a brief description of what you've found.

2. What did you discover about computer graphics that you didn't know before? What resources did you find that might help you with future writing projects? Did you see anything visually arresting that gave you ideas for illustrating your own work? If you did, what was it? Did you find anything that you disliked or that confused you? If so, why do you think it failed (unless that was its purpose)?

Part 4 A Case for Critical Thinking

YAHOO! THE LITTLE SEARCH ENGINE THAT COULD

The Beginning

Chug, chug, puff, puff, went young Sanford engineers David Filo and Jerry Yang as they climbed the hill of success. These Ph.D. candidates weren't looking to make multimillions. They were just having some fun with computers—and procrastinating from writing their doctoral dissertations.

Nevertheless, they were happy budding engineers, living in a trailer filled with life's little necessities: golf clubs, sleeping bags, computers, and half-empty food containers. There they spent their days adding new Web sites to their list of favorites—one by one. Soon their lists became unmanageable. So the engineers wrote some software to group their favorite Web sites into different subject areas. Then they posted their lists on the Web—for fun. Hurray! Hurray! cried all the surfers in cyberspace. They even sent the tired engineers e-mail messages, letting them know how much these lists helped surfers find information on the Web. This response, of course, encouraged Filo and Yang to work even harder, sometimes 20 hours a day.

It was the spring of 1995. Net mania was just beginning to flower, and Filo and Yang realized they were onto something big. So they ditched their dissertations, launched a company, named it Yahoo! (an acronym for "Yet Another Hierarchical Officious Oracle"), got some financing, turned down an offer to be absorbed by America Online (AOL), and went on with their business. That is, they developed an organized way for surfers to access the tangled mess of information on the Web.

The Human Touch

Meanwhile, big, sprawling spiders such as Infoseek and Excite were busy spinning their Webs. These search engines were bigger and faster than Yahoo! because they automated their process. But Filo and Yang weren't envious. They wanted Yahoo! to deliver the *best* of the Web, not its entirety—a philosophy from which the company has never veered. Intuitively, they knew that people liked to move around a bit and discover things on their own. And, even though the automated search engines could deliver thousands of listings in a flash—far more than Yahoo!—people still had to sift through all the dreck.

So instead of automating Yahoo!, Filo and Yang hired humans from all corners of the world to filter, categorize, and add Web sites to their lists (having humans cull the sites is the main difference between a directory and a search engine, which indexes Web sites automatically by robot software). As soon as one subject category grew too large, they created subcategories, then subsubcategories, and so on. Still, not everything on Yahoo! is an award-winning site. That's because Filo and Yang want Yahoo! to appeal to a variety of users.

The Big Climb

Knowing that word of mouth could push Yahoo! only so far, in 1996 Filo and Yang paid Netscape $5 million for the distinction of being one of Netscape's five featured search engines. This association gave Yahoo! a big push uphill. To keep the cyber population happy, Filo and Yang packed their engine with lots of goodies: stock quotes, maps, chat rooms, news, weather, sports, Yellow Pages, classifieds, dream homes, and more. In fact, every time Web surfers returned to the Yahoo! site, there was another new, cool—and free—feature. More and more surfers were climbing on board.

Overnight, it seems, Yahoo! morphed from a tiny directory into a dizzying array of Internet services and information. Then one day it raced all the shiny new search engines to the top of the hill—and it won. Yahoo! was the first to have its stock go public, the first to turn an annual profit, and the first to slap its name on television. In fact, pretty soon the Yahoo! name was everywhere—on parachutes, skateboards, sailboats, surfboards, hockey rinks, yo-yos, kazoos, and golf balls. One employee even tattooed it on his behind. In less than three years Yahoo! had become a be-all, do-all of the Net. Dubbed the most successful Internet company, its stock soared heavenward—23 times its original offering price.

But this is not the end of the line for Filo and Yang. These engineers have loftier ambitions. They want Yahoo! to become the primo portal of cyberspace. How? By making the directory accessible from all kinds of devices—telephones, televisions, pagers, hand-held organizers, and more. By making it easier to purchase goods on the Internet. And by closely monitoring each user's preferences and purchasing behavior so that My Yahoo! (the site's personal agent) can push even more tailored information and Web material right to a user's desktop.

Leader of the Pack

Even though Yahoo! currently leads the portal pack (over 18 million consumers are registered on My Yahoo!), some think this engine has a long way to go before it can truly call itself a successful portal. Others fear that the company is a mouse click away from be-

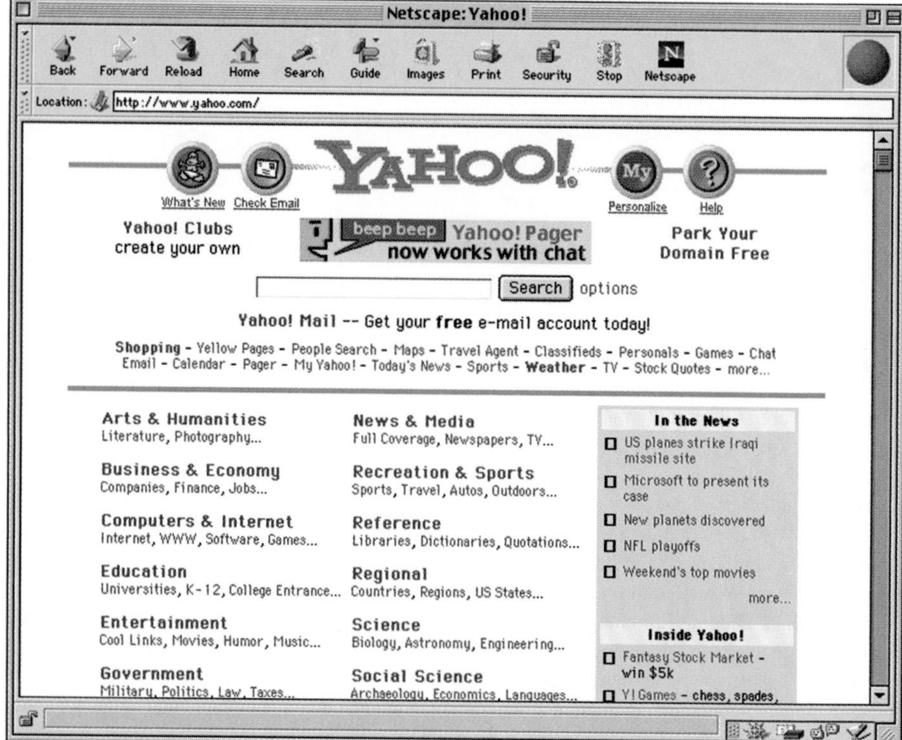

Over 32 million people visit Yahoo's Web site each month.

coming a has-been. After all, competition among portals is pretty tough these days. Not only must Yahoo! constantly duke it out with big-league players like AOL, Microsoft Network (MSN), and other wannabe cyberspacers, but Yahoo! can't match the big boys in marketing dollars. So to survive, Filo and Yang must surpass them in cleverness. Will saying "I think I can, I think I can, I think I can" be enough to get this little engine to the top and keep it there?

1. To make personal agents such as My Yahoo! even more personalized, Web sites must gather as much information as possible about each user's preferences. Divide the classroom into two groups: privacy advocates and freedom-of-information advocates. Use the Internet or library to gather information to support your assigned argument (pro or con Internet user privacy). Once you've completed your research, debate this topic in class as directed by your instructor.
2. If you were to use a directory such as Yahoo! to gather information on a specific company what else might you need to know besides the company's name to get started in the right direction?
3. Suppose you were thinking about starting your own business. What can you learn from David Filo and Jerry Yang's experience that might help you with your undertaking?
4. Visit the Yahoo! Web site and some of the other search engine sites listed in Table 10.1 (see page 346). Perform a search using the same key words on Yahoo! and on the other search engines. What difference, if any, do you notice in the results produced by Yahoo! and the others? Now try to access similar information by clicking on the appropriate Yahoo! Web site categories. Which method provides more usable results, searching or clicking? Which method do you like better? Why?

PART

Reports and Oral Presentations

CHAPTER 13
Communicating Through Reports

CHAPTER 14
Planning, Organizing, and Writing Reports and Proposals

CHAPTER 15
Completing Formal Reports and Proposals

CHAPTER 16
Giving Speeches and Oral Presentations

COMMUNICATING THROUGH REPORTS

AFTER STUDYING THIS CHAPTER, YOU WILL BE ABLE TO

1 Define what is meant by a business report
2 Discuss why businesses need reports and highlight the six general purposes of reports
3 Distinguish between informational and analytical reports
4 Describe four types of informational reports and provide examples of each
5 Describe three types of analytical reports and briefly explain how each is used
6 Cite the advantages and disadvantages of electronic reports

COMMUNICATION CLOSE-UP AT NARADA PRODUCTIONS

"It comes down to information management," says Wesley Van Linda, president of Narada Productions. Founded in 1983 by Van Linda's partner, John Morey, the Milwaukee-based company is a "small boutique specialty label" among the giants of the recording industry. With annual sales in the range of $10 million to $30 million, Narada produces contemporary instrumental, New Age, jazz, and electronic music. Van Linda relies on reports from every department (from sales to shipping) to track performance and to make managerial decisions based on current needs.

Van Linda says his system for using reports was developed by necessity as Narada grew rapidly from a small distribution company into two distinct companies: Narada Productions (which records and sells the music of David Lanz, David Arkenstone, Michael Jones, and other New Age artists) and Music Design (which distributes children's music, meditation music, environmental sounds, and unusual recordings by other record producers). These recordings don't get a lot of radio play, so Narada first sold tapes and CDs through mail-order catalogs, then in gift stores and bookstores (where in-store play helped acquaint customers with the new sounds), and later in local record stores. This market diversity saved the company during a tough economy, but it also made Van Linda's job harder—with so much sales information coming from so many directions.

Wesley Van Linda

The reports Van Linda receives include daily sales reports from his staff, monthly sales reports from MCA (which distributes Narada-label recordings), and weekly reports from Soundscan (a computerized cash-register-monitoring service for the music industry from which popularity charts are derived). To put all his reports into perspective, he developed a computerized spreadsheet program. Now he takes a few minutes every day to enter the facts from each of these reports into his personal computer, and at a glance, he can analyze everything from how well a particular artist's recordings are selling to how long custo-

At Narada Productions, reports of all kinds are used to track product performance as well as to assemble the information needed for making managerial decisions. Electronic reporting helps Narada president Wesley Van Linda quickly review the mountain of sales information he must sort through.

mers have to wait before their phone calls are returned. If something isn't right, he can fix it immediately.

Van Linda believes that good reports and good management go hand in hand, and one key is having enough historical information available to compare with the company's current performance. "If you know where you've been, you can project where you're going, based on the current information," he says. The spreadsheet program allows him to compare current monthly figures with monthly figures dating back seven years. He can quickly determine whether his business is growing or declining and what sort of pattern is developing for the year. He uses this information to make smarter decisions about the company's needs.

"I'm a firm believer in summary reports for a manager," says Van Linda. "Managers should know what's going on in their company but should also allow people the space and flexibility to do the job that they know how to do." For example, when his in-house computer specialist suggested that their system required an upgrade, Van Linda sent her off to do extensive research and analysis so that she could write a report for him, summarizing her findings and backing up her recommendations with hard facts. She spent three months evaluating Narada's current system, meeting with vendors, and working with a financial consultant to develop a justification report for purchasing a new computer system.

Her report opened with a brief overview that Van Linda could read quickly (an executive summary). It included sections on hardware and software options, diagrams of the new system, information and data flow diagrams and descriptions, a financial impact analysis, and her own conclusions and recommendations. The report was well researched and clearly presented, which helped Van Linda reach the determination he believed was best for the company: He decided the new system would be "overkill."

Although his decision probably wasn't what his computer specialist wanted to hear, Van Linda relied on her expertise to help him make the right choice. "Usually someone who knows how to write well," says Van Linda, "also knows how to think well and clearly and creatively." He believes that good reports are essential for keeping a business on track—and that good report writers are invaluable.[1] ■

WHY BUSINESSES NEED REPORTS

Even the most capable managers must rely on other people to observe events or to collect information for them. Like Wesley Van Linda, they are often too far away to oversee everything themselves. In addition, they often lack the time and the specialized background required to research and evaluate certain subjects. So they rely on reports prepared by others for making decisions and solving problems.

You may be surprised at the variety of messages that qualify as reports. The term covers everything from a fleeting image on a computer screen to preprinted forms to informal letters and memos to formal three-volume bound manuscripts. Many reports are delivered orally, as discussed in Chapter 16. In general, however, most businesspeople think of **reports** as written, factual accounts that objectively communicate information about some aspect of the business. Because business reports are a managerial tool intended to inform or to contribute to the decision-making and problem-solving process, they must be accurate, complete, and unbiased.

A business report is any factual, objective document that serves a business purpose.

The goal in developing a report is to make the information as clear and convenient to use as possible. Because time is precious, you tell your readers what they need to know—no more, no less—and you present the information in a way that is geared to their needs (Chapter 14 will discuss report organization in detail). Reports can be printed on paper or distributed electronically. Wesley Van Linda likes to use a computer to compare information from the reports he receives.

Select a format, a style, and an organization that reflect the reader's needs.

How Companies Use Reports

Reports are like bridges, spanning time and space. Organizations use them to provide a formal, verifiable link among people, places, and times. Some reports are used for internal communication; others are vehicles for corresponding with outsiders. Some serve as a permanent record; others solve an immediate problem or answer a passing question. Many move upward through the chain of command to help managers monitor the various units in the organization; some move downward to explain managerial decisions to lower-level employees responsible for day-to-day operations.

Before you start writing a report, ask yourself why it's being prepared.

Although business reports serve hundreds of purposes, most reports are used for one of the following six general purposes:

- To monitor and control operations
- To help implement policies and procedures
- To comply with legal or regulatory requirements
- To document work performed for a client
- To guide decisions on particular issues
- To obtain new business or funding

Each of these purposes imposes its own requirements on the report writer (see Table 13.1). If your readers need information to oversee an operation, you would present your message differently than if you were contributing to a decision on a complex issue. In other words, the purpose of a report affects its form.

How Business Reports Are Classified

Reports are commonly classified by who initiated the report, why it is being prepared, when it is prepared, and where it is being sent. In Chapter 14, we'll discuss how a report's format, style, and organization are frequently dictated by its classification. In this chapter we'll dis-

TABLE 13.1

THE SIX MOST COMMON USES OF REPORTS

Purpose of Report	Common Examples	Distribution	Features
To monitor and control operations	Plans, operating reports, personal activity reports	Internal reports move upward on a recurring basis; external reports go to selected audiences.	**Format:** Standard memo or preprinted form **Style:** Telegraphic **Organization:** Topical **Order:** Direct
To implement policies and procedures	Lasting guidelines, position papers	Internal reports move downward on a nonrecurring basis.	**Format:** Matches policies and procedures manual **Style:** Fully developed text **Organization:** Topical **Order:** Direct
To comply with regulatory requirements	Reports for IRS, SEC, EEOC, Revenue Canada, Canadian Human Rights Commission, and other industry regulators	External reports are sent on a recurring basis.	**Format:** Standardized; perhaps preprinted or electronic form **Style:** Skeletal **Organization:** To follow reader's instructions **Order:** Direct
To document work for a client	Interim progress reports, final reports	External reports are sent on a nonrecurring basis.	**Format:** Letter or manuscript **Style:** Fully developed text **Organization:** Around sequential steps or key findings **Order:** Usually direct
To analyze information and guide decisions	Research reports, justification reports, troubleshooting reports	Internal reports move upward on a nonrecurring basis.	**Format:** Memo or manuscript **Style:** Fully developed text **Organization:** Around conclusions or logical arguments **Order:** Direct or indirect
To obtain new business or funding	Sales proposals	External reports are sent on a nonrecurring basis.	**Format:** Letter or manuscript **Style:** Fully developed text **Organization:** Problem-solution **Order:** Commonly direct

cuss the different types of business reports and their many uses. Here are some common report classifications:

- *Voluntary reports versus authorized reports.* **Voluntary reports** are prepared on your own initiative. Thus, they usually require more detail and support than **authorized reports,** which are prepared at the request of someone else. When writing a voluntary report, you give more background on the subject, and you explain your purpose

Reports may be classified in several ways:
- Voluntary or authorized
- Routine or special
- Internal or external
- Short or long
- Formal or informal
- Informational or analytical

more carefully. An authorized report, on the other hand, is organized to respond to the reader's request.

- *Routine reports versus special reports.* **Routine,** or **periodic, reports** are submitted on a recurring basis (daily, weekly, monthly, quarterly, annually), as are the reports that Wesley Van Linda receives at Narada Productions. They require less introductory and transitional material than do **special reports,** nonrecurring reports that deal with unique situations or one-time events. Routine reports are often prepared on preprinted or computerized forms (either of which the writer simply fills in), or they're organized in a standard way.
- *Internal versus external reports.* **Internal reports** (used within the organization) are generally less formal than **external reports** (sent to people outside the organization). Many internal reports, especially those under ten pages, are written in memo format. On the other hand, external reports may be in letter format (if they are no longer than five pages) or in manuscript format (if they exceed five pages).

In addition to these categories, a report can be short or long, formal or informal. Keep in mind that a single report may have several classifications. For instance, a monthly sales report is generally an authorized, internal, routine, informal report. Nevertheless, most reports can be placed in two broad categories: *informational reports* and *analytical reports.*

The purpose of informational reports is to explain, whereas analytical reports are meant to convince the audience that the conclusions and recommendations developed in the text are valid.

Informational reports focus on facts and are intended mainly to educate readers. In contrast, **analytical reports** provide data analyses, interpretation, and a conclusion. Information in analytical reports plays a supporting role; it is a means to an end rather than an end itself.

Typically, an analytical report ends by presenting a decision (or a solution) to a problem or by recommending a number of actions. The body of the report presents all the facts (both good and bad) and persuades readers to accept a stated decision, an action, or the recommendations detailed throughout the report. To persuade the reader, the writer carefully analyzes the facts and organizes, or presents, an argument in one of several ways, generally around conclusions, recommendations, or logical arguments. Informational reports, on the other hand, are usually organized around subtopics. (Chapter 14 will discuss how to organize and present arguments in reports.)

INFORMATIONAL REPORTS

Informational reports include those for monitoring and controlling operations, statements of policies and procedures, compliance reports, and progress reports.

Reports for Monitoring and Controlling Operations

Monitor/control reports help managers find out what's happening in the operations under their control.

One of the most common applications for business reports is to monitor and control the operations of the organization. Because managers cannot be everywhere at once, they rely on reports to find out what's happening to the operations under their control.

Monitor/control reports focus on data. If you're new in an organization, construct your reports by using previous reports of the same type as examples. Your objective is to make your report similar in appearance, style, and organization to the reports your boss is familiar with so that he or she can easily absorb the information.

Monitor/control reports expose any problems that exist.

Pay special attention to the accuracy, thoroughness, and honesty of monitor/control reports. It is tempting to cover up the bad news and emphasize only the accomplishments, but such distortions defeat the purpose of a monitor/control report. Be objective. In the final analysis, the problems will show up anyway, so you might as well get them out in the open.

Three types of reports used for monitoring and controlling operations are plans, operating reports, and personal activity reports. In general, plans are written for both internal and

Jon Martin and Chance Miller own five Smoothie King franchise stores and are among Smoothie King's top producers. Each month, Martin and Miller must send their franchisor a variety of informational reports.

external audiences. However, operating reports and personal activity reports are usually written for internal audiences only.

Plans

Plans help managers
- Coordinate the various activities of a business
- Guide the distribution of resources
- Motivate employees

One of the most widely used monitor/control reports is the **plan,** a written report that establishes guidelines for future action. Plans come in all shapes and sizes: annual budgets, five-year plans, strategic plans, sales plans, recruiting plans, production plans, and so on. Just about every functional area of a company develops a plan to direct its activities. These plans are generally used by internal audiences to improve organizational coordination, to guide the distribution of money and material, and to motivate employees.

One particular type of plan, the *strategic plan,* documents an organization's overall goals and the operational methods it will use to reach those goals. Such plans help guide internal operations and provide benchmarks for measuring progress toward goals.[2] Small businesses, divisions of larger businesses, and entrepreneurial start-ups write *business plans* to obtain financing or to contract for managerial support services.[3] Similarly, companies write *marketing plans* to identify their customers and how they will serve them. Although marketing plans are similar to business plans (both contain a well-supported forecast, a thorough description of the business proposition, and financial projections), a marketing plan assumes that the money required for implementation is available, whereas a business plan usually includes strategies for raising capital. Furthermore, a marketing plan includes a more in-depth analysis of the market conditions than is normally found in a business plan.[4]

Operating Reports

A management information system (MIS) comprises many operating reports that provide managers with statistics on company performance.

Many managers get detailed information about operations from a management information system (MIS), which captures statistics about everything happening in the organization. In most companies the MIS is computerized, but operating reports can be created manually as well. In either case, someone must decide what facts to gather and in what form to report them. Either system then provides a constant stream of statistics on all operations of the company—sales, production, inventory, shipments, backlogs, costs, personnel—whatever management is interested in measuring. All this information can be given to management in its

BEST OF THE WEB

How to Write a Business Plan

At its Web site, Tikkanen-Bradley Consulting Group shares 12 important pointers for writing a polished business plan. Included are directions for creating a plan, specific tips on organizing and preparing information, and succinct statements about why and when each pointer is a good idea. Be sure to review these pointers before drafting a business plan. They might make the difference.

http://www.mortimer.com/consult/tips.htm

raw state through computer terminals, printouts, or pages of accounting numbers, or it can be analyzed and reported in paragraph form by staff members.

Periodic reports are recurring monitor/control reports that keep managers informed about departments that report to them.

A periodic report describes what has happened in a department or division during a particular period. Corporate annual reports are periodic reports that are formal and polished. Monthly sales reports are another example. The purpose of these recurring documents is to provide a picture of how things are going so that corporate managers will be up-to-date and can take corrective action if necessary.

The periodic report in Figure 13.1 was prepared by Roger Watson, real estate director for a San Francisco coffee retailer. According to Watson, "Real estate scouting is a crucial activity for our company as we expand eastward from our California base. My manager needs to know that my department is making good decisions when we select new store locations."

Personal Activity Reports

Personal activity reports describe the facts and decisions that emerge during conversations, trips, and business meetings.

A *personal activity report* is a form of monitor/control report that calls for a person's description of what occurred during a conference, convention, trip, or other activity. It's intended to provide management with any important information or decisions that emerged during the activity.

In addition to reporting on special activities, personal activity reports help companies keep track of what is happening in the marketplace or with customers. Sales-call reports are one example. In a sales-call report, the salesperson summarizes the events that occurred during an appointment with a customer. The report outlines the topics that were discussed and gives the salesperson's evaluation of the prospects for a sale, together with plans for follow-up action.

Marilyn Ounjian, the owner and chief executive officer of Careers USA, a fast-growing personnel-placement service based in Philadelphia, reads sales-call reports to track her salespeople's effectiveness and to check sales trends in 21 offices spread across nine states. "I want to know what's happening now," she says. "Salespeople are on the front lines. If they're not growing, we're not growing."[5]

Other examples of personal activity reports are expense reports, performance reviews, recruiting reports, and any other document intended to keep management posted on the activities of individuals. Figure 13.2 is a personal activity report prepared by Carrie Andrews, the human resources manager of a small Indianapolis insurance firm. Her report summarizes the highlights of a seminar on legal issues.

Case Study: Juan Martinez's Annual Recruiting Report

Juan Martinez is in charge of hiring for a Seattle-based software company. Part of his job in the human resources department is to keep statistics and write reports on the company's employees. Some of the reports are for internal information; others are submitted to the federal

Roger Watson doesn't want to burden his boss with a lot of details about every one of the potential sites being investigated. His monthly reports are concise and presented in a summary format. "If Joan has questions about a specific location and needs more information," says Watson, "we usually just talk by phone after she gets my report."

Figure 13.1
In-Depth Critique: Sample Periodic Informational Report

MEMO

TO: Joan Chen, V.P.
New Business Development
FROM: Roger Watson,
Real Estate Director

DATE: August 1, 2000
SUBJECT: July location scouting

During the last two weeks of July, I scouted four Denver locations for our coffee outlets. George Spindle recommended these sites in his business development report (which is on the intranet under "Regional reports" if you'd like to review it). All four sites are in existing office buildings.

HOW THE DENVER SITES COMPARE

Here's a quick look at the basic aspects of each site. Lease rates are comparable at all four locations, ranging from $34 to $38 a square foot.

Site	Space	Availability	Competition	Visibility
Lakewood	260 square feet	Now	Starbucks has begun construction 4 blocks north; no other stores within a 16-block radius	None; on the second of two retail floors in this building
Glendale	525 square feet; with additional 150 square feet in one year	January	2 Starbucks (2 blocks south and 8 blocks west); Chicago Blues (across street, but poor visibility)	
McNichols Arena	420 square feet	December	JavaLand 3 blocks east; Starbucks 4 blocks south	
University of Denver	Two options: 340 square feet, 655 square feet	Now for the smaller site; March for the larger	Five independents in the immediate area; Starbucks on campus (2 blocks west)	

SCOUTING PLANS FOR SEPTEMBER

Our schedule has been pretty tight for the last six months. Following are the plans for our efforts in September:

Denver: I'll contract Shure Research to conduct foot traffic counts at all four sites (we should have those numbers in 10 days). I've asked George's team to do a permits search to study future building plans in each location. I'll be talking with Melissa Hines next week about construction restrictions. (She's the Smith, Allen broker who helped us with the Grand Junction sites last year.)

Minneapolis: Jean-Luc Goddard wants us to review several sites he's had his eye on. I'll send Margie or visit them myself if my schedule permits.

The brief introduction orients the reader but doesn't waste time with unnecessary explanations.

Headings stand out to make report review easier for the reader.

The table organizes summary information in the most time-saving format.

Details of upcoming efforts help the reader maintain a timely overview of progress.

government to document the company's compliance with federal employee regulations. One of Martinez's responsibilities is to organize on-campus recruiting interviews. Every spring, company representatives visit several colleges and universities to interview and recruit new employees.

Figure 13.2
In-Depth Critique: Sample Personal Activity Report

Carrie Andrews attended a seminar on legal issues in employee recruiting and interviewing. Says Andrews, "I prepared this report for my boss, the company president, and the four people who work for me. We can't afford to send everyone in the department to seminars such as this, so it's important that I share the information I received with the people who couldn't attend."

MEMO

TO: Jeff Balou; all members of HR staff
DATE: March 14, 2000
FROM: Carrie Andrews
SUBJECT: Recruiting and hiring seminar

As you all know, the process of recruiting, screening, and hiring new employees can be a legal minefield. Because we don't have an in-house lawyer to help us make every decision, it's important for all of us to be aware of what is legally acceptable and what isn't.

Last week I attended an American Management Association seminar on this subject. I got enough useful information to warrant updating our online personnel handbook and perhaps developing a quick training session for all interviewing teams. First, here's a quick look at the things I learned.

AVOIDING LEGAL MISTAKES

- How to write recruiting ads that accurately portray job openings and that don't discriminate
- How best to comply with the Americans with Disabilities Act
- How to use an employment agency effectively and safely (without risk of legal entanglements)

SCREENING AND INTERVIEWING MORE EFFECTIVELY

- How to sort through résumés more efficiently (including looking for telltale signs of false information)
- How to avoid interview questions that could get us into legal trouble
- When and how to check criminal records

MEASURING APPLICANTS

- Which types of preemployment tests have been proven most effective
- Which drug-testing issues and recommendations affect us

As you can see, the seminar addressed a lot of important information. We cover the basic guidelines for much of this already, but a number of specific recommendations and legal concepts should be emphasized.

It will take me a couple of weeks to get the personnel handbook updated, but we don't have any immediate hiring plans anyway. I'll keep the seminar handouts and my notes on my desk, in case you want to peruse them. After I've updated the handbook, we can get together and decide whether we need to train the interviewing team members. Although we have a lot of new information, I think we can highlight what people need to be aware of and let them read the new sections as their schedules allow.

If you have any questions in the meantime, don't hesitate to e-mail me or drop by for a chat.

The introduction states Andrews's reason for attending the seminar.

The organization of this report around the three areas of knowledge gained by Andrews helps readers focus on what is important.

Bullets make the new knowledge stand out for easy reader reference.

Although reporting on personal activity, this report wastes no time on unimportant activities such as how many sessions were offered during the seminar or what was served for lunch. Rather, the report is full of the information needed by department members and the plans for how to disseminate it.

Although headquartered in Seattle, the company has divisions in Europe and Asia, and some of its software products are joint efforts of programming teams in several countries. Language differences can be a barrier to communication, so the company prefers to hire programmers who are fluent in at least one language besides English. "Our most recent product was developed collaboratively by teams in the United States, Germany, and Japan," says

After this year's Comdex trade show, many company representatives submitted informational reports to their superiors to communicate what they learned at the show.

Martinez. "The U.S. team included two members fluent in German and one who is fairly comfortable in Japanese. The team members in Germany and Japan all speak some English, but I believe the development cycle was shortened considerably by the U.S. team's ability to communicate with the other teams in their native languages. Hiring programmers who speak the language of one of our international divisions makes sense in a couple of ways. It conveys a message to these other divisions that they are important to the corporation. It also saves the company money in shortened product development cycles."

Each summer, after college interviewing and hiring is finished, Martinez analyzes statistics about the interviews and includes the information in his annual report to the company's human resources director (see Figure 13.3). The information in the report includes how many students applied, how many were interviewed on campus, how many of those were flown to corporate headquarters for further interviews, and how many were eventually hired. Also included in the report are recruiting costs, broken down by college, company department, and new employee. Besides documenting expenses, the report helps the company determine which institutions are most appropriate for recruiting in the future.

Reports for Implementing Policies and Procedures

Policy/procedure reports help managers communicate the company's standards.

Another common type of informational business report is one that documents and explains company policies and procedures. Like reports for monitoring and controlling operations, reports that discuss policies and procedures are necessary because managers cannot be everywhere at once. They need to communicate with employees, but they aren't usually able to talk firsthand with every person in the organization. Written policies and procedures can be read and reread by anyone who needs to know about a particular issue. Some of these documents are preserved as lasting guidelines; others are one-time explanations.

In general, make statements of policies and procedures as broad and simple as possible.

Reports for implementing policies and procedures have a straightforward organization, but they can be difficult to write well. The goal is to strike the right balance between the general and the specific. You may be tempted to answer every question that every possible reader might have, but this approach often creates more confusion than illumination. Try to keep the policies broad and the procedures as simple as possible. Nordstrom, one of the country's

Figure 13.3
In-Depth Critique: Juan Martinez's On-Campus Interview Report (Monitor/Control Excerpt)

Because this report includes so much data, Martinez has organized it mostly in tables. Also, he has wasted no time with extensive introductory material, since the human resources director is already familiar with the purpose and general content of the report.

MEMO

TO: **Stephanie Brogan**
FROM: **Juan Martinez**
DATE: **July 15, 2000**
SUBJECT: **2000 U.S. On-Campus Recruiting Report**

Being routine and recurring, this report needs little introductory and transitional material.

For the first time in five years, our projections for U.S. on-campus recruiting efforts have surpassed the previous year's. With our first-quarter 2000 sales nearly doubling from first-quarter 1999, we've had to scramble to fill positions in marketing, production, and product development. Programmers have been especially difficult to come by this year, but we have succeeded in filling all crucial positions. Following is a general overview of our U.S. on-campus recruiting efforts:

For readers' ease in tracking the results and cost of the entire effort, Martinez presents a summary first.

SUMMARY	
Campuses visited	27
Applications received	810
Campus interviews	725
Corporate interviews	540
Offers tendered	216
Offers accepted	198
Total cost	$686,664
Cost per new employee	$3,468

As you can see from the following information, our ratio of hires to corporate interviews is very high, and our ratio of hires to campus interviews isn't bad either.

The high degree of standardization allows readers to compare one report with another.

The table helps the reader by efficiently providing details of hiring statistics on each campus.

INFORMATION BY CAMPUS VISITED

						New hires fluent in another language		
Campus	Applications received	Campus interviews	Corporate interviews	Offers tendered	Offers accepted	French	German	Italian
Minnesota Central	57	35	15	13	12	4	2	2
Ohio Southern	43	20	9	7	5	1	0	0
Georgia A&M	23	17	14	12	11	4	3	1

most respected retailing chains, has carried simplification to the extreme. Its policy manual is one sentence: "Use your best judgment at all times."[6]

Lasting Guidelines

Some policies and procedures provide lasting "recipes" for how things should be done.

Each organization typically has a collection of lasting policies and procedures. The head of personnel might write a memo announcing a new reimbursement program for employees who continue their education; the head of production might develop guidelines for standardizing quality-control procedures; the office manager might issue a memo explaining how to reserve the conference room for special meetings; the assistant to the president might draft a policy on business ethics for use in international operations. Many companies distribute a written report of their ethics policy to employees on their first day of work. Such reports on policies and procedures then become part of the company's large body of lasting guidelines for doing things a certain way.

Position Papers

In contrast to lasting guidelines, *position papers* treat less permanent issues. They explain management's views on particular issues or problems as they arise. An office manager might write a report on the need for extra security precautions after a rash of burglaries in the area. Countless other situations also call for written statements aimed at informing various groups about management's position on special, nonrecurring events.

Other policies and procedures explain management's position on passing events.

Case Study: William Lawson's Building Access Policy

William Lawson is in charge of security for a medical research lab. Many of the scientists employed there work odd hours—late at night or on weekends—especially when a deadline approaches or when experiments require constant monitoring. During normal working hours, a company receptionist sits at the front desk, greeting everyone who enters the building. At night and on weekends, no one is at the front desk. Employees who need to work during those hours are issued a key to the outside door so that they can get into the building.

Until last year, only ten scientists and technicians worked in the lab, and the receptionist at the security desk recognized them on sight. This year the company served several new government contracts and tripled its number of employees. Moreover, the new receptionist couldn't be expected to recognize everyone who works in the lab. So Lawson believed it was time to establish a more formal procedure for entering the building (see Figure 13.4).

Reports for Complying with Government Regulations

Government regulation of business requires another common type of report: the *compliance report*. All compliance reports are written in response to regulations of one sort or another, most of them imposed by government agencies. In a sense, compliance reports are monitor/control reports for the government. These reports play a major role in relations between private industry and government agencies. (In fact, government reporting requirements are often a major point of dissatisfaction among business owners and managers because of the time and attention those reports require.)

Compliance reports explain what a company is doing to conform to government regulations.

The regulatory agency issues instructions on how to write compliance reports; the important thing is to be honest, thorough, and accurate. Remember that these reports are required by law, that they generally serve the public interest, and that you and your company can get into trouble if you're caught being dishonest. Depending on its size and industry, a company may also encounter more specialized reporting requirements. For example, the Food and Drug Administration regulates pharmaceutical companies operating in the United States, while the Interstate Commerce Commission watches over transportation companies that do business across state lines.

Annual Compliance Reports

Perhaps the most common example of an annual compliance report is the income tax return. Also, both the U.S. Internal Revenue Service and Revenue Canada require a yearly report from every corporation that has a pension plan. Another common compliance report that must be prepared every year by companies selling stock to the public is the annual report to the shareholders. This report is required in the United States by the Securities and Exchange

Many compliance reports are prepared on an annual basis.

Figure 13.4
In-Depth Critique: William Lawson's Building Access Policy (Policy/Procedure Excerpt)

The following excerpt is from the policy report prepared by Lawson. "In the past we got by with a loose, informal policy," explains Lawson. "There were only a few people working in the lab, and everyone knew everyone else. Anyone working in the building would recognize an unauthorized visitor and report the matter to security. Since we have expanded, we need to formalize a policy regarding building access. With so many new faces, it would be too easy for an unauthorized person to walk right in."

BUILDING ACCESS PROCEDURES

PURPOSE

The nature of our business demands a balance between free access to lab facilities and security for both equipment and information. One of the implications of our success in recent years is a dramatic increase in the number of employees, so much so that we can no longer rely on an informal approach to security. We've designed this new program to minimize the burden on employees while maximizing security. The program involves four elements:

- Photo ID badges for all employees
- A building access checkpoint
- A procedure for reporting unauthorized or suspicious entry
- Policies regarding personal guests and professional visitors

Employee ID Badges

To make personnel identification both easy and accurate, each employee will be issued a photo ID badge that must be worn at all times while in the building. The Human Resources Department will arrange photo sessions for all current employees. Badges for future new hires will be made during the new-employee orientation session.

Access Checkpoint

During normal working hours, 8:00 a.m. to 5:00 p.m. Monday through Friday, all employees will enter the building through the front door. Employees must show their photo ID badge to the receptionist before entering the lab.

For access after hours, all department heads will identify which employees need to enter the building outside normal working hours. A list of these employees will be kept at the receptionist's desk. After hours and on weekends the desk will be manned by a security guard. Each employee wanting to enter the building must show the guard a valid company ID card and must be included on the authorization list. If the employee is not on the list, the security guard will deny access.

Reporting Unauthorized or Suspicious Entry

We all stand to benefit from improved security, so the company considers it everyone's responsibility to watch for and report unauthorized or suspicious entry to the building.

Commission (SEC) and in Canada by the provincial securities commissions. Annual reports also serve a public relations function. The second half of annual reports must conform to information requirements laid out by the SEC, but the first half gives corporations a forum for educating and persuading readers about everything from corporate strategy to public misperceptions of company business. In fact, some companies show remarkable creativity and playfulness with their annual reports. Eskimo Pie produced a report in the shape of a popsicle, Comcast had a jigsaw puzzle for a front cover, and Oracle put its annual report on CD-ROM.[7] Many other annual and quarterly documents are required as well, all of which contain financial information related to a company's stock and bond offerings.

Companies that do business with the U.S. government are required to submit a yearly report to the Equal Employment Opportunity Commission describing the composition of their work force and their plans for ensuring full use of qualified women, minorities, and other protected groups. The Canadian Human Rights Commission has similar reporting requirements.

Case Study: Tai Chen's Child-Care Facility Report

Tai Chen operates a child-care facility in her home. To keep her state license current, she must submit regular reports on how her facility meets various state requirements. The report lists such things as the size of the facility, number of bathrooms, whether the outdoor play area is fenced, and the number of staff members.

"I started my day-care center when I had my first child," Chen said. "That way I can stay home with my own children while still earning an income. Before I applied for my license, I had no idea how many regulations apply to child care and how much paperwork is involved. Even though I care for only five children, I have to submit the same reports as a larger facility." Figure 13.5 provides an excerpt.

Reports for Documenting Progress

Reports documenting progress on a contract provide all the information the client needs.

Winning a contract or participating in a company project often marks the beginning of another stage of writing, as the company must now document the progress of its work to others. Reports that document progress vary in importance and complexity. Some are a mere formality; others are a vital element in the relationship with the client. These reports may be difficult to write, particularly if the work is not going well or if the customer is unusually demanding. Whether you're writing a progress report for a client or for your boss, it's important to anticipate the reader's needs and to provide the required information clearly and tactfully.

Progress reports are generally submitted on a regular basis. They may be required monthly or weekly, or they may be keyed to phases of the project. In many cases these periodic progress reports are followed by a final report at the conclusion of the contract.

Interim Progress Reports and Final Reports

A long or complex project is documented with periodic updates on the progress that has been made.

Interim progress reports naturally vary in length, depending on the period covered and the complexity of the contract. Their purpose is to give others an idea of the work that has been accomplished to date. Making such reports available whenever they're needed can give a company an important competitive edge.

Interim progress reports are often keyed to the work plan that was established at the beginning of the contract or project. The writer states what tasks have been accomplished, identifies problems, outlines future steps, and summarizes important findings. If a strict deadline is involved, including a Gantt chart similar to the one displayed in Chapter 12 (see Figure 12.8 on page 409) can be an effective way to visually display whether the project is on schedule.

At the end of the project, a final report provides a wrap-up of results.

Final reports are generally more elaborate than interim reports and serve as a permanent record of what was accomplished. They focus on results rather than on progress. They deal with what was done, not with how it got done.

Figure 13.5
In-Depth Critique: Tai Chen's Child-Care Facility Report (Compliance Excerpt)

Chen's report is straightforward and takes little time to prepare from the records that Chen keeps.

Because Chen's report is required and routine, it needs no lengthy introductions.

Chen follows the format dictated by the regulatory agency's instructions.

The language is impersonal and legalistic, emphasizing concise detail, not broad concepts.

This report is highly standardized and is prepared for external readers who review many reports of the same type.

DEPARTMENT OF HEALTH AND SOCIAL SERVICES
ANNUAL COMPLIANCE REPORT

State law requires that all day-care facilities file this form by March 31 of each year. Failure to complete this form fully and accurately may result in loss of your day-care license. All questions on the form must be answered; if you need to speak with a licensing advisor before submitting the form, call the Department of Health and Social Services at 555-1754.

FACILITY	
Type of facility:	Private home
Owner:	Tai and Hoa Chen
Type and age of building:	Brick, 14 years
Street address:	1625 Grandview
City:	Peterborough
Hours of operation:	7:00 a.m. to 6:00 p.m. Monday through Friday
Square footage of facility:	2,300 sq. ft total; 600 sq. ft used for child care
Play area provided:	600 sq. ft indoor playroom; 2,000 sq. ft fenced backyard
Number of bathrooms: Location of emergency exits:	2.5 total, 1 opening directly off playroom Door leads directly from room to fenced backyard
Number of children cared for:	Five
Age range:	2 to 9 years old
Meals provided:	Breakfast, lunch, snacks
STAFF	
Number of staff:	One
Education level:	B.A. in Elementary Education
Medical training:	Certified in first aid and CPR

DID YOU KNOW?

The increasing length of interim reports reflects the growing demand for information, driven by sophisticated financial analysis that no longer focuses solely on profits.

Case Study: Carlyce Johnson's Progress Report

Carlyce Johnson runs the office for her family's landscaping business. She works with a landscape architect to design landscaping for homes and businesses. The jobs vary from replanting a few beds to installing thousands of square feet of new lawn and beds. Each cus-

Johnson explains, "Our landscaping jobs vary in length from part of a day to several months. Often the only report required is a short final report sent to the customer with the billing for the job. For longer jobs, I send the customer weekly or monthly progress reports. The reports can vary from a single page to 20 pages, depending on the complexity of the installation."

Figure 13.6
In-Depth Critique: Carlyce Johnson's Progress Report (Interim Progress Excerpt)

Johnson Landscaping

1500 Dakota, Seattle, WA 98105 • (206) 745-8636 / Fax: 745-6361

May 31, 2000

Steve Gamvrellis, Facilities Manager
United Food Processing
9000 235th St. SW
Everett, WA 98204

Dear Mr. Gamvrellis:

This report will bring you up to date on the landscaping done for your company by Johnson Landscaping during the month of May 2000.

Ground Preparation and Sprinkler System Installation

Initial ground preparation is complete. We cleared, tilled, leveled, and raked 25,000 square feet for lawn and beds. Installation of the sprinkler system for 15,000 square feet of lawn and beds was completed on May 20.

Bed Planting

From May 21 to May 30, shrubs and ornamental perennials were planted in 7,000 square feet of beds. Beds were prepared for 3,000 square feet of annuals.

Problem Areas

We've resolved the flooding problem discovered last month near the south end of the shipping and receiving dock. It appears that an old plumbing repair had begun to come apart under the employee cafeteria, causing water to flow under the building and occasionally flood a small portion of the new lawn area.

Unfortunately, we have uncovered a potential problem in several of the perennial borders we've created along the east side of the main building. A series of soil samples indicates an extremely high level of acidity, much higher than would occur under natural

(continued)

Johnson's interim progress report uses the direct order, emphasizing what has been accomplished during the reporting period. If it were a final report, Johnson would focus on results rather than on progress.

Interim reports are often in memo format and tend to be brief. Final reports are generally longer and often in manuscript form. Main paragraph headings correspond to the tasks performed.

tomer must approve the design before installation can begin, and Johnson is responsible for monitoring and reporting progress on every job. For an excerpt from one of Johnson's interim progress reports, see Figure 13.6.

Figure 13.6, continued

These reports are written for outsiders and are submitted over the life of a contract. As many as five or six progress reports are followed by a final report.

The final section outlines plans for the coming period.

Mr. Steve Gamvrellis, May 31, 2000, Page 2

conditions. We suspect that the problem may have been caused by a small chemical spill at some point in the past. We'll try to resolve the problem next month, and I'll contact you if the solution to this problem is likely to affect your budget planning.

Plans for June

1. Distribute beauty bark and plant remaining annuals.
2. Resolve the soil quality issue in the perennial bed and make soil amendments as needed.
3. Monitor and adjust the automated sprinkling system to ensure adequate watering.

ANALYTICAL REPORTS

Reports that help managers make decisions about problems and opportunities are especially interesting to write.

In many respects, the most interesting business reports are those that help the managers in your organization make major decisions. Many managers rely on analytical reports from lower-level staff members to provide them with information, analyses, and recommendations. Frequently these types of reports are requested as a result of facts contained in informational reports. For instance, after studying a series of monthly sales and activity informational reports, a manager might request a special report analyzing why sales are declining. He or she might even ask that the report include recommendations for new programs to help turn things around.

Of course, before responding to problems or opportunities, most managers study the pros and cons of alternatives. This means that analytical reports require a strong foundation of facts combined with good insight and excellent communication skills on the part of the writer. When you prepare one of these reports, you have the chance to present your skills to top management. Naturally, you'll want to give these assignments your best effort.

Although analytical reports vary greatly, all of them tend to have a "should we or shouldn't we" quality: Should we expand into this market? Should we reorganize the research department? Should we invest in new equipment? Should we close this plant? Should we replace our computer system? Should we hire additional sales representatives? Should we make Minoru Yoshida a vice president? Because people performing the many functions of a company make many kinds of decisions, they require a variety of analytical or decision-oriented reports. Some of the more common types are problem-solving or troubleshooting reports, justification reports, and a special type of report called a proposal.

Problem-Solving Reports

Problem-solving reports provide management with background information and analysis of options.

People in management rely heavily on reports that analyze the advantages and disadvantages of various actions. Perhaps your company has to decide whether to launch a new product, expand into a new territory, change its pricing strategy, withdraw from a business venture, redesign a product, or acquire another company. At Narada Productions, for example, Wesley Van Linda relied on a report prepared by his computer specialist to decide whether he should invest in a new computer system.

When making these and similar decisions, managers need both basic information and analysis of the various options. Most problem-solving reports require research or internal information that may cover topics such as product demand, growth projections, competitor profiles, company strengths and weaknesses, and so on. If the report is prepared on a computer, it might include a financial model that allows managers to compare various scenarios by plugging in different assumptions and projections.

Troubleshooting reports are a type of problem-solving report prepared for submission to top management. Whenever a problem exists, somebody has to investigate it and propose a solution. The vehicle for communicating this analysis is the troubleshooting report. Regardless of the specific problem at hand, these reports deal with the same basic research questions: How did this problem arise, what's the extent of the damage, and what can we do about it? These reports usually start with some background information on the problem, then analyze alternative solutions, and finally recommend the best approach.

Troubleshooting reports analyze problems and propose solutions.

SHARPENING YOUR SKILLS

SEVEN ERRORS IN LOGIC THAT CAN UNDERMINE YOUR REPORTS

For your report to be effective, it must be logical. If you learn how to think logically, you'll also write more logically. Here are some common errors to avoid.

1. *Lack of objectivity.* Seeing only the facts that support your views and ignoring any contradictory information:

   Although half the survey population expressed dissatisfaction with our current product, a sizable portion finds it satisfactory. (*You may be tempted to ignore the dissatisfied half instead of investigating the reasons for their dissatisfaction.*)

2. *Hasty generalizations.* Forming judgments on the basis of insufficient evidence or special cases:

   Marketing strategy Z increased sales 13 percent in Atlanta supermarkets. Let's try it in Fairbanks. (*Atlanta and Fairbanks are probably vastly different markets.*)

3. *Hidden assumptions.* Hiding a questionable major premise:

   We are marketing product X in trade journals because we marketed product Y in trade journals. (*Who says product X and product Y should be marketed the same way?*)

4. *Either-or.* Setting up two alternatives and not allowing for others:

   We must open a new plant by spring, or we will go bankrupt. (*Surely there are other ways to avoid bankruptcy.*)

5. *False causal relationships.* Assuming that event A caused event B merely because A preceded B:

   Sales increased 42 percent as soon as we hired the new sales director. (*Something besides the new sales director might have been responsible for increased sales.*)

6. *Begged questions.* Assuming as proven what you are seeking to prove:

   We need a standard procedure so that we will have standard results. (*But why is standardization important?*)

7. *Personal attacks or appeals to popular prejudice.* Sinking people or ideas you don't like by chaining them to irrelevant but unpopular actions or ideas:

   Ellen mishandled the budget last year, so she can't be expected to motivate her staff. (*Ellen's accounting ability may have nothing to do with her ability to motivate a staff.*)

   It's un-American to impose government regulations. (*Regulations are unpopular, but they do exist in the United States.*)

1. Discuss some newsworthy business problem that arose from errors in logic. For example, Huffy tried to sell a combination mountain-and-racing bicycle through Kmart and other large stores that sold Huffy bicycles. Unfortunately, the reasoning that this special bike (priced higher than other Huffy models) could be sold by salespeople who weren't knowledgeable about bicycles was faulty, and Huffy lost $5 million on the product.
2. Go through the "Letters to the Editor" columns in recent newspapers or news magazines. Examine the arguments made, and point out errors in logic.

Justification Reports

A justification report is a proposal to upper-level management from lower- or middle-level management.

Another common type of analytical report is the *justification report* (or feasibility report), which is used to persuade top management to approve an investment in a project. A capital appropriation request is a specific type of justification report that deals with a request for facilities or equipment such as a new plant or an automated warehouse system. Most capital appropriation requests are aimed at justifying the investment from a financial standpoint. In many organizations these requests are submitted on a standardized form so that all projects can be evaluated according to the same financial criteria.

Not all justification reports deal with the acquisition of tangible assets, however. The proposed project might be the reorganization of a department, the revision of recruiting procedures, a change in the company's training programs, the redesign of the information storage and retrieval system, or any one of hundreds of other ideas for improving the operations of a company that do not require the addition of physical assets. In either case, a good justification report will explain why the project is needed, what it will involve, how much it will cost, and what the benefits will be. Remember, even if a justification report is intended to persuade others to do something, the report must always be unbiased.

Look at Shandel Cohen's report (Figure 13.7), for example. Cohen manages the customer response section of the marketing department for a Midwest personal computer manufacturer. Her section is responsible for sending out product information requested by customers and the field sales force. Over the last two years the company has introduced a new line of computers and several upgrades to existing lines. Cohen has observed that the demand for information fluctuates significantly, with greater demand when a new product is released and diminishing demand as the product matures. This varying demand causes drastic changes in her section's work load.

"It seems that in our unit, it's either feast or famine. We either have more work than we can possibly handle, or we don't have enough to keep us busy. I don't want to get into a hiring-and-firing cycle to deal with the fluctuating work load." Cohen is also concerned about the amount of printed material that is discarded when products are upgraded or replaced. She believes that she has found a viable solution to both problems.

Proposals for Obtaining New Business or Funding

Proposals are reports written to get products, plans, or projects accepted by outside business or government clients.

A **proposal** is a special type of analytical report designed to get products, plans, or projects accepted by outside business or government clients. Proposals to outsiders are similar to justification reports (which solicit approval of projects within an organization). However, proposals have some important differences:

- Unlike justification reports, proposals are legally binding, so they are prepared with extreme care. Sales proposals spell out precisely what the seller will provide under specific terms and conditions. If the proposal is accepted, it becomes the basis of a contract between the buyer and the seller. For example, if you propose to sell 500 units at a price of $250 each, you are bound to deliver at that price, come what may.
- Proposals often compete for a client's business; justification reports do not. In a proposal, you try to convince the buyer that your organization is the best source of the product. So you devote a considerable amount of space to explaining your experience, qualifications, facilities, and equipment. Also, to be persuasive, you try to prove that you clearly understand the buyer's problem or need.[8]

The two basic types of proposals are those solicited by a prospective client and those sent without a specific invitation from a prospective client.

Cohen's proposal is to install an automatic mail-response system. Because the company manufactures computers, she knows that her boss will have no objections to a computer solution to the problem. She also knows that company profits are always of concern, so her report emphasizes the financial benefits of the proposed system. Her report describes the problem, her proposed solutions, and the benefits to the company.

Figure 13.7
In Depth Critique: Shandel Cohen's Justification Report (Guiding Decisions Report)

MEMO

TO:	Jamie Engle
FROM:	Shandel Cohen
DATE:	July 8, 2000
SUBJECT:	Proposed automatic mail-response system

THE PROBLEM:
SLOW RESPONSE TO CUSTOMER REQUESTS FOR INFORMATION

Our new product line has been very well received, and orders have surpassed our projections. This very success, however, has created a shortage of printed catalogs and data sheets, as well as considerable overtime for people in the customer response center. As we introduce upgrades and new options, our printed materials quickly become outdated. If we continue to rely on printed materials for customer information, we have two choices: Distribute existing materials (even though they are incomplete or inaccurate) or discard existing materials and print new ones.

Cohen carefully describes the problem in a positive light—the company's success.

THE SOLUTION:
AUTOMATED MAIL-RESPONSE SYSTEM

With minor modifications to our current computer system and very little additional software, we can set up an automated mail-response system to respond to customer requests for information. This process can save us time and money and can keep our distributed information current.

Automated mail-response systems have been tested and proven effective. Many companies already use this method to respond to customer information requests, so we won't have to worry about relying on untested technology. Both customer and company responses have been positive.

Ever-Current Information

She uses report headings to highlight the benefits of her solution.

Rather than discard and print new materials, we would need to update only the electronic files. We would be able to provide customers and our field sales organization with up-to-date, correct information as soon as the upgrades or options are available.

Instantaneous Delivery

Within a very short time of requesting information, customers would have that information in hand. Electronic delivery would

(continued)

Solicited Proposals

Solicited proposals are prepared at the request of clients who need something done or want a certain product manufactured. The solicitation, or invitation to bid on the contract, is called a *request for proposal* (RFP). You respond to an RFP by preparing a proposal that shows how you would meet the potential customer's needs.

A solicited proposal demonstrates that your organization is better qualified than competitors to handle a particular contract.

Short paragraphs and good use of white space make this memo easy to read.

Cohen carefully explains the costs of her proposal, which she justifies by detailing the projected annual savings.

Rather than trying to anticipate management's questions and include unnecessary detail, she closes by offering to answer any questions management may have.

2

be especially advantageous for our international customers. Regular mail to remote locations sometimes takes weeks to arrive, by which time the information may already be out of date. Both customers and field salespeople will appreciate the automatic mail-response system.

Minimized Waste

With our current method of sending printed information, we discard virtually tons of obsolete catalogs, data sheets, and other materials.

By maintaining and distributing the information electronically, we would eliminate this waste. We would also free up a considerable amount of floor space and shelving that is required for storing printed materials.

Of course, some of our customers may still prefer to receive printed materials, or they may not have access to electronic mail. For these customers we could simply print copies of the files when we receive requests.

Lower Overtime Costs

Besides savings in paper and space, we would also realize considerable savings in wages. Because of the increased interest in our new products, we must continue to work overtime or hire new people to meet the demand. An automatic mail-response system would eliminate this need, allowing us to deal with fluctuating interest without a fluctuating work force.

Setup and Operating Costs

The necessary equipment and software costs approximately $15,000. System maintenance and upgrades are estimated at $5,000 per year.

We expect the following annual savings from eliminating printed information:

3

$100,000	Printing costs
25,000	Storage costs
5,000	Postage
20,000	Wages
$150,000	

CONCLUSION

I will be happy to answer any questions you have about this system. I believe that this system would greatly benefit our company, in terms of both cost and customer satisfaction. If you approve the system, we can have it installed and running in six weeks.

Say that the National Aeronautics and Space Administration (NASA) decides to develop a new satellite. Nobody makes this particular satellite yet; it hasn't been invented. Nevertheless, NASA knows what the satellite ought to do and wants to get the best design at the lowest cost. Typically, NASA first prepares an RFP that specifies exactly what the satellite should accomplish. The agency sends this RFP to several aerospace companies and invites them to bid on the job.

NASA isn't the only branch of the U.S. government that awards contracts on the basis of written proposals. Every agency from the Library of Congress to the Department of Health and Human Services issues RFPs, as do many states, provinces, counties, and cities. The federal government publishes RFPs both on paper and in electronic format, making it easy for firms to search for contracts of interest.

In addition, private industry awards major contracts on the basis of proposals. The items procured in this fashion range from office equipment to power plants. Whenever a customer is spending a lot of money—especially for something that is unique, sophisticated, and difficult to produce—the managers involved want to know as much as possible about potential suppliers and their ability to deliver the desired solution.

When a company gets an RFP, the managers have to decide whether they are interested in the job and whether they have a reasonable chance of winning the contract. If they decide to submit a bid, the proposal effort begins in earnest. The company reviews the requirements, defines the scope of the work, determines the methods and procedures to be used, and estimates time requirements, personnel requirements, and costs. Then the proposal writers put it all on paper, responding meticulously to every point raised by the RFP—and following the exact format specified by the RFP.[9]

Most proposals are organized in the same way: They begin with an introductory section that states the purpose of the proposal, defines the scope of the work, presents background information, and explains any restrictions that might apply to the contract. The body of the proposal gives details on the proposed effort and specifies what the anticipated results will be. The discussion covers the methods, schedule, facilities, equipment, personnel, and costs that will be involved in the contract. A final section generally summarizes the key points of the proposal and asks for a decision from the client.

Unsolicited Proposals

An unsolicited proposal establishes the value of funding your project.

The other major type of proposal, the unsolicited proposal, is initiated by an organization that is attempting to obtain business or funding on its own, without a specific invitation from a potential client. Unsolicited proposals differ from solicited proposals in one important respect: The recipient has to be convinced of the benefits of buying (or funding) something. As a consequence, unsolicited proposals generally spend considerable time explaining why the recipient should take action.

Unsolicited proposals vary widely in form, length, and purpose. A university seeking funding for a specific research project might submit an unsolicited proposal to a large local corporation. To be convincing, the proposal would show how the research could benefit the corporation, and it would demonstrate that the university has the resources and expertise to conduct the research.[10] As another example, an entrepreneur seeking funding for a new venture might modify a business plan to create a proposal showing potential investors the return they should expect in exchange for the use of their funds. Of course, such a proposal would try to convince investors of the viability of the new business.

In most cases, business plans (and supporting documents such as marketing plans and engineering plans) are considered highly confidential and are released to outsiders very selectively. External readers are frequently asked to sign a *nondisclosure agreement* to prevent them from using or sharing anything they read.

Case Study: Bruce Rogow's Business Plan Proposal

Bruce Rogow was a junior engineering major at San Diego State University when he was first struck by the idea of leading a team of students to design, build, and race a solar car at the World Solar Challenge race across the Australian outback. The race itself would be the least of Rogow's challenges: First he had to convince students and faculty of the project's benefits; then he had to keep them motivated (and working long, hard hours) while he tackled administrative and engineering roadblocks that even he couldn't predict.

Ultimately, the SDSU Solar Car Project succeeded, and it drew involvement from various academic departments, dozens of student volunteers, several corporate benefactors, and many news organizations. Rogow challenged science, engineering, and computer students to design and test *Suntrakker* (as the car was named). But he also challenged SDSU's business students to come up with a proposal that would help him raise the support *Suntrakker* required.

"We needed to raise $145,000," Rogow recalls. "And since we had no faculty support in the beginning, we had to have something that would give us credibility. The business plan gave us much more than that."

Three students from an entrepreneurship class agreed to work with Rogow on a plan that eventually filled over 70 pages. "The business plan mapped out every detail of our project, from start to finish, and made us look at things we had not considered. It also earned us respect from the faculty and was responsible for a $5,000 donation from our local power company." Rogow now believes that the business plan made the difference between "thriving and just surviving" (see Figure 13.8).

With the students' combined skills and Rogow's determined leadership, *Suntrakker* gave an impressive showing in Australia. In fact, the futuristic-looking solar car now tours schools as part of a university recruiting program, and both a book and a documentary film (*Warriors of the Sun*) have been produced about the project. Meanwhile, the Solar Car Project's business plan is still at work, helping students produce a second-generation *Suntrakker* for the next World Solar Challenge.

Bruce Rogow with Suntrakker *in Australia. Rogow wrote his business plan proposal to raise financial and team support for designing, building, and racing* Suntrakker. *The project involved 35 students, who raised $145,000. Their solar car finished 42nd out of 52 cars in Australia's World Solar Challenge race.*

Bruce Rogow's business plan is a type of unsolicited proposal, with the benefits up front and the financial information at the close. Detailed and thorough, it includes sections describing the vehicle, the management team, and even "Critical Risks." Appendixes include an organization chart, résumé, design schematics, letters of support, lists of volunteers and contributors, and a telemarketing script. Here is an excerpt from the executive summary (a miniversion of the report that gives busy executives a detailed overview).

Figure 13.8
In-Depth Critique: Bruce Rogow's Proposal (Business Plan Excerpt)

THE EXECUTIVE SUMMARY

Purpose of the Plan

This document will acquaint the reader with three principal topics by

- Showing what the San Diego State University (SDSU) SUNTRAKKER project is
- Showing that the team-oriented, interdepartmental disciplines at SDSU possess the tenacity and know-how to build and race a solar-powered vehicle in the World Solar Challenge Race in Australia in 1993
- Defining and articulating how this business team expects to promote and generate the necessary support, funds, and materials from the student body, alumni, community, and local businesses to seize and execute this opportunity

Project Profile

The SUNTRAKKER Solar Car project was conceived in July 1990 when a small group of San Diego State University engineering students, motivated by the successes of the General Motors Sunrayce, committed themselves to designing and building a superior solar-powered vehicle to compete in the World Solar Challenge.

From modest beginnings, the SUNTRAKKER project quickly evolved into a cross-disciplinary educational effort encompassing students from many colleges of San Diego State University. The project has provided student participants and volunteers with valuable real-life experiences and has brought them together in an effort that benefits not only the students and the university but also the environment.

Sponsors of this project are not only contributing to the success of the overall SUNTRAKKER project but will also enhance their goodwill, advertising, and name promotion by association with the project. In addition, the SUNTRAKKER offers a unique opportunity for the companies that can donate parts and accessories to showcase their name and field test their products in this highly publicized international contest.

The Nature and Value of the Project

The explicit purpose of the project is to design, build, test, and race a world-class solar-powered car with the express purpose of spurring the technological development of energy-efficient vehicles. Although winning the World Solar Challenge is the explicit focus of the project, the implicit goal is to promote ongoing technological research in the field of alternative energy sources, with a view toward conserving the earth's precious nonrenewable natural resources and encouraging international cooperation.

Competitions such as the World Solar Challenge are catalysts for innovation; they provide focus and expand our perspectives beyond the present technology horizon in many different disciplines. The competition stimulates development of seemingly impractical vehicles, yet actually promotes interest and involvement in real-life educational and practical experiences culminating in tangible benefits to the global community. Futuristic and evolutionary projects such as the SUNTRAKKER provide a stimulus to researchers and forward-thinkers to strive toward the common goal of making alternative energy sources a viable reality.

Remember to answer questions about *who* (voluntary), *what* (business plan), *when* (special, nonrecurring), *where* (external), *why* (analytical), and *how* (receptive readers).

For a business plan intended to raise funds, use the indirect approach to introduce your objectives, justification, and benefits. Include ample details supported by facts, figures, personnel qualifications, endorsements, and so forth.

Convey a confident tone by writing thoughtful, well-developed paragraphs. Provide good introductions and transitions, headings, and lists.

Business plans may be prepared for external and internal readers. Not usually compared with competing plans (as are solicited proposals or bids), business plans must still motivate readers to invest or contribute. Many businesses periodically update their plans as their objectives change and as they seek funding from new sources.

(continued)

Figure 13.8, continued

Subheads make it easy for readers to locate particular points.

Sections in the executive summary correspond to major sections in the report and summarize the information provided there.

2

Form of Organization

The SDSU SUNTRAKKER project has been founded as a tax-exempt, nonprofit student organization. The organization's primary purposes are to build the SUNTRAKKER and to represent SDSU in the World Solar Challenge Race in 1993.

The SUNTRAKKER project is organized by function, with directors of marketing, design, production, logistics, public relations, and finance. Together, the departments constitute the management review committee in charge of all activities. Each department director reports to the project manager, Bruce Rogow. In turn, Mr. Rogow, who is responsible for coordinating the whole team effort, reports to a board of advisers. The advisory board, headed by Dr. William Guentzler, oversees the project and acts as a resource think tank to assist in critical problem solving. (See Appendix AS for an organizational chart of the SUNTRAKKER project.)

Growth Trend of Market

Technology developed from the SUNTRAKKER project has direct applicability to the coming hybrid electric and solar-powered vehicle markets throughout the world, especially here in southern California. Because of massive pollution problems and rising population growth rates, transportation needs mandate that we find alternatives to the fossil-fueled vehicles now in popular use.

In many areas of California, pollution has become the driving factor in the search for alternative vehicle power sources. The South Coast Air Quality Management District, encompassing the greater southern California area, has enacted a plan to replace 40 percent of gasoline-powered vehicles now operating in metropolitan areas with nonemissions vehicles. The plan directs that government and commercial fleets greater than 15 vehicles be required to buy alternative-powered vehicles if they want to increase their fleet size.

SUMMARY REPORTS

Businesspeople are bombarded with masses of information, and at one time or another, everyone in business relies on someone else's summary of a situation, publication, or document. To write a summary report, gather the information (whether by reading, talking with others, or observing circumstances), organize that information, and then present it in your own words. Although many people assume that summarizing is a simple skill, it's actually more complex than it appears. A well-written summary has at least three characteristics.

Three characteristics of a well-written summary:

- Accuracy
- Comprehensiveness and balance
- Clear sentence structure and good transitions

First, as with any business document, the content must be accurate. If you're summarizing a report or a group of reports, make sure you present the information without error. Check your references, and then check for typos.

Second, the summary should be comprehensive and balanced. The purpose of writing your summary is usually to help colleagues or supervisors make a decision, so include all the information necessary for your readers to understand the situation, problem, or proposal. If the issue you're summarizing has more than one side, present all sides fairly and equitably. Make sure you include all the information necessary. Even though summaries are intended to be as brief as possible, your readers need a minimum amount of information to grasp the issue being presented.

Third, clear sentence structure and good transitions are essential.[11] The only way your summary will save anyone's time is if your sentences are uncluttered, made up of well-chosen words, and proceed logically. To help your readers move from one point to the next, your transitions must be just as clear and logical. Basically, when writing your summary, be sure to cut through the clutter. Identify those ideas that belong together, and organize them in a way that's easy to understand.[12]

How Electronic Technology Affects Business Reports

Electronic reports are becoming more popular.

Reports aren't necessarily confined to paper in today's business environment. Virtually all of the reports discussed in this chapter can be adapted to computerized formats. Businesses have envisioned the *paperless office* for years, and it's finally coming true for many organizations. People in the United States can now file their taxes electronically, the SEC actually requires corporations to file reports electronically, and thousands of companies have set up electronic reporting procedures to communicate with employees, customers, and suppliers.[13] Look at Isis, a small pharmaceutical company. Because being first to introduce a new drug in the market is critical in the pharmaceutical industry, Isis files its 40,000-page reports with the U.S. Food and Drug Administration in one-third the time by compressing the information onto one CD-ROM.[14] (See "Keeping Pace with Technology: Gain the Competitive Edge with Online Reporting.")

Did You Know?

In 1998 more than 25 million taxpayers filed their Federal income tax returns electronically.

KEEPING PACE WITH TECHNOLOGY

Gain the Competitive Edge with Online Reporting

Mrs. Fields uses them. Mrs. Paul's uses them. However, you don't have to be in the cookie or fish business to work with electronic reports. Today more and more managers and employees are using computers to write and send reports for virtually every business purpose. Computerized cash registers in Mrs. Fields cookie outlets are the heart of a sophisticated reporting system for monitoring and controlling operations. Rather than taking the time to write reports by hand, store managers enter data into the computer system by following report formats on their screen. Then they electronically transmit these reports to corporate headquarters in Park City, Utah. The computer system also serves as a two-way communication device, allowing store and corporate personnel to send messages back and forth in seconds. So Mrs. Fields corporate managers can quickly receive the information they need in order to track sales and productivity trends—and to spot potential problems—in more than 500 outlets around the world.

At Mrs. Paul's, a computerized reporting system allows production managers to continuously monitor and control the yield from the company's fish-processing operation. The system calculates the production yield using the weight of the fish before it's processed, the weight of any scraps, and the weight of the finished fish meals. If the reports show that the actual yield drops below the expected yield, the managers can immediately adjust the equipment to improve the yield. The production managers have instant access to electronic monitor and control reports at each stage of the operation, so they can find and fix problems more quickly than if they had to wait for printed reports.

Federal Express, the well-known package-shipping firm, uses electronic reporting to let customers know the status of their shipments at any time. It has one of the most popular sites on the World Wide Web. The company uses extensive satellite and computer technologies to track the location of every package in the system, and customers can log onto the FedEx site to find out where their packages are. This tracking system not only helps the company serve its customers better but also cuts down on costs because FedEx doesn't need to have so many people on the phones answering questions for customers.

1. What advantages and disadvantages do you see in asking store managers at Mrs. Fields to file troubleshooting reports immediately by entering data into the computerized cash register system?
2. How would an electronic reporting system help a company track the activity of personnel who frequently travel to customer sites or other locations?

Electronic reports fall into two basic categories: First are those that essentially replace paper reports. You simply draft a report using your word processor as usual, but instead of printing it and making copies, you distribute the file electronically. Most e-mail systems now have the ability to attach files to support electronic document distribution. The other category of electronic reports includes those that are unique to the electronic format. For example, an intranet site can offer text, video, and sound in a single integrated "report."

Report-writing software can pull information out of computerized databases and organize it in any format you want.

If you explore software for electronic reports, you'll discover a class of software known as *report writers* or *reporting tools*. Unfortunately, these tools don't magically write business reports for you. They are designed to extract and format data from computerized databases. For instance, you can use a personnel database to generate a report that ranks employees by income or a customer database to generate mailing labels for all your customers. Once the report is generated, you can print it or distribute it electronically. Also, some report writers allow you to work interactively with the database, in effect creating a "live" report that responds to your queries and inputs.[15]

Electronic reports offer both advantages and disadvantages when compared with their paper counterparts. The advantages include

Electronic reports have distinct advantages.

- *Cost savings.* After the initial expenditure for hardware and software, electronic reports can save a significant amount of money in terms of paper, printing or photocopying, and distribution.
- *Space savings.* A basic CD-ROM can hold the equivalent of hundreds of pages of text (and higher-capacity CD-ROMs and other massive storage devices are on the way), so electronic reports can be stored in far less space than paper reports. This can be a significant advantage for large businesses, businesses with heavy government reporting requirements, and businesses that must keep historical records for many years.
- *Faster distribution.* Electronic documents can reach their audiences in a few seconds, compared with the hours or days it can take to send paper documents to other locations.
- *Multimedia communication.* You can integrate sound and video with some electronic reports, bringing text to life.
- *Easier maintenance.* Documents on intranet and Internet Web sites are great examples of how much easier it is to correct and update electronic documents. If a single figure changes in a sales report after you've distributed it, your options with a paper report are to reprint and redistribute the entire thing, send out a corrected page, or send a memo to all the recipients asking them to pencil in the correction by hand. With an electronic report, you simply make the change and let everyone know via e-mail. When you offer your readers access to an electronic report on an intranet site, you have an added bonus: The only existing copy of the report is always current, so you don't have to worry about people hanging on to obsolete or incorrect information.

DID YOU KNOW?

The SEC now requires corporations to file their annual reports electronically via a system called EDGAR (Electronic Data Gathering, Analysis, and Retrieval). This system makes it possible to use a computer to find out what's in an annual report without obtaining a printed copy from the company.

Electronic reports have their disadvantages as well.

For all their advantages, however, electronic reports are not a cure-all for business communication problems, nor are they without some risks and disadvantages:

- *Hardware and software costs.* Naturally, you need some kind of computer equipment to distribute electronic documents. If those systems aren't already in place, their purchase, installation, and maintenance is an extra expense.
- *System incompatibility.* As discussed in Chapter 10, corporate intranets are helping businesspeople get around the computer compatibility problem, but companies that lack intranets may find themselves with incompatible computer systems that preclude the use of electronic documents.

- *Training needs.* Beyond the ability to read, there is little training involved in reading most paper business reports. However, reading electronic reports can require training in using Web browsers, accessing databases, or other skills.
- *Risks to data security and integrity.* Because information in electronic reports is not fixed on paper, it's vulnerable to tampering and inadvertent corruption. Even innocent computer errors can affect electronic reports and cause your carefully crafted document to end up as electronic rubbish.[16]

Many businesses see electronic documents as a way to cut costs while improving worker productivity and customer service, so expect to write and read many such reports on the job.

COMMUNICATION CHALLENGES AT NARADA PRODUCTIONS

Now that the daily reporting system has helped smooth the wrinkles from Narada's operations, Wesley Van Linda has time to focus on other important issues. One of them involves a marketing test he wants to conduct to determine how cover art affects the sales of a compact disc or audiocassette. Although other companies have conducted similar research into the dynamics of consumer buying and package design, Van Linda wants to know whether the buying habits of Narada listeners differ from those of conventional listeners, since they're choosing music that is unconventional. To conduct the test, Van Linda plans to issue one recording by pianist David Lanz with two distinct covers throughout the country.

INDIVIDUAL CHALLENGE: Van Linda has asked you to help with the project by recommending a reporting method for tracking how the cover designs affect sales. Van Linda explains: "Here's what we need to know: Does one cover sell better than the other? Are there regional distinctions? In other words, do this artist's fans respond positively to the same artwork no matter where they live, or do West Coast buyers differ from East Coast buyers? If so, this could affect how we issue future releases. Don't worry about the psychology behind the choices of artwork—we'll let marketing handle that. I want you to determine what kinds of reports we'll need for tracking the sales patterns, who should write them, and what information they should include. Let me have your recommendations as soon as possible."

TEAM CHALLENGE: Another possibility might be to incorporate the marketing test into reports Van Linda is already receiving from the field. He's asked your group to look into it. Refer to the chapter-opening vignette for descriptions of these operational reports, and discuss with your team how they might be used. Would using these existing reports be more efficient than devising new ones? Why or why not? What would be the advantages and disadvantages of handling the marketing test through a separate set of reports?[17] ■

SUMMARY OF LEARNING OBJECTIVES

1. **Define what is meant by a business report.** A business report is a factual, objective document that serves a legitimate business purpose. It may be 3 pages or 300 pages long. It may be a preprinted form, a memo, a letter, a manuscript, or an electronic form. The length, format, style, and organization of a business report all depend on who originates it, the subject of the report, when and why it is prepared, where it is sent, and how receptive the reader is.
2. **Discuss why businesses need reports and highlight the six general purposes of reports.** Businesses need reports to provide a variety of information to internal and external users. They are especially helpful to busy managers who can't oversee every operation themselves. The six general purposes of reports are to monitor and control operations, to help implement policies and procedures, to comply with legal and regulatory requirements, to document work performed for a client, to guide decisions on particular issues, and to obtain new business or funding.
3. **Distinguish between informational and analytical reports.** Informational reports focus on facts and are intended mainly to educate readers, whereas analytical reports provide data analyses, interpretation, and a conclusion. Many analytical reports are designed to persuade readers to accept a decision, action, or recommendations. Information in analytical reports plays a supporting role rather than being the primary focus.
4. **Describe four types of informational reports and provide examples of each.** Typical informational reports include reports for monitoring and controlling operations, such as plans, operating

reports, and personal activity reports; reports for implementing policies and procedures, such as lasting guidelines and position papers; compliance reports, such as annual reports to the SEC and income tax reports; and reports to document the progress of a project.

5. **Describe three types of analytical reports and briefly explain how each is used.** Three types of analytical reports are problem-solving or troubleshooting reports, which are used to assist with decision making; justification or feasibility reports, which are used for asset acquisitions or operational improvements; and proposals, which are used to obtain new business or funding.
6. **Cite the advantages and disadvantages of electronic reports.** The potential advantages include cost savings, space savings, faster distribution, and easier maintenance. The disadvantages include the cost of additional hardware, software, and training; the potential for system incompatibility; and the possible threat to data security and integrity due to tampering and inadvertent corruption.

CRITICAL THINKING QUESTIONS

1. If you want to make a specific recommendation in your research report, should you include information that might support a different recommendation? Explain.
2. Could the increased speed of electronic reporting create any problems with the quality of the information people see or the decisions they make? Explain your answer.
3. What are the advantages and disadvantages of asking your employees to "fill in the blanks" on standardized reporting forms? Briefly explain.
4. If you want to use your strategic or marketing plan as an unsolicited proposal for obtaining funds for a new business venture, what changes would you have to make to the report? Think about the who, what, when, where, why, and how of both types of reports, and explain your answer.
5. If you were writing a troubleshooting report to help management decide how to reduce quality problems at a manufacturing plant, what ethical issues might you face? How might these ethical issues conflict with your need to report all the relevant facts and to offer evidence for your conclusions? Explain briefly.
6. Discuss one internal issue and one external issue that might spark managers to draft a position paper. Identify the audience for each position paper you discuss.
7. If your report includes only factual information, is it objective? Please explain.
8. Discuss the advantages and disadvantages of using prepackaged software for writing business plans or proposals.

EXERCISES

1. Using the information presented in this chapter, identify the type of report represented by each of the following examples. In addition, write a paragraph about each, explaining who the audience is likely to be, what type of data would be used, and whether conclusions and recommendations would be appropriate.
   a. A statistical study of the pattern of violent crime in a large city during the last five years
   b. A report prepared by a seed company demonstrating the benefits of its seed corn for farmers
   c. A report prepared by an independent testing agency evaluating various types of cold remedies sold without prescription
   d. A trip report submitted at the end of a week by a traveling salesperson
   e. A report indicating how 45 acres of undeveloped land could be converted into an industrial park
   f. An annual report to be sent to the shareholders of a large corporation
   g. A report from a U.S. National Park wildlife officer to Washington, D.C., headquarters showing the status of the California condor (an endangered species)
   h. A written report by a police officer who has just completed an arrest
2. Call the public affairs department of a nearby company and ask for a copy of the policy statement concerning one of the following three topics:
   a. Environmental affairs
   b. Equal opportunity employment practices
   c. Buy-American policies

   Then write a one-page report discussing whether the policy offers sufficient guidance without being too specific to be implemented. How can you improve the way this policy statement communicates with employees?
3. Interview several people working in a career you might like to enter, and ask them about the types of written reports they receive and prepare. How do these reports tie in to the decision-making process? Who reads the reports they prepare? Summarize your findings in writing, give them to your instructor, and be prepared to discuss them with the class.
4. Find a copy of *Commerce Business Daily* through your library, or check your local newspaper for advertisements placed by government agencies that are issuing RFPs on construction contracts or other projects. Call or write for a copy of the RFP guidelines. Does the RFP specify a particular format for company bids? Is any specialized language used in the RFP form? What restrictions are mentioned? What financial points must be covered in each bid?
5. Imagine you're the manager of campus recruiting for Nortel, a Canadian telecommunications firm. Each of your four recruiters interviews up to 11 college seniors every day. What kind of personal activity report can you design to track the results of these interviews? List the areas you would want each recruiter to report on, and explain how each would help you manage the recruiting process (and the recruiters) more effectively.

6. You're the vice president of operations for a Florida fast-food chain. In the aftermath of a major hurricane, you're drafting a report on the emergency procedures to be followed by personnel in each restaurant when storm warnings are in effect. Answer who, what, when, where, why, and how, and then prepare a one-page draft of your report.

7. Visit the Narada Productions home page at http://www.narada.com, and consider the factual information it provides: company intentions, products, services, background, and so forth. On the basis of this information, prepare a short memo to Wesley Van Linda in which you justify the cost and effort of maintaining this Web site—its fulfillment of company goals, its effectiveness with Web browsers, its usefulness to customers. (Create any details necessary to complete your memo.)

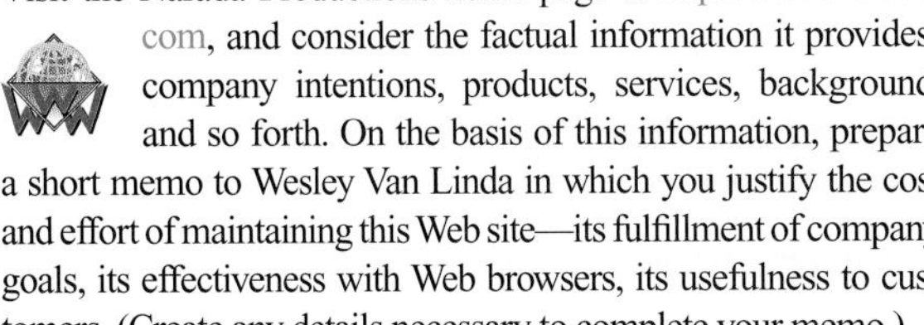

8. As the director of your college's placement office, you're always searching for employers who will hire students part-time during the school year. However, because three other colleges are located within 25 miles of your campus, most area employers are bombarded with similar requests. Now you're planning to send an unsolicited proposal to the nearby American Airlines reservations office. Your proposal must convince the airline that students from your college are better qualified to serve as reservations operators than students from other colleges. Make a list of the specific points you'll cover to be convincing; then note any restrictions you may have to mention in such a proposal.

9. You're an engineer training your assistant to write monthly progress reports. The current report is on a project in Singapore that's behind schedule. This report will go to Singapore government officials as well as to your own supervisors at corporate headquarters. Is it a voluntary report or an authorized report? What information should you ask your assistant to report? In what order should this information be presented? How formal do you want this report to be? Will the report be organized around conclusions or subtopics? Draft a brief (one- to two-page) memo, giving your assistant instructions on how to prepare this report.

10. Like any business message, a good report defines the main idea, states the major points, and illustrates each major point with evidence. Review the discussion in Chapter 5 under the heading "How Good Organization Is Achieved" (see page 128).
    a. Using Figure 5.3 (see page 133) as a guideline, analyze the Boeing case study on pages 333–334. What is the case study's main idea? What are the major points of the report? What supporting evidence is provided?
    b. Using some of the resources listed in Chapter 11, find current information on Boeing. Has the company solved its production problems? If so, how? If not, what are some challenges Boeing currently faces? Write a summary report (memo format) discussing Boeing's current operational status.

Exploring the Best of the Web

How to Write a Business Plan, page 444

In addition to posting 12 tips on writing business plans, the Tikkanen-Bradley Consulting Group provides Internet access to a full report, "Creating Successful Business Plans," in the archive section of the Web site. The report notes that "a good business plan answers five key questions regarding your business: (1) whether the proposed business venture is realistic, (2) whether the product-market fit is appropriate, (3) how the firm intends to achieve a sustainable competitive advantage, (4) what level of returns the business is expected to yield and when, and (5) whether the players involved in the business are capable of attaining the returns."

1. Which of those questions does the excerpt from Bruce Rogow's proposal (see Figure 13.8) address? Are any left unanswered?
2. If you were seeking support for *Suntrakker,* would you make any changes in the Rogow proposal?

PLANNING, ORGANIZING, AND WRITING REPORTS AND PROPOSALS

AFTER STUDYING THIS CHAPTER, YOU WILL BE ABLE TO

1 Differentiate between a problem statement and a statement of purpose
2 Identify at least five elements commonly included in a formal work plan
3 Explain the difference between a conclusion and a recommendation
4 List six ways to structure informational reports
5 Describe three basic organizational approaches to use when focusing on logical arguments, and briefly discuss when it's best to use each
6 Identify five tools writers can use when preparing a long report to help readers stay on track

COMMUNICATION CLOSE-UP AT THE SAN DIEGO WILD ANIMAL PARK

Whether encountering a cheetah, feeding a giraffe, or crossing a floating bridge to a "field biologist's research island," visitors to the San Diego Wild Animal Park aren't likely to be thinking about business proposals. But if it hadn't been for a dedicated team of five park employees and a particularly impressive proposal, the park's brand-new, 30-acre "Heart of Africa" safari tour would not exist. Hardy tourists would not be trekking through the artificially created African forestland, savanna, wetlands, waterholes, and islands to enjoy raging waterfalls, African plants, and lots of animals—grazing antelope, wattled cranes, sacred ibis, colobus monkeys, rhinos, wildebeests, gazelles, and some 250 other species of mammals and birds. If those determined park employees hadn't put their communication skills to work to sell a concept that was initially vetoed by the park's brainstorming committee, there would be no interpretive guides posing as "research scientists" and no demonstrations of radio telemetry tracking.

Deirdre Ballou

This is a communication success story. As education manager for the Wild Animal Park, Deirdre Ballou was part of the enthusiastic group that rescued the Heart of Africa concept from its early rejection. "We felt the idea was good and that if we carried it out a little bit more, we could try again." In addition to Ballou, this group included the park's public relations manager and the curators of birds, mammals, and zoology. These five colleagues agreed among themselves to meet on their own time to develop a proposal that the rest of the committee just couldn't refuse. They would do their homework, they vowed, and then return with a comprehensive, clear, impressive, and persuasive proposal for the Heart of Africa project.

Whether working on new concepts such as the Heart of Africa project, raising funds, or educating sponsors and visitors, Deirdre Ballou often finds herself writing reports and proposals. Ballou pays special attention to her communication skills in order to do her best while researching, organizing, analyzing, and presenting her ideas.

Ballou says their smartest move was to first identify the best skills of everyone in the group. The public relations manager was a sparkling presenter, and the three curators were extremely knowledgeable about the park's animal collection. Ballou contributed her knowledge of education and interpretation, as well as her proposal-writing experience. Identifying their individual strengths "was really key" to the team's success, says Ballou.

The next step was to write an evocative scenario using "very creative words" to walk committee members through an imaginary tour of the team's vision for the Heart of Africa. They put the sizzle before the steak, as the old adage goes (also known as using the indirect approach). All contributed their expertise to the scenario, but the team's "best writer" did the honors, says Ballou.

The park committee liked the scenario and challenged the team to take the next step: a slide-show presentation for the committees of the board of trustees of the Zoological Society of San Diego, nonprofit owner of the Wild Animal Park. Now Ballou and her colleagues really knuckled down, researching statistics published by zoo and museum professional organizations and drawing on their own experience working with the public and with the park's animal collections. They poured this information into a script that began with an overview to be presented by their best speaker, the public relations manager, followed by detailed information from the animal curators. Ballou came next with information about the terrific educational opportunities at the research island and with justification for hiring interpretive staff to portray field researchers. The public relations manager closed the presentation, reemphasizing the selling points of the Heart of Africa and research island project, reminding committee members how well it would fulfill the park's stated mission and purpose. The team knew the committee members' preference for short presentations, so they kept the report under 20 minutes, concluding with questions and answers.

"Committees and board members respect and will listen to people who have done their homework," Ballou says now, remembering the excitement of winning the committees' approval. Before long, she was out in the middle of a human-made lagoon in jeans and T-shirt, helping builders complete the final details in time for the Heart of Africa's official opening.

Ballou still routinely writes dozens of reports and proposals—funding proposals, budget and labor reports, and project status reports. And she still starts by asking: Will my audience be receptive? Have we met with them before? Are they expecting a formal presentation or a more casual approach? Then she chooses the right format, length, order, and tone to meet their expectations. But she also recalls with great fondness her participation on the team that saved the Heart of Africa and research island project. Who would have thought that preparing an ordinary business proposal could be so much fun—and so rewarding?[1] ■

STEP 1: PLANNING REPORTS AND PROPOSALS

As Deirdre Ballou knows, writing a report involves careful planning. Before putting a single word on the page, she follows a series of steps that form the foundation of any report:

1. Define the problem.
2. Develop a statement of purpose.
3. Prepare a work plan.
4. Collect, analyze, and interpret data, drawing conclusions and developing recommendations.

Informational reports seldom involve analysis.

The relative importance of these four steps depends on the type of assignment. Informational reports, which contain facts alone, require little in the way of analysis, interpretation, conclusions, or recommendations. In fact, if you're preparing an informational report, you'll probably only have to develop a statement of purpose, prepare a brief work plan, collect the facts, arrange them into a logical order, and write the report. Analytical reports, on the other hand, require a bit more effort, because they include interpretations, conclusions, and recommendations.

Defining the Problem

If you're writing an informational report, your assignment may be as simple as gathering last month's sales figures and submitting them to management in a table format. In fact, most informational reports don't go beyond submitting the facts. This is not the case, however, for analytical reports. If you're writing an analytical report, your assignment will likely involve solving a problem. So you begin the analytical report process by developing a *problem statement*—that is, by defining the particular problem that is to be solved by your report.

The first step in writing an analytical report is developing a problem statement.

In Chapter 11 we explained that a problem statement defines the problem you need to resolve. This problem can be negative or positive—it may deal with shrinking sales or the need for more child-care facilities. Whatever the problem, solving it will require research. Be careful not to confuse a simple topic (campus parking) with a problem (the lack of enough campus parking). Another thing to remember is that if you're the only person who thinks this issue is a problem, the audience won't be very interested in your solution. So be sure to consider the company's perspective and the individual perspectives of the people who will read your report.[2] You may have to spend some time convincing people that a problem exists.

Limiting the Scope of the Study

Linda Moreno is the cost accounting manager for Electrovision, a high-technology company based in Los Gatos, California. She was asked recently to find ways of reducing employee travel and entertainment costs (her complete report appears in Chapter 15). As in Moreno's case, the problem is often defined for the writer by the person who authorizes the report. To ensure that she understands exactly what is required of her, Moreno begins by discussing the objectives of her report with the person who requested and authorized the investigation. Specifically, she tries to answer the following questions:

- What needs to be determined?
- Why is this issue important?
- Who is involved in the situation?
- Where is the trouble located?
- When did it start?
- How did the situation originate?

Verify your assignment with the person authorizing the report.

Of course, not all these questions apply in every situation, but asking them helps limit the scope of the problem and clarify the boundaries of the investigation. You can then draft a written statement that will serve as a guide to whatever problem you're trying to solve or whatever question you're trying to answer in the report.[3]

Besides asking questions, another effective way to limit the scope of your study is to break the problem into a series of logical, connected questions that try to identify causes and effects. This process is sometimes called **problem factoring**. You probably subconsciously approach most problems this way. When your car's engine won't start, what do you do? You use the available evidence to organize your investigation, to start a search for cause-and-effect relationships. If the engine doesn't turn over at all, for instance, you might suspect a dead battery. If the engine does turn over but won't fire, you can conclude that the battery is okay but perhaps you're out of gas. When you speculate on the cause of a problem, you're forming a **hypothesis**, a potential explanation that needs to be tested. By subdividing a problem and forming hypotheses based on available evidence, you can tackle even the most complex situations.

Problem factoring is an effective way to limit the scope of your study.

Studies that focus on problem solving may be structured around hypotheses that the report writer plans to prove or disprove during the investigation.

Linda Moreno used the factoring process to structure her investigation into ways of reducing travel and entertainment costs at Electrovision. "I began with a two-part question," says Moreno. "Why have our travel costs grown so dramatically, and how can we reduce them? Then I factored that question into two subquestions: Do we have adequate procedures for tracking and controlling costs? Are these procedures being followed?

"Looking into cost-control procedures, I speculated that the right kind of information was not reaching the executives who were responsible for these costs. From there, the questioning naturally led to the systems and procedures for collecting this information. If we didn't have the right procedures in place or if people weren't following procedures, the information wouldn't reach the people in charge."

Once Moreno had determined what was wrong with Electrovision's cost-control system, she could address the second part of the main question: the problem of recommending improvements. This factoring process, or breaking a problem into a series of subproblems, enabled Moreno and her colleagues to approach the task methodically.

Outlining Issues for Investigation

As you go through the factoring process, you may want to use an outline format to represent your ideas. For example, if your problem is to determine why your company is having trouble hiring secretaries, you'll begin by speculating on the causes. Then you'll collect information to confirm or disprove each reason. Your outline of the major issues might look something like this:

Use an outline format when factoring complex problems.

Why are we having trouble hiring secretaries?

1. Are salaries are too low?
   a. What do we pay our secretaries?
   b. What do comparable companies pay their secretaries?
   c. How important is pay in influencing secretaries' job choices?

2. Is our location poor?
   a. Are we accessible by public transportation and major roads?
   b. Is the area physically attractive?
   c. Are housing costs affordable?
   d. Is crime a problem?
3. Is the supply of secretaries diminishing?
   a. How many secretaries were available five years ago as opposed to now?
   b. What was the demand for secretaries five years ago as opposed to now?

If a few notes are enough to guide you through a short, informal report in memo form, an outline might not be necessary. Nevertheless, it's worth noting that the way you outline an investigation may be different from the way you outline the resulting report. Solving the problem is one thing; "selling" the solution is another. During your investigation, you might analyze five possible causes of a problem and discover that only two are relevant. In your report, you might not even introduce the three unrelated causes. (Chapter 11 discusses how to prepare and format outlines. Later in this chapter, we'll discuss the benefits of preparing a final writing outline.)

Developing the Statement of Purpose

Once you've determined the problem and limited its scope, you're ready to develop a **statement of purpose,** which defines the objective of the report. In contrast to the problem statement, which defines *what* you are going to investigate, the statement of purpose defines *why* you are preparing the report (see Table 14.1).

The most useful way to phrase your purpose is to begin with an infinitive phrase. For instance, in an informational report, your statement of purpose can be as simple as these:

- To update clients on the progress of the computer-programming project (interim progress report)
- To develop goals and objectives for the coming year (strategic plan)
- To identify customers and explain how the company will service them (marketing plan)
- To submit monthly sales statistics to management (periodic operating report)
- To summarize the events that occurred at the annual sales conference (personal activity report)
- To explain the building access procedures (policy implementation report)
- To submit required information to the SEC (compliance report)

BEST OF THE WEB

Construct an Outline with Confidence

The Purdue University Online Writing Lab (OWL) offers a variety of resources and direct assistance for any writer in need of help. Over 100 valuable handouts are available for your use. For information about outlining, start on the home page, then under "Resources for Writers," click on "Handouts" and then "Developing an Outline" for information that will reinforce the points made in this chapter.

http://owl.english.purdue.edu

TABLE 14.1

PROBLEM STATEMENTS VERSUS PURPOSE STATEMENTS

Problem Statement	Statement of Purpose
■ Our company's market share is steadily declining.	■ To explore different ways of selling our products and to recommend the ones that will most likely increase our market share.
■ Our current computer network system is inefficient and cannot be upgraded to meet our future needs.	■ To analyze various computer network systems and to recommend the system that will best meet our company's current and future needs.
■ We need $2 million to launch our new product.	■ To convince investors that our new business would be a sound investment so that we can obtain desired financing.
■ Our current operations are too decentralized and expensive.	■ To justify the closing of the Newark plant and the transfer of East Coast operations to a single Midwest location in order to save the company money.

Using an infinitive phrase (*to* plus a verb) encourages you to take control and decide where you're going before you begin. When you choose an infinitive phrase—*to inform, to confirm, to analyze, to persuade, to recommend*—you pin down your general goal in preparing the report.

Of course, the statement of purpose for analytical reports is often more comprehensive. Look at Linda Moreno's statement of purpose. Because she was supposed to suggest specific ways of reducing costs, she phrased her statement like this:

Statements of purpose for analytical reports are often more complex than are those for informational reports.

> . . . to analyze the T&E [travel and entertainment] budget, evaluate the impact of recent changes in airfares and hotel costs, and suggest ways to tighten management's control over T&E expenses.

If Moreno had been given an informational assignment instead, she might have stated her purpose this way:

> To summarize Electrovision's spending on travel and entertainment.

You can see from these two examples how much influence the purpose statement has on the scope of your report. If Moreno's manager had expected her to suggest ways to reduce costs but she had only collected cost data, her report would have failed to meet expectations. Because she was assigned an analytical report rather than an informational report, Moreno had to go beyond merely collecting data to drawing conclusions and making recommendations.

Remember, the more specific your purpose, the more useful it will be as a guide to planning and writing the report. Furthermore, always double-check your statement of purpose with the person who authorized the report. When the authorizer sees the purpose written down in black and white, she or he may decide to point the study in another direction.

Prepare a written statement of your purpose; then review it with the person who authorized the study.

Preparing the Work Plan

Once you've defined the problem and the purpose of your report, you are ready to establish a work plan. In business, most report-writing situations involve a firm deadline and finite resources to get the job done. In other words, you not only have to produce quality reports, you have to do so quickly and efficiently. A carefully thought-out work plan is the best way to make sure you produce quality work on schedule.

When SBC Communications and Ameritech announced a proposed merger, the Federal Communications Commission and the U.S. Department of Justice set firm deadlines for the thousands of pages of reports these companies would be required to file. As such, the work plans for each of these companies would discuss the necessity for the timely preparation of formal studies to prove that the proposed merger would not negatively impact industry competition.

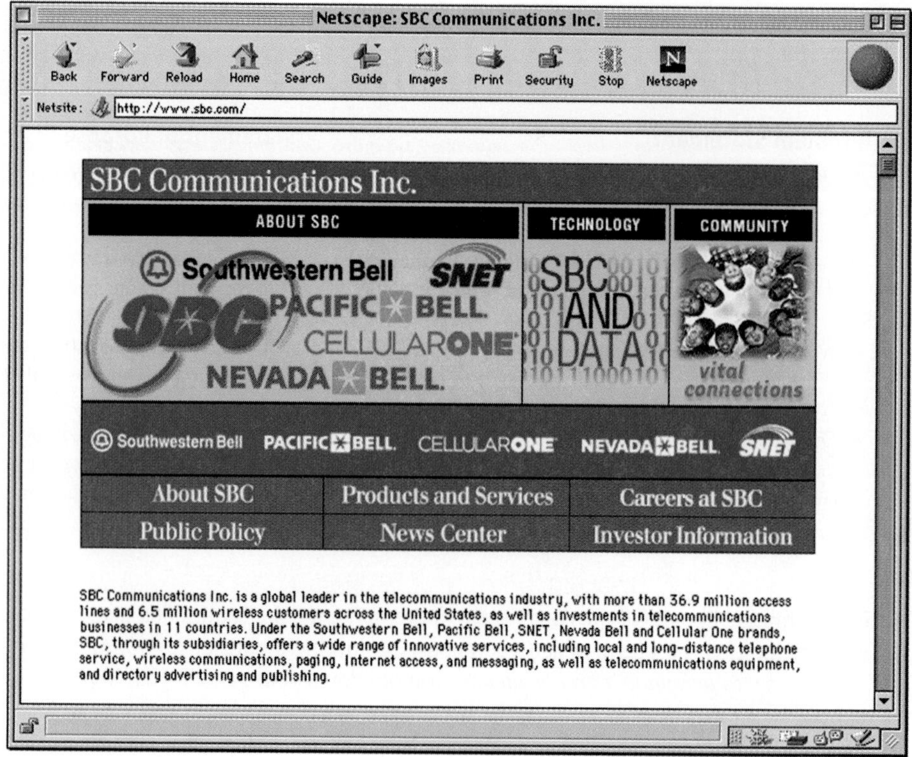

Prepare a work plan that identifies the tasks you will perform.

If you are preparing this work plan for yourself, it can be relatively informal: a simple list of the steps you plan to take, an estimate of their sequence and timing, and a list of the sources of information you plan to use. If you're conducting a lengthy, formal study, however, you'll want to develop a detailed work plan that can guide the performance of many tasks over a span of time. Most proposals require a detailed work plan, which becomes the basis for a contract if the proposal is accepted. A formal work plan might include these elements (especially the first two):

- *Statement of the problem.* Include the problem statement so that anyone working with you is clear about the nature of the challenge you face. Including the problem statement can also help you stay focused on the core problem and avoid distractions that are likely to arise during your investigation and writing.
- *Statement of the purpose and scope of your investigation.* By describing what you plan to accomplish with this report, you define the boundaries of your work. Stating which issues you will cover and which issues you won't cover is especially important with complex, lengthy investigations. If you've ever misunderstood a homework assignment and delivered something that didn't meet expectations, you know how frustrating such misunderstandings can be for both the writer and the reader. As with homework, you usually won't have time to rework business reports if you discover at the last minute that you're on the wrong track.
- *Discussion of the sequence of tasks to be accomplished.* Indicate sources of information, required research, and any restrictions or constraints (on time, money, personnel, or data). For simple reports, the list of necessary tasks will be short and probably obvious. Longer reports and complex investigations, however, require thorough

planning. You may need to reserve time with customers or executives or schedule outside services such as telephone researchers or print shops.

- *Description of the end products that will result from the investigation.* In many cases, the output of your efforts will be the report itself. In other cases, though, you'll need to produce something above and beyond a report, such as a new marketing plan, some improvements to a business process, or even a tangible product. As you do for the rest of your work plan, make sure these expectations are clear at the outset, and make sure you've scheduled enough time and resources to get the job done.
- *Review of project assignments, schedules, and resource requirements.* Indicate who will be responsible for what, when tasks will be completed, and how much the investigation will cost. You may also want to include a brief section on coordinating the writing and production of the report if more than one person will be involved. Collaborative writing has some important advantages over writing a report by yourself. For instance, a collaborative effort draws on the talents and experiences of many individuals, incorporates the viewpoints of many, and often results in a better finished product in less time. Still, making sure everyone works together productively can be a challenge. (Collaborative writing is discussed in detail in Chapter 6. See "Writing in Groups and Critiquing the Writing of Another.")

Collaborative writing has many advantages.

- *Plans for following up after the report is delivered.* Follow-up can range from something as simple as making sure people received the information they needed to something as complex as conducting additional research to evaluate the results of proposals contained in the report. Even if follow-up isn't required or expected, doing some informal follow-up can help you find ways to improve your future reports. Following up is also a good way to communicate to your audience that you care about the effectiveness of your work and the impact you can have on the organization.

Some work plans also include a tentative outline of the report (see Figure 14.1). With a plan in place, you're ready to get to work, which in some cases means starting with research.

Collecting, Analyzing, and Interpreting Data

If your report requires you to perform research, follow steps 1 through 5 of the research process outlined in Chapter 11 to gather, analyze, and interpret data. Once you have gathered the information you need, the next step is to use this information to draw conclusions and develop recommendations (if requested).

Follow the research process discussed in Chapter 11 to collect and analyze data.

Drawing Conclusions

Regardless of how much evidence you amass, at some point in every analysis you move beyond hard facts that can be objectively measured and verified. When you reach that point, you begin to formulate a **conclusion**, which is a logical interpretation of the facts in your report. Reaching good conclusions based on the evidence at hand is one of the most important skills you can develop in your business career. A sound conclusion meets the following criteria:

Conclusions are interpretations of the facts.

- *It must fulfill the original statement of purpose.* After all, this is why you took on the project in the first place.
- *It must be based strictly on the information included in the rest of the report.* In other words, the conclusion must consider all the information in the report and no information not included in the report. While drawing a conclusion, you can introduce no new information. (If it's that important, it should be in the body of the report.) Nor can you ignore any information in your report that doesn't support your conclusion.

Figure 14.1
In-Depth Critique: Work Plan for a Formal Study

This work plan was developed for a report on whether to launch a company newsletter.

The problem statement is clear enough for anyone to understand without background research.

The statement of purpose is specific, delineating exactly what will be covered in the report.

The tasks to be accomplished are clearly laid out.

Although no description of the end product is included here, a preliminary outline is presented for guidance.

This plan includes no provisions for following up, but it clearly states the assignments and the schedules for completing them.

STATEMENT OF THE PROBLEM
The rapid growth of our company over the past five years has reduced the sense of community among our staff. People no longer feel like part of an intimate organization where they matter as individuals.

PURPOSE AND SCOPE OF WORK
The purpose of this study is to determine whether a company newsletter would help rebuild employee identification with the organization. The study will evaluate the impact of newsletters in other companies and will attempt to identify features that might be desirable in our own newsletter. Such variables as length, frequency of distribution, types of articles, and graphic design will be considered. Costs will be estimated for several approaches. In addition, the study will analyze the personnel and the procedures required to produce a newsletter.

SOURCES AND METHODS OF DATA COLLECTION
Sample newsletters will be collected from 50 companies similar to ours in size, growth rate, and types of employees. The editors will be asked to comment on the impact of their publications on employee morale. Our own employees will be surveyed to determine their interest in a newsletter and their preferences for specific features. Production procedures and costs will be analyzed through conversations with newsletter editors and printers.

PRELIMINARY OUTLINE

I. Do newsletters affect morale?
   A. Do people read them?
   B. How do employees benefit?
   C. How does the company benefit?
II. What are the features of good newsletters?
   A. How long are they?
   B. What do they contain?
   C. How often are they published?
   D. How are they designed?
III. How should a newsletter be produced?
   A. Should it be written, edited, and printed internally?
   B. Should it be written internally and printed outside?
   C. Should it be totally produced outside?
IV. What would a newsletter cost?
   A. What would the personnel costs be?
   B. What would the materials costs be?
   C. What would outside services cost?
V. Should we publish a company newsletter?
VI. If so, what approach should we take?

WORK PLAN

Collect/analyze newsletters	09/01-09/14
Interview editors by phone	09/16-09/20
Survey employees	09/14-09/28
Develop sample	09/28-10/05
Develop cost estimates	10/07-10/10
Prepare report	10/10-10/24
Submit final report	10/25

- *It must be logical.* People sometimes toss the word *logical* into a conversation without thinking much about its true meaning. For the purposes of writing a business report, a logical conclusion is one that follows accepted patterns of reasoning.

Check the logic that underlies your conclusions.

Conclusions need to be logical, but this doesn't mean they automatically flow from the evidence. Most business decisions require assumptions and judgment; relatively few are based strictly on the facts. Your personal values or the organization's values may also influence your conclusions; just be sure that you are conscious of how these biases may be affecting your judgment. Nor can you expect members of a team to examine the evidence and all arrive at the same conclusion. One of the key reasons for bringing additional people into a decision is to gain the value of their unique perspectives and experiences.

Developing Recommendations

Drawing a conclusion is one thing; deciding what to do about it and then recommending action is another. Recall that a conclusion is an opinion or interpretation of the facts; a **recommendation** suggests what ought to be done about the facts. Here's an example of the difference:

Recommendations are suggestions for action.

CONCLUSION	RECOMMENDATION
I conclude that, on the basis of its track record and current price, this company is an attractive buy.	I recommend that we write a letter to the president offering to buy the company at a 10 percent premium over the market value of its stock.

When you've been asked to take the final step and translate your conclusions into recommendations, be sure to make the relationship between them clear. Most people use this six-step process to generate solutions or recommendations to a problem:[4]

1. Define and limit the problem.
2. Analyze the problem and gather data about it.
3. Establish criteria for possible solutions.
4. Brainstorm possible solutions.
5. Choose the best possible solution, based on the criteria you set in step 3.
6. Implement the chosen solution.

You won't cover all six steps in every report you write, of course, but knowing how to solve problems will help you make better decisions and recommendations in your reports. Remember, recommendations are inappropriate in a report when you're not expected to supply them.

When you develop recommendations of your own, try not to let your assumptions and personal values influence them. To be credible, recommendations must be based on logical analysis and sound conclusions. Furthermore they must be practical and acceptable to your readers, the people who have to make the recommendations work. Finally, when making a recommendation, be certain that you have adequately described the steps that come next. Don't leave your readers scratching their heads and saying, "This all sounds good, but what do I do on Monday morning?"

Good recommendations are
- Practical
- Acceptable to readers
- Explained in enough detail for readers to take action

STEP 2: ORGANIZING REPORTS AND PROPOSALS

Planning reports and proposals is an important step in the reporting process. So is organizing the material you've collected into a logical order that meets your audience's needs. That's why, before Deirdre Ballou drafts even the first word of her first sentence, she carefully analyzes her audience before she chooses an order, format, length, and structure for her report.

DID YOU KNOW?

When a survey by *CFO* magazine asked executives to assign a grade to the personal communication skills of MBA graduates, fully 70 percent awarded a C or a D.

Meeting Your Audience's Needs

One of the first things to consider when planning and organizing a report is your audience's needs.

When deciding on the content of your report, first put yourself in the audience's position. You want to make the information in your report as clear and convenient as possible. Because time is precious, you tell your readers what they need to know—no more, no less—and you present the information in a way that is geared to their needs. What major questions do you think your audience has about the subject? Use any of the brainstorming techniques discussed in Chapter 5 to think ahead to the questions your readers may have and anticipate their sequence. Your objective is to answer all those questions in the order that makes the most sense.

Identify the main questions your audience wants answered.

Your audience usually has one main question of greatest importance: "Why are we losing money?" "What's the progress on this project?" At the San Diego Wild Animal Park, Deirdre Ballou's audience was the brainstorming committee, and members had one major question: "Why should the Wild Animal Park pursue the Heart of Africa concept?" Be sure to define the main question as precisely as you can before you begin formulating your answer. Nine times out of ten, the main question is simply the reason you've been asked to write the report or make the presentation.

Once you've defined the main question, you can sketch a general answer, based on the results of your research. Then you can determine what additional questions your audience is likely to ask, and so on. When you've identified and answered all your audience's probable questions, you've defined the content of your report or presentation. Remember, for every piece of information you are tempted to include, ask why the audience needs it and how it is related to the main question.

FOCUSING ON ETHICS

DO YOU MAKE THESE COSTLY MISTAKES WHEN WRITING BUSINESS REPORTS?

When you write a report, or even a simple memo, you're creating a permanent record that may be read by an unintended audience. Once the document leaves your hands, it leaves your control. So don't expect the contents to remain confidential. Put nothing in writing that you're unwilling to say in public, and write nothing that may embarrass or jeopardize your employer.

Does this mean you should cover up problems? No, of course not. However, when you're dealing with sensitive information, think about what you're going to write. Maybe the best course is to present the information orally. However, if a written record is required, be discreet. Focus on presenting the information in such a way that it will help the reader resolve the problem. Avoid personal gripes, criticisms, alibis, attempts to blame other people, sugar-coated data, and unsolicited opinions.

To be useful, the information must be accurate, complete, and honest. However, being honest is not always a simple matter. Each of us sees reality a little differently, and we describe what we see in our own way. To restrict the distortions introduced by differences in perception, follow these guidelines.

- *Describe facts or events in concrete terms.* It's better to say "Sales have increased from $400,000 to $435,000 in the past two months" rather than "Sales have skyrocketed." Indicate quantities whenever you can. Be specific.
- *Report all the relevant facts.* Regardless of whether these facts will support your theories or please your readers, they must be included. Omitting the details that undermine your position might be convenient, but it isn't accurate. Readers will be misled if you hesitate to be the bearer of bad news and leave out unpleasant information.
- *Put the facts in perspective.* If you tell readers, "The value of the stock has doubled in three weeks," you are giving only a partial picture. They will have a much clearer understanding if you say, "The value of the stock has doubled in three weeks, rising from $2 to $4 per share on the rumor of a potential merger." Taken out of context, even the most concrete facts can be misleading.
- *Give plenty of evidence for your conclusions.* You can't expect readers to fully understand your conclusions unless you offer substantial supporting evidence. Statements such as "We have to reorganize the sales force or we're bound to lose market share" may or may not be true.

As you make decisions about the content, format, style, and organization of the report, keep your readers' needs in mind—especially when choosing the organizational approach.

Choosing the Direct or Indirect Approach

What psychological approach is best for your particular readers? As Chapter 5 explains, when the audience is considered either receptive or open-minded, use the direct approach: Lead off with a summary of your key findings, conclusions, and recommendations. This "up-front" approach is by far the most popular and convenient order for business reports. Direct order saves time and makes the rest of the report easier to follow. For those who have questions or want more information, later parts of the report provide complete findings and supporting details.

The direct approach saves time and makes the report easier to understand by giving readers the main idea first.

The direct approach also produces a more forceful report. You sound sure of yourself when you state your conclusions confidently at the outset. However, confidence may sometimes be misconstrued as arrogance. If you're a junior member of a status-conscious organization or if your audience is skeptical or hostile, you may want to use indirect order: Introduce the complete findings and supporting details before the conclusions and recommendations, which come last. The indirect approach gives you a chance to prove your points and gradually overcome your audience's reservations. Deirdre Ballou's team used this approach to pull their audience into their presentation. By deferring the conclusions and recommendations, you imply that you've weighed the evidence objectively without prejudging the facts. You also imply that you're subordinating your judgment to that of the audience, whose members are capable of drawing their own conclusions when they have access to all the facts.

The indirect approach helps overcome resistance by withholding the main idea until later in the report.

Readers have no way of knowing unless you provide enough data to support your claim.

- *Present only objective evidence and verifiable conclusions.* Of course, your facts and figures must be checked, and your sources must be reliable. In addition, try to avoid drawing conclusions from too little information. Just because one sales rep reports that customers are dissatisfied with your product doesn't mean that all customers are dissatisfied. Also, don't assume that a preceding event was the cause of what followed. The fact that sales declined right after you switched ad agencies doesn't necessarily mean that the new agency was to blame. Other factors may be responsible, such as the general state of the economy.

- *Keep your personal biases in check.* Even if you have strong feelings about the subject of your report, try to keep those feelings from influencing your choice of words. Don't say, "Locating a plant in Kraymore is a terrible idea because the people there are mostly students who would rather play than work and who don't have the ability to operate our machines." Such language not only offends but also obscures the facts and provokes emotional responses.

1. When would you use vague language instead of concrete detail? Would this action be unethical or merely one form of emphasizing the positive?
2. Describe each of the following situations in a single sentence that reveals nothing about your personal feelings or prejudices but that clearly shows your position.
   a. Your competitor has been dumping toxic waste into the local river for years, and local government has ordered your company to share in the cost of cleanup—a cost that accounts for a major part of next year's budget. You're writing a report on the financial impact for your CEO.
   b. An employee in your department has been taking supplies from company storage and selling them wholesale to unsuspecting small businesses. This employee's activities have cost your department a bundle in overhead expenses. You're writing a brief report on the inventory discrepancy for upper management.
   c. Recent budget cuts have endangered the day-care program at your local branch of a national company, and the effect on employees is grave. You're writing a report for headquarters about the impact on employees.

Figure 14.2
Direct Approach versus Indirect Approach in an Introduction

THE DIRECT APPROACH	THE INDIRECT APPROACH
Since the company's founding 25 years ago, we have provided regular repair service for all our electric appliances. This service has been an important selling point as well as a source of pride for our employees. However, we are paying a high price for our image. Last year, we lost $500,000 on our repair business. Because of your concern over these losses, you have asked me to study the pros and cons of discontinuing our repair service. With the help of John Hudson and Susan Lefkowitz, I have studied the issue for the past two weeks and have come to the conclusion that we have been embracing an expensive, impractical tradition. By withdrawing from the electric appliance repair business, we can substantially improve our financial performance without damaging our reputation with customers. This conclusion is based on three basic points that are covered in the following pages: • It is highly unlikely that we will ever be able to make a profit in the repair business. • Sevice is no longer an important selling point with customers. • Closing down the service operation will create few internal problems.	Since the company's founding 25 years ago, we have provided repair service for all our electric appliances. This service has been an important selling point well as a source of pride for our employees. However, the repair business itself has consistently lost money. Because of your concern over these losses, you have asked me to study the pros and cons of discontinuing our repair service. With the help of John Hudson and Susan Lefkowitz, I have studied the issue for the past two weeks. The following pages present our findings for your review. Three basic questions are addressed: • What is the extent of our losses, and what can we do to turn the business around? • Would withdrawal hurt our sales of electrical appliances? • What would be the internal repercussions of closing down the repair business?

Although the indirect approach has its advantages, some report readers will always be in a hurry to get to "the answer" and will flip to the recommendations immediately, thus defeating your purpose. For this reason, consider length when deciding on direct or indirect order. In general, the longer the message, the less effective an indirect approach is likely to be. Furthermore, an indirect argument is harder to follow than a direct one.

Because both the direct and indirect approaches have merit, businesspeople often combine them. They reveal their conclusions and recommendations as they go along, rather than putting them either first or last. Figure 14.2 presents the introductions from two reports with the same general outline. In the direct version, a series of statements summarize the conclusion reached in relation to each main topic on the outline. In the indirect version, the same topics are introduced (in the same order) without drawing any conclusions about them. The conclusions appear within the body of the report instead. So is this second report direct or indirect? Business reports are often difficult to classify.

DID YOU KNOW?

A good business plan should be no more than 40 pages long. All detailed supporting information and exhibits should be included in a second volume titled the appendix.

Deciding on Format and Length

When you're writing a report, decisions about format and length may be made for you by the person who requests the document. Such guidance is often the case with monitor/control reports, justification reports, proposals, progress reports, and compliance reports. In general, the more routine the report, the less flexibility you have in deciding format and length. Monthly status reports, for example, are usually pretty routine, so they will have the same basic appearance and structure. Within that framework, however, there is room for flexibility, depending on the nature of the information being reported.

Periodic reports are usually written in memo format and don't need much of an introduction; a subject line on the memo is adequate. They should follow the same general for-

Because Julie Beckman at Buckingham Real Estate receives piles of reports, she will often hunt for the report's bottom line before spending the time required to read the detail.

mat and organization from period to period. Personal activity reports are also written in memo format, but because they're nonrecurring documents, they require more of an introduction than periodic reports.

When you do have some leeway in length and format, base your decisions on your readers' needs. As the Wild Animal Park's Deirdre Ballou can attest, your goal is to tell your audience what they need to know in a format that is easy for them to use. When selecting a format for your report, you have four options:

You may present a report in one of four formats: preprinted form, letter, memo, or manuscript.

- *Preprinted form.* Used for "fill in the blank" reports. Most are relatively short (five or fewer pages) and deal with routine information, often mainly numerical. Use this format when it's requested by the person authorizing the report.
- *Letter.* Common for reports of five or fewer pages that are directed to outsiders. These reports include all the normal parts of a letter, but they may also have headings, footnotes, tables, and figures.
- *Memo.* Common for short (fewer than ten pages) informal reports distributed within an organization. Memos have headings at the top: *To, From, Date,* and *Subject.* In addition, like longer reports, they often have internal headings and sometimes include visual aids. Memos exceeding ten pages are sometimes referred to as *memo reports* to distinguish them from their shorter cousins. They also begin with the standard memo headings. The Checklist for Short Informal Reports provides guidelines for preparing memo reports and other short informal reports.
- *Manuscript.* Common for reports from a few pages to several hundred pages that require a formal approach. As their length increases, reports in manuscript format require more elements before the text of the report (prefatory parts) and after the text (supplementary parts). Chapter 15 explains these elements and includes additional instructions as well as a checklist for preparing formal reports.

Component Chapter A, "Format and Layout of Business Documents," contains more specific guidelines for physically preparing reports.

Length depends on
- Your subject
- Your purpose
- Your relationship with your audience

The length of your report obviously depends on your subject and purpose, but it's also affected by your relationship with your audience. If they are relative strangers, if they are skeptical or hostile, if the material is nonroutine or controversial, you usually have to explain your points in greater detail, resulting in a longer document. You can afford to be brief if you are on familiar terms with your readers, if they are likely to agree with you, and if the information is routine or uncomplicated. Short reports are more common in business than long ones, and you'll probably write many more 5-page memos than 250-page formal reports.

Regardless of whether you use the direct or indirect approach or a memo or letter format, you must still deal with the question of how your ideas will be subdivided and developed. Suppose you're writing a controversial report recommending that your company revise its policy on who reports to whom. You know that some of your readers will object to your ideas, so you decide to use indirect order. How do you develop your argument? Your job is to choose the most logical structure—the one that suits your topic and goals and that makes the most sense to your audience.

Structuring Informational Reports

Informational reports are the easiest to organize because they provide nothing more than facts.

When writing informational reports, you don't usually have to be too concerned about reader reaction. Most readers will presumably respond unemotionally to your material, so you can present it in the most direct fashion possible. What you do need to be concerned about, however, is reader comprehension. The information must be presented logically and accurately so that readers will understand exactly what you mean and be able to use the information in a practical way.

Topical organization is based on order of importance, sequence, chronology, spatial relationships, location, or categories.

When structuring an informational report, you can let the nature of whatever you're describing serve as the point of departure. If you're describing a machine, each component can correspond to a part of your report. If you're describing an event, you can approach the discussion chronologically. And if you're explaining how to do something, you can describe the steps in the process. In general, informational reports use a **topical organization,** which means they are arranged in one of these ways:

- *According to importance.* If you're reviewing five product lines, you might organize your study in order of the sales for each product line, beginning with the line that produces the most revenue and proceeding to the one that produces the least revenue.
- *According to sequence.* If you're studying a process, proceed step by step—1, 2, 3, and so on.
- *According to chronology.* When investigating a chain of events, organize the study according to what happened in January, what happened in February, and so on.
- *According to spatial orientation.* If you're explaining how a physical object works, describe it left to right (or right to left in some cultures), top to bottom, outside to inside.
- *According to geography.* If location is important, factor your study geographically, such as by regions of the United States or by areas within a city.
- *According to category.* If you're asked to review several distinct aspects of a subject, look at one category at a time, such as sales, profit, cost, or investment.

There are other bases for organization. Because some informational reports, especially compliance reports and internal reports, are prepared on preprinted forms, they are organized according to instructions supplied by the person requesting the information. In addition, many proposals conform to an outline specified in the request for proposal issued by the client, which might include statement of the problem, background, scope of work, restrictions, sources and methods, work schedule, qualifications of personnel, facilities, anticipated costs, and expected results.

CHECKLIST FOR SHORT INFORMAL REPORTS

A. Format and Style
  1. For brief external reports, use letter format, including a title or a subject line after the reader's address that clearly states the subject of the document.
  2. For brief internal reports, use memo or manuscript format.
  3. Present all short informal reports properly.
     a. Single-space the text.
     b. Double-space between paragraphs.
     c. Use headings where helpful, but try not to use more than three levels of headings.
     d. Call attention to significant information by setting it off visually with lists or indention.
     e. Include visual aids to emphasize and clarify the text.
  4. Use an appropriate writing style.
     a. Use an informal style (*I* and *you*) for letter and memo reports, unless company custom calls for the impersonal third person.
     b. Use an impersonal style for more formal short reports in manuscript format.
  5. Maintain a consistent time frame by writing in either the present or the past tense, using other tenses only to indicate prior or future events.
  6. Give each paragraph a topic sentence.
  7. Link paragraphs by using transitional words and phrases.
  8. Strive for readability by using short sentences, concrete words, and terminology that is appropriate for your readers.
  9. Be accurate, thorough, and impartial in presenting the material.
  10. Avoid including irrelevant and unnecessary details.
  11. Include documentation for all material quoted or paraphrased from secondary sources, using a consistent format.

B. Opening
  1. For short, routine memos, use the subject line of the memo form and the first sentence or two of the text as the introduction.
  2. For all other short reports, cover these topics in the introduction: purpose, scope, background, restrictions (in conducting the study), sources of information and methods of research, and organization of the report.
  3. If using direct order, place conclusions and recommendations in the opening.

C. Body (Direct or Indirect Order)
  1. Use direct order for informational reports to receptive readers, developing ideas around subtopics (chronologically, geographically, categorically).
  2. Use direct order for analytical reports to receptive readers, developing points around conclusions or recommendations.
  3. Use indirect order for analytical reports to skeptical or hostile readers, developing points around logical arguments.

D. Ending
  1. In informational reports summarize major findings at the end, if you wish.
  2. Summarize points in the same order in which they appear in the text.
  3. In analytical reports using indirect order, list conclusions and recommendations at the end.
  4. Be certain that conclusions and recommendations follow logically from facts presented in the body.
  5. Consider using a list format for emphasis.
  6. Avoid introducing new material in the summary, conclusions, or recommendations.

Structuring Analytical Reports

It is more difficult to organize analytical reports and presentations that contain analyses and are designed to lead the audience to specific conclusions and recommendations. Because your audience may respond in one of two ways to your material, your choice of organizational approach should depend on the reaction you anticipate:

- If you expect your audience to agree with you, use a structure that focuses attention on conclusions and recommendations.

TABLE 14.2

COMMON WAYS TO STRUCTURE ANALYTICAL REPORTS

	Conclusions or recommendations	Logical		
		2 + 2 = 4	Scientific	Yardstick
Reader	Likely to accept	Hostile or skeptical; needs convincing	Needs most convincing	Needs most convincing
Approach	Direct	Indirect	Indirect	Indirect
Writer's credibility	High	Low	Low	Low
Advantages	Readers grasp conclusions or recommendations quickly	Readers can follow writer's thinking pattern	Readers draw their own conclusions	Alternatives measured against same standards (criteria)
Drawbacks	May make things seem too simple	Makes report longer	Must discuss each alternative; very long	Must agree on criteria; can be boring; very long

- If you expect your audience to be skeptical about your conclusions and recommendations or hostile toward them, use a structure that focuses attention on the rationale that supports your point of view.

Three popular ways to organize analytical reports:
- By conclusions
- By recommendations
- By logical arguments

The three most common structural approaches for analytical reports are (1) focusing on conclusions, (2) focusing on recommendations, and (3) focusing on logical argument (see Table 14.2).

Focusing on Conclusions: A Research and Analysis Report

Analytical reports may be organized around conclusions and recommendations (direct approach) when the audience is receptive.

When writing an analytical report for people from your own organization who have asked you to study something, you're writing for your most receptive readers. They may know from experience that you'll do a thorough job, and they may trust your judgment. So they're likely to accept your conclusions, and you can usually organize your report around conclusions or recommendations using a direct approach.

The direct organizational approach does have some drawbacks, however. If your readers have reservations about either you or your material, strong statements at the beginning may intensify their resistance. Focusing on conclusions and recommendations may also make everything seem too simple. Your readers could criticize your report as being superficial: "Why didn't you consider this option?" or "Where did you get this number?" You're generally better off taking the direct approach in a report only when your credibility is high—when your readers trust you and are willing to accept your conclusions and recommendations.

Cynthia Zolonka works on the human resources staff of a bank in Houston, Texas, that decided to have an outside firm handle its employee training. A year after the outsourcing arrangement was established, Zolonka was asked to evaluate the results. She explains: "Moving our training programs to an outside supplier was a tough—and controversial—decision for the entire company. Some people were convinced outsourcing would never work, while others thought it might save money but hurt training quality. I took special care to do a thorough analysis of the data, and I supported my conclusion with objective answers not personal opinions." Consider Zolonka's outline in Figure 14.3 and an excerpt from her report in Figure 14.4.

The audience for Cynthia Zolonka's report on outsourcing employee training included some skeptical readers who assumed that the outsourcing experiment would fail. Zolonka's analysis showed that it was a success. She decided to organize her report in three main sections, as this outline illustrates.

Figure 14.3
In-Depth Critique: Outline of a Research Report Focusing on Conclusions

I. Introduction
II. Conclusion: Outsourcing employee training has reduced costs and improved quality
III. Cost reductions
  A. Cost reduction goal was 15 percent over the first year
  B. Actual reduction achieved was 22 percent
  C. Reassigned the three staffers who used to work on training full-time
  D. Reduced the management time needed to oversee training
  E. Sold the computers that used to be reserved for training and eliminated the equipment budget for next year
IV. Quality improvements
  A. Employees say they are more confident in seven out of ten key skill areas
  B. Measurable mistakes have dropped by 12 percent
V. Areas needing improvement
  A. Two trainers received approval ratings below 80 percent
  B. The outside trainers aren't always up to speed on internal company issues
  C. We've lost some flexibility for scheduling courses
VI. Summary

The conclusion is stated first: the outsourcing was successful because it met most of the goals established for the program.

The next two sections explore the two categories of goals: cost reductions and quality improvements.

The last main section discusses some areas of concern.

You can use a similar organization whenever you're asked to analyze a problem or an opportunity. Readers who are interested mainly in your conclusions can grasp them quickly, and readers who want to know more about your analysis can look at the data you provide.

When the reader is concerned with conclusions, use them as the main points.

Focusing on Recommendations: A Justification Report

A slightly different approach is useful when your readers want to know what they ought to do as opposed to what they ought to conclude. You'll often be asked to solve a problem rather than just study it. If so, the actions you want your readers to take become the main subdivisions of your report.

When the reader is concerned about what action to take, use recommendations as the main points.

When organizing a report around recommendations, you usually follow five steps:

1. Establish the need for action in the introduction, generally by briefly describing the problem or opportunity.
2. Introduce the benefit that can be achieved, without providing any details.
3. List the steps (recommendations) required to achieve the benefit, using action verbs for emphasis.
4. Explain each step more fully, giving details on procedures, costs, and benefits.
5. Summarize the recommendations.

Alycia Jenn, the business development manager at a Chicago-based retail chain, was asked by the company's board of directors to suggest whether the company should set up a

Figure 14.4
In-Depth Critique: Excerpt Showing the Development of Conclusions in an Analytical Report

The following is an excerpt from Cynthia Zolonka's report on outsourcing employee training. The excerpt is taken from the beginning of the section describing the quality improvements.

Zolonka introduces this main section and its two subsections with statements describing the success of the program (which support her overall conclusion at the beginning of the report).

Zolonka does not gloss over the lack of improvement in employee confidence in three areas. Moreover, she emphasizes what's being done to bring those numbers up.

Tables make it easy for readers to make comparisons.

21

MEASURING QUALITY IMPROVEMENTS

As you know, we survey employees once a year on training issues, and two of the areas we measure are confidence levels employees have in job-related skills and error rates in each job task. The numbers this year look quite favorable when compared with last year's.

Employee Confidence

The following table demonstrates the success of our new training programs in boosting employee confidence; the numbers indicate the percentage of employees who feel "confident" or "very confident" in the skills indicated.

	1/14/99	1/12/00		1/14/99	1/12/00
Order entry	95%	98%	Shipping	91%	93%
Refunds	85	91	Receiving	82	88
Restocking	97	99	Reordering	85	84
Troubleshooting	88	93	Negotiating	72	68
Kitting	95	98	Discounting	64	62

Naturally, we'd like to make improvements in the last three areas as well. We're working with Temple & Associates to find out why the training hasn't improved the scores here.

Error Rates

We want confidence to translate into improved performance, of course, so another important quality-control measurement is error rates. The following table shows that error rates decreased in every category, as measured during first-quarter quality audits.

	Q1 99	Q1 00		Q1 99	Q1 00
Order entry	5%	3%	Shipping	4%	3%
Refunds	8	7	Receiving	2	0
Restocking	4	1	Reordering	5	4
Troubleshooting	12	9	Negotiating	11	5
Kitting	8	5	Discounting	8	6

retailing site on the World Wide Web and, if so, how to implement the site. As Jenn noted, "Setting up shop on the Internet is a big decision for our company. We don't have the big computer staffs that our larger competitors have, and our business development team is stretched rather thin already. On the other hand, I know that more and more people are shopping online, and we don't want to be left out if this mode of retailing really takes off. After studying the issue for several weeks, I concluded that we should go ahead with a site, but we had to be careful about how we implement it." Her memo appears in Figure 14.5.

In her justification report, Alycia Jenn uses her recommendations to organize her thoughts. Because the board of directors wouldn't be interested in a lot of technical detail, she keeps her discussion at a fairly high level. She also maintains a formal and respectful tone for this audience.

Figure 14.5
In-Depth Critique: Sample Justification Report Focusing on Recommendations

MEMO

TO: Board of Directors, Executive Committee members
FROM: Alycia Jenn, Business Development Manager
DATE: July 6, 2000
SUBJECT: World Wide Web retailing site

In response to your request, my staff and I investigated the potential for establishing a retailing site on the World Wide Web. After analyzing the behavior of our customers and major competitors and studying the overall development of electronic retailing, we have three recommendations:

1. Yes, we should establish an online presence within the next six months.
2. We should engage a firm that specializes in online retailing to design and develop the Web site.
3. We must take care to integrate online retailing with our store-based and mail-order operations.

WE SHOULD SET UP A WEB SITE

First, does a Web site make financial sense today? Studies suggest that our competitors are not currently generating significant revenue from their Web sites. Stallini's is the leader so far, but its sales haven't broken the $1 million mark. Moreover, at least half of our competitors' online sales are from current customers who would have purchased the same items in-store or by mail order. The cost of setting up a retailing site is around $120,000, so it isn't possible to justify a site solely on the basis of current financial return.

Second, do we need to establish a presence now in order to remain competitive in the future? The online situation is too fluid and unpredictable to answer this question in a quantitative profit-and-loss way, but a qualitative view of strategy indicates that we should set up a site:

- As younger consumers (more comfortable with online shopping) reach their peak earning years (ages 35–54), they'll be more likely to buy online than today's peak spenders.
- The Web is erasing geographical shopping limits, presenting both a threat and an opportunity. Even though our customers can now shop Web sites anywhere in the world (so that we have thousands of competitors instead of a dozen), we can now target customers anywhere in the world.
- If the growth in online retailing continues, this will eventually be a viable market. Establishing a site now and working out any problems will prepare us for high-volume online business in the years ahead.

WE SHOULD ENGAGE A CONSULTANT TO IMPLEMENT THE SITE

Implementing a competitive retailing site can take anywhere from 1,000 to 2,500 hours of design and programming time. We have some of the expertise needed in-house, but the marketing and information systems departments have only 300 person-hours in the next six months. I recommend that we engage a Web-design consultant to help us with the design and to do all of the programming.

Jenn clarifies the purpose and origin of the report in the introduction.

For clarity, her recommendations are simple and to the point.

Her reasons for recommending that the firm establish a Web site are logically and clearly presented.

Her recommendations include not only establishing a Web site but also hiring a consultant to implement it and making sure to integrate it with existing systems.

(continued)

Focusing on Logical Arguments

Focusing on conclusions or recommendations is the most forceful and efficient way to organize an analytical report, but it isn't the best solution for every situation. Sometimes you can achieve better results by encouraging readers to weigh all the facts before you present your conclusions or recommendations.

Analytical reports may be organized around logical arguments (indirect approach) when the audience is unreceptive.

Figure 14.5, continued

2

WE MUST INTEGRATE THE WEB INTO EXISTING OPERATIONS

The studies we reviewed showed that the most successful Web retailers are careful to integrate their online retailing with their store- and mail-based retailing. Companies that don't integrate carefully find themselves with higher costs, confused customers, and Web sites that don't generate much business. Before we begin designing our Web site, we should develop a plan for integrating the Web into our existing marketing, accounting, and production systems. The online site could affect every department in the company, so it's vital that everyone has a chance to review the plans before we proceed.

SUMMARY

Her close briefly summarizes her recommendations and the reasons behind them.

1. Yes, establish a Web site now even though it doesn't make immediate financial sense, because we might lose business if we don't have a site in the near future.
2. Use the services of a Web designer, because we don't have enough person-hours available in-house.
3. Integrate the Web site with existing operations, particularly in marketing, accounting, and production.

Logical organization is based on logical arguments that reflect the reasoning process behind the conclusions and recommendations.

Three organizational approaches are useful for convincing skeptical readers that your conclusions and recommendation are well founded: the 2 + 2 = 4 approach, the scientific method, and the yardstick approach.

When your purpose is to collaborate with your audience and solve a problem or persuade them to take a definite action, your organizational approach must highlight logical arguments or focus the audience's attention on what needs to be done. You want your audience to concentrate on why your ideas make sense, so you use a **logical organization:** you arrange your ideas around the reasoning behind the report's conclusions and recommendations. In other words, you make the organization of your material reflect the thinking process that will lead readers to your conclusions.

Three basic organizational approaches may be used to argue your case: the 2 + 2 = 4 approach, the scientific method, and the yardstick approach. Bear in mind that these three approaches are not mutually exclusive. Essentially, you choose an organizational approach that matches the reasoning process you used to arrive at your conclusions. This way you can lead readers along the same mental pathways you used in hopes they will follow you to the same conclusions.

In a long report, particularly, you may find it convenient to use differing organizational approaches for various sections. In general, however, simplicity of organization is a virtue. You need a clear, comprehensible argument in order to convince skeptical readers to accept your conclusions or recommendations.

Use reasons as the main divisions in your outline to gradually build a case for your conclusions and recommendations.

The 2 + 2 = 4 Approach: A Troubleshooting Report The 2 + 2 = 4 approach essentially convinces readers of your point of view by demonstrating that everything adds up. The main points in your outline are the main reasons behind your conclusions and recommendations. You support each reason with the evidence you collected during your analysis.

Binh Phan, the national sales manager of a New Hampshire sporting goods company, was concerned about his company's ability to sell to its largest customers. His boss, the vice president of marketing, shared these concerns and asked Phan to analyze the situation and recommend a solution. As Phan says, "We sell sporting goods to retail chains across the country. Large nationwide chains with superstores modeled after Toys "R" Us have been revolutionizing the industry, but we haven't had as much success with these big customers as we've had with smaller companies that operate on only a local or regional basis. With more and more of the industry in the hands of the large chains, we knew we had to fix the situation."

Phan's troubleshooting report is outlined in Figure 14.6. The main idea is that the company should establish separate sales teams for these major accounts, rather than continuing to service them through the company's four regional divisions. However, Phan knew his plan would be controversial because it required a big change in the company's organization, so he used the 2 + 2 = 4 approach to focus on his reasons. Figure 14.7 is a copy of Phan's report.

Because of its naturalness and versatility, the 2 + 2 = 4 approach is generally the most persuasive and efficient way to develop an analytical report for skeptical readers. When writing your own reports, try this structure first. You'll usually find that your arguments fall naturally into this pattern. However, not every problem or reporting situation can be handled with this organizational approach.

The 2 + 2 = 4 approach works well when you have many reasons for your point of view but no single reason is overwhelming.

The Scientific Method: A Proposal When you're trying to discover whether an explanation is true, whether an option will solve your problem, or which one of several solutions will work best, you're likely to find the scientific method useful. Every day hundreds of managers ask

Binh Phan's proposal would change the way his company's sales representatives are paid, and that's obviously an important personal issue for everybody. Plus, there was some risk to the company as a whole because Phan was suggesting a fairly major change to the way it does business. Consequently, Phan's analysis had to be thorough and objective, and his thinking had to be clear and easy to follow.

Figure 14.6
In-Depth Critique: Outline of a Troubleshooting Report Using the 2 + 2 = 4 Approach

Main Idea: We should set up a national account team to sell to customers that are located in more than one region, and our sales commissions should reflect this change.

I. Introduction

II. Reason 1: Our sales department is not organized to match our customer base.

A. The sales force is now organized into four separate regions, but some of our biggest accounts are national companies with operations in two or more regions.

B. Sales reps from two or more regions often end up competing with each other by pursuing the same customers from different locations.

C. National customers are sometimes confused and frustrated; they want a single contact point with us.

III. Reason 2: Our sales commission program isn't providing the right kind of motivation and reward.

A. Salespeople in one region can invest a lot of time in pursuing a sale, only to have the customer place the order in another region. Moreover, the sales rep in the second region ends up with a commission that was earned by someone in the first region.

B. Sales reps occasionally don't pursue leads in their regions if they think a rep in another region will get the commission.

IV. Recommendation: Establish national account teams that cross all four regions, and change the compensation plan to encourage team selling.

V. Summary

Phan has made his main points the very reasons for his recommendations.

Each main point is supported with concrete evidence.

His recommendation is a logical culmination of the main points he has presented so carefully.

Figure 14.7
In-Depth Critique: Sample Troubleshooting Report Using the 2 + 2 = 4 Approach

Binh Phan's troubleshooting report would definitely stir emotions, so he had to make sure the logic was solid. Moreover, he was careful that his introduction didn't reveal his position.

MEMO

TO: Robert Mendoza, Vice President of Marketing
FROM: Binh Phan, National Sales Manager
DATE: September 12, 1999
SUBJECT: Major accounts sales problems

INTRODUCTION

Instead of summarizing his recommendations, Phan begins by discussing the report's purpose and scope, the background of the study, and his methods of research.

This report outlines the results of my investigation into the recent slowdown in sales to major accounts and the accompanying rise in sales- and service-related complaints from some of our largest customers.

As we discussed at last quarter's management retreat, major account sales dropped 12 percent over the last four quarters, whereas overall sales were up 7 percent. During the same time, we've all noticed an increase in both formal and informal complaints from larger customers regarding how confusing and complicated it has become to do business with us.

My investigation started with in-depth discussions with the four regional sales managers, first as a group and then individually. The tension I felt in the initial meeting eventually bubbled to the surface during my meetings with each manager. Staff members in each region are convinced that other regions are booking orders they don't deserve, with one region doing all the legwork only to see another region get credited with the sale and, naturally, the commission and quota credit.

I followed up the sales manager discussions with informal talks and e-mail exchanges with several sales reps from each region. Virtually everyone who is involved with our major national accounts has a story to share. No one is happy with the situation, and I sense that some reps are walking away from major customers because the process is so frustrating.

ORGANIZATIONAL ISSUES

When we divided the national sales force into four geographical regions last year, the idea was to focus our sales efforts and clarify responsibilities for each prospective and current customer. The regional managers have gotten to know their market territories very well, and sales have increased beyond even our most optimistic projections.

Unfortunately, while solving one problem, we seem to have created another. In the past 12 to 18 months, several regional customers have grown to national status. In addition, a few national retailers have taken on (or expressed interest in) our products. As a result, a significant portion of both our current sales and our future opportunities lie with these large national accounts.

I uncovered more than a dozen cases in which sales reps from two or more regions found themselves competing with each other by pursuing the same customer from different locations.

Moreover, the complaints from our major accounts about overlapping or nonexistent account coverage are a direct result of the regional organization. In some

When organizing a report to reflect the scientific method, you discuss, one by one, hypothetical solutions to the problem.

themselves, "What's wrong with this operation, and what should we do about it?" They approach the problem by coming up with one or several possible solutions (hypotheses) and then conducting experiments or gathering information to find the most effective one.

Reports based on the scientific method begin with a statement of the problem and a brief description of the hypothetical solution or a list of possible solutions. The body of the report discusses each alternative in turn and offers evidence that will either confirm the alternative

Figure 14.7, continued

2

cases, customers aren't sure which of our reps they're supposed to call with problems and orders. In others, no one has been in contact with them for several months.

An example should help illustrate the problem. AmeriSport, with retail outlets across the lower tier of the country, was being pitched by reps from our West, South, and East regions. Because we give our regional offices a lot of negotiating freedom, the three reps were offering the client different prices. But all of AmeriSport's buying decisions are made at their headquarters in Tampa, so all we did was confuse the customer.

The irony of this situation is that we're often giving our weakest selling and support efforts to the largest customers in the country.

COMMISSION ISSUES

The regional organization issues are compounded because of the way we assign commissions and quota credit. Salespeople in one region can invest a lot of time in pursuing a sale, only to have the customer place the order in another region. So some sales rep in the second region ends up with the commission on a sale that was partly or even entirely earned by someone in the first region.

Also, sales reps sometimes don't pursue leads in their regions if they think that a rep in another region will get the commission. For example, Athletic Express, with outlets in 35 states spread across all four regions, finally got so frustrated with us that the company president called our headquarters. Athletic Express has been trying to place a large order for tennis and golf accessories, but none of our local reps seem interested in paying attention. I spoke with the rep responsible for Nashville, where the company is headquartered, and asked her why she wasn't working the account more actively. Her explanation was that last time she got involved with Athletic Express, the order was actually placed from their L.A. regional office, and she didn't get any commission after more than two weeks of selling time.

In the body, Phan presents the facts and his observations in an objective tone, without revealing his own point of view.

RECOMMENDATION

Our sales organization should reflect the nature of our customer base. To accomplish that goal, we need a group of reps who are free to pursue accounts across regional borders—and who are compensated fairly for their work. The most sensible answer is to establish a national accounts group. Any customers whose operations place them in more than one region would automatically be assigned to the national group.

Further, we need to modify our commission policy to reward people for team selling. I'll talk with the sales managers to work out the details, but in general, we'll need to split commissions whenever two or more reps help close a sale. This policy will also involve a "finder's fee" for a rep who pulls in leads at the regional level that are passed on to the national account team.

He saves his recommendations for the fourth section, where he adds up the reasons (2 + 2 = 4).

3

SUMMARY

The regional sales organization is working at the regional and local levels but not at the national level. We should establish a national accounts group to handle sales that cross regional boundaries.

To make sure that the sales reps (at both the regional and national levels) are adequately motivated and fairly compensated, we need to devise a system of commission splitting and finders' fees. We'll then have one set of reps who are focused on the local and regional levels and another set who are pursuing national accounts. The two groups will have incentives to work together rather than against each other, as is now the case.

or rule it out. Because many problems have multiple causes and complex solutions, several alternatives may be relevant. The final section of the report summarizes the findings and indicates which solution or solutions are valid. The report concludes with recommendations for solving the problem or eliminating the causes.

A proposal using a variation of the scientific method was prepared by Fredrik Swensen, an executive with a Miami restaurant management firm (see the outline in Figure 14.8).

Figure 14.8
In-Depth Critique: Outline of a Proposal Using the Scientific Method

The purpose of Fredrik Swensen's proposal was to help the company decide which of four franchise operations to invest in. "We wanted to buy 45 or 50 more franchise outlets across the country, so this was a major investment decision. Our company already owns several hundred fast-food franchises, so we have a good idea of how to evaluate which ones are right for us."

This report covered two major steps: (1) establishing the decision criteria and (2) testing each of four alternatives against those criteria.

Each of the four alternatives is assigned to appropriate subdivisions: description, pros, cons, and conclusion (priority).

The decision is never black and white, of course, but it's Swensen's job to present the alternatives objectively.

Main Idea: We should purchase the 45 franchises currently for sale in the Burger World chain.

I. Statement of problem and purpose of this proposal
II. Scope of the investigation
III. Method used to compare the business opportunities
- **A. Establish decision criteria**
- **B. Get input from consultants**
- **C. Gather secondary research**
- **D. Conduct market surveys for primary research**
- **E. Meet with franchisor management teams**
- **F. Analyze quantitative and qualitative data**
- **G. Prioritize and select the best opportunity**

IV. Analysis of the four franchise operations
- **A. Wacky Taco**
  - **1. Description: Low-fat Mexican food; most locations in malls**
  - **2. Pros: 58 units available within a year; consultants believe the concept has significant growth potential; operations easy to manage**
  - **3. Cons: Company recently hit with employment discrimination lawsuit; franchise fees are 30 percent above average**
  - **4. Conclusion: Priority = 3; lawsuit may be indicative of mismanagement; fees too high**
- **B. Thai in the Sky**
  - **1. Description: Thai food served in New Age settings**
  - **2. Pros: Healthy and interesting food; unusual theme concept; no franchised competition**
  - **3. Cons: Complexity of food preparation; only 40 franchises available; franchisor's top management team replaced only six months ago**
  - **4. Conclusion: Priority = 4; too risky and not enough units available**
- **C. Dog Tower**
  - **1. Description: Gourmet hot dogs**
  - **2. Pros: No nationwide competition; more than 60 franchises available within a year; easy to manage; fees lower than average**
  - **3. Cons: Limited market appeal; many stores need updating**
  - **4. Conclusion: Priority = 2; needs too much investment**
- **D. Burger World**
  - **1. Description: Mainstream competitor to McDonald's and Burger King**

Figure 14.8, continued

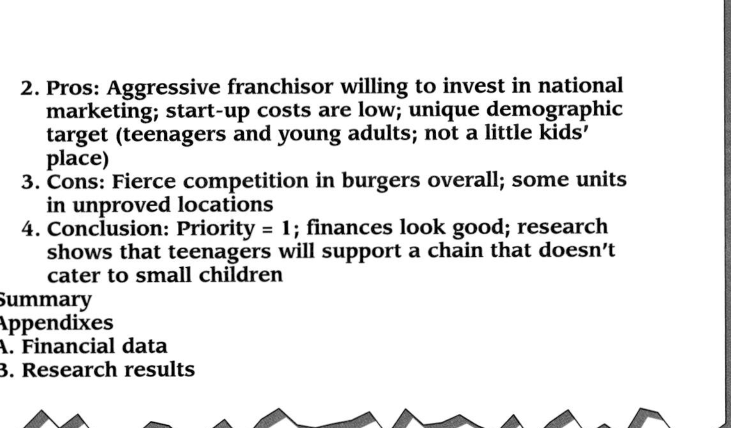
2. Pros: Aggressive franchisor willing to invest in national marketing; start-up costs are low; unique demographic target (teenagers and young adults; not a little kids' place)
3. Cons: Fierce competition in burgers overall; some units in unproved locations
4. Conclusion: Priority = 1; finances look good; research shows that teenagers will support a chain that doesn't cater to small children

V. Summary
VI. Appendixes
A. Financial data
B. Research results

Swensen's approach, analyzing each alternative, is useful when you're trying to unify a divided audience. Your chances of bringing about a consensus are much better when you show the strengths and weaknesses of all the ideas. The main drawback to the scientific method is that many of the alternatives may turn out to be irrelevant or unproductive, but you still have to discuss them all. The more ideas you discuss, the more confused your readers may become and the more trouble they may have comparing pros and cons.

When readers have their own ideas about how to solve a problem, you have to discuss those notions before you can sell your own solutions.

The Yardstick Approach: A Problem-Solving Report One way to reduce the confusion presented by having a lot of alternatives is to establish a yardstick for evaluating them. You begin by discussing the problem, as with the scientific method, but then you set up the conditions that must be met to solve the problem. These are the criteria against which you evaluate all possible solutions. The body of the report evaluates those alternatives in relation to the criteria. The main points of the outline are either the criteria themselves or the alternatives.

With the yardstick approach, the report is organized around criteria; the solution is the alternative that best meets the criteria.

Yardstick reports are similar in some respects to those based on the scientific method, but in criteria-based reports, all the alternatives are reviewed against the same standards. Another distinction is that criteria-based reports can be used to prove the need for action: The current situation can be measured against the criteria and shown to be wanting.

The yardstick approach is useful for certain kinds of proposals because the client who requests the proposal often provides a list of criteria that the solution must meet. Say that your company has been asked to bid on a contract to install a computer for a large corporation. The client has listed the requirements (criteria) for the system, and you've developed a preliminary design to meet them. In the body of your proposal, you could use the client's list of requirements as the main headings and under each one explain how your preliminary design meets the requirement.

Some proposals are best organized by using the client's criteria as the main points.

Figure 14.9 is an outline of a yardstick report that was provided by J. C. Hartley, a market analyst for a large Sacramento company that makes irrigation equipment for farms and ranches. "We've been so successful in the agricultural market that we're starting to run out of customers to sell to. To keep the company growing, we needed to find another market. Two obvious choices to consider were commercial buildings and residences."

Of course, if there is any disagreement on the decision criteria, you'll spin your wheels if you try to push forward to a decision. In Hartley's case, the criteria had been agreed to before she began her investigation, so her goal in including the criteria here was to remind her readers and make it easy for them to evaluate the options available.

For the yardstick approach to work, readers must accept your criteria.

Figure 14.9
In-Depth Critique: Outline of a Research Report Using the Yardstick Approach

J. C. Hartley knows that moving into a new market is not a trivial decision: "I had a responsibility to make careful recommendations," she says. "Even though I don't make the final decision, the information and professional opinion that I provide in my report both weigh heavily in the decision process."

After introducing the report and explaining the scope of her investigation, Hartley defines the criteria for evaluating and choosing the market opportunities.

The section on irrigation equipment trends gives readers valuable background information for understanding this report and its recommendations.

Communicating the decision criteria is particularly important in yardstick evaluation reports because you want readers to evaluate the options using a consistent and conscious set of factors.

Main Idea: We should move into the commercial irrigation equipment market but not into the residential market.

I. Introduction
II. Criteria for entering new markets
- **A. Size and growth**
- **B. Profit potential**
- **C. Ability to compete**
- **D. Distribution costs and opportunities**
- **E. Fit with current capabilities**

III. Irrigation equipment trends
- **A. Water shortages leading to demand for more efficient irrigation**
- **B. Labor costs encouraging automation**
- **C. More homeowners attempting do-it-yourself projects**

IV. Comparison of new market opportunities
- **A. Commercial landscapers and building owners**
  - **1. Size and growth**
  - **2. Profit potential**
  - **3. Ability to compete**
  - **4. Distribution costs and opportunities**
  - **5. Fit with current capabilities**
- **B. Residential landscapers and homeowners**
  - **1. Size and growth**
  - **2. Profit potential**
  - **3. Ability to compete**
  - **4. Distribution costs and opportunities**
  - **5. Fit with current capabilities**

V. Recommendations
- **A. Enter the commercial segment**
  - **1. Select a test market**
  - **2. Learn from the test and refine our approach**
  - **3. Roll out product marketing nationwide**
- **B. Do not attempt to enter the residential market at this point**

Tables are useful in the yardstick approach
- To avoid repetition
- To make the options easier to compare

The yardstick approach has one other drawback: It can be a little boring. You may find yourself saying the same things over and over again: "Opportunity A has high growth potential; opportunity B has high growth potential; opportunity C has high growth potential," and so on. One way to minimize the repetition is to compare the options in tables and then highlight the more unusual or important aspects of each alternative in the body so that you get the best of both worlds. This way you compare all the alternatives against the same yardstick but call attention to the most significant differences among them.

Preparing the Final Outline[5]

Once you've decided on the proper structure for your material, you can prepare a final report outline. A final outline gives you a visual diagram of the report, its important points, the order in which they will be discussed, and the detail to be included. Sometimes you can use the preliminary outline that guided your research as a final blueprint for the report. More often, however, you have to rework the preliminary outline to take into account your purpose, your audience's probable reactions, and the things you learned during your study. Furthermore, you'll want to include only the items you plan to discuss in your report (your research outline may have additional topics).

Before you write your report, you may have to revise the outline you used to guide your research effort.

Aside from guiding you in the writing effort, preparing a final outline forces you to reevaluate the information you have selected to include and the order in which you present it. You may notice, once you look at the outline, that your discussion is too light in one area or too heavy in another. In fact, you may decide to use an indirect instead of a direct approach, because now that you see the conclusions up front, you think it might be too forceful for your audience. In other words, think of your final report outline as a working draft that you'll revise and modify as you go along.

A final outline is a work in progress.

As is often the case, you'll phrase your final outline so that the points on the outline can serve as headings that appear in the report (report headings are discussed later in this chapter). Bear in mind that the way you phrase outline headings will affect the tone of the report. If you want a hard-hitting, direct tone, use informative phrasing. If you prefer an objective, indirect tone, use descriptive phrasing. Be sure to use parallel construction when wording the points on the outline. (See "Developing Subquestions and Outlining Your Approach" in Chapter 11 for a more in-depth discussion of constructing outlines.)

Soften the force of controversial points by using descriptive (not informative) headings.

Once you've prepared a final outline, you can begin to identify which points can be, and should be, illustrated with visual aids—tables, graphs, drawings, flowcharts, and so on. (See Chapter 12 for details on constructing and placing visual aids.) Ask yourself whether there is some way to visually dramatize the key elements of your message. You might approach the problem as though you were writing a picture book or making a movie. Think of each main point on your outline as a separate scene. Your job is to think of a "picture," a chart or a graph, that will communicate that point to the audience. Keep in mind that if you use visual aids to illustrate a minor point, you may be sending a misleading message about its significance. Furthermore, including too many visuals in your report can be distracting.

Use your final outline to strategically place your visual aids.

STEP 3: WRITING REPORTS AND PROPOSALS

Besides choosing a format, length, and basic organizational approach for your report, you need to make several other decisions that will affect the way your report is received and understood by readers. You need to set the degree of formality, establish a consistent time perspective, and insert appropriate structural clues.

Choosing the Proper Degree of Formality

The issue of formality is closely related to considerations of format, length, and organization. If you know your readers reasonably well and if your report is likely to meet with their approval, you can generally adopt a fairly informal tone. In other words, you can speak to readers in the first person, referring to yourself as *I* and to your readers as *you*. This personal approach is often used in brief memo or letter reports, although there are many exceptions.

Write informal reports in a personal style, using the pronouns *I* and *you*.

Longer reports, especially those dealing with controversial or complex information, are traditionally handled in a more formal vein. You'll also tend to use a more formal approach when writing a report to be sent beyond your own work area to other parts of the organization, customers, and suppliers. Communicating with people in other cultures often calls for more formality, for two reasons. First, the business environment outside the United States tends to be more formal in general, and that formality must be reflected in your communication style. Second, the things you do to make a document informal, such as using humor and idiomatic language, are the hardest to transfer from culture to culture. Less formality in these cases increases the risk of offending people and of miscommunicating.

You achieve a formal tone by using the impersonal style, eliminating all references to *I* (including *we, us,* and *our*) and *you*. The style is borrowed from journalism, which stresses the reporter's objectivity. However, be careful that avoiding personal pronouns doesn't lead to overuse of such phrases as *there is* and *it is*, which are both dull and wordy. Also, avoiding personal pronouns makes it easier to slip into passive voice, which can also be dull and wordy. Instead of saying "I think we should buy TramCo" you might end up saying "It is recommended that the company buy TramCo."

Being formal means putting your readers at a distance and establishing an objective, businesslike relationship.

When you write in a formal style, you impose a certain distance between you and your readers. You remain businesslike, unemotional, and objective. You eliminate your own opinions and perceptions and retain only the provable facts. You use no jokes, no similes or metaphors, and very few colorful adjectives or adverbs. You can easily destroy your credibility by exaggerating and using overblown language: "The catastrophic collapse in sales, precipitated by cutthroat pricing on the part of predatory and unscrupulous rivals, has jeopardized the very survival of the once-soaring hot-air balloon division." That sentence has no personal references, but the colorful adjectives make its objectivity highly questionable.

You are not being objective if you

- Use exaggerated language
- Omit crucial evidence

Nor does the formal style guarantee objectivity of content. The selection of facts is far more important than the way they're phrased. If you omit crucial evidence, you're not being objective, even though you're using an impersonal style.

Despite its drawbacks, the impersonal style is a well-entrenched tradition in many business organizations. You can often tell what tone is appropriate for your readers by looking at other reports of a similar type in your company. If all the other reports on file are impersonal, you should probably adopt the same tone yourself, unless you're confident that your readers prefer a more personal style. Most organizations, for whatever reasons, expect an unobtrusive, impersonal writing style for business reports.

Establishing a Time Perspective

Be consistent in the verb tense you use.

In what time frame will your report exist? Will you write in the past or present tense? The person who wrote this paragraph never decided:

> Twenty-five percent of those interviewed report that they are dissatisfied with their present brand. The wealthiest participants complained most frequently, but all income categories are interested in trying a new brand. Only 5 percent of the interviewees say they had no interest in alternative products.

By flipping from tense to tense when describing the same research results, you only confuse your readers. Is the shift significant, they wonder, or are you just being sloppy? Such confusion can be eliminated by using tense consistently.

Follow a proper chronological sequence in your report.

Also be careful to observe the chronological sequence of events in your report. If you're describing the history or development of something, start at the beginning and cover each event in the order of its occurrence. If you're explaining the steps in a process, take each step in proper sequence.

Helping Readers Find Their Way

As you begin to write, remember that readers have no concept of how the various pieces of your report are related to one another. Because you have done the work, you have a sense of its wholeness and can see how each page fits into the overall structure, but readers see the report one page at a time (see Figure 14.10). As you begin to write, your job is to give readers a preview or road map of the report's structure so that they can see how the parts of your argument are related. These directions are particularly important for people from other cultures and countries, whose language skills and business expectations may differ from yours.

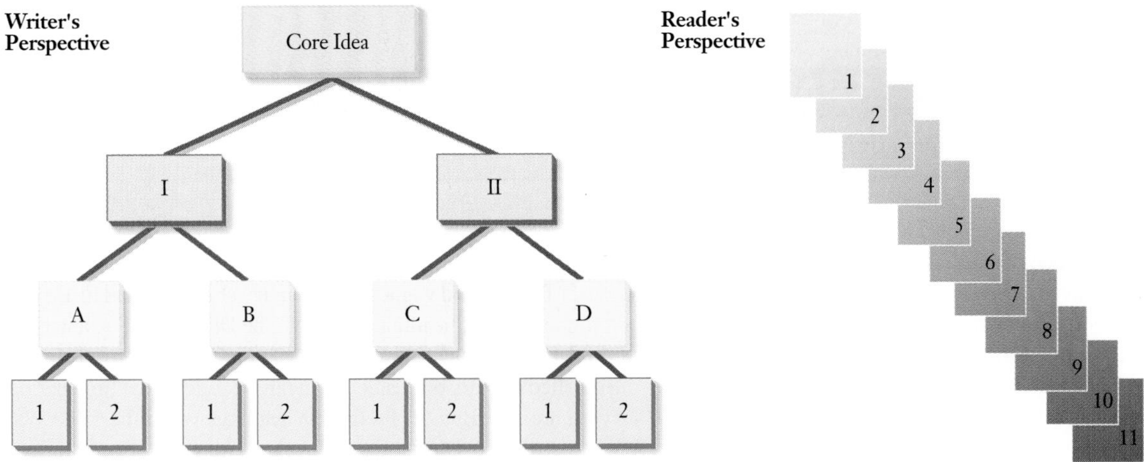

Figure 14.10
Differences in the Perspective of Writer and Reader

In a short report, readers are in little danger of getting lost. As the length of a report increases, however, so do readers' opportunities for becoming confused and losing track of the relationships among ideas. If you want readers to understand and accept your message, help them avoid confusion. Five tools are particularly useful for giving readers a sense of the overall structure of your document and for keeping them on track as they read along: the opening, headings and lists, smooth transitions, previews and reviews, and the ending.

The Opening

As the name suggests, the **opening** is the first section in any report. A good opening accomplishes at least three things:

- It introduces the subject of the report.
- It indicates why the subject is important.
- It previews the main ideas and the order in which they will be covered.

In the opening, tell readers what to expect, tell them why your subject is important, and orient them toward your organizational approach.

If you fail to provide readers with these clues to the structure of your report, they'll read aimlessly and miss important points, much like drivers trying to find their way through a strange city without a map.

If your audience is skeptical, the opening should downplay the controversial aspects of your message while providing the necessary framework for understanding your report. Here's a good example of an indirect opening, taken from the introduction of a memo on why a new line of luggage has failed to sell well. The writer's ultimate goal is to recommend a shift in marketing strategy.

> The performance of the Venturer line can be improved. In the two years since its introduction, this product line has achieved a sales volume lower than we expected, resulting in a drain on the company's overall earnings. The purpose of this report is to review the luggage-buying habits of consumers in all markets where the Venturer line is sold so that we can determine where to put our marketing emphasis.

This paragraph quickly introduces the subject (disappointing sales), tells why the problem is important (drain on earnings), and indicates the main points to be addressed in the body of the report (review of markets where the Venturer line is sold), without revealing what the conclusions and recommendations will be.

DID YOU KNOW?

When assessing business plans, investors are turned off by three things:

1. Infatuation with the product or service rather than familiarity with and awareness of marketplace needs
2. Growth projections out of touch with reality
3. Financial projections that deviate excessively from industry norms

SHARPENING YOUR SKILLS

WRITING HEADINGS THAT SPARK READER INTEREST

Headings help your audience follow the main points presented in your report, and when carefully developed, headings do much more. They capture your readers' attention and interest, inform them, and make them want to read the whole report. They show your reader at a glance how your document is organized. They label the parts of your document and help your readers find the parts they need to read. And they help you organize your writing.

Each heading offers you an opportunity to make an important point. For example, instead of "Introduction," your opening section might be called "An Insight into the Need for Better Communication." This title catches attention and sparks interest. The title "Chart of Proposed Organization" gains impact when reworded as "Organizing for Results." So does "Cost Considerations" when retitled "A New Way to Cut Costs."

Headings fall into two categories. Descriptive (topical) headings, such as "Cost Considerations," identify a topic but do little more. However, they are fine for routine reports and in controversial reports, where they may defuse emotional reactions. Informative (talking) headings, such as "A New Way to Cut Costs," convey more information about the main theme or idea of the report. They are helpful because they guide readers to think in a certain way about the topic. For more effective reports, concentrate on developing informative headings rather than descriptive ones. However, be aware that informative headings are more difficult to create.

Try to avoid vague headings. In a chronological history of your company, headings such as "The Dawning of a New Era" and "The Times They Are a-Changin'" may sound distinguished or cute, but readers will have no idea what time period you are referring to. Preferable headings would be "The War Years: Gebco Outfits Our GIs" or "The 1990s See International Expansion."

Whatever types of headings you choose, try to keep them grammatically parallel. For example, this series of headings is parallel: "Cutting Costs," "Reducing Inventory," "Increasing Profits." This series of headings is not: "Cutting Costs," "Inventory Reduction," "How to Increase Profits."

1. Think about the headlines in a newspaper. What functions do they perform? How are they usually phrased? What can you learn from journalistic headlines that applies to report writing?
2. For practice in writing headings, collect some brochures, newsletters, or similar items and rewrite the headings to convey more information about the theme or main idea. Can you draw any conclusions about what works best?

Headings and Lists

Use headings to give readers the gist of your report.

A **heading** is a brief title at the start of a subdivision within a report that cues readers about the content of the section that follows. Headings are useful markers for clarifying the framework of a report. They visually indicate shifts from one idea to the next, and when *subheadings* (lower-level headings) and headings are both used, they help readers see the relationship between subordinate and main ideas. In addition, busy readers can quickly understand the gist of a document simply by scanning the headings. (See "Sharpening Your Skills: Writing Headings That Spark Reader Interest.")

Phrase all same-level headings within a section in parallel terms.

Headings within a given section that are of the same level of importance should be phrased in parallel form, as they are in outlines. In other words, if one heading begins with a verb, all same-level headings in that section should begin with a verb. If one is a noun phrase, all should be noun phrases. Putting comparable ideas in similar terms tells readers that the ideas are related. The only exception might be such descriptive headings as "Introduction" at the beginning of a report and "Conclusions" and "Recommendations" at the end. Many companies specify a format for headings. If yours does, use that format. Otherwise, you can use the scheme shown in Figure 14.11.

Use lists to set off important ideas and to show sequence.

Lists are another effective way to set off important ideas and provide the reader with clues. (Bullets and lists are discussed in detail in Chapter 5.) Like headings, lists are phrased

Figure 14.11
Heading Format for Reports

TITLE

The title is centered at the top of the page in all capital letters, usually boldfaced (or underlined if typewritten), often in a large font (type size), and often using a sans serif typeface. When the title runs to more than one line, the lines are usually double-spaced and arranged as an inverted pyramid (longer line on the top).

FIRST-LEVEL HEADING

A first-level heading indicates what the following section is about, perhaps by describing the subdivisions. All first-level headings are grammatically parallel, with the possible exception of such headings as "Introduction," "Conclusions," and "Recommendations." Some text appears between every two headings, regardless of their levels. Still boldfaced and sans serif, the font may be smaller than that used in the title but still larger than the typeface used in the text and still in all capital letters.

Second-Level Heading

Like first-level headings, second-level headings indicate what the following material is about. All second-level headings within a section are grammatically parallel. Still boldfaced and sans serif, the font may either remain the same or shrink to the size used in the text, and the style is now initial capitals with lower case. Never use only one second-level heading under a first-level heading. (The same is true for every other level of heading.)

Third-Level Heading

A third-level heading is worded to reflect the content of the material that follows. All third-level headings beneath a second-level heading should be grammatically parallel.

Fourth-Level Heading. Like all the other levels of heading, fourth-level headings reflect the subject that will be developed. All fourth-level headings within a subsection are parallel.

Fifth-level headings are generally the lowest level of heading used. However, you can indicate further breakdowns in your ideas by using a list:

1. *The first item in a list.* You may indent the entire item in block format to set it off visually. Numbers are optional.
2. *The second item in a list.* All lists have at least two items. An introductory phrase or sentence may be italicized for emphasis, as shown here.

in parallel form. A list that uses bullets or letters instead of numbers indicates choices without implying order or hierarchy:[6]

A. Convert an existing conference room
B. Build an add-on room
C. Lease space in an existing day-care center

When you use lists, make sure to introduce them clearly so that people know what they're about to read. You might want to consider using multilevel lists, with subentries below each major item (much like an outline). If necessary, add further discussion after the lists (as this paragraph is doing). Moving your readers smoothly into and out of lists requires careful use of transitions—the subject of the next section.

Transitions

Use transitions consisting of a single word, a few words, or a whole paragraph to provide additional structural clues.

Such phrases as *to continue the analysis, on the other hand,* and *an additional concept* are another type of structural clue. These are examples of **transitions**, words or phrases that tie ideas together within a report and keep readers moving along the right track. Good writers use transitions to help readers move from one section of a report to the next, from one paragraph to the next, and even from one sentence to the next. (For example, the last sentence in the previous paragraph was a transition to help you move from the subject of lists to the subject of transitions.) Here is a list of transitions frequently used to move readers smoothly between sentences and paragraphs:

Additional detail: moreover, furthermore, in addition, besides, first, second, third, finally

Causal relationship: therefore, because, accordingly, thus, consequently, hence, as a result, so

Comparison: similarly, here again, likewise, in comparison, still

Contrast: yet, conversely, whereas, nevertheless, on the other hand, however, but, nonetheless

Condition: although, if

Illustration: for example, in particular, in this case, for instance

Time sequence: formerly, after, when, meanwhile, sometimes

Intensification: indeed, in fact, in any event

Summary: in brief, in short, to sum up

Repetition: that is, in other words, as I mentioned earlier

Although transitional words and phrases are useful, they're not sufficient in themselves to overcome poor organization. Your goal is first to put your ideas in a strong framework and then to use transitions to link them together even more strongly.

Consider using a transition device whenever it might help the reader understand your ideas and follow you from point to point. You can use transitions inside paragraphs to tie related points together and between paragraphs to ease the shift from one distinct thought to another. In longer reports transitions that link major sections or chapters are often complete paragraphs that serve as mini-introductions to the next section or as summaries of the ideas presented in the section just ending. Here's an example:

> Given the nature of this problem, the alternatives are limited. As the previous section indicates, we can stop making the product, improve it, or continue with the current model. Each of these alternatives has advantages and disadvantages. The following section discusses pros and cons of each of the three alternatives.

Previews and Reviews

You may have heard the old saying "Tell 'em what you're going to tell 'em, tell 'em, then tell 'em what you just told 'em." The more formal way of giving this advice is to tell you to use *preview sections* before and *review sections* after important material in your report. Using a preview section to introduce a topic helps readers get ready for new information. Previews are particularly helpful when the information is complex or unexpected. You don't want the reader to get halfway into a section before figuring out what it's all about.

Review sections, obviously enough, come after a body of material and summarize the information for your readers. For example, the summary section at the end of this chapter is a review section. Long reports and reports dealing with complex subjects can often benefit from multiple review sections, and not just a single review at the very end.

Swimming is a good analogy for using preview and review sections. Before you jump into the water, you look around, get your bearings, and get an idea of what you're about to dive into. A preview section serves the same purpose for your reader. After you dive in and swim for a few moments, you come back up for air. You look around and get your bearings again. This is like a review section. Whenever you've had your readers "swimming in details" for any length of time, bring them back to the surface with a review section so that they can get their bearings again.

The Ending

Reemphasize your main ideas in the ending.

Research shows that the **ending**, the final section of a report, leaves a strong and lasting impression. That's why it's important to use the ending to emphasize the main points of your message. In a report written in direct order, you may want to remind readers once again of your key points or your conclusions and recommendations. If your report is written in indirect order, end with a summary of key points (except in short memos). In analytical reports, end with conclusions and recommendations as well as key points. Be sure to summarize the benefits to the reader in any report that suggests a change of course or some other action. In general, the ending refers back to all the pieces and reminds readers how those pieces fit together. It provides a final opportunity to emphasize the wholeness of your message. Furthermore, it gives you one last chance to check that the report says what you really wanted to say.[7]

COMMUNICATION CHALLENGES AT THE SAN DIEGO WILD ANIMAL PARK

Deirdre Ballou often helps the Zoological Society of San Diego's development department solicit funding for the nonprofit organization. Educational projects are a favorite among corporate sponsors, so Ballou's expertise is invaluable. For the past three years, one corporation has underwritten an annual Educators' Event at the Wild Animal Park (WAP), which allows Ballou and staff to host and inform groups of teachers about the unique educational opportunities the park offers. For example, imagine trying to get schoolkids excited about keeping a detailed information log. Then picture them visiting the park's simulated research station and learning about logs from a guide portraying a real scientist who is tracking and recording the behavior of colobus monkeys that inhabit a nearby island.

Although some sponsors want only the facts about a project (proposal followed by preliminary, interim, and final reports), Ballou knows that this particular company likes colorful proposals and reports, describing everything from the menu served at the event to what the weather was like. But they also want to see a proposed timeline and budget spreadsheets. For this year's event, Ballou is planning a behind-the-scenes tour led by WAP animal experts, culminating in a visit to the research island, where interpretive guides will demonstrate how they entertain and inform visitors with their lab equipment, charts, maps, logs, microscopes, centrifuges, water purification equipment, discovery scopes, and radio telemetry tracking—not to mention their hand-reared animals. An aardvark is a permanent resident on the island, and ten other creatures—including a pygmy falcon, a lilac-breasted roller, a leopard tortoise, a springhaas (of the rodent family), and a fennec fox—are brought to the station throughout each day for demonstrations.

INDIVIDUAL CHALLENGE: Ballou is meeting again with company representatives, and she wants to take along a preliminary proposal for this year's Educators' Event. Use what you've learned in this chapter to suggest an outline for Ballou's preliminary proposal. Make up any details you need to make your outline authentic. Suggest a length, format, organization, and level of formality.

TEAM CHALLENGE: Ballou will also need to convince park management that hiring extra interpretive guides for a new exhibit is a necessity. Trouble is, because of their special knowledge and training, their hourly rate is higher than that of other park personnel, and keeping labor costs low is a primary concern for the general manager. Brainstorm ideas for solving Ballou's dilemma. How should she broach the subject and convince the general manager that the cost is justified? Make detailed notes explaining and justifying your recommended strategy.[8] ■

SUMMARY OF LEARNING OBJECTIVES

1. **Differentiate between a problem statement and a statement of purpose.** A problem statement defines what you are going to investigate, whereas a statement of purpose defines *why* you are preparing the report.
2. **Identify at least five elements commonly included in a formal work plan.** A formal work plan generally includes a statement of the problem, a statement of the purpose of your report and scope of your study, the sequence of tasks to be accomplished, a description of the end product that will result from your study, and a review of the assignment, schedules, and resource requirements.
3. **Explain the difference between a conclusion and a recommendation.** A conclusion is the writer's analysis of what the findings mean (an interpretation of the facts) whereas a recommendation is the writer's opinion (based on reason and logic) about the course of action that should be taken.
4. **List six ways to structure informational reports.** Six common ways to structure informational reports are according to (1) importance, (2) sequence, (3) chronology, (4) spatial orientation, (5) geography, and (6) category.
5. **Describe three basic organizational approaches to use when focusing on logical arguments, and briefly discuss when it's best to use each.** Use the 2 + 2 = 4 approach when readers are skeptical and when you want them to follow your thinking pattern. Use the scientific approach when readers need a lot of convincing and when you want them to draw their own conclusions. Use the yardstick approach when readers need a lot of convincing and you want them to measure the alternative solutions against a consistent set of criteria.
6. **Identify five tools writers can use when preparing a long report to help readers stay on track.** You can help readers navigate a report by using these five tools: (1) An opening that introduces the subject of the report, indicates why it's important, and previews the key points in the order they will be discussed; (2) headings and lists to set off important ideas and provide the reader with clues; (3) transitions to tie ideas together and keep readers moving along; (4) previews and reviews to prepare readers for new information and to summarize previously discussed information; (5) an ending to summarize the key points, conclusions, or recommendations.

CRITICAL THINKING QUESTIONS

1. After an exhaustive study of an important problem, you have reached a conclusion that you know your company's management will reject. What do you do? Explain your answer.
2. Put yourself in the position of a manager who is supervising an investigation but doing very little of the research personally. Why would a work plan be especially useful to the manager? To the researcher? Explain.
3. If you have a clear and detailed statement of purpose, why do you need a problem statement as well? Would it be a good idea to combine the two? Why or why not?
4. Would you use an opening, headings, and a closing in informal reports that stay within your own department? In routine status reports to your manager? Explain your answers.
5. Should a report always explain the writer's method of gathering evidence or solving a problem? Why or why not?
6. Would you use the direct or indirect approach to document inventory shortages at your manufacturing plant? To propose an employee stock-option plan? Why?
7. Why do you think some organizations prefer a formal tone for internal reports? What are the advantages and disadvantages of such a tone? Explain briefly.
8. What tense is better for most business reports, past or present? Explain.

EXERCISES

1. You are writing a report on the U.S. sales of your newest product. Of the following topics, identify those that should and should not be included in your report (please explain your choices):
   a. Regional breakdowns of sales across the country
   b. Sales figures from competitors selling similar products worldwide
   c. Predictions of how the struggling U.S. economy will affect sales over the next six months
   d. The impact of similar products being sold in the United States by Japanese competitors
   e. An evaluation of your company's selling this product internationally
2. You're getting ready to launch a new lawn-care business offering mowing, fertilizing, weeding, and other services. The lawn surrounding a nearby shopping center looks as if it could use better care, so you target that business for your first sales proposal. To help prepare this proposal, write your answers to these questions:
   a. What problem statement and statement of purpose would be most appropriate? (Think about the reader's viewpoint.)
   b. What questions will you need answered before you can write a proposal to solve the reader's problem? Be as specific as possible.
   c. What conclusions and recommendations might be practical, acceptable to the reader, and specific enough for the shopping center to take action? (Think about the purpose of the report.)
3. Now turn the situation around and assume that you're the shopping center's facilities manager. You report to the general manager, who must approve any new contracts for lawn service. Before you contract for lawn care, you want to prepare a formal study of the current state of your lawn's health. The re-

port will include conclusions and recommendations for your boss's consideration. Draft a work plan, including the problem statement, the statement of purpose and scope, a description of what will result from your investigation, the sources and methods of data collection, and a preliminary outline.

4. The college administration has asked you to head a student committee that will look into how the bookstore can ease the long lines during the first two weeks of every term, when students need to buy books. Select two other students to serve on your committee and help plan a feasibility study and an analytical report showing your recommendations. As a first step, your committee should prepare a brief memo to the administration. The memo should accomplish the following:
   a. Identify the problem (problem statement) and the purpose (statement of purpose).
   b. Identify two or three likely alternatives to be investigated.
   c. Clearly identify the criteria for selecting among the options.
   d. Identify the primary and secondary sources of information to be used in the study.
5. You're the advertising manager at a regional ice cream company. Your boss, the director of marketing, has asked you to report on how the company should use advertising to support new-product introductions, using this statement of purpose:

   Statement of purpose: To analyze various methods of advertising new products when they are introduced and to recommend the most effective and cost-efficient program

   a. How should you factor this problem? Will you use descriptive or informative headings for your preliminary outline?
   b. Develop an outline, following the rules of division.
   c. Exchange outlines with a student in your class and critique each other's work. Comment on the organization, logic, consistency, and completeness of the other student's outline. On the basis of the suggestions you receive, revise your own outline.
6. Look through recent issues (print or online) of *Business Week, Fortune,* or other business publications for an article that describes how an executive's conclusions about his or her company's current situation or future opportunities led to changes in policy, plans, or products. Construct an outline of the material, using (a) direct order and (b) indirect order. Which approach do you think the executive would use when reporting these conclusions to stockholders? When reporting to other senior managers? Explain your answers.
7. Of the organizational approaches introduced in the chapter, which is best suited for reporting on each of the following problem statements? Briefly explain why.
   a. In which market segment—root beer, cola, or lemon-lime—should Fizz Drinks, Inc., introduce a new soft drink to take advantage of its enlarged research and development budget?
   b. Should Major Manufacturing, Inc., close down operations of its antiquated Bellville, Arkansas, plant despite the adverse economic impact on the town that has grown up around the plant?
   c. Should you and your partner adopt a new accounting method to make your financial statements look better to potential investors?
   d. Should Grand Canyon Chemicals buy disposable test tubes to reduce labor costs associated with cleaning and sterilizing reusable test tubes?
   e. What are some reasons for the recent data loss at the college computer center, and how can we avoid similar problems in the future?
8. Go to the library or visit the Internet site http://www.annualreportservice.com and review the annual reports recently released by two corporations in the same industry. Analyze each report and be prepared to discuss the following questions in class:

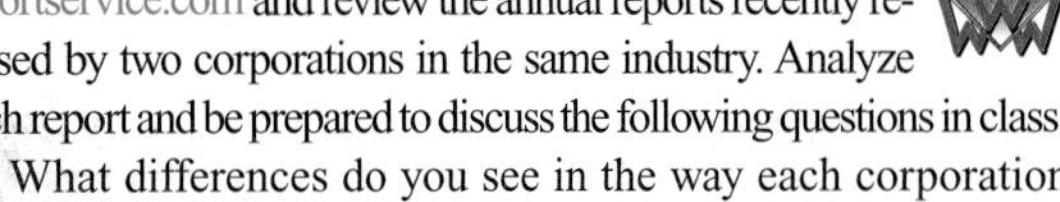

   a. What differences do you see in the way each corporation reports its financial data? Are the data presented clearly so that shareholders can draw conclusions about each corporation's financial results?
   b. What goals, challenges, and plans do top managers emphasize in their discussion of results?
   c. How do the format and organization of each report enhance or detract from the information being presented?
9. Your boss, Len Chow (vice president of corporate planning), has asked you to research opportunities in the cosmetics industry and to prepare a report that presents your findings and your recommendation for where you think the company should focus its marketing efforts. Here's a copy of your notecards:

Sub: Demand ref: 1.1 Industry grew through 1970s, 1980s, and early 1990s fueled by per capita consumption
Sub: Competition ref: 1.2 700 companies currently in cosmetics industry
Sub: Niches ref: 1.3 Focusing on special niches avoids head-on competition with industry leaders
Sub: Competition ref: 1.4 Industry dominated by market leaders: Revlon, Procter & Gamble, Avon, Gillette
Sub: Demand ref: 1.5 Industry no longer recession proof: Past year, sales sluggish; consumer spending is down; most affected were mid- to high-priced brands; consumers traded down to less expensive lines
Sub: Competition ref: 1.6 Smaller companies (Neutrogena, Mary Kay, Soft Soap, and Noxell) survive by: specializing in niches; differentiating product line; focusing on market segment

Sub: Demand ref: 1.7 Consumption of cosmetics relatively flat for past five years
Sub: Competition ref: 1.8 Prices are constant while promotion budgets are increasing
Sub: Niches ref: 1.9 Men: 50% of adult population; account for one-fifth of cosmetic sales; market leaders have attempted this market but failed
Sub: Demand ref: 1.10 Cosmetic industry is near maturity but some segments may vary. Total market currently produces annual retail sales of \$14.5 billion: Cosmetics/lotions/fragrances—\$5.635 billion; Personal hygiene products—\$4.375 billion; hair-care products—\$3.435 billion; shaving products—\$1.055 billion
Sub: Niches ref: 1.11 Ethnic groups: Some firms specialize in products for African Americans; few firms oriented toward Hispanic, Asian, or Native Americans, which tend to be concentrated geographically
Sub: Demand ref: 1.12 Average annual expenditure per person for cosmetics is \$58
Sub: Competition ref: 1.13 Competition is intensifying and dominant companies are putting pressure on smaller ones
Sub: Demand ref: 1.14 First quarter of current year, demand is beginning to revive; trend expected to continue well into next year
Sub: Niches ref: 1.15 Senior citizens: large growing segment of population; account for 6% of cosmetic sales; specialized needs for hair and skin not being met; interested in appearance
Sub: Demand ref: 1.16 Demographic trends: (1) Gradual maturing of baby-boomer generation will fuel growth by consuming greater quantities of shaving cream, hair-coloring agents, and skin creams; (2) Population is increasing in the South and Southwest, where some brands have strong distribution

Using Figure 5.3 "Organizational Chart for Organizing a Message" on page 133 as a model, reorganize your notes: Determine the main idea (your recommendation), major points (your conclusions), and supporting evidence. Then construct a final report outline with first- and second-level informative headings focusing on your conclusions. Because Chow requested this report, you can feel free to use the direct approach. Finish by writing a memo report to Chow.

10. Three years ago, your company (a carpet manufacturer) modernized its Georgia plant in anticipation of increasing demand for carpets. Because of the depressed housing market, the increase in demand for new carpets has been slow to materialize. As a result, the company has excess capacity at both its Georgia and California plants. On the basis of your research, you are recommending that the company close the California plant. The company president, J. P. Lawrence, has asked you to prepare a justification report to support your recommendation. Here are the facts you gathered by interviewing the respective plant managers:

Operational Statistics

- Georgia plant: This plant has newer equipment, productivity is higher, employs 100 non-union production workers, and ships \$12 million in carpets a year. Hourly base wage is \$16.
- California plant: California plant employs 80 union production workers and ships \$8 million in carpets a year. Hourly base wage is \$20.

Financial Implications

- Savings by closing California plant: (1) increase productivity by 17% ; (2) reduce labor costs by 20% (total labor savings would be \$1 million per year; see assumptions); (3) annual local tax savings of \$120,000 (Georgia has a more favorable tax climate).
- Sale of Pomona, California land: Purchased in 1952 for \$200,000. Current market value \$2.5 million. Net profit (after capital gains tax) over \$1 million.
- Sale of plant and equipment: Fully depreciated. Any proceeds a windfall.
- Costs of closing California plant: One-time deductible charge of \$250,000 (relocation costs of \$100,000 and severance payments totaling \$150,000).

Assumptions

- Transfer 5 workers from California to Georgia.
- Hire 45 new workers in Georgia.
- Lay off 75 workers in California.
- Georgia plant would require a total of 150 workers to produce the combined volume of both plants.

a. Which logical approach will you use to structure your report to the president? Why?
b. Suppose this report were to be circulated to plant managers and supervisors instead. What changes, if any, might you make in your approach?
c. Review Chapter 11, "Step 3: Evaluating and Finalizing Your Sources." What concerns, if any, might you have about the information you obtained from the plant managers? What could you do to satisfy your concerns?
d. Using the structure you selected for your report to the president, draft a final report outline with first- and second-level informative headings.

Exploring the Best of the Web

Construct an Outline with Confidence, page 472

Review the "Sample Outline" at the Purdue University Online Writing Lab; then try your hand at drafting an outline. For your subject matter, select a report that you're going to write as part of your study of this chapter, as another class project, or as an exercise assigned by your instructor. Develop the idea only as far as its organization.

CASES

INFORMAL INFORMATIONAL REPORTS

1. **My progress to date: Interim progress report on your academic career** As you know, the bureaucratic process involved in getting a degree or certificate is nearly as challenging as any course you could take.

Your task: Prepare an interim progress report detailing the steps you've taken toward completing your graduation or certification requirements. After examining the requirements listed in your college catalog, indicate a realistic schedule for completing those that remain. In addition to course requirements, include such steps as completing the residency requirement, filing necessary papers, and paying necessary fees. Use memo format for your report, and address it to anyone who is helping or encouraging you through school.

2. **Here's why: Personal report on how a class influenced a life decision** Think of a class or course you've taken that has helped influence a life decision. For example, you may have decided to pursue finance as a career because of a particularly dynamic professor. Or you may have decided never again to use products tested on animals after learning about the issue in a presentation by a fellow student in business communication.

Your task: Prepare an e-mail memo in which you explain your decision. Consider your target audience (your family or friends) as you decide on pertinent details to include. Remember that your task is not to persuade them to follow your decision but to inform them of the reasoning that led to your own.

3. **Gavel to gavel: Personal activity report of a meeting** Meetings, conferences, and conventions abound in the academic world, and you have probably attended your share.

Your task: Prepare a personal activity report on a meeting, convention, or conference that you recently attended. Use memo format, and direct the report to other students in your field who were not able to attend.

4. **With an eye toward change: Informational report on converting a building to a new use** The company you work for, Video Vendors, Inc., has just bought an abandoned fast-food restaurant with the intention of converting it to an outlet for renting and selling videotapes and video equipment. You are a planning specialist with Video Vendors, and it's your job to outline the architectural changes that will be necessary for successful remodeling.

Your task: Visit any fast-food restaurant in your area and draw a diagram that shows its current use of indoor and outdoor space. Next determine the architectural changes that will be necessary to convert the building into a video outlet, the major fixtures that must be removed, and the major items that must be purchased. Present your findings in a memo to Angelica Smythe, vice president of planning for Video Vendors, Inc. Include a diagram showing the proposed layout of the video outlet.

5. **Prospects for growth: Report describing a small firm** Choose a small independent business in your area, and assume that the owners have hired you to help them approach a local bank for financial help with their expansion. The bank will require a complete financial statement and a brief narrative description of the business, covering such topics as the length of time it has been operating, its chief product lines and services, the size of its market area, its usual mix of customers, and the general prospects for growth in its neighborhood.

Your task: Draft the report that you will submit to the bank for your client. Several paragraphs of objective writing will be sufficient, and no financial figures are necessary because they will appear in accompanying financial statements. Remember that your job is to describe the business, not to recommend that the bank lend money to it.

6. **Check that price tag: Informational report on trends in college costs** Are tuition costs going up, going down, or remaining the same? Your college's administration has asked you to compare your college's tuition costs with those of a nearby college and

determine which has risen more quickly. Research the trend by checking your college's annual tuition costs for each of the most recent four years. Then research the four-year tuition trends for a neighboring college. For both colleges, calculate the percentage change in tuition costs from year to year and between the first and fourth year.

Your task: Prepare an informal report (using the letter format) presenting your findings and conclusions to the president of your college. Include graphics to explain and support your conclusions.

7. Preparing for the worst: Policy report on crisis management When the anonymous call came in, Campbell Soup officials refused to take any chances. The caller claimed to have put poison in Campbell's tomato juice cans at a New England supermarket. The company quickly decided to yank the product from 84 area stores. Even though the call turned out to be a hoax, Campbell Soup believes it's best to be prepared for the worst. Moreover, an important part of any crisis-management plan is the way company officials tell the public about the situation.

Your task: You're a public relations consultant with special expertise in crisis management. You've been asked to develop a policy recommending how and when Campbell Soup should reveal product threats to the public. In addition, you want to suggest ways of reassuring consumers that Campbell Soup products are pure and completely safe. Draft the outline for a policy report to CEO David W. Johnson that includes your recommendations and the justifications for those recommendations. Be sure the headings you choose show what your report will cover, including the need for action, the benefits to be achieved, the list of recommendations (without details), and a summary.[9]

8. Sampling success: Operating report on a program to promote a new cracker To help food manufacturers promote their new products, Sample U.S.A. offers supermarket shoppers bite-size samples of everything from cheese and ice cream to pretzels and cookies. This month Sample U.S.A. gave away a total of 12,800 samples of Cheezy sesame crackers in 11 New Orleans supermarkets. The Cheezy Company wants Sample U.S.A. to give away 14,000 sesame cracker samples in 13 Houston supermarkets during the coming month. However, one large supermarket chain hasn't yet agreed to let Sample U.S.A. set up a tasting booth.

Your task: As the Southwest regional manager for Sample U.S.A., you send your clients a monthly operating report on results and future sampling plans. Prepare this month's report to Jacques D'Aprix, the director of marketing at the Cheezy Company. Be sure to include future plans as well as any problems that may affect next month's activities.

BUSINESS SUMMARY

9. How did Nike do it? Summary of a PR disaster Jill Montaine has been the proud owner of Jill's Jackets in Los Angeles for seven years, ever since her designs started showing up on celebrities at the best parties in Beverly Hills. Word of mouth spread so fast that it wasn't long before she moved out of her converted garage studio and into her own showcase shop on Rodeo Drive. Now she's worried.

"I don't know what I'm going to do. This could ruin me," she confesses to you (her store manager). She showed up early one morning shortly before you opened the shop for business. You sympathize. Montaine started out sewing all her own designs and selling them on consignment at local boutiques. When her popularity grew, she hired subcontractors outside the United States, most recently in Southeast Asia, to keep up with the order demands. Yesterday she learned that one of her overseas subcontractors was imposing new, harsh rules on his workers. Long hours, no breaks, unsanitary and hazardous working conditions—in common lingo, he'd turned the operation into the worst kind of overseas sweatshop. And Jill's Jackets was his only client.

Concerned about how much of her money had gone into his pockets instead of workers' paychecks, Montaine had already taken steps to replace him with another subcontractor. Now she's worried about how quickly this news might spread and destroy her reputation in the United States. Word of mouth is everything in the upscale fashion business, and similar stories had nearly ruined others—including some more famous than Jill's Jackets.

"Why don't you find out how other companies have handled this kind of situation?" you suggest gently.

"Oh, you're right! That's a great idea." Relief spreads quickly over Montaine's face. "What did Nike do? Can you find out? How did they handle this kind of PR disaster?"

Your task: Grateful for your suggestion, Montaine has left the shop in haste, heading off to a luncheon fashion show that she hopes will take the sting out of the bad publicity. Meanwhile, she's asked you to leave the clerks in charge of the store and zip over to the library. She wants you to read up on Nike's response to the accusations of overseas labor abuse that arose during the spring of 1997. Then you are to write up a summary of your findings and fax it to her home machine.[10]

INFORMAL ANALYTICAL REPORTS

10. My next career move: Justification report organized around recommendations If you've ever given yourself a really good talking-to, you'll be quite comfortable with this project.

Your task: Write a memo report directed to yourself and signed with a fictitious name. Indicate a possible job that your college education will qualify you for, mention the advantages of the position in terms of your long-range goals, and then outline the actions you must take to get the job.

11. Staying the course: Proposal using the 2 + 2 = 4 approach Think of a course you would love to see added to the core curriculum at your school. Conversely, if you would like to see a course offered as an elective rather than being required, write your e-mail report accordingly.

Your task: Write a short e-mail proposal using the 2 + 2 = 4 approach. Prepare your proposal to be submitted to the academic dean by e-mail. Be sure to include all the reasons supporting your idea.

12. Planning my program: Problem-solving report using the scientific method Assume that you will have time for only one course next term.

Your task: List the pros and cons of four or five courses that interest you, and use the scientific method to settle on the course that is best for you to take at this time. Write your report in memo format, addressing it to your academic adviser.

13. Section A, section B: Justification report using the yardstick approach Choose a course that is taught by at least two instructors at different times, either a course that you actually need to take or one that interests you. Justify your decision to enroll in one section rather than the other.

Your task: Write a memo to your academic adviser that explains which section you plan to enroll in and why you chose it. Use three or four important criteria as a basis for analyzing the two sections or instructors.

14. "Would you carry it?" Unsolicited sales proposal recommending a product to a retail outlet Select a product you are familiar with, and imagine that you are the manufacturer trying to get a local retail outlet to carry it.

Your task: Write a sales proposal in letter format to the owner (or manager) of the store, proposing that the item be stocked. Making up some reasonable figures, tell what the item costs, what it can be sold for, and what services your company provides (return of unsold items, free replacement of unsatisfactory items, necessary repairs, and the like).

15. Selling something special: Unsolicited proposal to a business Pick a company or business that you know something about. Now think of a customized item or service that you believe the business needs. Examples might be a specially designed piece of equipment, a workshop for employees on improving their communication skills, a program for curtailing shoplifting, a catering service to a company's construction site, or a customized word-processing system, to name just a few possibilities.

Your task: Write an unsolicited proposal to the owners or managers of this business. Convince them that they need the product you're selling. Include a statement of the problem, the purpose (benefits), the scope (areas in which your product will help the business), methods and procedures, the work plan and schedule, your qualifications, projected costs, and any other pertinent information. Use a letter format.

16. Who's best? Problem-solving report comparing job candidates Imagine that a family from another country (pick any country) has engaged you to help find a tutor for their two children (ages 9 and 11). You have just interviewed four people for the position.

Your task: Write a report in memo format to the parents. In it, describe the four candidates (use four friends) and recommend them, in rank order, for the position. Consider at least the following areas for comparison of the candidates: education, experience, and personal attributes. Analyze the pros and cons of each candidate using the yardstick method.

17. Restaurant review: Troubleshooting report on a restaurant's food and operations Visit any restaurant, possibly your school cafeteria. The workers and fellow customers will assume that you are an ordinary customer, but you are really a spy for the owner.

Your task: After your visit, write a short memo to the owner, explaining (a) what you did and what you observed, (b) any violations of policy that you observed, and (c) your recommendations for improvement. The first part of your report (what you did and what you observed) will be the longest. Include a description of the premises, inside and out. Tell how long it took for each step of ordering and receiving your meal. Describe the service and food thoroughly. You are interested in both the good and bad aspects of the establishment's decor, service, and food. For the second section (violations of policy), use some common sense. If all the servers but one have their hair covered, you may assume that policy requires hair to be covered; a dirty window or restroom obviously violates policy. The last section (recommendations for improvement) involves professional judgment. What management actions will improve the restaurant?

18. Mansfield Center or Cat Spring? Feasibility report comparing potential plant locations Current plant capabilities are inadequate for manufacturing Victory Valve's new line of gate valves, globe valves, check valves, ball valves, and butterfly valves. The company is seeking a new location removed from the strains of rapid urbanization and union pressures but still close to potential markets. Two locations have been proposed: Mansfield Center, Connecticut, and Cat Spring, Texas. Fellow members of the site-selection committee (you're in charge) submitted the following raw data about these two locations:

- *Mansfield Center, Connecticut.* An attractive town of about 5,000 near the Mansfield Hollow Reservoir, with rivers and forested recreation areas. Good schools, with moderately expensive housing available. Tax rates generally low and subject to negotiation; the town might forgive taxes during a three- to five-year start-up period. Adequate rail and road transportation available. Located within 50 miles of markets in Hartford, Providence, Springfield, Worcester, and New Haven. Energy costs ranging from average to high and rising. Experienced factory workers available. Steel must be brought in by rail, probably from Pennsylvania or the Chicago-Gary area. Moderate climate. The University of Connecticut, at nearby Storrs, might provide research facilities and assistance, as well as a supply of seasonal workers. In this heavily industrialized area, valves are in constant demand, but the presence of nearby competitors would force heavy price competition.

- *Cat Spring, Texas.* A tiny town about 50 miles from the Gulf of Mexico; conveniently located on the Houston–Fort Worth rail line. Real estate prices low and taxes minuscule. Adequate labor available from the Houston and Dallas–Fort Worth areas, but housing would have to be built to accommodate the influx of workers. Local schools currently inadequate for any increase from workers' families but could presumably be expanded. Steel from Europe arrives at the port of Houston and could be delivered economically by rail to Cat Spring. The climate is hot and dry nine months of the year, making air-conditioning of the plant necessary. Markets in Houston, Waco, Fort Worth, Dallas, and Austin are all about 200 miles away. The need for our type of valves appears to be growing as industrialization increases in southern Texas. Electricity and water expensive, although recent developments in solar power appear to be reducing the costs of air-conditioning.

Your task: Write a memo in which you recommend one of the two locations and justify your recommendation. The report has been requested by Ron Wasserman, chief executive officer of Victory Valves, Inc.

19. On the books: Troubleshooting report on improving the campus bookstore Imagine that you are a consultant hired to improve the profits of your campus bookstore.

Your task: Visit the bookstore and look critically at its operations. Then draft a memo offering recommendations to the bookstore manager that would make the store more profitable, perhaps suggesting products it should carry, hours that it should remain open, or added services that it should make available to students. Be sure to support your recommendations.

20. Fishing for more revenue: Troubleshooting report for a nonprofit organization The Historic Fishing Village of Puget Sound has asked you to determine why revenues have been lower than expected and to suggest how to improve revenues. You've found two probable causes for the low revenue: (1) unusually bad weather during prime tourism periods and (2) shoddy, inexpensive merchandise in the gift shop.

Your task: Draft a two-page troubleshooting report to present to the nonprofit's trustees. Use the 2 + 2 = 4 approach to support your conclusions, and address the report to the trustees as a group. Make up whatever details you need about the merchandise and about ways to improve revenues. Bear in mind that the trustees originally approved the purchase of the merchandise that's in the gift shop, so you'll want to use objective language to avoid offending them.

21. Press 1 for efficiency: Unsolicited proposal on a telephone interviewing system How can a firm be thorough yet efficient when considering dozens of applicants for each position? One tool that just may help is IntelliView, a ten-minute question-and-answer session conducted by Touch-Tone telephone. The company recruiter dials up the IntelliView computer and then leaves the room. The candidate punches in answers to roughly 100 questions about work attitudes and other issues. In a few minutes, the recruiter can call Pinkerton, which offers the service, and find out the results. On the basis of what the IntelliView interview revealed, the recruiter can delve more deeply into certain areas and, ultimately, have more information on which to base the hiring decision.

Your task: As a recruiter for Curtis Box and Crate, you think that IntelliView might help your firm. Write a brief memo to Wallace Jefferson, the director of human resources, in which you suggest a test of the IntelliView system. Your memo should tell your boss why you believe your firm should test the system before making a long-term commitment.[11]

22. The check's in the mail: A troubleshooting report on collecting overdue tuition payments As student representatives on your college's campus administration committee, you and three classmates are considering ways to collect from students who are late in paying their tuition bills. Decide on the criteria you'll use to evaluate alternatives; then come up with at least four ideas.

Your task: Weigh each idea against the criteria. Then draft a research report about your findings and address it to Heather Anderson, who heads the committee.

23. Day and night: Problem-solving report on stocking a 24-hour convenience store When a store is open all day, every day, when's the best time to restock the shelves? That's the challenge at Store 24, a retail chain that never closes. Imagine you're the assistant manager of a Store 24 branch that just opened near your campus. You want to set up a restocking schedule that won't conflict with prime shopping hours. Think about the number of customers you're likely to serve in the morning, afternoon, evening, and overnight hours. Consider, too, how many employees you might have during these four periods.

Your task: Using the scientific approach, write a problem-solving report in letter form to the store manager (Isabel Chu) and the regional manager (Eric Angstrom), who must agree on a solution to this problem. Discuss the pros and cons of each of the four periods, and include your recommendation for restocking the shelves.

24. Must be attractive and experienced: Yardstick report on selecting an architect You threw down your gavel, and said, "That's a wrap." Now, as chairperson of the design review committee, you must communicate the committee's recommendation for an architectural firm to design the company's new corporate headquarters. Three firms submitted plans for the facility: Wilson and Waugh, Kaufmann and Loew, and Mosely Associates. All three were workable designs. To guide the deliberations, your committee used four criteria:

1. Design must be functionally sound. (It should take into account that people work in teams and that small and large group meetings take place regularly.)
2. Cost must be within budget ($4 million).

3. Building must be attractive (internally and externally).
4. Architect must have experience with similar projects.

Here are the committee's findings:

Wilson and Waugh

- *Design.* Interior design meets needs but is built around inflexible individual small offices, with storerooms, laboratories, and secretarial offices in the center of each floor; technical and management offices arranged around the building perimeter. Cafeteria and gymnasium in separate wing of first floor.
- *Cost.* Project bid costs ($4.8 million) exceed budget. Eliminating the employee gymnasium and using lower-quality materials would lower the bid to $4.3 million.
- *Attractiveness.* Exterior design is conventional box, three stories high and faced with brick; overall design lacks imagination.
- *Experience.* Company in business over 35 years. Other projects include Union Bank Building, Mutual Insurance and Life Building, Westek Corporate Headquarters, Civic Center, downtown library, other notable landmarks.

Kaufmann and Loew

- *Design.* Interior design arranges technical offices and laboratories in open pattern on first floor; managerial, administrative, clerical, and secretarial offices clustered on second floor; cafeteria-auditorium and gymnasium on dramatic third floor. Design also provides three small meeting rooms but has little storage space. Floor plan is smaller by 5,000 square feet than Wilson and Waugh's.
- *Cost.* Project bid of $3.8 million is within budget.
- *Attractiveness.* Exterior design is startling, unconventional, and dramatic. One employee said, "Looks like a flying potato chip on top of a soda bottle." Comments from design review committee: four said it was "outlandish"; two said it was an "outstanding exercise in creativity."
- *Experience.* Fifteen years' experience and recipient of AIA and CCMA awards for excellence in urban design. Plan for East Hills Clinic featured in last June's *Architectural Review.* Projects include RobenHass Department Store, Prudential Tower, the *Dispatch-Sun* Building, and waterfront Cultural Complex.

Mosely Associates

- *Design.* Interior design uses modular offices, mobile walls, and open floor plan; some private offices. Two meeting rooms (one small, one large) on each floor. Employee cafeteria, gymnasium, and technical library on first floor. Technical offices and laboratories on second floor. Additional private management offices and administrative/clerical facilities on third floor. Floor plan is 3,000 more square feet than Wilson and Waugh's and 8,000 more square feet than Kaufmann and Loew's.
- *Cost.* Project bid ($4.0 million) is within budget. To keep in budget, design calls for adequate outdoor lot rather than underground parking garage.
- *Attractiveness.* Most attractive design. Exterior, a three-story structure inspired by mission architecture of the Southwest, is extremely attractive but lacks drama of the Kaufmann and Loew design. High-quality materials. Use of interior courtyard provides natural light to all interior spaces.
- *Experience.* Not as experienced as other two. Firm is only three years old. Projects include Teletec corporate headquarters, the IVET Building, the Warwick Commercial Center, and some custom houses. Owner, John Mosely, has ten years' experience on staff of Bolt Construction, where he was responsible for North Valley Shopping Center, Clairmont Hotel, and new science building at Overton College.

Your task: On the basis of these findings, the committee has recommended Mosely Associates. Construct an informative outline of the committee's logic using the yardstick approach. Use the four criteria as level-one headings and the three firms as level-two headings. Then prepare a yardstick report to the company president, Veronica Payne, justifying your selection.

Completing Formal Reports and Proposals

After studying this chapter, you will be able to

1 List the seven prefatory parts of a formal report
2 Explain the function of an executive summary
3 Describe four important functions of the introduction to a formal report
4 Identify eight topics you might include in the introduction of a formal report
5 Define the goal of most formal proposals
6 Name the four types of information that must be covered in the body of a proposal

Communication Close-up at Corporate Dynamics

In business, the phrase "dog and pony show" is sometimes used to describe a report or presentation that looks attractive on the surface but lacks substance. As president of Corporate Dynamics, Mark Landiak developed a sales proposal for one potential client by capitalizing on that expression: He put a tiny image of a toy dog and pony on the report cover and titled the report "Corporate Dynamics: Not Your Typical Dog and Pony Show." This creative strategy "worked like a charm," says Landiak. "It made the client laugh, and it made us really stand out."

In fact, standing out, or differentiation, is what Corporate Dynamics is all about. Founded in 1989 by Landiak, this Chicago-based company provides clients, both large and small, with innovative training and consulting in sales, customer service, and management applications. Landiak's team begins by holding one- to two-day "workout sessions" with senior managers from various parts of the client company. The group discusses the challenges the firm is facing, as well as the company's goals and specific needs. Then Landiak's team further researches these issues, including details on the client's market, competitors, and so on.

Mark Landiak

After weeks—even months—of analysis, Corporate Dynamics sums up its findings in a formal report or proposal. Such reports generally detail the client's current position, describe any problems being faced or situations requiring change, state future objectives, point out barriers to success, and recommend strategies for productive organizational change. All the information is useful—especially the final recommendation, which usually suggests training from Landiak and his staff of experts. Landiak knows, however, that to convince clients to use his company's services, he must provide a compelling argument or purpose—the key to a successful report.

Mark Landiak builds corporate success strategies for his clients one page at a time. By gathering critical data from clients during joint "workout sessions," Landiak identifies critical issues and makes sure that each issue is adequately addressed in his final report to the client.

For example, during one workout session, Landiak identified $40 million in potential profits that his client could recoup in three key areas. This information made a compelling opening in the report's introduction. Landiak followed that with a list of the critical issues that would be discussed in the body of the report: where profits were being lost, where productivity could be improved, where time was being wasted, and how customers could be better served. Finally, Landiak offered his recommendations for capturing the additional $40 million. Similar organizational strategies have proved successful for Landiak time and again.

Corporate Dynamics' reports can be as short as five pages or as long as 30, depending on the client's needs and the issues involved. Report formats also vary. Many clients have their own reporting styles, and Landiak tries to imitate them so that his reports feel familiar and are thus easy for clients to read. He even asks managers for a report template to work from. Landiak is also careful to use language that is familiar to his audience. "One client may call a goal a 'strategic imperative,' " he explains, "while another may call it a 'critical issue.' You have to align yourself with the clients' terminology and use their jargon rather than creating a new vocabulary."

Even so, Landiak is careful to avoid using too much technical language or detail. "If you dance around the issue, you will lose your audience," he says. That's why Landiak and his team strive to make their reports straightforward and concise. "A lot of people make the mistake of including too much ancillary material," he says. "If you put in extraneous information, the reader will turn to the back looking for the bottom line."

How does Landiak find the right balance between too much information and just enough? With a lot of effort. "Someone has to be willing to go the extra mile to produce a good report," Landiak says. Going the extra mile means paying close attention to detail and proofreading carefully. Consequently, members of Landiak's team regularly review each other's work to ensure that the final product is as clear as it can be.

Still, Landiak believes that beyond being clear and concise, a report's unique touches are what really grab his audience's attention. "Report writing is an extension of you, your organization, and the job you will do," he advises. "If a report is average, the image you project is to the client is average. Dare to be different!"[1] ■

REPORT PRODUCTION

Experienced business communicators such as Mark Landiak realize that planning a report or proposal, conducting the necessary research, developing visual aids, organizing the ideas, and drafting the text are demanding and time-consuming tasks. They also know that the process of writing a report or proposal doesn't end with these steps. After careful editing and rewriting, you still need to produce a polished final version.

In organizations that produce many reports and proposals, the preparation process involves teamwork.

How the final version is actually produced depends on the nature of your organization. The traditional approach was usually a team effort, with secretaries or other support personnel handling the typing, formatting, and other tasks. For important, high-visibility reports, a graphics department could sometimes help with charts, drawings, covers, and other visual elements.

Personal computers can handle many of the mechanical aspects of report preparation.

However, as personal computers have become commonplace in the business office, more and more employees are expected to handle most or even all of the formatting and production of their own reports. In fact, many of the advances in computer hardware and software in recent years have been designed specifically to give all businesspeople the ability to produce great-looking reports by themselves. The good news is that these computer tools are now generally easy enough for the average businessperson to use productively. A software "suite" such as Microsoft Office makes it easy to produce reports that incorporate graphics, tables, spreadsheet data, and even database records. Even advanced report features such as photography are relatively simple these days, with the advent of low-cost color desktop scanners. And inexpensive color printers with near-photo-quality output have put color reports within just about everybody's reach. Used effectively, color helps improve both the reader's interest in your material and the effectiveness of your message.

The bad news is that continually improving computer tools increase your audience's expectations. People are influenced by packaging, and a handsomely bound report with full-color graphics will influence many readers more than a plain, typewriter-style report containing the same information. To make matters even more challenging, paper reports are starting to compete with various multimedia electronic reports, such as Web sites and CD-ROMs. More and more computers are connected to the Internet and able to read CD-ROMs, and the cost and skill requirements for creating both options continue to drop. Instead of producing a lengthy report full of tables and other information, you can now provide the information electronically and let readers pick and choose what they want to read. And when it

Avoid Embarrassment by Avoiding Common Errors

Report and proposal writers will definitely want to take advantage of Professor Paul Brians' "Common Errors in English" Web site, which is designed to help American writers and speakers avoid embarrassing mistakes. Brians says he built the site "to help avoid low grades, lost employment opportunities, lost business, and titters of amusement at the way you write or speak." You'll find an easy-reference list of common errors, along with an intriguing list of "non-errors" that might upset your beliefs about "right" and "wrong" in English usage.

http://www.wsu.edu:8080/~brians/errors/index.html

comes to razzle-dazzle, sending a potential client a custom-made CD-ROM with your new business proposal might be a lot more effective than providing a paper report.

No matter which tools you use, make sure you leave enough time for formatting and production. Murphy's law (which says that if something can go wrong, it will) applies to just about every aspect of using computers. Data communication problems, incompatible or corrupted disk files, printing problems, and other glitches can consume hours. You don't want computer trouble to sabotage all your thinking, planning, and writing, so make sure you can create and produce the report before the deadline.

Be sure to schedule enough time to turn out a document that looks professional.

Once you've completed a major report and sent it off to your audience, you'll naturally expect a positive response, and quite often you'll get one—but not always. You may get half-hearted praise or no action on your conclusions and recommendations. Even worse, you may get some serious criticism. Try to learn from these experiences. Sometimes you won't get any response at all. If you don't hear from your readers within a week or two, you might want to ask politely whether the report arrived. In hopes of stimulating a response, you might also offer to answer any questions or provide additional information.

Ask for feedback, and learn from your mistakes.

Regardless of how the final product is produced, it will be up to you to make sure that all necessary components are included. Depending on the length and formality of your report, various prefatory and supplementary parts may be necessary. The more formal your report, the more components you'll include.

Components of a Formal Report

A formal report's manuscript format and impersonal tone convey an impression of professionalism. A formal report can be either short (fewer than ten pages) or long (ten pages or more). It can be informational or analytical, direct or indirect. It may be directed to readers inside or outside the organization. What sets it apart from other reports is its polish.

A formal report conveys the impression that the subject is important.

The parts included in a report depend on the type of report you are writing, the requirements of your audience, the organization you're working for, and the length of your report. At Corporate Dynamics, Mark Landiak pays close attention to his clients' needs; from the style of the report to the language used, Landiak targets his clients' preferences and familiarity and includes only the parts that are appropriate for each client. The components listed in Figure 15.1 fall into three categories, depending on where they are found in a report: prefatory parts, text of the report, and supplementary parts. For an illustration of how the various parts fit together, see Linda Moreno's Electrovision report in "Sharpening Your Skills: In-Depth Critique: Analyzing a Formal Report," beginning on page 524.

The three basic divisions of a formal report:

- Prefatory parts
- Text
- Supplementary parts

Figure 15.1
Parts of a Formal Report

PREFATORY PARTS	TEXT OF THE REPORT	SUPPLEMENTARY PARTS
Cover	Introduction	Appendixes
Title fly	Body	Bibliography
Title page	Summary	Index
Letter of authorization	Conclusions	
Letter of acceptance	Recommendations	
Letter of transmittal	Notes	
Table of contents		
List of illustrations		
Synopsis or executive summary		

Many of the components in a formal report start on a new page, but not always. Inserting page breaks consumes more paper and adds to the bulk of your report (which may be a significant financial concern if you plan to distribute many copies). On the other hand, starting a section on a new page helps the reader navigate through the report and recognize transitions between major sections or features of the report.

When a particular section is designed to stand apart, it generally starts on a new page, and the material after it starts on a new page as well. Most prefatory parts (such as the table of contents) should be placed on their own pages. However, the various parts in the text of the report often may not need to stand alone. If your introduction is only a paragraph long, don't bother with a page break before moving into the body of your report. If the introduction runs longer than a page, however, a page break can signal the reader that a major shift is about to occur in the flow of the report.

You can use this textbook as a model for deciding where to put page breaks. Each chapter starts on a new page, which provides a clear break between chapters. On the other hand, the opening vignettes, which come at the beginning of each chapter, flow right into the body of the chapter without a page break—because they are designed to lead readers into the chapter.

Prefatory Parts

Prefatory parts may be written after the text has been completed.

Although the prefatory parts are placed before the text of the report, you may not want to write them until after you've written the text. Many of these parts—such as the table of contents, list of illustrations, and executive summary—are easier to prepare after the text has been completed because they directly reflect the contents. Other parts can be prepared at almost any time.

Cover

Many companies have standard covers for reports, made of heavy paper and imprinted with the company's name and logo. Report titles are either printed on these covers or attached with gummed labels. If your company has no standard covers, you can usually find something suitable in a good stationery store. Look for a cover that is appropriate to the subject matter, attractive, and convenient. Also, make sure it can be labeled with the report title, the writer's name (optional), and the submission date (also optional).

Put a title on the cover that is informative but not too long.

Think carefully about the title you put on the cover. A business report is not a mystery novel, so give your readers all the information they need: the who, what, when, where, why, and how of the subject. At the same time, try to be reasonably concise. You don't want to intimidate your audience with a title that's too long or awkward. You can reduce the length of your title by eliminating phrases such as *A Report of, A Study of,* or *A Survey of.* You can also make the title more explanatory by using a substitute.

Title Fly and Title Page

The **title fly** is a plain sheet of paper with only the title of the report on it. You don't really need one, but it adds a touch of formality to a report.

The title page usually includes four blocks of information.

The **title page** includes four blocks of information, as shown in Moreno's Electrovision report: (1) the title of the report; (2) the name, title, and address of the person, group, or organization that authorized the report (usually the intended audience); (3) the name, title, and address of the person, group, or organization that prepared the report; and (4) the date on which the report was submitted. On some title pages the second block of information is preceded by the words *Prepared for* or *Submitted to*, and the third block of information is preceded by *Prepared by* or *Submitted by*. In some cases the title page serves as the cover of the report, especially if the report is relatively short and intended solely for internal use.

Letter of Authorization and Letter of Acceptance

If you were authorized in writing to prepare the report, you may want to include in your report the letter or memo of authorization (and sometimes even the letter or memo of acceptance). The **letter of authorization** (or *memo of authorization*) is a document requesting that a report be prepared. It normally follows the direct-request plan described in Chapter 5, and it typically specifies the problem, scope, time and money restrictions, special instructions, and due date.

A letter of authorization usually follows the direct-request plan.

The **letter of acceptance** (or *memo of acceptance*) acknowledges the assignment to conduct the study and to prepare the report. Following the good-news plan, the acceptance confirms time and money restrictions and other pertinent details. This document is rarely included in reports.

Use the good-news plan for a letter of acceptance.

Letter of Transmittal

The **letter of transmittal** (or *memo of transmittal*) conveys your report to your audience. (In a book, this section is called the preface.) The letter of transmittal says what you'd say if you were handing the report directly to the person who authorized it, so the style is less formal than the rest of the report. For example, the letter would use personal pronouns (*you, I, we*) and conversational language. Moreno's Electrovision report includes a one-page transmittal memo from Moreno to her boss (the person who requested the report).

Use a less formal style for the letter of transmittal than for the report itself.

The transmittal letter usually appears right before the table of contents. If your report will be widely distributed, however, you may decide to include the letter of transmittal only in selected copies, in order to make certain comments to a specific audience. If your report discusses layoffs or other issues that affect people in the organization, you might want to discuss your recommendations privately in a letter of transmittal to top management. If your audience is likely to be skeptical of or even hostile to something in your report, the transmittal letter is a good opportunity to acknowledge their concerns and explain how the report addresses the issues they care about.

The letter of transmittal follows the routine and good-news plans described in Chapter 7. Begin with the main idea, officially conveying the report to the readers and summarizing its purpose. Such a letter typically begins with a statement such as "Here is the report you asked me to prepare on . . ." The rest includes information about the scope of the report, the methods used to complete the study, and the limitations that became apparent. In the middle section of the letter you may also highlight important points or sections of the report, make comments on side issues, give suggestions for follow-up studies, and offer any details that will help readers understand and use the report. You may also wish to acknowledge help given by others. The concluding paragraph is a note of thanks for having been given the report assignment, an expression of willingness to discuss the report, and an offer to assist with future projects.

Use the good-news plan for a letter of transmittal.

If the report does not have a synopsis, the letter of transmittal may summarize the major findings, conclusions, and recommendations. This material would be placed after the opening of the letter.

The synopsis of short reports is often included in the letter of transmittal.

Table of Contents

The table of contents indicates in outline form the coverage, sequence, and relative importance of the information in the report. In fact, the headings used in the text of the report are the basis for the table of contents. Depending on the length and complexity of the report, your contents page may show only the top two or three levels of headings or only first-level headings. Of course, the exclusion of some levels of headings may frustrate readers who want to know where to find every subject you cover. On the other hand, a simpler table of

The table of contents outlines the text and lists prefatory and supplementary parts.

contents helps readers focus on the major points. No matter how many levels you include, make sure readers can easily distinguish between them (see Figure 14.11 on page 499 for examples of various levels of headings).

Be sure the headings in the table of contents match up perfectly with the headings in the text.

The table of contents is prepared after the other parts of the report have been typed so that the beginning page numbers for each heading can be shown. The headings should be worded exactly as they are in the text of the report. Also listed on the contents page are the prefatory parts (only those that follow the contents page) and the supplementary parts. If you have fewer than four visual aids, you may wish to list them in the table of contents, too; but if you have four or more visual aids, create a separate list of illustrations.

List of Illustrations

For simplicity's sake, some reports refer to all visual aids as illustrations or exhibits. In other reports, as in Moreno's Electrovision report, tables are labeled separately from other types of visual aids, which are called figures. Regardless of the system used to label visual aids, the list of illustrations gives their titles and page numbers.

Put the lists of figures and tables on separate pages if they won't fit on one page with the table of contents.

If you have enough space on a single page, include the list of illustrations directly beneath the table of contents. Otherwise, put the list on the page after the contents page. When tables and figures are numbered separately, they should also be listed separately. The two lists can appear on the same page if they fit; otherwise, start each list on a separate page.

Synopsis or Executive Summary

Provide an overview of the report in a synopsis or an executive summary.

A **synopsis** is a brief overview (one page or less) of a report's most important points, designed to give readers a quick preview of the contents. It's often included in long informational reports dealing with technical, professional, or academic subjects and can also be called an *abstract.* Because it's a concise representation of the whole report, it may be distributed separately to a wide audience; interested readers can then order a copy of the entire report.

An informative synopsis summarizes the main ideas; a descriptive synopsis states what the report is about.

The phrasing of a synopsis can be either informative or descriptive, depending on whether the report is in direct or indirect order. In an informative synopsis, you present the main points of the report in the order in which they appear in the text. A descriptive synopsis, on the other hand, simply tells what the report is about, in only moderately greater detail than the table of contents; the actual findings of the report are omitted. Here are examples of statements from each type:

INFORMATIVE SYNOPSIS	DESCRIPTIVE SYNOPSIS
Sales of super-premium ice cream make up 11 percent of the total ice cream market.	This report contains information about super-premium ice cream and its share of the market.

Use a descriptive synopsis for a skeptical or hostile audience, an informative synopsis for most other situations.

The way you handle a synopsis reflects the approach you use in the text. If you're using an indirect approach in your report, you're better off with a descriptive synopsis. An informative synopsis, with its focus on conclusions and key points, may be too confrontational if you have a skeptical audience. You don't want to spoil the effect by providing a controversial beginning. No matter which type of synopsis you use, however, be sure to present an accurate picture of the report's contents.[2]

Put enough information in an executive summary so that an executive can make a decision without reading the entire report.

Many business report writers prefer to include an **executive summary** instead of a synopsis or an abstract. Whereas a synopsis is a prose table of contents that outlines the main points of the report, an executive summary is a fully developed "mini" version of the report itself, intended for readers who lack the time or motivation to study the complete text. So an executive summary is more comprehensive than a synopsis, often as much as 10 percent as long as the report itself.

Unlike a synopsis, an executive summary may contain headings, well-developed transitions, and even visual aids. It is often organized in the same way as the report, using a direct or an indirect approach, depending on the audience's receptivity. However, executive summaries can also deviate from the sequence of material in the remainder of the report.

Linda Moreno's Electrovision report provides one example of an executive summary. After reading the summary, audience members know the essentials of the report and are in a position to make a decision. Later, when time permits, they may read certain parts of the report to obtain additional detail. However, from daily newspapers to Web sites on the Internet, businesspeople are getting swamped with more and more data and information all the time. They are looking for ways to cut through all the clutter, and reading executive summaries is a popular shortcut. Because you can usually assume that many of your readers will not read the main text of your report, make sure you cover all your important points (along with significant supporting information) in the executive summary.

DID YOU KNOW?

The most important part of the business plan is the executive summary. It must make the reader fascinated enough to read further; otherwise he or she will move on to the next business plan.

Of course, many reports require neither a synopsis nor an executive summary. Length is usually the determining factor. Most reports of fewer than ten pages either omit such a preview or combine it with the letter of transmittal. However, if your report is over 30 pages long, you'll probably include either a synopsis or an executive summary as a convenience for readers. Which one you'll provide depends on the traditions of your organization.

Text of the Report

Apart from deciding on the fundamental issues of content and organization, you must also make decisions about the design and layout of the report. You can use a variety of techniques to present your material effectively. Many organizations have format guidelines that make your decisions easier, but the goal is always to focus readers' attention on major points and on the flow of ideas. Headings, typographical devices (such as capital letters, italics, and boldface type), white space, and so on are useful tools, as are visual aids. Also, as discussed in Chapter 14, you can use preview and review statements to frame sections of your text. This strategy keeps your audience informed and reinforces the substance of your message.

Aids to understanding the text of a report:
- Headings
- Typographical devices
- Visual aids
- Preview and summary statements

Introduction

An introduction has a number of functions and covers a wide variety of topics.

The introduction of a report serves a number of important functions:

- Puts the report in a broader context by tying it to a problem or an assignment
- Tells readers the purpose of the report
- Previews the contents and organization of the report
- Establishes the tone of the report and the writer's relationship with the audience

The length of the introduction depends on the length of the report. In a relatively brief report, the introduction may be only a paragraph or two and may not be labeled with a heading of any kind. On the other hand, the introduction to a major formal report may extend to several pages and can be identified as a separate section by the first-level heading "Introduction." (See Linda Moreno's Electrovision report.)

Here's a list of topics to consider covering in an introduction, depending on your material and your audience:

- *Authorization.* When, how, and by whom the report was authorized; who wrote it; and when it was submitted. This material is especially important when no letter of transmittal is included.

- *Problem/purpose.* The reason for the report's existence and what is to be accomplished as a result of the report's being written.
- *Scope.* What is and what isn't going to be covered in the report. The scope indicates the report's size and complexity.
- *Background.* The historical conditions or factors that led up to the report. This section enables readers to understand how the problem developed and what has been done about it so far.
- *Sources and methods.* The secondary sources of information that were used and the surveys, experiments, and observations that were carried out. This section tells readers how the sample was selected, how the questionnaire was constructed (a sample questionnaire and cover letter should be included in the appendix), what follow-up procedures were used, and the like. It provides enough detail to give readers confidence in the work and to convince them that the sources and methods were satisfactory.
- *Definitions.* A brief introductory statement leading into a list of terms used in the report and their definitions. Naturally, if your audience is familiar with the terms you've used throughout the report, a list of definitions isn't necessary. Moreno's Electrovision report doesn't include a list of definitions because the topic doesn't involve any unfamiliar terminology. However, if you have any question about your readers' knowledge, be sure to include definitions of any terms that might lead to misinterpretation. In addition, if you've used familiar or general terms in a specific way, be sure to explain exactly what you mean. For example, the term *market* could mean any of a number of things, from a physical location to a collection of potential customers. Note that terms may be defined in other places as well: in the body (as the terms are used), in explanatory footnotes, or in a glossary (an alphabetical listing of terms placed at the end of the report).
- *Limitations.* Factors affecting the quality of the report, such as a budget too small to do all the work that should have been done, an inadequate amount of time to do all the necessary research, unreliability or unavailability of data, or other conditions beyond your control. This is the place to mention doubts about any aspect of the report. Although candor may lead readers to question the results, it will also enable them to assess the results more accurately and help you maintain the integrity of your report. However, limitations are no excuse for conducting a poor study or writing a bad report.
- *Report organization.* The organization of the report (what topics are covered and in what order), along with a rationale for following this plan. This section is a road map that helps readers understand what's approaching at each turn of the report and why.

DID YOU KNOW?

Different cultures approach report organization differently. For example, Japanese businesspeople tend to organize all reports in chronological order.

Some of these items may be combined in the introduction; some may not be included at all. Consider the items included in the 44-page introduction to *Management Education and Development: Drift or Thrust into the 21st Century?* This report on the future of business education was sponsored by the American Assembly of Collegiate Schools of Business (AACSB). Part 1 of the introduction discusses the background and objectives of the project, the issues addressed, the project's design (including limits to the project's scope), and the report's structure. Part 2 offers some background on various views of the future (including a brief overview of what other writers see for the future); an examination of future trends in economics, demographics, and societal variables; and a commentary about anticipating and responding to future changes.[3]

You can decide what to include by figuring out what kind of information will help your readers understand and accept the report. Also give some thought to how the introduction relates to the prefatory parts of the report. In longer reports you may have a letter of transmittal, a synopsis or an executive summary, and an introduction, all of which cover essentially the same ground. To avoid redundancy, balance the various sections. If the letter of transmittal and the synopsis are fairly detailed, for example, you might want the introduction to be relatively brief.

However, remember that some people may barely glance at the prefatory parts, so be sure your introduction is detailed enough to provide an adequate preview of your report. If you feel that your introduction must repeat information that has already been covered in one of the prefatory parts, simply use different wording.

Body

The body of the report follows the introduction. It consists of the major sections or chapters (with various levels of headings) that present, analyze, and interpret the findings gathered as part of your investigation. These chapters contain the "proof," the detailed information necessary to support your conclusions and recommendations. (See the body of Linda Moreno's Electrovision report.)

One of the decisions to make when writing the body of your report is how much detail to include. Your decision depends on the nature of your information, the purpose of your report, and the preferences of your audience. Some situations call for detailed coverage; others lend themselves to shorter treatment. In general, provide only enough detail in the body to support your conclusions and recommendations, and put additional detail in tables, charts, and appendixes.

Restrict the body to those details necessary to prove your conclusions and recommendations.

You can also decide whether to put your conclusions in the body or in a separate section or both. If the conclusions seem to flow naturally from the evidence, you'll almost inevitably cover them in the body. However, if you want to give your conclusions added emphasis, you can include a separate section to summarize them. Having a separate section is particularly appropriate in long reports; the reader may lose track of the conclusions if they're given only in the body.

Summary, Conclusions, and Recommendations

The final section of the text of a report tells readers "what you told them." In a short report, this final wrap-up may be only a paragraph or two. A long report generally has separate sections labeled "Summary," "Conclusions," and "Recommendations." Here's how the three differ:

Summaries, conclusions, and recommendations serve different purposes.

- *Summary.* The key findings of your report, paraphrased from the body and stated or listed in the order in which they appear in the body.
- *Conclusions.* An analysis of what the findings mean. These are the answers to the questions that led to the report.
- *Recommendations.* Opinions, based on reason and logic, about the course of action that should be taken. The author of the Electrovision report lists four specific steps the company should take to reduce travel costs.

If the report is organized in direct order, the summary, conclusions, and recommendations are presented before the body and are reviewed only briefly at the end. If the report is organized in indirect order, these sections are presented for the first time at the end and are covered in detail. Many report writers combine the conclusions and recommendations under one heading because it seems like the natural thing to do. It is often difficult to present a conclusion without implying a recommendation. (See Moreno's Electrovision report.)

Whether you combine them or not, if you have several conclusions and recommendations, you may want to number and list them. An appropriate lead-in to such a list might be, "The findings of this study lead to the following conclusions." A statement that could be used for a list of recommendations might be, "Based on the conclusions of this study, the following recommendations are made." Present no new findings either in the conclusions or in the recommendations section.

In action-oriented reports, put all the recommendations in a separate section and spell out precisely what should happen next.

In reports that are intended to lead to action, the recommendations section is particularly important; it spells out exactly what should happen next. It brings all the action items together in one place and gives the details about who should do what, when, where, and how. Readers may agree with everything you say in your report but still fail to take any action if you're vague about what should happen next. Your readers must understand what's expected of them and must have some appreciation of the difficulties that are likely to arise. So providing a schedule and specific task assignments is helpful because concrete plans have a way of commanding action.

Source Documentation

Give credit where credit is due.

When writing the text of the report, you need to decide how to acknowledge your sources. You have an ethical and a legal obligation to give other people credit for their work. Acknowledging your sources also enhances the credibility of your report. By citing references in the text, you demonstrate that you have thoroughly researched the topic. Mentioning the names of well-known or important authorities on the subject also helps build credibility for your message. In fact, it's often a good idea to mention a credible source's name several times if you need to persuade the audience.

On the other hand, you don't want to make your report read like an academic treatise, dragging along from citation to citation. The source references should be handled as conveniently and inconspicuously as possible. One approach, especially for internal reports, is simply to mention a source in the text:

> According to Dr. Lewis Morgan of Northwestern Hospital, hip replacement operations account for 7 percent of all surgery performed on women age 65 and over.

However, if your report will be distributed to outsiders, include additional information on where you obtained the data. Most college students are familiar with citation schemes suggested by the Modern Language Association (MLA) or the American Psychological Association (APA). *The Chicago Manual of Style* is a reference often used by typesetters and publishers. All of these encourage the use of *in-text citations*, in which you insert the author's last name and a year of publication or a page number directly in the text. An alternative is to use numbered footnotes (bottom of the page) or endnotes (end of the report). (Linda Moreno's Electrovision report uses the author-date system, whereas this textbook uses endnotes.) For more information on citing sources, see Component Chapter B, "Documentation of Report Sources."

Supplementary Parts

Put into an appendix materials that are

- Bulky or lengthy
- Not directly relevant to the text

Supplementary parts follow the text of the report and include the appendixes, bibliography, and index. They are more common in long reports than in short ones.

An **appendix** contains materials related to the report but not included in the text because they're too lengthy or bulky or because they lack direct relevance. However, as Mark

Landiak warns, be sure not to include too much ancillary material. Keep your reports straightforward and concise.

Frequently included in appendixes are sample questionnaires and cover letters, sample forms, computer printouts, and statistical formulas; a glossary may be put in an appendix or may stand as a separate supplementary part. The best place to include visual aids is in the text body nearest the point of discussion. If any graphics are too large to fit on one page or are only indirectly relevant to your report, they too may be put in an appendix. In fact, some organizations specify that all visual aids be placed in an appendix.

Each type of material deserves a separate appendix. Identify the appendixes by labeling them, for example, "Appendix A: Questionnaire," "Appendix B: Computer Printout of Raw Data," and the like. All appendixes should be mentioned in the text and listed in the table of contents.

List your secondary sources in the bibliography.

A **bibliography** is a list of secondary sources consulted when preparing the report. Linda Moreno labeled her bibliography "Works Cited" in her Electrovision report because she listed only the works that were mentioned in the report. You might call this section "Sources" or "References" if it includes works consulted but not mentioned in your report. The construction of a bibliography is shown in Component Chapter B.

An **index** is an alphabetical list of names, places, and subjects mentioned in the report and the pages on which they occur, as in the index for this book. An index is rarely included in unpublished reports.

Components of a Formal Proposal

As discussed in Chapter 13, certain analytical reports are called proposals, including bids to perform work under a contract and pleas for financial support from outsiders. Such bids and pleas are nearly always formal. As Mark Landiak knows only too well, the goal of a proposal is to impress the potential client or supporter with your professionalism, to make your service and your company stand out. This goal is best achieved through a structured and deliberate approach.

Formal proposals contain many of the same components as other formal reports (see Figure 15.2). The difference lies mostly in the text, although a few of the prefatory parts are also different. With the exception of an occasional appendix, most proposals have few supplementary parts.

Figure 15.2
Parts of a Formal Proposal

PREFATORY PARTS	TEXT OF THE PROPOSAL	SUPPLEMENTARY PARTS
Cover Title fly Title page Letter of transmittal Letter of acceptance Table of contents List of illustrations Synopsis or executive summary	Introduction Body Summary	Appendixes

Prefatory Parts

Formal proposals contain most of the same prefatory parts as other formal reports.

The cover, title fly, title page, table of contents, and list of illustrations are handled the same as in other formal reports. However, other prefatory parts are quite different:

Use a copy of the request for proposal in place of the letter of authorization.

- *Copy of the RFP.* Instead of having a letter of authorization, a formal proposal may have a copy of the request for proposal (RFP), which is a letter or memo soliciting a proposal or a bid for a particular project. The RFP is issued by the client to whom the proposal is being submitted and outlines what the proposal should cover. If the RFP includes detailed specifications, it may be too long to bind into the proposal; in that case, you may want to include only the introductory portion of the RFP. Another option is to omit the RFP and simply refer to it in your letter of transmittal.

Use the good-news pattern for the letter of transmittal if the proposal is solicited; use the persuasive plan if the proposal is unsolicited.

- *Letter of transmittal.* The way you handle the letter of transmittal depends on whether the proposal is solicited or unsolicited. If the proposal is solicited, the transmittal letter follows the pattern for good-news messages, highlighting those aspects of your proposal that may give you a competitive advantage. If the proposal is unsolicited, the transmittal letter takes on added importance; in fact, it may be all the client reads. The letter must persuade the reader that you have something worthwhile to offer, something that justifies the time required to read the entire proposal. The transmittal letter for an unsolicited proposal follows the pattern for persuasive messages (see Chapter 9).

Most proposals do not require a synopsis or an executive summary.

- *Synopsis or executive summary.* Although you may include a synopsis or an executive summary for your reader's convenience if your proposal is quite long, these components are somewhat less useful in a formal proposal than they are in a formal report. If your proposal is unsolicited, your transmittal letter will already have caught the reader's interest, making a synopsis or an executive summary pointless. It may also be pointless if your proposal is solicited, because the reader is already committed to studying the text to find out how you propose to satisfy the terms of a contract. The introduction to a solicited proposal would provide an adequate preview of the contents.

Text of the Proposal

A proposal is both a selling tool and a contractual commitment.

The text of a proposal performs two essential functions: It persuades the client to award you a contract, and it spells out the terms of that contract. The trick is to sell the client on your ideas without making promises that will haunt you later.

Follow the instructions presented in the RFP.

If the proposal is unsolicited, you have some latitude in arranging the text. However, the organization of a solicited proposal is governed by the request for proposal. Most RFPs spell out precisely what you should cover, and in what order, so that all bids will be similar in form. This uniformity enables the client to evaluate the competing proposals in a systematic way. In fact, in many organizations a team of evaluators splits up the proposals and looks at various sections. An engineer might review the technical portions of all the proposals submitted, and an accountant might review the cost estimates.

Introduction

In the introduction, establish the need for action and summarize the key benefits of

The introduction orients readers to the rest of the proposal. It identifies your organization and your purpose and outlines the remainder of the text. If the proposal is solicited, the introduction should refer to the RFP; if not, it should mention any factors that led you to submit the bid. You might mention mutual acquaintances, or you might refer to previous conversations you've had with the client, just as Mark Landiak would refer to the "workout sessions" his team conducts with each client. Subheadings in the introduction often include the following:

- *Background or statement of the problem.* Briefly reviews the client's situation, worded to establish the need for action. In business selling situations, the reader may not have the same perception of the problem the writer has. With unsolicited proposals, potential clients and other readers may not even think they have a problem. You have to convince them a problem exists before you can convince them to accept your solution. You can do this by discussing the reader's current situation and explaining how things could be better—in a way that is meaningful to your reader.
- *Overview of approach.* Highlights your key selling points and their benefits, showing how your proposal will solve the client's problem. The heading for this section might also be "Preliminary Analysis" or some other wording that will identify this section as a summary of your solution to the problem.
- *Scope.* States the boundaries of the study—what you will and will not do. This brief section may also be labeled "Delimitations."
- *Report organization.* Orients the reader to the remainder of the proposal and calls attention to the major divisions of thought.

Body

The core of the proposal is the body, which has the same purpose as the body of other reports. In a proposal, however, the body must cover some specific information:

- *Proposed approach.* May also be titled "Technical Proposal," "Research Design," "Issues for Analysis," or "Work Statement." Regardless of the heading, this section is a description of what you have to offer: your concept, product, or service. If you're proposing to develop a new airplane, you might describe your preliminary design by using drawings or calculations to demonstrate the soundness of your solution. To convince the client that your proposal has merit, focus on the strengths of your product in relation to the client's needs. Point out any advantages that you have over your competitors. In this example, you might describe how your plane's unique wing design provides superior fuel economy, a particularly important feature specified in the client's request for proposal.

In the approach section, demonstrate the superiority of your ideas, products, or services.

- *Work plan.* Describes how you will accomplish the work that must be done (necessary unless you're proposing to provide a standard, off-the-shelf item). For each phase of the work plan, describe the steps you'll take, their timing, the methods or resources you'll use, and the person or persons who will be responsible. Indicate dates for completion of critical portions of the work. If your proposal is accepted, the work plan will become contractually binding. Any slippage in the proposed schedule may jeopardize the contract or cost your organization a considerable amount of money. Therefore, don't promise to deliver more than you can realistically achieve within a given period.

Use the work plan to describe the tasks to be completed under the terms of the contract.

- *Statement of qualifications.* Describes your organization's experience, personnel, and facilities in relation to the client's needs. If you work for a large organization that frequently submits proposals, you can usually borrow much of this section intact from previous proposals. Be sure, however, to tailor any of this boilerplate material to suit the situation. The qualifications section can be an important selling point, and it deserves to be handled carefully.

In the qualifications section, demonstrate that you have the personnel, facilities, and experience to do a competent job.

- *Costs.* Typically has few words and many numbers but can make or break the proposal. If your price is out of line, the client will probably reject your bid. However,

The more detailed your cost proposal is, the more credibility your estimates will have.

before you deliver a low bid, remember that you'll have to live with the price you quote in the proposal. It's rarely worthwhile to win a contract if you're doomed to lose money on the job. Because it's often difficult to estimate costs on experimental projects, the client will be looking for evidence that your costs are realistic. Break down the costs in detail so that the client can see how you got your numbers: so much for labor, so much for materials, so much for overhead.

In a formal proposal it pays to be as thorough and accurate as possible. Carefully selected detail enhances your credibility. So does successful completion of any task you promise to perform.

Summary or Conclusion

You may want to include a summary or conclusion section because it's your last opportunity to persuade the reader to accept your proposal. Summarize the merits of your approach, reemphasize why you and your firm are the ones to do the work, and stress the benefits. Make this section relatively brief, assertive, and confident. To review the ideas and procedures presented in this chapter, consult this chapter's Checklist for Formal Reports and Proposals on pages 543–544.

SHARPENING YOUR SKILLS

IN-DEPTH CRITIQUE: ANALYZING A FORMAL REPORT

The report presented in the following pages was prepared by Linda Moreno, manager of the cost accounting department at Electrovision, a high-tech company based in Los Gatos, California. Electrovision's main product is optical character recognition equipment, which is used by the U.S. Postal Service for sorting mail. Moreno's job is to help analyze the company's costs. She has this to say about the background of the report:

"For the past three or four years, Electrovision has been on a roll. Our A-12 optical character reader was a real breakthrough, and the post office grabbed up as many as we could make. Our sales and profits kept climbing, and morale was fantastic. Everybody seemed to think that the good times would last forever. Unfortunately, everybody was wrong. When the Postal Service announced that it was postponing all new-equipment purchases because of cuts in its budget, we woke up to the fact that we are essentially a one-product company with one customer. At that point management started scrambling around looking for ways to cut costs until we could diversify our business a bit.

"The vice president of operations, Dennis McWilliams, asked me to help identify cost-cutting opportunities in the travel and entertainment area. On the basis of his personal observations, he felt that Electrovision was overly generous in its travel policies and that we might be able to save a significant amount by controlling these costs more carefully. My investigation confirmed his suspicion.

"I was reasonably confident that my report would be well received. I've worked with Dennis for several years and know what he likes: plenty of facts, clearly stated conclusions, and specific recommendations for what should be done next. I also knew that my report would be passed on to other Electrovision executives, so I wanted to create a good impression. I wanted the report to be accurate and thorough, visually appealing, readable, and appropriate in tone."

When writing the analytical report that follows, Moreno used an organization based on conclusions and recommendations, presented in direct order. The first two sections of the report correspond to Moreno's two main conclusions: that Electrovision's travel and entertainment costs are too high and that cuts are essential. The third section presents recommendations for achieving better control over travel and entertainment expenses. As you review the report, analyze both the mechanical aspects and the way Moreno presents her ideas. Be prepared to discuss the way the various components convey and reinforce the main message.

REDUCING ELECTROVISION'S TRAVEL AND ENTERTAINMENT COSTS

Prepared for
Dennis McWilliams,
Vice President of Operations
Electrovision, Inc.

Prepared by
Linda Moreno, Manager
Cost Accounting Services
Electrovision, Inc.

February 15, 2000

Capitalize the title; use uppercase and lowercase letters for all other lines.

Follow the title with the name, title, and organization of the recipient.

Balance the white space between the items on the page.

When centering the lines horizontally on the title page, allow an extra 1/2-inch margin on the left side if it's a left-bound report.

For future reference, include the report's publication date.

The "how to" tone of Moreno's title is appropriate for an action-oriented report that emphasizes recommendations. A more neutral title, such as "An Analysis of Electrovision's Travel and Entertainment Costs," would be more suitable for an informational report.

Use memo format for transmitting internal reports, letter format for transmitting external reports.

Present the main conclusion or recommendation right away if you expect a positive response.

Use an informal, conversational style for the letter or memo of transmittal.

Acknowledge any help that you have received.

Close with thanks, an offer to discuss results, and an offer to assist with future projects, if appropriate.

MEMORANDUM

TO: Dennis McWilliams, Vice President of Operations

FROM: Linda Moreno, Manager of Cost Accounting Services

DATE: February 15, 2000

SUBJECT: Reducing Electrovision's Travel and Entertainment Costs

Here is the report you requested January 30 on Electrovision's travel and entertainment costs.

Your suspicion was right. We are spending far too much on business travel. Our unwritten policy has been "anything goes," leaving us with no real control over T&E expenses. Although this hands-off approach may have been understandable when Electrovision's profits were high, we can no longer afford the luxury of going first class.

The solutions to the problem seem rather clear. We need to have someone with centralized responsibility for travel and entertainment costs, a clear statement of policy, an effective control system, and a business-oriented travel service that can optimize our travel arrangements. We should also investigate alternatives to travel, such as videoconferencing. Perhaps more important, we need to change our attitude. Instead of viewing travel funds as a bottomless supply of money, all traveling employees need to act as though they were paying the bills themselves.

Getting people to economize is not going to be easy. In the course of researching this issue, I've found that our employees are exceedingly attached to their first-class travel privileges. I think they would almost prefer a cut in pay to a loss in travel status. We'll need a lot of top management involvement to sell people on the need for moderation. One thing is clear: People will be very bitter if we create a two-class system in which top executives get special privileges while the rest of the employees make the sacrifices.

I'm grateful to Mary Lehman and Connie McIlvain for their help in collecting and sorting through five years' worth of expense reports. Their efforts were truly herculean.

Thanks for giving me the opportunity to work on this assignment. It's been a real education. If you have any questions about the report, please give me a call.

In this report Moreno decided to write a brief memo of transmittal and include a separate executive summary. Short reports (fewer than ten pages) often combine the synopsis or executive summary with the memo or letter of transmittal.

CONTENTS

iii

Include no element that appears before the "Contents" page.

Word the headings exactly as they appear in the text.

Include only the page numbers where sections begin.

Moreno included only first- and second-level headings in her table of contents, even though the report contains third-level headings. She prefers a shorter table of contents that focuses attention on the main divisions of thought. She used informative titles, which are appropriate for a report to a receptive audience.

LIST OF ILLUSTRATIONS

iv

Number the contents pages with lowercase roman numerals centered at the bottom margin.

Because figures and tables were numbered separately in the text, Moreno listed them separately here. If all had been labeled as exhibits, a single list of illustrations would have been appropriate.

EXECUTIVE SUMMARY

This report analyzes Electrovision's travel and entertainment (T&E) costs and presents recommendations for reducing those costs.

Travel and Entertainment Costs Are Too High

Travel and entertainment is a large and growing expense category for Electrovision. The company spends over $16 million per year on business travel, and these costs have been increasing by 12 percent annually. Company employees make roughly 3,390 trips each year at an average cost per trip of $4,720. Airfares are the biggest expense, followed by hotels, meals, and rental cars.

The nature of Electrovision's business does require extensive travel, but the company's costs appear to be excessive. Every year Electrovision employees spend more than twice as much on T&E as the average business traveler. Although the location of the company's facilities may partly explain this discrepancy, the main reason for Electrovision's high costs is the firm's philosophy and managerial style. Electrovision's tradition and its hands-off style almost invite employees to go first class and pay relatively little attention to travel costs.

Cuts Are Essential

Although Electrovision has traditionally been casual about travel and entertainment expenses, management now recognizes the need to gain more control over this element of costs. The company is currently entering a period of declining profits, prompting management to look for every opportunity to reduce spending. At the same time, rising airfares and hotel rates are making travel and entertainment expenses more important to the bottom line.

Electrovision Can Save $6 Million per Year

Fortunately, Electrovision has a number of excellent opportunities for reducing its travel and entertainment costs. Savings of up to $6 million per year should be achievable, judging by the experience of other companies. American Express suggests that a sensible travel-management program can save companies as much as 35 percent a year (Gilligan 39–40). Given that we purchase many more first-class tickets than the average company, we should be able to achieve even greater savings. The first priority should be to hire a director of travel and entertainment to assume overall responsibility for T&E spending. This individual should establish a written travel and entertainment policy and create a budget and a cost-control system. The director should also retain a nationwide travel agency to handle our reservations and should lead an investigation into electronic alternatives to travel.

v

Begin by stating the purpose of the report.

Present the points in the executive summary in the same order as they appear in the report; use subheadings that summarize the content of the main sections of the report without repeating those that appear in the text.

Type the synopsis or executive summary in the same manner as the text of the report. Use single spacing if the report is single-spaced, and use the same format as is used in the text for margins, paragraph indentions, and headings.

Moreno decided to include an executive summary because her report was aimed at a mixed audience. She knew that some readers would be interested in the details of her report and some would prefer to focus on the big picture. The executive summary was aimed at the big-picture group. Moreno wanted to give these readers enough information to make a decision without burdening them with the task of reading the entire report.

The hard-hitting tone of this executive summary is appropriate for a receptive audience. A more neutral approach would be better for hostile or skeptical readers.

At the same time, Electrovision should make employees aware of the need for moderation in travel and entertainment spending. People should be encouraged to forgo any unnecessary travel and to economize on airline tickets, hotels, meals, rental cars, and other expenses.

In addition to economizing on an individual basis, Electrovision should look for ways to reduce costs by negotiating preferential rates with travel providers. Once retained, a travel agency should be able to accomplish this.

Finally, we should look into alternatives to travel. Although we may have to invest money in videoconferencing systems or other equipment, we may be able to recover these costs through decreased travel expenses. I recommend that the new travel director undertake this investigation to make sure it is well integrated with the rest of the travel program.

These changes, although necessary, are likely to hurt morale, at least in the short term. Management will need to make a determined effort to explain the rationale for reduced spending. By exercising moderation in their own travel arrangements, Electrovision executives can set a good example and help other employees accept the changes. On the plus side, cutting back on travel with videoconferencing or other alternatives will reduce the travel burden on many employees and help them balance their business and personal lives much better.

vi

Number the pages of the executive summary with lowercase roman numerals centered about 1 inch from the bottom of the page.

This executive summary is written in an impersonal style, which adds to the formality of the report. Some writers prefer a more personal approach. In general, you should gear your choice of style to your relationship with the readers. Moreno chose the formal approach because several members of her audience were considerably higher up in the organization. She did not want to sound too familiar. In addition, she wanted the executive summary and the text to be compatible, and her company prefers the impersonal style for formal reports.

REDUCING ELECTROVISION'S TRAVEL AND ENTERTAINMENT COSTS

INTRODUCTION

Electrovision has always encouraged a significant amount of business travel, believing that it is an effective way of operating. To compensate employees for the inconvenience and stress of frequent trips, management has authorized generous travel and entertainment (T&E) allowances. This philosophy has been good for morale, but the company has paid a price. Last year Electrovision spent $16 million on T&E—$7 million more than it spent on research and development.

This year the cost of travel and entertainment will have a bigger impact on profits, owing to changes in airfares and hotel rates. The timing of these changes is unfortunate because the company anticipates that profits will be relatively weak for a variety of other reasons. In light of these profit pressures, Dennis McWilliams, Vice President of Operations, has asked the accounting department to take a closer look at the T&E budget.

Purpose, Scope, and Limitations

The purpose of this report is to analyze the T&E budget, evaluate the impact of recent changes in airfares and hotel costs, and suggest ways to tighten management's control over T&E expenses. Although the report outlines a number of steps that could reduce Electrovision's expenses, the precise financial impact of these measures is difficult to project. The estimates presented in the report provide a "best guess" view of what Electrovision can expect to save. Until the company actually implements these steps, however, we won't know exactly how much the travel and entertainment budget can be reduced.

Sources and Methods

In preparing this report, the accounting department analyzed internal expense reports for the past five years to determine how much Electrovision spends on travel and entertainment. These figures were then compared with average statistics compiled by Dow Jones (publisher of *The Wall Street Journal*) and presented as the Dow Jones Travel Index. We also analyzed trends and suggestions published in a variety of business journal articles to see how other companies are coping with the high cost of business travel.

1

Center the title of the report on the first page of the text, 2 inches ($2\frac{1}{2}$ inches if top-bound) from the top of the page.

Begin the introduction by establishing the need for action.

Mentioning sources and methods increases the credibility of a report and gives readers a complete picture of the study's background.

Use the arabic numeral 1 for the first page of the report; center the number about 1 inch from the bottom of the page.

In a brief introduction like this one, some writers would omit the subheadings within the introduction and rely on topic sentences and on transitional words and phrases to indicate that they are discussing such subjects as the purpose, scope, and limitations of the study. Moreno decided to use headings because they help readers scan the document. Also, to conserve space, Moreno used single spacing and 1-inch side margins.

Using arabic numerals, number the second and succeeding pages of the text in the upper right-hand corner where the top and right-hand margins meet.

2

Report Organization

This report reviews the size and composition of Electrovision's travel and entertainment expenses, analyzes trends in travel costs, and recommends steps for reducing the T&E budget.

THE HIGH COST OF TRAVEL AND ENTERTAINMENT

Although many companies view travel and entertainment as an "incidental" cost of doing business, the dollars add up. At Electrovision the bill for airfares, hotels, rental cars, meals, and entertainment totaled $16 million last year. Our T&E budget has increased by 12 percent per year for the past five years. Compared with the average U.S. business's travel expenditures, Electrovision's expenditures are high, largely because of management's generous policy on travel benefits.

$16 Million per Year Spent on Travel and Entertainment

Electrovision's annual budget for travel and entertainment is only 8 percent of sales. Because this is a relatively small expense category compared with such things as salaries and commissions, it is tempting to dismiss T&E costs as insignificant. However, T&E is Electrovision's third-largest controllable expense, directly behind salaries and information systems.

Last year Electrovision personnel made about 3,390 trips at an average cost per trip of $4,720. The typical trip involved a round-trip flight of 3,000 miles, meals and hotel accommodations for two or three days, and a rental car. Roughly 80 percent of the trips were made by 20 percent of the staff—top management and sales personnel traveled most, averaging 18 trips per year.

Place the visual aid as close as possible to the point it illustrates.

Figure 1 illustrates how the travel and entertainment budget is spent. The largest categories are airfares and lodging, which together account for $7 out of every $10 that

The titles of visual aids should be placed as consistently as possible throughout a report, either above, below, or beside the visual aid.

Give each visual aid a title that clearly indicates what it's about.

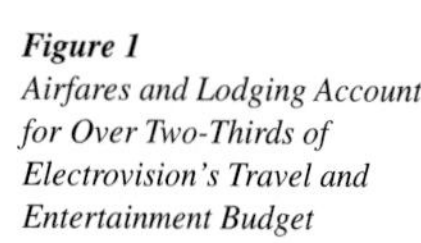

Figure 1
Airfares and Lodging Account for Over Two-Thirds of Electrovision's Travel and Entertainment Budget

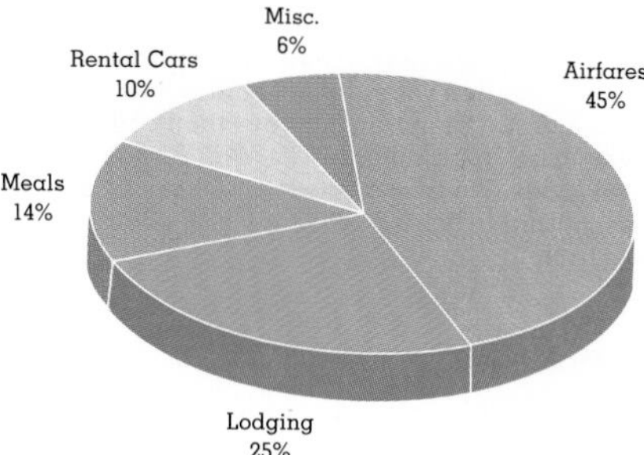

Moreno opened the first main section of the body with a topic sentence that introduces an important fact about the subject of the section. Then she oriented the reader to the three major points developed in the section.

3

employees spend on travel and entertainment. This spending breakdown has been relatively steady for the past five years and is consistent with the distribution of expenses experienced by other companies.

Although the composition of the T&E budget has been consistent, its size has not. As mentioned earlier, these expenditures have increased by about 12 percent per year for the past five years, roughly twice the rate of the company's growth in sales (see Figure 2). This rate of growth makes T&E Electrovision's fastest-growing expense item.

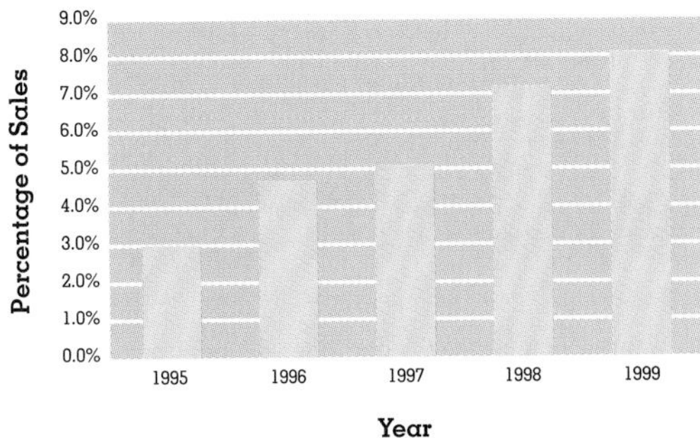

Figure 2
Travel and Entertainment Expenses Have Increased as a Percentage of Sales

Insert visual aids after the relevant text discussion, and indicate what readers should notice about the data.

Number the visual aids consecutively, and refer to them in the text by their numbers. If your report is a book-length document, you may number the visual aids by chapter: Figure 4-2, for example, would be the second figure in the fourth chapter.

Electrovision's Travel Expenses Exceed National Averages

Much of our travel budget is justified. Two major factors contribute to Electrovision's high travel and entertainment budget:

- With our headquarters on the West Coast and our major customer on the East Coast, we naturally spend a lot on cross-country flights.
- A great deal of travel takes place between our headquarters here on the West Coast and the manufacturing operations in Detroit, Boston, and Dallas. Corporate managers and division personnel make frequent trips to coordinate these disparate operations.

However, even though a good portion of Electrovision's travel budget is justifiable, our travelers spend considerably more on travel and entertainment than the average business traveler (see Figure 3).

Moreno originally drew the bar chart in Figure 2 as a line chart, showing both sales and T&E expenses in absolute dollars. However, the comparison was difficult to interpret because sales were so much greater than T&E expenses. A bar chart expressed in percentage terms made the main idea much easier to grasp.

4

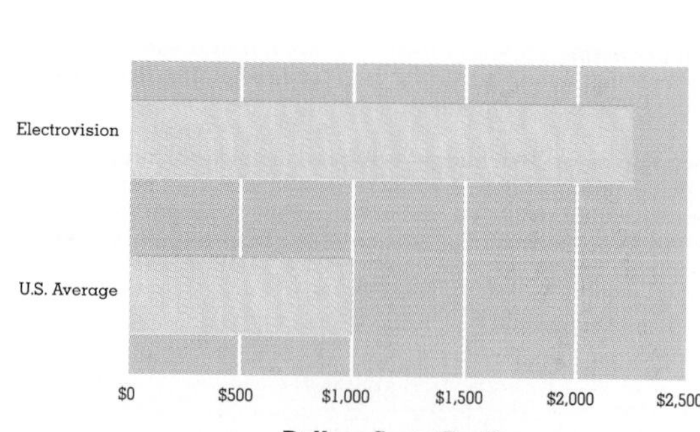

Figure 3
Electrovision People Spend Over Twice as Much as the Average Business Traveler
Source: *The Wall Street Journal* and company records

The Dow Jones Travel Index calculates the average cost per day of business travel in the United States, based on average airfare, hotel rates, and rental car rates. The average fluctuates weekly as travel companies change their rates, but it has been running at about $1,000 per day for the last year or so. In contrast, Electrovision's average daily expense over the past year has been $2,250—125 percent higher than average. This figure is based on the average trip cost of $4,720 listed earlier and an average trip length of 2.1 days.

Leaving a bit more white space above a heading than below it helps readers associate that heading with the text it describes.

Spending Has Been Encouraged

Although a variety of factors may contribute to this differential, Electrovision's relatively high T&E costs are at least partially attributable to the company's philosophy and management style. Because many employees do not enjoy business travel, management has tried to make the trips more pleasant by authorizing first-class airfare, luxury hotel accommodations, and full-size rental cars. The sales staff is encouraged to entertain clients at top restaurants and to invite them to cultural and sporting events.

The cost of these privileges is easy to overlook, given the weakness of Electrovision's system for keeping track of T&E expenses:

- The monthly financial records provided to management do not contain a separate category for travel and entertainment; the information is buried under Cost of Goods Sold and under Selling, General, and Administrative Expenses.

Moreno was as careful about the appearance of her report as she was about its content. The chart in Figure 3 is very simple, but it creates an effective visual comparison. Moreno included just enough data to make her point.

- Each department head is given authority to approve any expense report, regardless of how large it may be.
- Receipts are not required for expenditures of less than $100.
- Individuals are allowed to make their own travel arrangements.
- No one is charged with the responsibility for controlling the company's total spending on travel and entertainment.

GROWING IMPACT ON THE BOTTOM LINE

During the past three years, the company's healthy profits have resulted in relatively little pressure to push for tighter controls over all aspects of the business. However, as we all know, the situation is changing. We're projecting flat to declining profits for the next two years, a situation that has prompted all of us to search for ways to cut costs. At the same time, rising airfares and hotel rates have increased the impact of T&E expenses on the company's financial results.

Lower Profits Underscore the Need for Change

The next two years promise to be difficult for Electrovision. After several years of steady increases in spending, the Postal Service is tightening procurement policies for automated mail-handling equipment. Funding for the A-12 optical character reader has been canceled. As a consequence, the marketing department expects sales to drop by 15 percent. Although Electrovision is negotiating several promising R&D contracts with nongovernment clients, the marketing department does not foresee any major procurements for the next two to three years.

At the same time, Electrovision is facing cost increases on several fronts. As we've known for several months, the new production facility now under construction in Salt Lake City, Utah, is behind schedule and over budget. Labor contracts in Boston and Dallas expire within the next six months, and plant managers there anticipate that significant salary and benefits concessions may be necessary to avoid strikes. Moreover, marketing and advertising costs are expected to increase as we attempt to strengthen these activities to better cope with competitive pressures. Given the expected decline in revenues and increase in costs, the Executive Committee's prediction that profits will fall by 12 percent in the coming fiscal year does not seem overly pessimistic.

Airfares and Hotel Rates Are Rising

Business travelers have grown accustomed to frequent fare wars and discounting in the travel industry in recent years. Excess capacity and aggressive price competition, particularly in the airline business, made travel a relative bargain.

However, that situation has changed, as weaker competitors have been forced out and the remaining players have grown stronger and smarter. Airlines and hotels are better at managing inventory and keeping occupancy rates high, and high occupancy

Bulleted lists make it easy for readers to identify and distinguish related points.

Informative headings focus readers' attention on the main points of the report. Thus they are most appropriate when the report is in direct order and is aimed at a receptive audience. Descriptive headings are more effective when a report is in indirect order and the readers are less receptive.

Because airfares represent Electrovision's biggest T&E expense, Moreno included a subsection that deals with the possible impact of trends in the airline industry. Airfares are rising, so it is especially important to gain more control over employees' air travel arrangements.

Documenting the facts adds weight to Moreno's argument.

Pointing out both the benefits and risks of taking action gives recommendations an objective flavor.

6

translates into higher prices because suppliers have less reason to compete on price. Last year saw some of the steepest rate hikes in years. Business airfares (tickets most likely to be purchased by business travelers) jumped over 40 percent in many markets. The trend is expected to continue, with rates increasing another 5 to 10 percent overall (Phillips 331; "Travel Costs Under Pressure" 30; Dahl B6).

Given the fact that airfare and hotel costs account for 70 percent of Electrovision's T&E budget, the trend toward higher prices in these two categories will have serious consequences on the company's expenses unless management takes action to control these costs.

METHODS FOR REDUCING TRAVEL AND ENTERTAINMENT COSTS

By implementing a number of reforms, management can expect to reduce Electrovision's T&E budget by as much as 40 percent. This estimate is based on the general assessment made by American Express (Gilligan 130–40) and the fact that we have an opportunity to significantly reduce air travel costs by reducing or eliminating first-class travel. However, these measures are likely to be unpopular with employees. To gain acceptance for such changes, management will need to sell employees on the need for moderation in travel and entertainment allowances.

Four Ways to Trim Expenses

By researching what other companies are doing to curb travel and entertainment expenses, the accounting department has identified four prominent opportunities that should enable Electrovision to save about $6 million annually in travel-related costs.

Institute Tighter Spending Controls

A single individual should be appointed director of travel and entertainment to spearhead the effort to gain control of the T&E budget. More than a third of all U.S. companies now employ travel managers in an effort to keep costs in line ("Businesses Use Savvy Managers" 4). The director should be familiar with the travel industry and should be well versed in both accounting and information technology. The director should report to the vice president of operations. The director's first priorities should be to establish a written travel and entertainment policy and to implement a system for controlling travel and entertainment costs.

Electrovision currently has no written policy on travel and entertainment, a step widely recommended by air travel experts (Smith D4). Creating a policy would clarify management's position and serve as a vehicle for communicating the need for moderation. At a minimum, the policy should include the following provisions:

- All travel and entertainment should be strictly related to business and should be approved in advance.

Moreno created a forceful tone by using action verbs in the third-level subheadings of this section. This approach is appropriate to the nature of the study and the attitude of the audience. However, in a status-conscious organization, the imperative verbs might sound a bit too presumptuous coming from a junior member of the staff.

7

- Except under special circumstances to be approved on a case-by-case basis, employees should travel by coach and stay in mid-range business hotels.
- The travel and entertainment policy should apply equally to employees at all levels in the organization. No special benefits should be allowed for top executives.

To implement the new policy, Electrovision will need to create a system for controlling travel and entertainment expenses. Each department should prepare an annual T&E budget as part of its operating plan. These budgets should be presented in detail so that management can evaluate how travel and entertainment dollars will be spent and recommend appropriate cuts.

To help management monitor performance relative to these budgets, the director of travel should prepare monthly financial statements showing actual travel and entertainment expenditures by department. The system for capturing this information should be computerized and should be capable of identifying individuals who consistently exceed approved spending levels. The recommended average should range between $2,000 and $2,500 per month for each professional employee, depending on the individual's role in the company. Because they make frequent trips, sales and top management personnel can be expected to have relatively high travel expenses.

The director of travel should also be responsible for retaining a business-oriented travel service that will schedule all employee business trips and look for the best travel deals, particularly in airfares. In addition to centralizing Electrovision's reservation and ticketing activities, the agency will negotiate reduced group rates with hotels and rental car agencies. The agency selected should have offices nationwide so that all Electrovision facilities can channel their reservations through the same company. By consolidating its travel planning in this way, Electrovision can increase its control over costs and achieve economies of scale. This is particularly important in light of the dizzying array of often wildly different airfares available between some cities. It's not uncommon to find dozens of fares along commonly traveled routes (Rowe 30).

The director should also work with the agency to explore low-cost alternatives, such as buying tickets from airfare consolidators (the air travel equivalent of factory outlet malls). In addition, the director can help coordinate travel across the company to secure group discounts whenever possible (Barker 31; Miller B6).

Reduce Unnecessary Travel and Entertainment

One of the easiest ways to reduce expenses is to reduce the amount of traveling and entertaining that occurs. An analysis of last year's expenditures suggests that as much as 30 percent of Electrovision's travel and entertainment is discretionary. The professional staff spent $2.8 million attending seminars and conferences last year. Although some of these gatherings are undoubtedly beneficial, the company could save money by sending fewer representatives to each function and by eliminating some of the less valuable seminars.

The bulleted list format not only calls attention to important points but also adds visual interest. You can also use visual aids, headings, and direct quotations to break up large, solid blocks of print.

When including recommendations in a report, specify the steps required to implement them.

Moreno decided to single-space her report to save space; however, double spacing can make the text of a long report somewhat easier to read, and it provides more space for readers to write comments.

Similarly, Electrovision could economize on trips between headquarters and divisions by reducing the frequency of such visits and by sending fewer people on each trip. Although there is often no substitute for face-to-face meetings, management could try to resolve more internal issues through telephone, electronic, and written communication.

Electrovision can also reduce spending by urging employees to economize. Instead of flying first class, employees can fly tourist class or take advantage of discount fares. Instead of taking clients to dinner, Electrovision personnel can hold breakfast meetings, which tend to be less costly. Rather than ordering a $50 bottle of wine, employees can select a less expensive bottle or dispense with alcohol entirely. People can book rooms at moderately priced hotels and drive smaller rental cars. In general, employees should be urged to spend the company's money as though it were their own.

Obtain Lowest Rates from Travel Providers

Apart from urging individual employees to economize, Electrovision can also save money by searching for the lowest available airfares, hotel rates, and rental car fees. Currently, few Electrovision employees have the time or specialized knowledge to seek out travel bargains. When they need to travel, they make the most convenient and most comfortable arrangements. However, if Electrovision contracts with a professional travel service, the company will have access to professionals who can more efficiently obtain the lower rates from travel providers.

Judging by the experience of other companies, Electrovision may be able to trim as much as 30 to 40 percent from the travel budget by looking for bargains in airfares and negotiating group rates with hotels and rental car companies. Electrovision should be able to achieve these economies by analyzing its travel patterns, identifying frequently visited locations, and selecting a few hotels that are willing to reduce rates in exchange for guaranteed business. At the same time, the company should be able to save up to 40 percent on rental car charges by negotiating a corporate rate.

The possibilities for economizing are promising, but it's worth noting that making the best arrangements is a complicated undertaking, requiring many trade-offs such as the following:

- The best fares might not always be the lowest. Indirect flights are often less expensive than direct flights, but they take longer and may end up costing more in lost work time.
- The cheapest tickets may have to be booked 30 days in advance, often impossible for us.
- Discount tickets may be nonrefundable, which is a real drawback if the trip has to be canceled at the last minute.

Electrovision is currently ill-equipped to make these and other trade-offs. However, by employing a business-oriented travel service, the company will have access to computerized systems that can optimize its choices.

Note how Moreno made the transition from section to section. The first sentence under the first heading on this page refers to the subject of the previous paragraph and signals a shift in thought.

9

Replace Travel with Technological Alternatives

We might be able to replace a significant portion of our interdivisional travel with electronic meetings that utilize videoconferencing, real-time document sharing on PC screens, and other alternatives. Naturally, we don't want to reduce employee or team effectiveness, but many companies are using these new tools to cut costs and reduce wear and tear on employees.

Rather than make specific recommendations in this report, I suggest that the new travel director conduct an in-depth study of the company's travel patterns as part of an overall cost-containment effort. A thorough analysis of why employees travel and what they accomplish will highlight any opportunities for replacing face-to-face meetings. Part of this study should include limited-scope tests of various communication systems as a way of measuring their impact on both workplace effectiveness and overall costs.

The Impact of Reforms

By implementing tighter controls, reducing unnecessary expenses, negotiating more favorable rates, and exploring "electronic travel," Electrovision should be able to reduce its travel and entertainment budget significantly. As Table 1 illustrates, the combined savings should be in the neighborhood of $6 million, although the precise figures are somewhat difficult to project.

TABLE 1

Electrovision Can Trim Travel and Entertainment Costs by an Estimated $6 Million per Year

Source of Savings	Amount Saved
Switching from first-class to coach airfare	$2,300,000
Negotiating preferred hotel rates	940,000
Negotiating preferred rental car rates	460,000
Systematically searching for lower airfares	375,000
Reducing interdivisional travel	675,000
Reducing seminar and conference attendance	1,250,000
TOTAL POTENTIAL SAVINGS	**$6,000,000**

To achieve the economies outlined in the table, Electrovision will incur expenses for hiring a director of travel and for implementing a T&E cost-control system. These costs are projected at $95,000: $85,000 per year in salary and benefits for the new employee and a one-time expense of $10,000 for the cost-control system. The cost of retaining a full-service travel agency is negligible because agencies normally receive a commission from travel providers rather than a fee from clients.

Pointing out possible difficulties demonstrates that you have considered all the angles and builds readers' confidence in your judgment.

The use of informative titles for exhibits is consistent with the way headings are handled and is appropriate for a report to a receptive audience. The use of complete sentences helps readers focus immediately on the point of the illustrations.

Even though estimated savings may be difficult to project, including dollar figures helps management envision the impact of your suggestions.

The table on this page puts Moreno's recommendations in perspective. Note how she called attention in the text to the most important sources of savings and also spelled out the costs required to achieve those results.

The measures required to achieve these savings are likely to be unpopular with employees. Electrovision personnel are accustomed to generous travel and entertainment allowances, and they are likely to resent having these privileges curtailed. To alleviate their disappointment

- Management should make a determined effort to explain why the changes are necessary.
- The director of corporate communication should be asked to develop a multifaceted campaign that will communicate the importance of curtailing travel and entertainment costs.
- Management should set a positive example by adhering strictly to the new policies.
- The limitations should apply equally to employees at all levels in the organization.

11

CONCLUSIONS AND RECOMMENDATIONS

Electrovision is currently spending $16 million per year on travel and entertainment. Although much of this spending is justified, the company's costs appear to be high relative to competitors', mainly because Electrovision has been generous with its travel benefits.

Electrovision's liberal approach to travel and entertainment was understandable during years of high profitability; however, the company is facing the prospect of declining profits for the next several years. Management is therefore motivated to cut costs in all areas of the business. Reducing T&E spending is particularly important because the impact of these costs on the bottom line will increase as a result of fare increases in the airline industry.

Electrovision should be able to reduce travel and entertainment costs by as much as 40 percent by taking four important steps:

1. *Institute tighter spending controls.* Management should hire a director of travel and entertainment who will assume overall responsibility for T&E activities. Within the next six months, this director should develop a written travel policy, institute a T&E budget and a cost-control system, and retain a professional, business-oriented travel agency that will optimize arrangements with travel providers.

2. *Reduce unnecessary travel and entertainment.* Electrovision should encourage employees to economize on travel and entertainment spending. Management can accomplish this by authorizing fewer trips and by urging employees to be more conservative in their spending.

3. *Obtain lowest rates from travel providers.* Electrovision should also focus on obtaining the best rates on airline tickets, hotel rooms, and rental cars. By channeling all arrangements through a professional travel agency, the company can optimize its choices and gain clout in negotiating preferred rates.

4. *Replace travel with technological alternatives.* With the number of computers already installed in our facilities, it seems likely that we could take advantage of desktop videoconferencing and other distance-meeting tools. This won't be quite as feasible with customer sites, since these systems require compatible equipment at both ends of a connection, but it is certainly a possibility for communication with Electrovision's own sites.

Because these measures may be unpopular with employees, management should make a concerted effort to explain the importance of reducing travel costs. The director of corporate communication should be given responsibility for developing a plan to communicate the need for employee cooperation.

Use a descriptive heading for the last section of the text. In informational reports, this section is generally called "Summary"; in analytical reports, it is called "Conclusions" or "Conclusions and Recommendations."

Emphasize the recommendations by presenting them in list format, if possible.

Do not introduce new facts in this section of the text.

Because Moreno organized her report around conclusions and recommendations, readers have already been introduced to them. Thus she summarizes her conclusions in the first two paragraphs. A simple list is enough to remind readers of the four main recommendations. In a longer report she might have divided the section into subsections, labeled "Conclusions" and "Recommendations," to distinguish between the two. If the report had been organized around logical arguments, this would have been the readers' first exposure to the conclusions and recommendations, and Moreno would have needed to develop them more fully.

List references alphabetically by the author's last name or, when the author is unknown, by the title of the reference. See Component Chapter B for additional details on preparing reference lists.

12

WORKS CITED

Barker, Julie. "How to Rein in Group Travel Costs." *Successful Meetings* Feb. 1999: 31.

"Businesses Use Savvy Managers to Keep Travel Costs Down." *Christian Science Monitor* 17 July 1998: 4.

Dahl, Jonathan. "1998: The Year Travel Costs Took Off." *Wall Street Journal* 29 Dec. 1998: B6.

Gilligan, Edward P. "Trimming Your T&E Is Easier Than You Think." *Managing Office Technology* Nov. 1999: 39–40.

Miller, Lisa. "Attention, Airline Ticket Shoppers." *Wall Street Journal* 7 July 1998: B6.

Phillips, Edward H. "Airlines Post Record Traffic." *Aviation Week & Space Technology* 8 Jan. 1999: 331.

Rowe, Irene Vlitos. "Global Solution for Cutting Travel Costs." *European* 12 Oct. 1998: 30.

Smith, Carol. "Rising, Erratic Air Fares Make Company Policy Vital." *Los Angeles Times* 2 Nov. 1999: D4.

"Travel Costs Under Pressure." *Purchasing* 15 Feb. 1999: 30.

Moreno's list of references follows the style recommended in *The MLA Style Manual.*

CHECKLIST FOR FORMAL REPORTS AND PROPOSALS

A. Quality of the Research
  1. Define the problem clearly.
  2. State the purpose of the document.
  3. Identify all relevant issues.
  4. Accumulate evidence pertaining to each issue.
  5. Check evidence for accuracy, currency, and reliability.
  6. Justify your conclusions by the evidence.
    a. Do not omit or distort evidence in order to support your point of view.
    b. Identify and justify all assumptions.

B. Preparation of Reports and Proposals
  1. Choose a format and length that are appropriate to your audience and the subject.
  2. Prepare a sturdy, attractive cover.
    a. Label the cover clearly with the title of the document.
    b. Use a title that tells the audience exactly what the document is about.
  3. Provide all necessary information on the title page.
    a. Include the full title of the document.
    b. Include the name, title, and affiliation of the recipient.
    c. Give the name, title, and affiliation of the author.
    d. Provide the date of submission.
    e. Balance the information in blocks on the page.
  4. Include a copy of the letter of authorization or request for proposal, if appropriate.
  5. Prepare a letter or memo of transmittal.
    a. Use memo format for internal documents.
    b. Use letter format for external documents.
    c. Include the transmittal letter in only some copies if it contains sensitive or personal information suitable for some but not all readers.
    d. Place the transmittal letter right before the table of contents.
    e. Use the good-news plan for solicited proposals and other reports; use the persuasive plan for unsolicited proposals.
    f. Word the letter to "convey" the document officially to the readers; refer to the authorization; and discuss the purpose, scope, background, sources and methods, and limitations.
    g. Mention any special points that warrant readers' attention.
    h. If you use direct order, summarize conclusions and recommendations (unless they are included in a synopsis).
    i. Acknowledge all who were especially helpful in preparing the document.
    j. Close with thanks, offer to be of further assistance, and suggest future projects, if appropriate.
  6. Prepare the table of contents.
    a. Include all first-level headings (and all second-level headings or perhaps all second- and third-level headings).
    b. Give the page number of each heading.
    c. Word all headings exactly as they appear in the text.
    d. Include the synopsis (if there is one) and supplementary parts in the table of contents.
    e. Number the table of contents and all prefatory pages with lower-case roman numerals centered at the bottom of the page.
  7. Prepare a list of illustrations if you have four visual aids or more.
    a. Put the list in the same format as the table of contents.
    b. Identify visual aids either directly beneath the table of contents or on a separate page under the heading "List of Illustrations."
  8. Develop a synopsis or an executive summary if the document is long and formal.
    a. Tailor the synopsis or executive summary to the document's length and tone.
    b. Condense the main points of the document, using either the informative approach or the descriptive approach, according to the guidelines in this chapter.
    c. Present the points in the synopsis in the same order as they appear in the document. An executive summary can deviate from the order of points made in the report.
  9. Prepare the introduction to the text.
    a. Leave a 2-inch margin at the top of the page, and center the title of the document.
    b. In a long document (ten pages or more), type the first-level heading "Introduction" three lines below the title.
    c. In a short document (fewer than ten pages), begin typing three lines below the title of the report or proposal without the heading "Introduction."

(continued)

   d. Discuss the authorization (unless it's covered in the letter of transmittal), purpose, scope, background, sources and methods, definitions, limitations, and text organization.

10. Prepare the body of the document.

   a. Carefully select the organizational approach (see Chapter 14).

   b. Use either a personal or an impersonal tone consistently.

   c. Use either a past or a present time perspective consistently.

   d. Follow a consistent format for headings of different levels, using a company format guide, a sample proposal or report, or the format in this textbook as a model (see Component Chapter A).

   e. Express comparable (same-level) headings in any given section in parallel grammatical form.

   f. Group ideas into logical categories.

   g. Tie sections together with transitional words, sentences, and paragraphs.

   h. Give ideas of equal importance roughly equal space.

   i. Avoid overly technical, pretentious, or vague language.

   j. Develop each paragraph around a topic sentence.

   k. Make sure all ideas in each paragraph are related.

   l. For documents bound on the left, number all pages with arabic numerals in the upper right-hand corner (except for the first page, where the number is centered 1 inch from the bottom); for top-bound documents, number all pages with arabic numerals centered 1 inch from the bottom.

11. Incorporate visual aids into the text.

   a. Number visual aids consecutively throughout the text, numbering tables and figures (other visual aids) separately if that style is preferred.

   b. Develop explicit titles for all visual aids except in-text tables.

   c. Refer to each visual aid in the text, and emphasize the significance of the data.

   d. Place each visual aid as soon after its textual explanation as possible, or group all visual aids at the ends of chapters or at the end of the document for easy reference.

12. Conclude the text of reports and proposals with a summary and, if appropriate, conclusions and recommendations.

   a. In a summary, recap the findings and explanations already presented.

   b. Place conclusions and recommendations in their order of logic or importance, preferably in list format.

   c. To induce action, explain in the recommendations section who should do what, when, where, and how.

   d. If appropriate, point up the benefits of action, to leave readers with the motivation to follow recommendations.

13. Document all material quoted or paraphrased from secondary sources, using a consistent format (see Component Chapter B).

14. Include appendixes at the end of the document to provide useful and detailed information that is of interest to some but not all readers.

   a. Give each appendix a title, such as "Questionnaire" or "Names and Addresses of Survey Participants."

   b. If there is more than one appendix, number or letter them consecutively in the order they're referred to in the text.

   c. Type appendixes in a format consistent with the text of the report or proposal.

15. Include a reference list if you used secondary sources that need to be identified, if it seems that readers would benefit, or if the document would gain credibility.

   a. Type the bibliography on a separate page headed "Bibliography" or "Sources."

   b. Alphabetize bibliography entries.

   c. Use a consistent format for the bibliography (see Component Chapter B).

COMMUNICATION CHALLENGES AT CORPORATE DYNAMICS

Corporate Dynamics is competing against six other consulting firms for a large contract to analyze and recommend improvements to the customer service organization of a major industrial materials manufacturer. Landiak wants to make sure that Corporate Dynamics' sales proposal stands out, so he sent his team to survey the marketplace and interview a few of the potential client's customers. After all, Landiak knows that one way to capture a client's attention is to use customer quotations in a report that discusses opportunities, challenges, and how Corporate Dynamics can help.

INDIVIDUAL CHALLENGE: Landiak's team came back with a lot of useful information about the potential client. Although many of the comments they received from customers were positive, the team also received some negative feedback, including (1) "The customer service representatives never seem to be able to answer my questions," (2) "The sales representative doesn't call on me as often as some of the competitors' representatives do," and (3) "I don't carry the company's products because my customers never ask for them." Although these may seem like problems, Landiak wants to present them as opportunities for positive change. Landiak has asked you, a member of his team, to draft a transmittal letter that will set a positive tone, explaining how and why the team obtained this customer information. Remember, this is your opportunity to say what you'd say if you were handing the report directly to the client.

TEAM CHALLENGE: Landiak has assigned your team the job of organizing and formatting a proposal to this potential client. Because Corporate Dynamics is competing with six other firms for the contract, you must concentrate on making your proposal different. Your first step is to decide what components to include in the proposal. For example, what visual aids might you include? Will you include appendixes? If so, what kind of material would be suitable for appendixes? Will you include an executive summary? Why or why not? Would it be more effective for your team to put your conclusions at the beginning or at the end of your report? Why?[4] ■

SUMMARY OF LEARNING OBJECTIVES

1. **List the seven prefatory parts of a formal report.** The seven prefatory parts of a formal report are the cover, title fly and title page, letter of authorization and letter of acceptance, letter of transmittal, table of contents, list of illustrations, and synopsis or executive summary.
2. **Explain the function of an executive summary.** An executive summary is generally included in long reports (over 30 pages) as a convenience for readers. This minireport highlights the essentials of the full report and gives readers enough information to make a decision. Those who want more detail can refer to the complete report.
3. **Describe four important functions of the introduction to a formal report.** Four important functions of introductions are putting the report in a broader context by tying it to a problem or an assignment, telling readers the report's purpose, previewing the report's contents and organization, and establishing the tone of the report and the writer's relationship with the audience.
4. **Identify eight topics you might include in the introduction of a formal report.** The topics that could be included in an introduction include authorization, problem/purpose, scope, background, sources and methods, definitions, limitations, and report organization.
5. **Define the goal of most formal proposals.** The goal of formal proposals is to impress the potential client or supporter with the report writer's professionalism, accomplished through a structured and deliberate approach.
6. **Name the four types of information that must be covered in the body of a proposal.** The body of a proposal must cover four types of specific information: the proposed approach, a work plan, a statement of qualifications, and the costs involved.

CRITICAL THINKING QUESTIONS

1. What are the advantages and disadvantages of having managers and professional staffers (such as lawyers, accountants, engineers, and consultants) use such computer tools as page-layout programs, graphic-design software, and scanners to produce reports? Explain your answer.
2. When businesspeople prepare unsolicited proposals, they often have to make assumptions about timing and other issues that are under the client's control. Where in the formal proposal should these assumptions be included? Why?
3. Under what circumstances would you include more than one index in a lengthy report? Explain your answer.
4. If you were submitting a solicited proposal to build an indoor pool, would you include as references the names and addresses of other clients for whom you recently built similar pools? Would you include these references in an unsolicited proposal? Where in either proposal would you include these references? Why?
5. How would you report on a confidential survey in which employees rated their managers' capabilities? Both employees and managers expect to see the results. Would you give the same report to employees and managers? What components would you include or exclude for each audience? Explain your choices.
6. Would you include a letter of authorization with a periodic personal activity report? With a letter of transmittal? Why or why not?
7. If you were writing an analytical report about your company's advertising policies, where would you include your recommendations—in the beginning of the report or at the end? Why?
8. If you included a bibliography in your report, would you also need to include in-text citations? Please explain.

EXPLORING THE BEST OF THE WEB

Avoid Embarrassment by Avoiding Common Errors, page 512

Review the "Common Errors in English" Web site and click on some of the "Common Errors" until you come across a mistake you've been making—or have made in the past. Now do the same with the "Nonerrors." Then take a look at the list of "Commonly Made Suggestions" by readers of Brian's Web site, along with the professor's rebuttals.

1. What did you find that changed your beliefs about what's right and wrong in English usage?
2. Since many common errors are believed to be correct and many correct constructions are believed to be wrong, how can you avoid appearing ignorant when you come across one of these instances in your report or proposal writing? That is, if the boss thinks it's right but you know it's wrong, or if the boss thinks it's wrong but you know it's right, should you fight or switch?

CASES

SHORT FORMAL REPORTS REQUIRING NO ADDITIONAL RESEARCH

1. What do frequent travelers want? Report using statistical data to analyze attitudes about lodging You are a research assistant for the American Hotel & Motel Association, which recently commissioned a survey of frequent travelers and their lodging satisfaction. The study's purpose was to provide member hotels and motels with up-to-date data on the demographics and lodging preferences of frequent travelers. The hotels could use this information to adapt their services to changing consumer needs.

The results presented in Tables 15.1, 15.2, and 15.3 were obtained from detailed questionnaires mailed to people identified as "frequent travelers": male or female heads of households who had stayed one or more nights at any hotel or motel five or more times in the previous 12 months.

Your task: Write a report to the president of your organization that explains the results of the survey and its implications for hotels that wish to cater specifically to frequent travelers. What trends should they be concerned about? What changes should they make? Justify your conclusions and your recommendations by referring to the data in the tables.[5]

2. Climbing the ladder: Report summarizing data about corporate opportunities for women As the assistant director of human resources for a large financial services firm, you hear the concerns of many different employees. Lately, increasing numbers of female employees have been complaining about being passed up for promotions and management positions. They feel that male employees receive preferential treatment, even though many females are more highly qualified.

TABLE 15.1

FREQUENT TRAVELER DEMOGRAPHICS: TRENDS OVER TIME

Demographic characteristics	1997	1998	1999
Age			
Under 35 years	22%	28%	22%
35–50 years	40	42	45
Over 50 years	38	30	33
Gender			
Male	68	64	61
Female	32	36	39
Annual Household Income			
Less than $20,000	26	16	5
$20,000–$29,999	30	18	12
$30,000–$49,999	32	40	31
$50,000 or more	12	26	52
Number of Trips			
5–10 trips	70	63	65
More than 10 trips	30	37	35
Number of Nights Stayed			
5–10 nights	19	10	8
11–20 nights	35	31	30
21–30 nights	21	21	25
31 or more nights	25	38	37
Type of Travel			
Business	73	74	69
Pleasure	27	26	31

TABLE 15.2

HOTEL SELECTION FACTORS

Factor	Rank in Initial Selection	Rank in Initial Decision
Clean appearance	1	1
Convenient location	2	3
Price/reasonable rate	3	4
Good service	4	2
Name/reputation	5	7
Security/safety	6	5
Company/family discount	7	6
Reservation service	8	8
Recommendation	9	10
Recreational facilities	10	9
Chain frequency program	11	11
Business facilities	12	13
Other	13	12

TABLE 15.3

IMPORTANCE OF HOTEL SERVICES

Facilities, Services, and Amenities	Like to Use All or Most of the Time		
	Total	*Male*	*Female*
Television	94%	95%	93%
Bar soap	89	89	86
Restaurant/coffee shop	83	81	85
More than 2 towels	81	79	84
Personal-care amenities	80	78	82
Choice of smoking/ nonsmoking room	78	76	82
Wake-up call	77	78	75
Complimentary newspaper	75	78	71
In-room refrigerator	63	59	68
In-room coffeemaker	59	57	62
Pool	49	48	52
Auto check-in	40	40	41
Hair dryer	36	32	43
Auto check-out	33	35	33
In-room safety deposit box	29	28	34
Bar/lounge	28	30	25
Room service	28	26	31
Robes	27	24	21
Pay TV	23	26	21
Exercise facilities	22	24	21
Check cashing	21	18	24
VCR	15	16	13
Executive-level rooms	14	16	10
Valet dry cleaning	10	12	8
Coin laundry	8	7	10
Video games	8	8	6
Fax machine	7	7	7
Typing services	3	3	2
Day-care facilities	2	1	4

TABLE 15.4

STATISTICS FOR MALE AND FEMALE MANAGERS

Employee Statistics	Female Managers	Male Managers
Average number of years with the company	12.3	9.5
Average number of years of management experience	7.2	6.9
Percentage who have an MBA or other advanced degree	74%	63%
Average annual salary	$76,000	$84,000
Average number of times promoted	4.2	4.4

Table 15.4 indicates the results of a research study conducted by your staff. The study displays several key statistics pertaining to the male and female employees working for your company. Table 15.5 depicts how executives in Fortune 1000 companies perceive the barriers to female advancement, and Table 15.6 shows why female executives feel that women should be given more opportunities in the corporate world. These studies may help shed light on what could be viewed as a pattern of sex discrimination by your company. Because your company believes in equitable treatment for all employees, regardless of their gender, you believe your boss will be interested in this information.

Your task: Write a report to the director of human resources interpreting and summarizing the information in these tables. Suggest a possible course of action to remedy the situation at your company.[6]

TABLE 15.5

WHY FEMALE EXECUTIVES DON'T ADVANCE INTO CORPORATE LEADERSHIP POSITIONS

Reason Cited	According to Female Executives	According to Male CEOs
Male stereotyping/ preconceptions	52%	25%
Exclusion from informal networks	49	15
Lack of general management/line experience	47	82
Inhospitable corporate culture	35	18
Women not in pipeline long enough	29	64

TABLE 15.6

WHY FEMALE EXECUTIVES THINK COMPANIES SHOULD INCREASE THE NUMBER OF FEMALE SENIOR MANAGERS

Reason	Agree	Strongly Agree
Women are large part of management talent pool	29%	69%
Women contribute unique perspective	32	61
Women are large part of consumer base	45	36
Companies have social responsibility	41	10
Shareholders want more executive women	41	7
Customers want more executive women	34	7
Lawsuits are increasing	40	5

TABLE 15.7

TOP FIVE REASONS DO-IT-YOURSELFERS PERFORM CAR MAINTENANCE TASKS

Reason	Percent
Saves money	67
Something I can do for myself	21
Saves time	12
Can make sure it's done right	10
Easy to do	9

3. Do it yourself: Report using statistical data to analyze industry trends Auto parts stores get a lot of their business from do-it-yourselfers, people who repair their cars themselves. Auto parts retailers would like to see the number of do-it-yourselfers increase. Auto mechanics, on the other hand, would prefer that drivers bring their cars into a repair shop when something goes wrong. As assistant to Rob Ebbin, a market analyst for the Automotive Parts and Accessories Association (APAA), you don't necessarily have a preference. After all, both do-it-yourselfers and professional mechanics have to buy auto parts. However, the APAA has asked you to summarize the results of some recent surveys aimed at better understanding the do-it-yourselfer segment of the auto parts market (see Table 15.7 and Figures 15.3–15.6). The report will be available to all association members.

Your task: Write a report to your boss that summarizes the survey results, pointing out some basic trends that would be of interest to both auto parts retailers and auto mechanics. Is the do-it-yourselfer segment growing? What are the key characteristics of this market segment? What products do they purchase most frequently? Be sure to acknowledge the source of any data in the tables and figures that you discuss in your summary.[7]

4. Sailing past the sunsets: Report using statistical data to suggest a new advertising strategy As manager of Distant Dreams, a travel agency in Waco, Texas, you are interested in the information in Table 15.8. It seems that dollar income is shifting toward the 35–44 age group. Tables 15.9 and 15.10 are also broken down by age group.

Figure 15.3
Percentage of U.S. Car Owners Who Purchased Selected Auto Parts in the Past Year.

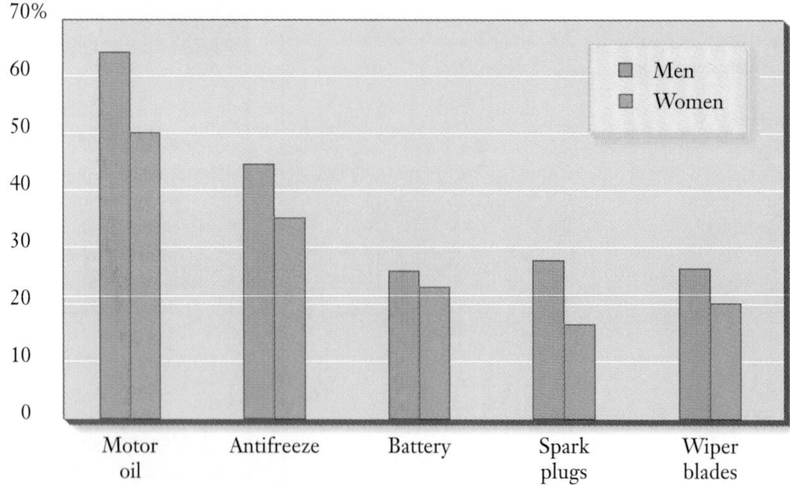

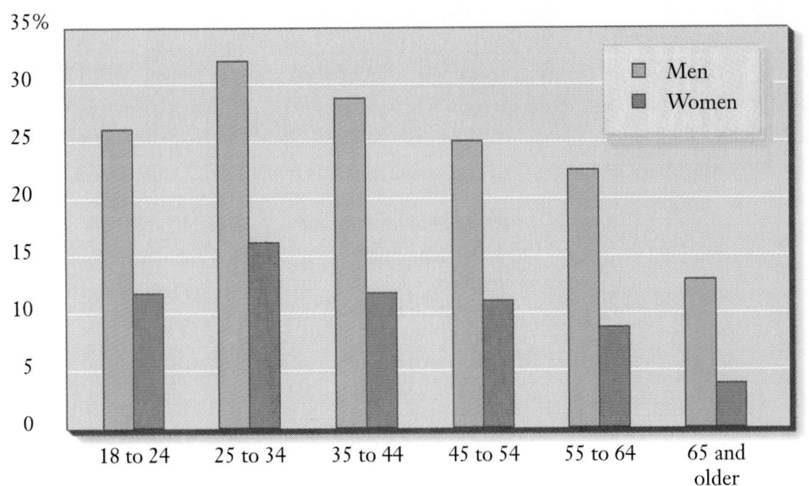

Figure 15.4
Percentage of Car Owners Who Perform Selected Maintenance Tasks Themselves, by Sex and Age (Note: Maintenance tasks include changing, adding, or installing any of the following: oil, oil filter, battery, antifreeze, spark plugs.)

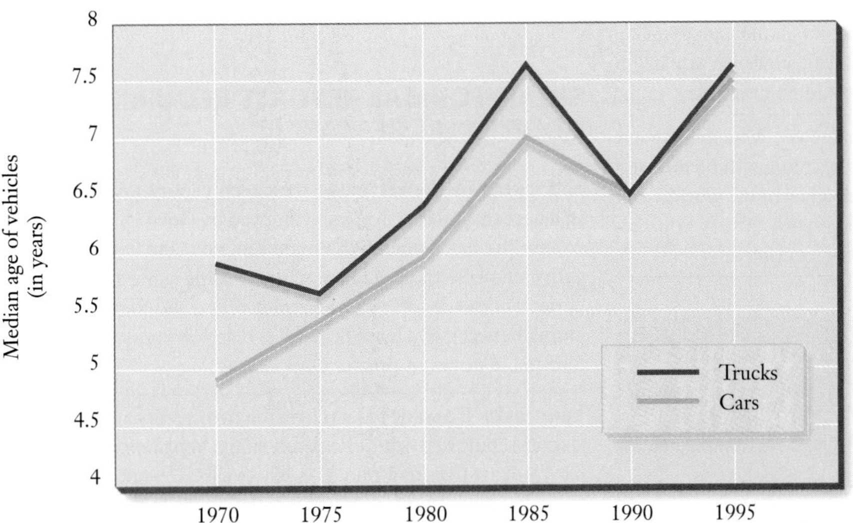

Figure 15.5
Median Age of Cars and Trucks in Operation in the United States, 1970–1995

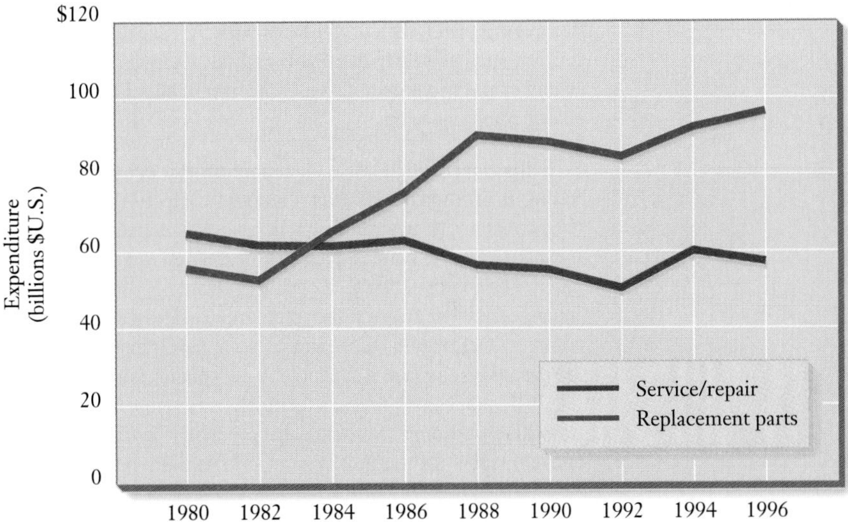

Figure 15.6
Billions of U.S. Dollars Spent on Replacement Parts and Service Repair, 1980–1996 (in 1996 dollars)

TABLE 15.8

PERCENTAGE OF TOTAL U.S. HOUSEHOLD INCOME EARNED BY VARIOUS AGE GROUPS

Age Group	1990	1995	2000*
25–34	23%	24%	26%
35–44	22	25	28
45–54	22	21	19
55–64	19	17	15
Over 65	14	13	12

*Projected.

Traditionally, your agency has concentrated its advertising on people nearing retirement, people who are closing out successful careers and now have the time and money to vacation abroad. After examining the three sets of data, however, you begin to think that a major shift in emphasis would be desirable.

Your task: Write a report to Mary Henderson, who writes your advertisements, explaining why future ads should still be directed to travelers who want to explore the far reaches of the world—but to people besides those in their fifties and sixties. Justify your explanation by referring to the data you have examined.

TABLE 15.9

PREFERENCES IN TRAVEL AMONG VARIOUS AGE GROUPS

	Age Group		
Travel Interests	18–34	35–54	55+
I am more interested in excitement and stimulation than rest and relaxation.	67%	42%	38%
I prefer to go where I haven't been before.	62	58	48
I like adventuresome travel.	62	45	32
I love foreign and exotic things.	41	25	21
Vacation is a time for self-indulgence, regardless of the cost.	31	16	14
I don't see the need for a travel agent.	67	63	52

TABLE 15.10

BASIC DESIRE FOR TRAVEL AMONG VARIOUS AGE GROUPS

	Age Group		
Attitude toward Travel	18–34	35–54	55+
Travel is one of the most rewarding and enjoyable things one can do.	71%	69%	66%
I love the idea of traveling and do so at every opportunity.	66	59	48
I often feel the need to get away from everything.	56	55	33

SHORT FORMAL REPORTS REQUIRING ADDITIONAL RESEARCH

5. Picking the better path: Research report assisting a client in a career choice You are employed by Open Options, a career-counseling firm, where your main function is to help clients make career choices. Today a client with the same name as yours (a truly curious coincidence!) came to your office and asked for help deciding between two careers, careers that you yourself had been interested in (an even greater coincidence!).

Your task: Do some research on the two careers and then prepare a short report that your client can study. Your report should compare at least five major areas, such as salary, working conditions, and education required. Interview the client to understand her or his personal preferences regarding each of the five areas. For example, what is the minimum salary the client will accept? By comparing the client's preferences with the research material you collect, such as salary data, you will have a basis for concluding which of the two careers is best. The report should end with a career recommendation.

6. Selling overseas: Research report on the prospects for marketing a product in another country Select (a) a product and (b) a country. The product might be a novelty item that you own (an inexpensive but accurate watch or clock, a desk organizer, or a coin bank). The country should be one that you are not now familiar with. Imagine that you are with the international sales department of the company that manufactures and sells the novelty item and that you are proposing to make it available in the country you have selected.

The first step is to learn as much as possible about the country where you plan to market the product. Check almanacs and encyclopedias for the most recent information, paying particular attention to descriptions of the social life of the inhabitants and their economic conditions. If your library carries the *Yearbook of International Trade Statistics, Monthly Bulletin of Statistics,* or *Trade Statistics* (all put out by the United Nations), you may want to consult them. Check the card catalog and recent periodical indexes for sources of additional information; look for (among other matters) cultural traditions that would encourage or discourage use of the product. If you have online access, check both Web sites and any relevant databases you can find.

Your task: Write a short report that describes the product you plan to market abroad, briefly describes the country you have selected, indicates the types of people in this country who would find the product attractive, explains how the product would be transported into the country (or possibly manufactured there if materials and labor are available), recommends a location for a regional sales center, and suggests how the product should be sold. Your report is to be submitted to the chief operating officer of the company, whose name you can either make up or find in a corporate directory. The report should include your conclusions (how the product will do in this new environment) and your recommendations for marketing (steps the company should take immediately and those it should develop later).

---

7. The new way to advertise: Report summarizing Internet demographics The number of Internet users continues to grow rapidly in the United States and around the world. For marketers, the Internet represents a veritable gold mine of potential customers. Unlike traditional print and broadcast media, an Internet site can be seen around the world at any time. The trick, however, is to get your target customers to take the time to visit your page.

As marketing strategist for a specialty foods mail-order company, you have been toying with the idea of going online for quite some time. Your company, Martha's Kitchen, has been selling its cakes, cheeses, fruit, and candy in printed catalogs for a little over a decade and has built up a loyal clientele. Most of your customers are affluent adults age 30 and over, and 75 percent of them are women. Of course, large portions of your sales come during the holidays.

As more and more customers ask about ordering on the Internet, you feel compelled to establish an Internet presence. Nevertheless, you have heard conflicting reports about whether companies actually make any money by selling over the Internet. Moreover, developing a top-notch Web site will likely cost a lot of money. How can you sort through the hype to find real answers?

Your task: Write a short formal report to the director of marketing explaining whether Martha's Kitchen should develop an Internet presence. You will need some solid figures about the demographics of Internet users, their surfing habits, the types of products they purchase online, and growth trends in online commerce. The following are good resources to help you get started.

- http://www.greenfieldcentral.com/dlrci/index.html
- http://www.nservices.com/internet.htm
- http://www.wilsonweb.com/webmarket/demograf.htm

These sites also contain links to other sites with additional useful information. As background, you may also find it helpful to look at some competitors' sites, such as Harry and David http://www.harryanddavid.com and Norm Thompson http://www.normthompson.com.

On the basis of your findings, how do you think an Internet site will improve the company's bottom line? Use your imagination to fill in the details about the company.

---

8. Hitting your target: Report on print advertising You are the manager of Le Couturier, an upscale women's clothing boutique that is part of a three-store chain in your area. Kathleen Bale, the owner, has decided to place print advertisements in local newspapers or other publications to increase her clientele. She has determined that the target market is educated women aged 30 or older with a higher-than-average household income. She has also determined that her competition includes other women's clothing boutiques and department stores.

Bale asks for your help in determining which local publication would best enable her to reach her target market. She would also like to know in which part of the publication to place the advertisement.

Your task: Visit your local library or newsstand and browse through the local newspapers and magazines. Identify (a) which publications are most likely to be read by your upscale clientele, (b) which publication(s) your competitors advertise in the most, (c) which other types of businesses generally advertise in each of the publications you've selected, and (d) which sections would be most widely read by your target market (for example, a fashion section). Browse through several issues of each publication to identify any patterns or changes.

Draft a formal report to Kathleen Bale that contains the results of your research and your conclusions and recommendations. If the report is successful, Le Couturier should be able to choose the appropriate publication in which to place its advertisements to reach new customers.

9. Language, literacy, and learning: Report on the need for English courses You are the program coordinator for the Literacy Learning Center (LLC), a neighborhood-based, not-for-profit organization that offers basic reading, writing, and computer skills to adult learners. Recently, a large number of non-native English speakers have come in requesting English-as-a-second-language (ESL) courses. Although the LLC does not currently offer such courses, they do seem to fit with the organization's mission of providing literacy skills that enable all people to fully participate in U.S. society. In addition, recent data collected by the city suggest that roughly 4 percent of the local population possess "limited English skills." Therefore, program director Anne Helmholz has asked you to further investigate the option of offering ESL classes.

Your task: Identify the current availability of ESL classes in your area. You might begin by looking in the Yellow Pages, contacting local community colleges, or searching the Internet. Find out which organizations offer ESL classes, as well as class times, cost, skill level, and frequency. Plot the locations of the classes on a map of your city and identify how accessible they are by public transportation to the different city neighborhoods.

Prepare a short formal report that summarizes your findings. On the basis of your research, make a recommendation as to whether the LLC should or should not offer ESL courses.

LONG FORMAL REPORTS REQUIRING NO ADDITIONAL RESEARCH

10. Software in a hard market: Report on selling software in China Breaking into the U.S. software market can be tough, especially when your product competes with well-known brands in

TABLE 15.11

PROFILES OF CHINA'S CONSUMERS

Market Segment	Nouveau Riche (Baofahu)	Yuppies (Dushi Yapishi)	Salary Men (Gongxin Jieceng)	Working Poor (Qionglaogong)
Size	200,000	60 million	330 million	800 million
Geographic location	Coastal urban areas	Major urban areas	Urban areas	Rural areas, small towns, urban areas
Average annual household income (in $U.S.)	Over $5,000	$1,800–$5,000	$1,150–$1,799	Less than $1,150
Age	30–65	25–45	18–60	15–65
Highest level of education	Various levels	College	High school	Elementary school
Type of employment	Commercial/ entrepreneurial, entertainment government	Managerial, professional, technical	Low-skilled office work, factory work, teaching	Manual labor, farming, migrant work
Lifestyle characteristics	Wheeling and dealing, wining and dining	Frequent travel and dining out	8-to-5 daily workweek, limited budget, few purchases	Struggling to make ends meet
Consumer readiness	High	Moderate	Low	Minimal
Innovativeness	Trend setters	Opinion leaders	Emulators	Laggards
Risk aversion	Low	Moderate	High	Very high

established categories. As marketing director for a small (22 employees) developer of financial management software, you are keenly aware of how difficult it is to take on domestic market leaders such as Quicken and Microsoft Money. Fortunately, you also know that greater opportunities may exist for you in international markets.

Your company is considering marketing its product in China, where consumers are less brand loyal and more likely to try new products. The Chinese economy has boomed over the past decade, growing at a rate of 9 percent per year. Research also indicates that a growing percentage of China's 1.2 billion consumers make more money today than ever before. In addition, software sales in China totaled $1.35 billion in 1997, representing a 23 percent jump over the previous year, and analysts expect the growth to continue. Because your product can be used for both business and home financial management, China looks like a ripe market.

Of course, the Chinese market also has its problems. Economic growth slowed this past year to about 7 percent, and studies show that consumers are feeling a sense of uncertainty as a result of volatility in Asian markets. Consumer saving this year is up 17 percent over last year, while retail sales growth has slowed from almost 40 percent to just under 10 percent.

On the other hand, the new financial concerns of Chinese consumers might actually present an opportunity for your company. After all, you are marketing software to help consumers and businesses manage their money more wisely. Greater concerns may be adapting your product to the Chinese language and competing with local companies. For example, one Chinese firm, User Friend, markets an accounting software package that commands 40 percent of the market. Another concern is avoiding software piracy. China has a reputation for being lax about enforcing patent and copyright laws. According to a 1997 study by the Business Software Alliance and the Software Publisher's Association, 96 percent of all software units in use in China are pirated.

TABLE 15.12

SELECTED RESPONSES TO A SURVEY OF 800 URBAN CONSUMERS IN CHINA

Purchase Practices of Respondents	Percent
Plan to buy or replace a personal computer in the next 3 years	26
Always look for new products when they shop	75
Try to cut down on expenses wherever they can	68
Saving more than they did a year ago	58
Try to buy Chinese brands whenever they can	71

TABLE 15.13

KEY CHINA ECONOMIC SECTORS AS A PERCENTAGE OF GDP

Sector	1976	1986	1996	1997
Agriculture	33.2%	27.1%	20.2%	19.7%
Industry (all)	42.3	44.0	49.0	50.8
Manufacturing industry	30.1	35.5	38.1	39.5
Services	24.5	28.9	30.8	29.5

Your task: Write an analytical report on the current market conditions in China. Make a recommendation as to whether your company should attempt to sell its financial management software in China. You have already gathered a lot of data from different sources (see Tables 15.11–15.14 and Figures 15.7–15.9). Now you must interpret the data and make clear recommendations. Identify your target customer and make projections about how much software you think the company can sell over the next three years. Assuming that the product sells for the equivalent of $45, how much revenue do you expect the Chinese market to generate for your company?[8]

11. Competitive crisis: Report on strategy to beat the competition As the regional manager of operations for Willco, a multistate chain of large hardware and home improvement stores, you are heavily involved in strategic planning. You are concerned because Home Depot recently began opening its hardware megastores in the larger markets in your state. Willco has had a loyal customer base for several years, but now, many customers are now migrating to Home Depot. To overcome this competitive challenge, Willco's management team feels that it must beat Home Depot in price, selection, or customer service.

As a first step, Willco recently conducted market research in your state to determine which factors have the greatest influence on where customers shop for hardware and building materials. The company surveyed 1,000 customers around the state who said they shop at both Willco and Home Depot. The results of this research are summarized in Tables 15.15 and 15.16.

Your task: Prepare a report that explains the data collected in Willco's market research. On the basis of the data, recommend whether Willco should attempt to compete with Home Depot on price, selection, or customer service. This will be a preliminary report, so in-depth strategies and their implementation will be the subject of future research. You might offer some initial suggestions for strategies to make Willco more competitive in the area you choose, but keep in mind that additional research will be necessary before a strategy can be developed. (For the purposes of

TABLE 15.14

ADDITIONAL ECONOMIC INDICATORS FOR CHINA

($ U.S. billions)	1976	1986	1996	1997
Gross domestic product (GDP)	148.8	295.7	825.0	935.0
Gross domestic investment/GDP	28.4	37.7	39.2	38.2
Gross domestic savings/GDP	29.0	35.2	41.3	42.2
($ U.S. millions)				
Exports of goods and services	7,383	29,583	171,700	207,800
Imports of goods and services	7,125	37,472	154,100	167,200

Source: U.S. Department of Commerce, *Big Emerging Markets Information Resource Page*, http://www.ita.doc.gov/bems/index.html, 28 August 1998, accessed 1 December 1998.

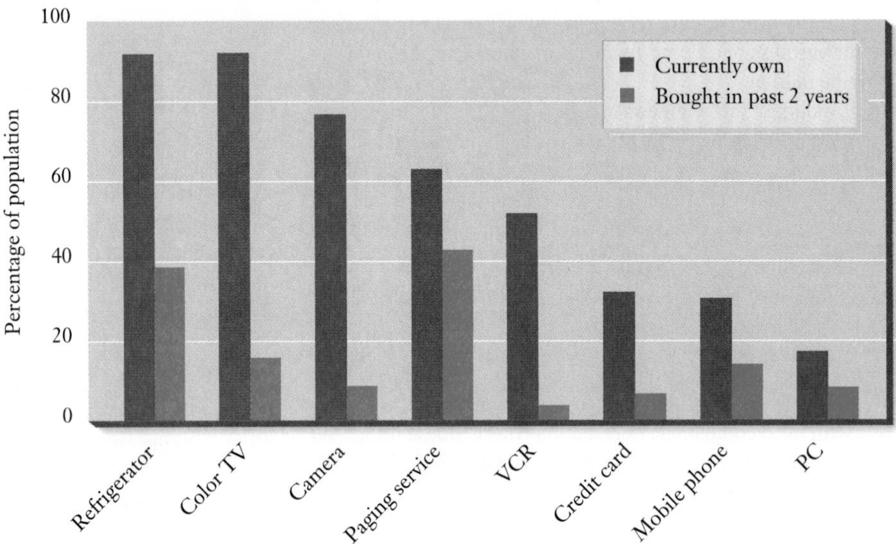

Figure 15.7
Percentage of Population That Uses Selected Durable Products, Beijing, Shanghai, Chengdu, and Guangzhou (major urban centers), 1998

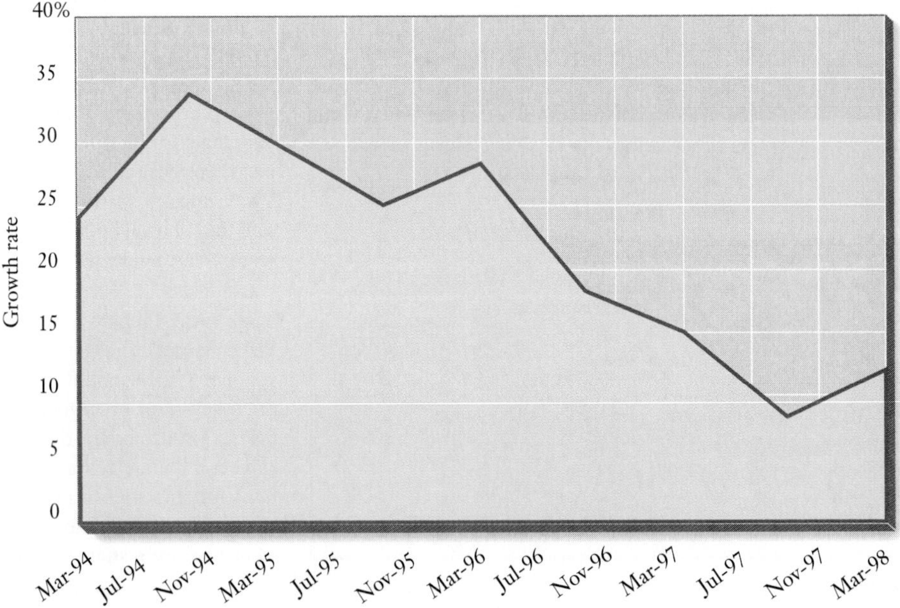

Figure 15.8
China's Retail-Sales Growth Rate

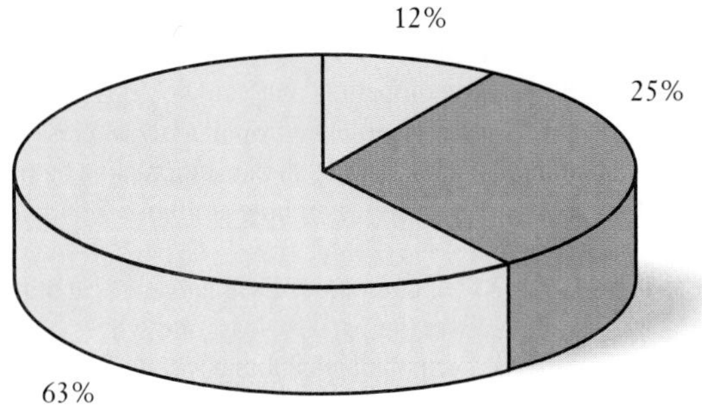

Figure 15.9
Software Market in China, 1997 (total software sales $1.35 billion)

this exercise, feel free to make up any facts you need regarding the company.)

LONG FORMAL REPORTS REQUIRING ADDITIONAL RESEARCH

12. Equipment purchase: Report on competitive product features Business is great at Dixie Electric Supply, a wholesaler of electrical equipment to building contractors, mines, high-tech manufacturers, and other businesses. The company plans to add ten new sales representatives this year, and it will supply each of them with a company car. As the fleet manager, you are assigned to determine which of six cars will give you the most bang for your buck. Fortunately, *Consumer Reports, Motor Trend,* and other magazines publish annual reviews of each of these vehicles:

- Ford Taurus
- Chevrolet Lumina
- Chrysler LHS
- Toyota Camry
- Nissan Altima
- Honda Accord

Your task: Write a long formal report to the purchasing manager describing the features of the above vehicles, listing the benefits and drawbacks of each, and making a clear recommendation. Be sure to include a discussion of the factors on which you've based your decision (including cost, reliability, resale value, fuel economy, and so on).

13. Is there any justice? Report critiquing legislation Plenty of people complain about their state legislators, but few are specific about their complaints. Here's your chance.

TABLE 15.15

FACTORS PEOPLE CONSIDER WHEN DECIDING WHERE TO SHOP FOR HARDWARE AND BUILDING MATERIALS

Factor	Percentage Who Said "Very Important"or "Important"
Selection	83%
Price	60
Knowledge level of staff	85
Courteousness of staff	79
Exchange/return policy	54
Sales/promotions	35
Quality of products	90
Store design (easy to find things)	75

TABLE 15.16

PERCENTAGE OF SHOPPERS WHO THINK HOME DEPOT OR WILLCO PERFORMS THE BEST IN THESE CATEGORIES

Category	Home Depot	Willco	The Two Are Equal
Selection	90%	7%	3%
Price	20	70	10
Knowledge level of staff	12	8	80
Courteousness of staff	18	19	63
Exchange/return policy	25	25	50
Sales/promotions	46	32	22
Quality of products	18	8	77
Store design (easy to find things)	35	25	40

Your task: Write a long formal report about a law that you believe should not have been enacted or should be enacted. Be objective. Write the report using specific facts to support your beliefs. Reach conclusions and offer your recommendation at the end of the report. As a final step, send a copy of the report to an appropriate state official or legislator.

14. Travel opportunities: Report comparing two destinations You are planning to take a two-week trip abroad sometime within the next year. Because there are a couple of destinations that appeal to you, you are going to have to do some research before you can make a decision.

Your task: Prepare a lengthy comparative study of two countries that you would like to visit. Begin by making a list of important questions you will need to answer. Do you want a relaxing vacation or an educational experience? What types of services will you require? What will your transportation needs be? Where will you have the least difficulty with the language? Using resources in your library, the Internet, and perhaps travel agencies, analyze the suitability of these two destinations with respect to your own travel criteria. At the end of the report, recommend the better country to visit this year.

15. Group effort: Report on a large-scale topic The following topics may be too big for any one person, yet they need to be investigated.

a. The success or failure of campaigns aimed at decreasing crime in your community
b. The quality and comprehensiveness of health benefits offered by the top employers in your area
c. The average amount of annual donations received by different social services agencies in your community
d. The percentage of people in your community who use public transportation and the frequency of use for each type
e. The attitudes students at your school have toward recycling
f. The number of small businesses in your community and the implications for your local economy
g. The availability and cost of retail space in the key retail areas of your city

Your task: Because these topics require considerable research, your instructor may wish to form groups to work on each. For all of the topics, be sure to reach conclusions and make recommendations in your report.

16. Secondary sources: Report based on library research Perhaps one of the following questions has been on your mind.

a. Which is the best college at which to pursue a graduate degree in business?
b. How can you organize a student group to make your campus safer at night?
c. Which of three companies that you would like to work for has the most responsible environmental policies?
d. What market factors led to the development of a product that you use frequently, and how are those factors different today?
e. Which three U.S. companies have had the best stock price performance over the past 30 years and why?
f. What are the best small-business opportunities available today?

Your task: Answer one of those questions, using secondary sources for information. Be sure to document your sources in the correct form. Give conclusions and recommendations in your report.

17. Doing business abroad: Report summarizing the social and business customs of a foreign country Your company would like to sell their products overseas. Before they begin negotiating on the international horizon, however, management must have a clear understanding of the social and business customs of the foreign countries where they intend to do business.

Your task: Choose a non-English-speaking country, and write a long formal report summarizing the country's social and business customs. Review Chapter 3 and use that chapter's Checklist for Doing Business Abroad as a guide for the types of information you should include in your report.

FORMAL PROPOSALS

18. Brewing up sales: Proposal to supply coffee to Peter's Doughnuts You are the president of Lighthouse Roasters, a small but growing coffee-roasting company. The company has made a name for itself by offering fresh, dark-roasted gourmet coffees. However, unlike Starbuck's and other competitors, Lighthouse Roasters does not operate its own stores. Instead, it sells roasted gourmet coffee beans to retailers such as restaurants, bakeries, and latte carts. These retailers then use the Lighthouse beans to make their coffee beverages.

Lighthouse's total cost to produce a pound of roasted gourmet coffee is $2.75. The company wholesales its roasted gourmet beans for an average price of $4.50 per pound. Competitors who sell nongourmet variety coffees typically charge about $3.00 per pound. However, the average price of a gourmet coffee beverage is $1.50, about $.50 more than beverages made with regular coffee (including both brewed coffee and espresso drinks). Each pound of coffee yields about 40 beverages.

Peter's Doughnuts, which owns 76 doughnut shops across 13 states, has seen its sales decline in recent months after Starbucks began opening stores in Peter's markets. Starbucks not only sells gourmet coffee, it carries a selection of delicious pastries that offer alternatives to doughnuts. Peter's management figures that by offering gourmet coffee, it will win back customers who like doughnuts but who also want darker-roasted coffees. Therefore, Peter's has invited you to submit a proposal to be its exclusive supplier of coffee. Peter's anticipates that it will need 400 pounds of coffee a month during the colder months (October–March) and 300 pounds during the warmer months (April–September). The company has said it wants to pay no more than $3.75 per pound for Lighthouse coffee.

Your task: Using your imagination to supply the details, write a proposal describing your plan to supply the coffee. Considering your costs, will you meet Peter's pricing demands, or will you attempt to gain a higher price?

19. Location is everything: Proposal to share retail space The average person in the United States eats at a fast-food restaurant six times a month. Research shows that factors influencing customer selection of fast-food restaurants include quality of food, speed of service, and menu selection. However, convenient location is the number one factor. This conclusion is reinforced by McDonald's own research, which shows that 75 percent of customers decide to eat at a McDonald's only five minutes before making their purchase.

McDonald's U.S. expansion slowed by a third in the early 1990s as the number of prime locations for its stores withered and competitors stepped up their own expansion efforts. As a result, McDonald's market share began to decline. To reverse the situation, the company began looking at smaller, nontraditional locations that were more conveniently located. In addition to opening these smaller, stand-alone stores, McDonald's began opening locations inside other retail businesses, such as Wal-Mart and Home Depot stores and Amoco and Chevron gas stations. These locations usually offer a limited menu of McDonald's most popular items. Nevertheless, many of the co-located stores serve just as many customers as traditional McDonald's stores. The reason? Shoppers get the food they want when they want it most, without having to make a separate stop. As an added benefit, McDonald's is able to share some of the costs normally associated with opening a new location.

As the director of retail development for Safeway Food Stores, you are intrigued by McDonald's new growth strategy. Research shows that the amount of every food dollar that consumers spend in grocery stores has fallen from $.70 to $.55 in the last 30 years. This drop is largely because customers are busier than ever before. As a result, they are purchasing more prepared foods, such as those offered by restaurants. Opening McDonald's locations in Safeway stores might be a great partnership for both companies. Safeway could benefit by luring customers who are seeking hot, ready-to-eat foods. At the same time, co-locating would offer McDonald's access to customers who have already made a stop to buy grocery items. However, there are also many issues to consider, such as the amount of counter space available, whether to offer seating (space in grocery stores is typically quite expensive), how to share costs, whether offering McDonald's food will cannibalize other Safeway food sales, how to share store signs, hours of operation (some Safeway stores are open 24 hours a day), compatibility of company images, and cleanliness standards.

Your task: Write a proposal to share retail space and direct it to Thomas Glasgow, McDonald's chief operating officer. Highlight the ways in which the partnership can benefit both companies. In addition, address any concerns that could limit the success of the partnership, and suggest ways to overcome them. Use your imagination to supply the details.[9]

20. Creative marketing: Proposal to sell educational/advertising materials to schools Reaching children poses significant challenges to marketers because children typically don't listen to the radio or read magazines or newspapers. They do watch television, but television ads can be very expensive. However, companies that market products to children have a new opportunity to get their messages out, thanks to Jeff Lederman. His company, Planet Report, targets youngsters by placing ads where they are most likely to be noticed—in the classroom. The ads are part of teaching materials that Planet Report distributes free to schools. These materials usually take the form of posters displaying information about current events. Each month, the company sends teachers a new poster containing tidbits of current news items and facts about science, politics, and culture. Along with this information are attractive ads for Disney movies, ABC television programs, Vans sneakers, and other products that appeal to young consumers. Lederman and an employee create two versions of each poster, one aimed at high school students and the other at elementary or middle school students. Teachers who use the posters also receive prepared questions they can use to test the students on the information in the posters. Besides questions about the factual information on the posters, the tests contain questions about the ads. Planet Report also distributes bookmarks with ads printed on them that teachers can give out as prizes or awards.

At a time when schools are facing tough financial constraints, Planet Report's strategy can be a real win-win situation. "Teachers get something they can use and a marketing purpose is served," says Lederman. Many teachers like the posters because they encourage students to read and learn. As one teacher who uses the posters says, "Whatever we can get that encourages voluntary reading is a plus."

However, not everyone supports the idea. Critics say that ads don't belong in the classroom. They complain that the posters distract students from their studies and encourage a commercial culture. Moreover, including test questions on the commercial content of the posters may cause confusion about what is most important for students to learn. One fourth-grade teacher points out that his students rarely miss questions about the ads, but they are likely to forget some of the other information.

Your task: Write a proposal that Jeff Lederman can use to convince school administrators to adopt Planet Report's posters in their schools. Provide details such as how the posters will benefit students. Keep in mind that not everyone supports the idea of advertising in schools, even if it is linked to effective learning materials. How will you address the concerns of your critics and convince your audience that your product is good for both students and schools?[10]

---

21. Put me in, Coach: Proposal to provide executive coaching services In today's fast-paced business world, companies are spending increasing sums of money on employee training and development. As part of this trend, many companies are turning to executive coaches to help make their managers more effective and productive. Coaches work with employees both one-on-one and in groups. They may provide guidance on how to communicate more effectively, build stronger leadership abilities, work with teams, develop career goals that mesh with company goals, embrace change, and develop the additional skills they need to move up the corporate ladder. Many companies offer coaching as a perk to managers. Some, such as financial services giant Chase Manhattan, even tie coaching to employee performance reviews. What's more, companies are willing to pay anywhere between $75 and $400 an hour for a coach's services.

Jean Isberg is an executive coach who has been increasing her clientele steadily for almost a decade. Isberg, a former sales executive in the information technology field, made a career change in the early 1990s by opening her own sales training business. After a while, she noticed that she was most effective at helping her clients understand themselves and their role in their organizations. Following her talents, Isberg began to coach executives about how to be more effective in their lives and in their work. Soon she began to focus exclusively on coaching female executives, and she named her company Executive Coaching for Women.

Isberg meets with her clients over a nine-week period in sessions lasting 60 to 90 minutes. She also gives reading, writing, and thinking exercises to be completed between sessions. And once each quarter, clients are invited to participate in group review sessions. Isberg tells her clients that to reach their career goals, they must know what they really want, make sure they have the training necessary to make their goals realistic, let others know they are capable, and let others help them achieve success.

Isberg operates her business from her home, renting office and conference space for meetings as needed. But low overhead doesn't necessarily mean a low price; Isberg's services start at $3,000.

Until now, Isberg has counseled clients on a one-on-one basis, with the client paying the cost herself. However, one of Isberg's clients, the vice president of marketing and sales at international telecommunications company Cable & Wireless USA, is so pleased with the coaching she received that she has asked Isberg to submit a proposal to provide coaching services to the company's top female managers. The client believes that many of these managers have yet to realize their full potential in their work and that with Isberg's help, they will become far more effective managers. However, Isberg will need a top-notch proposal in order to get the rest of the company's top brass to buy in and foot the bill. Isberg has delegated the task of drafting the proposal to you, her business development coordinator.

Your task: Jean Isberg has given you the important information about her skills and about the clients she is seeking. Now she needs you to draft a proposal that will land her the Cable & Wireless contract. Give special consideration to how you can help Isberg distinguish herself from other executive coaches the company has dealt with. Use your imagination to fill in the details.[11]

---

22. Competitive crisis: Proposal to win back customers Willco is the chain of hardware stores whose customer defections to Home Depot were the subject of case 11. After the company president read your report, she agreed that something must be done immediately to win back old customers and to stop current customers from defecting.

Your task: Write a proposal to implement the strategy you recommended in your report (competing on price leadership, best selection, or excellent customer service). For the purposes of this exercise, assume that Willco has conducted additional research based on your preliminary report, and use your imagination to supply facts that will back up your proposal. Focus on immediate measures to minimize customer defections as well as on a long-term plan to win customers back. Consider all aspects of the potential solution, including changes in the company's culture and changes to daily operations, employee hiring and training, store design, and so on. Some library research will help you find examples of companies that have overcome challenges from tough competitors.

GIVING SPEECHES AND ORAL PRESENTATIONS

AFTER STUDYING THIS CHAPTER, YOU WILL BE ABLE TO

1. Identify four basic purposes for giving a speech or presentation
2. Name the five elements that go into planning your speech or presentation
3. Discuss one benefit and one challenge of using the oral communication channel
4. Explain three important goals you must accomplish in the introduction of your speech or presentation
5. Describe three ways to hold your audience's attention
6. List at least eight techniques for overcoming anxiety

COMMUNICATION CLOSE-UP AT ANDERSON BUSINESS RESOURCES

When Leanne Anderson prepares a speech, she doesn't worry about whether her audience is going to like her. Instead she focuses on whether she will offer useful information to her audience. As the owner of Anderson Business Resources, she helps businesspeople enhance their image and become better public speakers. Whether Anderson is speaking to an audience in Bangkok about how to do business in the United States, consulting with clients on how to project a favorable image, or lecturing to college students about how to survive after they graduate, Anderson always focuses on giving something of value to her audience.

In fact, Anderson believes that knowing your audience is the most important element of a successful speech. "If you don't know whom you are talking to," she says, "the content becomes much less important and your message won't be heard." Anderson learned this lesson firsthand when delivering a speech in Cairo about improving corporate image. "I spent too much time on domestically oriented topics," she recalls, "so my message wasn't global enough for the audience." Anderson admits that doing more homework in advance would have allowed her to better meet the audience's needs. By understanding the members of your audience, "you can create examples specifically for them, personalize your message, avoid sensitive topics, and appeal to the most important issues on their minds."

Leanne Anderson

Of course, it also helps to be familiar with who else is speaking, the room setup, and so on. Anderson learned this the hard way when she once had the difficult task of delivering a speech immediately after a talk by presidential candidate Ross Perot. He was a tough act to follow, and Anderson was not prepared. Now Anderson tries to find out about the other speakers in advance—especially their styles and messages. This preparation allows her to tailor her own presentation so that it is fresh and interesting for the audience. "If you follow a great speaker and you don't have that same punch," she advises, "don't compete—be different."

No matter what personal or professional goals you set, you can use public speaking to make a difference.

Anderson is fond of using anecdotes, stories, quotations, and statistics to distinguish herself and hold her audience's attention. Another favorite tactic is to get her audience to participate in the presentation by asking questions or soliciting opinions. "If you ask their opinions," she says, "99 times out of 100 they'll go along with what you have to say." Soliciting audience input can also build a speaker's own credibility. Anderson advises that if you don't know as much about a topic as the audience does, "admit it so that you give credit to their own knowledge." Then you can tell the audience about your own expertise and how it can build on theirs.

Anderson also advocates being a ruthless editor. "Most of us fall in love with our own words, and our presentations get too long and complicated. A good speech is built on an intriguing introduction, a substantive body, and a memorable conclusion." That's why she advises speakers to eliminate anything that is not absolutely necessary. Anderson organizes her speech by creating a storyboard, much as advertisers do when developing a commercial. This approach allows her to examine each part of the speech and determine whether and how it is related to her core message. If it isn't relevant, she cuts it. "Economy of language is the real key to good communication," she says. "That means choosing the best way of saying something to get the desired result."

In fact, getting results is one of the many reasons Anderson's clients seek her advice. "If entrepreneurs knew how much they could improve the health of their businesses by becoming effective public speakers," she says, "more of them would jump on the bandwagon." So Anderson offers this advice: "Fine-tune your public speaking skills. . . . Don't wing it. Practice at least eight times by yourself and in front of others who will be honest with you. The more you practice, the more confident and relaxed you will be." And to make a really lasting impression, Anderson suggests injecting your personality into the speech. "Have some fun with it. Stop concentrating on 'will they like me?' and instead focus on 'what will they gain from hearing me?' "[1] ■

Speaking and Presenting in a Business Environment

As Leanne Anderson will tell you, giving speeches and oral presentations can be an integral part of your business career. Chances are you'll have an opportunity to deliver a number of speeches and presentations throughout your career. You may not speak before large audi-

The most common business presentation occurs in a conference room in front of a few people.

ences of employees or the media, but you'll certainly be expected to present ideas to your colleagues, make sales presentations to potential customers, or engage in other kinds of spoken communication. In fact, the most common type of business presentation, by far, is one that occurs in a conference room in front of only a few people.[2] Whether you're delivering a speech to associates, giving a formal presentation to clients, or simply explaining how to solve a business problem to your boss, you'll follow three general steps:

Three steps for delivering a speech are
1. Prepare to speak
2. Develop your speech
3. Deliver your speech

1. Prepare to speak (by defining your purpose, analyzing your audience, and planning your speech's content, length, and style).
2. Develop your speech or presentation (including the introduction, body, close, question-and-answer period, and visual aids).
3. Deliver your speech or presentation.

STEP 1: PREPARING TO SPEAK

Preparing speeches and presentations requires some special communication techniques to ensure your audience hears what you say.

Preparing speeches and oral presentations is much like preparing any other business message. However, because speeches and presentations are delivered orally under relatively public circumstances, they require a few special communication techniques. For one thing, a speech is a one-time event; your audience cannot leaf back through printed pages to review something you said earlier. You must make sure that audience members will hear what you say and remember it. To do so, you must capture their interest immediately. Otherwise, you'll lose them, and chances are you won't get them back. So when you prepare your speech or presentation, be sure to define your purpose clearly, analyze your audience as thoroughly as possible, and plan your speech carefully.

Defining Your Purpose

During your career you may be called on to give speeches and presentations for all sorts of reasons. If you're in the human resources department, you may give orientation briefings to new employees or explain company policies, procedures, and benefits at assemblies. If you're a department supervisor, you may conduct training programs. If you're a problem solver or consultant, you may give analytical presentations on the merits of various proposals.

The content and style of speeches and presentations vary, depending on your purpose.

These speeches and presentations can be categorized according to their purpose, which helps you determine content and style. The four basic reasons for giving a speech or presentation are to inform, to persuade, to motivate, and to entertain. Here are sample statements of purpose for business speeches:

- To inform the accounting department of the new remote data-access policy
- To explain to the executive committee the financial ramifications of OmniGroup's takeover offer
- To persuade potential customers that our bank offers the best commercial banking services for their needs
- To motivate the sales force to increase product sales by 10 percent

Many of your business speeches and presentations will be informative; if you're involved in a marketing or sales position, you'll need to do persuasive presentations as well. Motivational speeches tend to be more specialized. Many companies bring in outside speakers who specialize in motivational speaking. Entertainment speeches are perhaps the rarest in the business world; they are usually limited to after-dinner speeches and speeches at conventions or retreats. But no matter which kind of speech you plan to make, you will need to understand your audience in order to be successful.

Analyzing Your Audience

Once you have your purpose firmly in mind, you can think about your audience. As Leanne Anderson points out, analyzing your audience is a particularly important element of your preparation because you'll be gearing the style and content of your speech to your audience's needs and interests. Be sure to review the discussion of audience analysis presented in Chapter 4. Then, as a summary, review this chapter's Checklist for Audience Analysis. For even more insight into audience evaluation (including emotional and cultural issues) consult a good public-speaking textbook.

The nature of the audience affects your strategy for achieving your purpose.

CHECKLIST FOR AUDIENCE ANALYSIS

A. Audience Size and Composition
   1. Estimate how many people will attend.
   2. Consider whether they have some political, religious, professional, or other affiliation in common.
   3. Analyze the mix of men and women, age ranges, socioeconomic and ethnic groups, occupations, and geographic regions represented.

B. Probable Audience Reaction
   1. Analyze why audience members are attending the speech or presentation.
   2. Determine the audience's general attitude toward the topic.
      a. Decide whether the audience is very interested, moderately interested, or unconcerned.
      b. Review how the audience has reacted to similar issues in the past.
      c. Determine which facets of the subject are most likely to appeal to the audience.
      d. Decide whether portions of your message will create problems for any members of the audience.
   3. Analyze the mood that people will be in when you speak to them: tired from listening to other presentations like yours or fresh because your presentation comes early in the agenda; interested in hearing a unique presentation or restless from sitting too long in one position and needing a minute to stretch.
   4. Figure out which sort of backup information will most impress the audience: technical data, statistical comparisons, cost figures, historical information, generalizations, demonstrations, samples, and so on.
   5. Predict audience response.
      a. List ways that the audience will benefit from your message.
      b. Formulate an idea of the most desirable audience reaction and the best possible result (what you want the audience to believe or do afterward).
      c. Anticipate possible objections or questions.
      d. Analyze the worst thing that might happen and how you might respond.

C. Level of Audience Understanding
   1. Determine whether the audience already knows something about the subject.
      a. Analyze whether everybody has about the same amount of knowledge.
      b. Consider whether the audience is familiar with your vocabulary.
   2. Estimate whether everybody is equally capable of understanding the message.
   3. Decide what background information the audience will need to understand the subject.
   4. Think about the mix of general concepts and specific details you will need to explain.
   5. Consider whether the subject involves routine, recurring information or an unfamiliar topic.

D. Audience Relationship with the Speaker
   1. Analyze how this audience usually reacts to speakers.
   2. Determine whether the audience is likely to be friendly, open minded, or hostile toward your purpose.
   3. Decide how the audience is likely to respond to you.
      a. Analyze what the audience expects from you.
      b. Think about your past interactions with the audience.
      c. Consider your relative status.
      d. Consider whether the audience has any biases that might work against you.
      e. Take into account the audience's probable attitude toward the organization you represent.
   4. Decide which aspects of your background are most likely to build credibility.

Gear the content, organization, and style of your message to the audience's size, background, and attitude.

In many cases you'll be speaking to a group of people you know very little about. Of course, you'll have a much better chance of achieving your purpose if you investigate the audience's characteristics before you show up to speak. "Research the audience—tons!" advises Leanne Anderson. If you're involved in selecting the audience, you'll certainly have information about their characteristics. You can also ask your host or some other contact person for help with audience analysis, and you can supplement that information with some educated estimates of your own.

Planning Your Speech or Presentation

What you know about your audience affects your main idea, organization, outline, length, and style.

Planning an oral message is similar to planning a written message: You establish the main idea, organize your message, prepare an outline, estimate the appropriate length, and decide on the most effective style. At every step, your work is driven by what you know about your audience. For example, if you're planning a sales presentation, focus on how much your product will benefit the people in your audience, not on how great the product is. If you're explaining a change in medical benefits for company employees, address the concerns your audience is likely to have, such as cost and quality of care.

Establishing the Main Idea

The main idea points out how the audience can benefit from your message.

What is the main idea, or theme, that you want to convey to your audience? In other words, what's the one message you want the audience to walk away with? Look for a one-sentence generalization that links your subject and purpose to the audience's frame of reference, much as an advertising slogan points out how a product can benefit consumers. Here are some examples:

- Demand for low-calorie, high-quality frozen foods will increase because of basic social and economic trends.
- Reorganizing the data-processing department will lead to better service at a lower cost.
- We should build a new plant in Texas to reduce operating costs and to capitalize on growing demand in the Southwest.
- The new health plan reduces our costs by 12 percent while maintaining quality coverage.

Using the "you" attitude makes your material relevant to your audience and helps keep their attention.

Each of these statements puts a particular slant on the subject, one that is positive and directly related to the audience's interests. This sort of "you" attitude helps keep the audience's attention and convinces people that your points are relevant. For example, a group of new employees will be much more responsive to your discussion of plant safety procedures if you focus on how the procedures can save a life rather than on how the rules conform to Occupational Safety and Health Administration guidelines.

Organizing Your Message

Structure a short speech or presentation like a letter or a memo.

With a well-defined main idea to guide you, you can begin to organize your message. If you have ten minutes or less to deliver your message, organize your thoughts much as you would for a letter or a brief memo: Use the direct approach if the subject involves routine information or good news and use the indirect approach if the subject involves bad news or persuasion. Plan your introduction to arouse interest and to give a preview of what's to come. For the body of the presentation, be prepared to explain the who, what, when, where, why, and how of your subject. In the final paragraph or two, review the points you've made, and close with a statement that will help your audience remember the subject of your speech (see Figure 16.1).

A human resources manager used this outline for a brief speech he delivered to persuade a group of executives to invest in an on-site fitness center for employees.

Figure 16.1
In-Depth Critique: Sample Outline for a Brief Speech

PHYSICAL FITNESS IS GOOD FOR BUSINESS

Purpose: To convince company officers to approve an on-site fitness center.

I. Introduction

Mention the words *computer programmer,* and the picture that comes to mind is a person sitting in a cubicle and pounding away at a keyboard for 12 or more hours a day. This may be the stereotype, but it is outdated. Programmers and employees in general are more and more aware that physical activity makes them healthier, happier, and more productive. Corporations have also learned the benefits of having healthy, fit employees.

This introduction will arouse interest and preview what is coming in the presentation.

II. The most obvious improvement is in lowered health costs. [slides]

A. People who are physically active generally are healthier and take fewer sick days.

B. Increased activity leads to better general health and fewer visits to the doctor, which means lower health insurance costs for the company and less absenteeism.

C. Better physical fitness results in a reduction in work-related injuries.

Items II, III, and IV support the main idea (that an on-site fitness center would be a good investment).

III. Improving employees' physical fitness increases company profitability.

A. Studies show that improved physical fitness increases employee productivity. [slide]

B. Physical activity also increases creativity.

IV. A survey of college seniors showed fringe benefits to be the second most important factor (after salary) **in choosing a company.**

V. Conclusion: Installing an on-site fitness center makes good business sense.

The conclusion will summarize all the evidence that makes the installation of the center such a good business decision.

Longer speeches and presentations are organized like reports. If the purpose is to entertain, motivate, or inform, use direct order and a structure imposed naturally by the subject (importance, sequence, chronology, spatial orientation, geography, or category—as discussed in Chapter 14). If the purpose is to analyze, persuade, or collaborate, organize your material around conclusions and recommendations or around a logical argument. Use direct order if the audience is receptive and indirect if you expect resistance (see Figure 16.2).

Organize longer speeches and presentations like formal reports.

Figure 16.2
In-Depth Critique: Sample Outline for a 30-Minute Presentation

Here is an outline for a 30-minute analytical presentation organized around conclusions and presented in direct order. This outline is based on Chapter 15's Electrovision report, written by Linda Moreno. This presentation follows the same basic organization as the report did.

The overall organization is logical and simple.

The introduction highlights the problem.

Items II through IV explain why the problem exists.

OUR TRAVEL AND ENTERTAINMENT COSTS ARE OUT OF CONTROL

Purpose: To explain why Electrovision's travel and entertainment (T&E) costs are so high and to propose a series of changes to bring them under control.

I. Introduction
Our T&E costs are way above average, and they pose a threat to the company's financial health; fortunately, we can fix the problem in four straightforward steps that could save as much as $6 million a year.

II. How we approached the investigation
- **A. We analyzed internal expense reports.**
- **B. We compared our cost data with nationwide averages.**
- **C. We analyzed published information on trends and cost-control suggestions.**

III. Analysis of spending patterns
- **A. The amount we've been spending on T&E:**
  1. **Airfares, hotels, rental cars, restaurants, and entertainment totaled $16 million last year.**
  2. **T&E budget has increased by 12 percent per year for the past five years.**
- **B. Where that money goes:**
  1. **We took 3,390 trips last year at an average cost per trip of $4,725.**
  2. **Airfares and lodging represent 70 percent of T&E expenses.**
- **C. How our spending compares with national averages:**
  1. **Facilities and customers spread from coast to coast force us to spend a lot on travel.**
  2. **However, we spend 125 percent more than the national average for every travel day.**
- **D. Why do we spend so much?**
  1. **First-class travel has been viewed as compensation for the demands of extensive travel.**
  2. **The sales staff is encouraged to entertain clients.**

(continued)

Of course, you may have to adjust your organization in response to feedback from your audience, especially if your purpose is to collaborate. You can plan ahead by thinking of several organizational possibilities (based on "what if" assumptions about your audience's reactions). Then if someone says something that undercuts your planned approach, you can switch smoothly to another one.

Figure 16.2, continued

3. T&E costs are hard for managers to view and study.
4. No one has central responsibility for controlling costs.

IV. Impact on profits
  A. T&E costs continue to rise, as do other company costs.
  B. Revenue is projected to decline in coming years.
  C. Bottom line: we're headed for trouble.

V. Solution
  A. We should institute tighter spending controls:
    1. Hire a travel manager to control costs and negotiate group discounts.
    2. Develop a formal, written policy to contain costs.
    3. Give departmental managers the data they need to make smarter decisions.
  B. We can reduce unnecessary travel and entertainment costs:
    1. Cut down on discretionary trips (seminars, etc.).
    2. Reduce the number of intracompany trips and employees sent on each trip.
    3. Encourage employees to economize.
  C. We can find lower travel rates:
    1. Negotiate corporate discounts.
    2. Plan trips more carefully to take advantage of lower fares.
  D. We can replace some travel with technological alternatives:
    1. Conference calls
    2. Videoconferences
    3. Other possibilities
  E. Potential impact of all these changes: as much as $6 million in reduced costs

VI. Conclusion
  We spend more on T&E than we should, and four fairly obvious steps will yield significant cost savings.

Item V provides the four-step solution mentioned in the introduction and makes a recommendation for implementing the steps.

Use a clear, direct organization to accommodate your listeners' limitations.

Regardless of the length of your speech or presentation, bear in mind that simplicity of organization is especially valuable in oral communication. If listeners lose the thread of your comments, they'll have a hard time catching up and following the remainder of your message. They can't review a paragraph or flip pages back and forth, as they can when reading. So look for the most obvious and natural way to organize your ideas, using a direct order of presentation whenever possible. Explain at the beginning how you've organized your material, and try to limit the number of main points to three or four—even when the speech or presentation is rather long.

To keep the audience's attention, be sure to include only the most useful, interesting, and relevant supporting evidence. "Ask yourself: 'Is this related to my core message?' "

advises Leanne Anderson. "If it isn't, cut it." In addition, at the end of each section, reorient the audience by summarizing the point you've just made and explaining how it fits into your overall framework.

Preparing an Outline

Use an outline as your "script," but be prepared to deviate in response to audience feedback.

A carefully prepared outline can be more than just the starting point for composing a speech or presentation—it will help you stay on task. You'll use it to make sure your message accomplishes its purpose, is audience centered, and can be delivered in the allotted time. If you plan to deliver your presentation from notes rather than from a written text, your outline can also become your final "script." For this reason the headings on the outline should be complete sentences or lengthy phrases rather than one- or two-word topic headings. Many speakers also include notes that indicate where visual aids will be used. You might also want to write out the transitional sentences you'll use to connect main points. Or you may even want to jot down notes about using a certain tone or body language. Cues such as "Pause here, speak slowly, give extra emphasis," and so on can be helpful when it comes to practicing and delivering your speech.[3] In fact, experienced speakers often use a two-column format that separates the "stage directions" from the content (see Figure 16.3).

Figure 16.3
In-Depth Critique: Excerpt from Sample Outline with Delivery Notes

This excerpt is taken from a presentation that was made to persuade a company's marketing department to reassess its strategies.

The introduction is geared to arouse interest.

Outline items are in complete sentences.

Each slide noted here highlights a point being made and can even be used by the speaker as a prompt during delivery.

The transition leads listeners to the second main point: a view of marketing techniques currently being used.

Slide 1: **Text** Overview	**INTRO:** Have our marketing techniques become stale?
Slide 2: **Web site screen** Highlight first point **Slide 3:** **Bar chart** Internet usage, 1985 to present **Slide 4:** **Bar chart** Internet advertising, 1995 to present **Slide 5:** **Table** Current costs versus Internet marketing estimates	I. The Internet and World Wide Web open up 24 B/B totally new marketing possibilities. A. Usage of the Internet has mushroomed since its introduction. 1. The number of business advertising outlets on the Internet has increased significantly in the last few years. 2. Selling products via the Internet is gaining popularity. B. Marketing via the Internet can increase profitability.
Slide 6: **Text** Preview second point	**Transition:** Compared with the excitement of the Internet, our marketing techniques seem dated.

Estimating Length

You'll need to tailor your material to the time allowed, which is often strictly regulated. You can use your outline to estimate how much time your speech or presentation will take. The average speaker can deliver about 125 to 150 words a minute (or roughly 7,500 to 9,000 words an hour), which corresponds to 20 to 25 double-spaced, typed pages of text per hour. The average paragraph is about 125 to 150 words in length, so most of us can speak at a rate of about one paragraph per minute.

The average speaker can deliver about one paragraph, or 125 to 150 words, in a minute.

Say you want to make three basic points. In a 10-minute speech, you could take about 2 minutes to explain each point, using roughly two paragraphs for each. If you devoted a minute each to the introduction and the conclusion, you would have 2 minutes left over to interact with the audience. If you had an hour, however, you could spend the first 5 minutes introducing the presentation, establishing rapport with the audience, providing background information, and giving an overview of your topic. In the next 30 to 40 minutes, you could explain each of the three points, spending about 10 to 13 minutes on each one (the equivalent of 5 or 6 typewritten pages). Your conclusion might take another 3 to 5 minutes. The remaining 10 to 20 minutes would then be available for responding to questions and comments from the audience.

Which is better, the 10-minute speech or the hour-long presentation? If your speech doesn't have to fit into a specified time slot, the answer depends on your subject, your audience's attitude and knowledge, and the relationship you have with your audience. For a simple, easily accepted message, 10 minutes may be enough. On the other hand, if your subject is complex or your audience is skeptical, you'll probably need more time. Don't squeeze a complex presentation into a period that is too brief, and don't spend any more time on a simple talk than necessary.

Be sure that your subject, purpose, and organization are compatible with the time available.

Deciding on Style

Another important element in your planning is style. Will you present a formal speech in an impressive setting, with professionally produced visual aids? Or will you lead a casual, roll-up-your-sleeves working session? Choose your style to fit the occasion. The size of the audience, the subject, your purpose, your budget, and the time available for preparation all determine the style.

In general, if you're speaking to a relatively small group, you can use a casual style that encourages audience participation. A small conference room, with the audience seated around a table, may be appropriate. Use simple visual aids. Invite the audience to interject comments. Deliver your remarks in a conversational tone, using notes to jog your memory if necessary. This is the approach taken by Edward McQuade, a vice president of Campbell Soup. He prefers a casual style, talking from notes rather than a script and emphasizing his main points by using hand gestures naturally—just as he would in a personal conversation.[4]

Use a casual style for small groups; use a formal style for large groups and important events.

On the other hand, if you're addressing a large audience and the event is an important one, you'll want to establish a more formal atmosphere. A formal style is well suited to announcements about mergers or acquisitions, new products, financial results, and other business milestones. Executives of Hewlett-Packard and other public companies regularly meet with securities analysts to discuss financial performance. Because the analysts are responsible for recommending particular stocks, companies are eager to make a good impression. During these formal presentations, the speakers generally stand on a stage or platform, positioned behind a lectern and using a microphone so that their remarks can be heard throughout the room. These speeches are often accompanied by multimedia presentations showcasing major products, technological breakthroughs, and other information that the speakers want audience members to remember.

In both formal and informal presentations, keep things simple.

Keep in mind that whether you're delivering a formal or an informal speech, you should always choose your words carefully. If you try to impress your audience with obscure or unfamiliar vocabulary, your message will be lost. Keep things simple. Here's a good rule to follow: If you repeatedly stumble over a word as you rehearse, use a different word. In addition, be able to define all the words you use.[5]

STEP 2: DEVELOPING YOUR SPEECH OR PRESENTATION

How formal speeches and presentations differ from formal reports:

- More interaction with the audience
- Use of nonverbal cues to express meaning
- Less control of content
- Greater need to help the audience stay on track

Developing a major speech or presentation is much like writing a formal report, with one important difference: You need to adjust your technique to an oral communication channel, which presents both an opportunity and a challenge. The opportunity lies in the interaction that is possible between you and the audience. When you speak before a group, you can receive information as well as transmit it, which means you can adjust both the content and the delivery of your message as you go along, editing your speech or presentation to make it clearer and more compelling. Instead of simply expressing your ideas, you can draw out the audience's ideas and use them to reach a mutually acceptable conclusion. However, to realize the benefits of oral communication, you need to plan carefully.

The challenge of using an oral communication channel is being able to control what happens. As you develop each part of your speech or presentation, stop and think about how you plan to deliver the information. The more you expect to interact with your audience, the less control you'll have. Halfway through your presentation a comment from someone in the audience might force you to shift topics. If you can anticipate such shifts, you'll have a chance to prepare for them as you develop each part of your speech: the introduction, the body, the close, and the question-and-answer period.

The Introduction

The introduction captures attention, inspires confidence, and previews the contents.

You'll have a lot to accomplish during the first few minutes of your speech or presentation, including arousing your audience's interest in your topic, establishing your credibility, and preparing the audience for what will follow. That's why developing the introduction often requires a disproportionate amount of your attention.

Arousing Interest

Some subjects are naturally more interesting than others. If you will be discussing a matter of profound significance that will personally affect the members of your audience, chances are they'll listen regardless of how you begin. All you really have to do is announce your topic ("Today I'm going to announce the reorganization of the company.").

Connect the topic to the listeners' needs and interests.

Other subjects call for more imagination. How can you get your audience to listen if you're explaining the pension program to a group of new clerical employees, none of whom will be full participants for another five years and most of whom will probably leave the company within two? The best approach to dealing with an uninterested audience is to appeal to human nature. Encourage people to take the subject personally. Show them how they'll be affected as individuals. You might plan to begin your address to new clerical employees like this:

> If somebody offered to give you $200,000 in exchange for $5 per week, would you be interested? That's the amount you can expect to collect during your retirement years if you choose to contribute to the voluntary pension plan. During the next two weeks, you will have to decide whether you want to participate. Although retirement is many years away for most of you, it is an important financial decision. During the next 20 minutes, I hope to give you the information you need to make that decision intelligently.

Experienced speakers always make sure that the introduction matches the tone of the speech or presentation. If the occasion is supposed to be fun, you may begin with something light; but if you're talking business to a group of executives, don't waste their time with cute openings. Avoid jokes and personal anecdotes when you're discussing a serious problem. If you're giving a routine oral report, don't be overly dramatic. Most of all, be natural. Nothing turns off the average audience faster than a trite, staged beginning. (See "Sharpening Your Skills: Tired of Being Ignored? Five Ways Guaranteed to Get Attention and Keep It.")

Match the introduction to the tone of your speech or presentation.

Building Credibility

One of the chief drawbacks of overblown openings is that they damage the speaker's credibility, and building credibility is probably even more important than arousing interest. A speaker with high credibility is more persuasive than a speaker with low credibility.[6] So it's important to establish your credentials—and quickly; people will decide within a few minutes whether you're worth listening to.[7] You want the audience to like you as a person, but more important, you want them to respect your opinion. You have to plan for that response while you're developing your speech.

You have only a few minutes to establish your credibility.

Establishing credibility is relatively easy if you're speaking to a familiar, open-minded audience. The difficulty comes when you try to earn the confidence of strangers, especially those predisposed to be skeptical or antagonistic.

One way to handle the problem is to let someone else introduce you. That person can present your credentials so that you won't appear boastful. However, make sure that the person introducing you doesn't exaggerate your qualifications. Some members of the audience are likely to bristle if you're billed as being the world's greatest authority on your subject.

If you're introducing yourself, plan to keep your comments simple. At the same time, don't be afraid to mention your accomplishments. Your listeners will be curious about your qualifications, so tell them briefly who you are and why you're there. Generally, you need mention only one or two aspects of your background; your position in an organization, your profession, and the name of your company. You might plan to say something like this:

Without boasting, explain why you are qualified to speak on the subject.

> I'm Karen Whitney, a market research analyst with Information Resources Corporation. For the past five years, I've specialized in studying high-technology markets. Your director of engineering, John LaBarre, has asked me to brief you on recent trends in computer-aided design so that you'll have a better idea of how to direct your R&D efforts.

This speaker established credibility by tying her credentials to the purpose of her presentation. By mentioning her company's name, her specialization and position, and the name of the audience's boss, she let her listeners know immediately that she was qualified to tell them something they needed to know. She connected her background to their concerns.

Previewing the Presentation

Giving your audience a preview of what's ahead adds to your authority and, more important, helps them understand your message. A reader can get an idea of the structure of a report by looking at the table of contents and scanning the headings. In an oral presentation, however, the speaker provides the framework. Without cues from the speaker, the audience may be unable to figure out how the main points of the message fit together.

Let the audience know what lies ahead.

In your introduction, summarize your main idea, identify the supporting points, and indicate the order in which you'll develop those points. Tell your listeners in so many words, "This is the subject, and these are the points I will cover." Once you've established the framework, you can be confident that the audience will understand how the individual facts and figures are related to your main idea as you move into the body of your presentation.

SHARPENING YOUR SKILLS

TIRED OF BEING IGNORED? FIVE WAYS GUARANTEED TO GET ATTENTION AND KEEP IT

In any speech or presentation (especially in a long formal one), using attention-getters throughout your speech maintains and revives the audience's interest. Here are five ways to get attention.

1. *Use humor.* The subject of most business presentations is serious. Nevertheless, you can still include a light comment now and then to perk up the audience. Just be sure the humor is relevant to the presentation. However, if you're not comfortable telling jokes, don't try to do it in a speech. Also, be very careful about offending your audience with inappropriate humor.
2. *Tell a story.* Most audiences will pay attention to a story, and you can generally find one that illustrates an important point. A speaker who was trying to explain his company's strategy of buying old, low-priced houses and fixing them up told this story: "One of the first properties we bought was in a very poor part of town, and we had serious reservations about buying it. We were especially worried about the motorcycle tracks on the wall, but we fixed that with a coat of paint. In fact, that house taught me the value of paint in general. Most of our properties don't look like much on the surface, but they are solid underneath. All they need is a few coats of paint, some basic carpentry, new landscaping, and *voilà!* The ugly duckling emerges as a beautiful swan."
3. *Pass around a sample.* Psychologists say that you can get people to remember your points by appealing to their senses. The best way to do that is to pass around a sample. If your company is in the textile business, let the audience handle some of your fabrics. If you sell chocolates, give everybody a taste.
4. *Ask a question.* Asking questions will get the audience actively involved in your speech and, at the same time, will give you information about them and their needs. A securities broker whose presentation was designed to arouse interest in tax-free municipal bonds used these questions at various points in her talk: "How many of you paid over $10,000 in taxes last year?" "What's the biggest risk you run when you invest in common stocks?" "How important is safety to your investment strategy?" "What kind of return do you want on your investments?" These questions made the audience think about what she was saying, and their answers helped her understand them.
5. *State a startling statistic.* People love details. If you can interject an interesting statistic, you can often wake up an audience. In a presentation on opportunities in the computer field, you might say, "Experts estimate that by the turn of the century, 80 percent of the gross domestic product will depend on computers in one way or another."

Regardless of the attention-getters you use, remember to use them in moderation and with good taste. If you're giving a serious business presentation, keep the tone of your remarks on a businesslike level.

---

1. Which of your lecture classes do you enjoy the most? What techniques does the instructor use to keep students interested?
2. Suppose you're giving a presentation on white-collar crime. By using creative thinking or by conducting research, come up with three attention-getters you might use to enliven your talk.

Body

Limit the body to three or four main points.

The bulk of your speech or presentation is devoted to a discussion of the three or four main points in your outline. Use the same organizational patterns you'd use in a letter, memo, or report, but keep things simple. Your goals are to make sure that (1) the organization of your speech or presentation is clear and (2) the speech keeps your audience's attention.

Connecting the Ideas

To show how ideas are related, a written report uses typographical and formatting clues: headings, paragraph indentions, white space, and lists. However, an oral presentation relies on words to link various parts and ideas.

For the small links between sentences and paragraphs, use one or two transitional words: *therefore, because, in addition, in contrast, moreover, for example, consequently, nevertheless, finally*. To link major sections of the speech or presentation, use complete sentences or paragraphs, such as "Now that we've reviewed the problem, let's take a look at some solutions." Every time you shift topics, be sure to stress the connection between ideas. Summarize what's been said, and then preview what's to come.

Help your audience follow your presentation by using clear transitions between sentences and paragraphs, as well as between major sections.

The longer your presentation, the more important the transitions become. If you plan to present many ideas, audience members may have trouble absorbing them and seeing the relationship among them. Your listeners need clear transitions to guide them to the most important points. Furthermore, they need transitions to pick up any ideas they may have missed. If you plan to repeat key ideas in the transitions, you can compensate for lapses in the audience's attention. When you actually deliver your speech, you might also want to call attention to the transitions by using gestures, changing your tone of voice, or introducing a visual aid.

Emphasize your transitions by repeating key ideas, using gestures, changing your tone of voice, or introducing a visual aid.

Holding the Audience's Attention

To communicate your points effectively, you must do more than connect your ideas with clear transitions. You also have to keep the audience's attention. Here are a few helpful tips for developing memorable speeches:

Make a special effort to capture wandering attention.

- *Relate your subject to the audience's needs.* People are interested in things that affect them personally. Plan to present every point in light of the audience's needs and values.
- *Use clear, vivid language.* People become bored quickly when they don't understand the speaker. If your presentation will involve abstract ideas, plan to show how those abstractions connect with everyday life. Use familiar words, short sentences, and concrete examples.
- *Explain the relationship between your subject and familiar ideas.* Plan to show how your subject is related to ideas that audience members already understand so that you give people a way to categorize and remember your points.[8]

Another effective way to hold the audience's attention is to "get them involved," says Leanne Anderson. Ask their opinions or pause occasionally for questions or comments. Audience feedback will help you determine whether the audience understands a key point before you launch into another section; it will also give the audience a chance to switch for a time from listening to participating. Plan your pauses, even going so far as to note them in your outline so that you won't forget to pause once you're on stage. Visual aids will also help clarify points and stimulate interest. Look back at Chapter 12 to review "Designing and Producing Visuals for Oral Presentations." Be sure to include visual aids in your speeches or presentations whenever they're appropriate.

The Close

The close of a speech or presentation is almost as important as the beginning because audience attention peaks at this point. Plan to devote about 10 percent of the total time to the ending. When developing your conclusion, begin by telling listeners that you're about to finish so that they'll make one final effort to listen intently. Don't be afraid to sound obvious. Consider saying something like "in conclusion" or "to sum it all up." You want people to know that this is the home stretch.

The close should leave a strong and lasting impression.

Restating the Main Points

Once you've decided how to announce your close, plan on repeating your main idea. Be sure to emphasize what you want your audience to do or to think, and state the key motivating factor. Finally, plan to reinforce your theme by repeating the three or four main supporting

Summarize the main idea, and restate the main points.

Public speakers sometimes face challenging circumstances. This speaker has to battle crowd noises and other distractions.

DID YOU KNOW?

The two most important parts of your speech are the first 30 seconds and the last 15 seconds. Everything else is utterly forgettable if the presentation starts or ends badly.

points. A few sentences are generally enough to refresh people's memories. Here's how one speaker ended a presentation on the company's executive compensation program:

> We can all be proud of the way our company has grown. If we want to continue that growth, however, we will have to adjust our executive compensation program to reflect competitive practices. If we don't, our best people will look for opportunities elsewhere. In summary, our survey has shown that we need to do four things to improve executive compensation:
>
> - Increase the overall level of compensation
> - Install a cash bonus program
> - Offer a variety of stock-based incentives
> - Improve our health insurance and pension benefits
>
> By making these improvements, we can help our company cross the threshold of growth into the major leagues.

The speaker repeated his four specific recommendations and then concluded with a memorable statement that would motivate the audience to take action.

Describing the Next Steps

Some speeches and presentations require the audience to reach a decision or to agree to take specific action. In such cases the close provides a clear wrap-up. If the audience agrees on an issue covered in the presentation, plan to review the consensus in a sentence or two. If they don't agree, make the lack of consensus clear by saying something like, "We seem to have some fundamental disagreement on this question." Then you'll be ready to suggest a method of resolving the differences.

Be certain that everyone agrees on the outcome and understands what should happen next.

If you expect any action to occur, you must explain who is responsible for doing what. One effective technique is to list the action items, with an estimated completion date and the name of the person responsible. Plan to present this list in a visual aid, and ask each person on the list to agree to accomplish his or her assigned task by the target date. This public commitment to action is the best insurance that something will happen.

BEST OF THE WEB

Speak Like a Pro

The Speaker's Companion Reference Page links you to dozens of sites containing valuable help for business speakers and presenters. If you're stuck for a topic, need a good quote, want some speaking advice, need ideas or support for your ideas, want to link your topic to current events overseas, or just want to browse the latest tips or borrow some techniques from the "experts," click on a few of the links provided here. Your mind will soon be filled with new material, and you'll have renewed enthusiasm for your speaking project.

http://www.1m.com/~chipp/spkrref.htm

If the required action is likely to be difficult, make sure that everyone understands the problems involved. You don't want people to leave the presentation thinking their tasks will be easy, only to discover later that the jobs are quite demanding. If that happens, they may become discouraged and fail to complete their assignments. You'll want everyone to have a realistic attitude and to be prepared to handle whatever arises. So when planning your presentation, use the close to alert people to potential difficulties or pitfalls.

Ending on a Positive Note

Your audience will be more likely to remember your final words if those words are enthusiastic and upbeat.

Make sure that your final remarks are encouraging and memorable. Even if parts of your speech are downbeat, plan to close on a positive note. You might stress the benefits of action or express confidence in the listeners' ability to accomplish the work ahead. An alternative is to end with a question or a statement that will leave your audience thinking.

Remember that your final words round out the presentation. Your task is to leave the audience with a satisfied feeling, a feeling of completeness. The close is not the place to introduce new ideas or to alter the mood of the presentation. And even though you want to close on a positive note, avoid using a staged finale. Keep it natural. As with everything else in your speech, plan your closing remarks carefully. You don't want to wind up on stage with nothing to say but, "Well, I guess that's it."

The Question-and-Answer Period

Along with the introduction, body, and close, be sure to plan for an opportunity for questions and answers. Otherwise, you might just as well write a report. If you don't expect to interact with the audience, you're wasting the chief advantage of an oral format.

In general, the important things to consider when developing your speech are the nature and timing of that audience interaction. (Specifics about handling questions from the audience are discussed next under the heading "Mastering the Art of Delivery.") Responding to questions and comments during the presentation can interrupt the flow of your argument and reduce your control of the situation. If you're addressing a large group, particularly a hostile or an unknown group, questions can be dangerous. Your best bet in such cases is to ask people to hold their questions until after you have concluded your remarks. On the other hand, if you're working with a small group and need to draw out ideas, encourage comments from the audience throughout the presentation.

Encourage questions throughout your speech if you are addressing a small group, but ask a large audience to defer questions until later.

Regardless of when you respond to questions, remember that they're one of the most important parts of your presentation. Questions give you a chance to obtain important information, to emphasize your main idea and supporting points, and to build enthusiasm for your point of view. Try to anticipate as many questions as you can, and rehearse your answers. The more you know about your audience, the better you'll be at anticipating both positive and negative questions.

STEP 3: MASTERING THE ART OF DELIVERY

Once you've planned all the parts of your presentation, including your visual aids, you're ready to begin practicing your delivery. You have a variety of delivery methods to choose from, some of which are easier to handle than others.

- *Memorizing.* Unless you're a trained actor, avoid memorizing an entire speech, particularly a long one. You're likely to forget your lines. Furthermore, a memorized speech often sounds stiff and stilted. And in many business speaking situations, you'll need to address questions and comments from the audience during your speech, so you have to be flexible and sometimes adjust your speech as you go. On the other hand, memorizing a quotation, an opening paragraph, or a few concluding remarks can bolster your confidence and strengthen your delivery.
- *Reading.* If you're delivering a technical or complex presentation, you may want to read it. Policy statements by government officials are sometimes read because the wording may be critical. If you choose to read your speech, practice enough so that you can still maintain eye contact with the audience. Triple-spaced copy, wide margins, and large type help too. You might even want to include stage cues for yourself, such as *pause, raise hands, lower voice*.

Speaking from notes is generally the best way to handle delivery.

- *Speaking from notes.* Making a presentation with the help of an outline, note cards, or visual aids is probably the most effective and easiest delivery mode. It gives you something to refer to and still allows for eye contact and interaction with the audience. If your listeners look puzzled, you can expand on a point or put it another way. (Generally, note cards are preferable to sheets of paper; nervousness is more evident in shaking sheets of paper.)
- *Impromptu speaking.* You might give an impromptu, or unrehearsed, speech in two situations: when you've agreed to speak but have neglected to prepare your remarks or when you're called on to speak unexpectedly. Avoid speaking unprepared unless you've spoken countless times on the same topic or are an extremely good public speaker. When you're asked to speak "off the cuff," take a moment or two to think through what you're going to say. Then avoid the temptation to ramble.

Regardless of which delivery mode you use, be sure that you're thoroughly familiar with the subject. Knowing what you're talking about is the best way to build your self-confidence. It's also helpful if you know how to get yourself ready for successful speaking, to overcome anxiety, to use visual aids, and to handle questions.

Getting Ready to Give Your Presentation

Before you speak
- Practice
- Prepare the location
- Consider cultural differences

In addition to knowing your material, you can build self-confidence by practicing, especially if you haven't had much experience with public speaking. Even if you practice in front of a mirror, try to visualize the room filled with listeners. Put your talk on tape to check the sound of your voice and your timing, phrasing, and emphasis. If possible, rehearse on videotape to see yourself as your audience will. Be sure to include your visual aids and coordinate them with your talk. Practice is crucial to effective speaking, but it isn't the only thing you need to do to get ready to speak.

One way to overcome nervousness is to practice your speech in front of a mirror.

Whenever you can, check the location for your presentation in advance. Look at the seating arrangements, and make sure they're appropriate for your needs. If you want the audience to sit at tables, be sure tables are available. Check the room for outlets that may be needed for your projector or microphone. Locate the light switches and dimmers. If you need a flip-chart easel or a chalkboard, be sure it's on hand. Check for chalk, an eraser, a pointer, extension cords, and any other small but crucial items you might need.

If you're addressing an audience that doesn't speak your language, consider using an interpreter. Working with an interpreter does add some constraints to your presentation—you must speak slowly enough for the interpreter to keep up with you, but not so slowly that the rest of the audience loses interest. Send your interpreter a copy of your speech—and any visual aids—as far in advance as possible. Of course, any time you make a speech or presentation to people from other cultures, you may need to adapt the content of your speech. And just as important, be sure to take into account any cultural differences in appearance, mannerisms, and other customs. If you are working with an interpreter, she or he will be able to suggest appropriate changes for a specific audience or particular occasion. When you're addressing a U.S. or Canadian audience with few cultural differences, follow the specific guidelines in this chapter.

DID YOU KNOW?

Asians are more formal than Westerners; older people are more formal than younger people; people in large organizations are more formal than people in small organizations; people in older industries (such as mining) are more formal than people in newer industries (such as computer technology).

Overcoming Anxiety

A little stage fright is normal.

If you're nervous about facing an audience, you're not alone. Even speakers with years of experience feel some anxiety about getting up in front of an audience (see "Sharpening Your Skills: Nerves Are Normal"). Although you might not be able to make nervous feelings disappear entirely, you can learn to cope with your anxiety. Nervousness shows that you care about the audience, the speech topic, and the occasion. If your palms get wet or your mouth goes dry, don't think of nerves, think of excitement. This approach can give you the energy you need to pep up your planning, preparation, and performance. To harness nervous energy and become a more confident speaker, try these techniques:[9]

Several techniques can help you become a more confident speaker.

- Prepare more material than necessary. Extra knowledge, combined with a genuine interest in the topic, will boost your confidence.

SHARPENING YOUR SKILLS

NERVES ARE NORMAL

What do Barbra Streisand, Willard Scott, Sidney Poitier, and Liza Minelli have in common? All are professional performers, and all admit to being nervous about public speaking. If the pros can feel fear, it's no wonder beginners are sometimes scared speechless. In fact, survey after survey has confirmed that public speaking is the number one fear in the United States—so if you're anxious about stepping in front of an audience, you're not alone.

Nervousness might make your hands tremble, your knees knock, your mouth feel dry, or your stomach churn. As bad as these symptoms can be, remember that nerves are a good indicator of your concern for the occasion, the topic, and the audience. If you didn't care, you wouldn't be anxious. A speaker who cares is more likely to seek out every method of communicating with the audience.

Remember also that you'll feel a little less nervous with every speech. Once you see how the audience responds to your first speech, you'll realize that you did better than you feared you would. Audience members can't see the butterflies fluttering; they're too busy paying attention and responding to your ideas. People in the audience want you to succeed; they're interested in learning from you or being inspired by your words, not in straining to hear the sound of your knees knocking together.

You can harness your nerves by focusing on what you want to accomplish. In the words of actress Carol Channing, "I don't call it nervousness—I prefer to call it concentration." Like Channing, you can concentrate your efforts on making that all-important connection with your audience. But don't make the mistake of expecting perfection. Put that nervous energy into planning, preparing, and practicing, and you'll be better equipped to face your audience, the first time and every time.

---

1. Think of any speeches, lectures, or presentations you've recently attended. Have you ever noticed a speaker's level of anxiety? Were any of the speakers successful in overcoming this fear? As an informed observer, describe the ways in which a particular speaker visibly conquered his or her nervousness. If that speaker failed, what techniques might have helped?
2. As a member of the audience, what can you do to help a speaker overcome his or her nervousness? Briefly explain.

- Rehearse until you're thoroughly familiar with your material.
- Think positively about your audience, yourself, and what you have to say. See yourself as polished and professional, and your audience will too.
- Be realistic about stage fright. After all, even experienced speakers admit that they feel butterflies before they address an audience. A little nervous excitement can actually provide the extra lift that will make your presentation sparkle.
- Visualize success. Use the few minutes while you're arranging your materials, before you actually begin speaking, to tell yourself you're on and you're ready.
- Before you begin to speak, take a few deep breaths.
- Have your first sentence memorized and on the tip of your tongue.
- If your throat is dry, drink some water.
- If you feel that you're losing your audience during the speech, don't panic. Try to pull them back by involving them in the action; ask for their opinions or pause for questions.
- Keep going. Things usually get better, and your audience will silently be wishing you success.

The best technique for overcoming your anxiety is to concentrate on your listeners and on their needs, rather than focusing on yourself.

Perhaps the best way to overcome stage fright is to concentrate on your message and on your audience, not on yourself. When you're busy thinking about your subject and observing the audience's response, you tend to forget your fears. Even so, as you deliver your presentation, try to be aware of the nonverbal signals you're transmitting. To a great degree, your effectiveness will depend on how you look and sound.

Seamless presentations start with your first minute at the podium. So don't rush. As you approach the speaker's lectern, breathe deeply, stand up straight, and walk slowly. Face the audience. Adjust the microphone. Count to three slowly; then survey the room. When you find a friendly face, make eye contact and smile. Count to three again; then begin your presentation.[10] Even if you feel nervous inside, this slow, controlled beginning will help you establish rapport.

Don't rush the opening.

Once your speech is under way, be particularly careful to maintain eye contact with the audience. Pick out several people positioned around the room, and shift your gaze from one to another. Doing this will make you appear to be sincere, confident, and trustworthy; moreover, it will help you perceive the impression you're creating.

Use eye contact, posture, gestures, and voice to convey an aura of mastery and to keep your audience's attention.

Your posture is also important in projecting the right image. Stand tall, with your weight on both feet and your shoulders back. Avoid gripping the lectern. In fact, you might step out from behind the lectern to help the audience feel more comfortable with you and to express your own comfort and confidence in what you're saying. Use your hands to emphasize your remarks with appropriate gestures. Meanwhile, vary your facial expressions to make the message more dynamic.

Finally, think about the sound of your voice. Studies indicate that people who speak with lower voice tones at a slightly faster than average rate are perceived as being more credible.[11] Speak in a normal, conversational tone but with enough volume so that everyone in the audience can hear you. Try to sound poised and confident, varying your pitch and speaking rate to add emphasis. Don't ramble or use meaningless filler words such as *um, you know, okay*, and *like.* Speak clearly and crisply, articulating all the syllables, and sound enthusiastic about what you're saying.

DID YOU KNOW?

Caffeine, found in chocolate, tea, and coffee, is a stimulant and may make you more nervous.

Using Visual Aids Effectively

As discussed in Chapter 12, visual aids can be an effective tool for the speaker as well as for the audience. Use them to guide your speech, in addition to maintaining and reviving audience interest. But be careful. Inexperienced speakers are often afraid of forgetting something, so they put nearly everything they want to say on each slide. As a result, they end up reading slides to the audience and losing their inflection. Furthermore, because they are reading rather than simply talking, their audience skims or ignores wordy slides, perhaps missing the message altogether. In these situations, many members of the audience eventually stop paying attention.[12]

Visual aids help both the speaker and the audience.

Avoid simply reading your visuals.

To make your slides more effective, keep them simple. Remember, if visual aids were meant to do all the communicating, you wouldn't need to speak. In addition, make sure your audience can grasp a visual's message in two or three seconds. If necessary, cull the pile. The fewer the visual aids, the more effective the presentation.[13]

Keep your visuals simple so that your audience can grasp each message in less than three seconds.

When you put up a slide or a transparency, or as you flip your flip chart to the next page, give your audience about five seconds to look at the visual before you start talking. Then introduce it, tell them what it represents, and direct them to the portion you want to talk about. Wait a few seconds for your audience to find your point of reference. If you're using a pointer, remember that it's a tool meant to guide your audience to a specific part of a visual. It is not a riding crop, conductor's baton, leg scratcher, or walking stick. Use the pointer only at the time you need it, then fold it and remove it from sight. If you are using a laser pointer that puts a focused dot of light on the desired part of your visual, don't overdo it. A laser pointer is an excellent tool if used judiciously, but in the hands of the overzealous presenter, it can become a distraction.[14]

Minimize your use of a pointer and remove it from sight when you're not using it.

If you must dim the lights to show your slides or transparencies, be sure to stand in a lighted area, rather than becoming the anonymous "offstage announcer."[15] Once you've finished with a slide, remove it. Try not to switch to the next visual aid right away.

Remember, as you speak, keep your eyes on the audience. Don't talk to the screen. Visual aids don't need your attention, the audience does. Knowing exactly what each slide contains will make it easier for you to keep your eyes on your audience.[16]

Handling Questions

Be ready with answers so that you can

- Emphasize your most important points
- Refer to material that didn't fit in the formal presentation
- Overcome audience resistance

The question-and-answer period is a valuable part of an oral presentation. It gives you a chance to emphasize points you made earlier, work in material that didn't fit into the formal presentation, and identify and try to overcome audience resistance. Many speakers do well delivering their speech or presentation, only to falter during the question-and-answer period. Spend time before your speech thinking about the questions that might arise—including abrasive or difficult ones. Then be ready with answers. In fact, some experts recommend that you hold back some dramatic statistics as ammunition for the question-and-answer session.[17] As mentioned in Chapter 12, you may even want to prepare some visuals in anticipation of your audience's needs for greater detail. However, bear in mind that circumstances may require some changes in the answers you prepare.

Keep your answers short and to the point.

When someone poses a question, focus your attention on that individual. Pay attention to body language and facial expression to help determine what the person really means. Nod your head to acknowledge the question; then repeat it aloud to confirm your understanding and to ensure that the entire audience has heard it. If the question is vague or confusing, ask for clarification. Then give a simple, direct answer. If you're asked to choose between two alternatives, don't feel you must do so. Offer your own choice instead, if that makes more sense. For instance, if someone asks, "Which policy do you favor, salary cuts or layoffs?" you could respond, "As a matter of fact, I don't like either of those solutions, which is why I've put together the proposal I'm presenting this afternoon."[18]

Be sure to answer the question you're asked. Don't sidestep it, ignore it, or laugh it off. Furthermore, don't say more than you need to if you want to have enough time to cover all

Speakers often use question-and-answer sessions to reinforce their ideas and credibility.

the questions. If giving an adequate answer would take too long, simply say, "I'm sorry, we don't have time to get into that issue right now, but if you'll see me after the presentation, I'll be happy to discuss it with you." If you don't know the answer, don't pretend that you do. Instead, say something like, "I don't have those figures. I'll get them for you as quickly as possible." Remember, you don't have to answer every question that is asked.

If the message you delivered is unpopular, be prepared for hostile questions. Treat them as legitimate requests for information. Maintaining your professionalism will improve your credibility.

Maintain control by stating some ground rules in the beginning of the question-and-answer session.

Finally, try to maintain control during the question-and-answer session by establishing some ground rules up front. Announce a time limit or question limit per person before you begin. Establishing limits will protect you from getting into a heated exchange with one member of the audience and from allowing one or two people to monopolize the question period. Give as many audience members as possible a chance to participate by calling on people from different parts of the room. If the same person keeps angling for attention, restate the question limit or say something like, "Several other people have questions; I'll get back to you if time permits."

If audience members try to turn a question into an opportunity to mount their own soapboxes, it's up to you to stay in control. One way to do so is to asking people to identify themselves before they ask questions. People are more likely to behave themselves when everyone present knows their name.[19] Another approach is to admit that you and the questioner have a difference of opinion and offer to get back to the questioner after you've done more research. Then call on someone else. Or you might even respond with a brief answer, thus avoiding a lengthy debate or additional questions.[20] Finally, you could thank the person for the question and then remind the questioner that you were looking for specific questions. Remember, don't indulge in put-downs. They may backfire and make the audience more sympathetic to the questioner.

Respond unemotionally to tough questions.

If a question ever puts you on the hot seat, remember to be honest, but keep your cool. Look the person in the eye, answer the question as well as you can, and try not to show your feelings. Don't get into an argument. Questioners who challenge your ideas, logic, or facts may be trying to push you into overreacting. Defuse hostility by paraphrasing the question and asking the questioner to confirm that you've understood it correctly. Break long, complicated questions into parts that you can answer simply. State your response honestly, accurately, and factually; then move on to the next question. Avoid postures or gestures that might seem antagonistic. Maintain a businesslike tone of voice and a pleasant expression.[21]

In case your audience is too timid or hostile to ask questions, you might want to plant some of your own. If a friend or the meeting organizer gets the ball rolling, other people in the audience will probably join in. You might also ask a question yourself: "Would you like to know more about . . ." If someone in the audience answers, act as if the question came from that person in the first place. When all else fails, say something like, "I know from experience that most questions are asked after the question period. So I'll be around afterward to talk."[22]

When the time allotted for your presentation is up, call a halt to the question-and-answer session, even if more people want to talk. Prepare the audience for the end by saying: "Our time is almost up. Let's have one more question." After you've made your reply, summarize the main idea of the presentation and thank people for their attention. Conclude the way you opened: by looking around the room and making eye contact. Then gather your notes and leave the podium, shoulders straight, head up. (The Checklist for Speeches and Oral Presentations is a reminder of the tasks involved in these types of oral communication.)

Finish up on time—even if people are enthusiastic to continue.

CHECKLIST FOR SPEECHES AND ORAL PRESENTATIONS

A. Planning the Speech or Presentation
  1. Define the purpose.
  2. Analyze the audience.
  3. Establish the main idea.
  4. Prepare an outline.
  5. Estimate the length
  6. Decide on the style.

B. Developing the Speech or Presentation
  1. The introduction
    a. Begin with an attention-getter.
    b. Build credibility.
    c. Preview the main points.
      i. Provide a clear road map.
      ii. Arouse expectations.
  2. The body
    a. Limit discussion to no more than three or four points.
    b. Explain who, what, when, where, why, and how.
    c. Tell the audience what's in it for them.
    d. Connect the ideas.
      i. Vary the transitions by using bridge words, asking questions, or repeating key ideas.
      ii. Reinforce transitions with physical gestures.
      iii. In longer presentations, include previews and summaries of major points as you go along.
    e. Include only the necessary material.
  3. The close
    a. Review the main points and make a memorable statement.
    b. Describe the next steps or assign responsibilities.
    c. End on a positive note.

C. Delivering the Speech or Presentation
  1. Practice, practice, practice.
    a. Establish eye contact.
    b. Speak clearly and distinctly.
    c. Do not go too fast.
    d. Be sure everyone can hear.
    e. Speak in your natural style.
    f. Stand up straight.
    g. Use gestures in a natural, appropriate way.
    h. Stress the most important words and phrases.
  2. Check out the room ahead of time and make sure the equipment works.
  3. Control anxiety and nervousness.
  4. Use visual aids effectively.
    a. Keep information simple and use large, readable type.
    b. Number all slides and transparencies.
    c. Build suspense before using the visual.
    d. Vary your transitions into visuals.
    e. Don't read your visuals—editorialize and enlighten.
    f. Keep your eyes focused on the audience.
  5. Encourage questions.
    a. Prepare for all possible questions and objections.
    b. Respond to questions without getting sidetracked.
    c. Show sufficient knowledge to maintain credibility.
    d. Keep control of the audience and the situation.
    e. Maintain control of your feelings despite criticism.
    f. Use answers to refocus on the theme or message.

COMMUNICATION CHALLENGES AT ANDERSON BUSINESS RESOURCES

Leanne Anderson's expertise as a business consultant and speaker have earned her professional success as well as a busy schedule. Anderson likes to prepare as much of her own speeches as possible. Nonetheless, she sometimes enlists others to help her analyze her audience, organize her message, check facts, and develop visual aids.

Anderson was recently asked to speak at an upcoming conference for small-business owners on the topic of how to deliver an effective presentation. This is a great opportunity for her to network with owners of growing companies who could become clients for Anderson Business Resources. Although she is excited by the opportunity, Anderson has already committed to other speaking engagements around the same time as the conference. It looks as if she will need some help preparing for this one.

INDIVIDUAL CHALLENGE: Anderson has asked you, an intern at Anderson Business Resources, to help her prepare for her speech to the small-business conference. Begin by making a list of the things you must do to prepare for the speech. Be sure to include the things you'll need to learn about the audience. What is the main idea that the speech should convey? What can Anderson do to establish credibility with this audience? Next, develop a rough outline for the speech based on your knowledge of how to deliver effective presentations. (Anderson is an expert on this topic, so your outline should not be overly detailed. Your main concern should be to outline the primary topics that she should address in a half-hour speech.)

TEAM CHALLENGE: In groups of three or more, discuss some of the techniques that Anderson could use to grab and hold her audience's attention during the presentation. Try to come to a consensus about which techniques would be most effective, given the audience and the subject. Then develop some specific ideas for how Anderson might execute the technique (for example, think of some stories, anecdotes, or facts that she could use to relate the material to her audience). Next, discuss some of the questions that might arise from the audience. Share your questions as a class and discuss possible answers as well as techniques for handling especially difficult questions.[23] ■

SUMMARY OF LEARNING OBJECTIVES

1. **Identify four basic purposes for giving a speech or presentation.** The four basic purposes for giving a speech or presentation are (1) to inform, (2) to persuade, (3) to motivate, and (4) to entertain.
2. **Name the five elements that go into planning your speech or presentation.** The five elements that go into planning a speech or presentation are (1) establishing the main idea, (2) organizing the message, (3) preparing the outline, (4) estimating the appropriate length, and (5) deciding on the most effective style.
3. **Discuss one benefit and one challenge of using the oral communication channel.** One benefit of using the oral communication channel is the interaction that is possible between the speaker and the audience, which allows the speaker to draw out and use ideas from the audience. One challenge of using the oral communication channel is controlling the amount of interaction between speaker and audience, thereby controlling what actually happens during the speech or presentation.
4. **Explain three important goals you must accomplish in the introduction of your speech or presentation.** Developing an introduction requires a disproportionate amount of attention because the speaker needs to (1) arouse the audience's interest, (2) establish credibility, and (3) preview the entire presentation.
5. **Describe three ways to hold your audience's attention.** You can hold your audience's attention in three ways: First, you must relate your subject to your audience's needs (people are interested in the things that affect them personally). Second, you must use clear, vivid language (so that listeners don't become bored with vague abstractions, unfamiliar words, or rambling sentences). And third, you must explain the relationship between your subject and familiar ideas (to show how your subject is related to ideas that listeners already understand).
6. **List at least eight techniques for overcoming anxiety.** Eight techniques for overcoming anxiety are (1) preparing more material than is necessary; (2) rehearsing your material; (3) thinking positively about the audience, yourself, and what you have to say; (4) visualizing success; (5) breathing deeply before speaking; (6) memorizing the first sentence of a speech; (7) trying not to panic if you feel you're losing the audience; and (8) persisting until things get better.

CRITICAL THINKING QUESTIONS

1. Would you rather (a) give a speech to an outside audience, (b) be interviewed for a news story, or (c) make a presentation to a departmental meeting? Why? How do the communication skills differ among those situations? Explain.
2. How might the audience's attitude affect the amount of audience interaction during or after a presentation? Explain your answer.
3. Have you ever attended a presentation or a speech in which the speaker's style seemed inappropriate? What effect did that style have on the audience? Briefly explain.
4. What similarities and differences would you expect to see in the introduction to a formal presentation and the introduction to a formal report? Explain.
5. How can you avoid some of the problems that can result from using visual aids during a speech? Briefly explain.
6. From the speaker's perspective, what are the advantages and disadvantages of responding to questions from the audience throughout a speech or presentation? From the listener's perspective, which approach would you prefer? Why?
7. If you were giving a speech on the need for more student parking, how might you make your topic relevant to an audience of neighborhood businesspeople? Please explain.
8. Using the information in this chapter, discuss the meaning of the following quotations.
   a. "Speak clearly, if you speak at all; carve every word before you let it fall."—*Oliver Wendell Holmes*
   b. "It usually takes more than three weeks to prepare a good impromptu speech." —*Mark Twain*

EXERCISES

1. For many years, Toastmasters has been dedicated to helping its members give speeches. Instruction, good speakers as models, and practice sessions aim to teach members to

convey information in lively and informative ways. Visit the Toastmasters Web site at http://www.toastmasters.org and carefully review the linked pages about listening, speaking, voice, and body. Evaluate the information and outline a three-minute presentation to your class telling why Toastmasters and its Web site would or would not help you and your classmates write and deliver an effective speech.

2. Attend a speech at your school or in your area, or watch a speech on television. Categorize the speech as one that motivates or entertains, one that informs or analyzes, or one that persuades or urges collaboration. Then compare the speaker's delivery and use of visual aids with the Checklist for Speeches and Oral Presentations. Write a two-page report analyzing the speaker's performance and suggesting improvements.
3. Analyze the speech given by someone introducing the main speaker at an awards ceremony, a graduation, or some other special occasion. Did the introduction fit the occasion; was it related to the audience's interests; did it grab attention? How well did the introduction motivate the audience to listen to the featured speaker? Did the introduction provide the information necessary for the audience to understand, respect, and appreciate the speaker's background and viewpoint? Put yourself in the shoes of the person who made that introduction. Draft your own brief (two-minute) speech that would prepare the audience for the featured speaker.
4. You've been asked to give an informative ten-minute talk on vacation opportunities in your home state. Draft your introduction, which should last no more than two minutes. Then pair off with a classmate and analyze each other's introductions. How well do these two introductions arouse the audience's interest, build credibility, and preview the presentation? Suggest how these introductions might be improved.
5. Pick a speech from *Vital Speeches of the Day,* a publication containing recent speeches on timely and topical subjects. Examine both the introduction and the close; then analyze how these two sections work together to emphasize the main idea. What action does the speaker want the audience to take? Prepare a brief (two-minute) oral presentation summarizing your analysis for your class.
6. Look again at the speech you selected in exercise 5. What nonverbal signals do you think the speaker would have used to emphasize key points? Mark specific phrases you think would be more persuasive or better understood if accompanied by gestures or other nonverbal cues. Which nonverbal signals would you suggest to enhance the delivery of those sections? Explain the effect you would expect the cues to have on the audience.
7. In the speech you selected for exercise 5, note all the transitional sentences or phrases that clarify the speech's structure for listeners. In particular, focus on the transitions that help the speaker shift between supporting points. Using these transitions as clues, list the main message and supporting points; then indicate how each transitional phrase links the current supporting point to the succeeding one.
8. Review the material in Chapter 12 under the heading "Types of Presentation Visuals." Which types of visual aids would you use to accompany each of the following speeches? Explain your answers.
   a. An informal ten-minute speech explaining the purpose of a new training program to 300 assembly-line employees.
   b. An informal ten-minute speech explaining the purpose of a new training program to five vice presidents.
   c. A formal five-minute presentation explaining the purpose of a new training program to the company's 12-member board of directors.
   d. A formal five-minute speech explaining the purpose of a new company training program to 35 members of the press.
9. For the next meeting of the student government, you're preparing a presentation about the diversity of your college's student population. Prepare an introduction using humor, an introduction using a story, and an introduction using a question. Swap introductions with a classmate and assess how well each of your introductions gets attention. Which works best? Why?
10. With three classmates, practice audience analysis by analyzing the audience of a particular television program. Note the age, gender, race, marital status, relationships, and occupations of the characters. Also pay attention to the commercials that run during the program. On the basis of these clues, who do you think watches this program? Now choose a topic that this audience is likely to feel strongly about. How would you prepare a speech on that topic if you believed the audience would probably be hostile? What would you do differently if you believed the audience would be sympathetic? Present your group's analysis to the class, and defend your answers.
11. Select one of the following main ideas and outline a brief (three- to five-minute) persuasive speech to your business communication class.
    a. As a requirement for graduation, every college student should demonstrate proficiency in basic writing skills by passing a standardized national test.
    b. College students should be given access to their confidential academic records at least once a year and should be allowed to submit a written statement disputing or correcting information in the files.
    c. Rather than ask all students to pay an activities fee to support campus sports, the school should require only those students who participate to pay a special sports fee.
    d. The campus computer laboratory should remain open 24 hours a day, seven days a week, to give students the opportunity to complete their assignments at their own convenience.
    e. All college students should be required to complete a period of community service during their junior or senior year.
12. Prepare a list of questions you might be asked during the question-and-answer period following one of the speeches in exercise 11. Highlight the two or three most difficult or controversial questions, and write your answers. Then team up with a

classmate to evaluate how well your answers might satisfy a hostile or skeptical questioner. What can you do to improve your answers?

13. Read the jacket of a book for information about the author. Analyze the author's biography to see how his or her credentials are established. Next, use this biographical information to draft a brief introduction you might use when presenting this speaker to an audience of people who haven't read the book. How can you build the speaker's credibility without exaggerating?
14. Review the material in Chapter 2 under the heading "The Types of Nonverbal Communication." Then examine the nonverbal signals sent by a political figure who is making a live or televised speech. How do the speaker's gestures, facial expressions, eye contact, vocal characteristics, personal appearance, and use of time and space contribute to the message? Do these nonverbal signals detract from your confidence in the speaker? Do you detect any signs of nervousness? Is there any aspect of his or her delivery that you think this speaker should work to improve? Explain your answer.
15. Review the material in Chapter 2 under the heading "Listening," but this time, read it from a speaker's point of view. Then briefly list how you can use what you know about the different types of listening, barriers to listening, and strategies for effective listening to prepare and deliver an effective speech or oral presentation.

EXPLORING THE BEST OF THE WEB

Speak Like a Pro, page 575

Take time to peruse some linked sites from the Speaker's Companion Reference Page.

1. Try something familiar—*Bartlett's Familiar Quotations* or the *World History Compass*—and then try something foreign—*Asahi.com* (Japanese news and current events) or *The St. Petersburg Press.* Explore new ideas and old ones. Take a look at some of the advice offered by the many experts found here. Look for material you can use in an upcoming speech. What did you find that you can incorporate into a classroom speaking project? How could you use what you learned from overseas news and events to bolster a premise or to refute an argument?
2. Did your perusal of this site and its linked sites cause you to make any changes in your speaking plans? What new ideas did you glean from this wealth of material? (If you didn't find anything to spark your interest, explain why.)

Part 5 A Case for Critical Thinking

A Case for Critical Think

DUPLICATING SUCCESS AT KINKO'S

Paul Orfalea knew he would run a big company someday. He just never envisioned Kinko's becoming that dream. At 22, Orfalea borrowed enough money to open a copying service near the University of California, Santa Barbara. The store was so small that he had to wheel the copier onto the sidewalk to make room for customers. Nevertheless, it serviced the needs of local college students.

By 1995 (some 25 years later), Kinko's, named after Orfalea's reddish, curly hair, had grown into a chain of 127 stores in five countries. Each store was operated as a separate partnership in which Orfalea retained a majority interest. But not all Kinko's were the same. And that was a problem. While some owners reinvested their earnings in high-tech equipment, others cashed in their profits. As a result, traveling customers would find color copiers and high-speed Internet access at spruced-up outlets in one city and would find dilapidated storefronts with little more than black-and-white Xerox machines in another. Orfalea knew that Kinko's loose management structure was hurting its growth.

He also knew that to succeed in a highly competitive marketplace, all Kinko's stores would have to look alike and offer comparable services. So he selected private investors Clayton. Dublier & Rice, to help him turn things around. And they did. Plunking down $219 million in exchange for a 30 percent share of Kinko's, Clayton, Dublier & Rice rolled the individual partnerships into a single corporate entity and centralized all management functions. Today you can go into any of the 902 Kinko's, anywhere in the world, and find the same equipment, supplies, and services.

With over 900 stores, Kinko's is the leader in the $7 billion copy-services market.

Need a business presentation done right away? No problem. Walk into any Kinko's, any time of the day or night, and you'll find it buzzing with college students typing papers, salespeople printing proposals, and job seekers copying résumés. In fact, with more and more businesspeople working wherever they happen to be—at home, in cars, in airports, or in other remote locations—Kinko's has become their office away from home. Which is why tens of thousands of people stop by a Kinko's store each day.

They come to print, fax, bind, or photocopy documents or to use equipment their home office doesn't have, such as ultrafast high-resolution color printers (which can cost $100,000 or more), computers, software, or high-speed Internet connections. They come to plug in their laptops and to print out copies of sales, progress, and activity reports. They come to put finishing touches on presentations and to create overheads rich in color and graphics. And they come to professionally bind winning proposals with color copies, tabs, and laminated covers.

"Proposals and presentations are a visual showcase of a company's capabilities," notes one Kinko's manager. "There are thousands of customers who need posters, banners, and other large prints to help spruce up their presentations. . . . We know how difficult they can be to assemble, especially under time constraints." So Kinko's has bundled together all the communication products and services businesspeople need from start to finish. And with Kinko's newest service, Kinkonet Web Order, customers can compose reports in New York and send them by modem to Amsterdam, where the Kinko's outlet will print and bind them in time for their meeting. This service eliminates the need for costly air freight or the inconvenience of lugging boxes on the airplane.

Another growing in-store business for Kinko's is videoconferencing. William Campbell, a buyer for Applebee's International restaurant chain, for example, relies on the local Kinko's videoconferencing site to conduct screening interviews with job candidates. Applebee's applicants simply show up at their local Kinko's, where they speak to a video camera while watching the interviewer on a television screen. Campbell estimates that these video sessions save Applebee's $250,000 in travel expenses each year.

Of course, growth is nothing new for Kinko's. Even though the company leads the pack in the $7 billion copy-services market, Kinko's is always looking for new ways to expand its market. Kinko's goal? To make corporate sales account for 30 percent of the company's total annual revenue (presently they account for about 15 percent). Orfalea wants busy executives all over the world to rely on Kinko's for cutting-edge document solutions. And that means convincing them that Kinko's is not just a copy shop anymore.

1. If you had only two hours and could spend your time either revising your formal report one last time or having it professionally bound, which would you choose?
2. Why is it important for all Kinko's stores to have the same equipment and offer comparable services?
3. Why would a large corporation want to outsource its document management (photocopying, binding, and so on) to Kinko's?
4. Visit Kinko's Web site at http//www.kinkos.com, and under the section "I want to create," click on "Reports," "Proposals," and "Presentations." Read the tips and follow the links. Which tips did you find most helpful?

PART

Employment Messages

CHAPTER 17
Writing Résumés and Application Letters

CHAPTER 18
Interviewing for Employment and Following Up

CHAPTER

WRITING RÉSUMÉS AND APPLICATION LETTERS

AFTER STUDYING THIS CHAPTER, YOU WILL BE ABLE TO

1 Identify several career-building activities
2 Differentiate between the functions of a résumé and an application letter
3 List the major components of a traditional résumé
4 Differentiate among the three organizational approaches for résumés
5 Explain the process involved in adapting your résumé to an electronic format
6 Discuss how to apply the AIDA organizational approach to written job application messages

COMMUNICATION CLOSE-UP AT RECREATIONAL EQUIPMENT INCORPORATED (REI)

What does it take to land a job interview at a company listed by *Fortune* magazine as one of the 100 best places to work in the United States? Just ask Doug Halm, employment manager of Recreational Equipment Incorporated (REI), a national outdoor gear and clothing cooperative. Halm receives over 400 résumés each month. His job is to determine whether the person represented by the résumé would make a good job candidate for REI. This isn't an easy task, but after 18 years in human resources management, Halm has become quite skilled at it.

First Halm makes sure the candidate has the kinds of skills and experience that the job demands. "Experience is the most important thing," he says. "I try to look behind the résumé's appearance to see what a person's knowledge, skills, and experience are and whether they fit the job." Halm is most concerned with a candidate's specific achievements in previous positions. "In your résumé and application letter you want to create a picture of what you really did and what you accomplished," he says. For example, one applicant included a "PAR sheet," which outlines Problems, Actions, and Results. The candidate identified problems she had encountered in previous jobs, explained actions she had pursued to solve the problems, and documented her results. This strategy got Halm's attention, and the content was substantive as well.

Halm also looks for well roundedness. "Show that you can handle responsibility, such as your previous positions in clubs or social groups. Someone who is a leader, who worked after school, and who understands teamwork may work better in an interactive culture like REI than someone who got good grades but didn't do these things."

Doug Halm

Of course, even if you have all these attributes, you probably won't get a call from Halm if your résumé doesn't look professional. That's because a good-looking résumé is one of the

When a position opens at an REI store, Doug Halm looks for candidates with specific skills in addition to a passion for outdoor activities.

first things Halm will notice. "The résumé should be laid out well and visually appealing. That means lots of white space, boldface headings, bullet points, and a font size that is easy to read," notes Halm. However, he cautions that even an attractive résumé will fall flat if it lacks substance.

Halm advises candidates to think of a résumé as a personal marketing document. It should get someone's attention without carrying things to the extremes. For example, one graphic artist distinguished herself by designing her résumé to look like a newspaper and wrapping it around a fake fish. That résumé was effective for an artist, but others often stand out for less desirable reasons. One computer programmer alienated potential employers by faxing his résumé with 15 pages of attachments.

Another quality that Halm looks for is attention to detail. Spelling errors, poor typing, and incomplete sentences are just a few of the mistakes that can cast a dark cloud over an otherwise attractive résumé. Surprisingly, inexperienced applicants aren't the only ones who make such errors. Halm recently received an application for a high-level international merchandising position from a qualified candidate who misspelled a number of words. Halm wasn't very forgiving, especially with the availability of computerized spell checkers these days. "The person in this position makes important decisions, represents the company, writes proposals, and develops marketing strategies—and he can't even get his own résumé right?" Halm's advice: "Proofread with a fine-toothed comb. And ask other people to review your résumé, preferably professionals or someone who has a good eye."

Of course, even the best résumé can't say all there is to know about a person's qualifications. That's why Halm believes that a well-written application letter is crucial. "The application letter lets you personalize the résumé and bring yourself alive in the recruiter's mind," he says. "It gives you the chance to say why you want the job and why you would be good for the job. It fills in the blanks, such as gaps in your work history, and it answers questions that your résumé might create."

Halm feels that a good application letter should be no longer than three paragraphs and should maintain a friendly, yet conversational tone. "The letter is a sales piece," Halm advises. "Look at the job advertisement and highlight the specific points the company is looking for. Show that you know the job." Halm stresses that knowing your audience and adopting the "you" attitude are just as important in your résumé and application letter as they are in any other type of business communication.[1] ■

THINKING ABOUT YOUR CAREER

As Doug Halm will tell you, getting the job that's right for you takes more than sending out a few résumés and application letters. Planning and research are important if you want to find a company that suits you. So before you limit your employment search to a particular industry or job, analyze what you have to offer and what you hope to get from your work. Then you can identify employers who are likely to want you and vice versa.

What Do You Have to Offer?

What you have to offer:
- Functional skills
- Education and experience
- Personality traits

What are your marketable skills? You can analyze them in three steps.

First, jot down ten achievements you're proud of, such as learning to ski, taking a prize-winning photo, tutoring a child, or editing the school paper. Look carefully at each of those achievements. What specific skills did they demand? For example, leadership skills, speaking ability, and artistic talent may have helped you coordinate a winning presentation to the college administration. As you analyze your achievements, you'll begin to recognize a pattern of skills. Which of them might be valuable to potential employers?

Second, look at your educational preparation, work experience, and extracurricular activities. What kinds of jobs do your knowledge and experience qualify you for? What have you learned from participating in volunteer work or class projects that could benefit you on the job? Have you held any offices, won any awards or scholarships, mastered a second language?

Third, take stock of your personal characteristics to determine the type of job you'll do best. Are you aggressive, a born leader? Or would you rather follow? Are you outgoing, articulate, great with people? Or do you prefer working alone? Make a list of what you believe are your four or five most important qualities. Ask a relative or friend to rate your traits as well.

If you're having trouble figuring out your interests and capabilities, consult your college placement office or career guidance center for advice. Many campuses administer a variety of tests designed to help you identify your interests, aptitudes, and personality traits. Although these tests won't reveal the "perfect" job for you, they'll help you focus on the types of work that best suit your personality.

What Do You Want to Do?

Knowing what you *can* do is one thing. Knowing what you *want* to do is another. Don't lose sight of your own values. Discover the things that will bring you satisfaction and happiness on the job.

Envision the ideal "day at the office." What would you enjoy doing every day?

- *Decide what you'd like to do every day.* Talk to people in various occupations. You might consult relatives, local businesses, or former graduates (through your school's alumni relations office). Read about various occupations. Start with your college library or placement office. Also consider how much independence you want on the job, how much variety you like, and whether you prefer to work with products, machines, people, ideas, figures, or some combination thereof. Do you like physical work, mental work, or a mix? Constant change or a predictable role?

- *Establish some specific compensation targets.* What do you hope to earn in your first year on the job? What kind of pay increase do you expect each year? What's your ultimate earnings goal? Would you be comfortable with a job that paid on commission, or do you prefer a steady paycheck? What occupations offer the kind of money you're looking for? Are these occupations realistic for someone with your qualifications? Are you willing to settle for less money in order to do something you really love? Consider where you'd like to start, where you'd like to go from there, and the ultimate position you'd like to attain. How soon after joining the company would you like to receive your first promotion? Your next one? What additional training or preparation will you need to achieve them?

How much do you want to earn, and how high do you hope to climb?

- *Consider the type of environment you prefer.* Think in broad terms about the size and type of operation you find appealing, the location you prefer, the facilities you envision, and especially the corporate culture you're most comfortable with. Do you like the idea of working for a small, entrepreneurial operation or a large company? A profit-making company or a nonprofit organization? Are you attracted to service businesses or manufacturing operations? Do you want regular, predictable hours, or do you thrive on flexible, varied hours? Would you enjoy a seasonally varied job such as education (which may give you summers off) or retailing (with its selling cycles)? Would you like to work in a city, a suburb, a small town, an industrial area, or an uptown setting? Do you favor a particular part of the country? A country abroad? Do you like working indoors or outdoors? Is it important to you to work in an attractive place, or will simple, functional quarters suffice? Do you need a quiet office to work effectively, or can you concentrate in a noisy, open setting? Is access to public transportation or freeways important?

What type of industry and organization do you want to work in?

DID YOU KNOW?

A recent survey by Telecommute America reported that roughly 11 million U.S. citizens telecommute at least once a month. A few are full-time telecommuters, but most are full-time employees who telecommute one to three days a week.

Perhaps the most important environmental factor is the corporate culture. Would you be happy in a well-defined hierarchy, where roles and reporting relationships are clear, or would you prefer a less structured situation? What qualities do you want in a boss? Are you looking for a paternalistic organization or one that fosters individualism? Do you like a competitive environment or one that rewards teamwork?

What type of corporate culture best suits you?

How Do You Build Toward a Career?

Having the right skills is one way to build toward a career. Employers such as Doug Halm seek people who are able and willing to adapt to diverse situations, who thrive in an ever-changing workplace, and who continue to learn throughout their careers. In addition, companies want team players with strong work records and leaders who are versatile. In fact, many companies are encouraging their managers to get more varied job experience.[2] In some cases, your chances of being hired are better if you've studied abroad or learned another language. At the least, employers expect college graduates to have a sound understanding of international affairs, and they're looking for employees with intercultural sensitivity as well as an ability to adapt in other cultures.[3] Keep these things in mind and try to gain skills you can market later on.

Your chances of getting a job are increased by career-building efforts:

- Gaining intercultural experience
- Developing an employment portfolio
- Taking interim or freelance jobs
- Participating in an internship program
- Networking with others in your field
- Expanding your life experience

Consider keeping an employment portfolio. Get a three-ring notebook and a package of plastic sleeves that open at the top. Collect anything that shows your ability to perform, such as classroom or work evaluations, certificates, awards, and papers you've written. This employment portfolio accomplishes two things: (1) It serves as an excellent resource when writing your résumé, and (2) it provides employers with tangible evidence of your professionalism.

As you search for a permanent job that fulfills your career goals, take interim job assignments and consider temporary work or freelance jobs. You can also gain a competitive

Baking low-fat, low-cholesterol muffins for coffeehouses and other clients in the Chicago area was a recipe for success for this brother and sister team who founded Little Miss Muffin, Trisha and Barry Malone. What's your recipe for success? What skills are you gaining to better market yourself in the future?

edge by participating in an internship program. Not only will these temporary assignments help you gain valuable experience and relevant contacts, but they will also provide you with important references and with items for your portfolio.[4] Bear in mind that employers will be more willing to find (or even create) a position for someone they've learned to respect, and your temporary or freelance work gives them a chance to see what you can do.

If you're unable to find actual job experience, work on polishing and updating your skills. Whenever possible, join networks of professional colleagues and friends who can help you stay abreast of where your occupation and industry are going. While you're waiting for responses to your résumé or to hear about your last interview, take a computer course, or use the time to gain some other educational or life experience that would be difficult to get while working full time. Become familiar with the services offered by your campus career center (or placement office). These centers offer individual placement counseling, credential services, job fairs, on-campus interviews, job listings, advice on computerized résumé-writing software, workshops in job-search techniques, résumé preparation, interview techniques, and more.[5]

Once an employer hires you and you're on the job, don't think you've reached the end of the process. The best thing you can do for your long-term career is to continue learning. Listen to and learn from the experienced people around you. Be ready and willing to take on new responsibilities, and actively pursue new or better skills. Employers appreciate applicants and employees who demonstrate a willingness and enthusiasm to learn, to listen, and to gain experience.

SEEKING EMPLOYMENT OPPORTUNITIES AND INFORMATION

Find out where the job opportunities are.

Whether your major is business, biology, or political science, once you know what you have to offer and what you want, you can start finding an employer to match. If you haven't already committed yourself to any particular career field, first find out where the job opportunities are. Which industries are strong? Which parts of the country are booming, and which specific job categories offer the best prospects for the future?

Sources of Employment Information

In Chapter 11 we discussed how to research and find information on individual companies and industries, and we provided a list of popular business resources. Begin your job search by reviewing those sources as well as professional and trade journals in the career fields that interest you. Talk to people in these fields. You may be able to network with executives in your field by joining or participating in student business organizations, especially those with ties to real-world organizations such as the American Marketing Association or the American Management Association.

In addition to reviewing journals and periodicals, you'll want to keep abreast of business and financial news. If you don't already do so, subscribe to a major newspaper and scan the business pages every day. Watch some of the television programs that focus on business, such as *Wall Street Week.* You can find information about the future for specific jobs in the *Dictionary of Occupational Titles* (U.S. Employment Service), the *Occupational Outlook Handbook* (U.S. Bureau of Labor Statistics), and the employment publications of Science Research Associates.

Make a list of desirable employers.

Once you've identified a promising industry and a career field, compile a list of specific organizations that appeal to you. To do so, consult directories of employers at your college library or placement center. Write to the organizations on your list and ask for an annual report and any descriptive brochures or newsletters they've published. Check to see if a company you're interested in maintains a Web site. Those that do generally include a company profile, press releases, financial information, and information on employment opportunities. If possible, visit some of the organizations on your list, contact their personnel departments, or talk with key employees.

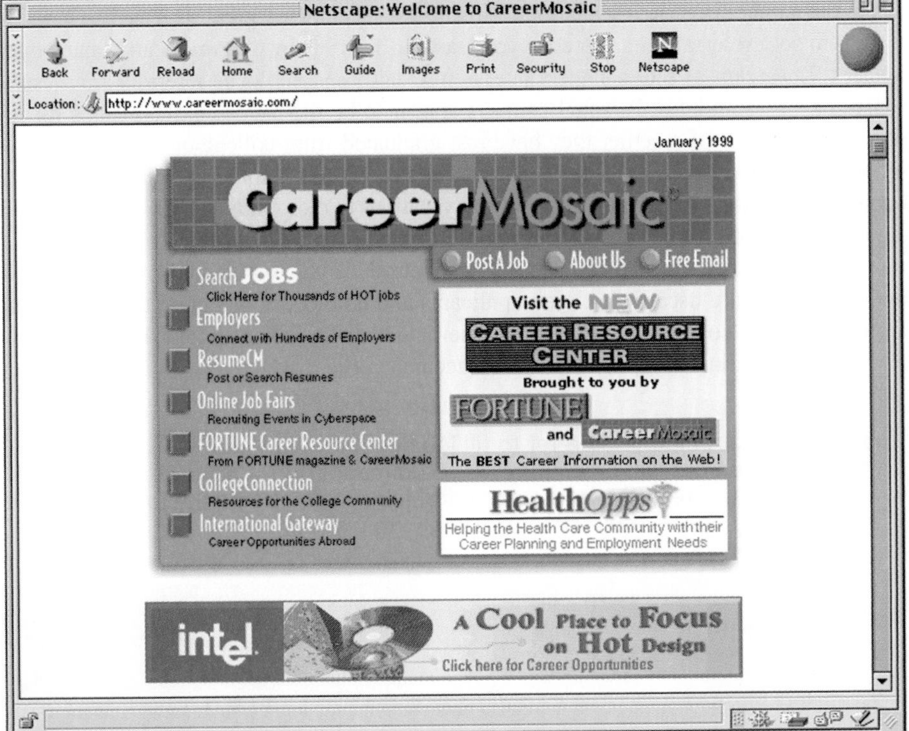

Career Mosaic is just one of the many Web sites job seekers turn to for advice, employer information, and company job postings.

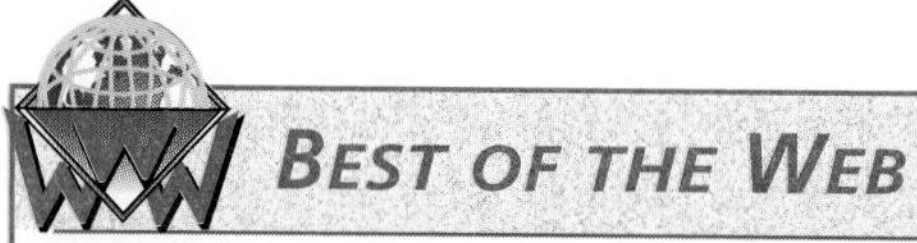

Link Your Way to a Better Job Search

Learn how to stand out in a crowded job market. Decide whether posting a résumé online is your best option. Maximize your job search by following Parachute's picks to the best Internet job listing sites, résumé advice, counseling assistance, key contacts, and company research. Take an interactive test to focus on career options that are a right fit for you. What color is your parachute?

http://www.tenspeed.com/parachute/front.htm

You can find ads for specific job openings by looking in local and major newspapers and by visiting your college placement office. Of course, a source of growing importance to your job search is the Internet, or more specifically the World Wide Web (see "Keeping Pace with Technology: High-Tech Job Hunting: The Secrets of Finding Employment on the World Wide Web"). An increasing number of large and small companies are posting job openings on the Internet. Look at Salestar. This San Francisco custom software developer didn't have the resources to advertise through traditional media, so the company posted an ad with an Internet recruiting service. Not only did the company find the right person in a relatively short time, but it saved two-thirds of the normal newspaper advertising costs.[6]

Employer Recruiting Practices

Employers find job candidates through
- Employee referrals
- On-campus interviews
- Placement agencies
- Unsolicited résumés
- Advertisements

An understanding of how employers approach the recruiting process can save you considerable time and effort when searching for the job you want (see Figure 17.1). The quickest route is to get a referral from someone you know. In a survey by the American Management Society, 70 percent of the managers interviewed said that employee referrals are a useful source of job candidates. Personal contacts appear to be the prime source of jobs for job seekers, regardless of whether they have just graduated from college or have been out of school for several years.[7] In fact, many companies pay their employees handsome referral bonuses—from mountain bikes to Caribbean vacations to thousands of dollars—if they recommend a candidate who subsequently is hired and stays for a designated period of time.[8]

Don't despair if you lack contacts who can introduce you to potential employers. A variety of avenues are used by both job applicants and employers. Many organizations send representatives to college campuses to interview students for job openings. These interviews are usually coordinated by the campus placement office, which keeps files containing

Figure 17.1
How Employers Approach the Recruiting Process

Studies show that employers prefer to fill job openings with people from within their organization or from an employee's recommendation. Placing want ads is often viewed as a last resort. In contrast, typical job-hunters begin the job-search process from the opposite direction (starting with want ads.)

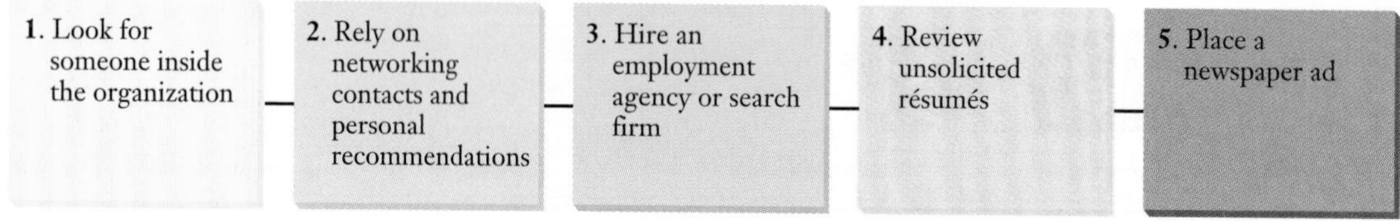

KEEPING PACE WITH TECHNOLOGY

High-Tech Job Hunting: The Secrets of Finding Employment on the World Wide Web

The World Wide Web offers an amazing amount of employment information. Is the Web the answer to all your employment dreams? Perhaps . . . or perhaps not. As the Web grows, the employment information it provides is constantly expanding. And you're fortunate, because you don't have to start from scratch like some intrepid adventurer. For helpful hints and useful Web addresses, you can turn to innumerable books, such as *What Color Is Your Parachute?* by Richard Nelson Bolles, or you can access this popular book online (see "Best of the Web" on page 594).

When you're dealing with the Internet, the one thing you can count on is rapid change. So exactly how using the Web will affect your job search depends on how well you prepare your job-search strategy, how many employers (especially in your field) come to accept the Web as a source of potential employees, and how quickly the resources already available expand and adapt to the ever-changing Web environment. The World Wide Web offers information not only from employers seeking applicants but also from people seeking work. You can use the World Wide Web for a variety of job-seeking tasks:

- *Finding career counseling.* Even when using the Web to locate particular job opportunities, you still need to analyze your skills and expectations. For example, you can begin your self-assessment with the *Keirsey Temperament Sorter,* an online personality test. The Web offers you job-seeking pointers and counseling from online career centers, many of which are run by colleges and universities that put a lot of effort into creating interesting and helpful sites. Other career centers are commercial and can run the gamut from award winning to depressing. So make sure the advice you get is both useful and sensible. One good commercial site is Mary-Ellen Mort's *Job-Smart.*
- *Making contacts.* You can use the Web to locate and communicate with potential employers. One way to locate people is through usenet newsgroups that are dedicated to your field of interest. Newsgroup members leave messages for one another on an electronic bulletin board and retrieve messages by visiting that Web site. Some employers even read through the postings to find the smartest comments. You might also try listservs (or Internet mailing lists). These discussion groups are similar to usenet newsgroups, except that the group mails each message to every member's e-mail address. Commercial systems such as Prodigy, America Online, and CompuServe have their own discussion groups (called Special Interest Groups, RoundTables, Clubs, Forums, or Bulletin Boards). These commercial groups are also devoted to a particular interest, but they make a profit from the time users spend accessing their services. Once you've located a potential contact, you can communicate quickly and nonintrusively by using e-mail to request information or to let an employer know you're interested in working for the company.
- *Researching employers' companies.* The Web is a good place to find information about the companies you might want to work for. Even companies that don't yet have a home page are in the process of getting one, and many companies are including job listings on their Web site. By visiting a company's Web site, you can find out about its mission, products, annual reports, employee benefits, and job openings. You can locate company Web sites by knowing the URL (or Web address), by using links from other sites, or by using a search engine such as Alta Vista, Lycos, or Excite.
- *Searching for job vacancies.* In addition to visiting company home pages, you can find job vacancies at sites that list openings from multiple companies. Table 17.1 provides a list of popular online indexes or job boards, many of which allow you to search by region, industry, job title, company, skills, or requirements. Of course, the World Wide Web offers no central, unified marketplace, so try to be selective in the sites you visit. If you narrow your search, the Web can work for you.
- *Posting your résumé online.* You can post your résumé online either through an index service or on your own home page. To post your résumé on an index service, you'll need to adapt it to an electronic format (discussed on page 608) and transmit it by mail, fax, modem, or e-mail. Once your information is input into the service's database, your résumé will be sent to any employers whose requests match key words in your information. Of course, it's up to the employer to decide whether to interview any of the people whose résumé they receive. When posting your résumé on your own home page, you can retain a

(continued)

nicer-looking format, and you can even include links to papers you've written, recommendations you've received, and sound or video clips.

Using the World Wide Web to seek employment allows you to respond directly to job postings (without going through recruiters), post résumés (that have been tailored to match exactly the skills and qualifications necessary to fill a particular position), send résumés through e-mail (which is faster and less expensive than printing and mailing them), send focused cover letters directly to the executives doing the hiring, and quickly gain detailed information about your prospective employers. Moreover, most campus placement offices are retooling to help you take advantage of Web opportunities. Still, experts predict that at least 10 million U.S. employers don't think of the Internet when it's time to hire. In short, the World Wide

TABLE 17.1

TWELVE PLACES TO START YOUR ONLINE JOB SEARCH

Web Site*	Description and Features
4Work http://www.4work.com	This is one of the few sites that includes listings of internships and volunteer opportunities.
America's Employers http://www.americasemployers.com	Maintained by career consultants, this site offers several thousand up dated listings and real-time seminars. Network forums help you develop new contacts and job leads. Includes chat room for online interviews.
America's Job Bank http://www.ajb.dni.us	On this government site, state agencies post an average of 5,000 new openings each day. Companies contribute another 3,000.
Career-Builder http://www.careerbuilder.com	Site offers a network of career services, job-search information, and tips on how to succeed once you're hired. Includes a database of 20,000 openings.
CareerMosaic http://www.careermosaic.com	More than 70,000 jobs are updated daily on this site. Includes a career resources center.
Careerpath.Com http://www.careerpath.com	Site offers classifieds from more than 65 newspapers, including the *New York Times, Los Angeles Times,* and *Boston Globe.*
HotJobs.Com http://www.hotjobs.com	Member-based site charges companies a hefty fee to post openings or to search through résumés. Job seekers can create a personal home page to manage their search and to collect statistics on how many companies have retrieved their résumé.
Job Trak http://www.jobtrak.com	This site has formed partnerships with 750 campuses nationwide and serves as a virtual career center for students and alumni. Many postings are aimed at entry-level candidates.
The Monster Board www.monster.com	Site posts more than 25,000 openings and more than 300,000 résumés. Heavily marketed, it brings a flood of employers—many with under 500 employees.
Nation.Job Network http://www.nationjob.com	Site posts more than 15,000 jobs nationwide, with an emphasis on those in the Midwest.
Online Career Center http://www.occ.com	Site offers numerous domestic and international job listings. Specializes in engineering, health care, and human resources.
Yahoo! Classifieds http://classifieds.yahoo.com/employment.html	Site offers extensive listing of companies by city in addition to a wealth of job-related information at the parent Web site, http://www.yahoo.com. Click on *Business & Economy/Jobs/Company Job Listings.*

*Direct links to these Web sites can be accessed at the Riley Guide at http://www.dbm.com/jobguide.

Web cannot replace other techniques for finding employment—it's just one more tool in your overall strategy.

1. Surfing the Web can chew up a disproportionate amount of your job-seeking time. So that you have plenty of time to spend on other sources, how can you limit the amount of time you spend on the Web and still make the Web work for you? Please explain.
2. When posting your résumé on the World Wide Web, you're revealing a lot of information about yourself that could be used by people other than employers (salespeople, people competing for similar positions, con artists). What sort of information might you leave off your Web résumé that would certainly appear on a traditional résumé?

college records, data sheets, and letters of recommendation for all students registered for the service.

Unsolicited résumés are a vital source of candidates for many organizations. Growing companies like to keep a steady flow of potential employees in mind. In tight labor markets, they recognize that whenever they happen upon a good candidate, they'll probably have a job for that person.[9] Thus, most companies will keep unsolicited résumés on file or scan them into a database.

Take Technology Solutions, a $3.3 million technology-staffing firm in Columbia, South Carolina. The company never throws away a résumé. Instead, every résumé is entered into a database. Then, every two years the company president reviews the database and sends out e-mail questionnaires to see what prospects have added to their résumés. If a job opens up, the database is one of the first places the company will look to fill it.

Employers also recruit candidates through employment agencies, state employment services, temporary staffing services, and the employment bureaus operated by some trade associations, and they post jobs through classified and display ads in newspapers, trade magazines, and campus publications. Some CEOs are even widening their advertising efforts to include such nontraditional recruiting media as radio and television.[10]

Of course, to get hired, you usually need an interview, and to get that interview, you usually need a résumé. In the next section we'll discuss how to write a résumé: what to include, how to choose the best organizational approach, and how to adapt it to an electronic format. Keep in mind that a well-written résumé can distinguish you from all the other people looking for work.

The purpose of the résumé is to get you an interview.

WRITING YOUR RÉSUMÉ

A **résumé** is a structured, written summary of a person's education, employment background, and job qualifications. Many people new to the job market have some misconceptions about résumés (see Figure 17.2). The fact is that a résumé is a form of advertising, designed to stimulate an employer's interest in meeting you and learning more about you. A good résumé inspires the prospective employer to pick up the phone and ask you to come in for an interview. Thus, your objective in writing your résumé is to create interest rather than to tell the reader everything about you. In fact, it's best to only hint at some things and leave the reader wanting more. That way, the potential employer will have even more reason to reach for the phone.[11]

Your résumé is a structured, written summary of your educational and employment background, and it shows your qualifications for a job.

One way to build the reader's interest is to call attention to your best features and to downplay your weaknesses, without distorting or misrepresenting the facts.[12] A good résumé conveys seven specific qualities that employers seek. It shows that a candidate (1) thinks in terms of results, (2) knows how to get things done, (3) is well rounded, (4) shows

DID YOU KNOW?

Only one interview is granted for approximately every 200 résumés received by the average employer.

Figure 17.2
Fallacies and Facts about Résumés

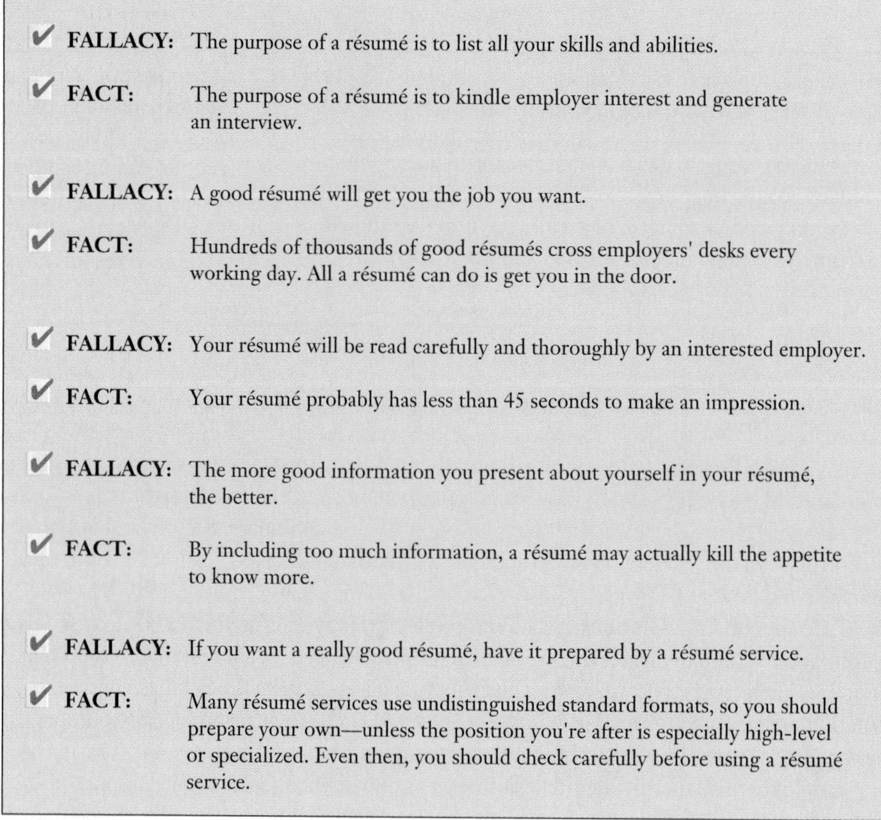

✔ **FALLACY:** The purpose of a résumé is to list all your skills and abilities.

✔ **FACT:** The purpose of a résumé is to kindle employer interest and generate an interview.

✔ **FALLACY:** A good résumé will get you the job you want.

✔ **FACT:** Hundreds of thousands of good résumés cross employers' desks every working day. All a résumé can do is get you in the door.

✔ **FALLACY:** Your résumé will be read carefully and thoroughly by an interested employer.

✔ **FACT:** Your résumé probably has less than 45 seconds to make an impression.

✔ **FALLACY:** The more good information you present about yourself in your résumé, the better.

✔ **FACT:** By including too much information, a résumé may actually kill the appetite to know more.

✔ **FALLACY:** If you want a really good résumé, have it prepared by a résumé service.

✔ **FACT:** Many résumé services use undistinguished standard formats, so you should prepare your own—unless the position you're after is especially high-level or specialized. Even then, you should check carefully before using a résumé service.

signs of progress, (5) has personal standards of excellence, (6) is flexible and willing to try new things, and (7) possesses strong communication skills. As you put your résumé together, think about how the format and style, content, and organization help you convey those seven qualities.

Controlling the Format and Style

Quick—you've got less than 45 seconds to make a good impression. That's the amount of time a typical recruiter devotes to each résumé before tossing it into either the "maybe" or the "reject" pile.[13] In fact, most recruiters scan rather than read a résumé from top to bottom. This means that if your résumé doesn't *look* sharp, and if you don't grab the reader's interest in the first few lines, chances are the recruiter won't read it long enough to judge your qualifications.

The key characteristics of a good résumé are
- Neatness
- Simplicity
- Accuracy
- Honesty

To give your résumé a sharp look, use a clean typeface on high-grade, letter-size bond paper (in white or some light earth tone). Make sure that your stationery and envelope match. Leave ample margins all around, and be certain any corrections are unnoticeable. Avoid italic typefaces, which can be difficult to read, and use a quality laser printer.

In general, try to write a one-page résumé. If you have a great deal of experience and are applying for a higher-level position, you may wish to prepare a somewhat longer résumé. The important thing is to give yourself enough space to present a persuasive but accurate portrait of your skills and accomplishments.

Lay out your résumé so that the information is easy to grasp.[14] Break up the text by using headings that call attention to various aspects of your background, such as your work experience and education. Underline or capitalize key points, or set them off in the left margin. Use indented lists to itemize your most important qualifications. Leave plenty of white space, even if doing so forces you to use two pages rather than one. Pay attention to mechanics and details. As Doug Halm notes, "It shows how you will present material in a corporate setting."[15] Check the headings and itemized lists to make sure they're grammatically parallel, and be sure that your grammar, spelling, and punctuation are correct.

Write in a simple and direct style to save your reader time. Use short crisp phrases instead of whole sentences, and focus on what your reader needs to know. Absolutely avoid using the word *I*. Instead start your phrases with active, impressive verbs such as these:[16]

accomplished	developed	maintained	resolved
achieved	directed	managed	saved
administered	established	motivated	served
approved	explored	operated	set up
arranged	forecasted	organized	simplified
assisted	generated	oversaw	sparked
assumed	identified	participated	streamlined
budgeted	implemented	performed	strengthened
changed	improved	planned	succeeded
chaired	initiated	presented	supervised
compiled	installed	proposed	systematized
completed	introduced	raised	targeted
coordinated	investigated	recommended	trained
created	joined	reduced	transformed
demonstrated	launched	reorganized	upgraded

For instance, you might say, "Coached a Little League team to the regional playoffs" or "Managed a fast-food restaurant and four employees."

Instead of This	Say This
Responsible for developing a new filing system	Developed a new filing system that reduced paperwork by 50 percent
I was in charge of customer complaints and all ordering problems	Handled all customer complaints and resolved all product order discrepancies
Won a trip to Europe for opening the most new customer accounts in my department	Generated the highest number of new customer accounts in my department
Member of special campus task force to resolve student problems with existing cafeteria assignments	Assisted in implementing new campus dining program allowing students to eat at any college dorm

Because your résumé has only 45 seconds to make an impression, adopt a "you" attitude by thinking about your résumé from the employers' perspective. Ask yourself: What key qualifications will employers be looking for? Which of these are your greatest strengths? What would set you apart from other candidates in their eyes? What are three or four of your greatest accomplishments, and what was produced as a result of these accomplishments? Then tailor your résumé to appeal to the employer's needs.

Tailoring the Contents

Most potential employers expect to see certain items in any résumé. The bare essentials are name and address, academic credentials, and employment history. Otherwise, make sure your résumé emphasizes your strongest, most impressive qualifications. It's up to you to combine your experiences into a straightforward message that communicates what you can do for your potential employer.[17] Think in terms of an image or a theme you'd like to project. Are you academically gifted? A campus leader? A well-rounded person? A creative genius? A technical wizard? If you know what you have to sell, you can shape the elements of your résumé accordingly. Don't exaggerate, and don't alter the past or claim skills you don't have, but don't dwell on negatives, either. By focusing on your strengths, you can convey the desired impression without distorting the facts.

Name and Address

The opening section shows at a glance
- Who you are
- How to reach you

The first thing an employer needs to know is who you are and where you can be reached: your name, address, and phone number (as well as your e-mail address or URL, if you have one). If you have an address and phone number at school and another at home, you can include both. Similarly, if you have a work phone and a home phone, list both and indicate which is which. Many résumé headings are nothing more than the name and address centered at the top of the page. You really have little need to include the word *Résumé*. Just make sure the reader can tell in an instant who you are and how to communicate with you.

Career Objective or Summary of Qualifications

Stating your objective or summarizing your qualifications helps the recruiter categorize you.

Experts disagree about stating a career objective on your résumé. Some argue that your objective will be obvious from your qualifications. They also point out that such a statement will only limit you as a candidate (especially if you would like to be considered for a variety of openings) because it labels you as being interested in only one thing. Other experts point out that employers will undoubtedly try to categorize you anyway, so you might as well be sure they attach the right label. Remember, your goal is to immediately generate interest. So if you decide to state your objective, make sure it's effective and be as specific as possible about what you want to do:

> A software sales position in a growing company requiring international experience
>
> Advertising assistance with print media emphasis requiring strong customer-contact skills

If you have two types of qualifications (such as a certificate in secretarial science and two years' experience in retail sales), prepare two separate résumés, each with a different objective. If your immediate objective differs from your ultimate one, combine the two in a single statement:

> A marketing position with an opportunity for eventual managerial status
>
> Proposal writer, with the ultimate goal of becoming a contracts administrator

As an alternative to stating your objective, you might want to summarize your qualifications in a brief statement that highlights your strongest points, particularly if you have had a good deal of varied experience. Use a short, simple phrase:

> Summary of qualifications: Ten years of experience in commission selling with track record of generating new customer leads through creative advertising and community leadership positions

Keep in mind that the career objective or summary may be the only section fully read by the employer, so make it strong, concise, and convincing.

Education

If education is your strongest selling point, discuss it thoroughly and highlight it visually.

If you're still in school, education is probably your strongest selling point. So present your educational background in depth, choosing facts that support your "theme." Give this section a heading, such as "Education," "Professional College Training," or "Academic Preparation." Then, starting with the school you most recently attended, list the name and location of each school, the term of your enrollment (in months and years) there, your major and minor fields of study, significant skills and abilities you've developed in your course work, and the degrees or certificates you've earned. If you are working on an uncompleted degree, include in parentheses the expected date of completion. Showcase your qualifications by listing courses that have directly equipped you for the job you are seeking, and indicate any scholarships, awards, or academic honors you've received.

The education section also includes off-campus training sponsored by business or government. Include any relevant seminars or workshops you've attended, as well as the certificates or other documents you've received. Mention high school or military training only if the associated achievements are pertinent to your career goals. Whether you list your grades depends on the job you want and the quality of your grades. If you choose to show grade-point averages for your total program or your major, be sure to mention the scale, especially if a 5-point scale is used instead of a 4-point scale.

Education is usually given less emphasis in a résumé after you've worked in your chosen field for a year or more. If work experience is your strongest qualification, save the section on education for later in the résumé and provide less detail.

Work Experience, Skills, and Accomplishments

Like the education section, the work experience section focuses on your overall theme. Tailor your description to highlight the relationship between your previous responsibilities and your target field. Call attention to the skills you've developed and the progression from jobs of lesser to greater responsibility.

DID YOU KNOW?

According to a recent survey by Accountemps (a staffing service), executives believe three out of every ten job applicants lie on their résumés.

When describing your work experience, you'll usually list your jobs in chronological order, with the current or last one first. Include any part-time, summer, or intern positions even if the jobs have no relation to your curent career objective. Employers will see that you have the ability to get and hold a job, which is an important qualification in itself. If you have worked your way through school, say so. Employers interpret this as a sign of character.

Each listing includes the name and location of the employer. Then, if the reader is unlikely to recognize the organization, briefly describe what it does. When you want to keep the name of your current employer confidential, identify the firm by industry only ("a large film-processing laboratory"), or use the name but request confidentiality in the application letter or in an underlined note ("Résumé submitted in confidence") at the top or bottom of the résumé. If an organization's name or location has since changed, state the present name or location and then "formerly . . ."

The work experience section lists all the related jobs you've had:

- Name and location of employer
- What the organization does (if not clear from its name)
- Your functional title
- How long you worked there
- Your duties and responsibilities
- Your significant achievements or contributions

Before or after each job listing, state your functional title, such as "clerk typist" or "salesperson." If you were a dishwasher, say so. Don't try to make your role seem more important by glamorizing your job title, functions, or achievements. You should also state how long you worked on each job, from month/year to month/year. Use the phrase "to present" to denote current employment. If a job was part-time, say so.

Be honest about the positions you've held, the companies you've worked for, and your dates of employment. You'll be courting trouble if you list jobs you never held, claim to have worked for a firm when you didn't, or change dates to cover up a gap in employment. Employers are checking on candidates' backgrounds more than they used to, so inaccuracies are likely to be exposed sooner or later (see "Focusing on Ethics: Warning: Deceptive Résumés Can Backfire").

Devote the most space to the jobs that are related to your target position. If you were personally responsible for something significant, be sure to mention it ("Devised a new collection system that accelerated payment of overdue receivables"). Facts about your skills and accomplishments are the most important information you can give a prospective employer, so quantify them whenever possible:

Quantify your accomplishments whenever possible.

FOCUSING ON ETHICS

WARNING: DECEPTIVE RÉSUMÉS CAN BACKFIRE

In an effort to put your best foot forward, you may be tempted to waltz around a few points that could raise questions about your résumé. For example, given your desire for a career in sales, you'd rather not explain why you quit your summer job as a door-to-door encyclopedia sales representative, so wouldn't it be better not to mention that three-week period at all? In addition, you may be inclined to dress up a few of your accomplishments. For instance, if advertising revenue increased by 25 percent shortly after you became advertising manager of the campus newspaper, do you really have to explain that most of the credit belongs to your predecessor, who laid the groundwork before she graduated?

As you weigh the alternatives, you may say to yourself: "Everybody else is probably shading the facts to make their résumés look good. I'd be a fool not to do the same." Statistics on the prevalence of résumé inflation are difficult to gather, but most recruiters agree that distortion is common. The best guess is that up to 40 percent of all résumés either omit potentially damaging information or exaggerate the candidate's accomplishments. The most frequent forms of deception include:

- *Claiming nonexistent educational credits.* Candidates may state (or imply) that they earned a degree when, in fact, they never attended the school or attended but did not complete the regular program. A typical claim might read, "Majored in business administration at Wayne State University."
- *Inflating grade-point averages.* Students who feel pressured to impress employers with their academic performance may claim a higher GPA than they actually achieved.
- *Stretching dates of employment to cover gaps.* Because periods of unemployment raise red flags for employers, many candidates try to camouflage gaps in their work history by giving vague references to dates of employment. For example, a candidate who left a company in January 1992 and joined another in December 1993 might cover up by showing that the first job ended in 1992 and the next began in 1993.
- *Claiming to be self-employed.* Another common way people cover a period of unemployment is by saying that they were "self-employed" or a "consultant." The candidate

---

Designed a new ad that increased sales by 9 percent

Raised $2500 in 15 days for cancer research

Include miscellaneous facts that are related to your career objective:

- Command of other languages
- Computer expertise
- Date you can start working

You may also want to include a section that describes other aspects of your background that pertain to your career objective. If you were applying for a position with a multinational organization, you would mention your command of another language or your travel experience. Other skills you might mention include the ability to operate a computer, word processor, or other specialized equipment. In fact, you might title a special section "Computer Skills" or "Language Skills" and place it near your "Education" or "Work Experience" section.

Keep in mind that a good résumé is a flexible marketing document that can be customized for different situations and different employers. Suppose you're applying for a marketing job at an international company such as Hewlett-Packard. If you speak a foreign language, you might want to list that skill first. However, if you're applying for a sales position at Frito Lay, you'll probably want to list your summer job of building product displays at a local grocery store before your foreign language skill. In fact, it's perfectly fine to have several résumés, each specifically crafted for a different type of position or company.

If samples of your work might increase your chances of getting the job, insert a line at the end of your résumé offering to supply them on request. You may put "references

claims to have operated an independent business during the period in question.

- *Leaving out any reference to jobs that might cause embarrassment.* Being fired from one or two jobs is understandable when corporate mergers and downsizing are commonplace. However, when a candidate has lost several jobs in quick succession, recruiters may jump to the conclusion that the person is a poor employee. To cover up a string of such job losses, candidates may decide to drop a few positions, particularly if a reference check could prove embarrassing. To cover the gap, candidates stretch the dates of employment for the jobs held before and after.
- *Exaggerating expertise or experience.* Candidates often inflate their accomplishments by using verbs somewhat loosely. Words such as supervised, managed, increased, improved, and created imply that the candidate was personally responsible for results that, in reality, were the outcome of a group effort.
- *Claiming to have worked for companies that are out of business.* Candidates who need to fill a gap in their work record sometimes say they worked for a firm that has gone out of business. Checking such claims is difficult because the people who were involved in the disbanded business are hard to track down.

Before trying one of these ploys yourself, think twice. Experienced recruiters are familiar with the games that candidates play to make themselves look better. Many employers have a policy of firing people who lied on their résumés. If your résumé raises suspicion, you may do yourself more harm than good by misrepresenting your background. Sure, it's fine to present your strongest, most impressive qualifications and to minimize your weaknesses. However, don't exaggerate, alter the past, or claim to have skills you don't have.

1. You'd rather not explain why you quit your summer job as a door-to-door encyclopedia sales representative. Describe how you might handle that period on your résumé. Should you omit it? Can you mention it without revealing why you quit?
2. Consider one or two positions you have held (whether in a club, in a volunteer organization, or with a business). Write a realistic description that doesn't inflate them but that presents them in a positive light.

available upon request" at the end of your résumé, but doing so is not necessary; the availability of references is usually assumed. Don't include actual names of references. List your references on a separate sheet and bring them to your interview.

Activities and Achievements

Your résumé should also describe any volunteer activities that demonstrate your abilities. List projects that require leadership, organization, teamwork, and cooperation. Emphasize career-related activities such as "member of the Student Marketing Association." List skills you learned in these activities, and explain how these skills are related to the job you're applying for. Include speaking, writing, or tutoring experience; participation in athletics or creative projects; fund-raising or community-service activities; and offices held in academic or professional organizations. (However, mention of political or religious organizations may be a red flag to someone with different views, so use your judgment.) Note any awards you've received. Again, quantify your achievements whenever possible. Instead of saying that you addressed various student groups, state how many and the approximate audience sizes. If your activities have been extensive, you may want to group them into divisions such as "College Activities," "Community Service," "Professional Associations," "Seminars and Workshops," and "Speaking Activities." An alternative is to divide them into two categories: "Service Activities" and "Achievements, Awards, and Honors."

Nonpaid activities may provide evidence of work-related skills.

Personal Data

Provide only the personal data that will help you get the job.

Experts advise that you leave personal interests off your résumé unless they would enhance the employer's understanding of why you would be the best candidate for the job.[18] For instance, REI's applicants may want to list outdoor activities among their personal interests. According to Doug Halm, this shows that they will fit in with the organization's culture.

Civil rights laws prohibit employers from discriminating on the basis of gender, marital or family status, age (although only persons aged 40 to 70 are protected), race, color, religion, national origin, and physical or mental disability. Thus, be sure to exclude any items that could encourage discrimination. Experts also recommend that you exclude salary information, reasons for leaving jobs, names of previous supervisors, Social Security number, and other identification codes. Save these items for the interview, and offer them only if the employer specifically requests them.

If military service is relevant to the position you are seeking, you may list it in this section (or under "Education" or "Work Experience"). List the date of induction, the branch of service, where you served, the highest rank you achieved, any accomplishments related to your career goals, and the date you were discharged.

Choosing the Best Organizational Approach

Select an organizational approach that focuses attention on your strengths.

Although you may want to include a little information in all categories, emphasize the information that has a bearing on your career objective and minimize or exclude any that is irrelevant or counterproductive. You do so by adopting an organizational approach—chronological, functional, or combination—that focuses attention on your strongest points. The "right" choice depends on your background and goals.

The Chronological Résumé

Most recruiters prefer the chronological plan: a historical summary of your education and work experience.

The most traditional type of résumé is the **chronological résumé.** When you organize your résumé chronologically, the "Work Experience" section dominates the résumé and is placed in the most prominent slot, immediately after the name and address and the objective. You develop this section by listing your jobs sequentially in reverse order, beginning with the most recent position and working backward toward earlier jobs. Under each listing, you describe your responsibilities and accomplishments, giving the most space to the most recent positions. If you are just graduating from college, you can vary the chronological approach by putting your educational qualifications before your experience, thereby focusing attention on your academic credentials.

The chronological approach is the most common way to organize a résumé, and many employers prefer it. This organizational approach has three key advantages: (1) Employers are familiar with it and can easily find things; (2) it highlights growth and career progression; and (3) it highlights employment continuity and stability.[19] Robert Nesbit, a vice president with Korn/Ferry International, speaks for many recruiters: "Unless you have a really compelling reason, don't use any but the standard chronological format. Your résumé should not read like a treasure map, full of minute clues to the whereabouts of your jobs and experience. I want to be able to grasp quickly where a candidate has worked, how long, and in what capacities."[20]

The chronological approach is especially appropriate if you have a strong employment history and are aiming for a job that builds on your current career path. This is the case for Roberto Cortez, whose résumé appears in Figure 17.3.

The Functional Résumé

A functional résumé focuses attention on your areas of competence.

A **functional résumé is** organized around a list of skills and accomplishments, and employers and academic experience are identified in subordinate sections. This pattern stresses individual areas of competence, and it's useful for people who are just entering the job mar-

Roberto Cortez calls attention to his most recent achievements by setting them off in list form with bullets. The section titled "Intercultural and Technical Skills" emphasizes his international background, fluency in Spanish, and extensive computer skills—all of which are important qualifications for his target position.

Figure 17.3
In-Depth Critique: Chronological Résumé

ROBERTO CORTEZ
5687 Crosswoods Drive
Falls Church, Virginia 22046
Home: (703) 987-0086 Office: (703) 549-6624

OBJECTIVE

Accounting management position requiring a knowledge of international finance

EXPERIENCE

March 1995 to present — Staff Accountant/Financial Analyst, Inter-American Imports (Alexandria, VA)

- Prepare accounting reports for wholesale giftware importer ($15 million annual sales)
- Audit financial transactions with suppliers in 12 Latin American countries
- Create computerized models to adjust accounts for fluctuations in currency exchange rates
- Negotiate joint-venture agreements with major suppliers in Mexico and Colombia

October 1991 to March 1995 — Staff Accountant, Monsanto Agricultural Chemicals (Mexico City, Mexico)

- Handled budgeting, billing, and credit-processing functions for the Mexico City branch
- Audited travel/entertainment expenses for Monsanto's 30-member Latin American sales force
- Assisted in launching an online computer system to automate all accounting functions

EDUCATION

1989 to 1991 — MBA with emphasis in international business
George Mason University (Fairfax, Virginia)

1985 to 1989 — BBA, Accounting
University of Texas (Austin, Texas)

INTERCULTURAL AND TECHNICAL SKILLS

- Fluent in Spanish and German
- Traveled extensively in Latin America
- Excel
- Access
- HTML
- Visual Basic

Cortez emphasizes his achievements by using an indented bulleted list.

The chronological organization highlights Cortez's career progress.

Cortez highlights his foreign language and technological skills by presenting them in a special skills section.

ket, people who want to redirect their careers, and people who have little continuous career-related experience. The key advantages of this organizational approach are that (1) it helps readers clearly see what you can do for them, rather than having to read through job descriptions to find out; (2) it allows job seekers to emphasize an earlier job experience; and

Figure 17.4
In-Depth Critique: Functional Résumé

Although Glenda Johns has not held any paid, full-time positions in retail sales, she has participated in work-experience programs, and she knows a good deal about the profession from doing research and talking with people in the industry. As a result, she was able to organize her résumé in a way that demonstrates her ability to handle such a position.

Glenda S. Johns

Home: 457 Mountain View Road
Clear Lake, IA 50428
(515) 633-5971

College: 1254 Main Street
Council Bluffs, IA 51505
(712) 438-5254

OBJECTIVE

Retailing position that utilizes my experience

RELEVANT SKILLS

- Personal Selling/Retailing
  - Led housewares department in employee sales for spring 1998
  - Created end-cap and shelf displays for special housewares promotions
  - Sold the most benefit tickets during college fund-raising drive for local community center
- Public Interaction
  - Commended by housewares manager for resolving customer complaints amicably
  - Performed in summer theater productions in Clear Lake, Iowa
- Managing
  - Trained part-time housewares employees in cash register operation and customer service
  - Reworked housewares employee schedules as assistant manager
  - Organized summer activities for children 6–12 years old for city of Clear Lake, Iowa—including reading programs, sports activities, and field trips

EDUCATION

- AA, Retailing Mid-Management (3.81 GPA / 4.0 scale), Iowa Western Community College, June 1998
- In addition to required retailing, buying, marketing, and merchandising courses, completed electives in visual merchandising, business information systems, principles of management, and business math

WORK EXPERIENCE

- Assistant manager, housewares, at Jefferson's Department Store during off-campus work experience program, Council Bluffs, Iowa (fall 1997–spring 1998)
- Sales clerk, housewares, at Jefferson's Department Store during off-campus work experience program, Council Bluffs, Iowa (fall 1996–spring 1997)
- Assistant director, Summer Recreation Program, Clear Lake, Iowa (summer 1996)
- Actress, Cobblestone Players, Clear Lake, Iowa (summer 1995)

LEADERSHIP EXPERIENCE

- Student Co-Chair for Clear Lake Women's Auxiliary Board Fashion Show 1998 (raised $45,000)
- President of Phi Kappa Phi Sorority 1997
- Student representive (high school) to Clear Lake Chamber of Commerce (2 years)

Because she is a recent graduate, the applicant describes her relevant skills first.

The use of action verbs enhances this résumé's effectiveness.

The applicant's sketchy work history is described but not emphasized.

The applicant calls attention to her leadership abilities and experience by listing her leadership positions in a separate section.

(3) it de-emphasizes lack of career progress or lengthy unemployment. Figure 17.4 illustrates how a recent graduate used the functional approach to showcase her qualifications for a career in retail. Bear in mind that many seasoned employment professionals are suspect of this résumé style; they assume that candidates who use it are trying to hide something.[21]

When Erica Vorkamp developed her résumé, she chose not to use a chronological pattern, which would focus attention on her lack of recent work experience. Instead, she used a combined approach that emphasizes her ability to organize special events.

Figure 17.5
In-Depth Critique: Combined Résumé

Erica Vorkamp

993 Church Street, Barrington, IL 60010
(847) 884-2153

OBJECTIVE

To obtain a position as a special events coordinator that will utilize my skills and experience

SKILLS AND CAPABILITIES

- Plan and coordinate large-scale public events
- Develop community support for concerts, festivals, and the arts
- Manage publicity for major events
- Coordinate activities of diverse community groups
- Establish and maintain financial controls for public events
- Negotiate contracts with performers, carpenters, electricians, and suppliers

SPECIAL EVENT EXPERIENCE

- Arranged 1999's week-long Arts and Entertainment Festival for the Barrington Public Library, involving performances by 25 musicians, dancers, actors, magicians, and artists
- Supervised the 1998 PTA Halloween Carnival, an all-day festival with game booths, live bands, contests, and food service that raised $7,600 for the PTA
- Organized the 1997 Midwestern convention for 800 members of the League of Women Voters, which extended over a three-day period and required arrangements for hotels, meals, speakers, and special tours
- Served as chairperson for the 1996 Children's Home Society Fashion Show, a luncheon for 400 that raised $5,000 for orphans and abused children

EDUCATION

- BA, Psychology, Northwestern University (Evanston, Illinois), Phi Beta Kappa

EMPLOYMENT HISTORY

- First National Bank of Chicago, 1983 to 1985, personnel counselor/campus recruiter; scheduled and conducted interviews with graduating MBA students on 18 Midwestern campuses; managed orientation program for recruits hired for bank's management trainee staff
- Northwestern University, 1981–1983, part-time research assistant for Professor Paul Harris (Science Department)

The capabilities and experience are all related to the specific job objective, giving a very selective picture of the candidate's abilities.

Vorkamp includes event attendance statistics and fundraising results to quantify her accomplishments.

This work history has little bearing on the candidate's job target, but she felt that recruiters would want to see evidence that she has held a paying position.

The Combination Résumé

A **combination résumé** includes the best features of the chronological and functional formats. As Figure 17.5 shows, this format emphasizes a candidate's skills and accomplishments while also including a complete job history. Nevertheless, it is not commonly used,

A combination résumé is a hybrid of the chronological and functional résumés.

and it has two major disadvantages: (1) It tends to be longer, and (2) it can be repetitious because you may have to list your accomplishments and skills in both the functional section and the chronological job descriptions.[22]

Adapting Your Résumé to an Electronic Format

Doing an electronic version of your résumé is helpful if it will be scanned or if you will be posting it on the Internet or submitting it via e-mail.

In the past, decisions about how to format a résumé were pretty basic. Plain white paper or buff. One page or two. But those days are gone. Today you need three differently formatted résumés: a traditional document such as the one we just discussed; a plain-text, or ASCII, document with descriptive key words designed for scanning or submitting electronically; and an HTML-coded document to post as a Web page should you choose to go that route.

Understanding the Scanning Process

Overwhelmed by the number of résumés they receive, most Fortune 1000 companies today encourage applicants to submit electronic or scannable résumés. By scanning these résumés into their electronic database, companies can narrow down the pile of applicants quickly. Because good scanning systems can cost up to $100,000, however, employers with fewer than 100 employees seldom use them.[23] If you're unsure whether an employer accepts scannable résumés, call and ask.

Because the required format is different from that for traditional résumés, it helps to understand how résumé scanning works. Special hardware and software are used to convert a paper résumé into an image on the employer's computer. Optical character recognition (OCR) software creates an electronic text document (similar to one you keyboard directly into a computer) by looking at the image to distinguish every letter and number. The electronic text is then downloaded into a company database that can be searched and sorted on key words, criteria, or just about anything the employer programs into the computer as a search strategy. For example, a manager might want to hire a marketing representative who speaks Spanish and who has five years' sales experience, a background in new product marketing, and experience in cold calling. The employer enters these key words plus others into the database program and performs a sort function on all the résumés in the database. The computer then provides a list of candidates whose résumés include these key words along with a percentage next to the candidate's name indicating how much of the hiring manager's wish list is reflected in the résumé.[24]

Changing the Format and Style

Electronic, or scannable, résumés should convey the same information as a traditional résumé, but the format and style must be made computer friendly. This means you must eliminate any graphics, boldface print, underlines, italics, small print, and formatting codes, such as tab settings, that were attached to your document by your software when you saved your traditional résumé document.[25] It's no longer necessary to confine your electronic résumé to one page, but don't get carried away. To change your traditional paper résumé into a scannable one, you convert it into plain-text (ASCII) format, provide a list of key words, and balance common language with jargon (see Figure 17.6).[26]

To make your résumé scannable

- Save it as an ASCII file
- Provide a list of key words
- Balance clear language with up-to-date jargon

Converting Your Résumé to ASCII Format ASCII is a common plain-text language that allows your résumé to be read by any scanner and accessed by any computer regardless of the word-processing software you used to prepare the document. All word-processing programs allow you to save files as plain text. To convert your résumé to an ASCII plain-text file, open your document and remove all formatting such as bolding, centering, bullets, and graphic lines. Then highlight all text and select a popular typeface such as Times, Helvetica, or

Because some of his target employers will be scanning his résumé into a database, and because he wants to submit his résumé via e-mail or post it on the Internet, Roberto Cortez created an electronic résumé by changing his formatting and adding a list of key words. However, the information remains essentially the same and appears in the same order.

Figure 17.6
In-Depth Critique: Electronic Résumé

Roberto Cortez
5687 Crosswoods Drive
Falls Church, Virginia 22046
Home: (703) 987-0086 Office: (703) 549-6624
RCortez@silvernet.com

KEY WORDS

Financial executive, accounting management, international finance, financial analyst, accounting reports, financial audit, computerized accounting model, exchange rates, joint-venture agreements, budgets, billing, credit processing, online systems, MBA, fluent Spanish, fluent German, Excel, Access, Visual Basic, team player, willing to travel

OBJECTIVE

Accounting management position requiring a knowledge of international finance

EXPERIENCE

Staff Accountant/Financial Analyst, Inter-American Imports (Alexandria, Virginia)
March 1995 to present
o Prepare accounting reports for wholesale giftware importer, annual sales of $15 million
o Audited financial transactions with suppliers in 12 Latin American countries
o Created a computerized model to adjust for fluctuations in currency exchange rates
o Negotiated joint-venture agreements with suppliers in Mexico and Colombia
o Implemented electronic funds transfer for vendor disbursements, improving cash flow and eliminating payables clerk position

Staff Accountant, Monsanto Agricultural Chemicals (Mexico City, Mexico)
October 1991 to March 1995
o Handled budgeting, billing and credit-processing functions for the Mexico City branch
o Audited travel/entertainment expenses for Monsanto's 30-member Latin American sales force
o Assisted in launching an online computer system to automate all accounting functions

EDUCATION

MBA with emphasis in international business, George Mason University (Fairfax, Virginia), 1989 to 1991

BBA, Accounting, University of Texas (Austin, Texas), 1985 to 1989

INTERCULTURAL AND TECHNICAL SKILLS

Fluent in Spanish and German
Traveled extensively in Latin America
Excel, Access, HTML, Visual Basic

An attractive and fully formatted hard copy of this document is available upon request.

Cortez removed all boldfacing, rules, bullets, and two-column formatting.

Cortez carefully selected key words that describe his skills and accomplishments, and he included specific attributes such as "team player" and "willing to travel" to single himself out from the crowd.

Cortez used a lowercase letter o in his indented lists and produced the indentions with the space bar rather than with the tab key.

Cortez used ample white space to make his résumé appear more readable.

Courier with a 10- to 14-point font size. Finally, save your document under a different name by using your word processor's "save as" option and selecting "text only with line breaks."

To help your electronic résumé appear more readable, open your new document, add some blank spaces (rather than tabs) to align text, add a few blank lines to create headings and separate paragraphs, and use an asterisk or a lowercase letter *o* to indicate a bullet. Be sure to use a lot of white space to allow scanners and computers to recognize when one topic ends and another begins. Make sure your name and address are the first lines on your résumé (with no text appearing above or alongside your name). When you print your résumé in this plain-text format, you'll see that it is indeed very plain but now is computer friendly.

Providing a List of Key Words When converting your résumé to a scannable format, you must emphasize certain key words that will help potential employers select your résumé from the thousands they scan. When employers scan résumés, they generally search for nouns because verbs tend to be generic rather than specific to a particular position or skill. To maximize the number of "hits," include a key word summary of 20 to 30 words and phrases that define your skills, experience, education, professional affiliations, and so on. Place this list right after your name and address. Here's an example of a possible key word summary for an accountant:

KEY WORD SUMMARY

Accountant, Corporate Controller, Fortune 1000, Receivables, Payables, Inventory, Cash Flow, Financial Analysis, Payroll Experience, Corporate Taxes, Activity-Based Accounting, Problem Solving, Computer Skills, Excel, Access, Networks, HTML, Peachtree, Quick Books, BA Indiana University—Accounting, CPA, Dean's List, Articulate, Team Player, Flexible, Willing to Travel, Fluent Spanish.

One way to identify which key words to include in your electronic summary is to underline all the skills listed in ads for the types of jobs your are interested in. Make sure that these ads match your qualifications and experience. Some job candidates try to beat the system by listing every conceivable skill and by guessing which words the computer is likely to be looking for. But that strategy seldom works. The computer may be looking for a Harvard Business School graduate who once worked at Netscape and lives in the 94024 zip code. If you went to Yale, worked at Yahoo! and live in Maine, you're out of luck.[27]

Balancing Common Language with Current Jargon To maximize matches (or hits) between your résumé and an employer's search, use words that potential employers will understand. For example, don't call a keyboard an input device. Also, use abbreviations sparingly, except for common ones such as BA or MBA. At the same time, learn the important buzzwords used in your field, and use them. Look for the current buzzwords in want ads in

An Internet classified ad placed by Salestar recruiting manager Jean E. West of San Francisco led to Kamran Lotfi of New York City taking a job as a product manager for the software firm.

major newspapers such as the *Wall Street Journal* and in other résumés in your field that are posted online. Be careful to check and recheck the spelling, capitalization, and punctuation of any jargon you include, and use only those words you see most often.

Submitting Electronic Résumés

If an employer gives you an option of submitting a scannable résumé by mail, by fax, or by e-mail, choose e-mail. Sending your résumé by e-mail in a plain-text format is preferable because e-mail puts your résumé directly into the employer's database, bypassing the scanning process. If you send your résumé in a paper format by regular mail or by fax, you still run the risk that an OCR scanning program will create an error when reading your résumé.

If you submit your résumé by e-mail, don't attach it as a separate document. Most human resources departments won't accept attached files (they are concerned about computer viruses). Instead, paste your résumé into the body of your e-mail message by putting your cursor in the body of the e-mail message and using the "insert text file" command to bring the ASCII-formatted résumé into the file. Always include reference numbers or job ad numbers in the subject line of your e-mail if they are available.

If you're posting your electronic résumé to an employer's online résumé builder, copy and paste the appropriate sections from your electronic file directly into the employer's form. This method avoids rekeying and eliminates errors.

If you fax your electronic résumé, set your machine to "fine" mode to result in a higher-quality printout on the receiving end. If you're mailing your résumé, you may want to send both a well-designed traditional résumé and a scannable one. Attach Post-It notes, labeling one copy "visual résumé" and the other "scannable résumé."

Building an Online Résumé

If you wish to showcase your abilities via a Web page résumé, keep in mind that many employers and recruiters will not take the time to use search engines to find your home page. So be sure to provide employers with your URL address.[28] As you design your Web site résumé, think of important key words to use as hyperlinks. Use words that will grab an employer's attention and make her or him want to click on that hyperlink to learn more about you. Do not use hyperlinks to organizations or other Web sites; they will take the employer's attention away from your credentials.

Remember, do not use photos or provide information that reveals your age, gender, race, marital status, or religion on your Web site résumé. Because a Web site is a public access area, you should also leave out the names of references and the names of previous employers. Simply say that references are available on request, or say nothing. Also be sure to refer to "a large accounting firm" or "a wholesale giftware importer" rather than naming companies. Finally, be sure to include an ASCII version of your résumé on your Web page that prospective employers can download into their company database, as well as a fully formatted résumé that can be read online and easily printed.

Writing the Perfect Résumé

The "perfect" résumé responds to the reader's needs and preferences and avoids some common faults.

Whether your résumé is electronic or paper, the key to writing the "perfect" résumé is to adopt the "you" attitude by thinking about what the prospective employer needs, then tailoring your résumé accordingly.

People like Doug Halm read thousands of résumés every year and complain about the following common résumé problems:

- *Too long.* The résumé is not concise, relevant, and to the point.
- *Too short or sketchy.* The résumé does not give enough information for a proper evaluation of the applicant.

- *Hard to read.* A lack of "white space" and of such devices as indentions and boldfacing makes the reader's job more difficult.
- *Wordy.* Descriptions are verbose, with numerous words used for what could be said more simply.
- *Too slick.* The résumé appears to have been written by someone other than the applicant, which raises the question of whether the qualifications have been exaggerated.
- *Amateurish.* The applicant appears to have little understanding of the business world or of the particular industry, as revealed by including the wrong information or presenting it awkwardly.
- *Poorly reproduced.* The print is faint and difficult to read.
- *Misspelled and ungrammatical throughout.* Recruiters conclude that candidates who make these kinds of mistakes don't have good verbal skills, which are important on the job.
- *Boastful.* The overconfident tone makes the reader wonder whether the applicant's self-evaluation is realistic.
- *Dishonest.* The applicant claims to have expertise or work experience that he or she does not possess.
- *Gimmicky.* The words, structure, decoration, or material used in the résumé depart so far from the usual as to make the résumé ineffective.

Guard against making these mistakes in your own résumé, and compare your final version with the suggestions in this chapter's Checklist for Résumés.

Also, update your résumé continuously. You'll need it whether you're applying for membership in a professional organization, working toward a promotion, or changing employers. People used to spend most of their career with one company. Today, however, the average person beginning a job in the United States will probably work in ten or more jobs for five or more employers before retiring.[29] So keeping your résumé updated is a good idea.

Whenever you submit your résumé, be sure to accompany it with a cover or application letter. This document lets your reader know what you're sending, why you're sending it, and how your reader can benefit from reading it. Because your application letter is in your own style (rather than the choppy, shorthand style of your résumé), it gives you a chance to make a good personal impression.

WRITING APPLICATION MESSAGES

The purpose of your cover letter is to get the reader interested enough to read your résumé. Always send the two together because each has a unique job to perform.

Before you write your application letter, learn something about the organization you're applying to. Then, when composing the letter, adopt the "you" attitude. Show that you've done your homework. Imagine yourself in the recruiter's situation and show how your background and talents will solve a particular company problem or fill a need. The more you can learn about the organization, the better you'll be able to capture the reader's attention and convey your desire to join the company.[30]

During your research, find out the name, title, and department of the person you're writing to. Reaching and addressing the right person is the most effective way to gain attention. Always avoid phrases such as "To Whom It May Concern" and "Dear Sir."

You write a solicited application letter in response to an announced job opening.

If you're sending a **solicited application letter**—one sent in response to an announced job opening—you'll usually know what qualifications the organization is seeking. However, you'll also have more competition because hundreds of other job seekers will have seen the

CHECKLIST FOR RÉSUMÉS

Traditional Résumé

A. Format and Style

1. Use short noun phrases and action verbs, not whole sentences.
2. Use facts, not opinions.
3. Adopt a "you" attitude.
4. Omit personal pronouns—especially the word *I*.
5. Omit the date of preparation, desired salary, and work schedule.
6. Use parallelism in listing multiple items.
7. Use positive language and simple words.
8. Keep it looking sharp by using plenty of white space, high-quality paper, and laser printing.

B. Content

1. Contact information
2. Career objective or skills summary (optional)
   - **a.** In stating a career objective, be specific and try to generate interest.
   - **b.** Prepare two different résumés if you can do two unrelated types of work.
   - **c.** For a skills summary, summarize your key qualifications, presenting the strongest ones first.
3. Education
   - **a.** List name and location of every postsecondary school you have attended, with the dates you entered and left and the degrees or certificates you obtained.
   - **b.** Indicate your major (and minor) fields in college work.
   - **c.** If your grade point average is impressive enough to list, be sure to include the numerical scale (4.0 or 5.0).
   - **d.** List any other related educational or training experiences, such as job-related seminars or workshops attended and certificates obtained. (Give dates.)
4. Work experience, skills, and accomplishments
   - **a.** List all relevant work experience, including paid employment, volunteer work, and internships.
   - **b.** List full-time and part-time jobs, with the most recent one first.
     - **i.** Provide the name and location of each firm that employed you, as well as the years (or months) you worked there.
     - **ii.** List your job title and briefly describe your responsibilities.
     - **iii.** Note on-the-job accomplishments and skills; quantify them when possible.
5. Activities and achievements
   - **a.** List all relevant offices and leadership positions.
   - **b.** List projects you have undertaken.
   - **c.** Show your abilities, such as writing or speaking, and mention any publications and community service.
6. Other relevant facts
   - **a.** List other information, such as your proficiency in languages other than English.
   - **b.** Mention your ability to operate any special equipment and all technical and computer skills (including software).
7. Personal data
   - **a.** Omit personal details that could be regarded negatively or be used to discriminate against you.
   - **b.** Leave personal interests off unless they are relevant to the position.
   - **c.** List a reference only if you have the person's permission to do so.

C. Organizational Approach

1. Use the chronological approach unless you have a weak employment history.
2. Use the functional approach if you are new to the job market, want to redirect your career, or have gaps in your employment history.
3. Use the combined approach to maximize the advantages of both chronological and functional résumés, but only when neither of the other two formats will work.

Modifications for Electronic Résumé

A. Style and Format

1. Eliminate any graphics as well as boldface, underlines, italics, small print, tabs, and other formatting codes.
2. Save file in plain-text (ASCII) format.
3. Add blank spaces, align text, and use asterisks for bullets.

B. Content

1. Add a "Key Word Summary" listing nouns that define your skills, experience, education, and professional attributes.
2. Mirror the job description when possible.
3. Add job-related jargon, but don't overdo it.

Modifications for Online Résumé

A. Provide employers with your URL and e-mail address.

B. Use keyword hyperlinks to the following:

1. ASCII version of your résumé that employers can download into an electronic database.
2. Fully formatted résumé that can be read online and printed.

You write an unsolicited application letter to an organization that has not announced a job opening.

listing and may be sending applications too. In some respects, therefore, an **unsolicited letter**—one that is sent to an organization that has not announced an opening—stands a better chance of being read and of receiving individualized attention. Regardless, the two types of letters present your qualifications similarly. The main difference is in the opening paragraph. In a solicited letter, you need no special attention-getter because you have been invited to apply. In an unsolicited letter, you need to start by capturing the reader's attention and interest.

Adopting the AIDA Approach

Follow the AIDA approach when writing your application letter: attention, interest, desire, action.

Like your résumé, your application letter is a form of advertising, so organize it as you would a sales letter: Use the AIDA approach, focus on the "you" attitude, and emphasize reader benefits (as discussed in Chapter 9). You need to stimulate your reader's interest before showing how you can satisfy the organization's needs. Make sure your style projects confidence; you can't hope to sell a potential employer on your merits unless you truly believe in them yourself and sound as though you do.

Of course, this approach isn't appropriate for job seekers in every culture. If you're applying for a job abroad or want to work with a subsidiary of an organization based in another country, you may need to adjust your tone. For instance, blatant self-promotion is considered bad form in some cultures. Other cultures stress group performance over individual contributions. And, as for format, recruiters in some countries (including France), prefer handwritten letters to printed or typed ones. So research a company carefully before drafting your application letter.

For U.S. and Canadian companies, let your letter reflect your personal style. Be yourself, but be businesslike too; avoid sounding cute. Don't use slang or a gimmicky layout. The only time to be unusually creative in content or format is when the job you're seeking requires imagination, such as a position in advertising.

Getting Attention

The opening of an unsolicited application letter captures attention and raises the reader's interest.

One way to spark attention in the opening paragraph is to show how your strongest work skills could benefit the organization. A 20-year-old in her third year of college might begin like this:

> When you need a secretary in your export division who can take shorthand at 125 words a minute and transcribe notes at 70—in English, Spanish, or Portuguese—call me.

Here's another attention-getter. It describes the applicant's understanding of the job's requirements and then shows how well his qualifications fit the job:

> Your annual report states that Mobil Corporation runs training programs about work force diversity for managers and employees. The difficulties involved in running such programs can be significant, as I learned while tutoring inner-city high school students last summer. My 12 pupils were enrolled in vocational training programs and came from diverse ethnic and racial backgrounds. The one thing they had in common was the lack of familiarity with the typical employer's expectations. To help them learn the "rules of the game," I developed exercises that cast them in various roles: boss, customer, new recruit, and co-worker. Of the 12 students, 10 have subsequently found full-time jobs and have called or written to tell me how much they gained from the workshop.

Mentioning the name of a person known to and highly regarded by the reader is bound to capture some attention:

> When Janice McHugh of your franchise sales division spoke to our business communication class last week, she said you often need promising new marketing graduates at this time of year.

References to publicized company activities, achievements, changes, or new procedures can also be used to gain attention:

> Today's issue of the *Detroit News* reports that you may need the expertise of computer programmers versed in robotics when your Lansing tire plant automates this spring.

Another type of attention-getting opening uses a question to demonstrate an understanding of the organization's needs:

> Can your fast-growing market research division use an interviewer with 1½ years of field survey experience, a BA in public relations, and a real desire to succeed? If so, please consider me for the position.

A catch-phrase opening can also capture attention, especially if the job sought requires ingenuity and imagination:

> Haut monde—whether said in French, Italian, or Arabic, it still means "high society." As an interior designer for your Beverly Hills showroom, not only could I serve and sell to your distinguished clientele, but I could do it in all these languages. I speak, read, and write them fluently.

Start a solicited application letter by mentioning how you found out about the open position.

Instead of using an attention-getter, a solicited letter written in response to a job advertisement usually opens by identifying the publication in which the ad ran and then describes what the applicant has to offer:

> Your ad in the April issue of *Travel & Leisure* for a cruise-line social director caught my eye. My eight years of experience as a social director in the travel industry would allow me to serve your new Caribbean cruise division well.

Note that all these openings demonstrate the "you" attitude, and many indicate how the applicant can serve the employer.

State in the opening paragraph which job you are applying for.

The opening paragraph of your application letter also states your reason for writing and the position you are applying for:

> Please consider my application for an entry-level position in technical writing.

> Your firm advertised a fleet sales position (on September 23, 1999, in the *Baltimore Sun*). With my 16 months of new-car sales experience, won't you consider me for that position?

Another way to state your reason for writing is to use a title at the opening of your letter:

> Subject: Application for bookkeeper position

After this clear signal, your first paragraph can focus on getting attention and indicating how hiring you may benefit the organization.

Building Interest and Increasing Desire

The middle section of an application letter

- Summarizes your relevant qualifications
- Emphasizes your accomplishments
- Suggests desirable personal qualities
- Justifies salary requirements
- Refers to your résumé

The middle section of your application letter presents your strongest selling points in terms of their potential benefit to the organization, thereby creating interest in you and a desire to interview you. If your selling points have already been mentioned in the opening, don't repeat them. Simply give supporting evidence. Otherwise, spell out your key qualifications, together with some convincing evidence of your ability to perform.

To avoid a cluttered application letter, mention only the qualifications that indicate you can do the job. Show how your studies and your work experience have prepared you for this job, or tell the reader about how you grew up in the business. Be careful not to repeat the facts presented in your résumé; simply interpret those facts for the reader:

> Experience in customer relations and college courses in public relations have taught me how to handle the problem-solving tasks that arise in a leading retail clothing firm like yours. Such important tasks include identifying and

> resolving customer complaints, writing letters that build good customer relations, and above all, promoting the organization's positive image.

When writing a solicited letter responding to a help-wanted advertisement, discuss each requirement specified in the ad. If you are deficient in any of these requirements, stress other solid selling points to help strengthen your overall presentation.

Stating that you have all the necessary requirements for the job is rarely enough to convince the reader, so back up assertions of your ability by presenting evidence. Cite one or two of your key qualifications; then show how you have effectively put them to use.

INSTEAD OF THIS	WRITE THIS
I completed three college courses in business communication, earning an A in each course, and have worked for the past year at Imperial Construction.	Using the skills gained from three semesters of college training in business communication, I developed a collection system for Imperial Construction that reduced its 1999 bad-debt losses by 3.7 percent, or $9,902, over those of 1998. Instead of using timeworn terminology, the new system's collection letters offered discount incentives for speedy payment.

This section of the letter also presents evidence of a few significant job-related qualities. The following paragraph demonstrates that the applicant is diligent and hard working:

> While attending college full-time, I trained 3 hours a day with the varsity track team. In addition, I worked part-time during the school year and up to 60 hours a week each summer in order to be totally self-supporting while in college. I can offer your organization the same level of effort and perseverance.

Other relevant qualities worth noting include the abilities to learn quickly, to handle responsibility, and to get along with people.

Another matter to bring up in this section is your salary requirements—but *only* if the organization has asked you to state them. The best strategy, unless you know approximately what the job pays, is to suggest a salary range or to indicate that the salary is negotiable or open. You might also consult the latest government "Area Wage Survey" at the library; this document presents salary ranges for various job classifications and geographic areas. If you do state a target salary, tie your request to the benefits you would provide the organization, much as you would handle price in a sales letter:

> For the past two years, I have been helping a company similar to yours organize its database. I would therefore like to receive a salary in the same range (the mid-20s) for helping your company set up a more efficient customer database.

Toward the end of this section, refer the reader to your résumé. You can do so by citing a specific fact or general point covered in the résumé:

> You will find my people skills an asset. As you can see in the attached résumé, I've been working part-time with a local publisher since my sophomore year, and during that time, I have successfully resolved more than a few "client crises."

Motivating Action

The final paragraph of your application letter has two important functions: to ask the reader for a specific action and to make a reply easy. In almost all cases, the action you ask for is an interview. Don't demand it, however; try to sound natural and appreciative. Offer to come to the employer's office at a convenient time or, if the firm is some distance away, to meet with its nearest representative. Make the request easy to fulfill by stating your phone number and the best time to reach you—or, if you wish to be in control, by mentioning that you will follow up with a phone call in a few days. Refer again to your strongest selling point and, if desired, your date of availability:

Close by asking for an interview and making the interview easy to arrange.

> After you have reviewed my qualifications, could we discuss the possibility of putting my marketing skills to work for your company? Because I will be on spring break the week of March 8, I would like to arrange a time to talk then. I will call in late February to schedule a convenient time when we could discuss employment opportunities at your company.

Once you have proofread and edited your application letter, mail it and your résumé promptly, especially if they have been solicited.

Writing the Perfect Application Letter

The "perfect" application letter accomplishes one thing: It gets the reader to read your résumé. It conforms to no particular model, because it's a reflection of your special strengths. Nevertheless, an application letter contains certain basic components. In the unsolicited letter for a retail position presented in Figure 17.7, the applicant gains attention by focusing on the needs of the employer. The letter in Figure 17.8, written in response to a help-wanted ad, highlights the applicant's chief qualifications and mirrors the requirements specified in the ad. Compare your own letters with the tasks in this chapter's Checklist for Application Letters.

Writing Other Types of Employment Messages

In your search for a job, you may prepare three other types of written messages: job-inquiry letters, application forms, and application follow-up letters.

Writing Job-Inquiry Letters

Some organizations will not consider you for a position until you have filled out and submitted an **application form,** a standardized data sheet that simplifies comparison of applicants' qualifications. A job-inquiry letter is sent to request such a form. To increase your chances of getting the form, include enough information about yourself in the letter to show that you have at least some of the requirements for the position you are seeking:

Use a job-inquiry letter to request an application form, which is a standardized data sheet that simplifies comparison of applicants' credentials.

> Please send me an application form for work as an interior designer in your home furnishings department. For my certificate in design, I took courses in retail merchandising and customer relations. I have also had part-time sales experience at Capwell's department store.

Instead of writing a letter of this kind, you may want to drop in at the office you're applying to. You probably won't get a chance to talk to anyone other than the receptionist or a human resources assistant, but you can pick up the form, get an impression of the organization, and demonstrate your initiative and energy.

Filling Out Application Forms

Your care in filling out application forms suggests to the employer that you will be thorough and careful in your work.

When filling out an application form, try to be thorough and accurate, because the organization will use it as a convenient one-page source for information about your qualifications. Be sure to have your résumé with you to remind you of important

Figure 17.7
In-Depth Critique: Sample Unsolicited Application Letter

In her unsolicited application letter, Glenda Johns manages to give a snapshot of her qualifications and skills without repeating what is said in her résumé (which appears in Figure 17.4).

Glenda S. Johns

Home: 457 Mountain View Road, Clear Lake, IA 50428 (515) 633-5971
College: 1254 Main Street, Council Bluffs, IA 51505 (712) 438-5254

June 16, 2000

Ms. Patricia Downings, Store Manager
Wal-Mart
840 South Oak
Iowa Falls, Iowa 50126

Dear Ms. Downings:

You want retail clerks and managers who are accurate, enthusiastic, and experienced. You want someone who cares about customer service, who understands merchandising, and who can work with others to get the job done. When you're ready to hire a manager trainee or a clerk who is willing to work toward promotion, please consider me for the job.

Working as a clerk and then as an assistant department manager in a large department store has taught me how challenging a career in retailing can be. Moreover, my AA degree in retailing (including work in such courses as retailing, marketing, and business information systems) will provide your store with a well-rounded associate. Most important, I can offer Wal-Mart's Iowa Falls store more than my two years' of study and field experience. You'll find that I'm interested in every facet of retailing, eager to take on responsibility, and willing to continue learning throughout my career. Please look over my résumé to see how my skills can benefit your store.

I understand that Wal-Mart prefers to promote its managers from within the company, and I would be pleased to start out with an entry-level position until I gain the necessary experience. Do you have any associate positions opening up soon? Could we discuss my qualifications? I will phone you early next Wednesday to arrange a meeting at your convenience.

Sincerely,

Glenda Johns

Glenda Johns

Enclosure

The applicant gains attention in the first paragraph.

The applicant points out personal qualities that aren't specifically stated in her résumé.

Knowledge of the company's policy toward promotion is sure to interest the reader.

Even though the last paragraph uses the word *I*, the concern and the focus of the letter are clearly centered on the audience and convey a "you" attitude.

information. If you can't remember something and have no record of it, provide the closest estimate possible. If the form calls for information that you cannot provide because you have no background in it, such as military experience, write "Not applicable." When filling out applications, use a pen (unless specifically requested to use a pencil) and print legibly.

Kenneth Sawyer grabs attention by focusing on a phrase the employer used in a want ad: "proven skills." Sawyer elaborates on his own proven skills throughout the letter, and he even mentions the term in the closing paragraph.

Figure 17.8
In-Depth Critique: Sample Solicited Application Letter

Kenneth Sawyer

2893 Jack Pine Road, Chapel Hill, NC 27514

February 2, 2000

Ms. Angela Clair
Director of Administration
Cummings and Welbane, Inc.
770 Campus Point Drive
Chapel Hill, NC 27514

Dear Ms. Clair:

In the January 31 issue of the *Chapel Hill Post*, your ad mentioned "proven skills." I believe I have what you are looking for in an administrative assistant. In addition to experience in a variety of office settings, I am familiar with the computer software that you use in your office.

The opening states the reason for writing and links the writer's experience to stated qualifications.

I recently completed a three-course sequence at Hamilton College on Microsoft Word and PowerPoint. I learned how to apply those programs to speed up letter- and report-writing tasks. A workshop on "Writing and Editing with the Unix Processor" gave me experience with other valuable applications such as composing and formatting sales letters, financial reports, and presentation slides.

These skills have been invaluable to me as assistant to the chief nutritionist at our campus cafeteria (please refer to my résumé). I'm particularly proud of the order-confirmation system I designed, which has sharply reduced the problems of late shipments and depleted inventories.

By discussing how his specific skills apply to the job sought, the applicant shows that he understands the job's responsibilities.

Because "proven skills" are best explained in person, I would appreciate an interview with you. Please phone me any afternoon between 3 and 5 p.m. at (919) 220-6139 to let me know the day and time most convenient for you.

In closing, the writer asks for an interview and facilitates action.

Sincerely,

Kenneth Sawyer

Kenneth Sawyer

Enclosure: Résumé

Application forms rarely seem to provide the right amount of space or to ask the right kinds of questions to reflect one's skills and abilities accurately. Swallow your frustration, however, and show your cooperation by doing your best to fill out the form completely. If you get an interview, you'll have an opportunity to fill in the gaps. You might also ask the person who gives you the form if you may submit a résumé and an application letter as well.

CHECKLIST FOR APPLICATION LETTERS

A. Attention (Opening Paragraph)

1. Open the letter by capturing the reader's attention in a businesslike way.
   - **a.** *Summary opening.* Present your strongest, most relevant qualifications, with an explanation of how they can benefit the organization.
   - **b.** *Name opening.* Mention the name of a person who is well known to the reader and who has suggested that you apply for the job.
   - **c.** *Source opening.* When responding to a job ad, identify the publication in which the ad appeared, and briefly describe how you meet each requirement stated in the ad.
   - **d.** *Question opening.* Pose an attention-getting question that shows you understand the organization's problem, need, or goal and have a genuine desire to help solve, satisfy, or meet it.
   - **e.** *News opening.* Cite a publicized achievement, contemplated change, or new procedure or product of the organization; then link it to your desire to work for the organization.
   - **f.** *Personalized opening.* Present one of your relevant interests, mention previous experience with the organization, or cite your current position or status as a means of leading into a discussion of why you want to work for the organization.
   - **g.** *Creative opening.* Demonstrate your flair and imagination with colorful phrasing, especially if the job requires these qualities.
2. State that you are applying for a job, and identify the position or the type of work you seek.

B. Interest and Desire, or Evidence of Qualifications (Next Several Paragraphs)

1. Present your key qualifications for the job, highlighting what is on your résumé: job-related education and training; relevant work experience; and related activities, interests, and qualities.
2. Adopt a mature, businesslike tone.
   - **a.** Eliminate boasting and exaggeration.
   - **b.** Back up your claims of ability by citing specific achievements in educational and work settings or in outside activities.
   - **c.** Demonstrate a knowledge of the organization and a desire to join it by citing its operations or trends in the industry.
3. Link your education, experience, and personal qualities to the job requirements.
   - **a.** Relate aspects of your training or work experience to those of the target position.
   - **b.** Outline your educational preparation for the job.
   - **c.** Provide proof that you learn quickly, are a hard worker, can handle responsibility, and get along well with others.
   - **d.** Present ample evidence of the personal qualities and the work attitudes that are desirable for job performance.
   - **e.** If asked to state salary requirements, provide current salary or a desired salary range, and link it to the benefits of hiring you.
4. Refer the reader to the enclosed résumé.

C. Action (Closing Paragraph)

1. Request an interview at the reader's convenience.
2. Request a screening interview with the nearest regional representative, if company headquarters is some distance away.
3. State your phone number (with area code) and the best time to reach you, to make the interview request easy to comply with, or mention a time when you will be calling to set up an interview.
4. Express appreciation for an opportunity to have an interview.
5. Repeat your strongest qualification, to help reinforce the claim that you have something to offer the organization.

Writing Application Follow-Ups

Use a follow-up letter to let the employer know you're still interested in the job.

If your application letter and résumé fail to bring a response within a month or so, follow up with a second letter to keep your file active. This follow-up letter also gives you a chance to update your original application with any recent job-related information:

> Since applying to you on May 3 for an executive secretary position, I have completed a course in office management at South River Community College. I re-

> ceived straight A's in the course. I now am a proficient user of MS Word, including macros and other complex functions.
>
> Please keep my application in your active file, and let me know when you need a skilled executive secretary.

Even if you have received a letter acknowledging your application and saying that it will be kept on file, don't hesitate to send a follow-up letter three months later to show that you are still interested:

> Three months have elapsed since I applied to you for an underwriting position, but I want to let you know that I am still very interested in joining your company.
>
> I recently completed a four-week temporary work assignment at a large local insurance agency. I learned several new verification techniques and gained experience in using the online computer system. This experience could increase my value to your underwriting department.
>
> Please keep my application in your active file, and let me know when a position opens for a capable underwriter.

Unless you state otherwise, the human resources office is likely to assume that you've already found a job and are no longer interested in the organization. In addition, organizations' requirements change. A letter like this demonstrates that you are sincerely interested in working for the organization, that you are persistent in pursuing your goals, and that you continue upgrading your skills to make yourself a better employee—and it might just get you an interview.

COMMUNICATION CHALLENGES AT RECREATION EQUIPMENT INCORPORATED (REI)

REI receives hundreds of unsolicited résumés each month. Doug Halm has recently revised the procedures for screening all résumés. Instead of reviewing them at REI's headquarters, Halm's staff now sorts the résumés and sends them directly to the human resources departments in the functional units that have specific openings. This procedure enables the people who actually do the hiring to evaluate the résumés. Although this method has several advantages, Halm is concerned about one possible problem: inconsistency in the evaluation process.

Individual Challenge: To ensure that all REI units use similar criteria to screen résumés, Halm wants to develop a guideline for evaluating the résumés of graduating students. The guideline will help REI's managers identify people who have good work habits, strong communication skills, commitment to teamwork, leadership potential, and a love for the outdoors. However, Halm wants to avoid imposing any rigid screening criteria that might arbitrarily eliminate promising candidates. He has asked you to develop the guideline and a one-page memo explaining how to use it. After you have done so, test the guideline by evaluating the résumés of three fellow students.

Team Challenge: Halm is planning a workshop on writing application letters for a Career Day at a nearby college. He wants to present letters that effectively portray limited work experiences in a positive light. He asks a group of you to draft letters that describe useful work skills and habits learned when (1) one applicant worked part-time as a supermarket cashier, (2) a second applicant worked as a camp counselor, and (3) a third applicant typed envelopes for a mailing service. Explain what employers may find relevant about the skills and habits described in each letter.[31] ■

SUMMARY OF LEARNING OBJECTIVES

1. **Identify several career-building activities.** Participating in internship programs, studying abroad, learning a foreign language, joining professional networks, and polishing and updating your skills are among the activities that will help you build toward a career.
2. **Differentiate between the functions of a résumé and an application letter.** The résumé is designed to create interest in a candidate and to get an interview, whereas an application letter is designed to get the recruiter to read your résumé.
3. **List the major components of a traditional résumé.** A traditional résumé should include contact information (name, address, telephone numbers), career objective and/or summary of qualifications, education, work experience, skills and accomplishments, activities and achievements, and job-related personal data.
4. **Differentiate among the three organizational approach for résumés.** The chronological résumé lists your employment history in reverse chronological order immediately after your name and objective, and it is the preferred organizational approach. The functional résumé stresses individual areas of competence and is used if you have little continuous career-related experience, if you want to redirect your career, or if you are just entering the job market. The combination résumé is a compromise between the other two formats and is used to emphasize skills and abilities.
5. **Explain the process involved in adapting your résumé to an electronic format.** First you eliminate all fancy printing, graphics, and formats such as boldface and italics. Then you save the résumé as a plain-text (ASCII) document, adding some blank spaces, blank lines, and asterisks to make it more readable. Finally, you provide a list of key words (nouns) that define your skills, experience, and education, adding current jargon characteristic of your field.
6. **Discuss how to apply the AIDA organizational approach to written job application messages.** You get attention in the opening paragraph by showing how your work skills could benefit the organization, explaining how your qualifications fit the job, or demonstrating an understanding of the organization's needs. You build interest and desire by showing how you can meet the job requirements. Finally, you motivate action by making your request easy to fulfill.

CRITICAL THINKING QUESTIONS

1. According to experts in the job-placement field, the average job seeker relies too heavily on the résumé and not enough on other elements of the job search. Which elements do you think are most important? Please explain.
2. How would you locate information about overseas employment opportunities in general? About job requirements at specific overseas companies? Explain briefly.
3. As an employer, what would you do to detect résumé inflation, such as misrepresented job qualifications, salaries, and academic credentials? Please explain.
4. Companies know that one of the disadvantages of résumé scanning is that some qualified applicants will be missed because the technology isn't perfect. Still, more and more companies are using this approach. Do you think that résumé scanning is a good idea? Please explain.
5. Stating your career objective might limit your opportunities by labeling you too narrowly. Not stating your career objective, however, might lead an employer to categorize you incorrectly. Which outcome is riskier? Do summaries of qualifications overcome such drawbacks? If so, how? Explain briefly.
6. It's getting pretty easy to build a personal Web site these days. What do you see as some of the advantages and disadvantages of online résumés?
7. When writing a solicited application letter and describing the skills requested in the employer's ad, how can you avoid using *I* too often? Explain and give examples.
8. How can you make your letter of application unique without being cute or gimmicky? Explain and give examples.

DOCUMENTS FOR ANALYSIS

Read the following documents; then (1) analyze the strengths or weaknesses of each document and (2) revise each document so that it follows the guidelines presented in this chapter.

Document 17.A: Writing a Résumé

SYLVIA MANCHESTER
765 BELLE FLEUR BLVD.
NEW ORLEANS, LA 70113
(504) 312-9504

PERSONAL: Single, excellent health, 5'8", 116 lbs.; hobbies include cooking, dancing, and reading.

JOB OBJECTIVE: To obtain a responsible position in marketing or sales with a good company.

Education: BA degree in biology, University of Louisiana. Graduated with a 3.0 average. Member of the varsity cheerleading squad. President of Panhellenic League. Homecoming queen.

WORK EXPERIENCE

FISHER SCIENTIFIC INSTRUMENTS, 1998 TO PRESENT, FIELD SALES REPRESENTATIVE. Responsible for calling on customers and explaining the features of Fisher's line of laboratory instruments. Also responsible for writing sales letters, attending trade shows, and preparing weekly sales reports.

FISHER SCIENTIFIC INSTRUMENTS, 1995–97, CUSTOMER SERVICE REPRESENTATIVE. Was responsible for handling incoming phone calls from customers who had questions about delivery, quality, or operation of Fisher's line of laboratory instruments. Also handled miscellaneous correspondence with customers.

MEDICAL ELECTRONICS, INC. 1992–95. ADMINISTRATIVE ASSISTANT TO THE VICE PRESIDENT OF MARKETING. In addition to handling typical secretarial chores for the vice president of marketing, I was in charge of compiling the monthly sales reports, using figures provided by members of the field sales force. I also was given responsibility for doing various market research activities.

NEW ORLEANS CONVENTION AND VISITORS BUREAU. 1988–91, SUMMERS. TOUR GUIDE. During the summers of my college years, I led tours of New Orleans for tourists visiting the city. My duties included greeting conventioneers and their spouses at hotels, explaining the history and features of the city during an all-day sight-seeing tour, and answering questions about New Orleans and its attractions. During my fourth summer with the bureau, I was asked to help train the new tour guides. I prepared a handbook that provided interesting facts about the various tourist attractions, as well as answers to the most commonly asked tourist questions. The Bureau was so impressed with the handbook they had it printed up so that it could be given as a gift to visitors.

UNIVERSITY OF LOUISIANA. 1988–91. PART-TIME CLERK IN ADMISSIONS OFFICE. While I was a student in college, I worked 15 hours a week in the admissions office. My duties included filing, processing applications, and handling correspondence with high school students and administrators.

Document 17.B: Writing an Application Letter

I'm writing to let you know about my availability for the brand manager job you advertised. As you can see from my enclosed résumé, my background is perfect for the position. Even though I don't have any real job experience, my grades have been outstanding considering that I went to a top-ranked business school.

I did many things during my undergraduate years to prepare me for this job:

- Earned a 3.4 out of a 4.0 with a 3.8 in my business courses
- Elected representative to the student governing association
- Selected to receive the Lamar Franklin Award
- Worked to earn a portion of my tuition

I am sending my résumé to all the top firms, but I like yours better than any of the rest. Your reputation is tops in the industry, and I want to be associated with a business that can pridefully say it's the best.

If you wish for me to come in for an interview, I can come on a Friday afternoon or anytime on weekends when I don't have classes. Again, thanks for considering me for your brand manager position.

Document 17.C: Writing an Application Letter

I saw your ad for a finance major in our paper last week. I hope the position isn't already filled because I'd like to interview for it. I've enclosed my résumé, which includes the work I've done since graduation.

Your ad said you were looking for a motivated person who wouldn't mind traveling. That would be me! I've also done the type of work you mentioned: budgeting, forecasting, and working with information systems. I know quite a bit about computers.

I know you get many résumés and mine is probably not all that special, but there's one thing that sets me apart: I'm friendly and eager to work. My present position is with a Silicon Valley company, which is in financial trouble. I'm afraid my whole division is going to be downsized, so I want to have something lined up in advance.

Could you send me some information about the financial stability of your company and its history of layoffs. I certainly wouldn't want to jump from the frying pan into the fire, so to speak. (Ha.) At any rate, thank you for considering my application and résumé. I hope you call me very soon.

Document 17.D: Writing Application Follow-Up Messages

Did you receive my résumé? I sent it to you at least two months ago and haven't heard anything. I know you keep résumés on file, but I just want to be sure that you keep me in mind. I heard you are hiring health-care managers and certainly would like to be considered for one of those positions.

Since I last wrote you, I've worked in a variety of positions that have helped prepare me for management. To wit, I've become lunch manager at the restaurant where I work, which involved a raise in pay. I now manage a wait-staff of twelve girls and take the lunch receipts to the bank every day.

Of course, I'd much rather be working at a real job, and that's why I'm writing again. Is there anything else you would like to know about me or my background? I would really like to know more about your company. Is there any literature you could send me? If so, I would really appreciate it.

I think one reason I haven't been hired yet is that I don't want to leave Atlanta. So I hope when you think of me, it's for a position that wouldn't require moving. Thanks again for considering my application.

EXERCISES

1. Using power verbs, change the following statements to make them more effective for a traditional résumé.
   a. Have some experience with database design.
   b. Assigned to a project to analyze the cost accounting methods for a large manufacturer.
   c. I was part of a team that developed a new inventory control system.
   d. Am responsible for preparing the quarterly department budget.
   e. Was a manager of a department with seven employees working for me.

f. Was responsible for developing a spreadsheet to analyze monthly sales by department.
g. Put in place a new program for ordering supplies.

2. Using your answers in exercise 1, make your statements stronger by quantifying them (make up any numbers you need).
3. Using the Document for Analysis 17.A (on page 622) develop a keyword summary for Sylvia Manchester's electronic résumé.
4. Use one of the prewriting techniques discussed in Chapter 5 to generate a list of your marketable skills. Include supporting evidence under each skill that would convince a recruiter that you indeed possessed that skill.
5. Perform an Internet job search for a career that interests you, using any of the Web sites listed in Table 17.1. Draft a memo to your instructor summarizing your general observations and findings. (*Hint:* Include such things as the number of job openings in your desired field, the types of experience and qualifications employers are looking for, and any helpful career information you could find.)

EXPLORING THE BEST OF THE WEB

Link Your Way to a Better Job Search, page 594

Follow the Parachute site's links and explore the wealth of information available on the Internet to help you with your job search.

1. Develop a personal Internet job search strategic plan. Briefly summarize (or list in steps) how you will incorporate the Internet into your future job search efforts.
2. Take one of the interactive career tests by following the links listed under "Career Sites." What did you find out about yourself that will be helpful when choosing a career? Were you surprised by your findings?

CASES

THINKING ABOUT YOUR CAREER

1. Taking stock and taking aim: Application package for the right job Think about yourself. What are some things that come easily to you? What do you enjoy doing? In what part of the country would you like to live? Do you like to work indoors? Outdoors? A combination of the two? How much do you like to travel? Would you like to spend considerable time on the road? Do you like to work closely with others or more independently? What conditions make a job unpleasant? Do you delegate responsibility easily, or do you like to do things yourself? Are you better with words or numbers? Better at speaking or writing? Do you like to work under fixed deadlines? How important is job security to you? Do you want your supervisor to state clearly what is expected of you, or do you like the freedom to make many of your own decisions?

Your task: After answering these questions, gather information about possible jobs that suit your profile by consulting reference materials (from your college library or placement center) and by searching the Internet (using some of the search strategies discussed in Chapter 11). Next, choose a location, a company, and a job that interests you. With guidance from your instructor, decide whether to apply for a job you're qualified for now or one you'll be qualified for with additional education. Then, as directed by your instructor, write one or more of the following: (a) a job-inquiry letter, (b) a résumé, (c) a letter of application, (d) a follow-up letter to your application letter.

2. Scanning the possibilities: Résumé for the Internet In your search for a position, you discover that CareerMosaic is a Web site that lists hundreds of companies advertising on the Internet. Your chances of getting an interview with a leading company will be enhanced if you submit your résumé and cover letter electronically. On the Web, explore http://www.careermosaic.com.

Your task: Prepare a scannable résumé that could be submitted to the site that best fits your qualifications, experience, and education. Print out the résumé for your instructor.

3. Online application: Electronic cover letter introducing a résumé *Motley Fool* is a "Generation X" online magazine accessed via the World Wide Web. Although its founders and writers are extremely creative and motivated, they lack business experience and need a fellow "X'er" to help them manage the business.

Among articles in a recent edition was one titled "The Soul of the Dead," about the influence of the Grateful Dead on more than one generation of concert-goers. Other articles deal with lifestyle issues, pop movies, music, and "trends for an old-young generation."

Your task: Write an e-mail message that will serve as your cover letter, and attach your résumé as a file to be downloaded. Address your message to Louis Corrigan, Managing Editor. Try to limit your message to one screen (about 23 lines). You'll need a creative "hook" and a reassuring approach that identifies you as the right person to help *Motley Fool* become financially viable.

WRITING A RÉSUMÉ AND AN APPLICATION LETTER

4. "Help wanted": Application for a job listed in the classified section Among the jobs listed in today's *Chicago Tribune* (435 N. Michigan Avenue, Chicago, IL 60641) are the following:

ACCOUNTING ASSISTANT
Established leader in the vacation ownership industry has immediate opening in its Northbrook corp. accounting dept. for an Accounting Assistant. Responsibilities include: bank reconciliation, preparation of deposits, AP, and cash receipts posting. Join our fast-growing company and enjoy our great benefits package. Flex work hours, medical, dental insurance. Fax résumé to Lisa: 847-564-2876.

ADMINISTRATIVE ASSISTANT
Fast-paced Wood Dale office seeks professional with strong computer skills. Proficient in MS Word & Excel, PowerPoint a plus. Must be detail oriented, able to handle multiple tasks, and possess strong communication skills. Excellent benefits, salary, and work environment. Fax résumé to 630-350-8649.

CUSTOMER SERVICE
A nationally known computer software developer has an exciting opportunity in customer service and inside sales support in its fast-paced downtown Chicago office. You'll help resolve customer problems over the phone, provide information, assist in account management, and administer orders. If you're friendly, self-motivated, energetic, and have 2 years of experience, excellent problem-solving skills, organizational, communication, and PC skills, and communicate well over the phone, send résumé to J. Haber, 233 North Lake Shore Drive, Chicago, IL 60641.

SALES-ACCOUNT MANAGER
MidCity Baking Company is seeking an Account Manager to sell and coordinate our programs to major accounts in the Chicago market. The candidate should possess strong analytical and selling skills and demonstrate computer proficiency. Previous sales experience with major account level assignment desired. A degree in business or equivalent experience preferred. For confidential consideration please mail résumé to Steven Crane, Director of Sales, Midcity Baking Company, 133 N. Railroad Avenue, Northlake IL 60614.

Your task: Send a résumé and an application letter to one of these potential employers.

WRITING OTHER TYPES OF EMPLOYMENT MESSAGES

5. Crashing the last frontier: Letter of inquiry about jobs in Alaska Your friend can't understand why you would want to move to Alaska. So you explain: "What really decided it for me was that I'd never seen the northern lights."

"But what about the bears? The 60 degree-below winters? The permafrost?" asks your friend.

"No problem. Anchorage doesn't get much colder than Buffalo does. It is just windier and wetter. Anyhow, I want to live near Fairbanks, which is near the gold-mining area—and the university is there. Fairbanks has lots of small businesses, like a frontier town in the West about 150 years ago. I think it still has homesteading tracts for people who want to do their own building and are willing to stay for a certain number of years."

"Your plans seem a little hasty," your friend warns. "Maybe you should write for information before you just take off. How do you know you could get a job?"

Your task: Take your friend's advice and write to the Chamber of Commerce, Fairbanks, AK 99701. Ask what types of employment are available to someone with your education and experience, and ask who specifically is hiring year-round employees.

INTERVIEWING FOR EMPLOYMENT AND FOLLOWING UP

AFTER STUDYING THIS CHAPTER, YOU WILL BE ABLE TO

1 Explain the dual purpose of an interview
2 Describe the function of a preliminary screening interview
3 Discuss three types of interview and explain their purpose
4 List several things you can do to prepare for a job interview
5 Name several things you should find out about a company before accepting a job offer
6 List six common types of message that follow an interview

COMMUNICATION CLOSE-UP AT MICROSOFT

At Microsoft—the world's largest software company—focus, enthusiasm, common sense, ambition, resourcefulness, and good analytical powers could get you a job—but only if you can demonstrate to your interviewer that you actually possess those traits. To do so successfully, explains Microsoft's college recruiting manager, Jodi DeLeon, you have to be able to think on your feet.

Like many other high-tech companies that conduct on-campus screening interviews, Microsoft sends managers who are trying to fill specific positions, not human resources specialists. Product managers interview potential product managers; software design engineers interview potential software design engineers. The engineers conducting those interviews may have helped design one or more of Microsoft's famous software products (MS-DOS, Windows98, Office97, Excel, PowerPoint, Internet Explorer), so don't try to impress them by saying, "Excel? Oh, I know everything about Excel." You could be in big trouble if your claim isn't true; Microsoft's interviewers like to dream up new queries to challenge such statements. In fact, you can expect technical questions even in the 30-minute screening interviews, where you'll be asked problem-solving questions designed to help you demonstrate whatever your résumé says you do best.

Jodi DeLeon

"We're not trying to intimidate or scare people at all," DeLeon explains. "We just want to find out as much as we can." If you do well in the screening interview, you're flown to Microsoft's headquarters in Redmond, Washington, for a full day of interviews. This second round of interviews is to determine whether you're a good "fit" for Microsoft—where the atmosphere may be easygoing, but the brainpower is intense.

DeLeon says Microsoft interviewers avoid the standard questions asked by many campus recruiters because such questions often elicit overrehearsed answers. Instead, "We just probe really deep." For example, DeLeon might ask students applying for a marketing position how they would penetrate their school with more Microsoft products, at both the stu-

Microsoft conducts on-campus interviews and participates in job fairs. Company representatives look for enthusiasm, excitement, and an ability to think logically. Students who do well in screening interviews are flown to headquarters in Redmond, Washington, for the next round of interviews.

dent and administration levels. However, she's not looking for a particular answer. "I look at how they focus their thoughts. I look at the steps they take to get from the beginning to the end. I look at all the resources they pull in, the implications that they think about. Do they ask me questions? Do they need to?"

She's been most impressed by candidates who have walked her through an idea using pen and paper or who have jumped up to sketch on a chalkboard. Such responses can't be faked. Good interviewers know when you're being genuine or just spouting off some pat, memorized response. "For instance," says DeLeon, "it's fine if you know Excel and admit, 'I think Excel is great, but it would be a lot easier if it had X, Y, or Z.' That's the kind of thing that the Microsoft person has to think about every day. Students shouldn't be afraid to say things like that."

When evaluating candidates, DeLeon asks how they set priorities for all the various projects they're currently working on. That's where demonstrating an ability to juggle school with extracurricular activities can help. She also looks at a student's drive and ambition, resourcefulness, and analytical ability. Good grades help, of course, but she's more interested in how well a person listens to and thinks through what she says.

Although companies differ, Microsoft doesn't consider it "cool" to dress like the interviewer, who may be in jeans and T-shirt. "Dress professionally," DeLeon advises. She adds that thank-you notes help, and follow-up phone calls (made after, not before, a promised answer date) are essential to demonstrate your continued interest in the job. Most of all, avoid attention-getting gimmicks. One of the worst blunders DeLeon ever encountered was a résumé sent in a pizza—and the candidate didn't stop there. "She just went above and beyond good judgment to get her foot in the door here," DeLeon recalls. After the pizza came fortune cookies with the applicant's qualifications in them, and then balloons. DeLeon finally had to write and ask her to stop.

The best way to prepare for an interview, suggests DeLeon, is to think about the job itself. "Ask yourself, what have I done in my life that is related to some aspect of this job?" Although that question may never be asked in the interview, your understanding of the answer will shine through every statement you make. Most important, she adds, be yourself and take your chances. "If you feel like you're taking a risk by telling the truth or being honest, you're probably doing the right thing," says DeLeon.[1] ■

UNDERSTANDING THE INTERVIEWING PROCESS

An interview helps both the interviewer and the applicant achieve their goals.

Companies take various approaches to recruiting, depending on their hiring needs. Successful applicants vary their job searches accordingly.

As Jodi DeLeon points out, the best way to prepare for a job interview is to think carefully about the job itself. Approach job interviews with a sound appreciation of their dual purpose. The organization's main objective is to find the best person available for the job; the applicant's main objective is to find the job best suited to his or her goals and capabilities. Even though the employer and the applicant approach the process from different angles, they both are heading toward the same goal—finding the perfect fit.

Because organizations approach the recruiting and interviewing process in different ways, you will need to adjust your job search accordingly. For instance, major corporations like Microsoft hire hundreds of new employees every year, so they take a more systematic approach to recruiting than small local businesses that add only a few new people each year. Table 18.1 contrasts the recruiting procedures of large companies with those of smaller companies and provides tips for increasing your chances of getting an interview with either type of employer. In general, the easiest way to connect with a big company is through your cam-

TABLE 18.1

RECRUITING PROCEDURES OF BIG COMPANIES VERSUS SMALL COMPANIES: THE BEST WAY TO GET YOUR FOOT IN THE DOOR

	Big Companies	Small Companies
Number and type of applicants sought	Consistently hire thousands of new emloyees each year; have relatively specific hiring criteria, depending on the position; tend to be highly selective	Hire a handful of new people each year, but requirements fluctuate widely depending on ups and downs in the business; may have specific requirements, but are often looking for flexibility, versatility; are often somewhat more open-minded than big corporations about candidate's background
Person or department in charge of recruiting	Handled by human resources or personnel department	Companies at large end of the small-company scale (500 employees) may have a specialized human resources department, but many depend on line managers to staff their own functions; in really small companies, the founder/top manager makes all hiring decisions
General recruiting and interviewing style	Governed by formal policies and procedures; typically involves series of several interviews on campus and at company facility; approach is generally systematic, well planned, and well financed	Conducted informally on an as-needed basis without a standard procedure; hiring decision may be made after first interview or may drag on for several months; company generally lacks budget/motive for conducting elaborate recruiting programs
Where/how they advertise	Use national and local newspapers, trade journals, campus placement offices, word of mouth, online job banks, company Web sites	Rely heavily on word of mouth and local newspapers; may post openings at local colleges or at a few colleges whose graduates have specific qualifications

pus placement office; the most efficient way to approach a smaller business is by contacting the company directly.

In either case, once you get your foot in the door, you move to the next stage and prepare to meet with a recruiter during an **employment interview**, a formal meeting during which both employer and applicant ask questions and exchange information to see whether the applicant and the organization are a good match. In fact, applicants often face a series of interviews, each with a different purpose. To be successful in your employment interviews, you can learn how to prepare and how to conduct yourself during the interview. But first, you need to understand the interviewing process. Is more than one interview required for a particular job? What types of interviews are there? Will you have to take any sort of preemployment tests? What do employers look for?

An employment interview is a formal meeting in which both employer and applicant ask questions and exchange information to learn more about each other.

The Typical Sequence of Interviews

Most employers interview an applicant two or three times before deciding to make a job offer. The first interview, generally held on campus, is the **preliminary screening interview**, which helps employers screen out unqualified applicants. Those candidates who best meet

Most organizations interview an applicant several times before extending a job offer.

TABLE 18.1, CONTINUED

	Big Companies	Small Companies
Use of employment agencies, search firms	Roughly 60 percent use employment agencies, whereas 40 percent use executive search firms; however, new college graduates are generally recruited directly without help of intermediaries	Agency use varies widely among small companies; cost may be a factor
Responsiveness to unsolicited résumés	Receive hundreds of unsolicited résumés, which typically get less attention than résumés obtained through department's own planned recruiting program; most companies will scan unsolicited résumés into a database if they maintain one; best to send résumé directly to line manager or potential co-worker in department where you want to work	Receive relatively few unsolicited résumés, so they pay close attention to them; however, given limited hiring needs, chances are slim that your résumé will arrive when company has a corresponding opening
Reliance on campus recruiting	Roughly 80 percent rely heavily on campus recruiting programs to fill entry-level professional, technical, and managerial positions; however, most limit their recruiting to a relatively small number of campuses	Companies at large end of small-company scale (500 employees) may have limited campus recruiting programs; the smaller the company, the less likely it is to recruit in this manner, and the fewer schools it is likely to visit
Best way for candidate to approach company	Use campus placement office to schedule interviews with companies that recruit on your campus; if these interviews are by invitation only, send a letter and résumé to company asking to be included on its schedule; if company does not recruit on your campus, call the person in charge of college recruiting, explain your situation, and ask for advice on best way to get an interview	Check with campus placement office; try to make direct personal contact with owner/manager or department head; get names and addresses from chamber of commerce, business directories, or local economic development agency; send résumé and application letter; follow up with phone call

the organization's requirements are invited to visit company offices for further evaluation. Some organizations make a decision at that point, but many schedule a third interview to complete the evaluation process before extending a job offer.

At Microsoft, line managers are responsible for conducting preliminary screening interviews on campus. However, many organizations assign this task to members of their human resources department, who may conduct hundreds of screening interviews each year. These interviews are fairly structured, so applicants are often asked roughly the same questions. Many companies use standardized evaluation sheets to "grade" the applicants so that all the candidates will be measured against the same criteria. Preliminary screening interviews enable an organization to sort through a large number of candidates efficiently—a practical necessity when, say, 50 people respond to a help-wanted ad or 50 students sign up for interviews through their campus placement office.

Your best approach to a screening interview is to follow the interviewer's lead. Keep your responses short and to the point. Talking too much can be a big mistake. As pointed out by Sandra Moersdorf, a recruiting manager for Procter & Gamble, "Some people are just motor mouths; they never shut up, and I'd like to be able to ask more than one question in the interview."[2] However, if an opportunity presents itself, emphasize the "theme" you used in developing your résumé. You want to give the interviewer a way to differentiate you from other candidates, while also demonstrating your strengths and qualifications.

The next round of interviews is designed to help the organization narrow the field a little further. Typically, if you're invited to visit a company, you will talk with several people: a member of the human resources department, one or two potential colleagues, and your potential supervisor. You might face a **panel interview**, meeting with several interviewers who ask you questions during a single session. Your interviewers will try to determine from your answers, actions, and attitudes whether you're right for the job. By noting how you listen, think, and express yourself, they can decide how likely you are to get along with colleagues. Your best approach during this round of interviews is to show interest in the job, relate your skills and experience to the organization's needs, listen attentively, ask insightful questions, and display enthusiasm.

In her efforts to find work, Marci Burkhart gets help from the Career Center at Syracuse University.

If the interviewers agree that you're a good candidate, you may receive a job offer, either on the spot or a few days later by phone or mail. In other cases, you may be invited back for a final evaluation by a higher-ranking executive who has the authority to make the hiring decision and to decide on your compensation. An underlying objective of the final interview is often to sell you on the advantages of joining the organization.

According to experts, it takes an average of 10 interviews to get one job offer. If you hope to have several offers to choose from, you can expect to go through 20 or 30 interviews during your job search.[3] Because interviewing takes time, start seeking jobs well in advance of the date you want to start work. Some students start their job search as much as nine months before graduation. Early planning is even more crucial during downturns in the economy, because many employers become more selective when times are tough. Moreover, many corporations reduce their campus visits and campus hiring programs during bad times, so more of the job search burden falls on you.

In a typical job search, you can expect to have 20 or 30 interviews before you accept a job offer.

Types of Interview

Companies use a variety of interviewing techniques to evaluate various attributes.

Different types of interview are used by organizations to discover as much as possible about applicants. A **structured interview** is generally used in the screening stage. Here the employer controls the interview by asking a series of prepared questions in a set order. Working from a checklist, the interviewer asks candidates each question, staying within an alloted time period. All answers are noted. Although useful in gathering facts, the structured interview is generally regarded as a poor measure of an applicant's personal qualities. Still, some companies, such as Ameritech Cellular Services, use them to create uniformity in their hiring process.[4]

By contrast, the **open-ended interview** is a less formal, unstructured interview with a relaxed format. The interviewer poses broad, open-ended questions and encourages the applicant to talk freely—perhaps even to divulge more than he or she should. This type of interview is good for bringing out an applicant's personality and is used to test professional judgment. Some candidates reveal too much, rambling on about personal or family problems that have nothing to do with their qualifications for employment, their ability to get along with co-workers, or any personal interests that could benefit their performance on the job. So be careful. You need to strike a delicate balance between being friendly and remembering that you're in a business situation.

Some organizations perform **group interviews**. They interview several candidates simultaneously to see how they interact; this type of the interview is useful for judging interpersonal skills. The Walt Disney Company uses group interviews when hiring people for its theme parks. During a 45-minute session, the Disney recruiter watches to see how three candidates relate to one another. Do they smile? Are they supportive of one another's comments? Do they try to score points at each other's expense?[5]

Perhaps the most unnerving type of interview is the **stress interview**, which is set up to see how well a candidate handles stressful situations (an important qualification for certain jobs). During a stress interview you might be asked pointed questions designed to irk or unsettle you. You might be subjected to long periods of silence, criticisms of your appearance, deliberate interruptions, and abrupt or even hostile reactions by the interviewer. For example, one executive would toss the keys to his car to the applicant and suggest they take a short spin around the neighborhood. Of course, initially, the interviewer wanted to see how the candidate would respond to the invitation, but he also used the car ride as a reasonable indicator of how the individual would handle surprise, since dealing with the unexpected was an important element of the job. Many corporate managers believe that stress interviews are inappropriate and unethical.[6]

Interviewing by video is becoming more popular as employers try to cut the costs and travel time associated with the interview process. Many large companies use videoconferencing systems to initially screen middle-management candidates or to interview new recruits at universities. Experts recommend that candidates prepare for a video interview a bit differently than for an in-person meeting. First, they suggest asking for a preliminary phone conversation to establish rapport with the interviewer. Second, they recommend arriving early enough to get used to the equipment and setting. During the interview, they suggest candidates speak clearly but not more slowly than normal. Other recommendations: Sit straight. Look up, but not down. And try to show some animation, but not too much because it will appear blurry to the interviewer.[7]

Another modern twist in interviewing candidates is asking behavioral or situational questions to determine how candidates would handle real-life work problems. In this approach, which has been used by companies such as Kraft Foods, Delta Air Lines, AT&T, and Procter & Gamble, an interviewer will describe a situation and ask, "How would you handle this?" Many companies use situational exercises because they've learned the hard way that no correlation exists between how well people interview and how well they perform on the job. Proponents of this approach claim that interviewing is not about where candidates see themselves in five years, their weaknesses or strengths, their most challenging experience or greatest accomplishments; rather, it's about the job. As a result, the situational interview is a hands-on, at-work meeting between an employer who needs a job done and a worker who must be fully prepared to do the work.[8]

Of course, this means preparation is mandatory. No more breezing into an interview and relying on charm and a good line of patter. Today's companies expect serious candidates to demonstrate an understanding of the company's operations, its market, and its strategic and tactical problems.[9] They might be asked to collaborate on a decision or to develop a group presentation. Trained observers evaluate the candidates' performance using predetermined criteria and then advise management on how well each person is likely to handle the challenges normally faced on the job.[10]

Regardless of the types of interview you may face, a personal interview is vital because a résumé can't show whether you are lively and outgoing or subdued and low-key, able to take direction or able to take charge. Each job requires a different mix of personality traits. The task of the interviewer is to find out whether a particular candidate will be effective in the job. To do so, most employers look for specific qualities and skills.

What Employers Look For

Herb Kelleher, CEO of Southwest Airlines, knows exactly what he's looking for in a potential employee. A sense of humor tops his list because Kelleher believes that people who don't take themselves too seriously are better able to cope with the stress of airline work. Kelleher also wants individuals who are self-motivated, enthusiastic, not afraid to make decisions, willing to take risks, intelligent, good communicators, and considerate of others.[11] Microsoft looks for candidates who demonstrate outstanding intelligence and creativity, ask insightful questions, and are able to collaborate successfully with colleagues.[12]

Interviewers try to determine what you can do and what kind of person you are.

Having the right personality traits for the job is important in today's workplace. As one executive put it, "You can teach skill sets, but you can't teach attitude."[13] In fact, current research shows that employees who possess certain attributes tend to be more successful at their job. As a result, many employers today seek candidates with a high "emotional intelligence," or EQ (emotional quotient). People with a high EQ generally possess these desirable attributes: self-awareness, good impulse control, persistence, confidence, self-

Figure 18.1
What's Your EQ?

Studies show that candidates with a high emotional quotient (EQ) have a greater chance of achieving career success. Here are some of the attributes characteristic of a person with a high EQ. How do you compare?

- ✔ Think clearly and stay focused on the task at hand while under pressure.
- ✔ Admit to your own mistakes.
- ✔ Meet commitments and keep promises.
- ✔ Hold yourself accountable for meeting your goals.
- ✔ Seek new ideas from a variety of sources.
- ✔ Handle multiple demands and changing priorities.
- ✔ Make sacrifices to meet an important organizational goal.
- ✔ Cut through red tape and bend outdated rules when necessary.
- ✔ Seek fresh perspectives, even if that means trying something totally new.
- ✔ Operate from an expectation of success rather than a fear of failure.
- ✔ Try to learn how to improve your performance.
- ✔ Set challenging goals and take calculated risks to reach them.

motivation, and empathy, as well as the abilities to persuade, articulate a mission, interpret the mood of a group, and communicate with people in terms they understand (see Figure 18.1).[14]

Of course, having a high EQ and a good sense of humor might make you more successful at the job, but when it comes down to it, every job has basic qualifications. So employers first look for two things: evidence that the person will fit in with the organization and proof that a candidate can handle a specific job.

A Good Fit with the Organization

Compatibility with the organization is judged on the basis of

- Appearance
- Personal background
- Attitudes and style

Interviewers try to decide whether the candidate will be compatible with the other people in the organization. Every interviewer approaches this issue a little differently. Some interviewers believe that personal background is an indication of how well the candidate will fit in with the organization, so you might be asked about your interests, hobbies, awareness of world events, and so forth. You can expand your potential along these lines by reading widely, making an effort to meet new people, and participating in discussion groups, seminars, and workshops.

Employers may also consider a candidate's personal style. Openness, enthusiasm, and interest are likely to impress an interviewer. So are courtesy, sincerity, willingness to learn, and a positive, self-confident style—all of which help a new employee adapt to a new workplace and new responsibilities.

Qualifications for the Job

Suitability for the specific job is judged on the basis of
- Academic preparation
- Work experience
- Job-related personality traits

Every position requires specific qualifications and skills. To become an auditor, for example, you must know accounting; to become a sales manager, you must have several years of sales experience. When you're invited to interview for a position, the interviewer may already have some idea of whether you have the right qualifications, based on a review of your résumé.

During the interview, you'll be asked to describe your education and previous jobs in more depth so that the interviewer can determine how well your skills match the requirements. In many cases, the interviewer will be seeking someone with the flexibility to apply diverse skills in several areas.[15] When describing your skills, be honest. If you don't know how to do something, say so. Given the high cost of hiring unsuitable employees, more and more companies are turning to preemployment testing to verify candidates' claims and to determine whether they have the necessary skills and psychological characteristics to handle a particular job.

Preemployment Testing

Preemployment tests attempt to provide objective, quantitative information about candidates' skills, attitudes, and habits.

According to a survey by the American Management Association, your chances of being asked to take some form of preemployment test are roughly 1 in 6 if you're applying for a managerial position and 1 in 4 if you're applying for a nonsupervisory job.[16] Even though many of the tests are related to specific job skills such as word-processing ability, the real growth is occurring in tests designed to weed out dishonest candidates and substance abusers.

Companies are concerned about these issues for good reason. The FBI and other law enforcement agencies estimate that white-collar crime costs U.S. businesses more than $400 billion a year and is increasing at a rate of 10 to 20 percent annually.[17] Moreover, studies show that substance abusers have two to four times as many accidents as do people who do not use drugs and that drug use can be linked to 40 percent of industrial fatalities.[18] Statistics like these are enough to worry any employer, particularly given the threat of being held liable for negligent hiring practices if an employee harms an innocent party on the job.

To combat such problems, approximately 45 percent of all companies now require applicants to undergo drug and alcohol testing.[19] Some companies administer medical and psychological exams, and some of the larger firms are even using gene testing to screen out applicants who may develop expensive and debilitating diseases.[20] Tests have their critics, of course. Some employers prefer not to go to the extra expense of administering them or feel that educated judgment works just as well. Some applicants question the validity of honesty and drug tests or consider them an invasion of privacy. However, used in conjunction with other evidence, such as reference checks, the tests attempt to provide an objective, quantitative measure of applicants' qualifications (see "Sharpening Your Skills: How to Check References—and Avoid Legal Traps"). To protect candidates' interests, employment tests must meet strict criteria of fairness set forth by the Equal Employment Opportunity Commission (EEOC).

DID YOU KNOW?

In a recent survey, 92 percent of employers indicated that they do speak to an applicant's former employer, but only 61 percent said that they verify educational information.

PREPARING FOR A JOB INTERVIEW

It's perfectly normal to feel a little anxious before an interview. So much depends on it, and you don't know quite what to expect. But don't worry too much; preparation will help you perform well. Before the interview, do some basic research, think ahead about questions, bolster your confidence, polish your interview style, plan to look good, and be ready when you arrive. Be sure to consider any cultural differences when preparing for interviews, and base your approach on what your audience expects. The advice in this chapter is most appropriate for companies and employers in the United States and Canada.

SHARPENING YOUR SKILLS

HOW TO CHECK REFERENCES—AND AVOID LEGAL TRAPS

Employers who hire people without adequately checking their backgrounds not only face the possibility of expensive hiring mistakes, they could also face legal action if problems arise. Some chilling examples include the building janitor with an unchecked criminal record who murdered a tenant, the school bus driver with an unchecked record of drunk driving arrests, and the "chemist" whose difficulties on his new job were finally explained by his forged college degree. More commonly, reference checks can reveal long employment gaps, inflated accomplishments, false claims about academic degrees, and potential interpersonal problems on the job.

Nevertheless, checking a job applicant's references is a challenging proposition because employee information is decentralized and difficult to obtain. Furthermore, former employers fear they will be sued over any remarks they might make. As a result, some companies verify only an employee's "name, rank, and serial number," and a few companies won't verify employment at all. Even though companies realize how much they need to share relevant information on employees, many executives are uncomfortable about committing their remarks to paper. Here's some advice from the most successful reference checkers.

- *Get applicants involved.* Ask candidates to provide a list of references to check. Have them sign a waiver releasing their references from legal liability for their statements, and ask each candidate to contact references beforehand to encourage them to speak freely.
- *Take your time, and don't delegate.* Checking references is an important task and should take about two hours for each candidate. Make your calls early in the morning or after five, when executives are likely to answer the phone themselves. (Be sure to check references before making a job offer so that the applicant won't blame his or her references if the job offer is withdrawn.)
- *Prepare your questions carefully.* Whether writing or calling references, pose open-ended, job-related questions that elicit information about *how* a candidate performed, not just what was accomplished. To avoid discrimination charges, ask similar questions for all applicants (don't inquire whether a female executive fears traveling alone if you wouldn't make the same inquiry about a male executive). Also, ask for referrals to others who can comment on the candidate's performance.
- *Know the laws in your state.* State and federal laws govern reference checks, and they're constantly being updated. In most states, it's illegal to ask direct or indirect questions about candidate's age, sex, religion, race, marital status, sexual orientation, disabilities, politics, pregnancy, drug use, medical history, or arrest records (unless the candidate will be working with minors). However, it's legal in most states to contact police departments and inquire about arrest records or to ask former employers if a person has ever been *convicted of* a crime. It's also legal (and recommended) to contact schools, or to have applicants sign requests for course transcripts to be mailed directly to the hiring company, at the applicant's expense.

You may have to rely on the telephone to check references. Prepare your questions carefully, and jot down the responses for your legal and personnel records. If your phone calls are unreturned, you might write a letter of request as a last resort. If you do have to write, politely explain that you can't make a job offer until you receive a reply.

1. Think about who you would supply as references on an employment application. Now assume the perspective of a potential employer, and prepare the questions you'd want those references to answer about you and your work.
2. You've interviewed a job candidate who has all the right answers and seems to have the right qualifications, but your intuition tells you something isn't quite right. What checking would you do to confirm or quell your concerns?

Do Some Basic Research

Learning about the organization and the job is important because it enables you to show the organization how you will meet its particular needs (see Table 18.2). With a little research, for instance, you would discover that Microsoft plans on investing heavily in the technical and marketing support of software developers as well as making things simpler for all users and

Be prepared to relate your qualifications to the organization's needs.

TABLE 18.2

FINDING OUT ABOUT THE ORGANIZATION AND THE JOB

Where to Look for Information	
■ *Annual report*	Summarizes year's operations; mentions products, significant events, names of key personnel
■ *In-house magazine or newspaper*	Reveals information about company operations, events, personnel
■ *Product brochures and publicity releases*	Provide insight into organization's operations and values (obtain from public relations office)
■ *Stock research reports*	Help you assess stability and prospects for growth (obtain from local stockbroker)
■ *Business and financial pages of local newspapers*	Contain news items about organizations, current performance figures
■ *Periodicals indexes*	Contain descriptive listings of magazine and newspaper articles about organizations (obtain from library)
■ *Better Business Bureau and Chamber of Commerce*	Distribute information about some local organizations
■ *Former and current employees*	Have insight into job and work environment
■ *College placement office*	Collects information on organizations that recruit and on job qualifications and salaries
What to Find Out About the Organization	
■ *Full name*	What the organization is officially known as (for example, 3M is Minnesota Mining & Manufacturing Company)
■ *Location*	Where the organization's headquarters, branch offices, and plants are
■ *Age*	How long the organization has been in business
■ *Products*	What goods and services the organization produces and sells
■ *Industry position*	What the organization's current market share, financial position, and profit picture are
■ *Earnings*	What the trends in the organization's stock prices and dividends are (if the firm is publicly held)
■ *Growth*	What changes in earnings and holdings the organization has experienced in recent years and its prospects for expansion
■ *Organization*	What subsidiaries, divisions, and departments make up the whole
What to Find Out About the Job	
■ *Job title*	What you will be called
■ *Job functions*	What the main tasks of the job are
■ *Job qualifications*	What knowledge and skills the job requires
■ *Career path*	What chances for ready advancement exist
■ *Salary range*	What the organization typically offers and what pay is reasonable in this industry and geographic area
■ *Travel opportunities*	How often, long, and far you'll be allowed (or required) to travel
■ *Relocation opportunities*	Where you might be allowed (or required) to move and how often you might be moved

system administrators.[21] Knowing these facts might help you pinpoint aspects of your background (such as the ability to simplify processes) that would appeal to Microsoft's recruiters.

Of course, one of the fastest ways to learn about a company is to visit its Web site. If you land an important interview and you need information on a company fast, you can use a Web search engine to find the location of information about mission statements, product descriptions, annual reports, and job listings. The largest companies also post press releases and employee news.[22]

Think Ahead About Questions

Most job interviews are essentially question-and-answer sessions: You answer the interviewer's questions about your background, and you ask questions of your own to determine whether the job and the organization are right for you. By planning for your interviews, you can handle these exchanges intelligently. (See "Sharpening Your Skills: Sixteen Tough Interview Questions: What to Say When You're Stopped in Your Tracks.")

Employers usually gear their interview questions to specific organizational needs, and many change their questions over time. In general, you can expect to be asked about your skills, achievements, and goals; your attitude toward work and school; your relationships with work supervisors, colleagues, and fellow students; and, occasionally, your hobbies and interests. For a look at the types of questions that are often asked, see Table 18.3 on page 640. Jot down a brief answer to each one. Then read the answers over until you feel comfortable with each of them. You may want to tape record them and then listen to make sure they sound clear and convincing. Although practicing your answers will help you feel prepared and confident, you don't want to memorize responses or sound overrehearsed. Another suggestion is to give a list of interview questions to a friend or relative and have that person ask you various questions at random. This method helps you learn to articulate answers and to look at the person as you answer.

Practice answering interview questions.

The questions you ask in an interview are just as important as the answers you provide. By asking intelligent questions, you can demonstrate your understanding of the organization and steer the discussion into those areas that allow you to present your qualifications to peak advantage. Before the interview, prepare a list of about a dozen questions you need answered in order to evaluate the organization and the job. Keep in mind that if you limit your questions to those you think will impress the interviewer, you'll deprive yourself of an opportunity to gather the information you'll need in order to make a wise decision if you are offered the job. Here's a list of some things you might want to find out:

You are responsible for deciding whether the work and the organization are compatible with your goals and values.

- *Are these my kind of people?* Look around. Observe the interviewer and other employees. If you can, arrange to talk to employees.
- *Can I do this work?* Compare your qualifications with the requirements described by the interviewer.
- *Will I enjoy the work?* To answer this one, you must know yourself and what is important to you. Is the work challenging? Will it give you feelings of accomplishment and satisfaction? Of making a real contribution?
- *Is the job what I want?* You may never find a job that fulfills all your wants, but the position you accept should satisfy at least your primary ones. Will the job make use of your best capabilities? Does it offer a career path to the long-term goals you've set for yourself?
- *Does the job pay what I'm worth?* Is the position comparable to those held by people with qualifications like your own? Is the pay in line with that for similar jobs in the field? By comparing jobs and salaries before you're interviewed, you'll know what's reasonable for someone with your skills in your industry.
- *What kind of person would I be working for?* You can find out quite a bit by watching how others interact with your interviewer (if the interviewer is the supervisor for the position), by tactfully querying other employees, or by posing a careful question or two during the interview. If the interviewer is not your prospective boss, ask who will be and find out her or his job title and responsibilities. Try to learn all you can, because that one person will have quite a bit to do with whether you'll like the job and whether it will lead you somewhere or nowhere.

- *What sort of future can I expect with this organization?* This is a key question to ask during the interview and to research on your own. How healthy is the organization? Can you look forward to advancement? Does the organization offer exciting career opportunities or fast salary improvement? What benefits does the organization offer (insurance, pension, vacation)?

Types of questions to ask during an interview:
- Warm-up
- Open-ended
- Indirect

Of course, bombarding the interviewer with these questions the minute you walk in the room would not be a good idea. Instead, use a mix of formats to elicit this information. Start with a warm-up question to help break the ice. You might ask recruiter Jodi DeLeon, "What Microsoft departments usually hire new graduates?" After that, you might build rapport by asking an open-ended question that draws out her opinion: for example, "How do you think the Internet's popularity will affect Microsoft's ability to continue growing?" Indirect questions are another approach. You can get useful information and show that you've prepared for the interview with comments like "I'd really like to know more about Microsoft's plans for handwriting-recognition software" or "That recent *Business Week* article about the com-

SHARPENING YOUR SKILLS

SIXTEEN TOUGH INTERVIEW QUESTIONS: WHAT TO SAY WHEN YOU'RE STOPPED IN YOUR TRACKS

The answers to challenging interview questions can reveal a lot about a candidate. You can expect to face several such questions during every interview. If you're prepared with thoughtful answers that are related to your specific situation, you're bound to make a good impression. Here are 16 tough questions and guidelines for planning answers that put your qualities in the best light.

1. *What was the toughest decision you ever had to make?* Be prepared with a good example, explaining why the decision was difficult as well as the process you followed to reach it. Chances are, the employer is more interested in following your thought process than in the actual decision.
2. *Why do you want to work for this organization?* This question tests whether you've done your homework about the company. It's your opportunity to show that you have by citing some of the things going on in the company that appeal to you.
3. *Why should we employ you?* Depending on your strengths, point to your academic preparation, job skills, and enthusiasm about the firm. Try to tie your specific skills to the employer's needs. Give examples of how you can learn and become productive quickly. If the job involves managerial responsibilities, refer to past activities as proof of your ability to get along with others and to work as part of a team.
4. *If we hire you, what changes would you make?* Watch out! No matter how bright you are, you can't know the right actions to take in a position before you settle in and learn about the job and company operations. Because you are still an outsider, you're best answer is to state that you will want to take a good hard look at everything the company is doing before making any recommendations.
5. *Can we offer you a career path?* Reply that you believe so, but you need to know more about the normal progression within the organization.
6. *What are your greatest strengths?* Here's your chance to really shine. Answer sincerely with a summary of your strong points: "I can see what needs to be done, and I do it" or "I'm willing to make decisions" or "I work well with others."
7. *What are your greatest weaknesses?* Describing a weakness so that it sounds like a virtue is a good way to honestly reveal something about yourself while showing how it works to an employer's advantage. If you say that you sometimes drive yourself too hard, you can also add that being driven has been helpful when you've had to meet deadlines.
8. *What didn't you like about previous jobs you've held?* State what you didn't like; then discuss what the experience taught you about your own abilities or the work-

pany was very interesting." Of course, any questions you ask should be put into your own words so that you don't sound like every other candidate. For a list of other good questions you might use as a starting point, see Table 18.4.

Take your list of questions to the interview on a notepad. If you need to, jot down brief notes during the meeting, and be sure to record the answer in more detail afterward. Having a list of questions should impress the interviewer with your organization and thoroughness. It will also show that you're there to evaluate the organization and the job as well as to sell yourself.

Bolster Your Confidence

By overcoming your tendencies to feel self-conscious or nervous during an interview, you can build your confidence and make a better impression. The best way to counteract apprehension is to try to remove its source. You may be shy because you think you have some flaw that will prompt other people to reject you. Bear in mind, however, that you're much more conscious of your limitations than other people are. If some aspect of your appearance or background

DID YOU KNOW?

Research shows that the first person interviewed gets the job only 17.6 percent of the time, whereas the last person interviewed is hired 55.8 percent of the time.

place. Avoid making slighting references to former employers.

9. *How do you spend your leisure time?* Mention a cross section of interests—active and quiet, social and solitary—rather than just one.
10. *Are there any weaknesses in your education or experience?* Take stock of your weaknesses before the interview. Practice discussing them in a positive light. You'll find that they're minor when discussed along with the positive qualities you have to offer.
11. *Where do you want to be five years from now?* This question tests two things: (1) if you are merely using this job as a stopover until something better comes along and (2) if you've given thought to your long-term goals and personal development. Of course, saying you'd like to be president of the company is unrealistic, yet few employers want people who are content to sit still. Your answer should reflect your long-term goals as well as the organization's advancement opportunities.
12. *What are your salary expectations?* If you're asked this at the outset, it's best to say, "Why don't we discuss salary after you decide whether I'm right for the job?" If the interviewer asks this after showing real interest in you, speak up. If you need a clue about salary levels, say, "Can you discuss the salary range with me?" Remember, do your homework. The more information you have, the better you'll be able to negotiate a fair salary.
13. *What would you do if . . .* This question is designed to test your resourcefulness. For example: "What would you do if your computer broke down during an audit?" Your answer isn't nearly as important as your approach to the problem, and a calm approach is best. You might give several alternatives: "I might . . . , or I might . . . "
14. *What type of position are you interested in?* Job titles and responsibilities vary from firm to firm. So state your skills instead, such as "I'm good with numbers," and the positions that require those skills, such as "accounts payable."
15. *Tell me something about yourself.* Say you'll be happy to talk about yourself, and ask what the interviewer wants to know. If this point is clarified, respond. If it isn't, say how your skills can contribute to the job and the organization. This question gives you a great opportunity to sell yourself.
16. *Do you have any questions about the organization or the job?* Employers like candidates who are interested in the organization. This is the time to convey your interest and enthusiasm.

Of course, many other responses might be appropriate, depending on your own circumstances. Just be sure that your answers are sincere, truthful, and positive. Take a moment to compose your thoughts before responding so that your answers are to the point.

---

1. What makes an effective answer to an interviewer's question? Consider some of the ways answers can vary: specific versus general, assertive versus passive, informal versus formal.
2. Think of four additional questions that pertain specifically to your résumé. Practice your answers.

TABLE 18.3

TWENTY-FIVE COMMON INTERVIEW QUESTIONS

Questions About College

1. What courses in college did you like most? Least? Why?
2. Do you think your extracurricular activities in college were worth the time you devoted to them? Why or why not?
3. When did you choose your college major? Did you ever change your major? If so, why?
4. Do you feel you did the best scholastic work you are capable of?
5. Which of your college years was the toughest? Why?

Questions About Employers and Jobs

6. What jobs have you held? Why did you leave?
7. What percentage of your college expenses did you earn? How?
8. Why did you choose your particular field of work?
9. What are the disadvantages of your chosen field?
10. Have you served in the military? What rank did you achieve? What jobs did you perform?
11. What do you think about how this industry operates today?
12. Why do you think you would like this particular type of job?

Questions About Personal Attitudes and Preferences

13. Do you prefer to work in any specific geographic location? If so, why?
14. How much money do you hope to be earning in five years? In ten years?
15. What do you think determines a person's progress in a good organization?
16. What personal characteristics do you feel are necessary for success in your chosen field?
17. Tell me a story.
18. Do you like to travel?
19. Do you think grades should be considered by employers? Why or why not?

Questions About Work Habits

20. Do you prefer working with others or by yourself?
21. What type of boss do you prefer?
22. Have you ever had any difficulty getting along with colleagues or supervisors? With other students? With instructors?
23. Would you prefer to work in a large or a small organization? Why?
24. How do you feel about overtime work?
25. What have you done that shows initiative and willingness to work?

If you feel shy or self-conscious, remember that recruiters are human too.

makes you uneasy, correct it or exercise positive traits to offset it, such as warmth, wit, intelligence, or charm. Instead of dwelling on your weaknesses, focus on your strengths so that you can emphasize them to an interviewer. Make a list of your good points and compare them with what you see as your shortcomings. Remember, too, that all the other candidates for the job are probably just as nervous as you are. In fact, even the interviewer may be nervous.

Polish Your Interview Style

Staging mock interviews with a friend is a good way to hone your style.

Confidence helps you walk into an interview, but the only way you'll walk out with a job is if you also give the interviewer an impression of poise, good manners, and good judgment. One way to develop an adept style is to stage mock interviews with a friend. After each prac-

TABLE 18.4

FIFTEEN QUESTIONS TO ASK THE INTERVIEWER

1. What are this job's major responsibilities?
2. What qualities do you want in the person who fills this position?
3. Do you want to know more about my related training?
4. What is the first problem that needs the attention of the person you hire?
5. What are the organization's major strengths? Weaknesses?
6. Who are your organization's major competitors, and what are their strengths and weaknesses?
7. What makes your organization different from others in the industry?
8. What are your organization's major markets?
9. Does the organization have any plans for new products? Acquisitions?
10. What can you tell me about the person I would report to?
11. How would you define your organization's managerial philosophy?
12. What additional training does your organization provide?
13. Do employees have an opportunity to continue their education with help from the organization?
14. Would relocation be required, now or in the future?
15. Why is this job now vacant?

tice session, have your friend critique your performance, using the list of interview faults shown in Table 18.5 to identify opportunities for improvement. You can even videotape these mock interviews and then evaluate them yourself. The taping process can be intimidating, but it helps you work out any problems before you begin actual job interviews.

Nonverbal behavior has a significant effect on the interviewer's opinion of you.

As you stage your mock interviews, pay particular attention to your nonverbal behavior. In the United States, you are more likely to be invited back for a second interview or offered a job if you maintain eye contact, smile frequently, sit in an attentive position, and use frequent hand gestures. These nonverbal signals convince the interviewer that you are alert, assertive, dependable, confident, responsible, and energetic.[23] Of course, some companies based in the United States are owned and managed by people from other cultures. So during your basic research, find out about the company's cultural background and preferences regarding nonverbal behavior.

The way you speak is almost as important as what you say.

Like other forms of nonverbal behavior, the sound of your voice can have a major impact on your success in a job interview.[24] You can work with a tape recorder to overcome voice problems. If you tend to speak too rapidly, practice speaking more slowly. If your voice sounds too loud or too soft, practice adjusting it. Work on eliminating speech mannerisms such as *you know, like,* and *um*, which might make you sound inarticulate. Speak in your natural tone, and try to vary the pitch, rate, and volume of your voice to express enthusiasm and energy. If you speak in a flat, emotionless tone, you convey the impression that you are passive or bored.

When nonverbal behavior is less of a concern, you can use live chat rooms on the Internet to simulate interviews. For example, by using the chat room function on America Online, CompuServe, or Prodigy, you can create a private room and invite other Internet users to meet you there for a one-on-one mock interview.[25] You'll be able to practice answering questions—but of course you'll have no way of evaluating gestures, voice, or appearance.

Plan to Look Good

To look like a winner
- Dress conservatively
- Be well groomed
- Smile when appropriate

When your parents nagged at you to stand up straight, comb your hair, and get rid of your gum, they were right. Physical appearance is important because clothing and grooming reveal something about a candidate's personality and professionalism. Consider this. One

TABLE 18.5

MARKS AGAINST APPLICANTS (IN GENERAL ORDER OF IMPORTANCE)

1. Has a poor personal appearance
2. Is overbearing, overaggressive, conceited; has a "superiority complex"; seems to "know it all"
3. Is unable to express self clearly; has poor voice, diction, grammar
4. Lacks knowledge or experience
5. Is not prepared for interview
6. Has no real interest in job
7. Lacks planning for career; has no purpose or goals
8. Lacks enthusiasm; is passive and indifferent
9. Lacks confidence and poise; is nervous and ill at ease
10. Shows insufficient evidence of achievement
11. Has failed to participate in extracurricular activities
12. Overemphasizes money; is interested only in the best dollar offer
13. Has poor scholastic record; just got by
14. Is unwilling to start at the bottom; expects too much too soon
15. Makes excuses
16. Is evasive; hedges on unfavorable factors in record
17. Lacks tact
18. Lacks maturity
19. Lacks courtesy; is ill-mannered
20. Condemns past employers
21. Lacks social skills
22. Shows marked dislike for schoolwork
23. Lacks vitality
24. Fails to look interviewer in the eye
25. Has limp, weak handshake

owner of a tax consulting firm admits to excusing himself in the middle of an interview to step into the parking lot where he inspects the car of the person he's interviewing. "If it's disheveled or dirty, I eliminate the candidate," he says bluntly. "I don't think you can separate your personal attire and organization from your business attire and organization."[26]

When it comes to clothing, the best policy is to dress conservatively. Wear the best-quality businesslike clothing you can, preferably in a dark, solid color. Avoid flamboyant styles, colors, and prints. Even in companies like Microsoft, where interviewers may dress casually, it's important to show good judgment by dressing (and acting) in a professional manner.

Good grooming makes any style of clothing look better. Make sure your clothes are clean and unwrinkled, your shoes unscuffed and well shined, your hair neatly styled and combed, your fingernails clean, and your breath fresh. If possible, check your appearance in a mirror before entering the room for the interview. Finally, remember that one of the best ways to look good is to smile at appropriate moments.

Be prepared for the interview:
- Take proof of your accomplishments
- Arrive on time
- Wait graciously

Be Ready When You Arrive

For the interview, plan to take a small notebook, a pen, a list of the questions you want to ask, two copies of your résumé protected in a folder, an outline of what you have learned about the organization, and any past correspondence about the position. You may also want

When Natalie Minton interviews potential employees for Texas Instruments in Fort Worth, Texas, she looks for people who communicate well. Part of good communication is being prepared with résumés and work samples; another part is knowing how to look. This graphic designer is showing more than her portfolio. She is also demonstrating her ability to communicate and her concern for a professional appearance.

to take a small calendar, a transcript of your college grades, a list of references, and a portfolio containing samples of your work, performance reviews, and certificates of achievement. Recruiters are impressed by such tangible evidence of your job-related accomplishments. In an era when many people exaggerate their qualifications, visible proof of your abilities carries a lot of weight.[27]

Did You Know?

Monday is, by far, the worst day of the week to be interviewed for a job. The worst time for a job interview is late afternoon.

Be sure you know when and where the interview will be held. The worst way to start any interview is to be late. Check the route you will take, even if it means phoning the interviewer's secretary to ask. Find out how much time it takes to get there; then plan to arrive early. Allow a little extra time just in case you run into a problem on the way.

Once you arrive, relax. You may have to wait a little while, so bring along something to read or occupy your time (the less frivolous or controversial, the better). If company literature is available, read it while you wait. In either case, be polite to the interviewer's assistant. If the opportunity presents itself, ask a few questions about the organization or express enthusiasm for the job. Refrain from smoking before the interview (nonsmokers can smell smoke on the clothing of interviewees), and avoid chewing gum in the waiting room. Anything you do or say while you wait may well get back to the interviewer, so make sure your best qualities show from the moment you enter the premises. That way you'll be ready for the interview itself once it actually begins.

Interviewing for Success

The way to handle the actual interview depends on where you stand in the interview process. If you are being interviewed for the first time, your main objective is to differentiate yourself from the many other candidates who are also being screened. Say you've signed up to talk with a recruiter on campus, who may talk with 10 or 15 applicants during the course of the day. Without resorting to gimmicks, you need to call attention to one key aspect of your background so that the recruiter can say, "Oh yes, I remember Jones—the one who sold used Toyotas in Detroit." Just be sure the trait you accentuate is relevant to the job in question. In addition, you'll want to be prepared in case an employer such as Microsoft expects you to demonstrate a particular skill (such as problem solving) during the screening interview.

Present a memorable "headline" during a screening interview.

Cover all your strengths during a selection interview.

If you progress to the initial selection interview, you should broaden your sales pitch. Instead of telegraphing the "headline," give the interviewer the whole story. Touch at least briefly on all your strengths, but explain three or four of your best qualifications in depth. At the same time, probe for information that will help you evaluate the position objectively. As important as it is to get an offer, it's also important to learn whether the job is right for you.

Emphasize your personality during a final interview.

If you're asked back for a final visit, your chances of being offered a position are quite good. At this point, you'll talk to a person who has the authority to make the offer and negotiate terms. This individual may already have concluded that you have the right background for the job, so she or he will be concerned with sizing up your personality. In fact, both you and the employer need to find out whether there is a good psychological fit. Be honest about your motivations and values. If the interview goes well, your objective should be to clinch the deal on the best possible terms.

Regardless of where you are in the interview process, every interview will proceed through three stages: the warm-up, the question-and-answer session, and the close.

The Warm-Up

The first minute of the interview is crucial.

Of the three stages, the warm-up is the most important, even though it may account for only a small fraction of the time you spend in the interview. Psychologists say that 50 percent of the interviewer's decision is made within the first 30 to 60 seconds, and another 25 percent is made within 15 minutes. If you get off to a bad start, it's extremely difficult to turn the interview around.[28]

Body language is important at this point. Because you won't have time to say much in the first minute or two, you must sell yourself nonverbally. Begin by using the interviewer's name if you're sure you can pronounce it correctly. If the interviewer extends a hand, respond with a firm but gentle handshake. Then wait until you are asked to be seated. Let the interviewer start the discussion, and listen for cues that tell you what he or she is interested in knowing about you as a potential employee.

The Question-and-Answer Stage

Questions and answers will consume the greatest part of the interview. During this phase, the interviewer will ask you about your qualifications and discuss many of the points mentioned in your résumé. You'll also be asked whether you have any questions of your own. Remember, let the interviewer lead the conversation, and never answer a question before he or she has finished asking it. The last few words of the question might surprisingly alter how you should respond.

As questions are asked, tailor your answers to make a favorable impression. Don't limit yourself to yes or no answers. Be sure you pause to think before responding if you're asked

Be Prepared for Challenging Interview Questions

Career magazine online presents excellent articles about job interviews, including "Behavioral Interviews: A Job Candidate's Toughest Obstacle," "Face-to-Face Interview Preparation," "How to Handle a Panel Interview," and "How to Answer Some of Those Awkward—and All Too Common—Interview Questions." The site also provides a career forum, job fair listings, and career links.

http://www.careermag.com/newsarts/interviewing.html

a difficult question. Consider the direction of the discussion, and guide it where you wish with your responses.

Another way you can reach your goal is to ask the right questions. If you periodically ask a question or two from the list you've prepared, you'll not only learn something but will demonstrate your interest as well. It's especially important to probe for what the company is looking for in its new employees. Once you know that, you can show how you meet the firm's needs. Also try to zero in on any reservations the interviewer might have about you so that you can dispel them.

Paying attention when the interviewer speaks can be as important as giving good answers or asking good questions. Listening should make up about half the time you spend in an interview. For tips on becoming a better listener, read Chapter 2. Be alert to nonverbal cues. The interviewer's facial expressions, eye movements, gestures, and posture may tell you the real meaning of what is being said. If the interviewer says one thing but sends a different message nonverbally, you may want to discount the verbal message. Be especially aware of how your comments are received. Does the interviewer nod in agreement or smile to show approval? If so, you're making progress. If not, you might want to introduce another topic or modify your approach.

Paying attention to both verbal and nonverbal messages can help you turn the question-and-answer stage to your advantage.

Bear in mind that employers cannot legally discriminate against a job candidate on the basis of race, color, gender, age (from 40 to 70), marital status, religion, national origin, or disability. Although questions that touch on these areas are not specifically prohibited by federal law, the Equal Employment Opportunity Commission considers such questions with "extreme disfavor." In general, the following topics should not be directly or indirectly introduced by an interviewer:[29]

Think about how you might respond if you are asked to answer unlawful interview questions.

- Your religious affiliation or organizations and lodges you belong to
- Your national origin, age, marital status, or former name
- Your spouse, spouse's employment or salary, dependents, children, or child-care arrangements
- Your height, weight, gender, pregnancy, or any health conditions or disabilities that are not reasonably related to job performance
- Arrests or criminal convictions that are not related to job performance

If your interviewer asks these personal questions, how you respond depends on how badly you want the job, how you feel about revealing the information asked for, what you think the interviewer will do with the information, and whether you want to work for a company that asks such questions. If you don't want the job, you can tell the interviewer that you think a particular question is unethical and mention that you plan to contact the proper government agency. You can also simply refuse to answer—a response that, in many cases, will leave an unfavorable impression on the interviewer.[30]

However, if you want the job (and you don't want to leave an unfavorable impression), you can choose a more tactful approach. You might (1) ask how the question is related to your qualifications for the job, (2) explain that the information is personal, (3) respond to what you think is the interviewer's real concern, or (4) answer both the question and the concern. Of course, if you answer an unethical or unlawful question, you still run the risk that your answer may hurt your chances, so think carefully before answering.[31]

When a business can show that the safety of its employees or customers is at stake, it may be allowed to ask questions that would seem discriminatory in another context. Despite this exception, if you believe that an interviewer's questions are unreasonable, unrelated to the job, or designed to elicit information in an attempt to discriminate, you may complain to the Equal Employment Opportunity Commission or to the state agency that regulates fair employment practices. To report discrimination on the basis of age or physical disability, contact the employer's equal opportunity officer or the U.S. Department of Labor. Be prepared to spend a lot of time and effort if you file a complaint—and remember that you may not win.[32]

The Close

Like the opening, the end of the interview is more important than its duration would indicate. In the last few minutes, you need to evaluate how well you've done and to correct any misconceptions the interviewer might have.

You can generally tell when the interviewer is trying to conclude the session by watching for verbal and nonverbal cues. The interviewer may ask whether you have any more questions, sum up the discussion, change position, or indicate with a gesture that the interview is over. When you get the signal, respond promptly, but don't rush. Be sure to thank the interviewer for the opportunity and express an interest in the organization. If you can do so comfortably, try to pin down what will happen next, but don't press for an immediate decision.

Conclude the interview with courtesy and enthusiasm.

If this is your second or third visit to the organization, the interview may culminate with an offer of employment. You have two options: Accept it or request time to think it over. The best course is usually to wait. If no job offer is made, the interviewer may not have reached a decision yet, but you may tactfully ask when you can expect to know the decision.

If you do receive an offer during the interview, you'll naturally want to discuss salary. However, let the interviewer raise the subject. If asked your salary requirements, say that you would expect to receive the standard salary for the job in question. If you have added qualifications, point them out: "With my 18 months of experience in the field, I would expect to start in the middle of the normal salary range."

Be realistic in your salary expectations and diplomatic in your negotiations.

If you don't like the offer, you might try to negotiate, provided you're in a good bargaining position and the organization has the flexibility to accommodate you. You'll be in a fairly strong position if your skills are in short supply and you have several other offers. It also helps if you're the favorite candidate and the organization is booming. However, many organizations are relatively rigid in their salary practices, particularly at the entry level. Still, in the United States and some European countries, it is acceptable to ask, "Is there any room for negotiation?"

Some applicants are finding the Internet to be a terrific resource for salary information. Thanks to the Internet, Holly Peckham negotiated herself a 21 percent pay increase when she switched public relations firms. Unsure about her worth at the outset of her job search, she found a U.S. salary database on a Web site created by a New York executive search firm and used the information to negotiate her starting salary. Keep in mind, however, that salary schedules don't always take into account company size, specific skills, geography, and market demand. Nevertheless, the information can at least tell you if your expectations are reasonable.[33]

The Internet is a good place to find salary information.

Even if you can't bargain for more money, you may be able to win some concessions on benefits and perquisites. The value of negotiating can be significant because benefits often cost the employer 25 to 45 percent of your salary. In other words, if you're offered an annual salary of $20,000, you'll ordinarily get an additional $5,000 to $9,000 in benefits: life, health, and disability insurance; pension and savings plans; vacation time; or even tuition reimbursement.[34] If you can trade one benefit for another, you may be able to enhance the value of the total package. For example, life insurance may be relatively unimportant to you if you're single, whereas extra vacation time might be very valuable indeed. Don't inquire about benefits, however, until you know you have a job offer.

Interview Notes

Keep a written record of your job interviews.

If yours is a typical job search, you'll have many interviews before you accept an offer. For that reason, keeping a notebook or binder of interview notes can be helpful. To refresh your memory of each conversation, as soon as the interview ends jot down the names and titles of the people you met. Next write down in capsule form the interviewer's answers to your questions. Then briefly evaluate your performance during the interview, listing what you handled well and what you didn't. Going over these notes can help you improve your performance in the future.[35] Whenever you need to review important tips, consult this chapter's Checklist for Interviews. In addition to improving your performance during interviews, interview notes will help you keep track of any follow-up messages you'll need to send.

CHECKLIST FOR INTERVIEWS

A. Preparation

1. Determine the requirements and general salary range of the job.
2. Research the organization's products, structure, financial standing, and prospects for growth.
3. Determine the interviewer's name, title, and status in the firm.
4. Prepare (but don't overrehearse) answers for the questions you are likely to be asked about your qualifications and achievements, your feelings about work and school, your interests and hobbies.
5. Develop relevant questions to ask, such as what training the organization might offer after employment, what type of management system the firm has, whether its executives are promoted from within, and why the position is vacant.
6. Plan your appearance.
   a. Dress in a businesslike manner, regardless of the mode of dress preferred within the organization. Choose traditional footware and a conventional hairstyle.
   b. Wear a minimum of jewelry, but wear a wristwatch to keep track of the time.
   c. Use fragrances sparingly, avoid excessive makeup, and clean and manicure your fingernails.
7. In a briefcase or portfolio, take a pen and paper, a list of questions, two copies of your résumé, and samples of your work (if appropriate).
8. Double-check the location and time of the interview.
   a. Map out the route beforehand, and estimate the time you'll need to get there.
   b. Plan your arrival for 10 to 15 minutes before the interview.
   c. Add 10 or 15 more minutes to cover problems that may arise en route.

B. Initial Stages of the Interview

1. Greet the interviewer by name, with a smile and direct eye contact.
2. Offer a firm but not crushing handshake if the interviewer extends a hand.
3. Take a seat only after the interviewer invites you to be seated or has taken his or her own seat.
4. Sit with an erect posture, facing the interviewer.
5. Listen for cues about what the interviewer's questions are trying to reveal about you and your qualifications.
6. Assume a calm and poised attitude.
7. Avoid gum chewing, smoking, and other displays of nervousness.

C. Body of the Interview

1. Display a genuine, not artificial, smile when appropriate.
2. Convey interest and enthusiasm.
3. Listen attentively so that you can give intelligent responses.
4. Take few notes, and expand on key points later.
5. Sell the interviewer on hiring you.
   a. Relate your knowledge and skills to the position you are seeking.
   b. Stress your positive qualities and characteristics.
6. Answer questions wisely.
   a. Keep responses brief, clear, and to the point.
   b. Avoid exaggeration, and convey honesty and sincerity.
   c. Avoid slighting references to former employers.
7. Avoid alcoholic drinks if you are interviewed over lunch or dinner.

D. Salary Discussions

1. Put off a discussion of salary until late in the interview, if possible.
2. Let the interviewer initiate the discussion of salary.
3. If asked, state that you would like to receive the standard salary for the position. (Know the standard salary for the position in your region of the country.)

E. Closing Stages of the Interview

1. Watch for signs that the interview is about to end.
2. Tactfully ask when you will be advised of the decision on your application.
3. If you're offered the job, either accept or ask for time to consider the offer.
4. Thank the interviewer for meeting with you, with a warm smile and a handshake.

FOLLOWING UP AFTER THE INTERVIEW

Touching base with the prospective employer after the interview, either by phone or in writing, shows that you really want the job and are determined to get it. It also brings your name to the interviewer's attention once again and reminds him or her that you're waiting to know the decision. As Jodi DeLeon at Microsoft points out, following up shows your continued interest in the job.

Six types of follow-up messages:
- Thank-you message
- Inquiry
- Request for a time extension
- Letter of acceptance
- Letter declining a job offer
- Letter of resignation

The two most common forms of follow-up are the thank-you message and the inquiry. These are generally handled by letter, but a phone call is often just as effective, particularly if the employer seems to favor a casual, personal style. The other four types of follow-up message—request for a time extension, letter of acceptance, letter declining a job offer, and letter of resignation—are sent only in certain cases. These messages are better handled in writing, because it's important to document any official actions relating to your employment. Regardless of your method of communicating, however, the principles outlined here will help you write better messages.

Thank-You Letter

Express your thanks within two days after the interview, even if you feel you have little chance for the job. Acknowledge the interviewer's time and courtesy, and be sure to restate the specific job you're applying for. Convey the idea that you continue to be interested. Then ask politely for a decision.

A note or phone call thanking the interviewer
- Is organized like a routine message
- Closes with a request for a decision or future consideration

Keep your thank-you message brief (less than five minutes for a phone call or only one page for a letter), and organize it like a routine message. Like all good business messages, it demonstrates the "you" attitude, and it sounds positive without sounding overconfident. You don't want to sound doubtful about your chances of getting the job, but you don't want to sound arrogant or too sure of yourself either.

The following sample thank-you letter shows how to achieve all this in three brief paragraphs:

After talking with you yesterday, touring your sets, and watching the television commercials being filmed, I remain very enthusiastic about the possibility of joining your staff as a television/film production assistant. Thanks for taking so much time to show me around.

The opening reminds the interviewer of the reasons for meeting and graciously acknowledges the consideration shown to the applicant.

During our meeting, I said that I would prefer not to relocate, but I've reconsidered the matter. I would be pleased to relocate wherever you need my skills in set decoration and prop design.

This paragraph indicates the writer's flexibility and commitment to the job if hired. It also reminds the recruiter of special qualifications.

Now that you've explained the details of your operation, I feel quite strongly that I can make a contribution to the sorts of productions you're lining up. You can also count on me to be an energetic employee and a positive addition to your crew. Please let me know your decision as soon as possible.

The letter closes on a confident and "you"-oriented note, ending with the request for a decision.

Even if the interviewer has said that you are unqualified for the job, a thank-you message like that shown in Figure 18.2 may keep the door open. A letter of this type will probably go into the file for future openings because it demonstrates courtesy and interest.

After Michael Espinosa's interview with Gloria Reynolds, he sent the following thank-you message.

Figure 18.2
In-Depth Critique: Thank-You Note

MICHAEL ESPINOSA
585 Montoya Road
Las Cruces, New Mexico 88005

January 5, 2000

Ms. Gloria Reynolds, Editor
Las Cruces News
317 N. Almendra Street
Las Cruces, NM 88001

Dear Ms. Reynolds:

Our conversation on Tuesday about your newspaper's opening for a food-feature writer was enlightening. Thank you for taking time to talk with me about it.

Your description of the profession makes me feel more certain than ever that I want to be a newspaper writer. Following your advice, I am going to enroll in an evening journalism course.

After I achieve the level of writing skills you suggested, I would deeply appreciate the chance to talk with you again.

Sincerely,

Michael Espinosa

Michael Espinosa

The main idea is the expression of thanks for the interviewer's time and information.

The writer specifically refers to points discussed in the interview. Enthusiasm and eagerness to improve skills are qualities that will impress the interviewer.

The letter closes with a specific and cordial request.

Letter of Inquiry

If you're not advised of the interviewer's decision by the promised date or within two weeks, you might make an inquiry. An inquiry is particularly appropriate if you have received a job offer from a second firm and don't want to accept it before you have an answer from the first. The following inquiry letter follows the general plan for a direct

An inquiry about a hiring decision follows the plan for a direct request.

request; the writer assumes that a simple oversight, and not outright rejection, is the reason for the delay:

When we talked on April 7 about the fashion coordinator position in your Park Avenue showroom, you said you would let me know your decision before May 1. I would still like the position very much, so I'm eager to know what conclusion you've reached.

To complicate matters, another firm has now offered me a position and has asked that I reply within the next two weeks.

Because your company seems to offer a greater challenge, I would appreciate knowing about your decision by Thursday, May 12. If you need more information before then, please let me know.

The opening paragraph identifies the position and introduces the main idea.

The reason for the request comes second. The writer tactfully avoids naming the other firm.

The courteous request for a specific action comes last, in the context of a clearly stated preference for this organization.

Request for a Time Extension

A request for a time extension follows the plan for a direct request but pays extra attention to easing the reader's disappointment.

If you receive a job offer while other interviews are still pending and you want more time to decide, write to the offering organization and ask for a time extension. Employers understand that candidates often interview with several companies. They want you to be sure you are making the right decision, and most of them are happy to accommodate you with a reasonable extension. Just be sure to preface your request with a friendly opening like the one shown in the following sample letter. Ask for more time, stressing your enthusiasm for the organization. Conclude by allowing for a quick decision if your request for additional time is denied. Ask for a prompt reply confirming the time extension if the organization grants it.

The customer relations position in your snack foods division seems like an exciting challenge and a great opportunity. I'm very pleased that you offered it to me.

Because of another commitment, I would appreciate your giving me until August 29 to make a decision. Before our interview, I scheduled a follow-up interview with another company. I'm interested in your organization because of its impressive quality-control procedures and friendly, attractive work environment. But I do feel obligated to keep my appointment.

If you need my decision immediately, I'll gladly let you know. However, if you can allow me the added time to fulfill the earlier commitment, I'd be grateful. Please let me know right away.

The letter begins with a strong statement of interest in the job.

The writer stresses professional obligations, not her desire to learn what the other company may offer. Specific reasons for preferring the first job offer help reassure the reader of her sincerity.

The expression of willingness to yield or compromise conveys continued interest in the position.

This type of letter is, in essence, a direct request. However, because the recipient may be disappointed, be sure to temper your request for an extension with statements indicating your continued interest.

Letter of Acceptance

A letter of acceptance follows the good-news plan.

When you receive a job offer that you want to accept, reply within five days. Begin by accepting the position and expressing thanks. Identify the job that you're accepting. In the next paragraph, cover any necessary details. Conclude by saying that you look forward to reporting for work.

I'm delighted to accept the graphic design position in your advertising department at the salary of $1,575 a month.

Enclosed are the health insurance forms you asked me to complete and sign. I've already given notice to my current employer and will be able to start work on Monday, January 18.

The prospect of joining your firm is very exciting. Thank you for giving me this opportunity for what I'm sure will be a challenging future.

The good-news statement at the beginning confirms the specific terms of the offer.

Miscellaneous details are covered in the middle.

The letter closes with another reference to the good news and a look toward the future.

As always, a good-news letter should convey your enthusiasm and eagerness to cooperate.

Be aware that a job offer and a written acceptance of that offer constitute a legally binding contract, for both you and the employer. So before you write an acceptance letter, be sure you want the job.

Written acceptance of a job offer is legally binding.

Letter Declining a Job Offer

After all your interviews, you may find that you need to write a letter declining a job offer. The best approach is to open warmly, state the reasons for refusing the offer, decline the offer explicitly, and close on a pleasant note, expressing gratitude. By taking the time to write a sincere, tactful letter like the one shown here, you leave the door open for future contact.

The bad-news plan is ideally suited to this type of letter.

A letter declining a job offer follows the bad-news plan.

One of the most interesting interviews I have ever had was the one last month at your Durham textile plant. I'm flattered that you would offer me the computer analyst position that we talked about.

During my job search, I applied to five highly rated firms like your own, each one a leader in its field. Both your company and another offered me a position. Because my desire to work abroad can more readily be satisfied by the other company, I have accepted that job offer.

I deeply appreciate the hour you spent talking with me. Thank you again for your consideration and kindness.

The opening paragraph is a buffer.

Tactfully phrased reasons for the applicant's unfavorable decision precede the bad news and leave the door open.

A sincere and cordial ending lets the reader down gently.

Letter of Resignation

If you get a job offer and are currently employed, you can maintain good relations with your current employer by writing a letter of resignation to your immediate supervisor. Make the letter sound positive, regardless of how you feel. Say something favorable about the organization, the people you work with, or what you've learned on the job. Then state your intention to leave and give the date of your last day on the job. Be sure you give your current employer at least two weeks' notice.

A letter of resignation also follows the bad-news plan.

My sincere thanks to you and to all the other Emblem Corporation employees for helping me learn so much about serving the public these past 11 months. You have given me untold help and encouragement.

An appreciative opening serves as a buffer.

You may recall that when you first interviewed me, my goal was to become a customer relations supervisor. Because that opportunity has been offered to me by another organization, I am submitting my resignation. I regret leaving all of you, but I can't pass up this opportunity.

I would like to terminate my work here two weeks from today but can arrange to work an additional week if you want me to train a replacement.

My sincere thanks and best wishes to all of you.

Reasons stated before the bad news itself and tactful phrasing help keep the relationship friendly, should the writer later want letters of recommendation.

An extra paragraph discusses necessary details.

A cordial close tempers any disappointment.

This letter follows the bad-news plan. By sending one like it, you show that you are considerate and mature, and you also help ensure the good feeling that may help you get another job in the future. Compare your messages with the suggestions in this chapter's Checklist for Follow-Up Messages.

CHECKLIST FOR FOLLOW-UP MESSAGES

A. Thank-You Messages
  1. Thank the interviewer in writing within two days after the interview, and keep your letter to one page.
  2. If you have no alternative, thank the interviewer by phone, keeping the message under five minutes.
  3. In the opening express thanks and identify the job and the time and place of the interview.
  4. Use the middle section for supporting details.
    a. Express your enthusiasm about the organization and the job.
    b. Add any new facts that may help your chances.
    c. Try to repair any negative impressions you may have left during the interview.
  5. Use an action ending.
    a. Offer to submit more data.
    b. Express confidence that your qualifications will meet the organization's requirements.
    c. Look forward to a favorable decision.
    d. Request an opportunity to prove that you can aid the organization's growth or success.

B. Inquiries
  1. Phone or write an inquiry if you are not informed of the decision by the promised date, especially if another organization is awaiting your reply to a job offer.
  2. Follow the plan for direct requests: main idea, necessary details, specific request.

C. Requests for a Time Extension
  1. Send this type of letter if you receive a job offer while other interviews are pending and you want more time before making your decision.
  2. Open with an expression of warmth.
  3. In the middle section explain why you need more time and express your continuing interest in the organization.
  4. Conclude by allowing for a quick decision if your request for more time is denied and by asking the interviewer to confirm the time extension if it is granted.

D. Letters Accepting a Job Offer
  1. Send this message within five days of receiving the offer. State clearly that you accept the offer with pleasure, and identify the job you're accepting.
  2. Fill out the letter with vital details.
  3. Conclude with a statement that you look forward to reporting for work.

E. Letters Rejecting a Job Offer
  1. Open a letter of rejection warmly.
  2. Fill out the letter with an explanation of why you are refusing the offer and an expression of appreciation.
  3. End on a sincere, positive note.

F. Letters of Resignation
  1. Send a letter of resignation to your current employer as soon as possible.
  2. Begin with an appreciative buffer.
  3. Fill out the middle section with your reasons for looking for another job and the actual statement that you are leaving.
  4. Close cordially.

COMMUNICATION CHALLENGES AT MICROSOFT

Cooking up new questions for interviews has become a favorite pastime at Microsoft (right up there with lunch-time Frisbee games). Says Jodi DeLeon, "You'll often walk down the hall and see a group of technical people bouncing a new idea for an interview question off each other." The challenge is to attract the best and brightest from the nation's campuses while making sure these candidates will fit in at Microsoft.

DeLeon believes it's important for every applicant to leave the screening interview with a positive feeling toward Microsoft. "They may not get a job here, but they may turn out to be a major consumer of our products." So she advises Microsoft interviewers to be fair and considerate, giving equal time to everyone and allowing candidates time to add information about their qualifications and to ask questions.

INDIVIDUAL CHALLENGE: Microsoft needs communication assistants in the busy Office Products division. Once hired, the new employees will help handle public relations for Microsoft Office, Word, Excel, PowerPoint, Access, and Outlook. The best candidates will know how to organize and write letters, memos, press releases, and possibly advertising copy, but they'll also be innovative in their thinking. DeLeon has come up with a problem-solving question for the campus interviews that she wants to test on you: What are some of the ways you might use written or spoken communications to promote Microsoft's Office software to teachers and administrators? Write your answer just as you would explain it in an interview, drawing on everything you've learned so far in this course.

TEAM CHALLENGE: To test your answers, divide your group so that one member role-plays the job candidate being interviewed by the others. Start by posing the problem-solving question. Then, if time allows, ask a few follow-up questions to determine more about the "applicant's" knowledge of good communication principles. Take turns until each of you plays the role of job candidate. This will give you some practice thinking on your feet and a chance to experience the interviewer's perspective.[36] ■

SUMMARY OF LEARNING OBJECTIVES

1. **Explain the dual purpose of an interview.** During an interview the organization's main objective is to find out whether you're the best person to fill a job opening; as the applicant, your main objective is to find a job that is best suited to your goals and capabilities.
2. **Describe the function of a preliminary screening interview.** Firms use preliminary screening interviews to sort through a large number of candidates efficiently and to eliminate unqualified applicants from the hiring process.
3. **Discuss three types of interview and explain their purpose.** The structured interview is a prepared series of questions that are generally asked in a set order and is used to create uniformity in the hiring process. The open-ended interview is unstructured and is used to encourage a free-flowing dialogue. It allows employers to customize the interview to learn as much as possible about the applicant's skills, personality, and critical success factors. The stress interview subjects applicants to a series of stressful situations that are designed to determine how well the applicant can handle job stress.
4. **List several things you can do to prepare for a job interview.** To prepare for a job interview, you should (1) do some basic research to learn as much as possible about the company and industry; (2) think about questions you might be asked, develop some answers, and practice your response; and (3) prepare a list of questions to ask the interviewer so you can better evaluate the organization and the job.
5. **Name several things you should find out about a company before accepting a job offer.** Before accepting a job, find out whether you will like working with the people and whether the company culture appeals to you. Determine whether you can perform the work and whether you will find it interesting and challenging. Learn about what kind of future you can expect with the company and whether there are opportunities for advancement. Finally, research what other companies are paying employees with your skills and experience.
6. **List six common types of message that follow an interview.** Follow-up messages include thank-you letters, inquiries, requests for a time extension to make a job decision, letters of acceptance, letters declining a job offer, and letters of resignation to your current employer.

CRITICAL THINKING QUESTIONS

1. How can you distinguish yourself from other candidates in a screening interview and still keep your responses short and to the point? Explain.
2. What can you do to make a favorable impression when you discover that an open-ended interview has turned into a stress interview? Briefly explain your answer.
3. Should applicants ask about preemployment testing during an interview? Explain your answer.
4. Why is it important to distinguish unethical or illegal interview questions from acceptable questions? Explain.

5. If you want to switch jobs because you can't work with your supervisor, how can you explain this situation to a prospective employer? Give an example.
6. If you feel you've gotten off to a bad start during a preliminary screening, what can you do to try to save the interview? Explain your answer.
7. During a group interview you notice that one of the candidates is trying to monopolize the conversation. He's always the first to answer, his answer is the longest, and he even interrupts the other candidates while they are talking. The interviewer doesn't seem to be concerned about his behavior, but you are. You would like to have more time to speak so that the interviewer could get to know you better. What should you do?
8. Why should you pay attention to the interviewer's nonverbal communication during an interview?

DOCUMENTS FOR ANALYSIS

Read the following documents; then (1) analyze the strengths or weaknesses of each document and (2) revise each document so that it follows this chapter's guidelines.

Document 18.A: Thank-You Letter

Thank you for the really marvelous opportunity to meet you and your colleagues at Starret Engine Company. I really enjoyed touring your facilities and talking with all the people there. You have quite a crew! Some of the other companies I have visited have been so rigid and uptight that I can't imagine how I would fit in. It's a relief to run into a group of people who seem to enjoy their work as much as all of you do.

I know that you must be looking at many other candidates for this job, and I know that some of them will probably be more experienced than I am. But I do want to emphasize that my two-year hitch in the Navy involved a good deal of engineering work. I don't think I mentioned all my shipboard responsibilities during the interview.

Please give me a call within the next week to let me know your decision. You can usually find me at my dormitory in the evening after dinner (phone: 877-9080).

Document 18.B: Letter of Inquiry

I have recently received a very attractive job offer from the Warrington Company. But before I let them know one way or another, I would like to consider any offer that your firm may extend. I was quite impressed with your company during my recent interview, and I am still very interested in a career there.

I don't mean to pressure you, but Warrington has asked for my decision within ten days. Could you let me know by Tuesday whether you plan to offer me a position? That would give me enough time to compare the two offers.

Document 18.C: Letter Declining a Job Offer

I'm writing to say that I must decline your job offer. Another company has made me a more generous offer, and I have decided to accept. However, if things don't work out for me there, I will let you know. I sincerely appreciate your interest in me.

EXERCISES

1. Divide the class into two groups. Half of the class will be recruiters for a large chain of national department stores looking to fill manager trainee positions (there are 15 openings). The other half of the class will be candidates for the job. The company is specifically looking for candidates who demonstrate these three qualities: initiative, dependability, and willingness to assume responsibility.
   a. Have each recruiter select and interview an applicant for ten minutes.
   b. Have all the recruiters discuss how they assessed the applicant against each of the three desired qualities. In other words, what questions did they ask or what did they use as an indicator to determine whether the candidate possessed the quality?
   c. Have all the applicants discuss what they said to convince the recruiters that they possessed each of these qualities.
2. Select a large company (one that you can easily find information on) where you might like to work. Use the Internet to perform some preliminary research on the company.

   a. What did you learn about the organization that would help you during an interview with that company?
   b. What Internet sources did you use to obtain this information?
   c. Armed with this information, what aspects of your background do you think might appeal to this company's recruiters?
3. Prepare written answers to ten of the questions listed in Table 18.3, "Twenty-Five Common Interview Questions" (see page 640).
4. You have decided to accept a new position with a competitor of your company. Write a letter of resignation to your supervisor announcing your decision.

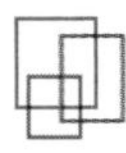

   a. Will you use the direct or the indirect approach? Please explain.
   b. Will you notify your employer that you are joining a competing firm?
   c. Will you send your letter by e-mail, send it regular mail, or place it on your supervisor's desk?
5. Write a short memo to your instructor discussing what you feel are your greatest strengths and weaknesses.

Exploring the Best of the Web

Be Prepared for Challenging Interview Questions, page 644

Explore the *Career* magazine Web site and then answer these questions.

1. Read one or more of the articles on interviewing techniques. Then with a classmate, role-play an interview situation and try out the tips you've gleaned from the articles. What did you learn?
2. By now, you've probably read about and practiced many approaches to job interviews, including what you've learned from this chapter and the *Career* magazine Web site. If you were going to write a "how-to" magazine article about job interviews and you didn't have space for everything, what interviewing advice would you include as the best and most important?

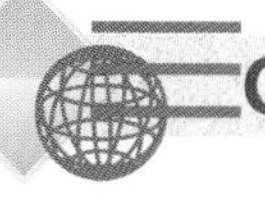

Cases

Interviewing with Potential Employers

1. Interviewers and interviewees: Classroom exercise in interviewing Interviewing is clearly an interactive process involving at least two people. So the best way to practice for interviews is to work with others.

Your task: You and all other members of your class are to write letters of application for an entry-level or management-trainee position requiring a pleasant personality and intelligence but a minimum of specialized education or experience. Sign your letter with a fictitious name that conceals your identity. Next polish (or prepare) a résumé that accurately identifies you and your educational and professional accomplishments.

Now, three members of the class who volunteer as interviewers divide among themselves all the anonymously written application letters. Then each interviewer selects a candidate who seems the most pleasant and convincing in his or her letter. At this time the selected candidates identify themselves and give the interviewers their résumés.

Each interviewer then interviews his or her chosen candidate in front of the class, seeking to understand how the items on the résumé qualify the candidate for the job. At the end of the interviews, the class may decide who gets the job and discuss why this candidate was successful. Afterward, retrieve your letter, sign it with the right name, and submit it to the instructor for credit.

2. Internet interview: Exercise in interviewing Using the Web 100 site at http://www.metamoney.com/w100, locate the home page of a company you would like to work for. Then identify a position within the company for which you would like to apply. Study the company using any of the online business resources discussed in Chapter 11, and prepare for an interview with that company.

Your task: Working with a classmate, take turns interviewing each other for your chosen positions. Interviewers should take notes during the interview. Once the interview is complete, critique each other's performance (interviewers should critique how well candidates prepared for the interview and answered the questions; interviewees should critique the quality of the questions asked). Write a follow-up letter thanking your interviewer and submit the letter to your instructor.

Following Up After the Interview

3. "Dear Mr. Chacon": Follow-up letter to straighten out possible confusion You have been interviewed for the position of assistant manager of a retail outlet in the In-a-Minute chain, consisting of company-owned stores that sell groceries, some medications, and petroleum products. The chain is successful, with new outlets opening regularly in Missouri, Kentucky, and Tennessee. You would appreciate a chance to join the firm.

During the interview, Roger Chacon asked you several questions about your academic record. Your answers, you feel, were somewhat scattered and left Mr. Chacon with no clear understanding of the courses you've taken, your proficiency in several key areas, or the date you expect to graduate—matters that he seemed most interested in.

Your task: Working with your own record, draft a follow-up letter to send to Mr. Chacon with a copy of your college transcript. Describe what you have accomplished in one or two academic areas. Mr. Chacon is with the human resources department at the corporation's headquarters, 99 Litzinger Lane, St. Louis, MO 63124.

4. A slight error in timing: Letter asking for delay of an employment decision You botched up your timing and applied for your third-choice job before going after what you really wanted. What you want to do is work in retail marketing with Neiman-Marcus in Dallas; what you have been offered is a similar job with Longhorn Leather and Lumber, 55 dry and dusty miles away in Commerce, just south of the Oklahoma panhandle.

You review your notes. Your Longhorn interview was three weeks ago with the human resources manager, R. P. Bronson, a congenial person who has just written to offer you the position. The store's address is 27 Sam Rayburn Dr., Commerce, TX 75428. Mr. Bronson notes that he can hold the position open for ten days. You have an interview scheduled with Neiman-Marcus next week, but it is unlikely that you will know the store's decision within this ten-day period.

Your task: Write to R. P. Bronson, requesting a reasonable delay in your consideration of his job offer.

5. Journey to Long Island City: Letter accepting a good job offer Today's mail brings you the following letter from Rhonda Frederick, Human Resources Director, Chesterton Ceramics, 3 Chesterton Place, Long Island City, NY 11101:

> We are pleased to offer you the position of chemical technician beginning 60 days from the date of this letter at a monthly salary of $1,650. Please let us know of your acceptance of this position within ten days.
>
> Your work will be given 6-month and 12-month reviews; we offer 4 percent salary increases at these points if the employee's work progress is satisfactory. As was indicated to you in the interview, employee participation in the company pension plan is voluntary during the first full year of employment; after that, participation is required. We will fund your moving expenses up to $850, with 50 percent of this amount sent to you in advance if you desire.
>
> We hope that you will accept this position. Your academic record and experience indicate that you should do well in our laboratories, and you will find that Long Island City provides easy access to Manhattan. We maintain a file of house and apartment listings; if you let me know your housing needs, I will send you whatever information you require.
>
> If you plan to join our pension program during your first year, please let me know so that I can start the paperwork before your arrival.
>
> Enclosed is our check for $232.76, covering your interview expenses.

Your task: Write a letter accepting the job and answering the questions that Ms. Frederick asked.

6. Job hunt: Set of employment-related letters to a single company Where would you like to work? Pick a real or an imagined company, and assume that a month ago you sent your résumé and application letter. Not long afterward, you were invited to come for an interview, which seemed to go very well.

Your task: Use your imagination to write the following: (a) a thank-you letter for the interview, (b) a note of inquiry, (c) a request for more time to decide, (d) a letter of acceptance, and (e) a letter declining the job offer.

Part 6 A Case for Critical Thinking

GAMES RECRUITERS PLAY

Warning! The gentle job interview is dead. These days, job candidates solve brainteasers and riddles, create art out of paper bags, spend a day acting as managers of make-believe companies, and solve complex business problems. They even answer questions such as "Why do they make manhole covers round? If you had your own company, what would you do?" "If previous co-workers were asked for key words to describe you, what would they say?"

While some candidates are caught off guard by these questions, others—such as Robert Bresky—are ready to play. For instance, when Bresky applied for an account executive position at a New York advertising firm, he didn't miss a beat when his interviewer reached into her desk drawer and tossed a hand grenade on the table. "If you're so good," she said, "sell me this." Bresky picked up the grenade and said: "Ma'am, if you're talking personal protection, this is the way to go. It's portable, it's easy to use, and it'll scare off even the toughest gang member." Bresky got the job.

Similarly, one software developer asked a candidate, "If I stood next to a skyscraper and gave you a barometer, how could you figure out how tall the building was?" He knew there wasn't a solution to this problem, but the interviewee created one: He'd find the building's janitor and offer him the barometer in exchange for information about the building's height. That candidate showed the type of creative thinking the interviewer was searching for.

Of course, these types of questions seldom have a right answer. "But there are lots of wrong ones," notes one Silicon Graphics manager. He often asks job candidates to talk about a time they hit a wall trying to push forward a great idea, "Whatever you do," he advises, "don't say you dropped your brilliant idea because no one listened."

Another way firms gauge an applicant's ability to perform is by constructing workplace simulation exercises. After all, people are often poor at describing their own process capabilities. For instance, good communicators with sensitive people skills will de-

Simulation interviews test job candidates' ability to perform on the job.

scribe themselves as average, whereas those with poor capability frequently think they're excellent because they don't notice the signals from others. So instead of asking candidates to describe their process skills, companies observe them in action.

Some companies even send applicants to specialized firms that construct job simulation exercises. Unisys, for example, sends its aspiring managers to Development Dimensions International (DDI) in Pittsburgh. There, job candidates pretend they are customer service managers for a fictional company called Pilot, Inc. It's their first day on the job and things are hectic already. Dozens of urgent e-mail and voice-mail messages await them. An important client is unhappy because his order is late. Another is frustrated because his equipment has failed. From a central control room filled with a dozen television monitors, DDI psychologists watch the candidates perform. "We take all the crises a manager might experience in a year and cram them into a day," notes DDI's founder.

Even though such job simulation exercises are becoming more popular, at $3,000 per person, they're still unaffordable to most companies. Furthermore, critics of the simulation process claim that these types of interviews can perpetuate the status quo.

Nevertheless, it takes more than rehearsing answers to land a job at a savvy company. Most companies don't want applicants merely to talk about their strengths and weaknesses anymore; they want proof that applicants can deliver the competencies they are looking for. Tired of hiring people with perfect résumés and outstanding references who were disasters, companies are continually experimenting with new ways to assess their job candidates. So expect the unexpected. And remember, while a high IQ may get you an interview, winning a job today takes creativity, intuition, flexibility, the ability to reason, and a good sense of humor.

1. How can job candidates prepare for job simulation interviews?
2. A recent study by Andersen Consulting discovered that one of the most important factors behind success is the ability to juggle a complicated schedule. Think about your own activities and experiences. What evidence could you provide to a future employer to demonstrate that you have this ability?
3. Why is it important to take courses both inside and outside your major area of study?
4. McKinsey & Company, a leading global consulting firm, has a company Web site full of information for job candidates. Go to the company's recruiting Web site at http://www.recruiting.mckinsey.com and click on "Case." Read the introduction and review the "buy and fly" case. Why does the company include this case study on their Web site?

Special Topics in Business Communication

Component Chapter A
Format and Layout of Business Documents

Component Chapter B
Documentation of Report Sources

COMPONENT CHAPTER A

FORMAT AND LAYOUT OF BUSINESS DOCUMENTS

An effective letter, memo, or report does more than store words on paper. It communicates with the right person, makes an impression, and tells the recipient who wrote it and when it was written. It may even carry responses back to the sender, if only to relate how and by whom it was received and processed.

Over the centuries certain conventions have developed for the format and layout of business documents. Of course, conventions vary from country to country, and, even within the United States, few hard-and-fast rules exist. Many organizations develop variations of standard styles to suit their own needs, adopting the style that's best for the types of messages they send and for the kinds of audiences that receive them. The conventions described here are more common than others. Whether you handle all your own communication on your computer or rely on someone else to handle it for you, knowing the proper form for your documents and knowing how to make them attractive to your readers are crucial.

FIRST IMPRESSIONS

A letter or other written document is often the first (sometimes the only) contact you have with an external audience. Memos and other documents used within an organization represent you to supervisors, colleagues, and employees. So it's important that your documents look neat and professional and that they're easy to read. Your audience's first impressions come from the paper you use, the way you customize it, and the general appearance of your document. These elements tell readers a lot about you and about your company's professionalism.

Paper

From your own experience, you know that a flimsy, see-through piece of paper gives a much less favorable impression than a richly textured piece. Paper quality is measured in two ways: The first measure of quality is weight, specifically the weight of four reams (each a 500-sheet package) of letter-size paper. The quality most commonly used by U.S. business organizations is 20-pound paper, but 16- and 24-pound versions are also used. The second measure of quality is the percentage of cotton in the paper. Cotton doesn't yellow over time the way wood pulp does, and it's both strong and soft. In general, paper with a 25 percent cotton content is an appropriate quality for letters and outside reports. For memos and other internal documents, lighter-weight paper and paper with a lower cotton content may be used. Also, airmail-weight paper may be more cost effective for international correspondence, but make sure it isn't too flimsy.[1]

In the United States the standard size of paper for business documents is 8½ by 11 inches. Standard legal documents are 8½ by 14 inches. Executives sometimes have heavier 7-by-10-inch paper on hand (with matching envelopes) for such personal messages as congratulations and recommendations.[2] They may also have a box of correspondence note cards imprinted with their initials and a box of plain folded notes for condolences or for acknowledging formal invitations.

Stationery may vary in color. Of course, white is standard for business purposes, although neutral colors such as gray and ivory are sometimes used. Memos are sometimes produced on pastel-colored paper so that internal correspondence can be more easily distinguished from external, and memos are sometimes printed or typed on various colors of paper for routing to separate departments. Light-colored papers are distinctive and often appropriate; bright or dark colors make reading difficult and may appear too frivolous.

Customization

For letters to outsiders, U.S. businesses commonly use letterhead stationery printed with the company's name and address, usually at the top of the page but sometimes along the left side or even at the bottom of the page. Other information may be included in the letterhead as well: the company's telephone number, fax number, cable address, Web site address, product lines, date of establishment, officers and directors, slogan, and symbol (logo). The idea is to give the recipient pertinent reference data and a good idea not only of what the company does but also of the company's image.[3] Nevertheless, the letterhead should be as simple as possible; too much information gives the page a cluttered look, cuts into the space needed for the letter, and may become outdated before all the letterhead has been used. If you correspond frequently with people in foreign countries, your letterhead can be misleading. If you do a lot of business abroad, be sure your letterhead is intelligible to foreigners, and make sure it includes the name of your country as well as your cable, telex, e-mail address, or fax information.

In the United States, company letterhead is always used for the first page of a letter. Successive pages are plain sheets of paper that match the letterhead in color and quality, or some companies use a specifically printed second-page letterhead bearing only the company's name. Other countries have other conventions. For example, Latin American companies use a cover page with their printed seal in the center.

Many companies also design and print standardized forms for memos and for reports that are written frequently and always require the same sort of information (such as sales reports and expense reports). These forms may be printed in sets for use with carbon paper or in carbonless copy sets that produce multiple copies automatically with the original. More and more, organizations are using computers to generate their standardized forms. These electronic forms can save money and time.[4]

Appearance

Most business documents are produced using either a letter-quality (not a dot matrix) printer or a typewriter. Some short informal memos are handwritten, and it's appropriate to handwrite a note of condolence to a close business associate. Of course, the envelope is handwritten, printed, or typed to match the document. However, even a letter on the best-quality paper with the best-designed letterhead may look unprofessional if it's poorly produced.

Companies in the United States make sure that documents (especially external ones) are centered on the page, with margins of at least an inch all around (unlike documents produced in Latin America, which use much wider margins and thus look much longer). Using word-processing or desktop publishing software, you can achieve this balanced appearance simply by defining the format parameters. If you are using a typewriter, such balance can be achieved either by establishing a standard line length or by establishing a "picture frame."

The most common line length is about 6 inches. Lines aren't usually right-hand justified because the resulting text can be hard to read, even with proportional spacing, and because the document generally looks too much like a form letter. Varying line length makes the document look more personal and interesting. If you're using a typewriter, the larger, pica type will give you 60 characters in a line; the smaller, elite type will give you 72 characters in a line. Sometimes a guide sheet, with the margins and the center point marked in dark ink, is used as a backing. The number of lines between elements of the document (such as between the date line and inside address in a letter) can be adjusted to ensure that a short document fills the page vertically or that a longer document extends to at least three lines of body on the last page.

Another important aspect of a professional-looking document is the proper spacing after punctuation. For example, U.S. conventions include (1) leaving one space after commas and semicolons and (2) leaving two spaces after periods at the ends of sentences and after colons (unless your typeface is proportional, requiring only one space). Each letter in a person's initials is followed by a period and a single space. Abbreviations for organizations, such as P.T.A., may or may not have periods, but they never have internal spaces. On computers and typewriters that have no special characters for dashes, use two hyphens with no space before, between, or after. Other details of this sort are provided in your company's style book or in most secretarial handbooks.

Finally, messy corrections are dreadfully obvious and unacceptable in business documents. Be sure that any letter, report, or memo requiring a lot of corrections is reprinted or retyped. Word-processing software and self-correcting typewriters can produce correction-free documents at the push of a button.

Letters

For a long time, letters have begun with some kind of phrase in greeting and have ended with some sort of polite expression before the writer's signature. In fact, books printed in the sixteenth century prescribed letter formats for writers to follow. Styles have changed some since then, but all business letters still have certain elements in common. Several of these elements appear in every letter; others appear only when desirable or appropriate. In addition, these letter parts are usually arranged in one of three basic formats.

Standard Letter Parts

All business letters typically include seven elements, in the following order: (1) heading, (2) date, (3) inside address, (4) salutation, (5) body, (6) complimentary close, and (7) signature block. The letter in Figure A.1 shows the placement of these standard letter parts.

Figure A.1
In-Depth Critique: Standard Letter Parts

The writer of this business letter had no letterhead available but correctly included a heading.

Heading	6412 Belmont Drive New Weston, OH 45348
Date	June 22, 2000
* * *	
Inside Address	Mr. Richard Garcia Director of Franchises Snack Shoppes 2344 Western Avenue Seattle, WA 98123
□	
Salutation	Dear Mr. Garcia:
□	
Body	Last Monday, my wife and I were on our way home from a long weekend, and we stopped at a Snack Shoppe for a quick sandwich. A sign on the cash register gave your address in the event customers were interested in operating a franchise of their own somewhere else. We talked about the idea all evening and into the night.
□	Although we had talked about changing jobs—I'm an administrative analyst for a utility company and my wife sells real estate—the thought of operating a franchised business had never occurred to us. We'd always thought in terms of starting a business from scratch. However, owning a Snack Shoppe is an intriguing idea.
□	We would appreciate your sending us full details on owning our own outlet. Please include the names and telephone numbers of other Snack Shoppe owners so that we can talk to them before we make any decision to proceed further. We're excited about hearing from you.
□	
Complimentary Close	Cordially,
□ □ □	Peter Simond
Signature Block	Peter Simond
* * * * * * *	

□ One blank space
* *Variable spacing depending on the length of the letter*

Heading

Letterhead (the usual heading) shows the organization's name, full address, and (almost always) telephone number. Executive letterhead also bears the name of an individual within the organization. Computers allow you to design your own letterhead (either one to use for all correspondence or a new one for each piece of correspondence). If letterhead stationery is not available, the heading consists of a return address (but not a name) starting 13 lines from the top of the page, which leaves 2 inches between the return address and the top of the page.

Date

If you're using letterhead, place the date at least one blank line beneath the lowest part of the letterhead. Without letterhead, place the date immediately below the return address. The standard method of writing the date in the United States uses the full name of the month (no abbreviations), followed by the day (in numerals, without *st*, *rd*, or *th*), a comma, and then the year: July 14, 1997 (7/14/97). The U.S. government and some U.S. industries place the day (in numerals) first, followed by the month (unabbreviated), followed by the year—with no comma: 14 July 1997 (14/7/97). This convention is similar to the one used in Europe, except that European convention replaces the U.S. solidus (diagonal line) with periods when the date appears all in numerals: 14 July 1997 (14.7.1997). The international standard places the year first, followed by the month and the day, separated by commas in the all-numeral form: 1997 July 14 (1997, 7,14). To maintain the utmost clarity, always spell out the name of the month in dates for international correspondence.[5]

When communicating internationally, you may also experience some confusion over time. Some companies in the United States refer to morning (A.M.) and afternoon (P.M.), dividing a 24-hour day into 12-hour blocks so that they refer to four o'clock in the morning (4:00 A.M.) or four o'clock in the afternoon (4:00 P.M.). The U.S. military and European companies refer to one 24-hour period so that 0400 hours (4:00 A.M.) is always in the morning and 1600 hours (4:00 P.M.) is always in the afternoon.[6] Make sure your references to time are as clear as possible, and be sure you clearly understand your audience's time references.

Inside Address

The inside address identifies the recipient of the letter. For U.S. correspondence, begin the inside address one or more lines below the date, depending on how long the letter is. Precede the addressee's name with a courtesy title, such as *Dr.*, *Mr.*, or *Ms.* The accepted courtesy title for women in business is *Ms.*, although a woman known to prefer the title *Miss* or *Mrs.* is always accommodated. If you don't know whether a person is a man or a woman (and you have no way of finding out), do not use a courtesy title. For example, Terry Smith could be either a man or a woman. The first line of the inside address would be just Terry Smith, and the salutation would be Dear Terry Smith. The same is true if you know only a person's initials, as in S.J. Adams.

Spell out and capitalize titles that precede a person's name, such as *Professor* or *General* (see Table A.1 for the proper forms of address). The person's organizational title, such as *Director*, may be included on this first line (if it is short) or on the line below; the name of a department may follow. In addresses and signature lines, don't forget to capitalize any professional title that follows a person's name:

Mr. Ray Johnson, Dean

Ms. Patricia T. Higgins
Assistant Vice President

However, professional titles not appearing in an address or signature line are capitalized only when they directly precede the name.

President Kenneth Johanson will deliver the speech.

Maria Morales, president of ABC Enterprises, will deliver the speech.

The Honorable Helen Masters, senator from Arizona, will deliver the speech.

If the name of a specific person is unavailable, you may address the letter to the department or to a specific position within the department. Also, be sure to spell out company names in full, unless the company itself uses abbreviations in its official name.

Other address information includes the treatment of buildings, house numbers, and compass directions. Capitalize the names of buildings, and if you specify a location within a building (suite, room, and so on), capitalize it and use a comma to separate it from the building name.

Empire State Building, Suite 1073

Use numerals for all house or building numbers, except the number *one*.

One Trinity Lane
637 Adams Avenue, Apt. 7

Spell out compass directions that fall within a street address, but abbreviate compass directions that follow the street address:

1074 West Connover Street
783 Main Street, N.E., Apt. 27

Also remember that apartment, suite, and room numbers always appear in numerals (as in the examples already listed in this paragraph). The following example shows all

TABLE A.1

FORMS OF ADDRESS

Person	In Address	In Salutation
	Personal Titles	
Man	Mr. [first & last name]	Dear Mr. [last name]:
Woman (marital status unknown)	Ms. [first & last name]	Dear Ms. [last name]:
Woman (single)	Ms. *or* Miss [first & last name]	Dear Ms. *or* Miss [last name]:
Woman (married)	Ms. *or* Mrs. [wife's first & last name] or Mrs. [husband's first & last name]	Dear Ms. *or* Mrs. [last name]:
Woman (widowed)	Ms. or Mrs. [wife's first name & last name] *or* Mrs. [husband's first & last name]	Dear Ms. *or* Mrs. [last name]:
Woman (separated or divorced)	Ms. or Mrs. [first & last name]	Dear Ms. *or* Mrs. [last name]:
Two men (or more)	Mr. [first & last name] and Mr. [first & last name]	Dear Mr. [last name] and Mr. [last name] *or* Messrs. [last name] and [last name]:
Two women (or more)	Ms. [first & last name] and Ms. [first & last name]	Dear Ms. [last name] and Ms. [last name] *or* Mses. [last name] and [last name]:
	or	
	Mrs. [first & last name] and Mrs. [first & last name]	Dear Mrs. [last name] and Mrs. [last name]: *or* Dear Mesdames [last name] and [last name] *or* Mesdames:
	Miss [first & last name] and Mrs. [first & last name]	Dear Miss [last name] and Mrs. [last name]:
One woman and one man	Ms. [first & last name] and Mr. [first & last name]	Dear Ms. [last name] and Mr. [last name]:
Couple (married)	Mr. and Mrs. [husband's first & last name]	Dear Mr. and Mrs. [last name]:
Couple (married with different last names)	[title] [first & last name of husband] [title] [first & last name of wife]	Dear [title] [husband's last name] and [title] [wife's last name]:
Couple (married professionals with same title & same last name)	[title in plural form] [husband's first name] and [wife's first name] [last name]	Dear [title in plural form] [last name]:

the information that may be included in the inside address and its proper order for U.S. correspondence:

Ms. Linda Coolidge, Vice President
Corporate Planning Department
Midwest Airlines
Kowalski Building, Suite 21-A
7279 Bristol Avenue
Toledo, OH 43617

Canadian addresses are similar, except that the name of the province is usually spelled out:

Dr. H. C. Armstrong
Research and Development
Commonwealth Mining Consortium
The Chelton Building, Suite 301
585 Second Street SW
Calgary, Alberta T2P 2P5

When addressing correspondence for other countries, follow the format and information that appear in the company's letterhead.[7] You want to be especially careful about the format of international correspondence because you want everything to be as clear as possible.[8] The

TABLE A.1, CONTINUED

Person	In Address	In Salutation
	Personal Titles	
Couple (married professionals with different titles & same last name)	[title] [first & last name of husband] [title] [first & last name of wife]	Dear [title] and [title] [last name]:
	Professional titles	
President of a college or university (doctor)	Dr. [first & last name], President	Dear Dr. [last name]:
Dean of a school or college	Dean [first & last name] *or* Dr., Mr., Mrs., Mrs., *or* Miss [first & last name] Dean of (title)	Dear Dean [last name]: Dear Dr., Mr., Ms., Mrs., *or* Miss [last name]:
Professor	Professor [first & last name]	Dear Professor [last name]:
Physician	[first & last name], M.D.	Dear Dr. [last name]:
Lawyer	Mr., Ms., Mrs., *or* Miss [first & last name]	Dear Mr., Ms., Mrs., *or* Miss [last name]:
Service personnel	[full rank, first & last name, abbreviation of service designation] (add *Retired* if applicable)	Dear [rank] [last name]:
Company or corporation	[name of organization]	Ladies and Gentlemen *or* Gentlemen and Ladies
	Governmental Titles	
President of the United States	The President	Dear Mr. *or* Madam President:
Senator of the United States	Honorable [first & last name]	Dear Senator [last name]:
Cabinet member Postmaster General Attorney General	Honorable [first & last name]	Dear Mr. *or* Madam Secretary: Dear Mr. *or* Madam Postmaster General: Dear Mr. *or* Madam Attorney General:
Mayor	Honorable [first & last name] Mayor of [name of city]	Dear Mayor [last name]:
Judge	The Honorable [first and last name]	Dear Judge [last name]:
	Religious Titles	
Priest	The Reverend [first & last name], [initials of order, if any]	Reverend Sir: (formal) *or* Dear Father [last name]: (informal)
Rabbi	Rabbi [first & last name]	Dear Rabbi [last name]:
Minister	The Reverend [first & last name] [title, if any]	Dear Reverend [last name]:

order and layout of address information vary from country to country, so follow the conventions of the country of the recipient. When you're sending mail from the United States, however, be sure that the name of the destination country appears on the last line of the address in capital letters. Also, use the English version of the country name so that your mail is routed from the United States to the right country. Then, to be sure your mail is routed correctly within the destination country, use the foreign spelling of the city name (using the characters and diacritical marks that would be commonly used in the region). For example, the following address uses Köln, instead of Cologne:

H. R. Veith, Director	Addressee
Eisfieren Glaswerk	Company name
Blaubachstraße 13	Street address
Postfach 10 80 07	Post office box
D-5000 Köln I	District, city
GERMANY	Country

Additional addresses might look similar to the following:

Mr. Toru Hasegawa
7-35 Kitashinagawa
6 Chrome—141 Shinagawa-ku
Tokyo
JAPAN

Cairo
Cleopatra
165 El Corniche Road
Mrs. Ahmed Abbas Zaki
EGYPT

Crédit Lyonnais
c/o Claude Rubinowicz
19, Boulevard des Italiens
75002 Paris
FRANCE

Sr. Ari Matos Cardoso
Superintendent of Human Resources and Personnel
Av. República do Chile, 65
Centro-Rio de Janeiro, RJ
CEP 20035
BRAZIL

Be sure to get organizational titles right when addressing international correspondence. Unfortunately, job designations vary around the world. In England, for example, a managing director is often what a U.S. company would call its chief executive officer or president, and a British deputy is the equivalent of a vice president. In France, responsibilities are assigned to individuals without regard to title or organizational structure, and in China the title *project manager* has meaning, but the title *sales manager* may not. To make matters worse, businesspeople in some countries sign correspondence without their names typed below. In Germany, for example, the belief is that employees represent the company, so it's inappropriate to emphasize personal names.[9]

Salutation

In the salutation of your letter, follow the first line of the inside address. That is, if the first line is a person's name, the salutation is *Dear Mr.* or *Ms. Name.* Base the formality of the salutation on your relationship with the addressee. If in conversation you would say "Mary," your letter's salutation should be *Dear Mary,* followed by a colon. In letters to people you don't know well enough to address personally, include the courtesy title and last name, followed by a colon. Presuming to write *Dear Lewis* instead of *Dear Professor Chang* demonstrates a disrespectful familiarity that a stranger will probably resent. If the first line is a position title such as Director of Personnel, then use *Dear Director;* if the addressee is unknown, use a polite description, such as *Dear Alumnus, Dear SPCA Supporter,* or *Dear Voter.* If the first line is plural (a department or company), then use *Ladies and Gentlemen* (look again at Table A.1). When you do not know whether you're writing to an individual or a group (for example, when writing a reference or a letter of recommendation), use *To whom it may concern.*

In the United States some letter writers use a salutopening on the salutation line. A salutopening omits *Dear* but includes the first few words of the opening paragraph along with the recipient's name. After this line, the sentence continues a double space below as part of the body of the letter, as in these examples:

Thank you, Mr. Brown,	Salutopening
for your prompt payment of your bill.	Body
Congratulations, Ms. Lake!	Salutopening
Your promotion is well deserved.	Body

Don't overlook an especially important point with personalized salutations: Whether they're informal or formal, make sure names are spelled right. A misspelled name is glaring evidence of carelessness, and it belies the personal interest you're trying to express.

Body

The body of the letter is your message. Almost all letters are single-spaced, with double spacing (one blank line) before and after the salutation or salutopening, between paragraphs, and before the complimentary close. The body may include indented lists, entire paragraphs indented for emphasis, and even subheadings. If it does, all similar elements should be treated in the same way. Your department or company may select a format to use for all letters.

Complimentary Close

The complimentary close begins on the second line below the body of the letter. Alternatives for wording are available, but currently the trend seems to be toward using one-word closes, such as *Sincerely* and *Cordially.* In any case, the complimentary close reflects the relationship between you and the person you're writing to. Avoid cute closes, such as *Yours for bigger profits.* If your audience doesn't know you well, your sense of humor may be misunderstood.

Signature Block

Leave three blank lines for a written signature below the complimentary close, and then include the sender's name (unless it appears in the letterhead). The person's title may appear on the same line as the name or on the line below:

Cordially,

Raymond Dunnigan
Director of Personnel

Your letterhead indicates that you're representing your company. However, if your letter is on plain paper or runs to a second page, you may want to emphasize that you're speaking legally for the company. The accepted way of doing that is to place the company's name in capital letters a double space below the complimentary close and the include the sender's name and title four lines below that:

Sincerely,

WENTWORTH INDUSTRIES

(Mrs.) Helen B. Taylor
President

If your name could be taken for either a man's or a woman's, a courtesy title indicating gender should be included, with or without parentheses. Also, women who prefer a particular courtesy title should include it:

Mrs. Nancy Winters
(Miss) Juana Flores
Ms. Pat Li
(Mr.) Jamie Saunders

Additional Letter Parts

Letters vary greatly in subject matter and thus in the identifying information they need and the format they adopt. The following elements may be used in any combination, depending on the requirements of the particular letter, but generally in this order:

1. Addressee notation
2. Attention line
3. Subject line
4. Second-page heading
5. Company name
6. Reference initials
7. Enclosure notation
8. Copy notation
9. Mailing notation
10. Postscript

The letter in Figure A.2 shows how these additional parts should be arranged.

Addressee Notation

Letters that have a restricted readership or that must be handled in a special way should include such addressee notations as *Personal, Confidential,* or *Please Forward.* This sort of notation appears a double space above the inside address, in all capital letters.

Attention Line

Although an attention line is not commonly used today, you may find it useful if you know only the last name of the person you're writing to. An attention line can also be used to direct a letter to a position title or department. An attention line may take any of the following forms or variants of them: *Attention Dr. McHenry, Attention Director of Marketing,* or *Attention Marketing Department.* You may place the attention line on the first line and use the company name as the second line of the inside address.[10] The address on the envelope should always match the style of the inside address shown in Figure A.2, to conform to postal specifications.

Subject Line

The subject line lets the recipient know at a glance what the letter is about; it also indicates where to file the letter for future reference. It usually appears below the salutation—against the left margin, indented as the paragraphs in the body of the letter, or centered on the line. Sometimes the subject line is placed above the salutation or at

Figure A.2
In-Depth Critique: Additional Letter Parts

This excerpt from a letter written by J. Elizabeth Spencer of the Worldwide Talent Agency includes many of the elements often appearing in business letters.

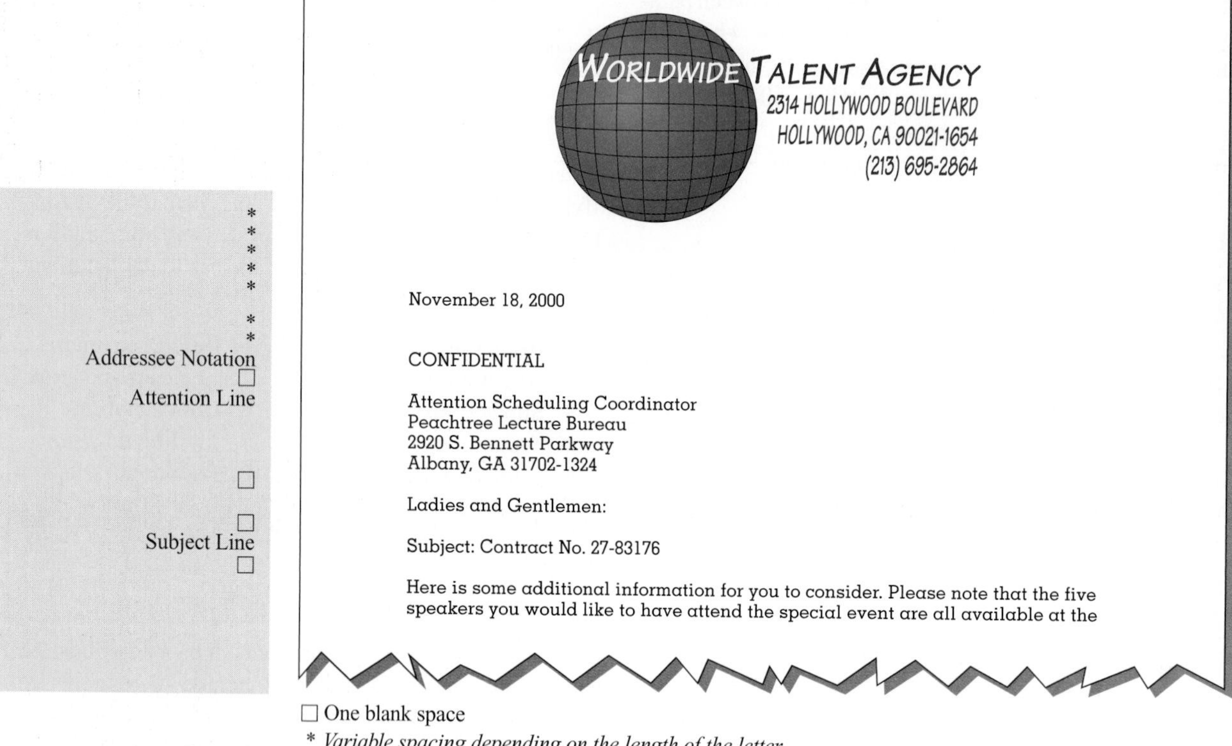

the very top of the page. The subject line may take a variety of forms, including the following:

> Subject: RainMaster Sprinklers
> About your February 2, 1998, order
> FALL 1998 SALES MEETING
> Reference Order No. 27920

Sometimes the subject line (or the last line of long subject "line") is underscored. Some writers omit the word *Subject* and put the other information all in capitals to distinguish it from the other letter parts. Organizations such as insurance and financial institutions, attorneys, and government offices may use the words *Re:* or *In re:* (meaning "concerning" or "in the matter of") rather than using the word *Subject.*

Second-Page Heading

If the letter is long and an additional page is required, use a second-page heading. Some companies have second-page letterhead, with the company name and address on one line and in a smaller typeface than on the regular letterhead. In any case, the second-page heading bears the name that appears in the first line of the inside address (the person or organization receiving the letter), the page number, and the date of the letter; you can also include a reference number. All the following are acceptable:

> Ms. Melissa Baker
> May 10, 1998
> Page 2

> Ms. Melissa Baker, May 10, 1998, Page 2

> Ms. Melissa Baker -2- May 10, 1998

Triple-space (leave two blank lines) between the second-page heading and the body. If a paragraph must be continued on a second page, make sure at least two lines of that paragraph appear on the first page and on the second page. Also, the closing lines of a business letter must never appear alone on a continued page. At least two lines of the body must precede the complimentary close or signature lines. And finally, don't hyphenate the last word on a page.

Figure A.2 (continued)

Peachtree Lecture Bureau
November 18, 1998
Page 2

This information should clarify our commitment to you. I look forward to good news from you in the near future.

Sincerely,

Worldwide Talent Agency

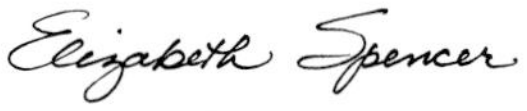

Elizabeth Spencer

J. Elizabeth Spencer
President

nt

Enclosures: Talent Roster
Commission Schedule

Copy to Everett Cunningham, Chairperson of the Board, InterHosts, Inc.

Special Delivery

PS: The lunch you treated me to the other day was a fine display of Southern hospitality. Thanks again.

Second-Page Heading

☐
☐

☐

☐
Company Name
☐
☐
☐

☐
Reference Initials
☐
Enclosure Notation

☐
Copy Notation
☐
Mailing Notation
☐
Postscript

*
*
*
*
*

☐ One blank space
* *Variable spacing depending on the length of the letter*

Company Name

If you include the company's name in the signature block, put it all in capital letters a double space below the complimentary close. You usually include the company's name in the signature block only when the writer is serving as the company's official spokesperson or when letterhead has not been used.

Reference Initials

Because it can happen in business that one person may dictate or write a letter and another person may produce it, reference initials are used to show who helped prepare the letter. Reference initials appear at the left margin, a double space below the last line of the signature block. When the writer's name has been included in the signature block, only the preparer's initials are necessary. If only the department appears in the signature block, both sets of initials should appear, usually in one of the following forms:

RSR/sm

RSR:sm

RSR:SM

The first set of initials is the writer's; the second set is the preparer's.

Sometimes the writer and the signer of a letter are different people. In that case, at least the file copy of a letter should bear both their initials as well as those of the typist: JFS/RSR/sm (signer, writer, preparer). When businesspeople keyboard their own letters, reference initials are not included, so such initials are becoming more and more rare.

Enclosure Notation

Enclosure notations also appear at the bottom of a letter, one or two lines below the reference initials. Some common forms:

Enclosure

Enclosures (2)

Enclosures: Résumé
Photograph

Attachment

Copy Notation

Copy notations may follow reference initials or enclosure notations. They indicate who's receiving a *courtesy copy (cc).* Some companies indicate copies made on a photocopier *(pc),* or they simply use *copy (c).* Recipients are listed in order of rank or (rank being equal) in alphabetical order. Among the forms used:

cc: David Wentworth

pc: Martha Littlefield

Copy to Hans Vogel

c: Joseph Martinez

In addition to the name of an individual, copy notations may include any combination of that person's courtesy title, position, department, company, and complete address, along with notations about any enclosures being sent with the copies.

On occasion, copies are sent to benefit readers other than the person who receives the original letter. In that case, place the notation *bc, bcc,* or *bpc* (for blind copy, blind courtesy copy, or blind photocopy) with the name where the copy notation would normally appear—but only on the copy, not on the original.

Mailing Notation

You may place a mailing notation (such as *Special Delivery* or *Registered Mail*) at the bottom of the letter, after reference initials or enclosure notations (whichever one is last) and before copy notations. Or you may place it at the top of the letter, either above the inside address on the left-hand side or just below the date on the right-hand side. For greater visibility, mailing notations may appear in capital letters.

Postscript

Letters may also bear postscripts: afterthoughts to the letter, messages that require emphasis, or personal notes. The postscript is usually the last thing on any letter and may be preceded by *P.S., PS., PS:,* or nothing at all. A second afterthought would be designated *P.P.S.,* meaning "post postscript."

Postscripts usually indicate poor planning, so generally avoid them. However, they're commonly used in sales letters, not as an afterthought but as a punch line to remind the reader of a benefit for taking advantage of the offer.

Letter Formats

Although the basic letter parts have remained the same for centuries, ways of arranging them do change. Sometimes a company adopts a certain format as its policy; sometimes the individual letter writer or preparer is allowed to choose the format most appropriate for a given letter or to settle on a personal preference. In the United States, three major letter formats are commonly used:

- *Block format.* Each letter part begins at the left margin. The main advantage is quick and efficient preparation (Figure A.3).
- *Modified block format.* Same as block format, except the date, complimentary close, and signature block start near the center of the page (Figure A.4). The modified block format does permit indentions as an option. This format mixes preparation speed with traditional placement of some letter parts. It also looks more balanced on the page than the block format does.
- *Simplified format.* Instead of using a salutation, this format often works the audience's name into the first line or two of the body and often includes a subject line in capital letters (Figure A.5). It also omits the complimentary close, so you sign your name after the body of

Rogers can be sure that her company's letterhead and the block format give her letter a crisp, businesslike appearance.

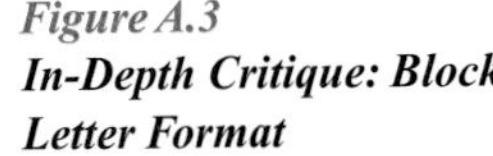

Figure A.3
In-Depth Critique: Block Letter Format

Beverly Hills Toys
3460 Rodeo Drive
Beverly Hills, California 90213
(310) 276-4839

September 5, 2000

Mr. Clifford Hanson
General Manager
The Toy Trunk
356 Emerald Drive
Lexington, KY 40501

Dear Mr. Hanson:

You should receive your shipment of Barbie dolls and accessories within two weeks, just in time for the holiday shopping season. The merchandise is being shipped by United Parcel Service. As the enclosed invoice indicates, the amount due is $352.32.

When preparing to ship your order, I noticed that this is your fifteenth year as a Mattel customer. During that period, you have sold over 3,750 Barbie dolls! We sincerely appreciate the part you have played in marketing our toys to the public.

Your customers should be particularly excited about the new Barbie vacation outfits that you have ordered. Our winter advertising campaign will portray Barbie trekking through the jungle in her safari suit, climbing mountains in her down parka, and snorkeling off a coral reef in her diving gear.

Next month, you'll be receiving our spring catalog. Notice the new series of action figures that will tie in with a TV cartoon featuring King Arthur and the Knights of the Round Table. As a special introductory incentive, you can receive a 15 percent discount on all items in this line until the end of January. Please send your order soon.

Sincerely,

Rhonda Rogers

Ms. Rhonda Rogers
Customer Service Representative

jhb

Enclosure

□ One blank space
* *Variable spacing depending on the length of the letter*

Figure A.4
In-Depth Critique: Modified Block Letter Format

O'Donnell's choice of a modified block format appears no less crisp or businesslike than the previous figure, but indenting the date and the signature block can make the letter appear somewhat more balanced.

JCPenney

June 3, 2000

Ms. Clara Simpson, President
League of Women Voters of Miami
P.O. Box 112
Miami, FL 33152

Dear Ms. Simpson:

Thank you for inviting us to participate in the League of Women Voters' Spring Fashion Show. We will be delighted to provide some clothing samples for the May 15 event.

You indicated that you would like us to supply about 12 outfits from our designer collection, all in size 6. We can certainly accommodate your request. To give your audience a representative overview of our merchandise, I suggest we provide the following: three tailored daytime dresses or suits, two dressy dresses, one formal ball gown, four casual weekend outfits, and two active sports outfits.

Please give me a call to schedule a "shopping" trip for you and your committee members. Together, I'm sure we can find exactly what you need to stage a well-rounded show. In the meantime, you might enjoy looking through the enclosed catalog. It will introduce you to some of the options.

Sincerely,

Vera O'Donnell

(Mrs.) Vera O'Donnell
Special Events Manager

bcg

Enclosure

J.C. Penney Company, Inc. 6501 Legacy Drive, Plano, Texas 75024

☐ One blank space
* *Variable spacing depending on the length of the letter*

Davis's use of the simplified format seems less personal than either the block or the modified block format.

Figure A.5
In-Depth Critique: Simplified Letter Format

PERFORMANCE TOOLS INTERNATIONAL
800 Superior Avenue • Cleveland Ohio 44114 • (216) 846-3286

May 5, 1998

Mr. Michael Ferraro
Pacific Coast Appliances
5748 Catalina Avenue
Laguna Beach, CA 92677

NEW PRODUCT INFORMATION

Thank you, Mr. Ferraro, for your recent inquiry about our product line. We appreciate your enthusiasm for our products, and we are confident that your customers will enjoy the improved performance of the new product line.

I have enclosed a package of information for your review, including product specifications, dealer prices, and an order form. The package also contains reprints of Performance Tools reviews and a comparison sheet showing how our products measure up against competing brands.

Please call with any questions you may have about shipping or payment arrangements.

Joanna Davis

JOANNA DAVIS
PRODUCT SPECIALIST

ek

Enclosures

the letter, followed by the printed (or typewritten) name (customarily in all capital letters). The advantages include convenience when you don't know your audience's name. However, some people object to this format because it seems mechanical and impersonal (a drawback that may be overcome with a warm writing style). In this format, the elimination of certain letter parts changes some of the spacing between lines.

These formats differ in the way paragraphs are indented, in the way letter parts are placed, and in some punctuation. However, the elements are always separated by at least one blank line, and the printed (or typewritten) name is always separated from the line above by at least three blank lines to allow space for a signature. If paragraphs are indented, the indention is normally five spaces.

The most common formats for intercultural business letters are the block style and the modified block style. Use either the U.S. or the European format for dates. For the salutation, use *Dear* (*Title/Last name*). Close the letter with *Sincerely* or *Cordially,* and sign it.

In addition to these three letter formats, letters may also be classified according to the style of punctuation they use. *Standard,* or *mixed, punctuation* uses a colon after the salutation (a comma if the letter is social or personal) and a comma after the complimentary close. *Open punctuation* uses no colon or comma after the salutation or the complimentary close. Although the most popular style in business communication is mixed punctuation, either style of punctuation may be used with block or modified block letter formats. Because the simplified letter format has no salutation or complimentary close, the style of punctuation is irrelevant.

ENVELOPES

The quality of the envelope is just as important for first impressions as the quality of the stationery. In fact, letterhead and envelopes should be of the same paper stock, have the same color ink, and be imprinted with the same address and logo. Most envelopes used by U.S. businesses are No. 10 envelopes (9½ inches long), which are sized to contain an 8½-by-11-inch piece of paper folded in thirds. Some occasions call for a smaller, No. 6¾, envelope or for envelopes proportioned to fit special stationery. Figure A.6 shows the two most common sizes.

Addressing the Envelope

No matter what size the envelope, the address is always single-spaced and in block form—that is, with all lines aligned on the left. The address on the envelope is in the same style as the inside address and presents the same information. The order to follow is from the smallest division to the largest:

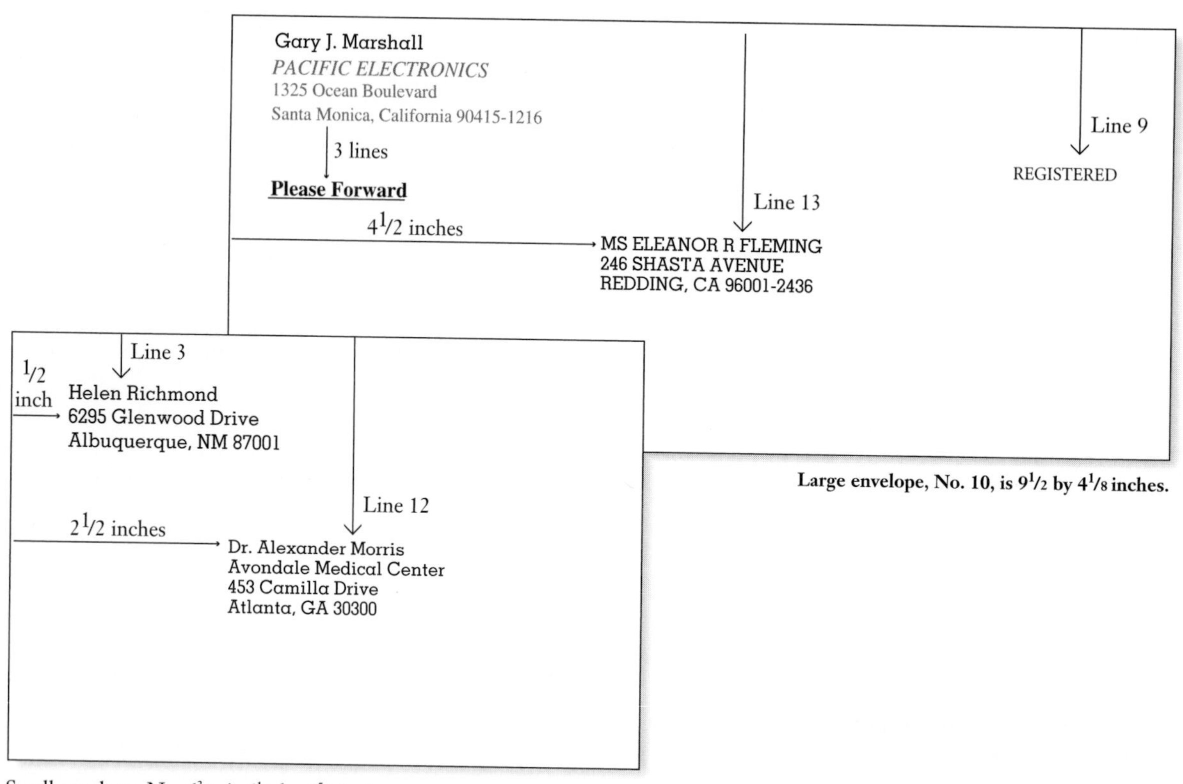

Large envelope, No. 10, is 9½ by 4⅛ inches.

Small envelope, No. 6¾, is 6½ by 3⅝ inches.

Figure A.6
Prescribed Envelope Format

1. Name and title of recipient
2. Name of department or subgroup
3. Name of organization
4. Name of building
5. Street address and suite number, or post office box number
6. City, state or province, and ZIP code or Postal Code
7. Name of country (if the letter is being sent abroad)

Because the U.S. Postal Service uses optical scanners to sort mail, envelopes for quantity mailings, in particular, should be addressed in the prescribed format. As in the mailing address on the No. 10 envelope in Figure A.6, everything is in capital letters, no punctuation is included, and all mailing instructions of interest to the post office are placed above the address area. Canada Post requires a similar format, except that only the city is all in capitals and the Postal Code is placed on the line below the name of the city. The post office scanners read addresses from the bottom up, so if a letter is to be sent to a post office box rather than to a street address, the street address should appear on the line above the box number. Figure A.6 also shows the proper spacing for addresses and return addresses.

The U.S. Postal Service and the Canada Post Corporation have published lists of two-letter mailing abbreviations for states, provinces, and territories (see Table A.2), to be used without periods or commas. Nevertheless, some executives prefer that state and province names be spelled out in full and that a comma be used to separate the city and state or province names. Thus the use of a comma between the name of the city and the state or province name is an unresolved issue. Most commonly,

TABLE A.2

TWO-LETTER MAILING ABBREVIATIONS FOR THE UNITED STATES AND CANADA

State/ Territory/ Province	Abbreviation	State/ Territory/ Province	Abbreviation	State/ Territory/ Province	Abbreviation
UNITED STATES					
Alabama	AL	Michigan	MI	Utah	UT
Alaska	AK	Minnesota	MN	Vermont	VT
Arizona	AZ	Mississippi	MS	Virginia	VA
Arkansas	AR	Missouri	MO	Virgin Islands	VI
American Samoa	AS	Montana	MT	Washington	WA
California	CA	Nebraska	NE	West Virginia	WV
Canal Zone	CZ	Nevada	NV	Wisconsin	WI
Colorado	CO	New Hampshire	NH	Wyoming	WY
Connecticut	CT	New Jersey	NJ		
Delaware	DE	New Mexico	NM	**CANADA**	
District of Columbia	DC	New York	NY	Alberta	AB
Florida	FL	North Carolina	NC	British Columbia	BC
Georgia	GA	North Dakota	ND	Labrador	LB
Guam	GU	Northern Mariana Is.	CM	Manitoba	MB
Hawaii	HI	Ohio	OH	New Brunswick	NB
Idaho	ID	Oklahoma	OK	Newfoundland	NF
Illinois	IL	Oregon	OR	Northwest Territories	NT
Indiana	IN	Pennsylvania	PA	Nova Scotia	NS
Iowa	IA	Puerto Rico	PR	Ontario	ON
Kansas	KS	Rhode Island	RI	Prince Edward Island	PE
Kentucky	KY	South Carolina	SC	Quebec	PQ
Louisiana	LA	South Dakota	SD	Saskatchewan	SK
Maine	ME	Tennessee	TN	Yukon Territory	YT
Maryland	MD	Trust Territories	TT		
Massachusetts	MA	Texas	TX		

the comma is included; sometimes, however, the comma is eliminated to conform with post office standards.

Quantity mailings follow post office requirements. For letters that aren't mailed in quantity, a reasonable compromise is to use traditional punctuation and uppercase and lowercase letters for names and street addresses but two-letter state or province abbreviations, as shown here:

Mr. Kevin Kennedy
2107 E. Packer Drive
Amarillo, TX 79108

For all out-of-office correspondence, use ZIP codes and Postal Codes, assigned to speed mail delivery. The U.S. Postal Service has divided the United States and its territories into ten zones, each represented by a digit from 0 to 9; this digit comes first in the ZIP code. The second and third digits represent smaller geographical areas within a state, and the last two digits identify a "local delivery area." Canadian Postal Codes are alphanumeric, with a three-character "area code" and a three-character "local code" separated by a single space (K2P 5A5). ZIP codes and Postal Codes should be separated from state and province names by one space. As an alternative, a Canadian Postal Code may be put on the bottom line of the address all by itself.

The U.S. Postal Service has added ZIP + 4 codes, which add a hyphen and four more numbers to the standard ZIP codes. The first two of these numbers may identify an area as small as a single large building, and the last two digits may identify one floor in a large building or even a specific department of an organization. The ZIP + 4 codes are especially useful for business correspondence. The Canada Post Corporation achieves the same result with special postal codes assigned to buildings and organizations that receive a large volume of mail.

Folding to Fit

Trivial as it may seem, the way a letter is folded also contributes to the recipient's overall impression of your organization's professionalism. When sending a standard-size piece of paper in a No. 10 envelope, fold it in thirds, with the bottom folded up first and the top folded down over it (Figure A.7); the open end should be at the top of the envelope and facing out. Fit smaller stationery neatly into the appropriate envelope simply by folding it in half or in thirds. When sending a standard-size letterhead in a No. 6 3/4 envelope, fold it in half from top to bottom and then in thirds from side to side.

International Mail

When sending mail internationally, remember that postal service differs from country to country. For example, street addresses are uncommon in India, and the mail there is unreliable.[11] It's usually a good idea to send inter-

Figure A.7
Letter Folds for Standard-Size Letterhead

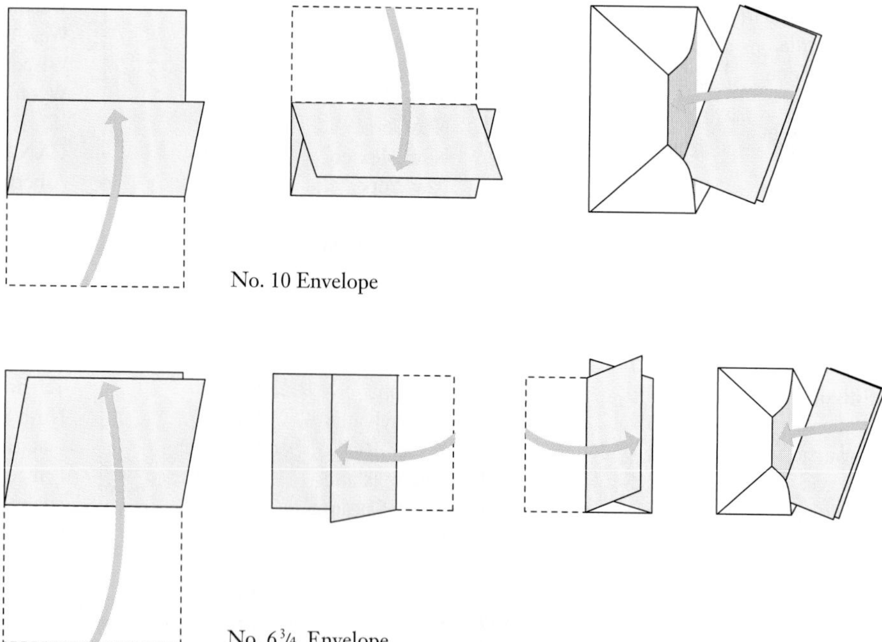

national correspondence by air mail and to ask that responses be sent that way as well. Also, remember to check the postage; rates for sending mail to most other countries aren't the same as the rates for sending mail within your own country.

Three main categories of international mail are the following:

- *LC mail.* An abbreviation of the French *Lettres et Cartes* ("letters and cards"), this category consists of letters, letter packages, aerograms, and postcards.
- *AO mail.* An abbreviation of the French *Autres Objets* ("other articles"), this category includes regular printed matter, books and sheet music, matter for the blind, small packets, and publishers' periodicals (second class).
- *CP mail.* An abbreviation of the French *Colis Postaux* ("parcel post"), this category resembles fourth-class mail, including packages of merchandise or any other articles not required to be mailed at letter postage rates.

The U.S. Postal Service also offers Express Mail International Service (EMS), a high-speed mail service to many countries; International Priority Airmail (IPA), an international service that's as fast as or faster than regular airmail service; International Surface Air Lift (ISAL), a service providing quicker delivery and lower cost for all kinds of printed matter; Bulk Letter Service to Canada, an economical airmail service for letters weighing 1 ounce or less; VALUEPOST/CANADA, a reduced postage rate for bulk mailings; International Electronic Post (INTELPOST), a service offering same- or next-day delivery of fax documents; International Postal Money Orders, a service for transferring funds to other countries; and several optional special services.

To prepare your mail for international delivery, follow the instructions in the U.S. Postal Service Publication 51, *International Postal Rates and Fees.* Be sure to note instructions for the address, return address, and size limits. Envelopes and wrappers must be clearly marked to show their classification (letter, small packet, printed matter, air mail). All registered letters, letter packages, and parcel post packages must be securely sealed. Printed matter may be sealed only if postage is paid by permit imprint, postage meter, precanceled stamps, or second-class imprint. Otherwise, prepare contents so that they're protected but in such a way that they won't hinder inspection. Finally, because international mail is subject to customs examination in the country of destination, the contents and value must be declared on special forms.

MEMOS

Interoffice memos aren't distributed outside the organization, so they may not need the best-quality paper. However, they still convey important information, so clarity, careful arrangement, and neatness are important. As do those for letters, the guidelines for formatting memos help recipients understand at a glance what they've received and from whom.

Many organizations have memo forms printed, with labeled spaces for the recipient's name (or sometimes a checklist of all departments in an organization or all persons in a department), the sender's name, the date, and the subject (see Figure A.8). If such forms don't exist, you can use plain paper.

Include a title such as *Memo* or *Interoffice Correspondence* (all in capitals) centered at the top of the page or aligned with the left margin. Also include the words *To, From, Date,* and *Subject*—followed by the appropriate

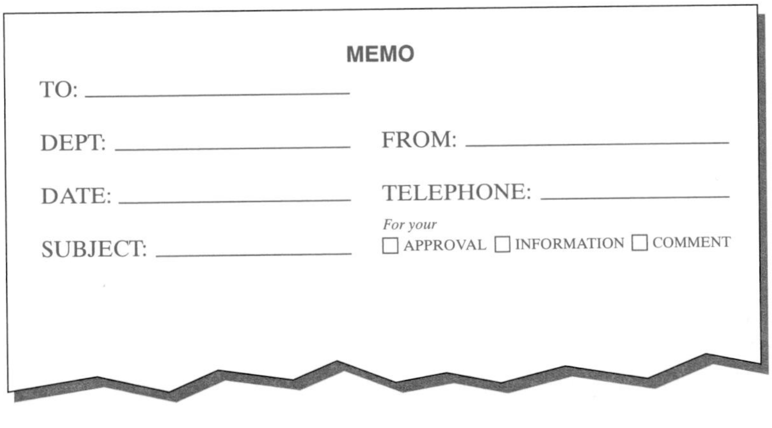

MEMO

TO: ____________

DEPT: ____________ FROM: ____________

DATE: ____________ TELEPHONE: ____________

SUBJECT: ____________ *For your* ☐ APPROVAL ☐ INFORMATION ☐ COMMENT

Figure A.8
Preprinted Memo Form

information—at the top with a blank line between, as shown here:

MEMO

TO:

FROM:

DATE:

SUBJECT:

Sometimes the heading is organized like this:

MEMO

TO:	DATE:
FROM:	SUBJECT:

You can arrange these four pieces of information in almost any order. The date sometimes appears without the heading *Date.* The subject may be presented with the letters *Re:* (in place of SUBJECT:) or may even be presented without any heading (but put it in capital letters so that it stands out clearly). You may want to include a file or reference number, introduced by the word *File.*

If you send a memo to a long list of people, include the notation *See distribution list* or *See below* in the *To* position at the top; then list the names at the end of the memo. Arranging such a list alphabetically is usually the most diplomatic course, although high-ranking officials may deserve more prominent placement. You can also address memos to groups of people—*All Sales Representatives, Production Group, Assistant Vice Presidents.*

You don't need to use courtesy titles anywhere in a memo; in fact, first initials and last names, first names, or even initials alone are often sufficient. As a general rule, however, use a courtesy title if you would use one in face-to-face encounters with the person.

The subject line of a memo helps busy colleagues find out quickly what your memo is about. Although the subject "line" may overflow onto a second line, it's most helpful when it's short (but still informative).

Start the body of the memo on the second or third line below the heading. Like the body of a letter, it's usually single-spaced. Separate paragraphs with blank lines. Indenting them is optional. Handle lists, important passages, and subheadings as you do in letters. If the memo is very short, you may double-space it.

If the memo carries over to a second page, head the second page just as you head the second page of a letter.

Unlike a letter, a memo doesn't require a complimentary close or a signature, because your name is already prominent at the top. However, you may initial the memo—either beside the name appearing at the top of the memo or at the bottom of the memo—or you may even sign your name at the bottom, particularly if the memo deals with money or confidential matters. Treat all other elements—reference initials, enclosure notations, and copy notations—as you would in a letter.

Memos may be delivered by hand, by the post office (when the recipient doesn't work at the same location as the memo writer), or through interoffice mail. Interoffice mail may require the use of special reusable envelopes that have spaces for the recipient's name and department or room number; the name of the previous recipient is simply crossed out. If a regular envelope is used, the words *Interoffice Mail* appear where the stamp normally goes so that it won't accidentally be stamped and mailed with the rest of the office correspondence.

Informal, routine, or brief reports for distribution within a company are often presented in memo form (see Chapter 14). Don't include such report parts as a table of contents and appendixes, but write the body of the memo report just as carefully as you'd write a formal report.

E-MAIL

Because e-mail messages can act both as memos (carrying information within your company) and as letters (carrying information outside your company and around the world), their format depends on your audience and purpose. You may choose to have your e-mail resemble a formal letter or a detailed report, or you may decide to keep things as simple as an interoffice memo. In fact, a modified memo format is probably appropriate for most e-mail messages.[12] All e-mail programs include two major elements: the header and the body (Figure A.9).

Header

The e-mail header depends on the particular program you use. Some programs even allow you to choose between a shorter and a longer version. However, most headers contain similar information.

The *To:* line contains your audience's e-mail address. The most common e-mail addresses are Internet addresses, like the following:

- NMAA.BETSY@C.SI.EDU Smithsonian Institution's National Museum of American Art
- webwsj@dowjones.com *Wall Street Journal*'s home page
- mailto: cc131@iway.fr Chamber of Commerce and Industry in Toulouse, France

E-Mail

Date: Tuesday, 17 May 2000, 9:34:27, PDT
X-Sender: KeithW@Bluecrane.com
To: bookco@artech.demon.co.uk
From: "Keith D. Wells" <keithw@bluecrane.com>
Subject: Please confirm shipping date

To: Jeffrey Coombs, International Sales Desk
Artech House, London

From: Keith Wells, Proprietor
Blue Crane Books, Laguna Beach

Re: Order # 1-SD-95466
Dated: 7 April 2000

Dear Jeffrey:

On 7 April 2000, we ordered the following books:
1 copy _Electronic Mail_
by Jacob Palme
(ISBN# 0-89006-802-X)

2 copies _Distance Learning Technology and Applications_
by Daniel Minoli
(ISBN# 0-89006-739-2)

Please confirm the date you shipped this order. My customers are eager to receive their copies and have been calling me almost daily.

You said in your last message that you would be shipping them UPS on 10 April, so I would have expected to receive them by now. Of course, I am used to ordering through your Boston office, so I may have misjudged the time it takes from London.

Anything you can tell me about when they were shipped will be most helpful.

Thank you,

Keith

Figure A.9
In-Depth Critique: A Typical E-Mail Message

HEADER (May vary from program to program)

Date: Includes the day, date, time, and time zone

To: Includes the recipient's address (perhaps addressee's proper name)

From: Includes your address (perhaps your proper name)

Subject (Re): Describes what your message concerns (an opportunity to gain interest)

Cc: Includes the address of anyone you want to receive a copy of the message

Bcc: Includes the address of anyone you want to receive a copy of the message but don't want listed as a receiver

Attachments: Includes the name of any files you have attached to your message

Greeting: Makes the message more personal

Message: Format depends on your audience and purpose. Can include headings, lists, and other common devices used in letters and memos

Closing: Personalizes your message and resembles simple closings in letters

Signature: Can be simply your name typed or can be a signature file

On the Internet, everything on the left side of the @ symbol is the user name; everything on the right side describes the computer where that user has an account. This machine name usually ends with a country code (such as fr for France, dk for Denmark, hk for Hong Kong, ca for Canada). But within the United States, the country code is replaced with the type of organization that operates that particular computer:[13]

- .com business and commercial users
- .edu educational institutions
- .gov nonmilitary government and related groups
- .mil military-related groups
- .net network providers
- .org organizations and nonprofit groups

Most e-mail programs will also allow you to send mail to an entire group of people all at once. First, you create a distribution list. Then you type the name of the list in the *To:* line instead of typing the addresses of every person in the group.[14]

The *From:* line contains your e-mail address. The *Date:* line contains the day of the week, date (day, month, year), time, and time zone. The *Subject:* line describes the content of the message and presents an opportunity for you to build interest in your message. The *cc:* line allows you to send copies of a message to more than one person at a time. It also allows everyone on the list to see who else received the same message. The *Bcc:* line lets you send copies to people without the other recipients' knowing—a practice considered unethical by some.[15] The *Attachments:* line contains the name(s) of the file(s) you attach to your e-mail message. The file can be a word-processing document, a digital image, an audio or video message, a spreadsheet, or a software program.[16]

Other lines containing more detailed information can be listed in your e-mail's header, including *Message-Id* (the exact location of this e-mail message on the sender's system), *X-mailer:* (the version of the e-mail program being used), and *Content type:* (a description of what kind of text and character set is contained in the message). Also, the *Received:* lines include information about each of the systems your e-mail passed through en route to your mailbox.[17] Most e-mail programs now allow you the choice of hiding or revealing this sort of detailed information.

Body

You might consider your mail program's header to be something like letterhead, because the rest of the space below the header is for the body of your message. In the *To:* and *From:* lines, some headers actually print out the names of the sender and the receiver (in addition to the e-mail addresses). Other headers do not. If your mail program includes only the e-mail addresses, you might consider including your own memo-type header, as was done in Figure A.9. The writer even included a subject line in his memo-type header that is more specific than the one in the mail program header. Although some may applaud the clarity such a second header providers, others may criticize the space it takes. Your decision depends on how formal you want to be.

Do include a greeting in your e-mail. As pointed out in Chapter 5, greetings personalize your message. Leave one line space above and below your greeting to set it off from the rest of your message. Again, depending on the level of formality you want, you may choose to end your greeting with a colon (most formal), a comma (conversational), or even two hyphens (informal).

Your message begins one blank line space below your greeting. Just as in memos and letters, skip one line space between paragraphs and include headings, numbered lists, bulleted lists, and embedded lists when appropriate. Limit your line lengths to a maximum of 80 characters by inserting a hard return at the end of each line.

One blank line space below your message, include a simple closing, often just one word. A blank line space below that, include your signature. Whether you type your name or use a signature file, including your signature personalizes your message.

TIME-SAVING MESSAGES

If there's a way to speed up the communication process, the organization stands to gain. Telephones and electronic mail systems are quick, as are mailgrams, telegrams, faxes, and the like. In addition, organizations have developed special formats to reduce the amount of time spent writing and typing short messages:

- *Fax cover sheets.* When faxing messages, you may use a fax cover sheet, which includes the recipient's name, company, fax number, and city; the sender's name, complete address, fax number, and telephone number; the number of pages being sent; a phone number to call if the faxed transmission isn't successful; and enough space for any brief message.[18] The format for this information varies widely. When a document is self-explanatory, a cover sheet may be unnecessary, so be sure not to waste paper or transmission time.
- *Memo-letters.* Printed with a heading somewhat like a memo's, memo-letters provide a space for an inside address so that the message may be sent outside the company (see Figure A.10). When the memo is folded prop-

Memo-letters such as this one are convenient for the writer, and, with the space for a reply message, they can be convenient for the recipient. However, they are much less formal than a business letter for outside correspondence.

Figure A.10
In-Depth Critique: Memo-Letter

MEMO

TO: Green Ridge Gifts
1786 Century Road
Nashua, NH 03060
USA

FROM: Whiteside Import/Export, Ltd.
1601 Ronson Drive
Toronto, Ontario M9W 3E3
CANADA

SUBJECT: Order for Royal Dorchester china completer sets

DATE: October 11, 1999

MESSAGE:

The six Wellington pattern completer sets that you ordered by telephone October 9 are on their way and should reach your shop by October 18.

The three Mayfield pattern completer sets are coming from the factory, however, and will not arrive here until October 26 or 27. That means you will get them around November 2 or 3.

Do you still want the Mayfield sets? Would you like us to bill you for the Wellington sets only so that you can pay for the Mayfield order separately? Please add your reply below, retain the yellow copy for your records, and send us the white and pink copies.

SIGNED: Barbara Hutchins

REPLY: PLEASE SEND THE MAYFIELD SETS AS SOON AS POSSIBLE. YOU MAY BILL FOR BOTH MAYFIELD AND WELLINGTON SETS.

DATE: OCT. 15, 2000

SIGNED: William L. Smith

* *
* *
* *
* *
* *
* □
* □
* □
* □
* □
* □
* □
* □
* □
* □
* □
* □
* □
* □
* *
* *
* *
* *
* *
* *

□ One blank space
* *Variable spacing depending on the length of the letter*

erly, the address shows through a window in the envelope, thereby eliminating the need to address the envelope separately. Memo-letters often include a space for a reply message so that the recipient doesn't have to print out or type a whole new letter in response; carbonless copy sets allow sender and recipient to keep on file a copy of the entire correspondence.

- *Short-note reply technique.* Popular in many organizations, this technique can be used even without a special form. The recipient of a memo (or sometimes a letter) simply handwrites a response on the original document, makes a copy for the files, and sends the annotated original back to the person who wrote it.
- *Letterhead postcards.* Ideal for short, impersonal messages, letterhead postcards are preprinted with a list of responses so that the "writer" merely checks the appropriate response(s) and slips the postcard into the mail. Organization such as mail-order companies and government agencies use these time-saving devices to communicate frequently with individuals by mail.

The important thing to realize about these and all other message formats is that they've developed over time to meet the need for clear communication and to speed responses to the needs of customers, suppliers, and associates.

REPORTS

You can enhance your report's effectiveness by paying careful attention to its appearance and layout. Follow whatever guidelines your organization prefers, but remember to be neat and consistent throughout. If it's up to you to decide formatting questions, the following conventions may help you decide how to handle margins, headings, spacing and indention, and page numbers.

Margins

All margins on a report page are at least 1 inch wide. Margins of 1 inch are customary for double-spaced pages, and margins of between $1^1/_4$ and $1^1/_2$ inches are customary for single-spaced pages. The top, left, and right margins are usually the same, but the bottom margins can be $1^1/_2$ times as deep as the others. Some special pages also have deeper top margins. Set top margins as deep as 2 inches for pages that contain major titles: prefatory parts such as the table of contents or the executive summary, supplementary parts such as the reference notes or bibliography, and textual parts such as the first page of the text or the first page of each chapter.

If you're going to bind your report at the left or at the top, add half an inch to the margin on the bound edge (Figure A.11). Because of the space taken by the binding on left-bound reports, make the center point of the page a quarter inch to the right of the center of the paper. Be sure that centered headings are centered between the margins, not centered on the paper. Of course, computers can do this for you automatically. Other guidelines for formatting a report can be found in the sample in Chapter 15.

Headings

Headings of various levels provide visual clues to a report's organization. Figure 14.11, on page 499, illustrates one good system for showing these levels, but many variations exist. No matter which system you use, be sure to be consistent.

Spacing and Indentions

The spacing and indention of most elements of a report are relatively easy. If your report is double-spaced (perhaps to ease comprehension of technical material), indent all paragraphs five character spaces (or about $^1/_2$ inch). In single-spaced reports, you can block the paragraphs (no indentions), leaving one blank line between them.

When using a typewriter, properly spacing the material on the title page is more complicated. For reports that will be bound on the left, start a quarter inch to the right of center. From that point, backspace once for each two letters in the line so that the line will appear centered once the report is bound.

To correctly place lines of type on the title page, first count the number of lines in each block of copy, including blank lines. Subtract the total from 66 (the total number of lines on an 11-inch page) to get the number of unused lines. To allocate these unused lines equally among the spaces between the blocks of copy, divide the number of unused lines by the number of blank areas (always one more than the number of blocks of copy). The result is the number of blank lines to devote to each section. Of course, a computer with a good word-processing program will do these calculations for you at the click of a mouse. As the title page of the sample report in Chapter 15 shows, the title page should look well balanced.

Page Numbers

Remember that every page in the report is counted but that not all pages have numbers shown on them. The first page of the report, normally the title page, is not num-

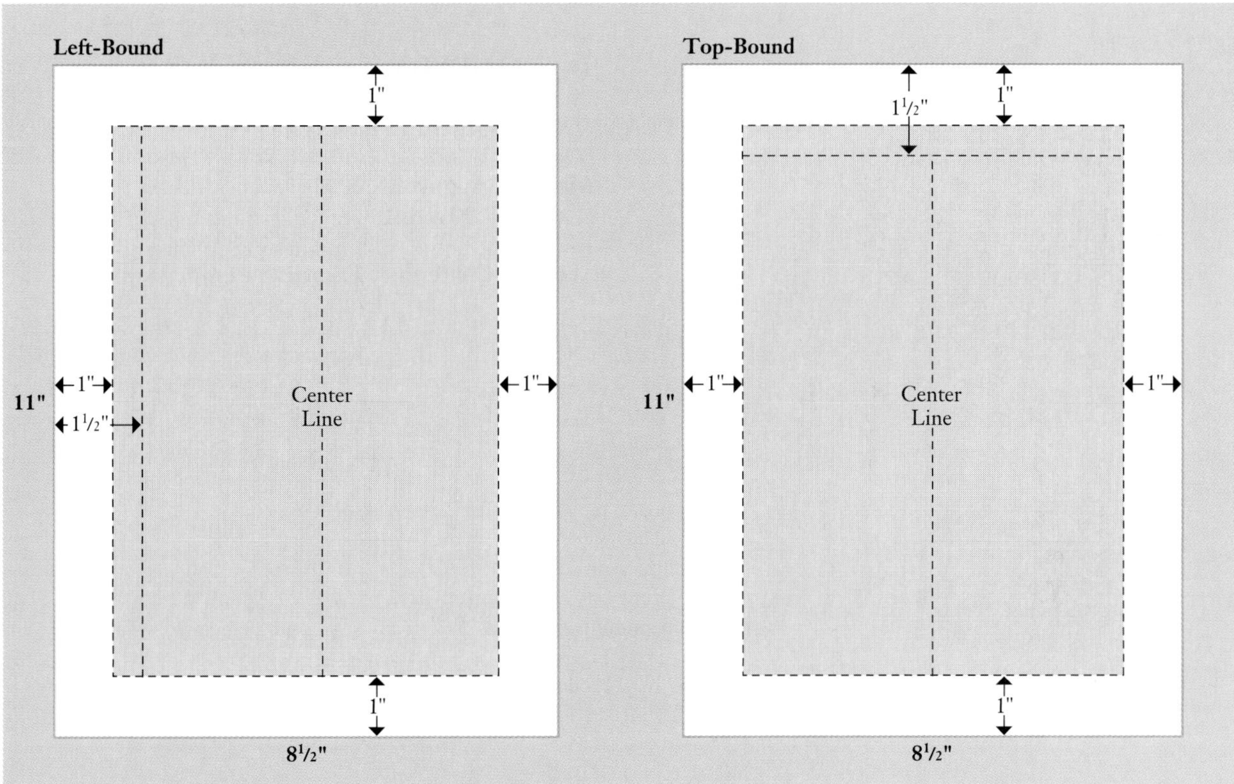

Figure A.11
Margins for Formal Reports

bered. All other pages in the prefatory section are numbered with a lowercase roman numeral, beginning with ii and continuing with iii, iv, v, and so on. The unadorned (no dashes, no period) page number is centered at the bottom margin.

Number the first page of the text of the report with the unadorned arabic numeral 1, centered at the bottom margin (double- or triple-spaced below the text). In left-bound reports, number the following pages (including the supplementary parts) consecutively with unadorned arabic numerals (2, 3, and so on), placed at the top right-hand margin (double- or triple-spaced above the text). For top-bound reports and for special pages having 2-inch top margins, center these page numbers at the bottom margin.

Meeting Documents

The success of any meeting depends on the preparation of the participants and on the follow-up measures they take to implement decisions or to seek information after the meeting. Meeting documents—agendas and minutes—aid this process by putting the meeting plan and results into permanent, written form. Although small informal meetings may not require a written agenda, any meeting involving a relatively large number of people or covering a lot of ground will run more smoothly if an agenda is distributed in advance. A written agenda helps participants prepare by telling them what will be discussed, and it helps keep them on track once the meeting begins. The typical agenda format (shown in Figure A.12) may seem stiff and formal, but it helps structure a meeting so that as little time as possible is wasted. It also provides opportunities for discussion, if that's what is called for.

The presentation, a special form of meeting that allows for relatively little group interaction, may also require an agenda or a detailed outline. Special visual aids such as flip charts help attendees grasp the message, and copies of the charts are often provided for future reference.

Figure A.12
Agenda Format

AGENDA

PLANNING COMMITTEE MEETING

Monday, August 21, 2000
10:00 A.M.

Executive Conference Room

I. Call to Order

II. Roll Call

III. Approval of Agenda

IV. Approval of Minutes from Previous Meeting

V. Chairperson's Report

VI. Subcommittee Reports
   A. New Markets
   B. New Products
   C. Finance

VII. Unfinished Business

VIII. New Business
   A. Carson and Canfield Data
   B. Reassignments

IX. Announcements

X. Adjournment

After a meeting the secretary who attended prepares a set of minutes for distribution to all attendees and to any other interested parties. The minutes are prepared in much the same format as a memo or letter, except for the heading, which takes this form:

MINUTES
PLANNING COMMITTEE MEETING
MONDAY, AUGUST 21, 1998

Present: [All invited attendees who were present are listed here, generally by rank, in alphabetical order, or in some combination.]

Absent: [All invited attendees who were not present are listed here, in similar order.]

The body of the minutes follows the heading, and it notes the times the meeting started and ended, all major decisions reached at the meeting, all assignments of tasks to meeting participants, and all subjects that were deferred to a later meeting. In addition, the minutes objectively summarize important discussions, noting the names of those who contributed major points. Outlines, subheadings, and lists help organize the minutes, and additional documentation (such as tables or charts submitted by meeting participants) are noted in the minutes and attached.

At the end of the minutes, the words *Submitted by* should be added, followed by a couple of blank lines for a signature and then the signer's printed (or typed) name and title (if appropriate). If the minutes have been written by one person and prepared by another, the preparer's initials should be added, as in the reference initials on a letter or memo.

An informal meeting may not require minutes. Attendees simply pencil their own notes onto their copies of the agenda. Follow-up is then their responsibility, although the meeting leader may need to remind them through a memo, phone call, or face-to-face talk.

COMPONENT CHAPTER B

DOCUMENTATION OF REPORT SOURCES

Documenting a report is too important a task to undertake haphazardly. When you provide information about your sources, you improve your own credibility as well as the credibility of the facts and opinions you present. Documentation gives readers the means for checking your findings and pursuing the subject further. Also, documenting your report is the accepted way to give credit to the people whose work you have drawn from.

What style should you use to document your report? Experts recommend various forms, depending on your field or discipline. Moreover, your employer or client may use a form different from those the experts suggest. Don't let this discrepancy confuse you. If your employer specifies a form, use it; the standardized form is easier for colleagues to understand. However, if the choice of form is left to you, adopt one of the styles described here. Whatever style you choose, be consistent within any given report, using the same order, punctuation, and format from one reference citation or bibliography entry to the next.

A wide variety of style manuals provide detailed information on documentation:

- American Psychological Association. *Publication Manual of the American Psychological Association,* 4th ed. Washington, D.C.: American Psychological Association, 1994. Details the author-date system, which is preferred in the social sciences and often in the natural sciences as well.
- *The Chicago Manual of Style.* 14th ed. Chicago: University of Chicago Press, 1993. Often referred to only as *Chicago* and widely used in the publishing industry; provides detailed treatment of documentation in Chapters 15, 16, and 17.
- Gibaldi, Joseph. *MLA Style Manual and Guide to Scholarly Publishing,* 2d ed. New York: Modern Language Association, 1998. Serves as the basis for the note and bibliography style used in much academic writing and is recommended in many college textbooks on writing term papers; provides a lot of examples in the humanities.
- Harnack, Andrew, and Eugene Kleppinger. *Online! A Reference Guide to Using Internet Sources.* New York: St. Martin's Press, 1997. Offers an approach to style for citing online references.
- Slade, Carol. *Form and Style: Research Papers, Reports, Theses,* 10th ed. Boston: Houghton Mifflin, 1997. Presents a comprehensive review of *Chicago, MLA,* and *APA* styles.
- Turabian, Kate L. *A Manual for Writers of Term Papers, Theses, and Dissertations,* 6th ed. Revised and expanded by Bonnie Birtwhistle Honigsblum. Chicago: University of Chicago Press, 1995. Based on the *Chicago Manual* but smaller and limited to matters of concern to report writers; contains many examples of documenting nonstandard references.
- Warren, Thomas L. *Words into Type,* 3d ed. Englewood Cliffs, N.J.: Prentice Hall, 1992. Presents useful information on the classic approach to scholarly notes and bibliographies.

Although many schemes have been proposed for organizing the information in source notes, all of them break the information into parts: (1) information about the author (name), (2) information about the work (title, edition, volume number), (3) information about the publication (place, publisher), (4) information about the date, and (5) information on relevant page ranges.

In the following sections, we summarize the major conventions for documenting sources in three styles: *The Chicago Manual of Style (Chicago),* the *Publication Manual of the American Psychological Association (APA),* and *The MLA Style Manual (MLA).*

CHICAGO STYLE

The Chicago Manual of Style recommends two types of documentation systems. The *documentary-note,* or *humanities,* style gives bibliographic citations in notes—either footnotes (when printed at the bottom of a page) or endnotes (when printed at the end of the report). The humanities system is often used in literature, history, and the arts. The other system strongly recommended by *Chicago* is the *author-date* system, which cites the author's last name and the date of publication in the text, usually in parentheses, reserving full documentation for the reference list (or bibliography). For the purpose of comparing styles, we will concentrate on the humanities system, which is described in detail in *Chicago.*

In-Text Citation—*Chicago* Style

To document report sources in text, the humanities system relies on superscripts—arabic numerals placed just above the line of type at the end of the reference:

> Toward the end of his speech, Myers sounded a note of caution, saying that even though the economy is expected to grow, it could easily slow a bit.[10]

The superscript lets the reader know how to look for source information in either a footnote or an endnote (see Figure B.1). Some readers prefer footnotes so that they can simply glance at the bottom of the page for information. Others prefer endnotes so that they can read the text without a clutter of notes on the page. Also, endnotes relieve the writer from worrying about how long each note will be and how much space it will take away from the page. Both footnotes and endnotes are handled automatically by today's word-processing software.

For the reader's convenience, you can use footnotes for **content notes** (which may supplement your main text with asides about a particular issue or event, provide a cross-reference to another section of your report, or direct the reader to a related source). Then you can use endnotes for **source notes** (which document direct quotations, paraphrased passages, and visual aids). Consider which type of note is most common in your report, and then choose whether to present these notes all as endnotes or all as footnotes. Regardless of the method you choose for referencing textual information in your report, both content notes and source notes are placed on the same page as visual aids.

Bibliography—*Chicago* Style

The humanities system may or may not be accompanied by a bibliography (because the notes give all the necessary bibliographic information). However, endnotes are arranged in order of appearance in the text, so an alphabetical bibliography can be valuable to your readers. The bibliography may be titled *Bibliography, Reference List, Sources, Works Cited* (if you include only those sources you actually cited in your report), or *Works Consulted* (if you include uncited sources as well). This list of sources may also serve as a reading list for those who want to pursue the subject of your report further, so you may want to annotate each entry—that is, comment on the subject matter and viewpoint of the source, as well as on its usefulness to readers. Annotations may be written in either complete or incomplete sentences. (See the annotated list of style manuals early in this component chapter.) A bibliography may also be more manageable if you subdivide it into categories (a classified bibliography), either by type of reference (such as books, articles, and unpublished material) or by subject matter (such as government regulation, market forces, and so on). Following are the major conventions for developing a bibliography according to *Chicago* style (see Figure B.2):

- Exclude any page numbers that may be cited in source notes.
- Alphabetize entries by the last name of the lead author (listing last name first). The names of second and succeeding authors are listed in normal order. Entries without an author name are alphabetized by the first important word in the title.
- Format entries as hanging indents (indent second and succeeding lines three to five spaces).
- Arrange entries in the following general order: (1) author name, (2) title information, (3) publication information, (4) date, (5) periodical page range.
- Use quotation marks around the titles of articles from magazines, newspapers, and journals—capitalizing the first and last words, as well as all other important words (except prepositions, articles, and coordinating conjunctions).
- Use italics to set off the names of books, newspapers, journals, and other complete publications—capitalizing the first and last words, as well as all other important words.
- For journal articles, include the volume number and the issue number (if necessary). Include the year of publication inside parentheses and follow with a colon and the page range of the article: *Journal of Business Communication* 36, no. 4 (1999): 72. (In this source, the volume is 36, the number is 4, and the page is 72.)
- Use brackets to identify all electronic references: [Online database] or [CD-ROM].
- Explain how electronic references can be reached: Available from CompuServe.
- Give the citation date for online references: Cited 23 August 1999.

Figure B.1
Sample Endnotes/ Footnotes*—Chicago *Style

Endnotes

Journal article with volume and issue numbers
1. James Assira, "Are They Speaking English in Japan?" *Journal of Business Communication* 36, no. 4 (Fall 1999): 72.

Brochure
2. BestTemp Staffing Services, *An Employer's Guide to Staffing Services,* 2d ed. (Denver: BestTemp Information Center, 1997), 31.

Newspaper article, no author
3. "Buying Asian Supplies on the Net," *Los Angeles Times,* 12 February 1997, sec. D, p. 3.

Annual report
4. Eurotec, *1998 Annual Report* (New York: Eurotec, Inc., 1998), 48.

Magazine article
5. Holly Graves, "Prospecting Online," *Business Week,* 17 November 1999, 43–45.

Television broadcast
6. Daniel Han, "Trade Wars Heating Up Around the Globe," *CNN Headline News* (Atlanta: CNN, 5 March 1999).

Internet, World Wide Web
7. "Intel—Company Capsule," *Hoover's Online* [cited 8 March 1999], 3 screens, available online from World Wide Web at http://www.hoovers.com/capsules/13787.html.

Book, component part
8. Sonja Kuntz, "Moving Beyond Benefits," in *Our Changing Workforce,* ed. Randolf Jacobson (New York: Citadel Press, 1998), 213–227.

Dissertation or thesis
9. George H. Morales, "The Economic Pressures on Industrialized Nations in a Global Economy" (Ph.D. diss., University of San Diego, 1998), abstract in *Dissertation Abstracts International* 52 (1998): 5436C–5437C.

Paper presented at a meeting
10. Charles Myers, "HMOs in Today's Environment" (paper presented at the Conference on Medical Insurance Solutions, Chicago, Ill., August 1998), 16–17.

Online magazine article
11. Preston Norwalk, "Training Managers to Help Employees Accept Change," in *Business Line* [online] (San Francisco, 1999 [updated 17 September 1999; cited 3 October 1999]); available from http://www.busline.com/news; INTERNET.

CD-ROM encyclopedia article, one author
12. Robert Parkings, "George Eastman," *The Concise Columbia Encyclopedia* (New York: Columbia University Press, 1995) [CD-ROM].

Newspaper article, one author
13. Evelyn Standish, "Global Market Crushes OPEC's Delicate Balance of Interests," *Wall Street Journal,* 19 January 1999, sec. A, p. 1.

Interview
14. Georgia Stainer, communications manager, Day Cable and Communications, interview by author, Topeka, Kansas, 2 March 1997.

Book, two authors
15. Miriam Toller and Jay Fielding, *Global Business for Smaller Companies* (Rocklin, Calif.: Prima Publishing, 1998), 102–103.

Government publication
16. U.S. Department of Defense, *Stretching Research Dollars: Survival Advice for Universities and Government Labs* (Washington, D.C.: GPO, 1999), 126.

APA STYLE

The American Psychological Association recommends the author-date system of documentation, which is popular in the physical, natural, and social sciences. When using this system, you simply insert the author's last name and the year of publication within parentheses following the text discussion of the material cited. Include a page number if you use a direct quote. This approach briefly identifies the source so that readers can locate complete

Figure B.2
Sample References—* Chicago *Style

Bibliography

Assira, James. "Are They Speaking English in Japan?" *Journal of Business Communication* 36, no. 4 (Fall 1999): 72. — Journal article with volume and issue numbers

BestTemp Staffing Services. *An Employer's Guide to Staffing Services,* 2d ed. Denver: BestTemp Information Center, 1997. — Brochure

"Buying Asian Supplies on the Net." *Los Angeles Times,* 12 February 1997, sec. D, p. 3. — Newspaper article, no author

Eurotec. *1998 Annual Report.* New York: Eurotec, Inc., 1998. — Annual report

Graves, Holly. "Prospecting Online." *Business Week,* 17 November 1999, 43–45. — Magazine article

Han, Daniel. "Trade Wars Heating Up Around the Globe." *CNN Headline News.* Atlanta: CNN, 5 March 1999. — Television broadcast

"Intel—Company Capsule." *Hoover's Online* [cited 8 March 1999]. 3 screens. Available online from World Wide Web at http://www.hoovers.com/capsules/13787.html. — Internet, World Wide Web

Kuntz, Sonja. "Moving Beyond Benefits." In *Our Changing Workforce,* edited by Randolf Jacobson, 213–227. New York: Citadel Press, 1998. — Book, component part

Morales, George H. "The Economic Pressures on Industrialized Nations in a Global Economy." Ph.D. diss., University of San Diego, 1998. Abstract in *Dissertation Abstracts International* 52 (1998): 5436C–5437C. — Dissertation or thesis

Myers, Charles. "HMOs in Today's Environment." Paper presented at the Conference on Medical Insurance Solutions, Chicago, Ill., August 1998. — Paper presented at a meeting

Norwalk, Preston. "Training Managers to Help Employees Accept Change." In *Business Line* [online]. San Francisco, 1999 [updated 17 September 1999; cited 3 October 1999]. Available from http://www.busline.com/news; INTERNET. — Online magazine article

Parkings, Robert. "George Eastman." *The Concise Columbia Encyclopedia.* New York: Columbia University Press, 1995. [CD-ROM]. — CD-ROM encyclopedia article, one author

Standish, Evelyn. "Global Market Crushes OPEC's Delicate Balance of Interests." *Wall Street Journal, 19* January 1999, sec. A, p. 1. — Newspaper article, one author

Stainer, Georgia, communications manager, Day Cable and Communications. Interview by author. Topeka, Kansas, 2 March 1997. — Interview

Toller, Miriam, and Jay Fielding. *Global Business for Smaller Companies.* Rocklin, Calif.: Prima Publishing, 1998. — Book, two authors

U.S. Department of Defense. *Stretching Research Dollars: Survival Advice for Universities and Government Labs.* Washington, D.C.: GPO, 1999. — Government publication

information in the alphabetical reference list at the end of the report. The author-date system is both brief and clear, saving readers time and effort.

In-Text Citation—*APA* Style

To document report sources in text using the *APA* style, insert the author's surname and the date of publication at the end of a statement. Enclose this information in parentheses. If the author's name is referred to in the text itself, then the number can be omitted from parenthetical material.

> Some experts recommend both translation and back-translation when dealing with any non-English-speaking culture (Assira, 1999).
>
> Toller and Fielding (1998) make a strong case for small companies succeeding in global business.

Figure B.3
Sample References—APA Style

References

Journal article with volume and issue numbers	Assira, J. (1999). Are they speaking English in Japan?" *Journal of Business Communication 36*(4), 72.
Brochure	BestTemp Staffing Services. (1997). *An employer's guide to staffing services,* (2d ed.) [Brochure]. Denver: BestTemp Information Center.
Newspaper article, no author	Buying Asian supplies on the net. (1997, February 12). *Los Angeles Times,* p. D3.
Annual report	Eurotec. (1998). *1998 annual report.* New York: Author.
Magazine article	Graves, H. (1999, November 17). Prospecting online. *Business Week,* 43–45.
Television broadcast	Han, D. (1999, March 5). Trade wars heating up around the globe. *CNN Headline News.* Atlanta, GA: CNN.
Internet, World Wide Web	Intel—Company Capsule. (1999). *Hoover's Online* [On-line]. Available: http://www.hoovers.com/capsules/13787.html Cited 1999, March 8.
Book, component part	Kuntz, S. (1998). Moving beyond benefits. In Randolph Jacobson (Ed.), *Our changing workforce* (pp. 213–227). New York: Citadel Press.
Dissertation or thesis	Morales, G. H. (1998). The economic pressures on industrialized nations in a global economy. (Doctoral dissertation, University of San Diego, 1998). *Dissertation Abstracts International, 52,* 5436C–5437C.
Paper presented at a meeting	Myers, C. (1998, August). *HMOs in today's environment.* Paper presented at the Conference on Medical Insurance Solutions, Chicago, IL.
Online magazine article	Norwalk, P. (1999, July 17). Training managers to help employees accept change. *Business Line* [On-line]. Available http://www.busline.com/news
CD-ROM encyclopedia article, one author	Parkings, R. (1995). George Eastman. *The concise Columbia encyclopedia.* [CD-ROM]. New York: Columbia University Press.
Newspaper article, one author	Standish, E. (1999, January 19). Global market crushes OPEC's delicate balance of interests. *Wall Street Journal,* p. A1.
Interview	*Cited in text only, not in the list of references.*
Book, two authors	Toller, M., & Fielding, J. (1998). *Global business for smaller companies.* Rocklin, CA: Prima Publishing.
Government publication	U.S. Department of Defense. (1999). *Stretching research dollars: Survival advice for universities and government labs.* Washington, DC: U.S. Government Printing Office, 1999.

Personal communications and interviews conducted by the author would not be listed in the reference list at all. Such citations would appear in the text only.

> Increasing the role of cable companies is high on the list of Georgia Stainer, communications manager at Day Cable and Communications (personal communication, March 2, 1999).

List of References—APA Style

The *APA* style recommends listing only those works actually cited in the text (so you would not include works for background or for further reading). Report writers must choose their references judiciously. Following are the major conventions for developing a reference list according to *APA* style (see Figure B.3):

- Format entries for publication by indenting the first line five to seven spaces. Students may wish to format entries as hanging indents to conform to the requirements of their university.
- List all author names in reversed order (last name first), and use only initials for the first and middle names.
- Arrange entries in the following general order: (1) author name, (2) date, (3) title information, (4) publication information, (5) periodical page range.
- Follow the author name with the date of publication in parentheses.
- List titles of articles from magazines, newspapers, and journals without underlines or quotation marks. Capitalize only the first word of the title and the first word to follow an internal colon.
- Italicize titles of books, capitalizing only the first word, any proper nouns, and the first word to follow a colon.
- Italicize names of magazines, newspapers, journals, and other complete publications—capitalizing all the important words.
- For journal articles, include the volume number (in italic) and, if necessary, the issue number (in parentheses). Finally, include the page range of the article: *Journal of Business Communication*, *36*(4), 72. (In this example, the volume is 36, the number is 4, and the page number is 72.)
- Include personal communications (such as letters, memos, e-mail, conversations) only in text, *not* in reference lists.
- Electronic references include author, date of publication, title of article, name of publication, electronic medium (*online* or *CD-ROM*), volume, series, page, and path.
- For electronic references, indicate the actual year of publication, the most recent update, or the exact date of your search.
- For electronic references, specify the method used to find the material (Telnet, FTP, Internet, etc.), the directory, and the file name. Leave periods off URLs (because stray punctuation in a path will hinder retrieval).

MLA Style

The style recommended by Modern Language Association of America is used widely in the humanities, especially in the study of language and literature. Like *APA* style, *MLA* style uses brief parenthetical citations in the text. However, instead of including author name and year, *MLA* citations include author name and page reference.

In-Text Citation—*MLA* Style

To document report sources in text using *MLA* style, insert the author's last name and a page reference inside parentheses following the cited material: (Matthews 63). If the author's name is mentioned in the text reference, the name can be omitted from the parenthetical citation: (63). The citation indicates that the reference came from page 63 of a work by Matthews. With the author's name, readers can find complete publication information in the alphabetically arranged list of works cited that comes at the end of the report.

> Some experts recommend both translation and back-translation when dealing with any non-English-speaking culture (Assira 72).
>
> Toller and Fielding make a strong case for small companies succeeding in global business (102–103).

List of Works Cited—*MLA* Style

The *MLA Style Manual* recommends preparing your list of works cited first so that you will know what information to give in the parenthetical citation (for example, whether to add a short title if you're citing more than one work by the same author, or whether to give an initial or first name if you're citing two authors who have the same last name). Your list of works cited appears at the end of your report, contains all the works that you cite in your text, and lists them in alphabetical order. Following are the major conventions for developing a reference list according to *MLA* style (see Figure B.4):

- Format entries as hanging indents (that is, indent second and succeeding lines by three to five character spaces).
- Arrange entries in the following general order: (1) author name, (2) title information, (3) publication information, (4) date, (5) periodical page range.
- List the lead author's name in reverse order (last name first), using either full first names or initials. List second and succeeding author names in normal order.
- Use quotation marks around the titles of articles from magazines, newspapers, and journals—capitalize all important words.
- Italicize the names of books, newspapers, journals and other complete publications, capitalizing all main words in the title.

Figure B.4
Sample References*—MLA *Style

Works Cited

Journal article with volume and issue numbers	Assira, James, "Are They Speaking English in Japan?" *Journal of Business Communication* 36.4 (1999): 72.
Brochure	BestTemp Staffing Services. *An Employer's Guide to Staffing Services,* 2d ed. Denver: BestTemp Information Center, 1997.
Newspaper article, no author	"Buying Asian Supplies on the Net." *Los Angeles Times* 12 Feb. 1997: D3.
Annual report	Eurotec. *1998 Annual Report.* New York: Eurotec, Inc., 1998.
Magazine article	Graves, Holly. "Prospecting Online." *Business Week* 17 November 1999: 43–45.
Television broadcast	Han, Daniel. "Trade Wars Heating Up Around the Globe." *CNN Headline News.* CNN. Atlanta. 5 Mar. 1999.
Internet, World Wide Web	"Intel—Company Capsule." *Hoover's Online.* 8 Mar. 1999 ⟨http://www.hoovers.com/capsules/13787.html⟩.
Book, component part	Kuntz, Sonja. *Moving Beyond Benefits. Our Changing Workforce.* Ed. Randolf Jacobson. New York: Citadel Press, 1998. 213–227.
Dissertation or thesis	Morales, George H. "The Economic Pressures on Industrialized Nations in a Global Economy." Diss. U of San Diego, 1998, *DAI 52* (1998): 5436C–5437C.
Paper presented at a meeting	Myers, Charles. "HMOs in Today's Environment." Conference on Medical Insurance Solutions. Chicago. 13 August 1998.
Online magazine article	Norwalk, Preston. "Training Managers to Help Employees Accept Change." *Business Line* 17 July 1999 ⟨http://www.busline.com/news⟩.
CD-ROM encyclopedia article, one author	Parkings, Robert. "George Eastman." *The Concise Columbia Encyclopedia.* CD-ROM. New York: Columbia UP, 1995.
Newspaper article, one author	Standish, Evelyn. "Global Market Crushes OPEC's Delicate Balance of Interests." *Wall Street Journal,* 19 Jan. 1999, p. A1.
Interview	Stainer, Georgia, communications manager, Day Cable and Communications. Telephone interview. Topeka. 2 Mar. 1997.
Book, two authors	Toller, Miriam, and Jay Fielding. *Global Business for Smaller Companies.* Rocklin: Prima Publishing, 1998.
Government publication	United States. Department of Defense. *Stretching Research Dollars: Survival Advice for Universities and Government Labs.* Washington: GPO, 1999.

- For journal articles, include the volume number and the issue number (if necessary). Include the year of publication inside parentheses and follow with a colon and the page range of the article: *Journal of Business Communication* 36.4 (1999): 72. (In this source, the volume is 36, the number is 4, and the page is 72.)
- Electronic sources are less fixed than print sources, and they may not be readily accessible to readers. So citations for electronic sources must provide more information. Always try to be as comprehensive as possible, citing whatever information is available.
- The date for electronic sources must contain both the date assigned in the source and the date accessed by the researcher.
- The URL for electronic sources must be as accurate and complete as possible, from access-mode identifier (http, ftp, gopher, telnet) to all relevant directory and file names. Be sure to enclose this path inside angle brackets: ⟨http://www.hoovers.com/capsules/13787.html⟩.

APPENDIX I

Fundamentals of Grammar and Usage

Grammar is nothing more than the way words are combined into sentences, and usage is the way words are used by a network of people—in this case, the community of businesspeople who use English. You'll find it easier to get along in this community if you know the accepted standards of grammar and usage. What follows is a review of the basics of grammar and usage, things you've probably learned but may have forgotten. Without a firm grasp of these basics, you risk not only being misunderstood but also damaging your company's image, losing money for your company, and possibly even losing your job.

1.0 Grammar

The sentence below looks innocent, but is it really?

> We sell tuxedos as well as rent.

You might sell rent, but it's highly unlikely. Whatever you're selling, some people will ignore your message because of a blunder like this. The following sentence has a similar problem:

> Vice President Eldon Neale told his chief engineer that he would no longer be with Avix, Inc., as of June 30.

Is Eldon or the engineer leaving? No matter which side the facts are on, the sentence can be read the other way. You may have a hard time convincing either person that your simple mistake was not a move in a game of office politics. Now look at this sentence:

> The year before we budgeted more for advertising sales were up.

Confused? Perhaps this is what you meant:

> The year before, we budgeted more for advertising. Sales were up.

Maybe you meant this:

> The year before we budgeted more for advertising, sales were up.

The meaning of language falls into bundles called sentences. A listener or reader can take only so much meaning before filing a sentence away and getting ready for the next one. So, as a writer, you have to know what a sentence is. You need to know where one ends and the next one begins.

If you want to know what a thing is, you have to find out what goes into it, what its ingredients are. Luckily, the basic ingredients of an English sentence are simple. They're called the parts of speech, and the content-bearing ones are nouns, pronouns, verbs, adjectives, and adverbs. They combine with a few functional parts of speech to convey meaning. Meaning is also transmitted by punctuation, mechanics, and vocabulary.

1.1 Nouns

A noun names a person, place, or thing. Anything you can see or detect with one of your other senses has a noun to name it. Some things you can't see or sense are also nouns—ions, for example, or space. So are things that exist as ideas, such as accuracy and height. (You can see that something is accurate or that a building is tall, but you can't see the idea of accuracy or the idea of height.) These names for ideas are known as abstract nouns. The simplest nouns are the names of things you can see or touch: car, building, cloud, brick.

1.1.1 Proper Nouns and Common Nouns

So far, all the examples of nouns have been common nouns, referring to general classes of things. The word *building* refers to a whole class of structures. Common nouns such as *building* are not capitalized.

If you want to talk about one particular building, however, you might refer to the Glazier Building. The name is capitalized, indicating that *Glazier Building* is a proper noun.

Here are three sets of common and proper nouns for comparison:

Common	Proper
city	Kansas City
company	Blaisden Company
store	Books Galore

1.1.2 Plural Nouns

Nouns can be either singular or plural. The usual way to make a plural noun is to add *s* to the singular form of the word:

SINGULAR	PLURAL
rock	rocks
picture	pictures
song	songs

Many nouns have other ways of forming the plural. Letters, numbers, and words used as words are sometimes made plural by adding an apostrophe and an *s*. Very often, *'s* is used with abbreviations that have periods, lowercase letters that stand alone, and capital letters that might be confused with words when made into plurals:

> Spell out all *St.*'s and *Ave.*'s.
>
> He divided the page with a row of *x*'s.
>
> Sarah will register the *A*'s through the *I*'s at the convention.

In other cases, however, the apostrophe may be left out:

> They'll review their *ABC*s.
>
> The stock market climbed through most of the 1980s.
>
> Circle all *the*s in the paragraph.

In these examples, the letters used as letters and words used as words are *italicized* (discussed later).

Other nouns, such as those below, are so-called irregular nouns; they form the plural in some way other than simply adding *s*:

SINGULAR	PLURAL
tax	taxes
specialty	specialties
cargo	cargoes
shelf	shelves
child	children
woman	women
tooth	teeth
mouse	mice
parenthesis	parentheses
son-in-law	sons-in-law
editor-in-chief	editors-in-chief

Rather than memorize a lot of rules about forming plurals, use a dictionary. If the dictionary says nothing about the plural of a word, it's formed the usual way: by adding *s*. If the plural is formed in some irregular way, the dictionary shows the plural or has a note something like this: *ples.*

1.1.3 Possessive Nouns

A noun becomes possessive when it's used to show the ownership of something. Then you add *'s* to the word:

the man's car | the woman's apartment

However, ownership does not need to be legal:

the secretary's desk | the company's assets

Also, ownership may be nothing more than an automatic association:

a day's work | a job's prestige

An exception to the rule about adding *'s* to make a noun possessive occurs when the word is singular and already has two *s* sounds at the end. In cases like the following, an apostrophe is all that's needed:

crisis' dimensions | Mr. Moses' application

When the noun has only one *s* sound at the end, however, retain the *'s:*

Chris's book | Carolyn Nuss's office

With hyphenated nouns (compound nouns), add *'s* to the last word:

HYPHENATED NOUN	POSSESSIVE NOUN
mother-in-law	mother-in-law's
mayor-elect	mayor-elect's

To form the possessive of plural nouns, just begin by following the same rule as with singular nouns: add *'s*. However, if the plural noun already ends in an *s* (as most do), drop the one you've added, leaving only the apostrophe:

the clients'~~s~~ complaints | employees'~~s~~ benefits

1.2 Pronouns

A pronoun is a word that stands for a noun; it saves repeating the noun:

> *Drivers* have some choice of weeks for vacation, but *they* must notify this office of *their* preference by March 1.

The pronouns *they* and *their* stand in for the noun *drivers.* The noun that a pronoun stands for is called the antecedent of the pronoun; *drivers* is the antecedent of *they* and *their.*

When the antecedent is plural, the pronoun that stands in for it has to be plural; *they* and *their* are plural pronouns because *drivers* is plural. Likewise, when the antecedent is singular, the pronoun has to be singular:

> We thought the *contract* had been signed, but we soon learned that *it* had not been.

1.2.1 Multiple Antecedents

Sometimes a pronoun has a double (or even a triple) antecedent:

> Kathryn Boettcher and Luis Gutierrez went beyond *their* sales quotas for January.

Kathryn Boettcher, if taken alone, is a singular antecedent. So is *Luis Gutierrez.* However, when together they are the antecedent of a pronoun, they're plural and the pronoun has to be plural. Thus the pronoun is *their* instead of *her* or *his.*

1.2.2 Unclear Antecedents

In some sentences the pronoun's antecedent is unclear:

> Sandy Wright sent Jane Brougham *her* production figures for the previous year. *She* thought they were too low.

To which person does the pronoun *her* refer? Someone who knew Sandy and Jane and knew their business relationship might be able to figure out the antecedent for *her.* Even with such an advantage, however, a reader might receive the wrong meaning. Also, it would be nearly impossible for any reader to know which name is the antecedent of *she.*

The best way to clarify an ambiguous pronoun is usually to rewrite the sentence, repeating nouns when needed for clarity:

> Sandy Wright sent her production figures for the previous year to Jane Brougham. *Jane* thought they were too low.

The noun needs to be repeated only when the antecedent is unclear.

1.2.3 Gender-Neutral Pronouns

The pronouns that stand for males are *he, his,* and *him.* The pronouns that stand for females are *she, hers,* and *her.* However, you'll often be faced with the problem of choosing a pronoun for a noun that refers to both females and males:

> Each manager must make up (his, her, his or her, its, their) own mind about stocking this item and about the quantity that (he, she, he or she, it, they) can sell.

This sentence calls for a pronoun that's neither masculine nor feminine. The issue of gender-neutral pronouns responds to efforts to treat females and males evenhandedly. Here are some possible ways to deal with this issue:

> Each manager must make up *his* . . .
>
> (Not all managers are men.)
>
> Each manager must make up her . . .
>
> (Not all managers are women.)
>
> Each manager must make up *his* or *her* . . .
>
> (This solution is acceptable but becomes awkward when repeated more than once or twice in a document.)
>
> Each manager must make up *her* . . . Every manager will receive *his* . . . A manager may send *her* . . .
>
> (A manager's gender does not alternate like a windshield wiper!)
>
> Each manager must make up *their* . . .
>
> (The pronoun can't be plural when the antecedent is singular.)
>
> Each manager must make up *its* . . .
>
> (*It* never refers to people.)

The best solution is to make the noun plural or to revise the passage altogether:

> Managers must make up *their* minds . . .
>
> Each manager must decide whether . . .

Be careful not to change the original meaning.

1.2.4 Case of Pronouns

The case of a pronoun tells whether it's acting or acted upon:

> *She* sells an average of five packages each week.

In this sentence *she* is doing the selling. Because *she* is acting, *she* is said to be in the nominative case. Now consider what happens when the pronoun is acted upon:

> After six months Ms. Browning promoted *her.*

In this sentence the pronoun *her* is acted upon. The pronoun *her* is thus said to be in the objective case.

Contrast the nominative and objective pronouns in this list:

NOMINATIVE	OBJECTIVE
I	me
we	us
he	him
she	her
they	them
who	whom
whoever	whomever

Objective pronouns may be used as either the object of a verb (such as *promoted*) or the object of a preposition (such as *with*):

> Rob worked with *them* until the order was filled.

In this example *them* is the object of the preposition *with* because Rob acted upon—worked with—them.

Here's a sample sentence with three pronouns, the first one nominative, the second the object of a verb, and the third the object of a preposition:

He paid *us* as soon as the check came from *them.*

He is nominative; *us* is objective because it's the object of the verb *paid; them* is objective because it's the object of the preposition *from.*

Every writer sometimes wonders whether to use *who* or *whom:*

(Who, Whom) will you hire?

Because this sentence is a question, it's difficult to see that *whom* is the object of the verb *hire.* You can figure out which pronoun to use if you rearrange the question and temporarily try *she* and *her* in place of *who* and *whom:* "Will you hire *she*?" or "Will you hire *her*?" *Her* and *whom* are both objective, so the correct choice is "*Whom* will you hire?" Here's a different example:

(Who, Whom) logged so much travel time?

Turning the question into a statement, you get:

He logged so much travel time.

Therefore, the correct statement is:

Who logged so much travel time?

1.2.5 Possessive Pronouns

Possessive pronouns are like possessive nouns in the way they work: They show ownership or automatic association.

her job	their preferences
his account	its equipment

However, possessive pronouns are different from possessive nouns in the way they are written. That is, possessive pronouns never have an apostrophe.

POSSESSIVE NOUN	POSSESSIVE PRONOUN
the woman's estate	her estate
Roger Franklin's plans	his plans
the shareholders' feelings	their feelings
the vacuum cleaner's attachments	its attachments

The word *its* is the possessive of *it.* Like all other possessive pronouns, *its* doesn't have an apostrophe. Some people confuse *its* with *it's,* the contraction of *it is.* Contractions are discussed later.

1.3 Verbs

A verb describes an action:

They all *quit* in disgust.

It may also describe a state of being:

Working conditions *were* substandard.

The English language is full of action verbs. Here are a few you'll often run across in the business world:

verify	perform	fulfill
hire	succeed	send
leave	improve	receive
accept	develop	pay

You could undoubtedly list many more.

The most common verb describing a state of being instead of an action is *to be* and all its forms:

I *am, was,* or *will be;* you *are, were,* or *will be*

Other verbs also describe a state of being:

It *seemed* a good plan at the time.

She *sounds* impressive at a meeting.

These verbs link what comes before them in the sentence with what comes after; no action is involved. (See Section 1.7.5 for a fuller discussion of linking verbs.)

1.3.1 Verb Tenses

English has three simple verb tenses: present, past, and future.

Present: Our branches in Hawaii *stock* other items.
Past: When we *stocked* Purquil pens, we received a great many complaints.
Future: Rotex Tire Stores *will* stock your line of tires when you begin a program of effective national advertising.

With most verbs (the regular ones), the past tense ends in *ed;* the future tense always has *will* or *shall* in front of it. But the present tense is more complex:

SINGULAR	PLURAL
I stock	we stock
you stock	you stock
he, she, it stocks	they stock

The basic form, *stock,* takes an additional *s* when *he, she,* or *it* precedes it.

In addition to the three simple tenses, there are three perfect tenses using forms of the helping verb *have.* The present perfect tense uses the past participle (regularly the past tense) of the main verb, *stocked,* and adds the present-tense *have* or *has* to the front of it:

(I, we, you, they) *have stocked.*

(He, she, it) *has stocked.*

The past perfect tense uses the past participle of the main verb, *stocked,* and adds the past-tense *had* to the front of it:

> (I, you, he, she, it, we, they) *had stocked.*

The future perfect tense also uses the past participle of the main verb, *stocked,* but adds the future-tense *will have:*

> (I, you, he, she, it, we, they) *will have stocked.*

Keep verbs in the same tense when the actions occur at the same time:

> When the payroll checks *came* in, everyone *showed up* for work.
>
> We *have found* that everyone *has pitched* in to help.

Of course, when the actions occur at different times, you may change tense accordingly:

> A shipment *came* last Wednesday, so when another one *comes* in today, please return it.

The new employee *had been* ill at ease, but now she *has become* a full-fledged member of the team.

1.3.2 Irregular Verbs

Many verbs don't follow in every detail the patterns already described. The most irregular of these verbs is *to be:*

TENSE	SINGULAR	PLURAL
Present:	I *am*	we *are*
	you *are*	you *are*
	he, she, it *is*	they *are*
Past:	I *was*	we *were*
	you *were*	you *were*
	he, she, it *was*	they *were*

The future tense of *to be* is formed in the same way that the future tense of a regular verb is formed.

The perfect tenses of *to be* are also formed as they would be for a regular verb, except that the past participle is a special form, *been,* instead of just the past tense:

Present perfect: you *have been*
Past perfect: you *had been*
Future perfect: you *will have been*

Here's a sampling of other irregular verbs:

PRESENT	PAST	PAST PARTICIPLE
begin	began	begun
shrink	shrank	shrunk
know	knew	known
rise	rose	risen
become	became	become
go	went	gone
do	did	done

Dictionaries list the various forms of other irregular verbs.

1.3.3 Transitive and Intransitive Verbs

Many people are confused by three particular sets of verbs:

lie/lay sit/set rise/raise

Using these verbs correctly is much easier when you learn the difference between transitive and intransitive verbs.

Transitive verbs convey their action to an object; they "transfer" their action to an object. Intransitive verbs do not. Here are some sample uses of transitive and intransitive verbs:

INTRANSITIVE	TRANSITIVE
We should include in our new offices a place to *lie* down for a nap.	The workers will be here on Monday to *lay* new carpeting.
Even the way an interviewee *sits* is important.	That crate is full of stemware, so *set* it down carefully.
Salaries at Compu-Link, Inc., *rise* swiftly.	They *raise* their level of production every year.

The workers *lay* carpeting, you *set* down the crate, they *raise* production; each action is transferred to something. In the intransitive sentences, one *lies* down, an interviewee *sits,* and salaries *rise* without (at least grammatically) affecting anything else. Intransitive sentences are complete with only a subject and a verb; transitive sentences are not complete unless they also include an object, or something to transfer the action to.

Tenses are a confusing element of the *lie/lay* problem:

PRESENT	PAST	PAST PARTICIPLE
I *lie*	I *lay*	I have *lain*
I *lay* (something down)	I *laid* (something down)	I have *laid* (something down)

The past tense of *lie* and the present tense of *lay* look and sound alike, even though they're different verbs.

1.3.4 Voice of Verbs

Verbs have two voices, active and passive:

Active: The buyer paid a large amount.
Passive: A large amount was paid by the buyer.

The passive voice uses a form of the verb *to be.*

Also, the passive-voice sentence uses eight words, whereas the active-voice sentence uses only six words to say the same thing. The words *was* and *by* are unnecessary to convey the meaning of the sentence. In fact, extra words usually clog meaning. So be sure to opt for the active voice when you have a choice.

At times, however, you have no choice:

Several items *have been taken,* but so far we don't know who took them.

The passive voice becomes necessary when you don't know (or don't want to say) who performed the action; the active voice is bolder and more direct.

1.3.5 Mood of Verbs

You have three moods to choose from, depending on your intentions. Most of the time you use the indicative mood to make a statement or to ask a question:

The secretary *mailed* a letter to each supplier.

Did the secretary *mail* a letter to each supplier?

When you wish to command or request, use the imperative mood:

Please mail a letter to each supplier.

Sometimes, especially in business, a courteous request is stated like a question; in that case, however, no question mark is required:

Would you *mail* a letter to each supplier.

The subjunctive mood, most often used in formal writing or in presenting bad news, expresses a possibility or a recommendation. The subjunctive is usually signaled by a word such as *if* or *that.* In these examples, the subjunctive mood uses special verb forms:

If the secretary *were to mail* a letter to each supplier, we might save some money.

I suggested that the secretary *mail* a letter to each supplier.

Although the subjunctive mood is not used as often as it once was, it's still found in such expressions as *Come what may* and *If I were you.* In general, it is used to convey an idea that is contrary to fact: If iron *were* lighter than air.

1.4 Adjectives

An adjective modifies (tells something about) a noun or pronoun:

an *efficient* staff	a *heavy* price
brisk trade	*poor* you

Each of these phrases says more about the noun or pronoun than the noun or pronoun would say alone.

Adjectives always tell us something we wouldn't know without them. So you don't need to use adjectives when the noun alone, or a different noun, will give the meaning:

a *company* employee

(An employee ordinarily works for a company.)

a *crate-type* container

(Crate gives the entire meaning.)

At times, adjectives pile up in a series:

It was a *long,* and *active* workday.

Such strings of adjectives are acceptable as long as they all convey a different part of the phrase's meaning.

Verbs in the *ing* (present participle) form can be used as adjectives:

A *boring* job can sometimes turn into a *fascinating* career.

So can the past participle of verbs:

A freshly *painted* house is a *sold* house.

Adjectives modify nouns more often than they modify pronouns. When adjectives do modify pronouns, however, the sentence usually has a linking verb:

They were *attentive.*	It looked *appropriate.*
He seems *interested.*	You are *skillful.*

Most adjectives can take three forms: simple, comparative, and superlative. The simple form modifies a single noun or pronoun. Use the comparative form when comparing two items. When comparing three or more items, use the superlative form.

SIMPLE	COMPARATIVE	SUPERLATIVE
hard	harder	hardest
safe	safer	safest
dry	drier	driest

The comparative form adds *er* to the simple form, and the superlative form adds *est.* (The *y* at the end of a word changes to *i* before the *er* or *est* is added.)

A small number of adjectives are irregular, including these:

SIMPLE	COMPARATIVE	SUPERLATIVE
good	better	best
bad	worse	worst
little	less	least

When the simple form of an adjective is two or more syllables, you usually add *more* to form the comparative and *most* to form the superlative:

SIMPLE	COMPARATIVE	SUPERLATIVE
useful	more useful	most useful
exhausting	more exhausting	most exhausting
expensive	more expensive	most expensive

The most common exceptions are two-syllable adjectives that end in *y:*

SIMPLE	COMPARATIVE	SUPERLATIVE
happy	happier	happiest
costly	costlier	costliest

If you choose this option, change the *y* to *i,* and tack *er* or *est* onto the end.

1.5 Adverbs

An adverb modifies a verb, an adjective, or another adverb:

Modifying a verb:	Our marketing department works *efficiently.*
Modifying an adjective:	She was not dependable,although she was *highly* intelligent.
Modifying another adverb:	His territory was *too* broadly diversified, so he moved *extremely* cautiously.

Most of the adverbs mentioned are adjectives turned into adverbs by adding *ly,* which is how many adverbs are formed:

ADJECTIVE	ADVERB
efficient	efficiently
high	highly
extreme	extremely
special	specially
official	officially
separate	separately

Some adverbs are made by dropping or changing the final letter of the adjective and then adding *ly:*

ADJECTIVE	ADVERB
due	duly
busy	busily

Other adverbs don't end in *ly* at all. Here are a few examples of this type:

often	fast	too
soon	very	so

1.6 Other Parts of Speech

Nouns, pronouns, verbs, adjectives, and adverbs carry most of the meaning in a sentence. Four other parts of speech link them together in sentences: prepositions, conjunctions, articles, and interjections.

1.6.1 Prepositions

Prepositions are words like these:

of	to	for	with
at	by	from	about

They most often begin prepositional phrases, which function like adjectives and adverbs by telling more about a pronoun, noun, or verb:

of a type	*by* Friday
to the point	*with* characteristic flair

1.6.2 Conjunctions, Articles, and Interjections

Conjunctions are words that usually join parts of a sentence. Here are a few:

and	but	because
yet	although	if

Using conjunctions is discussed in sections 1.7.3 and 1.7.4.

Only three articles exist in English: *the, a,* and *an.* These words are used, like adjectives, to specify which item you are talking about.

Interjections are words that express no solid information, only emotion:

Wow!	Well, well!
Oh, no!	Good!

Such purely emotional language has its place in private life and advertising copy, but it only weakens the effect of most business writing.

1.7 Sentences

Sentences are constructed with the major building blocks, the parts of speech.

> Money talks.

This two-word sentence consists of a noun (*money*) and a verb (*talks*). When used in this way, the noun works as the first requirement for a sentence, the subject, and the verb works as the second requirement, the predicate. Now look at this sentence:

> They merged.

The subject in this case is a pronoun (*they*), and the predicate is a verb (*merged*). This is a sentence because it has a subject and a predicate. Here is yet another kind of sentence:

> The plans are ready.

This sentence has a more complicated subject, the noun *plans* and the article *the;* the complete predicate is a state-of-being verb (*are*) and an adjective (*ready*).

Without these two parts, the subject (who or what does something) and the predicate (the doing of it), no collection of words is a sentence.

1.7.1 Commands

In commands, the subject (always *you*) is only understood, not stated:

> (You) Move your desk to the better office.
>
> (You) Please try to finish by six o'clock.

1.7.2 Longer Sentences

More complicated sentences have more complicated subjects and predicates, but they still have a subject and a predicate verb. In the following examples, the subject is underlined once, the predicate verb twice:

> Marex and Contron enjoy higher earnings each quarter.
>
> (*Marex* [and] *Contron* did something; *enjoy* is what they did.)
>
> My interview, coming minutes after my freeway accident, did not impress or move anyone.
>
> (*Interview* is what did something. What did it do? It *did* [not] *impress* [or] *move.*)
>
> In terms of usable space, a steel warehouse, with its extremely long span of roof unsupported by pillars, makes more sense.
>
> (*Warehouse* is what *makes*.)

These three sentences demonstrate several things. First, in all three sentences the subject and predicate verb are the "bare bones" of the sentence, the parts that carry the core idea of the sentence. When trying to find the subject and predicate verb, disregard all prepositional phrases, modifiers, conjunctions, and articles.

Second, in the third sentence the verb is singular (*makes*) because the subject is singular (*warehouse*). Even though the plural noun *pillars* is closer to the verb, *warehouse* is the subject. So *warehouse* determines whether the verb is singular or plural. Subject and predicate must agree.

Third, the subject in the first sentence is compound (*Marex* [and] *Contron*). A compound subject, when connected by *and,* requires a plural verb (*enjoy*). Also in the second sentence, compound predicates are possible (*did* [not] *impress* [or] *move*).

Fourth, the second sentence incorporates a group of words—*coming minutes after my freeway accident*—containing a form of a verb (*coming*) and a noun (*accident*). Yet this group of words is not a complete sentence for two reasons:

- *Accident* is not the subject of *coming*. Not all nouns are subjects.
- A verb that ends in *ing* can never be the predicate of a sentence (unless preceded by a form of *to be,* as in *was coming*). Not all verbs are predicates.

Because they don't contain a subject and a predicate, the words *coming minutes after my freeway accident* (called a phrase) can't be written as a sentence. That is, the phrase can't stand alone; it can't begin with a capital letter and end with a period. So a phrase must always be just one part of a sentence.

Sometimes a sentence incorporates two or more groups of words that do contain a subject and a predicate; these word groups are called clauses:

> My interview, because it came minutes after my freeway accident, did not impress or move anyone.

The independent clause is the portion of the sentence that could stand alone without revision:

> My interview did not impress or move anyone.

The other part of the sentence could stand alone only by removing *because:*

> (because) It came minutes after my freeway accident.

This part of the sentence is known as a dependent clause; although it has a subject and a predicate (just as an independent clause does), it's linked to the main part of the sentence by a word (*because*) showing its dependence.

In summary, the two types of clauses—dependent and independent—both have a subject and a predicate. Dependent clauses, however, do not bear the main meaning of the sentence and are therefore linked to an independent clause. Nor can phrases stand alone, because they lack both a subject and a predicate. Only independent clauses can be written as sentences without revision.

1.7.3 Sentence Fragments

An incomplete sentence (a phrase or a dependent clause) that is written as though it were a complete sentence is called a fragment. Consider the following sentence fragments:

> Marilyn Sanders, having had pilferage problems in her store for the past year. Refuses to accept the results of our investigation.

This serious error can easily be corrected by putting the two fragments together:

> Marilyn Sanders, having had pilferage problems in her store for the past year, refuses to accept the results of our investigation.

Not all fragments can be corrected so easily. Here's more information on Sanders's pilferage problem.

> Employees a part of it. No authority or discipline.

Only the writer knows the intended meaning of those two phrases. Perhaps the employees are taking part in the pilferage. If so, the sentence should read:

> Some employees are part of the pilferage problem.

On the other hand, it's possible that some employees are helping with the investigation. Then the sentence would read:

> Some employees are taking part in our investigation.

It's just as likely, however, that the employees are not only taking part in the pilferage but are also being analyzed:

> Those employees who are part of the pilferage problem will accept no authority or discipline.

In fact, even more meanings could be read into these fragments. Because fragments can mean so many things, they mean nothing. No well-written memo, letter, or report ever demands the reader to be an imaginative genius.

One more type of fragment exists, the kind represented by a dependent clause. Note what *because* does to change what was once a unified sentence:

> Our stock of sprinklers is depleted.
>
> Because our stock of sprinklers is depleted.

Although the second version contains a subject and a predicate, adding *because* makes it a fragment. Words such as *because* form a special group of words called subordinating conjunctions. Here's a partial list:

since	though	whenever
although	if	unless
while	even if	after

When a word of this type begins a clause, the clause is dependent and cannot stand alone as a sentence. However, if a dependent clause is combined with an independent clause, it can convey a complete meaning. The independent clause may come before or after the dependent clause:

> We are unable to fill your order because our stock of sprinklers is depleted.
>
> Because our stock of sprinklers is depleted, we are unable to fill your order.

Another remedy for a fragment that is a dependent clause is to remove the subordinating conjunction. That solution leaves a simple but complete sentence:

> Our stock of sprinklers is depleted.

The actual details of a transaction will determine the best way to remedy a fragment problem.

The ban on fragments has one exception. Some advertising copy contains sentence fragments, written knowingly to convey a certain rhythm. However, advertising is the only area of business in which fragments are acceptable.

1.7.4 Fused Sentences and Comma Splices

Just as there can be too little in a group of words to make it a sentence, there can also be too much:

> All our mail is run through a postage meter every afternoon someone picks it up.

This example contains two sentences, not one, but the two have been blended so that it's hard to tell where one ends and the next begins. Is the mail run through a meter every afternoon? If so, the sentences should read:

> All our mail is run through a postage meter every afternoon. Someone picks it up.

Perhaps the mail is run through a meter at some other time (morning, for example) and is picked up every afternoon:

> All our mail is run through a postage meter. Every afternoon someone picks it up.

The order of words is the same in all three cases; sentence division makes all the difference. Either of the last two cases is grammatically correct. The choice depends on the facts of the situation.

Sometimes these so-called fused sentences have a more obvious point of separation:

> Several large orders arrived within a few days of one another, too many came in for us to process by the end of the month.

Here the comma has been put between two independent clauses in an attempt to link them. When a lowly comma separates two complete sentences, the result is called a comma splice. A comma splice can be remedied in one of three ways:

- Replace the comma with a period and capitalize the next word: ". . . one another. Too many . . ."
- Replace the comma with a semicolon and do not capitalize the next word: ". . . one another; too many . . ." This remedy works only when the two sentences have closely related meanings.
- Change one of the sentences so that it becomes a phrase or a dependent clause. This remedy often produces the best writing, but it takes more work.

The third alternative can be carried out in several ways. One is to begin the blended sentence with a subordinating conjunction:

> Whenever several large orders arrived within a few days of one another, too many came in for us to process by the end of the month.

Another way is to remove part of the subject or the predicate verb from one of the independent clauses, thereby creating a phrase:

> Several large orders arrived within a few days of one another, too many for us to process by the end of the month.

Finally, you can change one of the predicate verbs to its *ing* form:

> Several large orders arrived within a few days of one another, too many coming in for us to process by the end of the month.

At other times a simple coordinating conjunction (such as *or, and,* or *but*) can separate fused sentences:

> You can fire them, *or* you can make better use of their abilities.

> Margaret drew up the designs, *and* Matt carried them out.

> We will have three strong months, *but* after that sales will taper off.

Be careful using coordinating conjunctions: Use them only to join simple sentences that express similar ideas.

Also, because they say relatively little about the relationship between the two clauses they join, avoid using coordinating conjunctions too often: *and* is merely an addition sign; *but is* just a turn signal; *or* only points to an alternative. Subordinating conjunctions such as *because* and *whenever* tell the reader a lot more.

1.7.5 Sentences with Linking Verbs

Linking verbs were discussed briefly in the section on verbs (Section 1.3). Here you can see more fully the way they function in a sentence. The following is a model of any sentence with a linking verb:

> A (verb) B.

Although words such as *seems* and *feels* can also be linking verbs, let's assume that the verb is a form of *to be:*

> A *is* B.

In such a sentence, A and B are always nouns, pronouns, or adjectives. When one is a noun and the other is a pronoun, or when both are nouns, the sentence says that one is the same as the other:

> She is president.

> Rachel is president.

When one is an adjective, it modifies or describes the other:

> She is forceful.

Remember that when one is an adjective, it modifies the other as any adjective modifies a noun or pronoun, except that a linking verb stands between the adjective and the word it modifies.

1.7.6 Misplaced Modifiers

The position of a modifier in a sentence is important. the movement of *only* changes the meaning in the following sentences:

> *Only* we are obliged to supply those items specified in your contract.

> We are obliged *only* to supply those items specified in your contract.

> We are obliged to supply *only* those items specified in your contract.

> We are obliged to supply those items specified *only* in your contract.

In any particular set of circumstances, only one of those sentences would be accurate. The others would very likely cause problems. To prevent misunderstanding, place modifiers such as *only* as close as possible to the noun or verb they modify.

For similar reasons, whole phrases that are modifiers must be placed near the right noun or verb. Mistakes in placement create ludicrous meanings.

> Antia Information Systems has bought new computer chairs for the programmers *with more comfortable seats.*

The anatomy of programmers is not normally a concern of business writers. Obviously, the comfort of the chairs was the issue:

> Antia Information Systems has bought new computer chairs *with more comfortable seats* for the programmers.

Here is another example:

> I asked him to file all the letters in the cabinet *that had been answered.*

In this ridiculous sentence the cabinet has been answered, even though no cabinet in history is known to have asked a question.

That had been answered is too far from *letters* and too close to *cabinet.* Here's an improvement:

> I asked him to file in the cabinet all the letters *that had been answered.*

In some cases, instead of moving the modifying phrase closer to the word it modifies, the best solution is to move the word closer to the modifying phrase.

2.0 Punctuation

On the highway, signs tell you when to slow down or stop, where to turn, when to merge. In similar fashion, punctuation helps readers negotiate your prose. The proper use of punctuation keeps readers from losing track of your meaning.

2.1 Periods

Use a period (1) to end any sentence that is not a question, (2) with certain abbreviations, and (3) between dollars and cents in an amount of money.

2.2 Question Marks

Use a question mark after any direct question that requests an answer:

> Are you planning to enclose a check, or shall we bill you?

Don't use a question mark with commands phrased as questions for the sake of politeness:

> Will you send us a check today.

2.3 Exclamation Point

Use exclamation points after highly emotional language. Because business writing almost never calls for emotional language, you will seldom use exclamation points.

2.4 Semicolons

Semicolons have three main uses. One is to separate two closely related independent clauses:

> The outline for the report is due within a week; the report itself is due at the end of the month.

A semicolon should also be used instead of a comma when the items in a series have commas within them:

> Our previous meetings were on November 11, 1998; February 20, 1999; and April 28, 2000.

Finally, a semicolon should be used to separate independent clauses when the second one begins with a word such as *however, therefore,* or *nevertheless* or a phrase such as *for example* or *in that case:*

> Our supplier has been out of part D712 for 10 weeks; however, we have found another source that can ship the part right away.

> His test scores were quite low; on the other hand, he has a lot of relevant experience.

Section 4.4 has more information on using transitional words and phrases.

2.5 Colons

Use a colon (1) after the salutation in a business letter, (2) at the end of a sentence or phrase introducing a list or (sometimes) a quotation, and (3) to separate two closely related independent clauses not joined by *and, but,* or *or.*

> Our study included the three most critical problems: insufficient capital, incompetent management, and inappropriate location.

In some introductory sentences, phrases such as *the following* or *that is* are implied by using a colon.

A colon should not be used when the list, quotation, or idea is a direct object or part of the introductory sentence:

> We are able to supply
>
> staples
> wood screws
> nails
> toggle bolts

> This shipment includes 9 videotapes, 12 CDs, and 14 cassette tapes.

2.6 Commas

Commas have many uses; the most common is to separate items in a series:

> He took the job, learned it well, worked hard, and succeeded.

> Put paper, pencils, and paper clips on the requisition list.

Company style often dictates omitting the final comma in a series. However, if you have a choice, use the final comma; it's often necessary to prevent misunderstanding.

A second place to use a comma is between independent clauses that are joined by a coordinating conjunction (*and, but,* or *or*) unless one or both are very short:

> She spoke to the sales staff, and he spoke to the production staff.

> I was advised to proceed and I did.

A third use for the comma is to separate a dependent clause at the beginning of a sentence from an independent clause:

> Because of our lead in the market, we may be able to risk introducing a new product.

However, a dependent clause at the end of a sentence is separated from the independent clause by a comma only when the dependent clause is unnecessary to the main meaning of the sentence:

> We may be able to introduce a new product, although it may involve some risk.

A fourth use for the comma is after an introductory phrase or word:

> Starting with this amount of capital, we can survive in the red for one year.

> Through more careful planning, we may be able to serve more people.

> Yes, you may proceed as originally planned.

However, with short introductory prepositional phrases and some one-syllable words (such as *hence* and *thus*), the comma is often omitted:

> Before January 1 we must complete the inventory.

> Thus we may not need to hire anyone.

> In short the move to Tulsa was a good idea.

Fifth, commas are used to surround nonrestrictive phrases or words (expressions that can be removed from the sentence without changing the meaning):

> The new owners, the Kowacks, are pleased with their purchase.

Sixth, commas are used between adjectives modifying the same noun (coordinate adjectives):

> She left Monday for a long, difficult recruiting trip.

To test the appropriateness of such a comma, try reversing the order of the adjectives: *a difficult, long recruiting trip*. If the order cannot be reversed, leave out the comma (*a good old friend* isn't the same as *an old good friend*). A comma is also not used when one of the adjectives is part of the noun. Compare these two phrases:

> a distinguished, well-known figure

> a distinguished public figure

The adjective-noun combination of *public* and *figure* has been used together so often that it has come to be considered a single thing: *public figure*. So no comma is required.

Seventh, commas should precede *Inc., Ltd.*, and the like:

> Cloverdell, Inc. Beamer, Ltd.

In a sentence, a comma also follows such abbreviations:

> Belle Brown, Ph.D., is the new tenant.

Eighth, commas are used both before and after the year in sentences that include month, day, and year:

> It will be sent by December 15, 1999, from our Cincinnati plant.

Some companies write dates in another form: 15 December 2000. No commas should be used in that case. Nor is a comma needed when only the month and year are present (December 2000).

Ninth, a comma may be used after an informal salutation in a letter to a personal friend. (In business letters, however, the salutation is followed by a colon.)

Tenth, a comma is used to separate a quotation from the rest of the sentence:

> Your warranty reads, "These conditions remain in effect for one year from date of purchase."

However, the comma is left out when the quotation as a whole is built into the structure of the sentence:

> He hurried off with an angry "Look where you're going."

Finally, a comma should be used whenever it's needed to avoid confusion or an unintended meaning. Compare the following:

> Ever since they have planned new ventures more carefully.

> Ever since, they have planned new ventures more carefully.

2.7 Dashes

Use a dash to surround a comment that is a sudden turn in thought:

> Membership in the IBSA—it's expensive but worth it—may be obtained by applying to our New York office.

A dash can also be used to emphasize a parenthetical word or phrase:

> Third-quarter profits—in excess of $2 million—are up sharply.

Finally, use dashes to set off a phrase that contains commas:

> All our offices—Milwaukee, New Orleans, and Phoenix—have sent representatives.

Don't confuse a dash with a hyphen. A dash separates and emphasizes words, phrases, and clauses more strongly than a comma or parentheses can; a hyphen ties two words so tightly that they almost become one word.

When typing a dash, type two hyphens with no space before, between, or after.

2.8 Hyphens

Hyphens are mainly used in three ways. The first is to separate the parts of compound words beginning with such prefixes as self-, ex-, quasi-, and all:

self-assured	quasi-official
ex-wife	all-important

However, hyphens are usually left out and the words closed up in words that have such prefixes as *pro, anti, non, un, inter,* and *extra*:

prolabor	nonunion
antifascist	interdepartmental

Exceptions occur when (1) the prefix occurs before a proper noun or (2) the vowel at the end of the prefix is the same as the first letter of the root word:

pro-Republican	anti-American
anti-inflammatory	extra-atmospheric

When in doubt, consult your dictionary.

Hyphens are also used in some compound adjectives, which are adjectives made up of two or more words. Specifically, you should use hyphens in compound adjectives that come before the noun:

an interest-bearing account	well-informed executives

However, you need not hyphenate when the adjective follows a linking verb:

> This account is interest bearing.
>
> Their executives are well informed.

You can shorten sentences that list similar hyphenated words by dropping the common part from all but the last word:

> Check the costs of first-, second-, and third-class postage.

Finally, hyphens may be used to divide words at the end of a typed line. Such hyphenation is best avoided, but when you have to divide words at the end of a line, do so correctly (see Section 3.4). A dictionary will show how words are divided into syllables.

2.9 Apostrophes

Use an apostrophe in the possessive form of a noun (but not in a pronoun):

> On *his* desk was a reply to *Bette Ainsley's* application for the *manager's* position.

Apostrophes are also used in place of the missing letter(s) of a contraction:

WHOLE WORDS	CONTRACTION
we will	we'll
do not	don't
they are	they're

2.10 Quotation Marks

Use quotation marks to surround words that are repeated exactly as they were said or written:

> The collection letter ended by saying, "This is your third and final notice."

Remember: (1) When the quoted material is a complete sentence, the first word is capitalized. (2) The final comma or period goes inside the closing quotation marks.

Quotation marks are also used to set off the title of a newspaper story, magazine article, or book chapter:

> You should read "Legal Aspects of the Collection Letter" in *Today's Credit.*

The book title is shown here in italics. When typewritten, the title is underlined. The same treatment is proper for newspaper and magazine titles. (Component Chapter B explains documentation style in more detail.)

Quotation marks may also be used to indicate special treatment for words or phrases, such as terms that you're using in an unusual or ironic way:

> Our management "team" spends more time squabbling than working to solve company problems.

When using quotation marks, take care to put in both sets, the closing marks as well as the opening ones.

Although periods and commas go inside any quotation marks, colons and semicolons go outside them. A question mark goes inside the quotation marks only if the quotation is a question:

> All that day we wondered, "Is he with us?"

If the quotation is not a question but the entire sentence is, the question mark goes outside:

> What did she mean by "You will hear from me"?

2.11 Parentheses

Use parentheses to surround comments that are entirely incidental:

> Our figures do not match yours, although (if my calculations are correct) they are closer than we thought.

Parentheses are also used in legal documents to surround figures in arabic numerals that follow the same amount in words:

> Remittance will be One Thousand Two Hundred Dollars ($1,200).

Be careful to put punctuation (period, comma, and so on) outside the parentheses unless it is part of the statement in parentheses.

2.12 Ellipses

Use ellipsis points, or dots, to indicate that material has been left out of a direct quotation. Use them only in direct quotations and only at the point where material was left out. In the following example, the first sentence is quoted in the second:

> The Dow Jones Industrial Average, which skidded 38.17 points in the previous five sessions, gained 4.61 to end at 2213.84.

> According to the Honolulu *Star Bulletin,* "The Dow Jones Industrial Average . . . gained 4.61" on June 10.

The number of dots in ellipses is not optional; always use three. Occasionally, the points of ellipsis come at the end of a sentence, where they seem to grow a fourth dot. Don't be fooled: One of the dots is a period.

2.13 Underscores and Italics

Usually a line typed underneath a word or phrase either provides emphasis or indicates the title of a book, magazine, or newspaper. If possible, use italics instead of an underscore. Italics (or underlining) should also be used for defining terms and for discussing words as words:

> In this report *net sales* refers to after-tax sales dollars.

> The word *building* is a common noun and should not be capitalized.

3.0 MECHANICS

The most obvious and least tolerable mistakes that a business writer makes are probably those related to grammar and punctuation. However, a number of small details, known as writing mechanics, demonstrate the writer's polish and reflect on the company's professionalism.

3.1 Capitals

You should, of course, capitalize words that begin sentences:

> *Before* hanging up, he said, *"We'll* meet here on Wednesday at noon."

A quotation that is a complete sentence should also begin with a capitalized word.

Capitalize the names of particular persons, places, and things (proper nouns):

> We sent *Ms. Larson* an application form, informing her that not all *applicants* are interviewed.

> Let's consider opening a branch in the *West,* perhaps at the *west* end of *Tucson, Arizona.*

> As *office buildings* go, the *Kinney Building* is a pleasant setting for *TDG Office Equipment.*

Ms. Larson's name is capitalized because she is a particular applicant, whereas the general term *applicant* is left uncapitalized. Likewise, *West* is capitalized when it refers to a particular place but not when it means a direction. In the same way, *office* and *building* are not capitalized when they are general terms (common nouns), but they are capitalized when they are part of the title of a particular office or building (proper nouns).

Titles within families, governments, or companies may also be capitalized:

> My *Uncle David* offered me a job, but I wouldn't be comfortable working for one of my uncles.

> We've never had a *president* quite like *President Sweeney.*

In addition, always capitalize the first word of the salutation and complimentary close of a letter:

> *Dear* Mr. Andrews: *Yours* very truly,

Finally, capitalize the first word after a colon when it begins a complete sentence:

> Follow this rule: *When* in doubt, leave it out.

Otherwise, the first word after a colon should not be capitalized (see Section 2.5).

3.2 Abbreviations

Abbreviations are used heavily in tables, charts, lists, and forms. They're used sparingly in prose paragraphs, however. Here are some abbreviations often used in business writing:

ABBREVIATION	FULL TERM
b/l	bill of lading
ca.	circa (about)
dol., dols.	dollar, dollars
etc.	et cetera (and so on)
FDIC	Federal Deposit Insurance Corporation
Inc.	Incorporated
L.f.	Ledger folio

ABBREVIATION	FULL TERM
Ltd.	Limited
mgr.	manager
NSF or N/S	not sufficient funds
P&L or P/L	profit and loss
reg.	regular
whsle.	wholesale

Because *etc.* contains a word meaning *and,* never write *and etc.*

3.3 Numbers

Numbers may correctly be handled many ways in business writing, so follow company style. In the absence of a set style, however, generally spell out all numbers from one to ten and use arabic numerals for the rest.

There are some exceptions to this general rule. First, never begin a sentence with a numeral:

> *Twenty* of us produced *641* units per week in the first *12* weeks of the year.

Second, use numerals for the numbers one through ten if they're in the same list as larger numbers:

> Our weekly quota rose from *9* to *15* to *27.*

Third, use numerals for percentages, time of day (except with *o'clock*), dates, and (in general) dollar amounts.

> Our division is responsible for *7* percent of total sales.

> The meeting is scheduled for *8:30* A.M. on August *2.*

> Add *$3* for postage and handling.

Use a comma in numbers with four digits (*1,257*) unless the company specifies another style.

When writing dollar amounts, use a decimal point only if cents are included. In lists of two or more dollar amounts, use the decimal point either for all or for none:

> He sent two checks, one for *$67.92* and one for *$90.00.*

3.4 Word Division

In general, avoid dividing words at the ends of lines. When you must, follow these rules:

- Don't divide one-syllable words (such as *since, walked,* and *thought*); abbreviations (*mgr.*); contractions (*isn't*); or numbers expressed in numbers (*117,500*).
- Divide words between syllables, as specified in a dictionary or word-division manual.
- Make sure that at least three letters of the divided word are moved to the second line: *sin-cerely* instead of *sincere-ly.*
- Do not end a page with more than three consecutive lines with hyphens.
- Leave syllables consisting of a single vowel at the end of the first line (*impedi-ment* instead of *imped-iment*), except when the single vowel is part of a suffix such as *-able, -ible, -ical,* or *-ity* (*re-spons-ible* instead of *re-sponsi-ble*).
- Divide between double letters (*tomor-row*), except when the root word ends in double letters (*call-ing* instead of *cal-ling*).
- Wherever possible, divide hyphenated words at the hyphen only: instead of *anti-inde-pendence,* use *anti-independence.*

4.0 VOCABULARY

Using the right word in the right place is a crucial skill in business communication. However, many pitfalls await the unwary.

4.1 Frequently Confused Words

Because the following sets of words sound similar, be careful not to use one when you mean to use the other:

WORD	MEANING
accede	to comply with
exceed	to go beyond
accept	to take
except	to exclude
access	admittance
excess	too much
advice	suggestion
advise	to suggest
affect	to influence
effect	the result
allot	to distribute
a lot	much or many
all ready	completely prepared
already	completed earlier
born	given birth to
borne	carried
capital	money; chief city
capitol	a government building
cite	to quote
sight	a view
site	a location

Word	Meaning
complement	complete amount; to go well with
compliment	to flatter
corespondent	party in a divorce suit
correspondent	letter writer
council	a panel of people
counsel	advice; a lawyer
defer	to put off until later
differ	to be different
device	a mechanism
devise	to plan
die	to stop living; a tool
dye	to color
discreet	careful
discrete	separate
envelop	to surround
envelope	a covering for a letter
forth	forward
fourth	number four
holey	full of holes
holy	sacred
wholly	completely
human	of people
humane	kindly
incidence	frequency
incidents	events
instance	example
instants	moments
interstate	between states
intrastate	within a state
later	afterward
latter	the second of two
lead	a metal
led	guided
lean	to rest at an angle
lien	a claim
levee	embankment
levy	tax
loath	reluctant
loathe	to hate
loose	free; not tight
lose	to mislay

Word	Meaning
material	substance
materiel	equipment
miner	mineworker
minor	underage person
moral	virtuous; a lesson
morale	sense of well-being
ordinance	law
ordnance	weapons
overdo	to do in excess
overdue	past due
peace	lack of conflict
piece	a fragment
pedal	a foot lever
peddle	to sell
persecute	to torment
prosecute	to sue
personal	private
personnel	employees
precedence	priority
precedents	previous events
principal	sum of money; chief; main
principle	general rule
rap	to knock
wrap	to cover
residence	home
residents	inhabitants
right	correct
rite	ceremony
write	to form words on a surface
role	a part to play
roll	to tumble; a list
root	part of a plant
rout	to defeat
route	a traveler's way
shear	to cut
sheer	thin, steep
stationary	immovable
stationery	paper
than	as compared with
then	at that time

WORD	MEANING
their	belonging to them
there	in that place
they're	they are
to	a preposition
too	excessively; also
two	the number
waive	to set aside
wave	a swell of water; a gesture
weather	atmospheric conditions
whether	if

In the preceding list only enough of each word's meaning is given to help you distinguish between the words in each group. Several meanings are left out entirely. For more complete definitions, consult a dictionary.

4.2 Frequently Misused Words

The following words tend to be misused for reasons other their sound. Reference books (including the *Random House College Dictionary,* revised edition; Follett's *Modern American Usage;* and Fowler's *Modern English Usage*) can help you with similar questions of usage.

a lot: When the writer means "many," *a lot* is always two separate words, never one.

correspond with: Use this phrase when you are talking about exchanging letters. Use *correspond to* when you mean "similar to." Use either *correspond with* or *correspond to* when you mean "relate to."

disinterested: This word means "fair, unbiased, having no favorites, impartial." If you mean "bored" or "not interested," use *uninterested.*

etc.: This is the abbreviated form of a Latin phrase, *et cetera.* It means "and so on" or "and so forth." The current tendency among business writers is to use English rather than Latin.

imply/infer: Both refer to hints. Their great difference lies in who is acting. The writer *implies;* the reader *infers,* sees between the lines.

lay: This is a transitive verb. Never use it for the intransitive *lie.* (See Section 1.3.3.)

less: Use *less* for uncountable quantities (such as amounts of water, air, sugar, and oil). Use *fewer* for countable quantities (such as numbers of jars, saws, words, pages, and humans). The same distinction applies to *much* and *little* (uncountable) versus *many* and *few* (countable).

like: Use *like* only when the word that follows is just a noun or a pronoun. Use *as* or *as if* when a phrase or clause follows:

She looks *like* him.
She did just *as* he had expected.
It seems *as if* she had plenty of time.

many/much: See *less.*

regardless: The *less* ending is the negative part. No word needs two negative parts, so it is illiterate to add *ir* (a negative prefix) at the beginning.

to me/personally: Use these phrases only when personal reactions, apart from company policy, are being stated (not often the case in business writing).

try: Always follow with *to,* never *and.*

verbal: People in the business community who are careful with language frown on those who use *verbal* to mean "spoken" or "oral." Many others do say "verbal agreement." Strictly speaking, *verbal* means "of words" and therefore includes both spoken and written words. Be guided in this matter by company usage.

4.3 Frequently Misspelled Words

All of us, even the world's best spellers, sometimes have to check a dictionary for the spelling of some words. People who have never memorized the spelling of commonly used words must look up so many that they grow exasperated and give up on spelling words correctly.

Don't expect perfection, and don't surrender. If you can memorize the spelling of just the words listed here, you'll need the dictionary far less often and you'll write with more confidence.

absence
absorption
accessible
accommodate
accumulate
achieve
advantageous
affiliated
aggressive
alignment
aluminum
ambience
analyze
apparent
appropriate
argument
asphalt

assistant
asterisk
auditor

bankruptcy
believable
brilliant
bulletin

calendar
campaign
category
ceiling
changeable
clientele
collateral
committee

comparative
competitor
concede
congratulations
connoisseur
consensus
convenient
convertible
corroborate
criticism

definitely
description
desirable
dilemma
disappear
disappoint
disbursement
discrepancy
dissatisfied
dissipate

eligible
embarrassing
endorsement
exaggerate
exceed
exhaust
existence
extraordinary

fallacy
familiar
flexible
fluctuation
forty

gesture
grievous

haphazard
harassment
holiday

illegible
immigrant
incidentally
indelible
independent
indispensable
insistent
intermediary
irresistible

jewelry
judgment
judicial

labeling
legitimate
leisure
license
litigation

maintenance
mathematics
mediocre
minimum

necessary
negligence
negotiable
newsstand
noticeable

occurrence
omission

parallel
pastime
peaceable
permanent
perseverance
persistent
personnel
persuade
possesses
precede
predictable
preferred
privilege
procedure
proceed
pronunciation
psychology
pursue

questionnaire

receive
recommend
repetition
rescind
rhythmical
ridiculous

salable
secretary
seize
separate
sincerely
succeed
suddenness
superintendent
supersede
surprise

tangible
tariff
technique
tenant
truly

unanimous
until

vacillate
vacuum
vicious

4.4 Transitional Words and Phrases

The following sentences don't communicate as well as they might because they lack a transitional word or phrase:

> Production delays are inevitable. Our current lag time in filling orders is one month.

A semicolon between the two sentences would signal a close relationship between their meanings, but it wouldn't even hint at what that relationship is. Here are the sentences, now linked by means of a semicolon, with a space for a transitional word or phrase:

> Production delays are inevitable; ___________, our current lag time in filling orders is one month.

Now read the sentence with *nevertheless* in the blank space. Now try *therefore, incidentally, in fact,* and *at any rate* in the blank. Each substitution changes the meaning of the sentence.

Here are some transitional words (called conjunctive adverbs) that will help you write more clearly:

accordingly	furthermore	moreover
anyway	however	otherwise
besides	incidentally	still
consequently	likewise	therefore
finally	meanwhile	

The following transitional phrases are used in the same way:

as a result	in other words
at any rate	in the second place
for example	on the other hand
in fact	to the contrary

When one of these words or phrases joins two independent clauses, it should be preceded by a semicolon and followed by a comma, as shown here:

> The consultant recommended a complete reorganization; moreover, she suggested that we drop several products.

APPENDIX II

CORRECTION SYMBOLS

Instructors often use these short, easy-to-remember correction symbols and abbreviations when evaluating students' writing. You can use them too, to understand your instructor's suggestions and to revise and proofread your own letters, memos, and reports. Refer to Appendix I for information on grammar and usage.

CONTENT AND STYLE

Acc	Accuracy. Check to be sure information is correct.
ACE	Avoid copying examples.
ACP	Avoid copying problems.
Adp	Adapt. Tailor message to reader.
App	Follow proper organization approach. (Refer to Chapter 5.)
Assign	Assignment. Review instructions for assignment.
AV	Active verb. Substitute active for passive.
Awk	Awkward phrasing. Rewrite.
BC	Be consistent.
BMS	Be more sincere.
Chop	Choppy sentences. Use longer sentences and more transitional phrases.
Con	Condense. Use fewer words.
CT	Conversational tone. Avoid using overly formal language.
Depers	Depersonalize. Avoid attributing credit or blame to any individual or group.
Dev	Develop. Provide greater detail.
Dir	Direct. Use direct approach; get to the point.
Emph	Emphasize. Develop this point more fully.
EW	Explanation weak. Check logic; provide more proof.
Fl	Flattery. Avoid compliments that are insincere.
FS	Figure of speech. Find a more accurate expression.
GNF	Good news first. Use direct order.
GRF	Give reasons first. Use indirect order.
GW	Goodwill. Put more emphasis on expressions of goodwill.
H/E	Honesty/ethics. Revise statement to reflect good business practices.
Imp	Imply. Avoid being direct.
Inc	Incomplete. Develop further.
Jar	Jargon. Use less specialized language.
Log	Logic. Check development of argument.
Neg	Negative. Use more positive approach or expression.
Obv	Obvious. Do not state point in such detail.
OC	Overconfident. Adopt humbler language.
OM	Omission.
Org	Organization. Strengthen outline.
OS	Off the subject. Close with point on main subject.
Par	Parallel. Use same structure.
Pom	Pompous. Rephrase in down-to-earth terms.
PV	Point of view. Make statement from reader's perspective rather than your own.
RB	Reader benefit. Explain what reader stands to gain.
Red	Redundant. Reduce number of times this point is made.
Ref	Reference. Cite source of information.
Rep	Repetitive. Provide different expression.
RS	Resale. Reassure reader that he or she has made a good choice.
SA	Service attitude. Put more emphasis on helping reader.

Sin — Sincerity. Avoid sounding glib or uncaring.
SL — Stereotyped language. Focus on individual's characteristics instead of on false generalizations.
Spec — Specific. Provide more specific statement.
SPM — Sales promotion material. Tell reader about related goods or services.
Stet — Let stand in original form.
Sub — Subordinate. Make this point less important.
SX — Sexist. Avoid language that contributes to gender stereotypes.
Tone — Tone needs improvement.
Trans — Transition. Show connection between points.
UAE — Use action ending. Close by stating what reader should do next.
UAS — Use appropriate salutation.
UAV — Use active voice.
Unc — Unclear. Rewrite to clarify meaning.
UPV — Use passive voice.
USS — Use shorter sentences.
V — Variety. Use different expression or sentence pattern.
W — Wordy. Eliminate unnecessary words.
WC — Word choice. Find a more appropriate word.
YA — "You" attitude. Rewrite to emphasize reader's needs.

Grammar, Usage, and Mechanics

Ab — Abbreviation. Avoid abbreviations in most cases; use correct abbreviation.
Adj — Adjective. Use adjective instead.
Adv — Adverb. Use adverb instead.
Agr — Agreement. Make subject and verb or noun and pronoun agree.
Ap — Appearance. Improve appearance.
Apos — Apostrophe. Check use of apostrophe.
Art — Article. Use correct article.
BC — Be consistent.
Cap — Capitalize.
Case — Use cases correctly.
CoAdj — Coordinate adjective. Insert comma between coordinate adjectives; delete comma between adjective and compound noun.
CS — Comma splice. Use period or semicolon to separate clauses.
DM — Dangling modifier. Rewrite so that modifier clearly relates to subject of sentence.
Exp — Expletive. Avoid expletive beginnings, such as it is, there are, there is, this is, and these are.
F — Format. Improve layout of document.
Frag — Fragment. Rewrite as complete sentence.
Gram — Grammar. Correct grammatical error.
HCA — Hyphenate compound adjective.
lc — Lowercase. Do not use capital letter.
M — Margins. Improve frame around document.
MM — Misplaced modifier. Place modifier close to word it modifies.
NRC — Nonrestrictive clause (or phrase). Separate from rest of sentence with commas.
P — Punctuation. Use correct punctuation.
Par — Parallel. Use same structure.
PH — Place higher. Move document up on page.
PL — Place lower. Move document down on page.
Prep — Preposition. Use correct preposition.
RC — Restrictive clause (or phrase). Remove commas that separate clause from rest of sentence.
RO — Run-on sentence. Separate two sentences with comma and coordinating conjunction or with semicolon.
SC — Series comma. Add comma before and.
Si — Split infinitive. Do not separate *to* from rest of verb.
Sp — Spelling error. Consult dictionary.
Stet — Let stand in original form.
S-V — Subject-verb pair. Do not separate with comma.
Syl — Syllabification. Divide word between syllables.
WD — Word division. Check dictionary for proper end-of-line hyphenation.
WW — Wrong word. Replace with another word.

Proofreading Marks

Symbol	Meaning	Symbol Used in Content	Corrected Copy
=	Align horizontally	meaningful re sult	meaningful result
||	Align vertically	1. Power cable 2. Keyboard	1. Power cable 2. Keyboard
(uc)	Capitalize	(uc) Do not immerse.	DO NOT IMMERSE.
≡	Capitalize	Pepsico, Inc.	PepsiCo, Inc.
	Close up	self- confidence	self-confidence
	Delete	harrassment ~~and abuse~~	harassment
(STET)	Restore to original	none ~~of the~~ (STET)	none of the
^	Insert	tirquoise shirts (u; and white)	turquoise and white shirts
^ ,	Insert comma	a, b and c	a, b, and c
⊙	Insert period	Harrigan et al ⊙	Harrigan et al.
/	Lowercase	TULSA, South of here	Tulsa, south of here
	Move left	Attention: Security	Attention: Security
	Move right	February 2, 2000	February 2, 2000
	Move down	Sincerely,	Sincerely,
	Move up	THIRD-QUARTER SALES	THIRD-QUARTER SALES
	Center	Awards Banquet	Awards Banquet
	Start new line	Marla Fenton, Manager, Distri- bution	Marla Fenton Manager, Distribution
	Run lines together	Manager, Distribution	Manager, Distribution
¶	Start paragraph	¶ The solution is easy to determine but difficult to implement in a competitive environment like the one we now face.	The solution is easy to determine but difficult to implement in a competitive environment like the one we now face.
#	Leave space	real estate testcase (# #)	real estate test case
	Spell out	(COD)	cash on delivery
(SP)	Spell out	(SP) Assn. of Biochem. Engrs.	Association of Biochemical Engineers
	Transpose	airy, light, casaul tone	light, airy, casual tone

REFERENCES

Chapter 1

1. Clarence Wooten Jr. and Andre Forde, founders of Metamorphosis Studios, personal communication, July 1996.
2. Raymond M. Olderman, *10 Minute Guide to Business Communication* (New York: Simon & Schuster, 1997), 1–2.
3. Joseph N. Scudder and Patricia J. Guinan, "Communication Competencies as Discriminators of Superiors' Ratings of Employee Performance," *Journal of Business Communication* 26, no. 3 (Summer 1989): 217–229; Joseph. F. Coates, "Today's Events Produce Tomorrow's Communication Issues," *IABC Communication World,* June–July 1991, 20–25.
4. Vanessa Dean Arnold, "The Communication Competencies Listed in Job Descriptions," *Bulletin of the Association for Business Communication* 40, no. 2 (June 1992): 15–17.
5. David Givens, "You Animal! How to Win Friends and Influence *Homo sapiens*," *Toastmaster,* August 1986, 9.
6. Stuart Berg Flexner, "From 'Gadzooks' to 'Nice,' the Language Keeps Changing," *U.S. News & World Report,* 18 February 1985, 59.
7. Michael H. Mescon, Courtland L. Bovée, and John V. Thill, *Business Today,* 9th ed. (New York: Prentice Hall, 1999), 214.
8. Augusta M. Simon, "Effective Listening: Barriers to Listening in a Diverse Business Environment," *Bulletin of the Association for Business Communication* 54, no. 3 (September 1991): 73–74; Phillip Morgan and H. Kent Baker, "Building a Professional Image: Improving Listening Behavior," *Supervisory Management,* November 1985, 35, 36.
9. Judith Valente and Bridget O'Brian, "Airline Cockpits Are No Place to Solo," *Wall Street Journal,* 8 February 1989, B1.
10. Joel Dreyfuss, "Workforce: The Three R's on the Shop Floor," *Fortune,* 28 May 1990, 86.
11. "An Ounce of Prevention," *American Management Association,* April 1995, 6; "AT&T Revamps Employee Communications to Emphasize 'New Direction' for '90s," *Public Relations Journal,* November 1990, 26, 41; Thomas J. Peters, "In Search of Communication Excellence," *Communication World,* February 1984, 12–15.
12. Gillian Flynn, "Pillsbury's Recipe Is Candid Talk," *Workforce*, February 1998, 56–57+.
13. J. David Pincus, Robert E. Rayfield, and J. Nicholas DeBonis, "Transforming CEOs into Chief Communications Officers," *Public Relations Journal,* November 1991, 22–27.
14. Joanne Cole, "Flying High at Southwest," *HR Focus*, May 1998, 8–9; James L. Heskett et al., "Putting the Service-Profit Chain to Work," *Harvard Business Review*, March/April 1994, 167.
15. Jim Braham, "A Rewarding Place to Work," *Industry Week,* 18 September 1989, 18.
16. Donald O. Wilson, "Diagonal Communication Links with Organizations," *Journal of Business Communication* 29, no. 2 (Spring 1992): 129–143.
17. Seth Lubove, "Destroying the Old Hierarchies," *Forbes,* 3 June 1996, 62–64.
18. Carol Hymowitz, "Spread the Word: Gossip Is Good," *Wall Street Journal,* 4 November 1988, B1; Donald B. Simmons, "The Nature of the Organizational Grapevine," *Supervisory Management,* November 1985, 40.
19. J. David Johnson, William A. Donohoe, Charles K. Atkin, and Sally Johnson, "Differences between Formal and Informal Communication Channels," *Journal of Business Communication,* 31, no. 2 (1994): 111–122.
20. Maureen Weiss, "Manager's Tool Kit: Tapping the Grapevine," *Across the Board,* April 1992, 62–63.
21. John Huey, "Wal-Mart: Will It Take Over the World?" *Fortune,* 30 January 1989, 56; Patricia Sellers, "Getting Customers to Love You," *Fortune,* 13 March 1989, 39; Stephen Phillips and Amy Dunkin, "King Customer," *Business Week,* 12 March 1990, 91; Charles Leerhsen, "How Disney Does It," *Newsweek,* 3 April 1989, 52; John Case, "Customer Service—The Last Word," *Inc.,* April 1991, 89–93.
22. Edmund L. Andrews and Laura M. Holson, "The Largest Acquisition of a Company in U.S. by a Foreign Buyer," *New York Times,* 7 May 1998, A1, C4.
23. Linda Grant, "How UPS Blew It," *Fortune,* 29 September 1997, 29–30.
24. "Presumed Guilty: Managing When Your Company's Name Is Mud," *Working Woman,* November 1991, 31; Judy A. Smith, "Crisis Communications; The War on Two Fronts," *Industry Week,* 20 May 1996, 136.
25. Edward A. Robinson, "America's Most Admired Companies," *Fortune,* 3 March 1997, 68, *Electric Library,* Online, accessed 2 September 1997; Susan Chandler, "Crisis Management: How TWA Faced the Nightmare," *Business Week,* 5 August 1996, 30; Kerri Selland, "Experts Say Corporations Ill-Prepared for Crises," *Reuters,* 23 July 1996, *Electric Library,* Online, accessed 2 September 1997; Thomas S. Mulligan, "TWA Garners Weak Marks for Crisis Management," *Los Angeles Times,* 20 July 1996, D1; Tom Incantalupo, "TWA's Image Polishing," *Newsday,* 23 July 1996, A49.
26. Some material adapted from Courtland L. Bovée, John V. Thill, Marian Burk Wood, and George P. Dovel, *Management* (New York: McGraw-Hill, 1993), 537–538.
27. Much of the material contained in the entire section on communication barriers has been adapted from Bovée, Thill, Wood, and Dovel, *Management,* 549–557.
28. Alice La Plante, "Still Drowning!" *Computerworld,* 10 March 1997, 69–70.
29. "Information Deluge Clogging Workplace," *Honolulu Advertiser,* 25 May 1998, B6; Stephen Barr, "Message Madness," *CFO,* May 1998, 25.
30. Diana Kunde, "Companies Get the Message: Workers Are Drowning in E-Mail," *San Diego Union-Tribune* 27 October 1997, C8.
31. Peter F. Drucker, "Management's New Paradigms," *Forbes,* 5 October 1998, 152–176.
32. J. Michael Sproule, *Communication Today* (Glenview, Ill.: Scott Foresman, 1981), 329.
33. Louis Hecht, corporate secretary of Molex, personal communication, May 1997; Matt Krantz, "Molex Inc.'s Fred Krehbiel," *Investor's Business Daily*, 7 January 1997, 1; Paul Conley, "Molex Sets Record-Breaking Global Pace," *Chicago Tribune*, 2 August 1996; Dave Savona, "The Billion-Dollar Globetrotter," *International Business*, November 1995, 52–56; Robert Knight, "How Molex, Inc. Connected in World Markets," *Chicago Enterprise*, July–August 1994, 24–27; Ronald E. Yates, "Firm's Growth Tied to Global Connections," *Chicago Tribune*, 6 February 1994, 8.
34. Carol Hymowitz, "If The Walls Had Ears You Wouldn't Have Any Less Privacy," *Wall Street Journal,* 19 May 1998, B1.
35. Kenneth Hein, "Hungry for Feedback," *Incentive,* September 1997, 9+.
36. John A. Byrne, "Jack," *Business Week,* 8 June 1998, 92–111.
37. A. Thomas Young, "Ethics in Business: Business of Ethics," *Vital Speeches,* 15 September 1992, 725–730.
38. Bruce W. Speck, "Writing Professional Codes of Ethics to Introduce Ethics in Business Writing," *Bulletin of the Association for Business Communication* 53, no. 3 (September 1990): 21–26; H. W. Love, "Communication, Accountability and Professional Discourse: The Interaction of Language Values and Ethical Values," *Journal of Business Ethics* 11 (1992): 883–892; Kathryn C. Rentz and Mary Beth Debs, "Language and Corporate Values: Teaching Ethics in Business Writing Courses," *Journal of Business Communication* 24, no. 3 (Summer 1987): 37–48.
39. David Grier, "Confronting Ethical Dilemmas: The View from Inside—A Practitioner's Perspective," *Vital Speeches,* 1 December 1989, 100–104.
40. Joseph L. Badaracco Jr., "Business Ethics: Four Spheres of Executive Responsibility," *California Management Review,* Spring 1992, 64–79;

Kenneth Blanchard and Norman Vincent Peale, *The Power of Ethical Management* (Reprint, 1989; New York: Fawcett Crest, 1991), 7–17.
41. Jules Harcourt, "Developing Ethical Messages: A Unit of Instruction for the Basic Business Communication Course," *Bulletin of the Association for Business Communication* 53, no. 3 (September 1990): 17–20; John D. Pettit, Bobby Vaught, and Kathy J. Pulley, "The Role of Communication in Organizations," *Journal of Business Communication* 27, no. 3 (Summer 1990): 233–249; Kenneth R. Andrews, "Ethics in Practice," *Harvard Business Review,* September–October 1989, 99–104; Priscilla S. Rogers and John M. Swales, "We the People? An Analysis of the Dana Corporation Policies Document," *Journal of Business Communication* 27, no. 3 (Summer 1990): 293–313; Larry Reynolds, "The Ethics Audit," *Business Ethics,* July–August 1991, 120–122.
42. Susan L. Fry, "How to Succeed in the New Europe," *Public Relations Journal,* January 1991, 17–21.
43. U.S. Bureau of Labor Statistics, *Occupational Outlook Quarterly, 1994.*
44. Christine Begole, "How to Get the Productivity Edge," *Working Woman,* May 1991, 47, 52, 54, 56, 58, 60.
45. Laurey Berk and Phillip G. Clampitt, "Finding the Right Path in the Communication Maze," *IABC Communication World,* October 1991, 28–32.
46. Clarence Wooten Jr. and Andre Forde, founders of Metamorphosis Studios, personal communication, July 1996.
47. "When Rumors Disrupt Your Staff," *Working Woman,* October 1992, 36.

Chapter 2

1. Virginia Johnson, director of human relations, 3M, personal communication, August 1993.
2. David Lewis, *The Secret Language of Success* (New York: Carroll & Graf, 1989), 67, 170.
3. Nido Qubein, *Communicate Like a Pro* (New York: Berkeley Books, 1986), 97.
4. Dale G. Leathers, *Successful Nonverbal Communication: Principles and Applications* (New York: Macmillan, 1986), 19.
5. Gerald H. Graham, Jeanne Unrue, and Paul Jennings, "The Impact of Nonverbal Communication in Organizations: A Survey of Perceptions," *Journal of Business Communication* 28, no. 1 (Winter 1991), 45–62.
6. Jill Neimark, "Reach Out and . . ." *Savvy,* February 1985, 42.
7. Graham, Unrue, and Jennings, "The Impact of Nonverbal Communication in Organizations"; Dianna Booher, *Communicate with Confidence* (New York: McGraw-Hill, 1994), 363–370.
8. Beverly Davenport Sypher, Robert N. Bastrom, and Joy Hart Seibert, "Listening, Communication Abilities, and Success at Work," *Journal of Business Communication* 26, no. 4 (Fall 1989): 293–301.
9. Robyn D. Clarke, "Do You Hear What I Hear?" *Black Enterprise,* May 1998, 129.
10. Soundview Executive Staff, *Skills for Success* (Middlebury, Vt.: Soundview Executive Book Summaries, 1989), 21–22.
11. Clarke, "Do You Hear What I Hear?" Dot Yandle, "Listening to Understand," *Pryor Report Management Newsletter Supplement* 15, no. 8 (August 1998): 13.
12. Augusta M. Simon, "Effective Listening: Barriers to Listening in a Diverse Business Environment," *Bulletin of the Association for Business Communication* 54, no. 3 (September 1991): 73–74.
13. Jennifer Lawson, "How I Did It: Persuading Staffers to Get with the Program," *Working Woman,* April 1991, 57–58, 60.
14. Bob Lamons, "Good Listeners Are Better Communicators," *Marketing News,* 11 September 1995, 13+; Phillip Morgan and H. Kent Baker, "Building a Professional Image: Improving Listening Behavior," *Supervisory Management,* November 1985, 35–36.
15. "An Added Joy of E-Mail: Fewer Face-to-Face Meetings," *Wall Street Journal,* 14 July 1998, A1.
16. J. Michael Sproule, *Communication Today* (Glenview, Ill.: Scott, Foresman, 1981), 69.
17. Sproule, *Communication Today*, 69.
18. Sproule, *Communication Today*, 69.
19. Lyman K. Steil, Larry L. Barker, and Kittie W. Watson, *Effective Listening: Key to Your Success* (Reading, Mass.: Addison-Wesley, 1983), 21–22; Sherwyn P. Morreale and Courtland L. Bovée, *Excellence in Public Speaking* (Orlando, Fla.: Harcourt Brace, 1998), 72–76.
20. Patrick J. Collins, *Say It with Power and Confidence* (Upper Saddle River, N.J.: Prentice Hall, 1997), 40–45.
21. Collins, *Say It with Power and Confidence,* 40–45.
22. Robert A. Luke Jr., "Improving Your Listening Ability," *Supervisory Management,* June 1992, 7; Madelyn Burley-Allen, "Listening for Excellence in Communication," *The Dynamics of Behavior Newsletter* 2, no. 2 (Summer 1992): 1; Lamons, "Good Listners Are Better Communicators."
23. Stephen P. Robbins, *Organizational Behavior,* 6th ed. (Upper Saddle River, N.J.: Prentice Hall, 1993), 343–345.
24. Michael H. Mescon, Courtland L. Bovée, and John V. Thill, *Business Today* (Upper Saddle River, N.J.: Prentice Hall, 1999), 203.
25. Richard L. Daft, *Management,* 4th ed. (Fort Worth: Dryden, 1997), 338.
26. Claudia H. Deutsch, "Teamwork or Tug of War?" *New York Times,* 26 August 1990, sec. 3, 27.
27. B. Aubrey Fisher, *Small Group Decision Making: Communication and the Group Process,* 2nd ed. (New York: McGraw-Hill, 1980), 145–149.
28. Julia Lawlor, "Videoconferencing: From Stage Fright to Stage Presence," *New York Times,* 27 August 1998, D6.
29. Heath Row, "The Joys of Togetherness," *Webmaster,* June 1997, 44–48.
30. Row, "The Joys of Togetherness."
31. Mary Beth Debs, "Recent Research on Collaborative Writing in Industry," *Technical Communication* (November 1991), 476–484.
32. Ruth G. Newman, "Communication: Collaborative Writing with Purpose and Style," *Personnel Journal,* April 1988, 37–38; William P. Galle Jr., Beverly H. Nelson, Donna W. Luse, and Maurice F. Villere, *Business Communication: A Technology-Based Approach* (Chicago: Irwin, 1996), 256.
33. Galle, Nelson, Luse, and Villere, *Business Communication*, 260.
34. Brenda Park Sundo, "Are You Noticing Too Many Yawns?" *Workforce,* April 1998, 16–17.
35. "Better Meetings Benefit Everyone: How to Make Yours More Productive," *Working Communicator Bonus Report,* July 1998.
36. Ken Blanchard, "Meetings Can Be Effective," *Supervisory Management,* October 1992, 5.
37. William C. Waddell and Thomas A. Rosko, "Conducting an Effective Off-Site Meeting," *Management Review,* February 1993, 40–44.
38. "Better Meetings Benefit Everyone."
39. Kathy E. Gill, "Board Primer: Parliamentary Procedure," *Association Management,* 1993, L-39.
40. Janis Graham, "Sharpen Your Negotiating Skills," *Sylvia Porter's Personal Finance,* December 1985, 54–58.
41. Jesse S. Nirenberg, *Getting Through to People* (Paramus, N.J.: Prentice Hall, 1973), 134–142.
42. Nirenberg, *Getting Through to People,* 134–142.
43. Nirenberg, *Getting Through to People,* 134–142.
44. Virginia Johnson, director of human relations, 3M, personal communication, August 1993.

Chapter 3

1. Michiru Tamanai, director of training, and Kayomi Kaneda, training administrator, Sheraton Hotels Hawaii, personal communications, August 1998.
2. President, Proclamation, "World Trade Week, 1997," *MSPress WIRE,* 22 May 1997, *Electric Library,* Online, accessed 17 July 1997; James Toedtman, "Battle over U.S. Trade Fought across 1,000 Fronts," *Newsday,* 1997, *Electric Library,* accessed Online, 17 July 1997.
3. President, Proclamation, "World Trade Week, 1997"; Toedtman, "Battle over U.S. Trade Fought across 1,000 Fronts."
4. Elizabeth Howard, "Going Global: What It Really Means to Communicators," *IABC Communication World,* April 1995, 12–15; Joel Russel, "NAFTA in the Real World," *Hispanic Business,* June 1996, 22–28.
5. "Eurostat: Total EU GDP Up by 2.5 Percent in 1995," *Xinhua News Agency,* 5 February 1997, *Electric Library,* Online, accessed July 1997; Edmund L. Andrews, "Europeans Clear Remaining Hurdle to Currency Unit—11 Nations Pass the Test," *New York Times,* 28 February 1998, A1, B2.
6. Bernard Wysocki Jr., "U.S. Firms Increase Overseas Investments," *Wall Street Journal,* 9 April 1990, A1; "U.S. Affiliates of Foreign Companies: Operations in 1988," *Survey of Current Business* 70 (July 1990): 127–143; Blayne Cutler, "Foreign Staff," *American Demographics,* August 1989, 16.
7. Much of the global trade information in this section is from David J. Rachman, Michael H. Mescon, Courtland L. Bovée, and John V. Thill, *Business Today* (Upper Saddle River, N.J.: Prentice Hall, 1999), Chapter 2.

8. Samuel Greengard, "How Technology Will Change the Workplace," *Workforce,* January 1998, 78–84.
9. Philip R. Harris and Robert T. Moran, *Managing Cultural Differences,* 3d ed. (Houston: Gulf, 1991), 394–397, 429–430.
10. Larry A. Samovar and Richard E. Porter, "Basic Principles of Intercultural Communication," in *Intercultural Communication: A Reader,* 6th ed., edited by Larry A. Samovar and Richard E. Porter (Belmont, Calif.: Wadsworth, 1991), 12.
11. John P. Fernandez, *Managing a Diverse Work Force* (Lexington, Mass.: Lexington Books, 1991), 5; Michael Mandel and Christopher Farrell, "The Immigrants," *Business Week,* 13 July 1992, 114–120, 122; David Jamieson and Julie O'Mara, *Managing Workforce 2000: Gaining the Diversity Advantage* (San Francisco: Jossey-Bass, 1991), 21.
12. Gus Tyler, "Tokyo Signs the Paychecks," *New York Times Book Review,* 12 August 1990, 7.
13. Kathleen K. Reardon, "It's the Thought That Counts," *Harvard Business Review,* September–October 1984, 141.
14. Otto Kreisher, "Annapolis Has a New Attitude toward Sexual Harassment," *San Diego Union,* 30 July 1990, A-6.
15. Tzöl Zae Chung, "Culture: A Key to Management Communication between the Asian-Pacific Area and Europe," *European Management Journal* 9, no. 4 (December 1991): 419–424.
16. James Calvert Scott, "Using an International Business-Meal Function to Develop Sociocultural Skills," *Business Communication Quarterly* 58, no. 3 (1995): 55–57.
17. Mary A. DeVries, *Internationally Yours* (New York: Houghton Mifflin, 1994), 194.
18. Robert O. Joy, "Cultural and Procedural Differences That Influence Business Strategies and Operations in the People's Republic of China," *SAM Advanced Management Journal,* Summer 1989, 29–33.
19. Hal Lancaster, "Workday Etiquette: Know the Right Fork and Watch That E-Mail," *Wall Street Journal,* 1 April 1998, B1.
20. "Pakistan: A Congenial Business Climate," *Nation's Business,* July 1986, 50.
21. David A. Victor, *International Business Communication* (New York: Harper-Collins, 1992), 234–239; Mohan R. Limaye and David A. Victor, "Cross-Cultural Business Communication Research: State of the Art and Hypotheses for the 1990s," *Journal of Business Communication* 28, no. 3 (Summer 1991): 277–299.
22. Carley H. Dodd, *Dynamics of Intercultural Communication,* 3d ed. (Dubuque, Iowa: Brown, 1991), 215.
23. Linda Beamer, "Teaching English Business Writing to Chinese-Speaking Business Students," *Bulletin of the Association for Business Communication* 57, no. 1 (1994): 12–18.
24. Edward T. Hall, "Context and Meaning," in *Intercultural Communication,* edited by Samovar and Porter, 46–55.
25. Beamer, "Teaching English Business Writing to Chinese-Speaking Business Students."
26. Dodd, *Dynamics of Intercultural Communication,* 69–70.
27. James Wilfong and Toni Seger, *Taking Your Business Global* (Franklin Lakes, N.J.: Career Press, 1997), 277–278.
28. Wilfong and Seger, *Taking Your Business Global,* 277–278.
29. Samovar and Porter, "Basic Principles of Intercultural Communication," 5–22; David A. Victor, personal communication, 1993.
30. Laray M. Barna, "Stumbling Blocks in Intercultural Communication," in *Intercultural Communication,* edited by Samovar and Porter, 345–352.
31. Jean A. Mausehund, Susan A. Timm, and Albert S. King, "Diversity Training: Effects of an Intervention Treatment on Nonverbal Awareness," *Business Communication Quarterly* 38, no. 1 (1995): 27–30.
32. Sharon Ruhly, *Intercultural Communication,* 2d ed., MODCOM (Modules in Speech Communication) (Chicago: Science Research Associates, 1982), 14.
33. Karen P. H. Lane, "Greasing the Bureaucratic Wheel," *North American International Business,* August 1990, 35–37; Arthur Aronoff, "Complying with the Foreign Corrupt Practices Act," *Business America,* 11 February 1991, 10–11; Bill Shaw, "Foreign Corrupt Practices Act: A Legal and Moral Analysis," *Journal of Business Ethics* 7 (1988): 789–795.
34. Harris and Moran, *Managing Cultural Differences,* 260.
35. Marita van Oldenborgh, "Court with Care," *International Business,* April 1995, 20–22.
36. J. Robert Carleton, "Cultural Due Diligence," *Training,* November 1997, 67–75.
37. Tim Jones, "Shrinking World Reshapes Auto Industry," *Chicago Tribune,* 10 May 1998, sec. 5, 1, 14; Edmund L. Andrews and Laura M. Holson, "Significant Risks—The Largest Acquisition of a Company in U.S. by a Foreign Buyer," *New York Times,* 7 May 1998, A-1, C-4; Robyn Meredith, "Two Auto Makers with Long Histories Attempt a Trans-Atlantic Marriage," *New York Times,* 7 May 1998, C-4.
38. Stephen Dolainski, "Are Expats Getting Lost in the Translation?" *Workforce,* February 1997, 32–39.
39. "Less Yiddish, More Tagalog," *U.S. News & World Report,* 10 May 1993, 16; Gary Levin, "Marketers Learning New Languages for Ads," *Advertising Age,* 10 May 1993, 33.
40. Victor, *International Business Communication,* 39; Harris and Moran, *Managing Cultural Differences,* 64.
41. Wilfong and Seger, *Taking Your Business Global,* 232.
42. Wilfong and Seger, *Taking Your Business Global,* 232.
43. Vern Terpstra, *The Cultural Environment of International Business* (Cincinnati: South-Western, 1979), 19.
44. Victor, *International Business Communication,* 36.
45. Geert Hofstede, *Cultures and Organizations* (London: McGraw-Hill, 1991), 211.
46. Richard W. Brislin, "Prejudice in Intercultural Communication," in *Intercultural Communication,* edited by Samovar and Porter, 366–370.
47. James S. O'Rourke IV, "International Business Communication: Building a Course from the Ground Up," *Bulletin of the Association for Business Communication* 56, no. 4 (1993): 22–27.
48. Jensen J. Zhao and Calvin Parks, "Self-Assessment of Communication Behavior: An Experiential Learning Exercise for Intercultural Business Success," *Business Communication Quarterly* 58, no. 1 (1995): 20–26; Dodd, *Dynamics of Intercultural Communication,* 142–143, 297–299; Stephen P. Robbins, *Organizational Behavior,* 6th ed. (Paramus, N.J.: Prentice Hall, 1993), 345.
49. Kevin J. Walsh, "How to Negotiate European Style," *Journal of European Business,* July–August 1993, 48.
50. Michele Marchetti, "Selling in China? Go Slowly," *Sales and Marketing Management,* January 1997, 35–36.
51. Susan A. Hellweg, Larry A. Samovar, and Lisa Skow, "Cultural Variations in Negotiation Styles," in *Intercultural Communication,* edited by Samovar and Porter, 185–192.
52. Doreen Mangan, "What's New in Language Translation: A Tool for Examining Foreign Patents and Research," *New York Times,* 19 November 1989, sec. 3, 15.
53. Mona Casady and Lynn Wasson, "Written Communication Skills of International Business Persons," *Bulletin of the Association for Business Communication* 57, no. 4 (1994): 36–40.
54. Michiru Tamanai, director of training, and Kayomi Kaneda, training administrator, Sheraton Hotels Hawaii, personal communications, August 1998.
55. Michael Copeland, specialist, international training, personal communication, January 1990.

Chapter 4

1. Jeff Hagen, director of consumer services, General Mills, personal communication, July 1997.
2. Mary Cullinan and Ce Ce Iandoli, "What Activities Help to Improve Your Writing? Some Unsettling Student Responses," *Bulletin of the Association for Business Communication* 54, no. 4 (December 1991): 8–10; Ruth Yontz, "Providing a Rationale for the Process Approach," *Journal of Business Communication* 24, no.1 (Winter 1987): 17–19; Annette Shelby, "Note on Process," *Journal of Business Communication* 24, no.1 (Winter 1987): 21.
3. Dianna Booher, *Communicate with Confidence* (New York: McGraw-Hill, 1994), 93.
4. Sanford Kaye, "Writing Under Pressure," *Soundview Executive Book Summaries* 10, no. 12, part 2 (December 1988): 1–8.
5. Peter Bracher, "Process, Pedagogy, and Business Writing," *Journal of Business Communication* 24, no.1 (Winter 1987): 43–50.
6. Mahalingam Subbiah, "Adding a New Dimension to the Teaching of Audience Analysis: Cultural Awareness," *IEEE Transactions on Professional Communication* 35, no. 1 (March 1992): 14–19; Ronald E. Dulek, John S. Fielden, and John S. Hill, "International Communication: An Executive Primer," *Business Horizons,* January–February 1991, 20–25; Dwight W. Stevenson, "Audience Analysis across Cultures," *Journal of Technical Writing and Communication* 13, no. 4 (1983): 319–330.
7. Iris I. Varner, "Internationalizing Business Communication Courses," *Bulletin of the Association for Business Communication* 50, no.4 (December 1987): 7–11.

8. Mary Munter, *Guide to Managerial Communication* (Paramus, N.J.: Prentice Hall, 1982), 9.
9. Elizabeth Blackburn and Kelly Belanger, "You-Attitude and Positive Emphasis: Testing Received Wisdom in Business Communication," *Bulletin of the Association for Business Communication* 56, no. 2 (June 1993): 1–9.
10. Annette N. Shelby and N. Lamar Reinsch, Jr., "Positive Emphasis and You Attitude: An Empirical Study," *Journal of Business Communication* 32, no. 4 (1995): 303–322.
11. Roger P. Wilcox, *Communication at Work: Writing and Speaking* (Boston: Houghton Mifflin, 1977), 30.
12. Judy E. Pickens, "Terms of Equality: A Guide to Bias-Free Language," *Personnel Journal,* August 1985, 24.
13. Lawrence W. Hugenberg, Renée M. LaCivita, and Andra M. Lubanovic, "International Business and Training: Preparing for the Global Economy," *Journal of Business Communication* 33, no. 2 (1996): 105–222.
14. Lisa Taylor, "Communicating about People with Disabilities: Does the Language We Use Make a Difference?" *Bulletin of the Association for Business Communication* 53, no. 3 (September 1990): 65–67.
15. Taylor, "Communicating about People with Disabilities."
16. Laurey Berk and Phillip G. Clampitt, "Finding the Right Path in the Communication Maze," *IABC Communication World,* October 1991, 28–32.
17. Al Schlachtmeyer and Max Caldwell, "Communicating Creatively," *IABC Communication World,* June–July 1991, 26–29.
18. Berk and Clampitt, "Finding the Right Path in the Communication Maze."
19. Raymond M. Olderman, *10 Minute Guide to Business Communication* (New York: Alpha Books, 1997), 19–20.
20. Mohan R. Limaye and David A. Victor, "Cross-Cultural Business Communication Research: State of the Art and Hypotheses for the 1990s," *Journal of Business Communication* 28, no. 3 (Summer 1991): 277–299.
21. Berk and Clampitt, "Finding the Right Path in the Communication Maze."
22. Berk and Clampitt, "Finding the Right Path in the Communication Maze."
23. Jeff Hagen, director of consumer services, General Mills, personal communication, July 1997.

Chapter 5

1. Julian Santoyo, chief financial officer, Community Health Group, personal communication, March 1996.
2. Carol S. Mull, "Orchestrate Your Ideas," *The Toastmaster,* February 1987, 19.
3. Susan Hall and Theresa Tiggeman, "Getting the Big Picture: Writing to Learn in a Finance Class," *Business Communication Quarterly* 58, no. 1 (1995): 12–15.
4. Bruce B. MacMillan, "How to Write to Top Management," *Business Marketing,* March 1985, 138.
5. MacMillan, "How to Write to Top Management."
6. Ernest Thompson, "Some Effects of Message Structure on Listener's Comprehension," *Speech Monographs* 34 (March 1967): 51–57.
7. Based on the Pyramid Model developed by Barbara Minto of McKinsey & Company, management consultants.
8. Philip Subanks, "Messages, Models, and the Messy World of Memos," *Bulletin of the Association for Business Communication* 57, no. 1 (1994): 33–34.
9. Mary A. DeVries, *Internationally Yours* (Boston: Houghton Mifflin, 1994), 61.
10. Susan Benjamin, *Words at Work* (Reading, Mass: Addison-Wesley, 1997), 136–137.
11. Randolph H. Hudson, Gertrude M. McGuire, and Bernard J. Selzler, *Business Writing: Concepts and Applications* (Los Angeles: Roxbury, 1983), 79–82.
12. Kathy M. Kristof, "Mutual Funds Try Something New: Plain English," *Los Angeles Times,* 1 November 1992, D4.
13. William M. Bulkeley, "Software Writers Try to Speak a Language Users Understand," *Wall Street Journal,* 30 June 1992, B6.
14. Peter Crow, "Plain English: What Counts Besides Readability?" *Journal of Business Communication* 25, no. 1 (Winter 1988): 87–95.
15. Portions of this section are adapted from Courtland L. Bovée, *Techniques of Writing Business Letters, Memos, and Reports* (Sherman Oaks, Calif.: Banner Books International, 1978), 13–90.
16. Robert Hartwell Fiske, *Thesaurus of Alternatives to Worn-Out Words and Phrases* (Cincinnati: Writer's Digest Books, 1994), 171.
17. Iris I. Varner, "Internationalizing Business Communication Courses," *Bulletin of the Association for Business Communication* 50, no. 4 (December 1987): 7–11.
18. Alinda Drury, "Evaluating Readability," *IEEE Transactions on Professional Communication* PC-28 (December 1985): 12.
19. DeVries, *Internationally Yours,* 168; Benjamin, *Words at Work,* 61, 140–141.
20. William Zinsser, *On Writing Well,* 5th ed. (New York: HarperCollins, 1994), 117.
21. Jill H. Ellsworth and Matthew V. Ellsworth, *The Internet Business Book* (New York: Wiley, 1994), 91.
22. David Angell and Brent Heslop, *The Elements of E-Mail Style* (Reading, Mass: Addison-Wesley, 1994), 10.
23. Lance Cohen, "How to Improve Your E-Mail Messages," http://galaxy.einet/galaxy/Business-and-Commerce/Management/Communications/How_to_Improve_Your Email.html.
24. Angell and Heslop, *The Elements of E-Mail Style,* 24.
25. Angell and Heslop, *The Elements of E-Mail Style,* 18–19.
26. Renee B. Horowitz and Marian G. Barchilon, "Stylistic Guidelines for E-mail," *IEEE Transactions on Professional Communication* 37, no. 4 (December 1994): 207–212; Cohen, "How to Improve Your E-Mail Messages."
27. Most of the material in this section is adapted from Angell and Heslop, *The Elements of E-Mail Style,* 21, 30, 117; Ellsworth and Ellsworth, *The Internet Business Book,* 99; William Eager, *Using the Internet* (Indianapolis: Que Corporation, 1994), 99; Cohen, "How to Improve Your E-Mail Messages"; William Eager, Larry Donahue, David Forsyth, Kenneth Mitton, and Martin Waterhouse, *Net.Search* (Indianapolis: Que Corporation, 1995), 225.
28. Angell and Heslop, *The Elements of E-Mail Style*, 20.
29. Horowitz and Barchilon, "Stylistic Guidelines for E-Mail"; Angell and Heslop, *The Elements of E-Mail Style,* 22.
30. Julian Santoyo, chief financial officer, Community Health Group, personal communication, March 1996.
31. Milton Moskowitz, Michael Katz, and Robert Levering, eds., *Everybody's Business: An Almanac* (San Francisco: Harper & Row, 1980), 131.
32. Randolph H. Hudson, Gertrude M. McGuire, and Bernard J. Selzler, *Business Writing: Concepts and Applications* (Los Angeles: Roxbury, 1983), 27.
33. Benjamin, *Words at Work,* 121.
34. Benjamin, *Words at Work,* 12.

Chapter 6

1. Adrianne Proeller, corporate communications manager, Turner Broadcasting System, personal communication, March 1993.
2. Iris I. Varner, "Internationalizing Business Communication Courses," *Bulletin of the Association for Business Communication* 50, no. 4 (December 1987): 7–11.
3. Kevin T. Stevens, Kathleen C. Stevens, and William P. Stevens, "Measuring the Readability of Business Writing: The Cloze Procedure versus Readability Formulas," *Journal of Business Communication* 29, no. 4 (1992): 367–382; Alinda Drury, "Evaluating Readability," *IEEE Transactions on Professional Communication* PC-28 (December 1985): 11.
4. Susan Benjamin, *Words at Work* (Reading, Mass: Addison-Wesley, 1997), 71.
5. William Zinsser, *On Writing Well,* 5th ed. (New York: HarperCollins, 1994), 126.
6. "Message Lost in Some Memos," *USA Today,* 25 March 1987, 1A.
7. Zinsser, *On Writing Well,* 7, 17.
8. Mary A. DeVries, *Internationally Yours* (Boston, Mass.: Houghton Mifflin, 1994), 160.
9. Zinsser, *On Writing Well,* vii–12.
10. Zinsser, *On Writing Well,* 9.
11. Joel Haness, "How to Critique a Document," *IEEE Transactions on Professional Communication* PC-26, no. 1 (March 1983): 15–17.
12. Charles E. Risch, "Critiquing Written Material," *Manage* 35, no. 4 (1983): 4–6.
13. Risch, "Critiquing Written Material."
14. "A Misspelling Proves Costly," *New York Times,* 23 November 1991, 29.
15. Stephen H. Wildstrom, "A Clipboard with a Memory," *Business Week,* 27 April 1998, 20; Jim Forbes and John D. Ruley, "Palm PCs Go Hand to Hand," *Windows Magazine,* August 1998, 194+.
16. William Wresch, Donald Pattow, and James Gifford, *Writing for the Twenty-First Century: Computers and Research Writing* (New York:

McGraw-Hill, 1988), 192–211; Melissa E. Barth, *Strategies for Writing with the Computer* (New York: McGraw-Hill, 1988), 108–109, 140, 172–177.

17. Portions of the following sections are adapted from Roger C. Parker, *Looking Good in Print,* 2d ed. (Chapel Hill, N.C.: Ventana Press, 1990).
18. Raymond W. Beswick, "Designing Documents for Legibility," *Bulletin of the Association for Business Communication* 50, no. 4 (December 1987): 34–35.
19. Patsy Nichols, "Desktop Packaging," *Bulletin of the Association for Business Communication* 54, no. 1 (March 1991): 43–45; Beswick, "Designing Documents for Legibility."
20. Beswick, "Designing Documents for Legibility."
21. "The Process Model of Document Design," *IEEE Transactions on Professional Communication* PC-24, no. 4 (December 1981): 176–178.
22. Eric J. Adams, "The Fax of Global Business," *World Trade,* August–September 1991, 34–39.
23. Adrianne Proeller, corporate communications manager, Turner Broadcasting System, personal communication, March 1993.

Chapter 7

1. Silva Raker, vice president of merchandise, The Nature Company, personal communication, February 1993; The Nature Company home page www.natureco.com, 13 June 1996.
2. Daniel P. Finkelman and Anthony R. Goland, "Customers Once Can Be Customers for Life," *Information Strategy: The Executive's Journal,* Summer 1990, 5–9.
3. Susan Stobaugh, "Watch Your Language," *Inc.,* May 1985, 156.
4. *Techniques for Communicators* (Chicago: Lawrence Ragan Communication, 1995), 34, 36.
5. John A. Byrne, "Jack," *Business Week,* 8 June 1998, 91–112.
6. Donna Larcen, "Authors Share the Words of Condolence," *Los Angeles Times,* December 20, 1991, E11.
7. Silva Raker, vice president of merchandise, The Nature Company, personal communication, February 1993; The Nature Company home page www.natureco.com, 13 June 1996.
8. Kendall Hamilton, "Getting Up, Getting Air," *Newsweek,* 13 May 1996, 68.
9. Adapted from Calvin Sims, "Reporter Disciplined for Reading His Coworkers' Electronic Mail," *New York Times,* 6 December 1993, A8.
10. "Shop Talk: Unauthorized Tardies Can Cut into Your Vacation Time," *Los Angeles Times,* 30 March 1997, D5.
11. Eben Shapiro, "Blockbuster Rescue Bid Stars Viacom Top Guns," *Wall Street Journal,* 7 May 1997, B1, B10.
12. *Red Herring News,* vol. 13, no. 2; http://www.RedHerringProductions.com accessed 3 September 1998.
13. Paul Dean, "Auto Makers Shift into New Gear," *Los Angeles Times,* 15 January 1997, E1, E6.
14. "Entrepreneurs across America," *Entrepreneur Magazine Online,* http://www.entrepreneurmag.com/entmag/50states5.hts, accessed 12 June 1997.
15. Associated Press, "Flood of Imports into Argentina Delights Shoppers, Riles Local Industry," *Los Angeles Times,* 6 January 1992, D4.
16. Michael M. Phillips, "Carving Out an Export Industry, and Hope, in Africa," *Wall Street Journal,* 18 July 1996, A8.
17. Joanne Lipman, "Do Toll Phone Services Play Fair by Advertising Directly to Kids?" *Wall Street Journal,* 7 July 1989, B1.
18. "Periscope: Beanie Mania," *Newsweek,* 3 June 1996, 8.
19. "Starters: Spearing the Best," *Bon Appétit,* March 1997, 20; Mary Alice Kellogg, "The Reel Dish," *Bon Appétit,* March 1997, 38.
20. "Technology: Sound Chamber," *Newsweek,* 13 May 1996, 10.
21. "How Microsoft Reviews Suppliers," Fast Company, no. 17; http://fastcompany.
com/online/17/msoftreviews.html accessed 3 September 1998.
22. William M. Bulkeley, "Office-Supply Superstores Find Bounty in the Boonies," *Wall Street Journal,* 1 September 1998, B1, B4.
23. Joseph Weber, "From Soup to Nuts and Back to Soup," *Business Week,* 5 November 1990, 114, 116; biography of Zoe Coulson from *Marquis Who's Who,* accessed online, 24 May 1992.
24. "Entrepreneurs across America," *Entrepreneur Magazine* Online; http://www.entrepreneurmag.com/entmag/50states5.hts#top accessed 12 June 1997.
25. Sal D. Rinalla and Robert J. Kopecky, "Recruitment: Burger King Hooks Employees with Educational Incentives," *Personnel Journal,* October 1989, 90–99.
26. Karen Kaplan, "Heard on the Beat: M-I-C, K-E-Y—Why? Because It's Disney," *Los Angeles Times,* 31 March 1997, D1, D6; http://www.disneyblast.com accessed 23 July 1997.
27. Sewell Chan, "In Frenzy to Recruit, High-Tech Concerns Try Gimmicks, Songs," *Wall Street Journal,* 9 August 1996, B1, 5.
28. Carl Quintanilla, "Work Week: Pizza, Pizza," *Wall Street Journal,* 18 August 1998, A1.

Chapter 8

1. Yia Eason, founder, Olmec Toys, personal communication, September 1996.
2. Mark H. McCormack, *On Communicating* (Los Angeles, Calif.: Dove Books, 1998), 87.
3. Ram Subramanian, Robert G. Insley, and Rodney D. Blackwell, "Performance and Readability: A Comparison of Annual Reports of Profitable and Unprofitable Corporations," *Journal of Business Communication* 30, no. 2 (1993): 49–61.
4. James Calvert Scott and Diana J. Green, "British Perspectives on Organizing Bad-News Letters: Organizational Patterns Used by Major U.K. Companies," *Bulletin of the Association for Business Communica-tion* 55, no. 1 (March 1992): 17–19.
5. *Techniques for Communicators* (Chicago: Lawrence Ragan Communication, 1995), 18.
6. Maura Dolan and Stuart Silverstein, "Court Broadens Liability for Job References," *Los Angeles Times,* 28 January 1997, A1, A11; Frances A. McMorris, "Ex-Bosses Face Less Peril Giving Honest Job References," *Wall Street Journal,* 8 July 1996, B1, B8.
7. Thomas S. Brice and Marie Waung, "Applicant Rejection Letters: Are Businesses Sending the Wrong Message?" *Business Horizons,* March–April 1995, 59–62.
8. Gwendolyn N. Smith, Rebecca F. Nolan, and Yong Dai, "Job-Refusal Letters: Readers' Affective Responses to Direct and Indirect Organizational Plans," *Business Communication Quarterly* 59, no. 1 (1996): 67–73; Brice and Waung, "Applicant Rejection Letters."
9. Judi Brownell, "The Performance Appraisal Interviews: A Multipurpose Communication Assignment," *Bulletin of the Association for Business Communication* 57, no. 2 (1994): 11–21.
10. Brownell, "The Performance Appraisal Interviews."
11. Stephanie Gruner, "Feedback from Everyone," *Inc.*, February 1997, 102–103.
12. Howard M. Bloom, "Performance Evaluations," *New England Business,* December 1991, 14.
13. David I. Rosen, "Appraisals Can Make—or Break—Your Court Case," *Personnel Journal,* November 1992, 113.
14. Patricia A. McLagan, "Advice for Bad-News Bearers: How to Tell Employees They're Not Hacking It and Get Results," *Industry Week,* 15 February 1993, 42; Michael Lee Smith, "Give Feedback, Not Criticism," *Supervisory Management,* 1993, 4; "A Checklist for Conducting Problem Performer Appraisals," *Supervisory Management,* December 1993, 7–9.
15. Jane R. Goodson, Gail W. McGee, and Anson Seers, "Giving Appropriate Performance Feedback to Managers: An Empirical Test of Content and Outcomes," *Journal of Business Communication* 29, no. 4 (1992): 329–342.
16. Craig Cox, "On the Firing Line," *Business Ethics,* May–June 1992, 33–34.
17. Cox, "On the Firing Line."
18. Yia Eason, founder, Olmec Toys, personal communication, September 1996.
19. Michelle Higgins, "The Ballet Shoe Gets a Makeover, But Few Yet See the Pointe," *Wall Street Journal,* 8 August 1998, A1, A6.
20. Pascal Zachary, "Sun Microsystems Apologizes in Letter for Late Payments," *Wall Street Journal,* 11 October 1989, B4.
21. Peter Fritsch, "It's Lighter Than Glass and Hurts Less When Thrown, But Can Plastic Stack Up?" *Wall Street Journal,* 24 July 1996, B1.
22. Patti Bond, "Hispanics Display Growing Muscle in Entrepreneurship," *Atlanta Journal-Constitution,* 11 July 1996, B1.
23. Leo W. Banks, "Not Your Average Joe," *Los Angeles Times*, 7 January 1997, E1, E6.
24. Sewell Chan, "A Seattle Blend Is Praised As Rich, Smooth, and Better Than Worms," *Wall Street Journal,* 16 July 1996, B1.
25. "Swimmer Invents Pool Tool," *The Coast News,* 13 August 1998, A-15.
26. Joseph Hanania, "Feeling Sheepish?" *Los Angeles Times,* 30 July 1996, E3.

27. International Tesla Society Museum Bookstore Catalog, Fall 1993.
28. Robert Johnson, "Your Little Monkey Is So Cuddly. Here, Let Me—OUCH!" *Wall Street Journal,* 2 December 1991, A1, A14.
29. Matt Murray, "Hey Kids! Marketers Want Your Help!" *Wall Street Journal*, 6 May 1997, B1, B8.
30. Barbara Foley, "Stepping into Something, Um, Ugly," *Los Angeles Times,* 18 December 1991, E1, E8.
31. Associated Press, "Is the Boss Watching? Surveillance Common at Work," *CNN Interactive*, http://cnn.com/US/9705/23/watching.workers.ap/index/html, accessed 30 May 1997.
32. Fleming Meeks, "Shakespeare, Dickens & Hillegass," *Forbes,* 30 October 1989, 206, 208, 209.
33. David Colker, "Rest in Space," *Los Angeles Times,* 25 July 1996, B2.
34. Wendy Bounds, "Here, Haute Couture Takes a Back Seat to the Front Row," *Wall Street Journal*, 9 May 1997, A1, A6.
35. "I.R.S. Error of $40 Million," *New York Times,* 7 February 1992, sec. C, 4.
36. Carla Koehl and Sarah Van Boven, "The Geek Squad Gets a Taste of Hollywood," *Newsweek*, 23 December 1996; Geek Squad Web site http://www.geeksquad.com, accessed 30 May 1997.
37. "Entrepreneurs across America," *Entrepreneur Magazine Online*, http://www.enterpreneurmag.com/entmag/50states2.hts, accessed 25 June 1997.
38. Jacquelyn Lynn, "Your Business: War and Pierce," *Entrepreneur,* June 1998, 104.
39. "Persicope: Color Me . . . Grossed Out," *Newsweek*, 20 November 1995, 8.
40. Reuters newswire, "U.S. Medical Journal Assesses Self, Ethics, Issues," CNN Interactive, 14 July 1998; http://customnews.cnn.com/cnews/pna.show_s...t_type=190294&p_subcate=Authors&p_category=, accessed 16 July 1998.
41. Gautam Naik, "These Guys Are Junk, and to Mark Tilden That's Just the Point," *Wall Street Journal,* 16 August 1996, A1.

Chapter 9

1. Jeanne Anderson, sales director, Language Line Services, AT&T, personal communication, December 1992.
2. Jay A. Conger, "The Necessary Art of Persuasion," *Harvard Business Review,* May–June 1998, 84–95; Jeanette W. Gilsdorf, "Write Me Your Best Case for . . ." *Bulletin of the Association for Business Communication* 54, no. 1 (March 1991): 7–12.
3. "Vital Skill for Today's Managers: Persuading, Not Ordering, Others," *Soundview Executive Book Summaries,* September 1998, 1.
4. Anne Fisher, "Success Secret: A High Emotional IQ," *Fortune,* 16 October 1998, 293–298.
5. Mary Cross, "Aristotle and Business Writing: Why We Need to Teach Persuasion," *Bulletin of the Association for Business Communication* 54, no. 1 (March 1991): 3–6.
6. Abraham H. Maslow, *Motivation and Personality* (New York: Harper & Row, 1954), 12, 19.
7. Robert T. Moran, "Tips on Making Speeches to International Audiences," *International Management,* April 1980, 58–59.
8. Conger, "The Necessary Art of Persuasion."
9. Raymond M. Olderman, *10-Minute Guide to Business Communication* (New York: Macmillian Spectrum/Alpha Books, 1997), 57–61.
10. Gilsdorf, "Write Me Your Best Case for . . ."
11. John D. Ramage and John C. Bean, *Writing Arguments: A Rhetoric with Readings,* 3d ed. (Boston: Allyn & Bacon, 1995), 102–117.
12. Ramage and Bean, *Writing Arguments,* 430–442.
13. Gilsdorf, "Write Me Your Best Case for . . ."
14. Conger, "The Necessary Art of Persuasion."
15. Dianna Booher, *Communicate with Confidence* (New York: McGraw-Hill, 1994), 110.
16. Tamra B. Orr, "Persuasion without Pressure," *Toastmaster,* January 1994, 19–22; William Friend, "Winning Techniques of Great Persuaders," *Association Management,* February 1985, 82–86; Patricia Buhler, "How to Ask For—and Get—What You Want!" *Supervision,* February 1990, 11–13.
17. Booher, *Communicate with Confidence,* 102.
18. Conger, "The Necessary Art of Persuasion."
19. Robert L. Hemmings, "Think Before You Write," *Fund Raising Management,* February 1990, 23–24.
20. Teri Lammers, "The Elements of Perfect Pitch," *Inc.,* March 1992, 53–55.
21. Kimberly Paterson, "The Writing Process—Sales Letters That Work," *Rough Notes,* April 1998, 59–60.
22. William North Jayme, quoted in Albert Haas Jr., "How to Sell Almost Anything by Direct Mail," *Across the Board,* November 1986, 50.
23. Paterson, "The Writing Process."
24. Hemmings, "Think Before You Write."
25. Hemmings, "Think Before You Write."
26. Conrad Squires, "How to Write a Strong Letter, Part Two: Choosing a Theme," *Fund Raising Management,* November 1991, 65–66.
27. Conrad Squires, "Getting the Compassion out of the Box," *Fund Raising Management,* September 1992, 55, 60.
28. Squires, "How to Write a Strong Letter."
29. Constance L. Clark, "25 Steps to Better Direct Mail Fundraising," *Nonprofit World,* July–August 1989, 11–13; Squires, "How to Write a Strong Letter."
30. Squires, "How to Write a Strong Letter."
31. Clark, "25 Steps to Better Direct Mail Fundraising."
32. Conrad Squires, "Why Some Letters Outpull Others," *Fund Raising Management,* January 1991, 67, 72.
33. Squires, "Why Some Letters Outpull Others"; Clark, "25 Steps to Better Direct Mail Fundraising"; Jerry Huntsinger, "My First $29\frac{1}{2}$ Years in Direct-Mail Fund Raising: What I've Learned," *Fund Raising Management,* January 1992, 40–43.
34. "The Ideal Collection Letter," *Inc.,* February 1991, 59–61.
35. Jeanne Anderson, sales director, Language Line Services, AT&T, personal communication, December 1992.
36. Albert R. Karr, "Work Week: Wake Up and Read This," *Wall Street Journal,* 6 May 1997, A1.
37. Monty Roberts and Lawrence Scanlan, with contributor Lucy Grealy, *The Man Who Listens to Horses* (New York. Random House, 1997); http://www.MontyRoberts.com/farm/fiuf.html, accessed 26 August 1998.
38. Jane Bryant Quinn, "A Primer on Downsizing," *Newsweek,* 13 May 1996, 50; Marshall Loeb, "What to Do If You Get Fired," *Fortune,* 15 January 1996, 38; "Urohealth Sets Sights on Eighth Acquisition," *Los Angeles Times,* 5 May 1996, B2.
39. Kevin M. Savetz, "Preventive Medicine for the Computer User," *Multimedia Online 2,* no. 2 (June 1996): 58–60.
40. John Case and Jerry Useem, "Six Characters in Search of a Strategy," *Inc.,* March 1996, 46–49.
41. Reuters Limited, "Kids Who Watch More TV Get Hurt More, Study Says," CNN Custom News, CNN Interactive, 14 July 1998; http://customnews.com/cnews/pna.show_s..t_type=190294&p_subcat=Authors&p_category, accessed 16 July 1998; Texas Classroom Teachers Association Web site, http://www.tcta.org/geninfo.htm, accessed 30 September 1998.
42. "US West Labor Strike Ends," CNNfn, CNN Interactive, http://cnnfn.com:80/hotsotreis/companies/9808/31/uswest/, accessed 31 August 1998.
43. Cathy Werblin, "Korean Business Owners Want Signs to Mark Area," *Los Angeles Times,* 29 March 1997, B3.
44. Terah Kathryn Collins, *The Western Guide to Feng Shui* (Carlsbad, Calif., Hay House, 1996), 200.
45. Joseph B. Cahill, "Regulators Discover There Is No There at a 'Virtual' Bank," *Wall Street Journal,* 1 September 1998, A1, A6.
46. Robert Cwiklik, " 'Honest, Mom, I Don't Even Know What Those @#$%& Words Mean,' " *Wall Street Journal,* 17 June 1998, B1.
47. Steve Bass, "ISDN Not; The Agony, the Ecstasy, the Migraines," *Computer Currents,* 7 May 1996, 43.
48. "Down These Aisles Is Matrimonial Bliss," *Los Angeles Times,* 22 March 1996, D3.
49. Anne Chalfant, "In the Genes: Progress, Perils of Disease Detection," *NurseWeek,* 27 July 1998; 13; National Public Radio broadcast, *All Things Considered,* 29 September 1998.
50. "Kelly Services Earns Gold Pentastar Award," *Workstyle,* Kelly Services newsletter, August 1998, 1, 2.
51. Ronaleen R. Roha, "Talk Is Cheaper," *Kiplinger Personal Finance Magazine,* May 1996, 105–107.
52. Interview with Bill Stevens, EnRoute Music, Janesville, Wisconsin, 28 July 1998; Ron Winslow, "Health Journal: Speed Is of the Essence in Reaping the Benefits of New Stroke Remedy," *Wall Street Journal,* 31 August 1998, B1.
53. Promotional mailing requesting volunteers, received from George Buys, buys@audio-tips.com, CEO, Audio International, via e-mail, 17 June 1998.
54. Tom Morganthau and Seema Nayyar, "Those Scary College Costs," *Newsweek,* 29 April 1996, 52–56; Jane Bryant Quinn, "Save First, Then Borrow," *Newsweek,* 29 April 1996, 67–68.
55. Edmund Sanders, "Subcontractors Still Waiting for Payoff from Giant Irvine Theater," *Orange County Register,* 9 May 1996, 2.

Chapter 10

1. Kim Daus, senior communications strategist, Silicon Graphics, personal communication, 28 July 1998; Micahel C. Brandon, "From Need to Know to Need to Know," *Communication World,* 20 October 1996, 18–19.
2. Paul Franson, *High Tech, High Hope* (New York: Wiley, 1998), 252.
3. Samuel Greengard, "How Technology Will Change the Workplace," *Workforce,* January 1998, 78–84.
4. Information for this section was taken in part from Michael Mescon, Courtland Bovée, and John Thill, *Business Today* (Upper Saddle River, N.J.: Prentice Hall, 1999), 639–647.
5. Anne Zieger, "Enterprise Computing: IP Telephony Gets Real," *Info-World* 20, 5 January 1998, *Electric Library,* accessed 10 March 1998; Laura Kujubu, "Telcos Answer Wake-Up Call from Internet," *InfoWorld* 19, 15 December 1997, *Electric Library,* accessed 10 March 1998.
6. "All about E-Mail: Use E-Mail to Communicate with Anyone, Anywhere," *Microsoft Magazine,* April–May 1996, 14–26.
7. Josh McHugh, "The Old Thing Behind the Next Big Thing," *Forbes,* 20 November 1998; Stephen H. Wildstrom, "Catching E-Mail on the Fly," *Business Week,* 26 October 1998, 19; "A New Little Pager That Also Handles E-Mail," *New York Times,* 26 November 1998, D3; John Markoff, "3Com to Offer a Palm Pilot with Wireless Capabilities," *New York Times,* 3 December 1998, C5.
8. Tim McCollum, "The Case for E-Mail," *Nation's Business,* May 1996, 61.
9. "Networked Meetings," *Business Week, Special Advertising Section,* 16 November 1998, 202.
10. Edward C. Baig, "A World of Talking Heads," *Business Week, Industrial/Technology*, 13 May 1996, 20–22.
11. Larry Long and Nancy Long, *Introduction to Computers & Information Systems,* 5th ed. (Paramus, N.J.: Prentice Hall, 1997), 208; David Morse, ed., *CyberDictionary: Your Guide to the Wired World* (Santa Monica, Calif.: Knowledge Exchange, 1996), 233.
12. Michael Mathiesen, *Marketing on the Internet* (Gulf Breeze, Fla.: Maximum Press, 1995), 11–12.
13. Vince Emery, *How to Grow Your Business on the Internet* (Scottsdale, Ariz.: Coriolis Group, 1996), 337; Mathiesen, *Marketing on the Internet,* 12–14; Michelle Rafter, "DejaNews Search Finds New Outlet on Web," *Chicago Tribune,* 15 March 1998, sec. 4, 7.
14. Morse, ed., *CyberDictionary,* 54.
15. Thomas E. Weber "Web's Vastness Foils Even Best Search Engines," *Wall Street Journal,* 3 April 1998, B1, B7; Matt Lake, "Desperately Seeking Susan OR Suzie NOT Sushi," *New York Times,* 3 September 1998, D1, D7; "How Search Engines Work," http://www.searchenginewatch.com/work.htm, accessed 18 January 1998.
16. "How Search Engines Work."
17. Thomas A. Stewart, "Internet Portals: No One-Stop Shop," *Fortune,* 7 December 1998, 235–236; James Coates, "Netscape, AOL May Form an Alliance," *Chicago Tribune,* 19 November 1998, sec. 3, 1, 3.
18. Leslie Ann Forrester, "Push Technology," *Legal Assistant Today,* May/June 1998, 36–37.
19. Andy Eddy, "Whither Push Technology," *Network World,* 3 August 1998, 27–30; Michael Marriott, "Happy Birthday, Your Team Won, Your Stock Crashed," *New York Times,* 17 September 1998, D1, D8.
20. Andrew Brown and Imran Kahn, "Internet Innovations Workshop '96: Internet Agents," http://www.cs.toronto.edu/~andy/IIW/ accessed 24 November 1998.
21. Marriott, "Happy Birthday, Your Team Won, Your Stock Crashed," D1, D8.
22. Michael Taylor, "Intranets—A New Technology Changes All the Rules," *Telecommunications,* January 1997, 39–40.
23. Diane Trommer, "Information Overload—Study Finds Intranet Users Overwhelmed with Data," *Electronic Buyers' News,* 20 April 1998, 98+.
24. Taylor, "Intranets."
25. Charlene Marmer Solomon, "Sharing Information across Borders and Time Zones," *Global Workforce,* March 1998, 13–18.
26. Taylor, "Intranets."
27. Don L. Boroughs, "Paperless Profits," *U.S. News & World Report,* July 17, 1995, 40.
28. Taylor, "Intranets."
29. Amy Cortese, "Here Comes the Intranet," *Business Week,* 26 February 1996, 76–84.
30. Cortese, "Here Comes the Intranet."
31. Charles Hoffman, "The Tao of Intranets," *Journal of Accountancy,* October 1998, 30–37.
32. Samuel Greengard, "Extranets Linking Employees with Your Vendors," *Workforce,* November 1997, 28–34.
33. "The Extranet Habit: The Web Becomes the New Business Platform," *Fortune, Technology Buyer's Guide,* Summer 1998, 243+.
34. Greengard, "Extranets Linking Employees with Your Vendors."
35. Greengard, "Extranets Linking Employees with Your Vendors.
36. Shari Caudron, "Virtual Manners," *Industry Week,* 6 July 1998, 52–53; Phil Waga, "Advanced Technology Sends Manners Back to the Stone Age," *Gannett Suburban Newspapers,* 1 August 1997, S09.
37. William R. Pape, "Becoming a Virtual Company," *Inc. Technology* 4 (1995): 29, 31.
38. Lisa Bransten, "Staying in Touch," *Wall Street Journal,* 16 November 1998, R14.
39. Stephanie N. Mehta, "MCI WorldCom to Launch Web Service via Traditional Copper Phone Lines," *Wall Street Journal,* 19 November 1998, B6; Chris DeVoney, "The Speed Is Great, If You Can Get It," *Computerworld,* 12 October 1998, 43, 45.
40. Otis Port, "Through a Glass Quickly," *Business Week,* 7 December 1998, 96–98.
41. "Don't Call Us, We'll Call You," *Newsweek,* 15 June 1998, 46.
42. Mike Bransby, "Voice Mail Makes a Difference," *Journal of Business Strategy,* January–February 1990, 7–10.
43. Neil Gross, Paul C. Judge, Otis Port, and Stephen H. Wildstrom, "Let's Talk," *Business Week,* 23 February 1998, 61–76.
44. Derrek Schartz, "Can We Talk?" *Communication News,* April 1998, 24+.
45. Gross, Judge, Port, and Wildstrom, "Let's Talk"; Michael J. Himowitz, "Dictating to Your PC," *Fortune,* New York, 9 November 1998, 240+.
46. Gross, Judge, Port, and Wildstrom, "Let's Talk"; Schartz, "Can We Talk?"
47. Gross, Judge, Port, and Wildstrom, "Let's Talk."
48. Jay Stuller, "Overload," *Across the Board,* April 1996, 16–22.
49. Stuller, "Overload," 16–22; Trommer, "Information Overload."
50. Taylor, "Intranets."
51. Mark Johnson, "Battling Information Overload," *Communication World,* April–May 1997, 26+.
52. Samuel Greengard, "How Secure Is Your Data?" *Workforce,* May 1998, 52–60, Nikhil Hutheesing and Philip E. Ross, "Hackerphobia," *Forbes,* 23 March 1998, 150–154.
53. Greengard, "How Secure Is Your Data?"
54. Elisa Deardorff, "With Voice Mail, You Never Know Who's Listening," *Chicago Tribune,* 1 June 1998, B1, B8.
55. Julie Deardorff, "With Voice Mail, You Never Know Who's Listening," *Chicago Tribune,* 6 July 1998, 1, 8.
56. Fernando Bartolome, *The Articulate Executive* (Boston, Mass: Harvard Business Review, 1993), xi.
57. Robyn Meredity, "Building 'Internet 2,' " *New York Times,* 2 February 1998, C3.
58. Fernando Bartolome, *The Articulate Executive* (Boston, Mass.: Harvard Business Review, 1993), xi.
59. Peter F. Drucker, "The Next Information Revolution," *Forbes ASAP,* 24 August, 1998, 47–58.
60. Kevin Maney, "Take the Internet with You in a Phone, Watch or Shoe," *USA Today,* 19 March 1998, B1.
61. Laton McCartney, "Getting Smart about Knowledge Management," http://www.industryweek.com, 4 May 1998.
62. Bob Filipezak, "Data-Mining: 16 Tons and What Do You Get?" *Training,* March 1998, 106–107.
63. Kim Daus, senior communications strategist, Silicon Graphics, personal communication, 28 July 1998; Brandon, "From Need to Know to Need to Know."

Chapter 11

1. Charles Shin, founder, Charley's Steakery, personal communication, June 1996.
2. Information for this section was obtained from "Finding Industry Information" http://www.pitt.edu/~buslibry/industries.htm, accessed 3 November 1998; Thomas P. Bergman, Stephen M. Garrison, and Gregory M. Scott, *The Business Student Writer's Manual and Guide to the Internet* (Upper Saddle River, N.J.: Prentice Hall, 1998), 67–80; Ernest L. Maier, Anthony J. Faria, Peter Kaatrude, and Elizabeth Wood, *The Business Library and How to Use It* (Detroit: Omnigraphics, 1996), 53–76; Sherwyn P. Morreale and Courtland L. Bovée, *Excellence in*

Public Speaking (Fort Worth: Harcourt Brace College Publishers, 1998), 166–171.

3. Sandy Whitely, ed., *The American Library Association Guide to Information Access* (New York: Random House, 1994), 4.
4. "The Research Sites Fairy Godmother Report," What Color Is Your Parachute Online, http://www.washingtonpost.com/wp~adv/classifieds/careerpost/parachute/reseajhg.htm, accessed 10 October 1998.
5. Thomas E. Weber, "Web's Vastness Foils Even Best Search Engines," *Wall Street Journal,* 3 April 1998, B1, B7.
6. Maier, Faria, Kaatrude, and Wood, *The Business Library and How to Use It,* 84–97; Matt Lake, "Desperately Seeking Susan OR Suzie NOT Sushi," *New York Times,* 3 September 1998, D1, D7.
7. "How to Design and Conduct a Study," *Credit Union Magazine,* October 1983, 36–46.
8. Morreale and Bovée, *Excellence in Public Speaking,* 177.
9. Morreale and Bovée, *Excellence in Public Speaking,* 178–180.
10. Morreale and Bovée, *Excellence in Public Speaking,* 182.
11. David A. Aaker and George S. Day, *Marketing Research,* 2d ed. (New York: Wiley, 1983), 88–89.
12. Robert E. Cason, *Writing for the Business World* (Upper Saddle River, N.J.: Prentice Hall, 1997), 102.
13. Bergman, Garrison, and Scott, *The Business Student Writer's Manual and Guide to the Internet,* 65.
14. "How to Paraphrase Effectively: 6 Steps to Follow," Researchpaper.com, http://www.researchpaper.com/writing_center/30.html, accessed 26 October 1998.
15. Cason, *Writing for the Business World,* 71–72.
16. Dorothy Geisler, "How to Avoid Copyright Lawsuits," *IABC Communication World,* June 1984, 34–37.
17. Robert W. Goddard, "The Crime of Copying," *Management World,* July–August 1986, 20–22.
18. Charles Shin, founder, Charley's Steakery, personal communication, June 1996.

Chapter 12

1. Curtis Symonds, executive vice president of affiliate sales and marketing, BET Holdings Group, personal communication, 23 July 1998; Karen Gutloff, "Show and Sell," *Black Enterprise,* July 1998, 106.
2. Alexander Petofi, "The Graphic Revolution in Computers," *The Futurist,* June 1985, 30.
3. Stephanie McKinnon, "Pictures, Signs and Symbols Prove to Be Powerful Tools," *Gannett Suburban Newspapers,* 27 September 1992, 12.
4. Sheri Rosen, "What Is Truth?" *IABC Communication World,* March 1995, 40.
5. Maureen Jones, "Getting Good Graphs," *PC Magazine,* 23 July 1985, 217.
6. Edward R. Tufte, *The Visual Display of Quantitative Information* (Cheshire, Conn.: Graphic Press, 1983), 113.
7. Courtland L. Bovée, Michael J. Houston, and John V. Thill, *Marketing,* 2d ed. (New York: McGraw-Hill, 1995), 250.
8. The staff of *Presentation Products Magazine,* "Better Presentations for a Better Bottom Line," *Fortune,* 9 October 1989, 24–25.
9. Kathleen K. Weigner, "Visual Persuasion," *Forbes,* 16 September 1991, 176; Kathleen K. Weigner, "Showtime!" *Forbes,* 13 May 1991, 118.
10. *How to Prepare and Use Effective Visual Aids,* Info-Line series, Elizabeth Lean, managing ed. (Washington, D.C.: American Society for Training and Develop-ment, October 1984), 2.
11. Kevin Daley, "Presentation Skills: How to Be Focused, Forceful, Passionate and Persuasive," *Information Executive,* September 1998, 7+.
12. Curtis Symonds, executive vice president of affiliate sales and marketing, BET Holdings Group, personal communication, 23 July 1998; Gutloff, "Show and Sell," 106.
13. *Advertising Age,* 29 September 1997, S63.

Chapter 13

1. Wesley Van Linda, president, Narada Productions, personal communication, June 1993.
2. Dan Steinhoff and John F. Burgess, *Small Business Management Fundamentals,* 5th ed. (New York: McGraw-Hill, 1989), 37.
3. Joan F. Vesper and Karl H. Vesper, "Writing a Business Plan: The Total Term Assignment," *Bulletin of the Association for Business Communication* 56, no. 2 (June 1993): 29–32.
4. Thomas P. Bergman, Stephen M. Garrison, and Gregory M. Scott, *The Business Student Writer's Manual and Guide to the Internet* (Upper Saddle River, N.J.: Prentice Hall, 1998), 266.
5. Elizabeth Conlin, "The Daily Sales Report," *Inc.,* January 1991, 73–75.
6. Tom Peters, "Don't Send Memos!" *Washington Monthly,* November 1987, 13.
7. Eric D. Randall, "Firms Serve Annual Reports with a Twist," *USA Today,* 17 May 1994, 6B; Patrick Flanagan, "Make Your Annual Report Work Harder," *Management Review,* October 1993, 52–58.
8. Tom Sant, *Persuasive Business Proposals* (New York: American Management Association, 1992), as summarized in *Soundview Executive Book Summaries* 14, no. 10, pt. 2 (October 1992), 3.
9. Iris I. Varner, *Contemporary Business Report Writing,* 2d ed. (Chicago: Dryden Press, 1991), 170.
10. Varner, *Contemporary Business Report Writing,* 178.
11. Claudia Mon Pere McIsaac, "Improving Student Summaries through Sequencing," *Bulletin of the Association for Business Communication* (September 1987): 17–20.
12. David A. Hayes, "Helping Students GRASP the Knack of Writing Summaries," *Journal of Reading* (November 1989): 96–101.
13. Susan L. Leach, "SEC Takes Next Leap into Computer Age," *Christian Science Monitor,* 7 June 1994, 8.
14. Michael H. Mescon, Courtland L. Bovée, and John V. Thill, *Business Today* (Upper Saddle River, N.J.: Prentice Hall, 1999), 135.
15. John Taschek, "New Report Writers Provide Improved Access to Data," *PC Week,* 6 February 1995, 81–85.
16. Stephan Manes, "E-Mail Troubles? You Have No Idea!" *PC World,* July 1996, 39.
17. Wesley Van Linda, president, Narada Productions, personal communication, June 1993.

Chapter 14

1. Dierdre Ballou, education manager, San Diego Wild Animal Park, personal communication, July 1997.
2. Bruce McComiskey, "Defining Institutional Problems: A Heuristic Procedure," *Business Communication Quarterly* 58, no. 4 (1995): 21–24.
3. Iris I. Varner, *Contemporary Business Report Writing,* 2d ed. (Chicago: Dryden Press, 1991), 135.
4. Maridell Fryar and David A. Thomas, *Successful Review Solving* (Lincolnwood, Ill.: NTC, 1989), 20.
5. This section is based on John V. Thill and Courtland L. Bovée, *Excellence in Business Communication,* 4th ed. (Upper Saddle River, N.J.: Prentice Hall, 1999), 314.
6. Eleanor Rizzo, "Document Design Basics," *Technical Communication,* Fourth Quarter 1992, 645.
7. A. S. C. Ehrenberg, "Report Writing—Six Simple Rules for Better Business Docu-ments," *Admap,* June 1992, 39–42.
8. Dierdre Ballou, education manager, San Diego Wild Animal Park, personal communication, July 1997.
9. Adapted from Nancy Jeffrey, "Preparing for the Worst: Firms Set Up Plans to Help Deal with Corporate Crises," *Wall Street Journal,* 7 December 1987, 23.
10. Adapted from "Group Accuses Nike of Vietnam Abuses," *Los Angeles Times,* 28 March 1997, D3; Greg Rushford, "Manager's Journal: Nike Lets Critics Kick It Around," *Wall Street Journal,* 12 May 1997; "Nike vs. Doonesbury," PEOPLE ONLINE Daily, http://pathfinder.com/@SX8oXwUA238MYHni/people/daily/pages/peephole.html, accessed 6 June 1997.
11. Adapted from Bob Smith, "The Evolution of Pinkerton," *Management Review,* September 1993, 54–58.

Chapter 15

1. Mark Landiak, president, Corporate Dynamics, personal communication, 20 August 1998.
2. Oswald M. T. Ratteray, "Hit the Mark with Better Summaries," *Supervisory Management,* September 1989, 43–45.
3. Lyman W. Porter and Lawrence E. McKibbin, *Management Education and Development: Drift or Thrust into the 21st Century?* (New York: McGraw-Hill, 1988), 1–44.
4. Mark Landiak, president, *Corporate Dynamics,* personal communication, 20 August 1998.

5. Adapted from American Hotel & Motel Association, "Lodging Guest Research Summary of Major Results," presented to International Hotel, Motel, and Restaurant Association Annual Convention, 14 November 1989.
6. Bickley Townsend, "Room at the Top," *American Demographics,* July 1996, 28–37.
7. Alison Stein Wellner, "Keeping Old Cars on the Road," *American Demographics,* July 1997, 53–58.
8. Gina Fraone, "China's Challenge," *Electronic Business* 24, no. 12 (1998): 24, downloaded from ABI/INFORM database, 1 December 1998; Trish Saywell, "Preparing for Take-Off," *Far Eastern Economic Review* 161, no. 48 (1998): 38, downloaded from ABI/INFORM database, 1 December 1998; Colin Bates, "The Many China Markets," *China Business Review* 25, no. 5 (1998): 26–29, downloaded from ABI/INFORM database, 1 December 1998; U.S. Department of Commerce, *Big Emerging Markets Information Resource Page,* http://www.ita.doc.gov/bems/index.html, 28 August 1998, accessed 1 December 1998; Trish Saywell, "Curious in China," *Far Eastern Economic Review* 161, no. 28 (1998): 74–76, downloaded from ABI/INFORM database, 1 December 1998; Catherine Gelb, "Installing a Software Sector," *China Business Review* 24, no. 5 (1997): 28–36, downloaded from ABI/INFORM database, 1 December 1998; Geng Cui, "The Different Faces of the Chinese Consumer," *China Business Review* 24, no. 4 (1997): 34–38, downloaded from ABI/INFORM database 1 December 1998.
9. Pamela Kasdan, "Fast Food for Thought," *American Demographics,* May 1996, 19–21; Greg Burns, "French Fries with That Quart of Oil?" *Business Week,* 27 November 1995, 86–87; David Fischer, "The New Meal Deals," *Business Week,* 30 October 1995, 66.
10. Denis Gellene, "Marketers Target Schools by Offering Facts and Features," *Los Angeles Times,* 4 June 1998, D1.
11. Sandra Evans, "First Come Goals, Then Guts and Glory," *Washington Post,* 5 October 1998, F10; Lisa Lee Freeman, "Getting Ahead May Mean Getting a Coach," *Investor's Business Daily,* 2 December 1997, A1; Anita Bruzzese, "Considering Taking a New Job?" *Gannett News Service,* 14 August 1997, S12.

Chapter 16

1. Leanne Anderson, founder of Anderson Business Resources, personal communications, 24 April 1997 and 23 July 1998; Leanne Anderson, "Speak Up," *Entrepreneur,* March 1997, 92–95.
2. Edward P. Bailey, *Writing and Speaking at Work* (Paramus, N.J.: Prentice Hall, 1999), 124.
3. Sherwyn P. Morreale and Courtland L. Bovée, *Excellence in Public Speaking* (Fort Worth: Harcourt Brace, 1998), 309.
4. Deirdre Fanning, "The Public Equivalent of a Root Canal," *New York Times,* 2 December 1990, sec. 3, 25.
5. "Choose and Use Your Words Deliberately," *Soundview Executive Book Sum-maries,* Vol. 20. no. 6, pt. 2 (June 1998):3.
6. Sherron B. Kenton, "Speaker Credibility in Persuasive Business Communication: A Model Which Explains Gender Differences," *Journal of Business Communication* 26, no. 2 (Spring 1989): 143–157.
7. Walter Kiechel III, "How to Give a Speech," *Fortune,* 8 June 1987, 180.
8. Communication and Leadership Program (Santa Ana, Calif.: Toast-masters International, 1980), 44, 45.
9. Morreale and Bovée, *Excellence in Public Speaking,* 24–25.
10. Judy Linscott, "Getting On and Off the Podium," *Savvy,* October 1985, 44.
11. Iris R. Johnson, "Before You Approach the Podium," *MW,* January–February 1989, 7.
12. Bailey, *Writing & Speaking at Work,* 162.
13. Pauline Gravier, "How to Speak So People Will Listen," *Planning,* December 1992, 15+.
14. Patrick J. Collins, *Say It with Power and Confidence* (Paramus, N.J.: Prentice Hall, 1997), 122–124.
15. Collins, *Say It with Power and Confidence,* 122–124.
16. Gravier, "How to Speak So People Will Listen."
17. Sandra Moyer, "Braving No Woman's Land," *The Toastmaster,* August 1986, 13.
18. "Control the Question-and-Answer Session," *Soundview Executive Book Summaries* 20, no. 6, pt. 2 (June 1998):4.
19. "Control the Question-and-Answer Session."
20. Teresa Brady, "Fielding Abrasive Questions During Presentations," *Supervisory Management,* February 1993, 6.
21. Robert L. Montgomery, "Listening on Your Feet," *The Toastmaster,* July 1987, 14–15.
22. Adapted from Ronald L. Applebaum and Karl W. E. Anatol, *Effective Oral Communication: For Business and the Professions* (Chicago: Science Research Associates, 1982), 240–244.
23. Leanne Anderson, founder of Anderson Business Resources, personal communications, 24 April 1997 and 23 July 1998; Anderson, "Speak Up."

Chapter 17

1. Doug Halm, manager, human resources, Recreational Equipment Incorporated, personal communication, August 1998.
2. Amanda Bennett, "GE Redesigns Rungs of Career Ladder," *Wall Street Journal,* 15 March 1993, B1, B3.
3. Robin White Goode, "International and Foreign Language Skills Have an Edge," *Black Enterprise,* May 1995, 53.
4. Nancy M. Somerick, "Managing a Communication Internship Program," *Bulletin of the Association for Business Communication 56,* no. 3 (1993): 10–20.
5. Cheryl L. Noll, "Collaborating with the Career Planning and Placement Center in the Job-Search Project," *Business Communication Quarterly* 58, no. 3 (1995): 53–55.
6. Roberta Maynard, "Casting the Net for Job Seekers," *Nation's Business,* March 1997, 28–29.
7. Robert J. Gerberg, Robert Gerberg's *Job Changing System,* summarized by Macmillan Book Clubs, Inc., in the "Macmillan Executive Summary Program," April 1987, 4.
8. Christoper Caggiano, "Recruiting Secrets," *Inc.,* October 1998, 29-42; Donna Fenn, "The Right Fit," *Inc.* 500, 1997, 104+.
9. Caggiano, "Recruiting Secrets."
10. Caggiano, "Recruiting Secrets."
11. Rockport Institute, "How to Write a Masterpiece of a Résumé," http://www.rockportinstitute.com/résumés.html, accessed 16 October 1998.
12. Pam Stanley-Weigand, "Organizing the Writing of Your Résumé," *Bulletin of the Association for Business Communication 54,* no. 3 (September 1991): 11–12.
13. Beverly Culwell-Block and Jean Anna Sellers, "Résumé Content and Format—Do the Authorities Agree?" *Bulletin of the Association for Business Communication 57,* no. 4 (1994): 27–30.
14. Janice Tovey, "Using Visual Theory in the Creation of Résumés: A Bibliography," *Bulletin of the Association for Business Communication 54,* no. 3 (September 1991): 97–99.
15. Doug Halm, manager, human resources, Recreational Equipment Incorporated, personal communication, August 1998.
16. Rockport Institute, "How to Write a Masterpiece of a Résumé."
17. Sal Divita, "If You're Thinking Résumé, Think Creatively," *Marketing News,* 14 September 1992, 29.
18. Rockport Institute, "How to Write a Masterpiece of a Résumé."
19. Richard H. Beatty and Nicholas C. Burkholder, *The Executive Career Guide for MBAs* (New York: Wiley, 1996), 133.
20. Adapted from Burdette E. Bostwick, *How to Find the Job You've Always Wanted* (New York: Wiley, 1982), 69–70.
21. Beatty and Burkholder, *The Executive Career Guide for MBAs,* 151.
22. Rockport Institute, "How to Write a Masterpiece of a Résumé."
23. Regina Pontow, "Electronic Résumé Writing Tips," http://www.proven-resumes.com/reswkshps/electronic/scnres.html, accessed on18 October 1998.
24. Ellen Joe Pollock, "Sir: Your Application for a Job Is Rejected; Sincerely, Hal 9000," *Wall Street Journal,* 30 July 1998, A1, A12.
25. William H. Baker, Kristen DeTienne, and Karl L. Smart, "How Fortune 500 Com-panies Are Using Electronic Résumé Management Systems," *Business Communi-cation Quarterly* 61, no. 3, September 1998, 8–19.
26. Bronwyn Fryer, "Job Hunting the Electronic Way," *Working Woman,* March 1995, 59–60, 78; Joyce Lane Kennedy and Thomas J. Morrow, *Electronic Resume Revolution,* 2d ed. (New York: Wiley, 1995), 30–33; Mary Goodwin, Deborah Cohn, and Donna Spivey, *Netjobs: Use the Internet to Land Your Dream Job* (New York: Michael Wolff, 1996), 149–150; Zane K. Quible, "Electronic Résumés: Their Time Is Coming," *Business Communication Quarterly 58,* no. 3 (1995): 5–9; Alfred Glossbrenner and Emily Glossbrenner, *Finding a Job on the Internet* (New York: McGraw-Hill, 1995), 194–197; Pam Dixon and Silvia Tiersten, *Be Your Own Headhunter Online* (New York: Random House, 1995), 80–83.

27. Pollock, "Sir: Your Application for a Job Is Rejected."
28. Pontow, "Electronic Résumé Writing Tips."
29. Louis S. Richman, "How to Get Ahead," *Fortune,* 16 May 1994, 46–51; Bruce Nussbaum, "I'm Worried about My Job," *Business Week,* 7 October 1991, 94–97.
30. William J. Banis, "The Art of Writing Job-Search Letters," *CPC Annual,* 36th Edition 2 (1992): 42–50.
31. Doug Halm, manager, human resources, Recreational Equipment Incorporated, personal communication, August 1998.

Chapter 18

1. Jodi DeLeon, college recruiting manager, Microsoft Corporation, personal communication, May 1993; Microsoft Web page <http://www.microsoft.com> 1998.
2. Paul Plawin, "Job-Hunting Blunders You Don't Have to Make," *Changing Times,* December 1988, 69.
3. Sylvia Porter, "Your Money: How to Prepare for Job Interviews," *San Francisco Chronicle,* 3 November 1981, 54.
4. Samuel Greengard, "Are You Well Armed to Screen Applicants?" *Personnel Journal,* December 1995, 84–95.
5. Charlene Marmer Solomon, "How Does Disney Do It?" *Personnel Journal,* December 1989, 53.
6. Barron Wells and Nelda Spinks, "Interviewing: What Small Companies Say," *Bulletin of the Association for Business Communication* 55, no. 2 (1992): 18–22; Clive Fletcher, "Ethics and the Job Interview," *Personnel Management,* March 1992, 36–39; Nancy K. Austin, "Goodbye Gimmicks," *Incentive,* May 1996, 241.
7. Marcia Vickers, "Don't Touch That Dial: Why Should I Hire You?" *New York Times,* 13 April 1997, F11.
8. Austin, "Goodbye Gimmicks."
9. Austin, "Goodbye Gimmicks."
10. Peter Rea, Julie Rea, and Charles Moonmaw, "Training: Use Assessment Centers in Skill Development," *Personnel Journal,* April 1990, 126–131; Greengard, "Are You Well Armed to Screen Applicants?"
11. "Southwest Is Picky," *Soundview Executive Book Summaries,* September 1998, 5.
12. "Look for Workers with Brains and Attitude," *Soundview Executive Book Summaries,* September 1998, 5.
13. Donna Fenn, "The Right Fit," *Inc.* 500, 1997, 1041.
14. Anne Fisher, "Success Secret: A High Emotional IQ," *Fortune,* 26 October 1998, 293–298.
15. Joel Russell, "Finding Solid Ground," *Hispanic Business,* February 1992, 42–44, 46.
16. Holly Rawlinson, "Pre-Employment Testing," *Small Business Reports,* April 1989, 20.
17. Josh Martin, "An HR Guide to White Collar Crime," *HR Focus,* September 1998, 1, 141.
18. "Substance Abuse in the Workplace," *HR Focus,* February 1997, 1, 41.
19. Tyler D. Hartwell, Paul D. Steele, and Nathaniel F. Rodman, "Workplace Alcohol-Testing Programs: Prevalence and Trends," *Monthly Labor Review,* June 1998, 27–34.
20. Michael P. Cronin, "This Is a Test," *Inc.,* August 1993, 64–68.
21. Microsoft 1997 Annual Report, http://www.microsoft.com, accessed 23 October 1998.
22. "Quick Click," *U.S. News & World Report,* 29 April 1996, 70.
23. Robert Gifford, Cheuk Fan Ng, and Margaret Wilkinson, "Nonverbal Cues in the Employment Interview: Links between Applicant Qualities and Interviewer Judgments," *Journal of Applied Psychology* 70, no. 4 (1985): 729.
24. Dale G. Leathers, *Successful Nonverbal Communication* (New York: Macmillan, 1986), 225.
25. Mary Goodwin, Deborah Cohn, and Donna Spivey, *Netjobs: Use the Internet to Land Your Dream Job* (New York: Michael Wolff, 1996), 170.
26. Nina Munk and Suzanne Oliver, "Think Fast," *Forbes,* 24 March 1997, 146–151.
27. Shirley J. Shepherd, "How to Get That Job in 60 Minutes or Less," *Working Woman,* March 1986, 119.
28. Shepherd, "How to Get That Job in 60 Minutes or Less," 118.
29. H. Anthony Medley, *Sweaty Palms: The Neglected Art of Being Interviewed* (Berkeley, Calif.: Ten Speed Press, 1993), 179.
30. Gerald L. Wilson, "Preparing Students for Responding to Illegal Selection Interview Questions," *Bulletin of the Association for Business Communication* 54, no. 2 (1991): 44–49.
31. Jeff Springston and Joann Keyton, "Interview Response Training," *Bulletin of the Association for Business Communication* 54, no. 3 (1991): 28–30; Gerald L. Wilson, "An Analysis of Instructional Strategies for Responding to Illegal Selection Interview Questions," *Bulletin of the Association for Business Communication* 54, no. 3 (1991): 31–35.
32. Stephen J. Pullum, "Illegal Questions in the Selection Process: Going Beyond Contemporary Business and Professional Communication Textbooks," *Bulletin of the Association for Business Communication* 54, no. 3 (1991): 36–43; Alicia Kitsuse, " 'Have You Ever Been Arrested?' " *Across the Board,* November 1992, 46–49; Christina L. Greathouse, "10 Common Hiring Mistakes," *Industry Week,* 20 January 1992, 22–23, 26.
33. Joann S. Lublin, "Web Transforms Art of Negotiating Raises," *Wall Street Journal,* 22 September 1998, B1, B6.
34. Marilyn Moats Kennedy, "Are You Getting Paid What You're Worth?" *New Woman,* November 1984, 110.
35. Harold H. Hellwig, "Job Interviewing: Process and Practice," *Bulletin of the Association for Business Communication* 55, no. 2 (1992): 8–14.
36. Jodi DeLeon, college recruiting manager, Microsoft Corporation, personal communication, May 1993.

Component Chapter A

1. Mary A. De Vries, *Internationally Yours* (Boston: Houghton Mifflin, 1994), 9.
2. Patricia A. Dreyfus, "Paper That's Letter Perfect," *Money,* May 1985, 184.
3. "When Image Counts, Letterhead Says It All," *The Advocate and Greenwich Time,* 10 January 1993, F4.
4. Mel Mandell, "Electronic Forms Are Cheap and Speedy," *D&B Reports,* July–August 1993, 44–45.
5. Linda Driskill, *Business & Managerial Communication: New Perspectives* (Orlando, Fla.: Harcourt Brace Jovanovich, 1992), 470.
6. Driskill, *Business & Managerial Communication,* 470.
7. Lennie Copeland and Lewis Griggs, *Going International: How to Make Friends and Deal Effectively in the Global Marketplace,* 2d ed. (New York: Random House, 1985), 24–27.
8. DeVries, *Internationally Yours,* 8.
9. Copeland and Griggs, *Going International,* 24–27.
10. U.S. Postal Service, *Postal Addressing Standards* (Washington, D.C.: GPO, 1992).
11. Copeland and Griggs, *Going International,* 24–27.
12. Renee B. Horowitz and Marian G. Barchilon, "Stylistic Guidelines for E-Mail," *IEEE Transactions on Profes-sional Communications,* 37, no. 4 (1994): 207–212.
13. Jill H. Ellsworth and Matthew V. Ellsworth, *The Internet Business Book* (New York: Wiley, 1994), 93.
14. William Eager, *Using the Internet* (Indianapolis: Que Corporation, 1994), 11.
15. Eager, *Using the Internet,* 10.
16. William Eager, Larry Donahue, David Forsyth, Kenneth Mitton, and Martin Waterhouse, *Net.Search* (Indianapolis: Que Corporation, 1995), 221.
17. Rosalind Resnick and Dave Taylor, *Internet Business Guide* (Indianapolis: Sams.net Publishing, 1995), 117.
18. James L. Clark and Lyn R. Clark, *How 7: A Handbook for Office Workers,* 7th ed. (Cincinnati: South-Western, 1995), 431–432.

ACKNOWLEDGMENTS

Text, Figures, and Tables

6 Adapted from Phillip Morgan and H. Kent Baker, "Building a Professional Image: Improving Listening Behavior." Reprinted by permission of the publisher, from *Supervisory Management,* November 1985, 34. © 1985 American Management Association, New York. All rights reserved. **9** Adapted from David J. Rachman and Michael H. Mescon, *Business Today,* 5th ed. (New York: McGraw-Hill, 1987), 127. Copyright © 1987 by McGraw-Hill, Inc. **10** Carol Hymowitz, "Spread the Word: Gossip Is Good," *Wall Street Journal,* 4 November 1988, B1; Donald B. Simmons, "The Nature of the Organizational Grapevine," *Supervisory Management*, November 1985, 40. **11** (PSSST! I Heard It through the Grapevine) Adapted from "Continental Achieves Buy-in through Communication," *Workforce,* July 1997, 8+; Bob Smith, "Care and Feeding of the Office Grapevine," *Management Review,* 1 February 1997, 6; Jitendra Mishra, "Managing the Office Grapevine," *Public Personnel Management,* 1 June 1990, 213; Frank Basile, "Pssst: Office Gossip Can Be a Productive Tool," *Indianapolis Business Journal,* 20 November 1995, 37A; William Hull, "Beating the Grapevine to the Punch," *Supervision,* August 1994, 17–20. **15** John V. Thill and Courtland L. Bovée, *Excellence in Business Communication* (New York: Prentice Hall, 1999), 10. **19** Adapted from Allan D. Frank, *Communicating on the Job* (Glenview, Ill.: Scott Foresman, 1982), 20. Used with permission of Allan D. Frank. **20** "Information Deluge Clogging Workplace," *The Honolulu Advertiser,* 25 May 1998, B6; Alex Markels, "Memo 4/8/97, FYI: Messages Inundate Offices," *Wall Street Journal*, 8 April 1997, B1. **24** (Ethical Boundaries: Where Would You Draw the Line?) Adapted from Ben Stein, "An Employer's Bill of Rights," *Business Month,* April 1990, 55; Thomas A. Young, "Ethics in Business: Business of Ethics," *Vital Speeches,* 15 September 1992, 725–730; "Business Ethics: What Are Your Personal Standards?" *Working Woman,* February 1990, 61–62; Kyle Herger, "One Communicator's Gold Star Is Another's Scarlet Letter," *IABC Communication World,* September 1989, 34–36; Barbara D. Langham, "Ethics: Where Do You Stand?" *IABC Communication World,* May 1989, 21–22, 24–25; Frank Yanacek, "A Question of Ethics," *Transportation and Distribution,* December 1988, 48–50. **26** Data from Richard W. Judy and Carol D'Amico, *Workforce 2020* (Indianapolis: Hudson Institute, 1997), 109. **28** G. A. Marken, "Think before You Click," *Office Systems,* March 1998, 44–46. **29** "The Myth of the Paperless Office," *Across the Board*, April 1996, 20. **36** Judith Light, "Keys to Successful Communication: More Than Words," *Journal of Management Consulting,* May 1998, 28–32. **37** Barbara Pachter, "When in Japan, Don't Cross Your Legs," *Business Ethics,* March–April 1996, 50. **38 (Actions Speak Louder Than Words All around the World)** Adapted from David A. Victor, *International Business Communication* (New York: HarperCollins, 1992); David Wallace, "Mind Your Manners," *World Trade,* October 1992, 52, 54–55; Hannele Duvfa, "Innocents Abroad: The Politics of Cross-Cultural Communication," *Communication and Discourse across Cultures and Languages,* 1991, 73–89; M. Katherine Glover, "Do's & Taboos: Cultural Aspects of International Business," *Business America,* 13 August 1990, 2–6; C. Barnum and N. Woniansky, "Taking Cues from Body Language," *Management Review,* June 1989, 59–60. **44** Copyright, Dr. Lyman K. Steil, president, Communication Development, Inc., St. Paul, Minn. Prepared for the Sperry Corporation. Reprinted with permission of Dr. Steil and Unisys Corporation. **47** Adapted from J. Michael Sproule, *Communication Today* (Glenview, Ill.: Scott, Foresman, 1981), by permission of J. Michael Sproule. Copyright J. Michael Sproule. **49 (Electronic Meetings: Work Together—Where-ver You Are—to Get the Results You Want)** Adapted from Elizabeth Niendorf, "High-Tech Meetings Help Timid Give Voice to Ideas," *Nashville Business Journal,* 18 November 1996, 20; Jim Clark and Richard Koonce, "Meetings Go High-Tech," *Training and Development,* 1 November 1995, 32+; Joseph G. Donelan, "Using Electronic Tools to Improve Meetings," *Management Accounting,* March 1993, 42–45; Brent Gallupe and George Fox, "Facilitated Electronic Meetings: Higher Quality, Less Time," *CMA Magazine,* April 1992, 29–32; Rosemary Hamilton, "Electronic Meetings: No More ZZZZ's," *Computerworld,* 14 September 1992, 109, 113; Michael Finley, "The Best of All Possible Meetings?" *Across the Board,* September 1991, 40–45; Michael Finley, "The New Meaning of Meetings," *IABC Communication World,* March 1991, 25–27; Stephen F. Friedman, "The Electronic Alternative," *Small Business Reports,* July 1991, 68–72; Robert Moskowitz, "Electronic Meetings Raise Effectiveness," *Office Systems,* August 1991, 30–36; Shawn Hartley Hancock, "Electronic Meetings: Ready for Prime Time," *Successful Meetings,* October 1988, 32–37; Ellen Muraskin, "Electronic Meetings," *Meetings & Conventions,* November 1988, 138; Sam Dickey, "Electronic Meetings: Substitutes with Substance?" *Today's Office,* July 1986, 40–46. **52** "Till They Meet Again," 1996 Newspaper Publishing P.L.C., 22 April 1996, 4; *Electric Library,* Online, accessed 17 July, 1998. **66 (Test Your Intercultural Knowledge)** Adapted from David A. Ricks, "International Business Blunders: An Update," *Business & Economic Review,* January–March 1988, 11–14, reprinted by permission; "Culture Quiz," *Workforce,* January 1998, 25; Valerie Frazee, "Keeping Up on Chinese Culture," *Global Workforce,* October 1996, 16–17; Valerie Frazee, "Establishing Relations in Germany," *Global Workforce,* April 1997, 16–17; James Wilfong and Toni Seger, *Taking Your Business Global* (Franklin Lakes, N.J.: Career Press, 1997), 282. **67** Classroom lecture material, "The Place of Honor," International Orientation Resources, Northbrook, Ill., February 1995. **71** J. Robert Carleton, "Cultural Due Diligence," *Training,* November 1997, 67–75. **72** Keith Denton and Charles Boyd, *Did You Know?* (Paramus, N.J.: Prentice Hall, 1994), 12. **74 (Should Companies Stress English Only on the Job?)** Adapted from Sam Howe Verhovek, "Clash of Cultures Tears Texas City," *New York Times,* 30 September 1997, A-10; Joseph D'Obrian, "Only English Speakers Need Apply," *Management Review,* January 1991, 41–45; Seth Mydans, "Pressure for English Only Job Rules Stirring a Sharp Debate across U.S.," *New York Times,* 8 August 1990, sec. A, 12; L. Erik Bratt and Fred Alvarez, "English Only Memo Outrages Employees," *San Diego Union,* 15 September 1990, C-1. **87 (Pillsbury's Recipe for Candid Talk)** Adapted from Gillian Flynn, "Pillsbury's Recipe Is Candid Talk," *Workforce,* February 1998, 56–57+; Thomas Petzinger Jr., "Two Executives Cook Up Way to Make Pillsbury Listen," *Wall Street Journal,* 27 September 1996, B1. **93** "Having the Write Skills," *Journal of Accountancy,* April 1998, 13. **94** (Send Me a Memo on It; or Better Yet, Don't) Adapted from Ruth Davidhizar and Sally Erdel, "Send Me a Memo On It; or Better Yet, Don't," *Health Care Supervisor,* June 1997, 42–47; Walter Kiechel III and John Paul Newport Jr., "Office Hours: Memo Punctilio," *Fortune,* 15 September, 1986, 185. **96** Adapted from Lenny Laskowski, "To Truly Customize Your Message, Research Your A.U.D.I.E.N.C.E.," *Presentations,* January 1998, 37–40. **101** Scott DeGraeve, president, Scotty's Home Market, personal communication, August 1998. **103** Mary A. DeVries, *Internationally Yours* (Boston, Houghton Mifflin: 1994), 61. **105** (Doublespeak: Why No One Knows What Anyone's Saying Anymore) Adapted from William Lutz, "Life under the Chief Doublespeak Officer," *USA Today,* 17 October 1996, 15A. **114** John S. Fielden, Jean D. Fielden, and Ronald E. Dulek, *The Business Writing Style Book* (Upper Saddle River, N.J.: Prentice Hall, 1984), 7. **115** Courtesy of General Mills, Inc. **142** Adapted from Susan Benjamin, *Words at Work* (Reading, Mass: Addison-Wesley, 1997), 136–137. **144** (Use Plain English, Please!) Adapted from Toddi Gutner, "At Last, the Readable Prospectus," *Business Week,* 13 April 1998, 11; Philip Maher, "One for the Writers," *Investment Dealers' Digest,* 17 November 1997, 4+; Ronald G. Shafer, "Government Bureaucrats to Learn a New Language: Simple English," *Wall Street Journal,* 2 June 1998, B1; Peder Zane, "For Investors, an Initial Public Offering of English," *New York Times,* 25 August 1996, 7; Dan Seligman, "The Gobbledygook Profession," *Forbes,* 7 September 1998, 174–175; Michael Weiss and James Hildebrandt, "Art of Clear Writing Lost in Sea of Legalese," *San Antonio Business Journal,* 28 October 1996, accessed online September 1998 at http://www.amcity.com/sanantonio/stories/102896/editorial2.html. **147** Webb Garrison, *Why You*

Say It (Nashville: Rutledge Hill Press, 1992), 21. **150** Charles Marsh, *A Quick and Not Dirty Guide to Business Writing* (Scottsdale, Ariz.: Gorsuch Scarisbrick Publishers, 1997), 22. **154** Susan Benjamin, *Words at Work* (Reading, Mass.: Addison-Wesley, 1997), 97. **169** Mark H. McCormack, On Communicating (Los Angeles: Dove Books, 1998), 54–57. **178 (How to Proofread Like a Pro)** Adapted from Philip C. Kolin, Successful Writing at Work, 2d ed., 102. Used with permission of D. C. Heath and Company; Dennis Hensley, "A Way with Words: Proofreading Can Save Cash and Careers," Dallas Magazine, May 1986, 57–58. Reprinted with permission. **180 (From Digits to Dust)** Adapted from Marcia Stepanek, "From Digits to Dust," *Business Week,* 20 April 1998, 128–130; Stephan H. Wildstrom, "Don't Be a Crash Dummy," *Business Week,* 13 April 1998, 15; Gary Sutton, "Backing Up Onsite—or Online: 25 Smart Ways to Protect Your PC from Data Disaster," *Computer Technology Review,* February 1998, 38, 421; Deborah Branscum and Jennifer Lach, "E-mail Scare," *Newsweek,* 10 August 1998, 10; Brooks Talley, "Killing Viruses Dead," *InfoWorld,* 10 August 1998, 1, 661; Stan Miastkowski, "Virus Killers," *PC World Online,* 1 March 1998; Philip Elmer-DeWitt, Scott Brown, and Thomas McCarroll, "Invasion of the Data Snatchers," *Time,* 26 September 1998, 621; James E. Hunton, "Facts and Fables about Computer Viruses," *Journal of Accountancy,* May 1998, 39–42. **182** Richard Gibson, "On the Dot: Fashion Dictates a New Life for the Lowly Period," *Wall Street Journal,* 9 July 1998, A1, A6; Grammatik 5, © 1986–93, Reference Software International, a wholly owned subsidiary of WordPerfect Corporation. All rights reserved. Used with permission. **183** Gary Sutton, "Backing Up Onsite—or Online: 25 Smart Ways to Protect Your PC from Data Disaster," *Computer Technology Review,* February 1998, 38, 421. **193 (Caution! E-Mail Can Bite)** Adapted from Steve Lohr, "Antitrust Case Is Highlighting Role of E-Mail," *New York Times,* 2 November 1998, C1, C4; Dan Goodin, "E-Mail Still Dangerous in Business," *The Net,* 20 January 1998, accessed from http://www.news.com/News/Item/0,4,18245,00.html on 9 September 1998; Bob Trott, "Microsoft Memos Tell the Story," *InfoWorld,* 25 May 1998, 91; Marcia Stepanek and Steve Hamm, "When the Devil Is in the E-Mails," *Business Week,* 8 June 1998, 72–74; Bryan Gruley, "Microsoft's Memos Bolster Government's Case," *Wall Street Journal,* 19 May 1998, A3, A15; John R. Wilke, "Old E-Mail Dogs Microsoft in Fighting Antitrust Suits," *Wall Street Journal,* 27 August 1998, B1, B8; John R. Wilke and Don Clark, "U.S. Adds to Case vs. Microsoft and Gates," *Wall Street Journal,* 2 September 1998, A3, A6; Michael R. Overly, "Is Your E-Mail Being Tapped?" *Business News,* Spring 1997, 51–52; June Kronholz and Rebecca Quick, "The Lewinsky Story Is a Tale Spun Out across Cyberspace," *Wall Street Journal,* 22 September 1998, A1, A10. **200** (How Direct Is Too Direct?) Adapted from Mary A. DeVries, *Internationally Yours* (Boston: Houghton Mifflin, 1994), 195; Myron W. Lustig and Jolene Koester, *Intercultural Competence* (New York: HarperCollins, 1993), 66–72; Mary Munter, "Cross-Cultural Communication for Managers," *Business Horizons,* May–June 1993, 69–78; David A. Victor, *International Business Communication* (New York: HarperCollins, 1992), 137–168; Larry A. Samovar and Richard E. Porter, *Intercultural Communication: A Reader,* 6th ed. (Belmont, Calif.: Wadsworth, 1991), 109–110; Larry A. Samovar and Richard E. Porter, *Communication between Cultures* (Belmont, Calif.: Wadsworth, 1991), 235–244; Carley H. Dodd, *Dynamics of Intercultural Communication,* 3d ed. (Dubuque, Iowa: Wm. C. Brown, 1989), 69–73. **213 A.** D. Keith Denton and Charles Boyd, *Did You Know?* (Paramus, N.J.: Prentice Hall, 1994), 27. **217 B.** D. Keith Denton and Charles Boyd, *Did You Know?* (Paramus, N.J.: Prentice Hall, 1994), 27. **222 C.** David A. Price, "Good References Pave Road to Court," *USA Today,* 13 February 1997, 11A. **224** (Recommendation Letters: What's Right to Write?) Adapted from Maura Dolan and Stuart Silverstein, "Court Broadens Liability for Job References," *Los Angeles Times,* 28 January 1997, A1, A11; David A. Price, "Good References Pave Road to Court," *USA Today,* 13 February 1997, 11A; Frances A. McMorris, "Ex-Bosses Face Less Peril Giving Honest Job References," *Wall Street Journal,* 8 July 1996, B1, B8; Dawn Gunsch, "Gray Matters: Centralize Control of Giving References," *Personnel Journal,* September 1992, 114, 116–117; Betty Southard Murphy, Wayne E. Barlow, and D. Diane Hatch, "Manager's Newsfront: Job Reference Liability of Employees," *Personnel Journal,* September 1991, 22, 26; Ross H. Fishman, "When Silence Is Golden," *Nation's Business,* July 1991, 48–49. **252** Richard M. Steinberg, "No, It Couldn't Happen Here," *Management Review,* September 1998, 70. **254 (Good Ways to Send Bad News Around the World)** Adapted from James Calvert Scott and Diana J. Green, "British Perspectives on Organizing Bad-News Letters: Organizational Patterns Used by Major U.K. Companies," *Bulletin of the Association for Business Communication* 55, no. 1 (March 1992): 17–19; Iris I. Varner, "A Comparison of American and French Business Correspondence," *Journal of Business Communication* 24, no. 4 (Fall 1988): 55–65; Susan Jenkins and John Hinds, "Business Letter Writing: English, French, and Japanese," *TESOL Quarterly* 21, no. 2 (June 1987): 327–349; Saburo Haneda and Hiosuke Shima, "Japanese Communication Behavior As Reflected in Letter Writing," *Journal of Business Communication* 19, no. 1 (1982): 19–32. **257** G. A. Marken, "Think before You Click," *Office Systems,* March 1998, 44–46. **267** David K. Lindo, "Are You Coaching the 'Bad News Bearers'?" *Supervision,* June 1998, 3–4+. **268** (How to Take the Sting out of Criticism and Foster Goodwill) Adapted from Les Giblin, *How to Have Confidence and Power in Dealing with People* (New York: Prentice Hall, 1956), 132–133. **289** Adapted from Abraham H. Maslow, *Motivation and Personality* (New York: Harper & Row, 1954), 12, 19, Copyright © 1970 by Abraham H. Maslow. Reprinted by permission of HarperCollins Publishers. **298** (Does Some Direct Mail Contain Deliberately Deceptive Copy?) Adapted from Galen Stilson, "Big Sales by Mail: Get the Order Now," *In Business,* October 1992, 44; Herschell Gordon Lewis, "The Future of 'Force-Communication': Power Communication," *Direct Marketing,* April 1991, 51–52; Annetta Miller, "My Postman Has a Hernia!" *Newsweek,* 10 June 1991, 41; Michael R. Hyman and Richard Tansey, "The Ethics of Psychoactive Ads," *Journal of Business Ethics,* February 1990, 105–114; Jill Smolowe, "Read This!!!!!!!!" *Time,* 26 November 1990, 62–67. **302** D. Keith Denton and Charles Boyd, *Did You Know?* (Paramus, N.J.: Prentice Hall, 1994), 28. **309** George Wachtel, "How to Write an Effective Sales Letter: Part 1," *Bank Marketing,* July 1996, 1091. **310** Rebecca Quick, "Measures to Rid Cyberspace of 'Spam' Run into Snags," *Wall Street Journal,* 18 May 1998, B1, B10. **314** (Canning Spam) Adapted from Rebecca Quick, "Sick of Junk E-Mail? Here Are Some Tips for Fighting Back," *Wall Street Journal,* 23 May 1998, B7; Jeri Clausing, "New Plan for Junk E-Mail Is Dividing Internet Camps," *New York Times,* 18 May 1998, C4; Rebecca Quick, "Measures to Rid Cyberspace of 'Spam' Run into Snags," *Wall Street Journal,* 18 May 1998, B1, B10. **333** (How Boeing Blew It—Almost) Adapted from James Wallace, "How Boeing Blew It," *Sales and Marketing Management,* February 1998, 52–57; Ronald Henkoff, "Boeing's Big Problem," *Fortune,* 12 January 1998, 96–103; John Greenwald, "Is Boeing Out of Its Spin?" *Time,* 13 July 1998, 67–69. **338** A. Gerard J. Holzmann, "Just the Fax," *Inc. Tech* (1998), 148. **342** (E-Mail Etiquette: Minding Your Manners Online) Adapted from Roberta Maynard, "Minding Your E-Mail Manners," *Nation's Business,* 1 August 1997, 10; Shari Caudron, "Virtual Manners," *Industry Week,* 6 July 1998, 52–53; Marian M. Extejt, "Teaching Students to Correspond Effectively Electronically," *Business Communication Quarterly* 61, no. 2 (1998): 57–67; Pamela Sebastian, "E-Mail Etiquette Starts to Take Shape for Business Messaging," *Wall Street Journal,* 12 October 1995, A1; David Angell and Brent Heslop, *The Elements of E-Mail Style* (Reading, Mass.: Addison-Wesley, 1994), 1–31, 66–69, 113–127; Renee B. Horowitz and Marian G. Barchilon, "Stylistic Guidelines for E-Mail," *IEEE Transactions on Professional Communications* 37, no. 4 (1994): 207–212; Lance Cohen, "How to Improve Your E-mail Messages," http://galaxy.einet/galaxy/business-and-commerce/management/communications/How_to_Improve_Your_E_mail.html. **346** (T10.1) Search Engines Fact and Fun http://searchenginewatch.internet.com/facts/major.html, accessed 11 March 1998; "Getting Started—What You Need to Know to Begin Using the Internet," *Fortune Technology Buyer's Guide*, Winter 1998, 232–240; Matt Lake, "Desperately Seeking Susan OR Suzie NOT Sushi," *New York Times,* 3 September 1998, D1, D7; "Notable Websites," *Fortune Technology Buyer's Guide,* Winter 1999, 238, 240. **350** (Create a Winning Web Site) Adapted from Brian Hurley and Peter Birkwood, *A Small Business Guide to Doing Big Business on the Internet* (Vancouver, B.C.: International Self-Counsel Press,1996), 124–134.; Melissa Campanelli, "Net Profits," *Entrepreneur,* October 1998, 49–50; "Selling on the Net," *Soundview Executive Book Summaries,* March 1997, 1–8. **351** B. Christine Lazuk, "The Voice Mail Advantage," http://www.smartbiz.com/sbs/arts/jrg7.thm, accessed 8 July 1998. **353** C. Laura Tangley, "Whoops, There Goes Another CD-ROM," *U.S. News & World Report,* 16 February 1998, 67–68. **355** Adapted from "Ten Steps to Caller-Friendly Voice Mail," *Managing Office Technology,* January 1995, 25. **369** Partially adapted from Michael Eisenberg and Robert Berkowitz, "Big Six" Model. Copyright 1998. http://big6.syr.edu/body.html, accessed 6 November 1998. **373** A. Kathy McGreevy, "How to Evaluate Information Resources," http://www.santarosa.edu/library/lib.guide.qual.shtml accessed 28 October 1998. **374** B. "Lost Information Costs Plenty," *Industry Week,* 20 July 1998, 68. **375** (The Tangled Web of Internet Copyrights) Adapted from *The Internet Unleashed,* 2d ed. (Indianapolis: Sams.net Publishing, 1995), 1056; Alice Bredin, "The Hard Drive: Analog Laws Can't Keep Up with Digital Technology," *Newsday,* 30 April 1995, 2; Ron Coleman, "Copycats on the Superhighway," *ABA Journal* 81 (1 July 1995): 68. **376** C. Ernest L. Maier,

Anthony J. Faria, Peter Kaatrude, and Elizabeth Wook, *The Business Library and How to Use It* (Detroit: Omnigraphics, 1996), 36. **382** Sherwyn P. Morreale and Courtland L. Bovée, *Excellence in Public Speaking* (Fort Worth: Harcourt Brace College Publishers, 1998), 176. **390** (How to Avoid Plagiarizing) Adapted from Daphne A. Jameson, "The Ethics of Plagiarism: How Genre Affects Writers' Use of Source Materials," *Bulletin of the Association for Business Communication* 56, no. 2 (June 1993): 18–28; Deni Elliott, "Plagiarism: It's Not a Black and White Issue," *The Quill,* November–December 1991, 15–16; Amy Gamerman, "Unfair Use: Copyright Decision Cramps Writers' Style," *Wall Street Journal,* 10 April 1990, A16; Pamela S. Zurer, "NIH Panel Strips Researcher of Funding after Plagiarism Review," *Chemical & Engineering News,* 7 August 1989, 24–25; Mark Fitzgerald, "Denver Post Art Critic Fired for Plagiarism," *Editor & Publisher,* 11 March 1989, 22. **392** Adapted from "Finding Industry Information," http://www.pitt.edu/~buslibry/industries.htm, accessed 3 November 1998; Thomas P. Bergman, Stephen M. Garrison, and Gregory M. Scott, *The Business Student Writer's Manual and Guide to the Internet* (Paramus, N.J.: Prentice Hall, 1998), 67–80; Ernest L. Maier, Anthony J. Faria, Peter Kaatrude, and Elizabeth Wood, *The Business Library and How to Use It* (Detroit: Omnigraphics, 1996), 53–76. **402** Jo Robbins, *High-Impact Presentations—A Multimedia Approach* (New York: Wiley, 1997), 116. **404** *Standard & Poor's Industry Surveys—Footware,* 1 December 1998, 26. **404** *Standard & Poor's Industry Surveys—Autos,* 5 March 1998, 16. **405** *Standard & Poor's Industry Surveys—Movies,* 12 November 1998, 30. **405** *American Demographics,* March 1998, 42. **406** (F12.6a, Where the College Students Are) *American Demographics,* March 1998, 47. **406** (F12.6b, Eating Occasions) *American Demographics,* January 1998, 58 **406** (F12.6c, Targeted Talks) *American Demographics,* February 1998, 52. **406** (F12.6d, Commercial Superhighway) *Wall Street Journal,* 7 December 1998, R4. **408** *Nation's Business,* April 1997, p. 34. **410** (F12.9, pie chart) *Frequent Flyer Magazine* and J. D. Power and Associates, 1998, Airline Customer Satisfaction Study—U.S. Flights. (F12.9, table) U.S. Department of Transportation http://www.dot/gov/airconsumer/9810del.htm, accessed 9 December 1998. **411** Iris I. Varner, *Contemporary Business Report Writing,* 2d ed. (Chicago: Dryden Press, 1991), 75. **412** http://www.census.gov/statab/ranks/pg05.txt. **412** "How the Networks Deliver the Goods," *Business Week,* 6 April 1998, 91–92. **414** (Creating Colorful Visual Aids with Computers for Maximum Clarity and Impact) Based on information from Hideaki Chijiwa, *Color Harmony* (Rockport, Mass.: Rockport Publishers, 1987), 139–141; Timothy N. Trainor and Diane Krasnewich, *Computers!,* 3d ed. (Watsonville, Calif: Mitchell McGraw-Hill, 1992), 198. **416** Jo Robbins, *High-Impact Presentations—A Multimedia Approach* (New York: Wiley, 1997), 128. **422** (Visual Aids that Lie: The Use and Abuse of Charts and Graphs) Adapted from A. S. C. Ehrenberg, "The Problem of Numeracy," *Admap,* February 1992, 37–40; Mary S. Auvil and Kenneth W. Auvil, *Introduction to Business Graphics: Concepts and Applications* (Cincinnati: South-Western, 1992), 40, 192–193; Peter H. Selby, *Using Graphs and Tables: A Self-Teaching Guide* (New York: Wiley, 1979), 8–9. **427** Lynn Kearny, *Graphics for Presenters* (Menlo Park, Calif.: Crisp Publications, 1996), 15. **433** (YAHOO! The Little Search Engine That Could) Adapted from Linda Himmelstein, "Meet the Grown-Up Voice of Reason at Yahoo!" *Business Week,* 7 September 1998, 67–76; Brad Stone, Jennifer Tanara, and Jennifer Bensko, "Surfers, Step Right Up!" *Newsweek,* 25 May 1998, 74–82; Jonathan Littman, "Driven to Succeed: The Yahoo Story," *Upside,* September 1998, 70–75+; "What Is Yahoo, Really?" *Fortune,* 22 January, 1998, C4; Randall E. Stross, "How Yahoo! Won the Search Wars," *Fortune,* 2 March 1998, 148–154; Mike Hewitt, "Chief Yahoo," *Marketing* (London), 30 October 1997, 23+; Paul Gibson, "Yahoo! Expands on Its Success," *Information World Review,* December 1997, 53–54; Thomas A. Stewart, "Internet Portals: No One-Stop Shop," *Fortune,* 7 December 1998, 235–236; Watty Piper, *The Little Engine That Could* (New York: Platt & Munk, 1981). **452** Hannah King, "What's the Latest on Interim," *Accountancy,* October 1997, 79. **455** (Seven Errors in Logic That Can Undermine Your Reports) Adapted from Christopher Power, "Flops," *Business Week,* 16 August 1993, 79; Mary Munter, *Guide to Managerial Communication,* 2d ed., © 1982, 31. Adapted by permission of Prentice Hall, Inc., Upper Saddle River, N.J. **463** IRS Electronic Services, http://www.irs.ustreas.gov/prod/elec_sus/index.html. **463** (Gain the Competitive Edge with Online Reporting) Adapted from Federal Express home page, http://www.fedex.com/svcs_online.html, accessed 14 June 1996; Jack Schember, "Mrs. Fields' Secret Weapon," *Personnel Journal,* September 1991, 56–58; Paul Kondstadt, "Ship 54—Where Are You?" *CIO,* May 1990, 80–81, 84, 86; Bruce G. Posner and Bo Burlingham, "The Hottest Entrepreneur in America," *Inc.,* January 1988, 44–48. **464** *Business Encyclopedia Illustrated* (Santa Monica, Calif: Knowledge Exchange, 1997), 39. **477** Stephen Barr and Roy Harris, "Incomplete Education" *CFO,* April 1997, 30–39 **478** (Do You Make These Costly Mistakes When Writing Business Reports?) Adapted from Joan Minninger, *The Perfect Memo* (New York: Doubleday, 1990), 169–170. Copyright © 1990 by Joan Minninger. Used by permission of Doubleday, a division of Bantam Doubleday Dell Publishing Group, Inc. **480** Stanley R. Rich and David E. Gumpert, *Business Plans That Win $$$* (New York: Harper & Row, 1987), 28. **497** Stanley R. Rich and David E. Gumpert, *Business Plans that Win $$$$* (New York: Harper & Row, 1987), 16–19. **517** Stanley R. Rich and David E. Gumpert, Business Plans That Win $$$ (New York: Harper & Row, 1987), 30–31. **518** Adapted from Iris I Varner, *Contemporary Business Report Writing,* 2nd ed. (Fort Worth: Dryden Press, 1991), 140. **547** Catalyst, New York, cited in Bickley Townsend, "Room at the Top," A*merican Demographics,* July 1996, 31. **548** Mediamark Research, Inc., New York, cited in Alison Stein Wellner, "Keeping Old Cars on the Road," *American Demographics,* July 1997, 54. **548** Catalyst, New York, cited in Bickley Townsend, "Room at the Top," *American Demographics,* July 1996, 33. **548** Automotive Parts & Accessories Association, Bethesda, Md., cited in Alison Stein Wellner, "Keeping Old Cars on the Road," *American Demographics,* July 1997, 57. **549** Mediamark Research, Inc., New York, cited in Alison Stein Wellner, "Keeping Old Cars on the Road," *American Demographics,* July 1997, 58. **549** The Polk Co., Detroit, cited in Alison Stein Wellner, "Keeping Old Cars on the Road," *American Demographics,* July 1997, 55. **550** Automotive Parts & Accessories Association, Bethesda, Md., cited in Alison Stein Wellner, "Keeping Old Cars on the Road," *American Demographics,* July 1997, 57. **552** Geng Cui, "The Different Faces of the Chinese Consumer," *China Business Review* 24, no. 4 (1997): 34–38, downloaded from ABI/INFORM database 1 December 1998. **553** Grey China, *The Grey ChinaBase Annual Consumer Study*, 1998, cited in Colin Bates, "The Many China Markets," *China Business Review* 25, no. 5 (1998): 26–29, downloaded from ABI/INFORM database 1 December 1998. **553** U.S. Department of Commerce, *Big Emerging Markets Information Resource Page,* http://www.ita.doc.gov/bems/index.html, 28 August 1998, accessed 1 December 1998. **553** U.S. Department of Commerce, *Big Emerging Markets Information Resource Page,* http://www.ita.doc.gov/bems/index.html, 28 August 1998, accessed 1 December 1998. **554** Grey China, *The Grey ChinaBase Annual Consumer Study,* 1998, cited in Colin Bates, "The Many China Markets," *China Business Review* 25, no. 5 (1998): 26–29, downloaded from ABI/INFORM database 1 December 1998. **554** China Economic Information Center, cited in Trish Saywell, "Preparing for Take-Off," *Far Eastern Economic Review* 161, no. 48 (1998): 38, downloaded from ABI/INFORM database 1 December 1998. **555** IGI Consulting, cited in Gina Fraone, "China's Challenge," *Electronic Business* 24, no. 12 (1998): 24, downloaded from ABI/INFORM database 1 December 1998. **572** (Tired of Being Ignored? Five Ways Guaranteed to Get Attention and Keep It) Adapted from Eric J. Adams, "Management Focus: User-Friendly Presentation Software," *World Trade,* March 1995, 92. **574** Steven Guarnaccia, *Fast Company*, February/March 1997, 127. **577** Joseph A. DeVito, *The Elements of Public Speaking,* 6th ed. (New York: Longman, 1997), 270. **578** (Nerves Are Normal) Adapted from Sherwyn P. Morreale and Courtland L. Bovée, *Excellence in Public Speaking* (Fort Worth: Harcourt Brace, 1998), 7; Leon Fletcher, "A Remedy for Stage Fright," *The Toastmaster,* June 1994, 8–10; Greg Dahl, "Fear of Fear," *The Toastmaster,* June 1994, 10–11; "A Survival Guide to Public Speaking," *Training & Development Journal,* September 1990, 15–16, 18–25. **579** Mary-Ellen Drummond, *Fearless and Flawless Public Speaking with Power, Polish, and Pizazz* (San Diego: Pfeiffer & Company, 1993), 22. **585** (Duplicating Success) Adapted from Kinko's Web site, http://www.kinkos.com/info, accessed 13 December 1998; Shawn Tully, "A Better Taskmaster Than the Market," *Fortune,* 26 October 1998, 277–286; Laurie J. Flynn, "For the Officeless, a Place to Call Home," *New York Times,* 6 July 1998, 1, 4; Michele Marchetti, "Getting the Kinks Out," *Sales and Marketing Management,* March 1997, 56–64; "Man of Few Words," *Sales and Marketing Management,* March 1997, 63; "Kinko's Improves Image of Business with Top-Notch Proposals and Presentations Capabilities; Presentations a Growing Percentage of Customer Work at Kinko's," *Business Wire,* 28 September 1997; "Kinko's Strengthens Office Product Assortment," *Discount Store News,* 17 November 1997, 6, 70; Ann Marsh, "Kinko's Grows Up—Almost," *Forbes,* 1 December 1997, 270–272; "Kinko's Strikes Deal for Mideast Growth," *Graphic Arts Monthly,* January 1988, 22. **591** John J. Xenakis, "Workers of the World, Disperse!" *CFO,* October 1997, 79+. **595** (High Tech Job Hunting: The Secrets of Finding Employment on the World Wide Web) Adapted from Richard Nelson Bolles, *The 1997 What Color Is Your Parachute?* (Berkeley, Calif.: Ten Speed Press, 1996), 129–166; Karen W. Arenson, "Placement Offices Leave Old Niches to Become Computerized Job Bazaars," *New York Times,* 17 July 1996, B12; Lawrence J. Magid, "Job

Hunters Cast Wide Net Online," *Los Angeles Times,* 26 February 1996, 20; Richard Van Doren, "On-Line Career Advice Speeds Search for Jobs," *Network World,* 4 March 1996, 54; Alex Markels, "Job Hunting Takes Off in Cyberspace," *Wall Street Journal,* 20 September 1996, B1, B2; Michael Chorost, "Jobs on the Web," *Hispanic,* October 1995, 50–53; Zane K. Quible, "Electronic Résumés: Their Time Is Coming," *Business Communication Quarterly 58,* no. 3 (1995): 5–9; Margaret Mannix, "The Home-Page Help Wanteds," *U.S. News & World Report,* 30 October 1995, 88, 90; Pam Dixon and Silvia Tiersten, *Be Your Own Headhunter Online* (New York: Random House, 1995), 53–69; Michele Himmelberg, "Internet an Important Tool in Employment Search," *San Diego Union-Tribune,* 7 September 1998, D2; Richard N. Bolles, "Career Strategizing, or What Color Is Your Web Parachute?" *Yahoo! Internet Life,* May 1998, 116–122; Valerie Frazee, "Online Job Services Explode," *Personnel Journal,* August 1996, 21. **597** Rockport Institute, "How to Write a Masterpiece of a Résumé," http://www.rockportinstitute.com/résumés.html, accessed 16 October 1998. **601** "Fibbing on the Résumé," *San Diego Union-Tribune,* 7 September 1998, D1. **602** (Warning: Deceptive Résumés Can Backfire) Adapted from Joan E. Rigdon, "Deceptive Résumés Can Be Door-Openers But Can Become an Employee's Undoing," *Wall Street Journal,* 17 June 1992, B1; Diane Cole, "Ethics: Companies Crack Down on Dishonesty," *Managing Your Career,* Spring 1991, 8–11; Nancy Marx Better, "Résumé Liars," *Savvy,* December 1990–January 1991, 26–29. **633** Adapted from Richard Nelson Bolles, *What Color Is Your Parachute?* (Berkeley, Calif.: Ten Speed Press, 1997), 67. **628** Adapted from Richard N. Bolles, "Career Strategizing or, What Color Is Your Web Parachute?" *Yahoo! Internet Life,* May 1998, 116, 121; Tara Weingarten, "The All-Day, All-Night, Global, No-Trouble Job Search," *Newsweek,* 6 April 1998, 17 ; Michele Himmelberg, "Internet an Important Tool in Employment Search," *San Diego Union-Tribune,* 7 September 1998, D2; Gina Imperato, "35 Ways to Land a Job Online," *Fast Company,* August 1998, 192–197; Roberta Maynard, "Casting the Net for Job Seekers," *Nation's Business,* March 1997, 28–29. **633** Adapted from Anne Fisher, "Success Secret: A High Emotional IQ," *Fortune,* 26 October, 1998, 293–298; Laura Lyne McMurchie, "Careers Can Rise and Fall with an EQ," *Computing Canada,* September 1998, 18, 21. **634** Samuel Greengard, "Are You Well Armed to Screen Applicants?" *Personnel Journal,* December 1995, 84–95. **635** (How to Check References—and Avoid Legal Traps) Adapted from James Krohe Jr., "Why Traditional Screening Doesn't Work," *Across the Board,* December 1997, 221; Frances A. McMorris, "Ex-Bosses Face Less Peril Giving Honest Job References," *Wall Street Journal,* 8 July 1996, B1, B8; Michael Kinsman, "Firm's Cost Cutting Left This Job-Seeker out in the Cold," *San Diego Union-Tribune,* 21 June 1996, C1; Samuel Greengard, "Are You Well Armed to Screen Applicants?" *Personnel Journal,* December 1995, 84–95; "Employers Find It More Difficult to Check References," *Personnel Journal,* May 1993, 20; Tim Weiner, "Fearing Suits, Companies Avoid Giving Job References," *New York Times,* 8 May 1993, 17, 29; David B. Kern, "Handling Reference Requests on Fired Employees," *Supervisory Management,* January 1993, 6; Paul W. Barada, "Check References with Care," *Nation's Business,* May 1993, 54, 56; Max Messmer, "Nothing But the Truth," *Small Business Reports,* March 1993, 11–14; "Managing People: Reference-Checking Tips," *Inc.,* November 1992, 38; James W. Fenton Jr. and Kay W. Lawrimore, "Employment Reference Checking, Firm Size, and Defamation Liability," *Journal of Small Business Management,* October 1992, 88–95; George D. Webster, "Background and Reference Checks," *Agency Sales Magazine,* October 1992, 26–28; Emily Leinfuss, "Reference Checks: The Truth Be Known," *Computerworld,* 22 April 1991, 88; Lois Vander Waerdt, "Take Nothing for Granted," *Management World,* March–April 1990, 5–10; Arthur Bragg, "Checking References," *Sales & Marketing Management,* November 1990, 68, 70, 73; James Braham, "Hiring Mr. Wrong," *Industry Week,* 7 March 1988, 31–34; Robert Half, "Reference Checking: A Critical Part of the Hiring Process," *Journal of Accountancy,* August 1988, 130–134. **638** (Sixteen Tough Interview Questions: What to Say When You're Stopped in Your Tracks) Adapted from "Career Strategies," *Black Enterprise,* February 1986, 122. Copyright © 1986, Black Enterprise Magazine, The Earl Graves Publishing Company, Inc., New York, NY. All rights reserved. **639** *Interviews That Win Jobs* (Garden City, NY.: Benci-Ventures, 1994), 13. **640** Adapted from *The Northwestern Endicott Report* (Evanston, Ill.: Northwestern University Placement Center). **641** Adapted from H. Lee Rust, *Job Search: The Completion Manual for Jobseekers* (New York: American Management Association, 1979), 56. **642** Adapted from *The Northwestern Endicott Report* (Evanston: Ill.: Northwestern University Placement Center). **643** *Interviews That Win Jobs* (Garden City, N.Y.: Benci-Ventures, 1994), 13. **656** (Games Recruiters Play) Adapted from Nina Munk and Suzanne Oliver, "Think Fast!" *Forbes,* 24 March 1997, 146–151; Christopher Caggiano, "Hands On," *Inc.,* October 1998, 117; Jonathan A. Segal, "Take Applicants for a Test Drive," *HR Magazine,* December 1996, 120–122.

Photos

1 Courtesy of Steve Niedorf/The Image Bank **2** Courtesy of Jim Caldwell/Metamorphosis Studios (both) **3** Courtesy of Metamorphosis Studios **14** Courtesy of Reuters/Jeff Christensen/Archive Photos **18** Courtesy of Michael Newman/PhotoEdit **19** Courtesy of Collins/Monkmeyer Press **22** Courtesy of Rob Crandall/Stock Boston **34** Courtesy of 3M Corpora-tion **35** Courtesy of 3M Corporation **39** Courtesy of Steven Rubin/The Image Works **42** Courtesy of Wayne Coltinuille/New England Stock Photo **46** Courtesy of Jay Daniel/Photo20-20 **50** Courtesy of Rick Friedman/Black Star **60** Courtesy of Kayomi Kaneda, Michiru Tamanai **61** Courtesy of ITT Sheraton Hotel Hawaii **68** Courtesy of Charles Thatcher/Tony Stone Images, Jeff Greenberg/Photo Edit **64** Courtesy of Mark Richards/Contact Press Images Inc. **75** Courtesy of Charles Gupton/Tony Stone Images **90** Courtesy of General Mills **97** Courtesy of Tom Wagner/SABA Press Photos,Inc. **99** Courtesy of Grant/Monkmeyer Press **109** Courtesy of Bachmann/New England Stock Photo **113** Courtesy of Don Heupel/AP/Wide World Photos **122** Courtesy of Julian Santoyo **123** Courtesy of Art Montes De Oca/FPG International LLC **129** Courtesy of Barry Staver **134** Courtesy of Jim Mendenhall **146** Courtesy of Linda Sue Scott **162** Courtesy of Adrianne Proeller **163** Courtesy of CNN Cable News Network, Inc. **168** Courtesy of Harry How/Allsport Photography (USA), Inc. **172** Courtesy of John R. Fulton, Jr. **175** Courtesy of T. Michael Keza/Nation's Business Magazine **179** Courtesy of Cross Pen Computing Group **194** Courtesy of Jeff Christensen,Ho/AP/Wide World Photos **197** Courtesy of Jose L. Pelaez/The Stock Market **198** Courtesy of The Nature Company **199** Courtesy of The Nature Company/Discovery Channel Retail DBA The Nature Company **203** Courtesy of Ed Reinke/AP/Wide World Photos **207** Courtesy of Rex Rystedt Photography **222** Courtesy of James Lemass/Index Stock Imagery, Inc. **226** Courtesy of Southwest Airlines Co. **227** Courtesy of Mark Peterson/SABA Press Photos, Inc. **236** Courtesy of D. Young Wolff/Photo Edit **237** Courtesy of Cindy Lewis/Cindy Lewis Photography **238** Courtesy of Leslye Bordon/Photo Edit **244** Courtesy of Yia Eason **245** Courtesy of Yia Eason **246** Courtesy of Marc Bryan-Brown Photography **267** Courtesy of Stephen Simpson/FPG International LLC **270** Courtesy of Reuters/John Hillery Archive Photos/Archive Photos **280** Courtesy of Celestis **283** Courtesy of D.Young-Wolff/PhotoEdit **286** Courtesy of AT&T Archives/Property of AT&T Archives, reprinted with permission of AT&T **287** Courtesy of AT&T Archives/Property of AT&T Archives, reprinted with permission of AT&T **292** Courtesy of T.Michael Keza/United States Chamber of Commerce **301** Courtesy of Felix Adamo **306** Courtesy of Mark Katzman/Ferguson and Katzman Photography, Inc. **312**Courtesy of Mark Katzman/Ferguson and Katzman Photography, Inc. **323** Courtesy of Westlight/Bill Ross/Westlight/Corbis **334** Courtesy of Matthew McVay/Stock Boston **327** Courtesy of Hay House **330** Courtesy of Esbin-Anderson/Photo20-20 **335** Courtesy of Jeff Zaruba/The Stock Market **336** Courtesy of Silicon Graphics, Inc. **337** Courtesy of Silicon Graphics, Inc. **338** Courtesy of Ariel Skelley/The Stock Market **349** Courtesy of Chris Stewart/Black Star **354** Courtesy of Ronnie Kaufman/The Stock Market **366** Courtesy of Charley Shin **367** Courtesy of Charley Shin **380** Courtesy of Bob Daemmrich/Stock Boston **398** Courtesy of Black Entertainment Television **399** Courtesy of Greg Miller Photography **415** Courtesy of Picture Perfect USA, Inc./© 1997 Picture Perfect **437** Courtesy of Taylor/Fabricius/Liaison Agency, Inc. **438** Courtesy of Narada Productions **439** Courtesy of Narada Productions **443** Courtesy of Ric Ferro/Fotobanc, Inc. **447** Courtesy of ZD Events **460** Courtesy of Raymond Guardiano/Bruce Rogow **481** Courtesy of Mug Shots/The Stock Market **510** Courtesy of Corporate Dynamics **511** Courtesy of Corporate Dynamics **551** Courtesy of Bill Truslow/Liaison Agency, Inc. **557** Courtesy of Frank Oberle/Image Quest **560** Courtesy of Shadowfax/Leann Anderson **561** Courtesy of Frank Herholdt/Tony Stone Images **574** Courtesy of Tom, Dee Anee McCarthy/The Stock Market **577** Courtesy of Rhoda Sidney/Stock Boston **580** Courtesy of Index Stock Imagery, Inc. **586** Courtesy of Churchill & Klehr Photography **587** Courtesy of Churchill & Klehr Photography **588** Courtesy of REI Recreational Equipment Inc. **589** Courtesy of REI Recreational Equipment Inc. **592** Courtesy of Todd Buchanan **610** Courtesy of Linda Sue Scott **626** Courtesy of Jodi DeLeon **627** Courtesy of Jodi DeLeon **630** Courtesy of The Image Works **643** Courtesy of Bob Daemmrich/The Image Works **657** Courtesy of Spencer Grant/Photo Edit

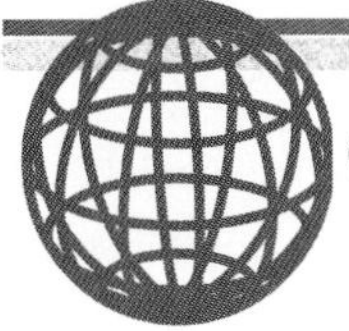

COMPANY, ORGANIZATION, AND BRAND INDEX

SUBJECT INDEX